For Beth, who took a
pile of Xerox paper
and turned it into
a book, with thanks —

Ken

LAW AND DEVELOPMENT
IN LATIN AMERICA

Published for the
UCLA LATIN AMERICAN CENTER
as Volume 28 in the
UCLA LATIN AMERICAN STUDIES SERIES
Series editor: Johannes Wilbert

BOOKS PUBLISHED BY THE UNIVERSITY OF CALIFORNIA PRESS
IN COOPERATION WITH THE UCLA LATIN AMERICAN CENTER

1. Kenneth Karst and Keith S. Rosenn, *Law and Development in Latin America: A Case Book*. Latin American Studies Series Volume 28, UCLA Latin American Center. 1975.

2. James W. Wilkie, Michael C. Meyer, and Edna Monzón de Wilkie, eds., *Contemporary Mexico: Papers of the IV International Congress of Mexican History*. Latin American Studies Series Volume 29, UCLA Latin American Center. 1975.

3. Arthur J. O. Anderson, Frances Berdan, and James Lockhart, *Beyond the Codices: The Nahua View of Colonial Mexico*. Latin American Studies Series Volume 27, UCLA Latin American Center. 1976.

(Except for the volumes listed above, which are published and distributed by the University of California Press, Berkeley, California 94720, all other volumes in the Latin American Studies Series are published and distributed by the UCLA Latin American Center, Los Angeles, California 90024.)

LAW AND DEVELOPMENT
IN LATIN AMERICA
A Case Book

Kenneth L. Karst

Professor of Law,
University of California, Los Angeles

Keith S. Rosenn

Professor of Law,
Ohio State University

UNIVERSITY OF CALIFORNIA PRESS
BERKELEY LOS ANGELES LONDON

University of California Press
Berkeley and Los Angeles, California
University of California Press, Ltd.
London, England
Copyright © 1975 by The Regents of the University of California
ISBN: 0-520-02955-0
Library of Congress Catalog Card Number: 74-30525
Printed in the United States of America

*To Smiley and Silvia
who were patient*

PREFACE

This book's extensive use of judicial decisions, statutes, notes, and questions reflects the book's primary objective, which is to serve as teaching materials for a law school course. Throughout this century, law teaching in the United States has emphasized the intensive analysis of concrete problems. This book is largely in that tradition. Its particularized exploration of legal-institutional materials in four diverse subject areas is bracketed by a chapter that places these materials in historical perspective and a concluding chapter that reexamines the same materials in the light of some general questions about the interrelation of the processes of law and development. The book may thus be of interest outside law school walls.

Parts of chapters II and III are revisions of material in K. Karst, Latin American Legal Institutions: Problems for Comparative Study (1966); once again we acknowledge with thanks the support and assistance acknowledged then.

For support of our work leading to the present book, we are indebted to a number of institutions: the Ohio State University College of Law; the UCLA School of Law; the Ford Foundation; the International Legal Center; and St. Antony's College, Oxford. The UCLA Latin American Center supported portions of the research with funds from its grants from the U.S. Agency for International Development.

Parts of a draft of Chapter I were read by Rafael Benítez and Boris Kozolchyk; we are grateful for their comments. We are also grateful for the research assistance of Thomas Roberts, Jess Sandoval, Carmen Slominski, Beth Ebey, and Jane Trapnell.

For preparation of the manuscript at UCLA, we thank P. Carolyn Kosche. For similar work at Ohio State, we thank Gladys Paulin, Linda Dixon, Judith Grasso, Karen Olson, Sue Gallogly, Sylvia Brown, Suzanne Sutphen, Susan Mayer, and Virginia Smith.

CONTENTS

TABLE OF CASES

(Principal cases are in italics.)

LIST OF FOREIGN ABBREVIATIONS

ARGENTINA

A.L.J.A.	Anuario de Legislación de Revista Jurisprudência Argentina
CN Civ.	Cámara Nacional de Apelaciones en lo Civil de la Capital Federal
CN Com.	Cámara Nacional de Apelaciones en lo Comercial de la Capital Federal
CN Paz	Cámara Nacional de Apelaciones de Paz Letrada de la Capital Federal
J.A.	Jurisprudencia Argentina

BRAZIL

A.C.	Ação Civil
Ag. M.S.	Agravo em Mandado de Segurança
Arch. Jud.	Archivo Judiciário
BNH	Banco Nacional de Habitações
Cam. Civ. Guan.	Câmara Civil Guanabara
Embs.	Embargos
E.M.S.	Embargo em Mandado de Segurança
H.C.	Habeas Corpus
M.S.	Mandado de Segurança
R.E.	Recurso Extraordinário
R.M.S.	Recurso de Mandado de Segurança
Rev. Dir.	Revista Direito
Rev. Dir. Admin.	Revista de Direito Administrativo
Rev. Fac. Dir. São Paulo	Revista da Faculdade de Direito de São Paulo
Rev. For.	Revista Forense
Rev. Juris. Guan.	Revista de Jurisprudência do Tribunal de Justiça do Estado da Guanabara
Rev. Procur. Ger.	Revista de Direito da Procuradoria Geral (Estado da Guanabara)
Rev. T.F.R. Juris.	Revista do Tribunal Federal de Recursos de Jurisprudência
R.T.J.	Revista Trimestral de Jurisprudência (an official reporter for the Supreme Federal Tribunal, publishing selected cases)
Rev. Trib.	Revista dos Tribunais
S.T.F.	Supremo Tribunal Federal
T.F.R.	Tribunal Federal de Recursos
T.J.S.P.	Tribunal de Justiça de São Paulo

CHILE

D.F.L.	Decreto con Fuerza de Ley
Rev. Der. Econ.	Revista de Derecho Económico
R.D.J.	Revista de Derecho y Jurisprudência

MEXICO

Rev. Fac. Derecho Mex.	Revista de la Facultad de Derecho de México
S.J.F.	Semanario Judicial de la Federación (The official reporter for the Supreme Court, now in its Sixth Epoch, which began in 1957)

INTRODUCTION

This book explores the interaction of the legal process and the process of development in Latin America. We focus on four subject areas: judicial control of governmental action; land reform; law and inflation; and a field study of the internal norms of some marginal squatter communities in Caracas. The selection of subjects, growing out of the editors' research interests, is arbitrary. Yet some selection is inescapable, and in combination our four topics present a considerable range of issues in the study of law and development.

Selection is also necessary at the level of theory. Both law and development are vast social phenomena, nearly as complex as the totality of human relationships; a comprehensive theory of law and development would be scarcely distinguishable from a comprehensive theory of society. We may take caution from Jorge Luis Borges' mythical land, where cartography reached such an art that the map of the kingdom was precisely the size of the kingdom itself. Social analysis, like any thought, requires abstraction. Abstraction, in turn, implies some distortion of reality; no witness ever tells "the whole truth." What is wanted is a map that will permit us to move over the terrain. The questions we raise in this book do not aim at eliciting a full-scale theory of law and development in Latin America, but at the more modest goal of articulating some of the issues that any such theory must confront.

We repeat: The "law" selected for study in this book assuredly does not touch the full range of legal principles and legal institutions relevant to the process of development. Omitted are such "law-and-economics" subjects as: the regulation of industry, labor law, the system of taxation, the control of foreign investment, the regulation of international trade, and the integration of national economies into such international communities as the Latin American Free Trade Area. Nor do we consider such "law-and-society" subjects as the legal status of women, or the role of law in affecting rates of population growth, or the law's place in promoting or retarding the integration of indigenous populations into the national societies. The four subject areas we consider are unified by a common theme, and that theme is "participatory development." Before we examine the meaning of that term, however, it will be well to examine the various meanings of development itself.

An economist can scarcely be blamed for thinking of "development" as synonymous with economic growth. Thus, in stating what is essential in development planning, Oscar Lange says:

> ... the essential consists in assuring an amount of productive investment which is sufficient to provide for a rise of national income substantially in excess of the rise in population, so that per capita income increases. The strategic factor is investment, or more precisely productive investment.[1]

---

[1] O. Lange, *Essays on Economic Planning* 11 (1960).

For the sociologist, however, even economic development is viewed against background of social change in spheres that are not primarily seen as economic:

> Development as a whole involves a complex series of changes in rates of growth — of output per capita, of political participation, of literacy, etc. — and major changes in those rates depend on the occurrence of fundamental changes in the social structure of the developing society. To complicate the study of development even more, changes in one institutional sector set up demands for changes in other sectors. Rapid economic development, for instance, establishes pressure for adjustment in the education and training of a new type of labor force. . . .
>
> Viewing development thus, we cannot escape the fact that persons must be shuttled through the social structure during periods of rapid development. Often they have to move to an urban setting. They must fill new occupational roles and positions of leadership. They must learn to respond to new rewards and deprivations and to accept new standards for effective performance.[2]

The sociologist's study of development thus emphasizes such questions as the differentiation of social roles, the integration of groups, the change from ascription of status to achievement orientation, or the impact of urbanization on attitudes. Correspondingly, political scientists tend to study such phenomena as the use of ideology or party structure to mobilize a population to seek certain "modernizing" goals, the changing role of the bureaucracy, changes in the forms of legitimacy of power, or the varieties of political participation.

What these various perspectives share, as their common object of study, is not a thing, but a process of social change. As we use the term "development," one of its dimensions is economic growth; another dimension includes those other social phenomena identified as causes or effects of economic growth. In these dimensions, "development" calls to mind such phenomena as child development or the growth of a camellia plant from seed to blossom. The term has a neutral and unilinear sound; it suggests gradual, incremental movement up a predetermined scale, and perhaps even inevitability.[3] But "development," in our view, has other dimensions as well, captured in this statement by Dudley Seers:

> The questions to ask about a country's development are therefore: What has been happening to poverty? What has been happening to unemployment? What has been happening to inequality? . . . If one or two of these central problems have been growing worse, especially if all three have, it would be strange to call the result "development," even if per capita income doubled.[4]

---

[2] Smelser and Lipset, "Social Structure, Mobility and Development," in N. Smelser and S. Lipset (eds.), *Social Structure and Mobility in Economic Development* at 1, 2 (1966).

[3] For a statement of such a unilinear theory, much criticized, see W. Rostow, *The Stages of Economic Growth* (1960).

[4] Seers, "The Meaning of Development," 11 *Int'l Development Rev.* 2, 3 (1969).

So conceived, development is anything but neutral; it implies not merely "more of the same," but structural changes, changes in the existing distribution of wealth, power and prestige. Seers' concerns about inequality may seem to some to be ideologically biased toward the value preferences of liberal democracy. We shall return to the issue of inequality, noting for the present that even the goals of reducing poverty and unemployment are not neutral. Development implies conflict.

The conflict may, in fact, be sudden and highly disruptive, producing immediate economic decline, not growth; presumably the hope of all revolutionaries is that after social and political relationships are drastically reordered, long-term economic growth will ensue. But the case of full-scale political revolution is not so much atypical of development as it is dramatically illustrative of the price of development. Development implies social change, and even incremental change implies wrenching discontinuities for some people. Technological unemployment is one example from our own affluent world; another is the growth of the leisure industry, which has been enormous overall, but selectively harsh — as the ex-managers of many now-defunct neighborhood cinemas would attest. Development implies dislocation.

Some kinds of social change probably are inevitable in a world of near-instantaneous communication. Thus, the members of the "stone-age" tribe recently discovered in the Philippines now use steel knives, and greet the anthropologists' helicopter with nondismay. They have experienced the first stirrings of their own "revolution of rising expectations." In some *very* long-range terms, too, it is a fair guess that a worldwide system of communication will tend to diminish disparities among the world's various societies' forms of social organization and levels of average income. But, in Lord Keynes' famous words, in the long run we shall all be dead. For hundreds of millions of humans alive today, there is nothing sure about development — even development conceived as *national* economic growth. Development is not inevitable.

Nor is development unilinear. Latin America has its own distinctive history as a region, and its separate national (and local) histories. There is no reason to assume a common destiny for Latin America and Asia or Africa, let alone Europe or North America. These materials do assume that Latin America can usefully be treated as an entity for some analytical purposes. Latin America as a region shares an Iberian tradition, a colonial tradition, and present-day patterns of social organization. More specifically, Latin America's nations share a considerable number of formal legal institutions, and its societies share a set of attitudes toward law. Colombia is not Mexico, and for that matter, Bogotá is not Medellín; the results of the process of development will be different not only from year to year but also from place to place. Yet the importance of a shared legal-institutional inheritance from the colonial period justifies a regional approach to analysis of the interrelation of law and development in Latin America.[5]

Development, in any of the senses thus far mentioned, is consistent with many forms of social organization. There are, however, two models, or perhaps styles, of development that may be contrasted by way of illuminating our general problem. One

---

[5] The colonial experience is considered in Chapters I and VI.

model can be called "top-down development." Given the conditions of scarcity, including scarcity of trained personnel, that characterize most developing countries, it is natural for the top-down approach to dominate most developmental planning. Governmental planners generally think in macroeconomic terms: the money supply, employment, health services, housing. A government's construction of high-rise apartments to house the poor typifies such thinking. Developmental decisions are made at the top and handed down; the ordinary person does not participate so much as acquiesce. In contrast, a decision by a resident of a squatter community to build or improve his or her own home exemplifies the other model, which is "participatory development." In this model, persons at all levels of society are involved in developmental decision making. The materials in this book emphasize the relation of law to participatory development.

In Latin America, the tendency toward a top-down approach to development is accentuated by a tradition of paternalism whose features are variously described as a patron-client[6] system, a corporative tradition or a patrimonial state. The archetypal institution, of course, is the classical great rural estate called the *hacienda*: One's status is ascribed at birth; loyalties run vertically in a community that is not merely stratified but also vertically segmented; discretion, not rule, characterizes the *patrón's* exercises of power; the dependent individual is protected *by* the *patrón,* but his or her only effective protection *against* the *patrón* is the sense of *noblesse oblige.* It is sometimes suggested that such a caricature portrays the dominant characteristics of Latin American society and government, seen as a giant pyramid of patronage. While there is much to be said for such a perspective, it bears emphasis that it *is* a perspective, and by no means the whole story of Latin American society. Paternalism is the enemy of participatory development, but it is not likely to destroy the roots of participation. We shall return to the problems of patronage as they arise in this book's various contexts. For now, it is sufficient to recognize that the influence of the tradition in Latin America is both broad and deep.

Whatever the form of social organization, development implies "the expansion of opportunities and the enhancement of human capacities needed to exploit them." [7] People must be mobilized, brought to participate in the process of change. A young Chinese woman, asked by a Western newspaper reporter in 1972 what she planned to do upon finishing college, replied with a smile that "the leadership" would decide where she would be most useful. The smile reminds us that even the most thoroughgoing top-down developmental program involves participation of a sort. To the extent that development rests on individual decisions, however, it depends on the creation and maintenance of developmental states of mind. The beliefs and attitudes to be encouraged are varied, but interrelated. Fundamental is the belief that the world is, to some minimum degree, understandable and susceptible to rational human manipulation, rather than ruled by fate or the gods. Change must be seen as legitimate, not something to be resisted just because it is change. One must assume that there will

---

[6] The clientship here discussed, of course, has nothing to do with the notion of "client" in a lawyer-client relationship.

[7] P. Dorner, *Land Reform and Economic Development* 15 (1972).

be a payoff for development-oriented activity — that rewards will be given for achievement, not ascribed on the basis of one's birth or other unearned status. Participatory development requires a time perspective that accepts the idea of deferring gratification. One should be alert to opportunities, and ready to take moderate risks to improve one's situation. Cooperation must be minimally acceptable, not merely for the success of collective ventures, but also for the efficient working of any market system that goes beyond the simple simultaneous exchange of goods. A market implies at least some willingness to "deal fairly with strangers,"[8] and to trust others. Cooperative work requires the abandonment of a belief that there is a limited amount of good in the world, so that one person's benefit necessarily means another's loss. There must similarly be a minimum acceptance of the government's organizing role in certain contexts — not submissiveness, but a willingness to entertain the idea of cooperation with the state.

Concern for these developmental states of mind does not imply a lapse into "psychologism" — an effort to find the causes of social phenomena in the properties of the individual psyche. Since such states of mind themselves have their causes in social relationships, psychologism is ultimately a circular path. Our task, instead, is to seek social explanations for developmental (or anti-developmental) attitudes, and in particular to examine into the role of law in shaping attitudes.

In fact, the law's main contribution to social life lies precisely in its influence on people's states of mind. Law, however we define it, operates by creating expectations. These materials thus emphasize the law's role in providing *security*. But security is not the only state of mind affected by law; we shall also be concerned with the law's impact on the *legitimacy* of power, and on the sense of *community*. To round out our discussion of the interrelation of law and development in Latin America, we shall consider the issues raised by *inequality*.

These four themes — security, legitimacy, community, and inequality — are treated explicitly in our final chapter, entitled "Perspectives on Law and Development." That chapter builds on the substantive materials of four individual chapters that explore the four subject areas mentioned in the opening paragraph of this Introduction. To place these materials in historical context, we begin with an historical introduction to law in Latin America.

---

[8] Parsons, "Institutional Aspects of Agricultural Development Policy," 48 *J. Farm Econ.* 1185, 1189 (1966). See also Kozolchyk, "Toward a Theory on Law in Economic Development: The Costa Rican USAID-ROCAP Law Reform Project," 1971 *Law and the Social Order* 681, 737-51.

Chapter I

HISTORICAL DEVELOPMENT OF
LATIN AMERICAN
LEGAL INSTITUTIONS

The science of the laws is like a fountain of justice and the world benefits from it more than from any other science.

Las Siete Partidas

The nations of Latin America are often classed with those of Asia and Africa as "underdeveloped" or "developing" countries. But Latin American law is not usually so characterized; the dizzying profusion of laws and lawyers suggests that a more appropriate word for law in Latin America might be "overdeveloped." The Latin American nations share with Europe a legal heritage that can be traced back to Rome. Roman influence is still manifest in much of Latin American law, particularly the basic codes. More importantly, Roman law and the particular medieval Iberian matrix in which it congealed have heavily colored Latin American attitudes and perceptions about law and legal processes. Some background in the development of Roman and Iberian law is essential for understanding the functioning of contemporary Latin American legal institutions.

A. Juridical Problem Solving in Latin America – A Preview

A preview of Latin American attitudes and perceptions about law and legal processes can be found in a modern Latin American jurist's solution to a typical legal problem: Should custody of minor illegitimate children be granted to the father or to the mother "when it is admitted that the children would be equally well off with either parent?" The following opinion, published in a leading Brazilian law review, was written by Dr. Caio Mário da Silva Pereira, a distinguished professor of civil law, and submitted to an appellate court for guidance in deciding this custody dispute. In the tradition of the ancient Roman jurisconsult, Dr. Pereira was acting as a disinterested, neutral legal expert, even though his fee was presumably paid by one of the litigants. In what ways does Dr. Pereira's opinion differ from what you would expect from his North American counterpart (one analogue might be the lawyer invited by an appellate court to submit an *amicus* brief) or from a common law judge? More particularly, what differences do you note with respect to:

(1) Concern for the specific facts of the case;
(2) Techniques of statutory interpretation;
(3) Use of deductive versus inductive reasoning;
(4) Concern for universal principles;
(5) Use of doctrine (scholarly writings);
(6) Use of judicial precedents;
(7) Relevance of comparative law.

C. PEREIRA, PÁTRIO PODER

214 Rev. For. 58 (1966)

Consultation

The Brazilian Civil Code of 1916 undoubtedly established the precedence of paternal over maternal rights ... with respect to the protection of children and the exercise of paternal power [*patria potestas* of Roman Law]. This orientation is manifested in the systematic interpretation of its dispositions, principally the following:
   (a) Article 326[1] ... ;
   (b) Article 360[2] ... ;
   (c) Article 380[3] ... ;
   (d) Article 393[4] ....

Decree-law No. 3.200 of April 19, 1941 opened a breach in the patriarchal system, establishing that the illegitimate child would remain under the father's power "unless the judge decided differently in the interest of the minor child" (art. 16).[5] This said, it is asked:

---

[1] Article 326. In the event of a legal separation [Brazil has no divorce] the minor children shall remain with the innocent spouse.

   1. If both should be at fault, the mother shall have the right to the custody of her daughters during their minority, and of her sons until the age of six.
   2. Sons above the age of six shall be delivered to the father's custody. [Eds.]

[2] Article 360. While still a minor, the acknowledged [illegitimate] child shall remain in the custody of the parent who has acknowledged him, and if both recognize him, in the custody of the father. [Eds.]

[3] Article 380. During a marriage the paternal power is exercised by the husband, as head of the family, and during his absence or impediment, by the wife. [Eds.]

[4] Article 393. The mother who remarries loses her rights of paternal power over the children of her prior marriage; however, she regains them upon becoming a widow. [Eds.]

[5] Decree-Law 3.200 of April 19, 1941:

   Article 16. While a minor, the natural child shall remain in the custody of the parent who

(1) Law No. 4.121 of August 27, 1962, having explicitly and directly modified articles 326(1), 380, and 393 of the Civil Code,[6] did the legislature not unequivocally desire, by such action, to exclude definitively the preponderance of paternal over maternal rights with respect to children?

(2) Has not article 360, already altered by Decree-law No. 3.200 in view of the interest of the minor, not lost its dispositive force in the face of the redaction given to articles 326(1) and 380 of the Civil Code?

Finally, (3) should a judge, in view of the orientation given the civil law by Law 4.121 of 1962, determine that minor illegitimate children stay in the custody of the father and not the mother, even when it is admitted that the children would be equally well off with either parent, . . . and without proof of any fact which would impede the mother from having them in her custody?

Opinion

Whoever observes the evolution of the institution of paternal power can verify the accentuated tendency in the whole civilized world to affirm the position of the children in relation to their parents. Starting from the condition stemming from the autocratic and patriarchal Roman family, when the absolute right over life and death over the children by the *pater-familias* was recognized — *ius vitae ac necis* — and assured perpetual authority (which did not even cease with death or the concession . . . of emancipation), we arrive at the stage which presently prevails, in which the person of the child overshadows all considerations and interests. . . .

The jurist who consults the sources . . . bequeathed by Roman civilization becomes

---

has acknowledged him, and if both acknowledge him, in the custody of the father, unless the judge decides differently in the interest of the minor child. (As amended by Decree-law No. 5.213 of January 21, 1943.) [Eds.]

[6] Law No. 4.121 of August 27, 1962.

    Article 1. Articles . . . 326, 380, 393 . . . of the Civil Code take effect with the following redactions:

    Art. 326. In the event of a legal separation, the minor children shall remain with the innocent spouse.

    1. If both spouses should be at fault, minor children shall remain in the custody of the mother, unless the judge finds that such disposition may prejudice the children's moral order . . . .

    Art. 380. During a marriage the paternal power belongs to both parents, being exercised by the husband with the collaboration of the wife. In the absence or impediment of one of the parents, its exercise shall pass exclusively to the other parent.

    Sole paragraph. If the parents disagree on the exercise of paternal power, the decision of the father shall prevail, reserving to the mother the right to appeal to the court to resolve the dispute.

    Art. 393. The mother who remarries does not lose her rights of paternal power over the children of her prior marriage, exercising such rights without any interference from her husband. [Eds.]

convinced that the Roman family was essentially based upon a permanent contrast: on one side, the father, invested with powers so extensive that they challenged the law of the City, and on the other side, the child who could invoke no power except that granted by paternal grace.

This organization was shattered by two influences. One was the penetration of the Germanic type family, in which the subjection of the child to the paternal *Munt* only nominally corresponded to the Roman *manus*. . . . The second was Christian spiritualization, much more profound in life than in the texts, as one infers from the admirable work of TROPLONG, "De l'Influence du Christianisme sur le Droit Privé des Romains." . . .

During the formative period of Portuguese law, whose offspring our law is, it was not the Roman family that was taken as the example. Rather it was a combination of three tendencies – Roman, Germanic, and Christian. This is why our family law, especially that part dealing with parental relations, is much more open and accessible to the penetration of reformist ideas than other systems which also constitute part of the great Western Roman-Christian family. This is why we admit . . . the influx of new tendencies that modern writers point out such as SAVATIER ("Du Droit Privé au Droit Publique," pages 15 et seq.), who shows that family law has moved appreciably from the realm of private law to that of public law, with social interest increasingly predominating.

Contemporaneous authors focusing particularly on the institution of parental power, such as RUGGIERO and MAROI ("Istituzioni di Diritto Privato," Vol. I, §66) note that the prevalence of the interest of the child and the burdens laid upon the parents are such that it would conform to modern orientation . . . to change parental power to *parental duty*.

Particularly in Brazilian law, the transformation has been radical. He who reads "The Rights of the Family" by LAFAYETTE, a book with all the classical titles, and compares it with the principles now prevailing, has the impression of viewing two diverse civilizations. Even reading CLÔVIS BEVILÁQUA [draftsman of Brazil's Civil Code], the author who, though much criticized, is always present, one has to be convinced that that law of the moment is unequivocally governed by principles which were not adhered to in the legislation and the doctrine of the first half of this century. Moreover, we live in an evolving period whose cycle has yet to be completed. . . .

The Civil Code of 1916 is marked by notorious paternalist reminiscences. The principle of domestic authority was concentrated in the father. It is he who exercises the paternal power. The mother who remarries loses her power over the children of the first marriage. When there is a legal separation, the minor children remain with the innocent spouse; however, if both spouses are blameworthy, the children above the age of six remain with the father. The husband is the head of the conjugal society, and at any time can revoke authorization to the wife for those acts which require such authorization. The requirement of parental consent for the marriage of children under the age of 21 can be satisfied by paternal consent in the event of a disagreement between the parents. These and other provisions display a constant tendency or orientation in the regime of civil law of 1916.

From subsequent legislative enactments stems a new tendency, a different orientation. No longer is the organization of the family determined in terms of paternal autocracy. The aim is to realize equality between spouses, and to promote a more democratic distribution in the behavior of the father and mother with respect to the children. Our positive law has shown a propensity to abandon the concept of paternal power upon which it was modeled, and to accept what one now purports to label *parental power.* This is the objective of Swiss law suggested by ROSSEL ET MENTHA, which should not be considered a local peculiarity, but a reflection of a new orientation with universalistic tendencies:

> Since it is exercised collectively by mother and father, it would be better to renounce the ancient terminology and to speak of paternal power as parental power. ROSSEL ET MENTHA, "Droit Civil Suisse," Vol. 1, page 431, No. 622.[7]

In effect, Law No. 4.121 of August 27, 1962 calls on the wife to collaborate: in heading the conjugal society (new art. 233), in the material and moral direction of the family (new art. 240), and in the exercise of the *patria potestas* (new art. 380). It also preserves parental power over children of a first marriage for the twice married woman (new art. 393). . . .

2.

One of the effects of acknowledgement, be it voluntary or compulsory, of illegitimate paternity, is the placing of the child *in potestate.* As we have developed in our monograph, "The Effects of Acknowledgement of Illegitimate Paternity," the linking of the illegitimate child to the family of his natural parents represents a real conquest. The statement that "les enfants naturels" were of no interest to the State has been attributed to the First Consul [*i.e.,* Napoléon]. In accordance with the evolutive line traced by RAOUL DE LA GRASSERIE, our law accompanied the others. . . .

It was soon verified that the rule of the Brazilian Civil Code automatically according custody of an illegitimate child to the father when and if he acknowledged the child was excessively rigid and severe. . . . The legislator returned to the subject with Decree-Law No. 3.200 of April 19, 1941. . . . [This] rule, as one can well see, is no more than that of 1916. . . . The innovation which subverted the traditional norm was giving the judge discretion to decide differently. . . .

3.

A categorical determination that the children had to remain in the custody of one of the parents, in accordance with an abstract standard, did not endure, even when the Code of 1916 was in full force. What mattered was the convenience of the minor child, his interests, the most suitable conditions of living, the best perspectives for the future,

---

[7] This quotation and the much longer one from Josserand on the following page appear in the original French without translation. It is common practice to quote English, French, Spanish, Italian and Latin sources without translation. [Eds.]

the conditions most favorable for the avoidance of conflicts in his education and upbringing. This was the path taken by the case law, inaugurating an interpretation which anticipated the legislator, and which decisively influenced him to adopt the spirit of the case law in making reforms.

Displaying concepts frankly liberated from Roman prejudices, the Tribunal of Justice of the Federal District (today the State of Guanabara) decided:

> Paternal power can no longer be considered as an absolute and discretionary right of the father, but rather as . . . a function of the interest of the child. (Revista dos Tribunais, Vol. 205, p. 528.)

Another decision of the same court, in which the reporter was the illustrious SERPA LOPES, contains passages revealing this elevated and modern thinking:

> Thus, the exercise of paternal power, which was formerly maintained beyond any control, is at the mercy of possible court intervention. . . . Consequently, there is no longer any place for paternal power in its Roman aspect, a paternal power governed by abstract discretion, protected by the apothegm — *"feci, sed iure feci."* (Revista dos Tribunais, Vol. 187, p. 892.)

A São Paulo decision enshrines the same principle:

> The law of custody is not inherent in paternal power. This right belongs to fathers as much as to mothers, without any order of precedence between them for its exercise. (Revista dos Tribunais, Vol. 194, p. 831.)

In a reference from which we can well draw a lesson, JOSSERAND discerned:

> It is up to modern law to recapture the Roman tradition, *mutatis mutandis*, in making paternal power a theatre of evolution, undoubtedly less profound, but incomparably more rapid than that followed by Rome over the course of a millenium. Although it has preferred to follow the mistakes of customary law, our civil code appeared to have compromised that power rigorously. Undoubtedly, the jurists asked themselves, on the day after its promulgation, if the codifiers were referring to the paternal power of our ancient customs, the power of protection for the child, or rather to the *patria potestas* which affected the allure of a power of domination and almost appropriation, at least in its origins and tendencies, and despite successive derogations which have profoundly tamed it. (JOSSERAND, "De l'esprit des lois et de leur Relativité, p. 96, no. 66.)

We can say almost the same thing about our law. The Code of 1916 reverted to a paternal power with characteristics . . . incompatible with our time. But, in half a century, the nation's juridical resources reacted. The writers understood and proclaimed the unreality and anachronism of this conception. And case law interpretation, legislative reform, and doctrinal ventilation transformed the institution of paternal power, clearly pruned of its Romanist excesses. . . .

What occurred was no mere modification of certain texts. The sociologist would say that one verifies a real revolution in customs in our times. . . . The jurist, in turn, encounters an authentic conceptual transformation and must extract from it a particular orientation governing application of the law.

At the time of applying the law, the judge ought never adhere to the understanding of a single text. . . . He must investigate the legislative tendencies of the whole province at a given time, on risk of being out of tune with the harmony present in the system. One cannot realize the precise interpretation of a proposition by proceeding with one's eyes turned to the past, or with one's thinking dominated by a structure overtaken by evolution. Grammatical interpretation, *ad unguem,* of an isolated text will not suffice; one must penetrate into the field of systematic interpretation, whose lines we have traced elsewhere:

> Systematic interpretation is denominated as that which takes the investigator further still, evidencing the subordination of the norm to a complex of dispositions of greater generalization, from which it may not and must not be disassociated. Here the interpretative force imposes the fixation of broad principles, guided by the system to which what is being interpreted pertains. . . . Systematic interpretation is also a logical process which operates in the vaster field of action. The interpreter starts from the proposition that a law does not exist in isolation, and therefore cannot be understood isolatedly. To comprehend it well, one must extract from the legislative complex the general ideas which inspired the legislation as a whole, or an entire juridical province, and by that light research the content of that provision. The interpreter must investigate what is *the dominant tendency of the various laws in existence on correlative matters,* and adopt that as his implicit premise for . . . the object of his research. . . . (CAIO MÁRIO DA SILVA PEREIRA, "Instituições de Direito Civil," Vol. I, no. 38.) . . .

In the face of the present orientation of our country's civil law, and bearing in mind that the institution of paternal power is destined to polarize the entire juridical complex towards the interest of the child, there is no reason for withdrawing the children from the mother's custody through the abstract and blind application . . . of an isolated text. What must be taken into account is the convenience of the minor children, indicating whose custody would be best for them.

If no fact occurs making it inadvisable, there is no reason for depriving minor children of maternal affection, for their interest and convenience outweigh any other factors.

Caio Mário da Silva Pereira, Professor of Law, University of Minas Gerais and the Catholic University of Rio de Janeiro.

As you read the following historical sketch of the development of Latin American legal institutions. consider to what extent these historical and cultural factors may account for the differences in approach and style between Dr. Pereira's opinion and North American legal writing.

B. A Brief Excursion into Roman Legal History

1. The Twelve Tables

It is customary to start with 450 B.C., the approximate date of the first known Roman code, the Twelve Tables. This was a crude sort of compilation of customary law and previous legislation, which — like our Restatements — could not resist the temptation to make a few changes. It was short; Cicero reports that the schoolboys of his day customarily memorized it. (It doesn't seem *that* short; it contains over 120 laws, or articles.) This code's planning and adoption, its structure, its interpretation and application — all of these resemble civilian experience with later codes, both in Europe and in Latin America.

The code was drafted by a commission of ten patricians over a period of about a year. (The agitation for a code had come primarily from plebeians, not patricians, but the patricians had no intention of turning over the rules of law to a debtor class.) A code of ten major parts was drafted; two further Tables were added a year later by a new group of commissioners. (The commissioners also administered the government in rotation, a day at a time, while they were in office; in this respect they are not typical of code drafters!) The legislative bodies duly adopted the code, which thereafter formed the core of Roman law for centuries, and which was the only comprehensive code to be enacted for a thousand years.

The first three of the Twelve Tables were devoted to what we should call procedural law. The explanation for this curious fact lies in the plebeian origins of the demand for a code. The judicial machinery and the law itself were in the hands of the patricians, who tended to be creditors; the tribunes (the plebeians' special governmental representatives) could not protect the plebeians' interests if the patrician magistrate could dredge up some old rule of law to suit the needs of the moment. The plebeians — most of them debtors — wanted some public statement of the limits on the discretion of the magistrates in devising legal remedies, and the first three Tables were apparently designed as such a statement. For example, Table III, Law IV provided: "In the case of an admitted debt or of awards made by judgment, 30 days shall be allowed for payment." That does not mean the code was soft on debtors. It was quite harsh enough. In default of settlement of the claim, the debtor could be kept in chains for 60 days. If the debtor still failed to come to terms with the creditor after three successive market days, the debtor could be reduced to slavery or sold beyond the Tiber. If a debtor was unfortunate enough to be delivered up to several creditors, after the third market day the creditors were entitled to divide the debtor's body; and any one that cut more or less than his just share was held guiltless.[8] That such a law should be regarded as an improvement shows the high store set on certainty by the plebeians, or perhaps the depth of their prior legal status.

The Tables also covered parental authority, inheritance and guardianship, contract, ownership, possession, real property, torts and crimes, some public — we should say constitutional — law ("No laws shall be proposed affecting individuals only"), along

---

[8] Table III, Laws V-X.

with detailed regulations for funerals and burial. But some of these subjects are "covered" only in the most generous sense of the word. For example, the Twelve Tables say nothing about the effect of mistake or error on contracts.

Such legislative omissions were filled in by the jurisconsults, a group of professional legal experts. They interpreted the code, and "by their process of interpretation, they extracted out of the XII Tables a good deal that was never in them."[9] The explanation for the assumption of this crucial role by the jurisconsults lies in the way in which the Romans decided cases. One of the most striking aspects of Roman justice through the classical period (27 B.C. – c. 235 A.D.) was the entrustment of judicial functions to laymen.[10] Proceedings in civil suits began with a hearing before a praetor, generally a lay judge elected to a one year term of office, to define the issues. Trial of the issues of law and fact took place in the second stage of the proceedings – the hearing before the *iudex*. The *iudex*, usually a high-ranking citizen with no formal legal training, was a cross between an arbitrator and a master. He was selected by the parties and empowered by the praetor to decide the dispute. The hearing before the *iudex* was relatively informal; there were no rules of evidence. Nor was there any appeal from his decision. Since he was appointed to serve only in a particular case, the *iudex* was not required to formulate the grounds for his decision in a written opinion. Despite the untrained and transient characteristics of their judiciary, during this period the Romans built up an impressive body of ordered adjudicatory rules. The opinions of the jurisconsults were written, collected, and considered authoritative. Indeed, during the second century A.D., the opinions of certain jurisconsults were binding on the judges.

The Roman jurists of the classical era were problem-solvers rather than jurisprudential theorists. They tended to avoid abstract formulations of general principles, preferring to reason on a case-by-case basis. But with the passage of time and the recurrence of similar problems, the opinions of the jurisconsults began to crystallize – just as English Equity later evolved from flexibility into formality – and the concerns of the leading jurists became increasingly detached from everyday legal problems. The annual praetorial edict, the principal technique through which the jurists influenced the growth and development of Roman law, was codified under the authority of the Emperor Hadrian shortly after 130 A.D., and the old system of civil procedure was gradually replaced by a system administered by permanent judges designated by the emperor. Appellate review was instituted, with the emperor sitting as a court of last resort. Imperial enactments (*constitutiones*), much of which were undoubtedly drafted by jurists in the emperor's employ, became the principal fount of Roman law.

---

2. The Institutes of Gaius

There were efforts to be more systematic. As early as the 2nd century, various

---

[9] W. Hunter, *Introduction to Roman Law* 6 (7th ed. 1909).
[10] This discussion is drawn largely from J. Dawson, *The Oracles of the Law* 101-07 (1968).

private attempts at compilation of imperial legislation were made. And one great treatise was written: the *Institutes of Gaius*. Gaius was virtually unknown during his lifetime; even today we do not know his surname. His treatise is in the nature of an introduction to the study of Roman law, and it has been pieced together under difficult circumstances by hundreds of scholars over the years. As the title suggests, it was an institutional treatise, arguably designed as a practice manual, but in any case highly systematic, stating the main principles of Roman law.

Gaius gave Europe its three-part division of private law: Persons, Things and Actions. (He may have borrowed the idea from earlier writers, but in any case it was his treatise which had great influence in later years.) Within the heading of Persons, Gaius treats status and family relationships; Things deals with ownership, inheritance, and obligation; and Actions deals with procedure. A look at the table of contents of a modern civil code discloses that the civil law still uses a similar classification structure, some 1,800 years later. Although Gaius lived in the 2nd century, his work focused on the Twelve Tables and on their elaboration by intermediate writings.

"True" codification, however, was not undertaken before Justinian's time. The Theodosian Code of 438 was instead a collection of imperial enactments (statute law) from Constantine's reign, rather like the United States Code, and did not purport to be a comprehensive codification of all private law. It remained for the Emperor Justinian to undertake the task of systematic arrangement and modernization of the whole body of private law. Even in the 6th century that was a monumental job.

---

3. The Justinian Legislation

The *Corpus Juris Civilis* of Justinian is unquestionably the most influential piece of legal scholarship the Western world has known. Justinian took the throne of the Eastern Empire at Constantinople in 527, half a century after the Western Empire had been overthrown. The Empire had lost its hold on the northern frontier; the Germanic tribes could not be kept from entering the Roman domain. The tribes had, at first, recognized the formal authority of the emperors, but eventually had cast aside even the pretense of subjection to Rome. The 5th century had seen the gradual dismemberment of the Empire in the west, ending in the displacement of the last Roman ruler of Rome itself in 476. Justinian's great wish was to re-establish the power and unity of the Empire "under one emperor, one church and one law."[11] He had partial success militarily, retaking Italy and northern Africa, and even some of southern Spain, nearly all of which were lost again after his death.

In addition to a reduced domain, Justinian inherited a legal system in bad disrepair. The Theodosian Code of a hundred years before had been supplemented by numerous imperial enactments. Various private compilations (such as the Gregorian and Hermogenian codes of the 4th Century) formed a new layer above the ancient

---

[11] H. Wolff, *Roman Law* 163 (1951).

praetorial edicts and the writings of the classical jurists. In all, the Empire was in a state of legislative confusion.

It had two outstanding law schools at Constantinople and at Beirut, however, in which scholars had been making exhaustive studies of the classical law. Their first task as codifiers was the consolidation of the old law. After a year's work by a ten-man commission the *Codex Vetus* (Old Code) was promulgated in 529; it brought together the law of the private compilations, the Theodosian Code and later imperial legislation. Then the scholars concerned themselves with the writings of the jurists; the result was the publication, over a four-year period, of the *Quinquaginta Decisiones* (Fifty Decisions) settling a number of points of dispute over the law of the jurists. These two tasks were largely preliminary to the main work; they are not included in the label *Corpus Juris Civilis.*

The *Corpus Juris* itself was prepared in a remarkably short time; the whole job took only four years. It was directed by Tribonian, the leading legal advisor to Justinian, and carried on by various committees of scholars and practicing lawyers. Three major works were produced: the Digest (or Pandects), the Institutes, and the Code; together, they formed the *Corpus Juris Civilis.*

That collection would have been about as difficult to use as could be imagined had it not included the Institutes, a school book founded on Gaius' *Institutes,* which sets out the elementary principles of the law in remarkably perspicuous order. But the Institutes form only between one thirtieth and one fortieth of the entire work and would assuredly not have made the fortune of Roman Law had they alone survived. The other portions are the Digest — the most important — which consists of extracts from the writings of the classical jurists, mainly of the second and third centuries A.D., and much altered by the compilers three hundred years later; the Codex, which is a collection of imperial enactments starting from about 120 A.D. but belonging mainly to the fourth, fifth, and sixth centuries; and the Novellae Constitutiones, or Novels, a string of Justinian's own enactments, which were afterwards added to the collection. The extracts from the classical jurists which form the Digest are almost all comments on the words of enactments or solutions of actual or hypothetical cases, supported at best by only so much reasoning as will connect them with other cases or with acknowledged principles of law. The Digest is, in fact, so far as its contents go, not at all unlike the digests of case law which are so familiar a feature of the Common Law on both sides of the Atlantic and of the Pacific. It is, however, not only casuistical in method, but extraordinarily ill-arranged. The titles, which are the main units, are in an order appropriate to a system of remedies existing in the classical period but hardly intelligible to the lawyers of Justinian's day, and not at all to those of the Middle Ages. It is very much as if we still arranged our legal encyclopedias according to the order of the old Register of Writs. Within each title, the order of the extracts gives little or no help to the student in search of his law. The imperial enactments in the Codex are anything but comparable to a modern code with its clear and complete enunciations of principle: they are for the most part decisions of cases, greatly inferior in quality to the opinions of jurists contained in the Digest, but otherwise hardly differing from them except that they rest on the authority of the emperor and not on conformity to a preexisting system of law. For practical purposes, their arrangement is perhaps even worse than that of the extracts in the Digest.

The Digest is the core of the *Corpus Juris,* and it is a world in itself. Of the same order of size as the Bible, it has meant different things to different ages, and is almost as inexhaustible.[12]

In the East, Justinian's legislation continued to be the principal source of law; theoretically it was *the* source, apart from later statutes, for Justinian forbade commentary on the Digest, except within closely defined limits, and repealed all legislation which had not been included in his *Corpus Juris.* In fact, the codification of Justinian survived the fall of Constantinople and the end of the Byzantine Empire in 1453.

---

4. The Desuetude of the Corpus Juris in Western Europe

In the West, however, the *Corpus Juris* was virtually buried for centuries after its promulgation. An exception was Italy, where the legislation of Justinian was introduced at the time of reconquest. Even in Italy, however, the Digest was not of great importance; such influence as the *Corpus Juris* had was limited to the Institutes, the Codes and the Novels.[13] When the Empire lost northern Italy again, the *Corpus Juris* faded from practical significance there. True, the West continued to be influenced by Roman law.

Yet the overall picture of Roman law in those centuries is one of progressive decay. The scanty literature of the period . . . shows us an increasing quantity of misconceptions, a complete lack of originality or ability to carry through doctrinal analysis, a further barbarization of institutions, and a greater mixture with elements of Germanic origin. However, from the standpoint of the historian of Roman law, the efforts of those centuries of decline are important, because they preserved the memory of, and respect for, Roman law until the revival of legal studies.[14]

Why did the Justinian legislation fail to make headway in the West? (The earlier Theodosian Code, for example, had been adopted into the Visigothic legislation, although it had been published after the Visigothic conquests.) The answer probably lies in the breakdown of communication between East and West which resulted from the Moslem occupation of Spain, the islands of the Mediterranean, and northern Africa. With the trade routes closed, other forms of East-West intercourse virtually

---

[12] F. Lawson, *A Common Lawyer Looks at the Civil Law* 10-12 (1953).

[13] See M. Cappelletti, J. Merryman, and J. Perillo, *The Italian Legal System* 11-12 (1967).

[14] H. Wolff, *supra* note 11, at 184-85.

ceased. Western society became provincial and agricultural. The need for a law of sales, for example, was much diminished; one seldom bought anything unless he had a bad year and could not feed his own.[15]

Still, legal learning did not die out altogether:

> It survived to some extent together with other remnants of ancient culture, more especially through the agency of the learned classes of those days — the clerical and monastic orders. The survivals in question, however, are not only slight and incoherent, but, as a rule, hopelessly mixed up with the attempt of the early Middle Ages to effect a kind of salvage of the general learning of antiquity. There are no definite traces of organized schools of law. What legal learning there is remains connected with exercises in grammar, rhetoric, and dialectics. A striking example of the kind of work carried on in the course of the seventh and eighth centuries is presented by the Etymologies or Origins of the Spanish Bishop, Isidor of Seville. It is an *Encyclopaedia* embracing all sorts of information collected from classical sources — on arts, medicine, Old and New Testament topics, ecclesiastical history, philosophy, and law. The legal sections comprise, firstly, generalizations on subdivisions of jurisprudence, on the aims and methods of law, on legislators and jurisconsults; and secondly, notices as to substantive law — on witnesses, on deeds, on the law of things, on crime and punishment, etc. All these matters are treated by excerpts from classical literature, from writings of jurisconsults, and from legal enactments. As is shown by the title, the author lays great stress on supposed etymologies for the explanation of institutions and rules. It is needless to say that the philological derivations compiled by him are sometimes fanciful in the extreme.[16]

The invading barbarian kings had earlier divided the land among their military chiefs, who had made further divisions among their followers; personal loyalties thus had been reinforced by mutual rights and obligations arising out of the resulting military-agrarian relationships. In feudal society, political power had become associated with land holdings. If a king wanted to expand his own power, he had to diminish that of the feudal lords. It was natural for him to turn to the merchants of the cities, who were happy to give him financial support in exchange for protection from the barons. The king's protection, in turn, encouraged trade. As trade expanded, so did cities and the power of kings. Thus it was that the need for a more sophisticated legal system coincided with an improvement in communication. By the end of the 11th century, the time was ripe for a revival of Roman law scholarship.

---

5. The Roman Law Revival

Bologna became a principal center of these studies. Students came from all over

---

[15] See A. Von Mehren, *The Civil Law System* 5 (1957).

[16] P. Vinogradoff, *Roman Law in Medieval Europe* 27-28 (1st ed. 1909).

Europe to study under teachers such as Irnerius, who made an examination of the text of a complete manuscript of Justinian's Digest, which had been discovered in Pisa. Irnerius and his followers concerned themselves with the text's "true" meaning and did not go beyond interpretation in this rather narrow sense. But even this limited task required them to harmonize apparent conflicts, and to state the more generalized legal principles that seemed to be the basis for the rather specific statements of the Digest. Their method for making comments was to make marginal notes — "glosses" — on the manuscripts which they examined, and they became known as the Glossators.

The Glossators focused their studies almost exclusively on the *Corpus Juris,* neglecting the blend of barbarized Roman and Germanic law then in force. There were basically two reasons for the Glossators' restrictive focus. First, the Glossators subscribed to the theory that the Holy Roman Empire of their time was the successor to the old Roman Empire; they therefore considered the *Corpus Juris* as the living law of the present-day Holy Roman Empire. As imperial legislation, it was backed by the authority of both the pope and the emperor, which made it far more important than any local legislation or custom. Second, the *Corpus Juris* was technically and intellectually much superior to the bastardized compilations that had been cranked out under the Germanic invaders. To these medieval academics Justinian's legislation was the only law worth studying, and study it they did — much as a Fundamentalist studies the Bible.

> By the end of the thirteenth century the method of the Glossators . . . had exhausted its purpose. The accumulation of glosses had suffocated the text, which was no longer studied directly, but only through its glosses. This state of affairs was ended by one of the great scholars, the Florentine Accursius (d. about 1260), who undertook to select the best of the glosses that his predecessors had produced. The task was enormous; the final selection amounted to about 96,000 glosses. Accursius' work had great success. It was called the *Glossa Ordinaria* or *Magna Glossa* and was regularly published with editions of the *Corpus Juris,* so that they were received together throughout the continent.[17]

By the latter half of the thirteenth century the Glossators had been displaced by a later group of scholars known as the Commentators, who were not content with literal exegesis of the texts of the *Corpus Juris.* Influenced by scholastic philosophy, this new school of legal scholars attempted to analyze legal problems systematically. In searching for the true rationale of a legal rule, they would go far beyond the literal techniques of interpretation of the Glossators. Instead of ignoring canon law and Italian statutory law, the Commentators sought to synthesize norms derived from these sources with the *Corpus Juris.* They began the scientific study of commercial and criminal law and concerned themselves with the development of case law. Best known of this school was Bartolus (1314-57), who commented upon all of the *Corpus Juris,* taught law at Pisa and Perugia, served as a jurisconsult, and wrote some 40 treatises on diverse subjects.

---

[17]M. Cappelletti et al., *supra* note 13, at 20.

During this period the study of canon law, a body of substantive and procedural rules developed by the Roman Catholic Church, became joined with the study of Roman law at Italian universities. "[T] he degree conferred on a student who had completed the full course of study was Juris Utriusque Doctor, or Doctor of Both Laws, referring to the civil law and the canon law. . . . Because the two were studied together . . ., there was a tendency for them to influence each other; and the canon law, as well as the Roman civil law, helped in the formation of the jus commune that was subsequently received by the European states."[18]

C. The Development of Spanish Law

The roots of Spanish law can be traced back to the customs of two tribes of early inhabitants of the Peninsula — the Celts and the Iberians. Both tribal groups were intruders; the Iberians appear to have crossed over from North Africa sometime prior to the sixth century B.C., while the Celts moved southward across the Pyrenees in the seventh and sixth centuries B.C. These ancient peoples gradually mixed with each other, and with the late-coming invaders — the Carthaginians, Romans, Visigoths, and Moors — to form the ethnic amalgam from which the modern Spaniard and Portuguese have developed.

Roman law first arrived about 250 B.C., when the Romans conquered the Peninsula. Though Roman law quickly dominated the area's public law, Celto-Iberian customary law continued to play a role, albeit minor, in the area's private law.

One is probably justified in assuming, in the absence of certainty, that as time went on, and partly too as a consequence of the judiciary applying Roman law, this law encroached to some considerable extent upon the sphere of Spanish native law. On the other hand, there is evidence of the continued vigour of native legal concepts at variance with those of Roman. . . . The impression remains that, during Spain's Roman period, Roman private law was the "official law," but that *de iure,* by the measure of its recognition of native law, and *de facto,* by the tenacity with which the population clung to its traditional usages, the importance of old customary law remained; "el hecho (the de facto law)," said Hinojosa, "se sobrepuso al derecho (superimposed itself on what was the official law)."[19]

In its tenacity, Roman law proved at least the equal of Celto-Iberian customary law. When, after some 650 years of Roman rule, Spain was invaded first by barbaric German tribes, and later by the more civilized Visigoths, a similar legal displacement did not occur.

---

[18] J. Merryman, *The Civil Law Tradition* 12 (1969).

[19] E. Van Kleffens, *Hispanic Law Until the End of the Middle Ages* 39-40 (1968).

1. The Visigothic Legislation

The Visigoths had encountered Roman law well before arriving in the Iberian Peninsula. The first known Visigothic codification, the Code of Euric (c. 475 A.D.), blended Gothic customary law with Roman law elements. Curiously, some thirty years later, Euric's son and successor, Alaric II, promulgated a new comprehensive code that set forth only pre-Justinian Roman law. The *Lex Romana Visigothorum,* also known as the Breviary of Alaric, was a crude and rather unsystematic restatement of Roman law dominated by excerpts from the Theodosian Code (promulgated by the Romans after the Visigothic conquest of Spain), sections of some of the Novels, an abridgment of the Institutes of Gaius, and other fragmented Roman sources. The Visigoths appear to have applied the principle of personal law, permitting the Hispano-Romans to live under the Roman law (as modified by custom) in all matters not prejudicial to the political supremacy of the conquerors. The Code of Euric and the Breviary of Alaric were in force simultaneously, with the former applying to the Visigoths and the latter to the Hispano-Romans.[20]

The law of Spain was thus divided: part corrupted Roman and part corrupted Gothic. The society was also divided between the Arian Visigoths and the Catholic Hispano-Romans. Intermarriage was prohibited. But such segregation was plainly an unsatisfactory way to run a kingdom. With the passage of time the two peoples drew closer. In the latter half of the sixth century, the Gothic king Leovigild (568-586) took a Catholic wife. His son Reckared (586-601) went even further. In 587, the year after assuming the throne, he converted to Catholicism. Unification of the nation became a prime royal concern, and part of the process was legal unification. King Chindasvinth (641-652) finally ended the dual legal system by abrogating the Breviary of Alaric and declaring that all his subjects should be governed by the same law. He sought to reconcile the interests of both peoples by compiling a new code that would blend Roman and Gothic law. The work was not published until 654, in the reign of Chindasvinth's son, Reckesvinth (652-672). Initially called the *Liber Judicorum,* this comprehensive compilation underwent frequent revision until 694, when it was promulgated in its final form. The code has since become known as the *Fuero Juzgo,* a corruption of the Latin *Forum Judicum,* and has displayed truly remarkable longevity.

The *Fuero Juzgo* drew heavily on Roman law, particularly with regard to inheritance, contracts, and prescription. But it specifically rejected the validity of any Roman law (or that of any foreign nation) not expressly stated in its text. Legislative lacunae were to be plugged by royal edicts. The *Fuero Juzgo* also drew upon ancient Gothic custom, acts of ecclesiastical councils, and assorted edicts of the Visigothic kings. It is superficially divided into 12 books, with 54 titles, subdivided into some 578 laws. "But the division has little practical significance, for the books as a whole are not arranged in a logical order nor are all related subjects treated in the same book.

---

[20] Altamira, "Spain," in *Assoc. of American Law Schools, A General Survey of Events, Sources, Persons and Movements in Continental Legal History* 579, 596 (1912). However, this theory has recently come under attack by several Spanish legal historians who maintain that both codes had territorial rather than personal application. See E. Van Kleffens, *supra* note 19, at 67-69.

In fact a plunge into the body of the work too often reveals a jumble of heterogeneous provisions occasionally interspersed with homilies and dissertations on legal policy."[21] The *Fuero Juzgo* is filled with paradox. Great pains are taken to inculcate enlightened ideals of justice, honesty, and freedom, and to soften some of the harsher aspects of the Roman laws, such as treatment of debtors. Yet the code abounds with savage punishments, tortures, and superstitions, and foreshadows the Inquisition in its religious intolerance. Nevertheless, the *Fuero Juzgo* continued in force as a supplemental source of Spanish law until 1889, when Spain finally adopted a Civil Code.

2. The Moorish Invasion

Very likely the reason the *Fuero Juzgo* reached "final" form at the end of the 7th Century was that there was no chance to revise it; Spain was overrun by the Moors soon thereafter. An exploratory invasion in 710 met so little resistance that the Moors planned a much larger one. A full-scale invasion began the next year and culminated in a battle in which 90,000 Goths were routed by a Moorish force one-fourth that size. The Moors stayed nearly 800 years.

The tenacity of Roman law was again demonstrated. The Moors applied their own law to their own people, but retained the old law — principally the *Fuero Juzgo* — for the Roman-Gothic population. The only substantive contribution of Islamic law which survived the expulsion of the Moors related to matters such as water and agrarian rights. The principal influence of the long Moorish occupation on Spanish law was the shattering of national unity attained at the close of the Gothic period. There was no Spain during this time, except as a geographic description; rather there was a multiplicity of small kingdoms and countries — all but a few subject to varying degrees of Moorish control — each with its own legislative jurisdiction.

3. The Reconquest

The Reconquest, which began in the latter half of the eighth century, was a period of great legal diversity. Starting almost on the heels of the Moors' conquest, and continuing for nearly the next eight hundred years, the Reconquest might be considered a more or less permanent state of near-war. It produced considerable legal diversity largely because of three factors: (a) the splintering of the reconquered territory into separate kingdoms, (b) the persistence of customary law, and (c) the practice of granting special privileges and jurisdictions.

[21] Lobingier, "The Forum Judicum (Fuero Juzgo)," 8 *Ill. L. Rev.* 1, 4-5 (1913).

(a) The Rise of Separate Christian Kingdoms

About 718 a small band of Visigoths, headed by Pelayo, withdrew to the Asturian mountains and set up a separate kingdom called Asturias. Beginning as a guerrilla resistance movement, the Asturians gradually grew in number and territory. By the early part of the tenth century, they had retaken sufficient land from the Moors to remove their kingdom's capital from the mountains to León. But as the Moors were pushed progressively southward, Christian Spain began to fragment into independent kingdoms. Catalonia, liberated by the Franks in the early part of the ninth century, declared its independence towards the close of that century. At his death in 910, Alfonso the Great (not to be confused with Alfonso the Wise, who ruled León and Castile in the 13th century) subdivided the Asturian kingdom for his sons: one received the parent kingdom of Asturias, the second León, and the third Galicia and northern Lusitania. In 1035 Aragón seceded from the ancient kingdom of Navarre; soon after, Castile separated from León. Political centrifugalism contributed to legal pluralism, for each king had his own concept of what should be decreed.

(b) The Persistence of Customary Law

A second important source of legal diversity was regional customary law. Despite the powerful centralizing forces unleashed by the Romans and the Visigoths, much of the ancient Celto-Iberian custom persisted. With the eclipse of a strong central government, the tendency to prefer custom to the formal Visigothic code was accentuated. An important reason for Castilian secession from León was the desire to substitute customary law for the *Fuero Juzgo,* then in force in León. After secession the Castilians decided to burn all copies of the *Fuero Juzgo,* which would have permitted appeals to the king of León from decisions of Castilian courts. The Castilian judges were instructed to decide cases submitted to them *ex aequo et bono.* Eventually, a crude and unsatisfactory system of precedents called *fazañas* developed.[22]

(c) Special Privileges and Jurisdictions

A third important source of legal diversity was the royal practice of granting special legal privileges to the multiplicity of corporate estates that constituted medieval Spanish society. Societal groups such as the nobility, military, clergy, university community, merchants, and various other guilds were generally exempted from the ordinary jurisdiction of the king's courts and largely governed by their own special systems of laws and courts, known as *fueros.* "Such privileged *fueros* or jurisdictions were the juridical expression of a society in which the state was regarded not as a community of citizens enjoying equal rights and responsibilities, but as a structure built of classes and corporations, each with a unique and peculiar function to perform."[23]

---

[22] See E. Van Kleffens, *supra* note 19, at 114-35.

[23] L. McAllister, *The "Fuero Militar" in New Spain* 5 (1957). See also, Wiarda, "Law and

Special legal privileges, embodied in municipal charters, also called *fueros*, were customarily granted to municipalities, particularly when freed from Moorish control. These were contractual in nature and varied widely. They generally set forth detailed rules and privileges for self-governance of the locale, often codifying local customs. They tended to restrict the king's arbitrary exercise of power by such measures as tax exemptions or basic guarantees of due process in criminal cases. The *fueros* of some cities, such as Toledo, were liberal and lengthy, virtually setting down a code of private law specifically to govern residents of that particular city. Both types of *fuero* were jealously guarded.

... [E]ven in cases where the succession did not involve any difficulty, the hereditary princes of the Peninsula's various States became kings with full powers only after having taken an oath to respect the *fueros*. In Spanish law, the oath created the power, and violation of the *fuero* effectively freed the subjects of their duty to obey. When a sovereign violated the *fuero* revolt almost always ensued, and sometimes the prince who had thus broken his convenant with his people was dethroned. At the end of the thirteenth century, the nobility and communes of Aragón tried to institutionalize this practice by compelling King Alfonso I to countersign a document which granted the Cortes [legislative assemblies in which the towns, cities, clergy, and nobility were represented] the right to depose a sovereign in the event of violation of the *fuero*. This charter was nullified in 1248, after a long period of upheaval, by an energetic and authoritarian monarch, Peter IV. The Basques of Vizcaya, on the other hand, succeeded in deposing their sovereign, King Henry IV of Castile, who had tried to force them to pay a tax for which the *fueros* did not provide.[24]

In addition to the special grants of jurisdiction embodied in the *fueros*, the Spanish kings, like other Western European sovereigns, made numerous feudal grants and donations of territory to their followers in return for service and tribute. The conditions of these grants varied widely, but they typically bestowed the right to exercise jurisdiction over the inhabitants of the granted lands. One form of grant widely used during the Reconquest to reward the military was the *encomienda*, which, in modified form, was transplanted to the New World and imposed on the Indians.[25]

The encomienda consisted in the temporary grant by the sovereign of territory, cities, towns, castles, and monasteries, with powers of government and the right to receive the revenues, or a stipulated part thereof, and the services owed to the Crown by the people of the areas concerned under fuero and custom. The grant was given for the lifetime of the recipient, for that of the sovereign, or at the will of the latter. In its jurisdictional aspect the encomienda was a charge of government, the comendador, or encomendero (*comer.dero*), exercising the authority of the Crown in the area involved.... The comendador, or

---

Political Development in Latin America: Toward a Framework for Analysis," 19 *Am. J. Comp. L.* 434, 439 (1971).

[24] E. Souchère, *An Explanation of Spain* 41-42 (1st Vintage ed. 1965).

[25] The tenurial implications of the *encomienda* are explored in Chapter III, *infra*.

encomendero, possessed no power to change the status of the people of the lands assigned, nor to alter the established tributes and services.[26]

The widespread use of the *encomienda* and similar institutions by which jurisdictional authority over the inhabitants of a region were subcontracted further accentuated the diversity of Spanish law.

(d) Alfonso the Wise and the Siete Partidas

A forceful reaction against this excessive legal diversity occurred during the reign of Alfonso X, known as *El Sabio* (the Wise), who ascended the throne of León and Castile in 1252. The fragmentation of Spanish law constituted a serious obstacle to the unity of his kingdom and to royal power. The Castilian nobility was virtually, although not theoretically, sovereign in many areas. Their broad privileges and rights had been confirmed in the 11th century in the *Fuero Viejo de Castilla* and in the following century by the *Fuero de Najera.* The cities and clerical orders were governed independently through their own *fueros.* The Jews, Mudéjars (Mohammedan residents of reoccupied lands), and Mozarabs (Spanish Christians living on lands occupied by the Moors) were governed by special rules. Such kingdom-wide legislation as there was dealt primarily with feudal relations, although there had been abortive attempts to codify private law.

Alfonso the Wise began the task of unification by continuing the practice instituted by his father, Ferdinand III, of granting the old *Fuero Juzgo* to newly liberated cities in place of the usual, custom-tailored *fueros.* But he soon decided that an updating was in order. In 1255 he promulgated the *Fuero Real* (Royal Code), a compilation of the existing laws and customs of Spain, and began granting it *in toto* in newly liberated communities as their *fuero.* The *Fuero Real* borrowed heavily from the Visigothic *Fuero Juzgo* and several of the Castilian municipal *fueros,* but it also introduced new elements borrowed directly from Roman law. Its importance has been far overshadowed by the *magnum opus* of Alfonso the Wise, the *Siete Partidas,* the first important compilation written in Spanish instead of the traditional Latin.

The *Siete Partidas* is one of the most influential documents of Iberian legal history. The Code takes its name from its septempartite division. Each part begins with one of the letters of Alfonso's name, making the document one of the world's most famous legislative acrostics. The *Siete Partidas* abound in homilies and much that is unrelated to what we now consider the business of codes, *i.e.,* rules of chivalry (how to dress a knight, how a knight should choose a horse, the knight's diet in peace and war) or how to play the role of king (a king should walk erect; eat and drink temperately at a proper time; not walk aimlessly or rapidly; choose a wife who is from good lineage, beautiful, rich and with good habits).[27] As Professor Morse has observed, "Though tinctured with Roman law, the *Partidas* were less Roman rules *for* conduct than medieval-type principles *of* conduct that approached being moral treatises."[28]

---

[26] Chamberlain, "Castilian Backgrounds of the Repartimiento-Encomienda," in *Carnegie Institution, 5 Contributions to American Anthropology and History* 21, 35 (No. 25, 1939).

[27] See Nichols, "Las Siete Partidas," 20 *Calif. L. Rev.* 260, 266-70 (1932); Lobingier, "Las Siete Partidas and its Predecessors," 1 *Calif. L. Rev.* 487 (1913).

[28] "Toward a Theory of Spanish American Government," 15 *J. History of Ideas* 71, 72 (1954).

The *Siete Partidas* represent a compromise between Hispano-Gothic and Roman sources, between codified custom and *ratio scripta* (written reason), between feudalism and the rising nation-state. But the balance struck was decidedly weighted in favor of Roman sources, *ratio scripta*, and the rising nation-state. Canon law (particularly in the area of procedure), the opinions of the Glossators and ecclesiastical writers, and a few of the municipal *fueros* constituted important sources, but heaviest borrowing was from the *Corpus Juris* of Justinian. Indeed the Third Partida, which deals with procedure and property, and the Fifth Partida, which deals with obligations and maritime law, were translated nearly verbatim from the *Corpus Juris.*

At the time of the drafting of the *Siete Partidas,* study of the Roman law of Justinian was much in vogue among European legal scholars. Many a Spanish student trundled off to study the recently discovered Roman law at Bologna and came back to teach or practice in his homeland. The diffusion of Roman and canon law concepts was greatly aided by the establishment of Spain's oldest university at Palencia early in the 13th century (removed to Salamanca in 1239). But one of the primary reasons for Alfonso's decided shift from traditional Hispano-Gothic sources to the *Corpus Juris* was surely the opportunity to utilize the technically superior Roman law as a vehicle for unification of Spain's excessively diverse legal structure. Another was to expand royal power by attempting to equate the position of the king as lawmaker with that of the Roman emperor. However, the unifying force of a single common law and expansion of royal power represented serious threats to the nobility, already aroused by Alfonso's precipitous abrogation of the *fueros* in 1254. (A revolt eventually restored these *fueros.*) The alien law of the *Siete Partidas* was also resented by the towns, which were concerned about the *Partidas'* variance with the *fueros* and local custom. Resistance by the nobility and the towns was so strong that Alfonso was never able to promulgate the *Partidas* with the force of law for his kingdom. Not until 1348, in the *Ordenamiento de Alcalá,* were the *Siete Partidas* given the force of law, and then only in a subsidiary fashion. Nevertheless, even in its unofficial capacity, the *Siete Partidas* exerted tremendous doctrinal influence on the courts, jurists and law students (frequently serving as a text).

(e) Canon Law

Even before the Visigothic invasion, the bishops of the Peninsula had begun holding ecclesiastical councils at important cities, frequently at Toledo. Initially, these councils were concerned only with spiritual matters. But after the reign of Reckared, the clergy was permitted to meddle in affairs of state. Visigothic rulers from time to time promulgated canons adopted by the councils, thereby enacting them into law.[29] Nearly 100 of these canons were enshrined in Gratian's *Decretum* (sometimes called *The Concordance of Discordant Canons*), the great medieval collection of canon law compiled in the middle of the 12th century.

---

[29] See C. Walton, *The Civil Law in Spain and Spanish America* 48-50 (1900).

Revival of an interest in Roman law in the 11th century coincided with revival of the influence of canon law, which was itself heavily Romanized. By the 12th and 13th centuries many of the institutions of Spanish law, such as marriage and the family, usury, and certain kinds of rents and contracts were governed by canon law.[30] The *Siete Partidas* expressly acknowledged the jurisdiction of the ecclesiastical courts in matters of church affairs, tithes, suits against the clergy, matrimony, legitimacy of children, executors of wills, adultery, perjury, and heresy.

(f) The Ordenamiento de Alcalá

By the middle of the 14th century when the *Ordenamiento de Alcalá* was promulgated for Castile and León by Alfonso XI, the great grandson of Alfonso the Wise, times had changed sufficiently to permit a new balance between Roman and traditional Hispano-Gothic law. Alfonso XI realistically recognized the strength of his people's attachment to traditional law, especially the cherished *fueros*. Instead of attempting to abolish the old rules and to impose Roman law principles directly, he adopted a compromise technique that has shaped the format of Spanish law until well into the 19th century (and which continues to the present day for parts of Spain) — the rank-ordering of sets of juridical norms. This compromise is set out below, and conveys some of the flavor of medieval Iberian legislation. In reading it, note who has the final word on questions of interpretation.

THE ORDENAMIENTO DE ALCALA, TITLE 28, LAW 1

It is our intention and desire that those born and living in our kingdoms remain in peace and in justice; since to that end it is necessary to give unequivocal laws in light of which lawsuits are to be decided in the disputes arising amongst them, and although in our own tribunal the *Fuero Real* is in use, and some townships under our authority have it as their *fuero*, while other cities and townships have various other *fueros* which enable them to decide only part of the lawsuits; but because there are many disputes and lawsuits, arising among men and current every day, which cannot be decided in the light of the *fueros;* therefore, wishing to remedy this situation as may be appropriate, we decree and command that the said *fueros* be kept in force as to the matters regarding which they were in actual use; except as we may find that they must be amended and improved, or as they may be against God and reason, or against the laws contained in this our book: by which laws of this our book we command that all civil and criminal proceedings be determined as a matter of priority. And we command that the proceedings and disputes which cannot be determined by the laws of this our book, or by the said *fueros,* be decided by the laws of the *Siete Partidas* which King Alfonso our great-grandfather ordered to be put in proper order, since hitherto they

---

[30] Altamira, *supra* note 20, at 634-36.

were neither promulgated by the King's command, nor in force and acknowledged as law. At the same time we command that they be examined and adjusted and amended in such aspects as seems advisable; and, thus adjusted and amended, we grant them as our laws, because they were derived and taken from the pronouncements of the Holy Fathers, and from the legal pronouncements of many scholars of olden times, and from *fueros* and ancient Spanish custom. And so that they may be unequivocal and that there be no reason to delete or change anything in them at will, we command that there be made two copies, one sealed with our seal in gold, the other with our seal in lead, to be kept in our chamber, so that on doubtful points you may resolve any discrepancy. And we wish them to be kept in force and validity from now on in the lawsuits and in the judgments of the courts and in all other matters dealt with in them, insofar as they are not contrary to the laws of this our book and to the aforesaid *fueros*. And since the members of the nobility of our kingdoms have in some districts the *fuero de albedrío* and other *fueros* by which they and their vassals are to be judged, we wish these *fueros* to be kept in force for them and their vassals, according to whatever *fuero* they possess, and in so far as it was in force for them previously. And furthermore, in matters of *riepto* [a special judicial action brought to redress insults among upper class equals], that usage or custom be kept in force which was observed and enforced in the days of the other Kings and in our own. And furthermore, we wish the *Ordenamiento* which we now make in these Cortes for the members of the nobility to be enforced, and this we wish to be put at the end of this our book. And because it is for the King, and because he has the authority, to give *fueros* and laws, and to interpret them and to explain and amend where he finds reason to do so, we decree that if in the said *fueros,* or in the book of the *Partidas,* or in this our book, or in one or more laws contained therein there is need of explanation or interpretation, or of amendment or addition or deletion or alteration, it should be done by us; and if any contradiction should become apparent in the aforesaid laws *inter se,* or in the *fueros,* or in any one of them, or if any doubtful point should be found in them, or any fact because of which no decision based on them can be taken, that we be notified thereof, in order that we may give an interpretation and decision or an amendment as we may deem appropriate, or give a new law as we may deem appropriate for the case concerned, so that justice and law be safeguarded. Yet, we desire and allow that the lawbooks written by the ancient scholars be read in the universities of our realm, for there is great wisdom in them, and we wish to promote the learning of our nationals, and that they be all the more honoured for it.

The *fueros* were sufficiently omissive that the Roman law principles of the *Siete Partidas* frequently became the basis for judicial decision. This tendency to apply Roman law was reinforced by legal professionals, whose training was primarily in Roman law principles. Indeed, until the 18th century the study of law in Spanish universities consisted entirely of Roman and canon law.[31]

The technique of the *Ordenamiento de Alcalá* became characteristic of both Spain and Portugal. Instead of abrogating old and obsolete texts, the Spanish and Portuguese

---

[31] M. Cappelletti et al., *supra* note 13, at 32.

issued recompilations. These attempted to bring some kind of order out of the chaos of accumulated legislation and decrees and to declare priorities in case of conflicts. Thus, legal research for the judge or lawyer involved searching through the various collections of laws in force, starting with the top of the hierarchy and working down until a rule might be found that fit the particular case.

D. The Development of Portuguese Law

The early history of Portuguese law is virtually indistinguishable from that of Spanish law. When Portugal achieved her independence in 1143 by separating from the Spanish kingdom of León and Castile, the *Fuero Juzgo* and the canons adopted by the various church councils remained in force as the new nation's general law.[32] Gradually the *Fuero Juzgo* fell into disuse, being displaced by local custom, *foraes* (the Portuguese version of *fueros*) and canon law, which came to be applied by civil as well as ecclesiastical tribunals in certain cases. Beginning in 1211 under King Alfonso II, the Portuguese monarchy promulgated general laws which modified and limited certain of the privileges of the clergy and nobility. As in Spain, the crown promoted legal unification to consolidate its power, and Roman law became a crucial instrument in this struggle. King Diniz (1279-1325) had the *Siete Partidas* translated into Portuguese and adopted as subsidiary legislation. He also ordered that the new university, founded in 1291 in Lisbon, teach courses in Roman law.[33]

Since Portuguese legislation and custom left large gaps, Roman law, as embodied in the *Siete Partidas* and the *Corpus Juris,* quickly became the basis of decision in the majority of cases before the Portuguese courts. The influx of Roman law was accentuated during the reign of King João I, who enacted by decree a large extract of the Justinian Code, complete with glosses of Accursius and the commentaries of Bartolus.[34]

By the 15th century Portuguese law was in a most confusing state. The plethora of sources of law, some of which were quite inaccessible, produced much uncertainty. Despite several abortive attempts, the first successful compilation of Portuguese law was not published until 1446. It was called the *Ordenações Afonsinas* and drew on a great many sources, including the general legislation of Portuguese kings since 1248, the resolutions of the Côrtes (parlimentary-like assemblies representing the clergy, nobility, and townspeople) sanctioned by the monarchy, customs, *foraes, façanhas* (the Portuguese equivalent of *fazañas*), opinions of various jurisconsults, and the *estilos* (procedural rules established by the *Casa de Suplicação,* a high court in Lisbon). But by far the most important sources were the *Siete Partidas,* canon law, and the

---

[32] J. Martins, Junior, *História do Direito Nacional* 74-75 (1895).

[33] *Id.* at 89-90.

[34] C. Tripoli, I *História do Direito Brasileiro* 64 (1936); Leme, "O Direito na Península Ibérica," 53 *Rev. Fac. Dir. São Paulo* 74, 79 (1958).

Corpus Juris, supplemented by the glosses of Accursius and the commentaries of Bartolus. Matters on which the statutes and supplementary legislation or interpretation were silent were to be referred to the king. In 1521 this compilation was revised, principally as to style and to include intervening legislation, by the *Ordenações Manuelinas,* which was in turn revised in 1603 by the *Ordenações Filipinas,* discussed *infra* at p. 36. These compilations were all based on the theory that Roman law, as distilled by the glossators and commentators, constituted the common law of the Portuguese kingdom.[35]

E. The Dualism of the Iberian Roman Law Heritage

Roman law was originally steeped in custom and experience, and displayed remarkable flexibility and adaptability. It "was a vital legal order which grew and developed as Rome herself grew and developed from a small agricultural community in central Italy to be the centre of a vast empire with a complex commercial economy and a multi-racial population."[36] However, by the time of the late Empire, Roman law had begun to be divorced from socio-economic reality and to take on an idealistic and rigid character. Much that Justinian had preserved in the *Corpus Juris* had had little relevance even for the Rome of his time. The revival of Roman law in the 11th century was based upon a slavish study of the texts of *Corpus Juris,* which had even less relevance to the Hispano-Gothic people upon whom it was imposed.

Thus, Spain and Portugal have a dual Roman law heritage. There was the living Roman law inherited from the six centuries of Roman occupation, in time modified by custom and Gothic superimpositions. This aspect of Roman law found its expression in the old *Fuero Juzgo* and the *Fuero Real.* There was also the idealized Roman law, culled by academicians from the texts of Justinian's *Corpus Juris.* It was this second aspect of Roman law that the Spanish and Portuguese kings found highly useful in their struggle to unify diverse legal systems and to expand their sovereign powers. This pattern of dualism — law as an ideal v. law as a practical system for ordering affairs — persists in Latin America today. We return to and further develop this theme in part K of this chapter.

F. The Fusion of Law and Religion

The idealism and unreality of Iberian law were accentuated by the manner in which law and religion were fused in the Peninsula. The Spanish and Portuguese monarchs were the beneficiaries of the "divine right of kings" theory of sovereignty, which had

---

[35]See generally Davidson, "The Brazilian Inheritance of Roman Law," in J. Watson (ed.) *Four Papers Presented in the Institute for Brazilian Studies Vanderbilt University* (1953).

[36]Thomas, "Roman Law," in J. Derrett (ed.) *An Introduction to Legal Systems* 1-2 (1968).

developed during the Middle Ages. In the Peninsula, as in the rest of Europe, the theory operated to strengthen royal power. Since the king was God's representative on earth, disobedience to royal command became sinful as well as unlawful. Obedience to the king as well as the church was a concept inculcated by a loyal clergy. Iberian colonial rule, therefore, was the product of an absolute monarchy, with "the King as its head, chief, father, representative of God on earth, supreme dispenser of all favors, and rightful regulator of all activities, even to all the personal and individual expressions of his subjects and vassals."[37] ". . . [T] he Christian monarch claimed total control in the name of God and the pursuit of justice. In the performance of the royal *officium,* he relied upon Christian dogma and his sense of equity. His duty was to promote the common good which, once translated into Christian terms, meant the salvation of the soul."[38]

Iberian political thought has long conceived of the primary purpose of government as the dispensation of justice on earth. The concept of owing allegiance to an abstract state has found Iberian soil infertile. Instead, the Iberian regarded the state as "a federal unity of the diverse yet interconnected interests of men, directed and held together by the sovereign who was to be the arbiter to resolve their conflicts and the dispenser of justice which should define the order in which they were to function. . . ."[39] This theory of the state was transmitted intact to the colonies.

Law, religion, and force of arms served as the bases for the Spanish and Portuguese conquests. Royal councils were continually concerned with the legal validity of claims to the Indies, the morality of waging war against relatively defenseless Indians, and the religious obligation to Christianize the infidels. Legal rationale for dominion over the Indies was based upon the bulls of Pope Alexander VI between May and September of 1492. But the monarchs of Castile and Portugal were plainly troubled by the morality and legality of the slaughter of thousands of hapless aborigines. Balm was applied to Christian consciences by requiring every *conquistador* to read a *Requerimiento* or proclamation through a notary and an interpreter as a condition precedent to the lawful commencement of hostilities or the taking of Indian territory. The text conveys some of the flavor of the Iberian blending of religion and legalism. Imagine the befuddlement of any Indian who might actually hear this proclamation.

REQUERIMIENTO (c. 1512)*

On the part of the King, Don Ferdinand, and of Doña Juana, his daughter, queen of Castile and León, subduers of the barbarous nations, we their servants notify and

---

[37] C. Prado Junior, *Formação do Brasil Contemporâneo* 297 (1942).

[38] F. Moreno, *Legitimacy and Stability in Latin America: A Study of Chilean Political Culture* 18-19 (1969).

[39] M. Madden, *Political Theory and Law in Medieval Spain* 14 (1930).

*Translation of Sir Arthur Helps, *The Spanish Conquest in America and Its Relation to the History of Slavery and to the Government of Colonies* 264-67 (Vol. 1, 1900) as adapted in C. Gibson, *The Spanish Tradition in America* 58-60 (1968).

make known to you, as best we can, that the Lord our God, living and eternal, created the heaven and the earth, and one man and one woman, of whom you and we, and all the men of the world, were and are descendants, as well as all those who come after us. But on account of the multitude which has sprung from this man and woman in five thousand years since the world was created, it was necessary that some men should go one way and some another, and that they should be divided into many kingdoms and provinces, for in one alone they could not be sustained.

Of all these nations God our lord gave charge to one man called St. Peter, that he should be lord and superior to all the men in the world, that all should obey him, and that he should be the head of the whole human race, wherever men should live, and under whatever law, sect, or belief they should be; and he gave him the world for his kingdom and jurisdiction.

And he commanded him to place his seat in Rome, as the spot most fitting to rule the world from; but also he permitted him to have his seat in any other part of the world, and to judge and govern all Christians, Moors, Jews, Gentiles, and all other sects. This man was called Pope, as if to say Admirable Great Father and Governor of men. The men who lived in that time obeyed that St. Peter and took him for lord, king, and superior of the universe. So also they have regarded the others who after him have been elected to the pontificate, and so has it been continued even till now, and will continue till the end of the world.

One of these pontiffs, who succeeded that St. Peter as lord of the world, in the dignity and seat which I have before mentioned, made donation of these islands and mainland to the aforesaid king and queen and to their successors, our lords, with all that there are in these territories, as is contained in certain writings which passed upon the subject as aforesaid, which you can see if you wish.

So their highnesses are kings and lords of these islands and mainland by virtue of this donation; and some islands, and indeed almost all of those to whom this has been notified, have received and served their highnesses, as lords and kings, in the way that subjects ought to do, with good will, without any resistance, immediately, without delay, when they were informed of the aforesaid facts. And also they received and obeyed the priests whom their highnesses sent to preach to them and to teach them our holy faith; and all these, of their own free will, without any reward or condition have become Christians, and are so, and the highnesses have joyfully and graciously received them, and they have also commanded them to be treated as their subjects and vassals; and you too are held and obliged to do the same. Wherefore, as best we can, we ask and require that you consider what we have said to you, and that you take the time that shall be necessary to understand and deliberate upon it, and that you acknowledge the Church as the ruler and superior of the whole world, and the high priest called Pope, and in his name the king and queen Doña Juana our lords, in his place, as superiors and lords and kings of these islands and this mainland by virtue of the said donation, and that you consent and permit that these religious fathers declare and preach to you the aforesaid.

If you do so you will do well, and that which you are obliged to do to their highnesses, and we in their name shall receive you in all love and charity, and shall leave you your wives and your children and your lands free without servitude, that you may do with them and with yourselves freely what you like and think best, and they shall not compel you to turn Christians unless you yourselves, when informed of the truth, should wish to be converted to our holy Catholic faith, as almost all the inhabitants of the rest of the islands have done. And besides this, their highnesses award you many privileges and exemptions and will grant you many benefits.

But if you do not do this or if you maliciously delay in doing it, I certify to you that with the help of God we shall forcefully enter into your country and shall make war against you in all ways and manners that we can, and shall subject you to the yoke and obedience of the Church and of their highnesses; we shall take you and your wives and your children and shall make slaves of them, and as such shall sell and dispose of them as their highnesses may command; and we shall take away your goods and shall do to you all the harm and damage that we can, as to vassals who do not obey and refuse to receive their lord and resist and contradict him; and we protest that the deaths and losses which shall accrue from this are your fault, and not that of their highnesses, or ours, or of these soldiers who come with us. And that we have said this to you and made this Requerimiento we request the notary here present to give us his testimony in writing, and we ask the rest who are present that they should be witnesses of this Requerimiento.

The three centuries of colonial rule produced a seemingly endless procession of laws attempting to secure better treatment for the Indians. But attempts to enforce these laws failed miserably, for they flew in the face of the realities of colonial power and economics.

G. The Laws of the New World Colonies

The discovery and settlement of the New World coincided with the development of an absolute, patrimonial[40] monarchy in Castile and substantive unification of Spain. The dynastic marriage of Ferdinand and Isabella in 1469 had united Spain's principal kingdoms, Aragón and Castile. The year 1492 significantly saw the first voyage of Columbus, the expulsion of the Jews, and the Battle of Granada, which finally expelled the Moors from Spanish soil. But royal power in the latter part of the 15th century was far from absolute. The foral rights (rights under *fueros*) of the aristocracy, church, municipalities, and other estates severely limited the king's prerogatives. So did the powers of the *Cortes.* Together Isabella and Ferdinand strove energetically to establish undisputed royal supremacy. Though never completely successful in Spain, they did succeed in the colonies, where no traditional institutions existed to curb the royal will.

The first expedition of Columbus was authorized and financed as a venture of Queen Isabella, and the profits of the venture accrued to her and her heirs as the

---

[40]Patrimonialism is a type of traditional authority in which the administration and the military

sovereigns of Castile. And from the outset the Indies were treated as the direct and exclusive possession of the crown.... The king possessed not only the sovereign rights but the property rights; he was the absolute proprietor, the sole political head, of his American dominions. Every privilege and position, economic, political, or religious, came from him. It was on this basis that the conquest, occupation and government of the New World were achieved.[41]

---

1. Spanish Legislation

Eventually, the Spanish monarchs enacted a sizeable body of special law to govern their new provinces. But underlying the special legislation was always the law of Spain itself, heavily Romanized, and increasingly unified (though never completely unified, even today). The pattern of royal encouragement of codification in order to achieve unification appears over and over in Spain, as elsewhere in continental Europe. In 1567 the *Nueva Recopilación de las Leyes de España* (New Recompilation of the Laws of Spain) was published; it was badly organized, and made no effort to do more than gather together the most important laws, leaving earlier compilations in force. Despite its defects, the compilation was retained, going through ten editions over the next 110 years.

An idea of the difficulties of legal research can be gleaned from Law No. 2, title 1, book II of the *Recopilación,* which provided:

> We ordain and command that in all cases ... which have not been decided, and which are not covered by the laws of this *Recopilación,* or by *cédulas,* provisions, and ordinances which have been promulgated for the Indies and remain unrevoked, ... shall be governed by the laws of our kingdom of Castile in accordance with the Laws of Toro....

The Laws of Toro consisted of 83 laws promulgated in 1505. The first of these laws reproduced the *Ordenamiento de Alcalá* in modified form, filling certain lacunae. The remainder of the provisions dealt with succession, marriage, prescription, contracts, and criminal law. Thus, to determine the applicable law, one had to sift through a mass of unindexed royal letters and ordinances, the Laws of Toro, the *Ordenamiento de Alcalá,* the municipal *fueros,* the *Fuero Real* (to the extent that one could prove it was in use), the *Fuero Juzgo,* and the *Siete Partidas.* In 1805 another attempt at compilation was published, this time called the *Novísima Recopilación de las Leyes de España* (Newest Recompilation of the Laws of Spain). This "Newest Recompilation" was, if anything, less satisfactory than its predecessor.

---

are purely personal instruments of the ruler. M. Weber, 1 *Economy and Society* 231 (G. Roth & C. Wittich eds. 1968). For the application of Weberian analysis to Latin America, see M. Sarfatti, *Spanish Bureaucratic-Patrimonialism in America* (1966).

[41] C. Haring, *The Spanish Empire in America* 5 (Harbinger edition 1963).

The need for gathering together the laws, orders, and administrative authorities governing the colonies was acute from the very beginning of colonial rule. No such compilation appeared, however, for nearly 200 years after discovery. By then legislative confusion had assumed chaotic proportions. Finally, after a number of unsuccessful attempts, there appeared in 1680 the *Recopilación de Leyes de los Reynos de Indias* (Compilation of the Laws of the Kingdoms of the Indies). This was not a code of private law; it was a distillation of about 400,000 royal *cédulas* (regulations issued from the home authorities to the colonial viceroys, letters to individual ministers ˙or churchmen, and the like), into approximately 6,400 items. While this effort alleviated the legislative confusion for a time, it was soon rendered obsolete by the steady outpouring of new laws and regulations.

Thus, determining the validity of any legal transaction during colonial times was a formidable undertaking. Transactions prior to 1505 were governed by the hierarchy of sources established in the *Ordenamiento de Alcalá*. For those occurring between 1505 and 1567, a lawyer had to refer first to the Laws of Toro and then to the hierarchy of the *Ordenamiento de Alcalá*. For those occurring between 1567 and 1805, the *Nueva Recopilación* was the primary reference, followed by the Laws of Toro and the rest of the hierarchy. After 1805, the primary source became the *Novísima Recopilación*. But the matter was even more complicated for the lawyer or judge in the New World, for he first had to consider whether the law of the case was governed by a precept in the special legislation of the Indies. He also had to consider whether a provision of Castillian law which appeared to govern the situation could be applied in the New World, for Law 40, Title 1, Book II, of the *Recopilación* of 1680 provided that no Spanish ordinance should apply in the colonies unless specifically made applicable by royal *cédula* and transmitted by the Council of the Indies.[42]

---

2. Portuguese Legislation

The Spanish New World does not, of course, include Brazil, which was settled by the Portuguese after some high-level politicking. In 1454, Pope˙ Nicholas V had conferred on Portugal the exclusive right to explore the only known route to the Indies, around the Cape of Good Hope. Columbus, seeking an alternate route for Spain, remained convinced that he had reached the Indies – Asia – until he died. When his "new route to Asia" was discovered, Spain claimed the right to exclusive exploration of that route. Pope Alexander VI agreed, and conferred on Spain exclusive title to lands beyond the Western Ocean. Exactly one day later, the representatives of Portugal protested, and the same Pope amended his ruling. He gave to Spain all the lands west of an imaginary line, running north to south a hundred leagues west of the Azores and the Cape Verde Islands. Since those islands are not even close to the same north-south line, confusion resulted. By treaty, the two powers compromised on a line running 370 leagues west of the Cape Verdes, or across the mouth of the Amazon.

---

[42] J. Ots Capdequí, Manual de Historia del Derecho Español en Las Indias 80 (1945).

(They did not know there *was* an Amazon then.) Portugal colonized around the northeast coast of South America, and Spain on the rest of the continent.

Less than a century after the voyages of Columbus, Spain and Portugal were united, with an assist from an invading army led by the Duke of Alba, under Philip II of Spain (Philip I of Portugal). During his reign (1580-98), Philip reorganized Portugal's judicial system. He also ordered Portugal's legal scholars to begin a recompilation of Portuguese law, which had been previously codified in 1446 in the *Ordenações Afonsinas* and in 1521 as the *Ordenações Manuelinas.* The new compilation was not published until 1603, during the reign of Philip III (Philip II of Portugal), under the title of *Ordenações Filipinas* (frequently referred to as the *Código Filipino*). Although improving the prior compilations somewhat, primarily through addition of subsequent legislation, the *Ordenações Filipinas* has been severely criticized as obsolete even at the time of promulgation. Something of the flavor of the *Ordenações,* as well as an awareness of the difficulties of legal research, can be gleaned from the Preamble to Title 64, Book 3 (dealing with sources of law), which is more lucid than many of its companion provisions. Note the similarity to the technique employed in the *Ordenamiento de Alcalá*.

> Whenever a case is commenced which is based upon any law of our Kingdoms, or procedure of our court, or custom in said Kingdoms or any part thereof, which custom has been followed for a long time, and which by law ought to be obeyed, such case shall be decided according to same, notwithstanding provisions to the contrary contained in imperial [Roman] laws relating to said case; for where the law, procedure or custom of our Kingdom apply, the other statutes and laws cease to apply. And when the case referred to is not solved by a law, procedure or custom of our Kingdom, we hereby ordain that it be decided, if involving matters of sin, by the holy canons. And when not involving matters of sin, it be decided according to imperial laws, although the holy canons provide otherwise. These laws we ordain to apply only because they are based upon sound reason.
> § 1 And when the case referred to in practice is not solved by the law, procedure or custom aforementioned, or imperial laws or holy canons, then we ordain the application of Acursio's [Accursius'] glosses as embodied in laws generally approved by Doctors; and when the glosses do not solve the case, then Bartolo's [Bartolus'] opinions shall apply because they ordinarily conform to sound reason, even though various Doctors think the opposite, unless the general opinion of Doctors writing after him is against said opinions.[43]

The *Ordenações Filipinas* was confirmed by João IV in 1643, soon after Portugal regained her independence. Despite being obsolete *ab initio* and promulgated by a foreign intruder, this compilation remarkably continued in force as Brazil's general law until adoption of the civil code in 1917, almost a century after independence and fifty years after Portugal had herself abandoned the *Ordenações*.

Why did the Brazilians muddle through until the beginning of the twentieth century

---

[43] Translated in Gomes, "Historical and Sociological Roots of the Brazilian Code," 1 *Inter-Amer. L. Rev.* 331, 332 (1959).

with such an outmoded hodge-podge at the core of their legal system? One reason the *Ordenações* survived so long as Brazil's basic law was the *Lei da Boa Razão* (Law of Good Sense), adopted by Portugal in 1769. This statute, in addition to rejecting the long discredited glosses and opinions of Accurius and Bartolus and relegating canon law exclusively to the ecclesiastical tribunals for religious matters only, directed the judiciary to apply Roman law to fill legislative lucunae only when in accord with "good human sense." "Good human sense," at least in theory, meant consistency with natural law, defined as "the essential, intrinsic and unalterable truths which Roman ethics had established, and which were given formal recognition by divine and human laws to serve as moral or legal rules of Christianity."[44] In practice this formula encouraged judges and lawyers to look to common sense, custom, natural law, or the legislation of other countries whenever the *Ordenações* were unclear or omissive, which was often the case. The effect of the *Lei da Boa Razão* was to increase substantially the doctrinal freedom and legal discretion of the Brazilian judiciary, which at times operated as *de facto* common law judges.

H. Colonial Administration

The manner in which Spain and Portugal administered their New World colonies also indelibly stamped the legal institutions of Latin America. Despite the new constitutions and codes which followed independence, general responses and attitudes towards law continue to be conditioned by this colonial heritage. The diversity of means for transmitting the royal will to the colonists was nearly matched by the diversity of means for colonial administrators to frustrate that will. The result was bureaucratic confusion, administrative delay, mistrust of government officials, and disrespect for law. This legacy from the colonial era has impeded a great many attempts at administrative reform in Latin American nations.

1. The Spanish Council of the Indies and the Portuguese Overseas Council

Directly subordinate to the king in the governance of the Spanish colonies was the Council of the Indies *(Real y Supremo Consejo de las Indias)*. Its size varied from 6 to 19 members, who were generally lawyers and clergy.

All laws and decrees relating to the administration, taxation, and police of the American dominions were prepared and dispatched by the council, with the approval of the king and in his name; and no important local scheme of government or of colonial expenditure might be put into operation by American officials unless first submitted to it for consideration and approval. . . . It

---

[44]*Id.* at 332 fn. 6.

proposed the names of colonial officials whose appointment was reserved to the king, and to it all such officers were ultimately accountable. It corresponded with the authorities in the New World, lay and ecclesiastical, and kept jealous watch over their conduct. Since by early papal bulls the tithes and the patronage of the Church in America were reserved to the Crown of Castile, the supervision of ecclesiastical matters also fell within the Council's jurisdiction. . . .

In its judicial capacity the Council sat as a court of last resort in important civil suits appealed from the colonial *audiencias* [royal courts, with some administrative functions], and in civil and criminal cases from the judicial chamber of the *Casa de contratación.* Reserved to it in the first instance were . . . all matters relating to *encomiendas* of Indians. . . .[45]

During the Spanish "captivity" of the Portuguese throne (1580-1640), Portugal adopted many Spanish colonial administrative practices. In 1604 a Portuguese Council of the Indies was created; in 1642 this became the Overseas Council *(Conselho Ultramarino).* Its role in superintending colonial life was similar to, though never as important as, its Spanish counterpart.

Both institutions were hardly paragons of efficient administration. Their paternalistic preoccupation with regulating all aspects of colonial life, down to the pettiest details, and their seemingly interminable procrastination, resulted in voluminous correspondence and intolerable delay. Professor Haring described the difficulties with the Council of the Indies in terms that also fit the Overseas Council.

An institution such as this, responsible collectively to an autocratic king, possessed the defects inherent in a conciliar system of government: on the one hand, absence of individual responsibility, on the other, growth of a spirit of routine which paralyzed procedure and made rapidity of decision and action difficult. Like other councils of Hapsburg Spain, it deliberated interminably. Matters were referred to the king, from the king back to the Council, and to the king again. There were instructions after instructions, memorials upon memorials, an endless accumulation of documents, useful as preserving precedents, and enlightening to the modern historical investigator, but serving only to clog the wheels of government. Moreover, the conciliar system threw greater responsibility back upon the sovereign, in whom alone resided any unity of control such as might have been exercised by a single minister of state. If the king lacked energy, character, decision, or was absent from the kingdom, the inevitable result was perpetual debate, procrastination, suspended judgment.[46]

---

[45] C. Haring, *supra* note 41, at 98.

[46] *Id.* at 100. For a similar description of the operations of the Overseas Council, see C. Prado Júnior, *Formação do Brasil Contemporâneo* 303 (1942).

2. Spanish Techniques for Controlling Colonial Administrators

A basic premise of Spanish colonial rule was the deep-seated suspicion that the king's distant representatives would misuse their authority unless closely watched. To guard against such abuses, an elaborate administrative system with overlapping grants of authority was designed. Until the 18th century, the New World colonies were divided into two viceroyalties, New Spain and Peru, each headed by a viceroy. The viceroyalties were subdivided into various *audiencia* districts headed by governors or captains-general who exercised powers similar to the viceroys. The viceroy wore several hats. In his *audiencia* district he served as governor and as captain-general (commander in chief of the military). He also served as presiding officer of the *audiencia*. In the other districts, captains-general fulfilled most of the viceroy's functions. Though ostensibly subordinate to the viceroy, the captains-general frequently behaved as co-equals.

The *audiencia* was a court composed of magistrates selected by the king. It exercised appellate jurisdiction unless the crown was a party, in which case its jurisdiction was original. The *audiencia* also acted as a kind of council of state, advising the viceroy or captain-general. When there was no viceroy or captain-general in the district, it also assumed his political functions.

Under the system of the *patronato,* the king's agents administered temporal aspects of the church, nominating the various members of the ecclesiastical hierarchy, while spiritual and doctrinal matters were governed by Rome. The viceroy acted as vice-patron of the Church in his district, but the clergy enjoyed a fair degree of autonomy. The officials of the royal exchequer formed still another hierarchy. While theoretically subordinate to the viceroy or governors, these officials constituted a co-ordinate authority where the king's finances were concerned.

Simplifying somewhat, there were four partly independent administrative hierarchies: the viceroys and captains-general, the *audiencias*, the Church, and the exchequer.[47] The jurisdictional conflicts resulting from their exercise of similar powers were frequently fierce. Each hierarchy reported directly to the Council of the Indies, whose interminable and ofttimes mutually contradictory directives constituted the cosmic glue that held this ungainly bureaucratic trapezoid together.

The crown employed two other devices to prevent its agents from misusing their authority: the *residencia* and the *visita.* A Spanish official's conduct in office was routinely reviewed at the end of his term in a judicial proceeding called a *residencia.* A specially designated judge held a public court of inquiry into all charges of misfeasance against the officeholder. Whenever the crown was displeased with the performance of particular officials, it would send out a special magistrate to hold a secret inquiry called the *visita.* Its aim was generally to prod colonial officials into taking more vigorous action or to remedy a specific situation which especially displeased the crown.

Still another control device was the direct appeal to the king. Subordinates were

---

[47]The lines of authority are diagrammed in much greater complexity in M. Sarfatti, *supra* note 40, at 22.

not only permitted, but actively encouraged, to appeal directly to the king whenever they disapproved of a superior's order. This practice was related to the curious Spanish administrative formula – "I obey but do not execute" – which has so frequently applied in the colonies. Law 24, Book II, title 1 of the *Recopilación* expressly recognized the right of Spanish viceroys and other officials to stay the execution of royal orders where special circumstances rendered their implementation inopportune. Writing in 1616, the great Spanish jurist, Castillo de Bavadilla, explained the reasoning underlying this formula:

> By laws of these realms it is provided that the royal provisions and decrees which are issued contrary to justice and in prejudice of suitors are invalid and should be obeyed but not executed . . . and the reason for this is that such provisions and mandates are presumed to be foreign to the intention of the Prince, who as Justinian has said, cannot be believed to desire by word or decree to subject and destroy the law established and agreed to with great solicitude.[48]

This convenient juridical formula provided colonial administrators with a much needed measure of flexibility and autonomy. Of course, there were limits as to how long administrators could avoid compliance with royal orders under this formula; its employment had to be justified immediately to the Council. But even if the Council decided to reissue the shelved order or decree, there was nothing to prevent colonial authorities from employing the formula again.[49]

3. The Portuguese Administrative Chaos

Though more poorly organized and less tightly controlled, Portuguese colonial administration was in many respects similar to the Spanish. Brazil too had her viceroys, captains-general, *patronato,* direct appeals to the king, *devassas (= visitas)* and *residencias;* the jurisdictional conflicts were just as fierce.[50] Portuguese rule was also authoritarian, paternalistic, and particularistic. Scanning the confused and contradictory mass of statutes, orders, opinions, regulations, letters patent, decrees, edicts, and instructions appropriately termed the *legislação extravagante* (literally, extravagant legislation) through which the sovereign's will was transmitted to the Brazilian colony, one is amazed that the administrative machinery functioned at all. There was not even an official compilation such as the Spanish *Recopilación* to attempt to bring order to this legal labyrinth. Probably the best capsule summary of Portuguese colonial administration is the following description by two Belgian scholars:

---

[48] Quoted in C. Haring, *supra* note 41, at 122-23.

[49] See Phelan, "Authority and Flexibility in the Spanish Imperial Bureaucracy," 5 *Admin. Science Q.* 47, 59-60 (1960).

[50] See D. Alden, *Royal Government in Brazil* 30-44 (1968); S. Schwartz, *Sovereignty and Society in Colonial Brazil* 263-79 (1973).

The institutions in the Portuguese colonies were mostly copied from those of the metropolis, without being, however, adapted to their new destination. Administrative organization never proceeded according to a uniform plan: it was determined by the march of events. The duties of the many officials, their hierarchy and relations of service, were not stipulated by laws or general rules, but by a mass of special decrees, some appointing functionaries for the places, others dealing with the solution of a transitory difficulty or the suppression of some abuse. Often the administrative machinery worked of itself, as a result of habit or routine, sometimes in accordance with the designs of the central government, other times against them.

If the Portuguese Kings since the reign of John II (1481-95) had their lawyers who gave the laws of the Kingdom the interpretation most suitable to the interests of the crown, the colonial governors also had their own legal authorities, who furnished the texts with the meaning most favorable to the power of the chiefs who respectively employed them. It is certainly not an easy task to describe this administrative machinery, even when one knows the text of the laws and decrees which have organized it, which is not always the case; but it is still more difficult to explain their real working. It is frequently impossible to distinguish with certainty the laws that were applied from those which were not applied, or which were not applied as they ought to have been, and it is not without difficulty that we are enabled to define with precision the duties of the several authorities.[51]

4. Failure to Develop Colonial Institutions of Self-Government

One of the most notable aspects of Iberian colonial rule was the failure to develop institutions of self-government. In sharp contrast with the English colonies, the Spanish and Portuguese monarchs insisted on interfering in and controlling every feature of colonial life. No aspect of colonial life was too trivial to escape the crown's concern. Local initiative was decidedly discouraged. In addition, the *creoles* (persons born in the New World) were discriminated against in favor of the *peninsulares* (persons born in Spain or Portugal) in holding governmental posts. "In the long list of over seven hundred and fifty viceroys, governors, and presidents of *audiencias,* less than twenty creoles appear."[52]

The only institution that is at all analogous to the colonial assemblies of the English colonies is the *cabildo* (*câmara* in Portuguese), a city or town council. But as a training ground for self-government, the *cabildo* left much to be desired. Any popular

---

[51] C. Lannoy and H. Van Der Linden, Histoire de L'Expansion Coloniale des Peuples Européens 87-88 (1907), cited in M. Lima, *The Evolution of Brazil Compared with That of Spanish and Anglo-Saxon America* 57-58 (1914).

[52] C. Jane, "Liberty and Despotism in Spanish America" 7 (1929).

character and autonomy these assemblies may have had was soon lost. Beginning with the reign of Phillip II, the crown sold the office of *cabildo* membership, along with a host of other colonial offices.

> Everywhere in Spanish America, except on the frontier and in the remoter agricultural areas, the activities of the *cabildo* were absorbed, or completely dominated by a royal representative. . . . The municipal councils were little aristocracies, consisting mainly of permanent cfficials who had purchased or inherited their posts, and who seemed to have little concern for their role as representatives of the people. As a repository of the people's liberty, a training school for the democratic system to be set up after independence the *cabildo* possessed no potency at all. It had little or no freedom in action or responsibility in government.[53]

This failure to develop self-government institutions and experience has been one of the most serious deficiencies of Latin America's colonial legacy.

I. Independence and Constitutionalism

For more than three hundred years the Spanish crown had been the symbol of legitimacy uniting the various parts of the Spanish empire. To be sure, the king was not always obeyed, but his authority, at least in theory, was always respected. Napoleon's seizure of Spain in 1808 created a legitimacy crisis from which parts of the former empire have not yet recovered. The Spanish kings, Carlos IV and his son Fernando, were forced to abdicate in favor of Napoleon's brother Joseph. The Spanish people refused to accept Joseph, who had no royal blood; instead local juntas were set up to direct resistance against the French. Since in the Spanish system, allegiance was owed to the person of the king, the ignominious abdication immediately beclouded the title to rule of the thousands of royal officials in the Spanish colonies.

Though some of the *penisulares* favored acceptance of the Bonaparte regime, creole leaders generally preferred to follow the path taken by the Spaniards, setting up juntas to rule in the name of the deposed Fernando. However, under the Spanish political system, the absence of a legitimate ruler justified assumption of power by the people, and a growing number of the creole elite began to contemplate independence. By 1822, after prolonged and bitter fighting, most of the Latin American nations had achieved or were on the verge of achieving independence.

Brazilian independence occurred without the violence or legitimacy crisis that marked the birth of her Hispanic neighbors. Instead of staying to greet Napoleon, the Portuguese royal family fled to Brazil. Even after Napoleon's ouster, the prince-regent, João, was in no hurry to return to Portugal. When crowned king in 1816, João VI proclaimed the joint kingdom of Portugal and Brazil, which he continued to rule from Rio de Janeiro. In 1821 Portuguese discontent with an absentee monarch forced his

---

[53] C. Haring, *supra* note 41, at 165.

reluctant return. But he left behind his son, Pedro, as regent, with instructions to declare Brazil independent if separation became necessary to preserve the dynasty. Pedro did just that the following year, and Portugal was in no position to dispute the issue.

The Constitution of 1824 declared Brazil to be a hereditary constitutional monarchy. It was in many ways a liberal document for its time, assuring individual freedom and equality before the law. The government was divided into the three conventional branches (executive, legislative, and judicial), but the Brazilian constitution introduced a fourth, called the moderating power, to be exercised by the emperor. Pursuant to this power, the emperor selected senators, ministers, bishops and presidents of the provinces; vetoed legislation; pardoned criminals; and even reviewed judicial decisions. This power recalls the medieval Iberian notion of the king as harmonizer of the conflicting interests of the various estates and the supreme dispenser of justice. The constitution proved durable, lasting until the fall of the monarchy in 1889.

Unfortunately, such easy transition was unavailable to the newly independent Hispanic nations, whose leaders were forced to cast about for new models upon which to build governments. Though some inclined towards monarchy, most found the emotional and philosophic appeal of the French and North American experiences irresistible, and opted for republican forms of government.

Both the United States and France greatly influenced the drafters of 19th century Latin American constitutions. Early constitutions of Venezuela and Mexico borrowed heavily from the United States; much of the Argentine Constitution of 1853 and the Brazilian Constitution of 1891 was literally copied from the American Constitution. All four of these countries imported the constitutional principle of federalism (today virtually abandoned in Venezuela and substantially modified in Argentina, Brazil, and Mexico). The concept of the separation of powers, derived both from Montesquieu and from the U.S. Constitution, was widely adopted in Latin America. Protection of individual liberties and private property was derived largely from the U.S. Bill of Rights and the French Declaration of the Rights of Man.

The institution of judicial review, as established by the U.S. Supreme Court in 1803 in *Marbury v. Madison,* also had great appeal to drafters of Latin American constitutions despite their civilian conceptions of the judiciary. We review some of these developments in Chapter II. Some, though by no means all, of the Latin American nations explicitly provided for judicial review in their constitutions. Brazil even sent a delegation to the United States specifically to study the operation of the Supreme Court before writing judicial review into her Constitution of 1891.

The debt of the framers of Latin American constitutions to France was perhaps greatest with respect to general theoretical notions about the nature of the state and sovereignty. The works of the 18th century French *philosophes,* particularly Rousseau, Voltaire, and Montesquieu, were highly influential with the creole elite, and were reflected in the strong emphasis placed upon human liberty, republicanism and equality in the basic documents. France was also the source of legal institutions such as the state of siege, council of state, and administrative court systems found in many Latin American constitutions.

As might be expected, numerous Spanish influences remained. The short-lived Spanish Constitution of 1812, which itself showed the influence of the French *philosophes,* was clearly an important source for early Latin American constitutions. Certain innovations of that constitution, such as the Standing Committee of the *Cortes* to oversee the observance of the constitution during parliamentary recesses, have survived in modern day Latin American constitutions. A number of Latin American constitutions impose restrictions on the president's leaving the country without Congressional permission or stipulate that he must remain in the country for a certain period after expiration of his term of office. Such requirements recall the colonial *residencia,* which required officials to remain on the scene after expiration of their commission until a royal inspector could complete an investigation of their administration. Another holdover from the colonial past reflected in Latin American constitutions has been the proliferation of special tribunals, a practice which dates back to the *fueros.* Despite the constitutional principle of the separation of powers, in practically all of the Latin American nations special courts or boards were set up, carving large exceptions from the jurisdiction of the ordinary judiciary.[54]

Although in good measure derived from the U.S. model, the first really innovative Latin American constitution was the Mexican Constitution of 1917. As a product of Latin America's first truly social revolution, the Mexican document differed sharply from 19th century constitutions. Instead of glorifying economic individualism and private property, it stressed economic nationalism, group obligations, and duties owed to society as a whole. Ownership of all land and water was declared vested originally in the Nation. The state's right to regulate private property in the public interest was set out in terms implying the "social function of ownership." (We explore this subject in Chapter III.) Land reform measures, prohibition of monopolies, and restrictions on competition from foreign labor were further innovations. Modern labor and social security legislation is provided for in almost statutory detail. The entire document is permeated with a paternalistic concern for the health, welfare, and cultural advancement of the poor, the illiterate, and the dispossessed.

The social justice provisions in this constitution have notably influenced subsequent Latin American constitutions, which generally include lengthy sections setting out socio-economic rights and obligations.

J. Codification

Independence stimulated the desire to remake basic legal structures. One reason was to stabilize and consolidate new national regimes. Another was that the former colonies had inherited legal systems in states of profound disarray. The preamble to the Argentine decree setting up a commission to draft new codes of law noted that the legislation presently in force "contains laws passed during a period of time extending

---

[54] See H. Clagett, *Administration of Justice in Latin America* 55-56 (1952).

over many centuries unknown to the people on whom they are binding, stored away in court archives or in private libraries of a few individuals fortunate enough to possess them as priceless curiosities; society at large, and very often jurisconsults and the judges themselves, are ignorant of their very existence. . . ."[55]

---

1. The Civil Codes

In Latin America, as in other civil-law countries, the heart of private law is expressed in the civil code. In theory a civil code is a systematic and harmonious set of general principles and specific rules governing legal relations among private persons. The code contains the rules governing contracts, domestic relations, damages, restitution, inheritance, legal personality and torts. Even when no provision appears to be specifically applicable, the civil code is frequently consulted as a source of general principle, serving to fill in gaps in other legislation in much the same way as the common law serves in Anglo-American jurisdictions.

The model that most appealed to the jurists designated to draft Latin American codes during the middle of the 19th century was the French Civil Code *(Code Napoléon),* enacted in 1804. The Code's newness, rationality, and clarity of style all recommended it to these new nations. Since it was heavily influenced by Roman law, its adoption would not require a complete break with the preexisting legal structure. In 1825 the first independent Latin American nation, Haiti, which had been a French colony, simply adopted the French Code. In turn the Haitians passed the French Code on to the Dominican Republic, which they forcefully annexed in 1822. When the Haitians withdrew in 1844, the Dominicans adopted the Haitian Code as their own. (Curiously, the Dominican Code was not translated into Spanish until 40 years later.) In 1831 Bolivia also adopted the French Civil Code in essence but reduced it from 2,281 to 1,556 articles and inserted a few provisions from the *Siete Partidas* and canon law.

Though derived principally from the French Civil Code, most Latin American codes are eclectic. In the area of family law, they have generally substituted Spanish for French custom. Some code articles are drawn from Roman law, either directly or

---

[55]Quoted in Eder, "Introduction" to *The Argentine Civil Code* xxii (Joannini trans. 1917). A distinguished Brazilian commentator described the snarl of his country's law preceding codification in the following colorful terms:

> Brazilian civil law was none other than a variable agglomeration of laws, orders, letters patent, resolutions and regulations, suppressing, repairing or sustaining the Ordenações do Reino, venerable antiquated monument, worn down by the action of a long course of uncultured and uncertain jurisprudence, whose high priests recited around it the cold texts of the Digest, read in the twilight glimmer of the Law of Good Reason [Sense]. Brazil was strangled in the accumulation, ever becoming greater, of a polychrome, confused and contradictory legislation, which had been piling up through the centuries; to find escape from such mortifying higgle-piggle was one of its most ardent aspirations. Dr. Paulo de Lacerda, quoted in Wheless, "Foreword" to *The Civil Code of Brazil* xiii-xiv (Wheless Trans. 1920).

indirectly (via the *Siete Partidas* or famous treatise writers). Many are derived from the civil codes of other countries or from drafts of civil codes. An idea of the depths and variety of sources can be gleaned from examination of a specific provision of the Argentine Civil Code. Article 923 provides: "Ignorance of the law, or an error of law, shall in no case prevent the legal effects of lawful acts, nor excuse responsibility for unlawful acts." The Code's principal draftsman, Dr. Vélez Sársfield, published annotations to explain his motives and identify his sources. His note to Article 923 includes quotations from Savigny, the famous 19th century German commentator on Roman law, and from several other commentators, principally French. It also includes these notations:

> L. 20, Tít. 1, Part. 1ª. – L.31, Tít. 14, Part. 5ª. – L. 24, Tít. 22, Part. 3ª. – Los arts. 1 y 2 del Título preliminar de las leyes. – L. 1, Tít. 6, Lib. 22, Dig. – L. 12, Tít. 18, Lib. 1, Cód. Romano. – Véase Cód. Francés, art. 1110 – Sardo, 1196 y 1197 – Holandés, 1357 – de Luisiana, 1813.

Decoded, this note means that Vélez Sársfield regarded as relevant authorities three references to the Siete Partidas (Book 20, Title 1, Partida 1ª, etc.); the first and second articles of his own Argentine Code, dealing with observance of the laws; a portion of Book 22 of the Digest of Justinian; a portion of Book 1 of the Justinian Code; and analogous articles in the civil codes of France, Sardinia, the Netherlands, and Louisiana. One enterprising commentator calculated the immediate sources from which Vélez Sársfield culled his draft: some 1200 articles were lifted from Teixeira de Freitas' draft code for Brazil (1856-65), an exhaustive, detailed work containing 4,908 articles; 700 came from Aubry and Rau, two Strasbourg law professors who published a still influential five-volume treatise on civil law between 1838 and 1847; 300 articles were taken from the only Spanish source, García Goyena, author of a four-volume draft and commentary of a civil code for Spain published in 1852; 170 articles were taken from the Chilean Civil Code; 145 articles came directly from the French Civil Code (though nearly half the Code appears in one form or another); 78 articles came from Zacharie, author of an 1808 German commentary on French civil law; 52 articles came from Louisiana's Civil Code; three French commentators, Demolombe, Troplong, and Chabot, contributed 52, 50, and 18 articles respectively; two Belgian commentators, Maynz and Molitor, contributed 15 and 12 articles respectively; 27 articles were borrowed from Acevedo's draft of a civil code for Uruguay; and the remaining articles were taken from miscellaneous codes and commentators.[56] Almost none of the Argentine Code's 4,051 articles are original.

This eclecticism was the natural result of viewing law as an abstract, universal science. The primary task of the codifier was to examine the legal rules set out in the laws of other countries or propounded by treatise writers to resolve certain problems and to choose that solution which, as a logical proposition, seemed "best" to him. His

---

[56]This analysis has been pieced together from E. Borchard, *Guide to the Law and Legal Literature of Argentina, Brazil, and Chile* 61-62 (1917) and Eder, "Introduction" to *The Argentine Civil Code* xxv-xxvi (Joannini trans. 1917).

secondary responsibility was to arrange the rules chosen into a precise, consistent, harmonious system.

There were three great Latin American codifications: (1) Andrés Bello's Chilean Code (drafted 1846-1855); (2) Vélez Sársfield's Argentine Code (drafted 1863-69); and (3) Teixeira de Freitas' draft code for Brazil (1856-65). The three have served as models for the civil codes of most Latin American countries. Thus, the Chilean Code was virtually adopted in its entirety in Ecuador and Colombia, and with slight modifications in El Salvador, Nicaragua, and Panama (until 1917). The Argentine Code has been in force in Paraguay since 1876. Though never adopted by any country, the Freitas draft heavily influenced the civil codes of Argentina, Brazil and Uruguay. (Cuba, which did not become independent until 1902, was the only Latin American nation to adopt the Spanish Civil Code of 1889, itself largely modeled after the French Civil Code.)

These codes reflected the rationalist, utopian, and highly individualistic values of the Enlightenment and the French Revolution. Heavy emphasis was placed upon freedom of contract, the sanctity of private property (particularly real property), and the family as the basic societal unit. They have been cogently criticized as ill-suited to 19th century Latin America, as well as anachronistic today.[57] They were enacted by and for a small, European-oriented upper class which paid little attention to the needs and desires of the illiterate, impoverished mass of the population. Pontes de Miranda's incisive indictment of the Brazilian Civil Code, adopted in 1917 and reflecting the influence of the German and Swiss codes, applies equally well to the 19th century codes of other Latin American nations:

> It is a law more concerned with the social circle of the family than with the social circle of the nation or its classes. When dealing with classes, it does so with a certain undisguised capitalism, which it is naively convinced will promote unity and social justice.[58]

Mexico's present Civil Code (in force in the Federal District and territories), enacted in 1928 after a profound social revolution, reflects a much heavier social emphasis than its French-inspired predecessors of 1870 and 1884. Moderate social limitations on the use of private property, protection of the obviously weaker party in certain bargaining situations, workmen's compensation for injuries without regard to fault, and an expanded protection of the rights of illegitimate children and women reflect the extensive supplementary legislation and code revisions modifying the civil codes of most Latin American nations.[59]

---

[57] R. David, *Traité Elémentaire de Droit Civil Comparé* 259-61 (1950); Wiarda, "Law and Political Development in Latin America: Toward a Framework for Analysis," 19 *Am. J. Comp. L.* 434, 442 (1971); Gomes, "Comments on the Reform of Civil Codes," 5 *Inter-Amer. L. Rev.* 137 (1963); Gomes, "Renovation of the Brazilian Civil Code," 8 *Inter-Amer. L. Rev.* 171 (1966).

[58] *Fontes e Evolução do Direito Civil Brasileiro* 489 (1928).

[59] A concise, English-language account of the changes that have taken place in the Chilean Civil Code appears in Matus Valencia, "The Centenary of the Chilean Civil Code," 7 *Amer. J. Comp. L.*

2. The Commercial Codes

European civil law systems of private law had split into two branches — commercial and "civil" (non-commercial) — well before the 19th century codification movement embedded the dichotomy in legislative concrete by creating separate codes of civil and commercial law. During the Middle Ages, merchants, like many other vocational groups, formed guilds and sought to regulate the conduct of their own profession. Eventually, like the church and the military, they received the right to establish a legal system of their own. Special judges called consuls, appointed by the guilds, came to exercise exclusive jurisdiction over mercantile disputes. Like maritime law, to which it is intimately related, the law merchant quickly took on an international flavor. The resurgence of commerce during the 11th and 12th centuries was accompanied by the growth of great commercial cities, particularly in Italy, which began to codify the customs being applied by their mercantile courts. The guilds' statutes are the source of much modern commercial law. Little of their content stems directly from Justinian's *Corpus Juris* or canon law; they were based upon the pragmatic considerations of mercantile custom rather than the legal sanction of any constituted polity, and their application was restricted to merchants.

Trade between Spain and her colonies was regulated by the *Casa de Contratación* (House of Trade) of Seville, established by royal decree in 1503. The *Casa* collected taxes and customs duties, licensed ships and merchants, and enforced laws regulating trade. It also functioned as a court, exercising jurisdiction over all civil suits arising from colonial trade and crimes committed during voyages. In 1543 a *consulado* (merchant guild) was established in Seville. The *consulado* quickly took over the resolution of virtually all civil disputes among guild members, including bankruptcy proceedings. The special tribunal of the *consulado* was a court of merchants for merchants, designed to settle commercial disputes rapidly. A distaste for the dilatory tactics of lawyers led to their being barred from practice before the *consulado*. In fact, the *consulado* at Barcelona went so far as to adopt the rule that an absent or incompetent party could be represented by anyone but a lawyer.[60]

The decisions and rulings of the *consulados* of Spain's commercial centers became the commercial law of the Spanish Empire. *Consulados* established in Mexico and Lima at the end of the 16th century were (at least in theory) obliged to follow the rules laid down by the *consulados* of Burgos and Seville. The collected rules of the *consulado* of Seville, known as the Ordinances of Seville, were enacted into positive law for all the Spanish colonies in 1680, constituting Book IX of the *Recopilación de Leyes de Los Reynos de Indias.* In 1737 the celebrated Ordinances of Bilbao, which

---

71 (1958). An overview of efforts to modify Latin American civil codes appears in De Gásperi, "El Futuro de la Codificación," 29 *Tulane L. Rev.* 223 (1955).

See also, "Le Code Civil Français et Son Influence en Amérique," in Travaux de la Semaine Internationale de Droit (Paris, 1950), *L'Influence du Code Civil dans le Monde* 723-78, 804-24 (1954).

[60]Smith, "Legal Foundations of the Spanish Consulado," 48 *Jurid. Rev.* 147 (1936). See also C. Haring, *supra* note 41, at 297-300.

were nearly as comprehensive as a modern commercial code, were given the force of general law for all mercantile matters in Spain's colonies. The Ordinances of Bilbao remained in force in Latin America until independence, and, in many countries, until long thereafter.

Portugal had little specialized commercial legislation prior to 1833, when she adopted a commercial code. Commercial transactions were regulated by the *Ordenações Filipinas* and a few specific laws about merchants and bankruptcy. However, after the *Lei da Boa Razão* of 1769 made the laws of Christian nations subsidiary sources of Portuguese law, Portuguese and Brazilian courts increasingly looked to the more developed laws of other countries for aid in resolving commercial disputes.[61]

The forces that led to codification of the civil law were also operating in the commercial arena. Here too the French codification (1807) served as an influential model, though not so influential as the more comprehensive Spanish Code of Commerce of 1829. The latter was copied almost verbatim by Ecuador, Paraguay, Peru, Costa Rica, and Colombia, while the former was copied by Haiti, the Dominican Republic, and Venezuela (1867 code). The most influential of the Latin American commercial codes were those of Brazil (1850), Argentina (1859), and Chile (1867). As with the civil codes, there was much borrowing and cross-fertilization. The Spanish Code was based upon the French Code, the Ordinances of Bilbao, Spanish consular decisions, and famous treatise writers, especially Pardessus of France. The Brazilian Code was based upon the French and Spanish Commercial Codes, as well as the Portuguese Commercial Code of 1833, which had been coauthored by a Brazilian jurist. Approximately one third of the Argentine Code, which was coauthored by a Uruguayan jurist, was borrowed from the Brazilian Code, but the Portuguese, Spanish, and Dutch Codes also served as important sources. The Argentine Code was adopted with slight modifications by Uruguay in 1866 and (with its 1889 modification) literally copied by Paraguay in 1903. The Chilean Code, drafted by an Argentine jurist, drew upon the commercial codes of Argentina, Spain, France, Portugal, Hungary, and Prussia, as well as the Ordinances of Bilbao. In turn, the Chilean Code heavily influenced subsequent commercial codes in Ecuador, Colombia, Venezuela, El Salvador, Guatemala, Honduras, Nicaragua, and Panama.[62]

Historically, commercial law developed as a special law for merchants, defined as members of the guilds. When the French guilds were abolished by the Edict of Turgot in 1776, jurists were forced to devise a means to determine when conduct should be regulated by civil or commercial law. The French developed the concept of "objective acts of commerce," which emphasizes the intrinsic nature of the transaction rather than the personal status of the parties. Thus, certain transactions constitute commercial acts regardless of the buyer's vocation. The French Commercial Code listed the types of acts defined as commercial. This approach has been more or less followed by the Latin American Codes, which generally define as commercial:

---

[61] J. Borges, *Curso de Direito Comercial Terrestre* 35 (3d ed. 1967).

[62] This discussion is largely drawn from J. Barrera Graf, *El Derecho Mercantil en la América* 26-34 (1963) and J. Olavarría, *Los Códigos de Comercio Latinoamericanos* 99-111 (1961).

purchases of goods for resale, banking and securities transactions, brokerage and agency, negotiable instruments, commercial bailments and warehousing, transport, business associations, and insurance. However, adoption of the objective theory of acts of commerce did not completely eliminate the need to consider the mercantile nature of the parties. Only transactions entered into with intent to make a profit are considered commercial, and an important means of proving profit motive is to show that one or more of the parties is a merchant. How does one determine whether a person is a merchant? The answer given by Latin American Codes is delightfully circular. A merchant is one who habitually engages in acts of commerce.[63]

Determining whether a contract should be governed by the civil or commercial code can be tricky, particularly if one party is a merchant and the other is not. In such circumstances some Latin American countries have taken the position that the commercial code applies to the merchant party and the civil code to the other party or that the personal status of the defendant determines which code applies. However, the more common rule is that the commercial code applies to the entire transaction.[64]

With the exception of Venezuela, the Latin American nations have abolished the special commercial courts inherited from Spain. However, the ordinary courts generally resort to special procedural rules when deciding cases governed by the commercial code. There has been strong doctrinal criticism of the continuation of the dichotomy between commercial and civil law, especially in the wake of Italy's unification of the two in 1942.[65]

The experience of Latin American countries with their commercial codes has generally been far less felicitous than with their civil codes. Though most countries have traded in their commercial codes several times, complaints about obsolescence are continually heard. For example, a Chilean law professor recently depicted his country's Commercial Code in the following terms:

> . . . [T]he Commercial Code almost has no modifications. In spite of having been based on navigation by sail in wooden ships and land transport by means of stage, this is true. Do not forget the obligation to change animals is expressly required at certain distances, and you must recall such anachronisms as the provision covering the collection of an additional fare for the newborn infant from a woman who gives birth during a trip. This is our Commercial Code.[66]

---

[63] See Cueto-Rúa, "Administrative, Civil and Commercial Contracts in Latin American Law," 26 *Ford. L. Rev.* 15, 29-31, 38 (1957). The difficulty is partially obviated by the Commercial Registry, in which all merchants and commercial associations are required to enroll. Failure to register may result in deprivation of evidentiary privileges and (for partnerships and corporations) limited liability privileges. Registration itself affords a rebuttable presumption as to one's merchant status.

[64] *Id.* at 32.

[65] Aztiria, "Commercial Law and Private Law in Countries Having a Continental Legal System," 1 *Inter-Amer. L. Rev.* 123, 129-33 (1959).

[66] Novoa Monreal, "The Crisis of the Law and of the Legal Profession" (translated by the Int'l Legal Center from the Boletín del Instituto de Docencia e Investigación Juridícas, Santiago, Chile, Jan. 1972).

Countries like Brazil and Chile, which have retained their original commercial codes, have been forced to modify them extensively. Despite the numerous modifications, Latin American commercial law has been trenchantly criticized as a stumbling block to speedy economic development.[67] Particularly with respect to corporations (i.e., protection of minority shareholders, issuance of no par shares, convertible debentures, stock options,) industrial property, bankruptcy, and credit instruments, Latin American commercial law has tended to lag far behind the needs of the economy. The entire field is presently changing rapidly as a result of pressures generated by rapid industrialization and economic growth.

---

3. Civil Procedure

The procedural law which the New World colonies inherited from Spain and Portugal was at least as confused and chaotic as the substantive law. The *Fuero Juzgo,* the *Fuero Viejo,* the *Siete Partidas,* the *Ordenações* and the various recompilations all contained detailed procedural rules derived largely from Roman, Germanic and canon law. The French Code of Civil Procedure of 1807, like its civil and commercial code counterparts, was highly influential in Latin America.

Although there are different procedural rules for commercial and administrative cases, the heart of Latin American procedural law is contained in the codes of civil procedure. The following thumbnail sketch of civil procedure represents a composite view, inaccurate in detail for any single Latin American jurisdiction, but a fair approximation of a hypothetical mean.[68] How many of the differences from Anglo-American procedure may be traced to the absence of the jury? How many to the lack of a trial in the common law sense?[69]

(a) The Pleading Stage

As in the United States, an action begins with the filing of a complaint (*demanda* in Spanish; *petição* in Portuguese). In the complaint, the plaintiff *(actor; autor)* must state the name of the court in which he is filing the action; his own name and address for the purpose of receiving notification concerning the suit; the name and address of

---

[67] J. Barrera Graf, *supra* note 62, at 45-46; Eder, "Law in Latin America," in, I *Law: A Century of Progress* 39, 59 (N.Y.U. ed. 1937); B. Kozolchyk, Law and the Credit Structure in Latin America (Rand Memo., RM-4918-RC March 1966); Kozolchyk, "Commercial Law Recodification and Economic Development in Latin America," 4 *Lawyer of the Americas* 189 (1972).

[68] For detailed English-language descriptions of individual jurisdictions, see Estellita, "Judicial Organization and Civil Procedure in Brazil, *N.Y.U. Comparative Judicial Administration Series* No. 1 (May 1959); Murray, "The New Code of Civil Procedure of Guatemala," 7 *Inter-Amer. L. Rev.* 303 (1965). See also Murray, "A Survey of Civil Procedure in Spain and Some Comparisons with Civil Procedure in the United States," 37 *Tulane L. Rev.* 399 (1963).

[69] See J. Merryman, *supra* note 18, at 120-31.

the defendant *(demandado; rêu);* what is in controversy and its value; an organized and succinct statement of the facts upon which his claim is based; the type of action being brought; and the legal basis of his claim. Frequently, documents supporting the claim must be filed along with the complaint.

If the judge thinks the complaint unclear, rather than wait for the defendant to request clarification, the court itself will order the plaintiff to clarify the doubtful portions; once the judge is satisfied, the complaint is accepted and filed with the secretary for the defendant's inspection. A summons is issued to the defendant to appear and answer. The defendant may be served within or without the jurisdiction. Personal jurisdiction (in the sense that it forms the basis of a personal judgment) does not require physical presence within the jurisdiction, but may be based upon other connections such as the performance of various acts within the jurisdiction, or even the intended performance of an obligation within the jurisdiction.

The defendant's answer *(contestación; contestação),* like the complaint, pleads both fact and law; there is no counterpart to the common law separation between demurrer and plea. There may or may not be subsequent pleadings (*réplica* for the plaintiff and *dúplica* for the defendant). The judge may then call a pre-trial conference for the purpose of asking the parties to stipulate certain facts and to limit the points on which evidence will be taken.

Discovery procedures tend to be rudimentary. However, this is not as serious a problem as it would be if there were the same kind of trial as in common law jurisdictions. The extended period for submitting evidence makes the likelihood of prejudice resulting from surprise relatively slight.

(b) Taking of Proof

There is no "trial" in the common law sense of the term. Instead there are a series of meetings and correspondence between counsel and court over a period of time during which evidence is presented, witnesses are heard, and procedural motions are made. All evidence is reduced to writing and added to the case's file by the clerk during the term for evidence. The judge does not study the evidence until the file is complete, and he is ready to decide the case. The decision is based upon examination of the written record and oral arguments of the attorneys at the final hearing.

Even if the judge is present at a hearing in which a witness is testifying, which is not always the case, he or she may pay little attention to the testimony until the written version is studied. Transcription of oral testimony often takes place simultaneously with its delivery; the clerk types while the witness talks. The parties submit their requests for examination of witnesses, along with the questions to be asked on direct or "cross examination," to the judge and opposing counsel prior to the hearing. The judge may screen the questions to eliminate those deemed improper, but only questions "contrary to law or morals" will be eliminated. There are no exclusionary rules of evidence such as the hearsay rule. The witness is examined by the judge or the clerk of the court. There is no cross-examination as we know it, but counsel for the other side is generally permitted to submit written interrogatories to the judge or clerk, who may, but need not, put them (or his own version of them) to the witness. The testimony is then read back to the witness by the clerk, who corrects any inaccuracies in the transcription process. If satisfactory, the statement is signed by the witness, certified by the clerk, and added to the file.

Documentary evidence is contained in either "public" or "private" documents. Public documents, which are issued by and recorded in public offices, are admissible without notice to the opposing party. Their authenticity may be attacked, but the issue is limited to a comparison of the certified copy in the evidence file with the original contained in the official record. Private documents are admitted only if their authenticity is stipulated by the parties or determined by the judge.

Proponents of the various propositions of fact must bear the burden of proof with respect thereto, be they plaintiff or defendant. The judge's power to evaluate evidence is much more circumscribed than that of the common law judge. The codes of civil procedure commonly set out detailed rules as to how the judge should weigh testimony, specifying considerations about motivation, precision, clarity, the witness' capacity to perceive, and his interest in the case. Latin American courts display a decided tendency to believe documents and to disbelieve people. The innate distrust of oral testimony is reflected in broad disqualifications of witnesses related to any of the parties. It is also reflected in laws like Article 141 of Brazil's Civil Code, which provides: "Unless expressly provided, exclusively testimonial proof is admissible only for contracts whose value does not exceed $Cr. 10.000,00 [worth U.S. $534 in 1952, when this statute was enacted, and worth only U.S. $1.35 in 1974]."

This orientation is slowly changing. A number of recently enacted codes and proposed drafts have foresaken the rigid, *a priori* criteria for evaluating evidence, leaving the trier of fact free to utilize his critical sense.[70]

(c) The Decision

The codes commonly contain detailed prescriptions about the format of the judge's decision. The opinion is to be clear and precise, and expressly decide the object of the action. The legal grounds for the decision must be clearly set out. (Unfortunately, there is no such admonition vis-à-vis the facts.) In some jurisdictions the judge will dictate an opinion to the clerk. The opinion will seldom be published unless the decision is appealed, in which event the lower court opinion may be published along with the appellate opinion. It is common to award costs, including attorneys' fees, to the winning party.

(d) Appellate Review

Latin American codes abound with procedural devices for securing review of judicial decisions, a legacy from a colonial past which demonstrated a distrust of inferior courts by permitting multiple appeals, with a final appeal to the king. Interlocutory appeals are frequently permitted. If a party asks for leave to appeal and

---

[70]Fix Zamudio, "Les Garanties Constitutionnelles des Parties dans le Procès Civil en Amérique

the judge of the first instance denies this request, that refusal may itself be appealed to the superior judge of the same court or to a higher court, which may or may not be the same appellate court to which the party seeks to appeal. Appeal may be taken to a higher court by any party who is not satisfied, or by a third person who has intervened in the suit, or by other interested persons aggrieved by the decision — e.g., a branch of the government. In some countries the judge of the first instance can also seek review to make sure that a decision is correct.

The appellate court, usually referred to as the court of second instance, is normally composed of three to five judges. It reviews the original file in the case, and does not feel bound by the lower court's factual determinations. Often it will order that new evidence be taken before it, obviating the necessity of remanding a case to the court of first instance for further proceedings. The court of second instance will affirm the decision below, reverse it, or modify it; in any case it will issue its own judgment. If the court of second instance unanimously affirms the lower court, the appellate process normally terminates. If there is a dissent or reversal, there is usually an appeal to a court of third instance, whose decision is final.

Complaints about lengthy procedural delays are commonly voiced in Latin America (as well as in many other countries, including the United States). While there is considerable variation, not only among countries and courts, but among judges of the same court, ordinary litigation in Latin America has frequently been characterized by delays of startling magnitude. Brazil's Federal Tribunal of Appeals only recently decided a case which began in 1892. Professor Ireland cites a case in which after fifty years the plaintiff made a motion mildly complaining that it was time for a decision.[71] Rapid growth of the population and economy has resulted in underpaid and overworked judges. Coupled with excessively fragmented procedural systems that permit almost any order to be appealed at any stage of the proceedings and appellate courts to try facts *de novo,* it is not hard to see why some cases appear to drag on interminably.

Another chronic complaint is the excessive cost of litigation. Notarial and filing fees, stamps and taxes, transcribing fees, and lawyers' fees quickly mount up, making the cost of litigation nearly prohibitive to all but the very poor or the very rich.[72]

Latine," in *Fundamental Guarantees of the Parties in Civil Litigation* 31, 82 (M. Cappelletti & D. Tallon eds. 1973).

[71] Cited in Eder, *supra* note 67, at 46-47.

[72] Legal aid is theoretically available in many Latin American nations free of charge to the poor in both criminal and civil cases. However, in many countries this theoretical legal right has been badly implemented. Fix Zamudio, *supra* note 70, at 72-73.

Briefs and other legal papers filed with the court must often be on stamped paper, which is usually expensive. Chile recently charged Anaconda $2300 a page to litigate its claim for compensation before the Special Copper Tribunal. Stern, "The Judicial and Administrative Procedures Involved in the Chilean Copper Expropriations," 66 *Am. J. Int'l. L.* 205, 210 (1972).

4. Codes of Criminal Law and Procedure

On the eve of independence Latin American criminal law was governed by the *Recopilación* (or the *Ordenações Filipinas* in Brazil), plus numerous royal *cédulas,* special laws, and the customary supplementary legislation back to the *Fuero Real* and the *Siete Partidas.* Much of this penal law was barbaric and outdated, with cruel and harsh penalties, obsolete offenses and superstitions, and differential treatment according to social class. Penal law reform naturally became a high priority concern in the new republics.

Here, too, the liberalizing, rationalizing, and modernizing influence of the French Revolution and the Napoleonic Penal Code of 1810 was plainly reflected in Latin American codification. Haiti and the Dominican Republic simply adopted the French Code of 1810, while the Brazilian Penal Code of 1830 drew extensively on the models of the French Code and the Neapolitan Code of 1819. The short-lived Spanish Code of 1822, which wrapped penal provisions of the *Fuero Juzgo* and the *Siete Partidas* in the cloak of the Napoleonic Code, provided the model for initial codes of Bolivia, Colombia (New Granada) and El Salvador. Far more influential was the Spanish Code of 1848, much of which was inspired by the Brazilian Code of 1830. The Spanish Code of 1848, as amended in 1850, was a prime source for the initial codifications of Argentina, Chile, Paraguay, Peru, Venezuela and Mexico. The Italian Code of 1889 was also an extremely influential source, particularly in Uruguay, Argentina, Panama, and Venezuela.[73]

Like the commercial codes, criminal codes have generally been short-lived in Latin America. No sooner is a code of criminal law enacted than drafts of a reform project begin to circulate. Most of the countries have gone through at least half a dozen penal codes since independence. Moreover, a great many criminal offenses are found elsewhere than in the criminal code, and are subject to frequent amendment.

The substantive provisions of a typical Latin American penal code do not differ greatly from those of a typical Anglo-American jurisdiction. There is a tendency to give more emphasis to crimes against honor and chastity in Latin American codes,[74] but the great bulk of offenses, defenses, and punishments do not differ markedly from those with which we are familiar in the United States.[75]

Latin American criminal procedure is another matter, differing in several important respects from Anglo-American procedure. Latin America adheres to the continental model frequently denominated as "inquisitorial." As applied to modern codes of criminal procedure, the term "inquisitorial" is likely to mislead; present-day continental criminal procedure is more accurately described as a mixed system,

---

[73] This brief account is drawn from L, Jiménez de Asúa, I *Tratado de Derecho Penal* 1077-1286 (2d ed. 1956); L. Jiménez de Asúa, I *Códigos Penales Iberoamericanos* 8-418 (1946).

[74] See Cooper, "Sexual Offenses in Peru," 21 *Am. J. Comp. L.* 86, 102-119 (1973).

[75] For an examination of some of the differences, see Schwenk, "Criminal Codification and General Principles of Criminal Law in Argentina, Mexico, Chile, and the United States; A Comparative Study," 4 *La. L. Rev.* 351 (1942).

blending elements of the "accusatorial" and "inquisitorial" systems. The following is a composite description of the salient features of Latin American criminal procedure.[76]

The typical Latin American criminal proceeding is divided into two stages: the investigative *(sumario* or *instrucción)* and the trial *(plenario* or *juicio oral).* The investigative stage is orchestrated by an examining magistrate, who conducts a complete, secret investigation into the facts surrounding the crime.[77] The police, at least in theory, work under the direction of the examining magistrate. The examining magistrate does not sit passively in a courtroom waiting for counsel to present evidence. One might say the magistrate makes house calls: interviewing witnesses, inspecting the scene of the crime, and interrogating the accused. Although the accused has the right to remain silent, the right is seldom exercised; the accused's silence is considered evidence of guilt, and is duly noted in the dossier compiled by the investigating magistrate. All the evidence (there are virtually no restraints on the admissibility of evidence) is carefully reduced to writing and entered in the dossier, along with a personal history of the accused. When the investigation is complete, the examining magistrate determines whether the defendant should stand trial or be exonerated. Exercise of this screening function is subject to the check of the prosecutor and ultimately the trial court, which must approve any order discharging the accused.

The trial generally takes place before a three-judge court, though in a number of Latin American jurisdictions, juries are used for certain offenses, particularly those involving the press.[78] At the relatively brief public trial (most are completed in less than an hour), the court, with the dossier before it, will interrogate witnesses and the accused, hear the arguments of the prosecutor and the defense counsel, determine guilt or innocence, and impose sentence. As in civil cases, opportunities to appeal abound.

The accused is entitled to counsel, and lawyers are appointed to represent indigents. The defendant is presumed innocent and entitled to the benefit of the doubt. *(In dubio pro reo.)* But the prosecutor does not have to prove guilt beyond a reasonable doubt; the burden of proof is similar to that of a plaintiff in a civil proceeding. Indeed, civil

---

[76] Detailed English language accounts of particular jurisdictions appear in Murray, "A Comparative Study of Peruvian Criminal Procedure," 21 *U. Miami L. Rev.* 607 (1967); Murray, "The Proposed Code of Criminal Procedure of Guatemala," 24 *La. L. Rev.* 728 (1964); Cooper, *supra* note 74, at 96-102. See also, Murray, "A Survey of Criminal Procedure in Spain and Some Comparisons with Criminal Procedure in the United States," 40 *N.D.L. Rev.* 7 and 131 (1964); Vouin, "The Protection of the Accused in French Criminal Procedure," 5 *Int'l. & Comp. L. Q.* 1 and 157 (1956).

[77] It has been estimated that in Peru about 95% of all criminal investigations involving poor defendants are conducted by the clerk rather than the magistrate, despite an express legal provision to the contrary. Cooper, *supra* note 74, at 98-99.

[78] See H. Clagett, *supra* note 54, at 117. Of course, the Latin American jury may bear little resemblance to the common law jury of 12. For example, in Colombia there are only three jurymen, and only a majority vote is needed for a verdict. Eder, "Introduction" to *The Colombian Penal Code* 8 (NYU Amer. Series of For. Penal Codes 1967).

suits for damages resulting from criminal acts are sometimes tried in conjunction with the criminal proceeding.

---

5. Labor Codes

Since 1931 almost all Latin American nations have enacted elaborate, comprehensive codes of labor law.[79] The typical labor code confers a great many modern benefits upon the worker, such as minimum wages, paid vacations, profit sharing, maternity benefits, bonuses, family allowances, free medical services, death and retirement benefits, job security, and special protection for women and children. Most of these benefits have been paternalistically bestowed by legislators eager to co-opt working-class political support by imitating the more advanced European nations; seldom have they reflected the economic power of the working class.[80] Matters which would be determined by collective bargaining in the United States are generally fixed by law in Latin America. Consequently, all too frequently the protective provisions of these codes have been circumvented by employers, sometimes with disastrous socioeconomic consequences.[81]

Enforcement of many provisions, such as minimum wage regulations, has been quite lax in most Latin American countries, due to a shortage of inspectors and surplus of unskilled labor. The problem of nonenforcement is particularly acute in the rural areas.[82]

K. Latin American Legal Culture

The preceding sketch of the formal aspects of Latin American legal institutions requires complementation with a sketch of the underlying legal culture. By legal culture is meant the generalized set of lay and professional values and attitudes

---

[79] The history of these codes is sketched in Cuban Economic Research Project, *Codification of Labor Law in Latin America, Cuba: A Case Study* (Univ. of Miami mimeo 1965).

[80] See Febres-Cordero, "A Look at the Scope of Venezuelan Labor Legislation," 5 *Inter-Amer. L. Rev.* 383 (1963).

[81] For example, the Brazilian Labor Code (until amendment in 1966) provided that an employee could not be discharged after ten years of service except for grave fault, duly proven before the labor courts. Employers reacted to this provision by routinely firing employees after nine and a half years of service. When the labor courts began to treat nine and a half years as the equivalent of ten, employers simply discharged employees sooner. Exposition of Motives of the Law of the Fund of Guaranty of Service, Law 5.107 of September 13, 1966; R. Alexander, *Labor Relations in Argentina, Brazil, and Chile* 121-22 (1962). See also S. Barraclough and A. Domike, "Agrarian Structure in Seven Latin American Countries," *infra* Chapter III, pp. 268-69.

[82] "Recent Trends in Labour Legislation for Hired Agricultural Workers in Latin America," 84 *Int'l. Lab. Rev.* 101 (1961).

towards law and the role of the legal process in society.[83] It is this complex of values and attitudes that largely determines which aspects of the formal legal structure work and which do not. Given the dearth of empirical studies of Latin American legal institutions and the very real differences among the legal systems of the score of republics comprising Latin America, this impressionistic description should be viewed with considerable caution. Like the composite pictures of criminal and civil procedure, it is inaccurate as to any single Latin American jurisdiction.

Where there is some gap between the law on the books and the law in practice in all countries, that gap is notoriously large in Latin America. Despite an impressive amount of concern for the appearance of legality, a strikingly large number of legal norms are honored only in the breach. Phanor Eder, a life-long student of Latin American law, put the paradox in these terms:

> How can we reconcile and understand the curious combination of an outward respect for legal formalities and rituals, evidencing a real reverence for law, and a complete disregard of the substance and essence of parts of the written law?[84]

Much of the explanation for this wide disparity between the law on the books and actual practice lies in a complex of historical and cultural factors that have conditioned Latin American attitudes towards law. Five of the most important of these factors are idealism, paternalism, legalism, formalism, and lack of penetration.

------

1. Idealism

Iberian legal culture has been heavily influenced by Roman law principles and tradition. As has been suggested, this Roman law heritage had a dual nature. Though originally solidly grounded in custom and experience, Roman law became increasingly abstract and idealized in the late Empire. The medieval Iberian jurist was most impressed with the detached, idealized aspects of Roman law, culled from Justinian's Digest. The revival of Roman law scholarship which began in the 11th century was primarily concerned with constructing a harmonious and universal system of ethical guides for conduct by reasoning deductively from abstract moral postulates.

> The Roman attempt to legislate on the basis of reason was an expression of idealistic thinking; they idealized the human reasoning ability. Idealism and universalism imbued the law with an essentially unrealistic character, and Roman legislation came to be identified with beautiful principles of conduct that were regularly more honored in the breach than in the observance.
>
> From its very beginning written Spanish law was far more an expression of ideals to be attained than a reflection of social customs and traditions. . . . As

------

[83] See Friedman, "Legal Culture and Social Development," 4 *Law & Soc. Rev.* 29, 35 (1969).
[84] *Supra* note 67, at 42-43.

the *Etymologies* of St. Isidore . . . show, the strength of ancient local habits was undermined by a legal system that claimed moral superiority. Law could only be understood in terms of justice. . . . What the Romans and Spaniards did was to establish the direct priority of justice over law. Specific legislation could be . . . superseded on the basis of . . . abstract moral conceptions. . . .[85]

In certain areas payment of lipservice to legal norms is a byproduct of the Church's influence on the formal legal structure. As indicated previously, law and religion went hand in hand in medieval Iberia, and canon law served as an important source of Spanish and Portuguese law. With its rigid dogmas, moral intolerance, and slowness to change, the Church has been responsible for the enactment into secular law of numerous ideal standards of behavior that many people, particularly in modern times, find impossible or distasteful to meet.

In a brilliant essay on Hispanic-American cultural history,[86] Richard Morse has suggested that the postmedieval jurist who most clearly recapitulated Hispanic-Catholic legal and political thinking during the formative period of the New World colonies was Francisco Suárez (1548-1617), a Jesuit professor of theology at the University of Coimbra in Portugal. The importance of Suárez's jurisprudential views lies primarily in their reflection of deep-seated attitudes towards law and assumptions about the relationship of man to the state which still pervade much of Latin American society. Suárez perceived of law as a moral system, grounded on eternal law. Eternal law is known to us through natural law, which in turn is known by the dictates of right reason. To be law, human law must accord with eternal truths. In other words, to be a law a rule must be moral and just. "Strictly and absolutely speaking, only that which is a measure of rectitude, viewed absolutely, and consequently, only that which is a right and virtuous rule, can be called law."[87] Suárez also theorized that the people do not delegate but alienate sovereignty to their prince. If, however, the prince acts tyrannically, the people have a right to rebel and seize control of the government.[88]

The implications of this view of law are continually reflected in Ibero-American experience. If each citizen is entitled to make an independent determination of the justice of any particular law, those entrusted with the task of administering the law feel few compunctions about amending legislation to conform with their own assessment of what is right or expedient. Indeed, the Crown expected colonial officials to invoke the "I obey but do not execute" formula when royal decrees were issued "contrary to justice." Hence the difficulty in collecting taxes; the casual attitude towards smuggling; the widespread requirement of "speed money" for routine public

---

[85] Moreno, "Justice and Law in Latin America: A Cuban Example," 12 *J. Interamer. Studies & World Affairs* 367, 374 (1970). See also, F. Moreno, *Legitimacy and Stability in Latin America: A Study of Chilean Political Culture* 6-11 (1969).

[86] "The Heritage of Latin America," in L. Hartz (ed.), *The Founding of New Societies* 123, 153 (1964).

[87] Cited in Scott, "Francisco Suárez: His Philosophy of Law and of Sanctions," 22 *Geo. L. J.* 405, 414 (1934).

[88] F. Suárez, 2 *Selections from Three Works* 854-55 (J. Scott ed. 1944).

services or bribes for special services; the sympathy shown for the perpetrators of crimes of passion; the blatant disregard of traffic laws; even down to the nearly universal disdain for "no smoking" signs in public places. The Spanish and Portuguese languages contain numerous maxims suggesting this attitude toward law. (*E.g.,* "For our friends, everything; for strangers, nothing; and for enemies, the law!" or "He who invented the law invented the way around it.") There is much truth in Angel Ganivet's half-jesting statement of the Spanish juridical ideal: that every Spaniard should carry around with him his own *fuero,* containing but a single line: "This Spaniard is entitled to do what he damn well pleases!"[89]

If the real source of law lies in "right reason," a natural law concept external to societal consensus, the notion that legislative enactments are to be obeyed because they represent the will of the majority must sled uphill. Important Latin American legislation has historically been drafted by distinguished jurists in an atmosphere far removed from the clamor of special interest groups. Draftsmen have typically consulted the various solutions to the problem that have been enacted in other countries (with little awareness of how these solutions operate in practice) and selected the solution that appeared best to them as a logical proposition. Seldom has there been a fact-finding inquiry about the peculiarly local economic, social, political, or administrative problems involved, or an attempt made to crystallize local custom or practice.[90] While there may be disputes among jurists and law professors about the particular rules that have been drafted, these are generally disputes of a technical, doctrinal nature. The end product of this process has been legislation of idealized standards of behavior, continuing a tradition that harks back to late Roman law.

If the legal culture emphasizes the right and duty of citizens to rebel against unjust governments, one can expect a high degree of political instability. While the tendency to overthrow governments by force rather than overhaul them by votes involves many factors, not the least among them is this natural law heritage.

---

2. Paternalism

The paternalism which stemmed from the Iberian monarchies and the extended patriarchial family still permeates Latin American society. The Brazilian civil code provisions on paternal power set out at the beginning of this chapter clearly display this traditional mentality. Paternalism is most commonly expressed in the traditional *patrón (patrão)* complex, under which a member of the local elite customarily looks after the interests of his employees, tenants, or debtors in return for fealty and service. The *patrón* plays the role of protector, interceding with the authorities when any of

---

[89] *Idearium Español y el Porvenir de España,* translated as *Spain: An Interpretation* 61 (1946).
[90] See e.g., Cooper, *supra* note 74, at 92-93.

his flock is in trouble or needs an official document or permission. The *patrón* system serves to personalize and particularize legal relations for the lower class. During the twentieth century the ultimate *patrón* has become the state, from which Latin Americans seem to expect just about everything. "From jobs, stable prices, credit, high wages, security, and transportation, to subsidies for carnival masquerades, there is hardly anything for which the government is not expected to provide."[91]

Historically, elites have paternalistically bestowed constitutions and laws upon the populace with little regard or awareness of the desires and capabilities of those governed. Thus legislation often is the product of what a small group imagines would be best for the people.[92] The labor legislation previously discussed is an egregious example of paternalism in the legislative process.

Almost all societies protect certain classes of people, like children and the insane, from suffering the legal consequences of their own folly. The classes of persons with a claim to such protection in Latin America is large, often including married women and the large numbers of indigenous peoples and illiterates. Moreover, beneficiaries of governmental largesse, such as the recipients of welfare or a distribution of land in an agrarian reform program, are prevented from making their own choices in many important respects. Successful plaintiffs in tort actions are likely to receive pensions rather than lump sum settlements to prevent squandering of the award. Latin American lawmakers seem to doubt the capacity of large numbers of persons to take care of their own affairs and/or the honesty of those who deal with such people. They also demonstrate a remarkable confidence in their own ability to discern what is best for the people.

---

3. Legalism

Latin American legal culture is highly legalistic; that is, society places great emphasis upon seeing that all social relations are regulated by comprehensive legislation. There is a strong feeling that new institutions or practices ought not be adopted without a prior law authorizing them. Laws, regulations, and decrees regulate with great specificity seemingly every aspect of Latin American life, as well as some aspects of life not found in Latin America. It often appears that if something is not prohibited by law, it must be obligatory.

Lawmakers are generally not content to set out desired conduct in general terms. In many areas they seem to try to preregulate all possible future occurrences with detailed, comprehensive, and occasionally incomprehensible legislation or decrees. Situations which in the United States would typically be left to judges or

---

[91] Willems, "Brazil," in *The Institutions of Advanced Societies* 525 (A. Rose ed. 1958).

[92] This phenomenon is by no means unknown to the United States. The U.S. Constitution is but one of many laws which have been characterized in this fashion.

administrators to work out on a case-by-case basis under the rubric of "reasonable-ness" or "fairness" tend to be preordained by statute or regulation in Latin America. The legislative style reflects a mistrust of those administering and interpreting the laws, as well as the entire legalistic and codifying tradition of the civil law, which exalts certainty as a supreme value.[93]

Another facet of this legalistic mentality is the apparent belief in the omnipotence of legal enactments. The faith that almost any social or economic ill can be cured by legal prescription seems boundless. Whether society is willing or able to shoulder the costs of enforcement or implementation seldom enters into legislative deliberations. The Spanish Crown used to issue, for a price, decrees of *gracias al sacar,* legally lightening the purchaser's skin color; the notion that the law can perform magic has persisted to this day. Latin American statute books abound with laws that would be difficult or impossible to administer, even with highly trained and efficient bureaucracies.[94]

4. Formalism

Closely related to legalism is the exaggerated concern with legal formalities. Every country has some formalistic behavior, but Latin American concern with authenticity and verification is both impressive and oppressive. There is an amazing proliferation of requirements for legal permissions and official documents in all sorts of legal relationships. The mere cashing of a traveler's check can become a complicated,

---

[93] J. Merryman, *supra* note 18, at 50-51. See generally H. Spiro, *Government by Constitution* 211-36 (1959); Weaver, "Bureaucracy During a Period of Social Change: The Case of Guatemala," in *Development Administration in Latin America* 314, 328-330 (C. Thurber & L. Graham, eds., 1973).

[94] One of Brazil's leading economists and former planning minister, Roberto de Oliveira Campos, caught this aspect of legalism nicely when he satirically proposed the following bill to reduce his country's high interest rates, the result of severe inflation and a shortage of credit:

Decree-Law No. 001 − Regulates the Law of Supply and Demand and prohibits the scarcity of money or merchandise.

Article 1 − The Law of Supply is maintained

Article 2 − The Law of Demand is repealed.

Article 3 − The natural or artificial scarcity of money or any other merchandise is permanently prohibited.

Article 4 − The just profit shall be equal to 10 percent per annum, because we are all born with ten fingers on our hands. "Os Pseudojuristas," in *Ensaios Contra a Maré* 47, 50 (1969).

In a similar vein, one of Brazil's most distinguished historians, Capistrano de Abreu, proposed the enactment of the following statute as a panacea for the country's juridical ills:

Article 1 − The law shall be obeyed.

Article 2 − All provisions to the contrary shall be revoked. Jornal do Brasil, Oct. 18, 1967, p. 6, 1st Caderno.

time-consuming operation, and dealing with customs agents is likely to be a Kafkaesque experience. There is a marked tendency to presume that every citizen is lying unless one produces written, documentary proof that one is telling the truth. The formal legal systems of Latin American countries, whether ascertaining criminal guilt or issuing employment benefits, display a decided tendency to believe only documents and not people.[95]

In much the same fashion as the *conquistadores* brought along notaries to certify the legality of the *requerimientos* read to the Indians,[96] present day Latin Americans display a prodigious concern with ascertaining the existence of formal legal authority for almost any act. Notaries do a land office business,[97] and even their signatures may occasionally have to be authenticated. Official forms typically come with half a dozen copies attached, all of which must be duly signed, authenticated, and stamped. Some of this is obviously bureaucratic featherbedding, but some of it is due to the old Iberian habit of requiring several persons to perform the same task, with each checking on the others.

Governmental action, even when plainly arbitrary or tyrannical, is likely to be spelled out in startling specificity in official gazettes. Latin American regimes frequently appear more concerned with ensuring the formal legality of their actions by putting them in black and white in an official gazette than concealing their arbitrariness. One explanation for exaggerated concern with legal formalities in modern Latin America has been offered by Professor Morse:

> It is because the lawmaking and law-applying processes in Latin America do not in the last instance receive their sanction from popular referendum, from laws and constitutions, from the bureaucratic ideal of "service," from tyrannically exercised power, from custom, or from scientific or dialectical laws. As Gierke said of the Middle Ages: "Far rather every duty of obedience was conditioned by the rightfulness of command." That is, in a patrimonial state, to which command and decree are so fundamental, the legitimacy of the command is determined by the legitimacy of the authority which issues it. Hence the importance of sheer legalism in Latin-American administration as constant certification for the legitimacy, not of the act, but of him who executes it.[98]

---

[95] An extreme example was the Brazilian requirement that a pensioner who appears personally to receive a pension must present certification from the police that he or she is still alive. It was finally abolished in 1968. O Globo, Aug. 24, 1970, p. 23.

[96] See pp. 31-33 *supra*. Another revealing example of the *conquistadores'* exaggerated concern with formality is Pedrarias Dávila's celebrated reenactment before notaries of Balboa's immersion in the Pacific so that the Spanish claim to possession of the new territory and sea would be entirely legal. E. Cruz, *Derecho, Desarrollo e Integración Regional en Centro América* 13-14 (1967).

[97] For a description of Colombia's notarial system in practice, see L. Arévalo-Salazar, The Legal Insecurity of Rural Property in Colombia: A Case Study of the Notarial and Registry Systems 6-16 (Univ. of Wis. Land Tenure Center Res. Paper No. 45, April 1972). See also Margadant, "The Mexican Notariate," 6 *Calif. W. L. Rev.* 218 (1970).

[98] Morse, *supra* note 86, at 174.

There is a pronounced tendency to honor form over substance. Elaborate simulations to bypass particular legal provisions are fairly common and authorities frequently manifest remarkable tolerance of such maneuvers. For example, Article 27 of the Mexican Constitution prohibits foreigners from acquiring ownership of land within fifty kilometers from the seacoast. Mexican corporations desiring to purchase land in the prohibited zone must obtain permission from the Ministry of Foreign Relations and expressly agree that no foreigner may be a shareholder of the corporation. However, if a wholly-foreign-owned Mexican corporation purchased land in the prohibited zone through a wholly-owned Mexican subsidiary, the sale was considered perfectly legal because the holding corporation was considered a Mexican national.[99]

However, it would be naive in the United States to assume that discrepancies between the law on the books and the law in action are always attributable to legislative miscalculation. It would be even more naive to make that assumption for Latin America. Some of these discrepancies are quite intentional. Formalism can be a useful strategy for averting social change or managing social conflict. In many countries, particularly those undergoing wrenching societal clashes, it is frequently easier and less socially divisive to prevent or limit implementation of redistributive or regulatory legislation inimical to powerful interest groups than to prevent the enactment of such legislation. Proponents of such legislation are afforded a symbolic victory, but in practice little or nothing changes, either because supporters of the *status quo* have sufficient political and economic power to stall enforcement at the administrative level, or, as is not infrequently the case, the means of producing a high level of enforcement have not been provided for. A number of Latin American agrarian reform statutes have been of this "lyrical" variety.[100] Occasionally, some of these "dead letter" laws are resuscitated and utilized as means for effectuating significant socio-economic change when reformist groups succeed in capturing the executive but not the legislature.[101] On other occasions formalism may serve as a strategy for promoting social change. Obviously unenforceable provisions may be written into constitutions and laws in the hope that some day social, economic, or

---

[99] H. Wright, *Foreign Enterprise in Mexico: Laws and Policies* 117 (1971). Several other simulations were also utilized to get around this constitutional norm, *id.* at 116-18, one of which has been formally legitimized by Mexico's Foreign Investment Law of March 9, 1973. The new statute requires all new acquisitions of land within the prohibited zone by foreigners to be made through trusts (with a maximum term of 30 years) with Mexican fiduciary institutions. Lacey & Sierra de la Garza, "Mexico − Are the Rules Really Changing?" 7 *Int'l. Lawyer* 560, 576 (1973).

A number of simulations commonly employed in Latin America are described in B. Kozolchyk, "Law and the Credit Structure in Latin America," 7 *Va. J. Int'l. L.* 1, 11-13, 34-5 (No. 2) (1967) and Rosenn, "The Jeito: Brazil's Institutional Bypass of the Formal Legal System and its Developmental Implications," 19 *Am. J. Comp. L.* 514 (1971).

[100] See, e.g., A. Hirschman, *Journeys Toward Progress* 107-58 (1963); Rosenn, *supra* note 99, at 533-34; Chapter III, *infra* p. 274.

[101] A striking example was the Allende regime's use of preexisting, formalistic legislation to nationalize a substantial part of Chile's economy, despite a hostile legislature. See Petras, "Political and Social Change in Chile," in *Latin America: From Dependence to Revolution* 9, 24-25 (J. Petras ed. 1973).

political conditions will evolve sufficiently to permit implementation. From time to time such essentially aspirational or hortatory provisions eventually bear fruit.[102]

---

5. Lack of Penetration

The formal legal systems of Latin American countries are modern, developed institutional structures. Disputes are resolved by a hierarchical arrangement of courts on the basis of the wording and legislative history of legal norms, scholarly doctrine, opinions of distinguished jurists, and prior court decisions. Official determinations of the rights and obligations are based upon the application of impersonal, universalistic principles by professionals trained in the system. However, this formal legal system has failed to penetrate very far into most Latin American societies. With the exception of the elite and the still relatively small but burgeoning middle class, the great bulk of the population does not actively avail itself of the formal legal system. Their disputes have been resolved by the *patrón, paterfamilias,* or local leaders.[103]

Even today penetration of the formal legal systems is quite limited. Some Latin Americans still live in remote and inaccessible areas, for all practical purposes outside the market economy. Much of the rural interior still is only nominally under the control of formal authorities; real power lies in the hands of local landholders. Typically, the latter have rendered justice to their friends, and applied the law to their enemies.

Not only in rural regions has the penetration of formal legal systems been limited. Millions of urban Latin Americans dwell in the squatter settlements that ring all major cities. Penetration of the formal legal structure into these settlements is often incomplete, perhaps in large part because such a settlement itself may be of doubtful formal legality.[104]

Penetration of the formal system into even the modern, urban sectors is greatly hampered by difficulties in ascertaining its provisions. Discovering the governing law in Latin America today often seems as perplexing and difficult a task as it was in colonial times. One looks in vain for comprehensive digests, citators, a key-number system, CCH- or PH-type loose-leaf services, or an index to legal periodicals. The official gazettes are typically unindexed and undigested.[105] Whether one finds a particular

---

[102] For example, Article 157 (IV) of Brazil's Constitution of 1946 provided for profit sharing in all Brazilian firms. However, implementing legislation was never enacted. The provision remained as Article 158 (V) of the 1967 Constitution, and finally germinated as the Program of Social Integration, Lei Complementar No. 7 of September 7, 1970, which finances a profit-sharing plan of sorts via a gross receipts tax.

[103] See e.g., Heath, "New Patrons for Old: Changing Patron-Client Relationships in the Bolivian Yungas," in *Structure and Process in Latin America* 101, 120 (A. Strickon & S. Greenfield eds. 1972).

[104] This problem is explored in greater detail in Chapter V, *infra*.

[105] It should be pointed out that the United States had no Federal Register until 1935. Brown, "Comment," 34 *Mich. L. Rev.* 91 (1935). The chaotic situation with respect administrative rules

law or decree frequently depends on luck and the caption's phraseology. Decisions of important tribunals, including many supreme court decisions, remain unpublished. Since there is no doctrine of *stare decisis,* it is not uncommon to find several decisions by the same court on different sides of an issue. Instead of amending basic code provisions, Latin American practice is generally to adopt supplemental legislation, which, in turn, is amended and reamended. Frequently, one is forced to read a host of separate statutes and decrees regulating a given subject (and many others as well) and then undertake the jigsaw job of piecing together the provisions still in force to find the governing law. Hence, it is quite common to discover that the authorities charged with administering a particular body of law are unaware of significant changes in the statutory or case law. Inertia, ignorance, and inability to keep abreast of rapid-fire legislative change frequently combine to produce substantial differences between the formal norm and the law actually being applied.

L. Legal Education

When a delegation of Latin American law students visits a law school in the United States, their North American counterparts tend to emerge from the encounter a bit bewildered. Here are youngsters, some only 17 or 18, and the legal subject they most want to talk about is Kelsen's Pure Theory of Law. These are law students? Yes and no; they are undeniably students in faculties of law or juridical science, but many are there primarily to obtain a university degree or a liberal education. For a great many students, law school training is not aimed at entry into practice, but rather provides background for a career in business or government. To be sure, there are such students in North American law schools, but their proportion is far greater in Latin America, as it is in Europe.

Latin American law students typically enter law school immediately after secondary school, or after a brief cram course to enable them to pass university entrance examinations. The only general liberal arts training they receive at the university comes during the first two years of law school, when political science, economics, history, and sociology courses are mixed with some perspective courses like Introduction to the Science of Law. The remaining three years are devoted almost exclusively to required legal subjects.

The full-time law professor is still a rarity in Latin America. Most law professors are busy practioners, who dash into the law school to give a lecture and disappear immediately thereafter. Absenteeism, both by professors and students, tends to be rather high. Examinations are generally oral. Since classes are large (there are 8,000 students registered in the first-year class of the law school of the University of Buenos Aires, and 1500-1800 in the same class at the National University of Mexico), and professors are busy, in an hour half a dozen students may be ground through exams,

---

and regulations that prevailed until then is described in Griswold, "Government in Ignorance of the Law – A Plea for Better Publication of Executive Legislation," 48 *Harv. L. Rev.* 198 (1934).

one at a time. Students are expected to master significant portions of the codes, as well as the theoretical constructs of the leading commentators, and to restate them when queried by the professor. During examination periods students can be observed in the corridors, reciting code provisions aloud to commit them to memory.

As is the case in an increasing number of law schools in the United States, a major piece of written work is likely to be required for graduation. Student theses tend to be in the scissors and paste tradition — back-to-back quotations from German, French, Italian, and Spanish authors. The law of the author's own jurisdiction may receive little attention, and rarely is there an attempt to appraise a particular legal rule against the background of the Latin American socio-economic scene.

While there may be a separate oral examination on the thesis or a comprehensive examination after completion of all courses, there is generally no bar examination.[106] The law school diploma makes the law student eligible to practice. Prior to graduation, it is probable that the student will have picked up some notion of the practice through practicums, legal aid work, apprenticeship programs, or by working in a law office while going through school.

With few exceptions, Latin American legal education is overwhelmingly formalistic. While an increasing number of law schools do require work in seminars or legal clinics, the great bulk of the course work is based on straight lecture. In these lectures, emphasis continues to be given to exegesis of the formal legislative texts, recalling the analytical and expository techniques of the Glossators and commentators. Professor Boris Kozolchyk described these techniques in the following terms:

> At root, these methods are scholastic That is, they rely almost exclusively on deductive techniques in the search for abstract concepts. Empiricism is rejected in favor of pure reason, and consequently the deduced legal concepts are devoid of socio-economic content except for that which is assumed in the wording of the major premises.
>
> As applied first to Justinian's *Corpus Iuris Civilis,* scholasticism brought about definitions, distinctions, and classifications of Roman legal institutions, many of which sprang from Aristotelian notions such as that of the essence or cause, and others from theologically inspired dichotomies such as the "external" and "internal," "perfect" and "imperfect," "personal" and "real," and "objective" and "subjective." As applied to the study of European-inspired codes in Latin America, these scholastic tools taught students to distinguish "civil" from "commercial" and "public" from "private" law, or to differentiate between a contract, a right in rem, and an administrative concession. . . . Similarly, in Latin America it was first sought to establish the meaning of codified rules through a rule-by-rule analysis of their grammatical and logical components *(exegesis),* and later by a synthetic or dogmatic formulation of underlying themes, as found ex-

---

[106] Brazil may be an exception. Law No. 4.215 of April 27, 1963, Art. 48 (III) restricted entrance to the Brazilian bar to law school graduates who had either passed a bar examination or served a two year clerkship, but the bar exam alternative does not appear to have been implemented.

clusively in the codes. . . . The shortcomings of this method are apparent. In the first place, it reduces conceptual legal reality to only what may be stated axiomatically, or to the point where systematic deductions are possible; a proposition that does not allow deductions related to the entire syllogistic system is unworthy of conceptual attention. This shortcoming is responsible for the rather scornful attitude developed by many Latin American professors toward the analysis of judicial or administrative decisions, which they dismiss as an inferior reasoning or as mere casuistry. In the second place, it tends to ignore the purpose of a legal institution by isolating it from its factual background. . . . The third and possibly most damaging shortcoming of scholastic conceptualization is that it commonly leads to what may be described as the fallacy of conceptual self-sufficiency or "reification." Concepts are deemed to have real existence simply because they can be formulated logically. Once they are seen as things, they are also endowed with the power to exclude inconsistent reality. . . . Clearly, the problem of such an educational approach is its failure to take into account the limitations of abstract or pure reason, particularly when used not merely as a descriptive but also as an evaluative tool. For the evaluation of legal institutions, from whatever standpoint, requires more information than that available in formal logic.[107]

Viewing law as a science and legal education as a means of teaching taxonomy and the true meaning of legal norms helps to perpetuate the divorce between the formal legal system and actual behavior. One of Brazil's leading jurists and law professors, Santiago Dantas, clearly perceived the problem:

In the study of abstract legal rules presented as a system one can easily lose the sense of the social, economic, or political relationships the law is intended to control. The legal system has a logical and rational value, autonomous, so to speak. The study we make of this system, with strictly deductive and *a priori* methods, leads to a condition of self-sufficiency which enables the jurist to turn his back on the society and lose interest in the matter regulated as well as in the practical significance of the legal solution.[108]

This situation is slowly changing; in a number of countries (most notably Brazil, Chile, Costa Rica, Colombia, and Peru),[109] some law schools have begun to use a more active method of teaching and to employ full time professors. They are also

---

[107]"Toward a Theory on Law in Economic Development: The Costa Rican USAID-ROCAP Law Reform Project," 1971 *Law & The Social Order* 681, 751-54.

[108]"A Educação Jurídica e a Crise Brasileira," 13-14 *Revista Jurídica* 7, 18 (1955).

[109]Some of these efforts are described in S. Lowenstein, *Lawyers, Legal Education, and Development: An Examination of the Process of Reform in Chile* (1970); Headrick, "Introducing the Method of Active Teaching in Latin America: Colombia's First Seminar on Legal Education," 23 *J. Leg. Educ.* 333 (1970); Rosenn, "The Reform of Legal Education in Brazil," 21 *J. Leg. Educ.* 251 (1969); Steiner, "Legal Education and Socio-Economic Change: Brazilian Perspectives," 19 *Amer. J. Comp. L.* 39 (1971).

making a greater effort to integrate legal training with insights derived from nonlegal disciplines. The impact of such reform efforts cannot yet be evaluated.

M. Inter-American Legal Institutions

Given the weakness of much of Latin American national law enforcement machinery, the universalistic, natural law perspective of the region's jurists, and the common legal, cultural and linguistic backgrounds of Latin America, it is not surprising that a substantial body of supranational Latin American law has evolved via a regional network of treaties and conventions. These agreements cover a wide range of topics, such as asylum, recognition of *de facto* governments, arbitration, conflict of laws (the Bustamante Code), patents, trademarks, and the political and civil rights of women.[110] Space limitations preclude treatment of this vast body of regional law. Instead, we briefly introduce three subject areas of these international agreements which seem especially important to the development process: (1) the Organization of American States (OAS), (2) economic integration, and (3) human rights. Interested students are invited to explore them individually.[111]

---

1. Organization of American States

In 1890 an international conference set up a permanent organization known as the International Union of American Republics, designed to collect and disseminate commercial information. By 1910 this organization became known as the Pan American Union, and its objectives broadened to include codification of international law, removal of trade barriers, and arbitration of disputes. Latin American unhappiness with Theodore Roosevelt's Corollary to the Monroe Doctrine produced repeated proposals for a convention with the United States accepting the principle of nonintervention into the internal affairs of the Latin American Republics. Not until President Franklin Roosevelt decided to substitute the "Good Neighbor Policy" for the "Big Stick" was such an accord possible. In 1936 at Buenos Aires the United States agreed to give up her role as policeman of the Hemisphere if the American Republics as a body would agree to assume collective responsibility for threats to Hemispheric peace. This vague agreement was given greater concreteness in Havana in 1940 when the American Republics agreed that an attack on one state would be considered as an attack on all.

---

[110]The Pan American Union publishes a pamphlet called "Inter-American Treaties and Conventions," setting out the current status of these agreements.

[111]Useful guides are H. de Vries, *Cases and Materials on the Law of the Americas* (1972) and H. de Vries and J. Rodríguez-Novás, *The Law of the Americas* (1965).

With the formation of the United Nations at the close of World War II, Latin Americans sought to preserve and reorganize the inter-American system. In 1947 the regional security resolutions were reduced to treaty form in the Inter-American Treaty of Reciprocal Assistance (known as the Rio Treaty). The following year the Charter of the Organization of American States was signed at Bogotá by representatives of the twenty Latin American countries and the United States, all of which subsequently ratified it. The OAS, whose Secretariat is the Pan American Union, was created as a permanent organization to implement the provisions of the Charter and the Rio Treaty.

The functions of the OAS, as defined in Article 2 of the Revised Charter, are:

(a) To strengthen the peace and security of the continent;

(b) To prevent possible causes of difficulties and to ensure the pacific settlement of disputes that may arise among the Member States;

(c) To provide for common action on the part of those States in the event of aggression;

(d) To seek the solution of political, juridical and economic problems that may arise among them; and

(e) To promote, by cooperative action, their economic, social and cultural development.

One U.S. writer suggests that there is an additional function that is perhaps more important than any of the stated functions — the OAS "constitutes a juridical system for protecting the security and promoting the interests of the Latin American countries vis-à-vis the power and resources of the United States."[112] However, despite the theoretical juridical equality among its member states, there is no semblance of one country, one vote. In reality, it is an organization of the United States and the Latin American countries, or as one Latin American vividly expressed it, an association of "the shark and the sardines."[113]

Though the OAS is in theory dedicated to ensuring "representative democracy" and the preservation of human rights, the governments of a good many of its members are neither democracies nor respecters of human rights. Maintenance of peace and security in the Hemisphere plainly requires a police force and intervention into the affairs of an offending state. Yet efforts to organize such a police force have been flatly refused, and no juridical principle would appear dearer to the Latin American nations than that of nonintervention into the internal affairs of other states. These built-in contradictions have resulted in institutional paralysis and breakdown in times of crisis, such as the Dominican intervention in 1965 and the Cuban crisis of 1962.[114]

---

[112] Dreier, "The Special Nature of Western Hemisphere Experience with International Organization," in R. Gregg (ed.) *International Organization in the Western Hemisphere* 9, 21 (1968).

[113] J. Arévalo, *The Shark and the Sardines* (1961).

[114] See generally R. Gregg, *supra* note 112; Interamerican Institute of International Legal Studies, *The Inter-American System* (1966).

2. Economic Integration

The economies of the Latin American republics were historically built around the export of primary products, i.e., copper, beef, bananas, coffee, or sugar. Consumer demands for manufactured goods were satisfied, or at least allayed, by imports from the industrialized nations, paid for with the foreign exchange earned from exports. Large capital outlays for infrastructure investments like railroads or power plants were generally financed by foreign investment, often in the form of bonds.

The Depression of the 1930's, which severely constricted commodity markets, created serious balance-of-payments problems for Latin America. The substantial drop in foreign-exchange earnings sharply curtailed the capacity of Latin American countries to import and to service their sizeable external debts. To conserve precious foreign currency for essential items, high tariffs, import quotas, and exchange controls were enacted. In the smaller nations, the lack of sufficiently large markets discouraged significant industrialization. But in the larger countries of Latin America factories sprang up behind such protective barriers to satisfy domestic demand for previously imported goods.

The process of import-substitution industrialization received considerable impetus during World War II, which cut off the flow of manufactured goods to Latin America. Though they were high-cost, inefficient operations, these industrial plants were largely responsible for the substantial economic growth experienced by most of Latin America in the decade following the Second World War. Moreover, industrialization became a source of nationalistic pride; for many it represented the key to economic independence from the swings of commodity prices.

During the early 1960's disenchantment with import-substitution industrialization began to set in. By then the larger countries were producing domestically the great bulk of previously imported consumer goods, leaving little new to substitute. Consequently, industrial growth slackened. Moreover, Latin American economies remained dependent upon the export of primary prod cts for foreign exchange. High cost and poor quality made Latin American manufacturers noncompetitive outside their own protective tariff barriers. To some extent, balance-of-payments problems worsened, because restricting importation of consumer goods during hard times is politically far more viable than import restrictions (on machinery, components, or raw materials) that necessitate shutting down factories and throwing men and women out of work.

One solution to this dilemma, seized upon by a number of Latin American *técnicos* and politicians, was regional economic integration. A regional tariff barrier would offer opportunities for industrial expansion by expanding markets. It would also permit economies of scale and greater technological advancement. And, by exposing monopolies and oligopolies to competition, it would stimulate greater economic efficiency.[115]

---

[115]This background sketch has been largely drawn from J. Grunwald et al., *Latin American Economic Integration and U.S. Policy* 20-29 (1972).

Though there had been numerous integrative efforts dating all the way back to Bolívar's Congress of American States in 1826, none achieved notable success prior to 1960. That year significantly marked the establishment of two important regional economic groups — the Central American Common Market (CACM) and the Latin American Free Trade Association (LAFTA). The original members of the CACM are El Salvador, Guatemala, Honduras, and Nicaragua, with Costa Rica joining in 1963. The original members of LAFTA are Argentina, Brazil, Chile, Colombia, Ecuador, Mexico, Paraguay, Peru, and Uruguay. Bolivia joined in 1966, as did Venezuela in the following year.

(a) The Central American Common Market

The economic integration movement in Central America began during the early 1950's with a series of bilateral free trade treaties. By 1958 the Central American states made a cautious effort to establish a free trade zone. The multilateral Treaty on Free Trade and Central American Economic Integration, signed in Tegucigalpa on June 10, 1958, committed the signatory states to setting up a free trade zone during a ten-year period. Simultaneously, an "integrated industries" program was adopted to encourage the development of industries requiring production on a larger scale than the markets of any one of the countries could absorb. Those plants designated "integrated" received tax incentives, free trade status within the CACM, and the right to import duty-free raw materials and component parts for a ten-year period.[116] In 1959 the Central American Agreement on the Equalization of Import Duties and Charges was signed, calling for a common external tariff within five years. Rates were to be low for capital goods, moderate for consumer goods, and high for goods produced or easily producible within the region.

This movement culminated in 1960 with the General Treaty on Central American Integration. The contracting countries agreed to establish a common market among themselves within five years and to set up a free trade zone. Approximately 75 percent of the formerly dutiable Central American products were freed from import duties immediately. By the late 1960's tariff exemption extended to 97 percent of the CACM's products. As a result, trade among the member countries in 1970 was nine times that of 1960. Foreign investment in the CACM more than tripled between 1960 and 1968. Part of this increase in economic growth has been attributable to economic integration.[117]

---

[116] No country is allowed to establish a second "integrated industry" until all CACM countries have at least one such industry. Quality and price controls were authorized to prevent unfair exploitation of the quasi-monopolistic positions of the "integrated industries." See generally Cochrane, "Central American Economic Integration: The Integrated Industries Scheme," 19 *Inter-Am. Econ. Affairs,* p. 63 (Aut. 1965).

[117] J. Grunwald et al., *supra* note 115, at 45-47. At least 1/7 of the economic growth in Central America during 1962 and 1965 has been traced to the expansionary effect of the CACM. *Id.* at 47-48.

Unfortunately, the CACM has been in a state of crisis since 1969, when the so-called "soccer war" erupted between El Salvador and Honduras. In 1970 Honduras withdrew from the CACM. In addition to the enmity between El Salvador and Honduras, dissatisfaction with the CACM has resulted from a feeling by Nicaragua and Honduras, the two least developed countries, that the lion's share of the benefits of economic integration have been going to the more developed nations of the CACM.

(b) The Latin American Free Trade Association

LAFTA, established by the Treaty of Montevideo in 1960, has made considerably less progress towards integration than the CACM. The LAFTA Treaty pledged its adherents to three courses of action: (1) elimination of intra-regional trade barriers over a twelve-year period, (2) establishment of industrial complementation agreements for zonal industries allowing two or more members to trade freely immediately in groups of products, and (3) preferential treatment for less developed countries within the group (Ecuador and Paraguay, joined by Bolivia). However, the wide disparities of income levels among the group's membership, and fear of domination by Argentine, Brazilian, and Mexican industries have forced the LAFTA countries to modify the Montevideo Treaty to extend the period for effectuating a free trade zone from 1973 to 1980. While some progress has been in reducing tariffs and establishing complementation agreements, the results have generally been disappointing.[118]

Dissatisfied with the slow rate of progress in LAFTA and fearful of being swallowed by the more industrially developed countries, the Andean countries (Bolivia, Chile, Colombia, Ecuador, and Peru) in 1969 signed a subregional integration agreement (Agreement of Cartagena), creating the Andean Common Market. The Agreement calls for the automatic annual tariff reductions of 10 percent beginning in 1971, with attainment of a customs union by 1980. The Andean nations have subsequently agreed upon a set of rules regulating foreign investment and multinational corporations.[119]

The Presidents of the Latin American Republics, meeting in Punta del Este in 1967, agreed to the establishment of a Latin American Common Market by 1985.

3. International Protection of Human Rights

Protecting basic individual rights via international convention has long appealed to jurists in Latin America, as it has in other parts of the world. In 1945 the Inter-American Conference on the Problems of War and Peace at Chapultepec adopted a resolution calling for the international protection of human rights. Three years later

---

[118] See generally J. Grunwald et al., *supra* note 115, at 50-56.

[119] See Furnish, "The Andean Common Market's Common Regime for Foreign Investment," 5 *Vand. J. Transnat'l. L.* 313 (1972); Swan, "The Andean Code: A Preliminary Appraisal," 5 *Lawyer of the Americas* 259 (1973). Venezuela joined the Andean Group in 1973.

the Bogotá Conference, in addition to adopting the Charter of the Organization of American States, also approved the American Declaration of the Rights and Duties of Man. Based largely on the draft of the U.N. Declaration of Human Rights, the American Declaration contained a series of articles dealing with basic civil and political rights. Its preamble proclaimed the hope that "the international protection of the rights of man should be the principal guide of an evolving American law."

However, no significant progress towards implementation of such aspirational statements occurred until the Fifth Meeting of the Consultation of Ministers of Foreign Affairs, held at Santiago in 1959. Resolution VIII of that conference requested the Inter-American Council of Jurists to draft a convention on human rights; part II of the Resolution created an Inter-American Commission on Human Rights.

The Commission on Human Rights has acted to carry out its mandate of furthering respect for human rights in the Americas by investigating complaints received concerning violations of fundamental rights. Though it has no power to impose sanctions, the Commission has had some modest successes in promoting respect for civil and political rights by working quietly behind the scenes with cooperative governments and by publishing reports exposing large scale violations by uncooperative governments.[120]

The American Convention on Human Rights ("Pact of San José, Costa Rica") was finally approved on November 21, 1969,[121] but delegates from only 12 countries signed it. The four most populous countries at the conference – Argentina, Brazil, Mexico, and the United States – conspicuously refrained from signing. The Convention is to become effective upon ratification by eleven of the members of the Organization of American States. To date only Costa Rica has deposited its instrument of ratification.

The American Convention in many ways resembles the European Convention on Human Rights, signed nineteen years earlier. But where the European Convention, as originally adopted, guaranteed only 13 categories of rights and freedoms, the American Convention guarantees 23 categories. Professor Buergenthal suggests two hypotheses to explain the broader coverage of the American Convention:

> The first is that the draftsmen of the European Convention were more realistic than their American colleagues about governmental attitudes towards international protection of human rights and, to assure its ultimate entry into force, kept its provisions to a bare minimum while leaving the door open to its subsequent enlargement by subsequent protocols. The second hypothesis is that the inhabitants of the American Continents urgently need international protection for many more rights than did their European brethren. Both

---

[120]The work of the Commission is described in detail in A. Schreiber, *The Inter-American Commission on Human Rights* (1970).

[121]The text appears at 9 *Int'l. Legal Materials* 673 (1970), and much of the legislative history can be found in the Report of the U.S. Delegation to the Inter-American Specialized Conference on Human Rights, 9 *Int'l. Legal Materials* 710 (1970).

hypotheses are probably valid and that does not bode well for the speedy entry into force of the American Convention.[122]

The preamble affirms the intention of the American states "to consolidate in this hemisphere . . . a system of personal liberty and social justice based upon respect for the essential rights of man" and that "the ideal of free men enjoying freedom from fear and want can be achieved only if . . . everyone may enjoy his economic, social and cultural rights as well as his civil and political rights. There are clauses guaranteeing protection against discrimination, the rights to life (from the moment of conception) and humane treatment, due process (plus the right to appeal and to be free from double jeopardy), right to vote, and the right to travel. There are, of course, certain peculiarly Latin American characteristics in the Convention, such as the guarantee of the right of asylum. There is also an escape clause, found in the European Convention as well, permitting derogation of the Convention's norms in times of war and public danger.

Implementation of the Convention is entrusted to the Commission on Human Rights, which is accorded both investigatory and adjudicatory functions for individual allegations of violations of fundamental rights by a signatory state. The Convention also creates a seven-judge Inter-American Court of Human Rights, whose jurisdiction is triggered by the coincidence of three factors. The defendant country must have adhered to the Court's jurisdiction; the dispute must have been submitted by a country or the Commission on Human Rights; and remedies before the Commission must have been exhausted. The Court has the power to order restoration of deprived rights and/or damages to the victim.

Whether the requisite additional ten ratifications will be forthcoming is uncertain. Even more problematic is whether some of the governments of the Organization of American States will be willing and able to respect the provisions of the Convention. As one author concluded with respect to the recent violations of the European Convention by Greece:

The Convention system can protect human rights in member states only when the states have the will to respect them on the level of municipal law, and when the rule of law is an operational reality. The Convention system is really able only to handle the aberration, the exceptional denial of justice that will occur in any democratic system.

In a situation where torture is government policy and dictatorship the system of government it is obvious that only by changing that regime is there a hope of respecting human rights.[123]

---

[122] Buergenthal, "The American Convention on Human Rights: Illusions and Hopes," 21 *Buff. L. Rev.* 121, 123 (1971).

[123] Becket, "The Greek Case before the European Human Rights Commission," 1 *Human Rights* 91, 113 (1970).

In the chapters which follow, we turn to four specific problem areas in Latin American law. Many of the themes introduced in this chapter reappear in these more particularized contexts. In Chapter VI, when we seek more general perspectives on the interaction of the processes of law and development, we shall return to our examination of the Latin American legal culture.

Chapter II

ROLE OF THE COURTS IN
CONTROLLING GOVERNMENTAL ACTION

This chapter examines the role of the judiciary in ensuring that the exercise of governmental power complies with constitutional norms and limitations. We focus on Brazil, Mexico and Argentina, three countries in which the judiciary has been assigned a major function in regularizing the acts of government officials. In none of those countries – indeed, nowhere in Latin America – does the judiciary wield significant political power. Is it then merely capricious to start here in our exploration of the interrelations of the processes of law and development in Latin America?

Professor Kalman Silvert suggests one possible response:

> ... [T]he rule of law itself is the central operational measure of the mitigation of class and other internecine conflict, and thus the rule of law permits the emergence of that general social interest within which the greater individual freedom and efficiency play. To the extent to which man is equal before the laws, he begins to escape the bondage of class and those other ascriptions which enslave him by limiting his power to act in ways that benefit both himself and his society. Liberty to be rational and to project oneself and an environment which opens to the individual opportunities for social confidence, equality before the laws, and the fraternity of an enlarged national community are still primary guides to the social and political requisites of development.[1]

This passage raises at least as many questions as it answers. Is the rule of law an essential ingredient of economic development? There is a wealth of recent historical experience to the contrary, some of it in Latin America. And if political development or social development are equated with the rule of law, then assertions which seem to be statements of fact turn out to be tautologies, or statements of value preferences, or both. It is even arguable that emphasis on the rule of law is anti-developmental, tending to protect existing interests against change. A heavy dose of skepticism is thus always appropriate when one thinks about the impact on development of a commitment to the rule of law – or, as it is sometimes called by its most privileged devotees, the Rule of Law.

Despite these cautionary remarks, it is undoubtedly true that strengthening the rule of law will bear on the developmental process, and often in a positive way. In

---

[1] K. Silvert, *The Conflict Society* 264 (Rev'd ed. 1966).

Chapter VI, we examine in detail some of the contributions of the rule of law to the process of development. Here we do no more than suggest some of those contributions:

(1) The most basic function of law is to provide security, and one possible variety is security against government itself. Government under law is government that is restrained from frustrating at least some expectations. Some kinds of developmental activity will never occur in the absence of this assurance embodied in law.

(2) Some developmental activities depend on the government's coordinating function. People must obey, and even cooperate; the likelihood that they will do so is increased if they perceive government to be legitimate. The rule of law provides government with one form of legitimacy.

(3) Various kinds of developmental activity are inconceivable in the absence of a sense of community. Law promotes the sense of community by making intra-group relationships more secure, and by legitimizing power; more basically, the very existence of law defines the boundaries of community.

(4) The problem of inequality, which is present in all societies, is especially severe in the developing countries. Some writers resolve the question of the relation between development and inequality by defining development partly in terms of increased equality. Others argue that inequality is a drag on development, even if development is narrowly conceived in purely economic terms. Still others argue that developmental activity tends to create greater inequality. If law creates power (and is power), then law and inequality are conceptually inseparable. Constitutionalizing governmental power may in some respects retard the movement toward greater equality, and may in other respects advance that movement.

This chapter begins with a look at some of the roots of authoritarianism in Latin America, and at the position of the Latin American judiciary. We then turn to recent experience with judicially-enforced constitutionalism in the three largest countries of Latin America. We close the chapter by examining the performance of Brazilian and Argentine judges under the stress of such phenomena as revolution and the suspension of constitutional guarantees.

---   •

A. Authoritarianism and the Latin American Judiciary

"Our poor Constitution — so virginal and so violated." This lament of a distinguished Argentine lawyer epitomizes not only much thinking about constitutionalism, but also a deeper skepticism about the place of law in Latin American society. In all societies, gaps are evident between the law on the books and the living law. In Latin America, that gap is a yawning abyss. Particularly in constitutional law, the social reality seems especially far removed from the guarantees found on paper. Nor are constitutions necessarily long-lived. After noting that from the time of Independence until 1959 twenty Latin American republics have had a total of 186 constitutions, one scholar concluded: "Nowhere are constitutions more elaborate and less observed."[2]

Those portions of Latin American constitutions which govern the succession of governments have been especially vulnerable. In consequence, governments in Latin America have regularly suffered from a deficiency of legitimacy. In much of the region, there has been little consensus as to government's "title to rule." Irving Louis Horowitz summarizes this state of affairs in a phrase: "the norm of illegitimacy."[3] The resulting political instability is often identified as an impediment to development in Latin America. But stumbling development and political instability stand in a chicken-egg relationship, for instability is also said to result from the failure to develop.[4]

The following three sections show the judiciary of three countries at work in the construction of systems of constitutional protections against arbitrary government. In this section, we set the stage with two formidable pieces of furniture. First, we look at the philosophical, historical and institutional origins of an authoritarian tradition that remains strong today. Next we consider the rather low estate of the judiciary in Latin America. This combination of a weak judiciary with a long history of government dominated by personalist leaders (*caudillos*), military juntas and single-party rule should give pause to any judicial review enthusiast. Yet, as the succeeding sections show, judges have played an important role in the creation and nurturing of constitutionalism in Latin America — and continue to play that role even under circumstances that are, to say the very least adverse. The theme of this chapter is epitomized at the end of this section in Professor Henry Hart's reply to Judge Learned Hand's famous disclaimer of judicial competence.

---

[2] Mecham, "Latin American Constitutions — Nominal and Real," 21 *J. Politics* 258 (1959). Calculating the number of constitutions which have been in force in Latin America is a perplexing task, for it is often difficult to tell whether a particular constitution was ever in force, or whether a constitution should be regarded merely as an amendment or a new constitution. Moreover, previously abrogated constitutions are occasionally resuscitated. The latest published count totals 247, an average of more than twelve per country. R. Fitzgibbon, *Latin American Constitutions: Textual Citations* 3 (1974).

[3] "The Norm of Illegitimacy: The Political Sociology of Latin America," in I. Horowitz, J. de Castro, and J. Gerassi, eds. *Latin American Radicalism* 3 (1969).

[4] Lipset, "Some Social Requisites of Democracy: Economic Development and Political Legitimacy, 53 *Amer. Pol. Sci. Rev.* 69 (1959).

1. The Roots of Authoritarianism

H. WIARDA, TOWARD A FRAMEWORK FOR THE STUDY OF POLITICAL CHANGE IN THE IBERIC-LATIN TRADITION: THE CORPORATIVE MODEL

25 *World Politics* 206, 210-212 (1973)*

If modern political analysis in the Northern European and Anglo-American tradition was to lead to the glorification of the accomplished fact and of political pragmatism, to materialism and the success theory, and to a unilinear, stage-by-stage conception of development, which was also derived principally from the experiences of these nations, then Iberic-Latin culture can surely claim as its basis a moral idealism, a philosophical certainty, a sense of continuity, and a unified organic-corporate conception of the state and society. This conception derives from Roman law (one can still profitably read Seneca for an understanding of the Iberic-Latin tradition), Catholic thought (Augustine, Aquinas), and the traditional legal precepts (the *fueros* or group charters of medieval times, the law of the *Siete Partidas* of Alfonso the Wise). In comprehending the Iberic-Latin systems, one must think in terms of a hierarchically and vertically segmented structure of class and caste stratifications, or social rank orders, functional corporations, estates, juridical groupings and *intereses* — all fairly well defined in law and in terms of their respective stations in life — a rigid yet adaptable scheme whose component parts are tied to and derive legitimacy from the authority of the central state or its leader. The foundations for these systems lie in what Morse has called the "Thomistic-Aristotelian notion of functional social hierarchy," and they find their major expression in the political thought of Spain's Golden Century . . . .

Vitoria and Suárez stand as the great system builders on which the Spanish empire and Iberic-Latin society were constructed. Their genius lay in fusing the older Thomistic conception and the system of juridical estates derived from Spanish customary law with the newer concept of absolute, state-building royal authority. There were important differences among the several writers mentioned, to be sure, but what is more striking are the common, unifying themes. All assume an ordered universe, all adopt the Thomistic hierarchy of laws, and all base their theories of state and society on Christian assumptions. All share, furthermore, a disdain for the common man; what they mean by popular government is feudal and aristocratic, based on a restoration of the privileges or *fueros* of the Middle Ages, the power of the traditional estates, dominated by "natural" elites, and without popular suffrage. Their view of society and the state is an organic one — that government is natural, necessary, and ordained by God for achieving harmony among men. This conception is an almost inherently conservative one. In contrast to contract theory which, except in Hobbes, is individualistic, democratic, liberal, and progressive, organic theory subordinates human law to natural and divine law, is more tolerant of authority, slights the individual in favor of group "rights" or a superior "general will," accepts and justifies the status quo, reserves extensive powers for traditional vested interests, and leads inherently

---

toward a corporate system which subordinates man to some allegedly higher end and unity.

The best form of government therefore is an enlightened monarchy or an all-powerful executive; there can be no "separation of powers" or "checks and balances" on the U.S. model. Rather, a monistic structure is required to keep peace and maintain the "natural" order. Extensive powers are also reserved for such corporate entities as the Church, the municipalities, the landed and commercial elites, the guilds, the military hierarchy, and other vested and chartered interests. Organic theory in both Church and state rejects liberal individualism and the materialistic and secular conceptions that accompanied development in northern Europe. Although this repudiation does not *necessarily* follow from the organic, Catholic, and scholastic premises, it certainly has a powerful basis in them.

C. ANDERSON, POLITICS AND ECONOMIC CHANGE IN LATIN AMERICA: THE GOVERNING OF RESTLESS NATIONS

Pp. 15-21, 23-26 (1967)*

With independence from Spain, the Latin American states came into existence. A new institution had been appended onto an old society, at the behest of a small part of the population who felt it relevant to its way of life. The form that the new nations took, with a few exceptions, notably Brazil, was the most modern available, that which was the product of the French and American revolutions. Certainly, such aspirations were not uncriticized. Some of the champions of independence, the most prominent being Simon Bolívar, remained skeptical of the applicability of democratic models to the Latin American situation, and such dissent was complicated by the fact that separation from the mother country was for some a defense of monarchical legitimacy, a reaction to the triumph of the Napoleonic armies in Spain. Experiments in state-creation on terms other than liberal democratic are an episode of Latin American independence. Iturbide established his short-lived empire in Mexico, the European courts were combed, unsuccessfully, for aspirants to Latin American thrones, and the achievements of the Portuguese monarchy's Brazilian captivity were not unworthy of the claims of those skeptical of the aspirations of the revolutionary leaders of the independence movements. Yet such experimentation with nondemocratic political forms appears historically, except in Brazil, as a curious counter-theme to the dominant tendencies of the times. The "most advanced nation" model has a fatal fascination for the builders of new nations. Thus, the relations of state to economy and society prescribed for the new republics of Latin America were to be those borrowed from the experience of the nineteenth-century nation-state in Europe, just as the relationship of economy and society to the state was to be structured in terms of the processes of constitutional democracy.

The establishment of the state nearly always precedes the development of corresponding national social and economic systems. It should be noted that the

---

*Copyright 1967. Reprinted by permission of D. Van Nostrand Company.

adoption of the physical and territorial form of the European state in Latin America poses no problem in itself. In contrast to the experience of, say, Eastern and Central Europe, the jurisdictional units established in Latin America have, after an initial period of sorting out, remained quite durable. The difficulty is rather that the particular models of constitutional democracy and economic liberalism, specifying the relationship of state and private society, did not work out as they had in the advanced Western nations.

We have attributed the plausibility of these models of the relationship between the state and corresponding, but discrete, social and economic systems, to the nation-integrating effects of absolutism and mercantilism in Western Europe. That the situation was different in Latin America may seem strange in view of the common conception that the Latin American colonial experience was mercantilistic, perhaps in its most extreme form. Yet from the point of view of Latin America, the experience of this continent with mercantilism was different from that which prevailed in Western Europe and North America

In the first place, Spanish policy toward Latin America did anything but stimulate semi-autonomous social and economic systems within the administrative units of empire that were later to declare themselves nations. Spanish imperial theory regarded the overseas dominions not as distinct units attached to the mother country, but as part of the mother country itself. The distinction was between *estos reinos* and *esos reinos,* "these" kingdoms and "those" kingdoms. The techniques of government and economic policy applied to the overseas dominions were not different from those enforced internally. Despite the reforms of the Bourbon period, the basic framework was one in which the Americas and the Iberian domains were identically involved in a centralized, bureaucratically regulated, absolutistic political economic system, in which the national community was the state, and the state the monarchy. . . .

. . . [T]he political economic system which assumed that the New World was an integral part of the home country nullified the presumed nationalizing effects of mercantilism and absolutism. The systems set in motion to the greater glory of the Spanish state tied Spain and the Americas rigidly together in working relationships. Independence became not a process of mitosis, in which prior interaction had led to the emergence of more or less self-sufficient organisms which could now go their separate ways, but a rending and tearing apart of the systemic substance about which social and economic life was organized.

Furthermore, the aggrandizement of state power through national integration and domestic productivity was a secondary concern to a Spanish crown grown wealthy through the exploitation of the precious metals of its overseas domains. Like many Latin Americans, the Colombian historian Nieto Arteta insists that Spain's intent was to suppress productive activity in the New World, to prevent Latin America from developing, so that the New World would be required to buy Spanish goods and pay for them with raw materials. However, to interpret Spanish policy as a classic case of colonialism misses the point somewhat. Spain's bullionist form of mercantilism seems to have constrained productive activity in the mother country in much the same way as it did in the Americas. Furthermore, as part of this policy of drawing wealth to the state, Spain had to create a viable economic base in the New World. While extractive industries certainly had first priority, attempts to improve industry and agriculture were not totally absent, and by the time of independence, the bulk of fabricated goods consumed in Hispanic America was produced there. Nonetheless, productive activity in the New World never represented more than the infrastructure for mineral exploitation. The economic development of the Americas as an objective in itself was never a central concern of the Spanish state.

Thus, Latin America did not undergo that nation-building experience of absolutism and mercantilism that was to pave the way for the particular conception of the nation-state institution that Latin America was to enact by *fiat*. The separation from Spain did not serve to disentangle a network of economic and social systems from the strict regulation of absolute monarchy. Rather, it severed the web of these relations, and left a ragged edge of broken strands. Furthermore, the types of socio-economic systems that had been constructed were not like those that had made plausible the revolutionary view of state and society which underlay the models of the state which inspired and guided the Latin American nation-builders.

The State's Economic Role in the Post-Independence Period

Most commentaries on the economic activities of the early independence period in Latin America are studies in the absence of events. Power struggles, civil war, the making and unmaking of constitutions are at the center of the historical stage. Economic life appears stagnant, a persistence of colonial patterns hampered by political turmoil; or change occurs so gradually that it escapes historical record. But the dominance of political events in the historical record does not mean that the economic role of the state was of little concern to the modernizing elites of that day, nor that they sought to minimize that role. Rather, as they tried to emulate the political systems of the most advanced nations, so they attempted to make the economic functions of the nation-state consistent with those implicit in the Western model. . . .

In one country or another, virtually all the techniques and tools of state economic activity which were available to the European and North American statesmen of the age were tested in the Latin American environment. Tariff policies were manipulated and revised as protectionists and free traders succeeded one another in decision-making authority. Schemes to attract immigration, colonization, and enterprise through liberal concessions of public lands and taxation advantages appear early in the records of many nations. *Latifundia* [great landed estates] concentration itself was often an unintentional by-product of early efforts to increase productivity by placing public lands, or Church lands, in the hands of private proprietors. Efforts to stimulate practical scientific and technological endeavor, in the best Enlightenment tradition, were to be found in patent laws, the establishment of academies, prizes, and awards. Lucas Alamáns's short-lived Banco Avío in Mexico, Rivadavia's national bank in Argentina and Paez's in Venezuela, were but examples of attempts to establish public financial institutions as a stimulus to enterprise. Advanced codes of commercial law, most based on the *Code Napoléon*,[5] were enacted. Although labor legislation was hardly a fundamental concern of any Western government of the time, the dedication

---

[5] *Code Napoléon* generally refers to the French Civil Code of 1804. Here the reference should be to the French Commercial Code of 1807. See Chapter I, *supra*, p. 49. [Eds.]

of Latin American statesmen to formulating a policy appropriate to a modern, liberal economic system is to be noted in the early abolition of slavery in most countries, particularly those where slavery was not an important economic factor.

It would hardly be accurate to report that all these efforts had no impact on economic life. Sporadically and spottily they found a respondent effect in the activities of private individuals. Some market agriculture was undertaken, some few industries began, a somewhat greater intensity of commercial transactions was to be seen. But only in the south of the continent, and perhaps in Peru, where foreign enterprise and foreign trade arrived early, did the first three or four decades of independence record any significant gains in economic activity.

Generally, the services that the state offered to the private economy fell on infertile ground. The economic function of the Western nation-state model adopted in Latin America was premised on the existence of an ongoing, dynamic, transactional network between private individuals which the state served to enhance, supplement and regulate. ... In the absence of such a dynamic and self-generating economic system operating primarily within the jurisdictional area of the state, the logic of economic liberalism simply did not apply.

Simply put, the nation-state in Latin America was imposed on an area where most people did not think of the nation as a critical arena of social or economic involvement. It existed in something of a vacuum. It was not called upon to perform any critical functions for a people involved in an integrated and interdependent way of life. Baltisario Betancur, the Colombian statesman, has put the matter most succinctly: "In the history of Colombia, it is easy to appreciate the divorce of state and society. The state existed for itself, abstracted from the fact that the reason for its existence was the nation."

For most of the people of Latin America, the most meaningful framework of human interaction has been either subnational or supranational. Involvement in such alternative social systems has been only loosely articulated with the nation. For most of the people of Latin America, most of the time, the nation-state's activities have appeared as an obstacle rather than a supplement to the achievement of social goals, to the reinforcement of desired patterns of interpersonal relations. Subsumed by the *fiat* boundaries of the "nation" have been a variety of social systems for whose effective functioning the activities of the nation-state have been most irrelevant.

The *latifundia,* or great estate, the not necessarily lineal descendent of the colonial *encomienda* or *repartimiento,* had become a virtually self-contained and self-sufficient political and economic system. The authority of the nation-state extended to its affairs only at the sufferance of the owners, and generally did not extend there at all. ...

The Latin American state was an appendage, attached to, but not part of, the social fabric of the New World. For most of the people of the society, what it did or did not do was a matter of considerable indifference. However, for a certain small part of the society, this transplanted institution became a critical focus of attention. With the establishment of the Latin American state, a locus of power and resources came to exist. Government derived resources from the society for functions it was not called upon to perform. Although the state was irrelevant to those it was structured to serve, it became relevant as a source of power, wealth, and social mobility for those who could not find or did not want a place in the subnational or supranational systems about which life was organized. . . .

Unbound by a responsibility to use public resources for public purposes, they found wealth in control of the nation-state. For many, the quest for El Dorado ended at the public purse. However, wealth was not all that was at issue for these "nationalized" groups. Isolated by indifference from society, they could fashion the nation-state as a total environment in which they could play out the roles and relationships prescribed for them in the European experience which they sought to emulate. With juristic ardour, they could dedicate themselves to the tasks of legislating for a body politic which had not consented to, in fact, which was for the most part unaware of, their authority. They could structure and assume positions and offices, imputing to them the prestige of their counterparts in other nations though such prestige did not rest on any real social responsibility. . . .

The quest for control of the nation-state was not only an alternative for these groups without place or status in the traditional order, it was virtually an imperative. Few other routes to prestige, wealth, and power were available to them. While in a society like the United States the energetic young have historically not found government service or politics an appealing career because business, the professions, and industry offer such great attractions, in the more rudimentary economies of Latin America such alternatives were simply not available. . . .

The high incidence of political violence, instability, and civil strife in Latin America has been explained in many ways, from class conflict to the "passionate nature" of the Hispanic race. However, it should also be noted that where the stakes of political success or failure are so very high, where the alternative possibilities for achievement so very low, to accept political defeat gracefully, or to be restrained in one's political activities by constitutional niceties, are virtues quite difficult to achieve. . . .

Public office may be a public trust, but the classic maxim of democracy is inoperative when so little is entrusted to public officials. In the absence of demands for responsibility by groups whose way of life was dependent on the effective operation of national socio-economic systems, those who did lay claim to that reservoir of powers and resources which was the state could dispose of these capabilities as they pleased.

The functional irrelevance of the Latin American nation to those whose consent it claimed but did not possess is a problem with many dimensions. The primordial function of the European nation-state was as a security system. Other activities came later, and were to a certain extent derivative. The state system emerged in Europe as an alternative to continental hegemony.

That the defensive function would be adopted as an integral part of the European model by the nation-builders of Latin America is obvious. In any event, the military institution as a legacy of the wars of independence was there, an indisputable social force. Yet history was to play a fateful trick on the newly established republics. In a very real sense, history bestowed an ironic blessing on Latin America. Due to the peculiar historical circumstances of the nineteenth century, the newly independent nations were seldom called upon to defend themselves by the use of armed force. England's balance of power strategy, the Monroe Doctrine "separation of the spheres," the entire complex of this "era of peace," served to insulate Latin America from international warfare. A second set of factors served to minimize intra-Latin American armed hostility. In the absence of credible threats or viable possibilities for armed expansion, the military function of the nation-state was more or less irrelevant to the life of the nation. The military became, at best, an institution in quest of a role (to be found perhaps, as "guardian of the constitution," or arbiter between other power contenders), at worst, as a residual but nonresponsible legatee of the powers inhering in that nation-state which had been decreed and established, but whose general social utility had not yet been discovered.

J. BUSEY, OBSERVATIONS ON LATIN AMERICAN CONSTITUTIONALISM

24 *The Americas* 46, 48-50, 53-56, 60 (1967)

Scholars have cited various causes as being responsible for the discrepancies between Latin American constitutional theory and political fact, and for the extreme fragility from which the basic documents suffer.

It is contended, first, that Latin American constitutions tend to be quite artificial, and divorced from the environments in which they are supposed to function. Because of their low level of previous experience, it is argued, the founders of Latin American republics were compelled to turn to other lands for their constitutional models. The Latin Americans borrowed freely from the United States, Spain, and France, and even imported some forms from Britain, Switzerland, and ancient Greek and Roman sources. The presidential system, the concept of separation of powers, the formalities of federalism where attempted, statements of individual rights, judicial structures, some tinkering with parliamentary devices – all these were lifted out of foreign constitutional documents, and were not native to the Latin American soil . . . .

Or, when not borrowed from abroad, the provisions in Latin American constitutional documents were quite artificial for another reason: They were and are creations of small, unrepresentative elites out of touch with their surroundings and moved by highly abstract, theoretical concepts unrelated to their environments. . . .

There is also a rather different kind of contention about the sources of Latin American constitutional anomalies. According to this view, the Latin American environments themselves were and are extremely hostile to the establishment of any sort of stable, constitutional government, no matter what the forms or origins.

Books have been written about these unfavorable elements of Latin American historical, physical, and social environment. . . . Suffice it to say here that many writers have lamented (1) the physical and social dissection of Latin America, which has made it difficult to agree upon the rules of the political game, (2) the intense poverty of large sectors of the Latin American population, which has deprived governments of the revenue needed for public education, communications, and general improvement, (3) the failure of leading sectors of many Latin American populations to regard government as having a social or public function, (4) the persistence of feudalistic relationships and attitudes which emerge out of patterns of land monopoly and prevent development of a sense of public responsibility, and (5) the paucity of self-disciplined, responsible, socially conscious leaders. . . .

Because of an understandable desperation which attaches to any attempt at rationalizing Latin American constitutions, another opinion is often expressed, and is designed to skirt the problem of causes for the inapplicability and fragility of Latin American constitutions. This is to the effect that Latin American framers never intended that their documents would really be put into practice or that they would reflect Latin American political reality. The constitutions, it is alleged, were only supposed to express hopeful aspirations, ideal goals, or noble dreams of their founders. Since there is little evidence that Latin American constitutional framers were in fact moved by such esoteric and unrealistic considerations, one cannot avoid the suspicion that much of this is rationalization after the fact. Nevertheless, there is doubtless much justification for assuming that after about the fifteenth or twentieth constitution, the statesmen of any country would probably develop a certain sense of unreality or even frivolity as they drearily set about their task another time. . . .

We can accept all these points of view, and still contend that there are features of Latin American constitutional content which have been inconsistent, self-defeating, and conducive to extreme governmental instability. . . . The broad outlines can be painted in easily and convincingly; and examples from a few representative documents can be cited.

It is frequently commented that though Latin American constitutional *policies* may be violated, their *forms* are usually observed. That is to say, there *are* presidents, congresses, systems of courts, and the like, and these more or less correspond to the constitutional dicta. However, Latin American governmental practice does not coincide with constitutional provisions for democratic and civilian government, free elections, independent judiciaries, effective and respected legislative bodies, limitation of the executive power, individual guarantees and civil rights, social reform, and the like.

Almost every constitution of Latin America makes some statement to the effect that the government is to be democratic, and that power is to emanate from the people. Elaborate provisions set up legislative bodies and provide in minutiae for the procedures whereby they will determine policy, as well as proclaim that no branch of government is to exercise the powers of others. And yet, the same documents provide their presidents with an incredible sweep of powers, permit them to declare states of siege and suspend constitutional guarantees, and provide only the most dubious protections against abuse of presidential authority. For example, the Mexican Constitution, Article 39, states that "the national sovereignty rests essentially and originally in the people," and in Article 40 proclaims that the republic is to be "democratic"; and there are many other phrases to the same effect. According to Article 49 "The supreme power of the Federation is divided, for its exercise, into Legislative, Executive, and Judicial" and "two or more of these Powers shall never be united in one single person or corporation," and so on. Articles 51-79 are devoted to every imaginable aspect of the legislative power; and then, Article 89 cuts the legislative power to pieces by granting to the President policy-making authority in areas which are unknown in most democratic systems. . . . In almost every Latin American constitution, sweeping legislative powers are granted to presidents, despite strong admonitions in the same constitutions against any fusion of two or more branches.

In the Mexican Constitution, as in most others of Latin America, the President is permitted to suspend constitutional guarantees throughout the republic or in determined places. His action is said (Article 29) to require "approval by the Federal Congress, and during adjournments of the latter [i.e., during eight months of each year – jlb] , of the Permanent Committee," which can be secured by the President *after* the guarantees have been suspended. Nothing of this sort is known to the Constitution of the United States, the Canadian Constitution, or to most of the constitutions of Western Europe.

In these matters, the Constitution of Mexico is no exception in Latin America. Rather, it represents the norm. Similar and occasionally even more striking provisions may be found in the documents of almost every republic south of the Río Bravo del Norte. . . .

It is said that the Constitution of Argentina, 1853, is closer to that of the United States than any other; and yet, features conducive to executive power were introduced in Argentina which are unknown to the U.S. document. Article 86 of the Argentine Constitution goes beyond anything to be found in our executive provisions of Article II, and includes (Section 19), a very broad and essentially unlimited power to suspend the constitutional guarantees. . . .

. . . [I] t must be stressed that the problem does not only lie in artificiality of origin or in unfriendliness of environment. The documents themselves include built-in conflicts of meaning and intent. They are likely to grant powers to executive and centralized authority which are enough to assure the establishment of dictatorships, with or without other causal factors; and the unsatisfactory, self-defeating content of the documents themselves would be reason enough for frequent change. Their own provisions often provide for violations of free government. Even ferocious dictators have carried on their rule without doing too much violence to their constitutions. Provisions could be found to permit every atrocity. Or, since the documents were so little worthy of respect, they could be easily changed to suit the whims of tyrants.

The fact is, that though there were widespread borrowings from abroad, and though narrow elites who were disconnected from reality did play important roles in Latin American constitution-making, much of the fault lies in the indigenous features of the constitutions themselves. It may even be said that *too much* of the Latin American environment went into them. That is, they omitted important protections, obfuscated statements of individual rights and added sections which could only subvert the democratic purposes that they were supposed to serve. Instead of protecting against some of the major threats in the Latin American environments – that is, *caudillismo, personalismo,* executive preëminence, weak rule of law, and the like – *the framers incorporated most of these features into the constitutional documents themselves.* For the achievement of stable democracy, environmental features demanded that radical and rigid protections be built into constitutions which would preserve and enhance, not weaken and destroy, the opportunities for development of free government. There is nothing unusual about the importation of ideas from abroad. This is the way all constitutions are built. What was unusual was that the Latin Americans would pay constitutional homage to the very dictatorial features of their environments which they were presumably trying to avoid.

Questions

1. The suspension of constitutional guarantees by the President may be unknown in the constitutional theory of the United States and Canada, but it is scarcely unknown in the experience of those two countries. How would Busey describe President Lincoln's constitutionally unauthorized suspension of habeas corpus, or Prime Minister Trudeau's 1970 suspension of constitutional guarantees in Canada? Apart from such rare and cataclysmic events, is it fair to suggest that "presidential government" is unknown in the United States? For example, what constitutional restrictions effectively limit the U.S. President's conduct of foreign affairs?

2. Is it possible that Latin America's constitution makers were *not* "presumably trying to avoid" presidential government?

3. How realistic is it to suppose that if the constitutions of countries like Argentina or Mexico had been identical to that of the United States, Argentine or Mexican political histories would have been substantially different?

---

2. The Civilian Image of the Judge

J. MERRYMAN, THE CIVIL LAW TRADITION

Pp. 36-39 (1969)*

... [I]n the civil law world, a judge ... is a civil servant, a functionary. Although there are important variations, the general pattern is as follows. A judicial career is one of several possibilities open to a student graduating from a university law school. Shortly after graduation, if he wishes to follow a judicial career, he will take a state examination for aspirants to the judiciary and, if successful, will be appointed as a junior judge. Before very long, he will actually be sitting as a judge somewhere low in the hierarchy of courts. In time, he will rise in the judiciary at a rate dependent on

---

*© 1969 by the Board of Trustees of the Leland Stanford Junior University. Reprinted with the permission of the publishers, Stanford University Press.

some combination of demonstrated ability and seniority. He will receive salary increases according to preestablished schedules, and will belong to an organization of judges that has improvement of judicial salaries, working conditions, and tenure as a principal objective.

Lateral entry into the judiciary is rare. Although provision is made in some civil law jurisdictions for the appointment of distinguished practicing attorneys or professors to high courts,[6] the great majority of judicial offices, even at the highest level, are filled from within the ranks of the professional judiciary. Judges of the high courts receive, and deserve, public respect, but it is the kind of public respect earned and received by persons in high places elsewhere in the civil service.

One of the principal reasons for the quite different status of the civil law judge is the existence of a different judicial tradition in the civil law, beginning in Roman times. The judge (*iudex*) of Rome was not a prominent man of the law. Prior to the Imperial period he was, in effect, a layman discharging an arbitral function by presiding over the settlement of disputes according to formulae supplied by another official, the *praetor*. The *iudex* was not expert in the law and had very limited power. For legal advice he turned to the jurisconsult. Later, during the Imperial period, the adjudication of disputes fell more and more into the hands of public officials who were also learned in the law, but by that time their principal function was clearly stated to be that of applying the emperor's will. The judge had no inherent lawmaking power. He was similarly limited in medieval times. One of the grievances against the French judiciary, which seems to have been the target of so many prerevolutionary complaints and postrevolutionary reforms, was that the judges were varying from the traditional Continental image of the judicial function by acting very much like English judges. They were interpreting creatively, building a common law that was a rival to the law of the central government in Paris, and even developing their own doctrine of *stare decisis.*

With the revolution, and its consecration of the dogma of strict separation of powers, the judicial function was emphatically restricted. The revolutionary insistence that law be made only by a representative legislature meant that law could not be made, either directly or indirectly, by judges. One expression of this attitude was the requirement that the judge use only "the law" in deciding a case, and this meant . . . that he could not base his decision on prior judicial decisions. The doctrine of *stare decisis* was rejected. Another expression of the dogma of strict separation of the legislative and judicial powers was the notion that judges should not interpret incomplete, conflicting, or unclear legislation. They should always refer such questions to the legislature for authoritative interpretation. It was expected that there would not be very many such situations, and that after a fairly brief period almost all the problems would be corrected and further resort to the legislature for interpretation would be unnecessary. . . .

The picture of the judicial process that emerges is one of fairly routine activity. The

---

[6] The manner in which Brazil's career judiciary is selected and the various provisions to ensure a certain percentage of appointments from practicing attorneys are described in Tácito and Barbosa Moreira, "Judicial Conflicts of Interest in Brazilian Law," 18 *Am. J. Comp. L.* 689, 690-92 (1970). [Eds.]

judge becomes a kind of expert clerk. He is presented with a fact situation to which a ready legislative response will be readily found in all except the extraordinary case. His function is merely to find the right legislative provision, couple it with the fact situation, and bless the solution that is more or less automatically produced from the union. The whole process of judicial decision is made to fit into the formal syllogism of scholastic logic. The major premise is in the statute, the facts of the case furnish the minor premise, and the conclusion inevitably follows. In the uncommon case in which some more sophisticated intellectual work is demanded of the judge, he is expected to follow carefully drawn directions about the limits of interpretation.

The net image is of the judge as an operator of a machine designed and built by legislators. His function is a mechanical one. The great names of the civil law are not those of judges (who knows the name of a civil law judge?) but those of legislators (Justinian, Napoleon) and scholars (Gaius, Irnerius, Bartolus, Mancini, Domat, Pothier, Savigny, and a host of other nineteenth- and twentieth-century European and Latin American scholars). The civil law judge is not a culture hero or a father figure, as he often is with us. His image is that of a civil servant who performs important but essentially uncreative functions.

It is a logical, if not a necessary, consequence of the quite different status of the civil law judge that he is not widely known, even among lawyers. His judicial opinions are not read in order to study his individual ways of thinking and his apparent preconceptions and biases. Although there are exceptions, the tendency is for the decisions of higher courts in civil law jurisdictions to be strongly collegial in nature. They are announced as the decision of the court, without enumeration of votes pro and con among the judges. In most jurisdictions separate concurring opinions and dissenting opinions are not written or published, nor are dissenting votes noted.[7] The tendency is to think of the court as a faceless unit.

The result is that although there is a superficial similarity of function between the civil law judge and the common law judge, there are substantial disparities in their accepted roles. In part the contemporary civil law judge inherits a status and serves a set of functions determined by a tradition going back to the *iudex* of Roman times. This tradition, in which the judge has never been conceived of as playing a very creative part, was reinforced by the anti-judicial ideology of the European revolution and the logical consequences of a rationalistic doctrine of strict separation of powers. The civil law judge thus plays a substantially more modest role than the judge in the common law tradition, and the system of selection and tenure of civil law judges is consistent with this quite different status of the judicial profession.

The establishment of rigid constitutions and the institution of judicial review of the constitutionality of legislation in some civil law jurisdictions has to some extent modified the traditional image of the civil law judge. In some jurisdictions (e.g. Italy and Germany), special constitutional courts have been established. These special courts, which are not part of the ordinary judicial system and are not manned by

---

[7] This generalization does not hold for a number of important Latin American jurisdictions. As will be seen later in this chapter, dissenting opinions are written and published in Argentina and Brazil, while the Mexican Supreme Court notes dissents. [Eds.]

members of the ordinary judiciary, were established in response to the civil law tradition that judges (i.e. *ordinary* judges — the modern successors of the Roman *iudex* and the civil judges of the jus commune) cannot be given such power. With the establishment of these special courts manned by specially selected judges, tradition is, at least in form, observed. Indeed, a few purists within the civil law tradition suggest that it is wrong to call such constitutional courts "courts" and their members "judges." Because judges cannot make law, the reasoning goes, and because the power to hold statutes illegal is a form of lawmaking, these officials obviously cannot be judges and these institutions cannot be courts. But even where, as in some nations in Latin America, the power of judicial review resides in ordinary courts, the traditional civil law image of the judge retains most of its power. Judicial service is a bureaucratic career; the judge is a functionary, a civil servant; the judicial function is narrow, mechanical, and uncreative.

Empirical studies of Latin American judiciaries are rare. One exception in English is Scheman, "The Social and Economic Origins of the Brazilian Judges," 4 *Inter-Am. L. Rev.* 44 (1962).

---

3. Independence of the Judiciary in Latin America

No Latin American judiciary enjoys the prestige, deference, and independence of the judiciary in Anglo-American countries. Some of the explanation for this disparity lies in factors mentioned in Professor Merryman's description of the differences in roles ascribed to judges in the civil law tradition. Part of the explanation stems from the economics of underdevelopment. Judicial salaries and the legally acceptable perquisites of judicial office are frequently meager, and salaries are not always paid on time, even in a comparatively wealthy country like Argentina.[8] It is not uncommon to find judges holding down several jobs in order to make ends meet. Although one can make out a good case for Latin America's having far too many law school graduates, in some countries the shortage of well-qualified judicial personnel, particularly in the outlying areas, has been an important cause of judicial incompetence, delay, and corruption.[9] In an imaginative, if misguided, attempt to circumvent the refusal of competent lawyers to serve as municipal judges, Colombia required all law students to serve as judges for a year after completion of their coursework. Since they still had to write a thesis and pass comprehensive examinations at the end of the year, law student

---

[8] Dana Montaño, "How to Improve the Administration of Justice in Latin America," 4 *Comp. Juridical Rev.* 155, 160 (1967).

[9] See Lott, "The Nationalization of Justice in Venezuela, 13 *Inter-American Economic Affairs*, No. 1, p. 3 (1959).

judges were seldom seen in their districts.[10] Even countries with a career judiciary seldom attract the most able law students, who find the gap between judicial salaries and the remunerations of private practice too great.[11]

In many Latin American nations these economic and legal-cultural explanations for a low level of judicial independence are overshadowed by political considerations. Chronic political instability and a proneness to dictatorship play havoc with judicial independence, particularly where fundamental political and civil rights are concerned. Thus, when the Dominican Supreme Court dared to uphold a claim of fraud in the 1930 election that brought Trujillo to power (the number of votes cast for Trujillo exceeded the number of eligible electors), the dictator's goon squad invaded the court's chambers and forced the judges to resign. Thereafter, Trujillo insisted upon holding undated resignations from all judges as well as other government officials.[12] When Ecuador's Supreme Court declared several controversial executive decrees unconstitutional in 1970, President Velasco Ibarra responded by abrogating the 1967 Constitution, reforming the Supreme Court, and seizing dictatorial powers.[13] Constitutional guarantees of judicial tenure still mean little in the wake of revolution, as evidenced by the 1966 and 1969 wholesale cashiering of the Argentine and Peruvian Supreme Courts following military *coups.*[14]

As the following selection indicates, the degree of independence and prestige of the judiciary varies greatly from country to country, and from regime to regime.

A. EDELMAN, LATIN AMERICAN GOVERNMENT AND POLITICS

Pp. 477-80 (Rev. Ed. 1969)*

As one of the three coequal branches of government, the judiciary according to law and theory should enjoy an independence of authority and function within its constitutionally allotted sphere of operation. To bolster or further this independence, various measures have been adopted in the several republics.

Selection on the basis of professional qualifications rather than political partisan-ship is becoming increasingly accepted in the region. The voice the supreme court often has in the selection of its own members and judges of the lower courts, also the requirement of competitive examinations in some nations, are commendable steps in

---

[10] For an account of the scandal surrounding the Colombian judiciary during the early 1960's, see S. Wurfel, *Foreign Enterprise in Colombia: Laws and Policies* 296-302 (1965).

[11] See Scheman, "Brazil's Career Judiciary," 46 *J. Amer. Judic. Soc'y* 134 (1962).

[12] H. Wiarda, *Dictatorship and Development: The Methods of Control in Trujillo's Dominican Republic* 64-65 (1968).

[13] See J. Martz, *Ecuador: Conflicting Political Culture and the Quest for Progress* 80 (1972).

[14] The Argentine case is discussed *infra,* p. 000. The Peruvian case is discussed in D. García Belaunde, *El Constitucionalismo Peruano y sus Problemas* (1970), Chap. 5; Cooper, "Peru's 'New Look' Judiciary," 55 *Judicature* 334 (1972).

*Reprinted by permission of the publisher, The Dorsey Press.

the right direction. They aim to make judicial service a professional career rather than the bailiwick of political favorites or hacks.

Permanence of tenure is likewise of great importance to the independence of the judiciary. Although only six of the nations provide for it at present, several others grant it to justices who have been re-elected successively.

In some of the nations, the courts have been able to achieve or approximate the independence of function the constitution envisaged. . . .

In Costa Rica the judiciary enjoys a degree of independence and respect seldom found in Latin America. "The Costa Rican Constitution uses all the ingenuity of human invention to guarantee the autonomy of the seventeen-member Supreme Court," says Busey. "There is no doubt that the Costa Rican judiciary is free of presidential control. . . . In Costa Rica, the judiciary functions as an independent branch, and can and does issue judgments which are contrary to presidential policy or design."

But in most of the other nations, the judiciary is not nearly so fortunate. There, independence is a high-sounding phrase in the paper constitution and bears little resemblance to reality.

As a part of the tripartite division of government, the courts have many highly significant relations with the other two branches of government. These relations afford the executive and the congress many opportunities to undermine the independence of the judiciary if they want to. . . .

In most of the other nations, however, the president is often accused not just of influencing the courts but of actually controlling them. Panama well typifies the situation in these nations. Say John and Mavis Biesanz:

> Even the Supreme Court appears to be putty in the president's hands. Although the five justices are appointed for ten-year terms, they rarely express a majority opinion contrary to that of the current president, for dissenters can be retired with pay. Only when he flagrantly violates the rules of the political game or arouses public opinion against him do the . . . justices venture to oppose him.

The congress has a number of controls over the judiciary. Sometimes, these are exercised in subservience to the president; sometimes, they represent quite independent expressions of congressional design. The congress may approve nominations for the court made by the president or may itself appoint the members. It also has the power to pass legislation regarding the organization and jurisdiction of the courts, thus being able to determine their structure, size, authorized agenda, and many other matters of fundamental importance. Control of the purse strings is also significant.

Congress' power of removal is in some nations a bludgeon for intimidating the judiciary. In Mexico, although the justices supposedly enjoy permanence of tenure, this is a blatant farce. . . .

Congress' power to amend the constitution, whether exercised independently or under presidential pressure, also has a critical bearing on the role and authority of the courts, as the experience of Guatemala shows. Nathan L. Whetten writes:

> The process of change is so simple in fact that a president in power who has complete control over his political party may change the Constitution almost at

will. The role of the Supreme Court as interpreter of the Constitution has therefore been relatively unimportant. It may declare laws unconstitutional but in the past this has had little significance because any powers desired by the government could easily be obtained through amendment of the law.

In most countries, the judiciary even in normal times find it an uphill battle to maintain its supposed independence. In times of repressive dictatorship, its chances of independence are far less.

Questions

1. In Edelman's second paragraph, he remarks on certain "commendable" steps to enhance the independence of judges in some Latin American countries. Was Edelman stepping out of the role of social scientist when he used that expression? Or does that sort of language merely convey candidly the value-loaded content of all such analysis? Can there be a value-free social science? More specifically, can there be a value-free analysis of the role of law in society? We return to these issues at several places in this book, and especially in Chapter VI.

2. What does the talismanic phrase "judicial independence" mean, and how is the existence or nonexistence of "judicial independence" relevant to development?

Consider J. Cohen, "The Chinese Communist Party and 'Judicial Independence' ": 1949-1959, 82 *Harv. L. Rev.* 967, 972-75 (1969):*

"Judicial independence" is not something that simply exists or does not exist. Each country's political-judicial accommodation must be located along a spectrum that only in theory ranges from a completely unfettered judiciary to one that is completely subservient. The actual situation in all countries lies somewhere in between.

Certainly we cannot say that American judges enjoy complete independence, even if we focus exclusively on federal judges, who are endowed with greater prestige and security than most of their brethren on state tribunals. "A judge," it has often been said, "is a lawyer who knew a governor." . . .

Not only are a federal judge's political connections and views frequently responsible for his initial appointment, but, as the Fortas case recently demonstrated, these factors, plus his record on the bench, also have a major bearing upon his prospects for promotion. Federal judges must also depend on the executive branch to enforce their decisions and on the legislative branch to finance their activities. Moreover, resort to the processes of amendment can nullify their constitutional interpretations, and simple legislation can overturn other rules of law. Legislation can reduce the jurisdiction of the courts. And if too impatient to await the opportunities created when vacancies occur, the President and Congress can alter the judiciary's political complexion by increasing the number of judges and filling the new positions with politically acceptable people.

---

*Copyright 1969 by the Harvard Law Review Association.

Despite these significant constraints, the Government of the United States is usually taken to be a good example of a government with an independent judiciary. Indeed, although one man's hero has sometimes been another's villain, the judge has generally played the role of hero in Anglo-American tradition, which may partially explain why formal checks on the judiciary are rarely invoked. Yet the unusual breadth of the powers enjoyed by American courts, particularly the power of judicial review, has disturbed many thoughtful persons, who have worried about the implications for democratic government of allocating these powers to officials who are insulated from the voters. An independent judiciary can frustrate effective democratic government as easily as it can frustrate effective totalitarian government, unless the judges are careful to exercise their powers responsibly, with due regard for the powers of the other branches of government.

Plainly enough, one cannot expect any country to staff its judiciary with men whose views and acts contradict the premises of that country's governmental system. Judges must implement many of the fundamental values and policies of their society as those values and policies are embodied in the constitution statutes, regulations, rules of decision, and other sources of law furnished by the state. But at a minimum, "judicial independence" means that political organs will not interfere with the application of these legal sources to the facts of particular cases. In principle, it should also mean that political organs will not inflict deprivations upon honest judges who make undesired decisions, nor reward those who make favored decisions. . . .

In practice every country probably fails to some extent to meet the standard of judicial independence that I have suggested. Because of the broad political power they enjoy, it was probably inevitable that the history of even the federal courts in the United States would reveal efforts by the executive and legislative branches to prevent judges from deciding certain cases,[15] to influence their decision making in individual cases, and to inflict deprivations upon them for past decisions.[16] Moreover, the impressionistic reports of persons familiar with the administration of justice in the United States suggest that unobtrusive

---

[15] Among the examples that come to mind are President Lincoln's suspension of the writ of habeas corpus and resort to summary arrests, . . .; Congressional removal of a case from the jurisdiction of the Supreme Court after the case had been argued but before it was decided, see *Ex parte* McCardle, 74 U.S. (7 Wall.) 506 (1869); and President Franklin D. Roosevelt's wartime closing of the courts to "all persons who are subjects, citizens, or residents of any nation at war with the United States . . . and who during time of war enter or attempt to enter the United States . . . and are charged with committing or attempting . . . to commit sabotage." . . . Congress recently came perilously close to reducing the Supreme Court's jurisdiction in retaliation for unpopular decisions. [Footnote by Cohen, renumbered.]

[16] For example, President Jefferson's attempt to purge the judiciary was in part a response to Federalist judges who had not only engaged in partisan political campaigning and imposed harsh punishments upon their Jeffersonian enemies in prosecutions for "sedition," but who had also recently asserted the power to frustrate governmental policies by invalidating acts of Congress. . . . Few have forgotten Franklin Roosevelt's attempt to "pack" a Supreme Court that had invalidated measures which the elected branches considered necessary. [Footnote by Cohen, renumbered.]

political interference with the courts may be as widespread as it is difficult to document. For example, in some cities it is not unusual for a "clubhouse lawyer" representing a political machine to which a judge owes his incumbency and future advancement to pay a private visit to the judge's chambers to discuss a pending case or to resort to more subtle forms of communication. Unresponsive state judges may face opposition at the next primary or general election for their office, and occasionally even a member of a state's highest court fails to win reelection because of an unpopular decision. Nor should we overlook instances when judges who have guided "political" trials to a popular conclusion are rewarded with promotion. It is apparent, therefore, that practices in the United States diverge considerably from our professed ideals. This must be borne in mind during our examination of the Chinese scene, since some American scholars of foreign law, particularly that of Communist countries, have tended to contrast our ideals with their practices.

3. Can you make a plausible argument that judicial independence during the early 1930's retarded economic development in the United States?

L. HAND, THE CONTRIBUTION OF AN INDEPENDENT JUDICIARY TO CIVILIZATION

in I. Dilliard (ed.), *The Spirit of Liberty*
Pp. 172, 181-82 (1952)

. . . I believe that for by far the greater part of their work it is a condition upon the success of our system that the judges should be independent; and I do not believe that their independence should be impaired because of their constitutional functions. But the price of this immunity, I insist, is that they should not have the last word in those basic conflicts of "right and wrong — between whose endless jar justice resides." You may ask what then will become of the fundamental principles of equity and fair play which our constitutions enshrine; and whether I seriously believe that unsupported they will serve merely as counsels of moderation. I do not think that anyone can say what will be left of those principles; I do not know whether they will serve only as counsels; but this much I think I do know — that a society so riven that the spirit of moderation is gone, no court can save; that a society where that spirit flourishes, no court need save; that in a society which evades its responsibility by thrusting upon the courts the nurture of that spirit, that spirit in the end will perish. What is the spirit of moderation? It is the temper which does not press a partisan advantage to its bitter end, which can understand and will respect the other side, which feels a unity between all citizens — real and not the factitious product of propaganda — which recognizes their common fate and their common aspirations — in a word, which has faith in the sacredness of the individual. If you ask me how such a temper and such a faith are bred and fostered, I cannot answer. . . . But I am satisfied that they must have the vigor within themselves to withstand the winds and weather of an indifferent and ruthless world; and that it is idle to seek shelter for them in a courtroom. Men must take that temper and that faith with them into the field, into the market-place, into the factory, into the council-room, into their homes; they cannot be imposed; they must be lived.

H. HART, COMMENT

in A. Sutherland (ed.), *Government Under Law*
Pp. 139, 140-41 (1956)*

My other footnote is prompted by a quotation which Judge Wyzanski makes, without protest, from Judge Learned Hand. "A society so riven that the spirit of moderation is gone, no court *can* save;... a society where that spirit flourishes no court *need* save." I cannot help believing that Judge Hand, when he wrote that, had his attention fixed on the turning of a phrase. But if the statement is projected into a serious discussion of constitutional government, something more needs to be said. It needs to be said that the statement is an example — a particularly clear example — of the fallacy of the undistributed middle.

What the sentence assumes is that there are two kinds of societies — one kind, over here, in which the spirit of moderation flourishes, and another kind, over here, which is riven by dissension. Neither kind, Judge Hand says, can be helped very much by the courts. But, of course, that isn't what societies are like. In particular, it isn't what American society is like. A society is a something in process — in process of becoming. It has always within it, as ours does, seeds of dissension. And it has also within it forces making for moderation and mutual accommodation. The question — the relevant question — is whether the courts have a significant contribution to make in pushing American society in the direction of moderation — not by themselves; of course they can't save us by themselves; but in combination with other institutions. Once the question is put that way, the answer, it seems to me, has to be yes.

B. From Habeas Corpus to Writ of Security in Brazil

The framers of Latin American constitutions were heavily influenced by the declaration of rights issued by the French revolutionaries, adopting the French precedent of explicitly setting out essential human rights. The hope was that if fundamental rights were identified and listed in the constitution, both the governed and the governors would be very much aware of these rights, so that their observance would be ensured.[17]

---

[17] Fix Zamudio, "Latin American Procedures for the Protection of the Individual," 9 *J. Int'l. Comm'n Jurists,* Dec. 1968, at 60-61.

Unfortunately, few were concerned about the development of effective procedural devices for ensuring compliance with constitutional guarantees. When it became apparent that those in power were not always governing their own behavior by the standards enshrined in the constitution, Latin American jurists turned to the Anglo-American nations for procedural remedies. Not surprisingly, the first remedial device to be imported was habeas corpus, which, under one label or another, has now been expressly or impliedly adopted, at least in theory, by every Latin American nation.[18]

P. EDER, HABEAS CORPUS DISEMBODIED:
THE LATIN AMERICAN EXPERIENCE

in K. Nadelmann, A. von Mehren & J. Hazard (eds.)
XXth Century Comparative and Conflicts Law 463, 465-69 (1961)*

Brazil was the first of the southern countries in our hemisphere to adopt habeas corpus. The lawyers who framed the Imperial Constitution of 1824 and the early legislation of the country, after independence from Portugal, were well versed in the law of England. That constitution, establishing a limited monarchy, followed the British pattern. The Penal Code of 1830, a progressive code for its day, made it a criminal offense for judges to refuse to issue or to delay a writ of habeas corpus, duly petitioned, or *ex officio* in a proper case (art. 183); for officers of justice to refuse or delay service of the writ; for the person to whom the writ was directed to refuse or delay presenting the prisoner at the time and place specified in the writ; to change the place of confinement or to hide the prisoner with intent to evade a writ of which the officer had notice, before service; to rearrest a person discharged under a writ for the same cause. . . .

These provisions were anticipatory of the provisions in the law of habeas corpus embodied in the Code of Criminal Procedure of 1832 (arts. 340-55). Every citizen who believes that he or another is suffering illegal imprisonment or restraint of his liberty is entitled to ask for an order of — Habeas Corpus — in his favor (art. 340). The petition should contain the name of the person under restraint and of the person causing it; the contents of the order of arrest or an explicit declaration that a copy was denied; the illegality claimed and signature and oath as to the truth of the allegations (art. 341). The writ contains an order to the detainer or gaoler to present the person before the judge or court at a stated time and place and to furnish a report as to the cause for detention (art. 343). A judge reliably informed of an illegal detention is under a duty to issue the writ *ex officio* without a petition (art. 344). If the judge finds that the prisoner is illegally detained, he shall release him; or, if the offense be bailable, shall admit him to bail (art. 352). Imprisonment is deemed illegal when there is no just

---

[18] Fix Zamudio, *supra* note 17, at 67.

*Reprinted by permission of the publisher, Sijthoff International Publishing Co.

cause therefor; for failure to be brought to trial within the time required by law; when the process is manifestly void; for lack of jurisdiction of the authority that ordered the arrest or when the grounds justifying imprisonment have terminated (art. 353).

The provisions of these two codes, it will readily be noted, were adopted from the Habeas Corpus Acts of 1640, 1689, and 1816 and the British practice as expounded by Blackstone or other authorities.

The Brazilian legislation was a logical corollary of a provision in the Imperial Constitution declaring the inviolability of the civil and political rights of Brazilian citizens based on liberty, individual security and property (art. 179 (8)). The Brazilian writers state that habeas corpus was congenial to Portuguese law which had something similar in the *cartas de seguro*.

In Brazil, the writ was amplified by Law 2073 of 1871, extending the privilege to aliens and, more important, including in its coverage *threats* to personal liberty, even where the petitioner had not yet suffered corporal constraint. This had already been established in practice by decisions of the courts. This was the first innovation. Under our law (except in cases of custody of children) actual imprisonment or restraint of freedom of movement is a necessary prerequisite to the writ.[19] Other extensions of the scope of the writ were soon to follow. Continued in Decree 848 of October 1890 of the Provisional Government after the overthrow of the monarchy, the writ was incorporated as a constitutional guarantee in the first Republican Constitution (1891). Article 72 (22) provided:

> Habeas Corpus is given whenever an individual suffers or is in imminent danger
> of suffering violence or coercion by reason of illegality or abuse of power.

Illegality includes unconstitutionality and the writ was frequently used, and still is, for judicial review of the constitutionality of statutes and executive acts. The language of the article, under the arguments of ingenious judges and lawyers, notably Rui Barbosa, gave rise to a remarkable extension of the writ to cover deprivation, actual or threatened, of any of the constitutional liberties. The "Brazilian" doctrine of habeas corpus evolved to an extent where the English father would have difficulty in recognizing his transatlantic offspring. The nomenclature was maintained, but the institution was adapted to meet new social or political needs. It supplied the need, in the absence of other remedies in the procedural codes, for effective rapid measures to cope with abuse of the public power. By 1893, the competence of the judiciary to examine, by habeas corpus, the legality of the acts of the executive was established. In 1898, the Supreme Court asserted its right to examine the constitutionality of political acts. A period of conflicting decisions as to the scope of the remedy ensued. Habeas corpus was granted against invasion of the home by sanitary inspectors; it was denied to protect the freedom of movement of street-walkers; it was granted to prevent examination of commercial books of account, to guarantee professional liberty, the exercise of elective officers, the practice of spiritualism, freedom of assembly. It was

---

[19] But see Hensley v. Municipal Court, San Jose Milpitas, 411 U.S. 345 (1973), holding that one released upon his own recognizance without any conditions curtailing his movements is "in custody" within the meaning of the federal habeas corpus statute. [Eds.]

applied in civil family controversies to permit a wife to join her husband against the opposition of her parents. In 1909, in a leading case, the Supreme Court extended the writ to permit aldermen (*intendentes municipaes*) to attend meetings of the Municipal Council to which they had been elected. The opinion by Pedro Lessa, reinforced by his book, a classic of constitutional law, pointed out that the Brazilian habeas corpus bore only a slight resemblance to its English progenitor. It is a procedural remedy to guarantee every certain and incontestable right which is directly or indirectly connected with freedom of movement. By being barred by the executive authorities from access to the municipal council, the aldermen's freedom of locomotion was being interfered with.

Since almost every right can be indirectly connected with freedom of movement, it was a short step to a further extension of the scope of the writ.

The Supreme Court in a decision of April 5, 1919, said:

> In effect, for the majority of the court, it is an accepted principle that habeas corpus is competent to protect the exercise of any right which is certain, liquid and incontestable.

Lessa maintained that freedom of locomotion being but a means to achieve an end, habeas corpus should be granted whenever the *end*, if lawful, presupposes freedom of locomotion and there is no reasonable doubt as to the petitioner's right to the action in question. Consequently habeas corpus became embodied in the law as a means to protect all political and electoral rights. It was used to reinstate the governor of a State who had been forced by federal troops to withdraw from the State House. The principle was frequently reiterated by the Supreme Court that habeas corpus was the proper remedy to enable duly elected deputies to assemble and exercise their functions. "Although a political question is involved, the Judicial Power cannot elude the duty to take cognizance of the justiciable question that is presented to it." This goes much further than our own Supreme Court has been willing to go.

Barbosa's theory went further; habeas corpus lies, irrespective of any question of locomotion, direct or indirect, in order to protect every certain and incontestable constitutional right. This became the view of the Court as we have noted from the above quotation. It was used not only to insure the right of elected officials to their office, but also to protect the rights of peaceable assembly and freedom of speech, the right of Congressmen to publish their speeches, as well as to prevent the removal of a state judge in violation of the provision for tenure during good behaviour, and to prevent peonage. A lower court even granted the writ to allow minors, under parental power, to take part in Carnival festivities.[20]

---

[20] Habeas corpus has undergone an even more striking expansion in Peru, which permits the use of habeas corpus for challenging the constitutionality of measures wholly unrelated to restraints on personal mobility such as an agrarian reform valuation. "Expediente" 16/64 of the Supreme Court, reproduced in D. García Belaunde, *El Habeas Corpus Interpretado* 307 (1971). See generally, Furnish, "The Hierarchy of Peruvian Laws: Context for Law and Development," 19 *Am. J. Comp. L.* 91, 98-103 (1971). [Eds.]

Lessa maintained, in contrast to Barbosa and the latter decisions of the courts, that habeas corpus was applicable only when freedom of movement was directly or indirectly but necessarily involved. There is no doubt that . . . the writ was abused. The courts were overwhelmed with habeas corpus proceedings. The President of the Republic urged reform. Lessa's theory was incorporated in the 1926 amendment to the Constitution which provided that habeas corpus was applicable only where one suffers or is in imminent danger of suffering violence by imprisonment or illegal constraint in his freedom of locomotion.

To protect those rights left unprotected when habeas corpus was cut back to cases involving threatened or actual restraints on personal movement, the Brazilians created a new juridical institution, the writ of security (*mandado de segurança*), which combines in a single writ the effective characteristics of the Anglo-American writs of mandamus, prohibition, quo warranto, and injunction. The present theoretical bases of habeas corpus and the writ of security are set out in Article 153 of the Constitution of the Federative Republic of Brazil (Emenda Constitucional No. 1 of October 17, 1969):

> 153. The Constitution assures Brazilians and foreigners residing in the country the inviolability of rights to life, liberty, security, and property, in the following terms: . . .
>
> §20. Habeas corpus shall lie whenever anyone shall suffer, or shall be threatened with suffering, violence or restraint in his freedom of movement, through illegality or abuse of power.[21] Habeas corpus shall not apply to disciplinary offenses.
>
> §21. The writ of security shall lie to protect a clear and certain right unprotected by habeas corpus, irrespective of the authority responsible for the illegality or abuse of power.

The writ of security embodies three essential procedural advantages over preexisting law that have made it a highly useful check on the actions of public authorities:

(1) It can function as affirmative or negative injunction — compelling an authority to perform or cease performing a particular act. Under prior law, the judiciary lacked the power to nullify unlawful administrative acts; an action for damages was ordinarily one's sole remedy.[22]

(2) It is a summary action that takes preference on court calendars over all other types of actions except habeas corpus. In theory, it should take but 20 days from the time of filing the action to the date of decision, though in practice it is usually closer to three months.

---

[21] The concept of "abuse of power" closely approximates "abuse of discretion" in United States administrative law. See Caio Tácito, "Desvio de Poder em Matéria Administrativa," p. 58 (Thesis presented for the *livre docente* in Administrative Law at the Faculdade de Direito do Rio de Janeiro (1951). *Cf.* E. Luna, *Abuso de Direito.* (1959) [Eds.]

[22] Buzaid, " 'Juicio de amparo' e Mandado de segurança," 56 *Rev. Fac. Dir. São Paulo* 172, 218 (1961).

(3) The judge may issue a preliminary injunction or restraining order to maintain the status quo while the matter is being determined. Given the numerous opportunities for delay in ordinary litigation, such a stay is frequently of crucial importance.

The basic regulatory statute, Law No. 1.533 is set out in the Appendix, pp. p. 711.

The following cases depict the actual functioning of the writ of security in present-day Brazil. They also give the student some of the peculiar flavor of judicial review (broadly defined) in a civil law system.

---

1. The Requirements of Certainty and Incontestability

CHAMPION CELULOSE S.A. v. PREFEITURA MUNICIPAL DE SÃO PAULO

Supreme Federal Tribunal of Brazil (en banc)
R.M.S. No. 17.132 (1967)
(Translated from certified copy of the opinion)

Report[23]

Minister Victor Nunes: The city government of São Paulo levied an industrial and professional tax of Cr$ 12.954.504 (old currency) [then about $U.S. 2500] on the appellant, Champion Celulose S.A., for fiscal year 1965. The levy was based upon economic activity, fixed at Cr$ 1.480,200.000 (old currency).

The company sought a writ of security, alleging that it carried on its activities in Mogi-Guaçu, producing its gross receipts there rather than in the municipality of São Paulo. This contention had previously served as the basis for obtaining a writ of security in the Supreme Federal Tribunal as to fiscal year 1962. . . . [The firm contends] that it should be protected by *res judicata,* as well as the case law of the Supreme Tribunal, which has determined that a tax may not be exacted on operations carried on in another municipality. RE 46.841, RE 53.344, RE 49.151.[24]

In a memorandum prepared for this appeal the company states that it obtained administratively the cancellation of levies relating to fiscal years 1962, 1963, and 1964.

[The City alleged that the company had moved a short distance away to avoid the tax, and had been using its São Paulo office to effect sales in São Paulo.]

The writ was denied by the court of first instance, because, in the words of the judge, "there is an unresolvable controversy about what activity was carried on in the

---

[23] Brazil's Supreme Federal Tribunal operates on a reporter system. The case is assigned to one minister (*relator*), who reviews the record and pleadings and reports the facts and conclusions of law to the rest of the court, which votes orally [Eds.]

[24] These are shorthand citations to Supreme Federal decisions, which are assigned permanent docket numbers according to the type of case. RE is an abbreviation for Recurso Extraordinário, the special appeal. The R.M.S. in the headnote stands for Revista Mandado de Segurança. [Eds.]

São Paulo office. In truth, unraveling the question would demand the production of evidence, including expert witnesses and the examination of books and documents." Moreover, the allegation of *res judicata* is improper, for it is based upon a decision concerning only fiscal year 1962. . . .

Vote of Minister Victor Nunes (Reporter): In our previous decision, referring to fiscal years 1962, . . . Minister Gonçalves de Oliveira . . . observed that the document . . . furnished by the Department of Property Receipts of the City of São Paulo expressly stated that "the principal place of business (*sede social*) [of the appellant firm] is in Mogi-Guaçu, where its economic activities occur." In São Paulo, it had only "an office used as a stockroom and a depositary for the receipt of a few packages destined for its place of business in the Municipality of Mogi-Guaçu." . . . [The fiscal authorities of Mogi-Guaçu also informed the Court that the appellant carried on its business there rather than in São Paulo.] The court thereupon determined that the appellant did not owe the São Paulo tax on industries and professions.

Keeping in mind the terms of that decision, restricted to fiscal year 1962, one cannot accept the argument of *res judicata* (*Súmula* 239.[25]) Even though the municipality has offered no proof thereof, it is possible that from 1962 to 1964 there has been a change in the activities of the appellant's office in São Paulo. One cannot presume . . . that the situation has remained the same.

The writ of security thus appears inadequate to resolve the controversy, leaving the appellant to an appropriate judicial means of demonstrating that it is being taxed upon operations carried on in another municipality. It is undoubtedly lamentable that the simple word of the fisc can bring this burden on the taxpayer; that is, the expeditious judicial remedy to protect its right, which is possibly being violated, will not lie, because there is a doubt concerning a question of fact. If the silence of the legislature with respect to this situation should continue for long, perhaps the case law will discover a solution for such cases through constructive interpretation.

Lacking such a construction, and bearing in mind the controversy existing in the pleadings, I vote to deny the appeal for lack of clarity and certainty.

Oral Addendum to the Vote

Minister Victor Nunes (Reporter): I really think that the [taxpayer] offered no proof with respect to the fiscal year in issue. But the City also offered no proof.

Minister Aliomar Baleeiro: In the Municipality of São Paulo . . . the tax on industries and professions, which began 8 or 10 years ago, is calculated on the basis of economic activity, defined by the local code as the gross volume of sales or receipts. . . . It is always possible to determine whether a firm has operated in that Municipality, for such operations are also subject to the sales tax. The City should not

---

[25] The *Súmula* is Brazil's concession to *stare decisis.* Since 1964, questions that have become firmly settled by the Supreme Court's decisions are published in capsule form, with a number assigned to each rule of law. These numbers of the *Súmula* are summarily cited to dispose of the issue in future litigation. Thus, *Súmula* 239 states: "A decision declaring a tax is unowed for a determined fiscal period does not constitute res judicata for later periods." The *Súmula* can be modified, but on constitutional issues the votes of at least 3 ministers are necessary to open the question. [Eds.]

have the slightest difficulty in proving that the firm sells in São Paulo, for the State Tax Collector would have the exact volume of these sales. . . .

Here, if we begin to adopt this practice of insisting that the writ of security will not lie because there is a question of proof, etc., one completely annuls a remedy which is in the Constitution and to which it gives the greatest emphasis. . . .

It is always difficult and practically impossible to prove a negative fact. I can prove that Manuel is married to Joana. If I am certain of this, I produce a certificate or an indirect document which establishes this juridical situation. But if I want to prove that Manuel is not married to Joana in any of the 3,000 municipalities of Brazil and their respective districts, or in no country in the world, this is practically impossible. . . .

The party says: I do not sell in São Paulo. The Municipality must prove if there are sales. And there are means to do so. . . .

Minister Eloy da Rocha: . . . But the fundamental consideration is whether or not one can grant a writ of security on the presumption that the allegation of the party seeking the writ be true.

Minister Adaucto Cardoso: If uncontested. The Public Power has the elements with which to contest it.

Minister Eloy da Rocha: The Public Power itself has the presumption of truth. The Municipality contested by responding to the allegations of the appellant, declaring that the tax is owed and under what circumstances. . . .

The appellee could not prove these circumstances in an action for a writ of security, which lacks a fact-finding procedure with all the techniques of proof. Hence, I do not recognize the existence of facts that are certain. It is my understanding that in such a case the writ of security will not lie . . . .

Minister Prado Kelly: Based upon the prior decision, one may infer that the preexisting situation has continued. . . . The eminent Reporter, perhaps with excessive caution, suggests that new facts may have occurred. But there is nothing in the pleadings in this respect. . . .

The levy is for 1965; the judicial decision is for 1962. For the intervening years there has been an express recognition by the taxing power that the tax was not owed. What new situation has been created for 1965? To this question the pleadings give no reply.

It would be impossible for the appellant to produce negative proof. Proving the contrary is exclusively the burden of the challenged authority.

For these reasons, Mr. President, I also vote to grant the appeal. . . .

Minister Evandro Lins: The concession of the previous writ of security is limited to the fiscal year 1962. . . . This is not extended into another year. In that writ, the Tribunal understood that the firm did not carry on economic activity in São Paulo, in view of the proofs there produced. In conformance with what I read in the writ, these facts were not disputed. It is possible that the City was not very diligent in defending its interests in that proceeding, in that it did not introduce the facts which it is now bringing to our attention.

Faced with Law 5.917 of São Paulo, which established the tax, . . . the firm transferred its office. The City alleges bad faith, simulation, and fraud. How are we going to decide these in an action for a writ of security?

Minister Aliomar Baleeiro: Allegation is one thing and proof is another.

Minister Victor Nunes (Reporter): Minister Evandro Lins, I stated that the City had not proved anything because it limited itself to allegations. If its functionaries had made such a verification, documents would have resulted. Where are these documents? They are not in the pleadings.

Minister Evandro Lins: I cannot doubt the official word if the firm has proved nothing to the contrary. I think the matter can be resolved by ordinary [judicial] means. The [taxpayer] will not be prejudiced. Denial of this writ does not imply a definitive solution. The firm can resort to the usual procedures, offer proof, and argue the issue *de novo*. With the respect due to those who think the contrary, I concur in the vote of the eminent Reporter and the eminent Minister Eloy da Rocha. . . .

Decision

[The full Tribunal decided to grant the writ of security over the dissenting votes of the Reporter, and Ministers Eloy da Rocha, Evandro Lins, and Adalício Nogueira. Sept. 20, 1967.]

Questions

1. To what extent does the writ of security resemble the U.S. procedure for summary judgment?

2. The 1934 Constitution used the expression "certain and incontestable right," which produced much controversy since lawyers were adept at finding some angle from which to contest almost any claim. The term "clear and certain right" was substituted in the 1946 Constitution and is generally interpreted to mean a legal right which cannot be fairly denied on a given set of facts. What is the function of the requirement of a "clear and certain right"?

3. Why should disputes about the payment of taxes be entitled to the benefits of summary procedure and docket preference?

---

2. The Writ of Security as a Substitute for Mandamus

ALEXANDRE VAZ v. JUÍZO DE DIREITO DA TERCEIRA VARA CÍVEL

3d Chamber of the Tribunal de Alçada Civil (Brazil)
390 Rev. Trib. 223 (1968)

. . . This case deals with an action for a writ of security against the act of the judge of the 3d Civil Chamber of the judicial district of Campinas, who conditioned the processing of an appeal taken by the petitioner, in a suit which decreed his eviction, upon full payment of the costs of the case.

. . . [Over the dissent of one judge] the writ is allowed in conformance with the case law of this Chamber,[26] according to which the measure will lie against a judicial decision. . . .

And, as to the merits, against the vote of Judge César de Moraes, consistent with reiterated decisions, . . . the judge cannot condition the transmittal of the record on payment of the costs, because Art. 56 § 2° of the Code of Civil Procedure imposes no penalty for non-compliance with its precept. It is unlawful for a magistrate to adopt a sanction not established in the law. In order to see his appeal go up, the petitioner is not obliged to settle all the costs of the proceeding incurred up to then, but need only . . . [prepare the necessary papers and pay] the expenses of the transmittal of the record to the higher court.

São Paulo, March 6, 1968.

---

3. Determining What Constitutes a Public Authority

ODARICO CARVALHO v. DIRECTOR DA FACULDADE DE DIREITO RIOPRETENSE

4th Civil Chamber of the Tribunal of Justice
of the State of São Paulo (Brazil)
398 Rev. Trib. 207 (1968)

This case deals with a writ of security sought against the dean of the Riopretense Law School by a student who completed the second year in 1967 and passed all of his courses.

The petitioner alleges that he was not permitted to matriculate in the third year of the law school course, because he was accused of being a subversive element creating unrest in the school. Having unsuccessfully appealed to the dean, [the student] sought the present writ and requested a preliminary injunction against the act which reputedly injures his clear and certain right to matriculate in the 3d year law course at the above school.

However, the judge below summarily decided against the petitioner on the ground that the party designated as the coercive authority was not a legitimate defendant. [The defendant] was neither a public authority nor equivalent thereto, but . . . [dean of] a private educational establishment. . . .

Despite the brilliant arguments of the appellant, the appealed decision must be wholly sustained, for it is supported by the best doctrine and the case law.

The new Federal Constitution of 1967, in assuring individual rights and guarantees in its Article 150, made no innovations with regard to the writ of security. . . .

---

[26]"Allowed" in this context means simply that the court has decided that the petitioner has invoked the correct procedure. [Eds.]

Consequently, I must agree that the provisions of Law No. 1.533 of 1951[27] continue in full force, such as was the case during the time the Federal Constitution of 1946 was in force.

From Art. 1, and its Section 1, one infers that a writ of security may only be brought against an act practiced by: (a) an authority or agent of the Public Power; (b) administrators or representatives of autarchic[28] entities; (c) administrators or representatives of individuals or legal entities with functions delegated by the public power.

One cannot place the dean of a private law school within any of these hypotheses. . . . He is not a public authority, nor does he exercise functions delegated by the Public Power. He does not represent any autarchy nor is he an administrator or representative of a company with functions delegated by the public power. He only directs a private educational establishment, a private, not a public, entity. It is unimportant that the school which he supervises is officially recognized and that its diplomas have the value of those issued by the official schools, maintained by the Public Power. . . . Recognition and delegation are distinct acts, of a diverse nature, without any equivalence. Hence, any private establishment may shut its doors at any time that its governing board so decides — something which does not happen in official educational establishments which require a law or statute [to authorize such an action.] . . .

[The Court then cites six decisions and two academic commentators maintaining the same position.]

On the other hand, neither can the argument be maintained that teaching, when carried on by a private party, can only be by delegation of the Public Power [constituting the private institution a supplementary public agency.]

If the legislator decrees that teaching may be public as well as private, this does not make their natures equivalent. [The legislature], not having instituted a state monopoly on education, admits the supplementary or complementary character of private initiative for the same educational mission, authorized. . . .

The function delegated by the Public Power stems from law or a concession contract of public service. By virtue of inspecting teaching and establishing its basic norms, the State does not transmit to the inspected, such as the school in question, any of its attributes or prerogatives. If the private institute does not fulfill the law, it is up to the Minister of Education to take the necessary measures.

In summary: an establishment of higher education, such as the Riopretense Law School, does not exercise the function of the Public Power and its dean is by no means a public authority nor the delegated agent of the Public Power. Such a private establishment only carries on an activity of public interest, which does not constitute a public function. . . .

Sao Paulo, July 25, 1968. [Two judges dissented.]

---

[27] Set out in Appendix A, pp. 711-12 *infra.*

[28] An autarchy, as the term is used here, is a semi-autonomous governmental administrative agency such as the Central Bank or the Brazilian Coffee Institute. [Eds.]

Questions

1. How much does this doctrinal limitation on use of the writ of security resemble the "state action" limitation on the 14th Amendment of the U.S. Constitution? Is it consistent with the constitutional language (Art. 153 §21), *supra* p. 102?

2. What is the utility of such a limitation in the Brazilian context?

Notes

1. There are decisions involving private schools which have held just the opposite. *Jorge Prates Paul v. União Federal*, RMS 10.173, 72 Rev. Dir. Admin. 206 (STF 1962); *Sérgio Luis Franklin v. União Federal*, Ag.M.S. 4.651, 62 Rev. Dir. Admin. 169 (TFR 1959).

2. "The relative rapidity of the judgment in the writ of security ... is creating problems in the courts and tribunals: the avalanche of such proceedings, prejudicing proper actions, and their constant invocation in the most common cases. Diverted from its purpose as the rapid heroic remedy, it serves for everything. . . .

"To verify how the heroic remedy is being vulgarized, petitions multiply for the correction of examination grades in our official institutes . . . . They extravagantly seek to misplace within the ambit of Justice the criteria which examiners ought to use to pass or fail the marginal student." Oliveira e Silva, "Uso e Abuso No Mandado de Segurança," 3 *Rev. Procur. Ger.* 133 (1956).

3. The following table shows the total number of writs of security which have been decided by the Supreme Federal Tribunal from 1963 to 1971, as well as the total number of civil cases decided by the tribunal in the same period.

	Writs of Security	Total Number of Civil Cases
1963	1448	6021
1964	1348	6652
1965	1028	5127
1966	2015	6780
1967	977	6617
1968	1324	8178
1969	135	8754
1970	73	5374
1971	59	5370

Source: Anuário Estatístico do Brasil

The sharp decline in 1969 was the result of Institutional Act No. 6 of February 1, 1969, which deprived the Supreme Federal Tribunal of ordinary appellate jurisdiction from denials of writs of security. See p. 215 *infra*.

---

4. Failure of Public Officials to Comply with the Writ

Issuance of the writ of security normally resolves the matter before the court. But, as in many countries, including the United States, the coercing public authority occasionally declines to abide by the court order, either out of self interest or conviction that the judge issuing the writ is wrong. S. Fadel, *Teoria e Prática do Mandado de Segurança* 159-60 (1966). While the American courts can use their contempt powers to assure respect for their orders, Brazilian courts have no such powers. Nor does the statute regulating the writ of security contain any efficient coercive measures to compel a rebellious public agency to comply with the writ. The following case arose during the chaotic years of the Goulart regime, whose principal support came from organized labor. Goulart was deposed by a military *coup* in April of 1964. This exercise in judicial judo demonstrates how imaginative and persistent Brazilian courts can be in their efforts to force public authorities to comply with the writ.

MANDADO DE SEGURANÇA No. 39.326-SP

Tribunal Federal de Recursos (Brazil)
5 Rev. T.F.R. Juris. 234 (1965)

[A group of non-union stevedores who were being denied the right to work in the port of Santos petitioned for a writ of security against the president of the stevedores' union and the Deputy for Maritime Labor (a representative of the Ministry of Labor) to assure their constitutional right to work. The judge of the first instance granted the writ, and the appellate court, the Tribunal de Recursos, affirmed, leaving the business of execution of the writ with the lower court. The writ was ignored, and the court of first instance took a series of measures designed to secure compliance. Against these very measures, the union itself ironically sought relief by writ of security. The judge of the first instance denied the union's request, and the Tribunal de Recursos affirmed on the opinion below, which follows.]

Dr. Francis Selwyn Davis —

On November 4, 1963 the President of the Union and the Deputy for Maritime Labor were officially notified of the court's decision, and initially agreed to abide by it. But . . . the plaintiffs were called to work only when no union member was available.

. . . On November 11, the plaintiffs complained to this court, which sought further information from the defendants. On November 13 the union president informed the court that work was being preferentially distributed to union members in accordance with article 1 of Decree No. 34.453 of November 4, 1953. The Deputy for Maritime Labor confessed his inertia and incapacity, stating that it was impossible to comply with the terms of the decision because of insufficient help, and that . . . police would be required.

On Dec. 18, 1963 the same plaintiffs brought a new action for a writ of security asking that they be guaranteed unionization. The measure was preliminarily granted, and that fact was communicated to the defendant authority on the following day. On Jan. 14 the writ was definitively granted. Notwithstanding, it has not been complied with until now. On Jan. 9, 1964, at the request of this court, a police force was placed at the disposition of the Deputy for Maritime Labor to the extent he deemed necessary. On Jan. 16, 1964 two officials sent by this court determined that the court's mandate was not being complied with. Affidavits to the same effect were taken. On Jan. 16 this court requested the Deputy for Maritime Labor to call people to work himself instead of leaving such function with the union inspectors, and to call all the stevedores irrespective of formal union membership. On Jan. 20 the Deputy for Maritime Labor once again stated his inability to comply with the determinations of the judiciary.

On Jan. 21 this court entered the order which is the object of the present writ of security and which in substance included:

(a) a request for a police inquiry against the president of the union for the crimes set out in articles 203 and 330 of the Penal Code,[29] and Article 31 of the Law No. 1.802 of 1953;[30]

(b) an official dispatch to His Excellency, the Minister of Labor, soliciting his intervention in the rebellious union and/or determination of responsibility for the failure of the Deputy for Maritime Labor to fulfill his obligations towards the plaintiffs;

(c) an official dispatch to banking establishments informing them that the balances in the accounts of the union or its directors may not be drawn upon without prior judicial authorization;

(d) an official dispatch to [employers] ... informing them all sums owed to the union and its members are to be deposited in the Bank of Brazil;

(e) an official dispatch to the distinguished Tribunal de Recursos, informing it of what this Court has done, to carry out its decision.

On January 31, the plaintiffs asked that they be paid the average wage earned by union members, starting from December 20, the date they were provisionally considered to be union members and prevented from being able to work. On February 3 this Court deferred the request, ... but authorized the Bank of Brazil to pay union members, with the exception of members of the union directorate, for the month of January.

Under these circumstances, no right, much less any clear and certain right, was violated by this Court. The only thing done was to carry out the decision of the distinguished Tribunal peacefully, in a manner designed to prevent the decision from

---

[29] Article 203 of the Penal Code makes it a crime, punishable by fine and up to a year's imprisonment, for anyone "to frustrate by fraud or violence any right assured by labor legislation." Article 330 of the Penal Code makes it a crime, punishable by fine and up to six months in jail, "to disobey a legal order of a public official." [Eds.]

[30] This provision increases the penalty which may be imposed for violation of Article 203 of the Penal Code for cases which threaten or subvert the political or social order. [Eds.]

becoming a true farce, due to the audacity of a few and the criminal complacency of the administrative authorities. The complaining union has no clear and certain right, for the simple reason that one who has maliciously opposed the law cannot claim its protection. Moreover, the measure imposed by this Court is expressly provided for in Article 922 of the Code of Civil Procedure, which states that "the payment of sums due may, upon request or *ex officio,* be ordered by the Judge, via judicial seizure of the goods or earnings of the debtor." . . .

In addition, this case involves defense of the very sovereignty of the Judicial Power. The civil judicial process does not stop with violent deployment of the police, with public scandal, or with the institution of criminal charges against administrative authorities who obstinately refuse to carry out court decisions. It is also necessary to complete execution in the civil arena to restore integrally the right violated. . . . Obviously, magistrates . . . cannot remain dependent upon the arbitrary discretion of the administrative authorities, of whatever position, to carry out their decisions. Execution of a judicial decision can only be stayed by appeal to a high court; never by the domination of occasional misuses of administrative fiat. With due respect, the words of the immortal Von Ihering are appropriate here: "The sword without justice is naked force; justice without the sword is impotent law." If in addition to the moral force of their decisions, judges do not have the coercive power to see them implemented, . . . in a short time the Judicial Power will be relegated to a secondary position within the division of powers, and citizens will have lost their ultimate protection, for as Rui [Barbosa] used to say, "The hope of the Judges is the ultimate hope."

5. Habeas Corpus, Writ of Security, and Representation: Overlapping Constitutional Remedies

Habeas corpus has retained much of its unusual elasticity in Brazil despite the development of the writ of security. Determining which writ is the proper remedy is no simple task, as the case of *Vieira Netto, infra,* demonstrates.

In addition to habeas corpus and the writ of security, Brazil has developed a third summary judicial procedure to ensure observance of constitutional guarantees. This is an action entitled "representation," which is initiated directly before the Supreme Federal Tribunal by the Procurator General. The representation was originally concerned solely with the maintenance of democratic government in the states. Article 7 (VII) of the 1946 Constitution authorized the federal government to intervene in state activities, *inter alia,* to assure observance of the following principles: (1) republican form of government, (2) independence and harmony of powers, (3) the temporariness of the holding of elective offices, (4) the prohibition against governors and mayors immediately succeeding themselves, (5) municipal authority, (6) rendering of administrative accounts, and (7) the guarantee of the power of the judiciary. Article 8 enpowered the Procurator General to submit to the Supreme Federal Tribunal for invalidation any state act deemed offensive to these seven constitutional principles. In December of 1965 the 16th Amendment to the 1946 constitution expanded the scope of representation to authorize the Procurator General to challenge "any federal or state law or normative act."

The following cases illustrate some of the overlap among the three summary constitutional procedures, and the difficulties in determining which writ is the proper remedy.

VIEIRA NETTO

Supreme Federal Tribunal of Brazil
H.C. No. 45,232, 44 R.T.J. 322 (1968)

[The petitioners, who are bankers, businessmen, and a lawyer, sought a writ of habeas corpus against the Substitute Auditor (under military jurisdiction a judge who determines criminal cases in the first instance) of the Fifth Military Region, who had suspended the petitioners from the exercise of their professional and business activities. Petitioners were accused of having violated the National Security Law. The suspension was decreed pursuant to Article 48 of this statute, which provides:

> Pretrial incarceration for those apprehended in *flagrante delicto* or the receipt of the accusation, in any of the cases provided for in this decree-law, shall simultaneously imply suspension of professional practice or employment with a private concern, as well as cessation of . . . [any governmental employment] until final decision.
>
> § 1° The head of the service or activity, employer, or person responsible for management, including schools, shall be subject to a fine of 100 to 1000 new cruzeiros if he permits violation of the provisions of this article, the fine being imposed by the judge in the principal case.
>
> § 2° Should there be a repeated violation, the penalty shall be that of the [principal] offense.

The petitioners initially sought a writ of habeas corpus from the Superior Military Tribunal, which declined to decide the case because the court was in recess. Since the matter was urgent, the petitioners brought the case directly before the Supreme Federal Tribunal.]

Vote of Minister Cavalcanti (Reporter):

The first question to be examined is whether the proper judicial relief has been requested, or whether the case is really one for the writ of security. Since the creation of [the writ] . . ., habeas corpus has been restricted to freedom of movement, with the writ of security being the proper remedy to safeguard other clear and certain rights unprotected by habeas corpus.

. . . However, a certain common area, a so-called gray zone, has remained in which the two institutions overlap in their application. This is in the conceptualization of what the Constitution itself defines as freedom of movement. Thus, habeas corpus initially would lie when freedom of movement (liberty to come and go *eunde ambulandi ulta citroque*) was necessary for the exercise of a right; however, this was not the case after the creation of the writ of security. Since then habeas corpus theoretically will be available only when the right to come and go is specifically necessary to the exercise of the right. However, this [condition] will not be met when the objective purpose of the petition is the examination of the legality of an act injuring that right.

But habeas corpus has also been expanded, for example, to the examination of just cause for a criminal prosecution, and in a general way, to all the diverse phases of the entire area of criminal procedure.

Thus, in the orthodox solution, the writ of security would be the proper and specific means to test the legality of an act . . . which violates a subjective right. Generally this is an administrative or executive act, or a legislative act applied by an administrative authority (never the law itself). Very exceptionally, through case law construction, it may be a judicial act, when there is no way of avoiding the damage caused by the act, the law failing to provide for any other recourse.

In the case at bar, however, the petition refers to a judicial act in a criminal prosecution, an act which carries with it a measure which has the character of a penalty under our criminal legislation, without a regular prosecution and prior to any judicial proceeding. Such a penalty is classified by Article 69 of our Penal Code as an ancillary sanction. . . .

I am certain that either of the two procedures would be appropriate in this case. The writ of security would have to be brought first in a lower court, with a slightly slower procedure, while habeas corpus could be brought initially in the Supreme Court. . . .

Given these two circumstances — the petition being against the determination of a judicial authority in a criminal prosecution and involving an examination of the legitimacy of a measure considered as an ancillary sanction — . . . I acknowledge that habeas corpus will lie.

On the merits certain questions deserve examination. . . .

I. The suspension from professional practice. In the case of pretrial incarceration it is obvious that the individual will not have conditions in which he can practice his profession, though he can operate through colleagues. But a mere accusation . . . cannot constitute an obstacle to the exercise of one's profession, depriving one of his means of sustenance and interrupting his professional activity simply because he is suspected of having committed a crime against national security. This prosecution, this simple accusation, may be totally unfounded. The course of the prosecution may be prolonged, and the professional will have suffered irreparable damage to his patrimony and professional activity. The accused incurs a veritable penalty, even prior to any determination of responsibility against him. . . .

II. The suspension of employment in a private concern is not an ancillary sanction, but constitutes an excessive intervention with a private concern, corresponding to the deprivation of the employee's means of sustenance, for no one will admit that the employer is obligated to continue to pay the salary of an employee suspended from work for an indefinite period. It is contrary to the free exercise of legitimate activity and restricts the employer's liberty of employment.

... It has been said that the National Security Law has changed the preexisting law. This it can do, but within limits. [Quoting from a book he has written on judicial review, the justice expounds a theory of constitutional interpretation bottomed upon viewing the Constitution as a harmonic whole in which the spirit as well as the letter of the law must be considered.] ... A [constitutional] guarantee does not have to be express; it is sufficient if it stems from the political system and the complex of expressed principles. I have no doubt that this occurs in the case at bar, for the rigors of the measures provided for in the law which we are examining cry out against the essence of human principles which are summed up in the right of survival. Only a finding of guilt can limit the right to work and the express norms which assure the right to exercise one's profession and the working relationship in the ambit of private enterprise.

... If the problem of unconstitutionality had to be supported by a rigid technique and in a purely legal fashion certainly Marshall would never have rendered his famous decision, today already classic, which constitutes the basis of the doctrine of unconstitutionality.

Then, which constitutional precept would have been violated by the norm under attack, that is, by Decree Law 314? The petitioner insists principally on 13, 14, and 15 of Article 150, as well as Paragraph 23 ....[31]

But the cited provisions do not seem entirely adequate to me for the unconstitutionality claimed. We would prefer to rest our vote on the right to live, mentioned at the beginning of Article 150 as the general source of the rights enumerated in the same article, as well as §35 of Article 150, which extends the guarantees set out in the same precept to other rights, as we shall attempt to show below.

Unfortunately, we do not have in our Constitution a provision corresponding to the Eighth Amendment of the American Constitution, which prohibits exacting excessive bail, excessive fines, and the imposition of cruel and unusual punishment. ... In Trop v. Dulles (1958), [Chief] Justice Warren observed (in my view, quite correctly) that the fundamental idea of the Eighth Amendment is the preservation of human dignity. We do not have an identical precept, but we do have §35 of Article 150, which is more generic and susceptible to a broader application. ... It provides: "The

---

[31] Constitution of 1967, Article 150:

The constitution assures to Brazilians and foreigners residing in the country the inviolability of rights to life, liberty and property, in the following terms: ...

§13. No penalty shall extend beyond the person of the delinquent. The law shall regulate individualization of punishment.

§14. All authorities are required to respect the physical and moral integrity of detained and imprisoned persons.

§15. The law shall assure accused persons an ample defense with the recourses inherent thereto. There shall be no privileged forum nor exceptional tribunals. ...

§23. The exercise of any employment, office, or profession shall be free, observing such conditions with regard to capacity as the law may establish. [Eds.]

specification of the rights and guarantees expressed in this Constitution does not exclude other rights and guarantees stemming from the regime and from the principles which it adopts."

Here, the present Constitution, as had its predecessors in the area of individual and social guarantees, tried to follow the exigencies of the perfectionism of man and respect for his physical and moral integrity. The preservation of his personality and its protection against infamous penalties, the condemnation without an adversary process, the suppression of certain penalties which were included in our old penal legislation, the affirmation that punishment was imposed only on the delinquent and not upon those who depended upon him, define an orientation which perfectly qualifies the regime and the fundamental principles of our Constitution. This precept comes from the Ninth Amendment of the American Constitution. . . .

In this respect, the expression – a "cruel" measure – which is found in the American text, characterizes well the norm in question, because it withholds from the individual the possibilities of professional activity, which permits him to maintain himself and his family. It is cruel also in respect to the disproportion between the situation of the accused and the consequences of the measure.

But not only Article 150 §35 may be invoked. The beginning of Article 150 is also relevant because it assures all who live here the right to life, individual liberty, and property. Hence, making it impossible to exercise an activity indispensable to permitting the individual to obtain the means of sustenance deprives him of a little of his life. . . .

Life is not only a complex of functions which resist death, but it is also a positive affirmation of the conditions which assure an individual and those who depend upon him of the indispensable means of sustenance.

This does not mean that the State must allocate these resources, but that it cannot deprive the individual of the exercising of activities from which he may obtain those resources without there having been at least a judicial decision legitimately depriving him of his liberty to exercise lawful activities. . . .

In the present case . . . I have no doubt considering this preventive measure as offensive to the inherent rights of life and of those rights fundamental to man.

Thus, I vote to grant . . . the order to the petitioners by considering unconstitutional that which refers to the exercise of liberal professions and of employment in private entities. . . .

Vote of Minister Eloy da Rocha:

. . . [With respect to the issue of the appropriateness of habeas corpus to protect the claimed right,] I diverge, with all due respect, from the eminent Reporter, for to my understanding the appropriate remedy is that of the writ of security. In his erudite vote, the eminent Reporter referred to the history of the writ of security, born in the evolution of habeas corpus, emphasizing that a gray zone may occur in which the rights cross, permitting either remedy. It appears to me, with all due respect, that this is not the case. . . .

As I see it, in this case freedom of movement is not at issue. In its broad sense, freedom of movement does not include the right to work or exercise one's profession, employment, or function. Cases which habeas corpus had evolved to cover today pertain to the writ of security. The protection of [professional activity] falls in the domain of the writ of security and not habeas corpus. As Pontes de Miranda teaches, the right to practice, in its entirety, is not protected by habeas corpus. . . .

Minister Gonçalves de Oliveira: Will the writ of security lie against a penal sanction?

Minister Eloy da Rocha: The provisional prohibition of the right does not result from conviction, which does not yet exist. Nor does the sanction's character as an anticipatory ancillary sanction preclude the writ of security. . . . [I]f the restriction on the exercise of professional activity presents itself as an isolated, autonomous [matter], when this restriction is imposed only as a provisional measure, then, in my opinion, the proper remedy is the writ of security. . . .

Thus, I am convinced that the proper remedy is the writ of security and not habeas corpus. One can raise an objection in dealing with a criminal judge, having in mind his coercive authority. But one does not contest, in theory, the possibility of the writ of security against an act of a penal judge. . . .

Vote of Minister Aliomar Baleeiro:

. . . I vote to grant the writ of habeas corpus. However, from the beginning, I have had in my own mind the doubt that . . . perhaps this is a case for the writ of security.

It is true that the illustrious counsel, [for the petitioners] in his brilliant explanation, tried to characterize [the case as involving] the right to go and come. The offices, including the building, would be the places in which these lawyers would be forbidden to set foot. But, Mr. President, I think that this case is most serious. I vote to grant the order in the terms of the eminent Reporter. . . .

Vote of Minister Evandro Lins:

Mr. President, the provision in Article 48 of the National Security Law is an excresence, even within the system of the Decree Law which contains it. . . .

The fact that one has been accused of an infraction of this provision of the National Security Law does not mean that he is incapable or has revealed any incapacity to exercise a liberal profession.

Minister Gonçalves de Oliveira: Especially because the prosecution has not yet imposed any penalty. The individual is presumed to be innocent until convicted.

Minister Evandro Lins: Thus, Mr. President, my vote is in the sense of declaring the unconstitutionality of all of Article 48, including its first two paragraphs, because, more excrescent than the Article itself, is its second paragraph coupled with the first, which . . . [impose the same punishment as that for the principal offense on] the employer or department head who consents to the exercise of a profession or employment. . . .

If the National Security Law does not impose the penalty of suspension of the exercise of a profession or employment . . . after the determination of the culpability of the accused, it cannot, logically, impose such [sanction] prior to sentence. That which offends logic so violently cannot be adopted as a valid juridical norm. The law cannot in this manner create preventive punishment without violating the general principles the system of guarantees and of rights safeguarded by the Constitution. . . .

Minister Luiz Gallotti (President): I ponder only the following: We are not judging unconstitutionality in theory in a representation but in a concrete case, in a petition for habeas corpus.

Minister Evandro Lins: But, Mr. President, why are we granting habeas corpus?

Minister Luiz Gallotti (President): It seems to me, being a judgment in a concrete case, the declaration of unconstitutionality has to be restricted to the matter dealt with [in the case] . . . .

Vote of Minister Gonçalves de Oliveira:

Mr. President, I am also in entire accord with the eminent Reporter when he votes to grant habeas corpus, for the case concerns a criminal prosecution. Really, the right of the accused to exercise his profession is clear and certain, and as this case grows out of a criminal prosecution, the petitioner may request . . . [habeas corpus]. The proper means of reparation has to be habeas corpus.

It is not only a case of the liberty to go and come, in which habeas corpus will lie. When a person is accused and the accusation is inappropriate, habeas corpus will lie. In short, all the implications and onus imposed on an accused in a criminal action are reparable through habeas corpus. . . .

Decision: . . . The preliminary objection to the appropriateness of habeas corpus was rejected over the vote of Minister Eloy da Rocha; in accordance with the vote of the Reporter, habeas corpus was granted in part, declaring unconstitutional Article 48 of Decree-Law 314 of March 13, 1967, which refers to the liberal professions and employment in private activities, with Minister Evandro Lins voting to grant habeas corpus *in totum* since he considers all of Article 48 unconstitutional. . . . Brasília, Feb. 21, 1968.

Questions

1. Why has part of Article 48 of the National Security Law been declared unconstitutional?

2. Has the Supreme Federal Tribunal invalidated the statute *erga omnes* or only as to the petitioners in this case? See *Engenharia Souza e Barker Ltda. v. Senado Federal, infra,* pp. 119-24.

3. Is this case a tropical variety of *Griswold v. Connecticut,* 381 U.S. 479 (1965)?

Notes

1. The Supreme Federal Tribunal's decision in the *Vieira Netto* case was one of several decisions which particularly angered military hardliners, who successfully forced a purge of three members of the Tribunal less than a year after the decision. See pp. 214-15 *infra.*

2. In the case of In re Gilson Soares de Freitas, 48 R.T.J. 245 (1968) a judge who refused to submit to a medical examination to determine his sanity sought relief through habeas corpus from the imminent issuance of an order suspending him from office. The Tribunal of Justice of Minas Gerais treated habeas corpus as the proper remedy, but denied the petition on the merits. Though there were doubts about whether habeas corpus was the proper procedure, the Supreme Court affirmed instead of dismissing the appeal. Minister Adaucto Cardoso, the Reporter, explained:

But it happens that the use of habeas corpus instead of the writ of security in this case does not constitute a gross error which would justify barring the path of the petitioner. The vacillating dividing line between the two procedural institutions, which the eminent Minister Gonçalves de Oliveira once called twin brothers, in this case raises doubts which [permit us to characterize the error as harmless,] especially considering the acute issue of liberty raised in this proceeding.

3. As the report of Minister Cavalcanti indicates, the writ of security will lie against an administrative act implementing a law, but not against the law itself. *Súmula* No. 266 of the Supreme Federal Tribunal states explicitly: "The writ of security will not lie against a law in the abstract." The theory is that the judiciary lacks the power to annul a law; it can only refuse to apply it in a concrete case. Even though a writ of security be conceded, the law continues in force. It simply may not be enforced against the party that sought the writ, as well as the similarly situated parties who may have legally joined in the action with him. Non-parties must bring their own writs of security if the administrative authority persists in applying the law.

However, the above paragraph is an over-simplification. There is a strong doctrinal current, which has some case law support, contending that the writ of security will lie against a self-executing law. Andréa Ferreira, *O Mandando de Segurança e o Ato Legislativo,* 231 Rev. For. 35 (1970). And, as the next case shows, the Brazilian constitutional system contains measures which permit nullification of laws declared unconstitutional by the Supreme Federal Tribunal. The votes also indicate appreciation of the great delicacy with which such powers must be exercised.

ENGENHARIA SOUZA E BARKER LTDA. ET AL. v. SENADO FEDERAL

Supreme Federal Tribunal of Brazil
RMS 16.512, 38 R.T.J. 5 (1966)

[The State of São Paulo levied a transaction tax on individuals or firms engaged in the construction or repair of buildings. In a 1961 case involving an architect who refused to pay, the Supreme Federal Tribunal declared the entire tax unconstitutional. However, the headnote stated only that the tax on professional service transactions was unconstitutional. In 1962 the President of the Tribunal sent to the Federal Senate copies of various decisions declaring laws and resolutions unconstitutional, including this particular decision. Article 64 of the 1946 Constitution (Art. 42 VII in the 1969 version of the Constitution) provided: "It is incumbent upon the Federal Senate to suspend the execution, wholly or in part, of any law or decree declared unconstitutional by final decision of the Supreme Federal Tribunal." Pursuant to this provision, the Senate in 1965 enacted a resolution suspending the entire tax. The Treasury of the State of São Paulo refused to consider the entire tax unconstitutional since that interpretation would mean that it would be unable to collect the tax from construction firms, and interpreted the court's decision as if the headnote were the entire opinion. The Governor of São Paulo asked the Senate to modify its resolution suspending the entire tax. Thereupon, the Senate revoked its original resolution and passed another, limiting the suspension of the transaction tax to professional service contracts.

[The petitioner and 27 other construction firms sought a writ of security against the second Senate resolution, alleging that it was unconstitutional and highly prejudicial to them. The Procurator General suggested that the writ of security would not lie to challenge the constitutionality of the Senate resolution, citing *Súmula* 266, set out on p. 000, *supra.*]

Vote of Minister Oswaldo Trigueiro (Reporter): . . .

Article 64 of the Constitution makes it incumbent on the Senate to suspend, in whole or in part, the execution of laws or decrees declared unconstitutional by final decision of the Supreme Tribunal. This measure, which originated in the 1934 Constitution, gives to the Senate in our political system the task of rendering inoperative, *erga omnes,* the laws and norms which the Judiciary refrains from applying, *in casu,* because of the defect of unconstitutionality.

The Senate in exercise of this power is subject to no sanction whatever, but one of the primary obligations of the Senate is to watch over the juridical order and preserve the harmony which ought to prevail for the Powers to live together.

Upon receiving the request for suspension of execution of an unconstitutional law or norm, it is proper for the Senate, if it has any doubts, either as to the form or even the meaning of the judicial declaration, to ask the Supreme Tribunal for the clarification which it deems necessary. However, it seems to me that after attending to the request of the Supreme Tribunal – promulgating the resolution suspending the unconstitutional law – the competence of the Senate is exhausted. It cannot review the matter, either to interpret the decision of the Supreme Tribunal without [the Tribunal] being heard, or to settle any doubts . . . about the partial validity of the questioned norm. In the first hypothesis it would be acting in the judicial sphere; in the second, it would be entering the field of state legislation.

In these conditions I believe the second Resolution inoperative . . . , without implying any disparagement of the Federal Senate, which proceeded as it understood its duty. . . .

Turning to the second question – the appropriateness of the writ of security – I do not see how it can be granted for the purpose sought in the petition. In the first place, the writ of security is inadmissable against a law in the abstract, . . . and for the purposes in view, I consider the Resolution of the Senate as equivalent to a law . . . .

Whatever be the reach of the challenged Resolution, in my view, it undoubtedly produces no immediate injury to a clear and certain right of the petitioners. Admitting that it may authorize a partial revival of the legal norm which was expunged from the fiscal legislation of the State of Sao Paulo since publication of Resolution 32, this only results in the possibility that the Public Treasury will exact the condemned tax in certain cases from certain taxpayers. As long as this levy does not materialize or does not present an immediate threat, there is no injury to a right that can be remedied via the writ. When this threat does exist, the writ will then lie against the state tax collectors. But in this case the remedy cannot be sought originally in the Supreme Tribunal. . . .

For these reasons, I vote not to grant the petition.

Vote of Minister Pedro Chaves:

. . . I do not consider the Resolution of the Senate a legislative act, nor do I consider the petition an affront to a law in the abstract. The act of the Senate of the Republic . . . is a mere secondary consequence of the execution of the provision of Article 64 of the Federal Constitution, which imposes on the Senate — imposes rather than giving it an option — [the duty of] carrying out the decisions of the Supreme Federal Tribunal. . . .

In a certain manner this suspension of the execution of a legislative act signifies the revocation of a law, and the Judicial Power does not have the competence to revoke laws; it has the competence to apply them. It is the Legislative Power that has the competence to revoke laws via another law.

A law declared unconstitutional can no longer be maintained effectively among the ranks of Brazilian legislation, because the Supreme Federal Tribunal, within its unique and exclusive competence, has said that the law was unconstitutional, and the Constitution obliges the Senate to suspend execution of the laws which the Supreme Federal Tribunal declares unconstitutional. . . . Consequently, when it performs this act, the Senate is the executor of a decision of the Supreme Tribunal. . . .

I vote to grant the writ of security.

Vote of Minister Aliomar Baleeiro:

I adopt the vote of the eminent Minister Oswaldo Trigueiro in the part in which he considers the writ of security inadequate for the purposes of the petitioner. . . . [A] resolution of the Senate to execute art. 64 of the Constitution is of the normative order — or, to use the expression of Minister Carlos Medeiros, "quasi-legislative." To revoke a law, to suspend the execution of a law, is a juridical act of the normative character.

In this case, on the same principle, the writ of security cannot be utilized, for it may not be employed against a norm in the abstract. . . .

In my opinion the Senate has the political discretion to suspend or not. If convenient, it suspends; if inconvenient, instead of giving prestige to a decision of the Supreme Tribunal, it may initiate a constitutional amendment, or take no action.

Minister Pedro Chaves: It was thus in the time of the 1937 Constitution.

Minister Aliomar Baleeiro:

. . . The eminent Minister Pedro Chaves cited the Constitution of 1937 which permitted the Legislative Power to annul decisions of the Supreme Tribunal with which it did not agree. And we know, unfortunately, that the dictator [Getúlio Vargas], exercising the functions of the Legislative Power with which he invested himself, in fact suspended at least one decision of the Supreme Tribunal, in 1939 or 1940.[32] If my memory does not fail me, it was a case in which the appellate judges of Bahia sought a judicial remedy against being required to pay income tax, which was introduced for magistrates by a decree law in March of that year. I remember very well . . . the eminent Minister Carlos Maxmiliano, . . . saying that he would issue no more judicial remedies, for it was not proper for the Supreme Court to issue [a decision] in order for it not to be carried out. . . . It was one of the most famous

---

[32] Decree-Law No. 1.564 of Sept. 5, 1939. [Eds.]

decisions in the history of the Supreme Federal Tribunal, and one of the most painful. . . .[33]

Now what I sustain is that the Senate has the right to suspend or not to suspend a law impugned as unconstitutional. It can observe whether the Supreme Tribunal has established a predominant course of decisions on the subject.

We cannot deny that, in the history of the Supreme Tribunal, with respect to countless theses, the case law has vacillated, and that we encounter within a short time, decisions . . . declaring that such a law is unconstitutional, and others declaring that it is constitutional. . . .

The Senate has the right, even after the *Súmula,* to wait for the case law to become settled . . . . It may be that the Senate prefers reform of the Constitution in order for the sense of the law to prevail . . . . It may also do nothing, cross its arms, and leave the matter a dead issue, for there is no sanction whatsoever for its resistence.

It is justifiable for it to do this, at times, for it is common knowledge that a tribunal of the level of the Supreme Federal Tribunal, or the Supreme Court of the United States or Argentina, legislates only in a concrete case. . . .

[I vote not to grant the writ of security.]

Vote of Minister Prado Kelly:

. . . The settled case law of the Supreme Federal Tribunal has denied extension of the effects of its decisions to interested third parties. The judgment has been . . . restricted to the question upon which the Court has focused. Only in habeas corpus . . . has the extension of the measure *erga omnes* been admitted.

Thus, quite naturally, juridical scholars pointed out the convenience of instituting an adequate means for the prompt suspension of the effects on third parties of laws or regulations declared unconstitutional by the Supreme Court. . . .

The mission which the Senate performs is political, and from a formal viewpoint is not to be confounded with its legislative function. . . . [To demonstrate] that it is not a law, it is sufficient to recall the Senate Rules. The expression used therein is "Resolution." It is not even a "legislative decree," which would correspond to the exclusive jurisdiction of the Congress, nor a "bill" which corresponds to acts subject to the presidential sanction. It is denominated "resolution" because the Senate found no better term with which to characterize it. . . .

What is the fundamental obstacle to the concession of the writ? It is argued that the writ is directed against a "law" or "quasi-law." But in my view, it deals neither with a "law" nor a "quasi-law." When the 1946 Constitution was in force, the competence of the Supreme Court to consider acts of the Senate was restricted, because under Art. 101, Section I(i), this Court could grant the writ of security only against an act of the President of the Republic, the House and Senate Executive Committees, and the President of the Court itself. But Amendment No. 16 expanded that jurisdiction, permitting pronouncements of this Court in writs of security against acts of the President of the Republic, the Senate and the House of Representatives. . . .

---

[33] There are two other notable cases in Brazilian legal history when the executive openly defied decisions of the Supreme Federal Tribunal; one occurred in 1911 and the other in 1915. L. Bittencourt, *O Contrôle Jurisdicional de Constitucionalidade das Leis,* 136-39 (2d ed. 1968). The paucity of cases is indicative of the respect normally accorded Brazil's highest court. [Eds.]

I vote to grant the writ of security because I regard it as the most expeditious means to make the authority of the Tribunal prevail in this case. . . .

Minister Victor Nunes: . . . When the Supreme Tribunal denies that the writ of security will lie against a law in the abstract, it uses the word *law* in its most ample sense, in the sense of a norm or a normative act. Thus, even in cases brought against ministerial directives (*portarias*) or decrees of the President of the Republic which have a normative character, we have not granted the writ of security.

Minister Evandro Lins: It depends on the case.

Minister Victor Nunes: What matters is the nature of the act, not its hierarchy. If the substance of the act is legislative, that is, normative, it does not yet take the form of an injury to an individual right. And it is the injury of an individual right, albeit imminent, that the writ of security protects. . . .

Now there exists, through the 16th Amendment, a constitutional procedure [the representation] which permits us to consider the constitutionality of normative acts in the abstract, independently of any injury to an individual right. . . . [T] he proceeding which we are now examining has all of the formal requirements of the representation of unconstitutionality, because it was taken over by the Procurator General, who has the initiative for the representation, and the authority whose act has been impugned — [the Senate] — has been heard. In view of this, if we agree to hear this case as a representation, we rid ourselves of all the difficulties as to whether . . . the writ of security lies, for it is beyond discussion that the procedure of representation will lie.

Minister Carlos Medeiros: There is no representation *ex officio*.

Minister Victor Nunes: Representation is always the initiative of the Procurator General, but His Excellency adopted the petition as a representation. A short time ago he made a lucid oral pronouncement, transforming his opinion into a representation of unconstitutionality . . . .

Minister Evandro Lins:

Mr. President, despite my understanding that the writ of security will lie, to obviate the difficulty . . ., I adhere to the suggestion made by the eminent Minister Victor Nunes, that if we do not concede the writ of security . . ., the petition be conceded as a representation . . . .

Vote of Minister Luiz Gallotti:

. . . I have always understood, and this Court has decided, that the fact that representation will lie does not exclude the use of other judicial remedies by interested parties. This is because the representation belongs exclusively to the Procurator General. His Excellency is free to use it or not. Hence, one ought not deprive interested parties of the possibility of resorting to other proper remedies.

The eminent Minister Aliomar Baleeiro has objected that the Senate can decline to comply with any decision that we may make against the challenged act without incurring any sanction, for none is provided for in the Constitution or the law. This reminds me of what happened when the unforgettable Epitácio Pessoa was President of the Republic. The President was in São Paulo, and the Rio newspapers thought it strange that a seat on the Supreme Court was still vacant as the legal time limit of thirty days for filling the post drew to a close. Epitácio telephoned Pires e Albuquerque, then Procurator General of the Republic, asking if the law fixed that period. Pires responded affirmatively. Then Epitácio asked, "But does the law provide for any sanctions if this time limit is not observed?" This is the response of Pires, which the intimacy between the two permitted — "The law provides no sanctions because it supposes that the President of the Republic will comply with the duty which it imposes on him."

In this case, annulling the second Resolution of the Senate will cause the first to prevail.

. . . [T]he Procurator General . . . agreed that the case should be a representation, endorsing it as such.

This permits us to grant the substance of the remedy if the Court decides not to grant the writ of security. . . .

I agree with the eminent Ministers Victor Nunes and Aliomar Baleeiro that the Senate, paying heed to reasons of convenience and expedience, may or may not suspend execution of a law declared unconstitutional, extending or not to everyone the effects of the Supreme Court decision. What it cannot do is, after suspension, to pass a new Resolution to interpret the Supreme Court's opinion restrictively. For this would mean that in this case the Senate could partially revive a state law (which it cannot) or in other cases, revive a federal law (which it also by itself cannot).

I decide in favor of the representation, given that the Court has decided to resolve the matter by that means . . . .

Decision

. . . The decision was the following: We have granted the petition as a Representation, and have decided in its favor, annulling the challenged act, against the votes of Ministers Aliomar Baleeiro and Hermes Lima on the merits.

Brasília, May 25, 1966.

Questions

1. Is the Brazilian method of protecting constitutional rights through the writ of security less likely to bring the judiciary into damaging conflicts with the political branches of government than the U.S. system? More specifically, compare the requirements for: (a) standing, (b) ripeness, (c) the effect of a declaration of unconstitutionality.

2. Is the Brazilian method of protecting constitutional rights through the representation likely to bring the Supreme Federal Tribunal into damaging conflicts with the political branches of the government? To what extent does the answer to this question depend on whether the Procurator General, who is appointed by the President, has complete discretion to refuse to bring a representation before the Supreme Tribunal? In *M.D.B. v. Procurador-Geral da República,* 59 R.T.J. 333 (STF *en banc* 1971) the opposition party brought suit against the Procurator General to compel him to institute a representation proceeding challenging the constitutionality

of a recent decree-law establishing prior censorship in the country. As one might have expected from dicta in the principal case, the Supreme Federal Tribunal held that the institution of a representation proceeding is within the complete discretion of the Procurator General. What would have been the implications of a contrary decision?

Note on the Popular Action

6. Note on the Popular Action

The Brazilian representation is similar to a nineteenth century Colombian system of judicial review, set out in Article 72 of the Colombian Constitution of 1863, which provided:

> On petition of the Procurator General or any citizen, the Supreme Court shall, by unanimous vote, suspend the enforcement of the legislative acts of the state assemblies, insofar as they may be contrary to the Constitution or laws of the Union, reporting in each case to the Senate so that the latter may decide definitively as to the nullity or validity of said acts.

By 1910 the Colombian counterpart to the Brazilian representation had evolved into an institution known as the "popular action" (*acción popular*), which permits any citizen to challenge the constitutionality of any law on its face. Article 214 (2) of the Constitution of 1886, as amended 1969. See Grant, "Judicial Control of the Constitutionality of Statutes and Administrative Legislation in Colombia: Nature and Evolution of the Present System," 23 *So. Calif. L. Rev.* 484, 496-504 (1950). The popular action has an extraordinarily simple procedure. Any citizen (defined loosely by the case law to include corporations and even aliens), irrespective of any personal stake in the outcome or the exhaustion of administrative remedies, may bring an action at any time directly before the Colombian Supreme Court by filing a simple written statement setting forth the asserted conflict between the law and the constitution. The Procurator General must then file an opinion on the issue with the court within 30 days; however, since the popular action is not considered an adversary proceeding, the Procurator's role is more analogous to an *amicus curiae* than to a respondent. The action goes directly to the constitutional chamber of the Supreme Court for an opinion and statement, which must be rendered within 30 days. No briefs or oral arguments are presented, and the action takes preference on the court's calendar. The Supreme Court sits *en banc,* exercising original and exclusive jurisdiction. The Court is not limited to the complainant's theory of the case; if it believes the law unconstitutional for reasons other than those set out in the complaint, the Court has the duty to invalidate the law. If the law is declared unconstitutional, the Court's decision has an *erga omnes* effect. However, technically this does not mean the law is annulled, nor that rights acquired under the law are invalidated. It simply means that the law cannot be enforced against anyone. The Court's decision is not appealable and cannot be reviewed in any later proceeding. L. Sachica, *Constitucionalismo Colombiano* 124-30 (2d Ed. 1966).

The popular action before the Colombian Supreme Court is limited to challenge of any public law or decree-law in force. Regulatory or administrative decrees or acts must be challenged before the Council of State, the highest administrative court. The Supreme Court has been roundly criticized for carving out two limitations on its broad jurisdictional grant: (1) laws approving treaties may not be challenged by popular action, (2) nor will the Court inquire into the procedural formalities with which a law was passed. F. Pérez, *Derecho Constitucional Colombiano* 446-49 (5th ed. 1962). However, in comparison with practice in other countries, these limitations upon the exercise of the power of judicial review seem quite minor. Consequently, one would imagine that the Supreme Court has been overwhelmed with popular actions, but apparently this has not been the case. The two volume work of Néstor Pineda, *Jurisprudencia Constitucional de la Corte Suprema de Justicia* (1963), which purports to collect all of the constitutional decisions of the Supreme Court sitting *en banc* from 1910 through 1962 contains only 329 cases. Three of these cases deal with permission for the Executive to leave the country; 25 deal with proposed legislation that has been vetoed by the President on constitutional grounds. Of the 301 popular actions, the Colombian Supreme Court avoided reaching the merits in 76. In 100 of about 225 popular actions decided on the merits, the Court declared the challenged legislation unenforceable (*inexequible*) either in whole or in part. A review of the cases involving contract claims appears in Grant, " 'Contract Clause' Litigation in Colombia; a Comparative Study in Judicial Review," 42 *Am. Pol. Sci. Rev.* 1103 (1948).

(b) The Popular Action in Other Latin American Countries

With slight modifications, the popular action has spread to Panama, Venezuela, and El Salvador. From 1931 until 1959 Cuba permitted the popular action, but required a petition signed by 25 citizens instead of an individual complaint. Article 133 of the Peruvian Constitution provides for a popular action to challenge the constitutionality of governmental decrees and regulations (not laws), but the Peruvian courts have been unwilling to permit its utilization. See Furnish, "The Heirarchy of Peruvian Laws: Context for Law and Development," 18 *Am. J. Comp. L.* 91, 107-110 (1971). Brazil also permits a popular action for the sole purpose of "annulling acts injurious to the patrimony of public entities." (Constitution of 1967, Art. 150 §31, regulated by Lei No. 4.717 of June 29, 1965).

Questions

1. What advantages does the popular action offer over the Brazilian writ of security and the U.S. system of judicial review? What disadvantages? See generally Grant, "Judicial Control of Legislation," 3 *Am. J. Comp. L.* 186 (1954).

2. What legal institutions in the United States perform functions analogous to those of the popular action? See L. Jaffe, *Judicial Control of Administrative Action* 459-500 (1965).

C. The Mexican Amparo

Judicial protection of constitutional rights developed quite differently in Mexico. The Constitution of 1824, the first following independence, explicitly delegated to Congress the exclusive power to resolve questions of constitutional interpretation. Though the Supreme Court was accorded jurisdiction over cases dealing with infractions of the Constitution, subject to procedures to be established by statute, such a statute was never enacted. Consequently, the judiciary perceived that it had no power to protect constitutional rights. When Mexico adopted its second constitution in 1836, a curious organ of government called the *Supremo Poder Conservador* (Supreme Conserving Power) was established as guardian of the constitution. Comprised of five members elected by the Senate, the *Supremo Poder Conservador* was granted the power to nullify any law, executive act, or Supreme Court decision that contravened the Constitution. It was also granted the power under certain circumstances to suspend the Supreme Court and Congress. In the event of revolution, the *Supremo Poder Conservador* was responsible for reestablishing the constitutional order. But the *Supremo Poder Conservador* lacked its own army, and could legally act only if requested to do so by one of the three branches of government. In its five-year existence, it was called to action only four times, none of which involved a defense of constitutional provisions.[34]

The frequent arbitrariness of local *caudillos* and the fiasco of the *Supremo Poder Conservador* produced a search for a new method of guaranteeing protection of constitutional rights. Influenced by the United States system of judicial review (particularly as described in De Tocqueville's *Democracy in America*), the drafters of an 1847 constitutional amendment, known as the Act of Reforms, accorded the federal judiciary the power to protect any person from infringement of his constitutional rights either by statute or executive action. The courts were to limit themselves "to affording protection in the special case to which the complaint refers, without making any general declaration as to the law or act on which the complaint is based." But Congress again failed to enact an implementing statute, and the Supreme Court refused to entertain any suits for protection of constitutional rights without such procedural legislation.

No further progress towards implementation of a remedy to protect constitutional rights occurred until adoption of a new Constitution in 1857. This Constitution grew out of the *Reforma* of Benito Juárez, whose forces had ousted the dictator Santa Anna only two years before. It was a "liberal" Constitution, not only in that it was dictated by the Liberal Party, but also because it reflected the dominant individualism of the

---

[34] R. Baker, *Judicial Review in Mexico: A Study of the Amparo Suit* 6-9 (1971).

century. The sharp contrast between the success of judicial review in the United States and the failure to safeguard the constitution in Mexico convinced the constitutional drafting committee that preservation of constitutional rights was best entrusted to the judiciary. There was, however, considerable debate about how the judiciary should protect the constitution. Should judges be limited to protecting individual rights in proceedings narrowly conceived for such protection, or should they be permitted to assume a broader political role, issuing general declarations of unconstitutionality which effectively repealed statutes? As can be seen from articles 101 and 102, which have been maintained virtually intact as articles 103 and 107 (paragraphs I and II) of the present Mexican Constitution, the 1857 Constitution resolved the issue by emphasizing the strictly judicial aspect of the protection of individual rights and by minimizing the legislative aspects of judicial review. The hope was that in this fashion "constitutional issues would cease to be incitements to insurrection."[35]

MEXICO, CONSTITUTION of 1917 (As amended, 1968)

ARTICLE 103. The federal courts shall decide all controversies which arise:

I. Because of laws or acts of authorities that violate the rights of individuals.

II. Because of laws or acts of the federal government that restrict or encroach on the sovereignty of the States;

III. Because of laws or acts of State authorities that invade the sphere of federal authority. . . .

ARTICLE 107. All controversies mentioned in article 103 shall follow the legal forms and procedures prescribed by law, in accordance with the following bases:

I. A trial in amparo shall always be granted upon the request of the aggrieved party.

II. The judgment shall only affect private individuals, being limited to according them the relief and protection pleaded for in the particular case, without making any general declaration as to the law or act on which the complaint is based. . . .

The code-like constitutional provisions set out in Appendix B, pp. 713-16 *infra,* have been fleshed out by a comprehensive, complementary statute known as the Law of Amparo. (In Spanish, *amparo* means "protection.") Like the Brazilian writ of security, the amparo is designed as a summary and speedy remedy, though it does not enjoy a similar preferred position on court dockets. A petition for amparo is to be filed within 15 days of the plaintiff's notification or awareness of the challenged action. Where one is challenging the constitutionality of a statute on its face, this period is extended to 30 days from the time the statute takes effect. The petition can be rather informal. A personal appearance by the plaintiff or his or her representative (or, in an emergency, even a telephone call or telegram to the judge) will suffice. The

---

[35]*Id.* at 36.

judge then makes a preliminary examination of the petition to see that it is in order and notifies the responsible authority, requesting justification for the act and setting the time and place for a hearing within 30 days. The judge is supposed to act within 24 hours after receiving the petition, and the authority is supposed to justify its action within five days, but in practice these brief time limitations are elastic.[36]

Unlike the Colombian Supreme Court in a popular action, the Mexican courts in an amparo proceeding are strictly limited to the allegations of the petition. If a party alleges that a statute is unconstitutional on one ground, and the court decides that the law is unconstitutional only on another, non-alleged theory, the court must deny the amparo. However, deficiencies in the petition can be liberally corrected in several instances, such as penal, labor, or agrarian matters, where the petitioner may be uneducated and ill-advised. The Mexican amparo resembles the Brazilian writ of security with regard to suspension of the challenged act. The Law of Amparo gives a judge the power to issue a temporary injunction or stay whenever execution of the challenged act may result in an injury that will be difficult or impossible to repair. In certain circumstances the amparo petitioner must provide a bond or suitable guarantee against damages resulting from issuance of the stay. However, the respondent may be able to avert the requested stay by posting a counterbond.

Unlike the writ of security, the amparo normally will not lie against a discretionary governmental act for an abuse of discretion. Recent case law has begun to develop a concept of the abuse of discretion, but the doctrine is still incipient.[37]

There are a substantial number of situations in which amparo will not lie. Most of these are set out in Article 73 of the Law of Amparo, which precludes, *inter alia,* the granting of amparo:

1. Against laws or acts which have been the basis of a final decree in another amparo proceeding involving the same parties.

2. Against acts which do not affect the legal interests of the petitioner.

3. Against laws which do not cause petitioner any injury by virtue of their enactment alone, but require the subsequent act of an authority to render them operative.

4. In political matters, such as against decisions of electoral officials.

5. Against resolutions or declarations of federal or state legislatures, electing, suspending, or removing functionaries, where the respective constitutions have conferred upon these bodies the discretion to do so.

6. Against acts consummated in an irreparable manner, or which are moot.

7. Against acts which have been consented to, either explicitly or implicitly.

8. Against judicial decisions where the law concedes an adequate remedy or defense.

9. Against administrative acts when administrative remedies have not been exhausted, unless such remedies do not provide for a stay of the challenged act, or impose greater requirements for issuance of a stay than does the Law of Amparo.

---

[36] Fix Zamudio, "Síntesis del Derecho de Amparo," in *Instituto de Derecho Comparado,* I *Panorama del Derecho Mexicano* 105, 135 (1965).

[37] See Fix Zamudio, "Judicial Protection of the Individual Against the Executive in Mexico," in 2 *Gerichtsschutz Gegen die Exekutive* 713, 750-51 (H. Mosler ed. 1970).

10. When an appeal is already pending in a matter in ordinary litigation.

11. Against decisions granting or restoring communal lands and water to villages, unless the proprietor has a certificate of nonaffectability.

To what extent are limitations of this nature simply logical consequences of the doctrine of the separation of powers? To what extent are they based upon considerations of convenience in judicial administration? In the United States, similar limitations on the judiciary are frequently considered necessary to protect it from damaging conflicts with the other branches of government. Are such limitations equally useful in the Mexican context?

The Mexican amparo is a complex institution. It can be used as a writ of habeas corpus, injunction, declaratory judgment, or appeal. One leading Mexican writer points out that the amparo combines the following five autonomous procedural functions: (1) the protection of life and liberty, (2) challenging unconstitutional laws, (3) resolution of conflicts stemming from administrative acts and decisions, (4) appeal of judicial decisions, and (5) protection of the rights of peasants subject to agrarian reform.[38] While there are many types of amparo, for our purposes it will suffice to subdivide amparo into two basic components: the legality amparo and the constitutional amparo.

------

1. The Legality Amparo (Amparo de la Legalidad)

Article 14 of the Mexican Constitution of 1857 contained a clause modeled after the due process clause of the Fifth Amendment to the Constitution of the United States: "No one can be tried or sentenced except by laws passed prior to the fact and exactly applied to it by the tribunal previously established by law." Before long this clause was being interpreted as establishing a constitutional right for each person to have the laws of the country correctly applied to his case. Any contention that a court had misapplied the law thereby became a constitutional question that could be reviewed by means of amparo. At first, the Mexican Supreme Court accepted this line of reasoning, reviewing state court decisions via amparo whenever there was an allegation of a violation of the constitutional right to have the law applied exactly to one's case.

There was considerable debate about the Supreme Court's practice. Not only did it open the floodgates to Supreme Court review of almost every case, but it practically eliminated the power of the state courts to interpret state law. Every question of state law was readily convertible into a federal constitutional question. From 1878 until 1882, while Ignacio Vallarta presided over the Mexican Supreme Court, this interpretation of Article 14 was sharply cut back in civil cases. Only in criminal cases

------

[38] Fix Zamudio, "El Problema de la Lentitud de los Procesos y su Solución en el Ordenamiento Mexicano," 21 *Rev. Fac. Derecho Mex.* 85, 116 (1971).

did amparo lie to review the correctness of any point of law. But after his death, the floodgates reopened.

In the 1917 constitutional convention, previous judicial abuses of Article 14 were criticized, but the new version of Article 14 contained the following clause: "In civil suits the final judgment shall be according to the letter or the juridical interpretation of the law; in the absence of the latter, it shall be based on general principles of law." Read literally, this clause would appear to establish a constitutional right to have all judicial decisions made correctly, in accord with the law, and that is precisely how the Mexican Supreme Court has read it. Thus, the Court has continued to exercise the power to review state court decisions whether or not they involve "federal questions." Article 14 is a means of appealing, by way of direct amparo, from the state courts to the Supreme Court, in almost any case. (The form remains that of an original action, but it is in effect an appeal.) Is such an interpretation consistent with a genuinely federal judicial system?

This kind of amparo is known as the "legality amparo" or the *amparo de la legalidad,* and its effect is to centralize the interpretation of all laws, be they state or federal, in the Supreme Court. It is also referred to as *amparo-casación,* showing its relationship to the power of cassation (quashing) conferred upon the highest courts in some civilian countries, most notably France. While the interpretation of facts is left with the state courts, every question of law can be converted into a federal constitutional question.

Direct Amparo. The legality amparo may be either "direct" or "indirect." One who feels that the final decision of a state or federal court incorrectly applied the law to his or her case may institute an amparo action directly before an appropriate chamber of the Supreme Court or the nearest Collegiate Circuit Court, depending on the severity of the sentence, the importance of the issue, or the monetary amount in conflict. Since 1951 awards of federal and state arbitral and conciliation boards have been treated as the equivalent of court decisions for the purpose of permitting direct amparo to the Labor Chamber of the Supreme Court. And since 1968, decisions of administrative tribunals may be challenged before the Administrative Chamber by direct amparo, giving taxpayers an automatic appeal to the Supreme Court against decisions of the Federal Fiscal Tribunal (analogue of the United States Tax Court).

Indirect Amparo. Indirect amparo may be brought against all other forms of illegal or unfair acts of governmental authorities. It is generally brought to compel or prevent actions of nonjudicial governmental agents, such as prosecutors, police, or public administrators, though an indirect amparo may be brought against a judge to challenge an unconstitutional or unlawful act committed apart from the trial, such as issuance of an arrest warrant. Instead of bringing the amparo action directly before a chamber of the Supreme Court, a complainant must first bring the action before a federal District Court, whose decision may be appealed to the Supreme Court or a Collegiate Circuit Court.

The legality amparo has been largely responsible for the enormous backlog of Supreme Court cases. As early as 1919 the Supreme Court's backlog exceeded 2,000, and within four years it had increased more than fivefold to 12,072 cases. The initial approach to dealing with this ever-increasing backlog was mathematical: division and addition. A 1928 reform divided the Supreme Court into three chambers (civil, criminal, and administrative), and increased the number of judges from eleven to sixteen. A 1934 reform added a fourth chamber (labor), and increased the number of judges to twenty-one. But despite these reforms, by 1946 the Supreme Court's backlog had grown to 27,000 cases.[39]

The reform of 1951 tried a somewhat different approach to the problem. Part of the Supreme Court's amparo jurisdiction was transferred to multi-judge circuit courts, whose decisions were non-appealable. A temporary Auxiliary Chamber, composed of five supernumerary judges, was set up to decide cases until the backlog was eliminated. While these measures reduced the backlog initially, by 1964 the Supreme Court was once again more than 10,000 cases behind. This led to further constitutional reform in 1967, transferring even more of the Supreme Court's amparo jurisdiction to the Collegiate Circuit Courts, and setting up an Auxiliary Chamber whose judges could substitute for absent regular judges, as well as whittle away at the backlog.

The 1967 reforms have made a serious dent in the Supreme Court's backlog, which exceeded 20,000 cases at the beginning of 1968.[40] By the beginning of December 1970, the Supreme Court reported a backlog in its chambers of only 2741 amparo cases, slightly less than half of the preceding year's backlog.[41] Of course, some of the Supreme Court's former backlog has simply been transferred to the Collegiate Circuit Court's backlog, which numbered 11,110 in December, 1970. The sheer volume of amparo litigation in the federal courts of Mexico is striking. From December of 1969 to December of 1970, more than 53,000 new amparo complaints were filed in the federal district courts alone.[42]

While the notion of giving the Supreme Court discretion to decide which cases it wants to review has enjoyed little support in Mexico, one of the 1967 reforms constitutes a significant innovation. In administrative amparo involving less than 500,000 pesos (about U.S. $40,000) the Supreme Court is given the discretion to hear cases which it considers "of transcendent importance for the interests of the Nation. . . ." (Law of Amparo, Art. 25, Sect. I(d).) If the backlog continues to remain a pressing problem, it is possible that this discretion may eventually be expanded to something resembling the certiorari jurisdiction of the United States Supreme Court.

---

2. The Constitutional Amparo (Amparo contra Leyes)

The facial constitutionality of certain laws, including executive decrees with the force of law, may be challenged by means of an amparo action brought in the federal

---

[39] Tena Ramírez, "La Reforma de 1968, en Materia Administrativa, al Poder Judicial de la Federación," *El Foro,* No. 10, Apr.-Je. 1968 (Quinta Epoca), pp. 55-56.

[40] Schwarz, "The Mexican Writ of Amparo: An Extraordinary Remedy Against Official Abuse of Individual Rights," Part II, 11 *Public Affairs Report,* Feb. 1970.

[41] "Informe Rendido a La Suprema Corte de la Nación por su Presidente" (First Part, 1970).

[42] *Ibid.*

district courts. In contradistinction to the legality amparo, where the issue is the correctness of the interpretation or application of the law to the plaintiff's case, the constitutional amparo is an attack on the law itself. Indispensable parties to the suit are the President or Governor who signed the law, the legislature that enacted it, and the departments that administer it. Only laws said to be "self-executing" may be challenged by the constitutional amparo. Though the issue is usually debatable, in general laws are considered "self-executing" when their promulgation alone, without any specific implementing act or application, requires immediate, detrimental compliance with their terms, or when they delineate a specific group to which their terms apply, i.e. an act imposing a tax on bachelors.

As a result of amendments to the Law of Amparo made in 1958, the Supreme Court was required to hear *en banc* all appeals involving the constitutional amparo. The motivation for this measure appears to have been the government's displeasure over the substantial amount of fiscal and economic legislation held unconstitutional by the Administrative Chamber of the Supreme Court. Since the Supreme Court had a backlog of more than two thousand constitutional amparos and had decided only eighteen of them in 1958, the result has been interminable delay in reaching final judgment.[43]

The 1967 reforms have attempted to clear some of this logjam by returning all appeals to the appropriate chamber whenever the Supreme Court has established a case law rule which governs the appeal. (See p. 137 et seq, *infra*.) However, it is unlikely that such a measure will appreciably unblock the jam.

Mexican amparo opinions tend to be summary; many are hardly more than a statement of a rule of law. The following cases convey some of the flavor and peculiarities of Mexican amparo litigation.

---

3. Determining What Constitutes a Public Authority

CORRAL, HILARIO

Supreme Court of Mexico (*en banc*)
6 S.J.F. 274 (5th Series 1920)

[The complainant's land was attached by one Avila Godina in a private action against a third person. The complainant brought this amparo action, complaining of the illegality of the attachment. The respondents are the judges of first instance who ordered and executed the attachment, and Sr. Avila Godina. The District Judge of the State of Durango rejected the complaint.]

---

[43] R. Baker, *supra*, note 34 at 72-76, 174.

Considering: The appealed decision is obviously contrary to law, insofar as it concerns the amparo requested against acts of the Judges of First Instance of Canatlán and the Municipality of Tepehuanes, because the Constitution, in the ninth paragraph of article 107, expressly permits amparo with respect to acts of the judicial authority, affecting persons outside the lawsuit, acts such as those of which the complainant complains in the present case. But the same cannot be said respecting amparo which, in the same complaint, is sought against acts of don Juan Avila Godina, because the amparo is allowable only against acts of authorities, in accordance with article 103 of the Constitution. Sr. Avila Godina does not have the status of an authority. Therefore, it is proper to modify the decision, affirming it insofar as it refers to the individual and reversing it insofar as it concerns the authorities, so that the complaint may be processed in accordance with the law. . . .

MEDRANO, ISAAC

Supreme Court of Mexico (*en banc*)
9 S.J.F. 407 (5th Series 1921)

Mexico, D.F. Decision of August 25, 1921.

The action of amparo of Isaac Medrano before the District Judge of Durango against acts of the Warden of "El Salto" [a prison, literally, "The Jump"] having been examined on appeal — acts consisting of the Warden's having established a sawmill on lands owned by the complainant, violating the guarantees established in article 16 of the Constitution; the statement of the Public Minister[44] before this Court, asking the dismissal of the action as unallowable, having been considered; and,

Considering: That from the record it appears that the person designated as the responsible authority is acting as a private individual, in the exercise of a right he believes legitimate. [Hence], the amparo complaint . . . is not allowable. Based on paragraph III of article 44 of the Regulatory Law of articles 103 and 104 of the Constitution, the action must be rejected and dismissed.

For the foregoing reasons, it is resolved:

First. — The decision of April 2 of this year, pronounced by the District Judge of Durango, is affirmed . . . .

Note

In the case of *Cía. de Luz y Fuerza de Pachuca, S.A.,* 15 S.J.F. 192 (5th Series 1924), the complaining electric company had cut off the electricity to some

---

[44] Article 5 (IV) of the law of Amparo states that the Federal Public Ministry, the Mexican equivalent of the Justice Department, shall be a party in every amparo suit unless the Ministry decides the case lacks public interest. The Ministry's participation is typically perfunctory,

government buildings in the state of Hidalgo, and had commenced a proceeding in amparo against various state officials. While the company was successful in the lower courts in this action, the District Judge nevertheless ordered the company to reconnect the electricity pending a final decision. The company successfully sought a direct amparo in the Supreme Court, which pointed out that amparo could not be brought against acts of private individuals, such as the electric company in this case.

CONTRERAS, ROGERIO

Supreme Court of Mexico (*en banc*)
15 S.J.F. 800 (5th Series 1924)

Mexico, D.F. Decision of September 27, 1924.

[The complainant brought an action in amparo against the General Manager and the Board of Directors of the Mexican National Railways, complaining that they had abrogated a contract with the complainant granting him a concession to sell goods on board trains. The District Judge granted the amparo, including an injunctive order (*suspensión*).]

Considering: Since the persons designated by the complainant as responsible authorities are not carrying on public functions, but only acting as contracting parties in the agreement which was declared ineffective, it is improper to grant the requested injunction. The action of amparo, according to the first paragraph of the first article of the Regulatory Law of articles 103 and 104 of the Constitution, has the objective of resolving every controversy raised by laws or acts which violate individual guarantees. Since the persons here designated as responsible for the acts . . . do not have the status of authorities, . . . there can exist no occasion for conceding the action of constitutional guarantees.

[The decision of the District Judge was unanimously reversed.]

Question

How does the approach of the Mexican Supreme Court in determining what constitutes a public authority differ from that of U.S. Supreme Court in dealing with the analogous problem of "state action" under the 14th Amendment to the U.S. Constitution?

---

generally being limited to a brief statement in support of the complainant or the respondent. The briefs which it files are said to be "frequently, if not customarily, ignored by the courts." R. Baker, *Judicial Review in Mexico: A Study of the Amparo Suit* 212 (1971). [Eds.]

Notes

1. Determination of whether a governmental agency is a "responsible authority" for the purposes of amparo jurisdiction is no simple matter. The Mexican Supreme Court has defined the term "authority" for the purposes of amparo jurisdiction as "every person who, *de jure* or *de facto*, exercises public power and is materially enabled thereby to operate as an individual who commits public acts . . . ." *Apéndice de Jurisprudencia de la Suprema Corte*, Tesis 179, p. 360. The Law of Amparo defines the term "responsible authority" as simply "one which decrees or orders, executes or attempts to execute, the complained of law or act." Application of these definitions, particularly to quasi-autonomous governmental corporations, has produced anomalous results. Thus, for example, the Mexican Social Security Institute is considered an "authority" with respect to the assessment of employer and employee contributions, but is considered a private organization with respect to its activities in granting or denying social security benefits. Fix Zamudio, "Judicial Protection of the Individual Against the Executive in Mexico," in 2 *Gerichtsschutz Gegen die Exekutive* 713, 721-22 (H. Mosler, ed. 1970). The National Autonomous University of Mexico, on the other hand, is considered a private organization for purposes of an amparo suit even though its juridical status would appear to be virtually the same as the Mexican Social Security Institute. Alcalá-Zamora y Castillo, "Judicial Protection of the Individual Against the Executive in Mexico," in 2 *Gerichtsschutz Gegen die Exekutive* 771, 777 (H. Mosler, ed. 1970).

2. Though the practice seems inconsistent with the basic principle that amparo exists for the protection of individual rights, in certain circumstances the complainant in an amparo suit can be the government. Article 9 of the Law of Amparo provides: "Official juridical entities (*personas morales oficiales*) may request amparo against the conduct of functionaries or representatives who determine the laws when the challenged act or law affects [the complainants'] patrimonial interests." Thus, the Labor Chamber of the Supreme Court has sustained the right of the government to bring amparo against awards of the Tribunal of Arbitration dealing with public employees. *Apéndice de Jurisprudencia de la Suprema Corte*, Tesis 451, p. 875. Similarly, the Supreme Court has determined that the government may request amparo against adverse judgments in nationalization or expropriation cases. *Apéndice de Jurisprudencia de la Suprema Corte*, Tesis 450, pp. 872-74. The theory is that when acting in a proprietary capacity, the government subjects itself to its own laws and should be able to exercise the same remedies as private litigants.

A cursory reading of Articles 103 and 107 of the Mexican Constitution (*supra*, p. 128) suggests that amparo should be available for resolution of federal-state conflicts. However, the Supreme Court has held that amparo will lie to challenge federal laws for encroaching on the sovereignty of the states, or state laws for encroaching on the sovereignty of the federal government, only when an individual complainant alleges violation of individual guarantees. *Apéndice de Jurisprudencia de la Suprema Corte*, Tesis 111, p. 246. Is such a result consistent with the constitutional text? *Cf.* R. Baker, *Judicial Review in Mexico: A Study of the Amparo Suit* 102-06 (1971).

---

4. The Role of Precedent

The *Contreras* case was the fifth decision of the Supreme Court to establish the principle that amparo will not lie against acts of private individuals. Therefore, under the terms of the Law of Amparo, this decision laid down a case law rule (*jurisprudencia*). It should be noted that the short opinion makes no reference to this fact. However, in the index to Volume 15 of the S.J.F., there is a section which indexes the various points on which case law rules have been established. At page 1627, the following entry appears:

> *Acts of individuals.* — They cannot be the object of an action of constitutional guarantees, which has been established in order to combat acts of the authorities that may be considered to violate the Constitution.

Vol. VI. —	Quintero, Román	884
	Corral, Hilario	274
Vol. IX. —	Medrano, Isaac	407
Vol. XV. —	Cía de Luz y Fuerza de Pachuca, S.A. .	192
	Contreras, Rogerio	800

Is it meaningful to list all these decisions as standing for the same proposition? What guidance is given for the decision of future cases by this statement of the Mexican Supreme Court's case law rule?

The nature and role of precedent in amparo litigation are governed by Articles 192-197 of the Law of Amparo (as amended, 1968).

> Article 192. The case law rule which the Supreme Court of Justice, functioning *en banc,* establishes as to the interpretation of the Constitution, laws, federal or local regulations, and international treaties celebrated by the Mexican State, is obligatory for the Court, as well as for the chambers of which it is composed; the single-judge and Collegiate Circuit Courts; District Judges; military tribunals; general law courts of the states, Federal District, and federal territories; and federal and local administrative or labor tribunals.
>
> The decisions of the Supreme Court of Justice, functioning *en banc,* constitute a case law rule whenever a result has been sustained in five consecutive decisions approved by at least fourteen ministers.
>
> Article 193. The case law rule established by the chambers of the Supreme Court of Justice as to the interpretation of the Constitution, federal or local law, and international treaties celebrated by the Mexican State, is obligatory for the same chambers and for the single-judge and Collegiate Circuit Courts; District

Judges; military tribunals; general law courts of the states, Federal District, and federal territories; and federal and local administrative or labor tribunals.

The decisions of the chambers of the Supreme Court of Justice constitute a case law rule whenever a result has been sustained in five consecutive decisions approved by at least four ministers.

Article 193 Bis. The case law rule established by the Collegiate Circuit Courts in matters of its exclusive jurisdiction is obligatory for the same Courts, as well as for the District Judges, general law courts, and administrative and labor tribunals which function within its territorial jurisdiction.

The decisions of the Collegiate Circuit Courts constitute a case law rule whenever a result has been sustained in five consecutive decisions approved by a unanimous vote of their judges.

Article 194. If established by the Court *en banc,* the case law rule ceases to have its obligatory character whenever a contrary decision is rendered by fourteen ministers; by four ministers, if established by a chamber; and by unanimous vote, if established by a Collegiate Circuit Court. . . .

In order to modify a case law rule, the same rules established for its formation by this law are to be observed. . . .

Article 197. The decisions of amparo and the individual votes of the ministers and judges of the Collegiate Circuit Courts related to those decisions, shall be published in the *Semanario Judicial de la Federación* whenever they meet the requirements to constitute or contradict a case law rule, along with the decisions . . . which expressly accord with them.

Questions

1. How does this concept of precedent differ from that prevailing in the United States?

2. What is the utility or disutility of the five-consecutive-decision requirement?

3. Does the Mexican judiciary in theory appear to have a more important role in interpreting the constitution than Chief Justice Marshall claimed for the United States' courts in *Marbury v. Madison*?

In practice the roles of the Mexican and U.S. Courts are quite different. Examination of the case law rules laid down by the Mexican Supreme Court reveals that almost all deal with technical aspects of constitutional and statutory interpretation.

Thus far, Mexican *jurisprudencia* affords nothing genuinely equivalent to the development by the Supreme Court of the United States of, for example, the commerce clause, the taxing power, or substantive due process. This is not to say that *jurisprudencia* is of no consequence, but that the Supreme Courts of Mexico and the United States are the heirs of substantially different legal and political traditions and, as a result, act within dissimilar environments and on different conceptions of the judicial role. From the practical point of view, *jurisprudencia* has been indisputably valuable as a device for clarifying the ambiguities and filling the gaps that neither statutory nor constitutional draftings can entirely avoid. In the doctrinal sense, it has defined the effective scope and limits of *amparo* and, consequently, determined the extent to which that institution can function as an effective constitutional defense.

... [S]ince the Mexican Constitution is no less ambiguous in its phrasing than that of the United States, there is no logically necessary or purely legal limit on the potential creativity of the Court in establishing *jurisprudencia.* ... [H]owever, it must be emphasized that tradition, a conception of the judicial function that excludes the idea of policy making, and the realities of the political process are the controlling factors, and there is no present indication of changes on any of these that would warrant an expectation that the Supreme Court will soon, or ever, embark on a more adventurous and independent course.[45]

COMPAÑIA MINERA DE SAN JOSE, S.A. DE C.V. et al.

Supreme Court of Mexico (2d Chamber)
48 S.J.F. 13 (6th Series 1961)

[In order to make assessments for an export tax, the Finance Ministry was authorized to set official export prices rather than accept the prices of the exporter. The Ministry set these prices in a monthly circular, which, though it purported to set the official price for that entire month, generally did not appear until the middle of the month.

[Five companies brought a consolidated amparo action in the Federal District Court, challenging the legality of a circular published on December 14, 1959, fixing the official price for amorphous graphite for the entire month of December. Similarly, they challenged a circular published on January 12, 1960, setting the official price for the month of January. The District Court granted the amparo because of a violation of the Constitution's Article 14, whose first sentence provides: "No law shall be given retroactive effect to anyone's prejudice." The government appealed to the Supreme Court.] ...

... [A]ppellants are mistaken in suggesting that an ordinary law operating on the past does not violate Article 14 of the Constitution unless a prior law exists, creating rights injured by application of the new law.

To be sure, the common case of retroactivity arises as a conflict of laws in time, as a controversy between two laws issued sequentially and regulating the same act, fact, or

---

[45] R. Baker, *supra,* note 34 at 253-54.

situation. But it is also true that the provisions of a law can be retroactive and violative of Article 14 when laying down rules for a particular question for the first time.

. . . [W]hen the conduct of the governed has not been controlled by the legislature in any way, . . . engaging in such conduct is the exercise of a "right" derived from the absence of any regulating law and protected by the Juridical Order. . . . Thus, the absence of norms limiting the activity of an individual is itself a right to be respected by authorities, including the legislator, and continues in force until enactment of a relevant legislative norm.

. . . [G]overnmental authorities can do only what the law empowers them to do; the governed can do anything which the law does not prohibit them from doing. . . .

When the problem is examined in light of opinions expressed by this Supreme Court, . . . we must conclude that the absence of any legal provisions requiring the complainants to act in a certain fashion left them free to export amorphous graphite at whatever price they deemed advisable. . . .

The reasoning of the lower court that the circulars under attack violate Article 14 of the Constitution because they purport to control a situation existing prior to their publication in the Official Gazette of the Federation is correct. . . . [T]hat decision is therefore affirmed.

Questions

1. Subsequent reports include two more decisions in which the Compañía Minera and the other complainants brought actions in amparo on the same facts. In each case the Supreme Court reached precisely the same result. 61 S.J.F. 36 (2d Chamber) (6th Series 1965) and 100 S.J.F. 21 (2d Chamber) (6th Series 1965). What do these suggest about the practices of the Ministry of Finance?

2. Is the court's opinion consistent with Article 107 (II) of the Mexican Constitution, *supra* p. 128?

3. Would the Ministry of Finance be obligated to behave differently if the Supreme Court had established a case law rule on the subject?

QUIMICA INDUSTRIAL DE MONTERREY, S.A.

Supreme Court of Mexico (2nd Chamber)
66 S.J.F. 25 (Sixth Series 1962)

[In 1944 President Avila Camacho issued an emergency executive decree requiring all foreigners and Mexican companies which had or might have foreign shareholders to obtain permission from the Ministry of Foreign Relations prior to entering into certain activities, such as industry, agriculture, stock raising, forestry, real estate, or minerals. Permission from the Ministry was also required to modify the charter of an existing Mexican company or to organize a new one where foreign shareholders were involved.

Acts performed in violation of the provisions of this emergency decree were considered null, and any property involved was subject to being forfeited to the Mexican government.

[The decree was promulgated pursuant to emergency powers assumed by the president in 1942, when he issued a decree suspending constitutional guarantees because of the Second World War. On September 28, 1945 the Mexican Congress issued a decree terminating the state of emergency declared in 1942 and restoring the constitutional order. Since the 1944 decree expressly limited the period of time for which permits would be required to the period that constitutional guarantees were suspended, it would appear that the postwar act of Congress would have terminated the 1944 decree. However, the Ministry of Foreign Relations went right on enforcing the provisions of the 1944 decree, arguing that the language in the 1945 Congressional decree ratifying executive decrees issued during the emergency justified its continued enforcement.

[The complainant is a Mexican corporation, organized in 1955 with the permission of the Ministry of Foreign Relations. To increase its capital from 2,500,000 pesos to 4,000,000, the corporation in 1958 sought and secured the permission of the Ministry. In 1961 the plaintiff sought to increase its capital to 4,500,000 pesos. The Ministry refused to grant its permission unless the corporation changed from bearer to nominative shares, and unless the corporation assured the Ministry that a majority of its board of directors were Mexicans and that the composition of the board would remain that way. The plaintiff refused to submit to these conditions and sought amparo in the federal district court.

[The district court granted the amparo, holding that the 1944 decree had been repealed in 1945. The Ministry appealed to the Supreme Court.[46]

[The representative of the Federal Public Ministry appeared in the proceedings and moved to dismiss the amparo on three grounds: (1) the plaintiff company's petition alleged that its shares are entirely owned by native-born Mexicans, which signifies that the company already complies with the decree's requirements and cannot claim injury from it; (2) that the plaintiff has consented to application of the decree by complying with its requirements when incorporating in 1955 and when increasing capital in 1958; and (3) that the plaintiff tacitly consented to the decree by failing to seek amparo when the decree was first applied to it in 1955.] . . .

[T]he first thing to determine in this matter is whether the grounds offered by the representative of the Federal Public Ministry for arguing that the amparo has been improperly brought can be sustained. . . .

[A]ll the arguments presuppose that an affirmative answer has already been given to a problem which is dialectically anterior to these arguments — whether the decree in issue is or is not in force. It is clear that these grounds do not take into account the fact that the decision below rests squarely on the proposition that the decree in question is no longer in force. . . .

The arguments for reversal relied upon by the responsible authority (the Secretary of Foreign Affairs) . . . are without justification. These arguments for reversal contend

---

[46]This statement of the facts is partially drawn from Laughran and Foster, "Foreign Investment in Mexico: The Emergency Decree of 1944," 39 *Tulane L. Rev.* 538 (1965). [Eds.]

that the decree in question (dated June 29, 1944) was ratified with the force of law by the provisions of Article 6 of the decree which lifted the suspension of guarantees decreed on July 1, 1942. It is said that Article 6 maintained in force those provisions, promulgated by the President during the period of emergency, which were related to the state's intervention in the economy . . . . Upon analysis, the foregoing arguments for reversal do not undermine the reasoning of the challenged decision — that control over the companies, according to Articles 1 and 2 of the Decree of June 29, 1944, is purely transitory and is limited to the time period for which the suspension of guarantees decreed on June 1, 1942 should remain in force. The arguments for reversal also fail to take account of the reasoning of the challenged decision concluding that the Decree of October 1, 1945, which lifted the suspension of guarantees, totally repealed the decree in question . . ., for Article 5 of the 1945 decree states: "Those provisions issued for the duration of the emergency or those from whose text it appears that they were based upon the suspension of one or more individual guarantees are not ratified." If the arguments for reversal placed before us fail to destroy the reasoning upon which the decision under review rests, and which is also, in the opinion of this court, legally correct, it is clear that these arguments cannot be sustained. Thus, the decision under review must be sustained, granting amparo to the complainant. . . .

Notes

1. "The potential foreign investor in Mexico would be relieved of the burdens and hazards of compliance with the Emergency Decree if the *Química Industrial* decision had accomplished what its holding indicates. However, . . . [t]he Ministry of Foreign Relations has continued to enforce the Emergency Decree as if *Química Industrial* had never been decided, and it is unlikely that the Ministry will voluntarily relinquish the sweeping discretionary powers it exercises under the decree. Direct presidential or congressional intervention is only a fairly remote possibility, considering that the Ministry will be exerting tremendous pressure in order to retain its powers and that almost twenty years of congressional and presidential inaction have already passed since termination in 1945 of the suspension of constitutional guarantees." Laughran and Foster, "Foreign Investment in Mexico: The Emergency Decree of 1944," 39 *Tulane L. Rev.* 538, 555-56 (1965).

2. One subsequent litigant, *Playtex de México,* also successfully challenged the 1944 Emergency Decree. *Amparo en revisión* 3596 (1964). The Ministry of Foreign Affairs has continued to apply the Decree's provisions, though on several occasions it has strategically retreated when threatened with amparo suits. H. Wright, *Foreign Enterprise in Mexico: Laws and Policies* 113 (1971). That these successful suits did not produce a flurry of amparo actions may have reflected a feeling on the part of foreign investors that the existing regulatory setup was a lesser evil than what might be likely to replace it if the matter were considered *de novo.* Recent legislation regulating foreign investment in Mexico would appear to justify such restraint in filing amparo

suits. See Lacy and Sierra de la Garza, "Mexico — Are the Rules Really Changing?" 7 *Int'l. Lawyer* 560 (1973).

---

5. Limitations on Amparo Review

GARCIA ALVAREZ

Supreme Court of Mexico (2d Chamber)
112 S.J.F. 586 (5th Series 1952)

[García Alvarez was denied a license to operate a bread distributorship in Mexico City. He brought an action in amparo against a number of federal officials, as noted below. The lower court granted the amparo.]

The argument of the appellant authorities [the President of the Republic, the Secretary of the Interior, the Chief of the Department of the Federal District, and the chiefs of certain offices of the District] is unfounded. The Supreme Court has laid down a case law rule respecting the matter in question:

It is true that the acts of expedition, promulgation, authentication and publication of a law are carried on in such form that they can no longer be made ineffective by an amparo decision (which by express constitutional provision shall be limited to protect individuals in the special case affected by the complaint, without any general declaration with respect to the law or act which motivates it). Nevertheless, it should be kept in mind that the said acts are soon put into effect as law, and the law in turn is applied to concrete cases, such as those complained of in the present action of amparo. Since those results of the law are imputable not only to the authorities who apply it but also to those from whom the law itself emanates or who have participated in the acts necessary to put it into effect, such results are susceptible of reparation in every concrete case. The unconstitutionality of the law can be asserted for this reason, not only against the Legislature which enacted it but also against the Executive which promulgated it and ordered it published, and against the Secretary of State who authenticated the promulgating accord and carried out the publication. Consequently, under the circumstances the ground of nonallowability established by article 73, par IX of the Law of Amparo does not apply.[47]

The foregoing is established in (among others) the decisions rendered in the actions of amparo on appeal numbers 6991-50, brought by Raúl Moreno Hernández; 2479-51, brought by Diego Alonso Hinojoso; 9043-50, brought also by the latter; and 2728-51, brought by Guadalupe Cuevas Vda. de García Sancho. Since the argument which the appellant authority has made is insufficient, the decision on appeal should be affirmed.

---

[47]That amparo is not allowable "against acts consummated in an irreparable manner." [Eds.]

For the foregoing reason, it is decided:

First. — The appealed decision is affirmed.

Second. — The Justice of the Union protects José García Alvarez from the acts of which he complains against the President of the Republic, Secretary of the Interior, Chief of the Department of the Federal District, and Chiefs of the Office of Licenses, Inspection of Regulations, and Censor of Infractions, subsidiaries of the Department of the Federal District, consisting in the enactment, promulgation, publication and authentication of the Regulation of the Bread Industry for the Federal District by the first three officers named and its application by the others, with respect to their delay in announcing the denial of a license to the complainant, and, therefore, in the possible closure of his bread distributorship, located in house no. 7 on Calle Soto in this city. . . .

Question

What is the role of the President in this litigation?

Note

The doctrine of mootness, established in paragraphs IX and XVI of article 73 of the Law of Amparo, has its typical application in a case such as *Segura,* 19 S.J.F. 18 (6th series 1959). In that case the complainant brought a direct amparo against the judge who had sentenced him to prison for a criminal offense. The amparo action originated in the First Chamber of the Supreme Court of Mexico, which dismissed the action on the ground that the complainant had already served his sentence.

HEREDIA, MARCELINO

Supreme Court of Mexico (*en banc*)
4 S.J.F. 862 (5th Series 1919)

Mexico, D.F., Decision of April 17, 1919 . . . .

Resulting: First: The complainant (in his own capacity and as representative of the political club "Melchor Ocampo") requested amparo and a temporary injunction before the District Judge of Michoacán, against the decree of last December 23, by the City Council of Maravatío. In that decree the council declared José L. Mandujano re-elected as Alderman and Secretary of said municipal corporation, despite the fact that the State Constitution prohibits the re-election of members of the municipal council. Complainant considers that said act is contrary to the provisions of articles 8, 14 and 35, par. 5, of the Federal Constition.

Second: The District Judge rejected the complaint as not allowable, on January 2 of the current year, considering that the prerogatives of a citizen, among which is that of being chosen to serve in popularly elected offices, are different from the natural rights of man, whose violation is the only permissible subject matter of the action of constitutional guarantees.

Third: The complainant appealed against the decision, ...

Considering: That as the District Judge maintains, in the appealed decision the political rights which the complainant says have been violated do not give rise to the action of constitutional guarantees, in conformity with the first paragraph of article 103 and in the first rule of article 107 of the Constitution; and since, on the other hand, the infraction of articles 8 and 14, allegedly committed by the responsible authority, cannot be considered to have been violated in prejudice of the complainant Marcelino Heredia, the latter lacks standing to bring this action of amparo, considering the provisions of the first paragraph of the cited article 107 of the Constitution; therefore, the decision of non-allowability, given by the lower court, must be affirmed . . . .

[By unanimous vote of all eleven ministers, the decision dismissing the complaint was affirmed.]

ARAGON, RAYMUNDO
Supreme Court of Mexico (*en banc*)
14 S.J.F. 1109 (5th Series 1924)

Mexico, D.F., Decision of March 28, 1924.

[The decision below] . . . rejects the complaint in amparo formulated by Srs. Raymundo Aragón and Alfredo Campaña against acts of the Congress of the State of Sinaloa, consisting in the refusal to recognize their status as acting substitute Aldermen of the Municipality of Cosalá. . . .

Considering: The complainants refer in their complaint to the fact that the Municipal Council of Cosalá, basing its action on Article 26 of the Municipal Charter of the locality, called them to act in their capacity as substitutes in place of the regular alderman, . . . and that, having taken the oath, they had taken office; that the legislature of the State of Sinaloa . . . refused to recognize said complainants as substitute aldermen, ordering that two other persons be named in their place. The complainants considered that the legislature's act violated the guarantees granted by article 14 of the Constitution, and they asked the assistance and protection of the Federal Judiciary. We consider that, in this case, the act is one which can be classified as a violation of individual political guarantees. The complainants assert that they have been deprived of remuneration to which they have a right, and of the exercise of the office to which they were legally elected. It is proper, therefore, to consider such acts as included in the first paragraph of article 103 of the Federal Constitution and to reverse the appealed decision, so that the complaint should be processed in the correct manner, and the proper decision rendered.

[The foregoing decision was joined by seven out of ten judges voting. The dissenters filed no opinion.]

PINEDA, FAUSTINO

Supreme Court of Mexico (2d Chamber)
63 S.J.F. 299 (5th Series 1940)

Mexico, D.F., January 13, 1940.

Considering: The District Judge [dismissed the complaint on the ground that] . . . the complainant has not exhausted the administrative remedies in Article 160, paragraph V, of the current Federal Fiscal Code. This article provides that the Divisions of the Fiscal Tribunal shall hear actions initiated against the administrative proceeding of execution [for unpaid taxes or penalties] by persons who . . . assert that they are entitled to attached goods, or that they are creditors preferred over the Treasury . . . . Since the complainant was able to resort to the said Tribunal in defense of his rights, the ground for non-allowability in paragraph XV of Article 73 of the Law of Amparo[48] exists and dismissal of the action is required . . . . The complainant alleges that in accordance with the thesis sustained by this High Tribunal in analogous cases, a person in his position has been permitted to resort to amparo, without having to exhaust previously the ordinary appeal referred to in the decision of the lower court. In reality the appellant is correct, having demonstrated . . . that he is a person outside the appealed administrative proceeding . . . . The tax officials admit that since they could not find the violator, Sr. Andrés González, they ordered coercive power exercised against the complainant, in his status as owner of the building in which was located the bar where González committed the infraction. As a third person outside the cited administrative proceeding, the appellant had the right to resort to the action of constitutional guarantees. This Second Chamber's interpretation of Article 107 of the General Constitution of the Republic refers to those cases in which the laws expressly establish ordinary appeals or means of redress . . . at the reach of the affected party, since in such a case one should not resort to the action of amparo until exhausting the defense established by ordinary laws. But it is not correct to accept these principles when the one who requests the amparo is a third person who does not have at his disposition such means of appealing. . . .

[The chamber unanimously voted to lift the attachment on the complainant's building.]

---

[48] Article 73 (XV) provides that amparo is not allowable "against acts of authorities other than the judiciary, when they should be revised *ex officio* according to the law governing them, or where they can be modified, revoked, or nullified by appeal, or some legal proceeding or defense, provided that the same law suspends the effects of said acts upon taking the appeal or legal defense . . . without imposing greater burdens than those required to grant a definitive injunction under the amparo law. [Eds.]

Note

The court seemed inclined to establish some precedent on this subject in a hurry. Within two months after the foregoing decision, the court had decided four other cases, on the same basis as that stated in this opinion. Thus the case law rule was established by March 13, 1940. See 63 S.J.F. 4742 (5th Series). Does such haste subvert the purpose of the requirement of five consecutive decisions to establish a binding precedent?

RUIZ, MANUEL

Supreme Court of Mexico (2d Chamber)
48 S.J.F. 2956 (5th Series 1936)

[Under the law of the State of Veracruz, municipal councils were authorized to force landowners to accept tenants under certain conditions. When the municipal president and council of Tlalixcoyán applied this law against Ruiz, he sought amparo against these authorities. The District Judge granted the amparo, and the municipal authorities have appealed.]

Considering: From the terms of the statement on appeal, . . . there need be examined in this decision only the ground of non-allowability invoked by the appellants . . . that the complainant, before resorting to the action of constitutional guarantees, should have made use of the remedy established in article 12 of Law No. 208 of the State of Veracruz, which serves as the basis for the forced tenancy which is the subject matter of this action. The argument . . . is groundless. On numerous occasions this Chamber has established that there is no obligation to exhaust ordinary remedies established in the law [authorizing] the act when the unconstitutionality of that law is asserted. In such a case it would be contrary to the principles of law for the complainants to resort to that statute, insofar as it benefits them, and attack it insofar as it causes them some prejudice. And since in the case in question the complainant attacked the constitutionality of the cited Law 208 of the State of Veracruz, under which certain lands that he possessed were given in forced tenancy, unquestionably he was empowered to resort directly to the action of constitutional guarantees, without having to make use of the ordinary means of defense established in the same law. Therefore, as there is no question about the [right to amparo on the merits], the appealed decision must be officially affirmed.

For the foregoing reasons and based on articles 103, par. I, and 107, par. IX, of the General Constitution of the Republic, it is decided [to affirm the decision of the District Judge granting the amparo and returning the land to the owner].

Note

Although it may not be necessary to exhaust one's administrative remedy before resorting to an action of amparo that attacks the constitutionality of legislation, if the complainant does choose to pursue his administrative remedy, he runs the risk of later discovering he has consented to the application of the law through his very resort to the remedy provided. For discussion of the general problem of exhaustion of administrative remedies in amparo, see Schwarz, "Exceptions to the Exhaustion of Administrative Remedies Under the Mexican Writ of Amparo: Some Possible Applications to Judicial Review in the United States," 7 *Calif. W. L. Rev.* 331 (1971). In *Palomeque de Hermida,* 5 S.J.F. 66 (6th Series 1957), the Second Chamber of the Mexican Supreme Court held that a landowner could not attack the constitutionality of the expropriation law of the State of Campeche via *amparo contra leyes* because he had (unsuccessfully) pursued his administrative remedy established by that law. Though it might appear that the complainant must choose between attacking the constitutionality of a statute on its face and attacking its applicability to him apart from constitutional considerations, in practice that is not the result. If the Supreme Court upholds the constitutionality of a law on its face in an *amparo contra leyes,* the case can be transferred to the appropriate circuit court or to the Supreme Court's Administrative Chamber for determination of the law's applicability. Cabrera and Headrick, "Notes on Judicial Review in Mexico and the United States," 5 *Inter-Amer. L. Rev.* 253, 260-63 (1963). Does such procedure seriously limit the Court's ability to avoid deciding constitutional issues by statutory construction?

---

6. Judicial Independence in Mexico

W. HEADRICK, BOOK REVIEW OF L. CABRERA, EL PODER JUDICIAL FEDERAL MEXICANO Y EL CONSTITUYENTE DE 1917

17 *American Journal of Comparative Law* 120, 122-23 (1969)

The power of protecting [Mexican] citizens against unconstitutional *acts* rests mostly in the hands of the district courts, and it takes an appreciable part of their efforts. The cases involve for the most part persons imprisoned or threatened with death where no criminal proceedings have been instituted against them; in some others a person may be exiled or his belongings confiscated. In such cases there is no time to lose, and the *amparo,* however cumbersome it may have become as a means of control over legality, is highly effective as a means of preventing these types of arbitrariness. . . . If he finds just cause, the district judge then orders the "responsible authorities" to "suspend the act complained of," pending a hearing in which it will be decided whether an *amparo* will be granted or not. But what is the sanction in case the official refuses to obey? Here we come to the edge of the political power of the federal courts. It is true that the *amparo* has so much prestige that an order of a federal judge is seldom disobeyed. But if it is, the district judge lacks the means to enforce his order by using public force. At most, he could denounce the guilty official to the Supreme Court which has the power to remove him from office. But this procedure is almost never used.[49]

The power of protecting citizens against unconstitutional *statutes* is an entirely different matter. The cases under this heading very seldom involve civil rights. They also very seldom have to do with the question of legislative jurisdiction, as between the federal Congress and the state legislatures. More than half of the cases are concerned with the question whether a new tax is "fair and equitable." These actions are brought mostly by wealthy or corporate taxpayers. Each taxpayer must bring an action if he wishes to be protected, because the *amparo,* even if granted to one taxpayer and holding the law unconstitutional in his case has no effect on the others. Hence these actions are brought by the thousands. The procedure is especially cumbersome. Here again we reach the edge of the political power of the federal courts. Why don't they have the power to annul a statute *erga omnes* when it is unconstitutional? The answer lies in history. Faced with the acts of arbitrariness of local *caudillos* in the last century, the Mexican liberals wanted a means to protect the person. They achieved this purpose without excessive interference with the government. On the other hand, annulment of a statute has vast consequences: it prevents the government from carrying out its policy. Although it seems desirable from a technical point of view to grant this power to the Supreme Court, as a way to avoid multiplicity of actions, it is not politically feasible. Almost no one in Mexico is in favor of it.

R. SCOTT, MEXICAN GOVERNMENT IN TRANSITION

Pp. 255, 262, 269-70, 272 (Rev'd Ed. 1964)

Mere listing of powers and responsibilities of governmental units in a constitution does not necessarily carry with it an inherent and automatic ability to exercise the assigned mandate; notwithstanding nominal federalism and presidential government, neither the national legislature nor the judiciary, much less any state government, has proved itself sufficiently capable to capture enough political authority to fulfill its governmental functions independently. In the present political system the other agencies of government do not perform the function of, and therefore cannot be considered as, independent, coequal, or sovereign units in relation to the national executive, particularly with regard to major policy questions.

Although a complete swing to strict constitutionalism has not yet been achieved, the complex social and economic relationships of modern society do demand orderly government, the mechanisms of which can provide access to policy-making for all the

---

[49] In Ingenio Santa Fé, 90 S.J.F. 12 (6th Series 1963) (*en banc*) the Supreme Court allowed a state governor, who had ordered a judgment against the state paid in monthly installments at a rate that would have required 140 years to satisfy the full amount, 24 hours to comply with the spirit of the judgment on threat of removal from office and institution of criminal charges. [Eds.]

major interests participating in national life, together with reasonable assurance that public policy will be more or less predictable and equitable for all elements in the society. In order to provide such government, Mexico's presidents have allowed — even forced — certain of the government agencies to perform their legal duties efficiently in relation to the day-to-day needs of the average citizen, but have been unable to allow them to assume their formal roles as independent or coequal units in the constitutional system because, for all its recent mushrooming, the broadly based national political value system has not yet become deeply enough institutionalized to assure loyal and coordinate cooperation without some firm directing hand. . . .

The constitutional unit that demonstrates most clearly just how widely yawns the gulf between legal form and actual political practice is the Congress of the Union because, as every informed Mexican knows, its principal function — policy- or law-making — has been assumed by the presidency almost *in toto*. Apart from their subordination to the executive on major policy issues, members of the national judiciary and state government officers maintain some freedom of action within the sphere of their official duties because the local units of government and the mechanisms for resolving local controversies between private persons must be able to exercise a certain amount of authority or the whole fabric of modern society would break down. As long as their acts or decisions do not run too strongly counter to the broad policy lines laid out by the executive therefore, judges and state officials may carry on their duties with reasonable independence and self-respect. . . .

The 1951 changes in the Law of the Judicial Branch also did much to professionalize the Mexican judiciary. The Supreme Court, appointed for life by the president with ratification of the Senate, not only has administrative jurisdiction over inferior courts, but appoints judges to the lower courts. If reappointed after a four-year term, these judges acquire permanent tenure. Furthermore, the tendency now is to name District Court judges from the J. P. courts, the so-called Public Ministry (prosecuting attorneys), and especially from among the clerks of the courts, and to appoint Circuit Court judges from the District Courts. Within the past few years, visitations by Supreme Court justices to District and Circuit Courts and much more careful scrutiny of inferior court activities have resulted in a notable improvement in judicial administration. In short, the courts seem both to provide an essential control function over the acts of the political branches of government and, at the same time, to be improving their personnel and techniques for acting effectively as the needs of the country for such service expand.

Undoubtedly the reason that the executive has been able to allow this growing judicial control over its activities is that in reality the court does not interfere in the basic policy questions decided by the executive. Even if the law of *amparo* did not specifically exclude all political matters from its jurisdiction, there is a great deal of evidence that the judges at all levels of courts would hesitate long before they attempted to act against a major policy decision of the president. No matter how strongly the constitution institutes the concept of balanced powers, the Mexican generally agrees with a justice of the Supreme Court of Justice (who later became its president) when he wrote that in his opinion "It is not true that the judicial power exists as an independent agency, with the characteristics of a real branch [of

government], as jurists seem to believe because of article 94 of the constitution. . . ."
This attitude stems not simply from the ease with which the executive can bring
pressure upon judges, though I have cited a number of examples of threats of
impeachment and the like in another study, but from the general acceptance of
political leadership by the president that is part of the political system. . . .

. . . [A]t present there is no real need to change the legal relationship of the court
with the other political branches of the government, because a satisfactory adjustment
of all three branches to each other and to the political system as it now operates
already exists. The average citizen is well aware of this; knowing that the real and
ultimate source of policy decisions, and the determination of their constitutionality as
well, resides with the person in whom real political authority resides, the chief
executive of the country, he looks to the courts for technical interpretation of the law
or for protection against arbitrary applications by capricious individuals, and to the
presidency when he wishes to influence basic policy.

A recent article by Professor David Helfeld, former Dean of the Law School at the
University of Puerto Rico, reflects a somewhat lower assessment of the integrity of the
lower levels of Mexico's judiciary.

A pervasive characteristic of the Mexican legal system is the extent of
corruption. Once again, corruption starts at the federal level and permeates large
segments of the political and judicial structure. Bribery, in the form of
gift-giving, is part of the national political tradition, and only supreme-court
justices are relatively immune to its effects. . . . The net effect of this pervasive
corruption is that a significantly large number of cases are not judged on their
own merits, short of a supreme-court decision. Helfeld, "Law and Politics in
Mexico," in *One Spark From Holocaust: The Crisis in Latin America* 81, 91
(E. Burnell, ed., 1972).

Pablo González Casanova, a leading Mexican political sociologist, offers empirical
evidence to support much the same conclusion reached by Professor Scott about the
independence of the Mexican judiciary. Consider to what extent the practice of
naming the President as a purely formal party in amparo suits challenging the
constitutionality of laws on their face undermines the value of the underlying data.

P. GONZALEZ CASANOVA, DEMOCRACY IN MEXICO

(Salti translation, paperback ed. 1972)*

. . . We analyzed the final decisions of the Supreme Court of Justice, in which the

---

*From *Democracy in Mexico* by Pablo González Casanova, translated by Danielle Salti.
Copyright © 1970 by Oxford University Press, Inc. Reprinted by permission.

President of the Republic appears as responsible for the suit. The immediate objective was to see how many claims have been made against the President, who made them, what issue they concerned, and what the Court's decision was. The ultimate goal was to measure the power of the Court, if any.

We found the following facts to be true from a study of the period from 1917 to 1960.

1. From 1917 to 1960 there was a total of 3,700 rulings in which the President of the Republic was expressly mentioned as being sued. The annual average of rulings in presidential regimes varied: 20 with Carranza, 35 during the provisional six-month rule of de la Huerta, 79 with Obregón, 62 with Calles, 53 with the Maximato, 78 with Cárdenas, 126 with Avila Camacho, 110 with Alemán, 95 with Ruiz Cortines, and 131 in each of the first two years of the term of López Mateos. . . .

2. Of all the rulings in the period 1917-60, 34 per cent are Court protections or suspensions granted the claimant. This means that of 3,700 rulings, in a little more than 1,200 the claimant's demands were satisfied. Of the remaining 66 per cent of the rulings, 34 per cent were denied protection or suspension of decision, 24 per cent were discontinued or received no ruling due to the claimant's waiving of his right or other causes, 9 per cent comprised other types of rulings.

3. In order to know who the claimants were and the nature of the contested rulings, we made different kinds of tabulations. The first tabulation included the cases from 1917 to 1940 by claimant, contested action, and ruling. Of a total of 1,470 claimants, 140 were oil companies, 186 were banks and other commercial companies, 644 were landowners, 30 were civil authorities and other public employees and functionaries, 27 were peasants, and 13 were workers. The remaining 430 are more difficult to categorize by social status or claims. From the above data it can be inferred that at least 66 per cent of the claimants are foreign and Mexican owners (of companies, banks, land, etc.), and it is very probable that a more detailed analysis would show an even higher percentage.

Of these Court cases in the period 1917-40, 44 per cent contested action taken by the Executive limiting the rights of the big owners — redistribution of latifundia (460), declarations relating to national waters (136), expropriations (52) — and 23 per cent contested the passing of laws, regulations, decrees, and agreements of the revolutionary governments, or tax levies. Claims relating to actions affecting property and utilities make up 67 per cent of the total. This percentage is the same as that of the claimants belonging to the owners category. Other motives for complaints, such as destitution from posts (23) and apprehensions and extraditions (21), have a lower rate of incidence.

The orientation of the Court in this period is reflected in its granting an average of 26 per cent rulings of protection and suspension of decisions and its denying 46 per cent. The remaining cases either were discontinued or they included diverse types of rulings that are less characteristic of acceptance or refusal.

4. Our second tabulation includes the cases in job matters for the period 1917-60. Court actions contested by employers amount to 150, of which the Court granted only 25, including both protections and suspensions. There were 24 cases of Court

actions contested by workers for the whole period, and the Court granted only 4 claims. Most were discontinued, and 2 were not heard.

5. Our third tabulation sums up cases in which the claimants were farmers and covers the period 1940-60. There were 210 cases of actions contested by farmers working on [ejidos,] communities, villages, small landowners, landless peasants, and other farmers. Twenty-seven per cent were granted, and 52 per cent were discontinued. The most frequent reasons for complaint were orders involving restitution of property to the original owners, expropriation of public lands, deprivation or denial of public land or agrarian rights generally, rulings affecting small properties, and cancellation of plot titles.

These data indicate that the Supreme Court of Justice operates with a certain degree of independence with respect to the executive power, sometimes exercising a controlling action over the President or his assistants. The Court subjects to judgment certain acts coming from the Executive. Its main political function is to provide hope for those groups and individuals who are able to utilize this recourse to protect their interests or rights. Among those claimants who go to the Court, there is a preponderance of owners and companies, old latifundists, and the new bourgeoisie. Businesses and members of the middle class are mainly occupied with complaints concerning fiscal legislation or tax enforcements. Compared to them, workers and peasants who appeal to the Court constitute a minority.

There is no doubt that the Supreme Court of Justice is endowed with power, yet it does generally follow the policy of the Executive, and in fact it serves to make the Executive more stable.

C. SCHWARZ, JUDGES UNDER THE SHADOW: JUDICIAL INDEPENDENCE IN THE UNITED STATES AND MEXICO

3 *Calif. W. Int'l L. J.* 260, 301-05, 307-08, 312-14, 317-18, 322-32 (1973)

The Supreme Court has thus far stood its ground in the face of such political pressure [to refrain from reviewing amparo challenges to laws or acts threatening the rights of small agricultural landholders] although it has conceded to the government on marginal issues involving agrarian policy. Federal courts in general have encountered great obstacles in some parts of the country when it comes to enforcing politically unpopular decisions. The President of the Court frankly complained about the lack of cooperation from some state governors and military zone commanders whose help was requested by federal district judges and the Supreme Court, but who failed to move promptly, if at all, against invasions by communal farmers onto lands possessed by small private owners supposedly protected by *amparo* injunctions.[50]

---

[50] Interview with Lic. Presidente Agapito Pozo, in Mexico City, August, 1968. Securing executive compliance of final amparo decrees is difficult, both politically and procedurally. If the responsible authority fails to comply with final suspension order, devices known as the *queja* (complaint), used in cases of excessive or deficient execution, and the *incidente de inejecución,* for

Two district judges interviewed in outlying towns expressed similar sentiment more intensely. On the other hand, a number of the Administrative Chamber's own cases indicate that the Federal Public Minister's Office is cooperating to some extent by bringing penal actions against responsible authorities and third-party *ejidos* who fail to carry out *amparo* judgments. . . .[51]

The Mexican Supreme Court's treatment of agrarian *amparo* cases, an area supposedly forbidden to judicial scrutiny, illustrates the increasing independence of the Mexican Federal Judiciary in deciding constitutional-rights cases on their merits. The *amparo* courts have expressed this independence mainly by demanding that all litigants be accorded a wider degree of procedural fairness in official decisions, whether such decision-makers be municipal officials, federal and state administrators, law enforcement officers, or judges.[52]

Insistence on proper administrative and judicial procedures in *amparo* litigation at times has borne down heavily on official discretion in politically sensitive areas. These have included state and federal taxation of income and real property; military control over pensions, housing, and non-service-connected crimes by soldiers; denials to aliens of professional licenses and due process in deportation actions; the application of international treaties to Mexican citizens; and methods of expropriating real property for public purposes, including the aforementioned agrarian reform programs. . . .

The Mexican position favoring taxpayers' suits represents an interesting contrast to the *Frothingham* pattern in the United States, especially since it comes from a judicial system based on the European civil law principle of "legislative supremacy:"

---

complete lack of execution, may be employed to order such compliance. *Law of Amparo* arts. 95-97, 105-08. These must be processed through the Plenary Court at the initiative of the plaintiff (*quejoso*) favored by the judgment. No federal district judge is empowered to issue his own contempt or non-compliance citation. . . .

If the offending authority continues to defy the judgment or repeats the enjoined acts, at the initiative of the original trial judge or interested parties, the Plenary Court can order his removal from office and his appearance before a district judge for appropriate criminal action as brought by the Public Minister. *Law of Amparo* art. 108. On conviction, the authority then can receive up to six years' imprisonment and a 1000-peso fine. *Id.* art. 199; *Federal Penal Code* 213. Such convictions are rare.

It should be noted that "there exists no particular statute nor immunity for public servants in civil conflicts." *Mexico Const.* art. 114. Further, the Supreme Court can demand suspension of immunity if the authority claims "constitutional status" to avoid removal from office. *Law of Amparo* art. 109. Many lawyers interviewed in Mexico, however, see the key problem of judicial enforcement as the lack of cooperation of the Federal Public Minister in bringing such criminal sanctions against the abusive official. See, e.g., Alcalá-Zamora y Castillo, *supra*, . . . who criticizes the exorbitant discretionary powers of the Public Minister in criminal prosecutions generally. [Footnote by Schwarz, renumbered.]

[51] See e.g., *Amparo en revisión de Comisariado Ejidal del Poblado Tumbiscatío* . . . 133 S.J.F. 6a época 15, 3a parte (Administrative) (1968). [Footnote by Schwarz, renumbered.]

[52] "[In Mexico] the average citizen . . . looks to the courts for technical interpretations of the law or protection against arbitrary applications by capricious individuals, and to the presidency when he wishes to influence basic policy." R. Scott, *supra* note 152, at 272. In light of the actual performance of *amparo* courts since 1940, however, this should be amended as follows: ". . . for the protection against arbitrary applications by capricious individuals and *non-elective agencies.*" [Footnote by Schwarz, renumbered.]

The Court is within its powers to judge the unconstitutionality of fiscal laws, just as it can that of any other law. This power may be exercised broadly, analyzing if there is insufficient generality [in the application of the law] ; if it contradicts its own principles; if the powers of other authorities are invaded; if the rights to a hearing for the litigants are not observed; if the laws are made retroactive; in sum, if the [fiscal laws] are within the general principles of individual guarantees [of the Constitution].

Perhaps the real reason behind the Mexican Court's marked independence in this area is the special relationship between the Administrative Chamber and the highly prestigious Federal Fiscal Tribunal. The Fiscal Tribunal is similar in function to the United States Tax Court but possesses broad review powers more like those of the French administrative tribunal, the *Conseil d' Etat.* The Mexican Tribunal oversees and screens for "illegality" all actions of the fiscal agencies of the Federal Government, including those operating the Federal District. It is known for its hard-headed review of administrative decisions for their substantive conformity with existing revenue statutes and the due process rights of taxpayers or other assessed citizens.[53] Thus, by the time the Government's case has reached the Administrative Chamber on direct appeal, it has been subjected to thorough and often critical scrutiny by the Tribunal. One survey revealed that the Chamber upheld the Tribunal against the federal fiscal authority in at least 60 per cent of the proceedings where the latter had appealed via the special *revisión fiscal* recourse.[54] This contrasts with greater percentages of "pro-government" decisions in the Civil, Criminal, and Labor Chambers of the Court.

The Mexican Supreme Court review of military courts-martial via the direct *amparo* procedure appears to be much broader as well as more common than in the United States. The issues cognizable by the Court range from whether the military tribunal correctly interpreted the Code of Military Justice to the accuracy of findings of fact. The Plenary Court also has forthrightly denied the military courts jurisdiction in competency disputes with civilian courts over soldiers charged with off-duty or non-military crimes. Finally, the Administrative Chamber of the Court has been under fire for upholding Fiscal Tribunal rulings against the Defense Secretariat in favor of revolutionary veterans and unmarried mothers in their claims for military pensions.

---

[53] "Organic Law Federal Fiscal Tribunal" arts. 228-30 (*as revised,* 1967). Herriman & Lee, *Financing Urban Development in Mexico* 39-47, 57-63 (1967). Reviewing only the legality and procedural sensitivity of fiscal agency decisions, and nullifying those not in accord with the Federal Fiscal Code, gives to the Fiscal Tribunal its "cassation" function. Unlike *amparo* courts, the Tribunal does not void such acts as unconstitutional nor substitute its own interpretation of the statute in the individual cases brought before it. See Fix Zamudio, *El Juicio Amparo* 327-28 (1964). . . . [Footnote by Schwarz, renumbered.]

[54] Interview with Carlos del Río Rodríguez, President, Federal Fiscal Tribunal (now Minister of the Supreme Court), in Mexico City, August, 1968. A perusal of the few *revisión fiscal* cases fully reported in S.J.F. for the period of January 1964-June 1966, and June through August, 1968, revealed that the President's estimate was, if anything, conservative. Of the 35 cases reported, the Administrative Chamber upheld Tribunal actions against Treasury officials in 30; three resulted in partial rulings for the government appellants, and only two affirmed the government's arguments against the Tribunal. [Footnote by Schwarz, renumbered.]

Protection and broad reviewability of a variety of aliens' claims to due process and legal equality by Mexican *amparo* courts is a third point of contrast with limited reviewability available in United States federal tribunals. Especially noteworthy are the successive *jurisprudencias* issued by the Mexican High Court against the constitutionality of the 1944 federal professional licensing law and state laws similarly discriminating against resident aliens. The Court has found that a commercial income tax levied as a requisite for practicing a "non-commercial profession" was a double, unequal tax compounding that already assessed on the plaintiff's income. Alien doctors and lawyers have benefited from *amparo* judges' "supplying the deficiency of the complaint," in other words correcting technical errors in their petitions, when appealing denials of licenses to teach or practice by the Federal Director-General of Professions. . . .

It may be concluded that the Mexican federal courts, especially in their exercise of *amparo* jurisdiction, are not as passively oriented to the Executive Branch as is commonly assumed. In a few areas, they are even more activist than their counterparts in the United States: most striking here is the broad reviewability of federal and state tax laws and military courts-martial. . . .

The Mexican Supreme Court has pressed officialdom vigorously in several key policy areas. *Amparo* courts appear willing to tackle almost every kind of procedural abuse in the administration and interpretation of laws as long as litigants meet the technical requisites for bringing the writ. Those subjected to rigorous constitutional standards via the *amparo* include judges, administrative tribunals, municipal officials, ordinary bureaucrats and agency chiefs, and law enforcement officers. In at least two ways, however, Mexican federal judges have relied on Professor Bickel's "passive virtues" falling short of declaring the question non-reviewable. One, the Supreme and District Courts rarely challenge basic governmental policies by upholding "constitutionality *amparos*" (called *amparos contra leyes*) against statutes, administrative regulations, and presidential decrees. Two, Mexican federal courts will defer to the discretion of responsible authorities in the face of certain politically sensitive issues, even while deciding on the merits.

The reluctance to void governmental enactments on constitutional grounds is primarily the result of an unfavorable congressional response in 1958 to this style of judicial activism: by granting monopoly jurisdiction over all "constitutionality *amparos*" [appeals] to the Plenary Court, the Congress ensured that it would be an awkward and rarely successful remedy. Fourteen out of a Court of twenty-one Ministers must now approve the five consecutive "theses" or decisions on the same legal point as necessary to establish *jurisprudencia* regarding the challenged law. This is required in a body already rendered unwieldy by its organization into four chambers dealing with highly disparate subject matter, whose members have little formal interaction with those of the other chambers. . . .

When the Court does sustain such challenges, it more often directs them against state rather than federal legislation. Rarely does it ever question laws assigned a priority by the President and his "ruling family" within the PRI.[55] . .

---

[55] Of this author's sample of 49 fully-reported *amparos* against the laws decided during a thirty-three month period in 1964-1968, only eight represented a victory for the complainant, and

Professor González's conclusion that the principal function of the Mexican Court is to provide haven for the propertied elites of Mexico should not be accepted without qualification. His finding is not wholly supportable in light of the over-all filings and decisional output of the Labor, Administrative, and Penal Chambers. His conclusions on the 1940-1960 period, for example, are based entirely on the occupational backgrounds of plaintiffs filing actions in labor and agrarian matters and naming the President as the defendant. But even in this limited sample he does not consider the Court's actual responses to the petitions presented. Thus, González's own data on agrarian-rights decisions indicates a higher percentage of suits won by *ejidos* and small rural proprietors, possessing certificates of inaffectability, than those won by private farmers of larger holdings, also with certificates. Moreover, an analysis of eighty fully reported *amparo* cases, decided by the Labor Chamber during a thirty-three-month period during the 1960's, revealed that employers and workers appeared as plaintiffs on approximately a 1-1 ratio.[56] Finally, and most significantly, criminal defendants appealing their convictions or sentences in state and federal courts constitute the greatest single portion of the Court's caseload; and about half of these are successful in *amparo* petitions to the Penal Chamber. Surely the vast majority of such petitioners have far from an aristocratic or even middle-class background.

. . . [T]he Mexican Supreme Court most sharply deviates from the norms of the other agencies of government when it decides complaints in criminal and administrative matters. The Administrative Chamber has developed an increasing independent posture in mandating procedural fairness in agrarian expropriation proceedings, state and federal tax administration, military decisions on pensions and salaries, and domestic applications of international treaties. Particularly striking in examining the decisional record is the frequency with which the Administrative Chamber decides against the federal "fiscal" authorities in such broad and important policy areas as federal disbursements, fines, and revenue levies. This phenomenon is perhaps attributable to the Chamber's unique relationship with the Federal Fiscal Tribunal whose numerous decisions against the government are regularly upheld by the Chamber.

The extent of the Mexican Supreme Court's independence in criminal *amparo* matters is less clear. Perhaps because it lacks a reinforcing buffer, or "lightning rod" of quasi-judicial specialists comparable to the Fiscal Tribunal, the Penal Chamber, more readily than the Administrative Chamber, appears to withdraw to its "passive virtues" when confronted with politically sensitive issues. Pressure from the criminal law profession, however, has influenced the Penal ministers toward a position of at least *deciding* most of these issues. Certainly the most salient and controversial example of

---

five of these involved state rather than federal laws. S.J.F. (January, 1964-July, 1966, June-August, 1968). [Footnote by Schwarz, renumbered.]

[56] Semanario Judicial de la Federación (January, 1964-July, 1966, June-August, 1968). These represent direct amparo cases brought against labor arbitration boards; because such boards are marginally sympathetic to employees and unions, it is generally the employer — including government agencies acting in a "patrimonial" capacity — who initiate the *amparos.* Direct labor *amparos* take up about 22 percent of the Supreme Court's total caseload (average filings for 1969-1971). [Footnote by Schwarz, renumbered.]

the Penal Chamber's judicial modesty was its decision on the former federal crime of "social dissolution" (*disolución social*). In 1966 the Penal Chamber of the Supreme Court finally ruled on nine separate *amparo* appeals from convictions under the anti-subversion statue and other crimes in federal trial courts. Most were radical labor leaders who had been in prison since their arrests in 1959 for fomenting a national strike against the government-operated railroads. That the President of the Court remitted the accumulated appeals to the Penal Chamber instead of the Plenary Court indicated the Court's overwhelming desire to avoid judging the constitutionality of the controversial statute, in spite of the fact that the plaintiffs had raised such a challenge. Regarding several of the cases, however, the unanimous opinions went far beyond the "legality" of the trial judge's interpretation of the statute in denying the merits of the *amparo* petitions. . . .

In their violent confrontations with federal riot police and the army during 1968 and 1969, university students commonly voiced demands that the President and Congress rescind the ambiguously phrased anti-subversion statute.[57] . . . Not surprisingly, the modesty of the Supreme Court and the legal profession in dealing with the ambiguities and "chilling effects" of the social dissolution statute was reflected in several federal trial court rulings on *amparo* petitions. After hundreds of students and other protesters had been arrested, jailed, and allegedly mistreated by police after the disturbances in 1968, one judge threw out no less than eighty-six such petitions in a single action; they were held inadmissible because the police acts "were not determined, nor imminent, nor probable in the future." Nineteen months after arrest uncounted persons remained imprisoned without trial.

The Plenary and Penal Chambers of the Court have occasionally responded with something like principle in dealing with politically significant cases. On the question of soldiers accused of non-service-connected crimes, for example, the Plenary Court has granted competency to civilian rather than military courts. The real record of the Court on criminal matters, however, is one of general and impartial availability to defendants aggrieved by errors in the day-to-day functioning of ordinary trial and appellate courts, errors vitally important perhaps only to the individuals affected. . . .

Essentially the same tribute could be paid to the other judicial components of the *amparo* system. . . .

For many Mexican attorneys and common people interviewed in 1968 and 1971, the Federal District Courts represent the "thin black line" against official abuse in the towns and countryside. They are undermanned — only fifty-five judges scattered throughout the nation — and woefully understaffed. Nonetheless, the district courts

---

[57]See K. Johnson, *Mexican Democracy: A Critical View,* at 152 and *passim.* The most challenged section of the statute read:

> [The penalties of this section will apply to any] foreigner or Mexican national who in written or spoken fashion, or by whatever other means, engages in political propaganda among foreigners or Mexican nationals, diffusing ideas, programs, or other norms of action of whatever foreign government which disturb the public order or affect the sovereignty of the State of Mexico.

Federal Penal Code art. 145 (pre-1970). [Footnote by Schwarz, renumbered.]

receive and process an enormous number of *amparo* petitions each year: some 58,000 filings in 1971, or 72 per cent of all *amparos* entering the Federal Judiciary that year. These trial judges in *amparo* cases deal primarily with appeals for help by criminal suspects and defendants claiming that their injuries at the hands of law enforcement cannot await final dispositions of ordinary trials or appellate proceedings. . . .

More than 62 per cent (36,500) of the district courts' caseload in 1971 comprised such emergency petitions for relief from criminal proceedings. The "little man" does therefore avail himself of the *amparo* writ, at the local level as well as at the Supreme Court Building in Mexico City. . . .

Before scoffing at the fact that only 12.5 per cent of criminal *amparo* petitions were granted on their merits, consider that less than 5 per cent of the applications for federal habeas corpus in the United States were decided by the Federal District Courts in favor of the applicant for the writ; the other 95 per cent were held to be without merit. . . .

The answer . . . is of necessity mixed and relative; much depends on the tribunal and issue area involved. Although both Supreme Courts rely on a doctrine of political questions as well as other forms of non-reviewability, the Mexican Court's restrictions primarily flow from specific constitutional and statutory provisions, and have not been so nearly fraught with exceptions as those of its United States counterpart. Furthermore, the two differ widely on the kinds of cases held to be almost or completely non-reviewable. Mexico broadly denies its courts *amparo* jurisdiction over cases involving free exercise of religion, challenges of electoral counting or administration, dismissals of certain "public functionaries," summary deportation of persons deemed undesirable by the President, direct review of most "decentralized agencies" at the federal level, and agrarian land expropriations. None of these would be immune from federal judicial review in the United States as long as individual rights under the Constitution or statute were properly raised. On the other hand, Mexican jurists would find it strange that United States Courts traditionally have abstained from, or severely restricted, review of state and federal tax laws, military courts-martial and administrative actions, administrative rationale for deportations, state practices adversely affecting the economic status of resident aliens, and the interpretation of international treaties and executive agreements.

As to those cases actually reviewed on the merits, there is no question that the Mexican federal courts have been reluctant to exercise their constitutional-rights jurisdiction in the independent, forthright, or comprehensive manner of the United States federal courts. [Statistics] . . . bear this out regarding the United States Supreme Court, as does a recent study finding that during the period of 1957 to 1968 the Court decided 70 per cent of the cases surveyed in a way favorable to the "civil rights and civil liberties" position. It would be safe to assume that the Penal and Administrative Chambers of the Mexican Court would not come close to such a figure in similar cases. The Mexican tribunal has particularly subordinated claims to constitutional protection on issues involving freedom of political and non-political expression, association, and demonstration. Relative to United States Supreme Court decisions in the first amendment area, the Mexican Court has strongly identified with the dominant political alliance, refusing to invalidate statutes where claims of vagueness or "chilling effects" on free expression were raised.

On the other hand, the Mexican *amparo* courts have increasingly chosen *not* to resort to Professor Bickel's passive virtues in certain issue areas. Both the Administrative Chamber and Plenary Court have broadly upheld the challenges of small private farmers, the *pequeñas propiedades,* against the confiscatory actions of agrarian reform commissions, an area formerly set off as a political question. Definitive *amparo* judgments against the government have also been rendered in cases raising the issues of income and property taxation; military jurisdiction over non-service-connected crimes; courts-martial generally; military policy toward pensions, housing, and salaries; aliens' rights to professional licenses; and criminal due process issues not involving the anti-subversive laws.

It is surprising, in fact, that the Mexican federal courts have largely charted their own courses, with or without political pressures from local *políticos* or national elites. The high percentages of cases won by *amparo* plaintiffs and the great volume of cases initiated each year demonstrate that the Mexican judiciary is an important allocator of values, scarce resources, and sanctions in the national political system. . . .

D. The Argentine Amparo

Prior to 1957, the Argentine courts afforded no generalized injunctive relief against unconstitutional official action. The writ of habeas corpus, known as the *recurso de amparo de la libertad,* gave fairly rapid protection against illegal or arbitrary restraints on physical liberty, but there was no comparable remedy for speedy protection of other constitutional rights. Aware of the dramatic expansion of the writ of habeas corpus in nearby Brazil and of the extraordinary versatility of the Mexican writ of amparo, Argentine lawyers quite naturally attempted to utilize the *recurso de amparo de la libertad* as a summary procedure to prevent denial of other constitutional rights. The courts of several of the Argentine provinces permitted the remedy of amparo in such cases, and a few federal Supreme Court cases appeared to permit such expansion of habeas corpus. However, the predominant position of the Supreme Court was expressed in the *Bertotto* case, where a publisher sought habeas corpus to compel the postal authorities to accept his newspaper for mailing:

> Neither in the letter, spirit, nor constitutional tradition of the institution of habeas corpus does one find any basis for applying it to liberty of property, commerce, industry, teaching, transport of correspondence, etc. . . . 41 J.A. 554, 559 (1933).

Subsequent attempts to expand habeas corpus prior to 1957 also came to naught.[58] Protection of constitutional rights not involving one's physical liberty was left to the

---

[58] See G. Bidart Campos, *Régimen Legal y Jurisprudencial del Amparo* 46-53 (1968).

ordinary course of administrative and judicial proceedings, which was arduous, expensive, and lengthy.[59]

By 1957 the Supreme Court was ready to reconsider this position. The Perón regime had virtually emasculated the court, impeaching all but one of its members in 1947. When Perón was overthrown in 1955, General Lonardi's provisional government promptly replaced Perón's appointees to the Court. It is probable that many years of living under a regime in which arbitrary governmental action was commonplace convinced the new judges of the necessity of creating a quick and effective judicial remedy to guard against the recurrence of such abuses. Beginning with the *Siri* case, which follows immediately, the Argentine Supreme Court set about fashioning such a remedy. The following cases, many of which are already referred to by the English term "leading cases," show the Argentine courts struggling to create rapidly a coherent body of law from the raw materials of individual cases. Consider the extent to which the Brazilian writ of security and the Mexican amparo have served as models. Also consider the likelihood that this new remedy will engage the Court in potentially damaging conflicts with the Executive.

---

1. Judicial Fashioning of the Amparo

SIRI

Supreme Court of Justice of Argentina
239 Fallos 459, 1958-II J.A. 478
89 La Ley 532 (1957)

Opinion of Procurator General of the Nation.

... I have already had the opportunity ("Fallos," vol. 236, p. 41) to state my opinion that habeas corpus protects only persons deprived of their physical liberty without the order of a competent authority. Therefore, if Your Honors decide to permit the ... appeal, I believe it would be proper to affirm what has been decided, insofar as it is appealed. — *Sebastián Soler.*

Buenos Aires, December 27, 1957. — [Considering]: In the proceedings ... the extraordinary appeal was permitted against the decision of the Chamber of Appeals (Penal) of Mercedes (Province of Buenos Aires), declaring that the newspaper "Mercedes," under the management and administration of Angel Siri, had been closed since the beginning of 1956, "by police custody of the premises," which act violated the freedoms of the press and of work as contained in arts. 14, 17, and 18 of the National Constitution, and arts. 9, 11, 13, 14, 23 and others of the Provincial Constitution. Siri asked that, pending the report of the Police Commissioner of the District of Mercedes concerning the present reasons for the custody of the newspaper

---

[59] See Bielsa, "Jurisdictional Protection and Other Remedies Against the Illegal Exercise or Abuse of Administrative Authority," in *United Nations, Remedies Against the Abuse of Administrative Authority — Selected Studies* 33, 57-60 (1964).

premises, he be accorded what was proper, consistent with the law and in accordance with the cited constitutional clauses.

[The Police Commissioner's report stated simply that, in accordance with an order from the National Directorate of Security, Siri had been arrested and the newspaper closed down. No reasons for closing the newspaper were given. Neither the Police Chief nor the Minister of the Interior of the Province of Buenos Aires knew why the order was issued nor which authority issued it. Nonetheless, the judge of the 1st Instance rejected the petition for habeas corpus on the ground that the writ protected only the physical liberty of individuals. The Chamber of Appeals (Penal) of Mercedes affirmed on the same ground.]

. . . In these conditions, it is clear that the right invoked by the petitioner to publish and administer the newspaper must be upheld.

[The plaintiff did not base his action on an expanded theory of habeas corpus, but simply relied on the guarantees of freedom of the press and of work.]

This confirmation of the constitutional violation is sufficient reason for the judges to re-establish in its entirety the constitutional guarantee that is invoked, and it may not be alleged to the contrary that there is no law regulating the guarantee. Individual guarantees exist and protect individuals by virtue of the single fact that they are contained in the Constitution, independently of regulatory laws . . . .

In consideration of the nature and order of importance of the principles of the Fundamental Charter in relation to individual rights, this Supreme Court (in its present composition and in the first opportunity when it must pronounce on the point) departs from the traditional doctrine declared by the tribunal, insofar as that doctrine relegated to the ordinary proceedings (administrative or judicial) the protection of guarantees not strictly included in habeas corpus . . . . Constitutional precepts as well as the institutional experience of the country jointly demand the enjoyment and full exercise of individual guarantees for the effective maintenance of a rule of law, and impose the duty of ensuring them upon the country's judges.

Therefore, the Procurator General having stated his opinion, the appealed sentence is revoked. And the proceedings are remanded to the tribunal of origin in order that . . . the police authority [be directed to terminate] the restriction imposed on the petitioner in his capacity as editor-owner of the newspaper that was shut down. – *Alfredo Orgaz. – Manuel J. Argañarás. – Enrique V. Galli. – Benjamín Villegas Basavilbaso. –* Dissenting: *Carlos Herrera.*

[The dissent of Dr. Herrera relied on admitted precedent and argued that the Court had exceeded its jurisdiction. Dr. Herrera argued that the Court had no authority, in the absence of legislation, to create the new remedy.]

2. Amparo Against "Private" Parties

SAMUEL KOT, S.R.L.

Supreme Court of Justice of Argentina
241 Fallos 291, 1958-IV J.A. 227
92 La Ley 626 (1958)

Buenos Aires, September 5, 1958. — . . . The firm of Samuel Kot (Society of Limited Responsibility), owner of a textile establishment . . ., has been involved in a conflict with its employees since last March 21. The strike by these workers was originally declared illegal by the San Martín Delegation of the Provincial Department of Labor on March 28. The [employer] therefore ordered the return of the workers to their jobs within 24 hours, with the exception of two union officials. A month and a half later, the president of the Provincial Department of Labor voided the decision of the San Martín Delegation and suggested to both parties that work be resumed. The company refused to reinstate the two workers it had fired. Thereupon, they and other workers occupied the factory on June 9 and have stayed there until now. [Although able to enter, the owners have been prevented from operating the factory since the start of the sit-in.]

[The business manager brought an action based on this usurpation of property, demanding the return of the plant. The judge dismissed the action because the occupation by the workers was not made with the object of assuming ownership of the property, but only in the course of the labor dispute. This decision was appealed to the 3d Chamber of Appeals (Penal) of La Plata, which affirmed the final dismissal. On the same day the attorney for the firm sought from the same chamber relief in the nature of amparo (*not* habeas corpus), relying the *Siri* case. This relief was also denied in the court of 2d Instance.]

Considering: First of all, it is proper to set aside the basis expressed by the court for rejecting the argument of the complainant, who did not rely on "habeas corpus" but rather on amparo, invoking the constitutional rights of freedom of work, of property and of free activity. That is, he alleged a different guarantee from the one protecting corporal freedom — one which, like "habeas corpus," obtains expeditious and rapid protection, coming directly from the Constitution. This Court so declared in the decision of December 27 of last year, in the case of "Angel Siri" (Fallos, vol. 239, p. 450), with grounds which are here incorporated by reference insofar as they are pertinent.

Although in the cited precedent the illegal restriction on liberty came from the public authority and not from acts of individuals, such distinction is not essential for the purposes of constitutional protection. If it be admitted that a tacit or implicit guarantee exists, protecting the various aspects of individual liberty (art. 33, National Constitution), no exception may be established that might exclude, absolutely and *a priori,* all such restrictions imposed by private persons.

. . . There is nothing in either the letter or the spirit of the Constitution that might permit the assertion that the protection of "human rights" — so called because they are the basic rights of man — is confined to attacks by official authorities. Neither is there anything to authorize the assertion that an illegal, serious, and open attack against any of the rights that make up liberty in the broad sense, would lack adequate constitutional protection because of the single fact that the attack comes from other private persons or organized groups of individuals. (This protection, of course, is in the form of habeas corpus and amparo, and not that of the ordinary proceedings. . . .) To attempt excessively technical constructions in order to justify this distinction would mean interpreting the Constitution in such a way that it would really appear to protect not basic rights, but open violations of those rights. The concrete facts of this case by themselves constitute a significant example.

This distinction is even less admissible, . . . considering the conditions in which social life of the past fifty years has developed. Besides individual persons and the State, there is now a third category of subjects . . .: consortiums, unions, professional associations, large businesses, which almost always accumulate enormous material or economic power. . . . [T]hese collective entities represent, with the material progress of society, a new source of threats for the individual and his basic rights.

. . . The Constitution does not forsake citizens in the face of such dangers, nor does it necessarily require them to resort to the slow and expensive defense of ordinary proceedings. Laws cannot be interpreted merely from an historical viewpoint, ignoring new conditions and needs of the community. Every law, by its nature, contains a vision of the future, and is intended to cover and govern acts that take place after its ratification. . . . The Constitution, which is the law of laws and to be found at the base of the entire positive juridical order, has the indispensable power to govern juridical relations born in social circumstances different from those that existed at the time of its ratification. This advance of constitutional principles, which is a part of natural development . . . is the real work of the interpreters, particularly of the judges, who must have the intelligence that will best assure the great objectives for which the Constitution was written. Among these great objectives and even of first importance among them, is "to secure the blessings of liberty to ourselves, to our posterity, and to all men of the world who may wish to inhabit Argentine soil" (Preamble).

[The court notes that habeas corpus, which comes from the Anglo-American tradition by way of the Constitution of the United States, has been interpreted broadly to protect physical liberty.]

The same breadth should be recognized for amparo, which this Court, in the aforementioned precedent [the *Siri* case], drew from the wise rule of art. 33 of the Constitution. . . . Habeas corpus and amparo are primarily concerned, not with the "origin" of the illegal restrictions of any of the fundamental rights of persons, but with those rights in themselves, for the purpose of safeguarding them. . . . The Constitution is irrevocably aimed at assuring to all citizens "the benefits of liberty," and this purpose . . . is weakened or damaged when distinctions are introduced that, directly or indirectly, become obstacles or delays to the effective fulfillment of rights. . . .

[The court also cites the 1948 Universal Declaration of Human Rights of the United Nations.]

Consequently, whenever it is clear and obvious that any restriction of basic human rights is illegal and also that submitting the question to the ordinary administrative or judicial procedures would cause serious and irreparable harm, it is proper for the judges to restore the restricted right immediately through the swift . . . remedy of amparo. . . . [J]udges must take special pains . . . not to decide, through the highly summary procedure of this constitutional guarantee, questions susceptible of greater debate and which should be resolved in accordance with the ordinary procedures. . . .

[In the present case, the Court found that the striking workers made no claim of a right to continue to occupy the factory and that their occupation of the factory deprived the owners of their property and their right to work.]

In these conditions, it is not appropriate to require the affected party to claim the return of his property through ordinary procedures. If, every time that a group of persons physically occupied a factory, a private teaching institution, or any other establishment, in connection with a conflict, the owners had no other recourse for defense of their constitutional rights than to bring a possessory action or one of ejectment, with multiple citations for each and every one of the occupants to appear in the action, with the power of each of the occupants to name his own attorney, to contest notices and documents, to offer and produce evidence, etc., anyone can see how the protection of rights given by the laws would be diminished and how the juridical order of the country would be subverted. In such situations, which include the present case, judicial protection of constitutional rights does not tolerate or consent to such a delay.

[By a vote of three to two, the decision of the court of 2d Instance was reversed, and the granting of the amparo was ordered. The two dissenting judges argued that the amparo was available only against official invasions of constitutional rights, and not against invasions of similar interests by private parties. The dissenters further argued that the decision would introduce considerable insecurity into the law. They suggested that the extension of the amparo to actions between private individuals would create an excessive discretionary power in all the judges in the country to grant amparo — *i.e.*, to decide private disputes — without using the normal means of hearing, proof, appeal, etc., which safeguard the rights of parties to ordinary litigation.]

GALVAN v. COUTO

Supreme Court of Justice of Argentina
246 Fallos 380 (1960)

[The plaintiff sought amparo against a private individual to secure fulfillment of his obligation to supply electricity. The lower courts rejected the complaint. 1960-III J.A. 30.]

Buenos Aires, May 30, 1960. . . .

As the foregoing opinion of the Procurator General points out, based on the case law of this Court, since the present case involves the non-fulfillment of a contractual obligation, amparo will not lie. The allegation that . . . the right to work will be infringed does not change the result. In effect, we deal with one form of exercise of that right, which presupposes the decision that there is a contractual obligation, and which, furthermore, is not unique. On the other hand [various procedural devices such as an order to maintain matters in status quo] , possible in an ordinary action, provide proceedings suitable for the protection of the right [to work] , which proceedings can be of assistance to the plaintiff.

Therefore, the Procurator General having given his opinion, the foregoing complaint is dismissed. . . .

Note

The leading case standing for the foregoing proposition is *Buosi* 244 Fallos 68, 1959-IV J.A. 36, 96 La Ley 709 (1959), involving a dispute over land and water rights. Similar rulings were made in the cases of *Magno Esquivel v. Corbiere de B.,* 247 Fallos 59, 99 La Ley 820 (1960) (contractual obligation to permit tenants to use an elevator), and *Precedo,* 253 Fallos 35, 1962-IV J.A. 334, 108 La Ley 328 (1962) (dispute over a labor contract).

MORIS

Federal Chamber of the Capital
(Contentious-Administrative Division) (Argentina)
1962-I J.A. 442 (1961)

2d Instance. – Buenos Aires, March 7, 1961. – [Following a minor disturbance at the headquarters of the Club Hípico Argentino, the plaintiff Moris, a member of the Club, was suspended from membership by order of the "intervenor," an official who had been appointed by the national government to manage the Club's affairs temporarily. (The propriety of the government's intervention is not in issue; all parties have treated the case as if the Club's own officers had suspended the plaintiff.) The plaintiff appealed from the decision of the intervenor to the Club's meeting, as he was entitled to do by the Club bylaws. This appeal was permitted, but his suspension continued in effect pending the next meeting. A successful appeal to the meeting, then, might simply wipe out the plaintiff's suspension after its period had terminated. The court of 1st Instance granted the amparo, ordering the intervenor to lift the suspension until the next meeting. The intervenor appealed to this court on several grounds, but particularly on the ground that the plaintiff's asserted constitutional right to freedom of association has not been injured.] . . .

. . . [T]he guarantee of "association for useful purposes" contained in art. 14 of the National Constitution is not to be understood as referring only to the act of forming an association and drawing up its bylaws, but must also necessarily include the power to exercise the rights that those bylaws confer, and to make use of the association in accordance with its rules. Thus, when one of the members is deprived of prerogatives that explicitly or implicitly arise from the provisions that govern the organization, it cannot be maintained validly that the constitutional guarantee is unaffected.

... [I]n the present case a sanction was applied to the plaintiff by an authority that was not one of those designated by the [Club] bylaw. As no one has questioned the right of the [national] Executive Power to intervene in the affairs of the Club, we need not consider the matter. Besides, the bylaws contain a complete, regulated procedure for disciplining members, which in this case was not observed because of lack of leadership in the competent organs, as the intervenor conceded. Nor is it proper to pass judgment in this respect, because within the Club a competent organ is provided to do so, that organ being the meeting of members.

But an appeal to that meeting exists – and this the intervenor conceded – notwithstanding which, he ordered . . . the suspension.

Accepting the legitimacy of this intervention, one cannot deny to the intervenor the power to adopt necessary means for maintaining the normal functioning of the Club. Among those means must be the minimum disciplinary power indispensable to that end.

In the present case one cannot see that Moris' conduct could be so serious as to compromise the normal functioning of the Club . . . . It follows that it is arbitrary to require him to comply with a sanction imposed without . . . awaiting the judgment of the meeting, which was the reasonable course. This illegality of the intervenor's conduct justifies judicial interference to safeguard the aforementioned constitutional guarantee ("Fallos," vol. 245, p. 542).

Furthermore, judicial [protection] becomes necessary because, as the judge of 1st Instance stated, the meeting might be delayed until after completion of the punishment, or at least until a good part of it had been completed. This possibility shows that relegating the question to the normal procedures can render the threatened constitutional guarantee illusory and cause Moris irreparable harm . . . .

For these considerations the appealed decision is affirmed. . . . The intervenor of the Club Hípico Argentino is ordered to suspend execution of the sanction applied to Gustavo A. Moris until such time as the meeting of members of the Club may vote on the matter. . . .

---

3. Limitations on Amparo Review

LUMELLI

Supreme Court of Justice of Argentina
242 Fallos 300, 1959-III J.A. 410
94 La Ley 210 (1958)

Buenos Aires, November 21, 1958. – The Customs Administration of Bahía Blanca charged Omar Pablo Lumelli with having brought an automobile into the country illegally . . . . The Administration ordered seizure of the automobile and detention of the accused. The latter's wife brought an amparo action, which was rejected by the Federal Judge of Bahía Blanca. She immediately appealed to the Federal Chamber of Appeals . . ., which ordered release of the accused, but affirmed the decision of the court of 1st Instance "insofar as it refused amparo against the order of seizure."

Lumelli's wife has filed an extraordinary appeal against the appellate decision, which she seeks to revoke on the ground that there has been a violation of the right to property and of various other provisions of the National Constitution.

As the Procurator General has certainly demonstrated, the complainant-appellant is not entitled to invoke the right of property. This circumstance bars the claim of amparo, in the absence of any rule to the contrary, such as that established by the procedural laws regarding *habeas corpus*. It is proper so to declare in this case, *a fortiori* since the owner of the seized automobile was himself in a position to defend his right, for the order of detention against him was inoperative prior to commencement of the present appeal.

Furthermore, the act against which the claim is asserted was executed by an administrative authority which, in the emergency, exercised jurisdictional powers given by [a 1956 law]. Because of this fact, the protection asked by the appellant could not be sought from agencies foreign to the case in which the seizure was ordered, but rather it had to be requested in compliance with the pertinent formal provisions of [the 1956 law]. These provisions, in principle, should be considered as excluding the exceptional remedy constituted by the claim of amparo.

[Amparo was denied.]

G. BIDART CAMPOS, REGIMEN LEGAL JURISPRUDENCIAL DEL AMPARO

Pp. 317-18 (1968)

Although, in principle, a person who requests amparo must establish the existence of a certain and incontestable right,[60] there are situations in which the existence of a mere legitimate interest suffices. . . . The notion of legitimate interest, rooted in administrative law, has served as the basis for a notable diffusion of the objective appeal or annulment [in judicial review of administrative action], and it is now invoked in constitutional law as a basis for complaints in amparo . . . .

When in its decision of December 9, 1960, the Federal Chamber of Rosario accepted the amparo brought by the Dean of the Faculty of Medical Sciences of the University of the Litoral against the occupation of the building by students, the court based its decision on the ground that such an occupation impeded the Faculty from developing its specific activity, and caused harm, "in prejudice of professors and students, to the right to teach and learn that is consecrated in art. 14 of the National

---

[60]The requirement of a certain and incontestable right has been drawn from the 1934 Brazilian Constitution's standards for the writ of security. [Eds.]

Constitution." It added "that it cannot be questioned that the Dean, as the indisputable authority of the mentioned Faculty, has the power to request the immediate reestablishment of the order which has been subverted, in order to make possible the normal functioning of the Faculty." (J.A. 1961-IV, p. 61.) In reality the constitutional right to teach and learn was not that of the Dean who requested amparo, but that of the professors and students . . . [T]he Dean was invested legally only with a legitimate interest, which was sufficient to confer standing on him in this summary action.

PAMPINELLA

Federal Chamber of the Capital
(Contentious-Administrative Division) (Argentina)
1961-II J.A. 62, 102 La Ley 312 (1959)

2d Instance. – Buenos Aires, November 18, 1959. – . . . [A social security fund appealed from an amparo decision ordering it to readjust a member's pension benefit.]

The Fund argues . . . that according to present doctrine and case law, amparo . . . will not lie unless there are no other procedures established by law for the protection of the rights claimed to be infringed. It maintains that, precisely for cases such as this, Law No. 14.236 instituted a specific procedure through which members may obtain a rapid and effective decision, without having to resort to other exceptional procedures, and that Pampinella has not followed this course.

In another line of argument, the appellant asserts that the amparo allowed in this case is also improper inasmuch as the alleged infringement of the member's right does not arise from an act contrary to the law, since the Fund has completely complied with the rules of Law No. 14.499. That law forbids it to liquidate [its obligation to pay a supplementary amount equalling 82% of the base pension figure] until the Executive Power issues the relevant regulations. [The law required the issuance of regulations within 90 days after its enactment, but some two years later, at the time of this action, no regulation had yet been issued.]

In accordance with the doctrine established by the Supreme Court [citations to the *Siri* and *Kot* cases], . . . in order for amparo to be allowable in cases such as this, it is necessary that: a) there be an illegal act, the existence of which is clear and manifest; b) one of the rights of liberty directly protected by the National Constitution be injured by that act; c) the injured person not have another legal means of defending his right or that the means provided by the laws be ineffective in avoiding serious and irreparable harm.

. . . [W]hile it is true that the Fund did not fulfill its obligation to readjust officially the pension of the petitioner Blas Pampinella, it is also true that the latter never complained of this conduct to the Directorate of the Fund, which is the organ in charge of "resolving all disputes concerning the granting of pensions," according to the function given to it in art. 11, par. (d), Law No. 14.236. Had he proceeded in this manner, assuming that the Directorate should deny his petition, he then had the legal possibility (art. 13) of bringing a revocation appeal in the same Fund, and of further appeal . . . to the National Institute of Social Security. From the decision of the latter, he still had the appeal foreseen by art. 14 before the labor court.

Since a complete procedure, regulated by law, exists to confirm petitions of the kind that has given rise to the present amparo, it is through that procedure and before the competent administrative and judicial authorities that the plaintiff . . . should have defended his rights. He did not need to use an exceptional method such as the one chosen, which is recognized as legitimate only for those cases in which any defense could prove illusory in the absence of an adequate procedural system.

By reason of these considerations, the appealed sentence is revoked insofar as it was the subject of this appeal. . . .

TRAVERSO

Federal Chamber of the Capital
(Contentious-Administrative Division) (Argentina)
1961-II J.A. 53 (1959)

2d Instance. – Buenos Aires, November 23, 1959. – . . .

[Conrado T. Traverso had been in the foreign service of the Argentine government since 1922. In 1946 he was appointed, with the consent of the Senate, to the position of Ambassador Extraordinary and Plenipotentiary. In 1947 his "resignation" – which he had never submitted – was accepted by the government. After the 1955 overthrow of the Perón regime, Traverso sought reinstatement. In 1958 he was appointed Ambassador to Venezuela, and later in the same year he was transferred to the Ministry of Foreign Relations, again with the title of Ambassador Extraordinary and Plenipotentiary. In 1959 he was removed from this post by an executive decree. He brought amparo against the enforcement of the decree, seeking restoration to his position as ambassador. He succeeded in the court of 1st Instance. The judge held that the decree which removed Traverso from his ambassadorial title was invalid, and that he must be reinstated. The effect of this decision was to leave him his title, but not to require the executive to use him in any particular ambassadorial post.]

The first issue to be decided is whether the proper procedural route has been chosen.

. . . [I]n accordance with the doctrine established by the Supreme Court, the following conditions must be present [to allow amparo:] . . . [a] that an illegal act take place, the illegality of which is clear and manifest; and [b] that this act damage one of the rights of liberty directly protected by the National Constitution. The final condition is [c] that the injured person not have available another legal means to defend himself or that the provisions of the laws be ineffective to prevent his suffering a serious and irreparable harm.

It is a matter of establishing, then, whether the present case fulfills the stated conditions . . . .

a) As Ambassador Traverso asserts, the National Constitution provides that the Executive Power "name and remove plenipotentiary ministers and chargés d'affaires with the agreement of the Senate" (art. 86, par. 10). Article 30 of Law 12.951, in accord with this higher rule, establishes: "The civil servant appointed with the agreement of the Senate shall retain his employment during good conduct and his removal must be carried out in the same manner [*i.e.*, with the consent of the Senate]."

[Traverso had reached the age and level of seniority which entitled him to a pension upon his removal from office. He refused to accept the pension, however, because the acceptance might be considered a waiver of his objections to being removed without the consent of the Senate.]

The *fiscal* of the chamber [a government attorney who advises the court] compares the status of diplomats to that of judges and military officers, maintaining that the ones who have true constitutional immunity from removal are the judicial magistrates. He says that military status does not prevent [compulsory] retirement of higher officers, for whose appointment the agreement of the Senate is necessary. This is said to be the case of Ambassador Traverso, whose active functions only have been terminated.

However, it does not seem that these three positions in the constitutional system are very similar. The Great Charter uses different rules in referring to each of them. . . . [The Constitution expressly requires the agreement of the Senate for their removal as well as their appointment.]

Neither can the argument be accepted that only active functions were taken away from this Ambassador, since that act involves depriving him of one of the essential rights belonging to a civil servant, . . . the right to discharge the duties of the office.

b) From what has been stated above, it also appears that the second requisite for allowability of amparo has been established in this case. . . . [S]ince the reform of 1957, the National Constitution assures stability of public employment.

c) It is asserted that an ordinary action is available to Traverso to protect the rights he claims. But he states that he has received neither salary nor pension, producing a true economic burden for him. Likewise he says that if he agrees to retire, it could be interpreted as waiver of the judicial action. He ends by saying that the "economic pressure, accentuated through the indefinite duration of an ordinary action, would be transformed into a kind of moral violence, in order to force me to acquiesce in the arbitrariness of the Executive Power."

It is clear that if this gentleman obtains the pension due him, via ordinary procedure, he will not be caused the serious and irreparable injury demanded for the allowability of the recourse of amparo. But to decide now that that attitude does not carry with it the waiver of the action of which he might avail himself . . . would mean prejudging a matter to be decided . . . by the tribunals that would hear the relevant actions. Naturally, such an occurrence should be avoided. . . .

The present case does not involve fact situations that require the evidentiary breadth of ordinary proceedings; neither is its juridical aspect intricate, so as to make fuller debate indispensable. In such conditions it is practical and equitable to ease the rigor of the requirement . . . and not to make dogmatic assertions for the sheer love of principles. This is clear where the illegality of the imputed behavior is not in doubt, as in the present case.

For these considerations the appealed judgment is affirmed.

Note

On April 7, 1961, the Supreme Court of Argentina reversed this decision on the ground that ordinary judicial remedies were avilable to Traverso. His assertion of "economic pressure" was said to be common to all litigants who seek economic relief, whether against private defendants or against the state. 249 Fallos 457, 1961-IV J.A. 502, 106 La Ley 415.

COMMUNIST PARTY

Federal Chamber of Resistencia (Argentina)
1960-V J.A. 531, 101 La Ley 576 (1960)

2d Instance. — Resistencia, February 25, 1960. — 1st. The decision of the court of 1st Instance, opposed by the *fiscal* of that instance, comes for consideration by this chamber. That decision allows the amparo brought by the Communist Party of [the Province of] Formosa, prejudiced by the resolution of the Ministry of the Interior of the Province, preventing the Party from holding public meetings in the electoral campaign preceding the national and provincial elections of next March 27. The plaintiff Party takes the position that such a measure violates the letter and spirit of the National and Provincial Constitutions, the Statute on Political Parties, and the laws and decrees of the present electoral system. It adds that its request for permission to hold public meetings was rejected in accordance with decree No. 4965/59, which, it asserts, is "patently unconstitutional," since neither the state of siege now in force (from which this decree arises), nor the decree itself, applies in Formosa Province, nor does the decree have any remote justification. . . .

2d. The federal judge of 1st Instance granted the requested protection, finding that because the Communist Party has electoral agents in Formosa and there has been no final decision on the pending request for cancellation of its corporate personality, and holding that Decree No. 4965/59 violates the decision of the electoral judge according the appellant Party all electoral rights. . . .

3d. This chamber in a similar opinion, opposed by the same party, has declared that it is clear from the presentation that the Party is trying to weaken or dispute the constitutional force of National Decree No. 4965/59 through the highly summary means of amparo. And this tribunal determined the impropriety of such an aim, since this exceptional method is to be used only when there is no procedure that might assure greater discussion [101 La Ley 572] . . . .

The demand of the appellant body that "our party be permitted to hold public meetings" and that "all the public meetings held by the Communist Party of Formosa in the current electoral campaign . . . be authorized on an equal plane with the other political groups," necessarily signifies a formal request for a declaration of unconstitutionality of a decree of the Executive Power. This issue cannot be determined through the very summary remedy of amparo, but rather through the normal means of the proper [ordinary] action. . . .

Therefore, the fiscal of the chamber having been heard, the decision that allows amparo is revoked. . . .

ASERRADERO CLIPPER, S.R.L.

Supreme Court of Justice of Argentina
249 Fallos 221, 1961-IV J.A. 108, 103 La Ley 315 (1961)

Buenos Aires, March 2, 1961. − . . . [The plaintiffs have succeeded in both the 1st and 2d Instances in their action of amparo against the National Directorate of Customs, based on an alleged administrative violation of a legislative decree. The customs officials have refused to hand over certain merchandise until the plaintiffs paid charges that the plaintiffs consider illegal.]

2d. The court below considers it possible to dispense with the requirement of prior payment of the duties questioned in this case, in exceptional instances in which the illegality of the charge is obvious. . . .

3d. Such a decision would mean a profound change of the system in force since the enactment of [a procedural statute], according to which the action for a declaration of unconstitutionality does not exist in the national procedural order. For, as this Court pointed out on a recent occasion (245 Fallos 552), "the application of the precepts of the laws of the Nation may not be hindered by an action for a declaration of unconstitutionality. This conclusion also accords with the presumption of validity that should be given to the acts of the constituted authorities and most particularly to the laws enacted by the Congress of the Nation. It also arises from the fact that, in the national procedural order, the prosecution of actions such as those giving rise to this complaint has not been provided for," that is, the impugning of the constitutionality of a law by means of a declaratory action.

4th. Since the decision of this Court . . . [in the *Siri* case], the institution of the action of amparo by decisional means has corresponded (as subsequent case law has repeatedly explained) to the necessity of giving due judicial protection to the human rights contained in the National Constitution, in those cases in which there is no legal means of according protection. Legitimate as this case law is when it fills an authentic vacuum, it is not legitimate when used to substitute another remedy, subjectively considered more appropriate by the Nation's judges, in place of the legislative criterion as to the form and means of the defense of property rights. Such substitution cannot be attempted without an obvious attack on the cardinal principle of the separation of powers and the preeminence . . . of Congressional laws, insofar as they may be enacted in accordance with the National Constitution. . . .

[The Court notes that according to clear precedent, the only way to attack a tax or other public tribute is to pay it and then sue for its recovery. The Court also notes the seriousness of the problem of evasion of customs duties in Argentina, a problem which requires prompt and effective administrative action.]

... [T]he action of amparo, whose procedure is most summary and does not permit sufficient discussion of the questioned tariffs, is capable of upsetting the system that the legislator provided for the control of imports. ... If it were accepted that the action of amparo might serve to fetter the activity of the State in such situations, the risk would be created that amparo, which is only a means for the protection of constitutional rights, could be converted to the opposite; that is, the failure to protect the right of each and every person from the behavior of those who deceitfully damage the national economy and offend the moral bases of the community. ...

Therefore, the Procurator General having expressed his opinion, the appealed decision is revoked and the complaint rejected. Costs will be apportioned in all instances.

Note

Compare the Supreme Court's treatment of amparo as a device for declaring statutes or decrees unconstitional in *J. Carlos Outon y otros, infra,* p. 179. For a thorough discussion of this issue, see G. Bidart Campos, *Régimen Legal y Jurisprudencial del Amparo* 119-161 (1968).

---

4. Codification of Amparo

Although there had been a series of proposals and draft statutes to eliminate the anomaly (to the civilian mind) of a judicially created juridical institution, it was not until the 1966 Revolution, when the President assumed the legislative power, that amparo was given statutory embodiment.

THE ACTION OF AMPARO – REGULATING LAW

Law 16.986, October 18, 1966
Law 16.986, October 18, 1967-A A.L.J.A., p. 500

The President of the Argentine nation sanctions and promulgates with the force of law:

Article 1 — The writ of amparo shall be admissible against every act and omission of public authority which, in its present or imminent form, injures, restricts, alters, or threatens, with manifest arbitrariness or illegality, the rights or guarantees explicitly or implicitly recognized by the National Constitution, with the exception of individual liberty protected by habeas corpus.

Article 2 — The writ of amparo shall not be admissible when:

(a) Judicial or administrative recourses or remedies exist which permit protection of the constitutional right or guarantee at issue;

(b) The challenged act emanates from an organ of the judicial power or has been adopted by the express application of Law 16.970 [The National Defense Law] ;

(c) Judicial intervention would directly or indirectly compromise the regularity, continuity and efficacy of performance of a public service, or the development of activities essential to the state;

(d) The determination of the eventual invalidity of the act requires greater amplitude of debate or proof, or declaring laws, decrees, or ordinances unconstitutional;

(e) The complaint has not been presented within 15 workdays, starting from the date on which the act was executed or ought to have taken effect.

Article 3 — If the writ is clearly inadmissible, the judge shall reject it summarily, ordering the proceedings to be filed in the archives.

Article 4 — The Judge of the First Instance with jurisdiction in the place where the act is manifested or has or could have effect, shall be competent to grant the writ of amparo. . . .

Article 5 — The writ of amparo may be brought, either personally on behalf of any individual or juridical entity or by attorney who considers himself (herself or itself) affected in conformance with provisions set out in Article 1. . . .

Article 6 — The complaint shall be in writing and shall set out:

(a) The name, surname, and real (and designated) domicile of the complainant;

(b) The identification, insofar as is possible, of the author of the challenged act or omission;

(c) Relation of the extreme circumstances which have produced or are about to produce injury to a constitutional right or guarantee;

(d) The relief requested, in clear and precise terms.

Article 7 — The complainant shall accompany the written complaint with the documentary proof at his disposal; if not within his control, he shall identify it and indicate the place where it may be found.

He shall also indicate other measures of proof upon which he intends to rely.

The number of witnesses may not exceed five for each party. . . .

Article 8 — When the suit is admissible, the judge shall require the corresponding authority to submit, within a prudently fixed period, a report setting forth the background and bases of the challenged measure. Failure to request such a report is cause for nullity of the process. . . .

When the report has been produced, or the period fixed for its submittal has elapsed, and the complainant has no proof to transmit, judgment conceding or denying amparo shall be entered within 48 hours.

Article 9 — If any of the parties have offered proof, its immediate production shall be ordered, with a date for the hearing to be fixed within three days. . . .

Article 11 — When the report referred to in Article 8 has been submitted, or, where called for, an evidentiary hearing has taken place, the judge shall render a decision within three days. . . .

Article 12 — A judgment which grants the writ shall contain:

(a) Concrete mention of the authority against whose resolution, act, or omission amparo has been conceded;

(b) Precise result of the conduct to be observed. . . .;

(c) The time by which the result must be carried out.

Article 13 — The final decision, which declares the existence or nonexistence of the injury, restriction, alteration or arbitrary or manifestly illegal threat to a constitutional right or guarantee, is *res judicata* with respect to the amparo, leaving unaffected the exercise of actions or recourses which the parties may have independent of amparo. . . .

Article 15 — Only final judgments, the determinations provided for in Article 3, and . . . [decisions with a suspensive effect] shall be appealable. The appeal shall be taken within 48 hours of notification of the result challenged and shall set forth reasons for the challenge. [The appeal shall be either denied or granted within 48 hours.] In the latter case, the matter shall be sent up to the respective appellate court within 24 hours of being granted. . . .

Article 18 — This law shall apply in the Federal Capital and in the territory of Tierra del Fuego, Antarctica, and the Isles of the South Atlantic.

It shall also be applied by federal judges in the provinces in cases in which the act challenged by writ of amparo stems from a national authority. . . .

Question

How does this statute modify the law of amparo as developed by the Argentine courts?

This 1966 statute raises issues parallel to those presented to the U.S. Supreme Court in *Sheldon v. Sill,* 8 How. 441 (1850), and *Ex Parte McCardle,* 7 Wall. 506 (1869).

Under the Argentine Constitution, to what extent does the Congress (or the Executive when acting as the legislature) have the power to regulate or restrict the jurisdiction of the courts in matters of amparo? Is the case for unrestricted power of the legislature to curtail judicial jurisdiction stronger in Argentina than in the U.S.? In answering these questions, consider the following constitutional provisions and cases.

CONSTITUTION OF ARGENTINA (1853)

Article 31 — This Constitution, the laws of the Nation enacted by the Congress in pursuance thereof, and treaties with foreign powers are the supreme law of the Nation; and the authorities in every Province are bound thereby, notwithstanding any provision to the contrary which the provincial laws or constitutions may contain. . . .

Article 94 — The Judicial Power of the Nation shall be vested in a Supreme Court of Justice and in such lower courts as the Congress may establish in the territory of the Nation.

Article 100 — The Supreme Court of Justice and the lower courts of the Nation have jurisdiction over and decide all cases dealing with matters governed by the Constitution and the laws of the Nation, with the exception made in item 11, article 67;[61] and by treaties with foreign nations; all suits concerning ambassadors, public ministers, and foreign consuls; of cases in admiralty and maritime jurisdiction; of suits in which the Nation is a party; of suits between two or more Provinces; between one Province and the citizens of another; between the citizens of different Provinces; and between one Province and its citizens against a foreign State or citizen.

Article 101 — In these cases the Supreme Court shall exercise appellate jurisdiction, according to rules and exceptions prescribed by Congress; but in all matters concerning ambassadors, ministers, and foreign consuls, and those in which any Province shall be a party, the Court shall exercise original and exclusive jurisdiction.

DIAZ COLODRERO

National Chamber of Appeals of Peace
of the Federal Capital (Argentina)
1967-II J.A. 356 (1966)

2d Instance. — Buenos Aires, November 25, 1966 — . . .

[Complainant was dismissed from membership by a committee of his union, without being afforded a hearing, for habitually keeping a messy room in violation of union rules. Considering the dismissal manifestly unjust and arbitrary, the member instituted an amparo action against the union, alleging that the dismissal violated his

---

[61] This exception refers to congressional power to enact civil, commercial, penal, mining, labor, and social security codes, which are not to alter local jurisdictions. [Eds.]

constitutional rights, and that he needed to be able to live in the quarters supplied by the union in order to continue residing in Buenos Aires. The lower court rejected his suit, and the complainant appealed.

[The appellate court is faced with the threshold issue of whether amparo will lie against an act of a private party, or an organized group of individuals, after the enactment of Law 16.986.]

Dr. Echegaray said: . . .

I consider, however, that despite its apparently all inclusive denomination ("Action of Amparo-Regulating Law"), the legal text intends only to regulate as to both substance and form, the right and the exercise of the action of amparo in certain types of proceedings — those in which the injury to a constitutionally declared liberty is attributable to the public authority — leaving the others (aggressions committed by individuals or private entities) governed by the guiding principles laid down by the doctrine and case law starting with the leading case of *Kot*. As a man of law and a magistrate, I cannot even suppose that through a simple omission, it was desired to disdain the conclusions . . . of prestigious judges and eminent treatise writers [as to the need] for the immediate preservation or the rapid reestablishment of essential rights guaranteed by the Constitution . . .; especially when that understanding does not contradict but rather concords with the purposes of the National Revolution, among whose declared objectives one finds "defending the dignity and respect for the human person, based upon an authentic liberty" . . . .

Thus one understands that the . . . said revolutionary purposes are not directed against the fundamental principles of the National Constitution, but, on the contrary, identify with them insofar as they have as their object, according to the emphatic declaration contained in the Preamble, "to secure the blessings of liberty to ourselves, to our posterity, and to all men of the world who may wish to inhabit Argentine soil." . . .

Since Law 16.986 has been limited to the regulation of the exercise of the . . . [amparo] action when the respondent is a "public authority," demonstrating that . . . there is nothing in the existing political order which opposes the implicit institutional guarantee upon which [amparo] is founded, it is evident that the amparo action directed against individuals or private entities has not been derogated by the said statute. Nor may it be properly inferred by application of the formal logical principle of non-contradiction ("inclusio unius est alterius exclusio"), since the legal text . . ., in declaring . . . [amparo] "admissible" under the enunciated supposition, has not signified that [amparo] ceases to be [admissible] in the non-legislated ambit (a non-state activity).

. . . [The message which accompanied the submission of the draft of the amparo statute to the President explicitly referred to the] "worthy antecedents . . . of the various provincial laws and the draft statutes on the theme," as well as to the "doctrinal and case law material elaborated with respect to the said institution." This clearly indicates that, in the absence of an express reservation, it was not intended to lay aside precedents so important as the Weidman project presented to the federal Senate or the laws in force in the Provinces of Buenos Aires, Santa Cruz, San Luis, and Mendoza, to whose regimes the public or private origin of the aggression is irrelevant.

Neither has the ample criterion which prevailed as to this aspect in the opinion of writers been abandoned, nor [has] the firm current in the same sense . . . in the case law starting with the *Kot* case. . . .

For all of these considerations, I am of the opinion that Law 16.986, which regulates the action of amparo, does not apply . . . [to the case] which is not directed against state authority. Consequently, since the basis of amparo is rooted in the Constitution itself, in the immediate operation of its implicit guarantees, . . . the case law doctrine is maintained in full effect . . . when the respondent of the action is an individual, an organized group of persons, or private law entity. . . .

[On the merits the court voted to deny the amparo for several reasons: *inter alia,* the appellant's constitutional rights had not been clearly and manifestly violated by the dismissal, which conformed to the union's by-laws, and the failure to afford appellant a hearing was not a violation of due process since the by-laws afforded him an opportunity to appeal to the general assembly of the union.]

CARLOS J. OUTON Y OTROS

Supreme Court of Justice of Argentina
267 Fallos 215, 1967-II J.A. 369, 126 La Ley 292 (1967)

[In 1964 the Executive issued a decree which in effect required all maritime workers to be members of a union in order to work. A number of maritime workers brought an amparo action to invalidate the decree as an unlawful interference with their constitutionally protected rights to work and of free association.

[The court of first instance conceded the amparo and ordered that the petitioners be allowed to work without showing evidence of union membership as required by the 1964 decree.

[The court of second instance reversed because the relief accorded by the lower court necessarily implied a declaration that the decree in question was unconstitutional, and several Supreme Court decisions had held that amparo was not the proper remedy to challenge the constitutionality of statutes or decrees. The dismissal of the action was without prejudice to make the same constitutional challenge via the extraordinary appeal (*recurso extraordinario*), a rather lengthy proceeding.]

Buenos Aires, March 29, 1967. . . .

The admission of this exceptional remedy [amparo] can engender the false belief that any litigious question can be resolved by this route; or worse yet, that via [amparo] it is possible to obtain precipitous declarations of unconstitutionality. Hence, the decisions of this Court have established that, in principle, the declaration of unconstitutionality in this type of proceeding is improper. . . .

Nevertheless, the principle should not be taken as absolute. Undoubtedly, it will govern the great majority of cases. But when the provisions of a law, decree, or ordinance clearly result in violations of any human rights, the existence of a regulation cannot constitute an obstacle to the immediate reestablishment . . . of the violated fundamental guarantee. Otherwise, an authority could resort to the device of preceding its arbitrary acts or omissions with a prior norm . . . in order to frustrate the possibility of obtaining immediate restitution of the . . . trampled right in court.

For this reason, and precisely because Law 16.986 . . . was intended to set out norms for this exceptional proceeding in order better to assure the exercise of individual guarantees against arbitrariness and manifest illegality, its article 2(d) must be interpreted as a reasonable measure designed to prevent the amparo action from being utilized capriciously to impede effective enforcement of laws and regulations dictated in accordance with the provisions of the Constitution. But [it should not be interpreted] as a measure tending to impede fulfillment of [its own] purposes. . . .

Although the letter of article 2(d) of Law 16.986 "prima facie" supports the proposition that the unconstitutionality of a norm never can be declared in an amparo proceeding, a correct interpretation — which takes into account not only the literal text but also the ends pursued . . . — ought to lead, in this case, to the conclusion that . . . in principle it is improper to declare unconstitutionality in a summary proceeding such as amparo. But this is not to be understood in an absolute sense, for to do so would be the equivalent of destroying the very essence of the institution, . . . safeguarding substantial personal rights when no other effective remedy exists.

. . . Whatever be the procedure through which a justiciable question is presented for judicial decision, no one can subtract from the sphere of action of the Judicial Power its inalienable prerogative and obligation — emanating directly from article 31 of the National Constitution [the Supremacy Clause, *supra,* p. 177] — to respect the Fundamental Law and, in particular, the personal guarantees recognized in its first part. [This is] without forgetting that article 100 expressly provides that "the Supreme Court and the lower courts of the Nation have jurisdiction over and decide all cases dealing with matters governed by the Constitution. . . ."

For this reason this Court declared in 33 Fallos 162 — where the constitutional validity of the law of expropriations of 1853 was questioned — . . . "it is elemental in our constitutional organization that the Tribunals of Justice have the prerogative and responsibility to examine the laws in concrete cases which are brought to their decision, comparing them with the text of the Constitution to determine whether they conform, and to abstain from applying [laws] opposed to the [Constitution] . This moderating prerogative constitutes one of the supreme and fundamental purposes of the national judicial power and one of the greatest guarantees . . . for assuring the rights set out in the Constitution against possible abuses . . . of public powers."

Consequently, there is no obstacle in the present case . . . to this Tribunal's examination and definitive resolution of whether the administrative decision based on . . . decree 280/64 . . . is contrary to the text and spirit of the National Constitution. . . .

In the case under examination there is no doubt about the nature of the rights which the complaint seeks to preserve, that is, the rights to work and to associate freely.

. . . When, as in the instant case, . . . the primary necessities of man are being compromised, one cannot argue about reasons of form if, in such way, one sacrifices a substantive right which must be safeguarded. . . .

The circumstance that the violation of fundamental rights is attributable to a decree of the Executive Power, which would give the act a presumption of legitimacy, cannot impede the progress of the amparo. Such presumption must be discarded when the illegitimacy of the act is clear because of its manifest contravention of a provision of the National Constitution. . . . The courts cannot deny amparo when there is no other way to invalidate the decree in such a way as to preserve the fundamental right and avoid opportunely grave and irreparable harm. . . .

[On the merits, the court held that the closed shop decree was an unconstitutional violation of the rights of the maritime workers to work and of free association. It therefore revoked the appealed decision and granted the amparo requested.]

Notes

1. The *Outon* case is discussed by Carlos Valiente Noailles in 126 La Ley 292 (1967).

2. The omission with regard to acts of private individuals in Law 16.986 was partially rectified in September of 1967 by passage of a new national Civil and Commercial Procedural Code, Law 17.454. Article 321 expressly provides for amparo against acts or omissions of individuals which injure constitutionally protected rights. However, this procedural code applies only to federal courts and those of the federal capital. It does not apply to the provincial courts, nor does it apply to certain specialized federal tribunals, such as the labor courts, criminal courts, or those which deal with crimes against the economy. G. Bidart Campos, *Régimen Legal y Jurisprudencial del Amparo* 109-110, 115-17 (1968).

3. For a general discussion of the implications of Laws 16.986 and 17.454, see Note, "The Writ of Amparo: A Remedy to Protect Constitutional Rights in Argentina," 31 *Ohio St. L. J.* 831 (1970).

4. The Argentine amparo is much more an extraordinary remedy than the Mexican amparo or the Brazilian writ of security. In sharp contrast to the thousands of amparo cases decided by the Mexican Supreme Court and the several hundred writ of security cases decided by the Brazilian Supreme Federal Tribunal, the Argentine Supreme Court has decided only a handful of cases each year. The table below shows the volume of amparo litigation in the Argentine Supreme Court from inception in 1957 to 1969.

Year	Number of Cases
1957	1
1958	6
1959	24
1960	37
1961	43
1962	30
1963	11

Year	Number of Cases
1964	17
1965	20
1966	18
1967	34
1968	28
1969 (thru October)	24

Compiled from Vocos Conesa, "La Demanda de Amparo en la Jurisprudencia de la Corte Suprema Nacional," 1969 *Reseñas J.A.,* p. 790.

E. Note on the Proliferation of Amparo

Many Latin American countries besides Mexico and Argentina have adopted the amparo as a device for protecting constitutional guaranties. In Costa Rica,[62] El Salvador,[63] and Panama,[64] amparo operates as a summary remedy to protect individual constitutional rights which are not protected by habeas corpus. Venezuela should perhaps be included within this grouping, but the present state of the law with respect to amparo is confusing.[65]

In Honduras[66] and Guatemala[67] amparo serves both as (1) a summary remedy to protect individual rights not protected by habeas corpus, and (2) a means of securing a speedy judicial declaration that a law or regulation does not apply to the plaintiff due to its unconstitutionality.

As a matter of form, the Nicaraguan amparo is closest to the Mexican amparo,[68] theoretically serving the functions of habeas corpus, protection of individual rights other than physical liberty, and challenging unconstitutional laws or decrees.[69] Nicaragua also, in theory, permits amparo to challenge the constitutionality of a law on its face.[70]

---

[62] Article 48 of the Constitution of 1949, regulated by Ley de Amparo (Ley No. 1161 of June 2, 1950, as modified August 9, 1952.)

[63] Article 221 of the Constitution of 1962; Ley de Procedimientos Constitucionales of Jan. 14, 1960, Articles 12-18.

[64] Article 49 of the Constitution of 1972, regulated by Ley sobre Recursos Constitucionales y de Garantía, Law No. 46 of Nov. 24, 1956. Of all the amparo statutes, this has the most summary procedure. The respondent authority is required to inform the court of its position within two hours after notification of the complaint and to suspend execution of the impugned act immediately. Articles 48 and 49. Decision is to be rendered within two days. Article 52.

[65] Article 49 (III) of the 1961 Constitution provides:

The courts shall protect (*ampararán*) every inhabitant of the Republic in the enjoyment and exercise of the rights and guaranties established by the Constitution, in conformance with the law (*Ley*). The procedure shall be brief and summary, and the proper judge shall have the power to restore immediately the infringed juridical situation.

Unfortunately, the legislature has never passed implementing legislation. When a litigant sought amparo in 1962, the Superior Court held that it had no power to concede amparo in the absence of

Three more Latin American countries adopted the amparo, at least as a matter of form, in 1967: Bolivia (Constitution of 1967, Article 19), Paraguay (Constitution of 1967, Article 77), and Ecuador (Constitution of 1967, Article 28 (15)). However, Ecuador's Constitution was abrogated in 1970, and constitutional guarantees have been suspended in Paraguay since 1947.

The procedural idiosyncracies of amparo in the various Latin American countries are described in Camargo, "The Right to Judicial Protection: 'Amparo' and Other Latin American Remedies for the Protection of Human Rights," 3 *Lawyer of the Americas* 191, 211-16 (1971); Fix Zamudio, "Latin American Procedures for the Protection of the Individual," 9 *J. Int'l Commission of Jurists,* No. 2, p. 60, 77-86 (December 1968); J. Othon Sidou, *Do Mandado de Segurança,* 131-178 (3rd ed. 1969). The multiplicity of usages ascribed to amparo in Hispanic-American legal lexicon is explored in Fix Zamudio, "Diversos Significados Jurídicos del Amparo en el Derecho Iberoamericano," 18 *Boletín del Instituto de Derecho Comparado de México* 119 (Jan.-April 1965).

F. Revolutions and Golpes

> *Treason doth never prosper; what's the reason?*
> *Why, if it prosper, none dare call it treason.*
>
> — Sir John Harrington (1561-1612), *Epigrams*

When visiting the Philadelphia Exposition in 1876, the Brazilian Emperor, Dom Pedro II, reputedly quipped that some of Brazil's neighbors had more revolutions per minute than many of the machines on exhibit. Dom Pedro's hyperbole was not excessive. "Venezuela is said to have experienced fifty-two major revolutions, in all, in the first century of its independent life, and Bolivia more than sixty — by 1952, indeed, more than one hundred and sixty."[71]

---

implementing legislation. Gutiérrez y Gutiérrez, 5 *Jurisprudencia Venezolana* 165 (1962). Seven years later, however, the same court reversed itself and granted amparo despite the absence of a regulatory statute. Manuel Beja Núñez en solicitud de Recurso de Amparo, 22 *Jurisprudencia Venezolana* 39 (1969). See also Procurador General de la República en recurso de amparo a favor de F. Wytack, 30 *Jurisprudencia Venezolana* 466 (Sup. Ct. 1971).

[66] Article 58 of the Constitution of 1965; Ley Constitucional de Amparo of April 14, 1936.

[67] Constitution of 1965, Articles 80-83, regulated by Ley de amparo, habeas corpus y constitucionalidad of April 28, 1966.

[68] See González Pérez, "El Processo de Amparo en Méjico y Nicaragua," 5 *Revista de Administración Pública* 297 (May-Aug. 1954).

[69] Ley de Amparo of Nov. 6, 1950, which, according to Article 323 of the Constitution of 1950 (as amended 1962), is a constitutional law. This Nicaraguan statute is peculiar in that it considers habeas corpus as part of amparo, yet on occasion refers to the institution of habeas corpus.

[70] Ley de Amparo of Nov. 6, 1950, Art. 5.

[71] R. A. Humphreys, *Tradition and Revolt in Latin America* 13 (1969).

The word "revolution" is used loosely and often in Latin America. With the exceptions of the Mexican Revolution of 1910, the Cuban Revolution of 1958, the short-lived Guatemalan Revolution of 1954, and arguably the Bolivian Revolution of 1952, the so-called Latin America "revolutions" have not been social revolutions, producing fundamental changes in societal structure or in the bases of power. Rather they have been more on the order of *coups d'état* (in Spanish, *golpes de estado*) in which essentially only the heads of government change. There are, of course, a great many variations on the theme of seizing power, ranging from the barracks revolt to the full-dress civil war.[72] In the context of this chapter the term revolution is used to refer to any successful change in government by extra-legal means.

Some Latin American nations do change their governments in accordance with constitutional procedures. Opposition parties have won in honest elections in countries like Chile, Costa Rica, and Uruguay.[73] Nevertheless, as the table below shows, the governments of nearly all Latin American nations have changed hands by extra-legal means several times in the years since 1930, which have witnessed more than 100 successful *golpes* in 19 Latin American nations.

Table 1 shows only a part of the extra-legal political process. It does not show the attempted *coups,* and for each successful *coup,* there were many more that were unsuccessful. For example, though the table shows no successful *coup d'état* in Bolivia in 1961, in that year there were 25 rebellions and 17 declarations of states of siege.[74] Nor does the table depict another common Latin American political phenomenon, *continuismo,* continuing an administration in power through constitutional manipulation and/or electoral fraud.[75] Thus, the long period of apparently constitutional rule in the Dominican Republic from 1930 to 1961 was the era of Trujillo, who blatantly rigged elections and ruthlessly exterminated opposition while paying elaborate lipservice to the forms of constitutionalism. Much the same sort of situation prevailed in neighboring Haiti, ruled from 1957 to 1971 by François Duvalier, a ruthless dictator who had himself declared "President for Life." Nicaragua has been under the iron-handed rule of the Somoza family since 1936; the 1947 *coup* was the result of a short-lived effort of a puppet president to assert his independence of the Somozas. Since 1954 Paraguay has been under the dictatorial rule of General Alfredo Stroessner, who has twice removed the constitutional barrier to the president's serving more than two terms. Finally, the table does not reflect the number of presidential assassinations or election frauds.

---

[72] See K. Silvert, *supra* note 1, at 19-24; Stokes, "Violence as a Power Factor in Latin American Politics," 5 *W. Pol. Q.* 445 (1952).

[73] Both Uruguay and Chile have recently undergone political and economic crises which threaten to shatter their democratic traditions. In July 1973, Uruguayan President Bordaberry, backed by the military, abolished congress; since then he has been ruling by decree. The efforts of the Allende regime to socialize Chile's economy by operating within the existing legal framework terminated in a bloody military *golpe* in September 1973. The Chilean congress has been disbanded, and the country is currently being ruled by a military junta.

[74] Estado de São Paulo, August 22, 1971, p. 3.

[75] See Fitzgibbon, " 'Continuismo' in Central America and the Caribbean," 2 *Inter-American Quarterly,* p. 56 (July 1940).

TABLE 1

SUCCESSFUL GOLPES IN LATIN AMERICA 1930-1975 (APRIL)

Country	Number	Dates
Argentina	9	9/30, 6/43, 2/44, 9/55, 11/55, 3/62, 6/66, 6/70, 3/71
Bolivia	13	6/30, 11/34, 5/36, 7/37, 12/43, 8/46, 5/51, 4/52, 11/64, 9/69, 10/70 (2), 8/71
Brazil	6	10/30, 10/45, 8/54, 11/55, 4/64, 8/69
Chile	4	7/31, 6/32, 9/32, 9/73
Colombia	2	6/53, 5/57
Costa Rica	1	5/48
Cuba	4	8/33, 9/33, 3/52, 1/59
Dominican Republic	5	2/30, 5/61, 1/62, 9/63, 4/65
Ecuador	13	8/31, 10/31, 8/32, 8/35, 10/37, 5/44, 8/47, 9/47, 11/61, 7/63, 3/66, 6/70, 2/72
El Salvador	6	12/31, 5/44, 12/48, 1/49, 10/60, 1/61
Guatemala	6	12/30, 7/44, 10/44, 6/54, 10/57, 3/63
Haiti	7	1/46, 5/50, 12/56, 2/57, 4/57, 5/57, 6/57
Honduras	5	12/54, 10/56, 10/63, 12/72, 4/75
Mexico	—	
Nicaragua	2	6/36, 5/47
Panama	5	2/31, 10/41, 11/49, 1/55, 10/68
Paraguay	7	2/36, 8/37, 6/48, 1/49, 2/49, 9/49, 5/54
Peru	6	8/30, 3/31, 10/48, 7/62, 3/63, 10/68
Uruguay	2	4/33, 7/73
Venezuela	4	10/45, 11/48, 12/52, 1/58

On the other hand, emphasizing the number of successful revolutions that have occurred in Latin America is likely to mislead with respect to dislocations of daily economic activity. A citizen's only notice that a revolution has occurred may be the newspaper headlines the following day. In some countries it is not unrealistic to regard revolution as the functional equivalent of the election process as a means of rotating high governmental offices.

A number of safeguards are built into the political system to reduce violence. The right of diplomatic asylum is highly developed in Latin America, in practice almost invariably respected by even the strongest *de facto* regimes.[76] While occasionally an ousted president suffers a violent end, it is far more common for the victims of a *golpe* to find sanctuary in a friendly embassy prior to fleeing the country. Efforts made by successful revolutionaries to impede the escape of those ousted from power are generally perfunctory. Few victims of a *golpe* need worry about economic security; most have sufficient funds stashed in foreign banks in anticipation of their eventual deposal. Occasionally, an ex-dictator can make a comeback; for example, Getúlio Vargas, ousted by a military *golpe* in 1945, returned as Brazil's constitutionally elected president in 1950. Juan Domingo Perón, ousted by a military *golpe* in 1955, returned to Argentina in 1973 after a decisive electoral sweep by Peronist candidates, and was elected President later that year.[77] So-called "enemies of the revolution" are more likely to be pensioned off or assigned to a relatively insignificant post abroad than to be shot or incarcerated. To be sure, a few Latin American revolutions have resulted in great losses of life, but they are atypical. Generally, actual bloodshed is kept to a minimum. What is crucial is the show of force, not the actual use of force.

The disappearance of the monarchy left a legitimacy vacuum in Latin America. The frequent unconstitutional changes of government are clear evidence that an acceptable surrogate has still not been found for much of Latin America. Under Spanish rule, legitimacy was based upon divine title. In theory, at least, the constitutions of the new Latin American republics substituted popular sovereignty. But popular sovereignty presupposes free and honest elections and a considerable measure of juridical and social equality among citizens. Neither characteristic has been conspicuous in much of Latin America.

The hope has long been nourished that the number of revolutions might be sharply reduced if other nations of the hemisphere were disposed to withhold recognition from governments coming to power through extralegal means. The Central American treaties of 1907 and 1923 provided:

> [T]he governments of the Contracting Parties will not recognize any other government which may come into power in any of the five Republics through a *coup d'état* or a revolution against a recognized Government, as long as the freely elected representatives of the people thereof have not constitutionally reorganized the country.

Venezuela's former President Betancourt and President Kennedy unsuccessfully tried variations on this theme.

On August 3, 1962, four months after the forcible removal of Frondizi, Argentine Chancellor Bonifacio del Carril sent U.S. Secretary of State Dean Rusk a note outlining a proposal for a new doctrine for international recognition of *de facto*

---

[76] C. N. Ronning, *Diplomatic Asylum: Legal Norms and Political Reality in Latin American Relations* 218-19 (1965); S. Sinha, *Asylum and International Law* 218-45 (1971).

[77] Other examples of this phenomenon are Rojas Pinilla's "near miss" at regaining the presidency of Colombia in 1972, and Velasco Ibarra's incredible feat of being chosen for and removed from the Presidency of Ecuador on five separate occasions between 1935 and 1972.

governments in Latin America. His point of departure was Article 5(d) of the Charter of the Organization of American States, which provides that "the solidarity of the American States and the high purposes pursued by it require that their political organization be based upon the effective exercise of representative democracy."

Carril's proposal called for distinguishing between revolutions designed to destroy representative democracy and those designed to restore it. To the traditional criteria for recognition of a *de facto* government (effective control over the territory of the nation, and willingness and ability to fulfill the state's international obligations), Carril would add a third:

3. Autolimitation of the *de facto* government, concretized in principle with the following four points:

a. Respect for human rights;

b. Setting of a prudential but precise termination for the mandate of those governing;

c. Independence of the Judicial Power;

d. Renewal of constitutional life in conformance with the principles of representative democracy and through realization of free elections.[78]

Do you think adoption of such a proposal would be useful? *Cf.* Fenwick, "The Recognition of De Facto Governments: Is There a Basis for Inter-American Collective Action?," 58 *Am. J. Int'l. L.* 109 (1964); Cowan, "Current U.S. Recognition Policy in Latin America: Diplomatic Albatross," 4 *Comp. Jur. Rev.* 193 (1967).

Several unsuccessful attempts have been made to secure acceptance of an Inter-American convention on the recognition of *de facto* governments. The closest the American republics have come to such an agreement has been adoption of a resolution setting out an informal procedure to be followed whenever an established government is overthrown by extralegal means. This procedure simply recommends that the member states exchange views on the subject, considering, *inter alia,* whether the *de facto* regime proposes to hold free public elections within a reasonable period, to fulfill the country's preexisting international obligations, and to respect the human rights set forth in the American Declaration of the Rights and Duties of Man.[79]

Current practice indicates a resurgence of the Estrada Doctrine, which treats revolutionary and duly elected governments alike.[80]

---

[78] Cited in García, "Reconocimiento De Los Gobiernos De Facto," 7 *J. Interamer. Studies* 449, 459 (1965).

[79] Resolution XXVI of the Second Special Inter-American Conference at Rio de Janeiro, November 17-30, 1965. For a discussion of the history of recognition doctrine in the Americas, see H. de Vries & J. Rodríguez-Novás, *The Law of the Americas* 37-43 (1965).

[80] See Cochran, "The Estrada Doctrine and United States Policy," 5 *Lawyer of the Americas* 27 (1973).

1. The Right of Revolution

THE DECLARATION OF INDEPENDENCE OF THE UNITED STATES

July 4, 1776

We hold these truths to be self-evident, that all men are created equal, that they are endowed by their Creator with certain unalienable rights, that among these are Life, Liberty and the pursuit of Happiness. That to secure these rights, Governments are instituted among Men, deriving their just powers from the consent of the governed, That whenever any Form of Government becomes destructive of these ends, it is the Right of the People to alter or abolish it, and to institute new Government, laying its foundation on such principles and organizing its powers in such form, as to them shall seem most likely to effect their Safety and Happiness. Prudence, indeed, will dictate that Governments long established should not be changed for light and transient causes; and accordingly all experience hath shown, that mankind are more disposed to suffer, while evils are sufferable, than to right themselves by abolishing the forms to which they are accustomed. But when a long train of abuses and usurpations, pursuing invariably the same Object evinces a design to reduce them under absolute Despotism, it is their right, it is their duty, to throw off such Government, and to provide new Guards for their future security.

EL SALVADOR, CONSTITUTION OF 1962

Article 5. . . . Alternation in the exercise of the Presidency is indispensable for the maintenance of the established form of Government. Violation of this norm requires insurrection.

Article 7. The people's right to insurrection is recognized. Exercise of this right shall in no case produce abrogation of the laws, and shall be limited in its effects to the removal, as may be necessary, of the functionaries of the Executive Power, who shall be replaced in the manner established by this Constitution.

GUATEMALA, CONSTITUTION OF 1945

Article 2. The people may have recourse to rebellion.

Questions

1. What is the source of the so-called "right of revolution?"
2. Does explicitly stating the existence of such a right in a constitution serve any useful purpose?
3. If you were entrusted with the task of drafting a constitution for a Latin American nation troubled with chronic revolutions, would you include a provision similar to Article 7 of El Salvador's 1962 Constitution? See R. Gallardo, *Estudios de Derecho Constitucional Americano Comparado* 139-42 (1961).

---

2. The Status of the Constitution in a Revolutionary Regime

Asking what happens to the constitution during a Latin American revolution is rather like Holden Caulfield's asking what happens to the ducks in Central Park during the winter. Both the ducks and the constitutions have puzzling ways of disappearing and reappearing. Some constitution makers have attempted to provide for the eventuality of revolution. Do the following provisions serve any useful purpose?

MEXICO, CONSTITUTION OF 1917

Article 136. This Constitution shall not lose its force and effect even if its observance is interrupted by rebellion. In the event that a Government contrary to the principles which [this Constitution] sanctions is established through any public disturbance, its observance shall be reestablished as soon as the people recover their liberty. . . .

VENEZUELA, CONSTITUTION OF 1961

Article 119. All usurped authority is ineffective, and its acts are null.

Article 120. Every decision agreed to because of direct or indirect application of force, or through the assemblage of people with a subversive attitude, is null. . . .

Article 250. This Constitution shall not lose its effect even if its observance is interrupted by force or it is repealed by extra-constitutional means. In such eventuality, every citizen, whether an authority or not, has the duty to collaborate in the reestablishment of its effective validity.

Those found responsible for the acts set out in the first sentence of the preceding paragraph and the principal officers of subsequently organized governments shall be judged in accordance with this Constitution and laws enacted in conformity with it, if they have not contributed to the reestablishment of its force and effect. Congress may decree, by resolution approved by an absolute majority of its members, confiscation of all or part of the property of such persons, as well as those unlawfully enriched under the protection of usurpation, in order to reimburse the Republic for damages suffered.

HONDURAS, CONSTITUTION OF 1957

Article 340. This constitution shall not lose its effect and force, even if, owing to some rebellion or *golpe de estado,* Congress does not meet on the date indicated herein, or if for any other reason its observance is interrupted.

In such cases any Power that may have continued functioning legally, Legislative, Executive, or Judicial, is under the obligation to dictate without delay the measures necessary to obtain due compliance with the constitutional provisions that have been violated.

Doctrinal writers in Latin America have been divided on the question whether constitutions ought to recognize the right of revolution, and whether it makes sense to talk about justifiable and nonjustifiable revolutions. It is probably no accident that the clearest denials of the right of revolution come from authors whose countries have shown the greatest recent stability, such as Mexico and (before 1973) Chile.[81] The legal philosopher who is probably most influential in Latin America today is Hans Kelsen. To what extent does Kelsen's theory about the basic norm of a legal order and revolutionary change underlie the practice of courts and lawmakers in legitimizing revolutions in Latin American nations?

H. KELSEN, GENERAL THEORY OF LAW AND STATE

Pp. 115-18 (1945)*

a. *The Basic Norm and the Constitution*

The derivation of the norms of a legal order from the basic norm of that order is performed by showing that the particular norms have been created in accordance with the basic norm. To the question why a certain act of coercion − e.g., the fact that one individual deprives another individual of his freedom by putting him in jail − is a legal act, the answer is: because it has been prescribed by an individual norm, a judicial decision. To the question why this individual norm is valid as part of a definite legal order, the answer is: because it has been created in conformity with a criminal statute.

---

[81] See generally, R. Gallardo, *Estudios de Derecho Constitucional Americano Comparado* 115-20 (1961).

*Copyright 1945, Harvard University Press.

This statute, finally, receives its validity from the constitution, since it has been established by the competent organ in the way the constitution prescribes.

If we ask why the constitution is valid, perhaps we come upon an older constitution. Ultimately we reach some constitution that is the first historically and that was laid down by an individual usurper or by some kind of assembly. The validity of this first constitution is the last presupposition, the final postulate, upon which the validity of all the norms of our legal order depends. It is postulated that one ought to behave as the individual, or the individuals, who laid down the first constitution have ordained. This is the basic norm of the legal order under consideration. The document which embodies the first constitution is a real constitution, a binding norm, only on the condition that the basic norm is presupposed to be valid. Only upon this presupposition are the declarations of those to whom the constitution confers norm-creating power binding norms. It is this presupposition that enables us to distinguish between individuals who are legal authorities and other individuals whom we do not regard as such, between acts of human beings which create legal norms and acts which have no such effect. All these legal norms belong to one and the same legal order because their validity can be traced back – directly or indirectly – to the first constitution. That the first constitution is a binding legal norm is presupposed, and the formulation of the presupposition is the basic norm of this legal order. The basic norm of a religious norm system says that one ought to behave as God and the authorities instituted by Him command. Similarly, the basic norm of a legal order prescribes that one ought to behave as the "fathers" of the constitution and the individuals – directly or indirectly – authorized (delegated) by the constitution command. Expressed in the form of a legal norm: coercive acts ought to be carried out only under the conditions and in the way determined by the "fathers" of the constitution or the organs delegated by them. This is, schematically formulated, the basic norm of the legal order of a single State, the basic norm of a national legal order. . . .

b. The Specific Function of the Basic Norm

That a norm of the kind just mentioned is the basic norm of the national legal order does not imply that it is impossible to go beyond that norm. Certainly one may ask why one has to respect the first constitution as a binding norm. The answer might be that the fathers of the first constitution were empowered by God. The characteristic of so-called legal positivism is, however, that it dispenses with any such religious justification of the legal order. The ultimate hypothesis of positivism is the norm authorizing the historically first legislator. The whole function of this basic norm is to confer law-creating power on the act of the first legislator and on all the other acts based on the first act. To interpret these acts of human beings as legal acts and their products as binding norms, and that means to interpret the empirical material which presents itself as law as such, is possible only on the condition that the basic norm is presupposed as a valid norm. The basic norm is only the necessary presupposition of any positivistic interpretation of the legal material.

The basic norm is not created in a legal procedure by a law-creating organ. It is not – as a positive legal norm is – valid because it is created in a certain way by a legal act, but it is valid because it is presupposed to be valid; and it is presupposed to be valid because without this presupposition no human act could be interpreted as a legal, especially as a norm-creating act.

By formulating the basic norm, we do not introduce into the science of law any new method. We merely make explicit what all jurists, mostly unconsciously, assume when they consider positive law as a system of valid norms and not only as a complex of facts, and at the same time repudiate any natural law from which positive law would receive its validity. That the basic norm really exists in the juristic consciousness is the result of a simple analysis of actual juristic statements. The basic norm is the answer to the question: how — and that means under what condition — are all these juristic statements concerning legal norms, legal duties, legal rights, and so on, possible?

c. The Principle of Legitimacy

The validity of legal norms may be limited in time, and it is important to notice that the end as well as the beginning of this validity is determined only by the order to which they belong. They remain valid as long as they have not been invalidated in the way which the legal order itself determines. This is the principle of legitimacy.

This principle, however, holds only under certain conditions. It fails to hold in the case of a revolution, this word understood in the most general sense, so that it also covers the so-called *coup d'état*. A revolution, in this wide sense, occurs whenever the legal order of a community is nullified and replaced by a new order in an illegitimate way, that is in a way not prescribed by the first order itself. It is in this context irrelevant whether or not this replacement is affected through a violent uprising against those individuals who so far have been the "legitimate" organs competent to create and amend the legal order. It is equally irrelevant whether the replacement is effected through a movement emanating from the mass of the people, or through action from those in government positions. From a juristic point of view, the decisive criterion of a revolution is that the order in force is overthrown and replaced by a new order in a way which the former had not itself anticipated. Usually, the new men whom a revolution brings to power annul only the constitution and certain laws of paramount political significance, putting other norms in their place. A great part of the old legal order "remains" valid also within the frame of the new order. But the phrase "they remain valid," does not give an adequate description of the phenomenon. It is only the contents of these norms that remain the same, not the reason of their validity. They are no longer valid by virtue of having been created in the way the old constitution prescribed. That constitution is no longer in force; it is replaced by a new constitution which is not the result of a constitutional alteration of the former. If laws which were introduced under the old constitution "continue to be valid" under the new constitution, this is possible only because validity has expressly or tacitly been vested in them by the new constitution. The phenomenon is a case of reception (similar to the reception of Roman law). The new order "receives," i.e., adopts, norms from the older order; this means that the new order gives validity to (puts into force) norms which have the same content as norms of the old order. "Reception" is an abbreviated procedure of law-creation. The laws which, in the ordinary inaccurate parlance, continue to be valid are, from a juristic viewpoint, new laws whose import coincides with that of the old laws. They are not identical with the old laws, because the reason for their validity is different. The reason for their validity is the new, not the old, constitution, and between the two continuity holds neither from the point of view of the one nor from that of the other. Thus, it is never the constitution merely but always the entire legal order that is changed by a revolution.

This shows that all norms of the old order have been deprived of their validity by revolution and not according to the principle of legitimacy. And they have been so deprived not only *de facto* but also *de jure*. No jurist would maintain that even after a successful revolution the old constituion and the laws based thereupon remain in force, on the ground that they have not been nullified in a manner anticipated by the old order itself. Every jurist will presume that the old order — to which no political reality any longer corresponds — has ceased to be valid, and that all norms, which are valid within the new order, receive their validity exclusively from the new constitution. It follows that, from this juristic point of view, the norms of the old order can no longer be recognized as valid norms.

d. Change of the Basic Norm

It is just the phenomenon of revolution which clearly shows the significance of the basic norm. Suppose that a group of individuals attempt to seize power by force, in order to remove the legitimate government in a hitherto monarchic State, and to introduce a republican form of government. If they succeed, if the old order ceases, and the new order begins to be efficacious, because the individuals whose behavior the new order regulates actually behave, by and large, in conformity with the new order, then this order is considered as a valid order. It is now according to this new order that the actual behavior of individuals is interpreted as legal or illegal. But this means that a new basic norm is presupposed. It is no longer the norm according to which the old monarchical constitution is valid, but a norm according to which the new republican constitution is valid, a norm endowing the revolutionary government with legal authority. If the revolutionaries fail, if the order they have tried to establish remains inefficacious, then, on the other hand, their undertaking is interpreted, not as a legal, a law-creating act, as the establishment of a constitution, but as an illegal act, as the crime of treason, and this according to the old monarchic constitution and its specific basic norm.

---

3. Judicial Legitimation: Argentina's De Facto Government Doctrine

Though there are notable exceptions, as a general rule Latin American revolutions leave the judiciary virtually intact. In such circumstances what should the role of the judiciary be? Should it declare the new revolutionary government illegitimate? Should it resign? Can it seek to cajole the new government into respecting constitutional guarantees? Should it attempt to distinguish between legitimate and illegitimate revolutions? For example, in determining whether to give formal recognition to a new regime, might the judiciary profitably consider the following factors:

(a) whether the ousted regime had come to power through force or through elections?

(b) whether the ousted regime had come to power or maintained itself in power by fraudulent elections?

(c) whether the ousted regime had respected the constitution?

(d) whether the ousted regime had been unable to control inflation or been otherwise incompetent?

(e) whether the new regime has sworn to respect the constitution?

(f) whether the new regime has been recognized by foreign governments?

(g) whether the new regime has promised to hold free elections within a reasonable period?

ACCORD (*Acordada*)

Supreme Court of Justice of Argentina
158 Fallos 290 (1930)

Meeting in extraordinary session on September 10, 1930 to consider the communication sent by the President of the Provisional Executive Power, Lt. General Uriburu, making known to this Court the formation of a provisional government for the Nation, the ministers of the Supreme Court state:

1. That the above cited communication places this Supreme Court in official recognition of the formation of a provisional government stemming from the triumphant revolution of September 7th of this year;

2. That this government finds itself with the military and police forces necessary to assure peace and order in the Nation and consequently to protect people's liberty, life, and property, and has declared, moreover, in public acts, that it will maintain the supremacy of the Constitution and the fundamental laws of the country in the exercise of its power;

3. That such antecedents undoubtedly characterize a *de facto* government . . . with all the consequences of a *de facto* government with respect to the possibility of validly accomplishing the acts necessary to carry out its purposes;

4. That this Court has declared that constitutional doctrine has become uniform with respect to *de facto* functionaries, in the sense of according validity to their acts, whatever the vice or deficiency in their nomination or election, based upon reasons of police and necessity in order to maintain protection of the public and of individuals whose interests may be affected. . . .

5. That the provisional government which has just been formed in this country is then a *de facto* government, whose title may not be judicially challenged successfully while it exercises administrative and police functions derived from its possession of force . . .;

6. That this notwithstanding, if once the situation is normalized, in developing the actions of the *de facto* government, its functionaries ignore individual guarantees, those of property, or others offered by this Constitution, the administration of justice, charged with accomplishing this, shall reestablish them with the same conditions and scope of the Executive Power under law; and this last conclusion, imposed by the very organization of the Judiciary, finds confirmation ... in the declarations of the provisional government, which, on assuming power, hastened to render an oath to uphold and execute the Constitution and fundamental laws of the Nation, a declaration which comports with the consequence of finding itself disposed to utilize the force it has to ensure that judicial decisions are carried out. . . .

Questions

1. How does the Argentine Supreme Court know that the provisional government "finds itself with the military and police forces necessary to assure peace and order in the Nation . . .?"

2. Assuming that the Argentine Court's jurisdiction is patterned on Article III of the U.S. Constitution (see p. 177 *supra*), is this Accord itself an unconstitutional pronouncement?

3. Does issuance of this type of Accord serve any useful purpose? Consider the following historical perspective:

> After the quick success of his coup amid general applause, General Uriburu set up a dictatorship and tried to convert Argentina into a corporative state under elite control. . . .
>
> The rock on which Uriburu foundered was political. As the only means of getting indispensable military and civilian support for his revolution, he had promised publicly to respect the Constitution. This won his regime a provisional but valuable endorsement by the nation's Supreme Court, which recognized it as the *de facto* government. The court's action then enabled him to issue a constitutionally valid declaration of a state of siege suspending all guarantees of individual rights. He issued the declaration at once, and maintained and enforced it throughout his brief administration. Moreover, it was soon apparent to all that he was determined to do everything in his power to scrap the Constitution in favor of his corporative system of government.
>
> Uriburu's power was not equal to the task. The stronger Justo military faction of liberal nationalists held him to his promise to change the Constitution only by Constitutional means, not by decree. This threw the question back into the civilian political arena . . . . Over-confident because of the public acclaim that had greeted his September coup, . . . he permitted a free election to be held in Buenos Aires in April, 1931, only seven months after the coup. The result was a disastrous defeat for the Uriburu ticket . . . . He canceled the election and set to work organizing para-military as well as political groups, but it was too late,

for his military and civilian foes only redoubled the pressure on him to restore normal constitutional government.

Too ill to hold out longer, Uriburu permitted a nationwide election to be held in November, 1931. A. Whitaker, *Argentina* 86-89 (1964).

Note

The Argentine Supreme Court has made substantially the same pronouncement in recognizing the "triumphant revolutions" of 1943 and 1955. 196 Fallos 6, 1943-II J.A. 522 (1943); 82 La Ley 398 (1956). On June 9, 1970, the Supreme Court officially recognized the action of the Junta of the Commanders in Chief of the Armed Forces in relieving Lt. General Juan Carlos Onganía of the presidency.

The Brazilian Supreme Federal Tribunal on October 27, 1930, similarly recognized the *de facto* government that brought Getúlio Vargas to power. 55 Rev. For. 359 (1930). However, this was an isolated event rather than a customary Brazilian practice.

MUNICIPALIDAD DE LA CAPITAL v. MAYER

Supreme Court of Justice of Argentina
1945-I J.A. 675, 38 La Ley 87 (1945)

Buenos Aires, April 2, 1945. . . .

[The *de facto* government of Juan Perón issued a decree amending the Expropriation Law to substitute, in cases in which the state was a party, a single, government-appointed valuation expert for the existing system of experts designated by the parties. The constitutionality of the decree was attacked on several grounds, *inter alia*: (a) as being beyond the competence of a *de facto* government and (b) as violating the principle of equality before the law.]

. . . [A] *de facto* government was constituted in the form of the Executive Power under the Constitution. Even though by reason of the force which supported it, the *de facto* government could have abrogated the Constitution and issued its own statute, it limited itself to toppling the executive and dissolving the legislature, swearing to comply with the Constitution and maintain the functioning of the constitutionally organized judiciary. Hence, the court . . . has continued to act in the full exercise of its functions . . . .

It is indisputable that the *de facto* government has all the powers that the National Constitution grants to the constitutional Executive . . . . It is also indisputable that the *de facto* government cannot exercise judicial functions . . . .

The question of the exercise of legislative powers is more complex. The legislature . . . is the genuine representative of the people and its character as a collegiate body is the fundamental guarantee of the faithful interpretation of the general will. The *de facto* government is unipersonal and lacks popular representation. If it maintains the Constitution in force, proposing (in well-known declarations) to restore it, the government is a temporary one, between two constitutional governments. However, factual necessity requires it to exercise those legislative powers which are indispensable to the maintenance of the functioning of the State and to fulfill the purposes of the revolution; the contrary would lead to chaos and anarchy. But these powers must be limited, keeping abrogation of the representative principle to a minimum . . . . To recognize broad legislative powers in one man or group of men is incompatible with the Constitution's being in force.

Also, the legislative powers of a *de facto* government are limited in time. Once the country has returned to normality, provisions of such character cease having future effects unless ratified by Congress, although they are valid as to accomplished facts. This is the doctrine which emerges from the decisions of the court . . . . In the first case we said: "It could happen that a revolutionary government, under the pressure of necessity, . . . and in the absence of a Congress with which to collaborate, might use legislative faculties to meet an exigency it considers vital, giving rise to what have been called decree-laws. . . ."

Consequently, the Executive Power has been able to promulgate Decree No. 17.920 of July 6, 1944, modifying Law 189 on Expropriation, to defend the interests of the State which, in its judgment, are poorly protected by the system of the law. Such decree is valid as to its origin and governs until the end of the *de facto* government which promulgated it.

However, article 6 of the cited decree is contrary to the guarantee of equality before the law, enshrined in article 16 of the National Constitution, insofar as it limits expert testimony to questions of fact related to the area and dimensions of the property taken and similar questions. . . . Experts are indispensable aids to justice and contribute to the correctness of judicial decisions . . .; the decree in question modifies Law 189 to preclude the intervention of experts in the expropriation of real property only in those cases in which the State is a party. . . . It thus creates an arbitrary distinction, depriving the litigant in those cases in which the State has a special interest, of a means of proof which the State accords him in its own legislation in analagous situations in all other cases. . . .

For these reasons . . . we declare that Decree 19.920 of July 6, 1944, which modifies Law 189 on Expropriation, is valid as to its origin, but that its article 6(a), insofar as it limits expert testimony to the sole purpose of deciding questions of fact relating to area and dimensions of the property taken and similar questions, is contrary to article 16 of the National Constitution. . . .

Concurring opinion of Dr. Repetto:

. . . [T]he *de facto* Executive lacks the powers to promulgate decrees with the effect of laws in matters of common or procedural legislation, because of limitations imposed by the revolution of June 4 itself on the exercise of its powers. . . .

The principal limitation of such kind flows from the words used by the President of the Republic, who, upon assuming his high office, hastened to manifest that "he was committing all his energy towards the reestablishment of the full force of the constitution and the security of its institutions." He made no concrete reference whatsoever to the possibility of promulgating, in general, decrees with the value of laws in matters of common or procedural law. . . .

The revolution closed down the Congress, but at no moment did it attribute to itself the legislative powers corresponding to that body. To have done so would have signified a change so unforeseen in the spirit and the letter of the Fundamental Charter, that . . . one might say that the federal, republican, representative regime provided for would have disappeared from the instrument notwithstanding the contrary proposition expressed so emphatically by the very authors of the revolutionary movement of June 4. . . .

It is the Constitution . . . to which one must look to know whether the Executive has the power to sanction the decree designed to modify Law 189 on Expropriation, in force since the year 1866. In accordance with the Constitution, among the powers of Congress figures that of promulgating penal, civil, commercial and mineral codes (art. 67(11)) and laws of general interest such as Law 189. . . .

Decree No. 17.920 . . . thus does not comply with the last part of the Accord of June 7, 1943 and specifically does not comply with the oath taken by the President and his ministers.

Such oath, in effect, had among its purposes the limitation of the powers with which the revolutionary government would avail itself to fulfill the purposes of the movement. It was an undertaking of honor by the President and his Ministers before the people of the Republic to carry out (and have carried out) the Constitution in all that was not strictly indispensable for the realization of those aims.

The sanction of new codes and statues or the modification or repeal of those in force is clearly not in the same category as electoral laws or those proposing the improvement of social conditions of the working classes or moral conditions of administration, which were the only purposes enunciated by the revolution as essential. . . . Equivalent to such purposes would be fiscal provisions imposed as necessary for the functioning of the Nation or those which respond to other urgent necessities . . ., a doctrine developed during the *de facto* government corresponding to the revolution of 1930. . . . Such a permissive doctrine applies only to cases of notorious urgency designed to fill a vital necessity of war or peace, . . . which has certainly not occurred in the case under examination.

Notes

1. The Supreme Court also invalidated several other decrees of the *de facto* regime, including one establishing a new court, 1945-I J.A. 684, 38 La Ley 51 (1945), and another ordering the transfer of a federal judge, 1945-I J.A. 686, 38 La Ley 53 (1945). The Court further irritated the *de facto* government by ordering the release of several political prisoners, though it prudently declined the petition of several hundred university professors requesting the court to rescind its 1943 accord recognizing the *de facto* government and assume the executive power itself. 39 La Ley 852 (1945).

2. Such displays of judicial independence spelled disaster for the Argentine

Supreme Court in 1946 when Juan Domingo Perón, a former leader of the *de facto* government, was constitutionally elected to the presidency. Perón's inaugural address to Congress was reminiscent of Franklin Delano Roosevelt's 1937 broadside attack on the U.S. Supreme Court: "I place the spirit of justice above the Judicial Power . . . and I consider that justice, besides being independent, must be efficient, and that it cannot be efficient when its ideals and principles do not conform to public feeling."

Shortly thereafter the Peronist-dominated Congress brought impeachment charges against all but one member of the Argentine Supreme Court. One of the most serious charges leveled against the court was that it had meddled in politics by legitimizing *de facto* governments in issuing the accords of 1930 and 1943! The Senate voted unanimously to remove the accused members of the court. See generally Leonhard, "The 1946 Purge of the Argentine Supreme Court of Justice," 17 *Inter-Amer. Econ. Affairs* No. 4, p. 73 (Spring 1964).

3. Much of the work of the Peronist Congress was devoted to ratifying decree-laws of the prior *de facto* regime. In 1946 some 500 decree-laws were ratified; in 1949 another 472 were ratified. Justo López, "Poder Legislativo," in *Argentina* 1930-1960, 108, 113 (J. Paita ed. 1961). The Perón appointees to the Supreme Court promptly reversed prior Court decisions limiting the legislative powers of *de facto* governments. *Arlandini, Enrique,* 47 La Ley 802 (1947). Since 1947 Argentine courts have been treating decree-laws of *de facto* governments as the equivalent of regularly enacted legislation even if not subsequently ratified by a duly elected Congress. *Ziella v. Smiriglio Hnos.,* 48 La Ley 361 (Sup. Ct. 1947). The Argentine cases dealing with *de facto* governments from 1865 to 1968 are discussed in 2 S. Linares Quintana, *Derecho Constitucional e Instituciones Políticas* 520-42 (1970). See also, Dana Montaño, "Los Gobiernos de Facto y la Legitimación de sus Actos Legislativos: Los Decretos Leyes," 7 *Cursos Monográficos* 93 (Acad. Inter-Amer. Der. Comp. 1959).

Now that the shoe is on the other foot the Peronists appear to have switched positions. The Peronist Procurator of the Treasury has recently challenged the correctness of the post-1947 Argentine cases on the legislative powers of *de facto* governments. La Prensa, July 12, 1973, p. 6, cols. 1-2.

4. Perón's wholesale dismissals of judges and the scandalous behavior of their replacements is detailed in Orgaz, "Poder Judicial," in *Argentina* 1930-1960, 124 (J. Paita ed. 1961).

The following two cases were the judicial culmination of an unhappy chapter in Argentine constitutional history. President Arturo Frondizi, constitutionally elected in 1958 with the support of the Peronists (who were barred from running their own candidates), permitted the Peronists to run in the congressional and gubernatorial elections of March 18, 1962. The Peronists won control of ten provinces, including Buenos Aires, plus 44 seats in the Chamber of deputies. Leading military officers were so disturbed by the specter of a Peronist resurgence that they pressed for cancellation of the elections and Frondizi's resignation. Frondizi refused to do either; instead he ordered military intervention in the provinces. On March 29, 1962 the military seized Frondizi and bustled him off to Martín García Island in the La Plata River. But though united in their decision to oust Frondizi, the armed forces had not reached agreement about what to do next. Just as it appeared that the commanders-in-chief of the army, air force, and navy were going to constitute themselves as a *junta* to rule the country, the president of the Senate, Dr. José María Guido promptly went before the Supreme Court and was hurriedly sworn in as the next president. (The vice president had resigned rather than attempt to succeed to the presidency under such circumstances.) In addition to performing the swearing-in ceremony, the Supreme Court issued an accord (*acuerdo*), one judge dissenting, confirming Guido's mandate on the theory that he had "validly assumed the National Executive Power, in a definitive character, in accordance with articles 1 and 3 of Law 252."[82] General Raúl Poggi, the commander-in-chief of the army, was reportedly so angered by the maneuver that he threatened Guido with a revolver in a futile attempt to force him to resign.[83] This extraordinary course of events was promptly challenged by an original action before the Supreme Court seeking a court order restoring Frondizi to the presidency.

PITTO

Supreme Court of Justice of Argentina
252 Fallos 177, 1962-II J.A. 514, 106 La Ley 123 (1962)

Buenos Aires, April 3, 1962. . . .
[The Court summarily rejected a request that its members recuse themselves.]
3d) The pleadings impugn acts performed by this court by virtue of the powers accorded to it in articles 1 and 4 of Law 252 [swearing in the new President]. It is asked, in addition, that the Tribunal restore Dr. Arturo Frondizi to the Presidency of the Nation.
4th) Both the oath of the then Provisional President of the Senate, Dr. José María Guido, and the confirmation of his mandate are strictly juridical and appropriate. . . . [H]e is the next in line in case of "headlessness [*acefalía*] of the Republic" (arts. 1st and 4th of the law 252) . . . . [S]aid headlessness occurred because of the "lack of a

---

[82]252 Fallos 8, 106 La Ley 68 (1962). To implement Article 75 of the Constitution, the Congress had enacted Law No. 252 of September 19, 1868:

Article 1. In the event that the Republic is without a head, for lack of a President and Vice President of the Nation, the Executive Power shall be vested in, first, the provisional President of the Senate, and secondly, in the President of the Chamber of Deputies, and if both of these are lacking, in the President of the Supreme Court. . . .

Article 3. The official called upon to exercise the national Executive Power in the cases mentioned in Article 1 shall call for a new election by the people of the Republic of a president and vice president within thirty days following his installation in office, provided the incapacity of those who held those offices is permanent.

Article 4. The official who is to exercise the Executive Power in the cases mentioned in Article 1 of this law shall, upon assuming office, take the oath prescribed by Article 80 of the Constitution, before Congress or, if it is adjourned, before the Supreme Court of Justice.

[83]E. Lieuwen, *Generals Vs. Presidents* 18 (1964).

President and Vice President of the Nation," and it is not incumbent on the Supreme Court to make any pronouncement concerning the reasons for this "lack." And, in turn, the challenged confirmation has been in a form adequate to confer full validity and power on assumption of the office, in conformance with art. 4th of the cited law.

5th) In addition, this Supreme Court, in performing the acts under examination, was carrying out a function invested in it. This function presupposes the duty of assuring the survival and continuity of the constitutional order, the only certain barrier against anarchy or despotism (Fallos: 205, p. 614, 248, p. 189). . . .

Therefore, the recusation interposed is rejected and the relief requested is denied. And since the terms underlined in blue on page 1 of the record seriously disturb the decorum with which one must act before this Court, let them be expunged by the Secretary. Let there be applied to the one who signed [the document in question] , by way of disciplinary sanction, . . . the maximum fine provided, 500 pesos. – *Benjamín Villegas Basavilbaso. – Julio Oyhanarte. – Pedro Aberastury. – Ricardo Colombres. – Esteban Imaz. – Ramón Lascano* [the Procurator General] .

[Dr. Luis M. Boffi Boggero had dissented from the acceptance of the oath of office from Dr. Guido, and did not participate in the decision of this case. Dr. Aristóbulo Aráoz de Lamadrid, who had agreed with the majority to accept the oath of office from Dr. Guido, also did not participate in this case.]

FRONDIZI

Federal Chamber of the Capital, Penal Division (Argentina)
1962-IV J.A. 404, 108 La Ley 682 (1962)

2d Instance. – Buenos Aires, June 15, 1962. [A habeas corpus petition was brought to secure the release of Frondizi, who remained a prisoner of the navy and air force until the election of July 1963. The judge of first instance rejected the petition, and this appeal was taken.

Omitted is a restatement of the facts concerning the deposing of Frondizi and the Supreme Court's role in swearing in Guido and confirming his mandate.]

. . . [T]hus, the Supreme Court of the Nation has understood that the situation contemplated in article 1, Law 252, "lack of a President and Vice President of the Nation" resulted in the case. Based upon this assumption, it deemed assumption of the position of President of the Nation by the provisional president of the Senate juridical and pertinent, points of view which it later ratified in the case of *Luis M. Pitto*. . . .

Having been proclaimed by the highest court of justice in the country . . ., such reasons . . . could, by themselves, serve to reject the appellant's attack. . . .

However, in the judgment of this tribunal, the solution provided by Law 252 in the event of the vacancy of the National Executive applies only to one of the suppositions contemplated in article 75 of the National Constitution: sickness, absence from the Capital, death, resignation, or removal. For obvious reasons, going to the substance of the regime created by the constitution, one cannot hold that our fundamental law provides for and permits removal by force, such as that presently witnessed in our country; rather it refers to the removal by impeachment (*juicio político*) referred to in arts. 45, 51 and 52.

. . . The inapplicability of law 252 still does not deprive Dr. José María Guido of a sufficiently valid title to serve as President of the Nation. . . . Such titles and their full validity derive from a rule, incorporated since ancient times into Argentine public law — governments constituted in the country as a consequence of some act of force, and which find themselves in fact capable "of insuring the peace and order of the Nation, and therefore of protecting the liberty, life and property of persons" and which declare, in addition, their purpose of maintaining "the supremacy of the Constitution and other laws of the country," have sufficient title to "carry out validly the acts necessary for the fulfillment of the ends pursued" (Sup. Ct., Accord of Sept. 10, 1930, Fallos, 158, 290). Based on this original situation of fact and in conformity with that jurisprudential precedent, the action of the present National Executive is also validated. In respect to that action the above-noted conditions are present and the government's title, as the Supreme Court of the Nation said on the noted occasion, "cannot be judicially questioned with success by anyone," which logically leads to recognition of full validity of the Executive's acts when performed within the orbit of its competence. Determination whether such acts are within that orbit is the function of the judiciary. . . .

Whether one or another of the expounded reasons be accepted as the more appropriate ground, and as it is a matter in the present action of examining only the validity of an act of exclusive jurisdiction of the President of the Nation, it is proper to conclude that the current detention of Dr. Arturo Frondizi under decree 2887/62 is fully constitutional. . . .

Notes

1. This case is noted by Aja Espil, *Presidente de "Jure" o Presidente de "Facto,"* 1962-IV J.A. 405 (1962). General background concerning the 1962 Argentine elections and the subsequent *golpe* can be found in R. Fagen and W. Cornelius, *Political Power in Latin America: Seven Confrontations* 105-153 (1970).

2. The decision of the Federal Chamber was affirmed by the Supreme Court on a quite different theory. Treating Frondizi as any other citizen detained pursuant to executive decree during a state of siege (*cf.* Trossi, *infra*, p. 225), the court stated that it had no power to substitute its judgment for that of the political authorities in determining whether a declaration of a state of siege was required for maintenance of the public peace, and that the record failed to disclose that the executive had clearly exceeded the extraordinary powers accorded by the Constitution to it during a state of siege. 254 Fallos 487 (1962).

Questions

1. Does it make any practical difference whether one adopts the theory of the Federal Chamber of the Capital or that employed by the Supreme Court in the *Frondizi* case?

2. Did Guido meet the standards the Supreme Court laid down in the 1930 Accord for recognition of *de facto* governments?

Judicial legitimation of *de facto* governments has been subjected to severe criticism. One Argentine political scientist recently blamed the Supreme Court's accords for contributing to general skepticism about the myth of constitutionalism, which in turn led to the military takeover in 1966.[84] After praising the French *Conseil d'Etat's* censure of Louis Napoleon Bonaparte's 1851 *coup d'état,* Dr. Rafael Bielsa, one of Argentina's leading jurists, ruefully observed:

> If the Argentine Supreme Court (and other courts as well) had taken the same attitude when constitutional powers were usurped by *de facto* regimes or, without passing judgment on that political development, had awaited the application of the constitutional law of acephalism [headlessness], many calamities would have been prevented which, not exactly attributable to government action during the 1930-1932 regime, were due rather to the precedent which once so to speak legitimated, was an incitement to the periodical repetition of the transgression of suppressing constitutional government.[85]

J. IRIZARRY Y PUENTE, THE NATURE AND POWERS OF A "DE FACTO" GOVERNMENT IN LATIN AMERICA

30 *Tulane Law Review* 15, 33-35, 66-68 (1955)

The note or communication of a Provisional Government is not a judicial case, controversy or suit between parties, which is all that the Courts are authorized to determine according to the Constitutions and laws of their respective countries. The notes of these governments do not seek merely to bring a *fait accompli* to the attention of the Courts, but they seek a recognition by the Courts of such governments, that is, to put their "constitutional seal" of approval upon them through a declaration outside the scope of a judicial proceeding.

---

[84] Puigbo, Prólogo, in *Instituto de Ciencia Política, La Revolución Argentina* 14 (1966).

[85] "Jurisdictional Protection and other Remedies Against the Illegal Exercise or Abuse of Administrative Authority," in *United Nations, Remedies Against the Abuse of Administrative Authority — Selected Studies* 33, 52 (1964).

The Courts cannot invoke a single constitutional or statutory provision in support of the practice of recognizing *de facto* governments.... [T]he Courts have undertaken to inquire into the strictly *political* question of the *de facto* existence of these governments and their possession of force, for the purpose of saying that their credentials cannot be successfully questioned in court by anyone. We feel justified in defending this practice only to the extent that the Courts have attempted to uphold a principle of juridical order by insisting on judicial control in the inevitable chaos of any revolution.

The Courts have been drawn by the *de facto* governments into the orbit of national politics, contrary to their own traditional position that questions of a general political character are outside the scope of the Court's function. Their decisions in all these cases, to the effect that the Provisional Government is "a *de facto* government with respect to its organization," and "that its title cannot be judicially questioned," are strictly political. If the Courts have authority to declare at what stage a revolutionary government becomes *de facto,* the reverse must be equally true: they should have authority to withdraw recognition at that stage in a government's life when it fails to live up to the conditions that the Courts think are essential to a *de facto* status, such as the failure to observe "institutional principles and individual rights." Then, again, if the Courts are convinced that their function is to ascertain whether a government *de facto* is or is not in possession of the force necessary to maintain peace and order for the purpose of saying "that the credentials of said authority cannot be *questioned judicially* with success," they should also have authority to determine the stage at which a *de jure* government lacks that force, and to declare its credentials void.

The Courts have been lured onto dangerous ground and into questionable doctrine, fraught with ominous consequences for the independence of the Judiciary. . . .

The view that the Judiciary retains its *de jure* status in the *de facto* government, which we might call the "split-personality" theory of government, would lead to unavoidable conflicts between the *de facto* authorities and the Judiciary, that is, between the surviving organ of a defunct constitutional and legal order and a triumphant revolutionary legal philosophy seeking to alter the political and social structure of the State. . . .

The tenure of office of the Judiciary in a *de jure* government should be presumed to have been voided by the fall of that government, and its tacit appointment by the *de facto* government should be presumed when it is allowed to continue in office as an agency of that government. The Judiciary's new title to office, though colorable, is sufficient for the extraordinary situation under which a *de facto* government functions, until its title is confirmed by the succeeding constitutional government.

We may infer from the fact that the judiciary now admits that the powers of a *de facto* government are not limited by the Constitution, and that it upholds the validity of executive, legislative and judicial acts of *de facto* governments, that it no longer claims that the judicial function under a *de facto* government is to safeguard institutional principles and individual rights. This change can be explained only on the theory that the Judiciary now regards itself as a *de facto* organ of a *de facto* government, required by the force of events to concur in the policy of that government, notwithstanding any constitutional limitations, assuming that the

Constitution remains in effect during the *de facto* period, that restrict the powers of government.

As long as the Judiciary claimed *de jure* status and its mission was to protect institutional principles, it could and did: (a) uphold the constitution, (b) define the limits of a *de facto* government, and (c) declare decree-laws unconstitutional. When it decided that a *de facto* government had legislative powers *in the measure necessary to govern* and that it did not have authority to declare decree-laws unconstitutional *by reason of their origin,* the Judiciary admitted, by implication: (a) that it is not, in the abnormal situation created by a revolutionary change, the vindicator of institutional principles of government and individual rights, (b) that it could not interfere with or obstruct the program of the revolution, (c) that it had become, qualitatively, a *de facto* agency of a *de facto* government, and (d) that the profession of a *de facto* government to support the Constitution, if that profession has been made, has become meaningless, and the Constitution itself non-existent for practical purposes.

Do you agree?

Consider the opinion of the late Nelson Hungría, former Minister of the Brazilian Supreme Federal Tribunal, in a writ of security appeal:

Against a successful armed insurrection, only a more forceful counter-insurrection will be valid, and this cannot positively be made by the Supreme Court, who would not be so naive as to quell an insurrection by means of a worthless declaration of principles. . . . The Supreme Court has never deserted from its constitutional function, which is not, precisely, that of quelling a successful insurrection. With the institution of the Republic, Brazil entered into the political cycle of Latin-America, in which the overthrow of regimes and of governments is often effected through military uprising against which it is not possible to use the force of law. Whether their intentions are good or bad, such uprisings silence the voice of law and of legal judgments. Against the historical fatalism of military uprisings the Judicial Power is of no avail. This is the truth of the matter and it cannot be denied by such as seem to think that instead of an arsenal of Law books, the Supreme Court has an arsenal of shrapnels and torpedoes available. Quoted in Basilio, "Judicial Power as a Guarantee of Individual Rights. Parallel Competence of the Legislative Power and the Judicial Power," in *Inter-American Bar Assoc., Proceedings of the Tenth Conference* 205, 211 (1957).

---

4. Autolegitimation: The Institutional Act

The institutional act whose preamble follows, was issued by the heads of the Brazilian Armed Forces, who successfully ousted the government of President João Goulart on March 31, 1964. How much of its theoretical base stems from Kelsen?

PREAMBLE TO BRAZIL'S FIRST INSTITUTIONAL ACT

April 9, 1964

It is indispensable to define the nature of the civil and military movement which has just opened a new perspective on Brazil's future. What has happened and what continues to happen at this moment, not only in the spirit and behavior of the armed forces, but in national public opinion, is an authentic revolution.

Revolution is distinguished from other armed movements by the fact that it carries with it, not the interest and will of a group, but the interest and will of the Nation.

The victorious revolution vests itself with the exercise of the Constituent Power [the basic powers of a constitutional convention], which manifests itself either by popular election or revolution. The latter is the most radical and most expressive form of the Constituent Power. Thus, the victorious revolution, like the Constituent Power, legitimates itself. It destroys the prior government and has the capacity to constitute a new government. It embodies the normative force inherent in the Constituent Power. It enacts juridical norms without the normative limitations existing prior to its victory. The leaders of the victorious revolution, thanks to the action of the Armed Forces and the unequivocal support of the Nation, represent the People and in their name exercise the Constituent Power, a power which belongs exclusively to the People. The Institutional Act which is today enacted by the Commanders in Chief of the Army, Navy, and Air Force, in the name of the revolution, which triumphed with the support of almost the entire Nation, is designed to assure the new government which will be formed the necessary means for the task of economic, financial, political, and moral reconstruction of Brazil, in a manner which will enable it to confront, directly and immediately, the grave and urgent problems on which restoration of internal order and the international prestige of our homeland depend. The victorious revolution has to institutionalize itself and speeds this institutionalization by limiting the complete powers which it effectively possesses.

The present Institutional Act could only be enacted by the victorious revolution represented by the commander-in-chief of the three armed services. . . . Constitutional processes were ineffective to remove the government, which was deliberately arranging to bolshevize the country. Only the revolution, which removed the prior government, can dictate the norms and processes of the new government and confer on it the powers or juridical instruments which will assure it the exercise of power in the exclusive interest of the country. To demonstrate that we do not intend to radicalize the revolutionary process, we have decided to maintain the Constitution of 1946, limiting ourselves to modifying it only with respect to the powers of the President of the Republic, in order to permit him to fulfill the mission of restoring economic and financial order in Brazil, as well as to take urgent measures to drain the large pocket of Communism, whose purulence has already infiltrated not only the highest echelons of the government, but its administrative dependencies. To further reduce the complete powers with which the victorious revolution finds itself invested, we resolve as well to maintain the National Congress, with the reservations with respect to its powers contained in the present Institutional Act.

Thus, it remains very clear that the revolution does not try to legitimate itself via the Congress. It is rather the Congress which receives its legitimation from this Institutional Act. . . .

The drafters of Brazil's Institutional Act limited its life to six months. Their expectation was that during that period "offensive" elements could be purged from the government, and the country could return to constitutional government with a president chosen by the military (and ratified by Congress). And, despite the last paragraph the Institutional Act, it is reasonably clear that the maintenance of an actively functioning Congress served as an important source of legitimacy for the military government.[86] However, in the following year cooperation between the Congress and the military, even after the quashing of a number of legislative mandates, was much less than the military had expected. The revolutionary government's candidates for governors were defeated at the polls in the important states of Guanabara (which includes the city of Rio de Janeiro) and Minas Gerais. The Supreme Federal Tribunal, which had been untouched by the revolution, had granted habeas corpus to such notorious enemies of the revolution as Francisco Julião, leader of the Peasant Leagues in the Northeast; Miguel Arraes de Alencar, former Governor of the state of Pernambuco; Mauro Borges, former Governor of the State of Goiás; and José Parsifal Barroso, former Governor of the State of Ceará.[87] Moreover, in a signed newspaper article, the President of the Court had invited "the military to return to the barracks and return the Nation to its own government."[88] The result was the promulgation of Institutional Act No. 2, which made several substantial constitutional changes. This act permitted the government to pack the Supreme Federal Tribunal, restricted the jurisdiction of civilian courts, and extended the jurisdiction of military courts over civilians. See pp. 214 *infra*. The preamble illustrates the constitutional theory for further tampering with the Constitution.

PREAMBLE TO BRAZIL'S SECOND INSTITUTIONAL ACT

October 27, 1965

. . . [The first Institutional Act] did not say that the Revolution was, but that it is and will continue. Hence its Constituent Power has not been exhausted, inasmuch as it is itself [part] of the revolutionary process, which has to be dynamic in order to achieve its objectives. . . .

---

[86] See Packenham, "Functions of the Brazilian National Congress," in *Latin American Legislatures: Their Role and Influence* 259, 270-73 (W. Agor ed. 1971).

[87] HC 42.560 of Sept. 29, 1965; HC 42.108 of April 19, 1965; HC 41.296 of Nov. 24, 1964; HC 41. 609 of Dec. 16, 1964.

[88] See Veja, Dec. 18, 1968, p. 23.

The autolimitation which the Revolution imposed in its Institutional Act of April 9, 1964 does not signify, however, that having the powers to limit itself, by this limitation it has denied or deprived itself of the burden of power which is inherent to it as a movement. . . .

The Revolution is alive and will not go backwards. It has promoted reforms and will continue to do so, patriotically insisting on its propositions of economic, financial, political, and moral recuperation of Brazil. For this it needs tranquility. Agitators of various shades and elements of the eliminated situation persist, however, in taking advantage of the . . . shortness of the period of the indispensable restriction of certain constitutional guarantees, and already threaten and challenge the very revolutionary order, precisely at the moment in which the revolution, attending to administrative problems, is trying to put before the people the practice and discipline of the exercise of democracy. Democracy supposes liberty, but it does not exclude responsibility nor does it imply the license to contradict the very political vocation of the Nation. One cannot undo the Revolution. . . .

Thus, the President of the Republic, as Chief of the Revolutionary Government and Supreme Commander of the Armed Forces, . . .

Considering that the Country needs tranquility to work in behalf of its economic development and well-being of the People, and that there cannot be peace without authority, which is also an essential condition of order;

Considering that the Constituent Power of the Revolution is intrinsic to it, not only to institutionalize itself, but also to ensure the continuity of its task which it has proposed,

Resolves to publish:

Institutional Act No. 2 . . . .

Even the military regime's adoption of a new constitution in 1967 in Brazil did not terminate the practice of amending the constitution by fiat in the name of the revolution. The process was startlingly simple: unconstitutional decrees were simply labeled "institutional acts" and signed by a few more generals. By October 14, 1969, 17 institutional acts had been issued. Three days later, the heads of the army, navy, and air force, using the powers conferred on them by the institutional acts, reissued the 1967 Constitution (with the intervening institutional acts integrated) as Constitutional Amendment No. 1, perhaps terminating a truly remarkable episode in bootstraps constitutionalism.

The Argentine Revolution of 1966 adopted much the same principle as the Brazilian Revolution with regard to autolegitimation. But the Argentine generals did not go through a long series of embarrassing institutional acts. They did not have to. The Statute of the Argentine Revolution, set out in Appendix C, pp. 717-18, *infra*, maintained the 1853 Constitution only insofar as it was not inconsistent with the aims and statute of the Argentine Revolution, and set no time limit for expiration of the term of office of the revolutionary government.

Questions

1. Do revolutions ever end?
2. Is autolimitation a significant limitation on the powers of a revolutionary government?
3. Why should *de facto* governments wish to limit their authority?

F. FOURNIER, COMMENT

in A. Sutherland (ed.), *Government Under Law* 83, 85 (1956)*

Finally, it might be interesting for you to know about a precedent that was recently established in my country [Costa Rica] in regard to these matters. In 1948, because of a revolution that we had against the Communists, the previous Constitution could not be enforced any more. The constitutional order had been broken. Then there was no constitution, and a *de facto* government was established. But that *de facto* government wished to limit its own authority and issued a decree declaring that the civil liberties chapter would remain in force until the new constitution was made. Then, some months after, one of the decrees of the same *de facto* government was challenged by somebody before the Supreme Court as unconstitutional. The government made the defense saying that it could not be unconstitutional because there wasn't any constitution. But the Supreme Court declared that as long as a government declares that there are certain fundamental principles of law which are superior, and that government had so declared, those principles were over any other law or decree, even though that second decree was coming from the same authority which had established its own self-limitations, and the court declared that second decree of the *de facto* government unconstitutional.

A. JANOS, AUTHORITY AND VIOLENCE: THE POLITICAL FRAMEWORK OF INTERNAL WAR

in *Internal War: Problems and Approaches* 130, 132-33
(H. Eckstein ed. 1964)**

Authority is related to two distinct elements: force and legitimacy. The two combine in specific institutional arrangements that define the relations between masses and élites and establish the scope and boundaries of political competition in society. The first element, force, implies a physical ability to compel someone . . . .

---

*Copyright 1956, Harvard University Press.

**Copyright © 1964. Reprinted by permission of MacMillan Publishing Co., Inc.

Legitimacy, the second element of authority, is the ability to evoke compliance short of coercion. It is a psychological relationship between masses and élites, involving acceptance by the mass of a claim by an élite to act in the name of the community. This claim is usually made in terms of principles representing "higher" truth or "inevitability." Insofar as the truth of these principles is accepted, legitimacy derives from compliance with certain processes — elections, hereditary succession — that are regarded as right and morally just ways of determining who should make decisions for the community and in what manner . . . .

It follows from this definition of force and legitimacy that the two elements of authority are, at least to some extent, interchangeable. The more legitimate the position of an élite is, the less it has to rely on force or the threat of force; the less widespread are habits of obedience rooted in a conviction of justness, the greater will be the need for the use of force. The lines of interchangeability cannot be easily determined, but authority without the element of force is "power of low weight," and some principle of legitimating force must exist in even the most ruthless of terroristic regimes. It is commonplace to say that the position of an élite must be legitimate at least in the eyes of those acting within the framework of organized force, then, sooner or later, the question of "who guards the guards" must be raised, with devastating implications to the authority of the élite.

Faced with mounting public unrest, disappointing economic performance, and a failure to institutionalize the "revolution," Argentine military leaders returned the country to civilian rule in 1973 by holding free public elections. Though Perón was not permitted to run personally, his proxy, Héctor Cámpora was elected handily. Shortly thereafter, Cámpora resigned, and Perón was once again elected to the presidency. (When Perón died in 1974, he was succeeded by his widow, María Estela Martínez de Perón, who had been serving as Vice President.)

On the other hand, the Brazilian military has derived a kind of legitimacy from impressively high economic growth rates. Despite difficulties in institutionalization, power has been peacefully transferred to four successive authoritarian "revolutionary" regimes.[89]

---

5. Judicial Review in a Revolutionary Ambiente — Walking the Tightrope in Brazil and Argentina

(a) The Judicial Tightrope — Brazilian Style

SÉRGIO CIDADE DE REZENDE
Supreme Federal Tribunal of Brazil
H.C. No. 40.910
5 Os Grandes Julgamentos do Supremo Tribunal Federal 7
(E. Costa ed. 1964)

[The accused, a professor in the College of Economic Sciences of the Catholic

University of Pernambuco, was accused of the crime of publicizing propaganda calling
for subversion of the political and social order by violent means. The judge of the 3d
Criminal Chamber of Recife ordered the arrest of the accused, who sought habeas
corpus in the Supreme Federal Tribunal.]

Minister Hahnemann Guimarães (Reporter).

The accusation says that the petitioner distributed to his students in his course in
introductory economics a manifesto propagandizing violent subversion of order and class
hatred, conduct which concords with his Communist ideas. In the exercise of his
professorial position in the Catholic University of Pernambuco, the accused wrote on a
piece of paper a subversive saying: "Viva o P.C." [Long live the Communist Party.]

In the manifesto, set out on page 41 of the record, the petitioner unfavorably
criticized the present political situation, emphasizing at the end that the students
"have a responsibility, have a part of the decision of the destiny of the society. Hence
they must opt between 'becoming gorillas' (*gorilizar-se*)[90] or remaining human. The
students have the honor to defend democracy and liberty."

There is nothing in the manifesto which can be considered propaganda for violent
subversion of the political or social order (Law No. 1.802, art. 11 A and §3) or
instigation of public disobedience of the law of public order (Law No. 1.802, art. 17).

Minister Evandro Lins: . . . I only want to remind the Distinguished Tribunal of the
words of William O. Douglas, justice of the Supreme Court of the United States, in his
recent book *The Right of the People.* . . . "Government may not deprive the citizens
of any branch of learning nor bar any avenue of research nor ban any type of
discourse. The prohibition extends to private discourse between citizens, public
discourse through any channel of communication, or teaching in any classroom. . . .
The spirit of free inquiry must be allowed to dominate the schools and universities. . . .
Teachers must be allowed to pursue ideas into any domain. There must be no terminal
points on discourse." . . .

In view of the constitutional guarantees of liberty of expression and academic
freedom, I concur in the vote of the eminent reporter to grant the order for lack of
just cause in the criminal proceeding. . . .

Minister Pedro Chaves:

I concur with the eminent reporter exclusively on legal grounds. On political-
ideological grounds, I disagree completely with the ideas set out in the vote of Minister
Evandro Lins . . . .

There is an evident contradiction in this revolution in which we are presently living.
. . . [I] f there are ideas which repel each other, . . . they are "the revolution" and the
"constitution." The Institutional Act, which sought to brighten up the Movement of
the 31st of March, says in Article No. 1 that "the Constitution of September 1946 is
in force." This Constitution of September 1946, like all constitutions inspired in
Democratic Liberalism, lacks means to defend national institutions. . . . Thus, there is

---

[89] See generally A. Stepan (ed.), *Authoritarian Brazil* (1973).

[90] *Gorila* is a term frequently applied to the hard-line military, particularly in Argentina, to
distinguish them from the *legalistas,* the military who prefer government according to the
constitution. [Eds.]

abuse of liberty of the press, abuse of liberty of thought, abuse of parliamentary immunity, and abuse of academic freedom. It could not have been the intention of the framers, honestly conscious of national necessities, to transform the right of academic freedom into the right to instill in students' minds ideas which are contrary to those proclaimed and consecrated by the Constitution.

Those who abuse liberty are primarily responsible for the present situation. They are ignorant or semi-illiterates — soldiers and sailors — who joined under the support of the prior government to engage in subversive propaganda. They do not know what Marxism is or what Marxist ideas are. They are men like this professor of introductory economics. . . . Was he expounding the subject of economics when he announced [these Marxist ideas]? No, he was distributing a manifesto, a memorial, to incite his young students to reflect on the present situation, and to avoid "becoming gorillas," because to him those that overthrew the Communism that was each day being implanted in this land were "gorillas." . . .

But . . . on a strictly juridical level, I concur in the vote of the eminent reporter, for the facts stated in the accusation do not really constitute the crime charged. I vote to grant the habeas corpus.

Minister Victor Nunes: . . .

[Omitted here is a detailed discussion of the U.S. Supreme Court case of *Sweezy v. New Hampshire,* 354 U.S. 234 (1957).]

In a certain period, Mr. President, there was a reactionary movement in the United States which did not protect university freedom. . . . During that period, Einstein was led to utter these melancholic words, "If I were young again and had to decide on my life, I would not try to be a scientist or university professor; I would prefer to be a plumber or salesman with the hope of enjoying the bit of the liberty which we still have." It was an expression of despair, obviously exaggerated. But it was also a symptom, and American statesmen perceived the danger in time. . . . I would not like to have young Brazilians able to repeat literally some day those melancholic words of Einstein, or compare our universities with those of countries submitted to dictatorship.

Minister Pedro Chaves: The melancholy of Einstein was entirely justified in the United States, a country which, because of economic structure and political conditions, enjoys the most ample liberties. . . . But there are no cancellations there of mandates [of elected representatives], or deprivations of constitutional guarantees, nor are there constant and repeated movements, as in Latin America, where we are accustomed to insurrections and revolutions. . . . I am always sad to hear Your Excellency invoking American culture, which is absolutely diverse from our culture, ways, and habits.

Minister Victor Nunes: . . . If I invoke the example of a more developed country, it is because it serves us as a model. . . .

Minister Hermes Lima: Will the cultural difference permit a person to be saddened in the United States by the lack of liberty and not permit a person to feel the same thing in Brazil? Will the cultural difference authorize the lack of liberty in Brazil? . . . Where do we go with this reasoning, what regime should we adopt here? Why do we have to adopt a democratic regime if this country, unlike the United States, is not mature enough for democracy? Then we would have to adopt a special regime, and this regime would signify . . . a curtailment of public liberties. The cultural difference would serve for this, precisely to prevent the country from rising to a higher level. . . .

Minister Victor Nunes: The risks of liberty of thought at the university are well compensated by the benefits that a free university brings to the people, to the economic development of the country, and to the moral and intellectual perfection of humanity. And it is thus that the Constitution seeks for in addition to consecrating the liberty of thought in general, it also guarantees, redundantly, academic freedom. (art. 168 VII).

I vote to grant the writ.

Minister Cândido Motta Filho: Mr. President, I am in complete accord with the eminent reporter. The preventive detention of the petitioner stemmed from the fact that he distributed to his students a manifesto critical of the revolution. This manifesto really is critical, but it is not subversive. In it one finds no appeal whatsoever to illegality.

I would also like to recall here a great Brazilian writer, Eduardo Prado, who said that the history of Brazil has been such that one never knows where revolution begins and legality ends. . . . And in this natural confusion of our history, . . . I prefer to remain with the Constitution; though for many it may not be in force, it is for us, for a judge can only reason within legality. Within this legality, I am proudly obliged to recognize liberty of thought and academic freedom.

I also vote to grant the habeas corpus.

Decision

Having viewed the pleadings in No. 40.910, the order sought for Sérgio Cidade de Rezende is granted, in conformance with the above notes.

Brasília, August 24, 1964.

Question

The debate among Ministers Pedro Chaves, Victor Nunes, and Hermes Lima is a familiar one in developing countries. Some critics of the formalism of their constitutional systems have blamed their elites for irresponsibly copying constitutional institutions and doctrines inappropriate for developing societies, while others have found formalism a useful defense against tyranny. A common argument is that constitutional guarantees of individual liberty are constantly being abused and deter speedy economic development; they are a luxury which only developed nations can afford. Does the argument given by Minister Hermes Lima adequately meet this contention? *Cf.* Trubek, "Toward a Social Theory of Law: An Essay on the Study of Law and Development," 82 *Yale L. J.* 1, 40-49 (1972).

Decisions such as *Sérgio Cidade de Rezende, Francisco Julião, Miguel Arraes de Alencar, Jose Parsifal Barroso, supra,* brought great pressure from the *linha dura,* the hard-line military officers, to do something about the judiciary's hamstringing of the revolution. The first assault on the judiciary's independence came with Institutional Act No. 2, which made three significant constitutional changes. Article 6 permitted the government to pack the Supreme Federal Tribunal, increasing the number of ministers from 11 to 16. The measure was thinly disguised as a way of relieving the court's tremendous workload, despite the protestations of the Court that increasing the number of ministers was not the way to accomplish that commendable task.[91] Article 8 provided that jurisdiction of the military courts could be extended to civilians in cases provided by statute for the repression of crimes against the national security or against military institutions. Law No. 314 of March 13, 1967, a draconic measure known as the Law of National Security, provided for this extension. Finally, Article 19 provided that any governmental acts based upon the first and second institutional acts were excluded from judicial review. This clause became boilerplate in all successive institutional acts.

While undeniably more favorably disposed toward the revolutionary government after its "packing," the Supreme Federal Tribunal was not converted into a mere rubber stamp for the executive. To their credit, Presidents Castelo Branco and Costa e Silva nominated to the Court a group, which, on the whole, consisted of capable jurists. Included among them was Adaucto Lúcio Cardoso, who had resigned as President of the House in 1965 in protest against Castelo Branco's quashing the mandates of six representatives and reputedly had helped no less notorious an enemy of the revolution than Francisco Julião flee from the military. Thus, despite the presence of ten ministers nominated after the 1964 Revolution, in the latter part of 1968 the Supreme Federal Tribunal had sufficient independence to grant habeas corpus to Darcy Ribeiro, former Minister of Education and deposed President Goulart's right-hand man; to Wladimir Palmeira, leader of the outlawed National Student Union (UNE); and to an entire group of students jailed for holding a forbidden meeting of UNE. It also invalidated parts of the Law of National Security. See *Vieira Netto, supra,* p. 113.

To be sure, in several cases the Court refused to interfere with extremely sensitive political issues, such as the confinement of ex-President Janio Quadros in the middle of the interior state of Goiás for 120 days for engaging in political discourse in open defiance of a revolutionary edict,[92] or the right of the government to prosecute Márcio Moreira Alves, an opposition representative from the State of Guanabara, who had severely denounced the military from the floor of the House. Alves' speech became a *cause célèbre* in the Congress, which handed the government a stinging rebuke by refusing to waive Alves' parliamentary immunity.

The military government's response was the promulgation of Institutional Act No. 5 of December 13, 1968, which removed virtually all institutional restraints on the

---

[91] See Nunes Leal, "Supremo Tribunal: A questão do número de juízes," 359 Rev. Trib. 7 (1965).

[92] HC 46.118, 52 R.T.J. 435 (1968).

executive's exercise of power. The President was given the power to suspend Congress; declare a state of seige; summarily quash elective mandates; deprive citizens of their political rights for ten years; dismiss or retire any government employee or office-holder despite constitutional guarantees of tenure; and exercise legislative power by himself. Article 10 suspended the writ of habeas corpus in all cases of political crimes against national security (a concept presently about as elastic in Brazil as the commerce power in the United States), as well as crimes against the social and economic order and the popular economy.

Institutional Act No. 5 touched off a witchhunt that the courts were powerless to prevent. A number of judges were themselves victims. Pursuant to Institutional Act No. 5, in closed, secret proceedings, three ministers of the Supreme Federal Tribunal (all appointed prior to the 1964 Revolution) were compulsorily retired. Several judges of the lower courts were also retired. The President of the Supreme Federal Tribunal, Antônio Gonçalves de Oliveira, resigned from the Tribunal in protest.[93] After another minister resigned because of age, still another institutional act (No. 6 of February 1, 1969) was promulgated, reducing the number of ministers from 16 to 11, cutting back on the Tribunal's jurisdiction to hear ordinary appeals from cases denying a writ of security, and eliminating ordinary appeals to the Tribunal from decisions of the military tribunals judging civilians for crimes against national security or military institutions.

The Fifth and Sixth Institutional Acts have severely curtailed the jurisdiction of the courts and have seriously interfered with judicial independence. Though badly shaken, the Brazilian Supreme Federal Tribunal has not been entirely cowed. As the next case and notes reveal, the Tribunal has been cautiously trying to minimize the restraints upon its independent operations.

JOÃO RODRIGUES CERQUEIRA

Supreme Federal Tribunal of Brazil
H.C. No. 46.881, 52 R.T.J. 160 (1969)

Minister Luiz Gallotti: Attorney Laercio Pellegrino requested habeas corpus for João Rodrigues Cerqueira from the Tribunal of Justice of the State of Guanabara against the General Secretary of Public Security, alleging: The petitioner was arrested on January 6 without having been in *flagrante delicto* and without issuance of a proper arrest warrant by any competent authority. He requested habeas corpus against the police, who informed the judge of the 3d Criminal Chamber that the petitioner had been arrested by the act of the Secretary of Public Security. The judge refused the request. This decision was appealed to the Tribunal of Justice. In addition to arresting the petitioner, the police impounded his car. Clarifications were solicited from the

---

[93] The background and details of the more general crisis surrounding Institutional Act No. 5 are examined in R. Schneider, *The Political System of Brazil* 266-78 (1971); A. Stepan, *The Military in Politics: Changing Patterns in Brazil* 259-62 (1971).

Secretary of Security, who communicated that the arrest was linked to Institutional Act No. 5. The Tribunal of Justice refused the request. From this refusal the present appeal was taken. I sent a dispatch requesting information from the Secretary of Security about the crime of which the petitioner is accused.

[The Secretary of Security responded as follows:]

. . . I have the honor of clarifying that the named alien was detained in this city because of criminal commerce in facilitating prostitution.

1. João Rodrigues Cerqueira is one of the many who derive a profit from the exploitation of prostitution by maintaining the Hotel Santarém on Avenue Mem de Sá in this city.

2. With the publication of Institutional Act No. 5 on December 13, 1968, it was once more made public that the Brazilian Revolution has not renounced its intentions of reestablishing an economic, moral, and social order befitting the country's civilization.

3. The unscrupulous commerce in prostitution under the protective mantle of a hotel license is one of the factors which most degrades the society, permitting the proliferation of prostitution, the gathering of marginals and the unemployed, and injury to the family and good people. . . .

4. It is worthwhile adding that from this stem other social anomalies, many times involving sectors of Public Administration in scandals of corruption and favors, which are not always proven.

5. One constant is that such "hotels" always belong to foreigners, which speaks well of the repulsion that the commerce in love causes the Brazilian businessman.

6. To inform you "what is the crime" imputable to the petitioner in terms of common penal legislation, appears to be, with due respect, an escape from the revolutionary reality.

7. The crime of João Rodrigues Cerqueira, like that of others, goes beyond the simple penal norm, because it constitutes a generic anti-social activity, which must be banished.

8. Hence, Mr. Minister, this Secretary of the State insists that the imprisonment of the petitioner has to escape judicial appreciation, for the measure which deprives João Rodrigues Cerqueira of his liberty is based upon the dispositions of articles 10 and 11 of Institutional Act No. 5 of Dec. 13, 1968. I hope that the Court will so decide.

Sincerely yours,

General Luiz França Oliveira
Secretary of the State

. . . [The representative of the attorney general's office recommended that the habeas corpus be denied because the imprisonment was linked to Institutional Act No. 5.]

Vote of Minister Luiz Gallotti (President and Reporter):

Article 10 of Institutional Act No. 5 provides: "The guarantee of habeas corpus is suspended in cases of political crimes, and crimes against national security, the social and economic order, and the popular economy."

The crime of facilitating prostitution, imputed to the petitioner, is not included in this enumeration. Hence, though as serious and respectable be the reasons invoked by the authorities, the guarantee of habeas corpus as to this crime is not suspended. . . .

On the other hand, one should observe that the concession of habeas corpus or the writ of security, remedies which lie against acts of an organ of the Public Power, does not signify that this organ loses prestige. . . . It signifies only that, though its aims be high, . . . it has erred in a concrete case as to its interpretation of the laws, or rather as to the fixing of the precise limits of its power. And it is the judiciary, in its turn, that fulfills its mission, for except in cases set out by the constitutional precepts in force, the rule is that its appreciation of the law cannot exclude any injury of a right. (Fed. Const. of 1967, Art. 150, §4). Judicial correction, when proper and accepted by the authority, maintains the authority's prestige intact, and even shows it by proving its respect for the judicial power.

One notes that the Revolution, in the Acts which it has promulgated, has suspended rights and excluded judicial appreciation in certain designated cases. But never has it annulled decisions rendered by the judiciary.

I vote to grant the appeal. Let the Tribunal of Justice of Guanabara recognize the request and judge it on its merits.

[The other members of the panel unanimously concurred in this decision.]
Brasília, June 3, 1969.

Notes

1. The Supreme Federal Tribunal also reversed a lower court decision which had denied a writ of security to a company whose eight-year tax exemption was summarily revoked. Revocation of the exemption had resulted from a state law that was complementary to an Institutional Act, and the lower court had reasoned that in accordance with the literal terms of the Institutional Act, later incorporated as a transitory provision in the 1967 Constitution, the judiciary was deprived of jurisdiction to review the constitutionality of such complementary legislation. The Supreme Federal Tribunal unanimously adhered to the vote of the Reporter, Minister Luiz Gallotti, who stated:

The precept of a Complementary Act is not, with due respect, a constitutional precept. The former complements the latter, but is not its equal or equivalent. . . .

If Complementary Acts which did not respect . . . [constitutional limitations] were approved and excluded from judicial appreciation, referring back to Institutional Acts which did not entirely support them, . . . according to the principle of the hierarchy of laws, the Institutional Acts have to prevail. . . .

The aforementioned exclusion from judicial review is aimed at acts of a political nature designed to assure the purposes and continuity of the revolution, and not at mere relations of tax law. . . . S. A. Metalúrgica Santo Antônio v. Estado de Minas Gerais, R. E. 68.661, Tribunal Pleno, (STF Dec. 3, 1969).

2. Similarly, Minister Gallotti was led to file a statement changing his vote in a recent case, taking the position that decree-laws issued by the President pursuant to Institutional Act No. 5 are not excluded from judicial review:

> What the Institutional Act sought to exclude from judicial appreciation were those exceptional acts which, normally, the Chief of the Government could not practice. . . . The Legislative Power conferred on the President during the recess of Congress is the same as that which the latter had. Thus, the Congress cannot enact laws contrary to the Constitution. Similarly, the President cannot do so when substituting for Congress during its recess.
>
> To understand differently would permit alteration of the Constitution and the Institutional Acts by decree-law. Rectification of vote in EMS 17.471, Diário de Justiça of June 25, 1969, p. 2817.

3. One byproduct of the 1969 redrafting of the 1967 Constitution was restoration of the Supreme Federal Tribunal's jurisdiction to hear ordinary appeals from decisions of the military tribunals in cases involving civilians accused of crimes against national security. Art. 118(II)b. The Supreme Federal Tribunal made use of this restoration of its jurisdiction to acquit Caio Prado Júnior, an eminent Marxist economic historian, convicted in the military courts of violating the National Security Law because of an interview given to a student magazine. R.O.C. No. 1.116, 59 R.T.J. 247 (1st Term STF 1971).

4. The case which has most shaken the Supreme Federal Tribunal recently was a suit brought by the opposition political party, MDB, to compel the Procurator General to bring a representation to test the constitutionality directly before the Supreme Federal Tribunal of a 1970 decree-law establishing prior censorship of books and periodicals. The Tribunal held that the Procurator General had discretion to decide whether to bring the representation and suggested that the constitutionality of the decree-law might be presented in a concrete case via the writ of security. Reclamação No. 849, 59 R.T.J. 333 (STF *en banc* 1971). Minister Audacto Cardoso, who had resigned as President of the House in 1965 in protest against the government's summary quashing of legislative mandates, took this opportunity to repeat his performance, stating:

> I believe that with the present decision the direct action for the declaration of unconstitutionality is dead. In the conditions in which the country now is, no private party will dare contest the constitutionality of laws of a political nature. One can do that only through representation via the Procurator General. And he has become the man who decides . . . whether the representation will proceed. This is the equivalent to making the Executive the judge of the constitutionality of the laws. Estado de São Paulo, March 11, 1971, p. 1, cols 2-4.

5. The ways in which the military have systematically contracted constitutional rights in Brazil are explored in considerable detail in Carl, "Erosion of Constitutional Rights of Political Offenders in Brazil," 12 *Va. J. Int'l L.* 157 (1972). See also, Steiner and Trubek, "Brazil — All Power to the Generals," 49 *Foreign Affairs* 464 (1971).

(b) The Judicial Tightrope — Argentine Style

The Act of the Argentine Revolution of July 8, 1966[94] was issued by the commanders-in-Chief of the three branches of the Armed Forces. Among other things, the Act abolished the mandates of the President, Vice President, Provincial Governors and Vice Governors; dissolved the National Congress and provincial legislatures; dismissed all of the members of the Supreme Court and the Procurator General, and designated their replacements; dissolved all political parties; and designated Lieutenant General D. Juan Carlos Onganía as the new president. The Act also required the new president to swear "to observe faithfully the Revolutionary goals, the Statute of the Revolution, and the Constitution of the Argentine Nation." The newly designated Supreme Court justices were obliged to swear to administer justice well and legally, "in conformity with what is prescribed in the Goals of the Revolution, the Statute of the Revolution, and the Constitution of Argentina." The Constitution remained in force, but only insofar as it did not conflict with the Aims of the Revolution. See the Statute of the Argentine Revolution, Appendix C, p. 717, *infra*. Despite such an unpropitious ambience for the effective operation of judicial review, the newly reconstituted Argentine Supreme Court, like its Brazilian counterpart, strove to maintain a measure of judicial autonomy, even on matters important to the executive.

In the *Outon* case, *supra* at p. 179, the Court deftly side-stepped a legislative attempt to restrict its amparo jurisdiction. The Court struck another blow for judicial independence the following year by invalidating Law 17.642, which imposed certain duties on the Court in conjunction with designating and serving on impeachment tribunals to try members of the provincial judiciary. Acting *sua sponte,* the Court unanimously issued an accord (*acordada*) stating that it would not comply with the statute because it exceeded the powers of the military government and was "incompatible with the federal principle of government established in the National Constitution and recognized by the Statute of the Revolution . . . ."[95]

The next case shows the Court more directly confronting the executive.

---

[94] 1966 A.L.J.A. 233. See Appendix C, p. 717, *infra.*
[95] 1968-II J.A. 118, 121.

SANCHEZ SORONDO ("AZUL Y BLANCO")

Supreme Court of Justice of Argentina
1968-IV J.A. 56, 130 La Ley 450 (1968)

Buenos Aires, April 30, 1968.

Considering:

1. The special appeal is properly taken from the decision of the civil and commercial division of the Federal Chamber of the Capital granting amparo, based upon the guarantee of freedom of the press, instituted against Decree 7954/67, ... which prohibited the printing, publication, and circulation of the periodical "Azul y Blanco."

2. Although the appellant does not reiterate at this stage its initial objection to the admissibility of the action (based upon non-exhaustion of administrative remedies), it is obvious that the Executive has plainly reaffirmed its intention to continue the challenged measure. ... Hence, the provision of article 2(a) of Law 16.986 [*supra*, p. 175] does not bar the means elected by the plaintiff to dispute the legitimacy of the decree which is in issue in this proceeding.

3. This Court has had the recent opportunity to refer to the reach of the guarantee at issue in its decision in *Calcagno R.R.,* Fallos 59.244, 128 La Ley 809 (decision of Oct. 30, 1967), in which it said that "the true essence of this right fundamentally stems from recognition that all men enjoy the ability to publish their ideas in the press without prior censorship ..., though not with subsequent impunity for the person who uses the press as a means to commit common crimes set out in the Penal Code." ...

5. If art. 14 of the National Constitution prohibits prior censorship, it is proper to conclude that it certainly does not permit the outright closing of a publication. ...

6. The purposes announced in the ... Act of the Revolution are not inconsistent with this conclusion, [The Act of the Revolution] ratifies safeguarding the essential liberties recognized by the Constitution: (1) by fixing as a General Objective the support of "our spiritual tradition inspired in the ideals of liberty and human dignity that are the heritage of western and Christian civilization," and (2) by fixing as a Special Objective in the ambit of internal politics, the restoration in the country of the "concept of authority, in the sense of respect for law and the command of true justice, in a republican regime in which the exercise of the obligations, rights, and individual liberties are in full force."

7. As this Court has said in its decisions of October 30, 1967 ..., "one must regard as an essential manifestation of the right of freedom of the press, free criticism of functionaries for governmental acts, since that is the very foundation of a republican form of government." ...

9. What has been said does not ignore the reproachable excesses which may have been committed by the authors of the periodical pages which gave rise to this amparo. But those excesses do not justify closure; only their eventual repression through judicial proceedings. For, in effect, it has been precisely in safeguarding the fundamental right debated in this case that the Constitution has proscribed the

measure of prior censorship, preferring to run the risk of the possible abuse of freedom of the press.

10. The motive of "security" also alleged . . . cannot prevail over these considerations. . . . Should there exist a real situation of necessity which compromises the security of the Nation with respect to external or internal order, the President has within his grasp — if the circumstances so require — the extreme remedy of suspending constitutional guarantees through invocation of a state of siege, authorized by art. 23 of the National Constitution.

Compare the decision of the United States Supreme Court in the "Pentagon papers" case, New York Times Co. v. United States, 403 U.S. 713 (1971).

Though Argentina's military government has complied with Supreme Court decisions which have curtailed important governmental actions, such respect has not always been accorded to the decisions of provincial courts. Severe *de facto* limitations on their use of amparo have been imposed, as evidenced by the federal government's recent intervention in the Province of Santa Fe.[96] When the police in Rosario, capital of the Province of Santa Fe, banned meetings by the Regional Committee for University Reform, the organizers filed amparo petitions in the provincial courts. Two courts issued writs of amparo declaring that the police actions violated the petitioners' constitutional right of peaceful assembly. The decisions were upheld by the Court of Appeal. Nevertheless, the police refused to comply with the writs of amparo. When the judges who issued the amparo personally appeared at the cordoned-off meeting places to inform the police of their duty to enforce court orders, the police brutally charged the group of lawyers, teachers, and students who had accompanied the judges. Several of the group were wounded, and one of the judges was physically assaulted.

Thereupon the Supreme Court of the Province of Santa Fe held an extraordinary session at which it declared the necessity of executing court orders whether they be right or wrong. The military government responded by promulgating the following decree law.

INTERVENTION IN THE PROVINCE OF SANTA FE

Law No. 17.782 (June 24, 1968)
ALJA, 1968-A, p. 605

The people of the Republic have been stupefied to see that two judges from the Province of Santa Fe, after having granted amparo to permit an act prohibited by the Executive Power, placed themselves at the forefront of what was unequivocally a political demonstration. . . .

---

[96] This statement of facts is drawn from "Argentina, Subjection of the Judiciary," 35 *Bull Int'l. Comm. Jurists* 13 (1968).

The maintenance of public order is an exclusive authority granted to the Executive; it is also the Executive's primary and most elemental duty, whose performance cannot be curtailed.

While respect for the independence of the judiciary is the inevitable basis for the Rule of Law, . . . such respect is owed only within the judiciary's proper authority. If this branch intends to meddle with the powers granted to the other branches of the state, the latter have a constitutional duty to prevent such excesses. One cannot confuse the independence of the judiciary with government by judges.

It is very important for a country to have honest and courageous judges. But, it is equally important that judges be thoroughly conscious of the limits of their authority. . . .

At no time could the Executive Power decline to exercise its authority in maintaining order; much less could it decline to do so at times like the present in which many countries are being shaken by a wave of violence instigated by extremist minorities seeking social dissolution and anarchy.

This movement of international magnitude intends to gain a foothold in this country, while the people want to work in peace and to continue enjoying their security and liberty.

This makes interference by these magistrates particularly serious, for they intended to prevent carrying out of measures indispensable for the maintenance of order.

If this matter were only an isolated act of the aforementioned magistrates, the problem could have been resolved through normal judicial proceedings. But, there has been an even more serious act. The Supreme Court of the Province, far from condemning such reproachable conduct, has supported it by unusual public declaration. . . . [I]nstead of waiting for the proceedings to come to it on appeal, the tribunal has issued, outside of the action, a declaration which not only constitutes a predetermination, but also has obvious political significance.

This demonstrates the obvious need for reorganizing the judiciary in that Province, using the exceptional remedy which Article 6 of the National Constitution provides. . . .

The president of the Argentine Nation sanctions and promulgates with force of law:

Article 1 — The Province of Santa Fe is hereby declared under "intervention" for the sole purpose of reorganizing its Judiciary.

Article 2 — The Commissioner, who shall be designated for such purpose, shall have the power to remove and replace the magistrates and judicial functionaries of the Province according to instructions given by the Ministry of the Interior. . . .

The day after this decree-law was promulgated, the entire Supreme Court of Santa Fe resigned. The intervention produced a number of protests in the Argentine press and in statements by bar groups. The supposed constitutional basis for the government's intervention, Article 6, which permits federal intervention "to guarantee a republican form of government," has been eviscerated in a brief article by one of Argentina's leading constitutional scholars.[97]

---

[97]Bidart Campos, "La Intervención Federal al Poder Judicial de la Provincia de Santa Fe," 131 La Ley 1287 (1968).

G. State of Siege

INTER-AMERICAN COMMISSION ON HUMAN RIGHTS (OAS), PRELIMINARY STUDY OF THE STATE OF SIEGE AND THE PROTECTION OF HUMAN RIGHTS IN THE AMERICAS

Pp. 1, 5-8 (1963)

During the decade 1950-1960, there were over one hundred occasions of the declaration or extension of a state of siege in the American states. During this period, the continent knew neither external war nor armed invasion. . . .

The state of siege is a constitutional measure, designed to provide for the security of the state in times of emergency due to external attack or serious disturbances of public order which the government is unable to control by ordinary measures. It sanctions the temporary granting of extraordinary powers to the executive branch of government and permits the suspension or restriction of certain constitutional rights and liberties of the individual. In practice, the institution suspends the separation of powers and temporarily invests the executive with discretionary powers ordinarily pertaining to the legislative and judicial branches. The execution of those powers must directly pertain to the maintenance of the public order. Several related institutions such as the state of assembly, state of emergency, state of national defense, or state of alarm, are essentially variations of the state of siege, and all will be treated here under the single generic term.

Although some commentators trace its origin to the time of the Roman Empire, in 501 A.D., when governmental powers were increased in the face of real emergencies, its modern history is generally dated to the French Revolution, to a law of July, 1791. As explained by the French Assembly, that law envisaged three different conditions: a state of peace, a state of war, and a state of siege. In the first situation, civilian authorities were completely independent of the military; in the second situation, the state of war, the civilian cooperated with the military; in the third, siege, the military dominated the civilian authority. Accordingly, siege was distinct from and more serious than the state of war and related directly to an armed attack on the territory of the nation. Article 11 of the original French law specified that the siege existed, "not only from the moment in which the enemy attacks commenced, but as soon as communications are severed, as a result of the encirclement, . . . to a distance of 1,800 *toises.*"

Napoleon, amending the French Constitution in 1815, added an important provision clarifying the declaration of the state of siege. It stated that, "no place, no part of the territory can be declared in state of siege, except in the case of foreign invasion or civil disturbances. . . . In the first instance, the declaration should be made by an Act of Government. . . . In the second instance . . . it can only be declared by law."

Thus, historically, the state of siege is intimately related to the necessities of armed battle carried on within the territory of one of the warring parties. It was to be invoked only when a city or locale is under actual siege, or, as described by Sánchez Viamonte, "only in the case of the gravest risk which could threaten a nation . . . . The state of siege is so serious a measure that it is not . . . authorized in case of war but when there is a foreign attack within our territory." Its use against civil disturbances, as specified in the Napoleonic amendment, implied its use against the very people whom the government is supposed to represent. For a democracy, this raises a myriad of problems. Some of these problems were provided for at that time by allowing it to be declared only by law in case of internal disturbance, that is, only with the approval of the people's own representatives. . . .

The modern state of siege bears but little resemblance to its historical precedent. Carlos Sánchez Viamonte points out the eclectic nature of the modern Latin American institution which combines the French and American concept [suspension of habeas corpus] and amplifies both of them by extending, sometimes without limit, the right to suspend specific constitutional guarantees. What exists in Latin America today, in many respects, appears to be a unique institution. It is sanctioned in the constitution for everything from epidemics and public calamities to "dangers to the national sovereignty." It has apparently evolved to serve entirely new purposes, with a wholly new juridical content. . . .

In France, where the state of siege can be declared only in the "event of imminent danger resulting from a foreign war or armed insurrection," the legislature, which has the power to declare and to end a state of siege, is the principal check against abuse of the institution. The courts will not review the legality of its declaration nor its continuance in force. Nor do the courts offer much in the way of protection from arbitrary governmental action taken during a state of siege.[98] But in many Latin American nations, where the state of siege is hardly an extraordinary event, courts have been under greater pressure to correct abuses of governmental action. The cases that follow show the development in Argentina of a cautious effort to impose judicial limitations upon the extraordinary powers granted to the executive during the state of siege.

CONSTITUTION OF ARGENTINA (1853)

Article 23. In the event of internal disorder or foreign attack endangering the operation of this Constitution and of the authorities created thereby, the Province or territory in which the disturbance of order exists shall be declared in a state of siege and the constitutional guarantees shall be suspended therein. But during such suspension the President of the Republic shall not convict or punish upon his own

---

[98] C. Rossiter, *Constitutional Dictatorship* 89 (1948).

authority. His power shall be limited, in such a case, with respect to persons, to arresting or transferring them from one point of the Nation to another, if they do not prefer to leave Argentine territory.

---

1. Arrest and Detention

TROSSI

Supreme Court of Justice of Argentina
247 Fallos 528 (1960)

Buenos Aires, August 26, 1960. [Twenty-eight plaintiffs sought release from detention by means of habeas corpus. They had been detained by the Executive under the terms of an act of Congress declaring a state of siege. The court of 1st Instance denied their petition.]

1st) [In this extraordinary appeal] , . . . the appellants' counsel maintains that the decision of the judge of 1st instance infringes arts. 14, 14 bis, 18, 23, and 29 of the Fundamental Law, because there is no demonstration that the detained persons, in whose favor the present habeas corpus was filed, "were found in situations such as those foreseen by art. 23 of the Constitution," so that the arrests ordered in this case violate the constitutional precepts mentioned. He argues, also, the unconstitutionality of law 14.785 [declaring the state of siege].

2d) As the record shows, the persons whose liberty is sought . . . have been detained by order of the President of the Nation, to "assure tranquility" and by virtue of the powers "conferred on him by the state of siege" . . . .

3rd) The substantial impropriety of the appeal under examination is apparent. As has been consistently decided, in these circumstances judges are prohibited from substituting themselves for the President of the Nation in considering the truth or error, the justice or injustice, of transitory measures of defense which he considers necessary to adopt in the exercise of the powers which art. 23 of the Constitution gives him exclusively. (Fallos: 243:504 and cases there cited.)

4th) Neither can we accept the challenge to law 14.785 . . ., for the act in which the Congress declared the existence of the state of siege is, in itself, not justiciable. (Decisions cited in the foregoing paragraph.)

On its merits, and the *Procurator General* having stated his opinion, the appealed decision is affirmed insofar as it has been the subject matter of the extraordinary appeal. – *Benjamín Villegas Basavilbaso.* – *Aristóbulo D. Aráoz de Lamadrid.* – *Julio Oyhanarte.* – *Pedro Aberastury.* – *Ricardo Colombres.*

MANUEL RODRIGUEZ

Federal Chamber of Appeals of La Plata, Sala I (Argentina)
138 La Ley 770 (1970)

[The petitioners were arrested on July 1, 1969, pursuant to an Executive Decree, issued during a state of siege. The only explanation for the arrest given in the Decree was that it was "necessary to assure public tranquility." Their petition for habeas corpus was denied in the court of 1st Instance, and the petitioners appealed.

[The appellate court refused to consider the first two questions raised — the propriety of the declaration of the state of siege and its duration — on the ground they were nonjusticiable political questions.]

2d Instance. — La Plata, August 19, 1969 — Is the appealed sentence just?

Dr. Alconada Aramburú said:

. . . [I] f article 23 of the National Constitution accords the Executive the power to arrest or transport persons during a state of siege, I understand that it cannot be interpreted so that such power is exercisable without any limitation. This would signify admitting the possibility that the National Constitution has invested the President of the Nation with an all-inclusive power that may be exercised above and even against the Constitution itself. This is what happens — in the opinion of the petitioners — when the decree which provides for the detention of a person gives no reasons or contains only the vague and general reference mentioned above. What the Supreme Court of Justice of the Nation declared in the case of the former national senator, Dr. Leandro N. Alem, bears recording: ". . . From this series of constitutional prescriptions one concludes that the powers of the state of siege, inasmuch as they refer to authorities created by the Constitution, must be exercised within the Constitution itself. . . ." (Fallos, t. 54, p. 432) Later on it asserts: ". . . [E] xercised discretionally and *without control,* this power which article 23 of the Constitution confers on the President may come to modify substantially the conditions of the Houses of Congress. . . ." (p. 459). This doctrine is applicable to the present case, inasmuch as it admits the power of the Judiciary to review the validity of detention in a concrete case. . . .

Summarizing all that has been expressed [in the doctrinal discussions here omitted], one can extract the following fundamental conclusions: (1) that it is the unrenounceable duty of the Judiciary of the Nation, upon petition of an interested party, to exercise due control over all detentions ordered by the Executive during a state of siege; and (2) that it is always necessary to have a basis for each order — especially when it restricts a person's liberty. This necessity cannot be seriously contested, at least in a Republic like ours. I sincerely believe that no one can reasonably maintain that anyone can decide the fate of a right or guarantee — even more so if it is a man's liberty — using a simple verbal expression as the sole and exclusive basis of his mandate. . . .

[F] rom September 6, 1930, up to the present date, a person might have been detained for 17 years, five months, and 18 days, for during that period, the state of siege, as well as other more serious measures (like the Conintes Plan, the state of internal war, martial law, etc.) was decreed no less than 11 times. On three of these occasions, it was extended for several years in succession (1941/1945; 1951/1955; and 1958/1963). . . . A person born on September 6, 1930, . . . could have been incarcerated for approximately 45 percent of his total existence. During all this time said person would have lacked all protection. For him there would have been no release, probation, parole, pardon, nor amnesty. That is to say, in a word, he would not have had even the hope of being accorded any of the benefits which are given to those accused or convicted of unlawful acts.

. . . It is my vote that it is the unrenounceable duty of the Judiciary to examine whether the order of detention is reasonable or not, and it is also my vote that in . . . [this case] the lack of any basis [for the detention] demonstrates the unreasonability of the measure in question. . . . [I] t was the inescapable obligation of the authority which issued [the order] to set out the bases which might eventually justify it.

[I] t is proper to decree the immediate liberty of the persons detained.

Dr. Masi said:

The absence of proof relating the arrest to the situation provided for in Article 23 of the National Constitution places this case within the exceptions in which doctrine considers habeas corpus unsuspended. Given our ignorance of reasons legitimately linking [the arrest to the state of siege] , . . . there is no alternative but to judge that there is *unreasonableness based on a misuse of power.*[99] Consequently the act is unconstitutional. . . .

I vote, then, for revocation of the appealed decision, for habeas corpus will lie . . .

Dr. Ríos Centeno said: . . .

According to the reiterated decisions of the Supreme Court, the concrete exercise of the powers inherent in the state of siege is reviewable only when it is manifestly clear that the powers bestowed by Article 23 of the National Constitution have been exceeded (Fallos, t. 252, p. 90). . . .

The . . . [record in this case] does not reveal that such powers have been exceeded, for the state of siege provided for in Law 18.262 was a response to a situation of perturbation, which is the reason that decree 3603 ordered the detention of the named parties. . . .

It is worth adding that the Supreme Court, in referring to the powers in issue accorded to the President of the Nation, has laid down the rule that the Judiciary cannot substitute its estimate of the measures required to preserve public peace for those of the political authorities. . . .

Furthermore, the power in issue, although of an exceptional character, is limited in its exercise, by the right of the persons arrested or transported by the Executive, to opt for leaving the country, an option which has not been made. In this situation it is proper to conclude that the ordered arrests are not susceptible to judicial review except in exceptional circumstances. [The circumstances are not exceptional in this case] , . . . for it appears to involve a reasonable exercise of the emergency powers of the Executive. . . .

---

[99] The Spanish term used is *desviación de poder,* which is essentially the same as the concept of abuse of power encountered in the Brazilian writ of security, *supra,* p. 102. [Eds.]

[Because the majority ordered immediate release of the petitioners, they did not reach the other issue in the case: the lawfulness of the conditions under which the prisoners were held.]

Since the detention of persons by virtue of the exceptional powers accorded by article 23 of the National Constitution does not affect their integrity, they certainly cannot be submitted to the same regime as an accused or condemned person. . . .

Consequently, I vote (1) to affirm the appealed decision insofar as it rejects the petition for habeas corpus brought in favor of Manuel Rodríguez and Edgar Pereyra García; (2) to modify the decision . . ., providing that within 48 hours the named citizens be placed in a situation and place which does not comport with imprisonment . . . .

[The decision below was reversed, and petitioners were ordered released.]

Notes

1. One factor that may be very significant in explaining the extensive use of the state of siege in Argentina is that military personnel are entitled to a 100 percent increase in their years of service for computing pensions for service during a state of siege, provided the President so states. See Law 14.777, Art. 69 (b), of Dec. 22, 1958.

2. The Supreme Court agreed to hear an extraordinary appeal from the decision in the foregoing case *sub nom. Del Río, Jorge B. y otros,* 138 La Ley 192 (1970). However, in December of 1969, while the appeal was pending before the Supreme Court, the Executive issued decrees releasing the detainees. The Procurator General suggested to the Supreme Court that in view of the mootness of these cases, it was proper to revoke the decision below conceding habeas corpus. The Court declined to follow this suggestion and simply declared its prior decision to hear the appeal unofficial. 140 La Ley 74 (1970).

The government was not content to let the matter rest. The *Canovi* case, which follows, became the government's vehicle for securing Supreme Court review.

RICARDO ALBERTO CANOVI

Supreme Court of Justice of Argentina
278 Fallos 337 (1970)

Buenos Aires, December 23, 1970. . . .

[Canovi, like Manuel Rodríguez in the preceding case, was arrested during a state of siege pursuant to an Executive Decree of June 30, 1969. Canovi obtained his release a month before Rodríguez and the others, because the judge of the 1st Instance granted his petition for habeas corpus. This decision was reversed by the National Chamber of Appeals of the Federal Capital, but Canovi's rearrest was not ordered. The Supreme

Court declined to dismiss the extraordinary appeal from the decision of the National Chamber of Appeals as moot.]

4. While it is true that the beneficiary of the present appeal is presently at liberty . . ., such circumstance does not require the result reached by this Court in the case D.73, *Del Río, J.B. y otros* of February 27 of the current year, because the pleadings . . . demonstrate that such liberty was conceded by the Executive to comply with the order of the judge of 1st Instance, who had issued the writ of habeas corpus, rather than because the Executive desisted from its intention to exercise the powers conferred by art. 23 of the National Constitution with respect to Canovi.

5. For many years this Court has held that the specific power conferred on the President of the Nation while a state of siege is in effect to arrest people or transfer them from one point of the Nation to another, assuming they do not prefer to leave Argentine territory, is not judicially reviewable, unless it goes beyond the limits set out in art. 23 of the National Constitution. . . . In this it differs from other types of measures, such as those which affect freedom of the press, which are susceptible to control for reasonableness (as was held *in re Primera Plana* [*infra,* p. 232] on March 3 of last year).

6. In practice the presidential powers to arrest or transfer persons in situations of emergency . . . lack any punitive connotation. They simply represent political security or transitory defense measures, to which one applies the title preventive. . . . Thus, the particular nature of these measures are exclusively ruled by political considerations. . . . If the judges could substitute their views for that of the President, in the final analysis it would be they rather than he who would come to exercise the powers of art. 23 of the Constitution. . . .

7. The preceding considerations certainly do not deny the legitimacy of judicial intervention in case of a measure which exceeds the powers conferred on the President by art. 23, as would occur if the President imposed a penalty or denied the option of leaving Argentine territory. But none of these situations is before us in this case.

Therefore, having heard the Procurator General, the appealed decision is affirmed insofar as it was the subject of the extraordinary appeal. Eduardo A. Ortiz Basualdo — Roberto E. Chute — Marco Aurelio Risolía (dissenting) — Luis Carlos Cabral — Margarita Argúas (dissenting).

Dissent of Ministers Risolía and Argúas: . . .

7. This Court has repeatedly held that the decision to arrest persons or transfer them . . . if they do not prefer to leave Argentine territory, is not reviewable by the tribunals of justice, unless it goes beyond the limits set out in art. 23 of the Supreme Law. . . .

8. However, the very peculiar aspects of this case should be set out: (a) Canovi was included in a general decree, which contained the names of 93 persons detained at the disposition of the Executive on June 30, 1969 . . .; (b) these persons regained their liberty in December of that year, with the exception of Canovi, who obtained his earlier . . . via habeas corpus on November 12, 1969 . . .; (c) the proof presented in this case, whose authenticity was not objected to by the government attorneys of the first and second instances . . . shows: (1) that Canovi has no police or court record; (2) that he was working for the firm of General Motors for several years, where he has

enjoyed a good reputation . . .; (3) that he is a student of the Law School of Buenos Aires, whose Dean indicated that Canovi had no disciplinary record and was not a student leader . . .; (4) that in a timely letter directed to the tribunal he affirms that he does not have, nor has he ever had, any political affiliation, and supposes the existence of a "lamentable error," which he asks the judge to clarify before the proper authority . . .; (5) that the testimony of witnesses corroborates that he is a correct person, who was studying and supporting his invalid father and his mother . . .; (6) that the only reference that could work against him comes from the police reports on pages 29 and 31, which, after stating that Canovi has no police or court record, add however, that he is accused by Federal Coordination of being an active militant of the Argentine Revolutionary Communist Party, although without setting out any date of affiliation or any facts supporting this active militancy.

9. In such conditions, . . . this Court has also held that the exercise of the power accorded by art. 23 of the National Constitution to arrest and transfer persons during a state of siege is not susceptible to judicial review *except under exceptional conditions of arbitrariness.* Fallos: 256:359, 531; causa A. 230-XV, Allende, Juan Manuel, s/recurso de amparo of September 6, 1963. . . .

11. The implantation of a state of siege . . . does not imply the submission of all guarantees to the discretion of the authorities of prevention. The operation of the constituted powers and their agents must not be arbitrary, "de legibus solutus," detached from any limiting constitutional or legal norm, under penalty of disavowing the very existence of a rule of law. The discretionary exercise of all public powers . . . must always respond to a reasoned and reasonable purpose, and may not adduce, as in this case, [reasons] which conflict with the evidence, . . . permitting the inference that it is a measure without basis or simply erroneous. . . .

[Under the peculiar circumstances of this case the dissenters consider the Executive's action unreasonable and would reverse the court below.]

Notes

1. The majority of the Supreme Court reached the same result in four recent cases presenting virtually the same issue as the *Canovi* case: *Jacobo Adrián Tieffemberg,* 279 Fallos 9 (1971); *Ricardo Holle,* 279 Fallos 305 (1971); *Agustín Tosco,* 12 J.A. 454 (Ser. cont. 1971); *Margarita Garbich de Todres,* 146 La Ley 30 (1972). Neither of the dissenters participated in *Tieffemberg*; only Minister Risolía participated in *Holle,* filing a dissenting opinion, and both dissented in *Tosco* and *Garbich de Todres.*

2. Equally interesting was a recent case the Supreme Court did not decide. In *Carlos Abelardo Garber y Otro,* 279 Fallos 193 (1971), during a state of siege the Executive had ordered the detention of a corporate officer and a director because of allegedly fraudulent business activities. The government's position, expressed in a note by the Minister of Justice to the Bar Association of Buenos Aires and in a public speech by the President of the Nation, was that the powers conferred by article 23 of the Constitution could be exercised to avoid illicit economic activities, which

disrupted the economy. This was too much for the Procurator General, who delivered a six-and-a-half page opinion to the Court urging issuance of the writ of habeas corpus on the ground that the Executive had exceeded the powers conferred by article 23. Soon after the Procurator General's opinion, the Executive released the detainees, and the Supreme Court dismissed the extraordinary appeal as moot.

The lower courts have split on this issue. See *Pasino, Angel y otros*, 10 J.A. 718, 720 (Ser. Cont.) (C. Fed. Córdoba 1971).

3. Recent responses of the Argentine courts of appeal to petitions for habeas corpus during a state of siege have been divided. The reported decisions generally agree that the judiciary has the power and obligation to determine whether specific detentions are reasonable in light of the circumstances, but they diverge with regard to the crucial question of burden of proof. Rarely does the government present the courts with substantial evidence that a particular detention is reasonable under the circumstances of the state of siege. The Criminal and Correctional Chamber of Appeals of the Federal Capital has been denying habeas corpus where the petitioner has failed to introduce sufficient proof that he should be freed. *Saguier, Eduardo y otros*, 138 La Ley 410 (1970); *Holle, Ricardo*, 141 La Ley 26 (1970); *Musella, Martha B.*, 141 La Ley 645 (1970); *Montenegro, José Oscar*, 13 J.A. 491 (Ser. Cont. 1971). The Federal Chamber of Appeals of Tucumán, on the other hand, has taken the same position as the Federal Chamber of Appeals of La Plata in the *Rodríguez* case, granting habeas corpus where the government failed to show why petitioner's detention was necessary to maintain public order. *Cheli, Guido C.* 141 La Ley 10 (1970).

4. The military regime promulgated two statutes designed to curtail the judiciary's power to release those the government wishes to see held. Law 18.232 of May 28, 1969 authorizes trial of civilians by courts martial for a substantial number of common crimes, primarily relating to destruction of property. Law 18.799 of October 5, 1970 denies release to anyone detained during a state of siege if an appeal from an order conceding habeas corpus is pending. A lower court has declared the former statute unconstitutional, *Espinoza, Jorge E. y otros*, 1969-3 J.A. 814, and both measures have been severely critized. See Morello, "Protección Procesal de los Derechos Humanos en la Argentina, en la Hora Actual," 12 *Revista del Colegio de Abogados de la Plata*, No. 25, p. 243, at 254, 266-67 (1970).

5. The extraordinary powers conveyed by the state of siege have been perenially abused by Argentine executives. Though Article 23 of the Argentine Constitution prohibits the President from convicting on his or her own authority, in practice this prohibition is frequently disregarded. Whether the "option" of leaving the country or being detained can be exercised depends upon executive decision. See Sánchez Viamonte, "Introducción a los Poderes del Gobierno," in J. Paita (ed.), *Argentina: 1930-1960*, 101 (1961).

2. Freedom of the Press

PRIMERA PLANA v. GOBIERNO NACIONAL

Supreme Court of Justice of Argentina
7 J.A. 301 (Ser. Cont. 1970), 138 La Ley 464 (1970).

[On August 5, 1969 the Executive issued a decree closing down Primera Plana, a weekly news magazine, and seizing all copies of the latest edition. The decree was issued pursuant to a continual state of siege declared for the entire country by Law 18.262. The owners of the magazine brought an action of amparo, challenging the constitutionality of the decree. The judge of the first instance granted the amparo, in part, invalidating the closure. The government appealed, and the court of 2d Instance reversed. From this decision, the newspaper owners appealed specially to the Supreme Court.]

Buenos Aires, March 3, 1970 — . . .

For a long time, this Supreme Court, in interpreting the limits of article 23 of the National Constitution, had invariably decided that the state of siege signified a suspension of individual guarantees — among them, freedom of the press. Consequently, it resolved that one could not question . . . the legitimacy of the seizure of editions of newspapers or periodicals, the prohibition of their circulation, or the closure of their offices. . . .

One may find support for this same position in . . . the refusal of the National Congress to enact bills tending to regulate article 23 of the Constitution to provide that the state of seige does not authorize the Executive to shut down presses, suspend periodicals, or prohibit their circulation. . . .

[S]tarting with the case "Antonio Sofía y otro," Fallos, t. 243, p. 504 (Rev. La Ley, t. 97, p. 533, Fallo 44.534) [1959] the case law has been oriented toward recognizing the power of the Judiciary to control the reasonableness of the acts of the Executive under the powers conferred by article 23 of the National Constitution. . . . Examination of the reasonableness of said acts may encompass . . . two aspects: (a) the relationship between the affected guarantee and the state of internal commotion, and (b) verification whether the act of the authority bears an adequate relationship to the purposes of the law declaring the state of siege. With respect to this last aspect, it should not be forgotten that it is beyond the judicial sphere — by virtue of the principle of separation of powers — to issue pronouncements on the basis of the convenience or inconvenience, or the correctness or incorrectness, of the authority's act. . . .

When examined in the light of such antecedents, decree 4179/69. by virtue of which the closure of the weekly "Primera Plana" has been ordered, does not show manifest unreasonableness. . . . [I]n the first place, one cannot say that the guarantee affected in the case is unrelated to the state of internal commotion which caused the establishment of the state of siege. Secondly, neither can one affirm — taking into account the content of the edition seized — that the challenged act lacks an adequate relationship to the ends of the law which adopted the extreme remedy authorized by article 23 of the National Constitution. It is evident that the enactment of Law 18.262

not only obeyed the necessity of acting against the dangers which threatened the Nation at the date of its enactment, but also of removing factors which might contribute to the creation of a perturbing lack of confidence or distrust in the peaceful development of public and private activities.

The argument that decree 4179/69 carries with it the imposition of a penalty equally lacks merit. The restrictions which article 23 of the National Constitution authorize . . . do not have a punitive sense, for they constitute only measures of security . . ., justified by the necessity of defending, in exceptional circumstances, public peace and tranquility.

Finally, wherein the appeal refers to the inability of the present government to decree a state of siege [because it is *de facto*], it is sufficient to refer to the result in Fallos, t. 270, p. 367. . . .

The appealed sentence is affirmed insofar as it has been specially appealed.

Eduardo A. Ortiz Basualdo. – Roberto E. Chute. – Marco A. Risolía (dissenting) – Luis C. Cabral. – José F. Bidau.

Dissent – . . .

[T]here are insurrectionist publications or those which perturb national security, capable of creating or aggravating, by virtue of their ends, a clear, present, or imminent danger, which justify the use of the powers referred to in article 23 of the Constitution with respect to freedom of the press. It is well understood that only by an appreciation of the circumstances of each case, which contemplates its specific peculiarities, can one reject or admit as reasonable the restriction imposed on the exercise of an essential right. . . .

There is no doubt that the publication . . . [in question] contains excesses which go beyond a temperate exercise of information and criticism, but no one, especially judges, as this Court has said – can take away from [the publication's] fulfillment of a public function within a republican order. . . . [I]f one considers the text of the publication which gave rise to these events and the general picture of what was contemporaneously happening in the country, . . . the closure ordered by decree 4179 of August 5, 1969 does not bear an adequate relationship to the spirit of article 23 of the National Constitution and the ends sought by Law 18.262. Let us admit that in this case the exigencies of legality are covered . . . and that while a state of siege is in force, the superior interest of the public peace must disallow the unscrupulous handling of facts, conjectures, or rumors capable of creating or fomenting a climate of agitation or subversion. Nevertheless, . . . the extreme measure of closure . . . directed against a weekly which has not identified itself as the organ of any action group, and extended for the length of an indeterminate period of emergency . . ., exceeds the character of an urgent security measure. . . .

[The dissenting judge was also disturbed by another decree, which forbade the company owning Primera Plana from printing any other publication substituting for Primera Plana.]

Notes

1. The *Sofía* case, relied on by the Supreme Court in the foregoing opinion, is a leading Argentine case on the suspension of constitutional guarantees during a state of siege. In that case, the chief of the Federal Police had refused a license to the Argentine League for the Rights of Man to hold a public meeting in a Buenos Aires theater to "analyze the present situation in Paraguay, regarding the state of the rights of man." The refusal was based on the existence of a state of siege, which had been declared throughout Argentina as a result of a series of "insurrectional" strikes, led by Peronist-dominated unions against the government that had succeeded Perón. The judge of 1st Instance denied the amparo sought by the League, and the Federal Penal Chamber of the Capital reversed, all within eight days after the refusal of the license.

On appeal, the Supreme Court, by a vote of 3-2, reversed once again, denying the League's right to amparo. The Court held, following established case law, that the decision to declare a state of siege was a political one, not susceptible to judicial review. The two opinions for the majority, however, agreed that during a state of siege the courts did have the power to review particular acts of the Executive branch, to determine whether they were, in the language of one opinion, "clearly and obviously unreasonable, [involving] methods that have no relation at all to the purposes of art. 23." The fact that the state of siege was originally declared with respect to labor unrest did not prevent the Court from taking notice of a more general political unrest which, the majority judges held, justified the suspension of the political rights which the League sought to exercise.

The two dissenting judges relied on the exceptional nature of the state of siege to argue that the suspension of guarantees must be closely related to the particular circumstances which motivated the declaration of the state of siege. That relation, they argued, was not present on the facts of the *Sofía* case.

What effect does the requirement of "reasonableness" of Executive action during a state of siege have on the substantive content of constitutional rights? On the role of the judiciary in maintaining those rights? Are these two questions different?

2. Even though the court has taken to examining the reasonableness of the closure of newspapers pursuant to a state of siege, the results of the cases have not changed. The government has been sustained in every case. The cases are collected and summarized in Valiente Noailles, *El control judicial de razonabilidad de medidas restrictivas de la libertad de prensa dictadas en virtud del estado de sitio,* 138 La Ley 465 (1970).

3. Professor Valiente Noailles suggests that the *Primera Plana* case marks a distinct advancement in the effectiveness of judicial control over the Executive's seizure of newspapers during a state of siege in that the court proceeded to read the edition that provoked the closure. "Until this decision, the control of the reasonableness of the measure in concrete cases might be considered somewhat perfunctory. In the case of 244 Fallos 59 [*Diarios "Norte" y "Voz Peronista,"* 97 La Ley 405, 1959-VI J.A. 334 (1959)] . . . the Court accepted the opinion of the Executive Power as to the insurrectional character of the publication that had been shut down. . . . In the case of 248 Fallos 529 [*Agosti, Héctor P.* (1960)] . . . the Court referred inexplicitly to the

content of the pages of the appellant. In the case of 250 Fallos 196 [*Marcos Kaplan,* 107 La Ley 121 (1961)] . . ., the Court went on the basis of a report in the pleadings, whose content was not explicit and which presumably stemmed from a security agency of the Executive Power. . . . [In the three cases prior to *Primera Plana* the Court either made no concrete reference to the content of the publication, or refused to consider the motives or circumstances surrounding the publication.]

"On the other hand, in the . . . [case of *Primera Plana*] there is a concrete reference to the subject matter of the issue seized. It is obvious that if the subject matter had been innocuous, in relationship to the internal commotion, the result of the opinion would have been different." 138 La Ley at 468.

4. The case law of the Argentine Supreme Court on state of siege from 1863 to June 30, 1970 has been abstracted by Vocos Conesa, in J.A. – Reseñas 233 (Ser. Cont. 1970).

One of the outstanding examples of the abuse of the state of siege in recent years has been Paraguay, where a state of siege has been in effect almost continuously since 1947. From 1954 Paraguay has been ruled by the dictatorial regime of General Alfredo Stroessner via the absolute powers derived from the state of siege provisions of the 1940 Constitution. In an act of rare courage, the Paraguayan bar association on May 7, 1965, issued the following formal condemnation of the continued abuse of the state of siege.

GOVERNING COUNCIL, PARAGUAYAN BAR ASSOCIATION

28 *Bull. Int'l. Comm. Jurists* 51-53 (1966)

. . . 3. That the state of emergency, considered in the light of its historical background and of its function as an extraordinary measure of defense for the preservation of the social order at times of grave and imminent peril – thus when an obviously exceptional situation obtains – constitutes an emergency measure which is *essentially transitory* in nature. When the danger (internal disturbance or international war) has been averted and constitutional order restored, the state of emergency should be lifted immediately. Article 52 of the 1940 Constitution observes this principle beyond all doubt in laying down the conditions under which a state of emergency may be declared. Nothing in the text permits of an interpretation by which a permanent state of emergency could be instituted, or by which the power to introduce such a provision could be implied solely on the grounds that the Article does not specify the duration of a state of emergency. . . . When the acts of the public authority do not comply with a "certain degree of reasonableness" and excesses and arbitrary actions result, overriding other constitutionally guaranteed rights such as the inviolable right to a defense lawyer, the right to be tried and sentenced exclusively by a court of law, the prohibition of arrest without a judicial order, the right to freedom of speech and freedom of assembly, etc., judicial control becomes a fundamental condition for the subsistence of constitutional order. The rights expressly formulated in the Constitution, which is the supreme law of the nation, are not mere theoretical pronouncements; they are imperative provisions, with obligatory force, which the judges must apply.

4. That the 1940 Constitution, despite its anti-liberal tendencies and the powerful means by which it has strengthened the powers of the Executive, did not go to the extreme of instituting dictatorship as a form of government. Apart from guaranteeing individual rights (Articles 19, 21, 26, 27, etc.), it expressly forbids the granting of extraordinary or supreme powers under which *the life, honour and property of Paraguayans would be at the mercy of the Government or any person* (Article 16). It makes categorical provision for the independence of the Judiciary (Article 87), forbids members of the Executive to arrogate to themselves judicial functions or to intervene in any way with the judgments of the courts, and institutes special exemptions for the protection of judges.

In pointing to these provisions, which are of universal validity, the intention is not to lend an aura of virtue to this "Political Charter," which is universally condemned by public opinion, nor are its inherent defects being overlooked . . . Nor again is it the intention to justify those now making use of the Constitution, since responsibility does not rest solely with those who drew up this operative instrument — it must be shared by those who use, and abuse it. No one doubts or disputes the need to change the Constitution, but until such time arrives it is the duty of lawyers to struggle to ensure that it be interpreted and applied in favour of freedom and human dignity.

5. That, faced with the present unforeseen reality of a state of emergency *sine die,* imposed continually year after year, with an emergency measure, essentially transitory in nature, being transformed into a normal system of government, it must be acknowledged that this unhappy anomaly is not a juridical creation of the 1940 Constitution but rather the manifestation of an obvious abuse of power. . . .

6. That the aim properly pursued in imposing a state of emergency is the preservation of the Constitution, not its destruction. But if this expedient is employed for other ends, purely oppressive in nature, if arrests are made without just cause and if detention can, without any intervention by a judge, last as long as a prison sentence, without the accused even knowing what the charge is or who is accusing him, then it can be affirmed with certainty that there has been a profound change in the constitutional order. . . .

7. That the crucial problem is that of translating these doctrines and constitutional provisions into practice in such a way that any violations of fundamental rights, resulting from illegal actions or proceedings on the part of the public authorities, may find a rapid and effective remedy through *habeas corpus* proceedings to put an end to illegal detention, and through the remedy of amparo to secure redress in respect of other violations of rights guaranteed by the Constitution.

8. That in order to achieve this result the effective independence of the judiciary is necessary; . . . judges must possess the qualities of probity, integrity and authority necessary to uphold the position of the judiciary in all circumstances. Judges, as interpreters of the laws and particularly of the Supreme Law, must jealously preserve

the rights and freedoms they are asked to uphold . . . Paraguay — irrespective of the defects its political charter may contain — maintains that it is organised as a constitutional State. Respect for human rights and guarantees is the teleological basis of the Constitution, which should be duly preserved by the judicial authority created to protect it.

H. Revolution, Constitutionalism, and Development

What are the developmental implications of frequent revolutionary changes of government and lack of respect for constitutional guarantees of individual liberties? We merely introduce these issues here, returning to them in Chapter VI.

RAPOPORT, COUP D'ÉTAT:
THE VIEW OF THE MEN FIRING THE PISTOLS

in C. Friedrich (ed.), *Revolution* 53, 69-74 (1966)*

Naudé notes that the final accomplishments of a single *coup d'état* depend on how extraordinary or unusual the event seems to be. When citizens believe that the safety of the state has been jeopardized by unique circumstances, a *coup d'état* will be fully accepted, but when *coups d'état* occur so often that they seem commonplace in the political world, men suspect the explanations offered, and are tempted to go outside the law themselves to secure their private purposes. A truly successful *coup d'état* — one that produces a lasting important change — must re-establish a law-abiding habit it has momentarily broken.

In this respect, it is worth noting the difference between Goodspeed's assessment of *coup d'état* and the one conventional among specialists in underdeveloped area studies. To the latter, the individual *coup d'état* rarely alters a body politic much; but to Goodspeed, whose examples come from twentieth-century Europe, a *coup d'état* is clearly the most economical way to achieve a revolution. The reasons for these two very different estimates are obvious. In Europe, where veneration for constituted authority is deeply embodied, only a profound crisis provides opportunity for *coup d'état*. Those who capture government, therefore, have captured an institution which commands respect. They are in a position to make laws which will be obeyed. In Latin America, where a comparatively insignificant incident can topple a government, an illegitimate regime will find it carries its predecessor's albatross.

Perhaps Naudé's major omission is his failure to speculate much about the effects of frequent *coups d'état* on a political system. Had he done so, we would have had some

---

ready-made leverage for a fair assessment of the view that in some countries the act is truly analogous to a constitutionally prescribed procedure – more specifically an election. . . . [B]efore any discussion of "constitutional equivalents" is completed, we need an analysis of the consequences of the compared acts on the capacities of the effected states to create agreement and carry on normal administrative functions. States experiencing frequent *coups d'état* notoriously have a low capacity in these respects, and the logical links between the practices and consequences are easy to grasp.

The major argument for the *coup d'état* as an "institutionalized" way of expressing public opinion rests on the undeniable fact that in some states they are common, and the more questionable assertion that they follow a regular, hence predictable pattern with reference to how many lives are lost, who will lose which office, etc. I cannot argue the statistics of the case, for they have not yet been published, but if the events alluded to do not involve the potential dangers, surprises, and suspense associated with *coups d'état* in our language, we ought to use more adequate descriptive terms. However, when Stokes tells us that a well-executed Latin-American *coup d'état* sheds little blood, while a badly bungled one may cost several thousand lives, Naudé's elaborations do not seem to be beside the point. At least, it is difficult to believe that Stokes is talking about procedures with clearly defined and well-understood rules.

Finally, even if regularity is demonstrated, institutionalization is not thereby established. Accidents and robberies can be treated statistically, but we do not then call them institutions. The distinction suggested is similar to the one the lawyer makes between practice and convention. To say that a convention exists is to imply that the parties to a transaction willingly accept it as the right way to manage affairs even though one party may suffer disadvantages. But there are practices no one considers binding. A government which has the sanction of convention in this sense possesses a right or mandate to rule or represent the citizenry within prescribed limits. A government which lacks a right to rule, whether it attains power through election or *coup d'état,* depends almost entirely on its ability to coerce. Its dilemma is poignantly illustrated by a recent *New York Times* photograph. The picture showed the Venezuelan President Betancourt embracing the Argentine President, and in Betancourt's hip pocket was a pistol! During his five-year administration, he frustrated fifty-six attempted revolts. His right to rule depended partly on his personal willingness to use that pistol, since many of the uprisings were led by men hired to protect his person and office. It takes unusual courage to keep a level head, and, indeed, to survive in such an atmosphere, and the pressures are bound, in time, to engulf the whole state.

. . . Members of a regime where *coups d'état* are commonplace know that they are likely to be deposed by violence; but before the actual event they do not know who the usurpers are, when they will strike, or what will be the consequences for the members' separate lives and fortunes. The implications of this uncertainty cannot be overestimated. The political world becomes the Hobbesian state of nature where one might be well advised to "shoot first and ask questions later." A prudent government will understand that those most likely to threaten it are posing as loyal supporters occupying positions of trust and protected by the strength of the regime. Its anxiety must obviously influence those who have no desire to overturn the status quo but have reason to think they are peculiarly vulnerable to an "unsteady trigger finger." In a state prone to *coup d'état* there can be little mutual confidence among officials, and since individual initiative, according to law, will breed suspicion, it cannot be permitted much scope. Can government in these circumstances face crises calmly when it does not know who its true supporters are, and when it does know that those who command its separate administrative tools may be able to save themselves by throwing their support to enemies whom the crises has spawned?

The mutual uncertainty of government officials must invariably affect the government's relationship with the public. In Naudé's view, after the limited objective of the *coup d'état* has been achieved, the logic of the situation compels the usurpers to seek public confirmation of their deed — a confirmation which no one can assume will be forthcoming automatically. But if popular approval is indicated, the value of this apparent approval must always be suspect. Members of the public will always have reason to hide their true feeling; the real strength and purposes of the usurpers are unknown; the examples of how the usurpers treated other officials — especially their confederates — and how the latter, in their time, handled their opposition are still fresh. By the same token, the knowledge that the public has reason to dissemble must sap the new officials' confidence in popular demonstrations. . . .

The more often *coup d'état* occurs, the more widespread lawlessness must become. A successful *coup d'état* illustrates how profitable it is to evade the law, and that those entrusted with its enforcement cannot be expected to treat their responsibilities seriously. The dilemma of an official wishing to abide by the law in such situations is readily imaginable. If he does his duty and attempts to put down subversion, stamp out corruption, and administer justice, that may be the very reason for his elimination when the government he serves is broken — a consideration he can never forget in a country like Venezuela, where there have been eighty illegitimate successions in a century and probably four hundred and eighty unsuccessful attempts.[100] On the other hand, the official who uses his position for private purposes is not easily detected in the great confusion and ineffective supervision implicit in perpetual instability.

In countries where governments succeed one another legitimately, and where the scope of the act vis-à-vis specific officeholders is defined ahead of time, successions may not breed much innovation; but what is more fundamental, though not so obvious, is that each government will receive its predecessors' powers — powers that have not been withered by disrespect, and powers ample enough to accomplish the state's purposes. Where there has been a long tradition of peaceful succession, we can learn much about the distribution of power simply by analyzing constitutions, but in states where *coup d'état* prevails we have learned to use the curious phrase "paper

---

[100]There are many reasons why it is virtually impossible for an American relying on newspaper reports published in this country to know the correct ratio of unsuccessful to successful *coup d'état* attempts. My six-to-one estimate, based entirely on information since 1945, is very conservative. In fact an eight- or nine-to-one ratio is probably more accurate. I have also assumed that the ratio remained constant throughout the nineteenth century, but I believe in that period the percentage of unsuccessful ones was even larger. [Footnote by Rapoport, renumbered.]

constitutions," which indicates fundamentally that we cannot specify rights and obligations.

When one cannot reckon on the authority of offices or institutions for protection, one will risk "loyalty" only because there seems to be a reason to think the intentions and ability of particular men are different from the type most men display, or because interest compels men to behave in a particular way. Where *coup d'état* is common, so are personal and corrupt regimes. But neither interest nor extraordinary personalities can afford stability and continuity. Interest devoid of the certainty of law varies with circumstance; when a regime is unchallenged, an official's interest is one thing; when it shows signs of crumbling, interest dictates another course. And the same conditions that make extraordinary personalities necessary in a "lawless" state make it immensely difficult for them to create something which will outlive them.

Everything an impersonal law nourishes is threatened by continuous *coups d'état*. The moral fiber disintegrates; injustice is widespread in all states with a tradition of *coups d'état*. The material world is also grossly affected. Rich men buried their gold in ancient despotisms plagued by *coups d'état*, and they sent it to Swiss banks from modern underdeveloped countries, where it is almost impossible to find three consecutive legitimate successions. In both cases the fear of arbitrary administrative events prevents a socially beneficial employment of capital.

Questions

1. What kind of market does Rapoport assume?
2. Why must a "truly successful *coup d'état*" re-establish a law-abiding habit?
3. Cannot law be used instrumentally to promote economic development without protecting individual liberties?

A Final Question

Do the materials of sections F, G and H throw any light on the "debate" between Judge Hand and Professor Hart, pp. 97-98, *supra*?

Chapter III

LAND REFORM

"Get off this estate."
"What for?"
"Because it's mine."
"Where did you get it?"
"From my father."
"Where did he get it?"
"From his father."
"And where did he get it?"
"He fought for it."
"Well, I'll fight you for it."

Carl Sandburg
The People, Yes 75 (1936)

A. Introduction

Land reform is a revolutionary process, implying fundamental changes in a structure of rights and powers. It is, in classic definition, "the redistribution of property or rights in land for the benefit of small farmers and agricultural labourers."[1] In Latin America, the expression "land reform" has sometimes been used to describe such diverse policies as the colonization of desert and jungle lands, the regulation of labor contracts or the introduction of new seeds and fertilizers. The term has also meant, in some countries, the adoption of legislation authorizing land redistribution without significant implementation of the new laws. In any of these non-redistributive senses, of course, "land reform" is not revolutionary, for it is not land reform:

> ... [L]and reform, for nations in which landownership is the central pillar of the structure of social privilege, is not a small concession to be wrung from landlording groups, but a profound and wrenching alteration of the very basis of wealth and power.[2]

However revolutionary the process of land reform may be, it is nonetheless a process that is closely bound to the institutional structure – the legal structure – of a

---

[1] D. Warriner, *Land Reform in Principle and Practice* xiv (1969).

[2] R. Heilbroner, *The Great Ascent: The Struggle for Economic Development in Our Time* 128-29 (1963).

developing society. Thus land reform is a fit subject for law study. This chapter, in focusing on issues of legislative-administrative policy, includes materials that are sometimes called "nonlegal." If any justification were necessary, it was provided ninety years ago by a jurist who had lived through the greatest institutional crisis in the history of the United States:

> In substance the growth of the law is legislative. . . . The very considerations which judges rarely mention, and always with an apology, are the secret root from which the law draws all the juices of life. I mean, of course, considerations of what is expedient for the community concerned.[3]

Land ownership in most of Latin America is highly concentrated. Studies in the early 1960s sponsored by the Inter-American Committee for Agricultural Development (ICAD) substantiate this statement, although ownership patterns vary from country to country. In Argentina, the ICAD study produced these figures:

Farm Size	% of Number of Farm Units	% of Total Area of Farms
Sub-family	43.2	3.4
Family	48.7	44.7
Medium Multi-Family	7.3	15.0
Large Multi-Family	0.8	36.9

(A *sub-family* unit is not large enough to provide employment for 2 people, assuming prevailing incomes, markets, and levels of technology and capital. A *family* unit is large enough to provide employment of 2 to 3.9 people. A *medium multi-family* unit can provide employment for 4 to 12 people. A *large multi-family* unit can provide employment for more than 12. These figures and those that follow are taken from Barraclough and Domike, "Agrarian Structure in Seven Latin American Countries," 42 *Land Economics* 391 (1966).)

Comparable figures from other countries show much higher levels of concentration of ownership. Here are the figures for Colombia:

Farm Size	% of Number of Farm Units	% of Total Area of Farms
Sub-family	64.0	4.9
Family	30.2	22.3
Medium Multi-Family	4.5	23.3
Large Multi-Family	1.3	49.5

[3] O. W. Holmes, Jr., *The Common Law* 35 (1881).

And for Peru (before any distributions under the 1969 land reform law):

Farm Size	% of Number of Farm Units	% of Total Area of Farms
Sub-family	88.0	7.4
Family	8.5	4.5
Medium Multi-Family	2.4	5.7
Large Multi-Family	1.1	82.4

This introductory section is designed to explore the social-economic-political implications of a land tenure system that concentrates ownership so dramatically. We begin with a look at the origins of the great estates in Latin America's colonial period. Then we turn to today's setting for land reform, briefly examining the social and economic context of reform proposals. Competing theories of indirect reform are then considered: colonization of new lands, contract regulation, taxation schemes, industrialization. A typical land reform statute is outlined, and lastly the subject of "counterreform" is introduced.

---

1. Colonial Origins of the Great Estates

The typical *conquistador* came to the New World not to escape religious persecution, nor to found a new society; he came to make his fortune, in the hope of taking it back to Spain where he might live like a lord. The Mayflower had brought wives and children to Plymouth, but the Cortez expedition brought only soldiers, seeking the legendary wealth of the Indies — wealth that was to be enjoyed in the patterns that had been established in the Iberian peninsula.

The conquest of New Spain (Mexico) and of Peru took up where the reconquest of Spain itself had left off; it will be recalled that the year 1492 marked not only the first voyage of Columbus, but also the final expulsion of the Moors from southern Spain. One of the institutions of the reconquest period had been the *encomienda*:

In Andalusia, villages, towns, castles, and lands had been "shared out" among the knights arriving from the north as alodiums [holdings that were absolute, not subject to feudal duties] to be held in perpetuity and with jurisdiction over the inhabitants. Slightly later the military orders had conferred on certain of their members encomiendas in conquered territory: They granted cities, lands, and vassals (owing tribute and personal services), with the stipulation that the beneficiaries maintain armed forced and support divine worship.

These encomiendas present striking similarities to the later ones in New Spain; the resemblance is visible even in such details as the wording of the deeds of grant or the ceremonies of investiture. By 1524 [five years after Cortez landed] the institution seemed clearly fixed: The Spaniards had a right to tribute and labor from the Indians, whose situation recalled indeed that of the men in feudal estates *(señoríos de solariego)* after the decadence of serfdom. In exchange the Spaniards had to maintain their weapons and a horse, and then evangelize the natives. Finally, they attempted to obtain grants in perpetuity.[4]

Cortez himself received an enormous allotment: "The areas claimed must have amounted to not less than 25,000 square miles and contained a total population of some 115,000 people. . . ."[5] While the quoted sentence suggests that the encomienda was a grant of land, in law it was not; it was, instead, "essentially conceived as a concession of the right to collect the king's tribute."[6] There were grants *(mercedes)* of land, often obtained by *encomenderos* (holders of encomiendas). But the encomienda itself granted not lands but Indians, who were "entrusted" to the encomenderos for purposes of Christianizing them — but also to work the encomenderos' lands and mines.

Historical interpretations have changed concerning the place of the encomienda in the formation of the *haciendas,* the great estates that came to flower in the 17th and 18th centuries. It is now generally accepted that in a juridical sense the encomienda and the hacienda are quite separate; the encomienda did not, in a legal sense, blend into the hacienda. But in a social and economic sense, the two institutions do blend together, as Lockhart shows in the article cited above: Both the encomendero and the hacendado were "patriarchs" who "ruled both the countryside and the city." "Each institution in its time was a family possession, the main resource of a numerous clan. Each gave rise to many entails; but, with or without legal devices of perpetuation, each had a strong tendency to remain in the family." The hacendado, like the encomendero, hired a majordomo to run his estate, along with lower-level supervisors; work was performed in each case by Indians. On the larger haciendas, there were live-in priests who performed the functions previously assigned to the *doctrinero,* the priest who ministered to the encomienda's Indians. "Both resident labor and nonresident labor, under both encomienda and hacienda, were still very close to pre-Columbian systems of periodic obligatory work." And, "by and large the great estate scheme was economically rational as well as socially desirable [for the landowner, Lockhart means] . . . . The desire to assemble a complete set of varied holdings was not inconsistent with a thoroughly commercial orientation. . . . The constant effort of the most acute commercial minds was to monopolize, drive out competition, and sell at high prices to the severely limited market. . . . Monopolizing the land discouraged the rise of competitors in the immediate neighborhood." Lockhart summarizes:

---

[4] F. Chevalier, *Land and Society in Colonial Mexico* 36 (Eustis transl. 1963).

[5] G. McBride, *The Land Systems of Mexico* 47 (1923).

[6] Lockhart, "Encomienda and Hacienda: The Evolution of the Great Estate in the Spanish Indies," 49 *Hispanic-American Hist. Rev.* 411, 415 (1969).

All in all, the replacement of the encomienda by the hacienda involved only a shift in emphasis, whatever the factual details of institutional development. A semigovernmental domain, serving as the basis of a private economic unit, gave way to a private estate with many characteristics of government.[7]

Thus the hacendado, while not the juridical descendant of the encomendero, was his social-economic-political heir.

The hacienda is only one of the two main types of great estate in Latin America. The other is the plantation. Where the hacienda prevailed in the first areas of Spanish conquest (Mexico and Peru), the plantation dominated in areas settled later by the Spaniards (Cuba, Venezuela and the Rio de la Plata area), and in Portuguese America. Here we shall look briefly at the example of Brazil.

The plantation — a large-scale commercial farming enterprise, usually producing an export crop — was a form of agricultural organization that originated in the Eastern Mediterranean area. The Portuguese had adapted it to use in their Atlantic islands, and carried it with them to the south Atlantic coast of Brazil. This was an underpopulated area, quite unlike Mexico and Peru, where the Spaniards had found large, settled agricultural populations. To provide labor, the Portuguese brought African slaves to Brazil; after 1600, slaves were the main labor force in the Brazilian sugar plantations.

Although the Brazilian plantations were oriented toward production for an export market, they, like the plantations in Spanish America, tended to be self-sufficient in the style of the hacienda. They raised cattle, and much of their own maize and wheat. The economic history of Brazil can be written in terms of successive booms and busts in mining and in plantation agriculture: sugar, gold, diamonds, rubber, and coffee. Sugar production fell off by the late 17th century, largely because the world market for sugar was also being supplied by competitors in the Dutch, French and English colonies of the Caribbean. Since the 1830s, coffee has been Brazil's leading export; coffee production has been the economic base for the development of southern Brazil, including the metropolis of São Paulo. One local study includes these comments:

> ... [T]he dominant families preserved and extended their holdings by inter-marriage within and between clans, by partnership arrangements... and later by consortiums ... set up among planters and their children. Concentration was further encouraged by the "immunity of land from taxation and the heavy tax on transfers."... Both the extension of coffee cultivation and progressive exhaustion of virgin soil fostered what one planter described as the "almost superstitious spirit ... of the individual agricultural proprietor whose general tendency is to augment his territorial property" and made of the município [county] an area where a few large family-proprietors controlled thousands of acres.[8]

---

[7] *Id.* at 425.

[8] S. Stein, *Vassouras: A Brazilian Coffee County, 1850-1900,* 16-17 (1957).

By the end of the 1880s, 20% of the owners in two parishes of this county owned 70% of the arable land.

The parallels between plantation and hacienda are easily seen: In both cases, land is a base for wealth and power; in both cases, oligopoly in land and agriculture tends to produce oligarchy in politics; in both cases, rural society tends to be rigidly stratified, with a small upper class, a large lower class and virtually no middle class. Labor is tied to the great estate, because there is no alternative employment in agriculture, owing to the scarcity of land outside the great estate. Paternalism and dependence are essential features of such a rural society. People at the bottom of the social-economic scale do not participate in government; locally, the *patrón* is the government. This description of the influence of the traditional great estate is in great measure as accurate today as it was 200 years ago. What is different is that today there are fewer traditional great estates.

---

2. The Modern Setting

A complex social phenomenon such as a land reform cannot be said to have an objective, or even a set of objectives. But land reforms are made by men and women who do have objectives. In this section we shall consider arguments for land reform in Latin America that appeal to such "neutral" and widely-shared values as increased agricultural production, or the creation of a more flexible market economy in agriculture. It would be mistaken, however, to assume that legislative decisions about land reform are primarily made in response to such considerations. Jacques Chonchol, an agricultural economist who headed Chile's Institute of Agricultural Development under President Frei and who was Minister of Agriculture in the government of President Allende, has written:

> In the last analysis agrarian reform is not a technical process, but basically a political process. The experts will no doubt have to play a very important role in agrarian reform, which consists in pointing out the economic and social implications of the various measures to be adopted and in recommending the technically most advisable courses of action for its success. But if we are objective, we have to recognize that nowhere in the world have successful agrarian reforms been carried out by technical experts. They have begun when certain favorable political conditions were present and when certain politicians made the decision to carry them out.[9]

Surely the primary short-range motives of effective land reformers over the years have been essentially political: to get power, to keep power, to reorder the bases of power for the future. Beyond such motives, or perhaps included in them, is the goal of

---

[9] J. Chonchol, *El Desarrollo de América Latina y la Reforma Agraria* 94-95 (1964), translated in *Agrarian Problems and Peasant Movements in Latin America* at 159, 162 (R. Stavenhagen ed. 1970).

creating a greater equality among members of society. Whether rights in land be regarded only in economic terms, or whether they be regarded as the base for political liberty or effective citizenship, their distribution is only instrumental, aimed at a greater social equality. Talk about land distribution in physical terms is common, but it is sterile, for it diverts attention from the fact that what is in issue is a series of relations among people, concerning land as a source of income and power.

The readings that follow explore the social-economic setting for land reform in Latin America. Professor Tannenbaum's description of the classical (and now dying) hacienda is useful not because it portrays a mythical "typical" great estate, but rather because it portrays the evils that are the principal targets of every modern land reform. At the other end of a spectrum of large rural estates in Latin America is the great commercial enterprise, which pays cash wages and produces a cash crop for market. Even such an enterprise may be the object of a reforming government's attention, for the reasons noted in the selection following Professor Tannenbaum's article. The third reading in this section is extracted from an article by two North American agricultural economists with long experience in Latin America, analyzing the economic impact of the concentration of land ownership. Next comes an abbreviated interpretive comment by a Mexican economist on the relation of land reform to economic development in that country. The section closes with Doreen Warriner's caution that land redistribution by no means assures economic development.

F. TANNENBAUM, TOWARD AN APPRECIATION OF LATIN AMERICA
in H. Matthews (ed.), *The United States and Latin America* at 33-39 (2d ed. 1963)*

The hacienda is not just an agricultural property owned by an individual. It is a society, under private auspices. The hacienda governs the life of those attached to it from the cradle to the grave, and greatly influences all of the rest of the country. It is economics, politics, education, social structure and industrial development. . . .

The hacienda as a society may be described by saying that it was — and is — an economic and social system that seeks to achieve self-sufficiency or autarchy on a local scale. It seeks this not as a matter of malice, but in the logic of a given institution to expand so as to have within its own borders all that it needs, salt from the sea, *panela* (black sugar) from its own fields, corn, barley and wheat, coconuts, bananas, apples and pears. All of this depends upon where the hacienda is located. If it can run from the seacoast to the mountain top, from the river bottom where sugar cane will grow to the snow line, then it can raise all of the crops that will grow in all of the climates. Not all haciendas — not any perhaps — satisfy this ideal completely, but that is the bent of hacienda organization: buy nothing, raise and make everything within the limits of your own boundaries. The big house is built from the timbers on the place — and these may be, as I have seen them, of mahogany. The furniture is made at home; the cloth is woven on the place from the sheep; the llamas that graze in the hills, the oxen, the

---

*© 1963 by The American Assembly, Columbia University. Reprinted by permission of Prentice-Hall, Inc., Englewood Cliffs, New Jersey.

horses, are raised and broken on the place; the saddles, bridles, harnesses, are made from the hides of the slaughtered animals. The wooden plow, the wagon, the windmill for the grinding of the corn, or the watermill for the grinding of cane are all made on the place. The table may be loaded at a meal with every kind of meat, grain and fruit — and all of these, the table itself, the house, and the servants as well, will all have been raised, contrived, conserved, grown on the place, including the tablecloth that covers the table, the sandals of the servants, if they are not barefooted. And perhaps even the Indian musician who sits behind the screen and plays his old songs on the homemade instrument is also of the plantation. I am recalling this from personal experience on a plantation in the Province of Ayacucho in Peru.

The people on the plantation are born there. They cannot leave because they may be in debt, or because there is no place to go, for this is home and every other place is foreign. And here too their fathers and grandfathers were born and are buried. If the place changes hands, they change with it. In 1948 the leading newspaper in La Paz, Bolivia, carried an advertisement offering for sale on the main highway a half hour from the capital of the country a hacienda with five hundred acres of land, fifty sheep, much water and *twenty peons.* And similar advertisements have appeared even more recently in Ecuador and Chile. (This I have from others, one a native scholar, the other an American political scientist.) The point is that what we are dealing with is a closed economic, social, political and cultural institution.

Its administrative organization is an interesting adaptation to an aristocratic agricultural society of a non-commercial economy. For the hacienda is a way of life rather than a business. It is not an investment. It was inherited. It is operated with the expenditure of as little cash as possible. If the hacienda is large there may be a couple of hundred or more families residing within its borders. These are scattered in groups of five or ten families in different parts of the hacienda, depending on the kind of land, crops, forest. The laborer usually has a hut which he has built, and a given amount of land, which he works or shares. The hacienda provides the land, the work animals and the seed; and the peon turns over, carrying to the granary by the big house, the share of the crop belonging to the hacendado. The share is determined by the crop, and the tradition of the hacienda. In addition, the Indian also owes the landlord a given number of days' work each week throughout the year. This practice varies. It might be one day's work a week for each hectare of land, or so many days a week for living on the land. The families might also owe a certain amount of service in the big house. The point is that the hacienda has its labor supplied to it without the use of money. If there are two hundred families on the hacienda and if they each owed only one day's work a week for each of two hectares allotted to each family, it would have 400 work days each week.

The labor at its disposal without expenditure of any money for wages is used by the hacienda for working those lands which it tills on its own account. These lands might be in sugar cane, from which it can either with oxen or water power in a small homemade *trapiche,* squeeze out the juice and make *panela,* a dark unrefined sugar, and manufacture rum as well. Or its cash crop may be coffee or cacao, or other products which can be carried to the market on the backs of mules, or on the backs of men, over steep mountain and narrow gorges, to the nearest railroad station, or more recently to the nearest automobile road, or to the nearest town. The cash crop will have been raised, harvested and delivered part or all of the way to the nearest market without the expenditure of any money.

In a curious way, the hacienda is largely beyond the reach of the money economy. Internally it provides, so far as it can, for all of its needs as a going concern as well as a community without recourse to the market. The seed the hacienda supplies to the sharecroppers comes out of the store houses in which it was deposited in the fall; if the laboring population living on the hacienda runs short of food or other supplies they can be purchased in the store — *tienda de raya,* in Mexican parlance, or *company store* in our own economic history. The peon will pay no cash for his purchase for he has no money. It will be written down in a little book by a storekeeper, usually some distant relative or *compadre* of the hacendado. The debt can be liquidated by labor, but it rarely is and serves to tie the laboring population to the hacienda, as they cannot leave without first paying off their debt. This has long been so. It has roots in the colonial system. It persisted all through the nineteenth century, and is still in full vigor wherever the hacienda system survives. It is as hard to kill as was the company store, token coin, or script [sic], in the mining and lumbering camps in the United States. And token coin has its use on the hacienda, for the payment of wages, for the extra labor which may be needed beyond that owed by the peons or for tasks which for some reason lie outside the traditional work the peons accept as theirs. These token coins, sometimes bearing the name of the hacienda, or a piece of metal stamped with *vale un día de trabajo* (it is worth one day's work) can only be exchanged in the hacienda store.

As the hacienda satisfies its own and its community's needs with as little recourse to the market as possible, it buys little, and it sells little as well. The distances, the poor roads, the primitive means of communication, make the transport of goods from one part of the country to another difficult and expensive. The relatively small income from the hacienda is, so to speak, net profit — taxes on land have always been low, the cost of production is at a minimum in monetary terms.

The hacienda is, however, not merely an economic enterprise. It is also a social, political and cultural institution. Socially it is a closed community living within its borders. Part of the hacienda population will be located near the big house, where the store, the church, the school (if there is one), the repair shops, granaries, the blacksmith, carpenter, harness shop will also be. The grist mill and the *trapiche* (sugar mill) will also, in all likelihood, be near the big house if there is water close by. The stables for the favorite horses, cows and other animals raised for household use or consumption will also be close by. The laborers about the big house tend to all these different functions. This is usually the larger part of the hacienda community. The others are scattered in small groups in different parts of the domain, tending different duties and raising crops appropriate to the altitude, the climate, moisture and heat. Each little *rancho* hamlet is isolated and far away. It may be anything from one to ten or more miles from the next hamlet, depending upon the size of the hacienda. Their contacts with the outside world are few indeed, and the paths on the hacienda lead to the center where the big house is located, and only one rarely used path goes off to another hacienda, and to still another until the neighboring town is reached, which may be ten, twenty, thirty or more miles away. . . .

Before closing this discussion of the hacienda, there are certain other elements which must be brought out. The hacienda both dominated the small neighboring city and prevented it from developing economically or politically. The complaint so often heard in the Latin American smaller town, that it has no "movement," that it is "dead," is true and no great mystery. The haciendas which surround this town for many miles about buy little. Their peons have no money. The town has no important distribution function. The hacienda sells relatively little, considering its size and the number of people living on it; and what it does sell is marketed, usually, on a wholesale basis, by some agent employed by the hacienda, or by a member of the family, and is sent on, if possible to a larger city at a distance, with the result that the smaller neighboring city is bypassed. Even the mule pack carrying the hacienda goods to the city or the nearest railroad belongs to the hacienda. . . .

If we now summarize the role of the hacienda in the development of Latin America we will see that it has been and has remained, where it still exists, an isolating and conservative influence. It lived by routine sharecropping methods which prevented the use of improved machinery, methods or seeds. It tied its labor force to the property and kept mobility down to a minimum. It was a dampening influence on commercial development by buying little in the open market and selling relatively little. Its huge areas and internal system of paths leading to the big house discouraged road building. It established and maintained — and still does — a system of dependence between the hacendado and his peons which perpetuated an authoritarian tradition of master and very humble servant (I saw in Bolivia the Indians on a plantation bend their knees and kiss the hands of the hacendado) which leads directly into *caciquismo* [bossism] and instability. It prevented the accumulation of capital, required no investment, called for no change, did nothing to prevent soil erosion or improve agricultural techniques. The hacienda family controlled the local political scene and set the tone socially. As a dominant influence, the hacienda paid little taxes, and neglected to, or was unable to, put all of its resources to good use.

K. KARST, LAND REFORM IN INTERNATIONAL LAW
in R. Miller and R. Stanger (eds.), *Essays on Expropriations* at 41, 45-50 (1967) *

The foreign-owned plantation produces for an overseas market. Indeed, the largest plantation owners may own their own marketing system so that their operations are vertically integrated, all the way from the planting of the crop to the selling to wholesale distributors, say, in New York or New Orleans. The natural tendency of such a system is toward specialization in one or two crops in any country in which a single company or a few companies own a large share of the productive land. This system of monoculture has a number of very far-reaching consequences. First, much of the country's land is devoted to production not destined for domestic food consumption. The country may, indeed, be required to import food. This is not to say that such a system is necessarily uneconomical; the cash crops sold overseas may produce enough foreign exchange so that it would be inefficient at present to give up the advantages of specialization. On the other hand, there are longer term disadvantages that no responsible government can ignore.

The population of virtually all the underdeveloped countries has been growing at a staggering rate, between 2.5 and 3 per cent a year, and it will grow at an increasing rate in the future. Whatever else can be said about that statistic, undeniably those people have to eat. The chances are that the sale of export crops will not be able to keep up. What is operating here is an economic "law" that is none the worse for bearing the name of Engels: "percentage expenditure on food is on the average a decreasing function of income," *i.e.,* a man who makes $50,000 a year will not spend one hundred times as much on food as one whose income is $500. The consumption of coffee or bananas in the United States may increase with the population, but this consumption will not increase at a higher rate than the rate of population growth; if the developed or "customer" countries do not grow in population at the rate of the underdeveloped or "producer" countries, exports will not produce enough foreign exchange to buy food for the producer country's people.

Another aggravating factor is the very economic development toward which nearly all governments claim to aspire. As incomes at the very bottom are raised, Engels' Law works in the other direction, so that more food is needed to supply the wants of those who have just emerged from the subsistence level than was needed before the increment to their incomes. Here is an example from the Chilean economist Jacques Chonchol: Suppose that the population is growing at the rate of 2.9 per cent per year, a reasonable estimate for much of the underdeveloped world over the next two decades. Suppose also that the development goal is to increase per capita income by 2.5 per cent a year, the goal set at the outset of the Alliance for Progress. Assume, as is not unreasonable, that half of the growth in per capita income will be spent on food; remember, we are dealing with the spending pattern of people at a level barely above subsistence. Half of the increase, then, will be 1.25 per cent; add that increased per capita demand to the population increase, and you have the appalling figure of 4.15 per cent as the rate of *yearly* growth in demand for food. The cash produced by export crops simply cannot be expected to maintain that growth rate, not because of any inability of the producers to increase the supply, but because of a lack of sufficient increase in demand in the developed countries.

Other disadvantages of monoculture are more obvious. The whole economy, governmental revenues in particular, is tied closely to the world commodity price for the dominant crop. Although much development of the economies of the former colonies and near colonies has taken place during periods of commodity-price boom, there are many responsible and influentially placed economists who argue that the long-range trend is toward steadily decreasing terms of trade for countries that produce raw materials for consumption overseas. If the export crops are expected to finance schemes for the country's industrial development, along with filling all those new mouths, it seems plain that something will have to give. Although crash programs to diversify agriculture may, as in the recent Cuban case, prove foolish, any government of a developing country must take a sober look at the long-range attractions of diversification. When anticolonial emotionalism adds its political influence to the mixture, the future of foreign investment in export-crop agriculture seems bleak indeed.

Whatever may be the future dangers of monoculture, the foreign-owned plantation has an interesting past. The tradition of the liberal orthodoxy is to emphasize the way that private companies from the colonial nations have dominated public affairs in the colonies and in formally independent banana republics. Although the greater part of the crude abuses of foreign owners would seem to belong to the past, there are occasional reminders that the tradition of political domination retains some substance. In Central America, for example, both Guatemala (1954) and Honduras (1963) have seen the adoption of land reform measures, soon followed by successful revolutions that have substantially changed the direction of the reforms. Nonetheless, the foreign developers of plantation agriculture have made some important and irreversible contributions to development. It should also be part of the liberal orthodoxy to examine both sides of the coin.

The foreign investors brought with them a substantial investment in the local economy, in both the production and the processing phases of their operation. Furthermore, they built railroads and communications networks — admittedly "colonial" railroads, geared to exports and not to internal development, but railroads nevertheless, which now may serve as a base for expansion to meet present needs. Transportation systems accelerate centralizing tendencies, both economic and political, helping national societies to emerge from formerly fragmented groups. The plantation developers also brought with them new skills, new tastes, and above all a "growth mentality," which emphasizes the value of investing today for tomorrow's profit. Many plantation crops take several years to mature; the plantation itself is thus an easily understood lesson in the need for security and long-range stability. By paying relatively attractive day wages, the plantation lured workers away from nearby estates and into the money economy.

Despite these past contributions, the attitude of a modern government toward the plantation is apt to be, "What have you done for us lately?" Along with the problems of monoculture, there are other problems associated with the plantation economy that cannot easily be resolved. Much of the plantation's need for labor is seasonal; that is to say, unemployment is also seasonal and regular as clockwork. Although automation may smooth out the seasonal needs for labor, the smoothing will replace seasonal unemployment with year-round unemployment in numbers that are likely to be too great for even an expanding industry to absorb.

S. BARRACLOUGH AND A. DOMIKE, AGRARIAN STRUCTURE IN SEVEN LATIN AMERICAN COUNTRIES

42 *Land Economics* 391 (1966), in *Agrarian Problems and Peasant Movements in Latin America* at 41 (R. Stavenhagen (ed.) 1970)*

... *Traditional Land Tenure Institutions.* In the absence of technological

---

*Reprinted by permission of Land Economics.

development, land is the main source of wealth in the traditional rural economy. Income from land, however, cannot be realized without labor. Rights to land have therefore been accompanied by laws and customs which assure the landowners a continuing and compliant labor supply.

These land-tenure institutions are a product of the power structure. Plainly speaking, ownership or control of land is power in the sense of real or potential ability to make another person do one's will. Power over rural labor is reflected in tenure institutions which bind workers to the land while conceding them little income and few continuing rights. In the countries studied, tenure institutions vary from *peonaje* and *inquilinaje,* through various forms of wage and share-hiring, to instances of "commercial" cash and share-tenancy contracts.

The most common technique used to tie the campesino [peasant] to the farm is to cede him a small parcel of land for his home and garden while seeing to it that he has no alternative opportunities to obtain land or employment. The system receives characteristic names according to the traditions of each country: *inquilinaje, huasipungo, yanaconazgo,* etc. The campesino is obliged to work for a low salary or often for nothing for a certain period of each year or to turn his production over to the owner at a low price. As is discussed below, "contracts" often contain repressive clauses.

The land concentration indexes reveal only one symptom of the problem and not the manner in which the traditional tenure structure impedes development. In order to comprehend the process it is necessary to understand the functioning of the traditional society and the forces which give the system cohesion. Sociologists and anthropologists have studied the ways in which local social systems, dominated by archaic tenure institutions, determine the opportunities, incentives and motivations of their members.[10]

The large landowners and their representatives are the richest and most influential members of their communities. The role they play is a key one in the nation as well as in the community. Their status and income are assured through traditional tenure institutions because they control most of the land. They also command the other resources necessary for efficient production such as water and credit.

Characteristically the larger farm owners have financial and commercial activities in the large cities, political responsibilities in the capital and professional or cultural interests far removed from the land. Agriculture as such is often only of secondary interest to them. Typically they maintain residence in the city or even abroad. Since

---

[10] For example, see Gilberto Freyre, *Casa Grande y Senzala [The Masters and the Slaves]* (Buenos Aires, Argentina: Emece Editores, 1943); Mario C. Vásquez, *Peonaje y Servidumbre en Los Andes Peruanos* (Lima, Peru: Editorial Estudios Andinos, 1961); Orlando Fals Borda, *Peasant Society in the Colombian Andes* (Gainesville, Fla.: University of Florida Press, 1955); Sol Tax, *Penny Capitalism, A Guatemalan Indian Economy* (Smithsonian Institution: United States Government Printing Office, 1953). One should not neglect the contribution of the novelists who have made some of the most penetrating analyses of Latin America's land tenure problems, such as Ciro Alegría, *El Mundo es Ancho y Ajeno* (Santiago, Chile: Ercilla, 1955). [Footnote by Barraclough and Domike, renumbered.]

they have easy access to the medical, educational and cultural facilities in modern urban centers they feel little compulsion to duplicate them in the rural communities where they hold land. Owning agricultural property not only gives status and income but it provides security against inflation and serves as a basis for obtaining cheap credit for nonagricultural pursuits. Innovations which might change present tenure relationships threaten the large landowners' traditionally privileged position.

In communities dominated by traditional latifundia [great estates], such as may be found in the Andean highlands, in much of Brazil, and in some parts of all the study countries, practically everyone is dependent on the landholder or *patrón*. Public officials including the police and army are commonly at his disposal; his influence at provincial and national political levels may make his continued good will necessary for their job security. Banks and marketing institutions operate for the large landowner's convenience as he is the only one with sufficient volume of business to support them profitably. Churches and schools must obtain the landowner's patronage if they are to prosper.

This power structure is perpetuated by systematic restriction of educational opportunities. The ICAD case studies, for example, found several large haciendas in Ecuador and Guatemala on which there were no elementary schools, nor were there any schools nearby although legally every large property owner is required to aid in providing elementary schooling for the residents of his estate. In all of the countries studied the levels of education and literacy were much lower in rural than in urban areas. An extreme case is given by Guatemala's central provinces where only 5 per cent of the population is literate.

Tenants and workers on the large estates depend upon the *patrón* for employment – there being no alternatives – and for a place to live. Wage and rental agreements can be adjusted to suit the landowner's convenience so that all productivity increases and windfall gains accrue to him. Permanent improvements such as buildings or fruit trees belong to the estate even when all the costs are borne by the tenant. On many large plantations residents are strictly forbidden to make improvements without permission for fear they would acquire vested interests in the land or take resources away from the production of the cash plantation crop. Residents of the large estates can be expelled at will in traditional areas where there is neither a strong central government nor a labor union to defend them. The ICAD researchers found haciendas in certain Andean regions which required that people of the neighboring communities work without pay in order to have the right to use the paths and bridges on the property. In some cases the administration's consent is required even to receive visitors from outside or to make visits off the property. Even though it was prohibited as long ago as the seventeenth century, the practice of "renting out" workers still persists. And corporal punishment is still occasionally encountered on some of the most traditional plantations and haciendas. Tenants and workers depend on the *patrón* for credit, for marketing their products and even for medical aid in emergencies. Food and clothing are frequently obtained through the estate's commissary and charged against wages or crops.

With the abolition of compulsory servitude during the last century *peones* and tenants now have the right to leave but, with few alternative job opportunities and little education, this possibility often appears to be as much of a threat as an opportunity for improving their lot.

The traditional minifundia [very small holdings] zones not directly dependent upon the large landholdings are characterized by tenure institutions that are scarcely more conducive to development than those found on the big estates. The minifundia communities are generally dependent for their contacts with the outside world upon a small group of town-dwelling politicians, landowners, merchants, secular and ecclesiastical officials. As a result these people have a great deal of power over the small holders. They are seldom interested in jeopardizing their influence by promoting other close contacts with the outside world or by encouraging technical innovations and education that would make the small holders more independent and mobile.

Within the minifundia communities themselves there is a strong resistance to change as the small holders have learned over the years that penetration by outsiders usually results in eventual loss of land and independence. In the face of mounting population pressures and a shortage of land, social institutions have developed which restrict the possibilities of individual community members accumulating disproportionate amounts of wealth at the expense of their neighbors. While these mechanisms help to preserve the community they also make change and technological improvement more difficult. To better one's social position by becoming a more efficient farmer, for instance, is practically unheard of and migration to the towns is the principal accepted means for personal advancement. Although small holders generally manage their parcels with skill and economic acumen, their limited opportunities and resources keep incomes low. In only a few cases, however, can technological advance overcome the desperate shortage of farm land in most minifundia areas.

. . . *Economic Productivity.* To the extent that tenure structure impedes full, efficient use of the land, the labor force and the other resources at the command of agriculture, economic progress is stifled. As part of the ICAD analysis, indicators of efficiency on farm units of different tenure types and scales were developed. These indices are limited, however, by the adequate quantity and quality of available data so that sophisticated analytical refinement is impossible. The preferred measure of theoretical economists is the marginal productivity of the various factors of production.[11] When resources are being used efficiently, marginal returns are about

---

[11] The marginal productivity of the various factors of production has been estimated for the central zone of Chile by Carlos O'Brien Fonck (see "An Estimate of Agricultural Resource Productivities by Using Aggregate Production Functions, Chile, 1954-55," Cornell University, M.S. thesis, 1966). The results obtained tend to confirm the conclusions presented in this report. Using a Cobb-Douglas production function and data from the Agricultural Census of 1955, he arrived at the following conclusions: The marginal productivity of the land in cultivation is very high; that is, natural pastures converted into cultivated land yield a high marginal return. Measures of marginal labor productivity were generally quite low but, in areas of intensive cultivation, the marginal returns are greater and the potential response to increased labor input appears to be higher on the large than small units. The marginal productivity and returns to investments in cattle and farm building were consistently higher than costs of capital. In brief, large farms have high potential marginal returns in relation to capital, to conversion of natural pastures to cultivation, and to increases in complementary labor force. Nonetheless, they have failed to intensify their production. [Footnote by Barraclough and Domike, renumbered.]

the same to a given factor, irrespective of the tenure system in which it is employed. For example, land of lower productive potential or poor location has less labor and capital combined with it than the better land. Consequently the marginal contribution of the better lands to the total production keeps diminishing until it is equal to that of the worst lands in use.

In theory, to compare the relative efficiency of large and small units, it would be necessary to determine the marginal productivity of all the different factors of production of both groups. The circumstances under which the large and small units are now exploited are so different and the markets so imperfect that it is doubtful that such comparisons have great validity.

Even after allowing for the measurement difficulties the general tendencies in resource use of the different tenure systems are clear. The two most important tenure groups – the minifundia and the latifundia – both appear to use resources wastefully. On small holdings labor is wasted by overuse on small pieces of land. Lands unsuitable for agriculture – frequently on hillsides, in gullies, or in deserts – are cultivated so intensely that output per hectarc is high even by the standards of modern agriculture. Yields appear even more remarkable when account is taken of the poor quality of the land, seed and other inputs. Minifundia consistently show much higher average returns per hectare than the large holdings whether comparisons are made on the basis of total farm land or area cultivated. . . . But the low level of technology means that average (and marginal) returns to labor are very low. Aggregate country data indicate that average production per agricultural worker is one-fifth to one-tenth as great on small holdings as on latifundia. Finally, many soils rapidly lose fertility and are eroded. This is particularly striking on the steep hillsides of Ecuador and Colombia and in the tropical rain forests of Brazil and Guatemala.

On large estate resources are also used wastefully but in a different way. At least half of the total farm land in the countries studied is in large holdings. These incorporate a high proportion of the best soils and the land most favorably located with regard to roads, markets and water supply. The owners have ready access to credit and technical assistance. Nonetheless, only one-sixth of the lands in estates in the seven countries is or has been in cultivation; the rest are left in native vegetation. Relatively much less labor is used on most large holdings than on small farms. Even while average production per worker is sometimes quite high, production per hectare is low compared to either technical potentials or to outputs achieved on smaller units.

Measured by commercial standards the management of large landholdings is typically deficient. For example, agronomists estimate that the large-scale producers of cocoa and coffee in Brazil could double production of many existing plantations with only nominal improvements in management and investment. In Argentina new investments on large cattle *estancias* are not made even though returns would be increased by 25-40 per cent because they require better management than is provided by their absentee owners. In case studies made in the coastal areas of Peru, capital-product ratios of 6.0 were estimated on large units indicating very low capital productivity. In the United States the ratio is typically about 2.5.

The economic behavior of the large and small units is explicable in terms of factors related to the tenure structure. Those who control the land in the large and small enterprises have different motivations and their reactions in the face of changes in markets and demographic pressures are quite different. There are three important classes of units: the minifundia, the traditional haciendas and the "modern" plantations. No special attention is given here to family-sized units because of their limited importance in the countries studied.

Minifundia, whether they are in communities, in fragmented independent holdings, or in a latifundia complex, have a fixed land base and virtually no access to productive factors other than labor. The principal motivation for production is survival. At the same time these people must find room for that part of the increasing population which does not migrate. In the highlands of Guatemala, for example, where population is increasing by nearly 3 per cent per year, one study shows average arable land per small farm to be 1.1 hectare [1 hectare = 2.47 acres] most of which is on steep hillsides. This is land enough to occupy only about one-fifth of the available family labor force even at the low levels of technology used. Under such circumstances labor is necessarily applied with increasing intensity to the fixed land base. In brief, the combination of rapid population growth, a rigid tenure structure, a paucity of technical aid or capital, and lack of employment alternatives explain the minifundia's high yields from land and low yields from labor. The predictable consequences are low gross labor incomes and disguised unemployment.

In contrast, the production possibilities of the large-scale units are not seriously limited by lack of resources— with the exception of administrative capacity. Some large farm enterprises are managed with a commercial orientation and modern technology and their results can be analyzed separately from those of the traditional farms. Nevertheless, in the ICAD-studied countries the traditional-oriented ones are in a large majority in number as well as in the proportion of the land resources that they control.

Traditional multi-family exploitations resemble minifundia in that their technology, capital investments and management are rudimentary so that their level of production is determined essentially by the quantity of labor they use. But the motivations of the latifundia managers are different from those of the minifundistas. The large landowners do not need to produce in order to survive nor are they obliged to find employment on the farm for cousins, brothers and other relatives. In effect, for the hacienda-owner to maintain his social and economic power it is necessary that he maintain the peasants (campesinos) in a situation where they have low incomes, insecure tenancy and few alternative sources of employment. He has a constant motive to limit rather than to raise his labor requirements. The economic results of this situation are that land directly administered by the large traditional enterprises is farmed extensively [*i.e.,* not intensively]. The possibilities for increasing employment and production are wasted and the excess labor supply on the neighboring minifundia is increased. It should be emphasized that this behavior is in complete agreement with the social and economic aspirations of the hacienda-owners although it does not bear out the idea generally held by economists of what is rational motivation.

The small group of large-scale estates using modern technology and management may, within the limits suggested below, contribute to the economic growth of the country. The best-operated units show high productivity for both the land and labor.

As producers of export crops and import substitutes they help to improve the national trade balance. As employers they provide some of the economic alternatives needed to break down traditional tenure systems. As demonstration units they may induce other estates to follow suit.

The bright possiblities of "modern" farming are seldom realized in full. For example, in order to reduce dependence on the local labor force and to limit "labor problems" many of these estates substitute capital for labor to such an extent that fewer work opportunities and lower gross wages are offered in the end than under traditional management. It is also a common practice on single-crop plantations to withdraw or withhold land suitable to cropping in response to special market forces or merely to hold land in reserve and thereby reduce employment opportunities for the campesinos. In Guatemala the "reserves" of the banana and coffee plantations were a special target of the frustrated agrarian reform of 1952-54. Many plantation owners retain or reinvest little of their profits in the country itself. In effect, the major benefit to the nation from these "pockets of efficiency" is likely to be the direct benefits of higher wage payments and higher taxes plus a possible demonstration effect.

Even an accelerated transformation of traditional land tenure systems would not mean that all lands would suddenly be intensively exploited and that there would be larger marginal returns to labor. Production patterns would need time to be adjusted to account for comparative economic advantage and market demands. In some regions the land would continue to be used extensively but the inevitable tendency would be to use the land as well as labor better and more economically. The true production potential could be reached only after having overcome customs which have been deeply rooted for centuries.

Serious estimates should be made of the misallocation of labor that is created by existing tenure systems. Unfortunately, sufficiently detailed data were not gathered in the ICAD country studies to permit such calculations. To have an idea of the magnitudes involved the average land per worker on the family-scale farms in each country may be used as an index. If this "desirable" land/labor ratio prevailed among minifundia only 700,000 of the 4.4 million workers on sub-family-scale farms in six of the countries studied (excluding Peru which had insufficient data) would be required. If the family-scale land/labor ratios were applied to only half the land in large-scale exploitations (on the generous assumption that half the land was of no economic potential), resources would exist for employing 25 million additional workers in the six countries. These admittedly rough guesses indicate the tremendous pressure on the land in minifundia and the ample possiblities for improvement of land and labor use on the large units.

. . . *Income Distribution and Investment.* The distorted distribution of land is a fundamental cause of the rural social stratification which in turn dates from the period of colonial conquest and slavery. In Chile, for example, the upper 3 per cent of the agricultural population now receives 37 per cent of the agricultural income while the bottom 71 per cent of the farm labor force receives only one-third of the income. In one zone studied in Colombia 85 per cent of the farm units received 9.3 per cent of the agricultural income.

The distribution of farm income, plus the fact that a large proportion of the population vegetates at close to subsistence conditions and suffers chronic under-employment, are evidence of a rigid class structure and are the major causes of the weak internal markets which impede industrial expansion. According to the ICAD studies the modal campesino income is the equivalent of about $300 annually except in the few regions where alternative employment exists or where the tenure structure is unusually good. Cash family incomes are much lower. In the Andean highlands, Brazil's northeast, and in much of Guatemala cash family incomes are typically far below the equivalent of $100 annually. From half to three-quarters of the family's income goes for food, leaving very little for clothing and other necessities. There is really no surplus income with which to buy the products of infant industries whose growth depends on expanding internal markets.

It has been estimated that the income of the large landowners is great enough to permit them to make substantial investments in industry and agriculture. With respect to Chile, Nicholas Kaldor affirms that "if the ratio of consumption to gross income from property were reduced to levels found in Great Britain, 30 per cent, the personal consumption expenditures of this group would fall from 21.1 to 10.3 per cent of the national income. The freed resources would be more than sufficient to double investments in fixed capital and inventories. This means that, according to official estimates, net investment would increase from 2 per cent to 14 per cent of net national income. . . ."

Instead, those who receive agricultural income spend a greater part of it on consumption than do the high-income receivers in developed countries. A considerable portion of these incomes is spent on foreign travel and consumption of imported articles. Investments, when they are made, are usually safe investments such as land, foreign stocks and bonds or in the construction of apartments and luxury hotels.

The conclusion seems inevitable that the seigneurial distribution of income is as antagonistic to economic development in Latin America as it has been in other regions in which large plantations and near-feudal conditions prevail.

W. ROSTOW, THE STAGES OF ECONOMIC GROWTH
Pp. 22-24 (1960)*

The point is that it takes more than industry to industrialize. Industry itself takes time to develop momentum and competitive competence. In the meanwhile there is certain to be a big social overhead capital bill to meet; and there is almost certain to be a radically increased population to feed. In a generalized sense modernization takes a lot of working capital; and a good part of this working capital must come from rapid increases in output achieved by higher productivity in agriculture and the extractive industries.

More specifically the attempt simultaneously to expand fixed capital — of long gestation period — and to feed an expanding population requires both increased food output at home and/or increased imports from abroad. Capital imports can help, of course, but in the end loans must be serviced; and the servicing of loans requires enlarged exports.

It is, therefore, an essential condition for a successful transition that investment be increased and – even more important – that the hitherto unexploited back-log of innovations be brought to bear on a society's land and other natural resources, where quick increases in output are possible.

Having made the general case in terms of requirements for working capital, look for a moment more closely at the question of agriculture and the food supply. There are, in fact, three distinct major roles agriculture must play in the transitional process between a traditional society and a successful take off.

First, agriculture must supply more food. Food is needed to meet the likely rise in population, without yielding either starvation or a depletion of foreign exchange available for purposes essential to growth. But increased supplies and increased transfers of food out of rural areas are needed for another reason; to feed the urban populations which are certain to grow at a disproportionately high rate during the transition. And, in most cases, increased agricultural supplies are needed as well to help meet the foreign exchange bill for capital development: either positively by earning foreign exchange, as in the United States, Russia, Canada, and several other nations which generated and maintained agricultural surpluses while their populations were growing (and their urban populations growing faster than the population as a whole); or negatively, to minimize the foreign exchange bill for food – like a whole series of nations from Britain in the 1790's to Israel in the 1950's.

The central fact is that, in the transitional period, industry is not likely to have established a sufficiently large and productive base to earn enough foreign exchange to meet the increments in the nation's food bill via increased imports. Population increases, urbanization, and increased foreign exchange requirements for fixed and working capital are all thus likely to conspire to exert a peculiar pressure on the agricultural sector in the transitional process. Put another way, the rate of increase in output in agriculture may set the limit within which the transition to modernization proceeds.

But this is not all. Agriculture may enter the picture in a related but quite distinctive way, from the side of demand as well as supply. Let us assume that the governmental sector in this transitional economy is not so large that its expanded demand can support the rapid growth of industry. Let us assume that some of the potential leading sectors are in consumers' goods – as, indeed, has often been the case; not only cotton textiles – as in England and New England – but a wide range of import substitutes, as in a number of Latin American cases. In addition, the modern sector can – and often should – be built in part on items of capital for agriculture: farm machinery, chemical fertilizers, diesel pumps, etc. In short, an environment of rising real incomes in agriculture, rooted in increased productivity, may be an important stimulus to new modern industrial sectors essential to the take-off.

The income side of the productivity revolution in agriculture may be important even in those cases where the transition to industrialization is not based on consumers' goods industries; for it is from rising rural incomes that increased taxes of one sort or another can be drawn — necessary to finance the government's functions in the transition — without imposing either starvation on the peasants or inflation on the urban population.

And there is a third distinctive role for agriculture in the transitional period which goes beyond its functions in supplying resources, effective demand or tax revenues: agriculture must yield up a substantial part of its surplus income to the modern sector. At the core of the *Wealth of Nations* — lost among propositions about pins and free trade — is Adam Smith's perception that surplus income derived from ownership of land must, somehow, be transferred out of the hands of those who would sterilize it in prodigal living into the hands of the productive men who will invest it in the modern sector and then regularly plough back their profits as output and productivity rise.

In their nineteenth-century land-reform schemes this is precisely what Japan, Russia, and many other nations have done during the transition in an effort to increase the supply of capital available for social overhead and other essential modernizing processes.[12]

It is sometimes said that land reform reduces the economic surplus obtainable from agriculture, by permitting the beneficiaries of the reform to consume more of this surplus. Yet substantial numbers of peasant children suffer from mental retardation as a result of malnutrition. The one thing that land reform undeniably does with the food supply is to redirect some of it to peasant consumption. If peasant children are avoiding malnutrition, and the peasant population of tomorrow is avoiding mental retardation, the gains in human capital may outweigh any loss of "surplus" available for feeding city dwellers and for export. Is it not at least odd to speak of a "surplus" obtainable from the agricultural sector when peasant children are not getting enough to eat?

E. FLORES, THE ECONOMICS OF LAND REFORM

92 *International Labour Review* #1 (July 1965), 30-31, 34[*]
in R. Stavenhagen (ed.), *Agrarian Problems and Peasant Movements in Latin America* at 139 (1970)

From the specialized viewpoint of economics, land reform can be defined as a redistributive measure: a capital levy on a few landlords that is distributed among many peasants and the State. This transfer changes resource allocation in agriculture through the redistribution of land and water rights; and it also changes the distribution of income and wealth in the economy as a whole. It therefore reduces the private demand of the landlords and releases resources which can then be applied simultaneously to raise the level of consumption of the peasants and to increase the rate of capital formation.

Land reform shares many common characteristics with a large family of redistributive instruments such as public finance, taxation, inflation, subsidies,

---
[12] See also P. Dorner, *Land Reform and Economic Development* (1972). [Eds.]

[*]Published by the International Labour Office, Geneva, Switzerland.

minimum wage policies, price supports, tariff protection, rationing, expropriation, nationalization, etc. Essentially, all these measures of public policy operate according to the same principles, and their study and application constitute a very important part of theoretical and applied economics.

The following two premises of redistributive policies are particularly relevant for the understanding of the economics of land reform:

(a) total income available for consumption and for capital formation in an economy is itself a function of the state of distribution;

(b) changes in the state of distribution may increase the size of the total income to be divided or they may decrease it.

Land reform gives mobility to the agricultural structure and makes it possible to shift savings and labor from agriculture to industrial and urban development; it exerts a powerful influence over the propensity to consume and the propensity to save, and affects the composition of imports and of exports and the general level of employment. In turn, the joint and cumulative effects of all these changes create favorable conditions and incentives for further growth.

In order to be effective, land reform has to fulfill the following conditions:

(1) It has to take *productive land* and its income, above a ceiling which is exempt from the reform and is determined by political considerations disguised as economics about the optimum size. Productive land must be taken *without immediate compensation*. Otherwise it is not a redistributive measure. To claim that landlords should be fully compensated is as absurd as to expect that taxpayers of advanced countries should receive cash compensation or bonds in an amount equal to their taxes.

(2) It must take place rapidly and massively: say, within one or two decades. Otherwise it will *not* generate the momentum for take-off. Instead, it will depress even further the performance of the agricultural economy and set in a process of disinvestment because of the spread of uncertainties.

(3) It must be accompanied by vigorous development policies within agriculture and outside it. In the agricultural sector a new, flexible and efficient pattern of resource allocation and use must be created. Simultaneously, there has to be a transfer to industry and trade of capital originally tied up in land. The determination of investment priorities accorded to agricultural development vis-à-vis overhead facilities, urban, industrial and service development is of critical importance. The availability of development capital, in fact, makes for significant differences in land reform policies and provides criteria for a typology of land reform. . . .

In 1917, when the land reform began, Mexico was a very backward and unstable nation. Less than 3 per cent of the landowners together owned over 90 per cent of the productive land; that meant that a correspondingly large proportion of *agricultural cash income* accrued to only a tiny proportion of the total population. Mines, oil wells and about 50 per cent of total investment belonged to foreign investors.

From 1917 to date, 120 million acres of all types of land have been granted to 2.2 million peasants. Land grants were freely given to communities called *ejidos*. The government issued bonds to compensate landlords, but only around 0.5 per cent of the total value of expropriated land was paid for. In other words, Mexico's land reform was confiscatory for lands in excess of 100 hectares. As a result of the land reform, the expropriation of the oil wells and the nationalization of public utilities, from 1910 to 1942 foreign capital did not go to Mexico. Instead, there was a flight of capital abroad.

For capital formation purposes, agriculture was subjected to a steady drain. The peasants tolerated the ensuing forced austerity because it came from the same government that was giving them free land and was engaged in unprecedented efforts to build dams, highways and schools.

For the last thirty years gross national product has increased at an average annual rate of 6.2 per cent and agricultural product at a rate of 5.4. Today Mexico has one of the most dynamic, diversified and self-sufficient agricultural structures in Latin America. There is no doubt that the high rates of capital formation for Mexico's industrial revolution in the early stages of the reform (1917-42) came from agriculture. Without the land reform, political stability, high rates of capital formation and increased agricultural production and productivity would have been impossible.

Since it can be soberly assumed that in most under-developed countries neither trade, nor aid, nor foreign investment will provide the major share of capital required to finance economic development and since, by definition, agriculture is one of their few sources of capital, we are led inescapably to the grim conclusion that, if these countries are ever going to develop, they will need to undertake land reforms such as the Mexican, in which the agricultural sector had to foot the development bill for a long time almost alone.

D. WARRINER, LAND REFORM IN PRINCIPLE AND PRACTICE
Pp. 262-67 (1969)*

Although there is so little sign of independent thought on national lines, there is a strong tendency to think of Latin America as a region, with common features and common problems, and to adduce arguments for reform which have been evolved in this regional setting. These arguments originate in the influential school of economic thought led by Dr. Raúl Prebisch. It is difficult, and perhaps impossible, to summarize the economic doctrines of this school; its central conception is that of 'balanced development'; and this may be identified with a planned economy, or a democratic society, or both. Its significance lies in the attempt to think out the implications of changing an economy which is still colonial, in that it exploits and wastes land and labour in the interests of the ruling class, into something different and something which can be interpreted in economic terms, rather than in terms of social values. It is not so much a doctrine as a part of the process of 'a mind in the making'.

Agrarian reform is advocated by this school as a condition of balanced development. It cannot, of course, be argued that there is a direct relationship between the rate of growth and agrarian reform (though sometimes the protagonists of the

*Copyright © 1969 Oxford University Press. Reprinted by permission of The Clarendon Press, Oxford.

school seem to suggest that agrarian reform will actually cause development to be faster than it is at present). If by economic development is meant the increase in national income *per capita,* and if land reform means land distribution, then the results in Mexico, Bolivia, and Cuba show that there is no empirical foundation for the belief that they are necessarily connected. In 1950-60 the rate of growth of gross product *per capita* in Latin America as a whole was 2 per cent per annum, a higher rate than that of the United States and several other advanced countries. Between the different countries there were marked contrasts in rates of growth, depending on the rate of expansion of their exports; those with the highest rates were Venezuela, Brazil, and Mexico, and those with the lowest were Argentina, Bolivia, Chile, Paraguay, and Uruguay. Among the fast developers, only Mexico had then had an agrarian reform, among the slow developers, only Bolivia.

But it is argued that this development, even where rapid, has been unbalanced, and that this unbalance characterizes all countries (not only those which are dualistic in structure on the Lambert classification). Agricultural production has not increased as fast as industrial production (though of course this contrast is not peculiar to Latin America) and agricultural output per head of total population is still below the level of the period 1936-40 (and this is true of Asia also). Since the Second World War, however, crop production (though not livestock) has kept pace with the very rapid growth of population and it is now increasing faster, chiefly as a result of tariff protection or other measures of agricultural price support. (In this respect the food situation is far better than it is in Asia.) However, the increase in crop production does not keep pace with the increased demand for food arising from increased incomes, apart altogether from meeting the food requirements of people who live in extreme poverty and who would increase their consumption of food if income distribution were more equal.

This failure to meet the food needs of a fast growing population is attributed to the land system. Production for export has priority over production for the internal market "mainly because the uneven distribution of income restricts demand, because the traditional agriculturists do not respond to the existing stimuli of the domestic market, and because there is little incentive to employ new and more efficient techniques. All these reasons are closely connected with the concentration of land in the hands of a few."

At the same time, the low level of wages in agriculture drives labour off the land into the cities in numbers far exceeding the increase in the number of jobs in industry, so that the services sector is uneconomically swollen, and labour is wasted. The rural exodus does not raise farm wages or stimulate more efficient production, because the number of workers on the land continues to increase: its effect is to reduce urban wages.

In this situation, it is contended, the reform of the agrarian structure has a key role to play:

The slow development of Latin American agriculture has up to now been one of the principal obstacles to the region's economic progress; production has failed to keep pace with the growing demand for foodstuffs and raw materials of an expanding and increasingly urbanized population with rising income levels. Moreover, because of its extremely low average income, the agricultural population does not offer an adequate market for industrial goods. Both factors act as a powerful brake on the balanced growth of the Latin American economy.

Among the reasons for this situation, one of the most important — because of the chain reaction which it produces — is undoubtedly the faulty agrarian structure prevailing in almost all Latin American countries. It is largely responsible for low agricultural labour productivity and the consequent miserable level and inequitable distribution of income, bad soil utilization, the poor rate of capital formation, the scarcity of up-to-date farming techniques, the archaic systems of labour remuneration and the low educational level of the rural population. It is thus apparent that these structures will have to be changed by means of land redistribution if resources are to be better utilized, farm techniques are to become more up to date and levels of productivity are to be raised. A far-reaching institutional change would be the only way to increase the average *per capita* product and to redistribute income so as to enable the agricultural sector to play the role which is expected of it in Latin American economic development.[13]

In this extreme form, the argument is an unrealistic oversimplification. In the first place, it is simply not true that 'a far-reaching institutional change' is the only way to increase product per head in agriculture, because there has been an increase in recent years, chiefly due to price supports and protection. In the second place, it obviously begs the key question of whether land reform *will* increase production, for if it does not, there will be no increase in agricultural employment to stem the flow of labour to the towns, and no rise in farm incomes to create a market for industrial goods. The Latin American experience to date shows that land reform alone, whether individual or collective, does not increase production; nor is it likely to do so unless it is reinforced by price and investment policy — unless, that is to say, the urban population is prepared to incur costs. The concomitants of the present land system — hoe cultivation, backward methods, and extensive land use — will persist, even after large estates are subdivided, and so will the attitudes fostered by them, the ambition of becoming a boss, the tendency to move on elsewhere, unless the new owners are given the opportunity of earning higher incomes in more highly capitalized farming, capable of development in countries which are developing. As expounded above, the balanced growth doctrine is a rather naive urban colonialism, keeping workers in the rural hinterland to provide food and raw materials and markets for urban consumers and producers, while preventing them from competing in the industrial labour market.

Still, in its Latin American context, so utterly urban and so hostile to social change, this attempt to prove that reform is needed for the sake of development is understandable. 'Development' is the fashionable thing, the only acceptable sanction in countries without a liberal tradition. The attempt is excusably disingenuous, because what its protagonists really mean by development is a different form of

---

[13] UN/ECLA, "Economic Survey of Latin America," 1959, 120, mimeo. [Footnote by Warriner, renumbered.]

society, and not a higher rate of growth of product *per capita*. But the danger of disingenuity is that the equally sophisticated opponents of reform can so easily turn the tables on its protagonists. If the object of reform — the only object — is development, then it follows that estates which are efficiently managed should be exempted from expropriation, since they are clearly not obstacles to development; so the rich can escape expropriation and only poor and uncultivated land need be distributed. This is casuistry, because it assumes that development, and not redistribution of income, is the purpose of reform. It is also sophistry, since it assumes that high profits are a test of efficiency, as they are under the existing conditions of underpaid labour and under-utilized land. But it is these conditions which should be changed and might be changed if land reform could be geared to higher productivity. There is truth in the balanced growth doctrine, since redistribution of income is a necessary condition of social progress; but there is also falsehood, since it is not a sufficient condition of development. The idea that reform is a *cheap* solution to economic problems is pernicious and pervasive.

As has already been emphasized, Latin American countries are far more heterogeneous in structure than the 'condition of development' static model suggests. In Chile the model seems to fit, because in the central zone there is a high degree of uniformity, and there is also stagnation. But in Brazil, Venezuela, and Peru the demand for reform arises because these countries are developing, and the 'have-nots' can claim a bigger share in the gains of economic progress: it may be that development is a condition of reform, and not vice versa.

Even more lacking in cogency are the arguments intended to show that reform will provide the *desiderata* of the American way of life. The Inter-American Committee for Agricultural Development has formulated the evils of the existing land tenure system, under four headings, in sociological jargon. In its economic aspect, the present land tenure system is considered to prevent rationalization of land use and employment, the introduction of more efficient technology, and higher productivity, higher consumption, more investment in agriculture. Socially, it causes rigid stratification. Culturally, it preserves among the dependent classes and ethnic groups "sub-cultures which operate to prevent change." Politically, it concentrates power, and excludes the primary producers from "participation and representation." In other words, the present system prevents efficiency, liberty, equality, and fraternity. But does it follow that its abolition will create all these things?

Of course it does not; these things take longer. Land reform is not a magic key to unlock all doors, or to wash whiter than white. It is a most difficult thing to carry through, precisely because there are so many obstacles. It must, in Latin American conditions, mean a fundamental change in the agrarian structure, because it represents the first step, but it does not mean transferring land to people who already know how to farm it better. If the impetus is found among the people who suffer from the oppressions of the land system, it may turn into a revolutionary movement.

To this, the American school will reply that reform must be integral and comprehensive, which in practice means that farmers should be given supervised credit and extension as well as land. But in the countries visited, belief in the possibility of planned reform was hard to sustain. States which cannot operate even rudimentary local government services are not likely to be able to plan agriculture. In Latin America no reforms will be carried out without some impetus from below, even though this impetus is fostered and generated from above. There must be a movement before there can be action, and a movement precludes planning in advance; it may well be anarchic.

So at present the outlook for reform is problematical. Sometimes the various influences are welded into an incongruous mixture of leftish impetus and 'credit-and-extension', and whether this odd hybrid can set a pattern remains to be seen. The questions which arise are whether Latin American governments will succeed in carrying through reforms at all, and if so, whether they can improve on the results achieved in the past.

3. Indirect Reforms

Since the redistribution of rights in land implies revolutionary structural change, it is not surprising that less drastic alternatives have been proposed for ameliorating the conditions of life for Latin America's rural dispossessed. Four such alternatives to land reform are considered in the following extract from the article by Barraclough and Domike, who conclude that each of the suggested alternatives is in fact a false one.

S. BARRACLOUGH AND A. DOMIKE, AGRARIAN STRUCTURE IN SEVEN LATIN AMERICAN COUNTRIES

42 *Land Economics* 391 (1966), in R. Stavenhagen (ed.),
Agrarian Problems and Peasant Movements in Latin America at 41 (1970)*

In none of the seven countries studied has an irreversible direct reform of tenure structure been achieved. Variations and blends of indirect reform programs have gained some political support. These programs include colonization, labor and tenant contract regulation, land and inheritance tax reforms and industrialization. The nature and success of such measures need to be studied carefully before considering the probable requisites of a program of direct reforms.

Colonization. Land settlement programs, particularly in unexploited jungles and disputed border regions, have been favored as an escape from the agrarian problem, particularly by the groups opposed to expropriation of privately held land but still concerned about rural discontent. Within the scope of settlement-programs must also be included assistance to spontaneous settlers and the opening of new agricultural zones through irrigation projects. These various programs have been promoted with two aims in mind: to reduce rural social tensions and to incorporate new wealth into the economies.

To judge from the experience of the study countries, such hopes are as yet unfulfilled. Attempts to colonize new areas have been slow and costly, leaving the agrarian problems unresolved. In Guatemala, for example, between 1954 and 1962

*Reprinted by permission of Land Economics.

only 6,000 families, many from the urban middle class received family-scale units in colonization zones. The number of families benefited was less than 7 per cent of the demographic increase of the rural population of the country. As is noted below, it would have been necessary to benefit 240,000 families during this period in order to transform the agrarian structure in a significant way. In the other countries official colonization activities have proceeded just as slowly at rates which do not even approximate the rate of formation of rural families, much less fulfill the objective of an effective reform.

Costs of colonization programs have to be high because land "on the agricultural frontier" can be cultivated only after costly clearing, drainage and road building. Actually there is not enough potentially good agricultural land outside the already populated areas to settle the "excess" rural population or even to take care of the present demographic increase in the rural areas. In none of the countries studied is more than a small part of the government-owned land suitable for intensive use while the rest is usable at best for forest and extensive pasture. Unless special precautions are taken land which becomes valuable after roads or improvements are made is immediately taken over by influential persons from outside the farm sector. . . .

The evidence indicates that official colonization activities do not compare favorably with settlement which occurs spontaneously without governmental aid. . . .

Tenure and Labor Contract Regulation. Two widely applied techniques for mitigating the bitter conflicts between landlords and campesinos are regulation of work and tenancy contracts, and social insurance schemes. The apparent aim of such schemes is to bring about a balance in the bargaining power between the two groups, a balance which the existing economic and social structure has not been able to generate. The popularity of such an approach is undeniable. In all the countries studied there exist laws which proscribe tenancy contract abuses and establish minimum wages and working conditions for workers. Special courts to hear cases of violations and to enforce the rules have been created. In several study countries farm workers participate in government retirement and health programs along with the urban groups.

None of these measures are new and untried. In all countries studied the laws have been in effect sufficient time so that their real impact can be ascertained. In Chile and Argentina regulations of tenancy contracts were established forty to forty-five years ago and the laws now in force were enacted in the mid-1940's. Since 1947-48 laws controlling Peru's system of *yanaconaje* as well as aspects of conventional tenancy contracts have been on the books. In Brazil, Ecuador, Colombia and Guatemala laws which stipulate the conditions under which farm operators are supposed to contract with farm workers and tenants have existed for a generation or more.

If these laws had been effective there would now exist greater security and higher shares of farm incomes for tenants and higher wages and improved social conditions for hired workers. As has already been indicated and described in ample detail in the various ICAD country studies, the evidence demonstrates that these laws have not achieved these objectives and at times act counter to the interests of the campesinos. Large proprietors and landowners continue to be assured of the bulk of the sector's earnings. In Chile, for example, field studies showed average *inquilino* family incomes ranging from 1/80 to 1/230 of the large proprietor's income from the farm. In Argentina the wage situation improved during the late 1940's but between the mid-1950's and 1965 controlled wages of farm workers in real terms fell by 30 per cent. Such amenities as education and health services are no more readily available to campesinos today than at the time the regulations were enacted in the 1930's and 1940's.

Although it has proved extremely difficult to determine the degree of compliance with minimum wage and tenancy-share laws, a 1957 survey in Brazil showed that farm workers in seven of eight important agricultural states studied were receiving wages one-third or more below the fixed minimum wage and were being overcharged for their housing. . . . Recent Chilean studies indicate a record of compliance with social laws of only 20 per cent. . . .

The effects of the laws in some cases have been negative. In Colombia, Peru and Argentina, for example, regulation of tenancy contracts is one of the major reasons why thousands of small tenants were evicted by landlords who sought to circumvent the effects of the laws. In Argentina there was a 25 per cent decline in the number of tenants in the decade following enactment of tenancy regulations in 1947. In Colombia the expulsion of campesinos from the large haciendas immediately followed passage of the law giving legal rights to those who had worked more than ten years on the property. Many observers agree that this move contributed importantly to the spread of rural violence in Colombia. In Brazil the attempts by the *ligas camponesas* and other campesino groups to force the latifundistas to respect the tenure rights of renters and other resident workers has led to serious conflicts, violence and assassinations. Unschooled campesinos have not proved to be difficult adversaries for landowners' lawyers.

Why have these measures suffered such repeated failures? What possibilities exist for putting real force into such laws? The problem, in part, lies in the lack of effective administration of existing laws. But it must be remembered that these laws are approved with the tacit agreement that they will not be vigorously enforced. In the best of cases they are meant to provide bargaining guidelines which fix acceptable limits to the aspirations of the campesinos. It is well recognized that the influence of the landlords prevents effective enforcement of the regulations since those who would suffer most are themselves frequently the politicians or government functionaries who are responsible for enforcing the law. Even when this is not the case a large and independent bureaucracy and powerful courts would be required to apply such complicated legal instruments. These requirements are beyond the technical capacity of even the richest of the countries studied. In those countries where the social and economic problems are most difficult, enforcement is almost impossible.

Tax Reforms. In several of the countries studied, fiscal reforms which put special emphasis on land, inheritance and income taxes were considered to be substitutes for agrarian reform. High land taxes (preferably progressive) can influence large landowners to use their properties more intensively or to sell it to those who will. Higher inheritance taxes, particularly where the "family corporation" loophole is closed, can also lead to more rapid subdivision of large estates. The benefits from such measures are expected to be higher farm output, lower land values, more land made available for sale and more government tax revenues for development and reform programs. But it cannot be claimed that higher taxes will, as such, overcome the social tensions in rural areas.

There is ample scope for agricultural tax reform. In all of the countries studied taxation penalizes the more productive farmers while leaving those with large, idle estates virtually tax-free. The bulk of the government revenues now derived from agriculture come from taxes on sales, on imports and exports and on farm wage payments. The farmers with most production carry the burden; meanwhile the tax take is negligible on land, capital, net incomes or inheritances. In Argentina, for example, the ICAD study indicates that only one-third of the total tax revenue collected from the agricultural sector was based upon income from land or from capital. In Peru land taxes are virtually nonexistent. In other countries land taxes and income taxes are constantly evaded by large property owners.

Some note has already been made of the slow rate of "natural subdivision" of large estates through the workings of inheritance laws. Landowning families tend to hold land in a corporate entity which is exempt from death duties and requires no more than redistribution of shares when one of the family dies. This has two negative effects. The economic pressure to subdivide large holdings is diluted and lost, and the government's revenues from inheritance taxes is diminished.

The benefits of a good tax system can be enjoyed only if the taxes are strictly and impartially enforced. Experience in the study countries indicates that land and inheritance taxes have the same weakness as regulation of tenancy contracts and minimum wages. The more immediate interests of the bureaucrats, legislators and politicians give them no motive for adopting or enforcing really effective regulations. In Latin America the public imagination is not to be captured by tax reforms. Although agrarian reforms can have the enthusiastic support of the campesinos, tax reform invariably produces intense opposition without garnering offsetting support. Politically, taxes are never popular, even among the potential beneficiaries.

Industrialization. The creation of a vigorous industrial sector is held by some to be the only realistic solution to the agrarian problems of developing countries. In the long run, this view is certainly correct but it is also tautological. Economic development involves by definition creation of new industry, new job opportunities, greater urbanization and the other attributes of a commercial society. Through the process of development a country's social and economic structure, including its land tenure relationships, is fundamentally transformed. Campesinos are emancipated from their inferior position because of wider job possibilities, higher political and social status and better health and education facilities. But having a destination is not the same as knowing the road. The question remains: how is it possible to achieve industrial growth quickly while simultaneously reducing social tensions and increasing production in the agricultural sector?

The arithmetic of development argues against the possibility of solving the agrarian problem simply by moving the rural poor into urban areas. In the study countries rural population could not be absorbed much more rapidly than at present, even if there were rapid forced-draft industrialization. In regions where the farm population lives under the full burden of the traditional land tenure institutions, industrialization cannot have much impact on employment opportunities for at least two generations. Celso Furtado recently estimated that the investments in Brazilian industry made between 1950 and 1960 did not change the occupational structure of the country; the number of industrial jobs increased at an annual rate of 2.8 per cent, which was below the rate of population increase and less than half the rate of increase in urban population. In Chile employment in industrial manufacturing increased by 21 per cent between 1950 and 1960 but the relative importance of such employment decreased as population increased by 30 per cent in the same period. A large proportion of the farm population entering the labor market during the next few decades must continue to seek employment in farming or in related rural industries.

The speed with which new industrial jobs can be created depends not simply on the rate of industrial growth but also upon the size and nature of the existing industrial base. Of the countries studied, only Argentina and Chile now have sufficient industrial development so that rapid growth — say, doubling manufacturing jobs over a decade — could have an appreciable effect on rural employment alternatives.

---

4. The Venezuelan Land Reform Law of 1960

After the overthrow of the military dictator Marcos Pérez Jiménez early in 1958, the first popularly elected President of Venezuela was Rómulo Betancourt. One of the chief goals of the Betancourt administration was agrarian reform. The commission that drafted the government's proposed legislation was (to put it conservatively) broadly based, including such diverse members as an Archbishop of the Catholic Church and a leader of the Communist Party. Land reform thus came to Venezuela based on an extraordinary political consensus. The result was the Agrarian Reform Law of 1960. The following summary of that law is intended to provide a broad outline of the provisions of a statute that is in many respects typical of Latin American land reform legislation of the 1960s.

Introductory Title: Principles of the Agrarian Reform

Article 1 of the law states the law's purposes:

The purpose of this Act is to transform the agrarian structure of the country and to incorporate its rural population into the economic, social and political development of the Nation, by replacing the latifundia system with an equitable system of land ownership, tenure and operation based on the fair distribution of the land, satisfactory organization of credit, and full assistance to agricultural producers, in order that the land may constitute, for the man who works it, a basis for his economic stability, a foundation for his advancing social welfare and a guarantee of his freedom and dignity.

This ambitious declaration announces that the Venezuelan reform is to be "integral," involving not only the distribution of rights in land but also such features as agricultural credit and marketing systems, irrigation schemes, rural education, technical assistance and the like. Venezuela, it should be noted, is one country that has very substantial governmental revenues, derived from petroleum.

Title I: Agricultural Property

Priorities are set out for the acquisition of land for purposes of the land reform. Public lands are to be used first, and in Venezuela there were enormous tracts of public lands available for settlement. General Juan Vicente Gómez, the dictator who died in 1935, was a notorious land-grabber. (Rómulo Betancourt once called him a *terrófago*, literally, a land-eater.) The government "inherited" the Gómez lands. Much of what is called land reform in Venezuela consists of the confirmation of titles to squatters on public land, a process that avoids the political trauma of expropriation of the holdings of private owners.

Such expropriations are, however, authorized, when private ownership does not fulfill its "social function." That term is defined largely in terms of two goals: to exploit agricultural lands efficiently, and to end indirect systems of exploitation by tenants on behalf of absentee owners. Expropriation is a judicial process, and compensation is to be paid for expropriated lands and waters (partly in bonds; see Title X, below). An owner is to be allowed to reserve a portion of his estate for his own personal operation.

The text of Title I is reprinted in Appendix D, p. 719, *infra*.

Title II: Allocation of Land

Land is to be distributed either in individual ownership or in collective ownership. Criteria are established for eligibility of beneficiaries, and priorities among eligible persons are set. The National Agrarian Institute is made responsible for supporting and supervising beneficiaries.

Title III: Farm Credit

An interim system of farm credit is outlined, pending the establishment of a special agency to run the credit system.

Title IV: Conservation and Development of Renewable Natural Resources

The Ministry of Agriculture is instructed to prepare soil/ecology maps of the country, to serve as the basis for a land classification system. The state declares the purpose to engage in a broad-scale conservation program. Research and agricultural extension services are declared as goals of the government.

Title V: Organization of the Market in Agricultural Products and Supplies

Interim responsibility for supervising the creation of a new marketing system is given to the Agricultural Bank. Minimum prices are to be guaranteed to farmers.

Title VI: Rural Housing

The National Agrarian Institute is charged with fostering the construction and improvement of rural housing. Employers on large farms are to be required to provide adequate housing for their workers.

Title VII: Agricultural Cooperatives

Such cooperatives are to be encouraged in such areas as credit, production, marketing and buying. Pilot cooperatives are to be established by the state.

Title VIII: Agricultural Contracts

Certain types of provisions in tenancy contracts are declared void: *e.g.,* an agreement by the tenant to receive supplies from the owner, or to sell his products through the owner. Advance payments of rent are not to be required. Upon expiration of a tenancy period, the owner must compensate the tenant for any fixed improvements on the land. Evictions must be approved by the National Agrarian Institute. Certain oppressive practices of owners are declared to be acts of "indirect eviction": *e.g.,* reducing the area which a tenant has been allowed to work, withholding approval of a chattel mortgage given by the tenant in order to get farm credit, allowing livestock to trample tenants' crops, etc.

Title IX: Agencies of the Agrarian Reform

An autonomous land reform agency, the National Agrarian Institute, is created, attached to the Ministry of Agriculture. The Directorate of the Institute is to include a President and four Directors, two of whom represent campesino organizations and one of whom is to be an agronomist. A national land registry is established; all landowners are required to register their lands.

Title X: Means of Execution

The Agrarian Debt is established. Three classes of bonds are to be created, for use in paying compensation to expropriated owners. The bonds vary in their terms; the most favorable bonds are to go to owners whose ownership has come the closest to performing its social function, as defined earlier. An Irrigation Institute is authorized; public waters may be declared to be part of a Hydraulic Reserve.

Title XI: Transitional Provisions; Title XII: Final Provisions

Various interim agencies are established, to carry on certain functions under the law until permanent agencies are in business. An interim land classification scheme is established. Miscellaneous housekeeping regulations are established.

---

5. "Counterreform"

A land reform statute is not a land reform. In Latin America, both the landlords and the campesinos understand this simple truth. A statute, in fact, can be an instrument for undermining a land reform movement, channeling reformist energies into "pilot projects," agricultural censuses, and other activities that do not imply fundamental structural change. John Kenneth Galbraith made a similar observation a full ten years before the Alliance for Progress was born:

> Unfortunately, some of our current discussion of land reform in the under-developed countries proceeds as though this reform were something that a government proclaims on any fine morning – that it gives land to tenants as it might reform the administration of justice. In fact, a land reform is a revolutionary step; it passes power, property and status from one group in the community to another. If the government of the country is dominated or strongly influenced by the landholding group – the one that is losing its prerogatives – no one should expect effective land legislation as an act of grace.[14]

To this caution we can add, in view of the Latin American experience of the 1960s, that neither should we expect land reform legislation to be carried out just because it has been enacted.

In an article published in 1970, Ernest Feder (an agricultural economist) severely criticizes much that has carried the name "land reform" in Latin America during the past decade. Feder's criticism is directed partly at the legal profession; the land reform laws, he says, "have been a playground for lawyers. . . ."[15] In the sections of this chapter that follow, we shall return to some of Feder's specific criticisms of "counterreform" practices. For now, it is sufficient to take note of his general points, which are representative of a growing body of "post-mortem" literature on the Alliance for Progress.

---

[14] Galbraith, "Conditions for Economic Change in Under-Developed Countries," 43 *J. Farm Econ.* 689, 695 (1951). For the remarkable view that land reform can be achieved in Latin America with essentially no redistribution of wealth (*i.e.,* with full compensation of expropriated landowners), see Prosterman, "Land Reform in Latin America: How to Have a Revolution Without a Revolution," 42 *Wash. L. Rev.* 189 (1966).

[15] Feder, "Counterreform," in *Agrarian Problems and Peasant Movements in Latin America* at 173, 177 (R. Stavenhagen ed. 1970).

Feder argues that the land reform legislation itself has defeated land reform, in a variety of ways: (a) The laws entrench delay, rejecting rapid and massive transformations of the agrarian structure in favor of piecemeal expropriations which themselves result only after lengthy studies. (b) The terms of the laws specifying which properties are to be expropriated are slippery, cast in language like "inefficient" management; thus there is opportunity for manipulation in the administration of the laws. (c) Exemptions are carved out for "well-managed" estates or estates up to a certain size (often very large); thus what starts out as land reform turns out to be colonization, settling campesinos on marginal lands (often governmentally owned). Beyond the terms of the laws, there are of course other ways to sabotage a land reform: underfinance the responsible agency; appoint landowners to direct the agency; transfer aggressive staff members to other jobs; attack the agency in the press for mishandling funds, etc. Feder's catalogue of such practices is continent-wide in its geographical scope.

The Alliance for Progress was a program intended to provide large-scale United States aid to social and economic development in Latin America. Born in 1961 as a response to the Cuban revolution, the Alliance was formally laid to rest in a presidential speech of October 31, 1969. Its basic document was the Charter of Punta del Este. On the subject of land reform, the Charter committed the signatory nations (the United States and the nations of Latin America except for Cuba):

> to encourage . . . programs of integral agrarian reform, leading to the effective transformation, where required, of unjust structures and systems of land tenure and use; with a view to replacing latifundia and dwarf holdings by an equitable system of property.[16]

By 1964 the tone and the substance of United States foreign policy had changed. On the third anniversary of the Charter, President Johnson said:

> Through land reform aimed at increased production, taking different forms in each country, we can provide those who till the soil with self-respect and increased income, and each country with increased production to feed the hungry and to strengthen its economy.[17]

This language reflects not only an emphasis on increasing the production of agricultural commodities, but also a de-emphasis of structural change. The net result is summarized by one leading (and not unfriendly) analyst of the Alliance: "In the region as a whole, progress in agrarian reform continued to be painfully slow or virtually non-existent."[18]

Given this history, why study Latin American land reform? It is only partly flippant to reply that medical students study dead bodies in order to understand the ills that plague the living. Land reform is a massive social transformation, in which law and lawyers can play — have played — crucial roles, both positive and negative. It is

---

[16] Title I, Objective 6, Charter of Punta del Este (1961).

[17] L. Johnson, *Third Anniversary of the Alliance for Progress* 8 (U.S. Dep't of State 1964).

[18] H. Perloff, *Alliance for Progress: A Social Invention in the Making* 70 (1969).

instructive to inquire into both the strengths and the limitations of a legal system in the face of such a challenge. And several land reforms in Latin America antedate the Alliance for Progress: Mexico (1915); Bolivia (1952); Cuba (1959); Venezuela (1960) — none an unqualified success, but each a success in some exceedingly important respects.

B. Mexico and the Theory of Restitution

Given the history of land-grabbing which resulted in the loss of village lands to the haciendas, it is not surprising that one of the earliest calls for land reform took the form of a demand for restitution. The land had been aggregated illegally, it was said, and should be restored to its true owners. Similar arguments have been heard in all the countries in which there is a large indigenous population, since in every such case it can be said that the land belonged to the people who held it before the Conquest. (The larger Indian populations of Latin America were settled rather than migratory, farmers rather than hunters.) Land reform thus began in Mexico on the basis of a "title" theory.

Pleas for the restoration of land to the villages were heard from early colonial times forward; the first royal decree ordering restitution of village lands came in 1535, only 19 years after the landing of Cortez. The Laws of the Indies themselves were partly addressed to the problem, although they were never really enforced in the villages' favor. Father Hidalgo, the first leader in Mexico's war for independence, called the countryside to arms in distinctly agrarian terms: "Will you make the effort to recover from the hated Spaniards the lands stolen from your forefathers three hundred years ago?"[19] But the hacendados soon captured the revolution. In the mid-19th century, some influential Mexican leaders sought to restore the rights of the villages. Here are the words of a member of the legislative committee which drafted the document which became the Constitution of 1857:

> And, limiting ourselves to the object which we have proposed, shall it be necessary in an assembly of public deputies, in a congress of representatives of this poor and enslaved people, to demonstrate the maldistribution of territorial property in the Republic, and the infinite abuses to which it has given place? . . . With good reason the public now feels that constitutions are born and die, that governments succeed each other, that codes are enlarged and made intricate, that pronouncements and plans come and go, and that after so many mutations and upheavals, so much inquietude and so many sacrifices, nothing positive has been done for the people, nothing advantageous for these unhappy classes, from which always emerge those who shed their blood in civil wars, those who give their quota for the armies, who populate the jails and labor in public works, and for which were made, finally, all the evils of society, and none of its goods.

---

[19] Quoted in E. Greuning, *Mexico and its Heritage* 30 (1928).

The miserable servants of the countryside, especially those of indigenous race, are sold and traded for their whole life, because the master regulates their salary, gives them the food and the clothing which he wishes to give, and at the price which is convenient for him, under the threat of putting them in jail, punishing them, tormenting them and dishonoring them, whenever they do not submit to the decrees and orders of the landowner. It should be understood that we are speaking in general terms, and that while we recognize many and very honorable exceptions, while we know that there exist respectable and even generous proprietors, who in their haciendas are nothing more than beneficent fathers and even charitable brothers of their servants, who help them in their misery, alleviate their suffering and cure their diseases; there are others — and they are more numerous — who commit a thousand arbitrarinesses and tyrannies, who make themselves deaf to the cries of the poor, who have not one sentiment of humanity, nor recognize any law beyond money, or any morals beyond avarice. . . .

He who may believe that we are exaggerating can read the important articles which our worthy companion Sr. Díaz Parriga published a few days ago in the "Monitor Republicano," which have been published in the press of Aguascalientes, San Luis Potosí and other States. Above all, he can visit the districts of Cuernavaca and others to the South of this capital, the banks of Rioverde in the State of San Luis, all the region of the Huasteca, and without going very far, see what is going on in the very Valley of Mexico. But what part of the Republic could he not choose to convince himself of what we are saying, without lamenting an abuse, without feeling an injustice, without being pained by the fate of the unfortunate workers of the countryside? In what tribunal of the country would he not see a people or an entire republic of indigenous citizens, litigating over lands, complaining of despoilments and usurpations, praying for the restitution of their forests and waters? Where would one not see congregations of villagers, small populations which do not grow, which barely live, growing smaller every day, surrounded as they are by the ring of iron which the landlords have placed around them, without permitting them the use of their natural fruits, or imposing on them heavy and exorbitant requirements? . . .[20]

The Constitution itself said nothing about restitution of village lands, nor did Juárez's Laws of Reform (1856) touch on the question (they were principally directed against the power of the clergy). Much less did Maximilian's imperial government (1862-67) show an interest in the claims of the villages. After Juárez' army had forced the French troops to withdraw, and after Maximilian had been shot, the Reform had a few more years left. But Juárez died in 1872, having done little for the villages' cause, and the Reform itself died in 1876 when Porfirio Díaz entered the capital with his army and arranged to be elected President.

The legislation of the Reform, forbidding corporate ownership of land, was applied during Díaz' long rule (1876-1910) to the villages' lands, and with a vengeance. Other

---

[20] Special vote (report) of Ponciano Arriaga, June 23, 1856, in F. Tena Ramírez, *Leyes Fundamentales de México, 1808-1957* at 573, 577-79 (1957).

legal devices for despoiling village lands during the Díaz regime were: (a) an 1894 law permitting any inhabitant to file a claim to land which had never been legally transferred by the government – which included most village lands, since under the 1856 reform laws villages were not eligible to hold land; (b) an 1888 law, later amended, the interpretation and application of which made it possible for politically influential persons to control the supply of water to village lands; and (c) the punishment of some villages on the ground that their people had participated in rebellion against the government. All these techniques are described in N. Whetten, *Rural Mexico* at 87-89 (1948).

The revolution of 1910, which Mexicans now call The Revolution, began not as an agrarian revolt but as a political one, against the prolongation of the Díaz regime. Díaz had previously given an interview to a New York journalist, in which he stated that he would not be a candidate for re-election. When he announced that after all he would run again, a mild sort of revolution was on, under the leadership of Francisco I. Madero, himself a landowner of some wealth and position. Madero announced as a candidate; when Díaz "won," the real revolution started. Madero's Plan of San Luis Potosí set the guidelines for the new government, and included a word concerning the restitution of village lands.

PLAN OF SAN LUIS POTOSI

3d.-- . . .

In abuse of the law of vacant lands, numerous small property owners, most of them indigenous, have been despoiled of their lands, either by rulings of the Ministry of Development, or by decisions of the Tribunals of the Republic. Since it is only just to restore to the former possessors (or to their heirs) the lands of which they were despoiled in such an immoral manner, let those lands be restored to their original owners, to whom shall also be paid an indemnity for prejudices suffered. Only in the case in which the lands may have passed to third persons, before the promulgation of this plan, the old owners shall receive indemnity from those in whose benefit the despoilment is proved. . . .

Effective Suffrage. No Reelection.

San Luis Potosí, October 5, 1910.

[Signed] Francisco I. Madero[21]

A year later, with the revolution apparently over and the government in Madero's hands, land reform became a central political issue. Emiliano Zapata, the great Indian

---

[21] *Id.* at 732, 736,739.

leader of the State of Morelos, attacked Madero for his failure to carry out the promised land reform. Zapata issued his own plan, the Plan of Ayala.

PLAN OF AYALA

4th. -- The Revolutionary Junta of the State of Morelos manifests to the Nation, under formal oath, that it adopts as its own the Plan of San Luis Potosí with the additions which are expressed below for the benefit of oppressed peoples, and that it will make itself the defender of the principles which they defend until it triumphs or dies. . . .

6th. -- As an additional part of the Plan which we invoke, we declare: that possession of the lands, forests and waters which have been usurped by the hacendados, *científicos* [a kind of palace guard of technocrats around the dictator Díaz] or bosses in the shadow of tyranny and venal justice, shall be given immediately to those villages or citizens who may have their respective titles to these properties, of which they have been despoiled by the bad faith of our oppressors. We shall resolutely maintain that possession, with arms in hand, and usurpers who may consider themselves to have a right to the lands shall allege such right before special tribunals which may be established upon the triumph of the Revolution.

7th. -- Since the immense majority of Mexican villages and citizens own no more than the ground which they tread, suffering the horrors of misery without being able to improve their social condition in any respect nor to dedicate themselves to industry or to agriculture because lands, forests and waters are monopolized in a few hands — for this reason one-third of these monopolies shall be expropriated from their powerful owners by means of prior compensation, to the end that the villages and citizens of Mexico may obtain *ejidos*, villages, legal estates for villages or fields to be sowed or worked, and so that poverty and privation may be remedied thoroughly for all Mexicans.

8th.--Hacendados, *científicos,* or bosses who may oppose the present plan directly or indirectly shall have their goods nationalized, and the two-thirds which correspond to them shall be destined for war indemnities, pensions for the widows and orphans of the victims who die in the struggle for this Plan.

9th. -- In order to carry out the proceedings with respect to the property above mentioned, the laws of mortmain and nationalization shall be applied as they may be appropriate, so that we may be served, by precept and example, by these laws put in force by the immortal Juárez for ecclesiastical property, which laws gave warning to the despots and conservatives who in every era have attempted to impose on us the ignominious yoke of oppression and backwardness. . . .

Liberty, Justice and Law.

Ayala, November 25, 1911. [Signed by Zapata as general in chief, and by seven other generals, twenty-seven colonels, five captains and others.][22]

---

[22] F. Tena Ramírez, *Leyes Fundamentales de México, 1808-1957,* at 740, 741-43 (1957); also

Over the next few years, various revolutionary forces contended for power. In 1914, General Venustiano Carranza, a former supporter of Díaz, asserted his authority as First Chief of the Constitutionalist Army. (It was called "constitutionalist" because it had supported the "constitutional" President, Madero, who had been elected in a special election in 1911 after the resignation and exile of Díaz. When Díaz resigned, no one had suggested that he be replaced by his vice-president, General Ramón Corral, "who was detested for his barbarity in selling Yaqui Indians from Sonora into slavery on the henequen plantations of Yucatán."[23]) Carranza, under fire from Zapata in the south and Francisco Villa in the north, issued a decree which became the basis for all of Mexico's modern agrarian legislation. The decree was in large part the product of Luis Cabrera, whose famous speech describing the despoiling of the villages had moved the Chamber of Deputies in 1912.

AGRARIAN LAW OF JANUARY 6, 1915

VENUSTIANO CARRANZA, First Chief of the Constitutionalist Army, Agent of the Executive Power of the Mexican Republic, and Chief of the Revolution, in use of the powers with which he is invested, and CONSIDERING:

That one of the most general causes of the ill-being and discontent of the agricultural populations of this country has been the despoilment of the communal property lands or allotment lands which had been conceded by the Colonial Government, as a means of assuring the existence of the indigenous class, and which, under the pretext of complying with the law of June 25, 1856, and other provisions which ordered the fractioning and reduction to private property of those lands, among the inhabitants of the villages to which they belonged, came to rest in the power of a few speculators;

That a multitude of other towns of different parts of the Republic find themselves in the same situation, and that so-called congregations, communities or settlements, had their origin in some family or families which possessed in common greater or lesser areas of land, which continued to be kept undivided for various generations, or rather originated in a certain number of inhabitants who came together in favorable places to acquire and jointly exploit waters, lands and forests, following the ancient and general custom of the indigenous peoples;

That the despoilment of the said lands was done, not only by means of alienations carried into effect by the political authorities in open contravention of the mentioned laws, but also by means of concessions, compositions or sales agreed upon with the Ministries of Development and Finance, or under the pretext of surveys and demarcations, to favor those who made denunciations of surplus lands and to the

---

in J. Silva Herzog, I *Breve Historia de la Revolución Mexicana* 240, 242-45 (2d ed. 1962). For a somewhat different translation from our own, see John Womack's excellent historical study, *Zapata and the Mexican Revolution* at 393, 402-03 (1969).

[23] H. Herring, *A History of Latin America* 352 (2d ed. 1961).

so-called border-marking companies; but in any case lands were invaded which for long years belonged to the villages and on which the latter based their subsistence;

That as may be inferred from existing litigation, the rights of the villages and communities have always been flouted. Since, under Article 27 of the Federal Constitution, the villages lacked capacity to acquire and possess real property, they were also held to lack juridical personality to defend their rights. On the other hand, it became entirely illusory to provide for the protection which the existing law of vacant lands attempted to grant them (by empowering the syndicates of the City Councils of Municipalities to reclaim and defend communal property in cases in which those properties might be confused with vacant lands), since as a rule the syndicates never bothered to fulfill this mission, because they lacked interest to stimulate them to work, and also because political chiefs and State governors were almost always interested in seeing that the spoliation of the lands in question be consummated;

That once the indigenous villages were deprived of lands, waters and forests which the colonial government had conceded to them, as well as the congregations and communities deprived of their undivided lands, and once the rural property of the rest of the country was concentrated in a few hands, the only recourse for the great mass of the population in the countryside has been for obtaining the necessities of life, than to hire out their labor to powerful landowners at a low price, which in turn inevitably produces the state of misery, abjection and effective slavery in which this enormous number of workers has lived and still lives;

That in view of the foregoing, it is obviously necessary to return to the villages the lands of which they have been despoiled, as an act of elemental justice and as the only effective manner of assuring peace and promoting the well-being and improvement of our poor classes, without hindrance from the interests created in favor of persons who presently possess the lands in question. Not only do those interests lack legal foundation, from the moment in which they were established in express violation of the mortmain laws which ordered only the distribution of the communal property among the residents themselves, and not their alienation in favor of strangers; neither have these rights become sanctioned or legitimate through long possession, since the aforementioned laws did not establish prescriptive rights with respect to these properties, and since the villages to whom they belong were unable to defend themselves for lack of the juridical personality necessary to take part in a lawsuit;

That it is probable that in some cases the restitution in question cannot be realized, either because the alienation of the lands which belonged to the villages may have been made in accordance with the law, or because the villages may have lost the title documents or because those which they have may be deficient, or because it may be impossible to identify the lands or fix their precise area, or, finally, for any other cause; but since the reason which prevents the restitution, however just and legitimate it may be, does not solve the difficult situation which so many villages find themselves in, nor much less justify the continuation of this painful situation, it is necessary to remove the difficulty in another manner which may be compatible with the interests of all;

That the manner of accommodating the necessity which has just been pointed out can be none other than to give authority to the superior military authorities acting in each locality, so that, carrying out the expropriations which may be indispensable, they may give sufficient lands to the villages which lack them, thus realizing one of the great principles inscribed in the program of the Revolution, and establishing one of the primary bases on which the reorganization of the country must rest;

That, in establishing the manner by which many villages may recover the lands of which they were despoiled, or may acquire those which they need for their well-being and development, there is no intention to revive the old indigenous communities, or to create other similar ones, but only to give that land to the miserable rural population which today lacks it, so that it may develop fully its rights to life and free itself from the economic servitude to which it has been reduced. It is to be noted that ownership of lands will not belong to the village in common, but that it must be divided in full ownership, although with the limitations necessary to prevent avid speculators, particularly foreigners, from speculating in this property easily, as almost invariably happened with the division legally made of the *ejidos* and legal estates of the villages as a result of the revolution of Ayutla [Juárez' revolution] .

Therefore,

I have considered it proper to issue the following DECREE:

Article 1st. The following are declared void:

I. All transfers of the lands, waters, and forests belonging to villages, *rancherías*, congregations, or communities made by local officials (*jefes políticos*), State governors, or other local authorities in violation of the provisions of the Law of June 25, 1856, and other related laws and rulings;

II. All concessions, compositions or sales of lands, waters, and forests made by the Secretariat of Development, the Secretariat of Finance, or any other federal authority from December 1, 1876 to date, which encroach upon or illegally occupy ejidos lands allotted in common, or lands of any other kind belong to villages, *rancherías*, congregations or communities, and

III. All survey or demarcation-of-boundary proceedings effected during the period of time referred to in the preceding sub-clause, by companies, judges, or other Federal or State authorities involving encroachments on or illegal occupation of the lands, waters, or forests of ejidos, lands held in common, or other holdings belonging to villages, *rancherías*, congregations or communities.

Article 2d. The division or allotment of land which may have been made legitimately among the inhabitants of a village, *ranchería*, congregation or community, and in which there may have been some defect [such as mistake, fraud, etc.] , may be nullified only upon the petition of two-thirds of the inhabitants or their representatives.

Article 3d. Villages which lack ejidos or which are unable to have them restored to them because of lack of title documents, because of impossibility of identification, or because they had been legally transferred, shall be granted sufficient lands and waters to reconstitute them, in accordance with the needs of the population; and for this purpose the land needed shall be expropriated, at the expense of the Federal Government, to be taken from lands adjoining the villages in question.

[Articles 4 through 9 establish the machinery for obtaining grants of land, or restitution of lands. Chief responsibility for handling the villages' petitions is given to

State governors and local military commanders. Ultimate approval is reserved for the President of Mexico.]

Article 10th. Interested persons who believe themselves to be prejudiced by the decision of the [President] may resort to the courts to assert their rights, within the period of one year, counting from the date of said decisions, but after this time no claim shall be admitted.

In cases in which claims are filed against restitutions and in which the interested party may obtain a judical decision declaring that the restitution made to a village is not proper, the judgment shall give only a right to obtain the appropriate compensation from the Government.

In the same period of one year, owners of expropriated lands may resort to the courts claiming the compensation owing to them. . . .

Transitory. This law shall begin to take effect from the date of its publication. So long as the present civil war shall not have concluded, the military authorities shall cause the present law to be published and proclaimed in each of the village squares or places which shall be occupied by them.

Constitution and Reforms. Given in Veracruz, January 6, 1915.

The First Chief of the Constitutionalist Army, Agent of the Executive Power of the Republic and Chief of the Revolution, Venustiano Carranza.

To the C. Engineer Pastor Rouaix, Managing Subsecretary of the Office of Development, Colonization and Industry. Present.

Much of the substance of the 1915 Law was written into the Constitution of 1917 — the Constitution that governs Mexico today. It is proper to regard the 1915 Law as the definitive agrarian legislation of the Revolution. But a social revolution is not neat and surgical, and so no one should be surprised to learn that land reform was carried out in a portion of Mexico under the authority of legislation that was entirely distinct from the 1915 Law. In the State of Morelos, just South of Mexico City, Zapata's forces carried out their own land reform, beginning with their early military successes in the months following the promulgation of the Plan of Ayala. Lands in Morelos were initially taken from the haciendas and given to the villages with nothing to guide the redistribution but the generalities of the Plan. By late 1915, however, the Zapatistas promulgated their own Agrarian Law, which was far more sweeping than the Law that Carranza had issued earlier in the same year — and more sophisticated, as well.

The Zapatista law provided for restitution of lands to villages that could show pre-1856 titles, and also the expropriation of *all* lands in excess of certain specified maximum areas (ranging from 100 hectares in the case of prime, irrigated land in warm climates to as much as 1500 hectares of uncultivated semi-desert land). Compensation was to be paid, except to landowners who were identified as Enemies of the Revolution; the amount of compensation was to be fixed according to evaluations on the property tax rolls. Preferences were established for potential beneficiaries. Lands once distributed were to be inalienable, but beneficiaries who did not cultivate their lands were to be dispossessed. The elements of an "integral" reform were recognized:

the law ordered the establishment of an agricultural credit agency, an extension service, and an agency to construct irrigation works.[24]

The Constitution of 1917, in Article 27, asserted original national ownership of all lands and waters in Mexico, providing that the Nation has "the right to transmit title thereof to private persons, thereby constituting private property." It contained the familiar guarantee that "Private property shall not be expropriated except for reasons of public use and subject to payment of indemnity [*mediante indemnización*]" The agrarian reform was specifically recognized, and the key provisions of the 1915 Law (articles 1st and 3d) were adopted almost verbatim in Article 27 of the Constitution. One exception was added: Persons who for more than ten years had held title to lands not exceeding fifty hectares in area, which title had been granted in conformity with the procedural requirements of the 1856 law of Juárez, were entitled to continue to hold their lands, even though the lands might otherwise fall under the nullity provisions of the 1915 Law, as incorporated into Article 27. And an important remedial provision was added: Landowners were denied *any* judicial relief in cases of expropriation; they were required to apply to the government for compensation, within one year of the decree ordering the taking of their lands. (We shall see later in this chapter that this limitation was amended in 1947 to permit judicial protection of owners of "small properties" against expropriations in violation of certain exemptions established in the same 1947 amendment to Article 27.)

Although it was Carranza who had called the convention that produced the 1917 Constitution, under his administration land reform principally took the form of wholesale transfers of land from the old *hacendados* to revolutionary generals and political chiefs. Yet another revolt formed, this time under Alvaro Obregón, the northern general and champion of social reform. In 1920, a year after he had caused Zapata's assassination, Carranza, having been deserted by his army, put his family, some friends, and large quantities of gold from the national treasury on a train for Veracruz. He was betrayed by an associate and assassinated. The fighting ended, and Obregón was elected President; the 1917 Constitution remained in force as it remains today.

Even so, the restitution of village lands proceeded slowly. "As long as this was the principal basis for distributing land, very little was restored. During the entire period from 1916 to 1944, only 6 per cent of the total land distributed was by the method of restitution."[25] (40 per cent of that 6 per cent had been distributed by 1927.) It is not hard to see why a title theory of land reform was insufficient to get much land distributed. Simpson recounts one typical case in the following extract from his outstanding early work on the Mexican land reform:

---

[24] The Zapatista law is translated in J. Womack, Jr., *Zapata and the Mexican Revolution* 405-11 (1969). Womack's biography details not only the life of Zapata but also the role of the villages of Morelos in the Revolution which was, for them, first and foremost an agrarian revolution. See also R. Quirk, *The Mexican Revolution, 1914-1915* (1963).

[25] N. Whetten, *Rural Mexico* 129 (1948).

E. SIMPSON, THE EJIDO: MEXICO'S WAY OUT
Pp. 465-66 (1937)

Among the very first of the agrarian communities to take advantage of Carranza's famous decree was Zacapan. On August 17, 1915, a petition was addressed by the citizens of Zacapan to the governor of the state which held: (a) that from time immemorial the village had been in pacific and uninterrupted possession of its land; (b) but that for over forty years the owners of the hacienda of Manantiales had been persecuting the village "even to the extent of starting armed combats" and that, during the Díaz regime, supported by the "dictatorial government of the time," the hacienda succeeded in absorbing most of the village land; (c) that the old Quiroga swamp was the property of Zacapan and neighboring villages and when the swamp was drained by Lorenzo Garza and his associates Zacapan was thus further despoiled; and (d) that, therefore, the village, encouraged by the promises of the revolution, hereby petitioned the government to restore to it the lands unlawfully taken away.

Unfortunately, when the time came for Zacapan to present its titles and other documents proving its ownership to the property claimed, the most that the village could do was to produce a map whereon were marked the lands which "according to the memory of the oldest inhabitant" had once belonged to the community. The *hacendados,* on the other hand, were able to bring forward all sorts of *testimonios, contratos, escrituras* and other legal documents to show their right to the land in dispute. Although some of the agrarian authorities believed there were grounds for "reasonable presumption that in truth the lands of the village had been invaded" by the *hacendados,* in the absence of documentary proof, there was nothing to do but declare Zacapan's petition for restitution *no procedente* [not allowable].

The village finally did get its land. In 1922, 450 hectares from three haciendas were granted in provisional possession; the final decree in 1924 increased the grant to 632 hectares for the 316 heads of families.[26] The case illustrates the progress of the Mexican land reform — early reliance on the restitution theory, followed by its gradual abandonment in favor of more far-reaching measures, which turned out to be almost equally confiscatory. Even so, the Mexican law still provides for restitution as one manner of distributing land to the villages.[27]

Questions

1. Why might a restitution principle be more appealing to a reforming government than a land reform based on the expropriation of land and its subsequent redistribution?

---

[26] Simpson, *supra* at 466-67.

[27] *Agrarian Code of 1943,* art. 46-49.

2. What lands were "restored" by the terms of the 1915 Law? Restored to whom? Were some kinds of "despoilment" of village lands left untouched by these provisions?

3. What are the justifications for limiting restitution to the lands specified in the 1915 Law?

4. Even assuming that restitution was ineffective as a means of redistributing land, might the *theory* of restitution nonetheless play a significant role in a system of land distribution based on confiscatory expropriation?

C. Expropriation: The Affectability of Land

A land reform based entirely on a theory of restitution, we have seen, (a) identifies the land to be taken in the reform, (b) avoids any payment to the "owner" who is dispossessed in favor of those who are held to be the true owners, and (c) identifies the beneficiaries of the reform. Even in Mexico, however, restitution was an insufficient basis for the redistribution of land; the earliest legislation recognized the need for the government to expropriate land in order to carry out the reform. In a reform based on expropriation, all three issues mentioned above must be faced. This section deals with the first question: which lands shall be "affectable," that is, subject to expropriation for the purposes of the reform. The next section considers issues related to the compensation of landowners who lose their land, and the final section of this chapter explores a variety of issues relating to the "new agrarian structure" – the institutions of ownership and management that emerge from the land reform.

This section begins with an examination of the legislative principle that ownership must fulfill a social function, and the corollary, crucial for our present purposes, that ownership interests which do not fulfill their social function should be expropriated by the state. Next, we shall consider a geographical principle for identifying land to be expropriated: the taking of land because it is near a village that lacks land. Then we shall look at legislation designed to attack the great landed estates for their very bigness, expropriating land holdings that exceed designated maximum areas. This section next inquires into the exemption of lands otherwise affectable, granted in order to assure an expropriated owner a reserve on which he can continue farming. The section closes with brief examination of the experience in Bolivia, where land reform preceded legislation, and in Puerto Rico, where the affectability of land had to be squared with the United States Constitution.

---

1. "The Social Function of Ownership"

When the Colombian dictator Gustavo Rojas Pinilla was deposed in 1957, a plebiscite was held to determine whether the public approved the retention of the constitutional reforms of 1936. The resulting affirmative vote adopted as Article 30 of the new Constitution these provisions, which had been established in the 1936 Constitution:

Private ownership is guaranteed along with other rights acquired by rightful title, in accord with civil laws, by natural or juridical persons, which rights shall not be ignored or injured by subsequent laws. When, because of the application of a law enacted for reasons of public purpose or social interest, the rights of individuals come into conflict with the necessity recognized by the law itself, the private interest shall give way to the public or social interest.

Ownership is a social function which implies obligations.

For reasons of public purpose or social interest, as defined by the legislature, there may be expropriation, by means of judicial decision and prior compensation.

Nevertheless, the legislature, for reasons of equity, shall have the power to determine those cases in which there shall be no compensation, by means of the favorable vote of an absolute majority of the members of both Houses.

Before 1964, about the only judicial gloss to be added to the words about "social function" was that the obligation in question was to use one's property "in such a form as not to prejudice the community."[28] This language is like a public-oriented version of the famous common law maxim: *sic utere tuo ut alienum non laedas* (use your own property in such a manner as not to injure that of another), and is equally unhelpful as a guide to decision. The language does, however, represent a shift of emphasis and mood: "What we have wanted to do, then, is to loosen the fetters which the Constitution of 1886 placed on the legislator with respect to private ownership. . .," said Darío Echandía, the Minister of Education and one of the leading advocates of the 1936 reform.[29]

In 1936, The Colombian Congress adopted Law 200, an important piece of legislation aimed at the elimination of private ownership of *uncultivated* land. But for a variety of reasons, political and administrative, little came of the law. Finally in late 1961, after very great difficulties, and at least in part in response to the prodding of officials of the Alliance for Progress, the Colombian Congress adopted a comprehensive land reform law.[30] The 1961 law reaffirms Law 200 of 1936, and gives its administration over to the newly-created Colombian Land Reform Institute (INCORA). The same Institute is given responsibility for administering a program of settlement of state-owned land, and also charged with the acquisition of private land for reform purposes. The key provisions relating to the affectability of privately owned land for expropriation are reproduced below. What meaning does this legislation give to the expression "social function of ownership"? Is this meaning constitutional? In 1964, Colombia's Supreme Court of Justice upheld the law. For excerpts from that decision, see p. 346, *infra.*[31]

---

[28] Supreme Court of Justice, Gaceta Judicial, vol. LV, pp. 349-400 (1943), quoted in O. Morales Benítez, *Reforma Agraria — Colombia Campesina* at 242-43 (1962).

[29] Quoted in Morales Benítez, *id.* at 243.

[30] See A. Hirschman, *Journeys Toward Progress,* Ch. II (1963).

[31] For further discussion of the content of the "social function" concept, see Karst, "Latin-American Land Reform: The Uses of Confiscation," 63 *Mich. L. Rev.* 327, 346-48 (1964).

COLOMBIA: ACT NO. 135 ON SOCIAL LAND REFORM

December 13, 1961, Diario Oficial No. 30691, Dec. 20, 1961, p. 801
(FAO translation)

54. The Colombian Land Reform Institute is hereby authorized to acquire privately-owned land in pursuance of the aims set forth in paragraphs 1, 2 and 4 of Article 1 of this Act, with a view to combatting soil erosion, carrying out reafforestation, facilitating irrigation and marsh reclamation work and improving transit and transport facilities in rural areas.

If the owners of land which it is deemed necessary to acquire fail to sell or transfer their land voluntarily, the Institute may compulsorily acquire such land in accordance with the provisions of the succeeding Articles. The acquisition of such land is hereby declared to be of social interest and public utility in accordance with Article 30 of the Constitution.

55. Except as otherwise specified in Article 58 of this Act, the Institute shall, in making dispositions of land, give preference to easily accessible common land which shall be granted to the peasants in the area. The land must, however, be entirely suitable for the establishment of settlement areas in accordance with Articles 43 *et seq.* of this Act.

If privately-owned land has to be acquired for the purposes of making such dispositions, this shall be done in accordance with the following order of priority:

1. Uncultivated land not covered by the rules on the termination of rights of ownership;
2. Inadequately-worked land;
3. Agricultural land which is totally or very largely farmed by tenant farmers or share-croppers, when in the case of sharecropping the owner does not himself manage the farm and is not, under the sharecropping agreement, responsible for any part of the expenses or operation of the farm. This shall not apply to farms owned by minors or persons without full legal capacity;
4. Properly farmed land not covered by sub-paragraph 2 above but whose owners are prepared to alienate it voluntarily in accordance with the terms of this Act.

56. For the purposes of sub-paragraph 1 of the preceding Article, uncultivated land shall be considered that which while being economically usable is visibly not used for organized crop-farming or stock-breeding. Account shall not be taken for this purpose of land covered with natural forest required for water conservation and the needs of the holding nor of forest plantations of useful timber varieties. In classifying an area of land as being inadequately farmed, the Institute shall take the following factors into consideration: situation in relation to large urban centers; relief; quality of the soil; possibility of irrigation and reclamation; possibility of continuous and regular use; type and intensity of farming; capital and labour employed on the farm; commercial

value and yield of the property and population density in the rural area where the property is situated.

57. In matters pertaining to the acquisition of privately-owned land, the Institute shall furthermore observe the following rules:

1. It shall give priority to those areas where concentration of land holdings is particularly high or where there is total or partial unemployment affecting a large rural population. It shall also give priority to other areas, including those suffering from active erosion, inequitable labour relationships or noticeably lower levels of living amongst the rural population than in other areas of the country.

2. The Institute shall acquire only such land as is suitable for small-scale crop-farming or stock-breeding. Land shall be considered suitable in this respect if it is irrigable or if without irrigation it normally has sufficient rainfall to grow crops or pasture to serve as a basis for the regular upkeep and profitable working of "family farms."

The Institute, may, however, acquire adjacent areas which do not have such characteristics to use them as communal pasture land where this seems suitable.

The acquisition of land in respect of which irrigation works, flood defence works and land or marsh reclamation works may make for economic exploitation or a substantial change in farming methods, shall be governed by the provisions of Articles 68 *et seq.* of this Act.

58. Well-farmed land may only be expropriated when it is proposed to put an area of small-holdings (*minifundios*) together with contiguous or nearby properties as part of land consolidation operations; well-farmed land may also be expropriated to enable small tenant farmers or share-croppers to acquire or extend the plots on which they have been working or to transfer to other land in the same area if such a course seems the most suitable; well-farmed land may also be expropriated when its acquisition is necessary to establish thereon small landowners, tenant farmers or share-croppers who are the occupiers of land that is no longer to be farmed; lastly, well-farmed land may be expropriated as provided in paragraph 3 of Article 55, or to facilitate the piping of water, the execution of land reclamation works and the provision of transit facilities in rural areas.

Each owner subject to expropriation shall, however, be entitled to retain an area of one hundred hectares [1 hectare = 10,000 m^2 = 2.47 acres. – Eds.] This right shall also apply to the owners of inadequately farmed land which the Institute has decided to expropriate under this Article.

Proviso. Small tenant farmers or share-croppers shall be considered to be those wh. occupy in that capacity areas not larger than that which they can themselves farm with the aid of their families. Such areas should not be covered with permanent plantations or if they are so covered, the plantations should be the property of the tenant farmers, share-croppers or settlers concerned and not of the landowner.

59. Except as otherwise specified in the foregoing Article, owners of inadequately farmed land shall, in the event of expropriation proceedings being instituted against

them, be entitled to retain an area of up to two hundred (200) hectares, not more than one hundred (100) of which may be suitable for crop farming.

In computing the above-mentioned area, account shall not be taken of land that is too steep to be cultivated, of natural forests required for water conservation and the needs of the holding nor of enclosed areas, lakes, and areas covered with roads and buildings. Nor shall account be taken of areas normally subject to periodic flooding and which for that reason can be used only during a part of the year. Artificial forest plantations of useful timber varieties shall also not be counted.

Questions

1. Suppose you are a lawyer in Colombia. You are asked by a leader of a local campesino organization whether a specified estate falls within the provisions of Article 56. How will you go about determining your answer to his inquiry?

2. Does your response to question 1 suggest any criticism of the legislative technique used in Article 56? What alternative techniques might be used for identifying lands subject to expropriation for purposes of the land reform? With respect to each such alternative, what difficulties might be involved in its use?

The expression, "the social function of ownership," originated early in this century in the writings of Léon Duguit, a French socialist. Later in this chapter we shall contrast Duguit's ideas about property with the ideas of other writers of the 19th and 20th centuries. For now it is enough for us to note that the "social function" idea has had great vogue among land reformers in Latin America and elsewhere. In Venezuela, as in Colombia, the phrase is expressly written into law. Article 2 of the 1960 Agrarian Reform Law

Guarantees and regulates the right of private land ownership, in accordance with the principle that such ownership should fulfill a social function. . . .

That lofty generality is given real force by the following articles of the Venezuelan law. (The full text of the Venezuelan law's provisions on affectability is reprinted in Appendix D, p. 719, *infra.*)

VENEZUELA: AGRARIAN REFORM LAW (1960)

19. For the purposes of the Agrarian Reform, private ownership of land fulfills its social function when it combines all the following essential elements:

(a) The efficient exploitation and profitable use of the land in such a manner as to bring usefully into play the productive factors thereof, according to the zone in which it is located and its special characteristics.

(b) Personal operation and management of, and financial responsibility for, the agricultural enterprise by the landowner, except in special cases of indirect exploitation for good reasons.

(c) Compliance with the provisions governing conservation of renewable natural resources.

(d) Compliance with legal provisions governing paid labor, other labor relations questions, and other farm contracts, under the conditions laid down in this Act.

(e) Registration of the rural property in the Office of the National Register of Land and Waters in accordance with appropriate legal provisions.

20. In particular, it shall be considered contrary to the principle of the social function of property and incompatible with the national welfare and economic development for uncultivated or unprofitable properties to exist and to be maintained, especially in economic development regions. Indirect systems of land exploitation, such as those carried out through leasing, the various types of sharecropping, day labor and squatting, shall also be considered contrary to the principle of the social function of property;

Provided, that the State shall in particular impose upon uncultivated or unprofitable properties a graduated tax scale to be prescribed in the appropriate enactments, without prejudice to expropriation in cases provided for under this Act. . . .

26. Rural properties which fulfill their social function in accordance with the provisions of Article 19 shall be immune from expropriation for the purposes of the Agrarian Reform, except as specifically provided otherwise by this Act.

27. Expropriation shall be resorted to when, at the site of allocation or at neighboring sites, there exists no public land or other rural properties mentioned in Title I, Chapter I, of this Act, or if such land or properties are inadequate or unsuitable, and if the National Agrarian Institute has been unable by any other means to acquire other land equally exploitable from an economic point of view.

Such expropriation shall be applied primarily to such land as fails to fulfill its social function, in the following order of priorities:

1) Uncultivated properties, and, in particular, those of the greatest area; properties exploited indirectly through tenants, sharecroppers, settlers and occupiers; and properties not under cultivation during the five years immediately prior to the initiation of expropriation proceedings.

2) Properties on which private land fragmentation programs have not been brought to completion, provided that if the National Agrarian Institute requests expropriation thereof after the said programs have been initiated, the rights of beneficiaries of such fragmentation already in occupation shall be safeguarded.

3) Crop lands being used for range livestock grazing.

Expropriation of other land shall be resorted to when the above possibilities have been exhausted and there is no other means of solving an agrarian problem of evident gravity; in such cases, the provisions of Article 33 of this Act shall apply. . . .

33. When it becomes necessary to organize land in a given place, and when the existence thereat of one or more properties forms a technical or economic obstacle to

proper execution of the scheme, the total or partial expropriation of such properties shall be authorized even when they fall within any of the classifications specified in articles 26 and 29 of this Chapter. [Art. 29 provides for an owner's exemption of 150 hectares.] In order to take such action, the Institute shall be required to prove, during the appropriate judicial proceedings, that the conditions laid down in this Article exist. In such cases, cash payment shall be made for existing useful improvements, livestock, mortgages or preferential debts incurred and used for development and improvement purposes. The balance shall be paid in Class "C" bonds in accordance with the provisions of Article 174 of this Act. [The Class "C" bonds carry the most favorable terms of all Agrarian Bonds authorized in the law. See p. 352, *infra.*] . . .

A comparison of Venezuela's Article 19 with Colombia's Articles 55-56 suggests that the draftsmen of the two laws had two targets in common: the inadequate cultivation of land and its indirect exploitation through tenancy or sharecropping arrangements. We shall consider the first of these problems in some depth, and the second more cursorily.

(a) Inadequate Cultivation

The Venezuelan law, in Article 19, establishes as one criterion of ownership's social function "the efficient and profitable use" of the land in question. What guidance does this provision give to landowners, to the government's land reform agency, or to judges who must decide on the propriety of expropriation? Would a more specific statement of the meaning of "efficient exploitation" be desirable? What would be gained by such a specification? What would be lost? How might a more specific provision be worded?

In Chile, the 1967 Agrarian Reform Law relied primarily on expropriation of lands for excessive size. However, the law also provided for the expropriation of lands that were "abandoned" or "badly exploited," whatever their area. Art. 4, Law No. 16,640, Diario Oficial, July 28, 1967. The draftsmen of the law defined those terms in Article 1 of the law:

> 1.(b) *Abandoned farm:* a farm that is not the object of positive acts of economic exploitation such as agricultural cultivation, cultivation of pastures, cattle raising, care and conservation of natural or artificial forests, or others of analogous economic significance. The fact that a farm may be fenced, or be in the charge of caretakers, or the existence of buildings or simple subsistence exploitation shall not alone constitute proof of economic exploitation.
>
> 1.(c) *Badly exploited farm:* a farm whose exploitation is carried on under inadequate economic, technical or social conditions.
>
> The Regulations shall determine the norms to be followed in establishing the economic, technical and social conditions under which a farm must be exploited in order for that farm not to be characterized as badly exploited; [the

Regulations] shall take into account factors of a technical order, such as the use of the land and waters, practices of administrration and social factors, such as wages, housing, education and health conditions.

In any case, a farm shall be considered badly exploited when annual or permanent crops, plantations or artificial pastures occupy a proportion less than 80% of its useful area of normal irrigation, or, in cases of dry, unirrigated land, the proportion of the useful area dedicated to annual or permanent crops, plantations, or improved artificial or natural pastures is less than 70%. For purposes of determining the useful area of normal irrigation, [the Regulations] shall take into account the degree of certainty that the farm will receive irrigation. . . .

In any event, a farm shall be considered to be badly exploited if, within two years prior to the [government's determination to proceed with expropriation], its owner has committed any of the following infractions on two or more occasions: improper appropriation of family allotments; firing of employees or workers without just cause [as defined in a 1966 law]; failure to make payments, in money or in kind, owing to workers, or to social security funds. Such infractions must be established by an executed judicial or administrative decision. Such an administrative decision must have been communicated personally to the owner or to his representative.

The Regulations envisioned in Article 1(c) were issued in 1968. Decree No. 281 of the Ministry of Agriculture, Diario Oficial, June 4, 1968. The Regulations established a point system, based on a scale of 1,000 points, of which 600 are assigned to economic and technical factors: use of natural resources, 200 points; general administrative practices, 220 points (the plan of exploitation, capital investments, etc.); and special administrative practices, 180 points (in the case of farming land: quality of seeds, pest control, timing of sowing, etc.; in the case of cattle-raising land: quality of feed, quality and condition of the cattle, etc.). The other 400 points are assigned to social factors: health and housing, 200 points; wages, 100 points; compliance with labor and social security laws, 100 points. Each factor in the list is explained in the Regulations, and some (*e.g.,* water conservation) are elaborated in considerable detail. Lands that are assigned fewer than 500 points in total, or fewer than 300 points on the "technical-economic" scale or 200 points on the "social" scale, are subject to expropriation as "badly exploited" lands. The burden of proof with respect to each such factor is on the owner.

What assumptions are implicit in the Chilean legislative scheme for identifying lands to be expropriated as "badly exploited"? Under what circumstances would you recommend the adoption of legislation like the Chilean Regulations? Under what circumstances would you recommend a general statement such as that in Venezuela's Article 19? (The Venezuelan Regulations, adopted in 1967, do little more than repeat the language of Article 19.)

The Venezuelan judicial proceeding from which the following extracts are taken illustrates the operation of Article 19 in a live dispute. As you read these documents, consider what differences you might expect in a Chilean expropriation proceeding based on allegations that an owner's lands were "badly exploited." (This case also involves issues of indirect exploitation through tenancy arrangements, and serves as an introduction to the next subsection of this chapter.)

NATIONAL AGRARIAN INSTITUTE v. MUÑOZ

Court of First Instance, Civil and Commercial
District of Paz Castillo
State of Miranda, Venezuela (1961)

[The record in this case has been published under the title of *Alegación y Prueba de la Función Social* (1962).]

Petition for Expropriation

Citizen Judge of the First Instance, Civil and Commercial, of the State of Miranda. His office. I, Leopoldo Márquez Añez, Attorney, resident of Caracas, identified by Identity Card No. 528,560, proceeding in my status as attorney for the National Agrarian Institute, . . . a representation proved by a power of attorney which is attached and marked "A," . . . appear before your competent jurisdiction to petition for the expropriation of the estates denominated "El Rosario" and "El Carmen" (or "La Haciendita"), both located in the municipality Reyes Cueta, District of Paz Castillo of the State of Miranda and included respectively within the following boundaries: [here follows a very long description of the properties by metes and bounds]. The ownership of the said estates belongs to citizen Juan José Muñoz in accordance with the document recorded in the sub-registry office of the District of Paz Castillo of the State of Miranda [stating the books in which the estates are registered]. This expropriation is petitioned in conformity with the provisions contained in the Third Section, Second Chapter, of the Agrarian Reform Law and based on the following reasons: FIRST: The derivation of this petition is based on Article 27 of the Agrarian Reform Law, in that the insufficiency or the inappropriate condition of publicly owned lands, described in the First Chapter of the cited Law, impedes the realization of gratuitous grants to beneficiaries of estates owned by the government, equally affected by the reform. In addition there is operating as a sufficient reason for the expropriation the first paragraph of the same Article 27, which expressly declares uncultivated lands to be subject to expropriation. SECOND: The absence in this case of grounds for inexpropriability which might impede the affecting of the property in accordance with Article 26 of the same Law. THIRD: In execution of the provisions of Article 35, my client has taken steps to acquire the described estates amicably, but without success. There are annexed to this petition, in fulfillment of the conditions outlined in Article 36, the following collected items: a) Certified Copy of the resolution of expropriation adopted by the Directorate of the Institute in session held the 13th day of April, 1961; b) certification of encumbrances executed by the competent Registry; and c) a report containing the general characteristics of the estates and their classification for purposes of the reservation of property for use of the owner. Based on the foregoing I request the admission of this petition, and that it be allowed. Los Teques, the 23rd day of the month of May, 1961. (Signed) Leopoldo Márquez Añez.

Answer

Citizen Judge of First Instance, Civil and Commercial. I, Antonio José Puppio, attorney, resident of Caracas and here as a transient, acting in representation of Citizen Juan José Muñoz, farmer and cattle raiser, adult, resident in the jurisdiction of the municipality Reyes Cueta, District of Paz Castillo of the State of Miranda, a representation which I exercise according to the Power which I attach marked "A," appear before you and declare in answer to the petition for expropriation formulated by the National Agrarian Institute before this Tribunal, and respecting the estates owned by my client, denominated "El Rosario" and "El Carmen" (or "La Haciendita"), both located in the jurisdiction of the municipality Reyes Cueta, District of Paz Castillo of the State of Miranda, and whose boundaries and other descriptions are stated in the said petition for expropriation: Chapter I. My client is the owner of the named estates whose expropriation has been petitioned for by the National Agrarian Institute. . . . Chapter II. It is true that a mortgage on the hacienda "El Carmen" (or "La Haciendita"), whose boundaries have been outlined in the petition for expropriation, did exist in favor of Sebastián Suárez, deceased, but the said mortgage was cancelled by means of payments which were made in various installments as the attached exhibits . . . show . . . . [The owner admits also that there is a mortgage on the other estate in favor of the Agricultural Bank amounting to some 38,000 Bolivars. From the time of this decision to the present time, one Bolivar has equalled approximately $.22 in United States money.] Chapter III. My client formally rejects the "Technical Report and Evaluation of the Estates of 'El Carmen' and 'El Rosario'" attached to the petition, and signed on September 28, 1960, by the agronomist, Juan Bta. Castillo and the agricultural expert Samuel Peralta, as well as its conclusions and amount. From this time forward my client states that the said Report and Valuation cannot be opposed to him and therefore can produce no legal effects against his rights and interest, and therefore, my client does not accept it, refuses to recognize it and rejects it, in particular with respect to the price, to the property [included] and the area of the estates, and the conditions of the same. Chapter IV. My client formally opposes the petition . . . insofar as it refers to the estate "El Carmen" (or "La Haciendita"), since, in respect to it, the said Institute took no steps, direct or indirect, before proceeding to petition for expropriation, to arrange an amicable settlement with my client, as Article 35 of the Agrarian Reform Law requires. Neither has the petitioner taken steps to secure said settlement after the petition. The representative of the National Agrarian Institute orally negotiated with my client for the acquisition, by means of a friendly settlement, of the estate "El Rosario," with the qualification that said negotiations were limited to asking him how much he wanted for said estate, without making him any offer and demonstrating little interest or seriousness in the matter, by reason of which my client is obliged to deny the affirmation contained in the petition, ... Chapter V. My client also formally opposes the petition . . . because in conformity with Article 26 of the Agrarian Reform Law, the lands of my client to which the petition refers . . . are inexpropriable for the purposes of the Agrarian Reform, since they fulfill their social function in conformity with Article 19 of the same. In effect, "El Rosario" and "El Carmen" (or "La Haciendita") are agricultural and cattle-raising estates. Their exploitation has been efficient and their income has always been very good. In "El Carmen" and in "El Rosario" cultivated pastures predominate, and my client has built stables, watering places (36) and lakes (6); on the estates there are maintained the greatest possible number of head of cattle – approximately 800 – in the least possible area, and without either the land or the animals suffering. There has been an average birth of 25 calves per month; because they are duly attended, almost all survive. The burning of fields has been abolished, and both estates are totally and completely fenced in an adequate manner. In "El Carmen" and "El Rosario" there are produced more than 250 liters of milk daily for sale by others, with the qualification that the calves are not deprived of their food. My client attends to and carries on personally the working and direction of his two estates, and he has the financial responsibility for the agricultural enterprise as well as the cattle-raising enterprise which he directs in "El Carmen" and "El Rosario." In addition, my client has always complied with the existing provisions for conservation of woods and waters and renewable natural resources, and has fulfilled all the provisions of the Law which regulates rural labor relations. . . . [The client is also taking steps to register his property in the correct Registry Office.] For the reasons expressed, my client is also obliged to reject categorically the affirmation contained in the petition according to which in the present case there are no "grounds for inexpropriability which might impede the affecting [of the property] in accordance with Article 26" of the Agrarian Reform Law. And he also denies and categorically rejects the affirmation of the petitioner according to which the aforementioned estates of my client are expropriable for the reason that they are uncultivated lands. Chapter VI. For the reasons expressed in the two foregoing Chapters, my client expressly requests the Citizen Judge that, on deciding the merits of this action, he declare: a) that the National Agrarian Institute did not fulfill the requirement demanded by Article 35 of the Agrarian Reform Law with respect to the estate "El Carmen," since it took no steps to arrange an amicable settlement with my client for the acquisition of the same; and b) that both the estate "El Rosario" and "El Carmen" whose expropriation has been petitioned by the Institute, are inexpropriable according to Article 26 of the Agrarian Reform Law because they fulfill their social function. And that in conformity with the same Article, only "by exception" should the total or partial expropriation of said estates be allowed, and always on the conditions and by means of the fulfillment and proof in the respective action, of the requirements set out in said provision [Article 33], whose application has not been invoked [by the Institute] . . . . *And in case that it be decided that the estates are expropriable, by exceptional means, according to the said Article 33 of the Agrarian Reform Law, my client requests that it be declared and ordered that the corresponding payment should be made in the form established by that provision.* [Emphasis in original. Article 33 is reprinted at pp. 291-92, *supra.*] Chapter VII. On the supposition that the Tribunal may declare that the expropriation requested is proper — either by the ordinary or exceptional means — I state that my client has decided to exercise and does exercise the right to reserve for himself in the estate "El Carmen" the respective area fixed as inexpropriable, all in conformity with Articles 29 and 30 of the Agrarian Reform Law. [Art. 29 and 30 are reprinted at p. 323, *infra*.] As the estate "El Carmen" is constituted by lands which in their conjunction — it is said — have been classified as of the fourth class, the reservation should amount to 500 hectares, which in this case are constituted by all the level lands of the estate "El Carmen," including the area where my client has constructed his dwelling house and other buildings, and to which there should be added the lands which (in accordance with the second part of Article 30 of the Agrarian Reform Law) are the object of an additional reservation, which my client also requests, and which are indispensable to him for the proper exploitation of the estate since they are destined for the pasturing of animals and for buildings, and they are covered with high woods which serve as protection zones for the conservation of waters and as windbreaks. At the opportune time my client will present further allegations in this respect. Chapter VIII. . . . [There is no petition for expropriation of livestock. This constitutes a partial expropriation, in violation of the Law of Expropriation for Reasons of Public or Social Utility.] Chapter IX. Article 23 of the Agrarian Reform Law provides that "the State shall provide incentives for those persons who utilize land in accordance with its social function and thus contribute to the economic development of the country." The petition for expropriation presents a tremendous irony and a painful drama for my client, Citizen Judge. During 29 years he has worked the lands whose expropriation have been petitioned for, without any more help than his own efforts, and with his product has maintained his family — 16 live children and four grandchildren — and has contributed to the economic development of the region and of the Country. And today he finds himself rewarded with a petition for expropriation. Will that be, Citizen Judge, the incentive created by the State and to which the cited legal provision refers? If the other provisions invoked did not aid him, that expressed in this Chapter would be sufficient to justify the opposition that my client formulates to the petition for expropriation. Chapter X. I ratify the opposition formulated in the foregoing Chapters to the petition for expropriation which has commenced this action, and for the expressed reasons I request that said petition be declared inadmissible and out of place, or at least that it be declared admissible only by virtue of the exception established in Article 33 of the Agrarian Reform Law, and that the payment be ordered corresponding to all the property which may be expropriated, as alleged in order that in the established form the cited Article 33 of the mentioned Law be effectuated. My client reserves the right to exercise any legal actions which may be appropriate. *Es justicia.* Los Teques, Jan. 14, 1961. (Signed) Dr. Antonio José Puppio.

[The next document in the record is a statement by the Secretary of the Court that the attorneys for the plaintiff and defendant appeared at a hearing on June 14, 1961, and that the answer was accepted by the Court, as the petition had been accepted previously. The Court declared open the period of proof provided by Article 36 of the Agrarian Reform Law.]

Offers of proof

[Counsel for both sides then requested that certain witnesses be called and asked certain specified questions. The attorney for the Institute requested that Dr. Merchán, an attorney, Dr. Villalba Villalba, an agronomist, and an agricultural expert named Baggio Baggio be called. They were to be asked these questions:]

A) The witness Doctor Antonio Merchán: 1st. If he knows by sight, dealings and communication the citizen Juan José Muñoz, defendant in the present action; 2nd. If in his capacity as a member of the Directorate of the National Agrarian Institute he carried on conversations with the mentioned citizen, directed to the amicable acquisition of the estates "El Carmen" and "El Rosario," in fulfillment of the requirements of Article 35 of the Agrarian Reform Law; 3d. If with such a purpose he ordered Doctor Jesús Villalba Villalba, the Chief of the Division of Lands of the National Agrarian Institute, to make a formal offer of purchase to the defendant in accordance with the amount of the valuation which is shown in the file of this case, and that the amicable acquisition was impossible because the owner demanded the quantity of 20 million Bolivars for both estates. B) The witness Doctor Jesús Villalba Villalba: 1st. If he knows by sight, dealings and communication the citizen Juan José Muñoz, defendant in the present action; 2nd. If in his capacity as Chief of the Division of Lands of the National Agrarian Institute and in execution of instructions of Doctor Antonio Merchán, Member of the Directorate, offered to the defendant for the two estates "El Carmen" and "El Rosario," the quantities which respectively represent the valuation of each estate and which are shown in the file; 3d. That the amicable acquisition was impossible because the owner asked for the quantity of 20 million Bolivars for both estates; 4th. That in the mentioned capacity as Chief of the Division of Lands of the National Agrarian Institute he clearly knows the agricultural capacity of the estates whose expropriation is requested and that, consequently, since the lands are devoted to cattle-raising, proper advantage has not been taken of them in accordance with the zone in which they are found, which is essentially agricultural. C) The witness Giuseppe Baggio Baggio: 1st. If he knows the estates "El Rosario" and "El Carmen," whose expropriation is petitioned; 2nd. If through such knowledge it is apparent to him that on those estates a cattle-raising enterprise is being carried on; 3d. If he knows their agricultural capacity; 4th. If, in consequence, the exploitation which is carried on there is in conformance with such capacity. . . . [Counsel for the Institute requests the admission of testimony along the foregoing lines.]

[Counsel for the defendant submits a copy of the request his client made for the registration of his ownership in the proper Registry Office. He also submits various communications from government officials relating to the manner of exploitation of his land. In addition he asks that five named men be called as witnesses to answer the following questions:] 1st. If they know my client, and if they have no impediment preventing them from testifying as witnesses in the present action. 2d. If it is true and evident to them that for 29 years my client has been promoting and developing agricultural and cattle-raising enterprises on the estates which he owns called "El Carmen" and "El Rosario." 3d. If it is true and evident to them that on the named estates there abound and predominate cultivated pastures; there exist more than 800 head of beef cattle which are adequately attended without harming the land; there exist six lakes and more than 30 watering places; the estates are completely fenced and there exist ditches and canals for irrigation; they are not uncultivated; and the fields are attended and sowed by using machines and not by burning. 4th. If it is true and evident to them that in the average month 25 to 30 calves are born, and all live, since mortality is practically nil because they are duly attended; and that in addition to the milk with which said calves are fed there are produced on the estates "El Carmen" and "El Rosario" from 200 to 250 liters of milk per day which are sold to outsiders. 5th. If it is true and evident to them that Sr. Muñoz personally directs his enterprises and works on them with his children; pays with his own money the wages of his workers and other expenses which the exploitation of the same may cost, that he sells trees only when competent authorities authorize it; that he replants trees in order to care for the woods and waters; and that he fulfills the obligations which the Labor Law imposes on him and other laws which regulate labor activities. . . . [The attorney for the defendant requests the admission of testimony along these lines, and also asks that the deposition of the President of the National Agrarian Institute be taken in Caracas, for the purpose of denying certain testimony to be expected from other officials of the Institute. He also asks that testimony be taken from four other men who are familiar with the operations of Sr. Muñoz, for the purpose of showing that Sr. Muñoz operates his lands directly and not through intermediaries, and that he takes personal direction of the management and financing of his operation, including taking the risks of loss. Finally, he requests that the Judge make a visual inspection of the two estates in order to verify that they are completely fenced and cultivated, that they include lakes and watering places as stated in his answer, that tractors and other machinery are used in the cultivation of the estates, etc.]

Completion of proof

[The Judge did visit the estates as requested by the defendant and made some neutral findings, avoiding conclusions concerning the degree of intensiveness with which the land was used or cultivated. The visit was carried out on July 6, 1961. On the same day, the testimony of the defendant's witnesses was taken, put in written form, and added to the record. It appears that the Judge was personally present during the taking of the testimony of each witness. All the witnesses for the defendant testified to the same effect, answering affirmatively to the leading questions set out above. A typical set of answers came from the witness Medardo Villegas, as follows:]

On the same date appeared in the Office of this Tribunal, by means of previous citation, the citizen Medardo Villegas; he gave the oath required by law, stated that he was named as noted above, that he was 50 years of age, a bachelor, by profession farmer, resident of this Municipality, bearer of Identity Card No. 2578509 and without any legal impediments to testify. Apprised of the purpose of this citation and having been read the offer of proof by the defendant, to the First question, he said: "Yes, I know Sr. Juan José Muñoz and I have no impediment to testify." To the

Second, he said: "Yes, it is true and evident to me because I have worked for 29 years with him." To the Third, he said: "Yes, it is true in all the parts of the question, and it is evident to me because I have seen all this in the 29 years that I have worked for Sr. Muñoz." To the Fourth he said: "Yes, it is true and evident to me in all respects and every part of the question put to me. Because since I work with Sr. Juan José Muñoz I know of all this. As to the average of 200 to 250 liters of milk daily, it varies." To the Fifth and last, he said: "This is true, because, as I said before, I worked for Sr. Muñoz for 29 years on the said estates." — He finished, he was read [an account of what he had stated] and in conformance he signed, the witness not doing it himself because he did not know how to write, but instead he stamped his fingerprints. . . .

[The plaintiff's witnesses had been interviewed on July 4, 1961, but their testimony appears following that of the defendant's witnesses in the record. Counsel for the defendant objected to permitting the officials of the Institute to testify, on the ground that they were interested in the litigation. The Judge did not rule on the objection at this time, but permitted the testimony to be taken. The Judge ultimately overruled the objection in his final decision of the case. The three witnesses for the plantiff all testified affirmatively to the questions listed in the offer of proof. Counsel for the defendant was permitted to formulate questions, which were put to the plaintiff's witnesses by the Secretary of the Court. All of these questions related to the possible interest of the witnesses in the outcome of the case, and were designed to show partiality. The witnesses denied any interest in the case other than an interest in seeing that the law be complied with.]

[The two best witnesses for the defendant appeared on July 7, 1961. They were both merchants, and both had worked for Sr. Muñoz previously. Luis Gabriel Rodríguez testified that he had worked for Sr. Muñoz from 1952 to 1960. He testified that Sr. Muñoz had exploited the estates directly and had complied with the obligations which various laws imposed on him. He also testified that Sr. Muñoz had personally run the financial risks of the operation, and that he had obtained a good return for his efforts, achieving an increase of about 500 head of livestock during the eight-year period described. He also testified that Sr. Muñoz ran a sugar mill, grew some sugar cane, and generally dedicated himself to the raising of livestock, both cattle and hogs. Heraclio Antonio Silva Valladares testified that he had worked for Sr. Muñoz from 1957 to 1960, and he verified the testimony of Sr. Rodríguez. Counsel for the Institute asked that certain questions be put to this witness, which questions and their answers are reproduced here:] First: Let the witness state whether the success and the income obtained by the owner refers exclusively to livestock raising, or also to agricultural exploitation. Answer: The success obtained during the time when I worked on the estate refers to both branches, to livestock and to agriculture. Another: Let the witness state whether extensive exploitation in relation to the area of the estates is presently maintained. Answer: [Question withdrawn by counsel.] Another: Let the witness state, up to the year 1960 and during the period in which he served the owner on the estates "El Carmen" and "El Rosario," what kind of cultivation was carried on and over what area. Answer: Sugar cane in a large area of land which I cannot describe precisely, and minor cultivation such as sweet potatoes, [and various other indigenous vegetables] and another large area of land which I cannot describe precisely. Another: Let the witness state whether with relation to the livestock exploitation now existing, what percentage approximately of the estates is occupied by agricultural exploitation. Answer: I cannot answer this question exactly; I quit working on the estate in 1960 and from that time forward I do not know in what condition the estates are, with relation to cattle raising and agriculture. When I worked on said estates 30% was devoted to agriculture and 70% to livestock. Another: Let the witness state whether the system of exploitation of those minor crops was by means of *conuco* [literally, a small plot of land; here used to refer to a form of tenant farming]. Answer: Cultivation was carried on in the form of *conuco* and in the form of *arado* [literally, plow; refers to another form of tenant farming]. Another: Let the witness state whether during the years he worked on the estates he received "utilities" [that is, services or other benefits in addition to a salary], considering the extraordinary income of the exploitation. Answer: The utilities were paid annually to all the employees in accordance with the production and income of the estates and in accordance with our salary. I am certain that I received utilities. Another: Let the witness state the salary obtained during the last year and the approximate amount of the utilities received. Answer: I received a salary of 300 Bolivars per month, and during this year they gave me a utility or bonus of 1,500 Bolivars. [Signed by the Judge, the witness, the Secretary, and the attorneys for both parties.]

Written arguments of counsel

[At the close of the period for submitting proof, each counsel submitted a written argument summarizing the evidence and drawing conclusions favorable to his side. The arguments dealt not only with the question of the social function of ownership, but with the other issues as well. Only the portions dealing with the social function of ownership are reproduced here.]

[Argument for the National Agrarian Institute:]

II. As was observed before, the burden of allegation and proof of the ground of inexpropriability established in Article 19 of the Agrarian Reform Law is on the defendant owner, who in this case so understands the article and consequently has offered various proofs directed to such end. For particular consideration in these arguments are the testimony and the visual inspection, opportunely offered and taken. A) *Testimonial proof.* Apart from the fact that only doubtfully can the proof of witnesses be considered proper for the demonstration of the requisites demanded in Article 19 of the Law, there should be particularly observed the negative result of the responses of the offered witnesses. In effect, the citizens who gave their declarations before the Judge of the District of Paz Castillo of the State of Miranda limited themselves in the most important particulars of the interrogatories (that is, numbers 2, 3, and 5), without exception, to grounding their affirmations on the fact that they had some 29 (and others 24) years of experience working with the owner of the estates "El Carmen" and "El Rosario"; and in similar terms those who gave their declarations before the Judge of the Municipality Chacao, District of Sucre of this State were also distinguished by their laconic and vague manner of expressing themselves. Especially the witness Heraclio Silva Valladares, cross-examined by the attorney for the plaintiff, shows an absolute failure to understand the exploitation of the estates, even to the point of referring to a system of *conuco,* whose significance is well understood to be contrary to rational systems of agricultural exploitation; this apart from declaring as a monthly salary the quantity of 300 Bolivars and 1,500 Bolivars by way of utilities, almost 40% of the total of annual salaries, when it is well known that the participation of the worker by way of utilities does not exceed the salary or wage of two months. In the record there is no offer of proof which concretely credits the owner with the fulfillment of the legal requirements with respect to rural wage labor. B) *Visual inspection.* This means of proof of superior fitness and certainty to demonstrate the social function of the land, has had for the offering party [the defendant] a constant negative result. It could not be shown that these estates are cultivated, since the report of the inspection says [that the area and quality of cultivation will be left to the expert reports in the case]; and 2d) neither was it demonstrated that among the pastures which exist the cultivated ones predominate, since such an estimate was naturally referred to the proper expert report. . . .

[Argument for the defendant:]

Chapter II. My client also opposes the expropriation of his estates "El Carmen" and "El Rosario." In conformity with Article 26 of the Agrarian Reform Law, *they are inexpropriable* because they fulfill their social function in conformity with Article 19. The expropriating agency has based its action on the strange affirmation, among others, that the said estates *are uncultivated lands,* and therefore expropriable. No proof has been offered in the record which demonstrates such an assertion. On the other hand, from the procedural record the alleged ground of inexpropriability has been clearly demonstrated, since the result of the visual inspection made by this Judge as well as the declarations of the witnesses [seven men named] and also, the documents attached to the offer of proof, prove that said estates have been exploited in an efficient form; that my client has personally worked and directed the enterprise, and has kept it under his financial responsibility; that my client has fulfilled and complied with the legal norms that regulate rural labor relations and has complied with the existing rules concerning the conservation of renewable natural resources; that the estates whose expropriation has been requested have been inscribed in the proper Registry Office; and that cultivated pastures predominate on them, they are completely fenced, and there exist lakes, stables, and watering places, and the cultivation is brought to effect by means of adequate machines and tools. The productivity of the estates and the existence on them of herds of livestock [beef cattle, horses, and hogs] also are demonstrated. Thus not only "El Carmen" but also "El Rosario" fulfill their social function and therefore are inexpropriable. Therefore it is evident, that in case expropriability should be decreed, it can be done only by means of the exceptional manner provided in Article 33 of the Agrarian Reform Law, and, in such a case, their price must be paid in the form and on the conditions provided in said provision. [Signed on July 17, 1961.]

Decision

[The Judge held for the Institute on all questions except the issue of partial expropriation. The Court ordered the estates expropriated, but referred the valuation question back to the expert appraisers, so that they might include the value of the cattle, etc. in the amount to be paid to Sr. Muñoz. Only that portion of the opinion dealing with the question of the social function of ownership is reproduced here.]

Now then, in the technical report and valuation of the estates "El Carmen" and "El Rosario" subscribed by the agronomist Juan Bautista Castillo and Manuel Peralta, and dated in Guarenas the 28th of September, 1960 (although said report has been rejected formally in Chapter III of the Answer of the defendant), . . . the following appears: "The natural vegetation of the region is generally of a shrubby character, with dry zones, except the banks of ravines and little streams where the vegetation is wooded. There predominate [various varieties of trees from which charcoal may be made]. Of the 2,200 hectares at which we estimate the area, the most irregular parts and the most level parts also are covered with this natural vegetation, there being realized on part of them a relatively slight pasture. The area under such conditions we estimate at 1,500 hectares of which some 500 are used for pasture. Of the remaining area, 700 hectares are cultivated as pastures and with sugar cane in very bad conditions. The estate "El Carmen" has a mill which is not in use. It is estimated that Sr. Muñoz presently has some 300 cattle of various ages and 25 pigs. He produces daily some 250 liters of milk. From the foregoing it can be clearly established that only on a very low scale do these estates fulfill the social function to which Article 19 of the Agrarian Reform Law refers. A few cattle, with some watering holes, without selection of livestock, without installations, with a few poorly paid workers, represent a very low investment of capital in a zone where the natural and social conditions deserve intensive exploitation, agricultural as well as of livestock." In the same report, with relation to the agricultural capacity of the estate, it is said: ". . . Capacity for use I.—Lands apt for agricultural use, with current conservation practices — 200 hectares. Capacity for use II.—Lands apt for agricultural use with simple conservation practices — 200 hectares. Capacity for use III.—Lands apt for agricultural use, intensive conservation practices — 160 hectares. Capacity for use IV.—Lands apt for occasional agricultural use and principally for permanent vegetation (pastures, woods) — 230 hectares. Capacity for use VI.—Use of permanent vegetation (pastures) with moderate restrictions — 110 hectares. Capacity for use VII.—Use of permanent vegetation (pastures, woods) with severe restrictions — 200 hectares. Total of hectares — 1,200 [sic]. [Similar figures for "El Carmen" total 1,000 hectares. The report goes on to place the land of these two estates in the fourth category of lands as described in Article 198 of the Agrarian Reform Law. It concludes that the ownership of this land is fulfilling barely 10% of its social function, considering the natural conditions of the land. The opinion in this case does not make clear the source of the figure of 10%, but it would seem that the report said that only some 10% of the land was being used at a level commensurate with its capacity to absorb investment, cultivation, etc.] *The Tribunal gives full probative value to the foregoing report, since it constitutes a document of vital importance for the characterization of the lands as fulfilling or not the social function in conformity with Article 19 of the Agrarian Reform Law.* [Emphasis in original.] ... Now then, as to the witnesses presented by the defense, apart from the fact that they appeared making declarations over various highly technical aspects, their statements are insufficient. [Here the Court reviews the testimony of those witnesses who simply answered affirmatively to the various leading questions about the manner of cultivation of the two estates.] *There are undoubtedly notions which, by reason of their evidently scientific flavor, somewhat escape the purposes of testimonial proof. It is clear that a witness, unless he be a technician in the subject, cannot appear declaring that an estate does or does not have cultivated pastures, that its owner has developed and forwarded agricultural and cattle-raising enterprises, that the lands are not uncultivated, etc., because to the contrary the expert testimony has denied these arguments, and it would be made very easy to impugn a technical report with testimonial proof, most often of easy elaboration and of foreseeable practical effects.* [The Court then notes that the witnesses Rodríguez and Silva Valladares were unable to state how much area was being used for crops, how much "utility" the estates were producing, etc., and that they did point out the indirect form of exploitation of the lands by means of *conuco* and *arado*. The Court concludes that the defendant's evidence is insufficient to overcome the technical report, and that there is no ground for the defendant's claim that his lands are not expropriable. The opinion is signed by the Judge and the Secretary, and dated November 7, 1961.]

Consider these questions about the Muñoz case:

1. What were the grounds for the decision that Muñoz's ownership had not fulfilled its social function?

2. Upon what evidence did the court base each ground?

3. Has the court established any standard for proof in such cases? To what extent does the court's position leave the question of social function to administrative discretion? To what extent does the court contribute its own elaboration of the statutory language? What can a landowner do to demonstrate the fulfillment of ownership's social function?

4. What was Muñoz' objective in this case? Did he expect to prevent the taking of his land?

Finally, with respect to legislation that calls for the expropriation of lands that are uncultivated or poorly exploited, consider Ernest Feder's criticisms:

[The typical Latin American land reform law] requires expropriation of estates on an individual basis, not of all estates in a given larger area or zone. In other words, the reform institute designates specific estates for expropriation and handles each estate and each owner individually. ... One of the more serious consequences is that even in a relatively small agricultural zone it does not result in an effective transformation of unjust structures and systems of land tenure. ...

Instead of permitting that reform be carried out on the best soils, in the best, most densely populated agricultural areas — as true land reformers would attempt to do — they have introduced a classification of farms and farm land for purpose of expropriation which relegates reform to distant, marginal areas where agriculture is still relatively undeveloped and have excluded from expropriation certain types of estates altogether. . . . [Such legislation] has transformed land reform into a colonization scheme. . . .

It is probably also no accident that [the Colombian law, Arts. 55-56] . . . does not talk about inadequately managed farms, but land. The effect of this is that if an estate owner cultivates only his best land as he usually does, so that it is difficult on legal grounds to pretend that this portion is "inadequately managed," only marginal areas of the estate would become available for expropriation and distribution to peasants. Hence, the legislator intended to relegate the beneficiaries of land reform to the poorest and least developed areas. . . . [32]

Are Feder's criticisms well founded? Is his reading of the Colombian law accurate? To what extent can his objections be met by technical revisions of the drafting of Articles 55-56, and to what extent do his criticisms imply a fundamental redefinition of the purposes of the Colombian reform? In 1968, the Colombian law was amended, and new regulations issued authorizing INCORA, the land reform agency, to acquire land without regard to the order of priority stated in Article 55. Law No. 1 of 1968; Decree No. 719 of 1968, Arts. 2, 3. Does this change meet Feder's objection?

Is Feder's criticism of Colombia's Articles 55-56 equally applicable to Venezuela's Articles 19, 20 and 26? The courts in Venezuela have read those articles to require the expropriation of an entire holding when most of the land is idle, but a portion is being cultivated efficiently. See Comment, "Expropriation and the Venezuelan Law of Agrarian Reform," 6 *Colum. J. Transnational L.* 273, 281 (1967).

Another perspective on the affectability provisions of the Venezuelan law is offered by Doreen Warriner, who suggests that the question of affectability is determined not by reference to the law, but according to political decisions made by the Campesino Federation (FCV), the national rural labor union associated with the two principal national political parties. A "syndicate," in the following discussion, is a local rural labor union.

---

[32] Feder, "Counterreform," in R. Stavenhagen (ed.), *Agrarian Problems and Peasant Movements in Latin America* 173, 182-85 (1970). Reprinted by permission of the publisher, Doubleday & Company, Inc. Copyright© 1970 by Rodolfo Stavenhagen.

D. WARRINER, LAND REFORM IN PRINCIPLE AND PRACTICE

Pp. 351, 355-57 (1969)*

The difficulty in assessing the results [of the Venezuelan land reform] arises because the reform has been carried out on two levels, the political and the administrative, which are not co-ordinated. On the one hand, there is the law itself, with its own conception, laying down the provisions which would allow for an integrated procedure. On the other, there is the strong political impetus arising from the syndicate movement, which decides what properties are to be taken over, and how they are to be managed, without much regard to the provisions of the law. This is not unfortunate; on the contrary, without this impetus, the law would never have been carried out at all. Venezuela is the only country where a trade union movement has carried out a land reform; and it is interesting to see what labour will make of it. . . .

[The provisions of the law governing affectability] are not at present of much practical importance, since there is no need to use compulsion. An estate may be taken over by an invasion, and IAN [the National Agrarian Institute] then proceeds to negotiate its purchase if it is private property. The law lays down the procedure by which local syndicates can petition the Institute for the expropriation and division of the estate; it also lays down the procedure for property valuation and the payment of compensation to landowners. . . . The chief concern of the Institute is to settle up with the landowners. It is an intermediary between them and the government, just as the Federation is the intermediary between the government and the rural workers. Since funds are available, agreement is easily reached; estates are purchased at their market value. Thus the initiative still rests with the syndicates, which continue to put forward petitions to FCV for land redistribution. . . . The extent to which petitions can be granted depends on whether the funds available are sufficient to undertake purchase. Under these conditions the estates purchased are likely to be those which landowners wish to sell. . . .

It is commonly asserted, by people who know, that the landowners themselves encourage syndicates to invade their estates, or to petition for purchase and division, in order to dispose of their property at a good price. . . . Of course, there is nothing wrong in buying out landowners at good prices, or settling people at high cost, though it is unusual, because few countries can afford to spend so much. But it seems that the landowners have gained more than the *campesinos*. . . . [T]he landowners are shifting their interests to urban building and speculation in urban land values; so that it must often be convenient to sell a derelict estate, and with the proceeds build a sky-scraper apartment block in Caracas.

(b) Indirect exploitation of land

The classical hacienda, described by Professor Tannenbaum earlier in this chapter, gets its labor without making cash payments. Sharecropping systems are at the heart of the hacienda, which would be destroyed by conversion to a system of cash wages. It is not surprising that both the Colombian and Venezuelan laws, quoted earlier, provide for the expropriation of estates on which these indirect systems of exploitation of the land are used. Compare Colombia's Article 55(3), page 288, *supra,* with Venezuela's Articles 19 and 20, pages 290-91, *supra.* Are there any cases that would be reached by one law but not by the other?

Is corporate ownership of land vulnerable to expropriation on the ground of indirect exploitation? The issue was raised explicitly in the Venezuelan Congress during the debates on the bill which became the 1960 law. During those debates, a leader of the government party who was also a leader of the Campesino Federation said that corporate management was not a form of indirect exploitation; he then suggested that Article 20 be cast in what is nearly its present form, listing the kinds of tenancy that were to be condemned. As a result of this discussion, the Congress discarded some general language to the effect that indirect exploitation was contrary to the principle of the social function of ownership; in place of this language, the Congress adopted what is now Article 20. In light of this history, can we say with confidence what the rule is in Venezuela concerning corporate ownership? See Comment, "Expropriation and the Venezuelan Law of Agrarian Reform," *6 Colum. J. Transnational L.* 273, 281-82 (1967). In Mexico, Article 27 of the 1917 Constitution expressly forbids corporate ownership or management of rural properties. Do you prefer such a prohibition, or the Venezuelan rule? Why?

(c) The social function of ownership: perspectives from legal philosophy

Here we pause to consider where the idea of expropriation stands in a system which protects rights of property. It is seldom helpful to ask questions like "What is property?" in a vacuum; but such questions can be useful if they are asked with concrete issues in mind, for the purpose of analyzing specific problems. With that caution, the following excerpted readings are offered: a classic of utilitarianism, an early 20th century socialist work, and a criticism which seems directed at them both. Morris Cohen's book review of the volume which contains these readings is followed by one of his own efforts at generalization. (An additional reading which may be helpful is F. S. Cohen, "Dialogue on Private Property," *9 Rutgers L. Rev.* 357 (1954).) The section closes with some comments on an early 20th century "institutional economist," directed specifically to expropriation. Can you relate all these general statements to land reform legislation based on assumptions about the social function of ownership?

J. BENTHAM, THEORY OF LEGISLATION

Pp. 109-13, 119-21

(Hildreth ed. 1871, translated from 1830 French ed. of Dumont)

Of Security

We come now to the principal object of law, —the care of security. That inestimable good, the distinctive index of civilization, is entirely the work of law. Without law there is no security; and, consequently, no abundance, and not even a certainty of subsistence; and the only equality which can exist in such a state of things is an equality of misery. . . .

Law alone has done that which all the natural sentiments united have not the power to do. Law alone is able to create a fixed and durable possession which merits the name of property. Law alone can accustom men to bow their heads under the yoke of foresight, hard at first to bear, but afterwards light and agreeable. Nothing but law can encourage men to labours superfluous for the present, and which can be enjoyed only in the future. Economy has as many enemies as there are dissipators — men who wish to enjoy without giving themselves the trouble of producing. Labor is too painful for idleness; it is too slow for impatience. Fraud and injustice secretly conspire to appropriate its fruits. Insolence and audacity think to ravish them by open force. Thus security is assailed on every side — ever threatened, never tranquil, it exists in the midst of alarms. The legislator needs a vigilance always sustained, a power always in action, to defend it against this crowd of indefatigable enemies.

Law does not say to man *Labor, and I will reward you;* but it says *Labor, and I will assure to you the enjoyment of the fruits of your labor — that natural and sufficient recompense which without me you cannot preserve; I will insure it by arresting the hand which may seek to ravish it from you.* If industry creates, it is law which preserves; if at the first moment we owe all to labor, at the second moment, and at every other, we are indebted for everything to law. . . .

Of Property

The better to understand the advantages of law, let us endeavor to form a clear idea of *property*. We shall see that there is no such thing as natural property, and that it is entirely the work of law.

Property is nothing but a basis of expectation; the expectation of deriving certain advantages from a thing which we are said to possess, in consequence of the relation in which we stand towards it.

There is no image, no painting, no visible trait, which can express the relation that constitutes property. It is not material, it is metaphysical; it is a mere conception of the mind.

To have a thing in our hands, to keep it, to make it, to sell it, to work it up into something else; to use it — none of the physical circumstances, nor all united, convey the idea of property. A piece of stuff which is actually in the Indies may belong to me, while the dress I wear may not. The aliment which is incorporated into my very body may belong to another, to whom I am bound to account for it.

The idea of property consists in an established expectation; in the persuasion of being able to draw such or such an advantage from the thing possessed, according to the nature of the case. Now this expectation, this persuasion, can only be the work of law. I cannot count upon the enjoyment of that which I regard as mine, except through the promise of the law which guarantees it to me. It is law alone which permits me to forget my natural weakness. It is only through the protection of law that I am able to inclose a field, and to give myself up to its cultivation with the sure though distant hope of harvest.

But it may be asked, What is it that serves as a basis to law, upon which to begin operations, when it adopts objects which, under the name of property, it promises to protect? Have not men, in the primitive state, a *natural* expectation of enjoying certain things, — an expectation drawn from sources anterior to law?

Yes. There have been from the beginning, and there always will be, circumstances in which a man may secure himself, by his own means, in the enjoyment of certain things. But the catalogue of these cases is very limited. The savage who has killed a deer may hope to keep it for himself, so long as his cave is undiscovered; so long as he watches to defend it, and is stronger than his rivals; but that is all. How miserable and precarious is such a possession! If we suppose the least agreement among savages to respect the acquisitions of each other, we see the introduction of a principle to which no name can be given but that of law. A feeble and momentary expectation may result from time to time from circumstances purely physical; but a strong and permanent expectation can result only from law. That which, in the natural state, was an almost invisible thread, in the social state becomes a cable.

Property and law are born together, and die together. Before laws were made there was no property; take away laws, and property ceases.

As regards property, security consists in receiving no check, no shock, no derangement to the expectation founded on the laws, of enjoying such and such a portion of good. The legislator owes the greatest respect to this expectation which he has himself produced. When he does not contradict it, he does what is essential to the happiness of society; when he disturbs it, he always produces a proportionate sum of evil. . . .

Opposition Between Security and Equality

In consulting the grand principle of security, what ought the legislator to decree respecting the mass of property already existing?

He ought to maintain the distribution as it is actually established. It is this which, under the name of *justice,* is regarded as his first duty. This is a general and simple rule, which applies itself to all states; and which adapts itself to all places, even those of the most opposite character. There is nothing more different than the state of property in America, in England, in Hungary, and in Russia. Generally, in the first of these countries, the cultivator is a proprietor; in the second, a tenant; in the third, attached to the glebe; in the fourth, a slave. However, the supreme principle of security commands the preservation of all these distributions, though their nature is so different, and though they do not produce the same sum of happiness. How make another distribution without taking away from each that which he has? And how despoil any without attacking the security of all? When your new repartition is disarranged — that is to say, the day after its establishment — how avoid making a second? Why not correct it in the same way? And in the meantime, what becomes of security? Where is happiness? Where is industry?

When security and equality are in conflict, it will not do to hesitate a moment. Equality must yield. The first is the foundation of life; subsistence, abundance, happiness, everything depends upon it. Equality produces only a certain portion of good. Besides, whatever we may do, it will never be perfect; it may exist a day; but the revolutions of the morrow will overturn it. The establishment of perfect equality is a chimera; all we can do is to diminish inequality.

If violent causes, such as a revolution of government, a division, or a conquest, should bring about an overturn of property, it would be a great calamity; but it would be transitory; it would diminish; it would repair itself in time. Industry is a vigorous plant which resists many amputations, and through which a nutritious sap begins to circulate with the first rays of returning summer. But if property should be overturned with the direct intention of establishing an equality of possessions, the evil would be irreparable. No more security, no more industry, no more abundance! Society would return to the savage state whence it emerged.

If equality ought to prevail today it ought to prevail always. Yet it cannot be preserved except by renewing the violence by which it was established. It will need an army of inquisitors and executioners as deaf to favor as to pity; insensible to the seductions of pleasure; inaccessible to personal interest; endowed with all the virtues though in a service which destroys them all. The leveling apparatus ought to go incessantly backward and forward, cutting off all that rises above the line prescribed. A ceaseless vigilance would be necessary to give to those who had dissipated their portion, and to take from those who by labor had augmented theirs. In such an order of things there would be only one wise course for the governed, that of prodigality; there would be but one foolish course, — that of industry. This pretended remedy, seemingly so pleasant, would be a mortal poison, a burning cautery, which would consume till it destroyed the last fiber of life. The hostile sword in its greatest furies is a thousand times less dreadful. It inflicts but partial evils, which time effaces and industry repairs.

L. DUGUIT, LES TRANSFORMATIONS GENERALES DU DROIT PRIVE

(Register transl.), in *The Progress of Continental Law in the 19th Century* 130-136 (1918)

Property under the Individualistic System. — How have the codes founded on the individualistic principle developed this social instrumentality? Very simply. In the first place, those who drafted the codes were not concerned with inquiring into the legality of property rights then in fact existing, nor with determining on what they were founded. They accepted existing facts and declared them inviolable. Furthermore, being profoundly individualistic, they had in mind only the application of wealth to individual ends, for this is the very fulfillment, the very cornerstone, as it were, of individual autonomy. They did not, and have not since, been able to understand anything but a *protection* thrown about the individualistic use of property. They believed that the only way of protecting such a use was to endow the holder with a subjective right, absolute in duration and in effect. The right attached to the thing appropriated, and the duty corresponding to this right rested on all persons other than the owner of the thing. In a word, they adopted the rigid legal construction of the Roman "dominium."

The declarations of principles which created this system are well known. Article 17 of the "Declaration of the Rights of Man" of 1789 begins: "Property being a sacred and inviolable right," etc. Article 17 of the Argentine Constitution declares that: "property is inviolable. . . ."

Consequences Rejected To-Day. — The consequences of the conception of property as a right are well known; it will be well, however, to recall the principal ones.

In the first place, the owner, having the right to use, benefit by, and to dispose of the thing which is the object of his ownership, has, for like reasons, the right *not to use it,* not to derive benefit from, and not to dispose of it, consequently to leave his lands uncultivated, his city lots unimproved, his houses untenanted and unrepaired, his capital consisting of personal property unproductive.

The right of property is *absolute.* It is absolute even as against public authority, which can, indeed, place upon it certain restrictions of a police nature, but cannot lay hands upon it, save after paying a just indemnity. It is absolute insofar as it affects individuals and, in the words of Baudry-Lacantinerie, the owner "may lawfully perform upon the object of his ownership acts even though he have no demonstrable interest in performing them," and if in so doing he injures another party, "he is not liable, because he is but acting with his right."

The right of ownership is also absolute *in duration.* Upon this attribute is based the right of transmitting property by will, because the owner or titleholder of an absolute right has logically the power of disposing of his property both during his life and also for a time after his death.

It is easy to show that as a matter of fact none of these consequences represents the truth; at least in certain countries, notably in France. To be less categorical, I will say that the entire individualistic system of property law is disappearing. This assertion is not unfounded; it is based upon a direct observation of facts, for both in statutory and in case-law there is appearing a body of principles directly opposed to the consequences of the individualistic system. Is this not proof that the legal system from which those consequences spring is breaking down and disappearing?

The general causes of this disappearance are again those that we have studied above, which are determining the direction of the general transformation of individualistic institutions.

First, property, as a subjective right, is a purely *metaphysical* conception, in radical opposition to modern positivism. To say that the possessor of capital has a right over it, is equivalent to saying that he has a power, of itself superior to, and prescribable upon, the will of other individuals. The "dominium" of the individual is no more intelligible as a right than the "imperium" of the Government as the seat of force.

Furthermore, the individualistic system of property is breaking down because it tends to protect *individual uses alone,* which are considered as sufficient in themselves. The system reflected perfectly the individualistic conception of the society of the period. It found a perfect medium of expression in Article 2 of the "Declaration of Rights of Man" of 1789: "The aim of every political association is the preservation of the natural and imprescriptible rights of man. These rights are: liberty, property, security, and resistance to oppression." If the application of wealth to private uses was protected, it was solely out of consideration of the individual; it was solely the utility to the individual that was kept in view. To-day there is a very clear sense abroad that the individual is not the end but the means; that the individual is only a wheel of a huge mechanism, the body social; and that his only reason to exist is the part which he performs in the labor of society. The individualistic system is seen, therefore, to be in open opposition to the temper of the modern conscience. . . .

Every individual is under an obligation to perform a certain function in the community, determined directly by the station which he occupies in it. The possessor of wealth, by reason simply of his possession, is enabled thereby to accomplish a certain work where others cannot. He alone can increase the general stock of wealth by putting his capital to use. For social reasons he is under a duty, therefore, to perform this work and society will protect his acts only if he accomplishes it and in the measure in which he accomplishes it. Property is no longer a subjective right of the owner; it is the social function of the possessor of wealth. . . .

I am anxious to avoid being misunderstood in this matter. I do not say, and I have never said or written, that private ownership as an economic institution is disappearing or should *disappear.* I maintain merely that the *legal notion* upon which protection of property is founded is *being modified.* Individual ownership, nevertheless, continues to be protected against all attacks, even those of the State. I will go even further and say that it is more strongly protected under the new than under the old conception.

I accept also as a fact the possession of capitalistic wealth by a limited number of individuals. There is no need to criticise or justify the fact; it would, indeed be labor lost, for the reason that it is a fact. Nor shall I inquire whether (as certain schools of thought assert) there is an irreconciliable conflict between those who possess wealth and those who do not, between capital and labor, and whether in this conflict capital is to be despoiled and annihilated. I cannot refrain, however, from voicing the opinion that these schools take an altogether erroneous view. The structure of modern society is not so simple. In France, in particular, many persons are both capitalists and laborers. It is a crime to preach the struggle of classes; I believe that we are moving, not toward the destruction of one class by another, but towards a society where there will be a coordination and a hierarchy of classes.

The Obligation to Cultivate Land. — The conception of property as a function, and the idea of society extending its protection to the application of wealth to certain uses, provide a very simple and clear explanation of the laws and decisions which are repugnant to the conception of property as a right.

An objection has been repeatedly raised to this explanation. Opponents have argued: "We understand your view; we even admit that society is moving toward a system of law in which the right of property will rest upon the duty of the owner to fulfill a certain function. But we have not yet reached that state; and the proof is that no statute yet imposes upon an owner the obligation to cultivate his field, repair his house, or utilize his capital. And yet that is the necessary and logical consequence of the conception of property as a function."

The objection does not embarrass me. From the fact that the law does not yet directly force the owner to cultivate his land or repair his houses or utilize his capital, it cannot be concluded that the idea of social function has not yet supplanted the idea of a subjective right of property. Such a law has indeed not made its appearance, because the need for it has not yet been felt. In France, for example, the amount of land left uncultivated by the owner or the number of houses which are unproductive is insignificant in comparison to the total capital in real estate which is being worked. But the fact that the question of such a law has been raised is itself evidence of the transformation that has taken place. Fifty years ago such a question was in no man's mind; to-day, it is everywhere agitated. And if, in a country like France, the time should come when the non-cultivation of the land became a serious problem, no one would then deny, certainly, the justification of intervention by legislation.

R. TAWNEY, THE ACQUISITIVE SOCIETY
Pp. 52-54 (1920)*

The application of the principle that society should be organized upon the basis of functions, is not recondite, but simple and direct. It offers in the first place, a standard for discriminating between those types of private property which are legitimate and those which are not. During the last century and a half, political thought has oscillated between two conceptions of property, both of which, in their different ways, are extravagant. On the one hand, the practical foundation of social organization has been the doctrine that the particular forms of private property which exist at any moment are a thing sacred and inviolable, that anything may properly become the object of property rights, and that, when it does, the title to it is absolute and unconditioned. The modern industrial system took shape in an age when this theory of property was triumphant. The American Constitution and the French Declaration of the Rights of Man both treated property as one of the fundamental rights for the protection of which Governments exist.

On the other hand, the attack has been almost as undiscriminating as the defense. "Private property" has been the central position against which the social movement of the last hundred years has directed its forces. The criticism of it has ranged from an imaginative communism in the most elementary and personal of necessaries, to prosaic and partially realized proposals to transfer certain kinds of property from private to public ownership, or to limit their exploitation by restrictions imposed by the State. But, however varying in emphasis and in method, the general note of what may conveniently be called the Socialist criticism of property is what the word Socialism itself implies. Its essence is the statement that the economic evils of society are primarily due to the unregulated operation, under modern conditions of industrial organization, of the institution of private property.

The divergence of opinion is natural, since in most discussions of property the opposing theorists have usually been discussing different things. Property is the most ambiguous of categories. It covers a multitude of rights which have nothing in common except that they are exercised by persons and enforced by the State. Apart from these formal characteristics, they vary indefinitely in economic character, in social effect, and in moral justification. They may be conditional like the grant of patent rights, or absolute like the ownership of ground rents, terminable like copyright, or permanent like a freehold, as comprehensive as sovereignty or as restricted as an easement, as intimate and personal as the ownership of clothes and books, or as remote and intangible as shares in a gold mine or rubber plantation. It is idle, therefore, to present a case for or against private property without specifying the particular forms of property to which reference is made. The journalist who says that "private property is the foundation of civilization" agrees with Proudhon, who said it was theft, in this respect at least that, without further definition, the words of both are meaningless. Arguments which support or demolish certain kinds of property may have no application to others; considerations which are conclusive in one stage of economic organization may be almost irrelevant in the next. The course of wisdom is neither to attack private property in general nor to defend it in general; for things are not similar in quality, merely because they are identical in name. It is to discriminate between the various concrete embodiments of what, in itself, is, after all, little more than an abstraction.

M. R. COHEN, BOOK REVIEW OF
THE RATIONAL BASIS OF LEGAL INSTITUTIONS
33 Yale Law Journal 892, 893-94 (1924)*

Almost all the selections on property — which fill nearly half of the volume — illustrate what philosophers call the fallacy of vicious abstraction. Property is discussed as if it were just one simple thing existing by itself. In view of the fact that almost everyone believes both (1) in some amount of government or limitation on the right of individuals to do as they please, and (2) in some sphere of individual freedom to dispose of things in accordance with our pleasure, the significant question is not whether you are for or against private property, but rather where you will draw the line between public and private things and affairs. May there be private property in

---

*Reprinted by permission of The Yale Law Journal Company and Fred B. Rothman & Company.

human beings (slavery), in public office, in the immoral use of things (intoxicants, etc.)? How far may a state expropriate an industry by entering into competition with it, or how far may it use the power of taxation to discourage undesirable enterprises? Questions of this sort are really more significant as to the meaning of private property than abstract arguments such as the one that private property is a guarantee of the desire for possession. For obviously the institution of private property is also a thwarting of this desire on the part of all who are not legal possessors. Indeed modern ownership of capital really amounts to a right to tax those who wish to use certain tools. This tax may be for the good of all in the long run but the argument that such a system sets examples of thrift sounds too ironic.

M. R. COHEN, PROPERTY AND SOVEREIGNTY

13 *Cornell Law Quarterly* 8 (1927)*

Anyone who frees himself from the crudest materialism readily recognizes that as a legal term "property" denotes not material things but certain rights. In the world of nature apart from more or less organized society, there are things but clearly no property rights.

Further reflection shows that a property right is not to be identified with the fact of physical possession. Whatever technical definition of property we may prefer, we must recognize that a property right is a relation not between an owner and a thing, but between the owner and other individuals in reference to things. A right is always against one or more individuals. This becomes unmistakably clear if we take specifically modern forms of property such as franchises, patents, good will, etc., which constitute such a large part of the capitalized assets of our industrial and commercial enterprises.

The classical view of property as a right over things resolves it into component rights such as the *jus utendi, jus disponendi,* etc. But the essence of private property is always the right to exclude others. The law does not guarantee me the physical or social ability of actually using what it calls mine. By public regulations it may indirectly aid me by removing certain general hindrances to the enjoyment of property. But the law of property helps me directly only to exclude others from using the things which it assigns to me. If then somebody else wants to use the food, the house, the land, or the plough that the law calls mine, he has to get my consent. To the extent that these things are necessary to the life of my neighbour, the law thus confers on me a power, limited but real, to make him do what I want. If Laban has the sole disposal of his daughters and his cattle, Jacob must serve him if he desires to possess them. In a regime where land is the principal source of obtaining a livelihood, he who has the legal right over the land receives homage and service from those who wish to live on it.

------

*©Copyright 1927 by Cornell University.

The character of property as sovereign power compelling service and obedience may be obscured for us in a commercial economy by the fiction of the so-called labour contract as a free bargain and by the frequency with which service is rendered indirectly through a money payment. But not only is there actually little freedom to bargain on the part of the steelworker or miner who needs a job, but in some cases the medieval subject had as much power to bargain when he accepted the sovereignty of his lord. Today I do not directly serve my landlord if I wish to live in the city with a roof over my head, but I must work for others to pay him rent with which he obtains the personal services of others. The money needed for purchasing things must for the vast majority be acquired by hard labour and disagreeable service to those to whom the law has accorded dominion over the things necessary for subsistence.

To a philosopher this is of course not at all an argument against private property. It may well be that compulsion in the economic as well as the political realm is necessary for civilized life. But we must not overlook the actual fact that dominion over things is also *imperium* over our fellow human beings.

The extent of the power over the life of others which the legal order confers on those called owners is not fully appreciated by those who think of the law as merely protecting men in their possession. Property law does more. It determines what men shall acquire. Thus, protecting the property rights of a landlord means giving him the right to collect rent, protecting the property of a railroad or a public-service corporation means giving it the right to make certain charges. Hence the ownership of land and machinery, with the rights of drawing rent, interest, etc., determines the future distribution of the goods that will come into being – determines what share of such goods various individuals shall acquire. The average life of goods that are either consumable or used for production of other goods is very short. Hence a law that merely protected men in their possession and did not also regulate the acquisition of new goods would be of little use.

From this point of view it can readily be seen that when a court rules that a gas company is entitled to a return of 6 percent on its investment, it is not merely protecting property already possessed, it is also determining that a portion of the future social product shall under certain conditions go to that company. Thus not only medieval landlords but the owners of all revenue-producing property are in fact granted by the law certain powers to tax the future social product. When to this power of taxation there is added the power to command the services of large numbers who are not economically independent, we have the essence of what historically has constituted political sovereignty. . . .

I have already mentioned that the recognition of private property as a form of sovereignty is not itself an argument against it. Some form of government we must always have. For the most part men prefer to obey and let others take the trouble to think out rules, regulations and orders. That is why we are always setting up authorities; and when we cannot find any we write to the newspaper as the final arbiter. But although government is a necessity, not all forms of it are of equal value. At any rate it is necessary to apply to the law of property all those considerations of social ethics and enlightened public policy which ought to be brought to the discussion of any just form of government.

OHIO: CONSTITUTION OF 1851
Article 1, Section 19

Private property shall ever be held inviolate but subservient to the public welfare. . . .

R. ELY, PROPERTY AND CONTRACT IN THEIR RELATIONS TO THE DISTRIBUTION OF WEALTH
Vol. 2, pp. 490-98 (1914)

The chief limitation of eminent domain as it exists in the United States is found in the concept "public" in public purpose; and when obstacles to a sufficiently wide scope of eminent domain are encountered, these may be traced back to a narrow view of public purpose.

Generally expropriation has been confined to real estate, but property in railways, water, dikes, mines, would come under this term in our own and other countries. When we come, however, to the transfer of property during a transition from one economic period to another, we find that expropriation has had a wider range and that rights have been expropriated in one way or another. For example, when we passed over from feudalism to modern industrialism, a great many rights were done away with, either with or without compensation. That was true in regard to serfdom. The old rights of the lords, the serf owners, were abolished in Russia with some compensation. It is generally held that the compensation was not a full one. The same is true with regard to slavery. This shows that in expropriation we have to go beyond real estate in order to accomplish economic purposes. Moreover, we cannot, as Stahl does, limit expropriation to public necessity as distinguished from public utility. What do we mean by necessity, and what do we mean by utility? We have simply different degrees of utility. Perhaps it can scarcely be said that there is any absolute necessity that any right of expropriation should be exercised. We could have lived without railways, but we could not have had them without exercising the right of expropriation. And as we could have lived without railways, how can we say that it was absolutely a case of necessity? We have only varying degrees of utility. . . .

It is time now for a definition of expropriation, and the author quotes Wagner's definition with the statement he makes, and also a statement of Professor von Ihering concerning expropriation. Wagner's definition is, — *"The right of expropriation is the right of the state to seize a specific object of property without the consent of the owner in order to employ it in a manner demanded by the public interest; or to limit the property right of the proprietor in order to place a servitude (easement) upon it; or to take the use of it in the public interest."* His statement in this connection is that "the proper economic and socio-political conception of expropriation regards it as the legal institution by means of which, when free contract fails, changes are compulsorily brought about in the division and ownership of specific pieces of capital and land among the various economic units *(Verteilung der individuellen Kapitalien und Grundstücke)* –, especially between compulsory public economies on the one hand and private economies on the other, and then among these last named with respect to one another, in order that there may be such a division and ownership of land and capital as the development of national life requires." . . .

Changes are brought about in the division and ownership of property among the various economic units, that is, among various persons. The units in economic society are natural and artificial persons, individuals, cities, etc., and this conception regards expropriation as a legal institution for use especially when it is desirable to bring about changes between compulsory public economies (political units, nations, state, city, etc.), on the one hand and private economies on the other. We must make this distinction, and we must also admit that sometimes it is necessary to exercise this right of eminent domain or expropriation in order to bring about a different distribution among various private persons. That was the case in the abolition of feudalism. There was then a different distribution of the rights of property effected among private units. So we do not have to deal simply with changes between political units on one hand and private units on the other, but with changes among the private units themselves. The purpose is that there may be such a division and ownership of land and capital as is required by the development of national life. The idea is growth, natural evolution, and these changes cannot be brought about in all cases by voluntary methods; consequently compulsion has resulted and is the lesser of two evils. Otherwise we would have the whole suffering for the sake of the few and we cannot consider that to be just. . . .

Expropriation is out of harmony with the absolute idea of property. Expropriation makes the interest of the individual conform to the social interest, to the growth and evolution of the ethical ends of society. It is, to use Wagner's expressive phase, a "postulate of the social coexistence of individuals." We cannot then establish any definite limit, but every age has its own needs of expropriation brought about by changes in the organisation of the national economy and by changes desired in individual productive processes.[33]

It still holds true that the chief use and requirement of expropriation is in land sales because it is in these chiefly but not exclusively that we need to exercise compulsion. We have already pointed out the needs which arose from the change from feudalism

---

[33]P. 497. J. B. Clark, "Capital and its Earnings," "Publications of the American Economic Association," Vol. III, No. 2, p. 67. "Eminent domain, by changing one capital in form, may preserve or increase a hundred others in substance. It is in the interest of value, the fruit of personal sacrifice, that the course is taken. If land, then, is anywhere dangerously monopolized, take it, pay for it, and use it as you will. Expediency here has much to say, but not equity. You will have guarded the essential wealth that, by your invitation and in your interest, has vested itself in this form. The evidence of *a priori* law, and the practical signs of the times, indicate that measures not a few for the diffusion of land ownership are in store for us in future eras. What our

into modern industrialism. The Reformation also had its needs, when there was a change from one religious order to another. When the idea concerning the ownership of property by religious bodies changed we had again need of expropriation. And in the case of the land of the Friars in the Philippines, if the owners had been unwilling to sell for a reasonable compensation, expropriation might have been desirable. The passage from slavery to freedom has frequently involved expropriation, and it is in that way alone that the change can be brought about in such a manner as to secure the greatest gain with the least harm. . . .

---

2. Affectability and Geographic Location

The theories thus far considered for taking property in a land reform have related to the manner in which the owner acquired his land, and the manner in which he has used it. There is, in the theory of restitution and in the social function theory, an element of fault or illegitimacy on the landowner's side, which may bring the theory into line with traditional ideas about the protections that should be given property interests. But land reforms normally take place in revolutionary settings, and political necessities have frequently caused revolutionary governments to meet the demand for land distribution for its own sake. The theories of economic development noted earlier made little distinction among the various legal rationalizations for redistributing wealth and income; it is the redistribution that counts. So it was that Peru's 1964 land reform law included as one ground of affectability: "Concentration of land in such a manner as to constitute an obstacle to the diffusion of small and medium rural ownership, and which causes extreme or unjust dependence of the rural population on the owner." (Art. 13 (b).)

Although the restitution theory of expropriation may have been conceived in part as a solution to the invasions or occupations by campesinos in Mexico, it became clear that any serious attempt to trace titles would be hopelessly inefficient to achieve the reforms required by political leaders for political reasons. The result, we have seen, was the early adoption of the principle that the villages deserved lands whether or not they could prove title to any lands in particular. Article 3d of the 1915 Decree of General Carranza and paragraph X of Article 27 of the 1917 Constitution provide the basis for a system of grants to the villages of land expropriated by the government for the purpose. The system, by which affectability is largely a geographical question, is now governed by the Agrarian Code.

---

government has already done it may do hereafter, though in the face of greater obstacles. It may divide lands and put owners and cultivators upon them, even though it cannot continue always to present a farm to every man who asks for it. The land reform of the future will curtail great holdings and multiply small ones, while protecting to the uttermost the value that is anywhere invested." [Footnote by Ely, renumbered.]

MEXICO: AGRARIAN CODE OF 1943

Affectable property

57. All estates whose borders are touched by a radius of 7 kilometers from the most densely populated part of the petitioning nucleus of population shall be affectable for granting to *ejidos* [village land holding units], under the terms of this Code.

58. Properties of the Federation, of the States or of Municipalities shall be affected in preference to private properties in order to make grants to or enlarge *ejidos* or to create new centers of agricultural population. . . .

The colonization of private properties is prohibited.

Nuclei of indigenous population shall have preference to be granted the lands and waters that they possess.

59. The grant [of land to the *ejido*] should preferably be made in affectable lands of the best quality and closest to the petitioning nucleus.

Under these provisions of the Mexican law, does the affectability of land depend on the conduct of the owner or the origins of his title? Suppose, for example, these two cases:

a. Owner A inherited his land, covering some 2500 hectares, from his grandfather, who had in turn inherited the land from *his* father. The latter had aggregated the estate by a series of purchases at bargain prices from individuals who had received their parcels when their village was required during the Díaz regime to divest itself of landholdings under the laws of the Juárez Reform. Owner A lives in a city far away; the estate is managed by a resident supervisor. Much of the land is idle; the rest is farmed non-intensively by tenant sharecroppers, who live close to the subsistence level.

b. Owner B was a day laborer who saved enough money to buy a small plot of land in 1925. He and his sons worked the land intensively, and with some of the profits bought additional land. In this manner, by 1950 Owner B came to own 200 hectares, which he and his sons have continued to work intensively. His only laborers are paid in cash at levels that are the highest in rural Mexico.

Which of these two estates is subject to expropriation under Article 57 of the Agrarian Code? Is any of the history of the two estates relevant to this determination?

These questions, largely rhetorical, are designed to point up the differences between the Mexican system of affectability and a system based on the social function theory. Now we need to ask whether the Mexican legislation is or is not more advantageous than, say, the Venezuelan provisions on affectability. What are the advantages of a principle that bases affectability on the location of the estate with respect to a needy rural population? What are the principle's disadvantages, as compared with a system of expropriation based on the social function theory? Consider Ernest Feder's criticism of legislation that limits expropriation to uncultivated or badly exploited lands. To what extent does the Mexican law meet those criticisms? At what costs?

Even a legislative scheme basing affectability on the social function theory may make provision for taking land on the basis of the reform's needs, as distinguished from the owner's performance of his social function. The 1968 amendments to the Colombian law, authorizing the land reform agency to depart from the priority list that starts with uncultivated land, are a concession to population pressures. Is the Colombian affectability scheme now the same in practical effect as the Mexican one?

In the *Muñoz* case, page 294, *supra,* we saw that the defendant landowner urged, as an alternative argument, that if his land was to be taken, it should be taken under the terms of Article 33 of the Venezuelan law. That article provides, in part:

> 33. When it becomes necessary to organize land in a given place, and when the existence thereat of one or more properties forms a technical or economic obstacle to proper execution of the scheme, the total or partial expropriation of such properties shall be authorized even when they fall within any of the classifications specified in Articles 26 and 29 of this Chapter. In order to take such action, the Institute shall be required to prove, during the appropriate judicial proceedings, that the conditions laid down in this Article exist. . . .

Article 29 provides for an exemption of 150 hectares, which the owner may claim as a reserve when his or her estate is taken. If the provisions of Article 33 apply, authorizing a taking of land even when the ownership is performing its social function (*i.e.,* despite Article 26), then the owner is paid cash for any improvements, improvement mortgages and livestock, and paid for the rest of the property in bonds which are relatively favorable in their terms: 10-year maturity, with interest at the market rate, and exemption of the interest from income taxation. If the court in the *Muñoz* case had held that the ownership was fulfilling its social function, the result would not have been to prevent the taking of land, but rather to require these favorable terms for compensating the owner. As it was, Muñoz was entitled to compensation in 20-year bonds that were non-transferable, bearing interest at 3%. (Issues relating to compensation are considered in Section D of this chapter, *infra.*)

Given the existence of Article 33, what answer can be given to the question: Which lands are affectable in the Venezuelan land reform? Which law, the Mexican or the Venezuelan, gives more protection to the landowner? What kinds of protection?

---

3. Affectability and Excessive Size

Chile's 1967 land reform law is a complex piece of legislative draftsmanship; it "contains 357 excruciatingly detailed and legalistic articles which, in addition, cross-refer to each other and to articles in other laws."[34] Despite this complexity, the Chilean law adopts as its main principle of affectability the rather uncomplicated principle of excessive size. Article 3 of the law states the principle:

---

[34] Thome, "Expropriation in Chile under the Frei Agrarian Reform," 19 *Am. J. Comp. L.* 489, 500 (1971).

3. Rural estates are subject to expropriation, whatever their location in the territory of the nation, and whatever their category of terrain, when they are owned by a single natural person and, alone or in conjunction, they exceed in area 80 basic irrigated hectares, calculated according to the conversion table established in Article 172. [This table covers the entire nation, and takes 8 pages to list. The equivalents range from 40 hectares of the best lands to 7,000 in the most inaccessible mountainous regions.]

When the total area of estates owned by a single natural person exceeds 80 basic irrigated hectares, any one of those estates shall be subject to expropriation, or part of one of them, or the totality of them shall be expropriable, without prejudice to the right of reserve which may be appropriate in conformity with this law.

Rural estates shall be affected by the provisions of this law when they are owned by two or more persons in common, and when their area is greater than that indicated in the first paragraph of this article, except in cases involving [certain special communities, including indigenous communities].

For purposes of expropriation on the ground established in this article, estates owned by married persons shall be considered as a [combined] whole, whether they are owned jointly or separately, even where the persons may be separated with respect to property, except in cases of permanently divorced persons.

Divisions made in anticipation of the land reform law are to be disregarded, under Article 5.[35]

The Peruvian law of 1969 similarly sets the maximum area permitted to be held by a single "legal entity," that is, a natural person, or a society (partnership or corporation). The area permitted varies, as in Chile, according to the region where the land is located. If a natural person owns or controls 40% or more of a corporation's shares or a partnership's participating interests, then he or she is considered to own any land held by that entity. And in the context of corporate or partnership ownership, there are rules attributing to an individual lands held by certain of his or her relatives. Agrarian Reform Law of Peru, Decree-Law No. 17716, Arts. 11, 23, 24 (1969). (Corporations are forbidden to own rural land. Art. 22. The attribution rules described above are designed to reach the holdings of individuals during the six-month transitional period when corporations are divesting themselves of their holdings.)

Why might the draftsmen of a land reform law choose the excessive size principle in preference to the social function theory embodied in the Venezuelan law? What are the disadvantages of the excessive size principle, as compared to the social function

---

[35] The political setting for the 1967 Chilean law is analyzed in R. Kaufman, *The Politics of Land Reform in Chile, 1950-1970* (1972). For preliminary evaluations of the law's impact, see Chonchol, "Poder y Reforma Agraria en la Experiencia Chilena," in *Chile Hoy* at 255 (1970); Thiesenhusen, "Agrarian Reform: Chile," in *Land Reform in Latin America: Issues and Cases* at 105 (P. Dorner ed. 1971).

principle? Similarly, compare the excessive size principle with Mexico's geographical principle of affectability. Are the two principles the same in practice? If there are differences, what are they? Which of these three competing theories would you select? Why?

It should be noted that the principles are not mutually exclusive, but may coexist in the same law. We have noted, for example, that the Chilean law not only authorizes expropriation of excessively large estates, but also authorizes the taking of any estate, large or small, which is inadequately farmed or indirectly operated through sharecroppers. The Peruvian law is similarly structured.

---

4. Exemptions and the Owner's Reserve

In the *Muñoz* case, page 294, *supra,* we saw that the owner claimed a reserve of 500 hectares under the provisions of Article 30 of the Venezuelan law. This reserve is granted to expropriated owners by way of effectuating the principle of the exemption created by Article 29:

> 29. Land or properties the area of which is not in excess of 150 hectares of the first category, or the equivalent thereof in land of other categories, in accordance with criteria to be laid down in Regulations, shall also be immune from expropriation.
>
> The equivalents referred to in this Article shall be included between 150 and 5000 hectares. . . .

(We noted earlier that Article 33 of the Venezuelan law permits the land reform agency to take land despite this exemption, provided that it pays compensation on Article 33's more favorable terms.) In Colombia, the reserve is set at 100 hectares, of crop land, and a 1968 amendment similar to Venezuela's Article 33 permits expropriation even of such areas when it is necessary for the accomplishment of certain purposes (*e.g.,* irrigation projects), or when the land expropriated has been "uncultivated" or worked by sharecroppers. Similar reserves are available, with similar limitations, in Peru and Chile.

The Mexican law, however, contains a powerful guarantee against expropriation of the "small property." Article 27 of the Constitution of 1917 was amended in 1947 to include the following paragraphs:

> XIV. . . . [The original 1917 Constitution denied to expropriated owners the right of judicial review or amparo proceedings. The 1917 provision is retained in the 1947 revision; an expropriated owner can claim only a right of compensation, and even that is not judicially enforceable.]
>
> Owners or occupants of agricultural or stockraising properties who have been issued or to whom there may be issued in the future certificates of non-affectability may institute *amparo* proceedings against any illegal deprivation or agrarian claims on their lands or water.

XV. The mixed commissions, the local governments and any other authorities charged with agrarian proceedings cannot in any case affect small agricultural or livestock properties in operation, and they shall incur liability for violations of the Constitution if they make grants which affect them. [This sentence was included in the 1917 Constitution, and remains in force.]

Small agricultural property is that which does not exceed one hundred hectares of first-class moist or irrigated land or its equivalent in other classes of land, under cultivation.

To determine this equivalence one hectare of irrigated land shall be computed as two hectares of seasonal land; as four of good quality pasturage (*agostadero*) and as eight of scrub land (*monte*) or arid pasturage.

Also to be considered as small holdings are areas not exceeding two hundred hectares of seasonal lands or pasturage susceptible of cultivation; or one hundred fifty hectares of land used for cotton growing if irrigated from fluvial canals or by pumping; or three hundred, under cultivation, when used for growing bananas, sugar cane, coffee, henequen, rubber, coconuts, grapes, olives, quinine, vanilla, cacao, or fruit trees.

Small holdings for stockraising are lands not exceeding the area necessary to maintain up to five hundred head of cattle *(ganado mayor)* or their equivalent in smaller animals (*ganado menor* – sheep, goats, pigs) under provisions of law, in accordance with the forage capacity of the lands.

Whenever, due to irrigation or drainage works or any other works executed by the owners or occupants of a small holding to whom a certificate of non-affectability has been issued, the quality of the land is improved for agricultural or stockraising operations, such holding shall not be subject to agrarian appropriation even if, by virtue of the improvements made, the maximums indicated in this section are lowered, provided that the requirements fixed by law are met.

The key to these provisions, reflected in the Agrarian Code and in a long regulation first issued in 1948, is the procedure for obtaining certificates of inaffectability. Every owner of 100 hectares may be issued such a certificate. Thus, by a judicious distribution of land among the members of a family, including babies and great-aunts, a sizeable estate may be covered by many certificates of inaffectability and yet operated as a unit. The 100-hectare figure, it will be seen, applies only to the best land; in cases of less desirable land, the inaffectable area may range much higher per person.[36] What is the purpose of the last paragraph of Article 27, par. XV, quoted above?

Is the certificate of inaffectability approach adaptable to the social function principle of expropriation? What problems might be encountered in an effort to use such certificates in, say, Venezuela?[37] The 1967 Chilean law includes provisions

---

[36] See generally L. Mendieta y Núñez, *El Problema Agrario de México,* ch. XXVII, XXVIII (9th ed. 1966); I. Burgoa, *El Amparo en Materia Agraria* 79-110 (1964).

[37] See Karst, "Latin-American Land Reform: The Uses of Confiscation," 63 *Mich. L. Rev.* 327, 352-53 (1964).

designed to accomplish this purpose. Article 20 provides that an owner who is subject to expropriation for excessive size or a corporation otherwise forbidden to own rural land may petition the land reform agency for a declaration that the owner's land is immune from expropriation, up to a maximum of 320 basic irrigated hectares (including the 80 basic hectares which the owner is entitled to reserve). The agency's board may, by a two-thirds vote, grant the petition and issue the declaration, provided that the owner has complied with a long, detailed list of obligations established in Article 21. For example, the owner must dedicate at least 95% of his or her irrigated land to annual or permanent crops or artificial pastures (or 80% of non-irrigated land); must exploit the land efficiently, according to regulations of the Ministry of Agriculture; must maintain good soil conservation practices; must pay twice the normal minimum wage established by law; etc. The immunity from expropriation conferred under Article 20 lasts only so long as the owner fulfills these obligations; in case of an asserted failure to fulfill the obligations, the land reform agency brings a proceeding in the local Agrarian Tribunal, which decides the issue.

---

5. The Case of Bolivia: Land Reform First, Then Law

R. PATCH, BOLIVIA: U.S. ASSISTANCE IN A REVOLUTIONARY SETTING
In *Social Change in Latin America Today*
at 108, 122-26 (1960)*

In the early months after the revolution the national government in La Paz paid little attention to the rising tide of peasant unrest.[38] It announced that the innocuous reforms decreed ten years before by the Villarroel government, which had placed certain restrictions on the exploitation of *pegujaleros* by latifundium owners, were again to be put into effect. The landowners were not much concerned over this mild gesture, and for a time the traditional landlord-peasant pattern seemed likely to remain unchanged by this as by so many previous revolts.

Then, on November 9, 1952, the syndicate [rural union] of Ucureña demanded the return of eleven parcels of land to *pegujaleros* who had been driven from one of the latifundia a few years before. The landowner refused. Thereupon, the syndicate called for a general uprising of the *campesinos* in the provinces of Cliza, Punata, and Tarata. It threatened to pillage the town of Cliza and burn the houses of the nearby landowners. This threat of direct action, reported to Cochabamba, the departmental capital, found the governor and his officials, with their limited forces, understandably reluctant to interfere. Only prompt action by the sub-prefect of Cliza finally succeeded in pacifying the *campesinos* and in preventing a general assault upon the

---

*New York: Harper and Row for the Council on Foreign Relations, 1960.

[38] For a discussion of the peasant movement in Bolivia both before and after the land reform, see G. Huizer, *Peasant Rebellion in Latin America* 48-61 (1973). [Eds.]

latifundia and the smaller towns. The *campesinos* had now come to realize their strength, and acts of violence became more frequent.

The uprising of the *campesinos* could not but arouse the national government to the necessity for drastic action. If far-reaching concessions could no longer control but only channel the emergence of the *campesinos,* they would at least demonstrate that the sympathies of the government were on the side of the now irresistible movement. Fortunately, the *campesinos* also had a direct channel to the national leaders of the MNR [the government party] in La Paz. The minister of *campesino* affairs, Ñuflo Chávez, was acutely aware of the government's dependence on the good will of the village population, and was in close contact with José Rojas and other *campesino* leaders. Ñuflo Chávez became an early and insistent advocate of an extreme type of agrarian reform. His concept, if carried out, would have divided all the land in areas of predominantly Indian population into *minifundios* (small parcels). A reform of this type would have converted the country's entire system of agriculture to subsistence farming, leaving little or no marketable surplus to feed the cities. Had the *campesinos* been left to their own devices this would assuredly have been the final upshot.

As it was, the syndicates rapidly took over the most accessible latifundia or *haciendas,* divided up the land among their members, and expropriated the vehicles, machinery, and houses of the former *patrones.* For example, at Ucureña the *casa hacienda,* or manor house, of one *patrón* was seized by the syndicate, which renamed it the "General Barracks" or village headquarters of Ucureña. Other houses were converted to serve as hospitals, schools or syndicate headquarters. By this time those landowners who had so far remained in the rural areas finally realized the full sweep of the revolution and fled for safety to the cities, especially to Cochabamba and La Paz. Since then most of them have not been able so much as to go near their former *haciendas.* Large areas of Bolivia have remained inaccessible for this class of *blancos,* often called *"la rosca,"* a bitter term applied to persons popularly believed to have used their wealth and power to exploit the Indians.

The Government and Agrarian Reform

The *campesino* uprising with its demand for agrarian reform posed several difficult questions to the MNR. As a political party, the MNR had risen to power as a congeries of groups each of which had its own purposes, and their amalgamation was not accompanied by a genuine unity of views or goals. The original inspirers of the MNR, leaders such as Víctor Paz Estenssoro and Wálter Guevara Arze, minister of foreign affairs until February 1956, were supporters of moderate, evolutionary "socialism." As such, they attempted to keep the use of force to a minimum. Hernán Siles, then vice-president and president of the republic from 1956 to 1960, also belonged to the moderates.

In the 1940's the moderate intellectuals had been joined by a group which called itself the Vanguardia of the MNR. The Vanguardia in turn was, in its origins, close to the RADEPA, an organization of younger army officers, veterans of the Chaco war, who had turned against the higher officers, holding them responsible for Bolivia's defeat.[39] However vague the political platform of the Vanguardia, its leaders were more conservative in social outlook than the Paz Estenssoro group, and also more willing to resort to force.

The Universities had been another source of recruits and ideas for the MNR. While some professors and students were close to the moderate views of the MNR, many other students, no longer attracted to the older MNR intellectuals, had formed their own groups. The Avanzadas Universitarias (Avant-Garde University Students), as they were called, were young enough to be strongly influenced by the Marxist thinking that had flourished at the universities in the 1930's and 1940's. These groups were far to the left of the rightist Vanguardia wing of the MNR, whose adherents were barely lukewarm toward agrarian reform. Other influential leaders within the MNR took strong positions for or against the peasants' demands. Among them, the very influential Juan Lechín was an advocate of extreme land reform.

As the pressure of the *campesinos* and their syndicates was rising explosively, President Paz Estenssoro decided to put the government and the MNR at the head of the movement. On January 20, 1953, he proclaimed Supreme Decree No. 3301, creating an agrarian reform commission to study the "agrarian-*campesino* problem" and suggest the best ways in which the reform could be carried out. The commission, headed by Vice-President Siles, was given 120 days in which to prepare a report and draft a decree dealing with all interrelated aspects of the reform. These included property and tenure patterns of agricultural and grazing lands; "an adequate redistribution of this land, in order to raise the standard of living of the *campesinos*, intensify agricultural and livestock production, and develop the national economy"; procedures for liquidating the latifundia and suppressing "semifeudal" exploitive practices in rural areas; the effect of these reforms on agricultural production, work patterns, and the payment and protection of the *campesinos*; *campesino* housing; technical assistance and credit for agricultural producers; conservation of natural resources. While Paz Estenssoro assigned responsibility for carrying out the decree jointly to the ministers of *campesino* affairs, agriculture, and finance, the primary responsibility, significantly enough, was assigned to the minister of *campesino* affairs, Ñuflo Chávez, an intimate of the Indian leader, José Rojas, rather than to the minister of agriculture, Germán Vera Tapia, one of the stronger leaders of the MNR's Vanguardia wing.

Within the stipulated period of four months the commission completed a series of reports and prepared a draft decree which Paz Estenssoro enacted into law by Supreme Decree No. 3464. On August 2, 1953, the decree was signed with much pomp and ceremony by the president and the entire cabinet before a huge convocation of *campesinos* held in the village of Ucureña.

---

[39] RADEPA stands for Razón de Patria. [Footnote by Patch, renumbered.]

BOLIVIA: LEGISLATIVE DECREE NO. 03464
RELATIVE TO AGRARIAN REFORM

August 2, 1953 (FAO translation)

1. The soil, the sub-soil and the waters of the territory of the Republic shall belong by original right to the Bolivian Nation.

2. The state shall recognise and guarantee private agrarian property where it serves a purpose benefiting the national community: it shall plan, regulate, supervise and organise the exercise thereof and shall promote the equitable distribution of the land in order to ensure the economic and cultural liberty and welfare of the Bolivian population. . . .

4. Considered as State domains shall be uncultivated lands reverting thereto owing to lapse of concession or for some other reason, vacant lands outside the urban radius of population centres, lands belonging to the organs and self-administering bodies of the States, forest lands under Government control and all property considered to be of such character under legislation in force.

5. Private agrarian property is that which is acknowledged and granted to natural or juridical persons in order that they shall exercise their right in accordance with the civil laws and the conditions of this Legislative Decree. The State recognises only those forms of private agrarian property enumerated in the following Articles.

6. The farm-house plot has the function of a rural residence, inadequate to satisfy the needs of a family.

7. The small property is that worked by the peasant and his family personally, the produce of which enables them reasonably to satisfy their needs. The personal labour of the peasant does not exclude the collaboration of possible assistants for certain tasks.

8. The medium property is that having an area larger than the small property as defined above, which while lacking the characteristics of the capitalist agricultural undertaking, is operated with the assistance of paid workers or with the aid of technical and mechanical equipment, the bulk of its produce being intended for the market.

9. The Indian community property is that acknowledged as such under legislation in force, on behalf of certain social groups of Indians.

10. The co-operative agrarian property is:

a) That property granted to farmers forming a co-operative association for the purpose of acquiring the land, putting it in order, cultivating it and settling thereon;

b) The lands of small and medium property owners, contributed for the establishment of the registered capital of the co-operative;

c) Lands of peasants who have received grants of land belonging to former latifundia and who have formed a co-operative society for their cultivation;

d) Lands belonging to agricultural co-operative societies under any other title not included in the foregoing paragraphs.

11. The agricultural undertaking shall be characterised by the investment of supplementary capital on a large scale, a system of paid labour and the use of

up-to-date technical methods, exception being made as regards the latter in the case of areas with an uneven terrain. The determination of these factors in detail shall be governed by special regulations.

12. The State does not recognise the latifundium which is a rural property of large area varying according to its geographical situation, either undeveloped or substantially under-developed, by the diffuse field-cropping system with the use of obsolete implements and methods resulting in the waste of human effort, or by the imposition of lease rent; it is also characterised as regards the use of the land in the inter-Andean zone by the grant of parcels, small plots *(pegujales)*, allotments *(sayañas)*, part holdings and other equivalent forms, so that its profitability owing to the disequilibrium [among] the factors of production, is fundamentally dependent upon the extra yield which is contributed by the peasants in their capacity of servants or tenant-farmers and which is taken by the landowner as rent in the form of service, thus constituting a system of feudal oppression reflected in agricultural backwardness and a low standard of living and culture of the peasant population. . . .

29. This Legislative Decree establishes the bases for the achievement of economic and political democracy in the rural area by the designation and grant of lands affected thereby as established under its provisions.

30. The latifundium shall be abolished. The possession of large corporative agrarian property or of other forms of large-scale concentration of land by private persons and by bodies which, by their legal structure, hinder its equitable distribution among the rural population, shall not be permitted.

31. Industrial capital investment in rural areas, for example in grain and sugar mills, cold storage plants and other forms of enterprise for manufacturing production shall be considered as beneficial wherever such enterprise exists side by side with medium and small properties and purchases their products at a fair price without arrogating to itself large areas of land. Large-scale capital investment which acquires extensive areas of land for itself shall be considered harmful, because besides retaining the source of wealth, it monopolizes the market and eliminates the independent farmer by unfair competition.

32. The small property is not affected by this Legislative Decree. . . .

33. The medium holding is not affected. It may, however, in exceptional cases, be affected in respect of those areas owned by farmers (allotments, small plots, etc.) the possession of which is assumed by the workers, without prejudice to the grant of land in other zones, to the extent of the minimum area of the small property. Where these areas, which are inalienable, become vacant by the departure of those workers to whom land has been granted, they shall be consolidated on behalf of the medium property holder to the extent of the maximum area of the medium property, subject to the requirement that compensation small be made for the improvements carried out by the worker.

34. Landed property defined as a latifundium in accordance with Article 12 shall be affected by this Legislative Decree to the extent of its entire area.

35. For the purposes of the preceding Article, property whereon the owner has invested capital in modern agricultural methods and machinery and which is worked by him personally or by his closest relatives shall not be considered as a latifundium.

In those regions where the topography of the cultivable land hinders the use of machinery, only the personal labour of the owner or of his closest relatives shall be stipulated.

This type of property as well as those properties having the characteristics referred to in Article 8 shall be reduced to the dimensions of the medium property with all the rights and duties devolving upon the owner of medium property.

36. The agricultural undertaking [which] on the date of proclamation of this Legislative Decree employs the mixed system of colonization and wage-payment shall not be affected if it has been ascertained that an amount of supplementary capital has been invested which is at least double that of the land capital and that up-to-date cultivation techniques have been employed thereon.

Given the history of the land reform in Bolivia as recounted by Patch, what was the purpose of enacting the 1953 law? What would be the likely role of government in the Bolivian reform after 1953? See Clark, "Problems and Conflicts over Land Ownership in Bolivia," 22 *Inter-Am. Econ. Affairs* 3 (1969). For a thorough analysis of the Bolivian land reform, see Clark, "Agrarian Reform: Bolivia" in P. Dorner (ed.), *Land Reform in Latin America: Issues and Cases* at 127 (1971).

---

6. Puerto Rico and the Public Use Doctrine in United States Constitutional Law

In 1900, the United States Congress enacted a joint resolution forbidding any corporation to own or control more than 500 acres of land in the territory of Puerto Rico. No sanction was specified, and many instances were recorded of corporate land ownership on the Island in excess of 500 acres. In 1935, the Puerto Rico territorial legislature authorized the Attorney General of Puerto Rico to bring a *quo warranto* proceeding in the territorial Supreme Court, to require any corporation owning excess land to divest itself of such land. In *Puerto Rico v. Rubert Hermanos, Inc.*, 309 U.S. 543 (1940), the United States Supreme Court upheld the application of the 1935 territorial legislation to the defendant company, rejecting the defense that the Congress had "occupied the field," pre-empting the territorial legislature.

For a discussion of the political context of efforts to enforce the 500-acre law, see T. Matthews, *Puerto Rican Politics and the New Deal* (1960). See also Rosenn, "Puerto Rican Land Reform: The History of an Instructive Experiment," 73 *Yale L. J.* 334 (1963). Rosenn's discussion of the Puerto Rican "proportional-profit farm" is extracted *infra* at page 385.

PEOPLE OF PUERTO RICO v. EASTERN
SUGAR ASSOCIATES

United States Circuit Court of Appeals, First Circuit
156 F.2d 316, cert. denied,
329 U.S. 772 (1946)

Before MAGRUDER, MAHONEY, and WOODBURY, Circuit Judges.

WOODBURY, Circuit Judge.

This appeal is from an order of the District Court of the United States for Puerto Rico dismissing a petition to condemn approximately 3,100 acres of land situated on the Island of Vieques owned by the appellee, Eastern Sugar Associates, subject to a mortgage held by the appellee, National City Bank of New York, on the ground that the petition fails "to state a public use or purpose for which private property may be acquired by eminent domain."

By Act No. 26 approved April 12, 1941, (Laws of Puerto Rico 1941, p. 388 et seq.) called the "Land Law of Puerto Rico," the insular Legislature launched a far-reaching program of agrarian reform. This law is long and rather complicated. At the moment it will suffice to say that after a lengthy "Statement of Motives" the Act creates a board in the "nature of a governmental agency or instrumentality of the People of Puerto Rico" in the Department of Agriculture and Commerce, to be called the "Land Authority of Puerto Rico," "for the purpose of carrying out the agricultural policy of The People of Puerto Rico as determined by this Act, and to take the necessary action to put an end to the existing corporative latifundia in this Island, block its reappearance in the future, insure to individuals the conservation of their land, assist in the creation of new landowners, facilitate the utilization of land for the best public benefit under efficient and economic production plans; provide the means for the agregados[40] and slum dwellers to acquire parcels of land on which to build their homes, and to take all action leading to the most scientific, economic and efficient enjoyment of land by the people of Puerto Rico." Then the Act goes on to make detailed provisions with respect to the organization, powers, and duties of the Land Authority, and to authorize it both to expropriate lands held in violation of the so-called 500 acre provision of the Organic Act (39 Stat. 964, 48 U.S.C.A. § 752) and also to request the Insular Government to acquire on its behalf by eminent domain "title to any real property or estate thereon (sic) which might be necessary or advisable for the purposes of the Authority." The act fully establishes the procedure to be followed in condemnation proceedings and provides, apparently adequately, for payment of "just compensation" for property so taken.

As this Land Law stood, after amendment, at the time the present condemnation proceedings were instituted, the Land Authority was authorized to dispose of lands which it acquired for three purposes: (1) in small parcels to individual agregados for

---

[40] An agregado, frequently referred to in Puerto Rico as a "squatter," is defined in § 78 of the Act as "any family head residing in the rural zone, whose home is erected on lands belonging to another person or to a private or public entity, and whose only means of livelihood is his labor for a wage." [Footnote by the court, renumbered.]

the erection of their dwellings, (2) in somewhat larger parcels to individual farmers for subsistence farms, and (3) in large parcels by lease to expert farmers, agronomists, or other qualified personsl with experience in agricultural management, for the operation of "proportional-profit" farms as described in detail in § § 64-73 of the Act.

Following enactment of the Land Law, the Insular Legislature by Act No. 90, approved May 11, 1944, popularly called the "Vieques Act," made specific provisions for the relief of economic distress which it said existed on the small outlying islands of Vieques and Culebra, both municipalities of Puerto Rico. In its "Statement of Motives" this statute refers to the condemnation of some 20,000 acres of land on Vieques by the United States for Naval purposes (see Baetjer et al. v. United States, 1 Cir., 143 F.2d 391), which it said paralyzed the sugar industry on that island and caused acute economic distress to its inhabitants which could only be relieved by a renewal of that industry there, and the establishment thereon of a distillery, and then it provides:

"Section 1. – The Land Authority is directed and empowered to acquire, through purchase or condemnation proceedings, or in any other form or by any other means compatible with the laws of Puerto Rico, the lands belonging to the Eastern Sugar Associates in the Islands of Vieques, as well as any other lands in the Island of Vieques, Puerto Rico, that may be necessary, in the judgment of the Land Authority of Puerto Rico, to carry out the provisions of this Act.

"Section 2. – As soon as the Land Authority acquires these lands from the Eastern Sugar Associates, it shall establish the consequent organization of the same and shall devote them principally to the planting of sugar cane and of any other products that may be necessary to develop in Vieques the sugar industry and the liquor industry."
. . .

[The petition for condemnation was granted by the insular District Court, whereupon Eastern Sugar Associates successfully sought to remove the case to the United States District Court for Puerto Rico. After removal, Eastern Sugar Associates moved to dismiss, principally on the ground that, in the words of Judge Woodbury, "the taking was not for a public use and purpose and thus violated rights guaranteed by the Fifth and Fourteenth Amendments to the Constitution of the United States and § 2 of the Organic Act of Puerto Rico, ..." The U.S. District Court dismissed the petition for condemnation, setting aside the order of the insular District Court.]

. . . The basic question presented is whether on the pleadings it can be said that the appellees' land is sought to be taken for a public use. And this requires consideration of the nature as public or private of four possible uses to which the land here involved may, if acquired, be put, to wit, the three specific uses enumerated in the Land Law and in addition the more general use permitted by the Vieques Act. . . . [If] any one of those uses, each considered, however, as part of a broad, integrated program of agrarian reform as will be pointed out hereafter, is not public, the petition was properly dismissed.

But the power of the Insular Legislature in the respect is not unlimited. In § 2 of the Organic Act, as already appears, Congress saw fit to allow the Insular Government to take or damage private property only for public use, and then only upon payment of just compensation, and furthermore in the same section it provided that "no law shall be enacted in Puerto Rico which shall deprive any person of life, liberty, or property without due process of law." ...

... It is therefore clear that the ultimate test imposed by § 2 of the Organic Act, as well as by the Fourteenth Amendment, is a due process test and thus it is immaterial whether the limiting criteria are stated in terms of "due process of law" or in terms of "public use." ...

The four contemplated uses for the land enumerated above are closely inter-related. Each use plays a part in a comprehensive program of social and economic reform. Thus we see no basis for analyzing each proposed use separately. Instead we think the entire legislation should be regarded "as a single integrated effort," United States ex rel. Tennessee Valley Authority v. Welch, 66 S. Ct. 718, to improve conditions on the island, and so viewed we think enactment of the statutes within the power of the Insular Legislature. ...

It does not follow from this, however, that a taking of property from one, for the purpose of transferring it to another, without anything more, conforms to due process of law. Some public benefit or advantage must accrue from the transfer and mere financial gain to the taker is not enough, since the Supreme Court has intimated that the power of eminent domain cannot be used by the taking authority in aid of "an outside land speculation." Brown v. United States, 263 U.S. 78, 84, 44 S. Ct. 92, 94, 68 L. Ed. 171. But the local Legislatures nevertheless have wide scope in deciding what takings are for a public use. ... In fact, in Old Dominion Co. v. United States, 269 U.S. 55, 66, ... the Supreme Court said that a legislative decision that a given use is public "is entitled to deference until it is shown to involve an impossibility."

In view of these principles we cannot strike down the legislative program for the Island of Vieques as in violation of the appellees' right to due process of law. That program in part, may be radical in that if carried out it will put the Insular Government in business in direct competition with the appellee Eastern Sugar Associates. This may be, as the appellees contend, "state socialism." But concrete cases are not to be decided by calling names. Our function is to pass upon the statutes before us without regard to our views of the wisdom of the political theory underlying them; (McLean v. Arkansas, 211 U.S. 539, 547, 29 S. Ct. 203, 53 L. Ed. 315) it is our duty to determine whether their enactment rested upon an arbitrary belief of the existence of the evils they were intended to remedy, and whether the means chosen are reasonably calculated to cure the evils reasonably believed by the Legislature to exist. ...

Puerto Rico, including its adjacent islands, is small in area and densely populated, and that congested population is largely dependent upon the land for its livelihood. Puerto Rico v. Rubert Hermanos, Inc., 309 U.S. 543, 548, 60 S. Ct. 399, 84 L. Ed. 916. But it is not directly dependent upon the land because the basic agricultural crop is sugar cane. Indeed it is no secret that sugar dominates the whole insular economy. And the exigencies of sugar cane growing and grinding, which must be done promptly after the cane is cut, are such that rural landholdings have tended to become large and the majority of the workers thereon employable for only a few weeks during the year. Then, in addition to the foregoing, the economy of the Island of Vieques has been disrupted by the withdrawal of a substantial part of its best agricultural land for naval purposes, see Baetjer et al. v. United States, 1 Cir., 143 F.2d 391, thereby rendering it commercially expedient to transport the relatively small amount of cane still grown on that island to Puerto Rico proper for grinding instead of grinding it locally as had been done in the past. Were it necessary we might even go further and point to the plight of Puerto Rico during the late war brought to our attention in Buscaglia v. District Court of San Juan, 1 Cir., 145 F.2d 274. But enough has been said to indicate both that the Puerto Rican Legislature's belief in the existence of a serious economic and social problem was not arbitrary, and that the program to provide not only homesteads and proportional profit farms for agregados and subsistence farms for more skilled farmers, on the Island of Puerto Rico proper, but, in addition to the foregoing, to provide for the renewal of sugar cane grinding and the development of the liquor industry on the Island of Vieques, embodied means reasonably calculated to deal with these problems.

One further point remains to be briefly considered. The appellees contend that the Land Authority which the People of Puerto Rico seek to vest with title to the 3,100 odd acres of land here in question lacks legal capacity to take title because of the five hundred acre provision of the Organic Act, referred to at the outset of this opinion. Their argument in a nutshell is that the Land Authority, although denominated "a governmental agency or instrumentality" in fact has all the essential attributes of a corporation and hence should be regarded as such, and as within the scope of the provision. We do not agree.

Even assuming, although we do not by any means decide, first, that the Land Authority is in fact a corporation, and second, that it is one "authorized to engage in agriculture," it does not seem to us to be the kind of a corporation intended to be included within the scope of the five hundred acre provision. Instead we are of the view from the wording of the provision that it was not intended to apply to governmental corporations created by the Insular Legislature to carry on a public function, but was intended to be limited in its application to private business corporations chartered by the insular government to engage in agriculture for profit, and clearly the Land Authority, whatever it may be, is not such an organization.

The order of the District Court is set aside and the case remanded to that Court for further proceedings not inconsistent with this opinion.

The *Eastern Sugar Associates* case was cited, and its results distinguished, by the United States District Court in the case of *Schneider v. District of Columbia,* 117 F. Supp. 705 (D.D.C. 1953). In the *Schneider* case, the owners of urban real property sought to enjoin the condemnation of their land and buildings, which condemnation was to be part of a general plan for the development of Southwest Washington, D.C. The court adopted the plaintiffs' argument that while a taking of slum property in order to do away with slums would be a taking for public use, a taking of property which was not a slum for the purpose of developing a better balanced community was not. The court did not hold the Redevelopment Act invalid; rather, it construed the

Act to authorize only the taking of slum property. In distinguishing the *Eastern Sugar Associates* case, the court pointed to "the public necessity for solution of the general and acute [economic] conditions" in Puerto Rico.

On appeal, the Supreme Court reversed, holding the Redevelopment Act applicable to non-slum property, including the plaintiffs', and holding the Act as so interpreted to be constitutional. *Berman v. Parker,* 348 U.S. 26 (1954). Mr. Justice Douglas, speaking for the Court, went to some length to show the breadth of "what traditionally has been known as the police power," *i.e.,* police power objectives. Finding that the attractiveness and balance of a community were within the scope of proper governmental objectives, Justice Douglas found no obstacle in the "public use" doctrine:

> Once the object is within the authority of Congress, the right to realize it through the exercise of eminent domain is clear. For the power of eminent domain is merely the means to the end. See *Luxton v. North River Bridge Co.,* 153 U.S. 525, 529-530; *United States v. Gettysburg Electric R. Co.,* 160 U.S. 668, 679. Once the object is within the authority of Congress, the means by which it should be attained is also for Congress to determine. Here one of the means chosen is the use of private enterprise for redevelopment of the area. Appellants argue that this makes the project a taking from one businessman for the benefit of another businessman. But the means of executing the project are for Congress and Congress alone to determine, once the public purpose has been established. . . . The public end may be as well or better served through an agency of private enterprise than through a department of government — or so the Congress might conclude. We cannot say that public ownership is the sole method of promoting the public purposes of community redevelopment projects. What we have said also disposes of any contention concerning the fact that certain property owners in the area may be permitted to repurchase their properties for redevelopment in harmony with the over-all plan. That, too, is a legitimate means which Congress and its agencies may adopt, if they choose. [348 U.S. at 33-34.]

What is left of the public use requirement, after this language is made the doctrine of the Court? To what extent does the doctrine of the *Berman* case, coupled with the language of legislation such as the Redevelopment Act ("blight," "sound development"), confide the question of public use to administrative discretion?

Is the question before a United States court in a public use case the same as the question before the Venezuelan court in the *Muñoz* case? Can you think of more fitting analogies in our law? Is there any reason why a court in the United States might be *less* concerned to protect against unjustifiable takings of property than its Latin American counterpart might be?

D. Expropriation: Compensation and Confiscation

1. The Rationale of Confiscation: To Compensate or Not?

O. W. HOLMES, JR., INTRODUCTION
in J. Wigmore and A. Kocourek (eds.), *Rational Basis
of Legal Institutions* xxxi-xxxii (1923)

. . . I will go no farther than to repeat that most even of the enlightened reformers that I hear or read seem to me not to have considered with accuracy the means at our disposal and to become rhetorical just where I want figures. The notion that we can secure an economic paradise by changes in property alone seems to me twaddle. . . . I can understand a man's saying in any case, I want this or that and I am willing to pay the price, if he realizes what the price is. What I most fear is saying the same thing when those who say it do not know and have made no serious effort to find out what it will cost, as I think we in this country are rather inclined to do.

The passion for equality is now in fashion and Mr. Lester Ward has told us of the value of discontent. Without considering how far motives commonly classed as ignoble have covered themselves with a high sounding name, or how far discontent means inadequacy of temperament or will, the first step toward improvement is to look the facts in the face.

Fidel Castro was trained as a lawyer. In October, 1953, in a hospital room in Santiago de Cuba, Castro was his own client, on trial for leading an attack on the Moncada Barracks in Santiago the preceding July 26. For five hours, Castro spoke in his own defense, closing with the words that are now commonly used as the title of his speech: "History will absolve me." The reporter's transcript of that speech has been published as the first major document of the Cuban revolution that culminated on January 1, 1959. That date marked the flight from Havana of Fulgencio Batista, the dictator who had ruled Cuba from 1933 to 1944, and again from 1952 until the success of Castro's revolutionary army.

The "History Will Absolve Me" speech was in major part an appeal to legality. One of its portions was a statement of the intentions of the revolutionary group, if their attack on the barracks had sparked a successful revolution. The 1940 Constitution was to be restored in the first of five revolutionary laws. Castro went on:

> The Second Revolutionary Law would have granted property, non-mortgageable and non-transferable, to all planters, non-quota planters, lessees, share-croppers, and squatters who hold parcels of five *caballerías* or less [1 *caballería* = 33-1/3 acres], and the State would indemnify the former owners on the basis of the [income] which they would have received for these parcels over a period of ten years.[41]

Critics of the Cuban revolution have pointed to statements such as these as evidence

---

[41] F. Castro, *History Will Absolve Me* 44 (1968 English ed.)

that Castro promised a moderate or liberal revolution, while in the event the revolution turned out to be radical and confiscatory.

One response might be that revolutions are not made of documents, even revolutions that are led by lawyers. The Mexican land reform, as finally reflected in the 1934 Agrarian Code, bears only a hazy resemblance to the Plan of San Luis Potosí and the Plan of Ayala. But a "lawyer's argument" might be added: Castro included in the same speech a projected fifth revolutionary law. This law

> would have ordered the confiscation of all holdings and ill-gotten gains of those who had committed frauds during previous regimes, as well as the holdings and ill-gotten gains of all their legatees and heirs. To implement this, special courts with full powers would gain access to all records of all corporations registered or operating in this country, in order to investigate concealed funds of illegal origin, and to request that foreign governments extradite persons and attach holdings rightfully belonging to the Cuban people.[42]

The theoretical basis for such a law is the same as that for the Mexican principle of restitution; it is, indeed, a theory that *defends* property interests by emphasizing the rights of rightful owners against those who steal from them. Similar laws of "illicit enrichment" have been enacted in Argentina (to reach the properties of Perón and his close associates), Venezuela (Pérez Jiménez), and the Dominican Republic (Trujillo). The crucial question with respect to such a law is not its justification in the abstract, but the fairness of its application. For a critical evaluation of the Cuban experience in the first years of the revolution, see *Cuba and the Rule of Law* (Int'l Comm'n of Jurists 1962).

In rejoinder to this claim of traditional legality, critics of Castro might argue that while some of the Cuban confiscations were directed against Batista and his henchmen, a greater proportion of them were directed against foreign owners, particularly United States interests, in violation of the rules of international law. It is true that the classical standard of international law is that an expropriating government must make "prompt, adequate and effective" compensation for its taking of property of foreign owners. While there is evidence that this standard is undergoing change, so as to permit deferral of payment in cases of takings for purposes of general economic and social reform, still some compensation remains the norm of international law. "The duty of a government to compensate in case of nationalization is almost universally recognized."[43]

Fidel Castro's speech, quoted above, also included this remark:

> More than half of the most productive land belongs to the foreigners. In Oriente, the largest province, the lands of the United Fruit Company and West Indian Company join the north with the south coasts.[44]

---

[42] *Ibid.*

[43] Domke, "Foreign Nationalizations," 55 *Am. J. Int'l L.* 585, 603 (1961). See also Sohn and Baxter, "Responsibility of States for Injuries to the Economic Interests of Aliens," 55 *Am. J. Int'l L.* 545 (1961).

[44] F. Castro, *History Will Absolve Me* 46 (1968 English ed.).

What would adherence to the classical rule of international law have meant to the Cuban land reform? Later in this section we shall see how reforming governments have compensated owners of expropriated land with bonds, or in other ways that fall short of the classical rule of international law, and we shall see how that rule is coming to be modified. The Cuban government did, in fact, offer to pay North American owners of expropriated property in bonds. The catch was that the bonds were to be financed only out of the proceeds of sugar sales to the United States – and the United States government had abandoned the Cuban sugar quota. In the first two years (1959-61), some 28% of the lands taken for purposes of the Cuban land reform were taken from North American owners without payment. Only 27% of those lands were taken from private owners pursuant to the Agrarian Reform Law of 1959.[45]

J. LE RIVEREND, CONCLUSIONES SOBRE LA REFORMA AGRARIA CUBANA

in *Les Problèmes Agraires des Amériques Latines* at 653, 655 (1967)

. . . The Cuban Agrarian Reform, like others, has had its costs. Nevertheless, the costs have been reduced substantially in comparison with the others, since we have obviated the payment of compensation for lands [taken]. Compensation is considered by many authors who are very learned in these matters to be a factor that totally impedes the possibility of an effective agrarian reform. We know well that the cause for the greatest debate lies precisely in this point which has excited the greatest opposition to the Cuban Agrarian Reform on the part of certain foreign and domestic economic interests. It is not appropriate for us to get entangled here in a theoretical or philosophical discussion about private property; but we do have something to say. Latifundia in Cuba, through continued exploitation for many years, have produced their original prices many times. . . . A global figure based on North American financial sources states that from 1946 to 1954, North American properties in Cuba, representing some 700 million dollars of investment, produced more than 600 million dollars of profit. Other data permit one to affirm that every ten or fifteen years the entire invested capital was wholly recaptured. Calculate the quantity of profits extracted during the course of sixty years! Obviously we owed nothing to the latifundistas, either individuals or companies. In any case, the efforts carried out by the Revolutionary Government to make compensation in a form that would not impede the real possibilities of development were airily rejected by the foreign companies, and even by the government of the United States. Now, then, the campesinos who were medium owners, expropriated by reason of possessing more than 76 hectares, are presently receiving compensation, in conformance with the law of October 13, 1963. Without the payment of great amounts of compensation, the nation

---

[45] See Chonchol, "Análisis Crítico de la Reforma Agraria Cubana," *El Trimestre Económico,* vol. XXX(I), No. 117, p. 69, at 97 (1963); Gutelman, "The Socialization of the Means of Production in Cuba," in *Agrarian Problems and Peasant Movements in Latin America* at 347, 355 (R. Stavenhagen ed. 1970).

can confront its future tasks serenely; if we had paid the abusive compensation which the latifundistas tried to recover, scarcely a minimum settlement of campesinos could have been accomplished, on infertile marginal lands or public lands. In other words, it would have been a reform with such a slow rhythm of realization that it doubtless would have been lost in the shadows of the future.

Confiscation is not unknown in United States history. The American Revolution produced its share of confiscations; laws confiscating or placing special taxes on property owned by Tories were enacted by every one of the thirteen colonies. See C. Van Tyne, *The Loyalists in the American Revolution* 275-81, 335-41 (1929) ("To prevent 'dangerous monopolies of land,' the estates were to be divided and sold in small tracts." p. 279.) The famous case of *Martin v. Hunter's Lessee,* 1 Wheat. 304 (1816), dealt with the validity of Virginia legislation confiscating Tory-owned land. During the Civil War, both sides enacted general legislation confiscating property owned by their opponents. Since the Union armies eventually penetrated deep into the South the question naturally arose: what to do with all the property that was coming into the government's hands, not only through confiscation, but also as a result of delinquencies in the "direct tax," an indirect form of confiscation? In 1864, William Whiting, Solicitor of the War Department, wrote a letter to the Committee on Public Lands of the House of Representatives, in which he advocated what we should now call a land reform. His letter is contained in W. Whiting, *War Powers Under the Constitution* 469-78 (43d ed. 1871). A far-reaching amnesty, proclaimed by President Andrew Johnson, prevented this proposal from reaching the proportions of a land reform. However, many of Whiting's recommendations were carried out on lands that remained in the hands of the government, through the operation of the Freedmen's Bureau Act, 14 Stat. 173 (1866), which authorized the sale of land at low cost and in small parcels to former slaves, which land was to be inalienable for six years.

The abolition of slavery was itself an uncompensated taking of property interests — although many proposals for compensating the slaveowners had been made before the Emancipation Proclamation and the 13th Amendment ended the debate. Emerson once commented that it was the slaves — not their owners — who deserved to be compensated. Compare Madero's Plan of San Luis Potosí, page 278, *supra,* which proposed just such a compensation for the Mexican villagers who were reclaiming their land.

Other examples of uncompensated destruction of property rights or their equivalents in North American law are the abatement of public nuisances, and the withdrawal of public utility franchises. Indeed, such regulations as zoning ordinances or minimum-wage laws are, in their economic effects, partial takings. Presumably all the examples mentioned have some basis in arguments that are analogous to the social function theory. Is it appropriate to say that confiscation is justified only when the ownership interest in question has failed to perform its social function? Recall the argument of Le Riverend, *supra,* that foreign investors in Cuba had already recouped their investments many times over when they lost their properties. Is that an argument based on the social function theory? Would a supporter of the Cuban revolution say that the land reform should have spared from confiscation any sugar plantation that was operating efficiently and paying cash wages to its labor force? If not, then is the social function theory inadequate to serve as a doctrinal justification for the Cuban land reform? Or does the Cuban experience suggest that the Venezuelan law's definition of the social function of ownership is too narrow?

An article that has had much vogue in underdeveloped countries is Bronfenbrenner, "The Appeal of Confiscation in Economic Development," 3 *Economic Development and Cultural Change* 201-13 (1955). The title alone has been a popular citation, despite the author's reminder that he was not advocating confiscation, but warning investor countries to expect it and defend against it.[46]

Bronfenbrenner's thesis is that confiscation is an attractive device for a government which wants to achieve rapid development "without sacrifice of the scale of living of the mass of the population . . . by shifting income to developmental investment from capitalists' consumption, from transfer abroad, and from unproductive 'investment' like luxury housing." He uses economic models to illustrate that confiscation gives the government control over the investment of the income from the confiscated property, and that even a highly inefficient investment for developmental purposes can produce substantial changes in per capita income growth over a generation. Even his figures for forced-draft industrialization on the Stalin model are gloomy, however, in relation to the expectations which have been awakened in the minds of many in the underdeveloped world. When it is added that he has used a very conservative net population growth figure (1.5% per year), the picture becomes even more discouraging; Latin America is expected to grow at a net rate of around 3% over the next generation. Even confiscation, given Bronfenbrenner's thesis and a 3% yearly population growth rate, will not produce substantial per-capita growth.

Despite the obvious attractions of confiscation, with the exception of Cuba, the tendency among the countries of Latin America which have experienced land reform has not been to confiscate openly. Without exception, the legislation provides for payment for expropriated land. This is not to say that the reforms have eschewed confiscation; it is to say, however, that the forms of compensation have been retained, and that confiscation has been somewhat disguised, although not very subtly. The principal techniques for disguising non-payment have been the use of deferred payment schemes — agrarian bonds — and the valuation of property at less than market values. The next two sections explore these techniques.

---

[46]See Bronfenbrenner, "Second Thoughts on Confiscation," 11 *Econ. Development and Cultural Change* 367 (1963).

2. **Deferred Compensation**

D. TOVAR CONCHA, LA TESIS CONSERVADORA SOBRE PROPIEDAD

in *Tierra:* 10 *Ensayos Sobre la Reforma Agraria en Colombia*
at 235, 242-43 (1961)

[These are remarks of a Senator, a member of the Conservative Party, before a Senate committee considering the bill which became the Colombian land reform law of 1961.]

We defend the thesis that compensation must be made prior to taking because the Constitution says so. And we defend the thesis that compensation must be paid in money, because we so understand the Constitution. The constitutional principle may be good or bad, but it is a constitution. If it is bad, we expect that an appropriate amendment will be presented, and at that time we shall consider the problem But for the moment what we desire is that the Constitution be respected. [Article 30 of the Colombian Constitution is reprinted at pp. 286-87, *supra.*]

Payment is proposed for the expropriated lands by means of bonds. That is to say that the requirement of "prior compensation" will be fulfilled in bonds. Is that constitutional? I do not believe so.

If compensation corresponds to "damages"; or if it corresponds to a *conditio juris,* the payment must be in money. And that is so because of what money is; because of its juridical nature.

If the Constitution of 1936 had contemplated non-monetary forms of compensation, it would have said so. The Senate should not forget that the Spanish Constitution of 1932, which had such an influence on ours of 1936, foresaw that situation when it said that the statute law would establish the forms of compensation. Is there something similar in our own Article 30? No. Consequently it must be accepted that compensation must be in money. . . .

C. LLERAS RESTREPO, ESTRUCTURA DE LA REFORMA AGRARIA

in *Tierra: 10 Ensayos Sobre la Reforma Agraria en Colombia*
at 11, 63-64 (1961)

[This is a very brief excerpt from a long report which was the principal official statement of position concerning the same bill, made by a Senator and member of the Liberal Party who was the single most influential individual in the enactment of the law, and who later served as President of Colombia from 1966 to 1970.]

Persons who are still not completely familiar with the constitutional reform of 1936, supported in referendum by the Colombian people in the plebescite of 1957, continue to argue that there can be no expropriation without full and previous compensation in cash. But such pretension has no support in the text of the Charter.

[The Senator quotes article 30 of the Constitution, which concludes: "Nevertheless, the legislative power, for reasons of equity, shall have the power to determine those cases in which there shall be no compensation, by means of the favorable vote of an absolute majority of the members of both Houses."]

Thus it is obvious that the legislature is also sovereign to determine when reasons of equity are present. Now then, if the statute law can say that in one case there is no need for compensation, with much greater reason it can say that compensation be only partial, that it be paid in instruments [bonds] of the State or that it be paid in installments. The greater includes the lesser power, according to a well known juridical axiom. And it should be remembered that in the course of the debates over the constitutional reform of 1936 precisely this point was raised, and not only Dr. Darío Echandía, co-author of the reform, but also the parliamentary representatives were in accord as to the indicated interpretation, and they left it so expressly.

There is not, then, any difficulty of a constitutional origin preventing the articles of the agrarian project from being converted into law.

A. LOPEZ MICHELSEN, HACIA UNA VERDADERA REFORMA QUE COMPLETE LA "REVOLUCION EN MARCHA"
in *Tierra: 10 Ensayos Sobre la Reforma Agraria en Colombia*
at 85, 93-94 (1961)

[This is a statement by the legislative chief of the Revolutionary Liberal Movement, in floor debate. In 1974, López was elected President of Colombia.]

In accordance with Article 30 of the Constitution, which pertains to the Reform of 1936, there exist two classes of expropriations: one for reasons of *public purpose* and *social interest,* another for reasons of *equity.* With respect to expropriation for reasons of public purpose and social interest, defined by the Legislature, expropriation is authorized, provided there be judicial decision and prior compensation. . . .

Then I affirm the following: When compensation is not prior, when it is made in five installments, or when it is made in bonds, the statute law should be based, not on the article requiring prior compensation, but on the article which requires reasons of equity, because, in accordance with the judicial principle that the greater includes the lesser power, and based on the power to expropriate the land without any compensation, it is obvious that expropriation with partial compensation or with compensation in installments can be made, based on this article.

[Lopez is concerned that an expropriation based on the theory of public purpose might be subject to judicial review, and might be held unconstitutional in the event that compensation should not be paid prior to the taking of the property.]

This possibility of expropriation for reasons of equity is particularly delicate, considered in the light of foreign investments, of the Alliance for Progress, and of "due process of law." . . . It is particularly delicate, because, as I say, and as [Senator Carlos Lleras Restrepo] says in his study of this agrarian reform project, equity is a concept which is not subject to review by the Supreme Court of Justice. All Colombian laws may be challenged before the Court on the ground of unconstitutionality, that is to say, making a comparison between the statute law and the Constitution. But when questions of equity are put in the hands of the Legislature, no one can complain before the Court against a law, arguing that it is inequitable and that the Court should decide whether there is equity or not, because the Court only decides on questions of law. Equity is discretionary with the Legislature, which is the branch with power to decide (and so the text states) when there is equity. Then, if an expropriation with bonds is presented, as this agrarian reform project suggests, the compensation is neither prior nor complete, because bonds are not the same as cash payment, and the expropriation must be based on the article concerning equity, since the greater includes the lesser power.

Doctor Carlos Lleras understands it thus, and in his exposition of purposes of the law he makes the same argument. But the truth is that in the very context of the law the invocation of equity is not defined, and above all there was no reference to the quorum required in cases of equity, which is that of an absolute majority. Whenever the equity argument is to be used, it is necessary to determine equity in each case and also to adopt the law with the absolute majority required in cases of equity. This would be the "due process of law" of which Senator [Hubert] Humphrey speaks, with respect to land ownership, in Colombia.

A. GOMEZ HURTADO, EL AUTENTICO CONTENIDO DE UNA REFORMA AGRARIA
in *Tierra: 10 Ensayos Sobre la Reforma Agraria en Colombia*
at 169, 192-94 (1962)

In the first place we have the so-called uncultivated lands. The determination that the land is "uncultivated" is made through a system that gives our colleagues the opportunity to make an analysis of the rectitude and efficiency of the systems which the project proposes. But once it is established that the lands are uncultivated, they are paid for in bonds of class B with 2% interest, over 25 years. I believe that, to begin, it is necessary to establish the current rate of interest. The country's rate of interest today is 10% in banks; in non-bank transactions it is 12%. In a magazine commonly distributed here, the "National Statistical Bulletin," we see how the mortgages given in Bogotá have even reached the usurious levels of interest of 18 and 24 per cent. But let us limit ourselves to the bank interest rate of 10% or the non-bank rate of 12%. . . . Then, how much is a bond worth which produces 2%? That is elementary. It is a matter of applying a simple rule of short division. Then we find that if the current interest is 12%, the bond is worth 16.66% of face value; if the interest is 10%, the bond is worth only 20%. That is to say, if a property owner given bonds with a nominal value of 100 pesos is going to sell them as a function of their income-producing capacity, he will sell them for 20 pesos. If we consider the current interest to be 12%, he will have to sell them for 16.66 pesos.

There is, then, a confiscation of 80% in the first case, or 83-1/2% in the second case. Why is there a confiscation? Because the bond has no market. It is very difficult to get anyone to buy a bond of 2% at 25 years. Because the bond has nothing except a possibility of being received at par by the Institute: for the payment of 15% of the principal [in payment for parcels] in some cases of colonization. . . . Then the person who receives those bonds, which for him have an income-producing capacity of scarcely 20%, has to suffer the consequences of devaluation. Instruments of fixed interest, as is well known, have no corrective power in the face of devaluation of the currency. Here I have figures from the Bank of the Republic, which show that the currency in the last eight years has lost 50% of its purchasing power. That means that in 25 years the bonds with which these uncultivated lands will be paid will value zero, and since they have had an income-producing capacity of 2% the confiscation has been practically 96.96% of the commercial value.[47]

COLOMBIA: ACT NO. 135 OF SOCIAL AGRARIAN REFORM
December 13, 1961, Diario Oficial No. 30961, December 20, 1961, p. 801,
as amended by Act No. 1, January 26, 1968 (FAO translation)

62. Land acquired by the Institute as a result of voluntary sale or expropriation shall be paid in the following manner:

1) for uncultivated land, in class B Agrarian Bonds issued in pursuance of this Act;

2) for improperly farmed land, in cash. An amount equivalent to 20 percent of the price shall be paid on the date of the transaction without, however, exceeding a maximum of one hundred thousand (100,000) Colombian pesos. The remainder shall be payable in twelve successive annual instalments of an equal value, the first of which shall fall due one year after the date of the transaction;

3) for land not accounted for under the two preceding paragraphs, in cash. An amount equivalent to 20 percent of the price shall be paid on the date of the transaction without, however, exceeding a maximum of three hundred thousand (300,000) Colombian pesos. The remainder shall be payable in five successive annual instalments of an equal value, the first of which shall fall due one year after the date of the transaction.

The payment term referred to in subparagraph 2 hereof shall be reduced to eight (8) years if the owner is able to demonstrate from his income returns and statements of property for the immediately preceding three (3) tax periods that he obtains from the land in question more than 70 percent of his liquid income and at the same time that the value of the said holding represents at least 50 percent of his negotiable property.

The amount of the payment to be made by the Institute at the time of completion of the transaction shall, in accordance with paragraphs 2 and 3 above, amount to up to seventy five thousand (75,000) and one hundred and fifty thousand (150,000)

---

[47]For a description of the political maneuvering required to enact the Colombian law, see A. Hirschman, *Journeys Toward Progress,* ch. II (1963). [Eds.]

Colombian pesos respectively, if the 20 percent referred to therein does not reach either of such figures as the case may be.

The Institute shall pay interest at the rate of 4 percent *per annum* on the amounts outstanding to its charge under paragraph 2 above and at the rate of 6 percent *per annum* on amounts outstanding under paragraph 3 of this Article. Such interest shall be paid at the expiry of each six-month period.

The Institute's liabilities whether in respect of capital or of interest shall be guaranteed by the State and may at the request of a creditor be divided into two or more promissory notes which shall not be negotiable in accordance with Act No. 46 of 1923 and shall not be issued for sums of less than fifty thousand (50,000) Colombian pesos. They may, however, be transferred and ceded as guarantee in accordance with the provisions of Title XXV, Book IV of the Civil Code.

The owners of land referred to in paragraphs 2 and 3 above shall be entitled to full payment by the Institute at the time of the conclusion of the transaction and to payment of any part outstanding to their credit thereafter in Class A Agrarian Bonds at face value. Any person to whom such credit rights have been transferred shall automatically thereby acquire this entitlement.

The Institute may refrain from making payment in bonds when such bonds as it has in its possession are of shorter term than that within which this Article lays down that payment of the value of the land that it acquires shall be completed. . . .

74. The Government is hereby authorized to issue Agrarian Bonds in the quantity and manner and of the type specified in this and the succeeding Articles.

An issue shall be made to the value of two thousand million (2,000 million) Colombian pesos of Class A Bonds and of up to six hundred million (600 million) Colombian pesos of Class B Bonds.

Class A Bonds shall be issued in successive annual series of two hundred million (200 million) Colombian pesos each and the first issue shall be made within sixty (60) days from the date on which the Colombian Land Reform Institute starts operation. The second issue shall be ordered by the Government in accordance with requests to the effect by the Managing Board of the Institute and after approval by the Ministry of Agriculture and shall go forward in successive series of not less than five million (5 million) Colombian pesos each.

Once the Bonds in each series have been issued, the Government shall deposit them in the *Banco de la República* making them payable to the order of the Institute, and from that moment forward they shall be deemed part of the Institute's property.

75. Agrarian Bonds shall be of the following types:

Class A carrying 7 percent interest *per annum* to be amortized over fifteen years.

Class B carrying 2 percent interest *per annum* to be amortized over twenty-five years.

Interest shall be payable at the conclusion of each quarterly period; the Bonds shall be amortized by the accumulative fund system of gradual amortization in sixty and one hundred quarters respectively depending on the class to which they belong, and with effect from the first three months following their issue through the drawing of lots at face value. Both the capital and the interest shall be free of all national, departmental and municipal tax other than income tax and other taxes assimilated thereto. . . .

77. The Institute shall issue class A Agrarian Bonds only when the owners of land which it acquires in pursuance of this Act request payment for their land in such Bonds or use them to pay off the credits made by the Institute as a result of the acquisition.

The Institute shall, however, use the funds it receives from the State in interest and amortization on the Bonds to meet any cash payments to which the acquisition of land gives rise, and it may also use such funds to prepare land for cultivation through irrigation works, the regulation of water courses and land reclamation works in accordance with Articles 68 *et seq.* of this Act.

The Institute may also use class A Agrarian Bonds as guarantee for any credit transactions which it carries out under the foregoing paragraph. It may also use any sums it is due to receive from the State on account of the Bonds for the same purpose.

78. Class A Agrarian Bonds shall be received by the Institute at face value as the price of land which it sells in organized settlements areas. Class A Agrarian Bonds may also be used for paying the capital part of the periodic payments which persons acquiring land in land partition or consolidation areas must make to the Institute; the outstanding amounts which the purchasers of land referred to in the third and fourth paragraphs of Article 70 must pay and the tax on the increased value of land referred to in subparagraph 4 of Article 68.

Class B Agrarian Bonds shall also be received by the Institute at par for the payments referred to in the final part of the third paragraph of Article 70 if the owner was paid for the land with class B Agrarian Bonds and in the proportion corresponding thereto.

Persons acquiring land in partition or consolidation areas shall also be entitled to make payment in class B Agrarian Bonds at par up to an amount equivalent to 15 percent on capital of the instalment payments which they must make to the Institute.

So as to facilitate payment by persons receiving plots in partitioned land of the amount corresponding to the principal of their debts, the Institute shall organize a revolving fund which it shall use for the purchase of bonds on the open market and it shall then sell such bonds to its debtors for the average purchase price in the amounts and proportions which they need to make their payments.

Any bonds which the Institute receives in payment for the lands it sells may be used by it again for the purchase of other land.

CASE OF CONSTITUTIONALITY OF LAW NO. 135

Supreme Court of Justice of Colombia (Plenary Session 1964)
VII Derecho Colombiano No. 37, p. 3 (1965)

[Under Colombia's procedure for testing abstract questions of the constitutionality of legislation (see p. 125, *supra*), a citizen challenged the 1961 Law of Social Agrarian Reform. He urged that various provisions of the Law violated the principle of separation of powers, and he made a number of other arguments based on the constitutional aspects of administrative law doctrine. The Court's discussion of those issues — all decided in favor of the Law's validity — is omitted here. The plaintiff also argued that the deferment of payment of compensation for expropriated land (articles 62 and 74 of the Law) violated article 30 of the Constitution. He contended first that the compensation was not "previous," and secondly that the last paragraph of article 30, authorizing uncompensated takings for "reasons of equity," was not applicable, since (a) the Congress, in considering the Law to provide compensation, had not relied on this paragraph; (b) the paragraph did not apply to takings for "reasons of public purpose or social interest"; and (c) takings for "reasons of equity" required case-by-case consideration by the legislature, and could not be authorized generally by statute. The Court was able to avoid these latter arguments by holding that the payment provided by the Law was "previous." Only the portions of the opinion dealing with the plaintiff's contentions under article 30 are reprinted here.]

The Court considers:

The political constitutions of Colombia without exception have established the principle of the superiority of public over private interest. It follows that they authorize the expropriation of private property for reasons of public purpose, with the correlative indemnification to the owner.

The constitutions of 1811, 1812, 1821, 1832 and 1842 did not specify that the indemnification must be *previous*,[48] but those of 1830, 1853, 1858, 1863 and 1886 and the Legislative Acts Nos. 3 of 1910 and 1 of 1936 did indeed so require.

Article 10 of [the 1936 Constitution — the present article 30] introduced to the constitution of 1886 a reform of the highest importance: *the social function of ownership*, in the common good. This source of the owner's obligations results from the process of the socialization of law begun in the middle of the 19th century and vigorously pursued after the First World War.

Between the individualist conception of property — the result of a Revolution directed at redeeming the "sacred, inalienable and imprescriptible" rights of man — and the collectivistic conception which negates private ownership, the "social function of ownership" is seen as an intermediate system. But in this system at the same time that one current abolishes property as a right, radically transforming it into a *function*, which is the responsibility of the owner (who is like a state functionary), another current maintains property to be a subjective right of the owner, but attributes to it an essential function imposed by the interests of the community.

The function has not been substituted for property rights merely because article 30 of the Constitution says that "ownership is a social function". . . . The first part of the same article 30 guarantees "private ownership," acquired with a proper title in accordance with the laws. This interpretation, besides, is the only one that is consistent with the individualistic structure of our democratic organization, and such has also been the uniform jurisprudence and doctrine of the country. . . .

Thus, to the classical characteristics of ownership — to be perpetual, exclusive, complete, etc. — is added that of having a social function. But while the former

---

[48] All the italicization in this opinion is in the original. [Eds.]

characteristics were set forth in former times, the latter is barely beginning its process of conformation, after having been established in Constitutions after the recent world wars, especially in America.

Neither the Constitution nor the law defines the social function. *Function* is a specific activity directed at an end, within the organism which it serves. In other words, this new characteristic of ownership affects the exercise of the owner's right. Since the right is composed of the elements *usus, fructus and abusus* [Latin in the original], in any given moment the function . . . can affect one or all of them. And if this functionalism has an object, that of being *social,* it is obvious that the function established in article 30 of the Supreme Law has no other purpose than the common good, based inevitably upon the prevalence of social interests over private ones, in all instances and circumstances.

The constitutional text provides help in defining the function. It says of the function that it "implies obligations," which can be none other than the responsibility of the owner . . . toward the community. What are these obligations? We know from the language of the precept only that they are a product of the new function, and that this function is revealed publicly and collectively through their performance. But, being a generic characteristic of ownership, the function cannot be manifested except through burdens which must be specified by the legislative branch, as the Court (Sala de Negocios Generales) has said in a decision of March 24, 1943 (vol. LV, pp. 1966 and 1997. 399. 2a.) and in the cassation decision of Aug. 31, 1954 (vol. LXXVIII, p. 2145, 432, 2a.) The Framers of the amendment themselves applied the new principle in the last part of Article 30, in authorizing expropriation without compensation, and shortly after the constitutional reform took effect, Law 200 of 1936 imposed upon landowners the obligation of working their lands economically under the threat of losing them.

The Court began the process of interpretation of the constitutional reform in the following terms, according to the decision of the Plenary Session on March 10, 1938:

> The Framers of the 1936 amendment made the fundamental right of ownership relative, accentuating its subordination to the interests of the community, and also accentuating limitations on the free choice of the owner.

> The Framers founded individual ownership on the social function that involves obligations, in accordance with the views of modern social function theorists who reject the fixed and ever identical form attributed to that institution by the [classical] economic schools, recognizing that, since ownership has taken very different forms throughout history and is susceptible to very great modifications, it is fully guaranteed through [the present article 30] only to the degree that it responds to the collective necessities of economic life.[49]

The social function, according to this doctrine, accentuated the subordination of ownership to community interests, to the point that the guarantee given in the Constitution in favor of property rights is conditioned on the extent to which the

---

[49] Vol. XLVI, p. 1934, 193. [Footnote by the court renumbered.]

rights correspond to the needs of the community. It is precisely this which must be determined in this part of the present decision: whether the statute law can introduce [new forms of payment of indemnification in cases of expropriation].

Article 62 of the Law contains the formula by which the State should attend to the compensation payment corresponding to the expropriation of land. The motives of public utility and social interest that justify it are stated in the Law. [The opinion quotes art. 54, p. 288, *supra,* and summarizes art. 62, p. 344, *supra.*]

The plaintiff challenges article 62, not because it orders payment for uncultivated land in bonds, but because it authorizes installment payments for the balances to be paid on [improperly farmed or other land]. The Procurator General agrees, but he adds that it is contrary to the text of the Constitution to make payment in bonds on the basis of their face value.

Article 30 of the Constitution does not specify that the indemnification must be made *in cash* or *immediately.* The text does provide that payment be *previous,* and so it must be determined whether by being in bonds (lands of group a), or part in money and the balance *in installments* (lands of groups b and c) *it is no longer previous.*

Previous indemnification is, primarily, the definition and recognition of the right of the owner before the expropriation, so that, on the one hand, there will not be arbitrary expropriations and on the other, the owner will be able to count on receiving commercial goods or paper, alienable and certain, equivalent to the damage caused.

A) In regard to uncultivated lands. – Class B bonds are commercial paper with the backing of the State. They earn interest, are negotiable, are redeemed quarterly by means of drawing lots, and besides, can be given to the Institute in payment for lands, according to article 78 of the law. . . .

In this case the Law substitutes for an unproductive property, the ownership of bonds, guaranteed by the State, which earn interest and represent the commercial valuation of the land (art. 61, par. 5, Law 135). The interest is in any case greater than the income from uncultivated land. The constitutional precept does not guarantee private ownership to the extreme of protecting persons who do not work their estates; thus the reversion of titles to the state is permitted as a sanction applied to owners who allow their lands to go unexploited for the periods established in article 6 of Law 200 of 1936 and article 10 of Law 100 of 1944. Thus, with regard to uncultivated lands, for which those periods have not yet terminated, the compensation prescribed by articles 62 and 74 of the Law amounts to generous treatment to those who maintain their land apart from the performance of the social function, in expectation of an increase in value owing to some outside force. . . . The depreciation that the bonds might suffer in the market does not affect their intrinsic worth as an indication of compensation, because this risk is a phenomenon from which no securities, governmental or commercial – indeed, no property of any kind – can escape.

B) In regard to lands of groups b) and c). – With respect to lands that are adequately or inadequately exploited, or whose exploitation is carried out by small sharecroppers or tenants without the direct participation of the owner, it is true that the compensation is not made *entirely in money and immediately,* but the balance is paid in goods that are equivalent to money, since the balances are *credits* guaranteed by the State and which produce respectively, interest of 4% and 6% annually, paid twice a year. Furthermore, upon being reduced to *private documents,* at the option of the expropriated party or creditor, these obligations can be transferred or mortgaged in accordance with the Civil Code; or if they prefer, the owners receive Class A bonds, guaranteed by the State, bonds that earn 7% interest annually, are negotiable, are redeemed through quarterly drawings at their nominal value and may be used to pay the Institute for lands, in the cases under the conditions specified by articles 70 and 78 of the Law.

Credits with or without documents, or bonds. – These constitute the performance of the obligation of the State, previously satisfied, because from the beginning they are added to the patrimony of the expropriated party, thus accomplishing previous compensation. The Constitution, in order to make expropriation an easier and more adequate instrument for the common good, does not require payment in money, but simply indemnification. . . .

[The Procurator General argues that] payment in bonds conforms to the constitutional precepts, "so long as the bonds represent irrevocable and certain notes of a fixed monetary value, liquid, commercially acceptable and transferable, with an adequate periodical income, . . . and that they serve to indemnify the value of the expropriated property." But, [he argues,] it is not so when the Institute pays with bonds, computing them *at their nominal value,* be it a case of expropriation of lands of group a), or of those included in groups b) and c). The censure of the Public Ministry does not refer, therefore, to payment in bonds, which it accepts as being in harmony with the statute, but rather to such payment based on the nominal value of the bonds. But the Procurator General fails to note that in cases involving lands in groups b) and c), the payment in bonds depends on the will of the owner or expropriated party or of his successors. And as for lands of group a), we deal with uncultivated, abandoned lands, almost subject to an uncompensated reversion of title to the State.

It is superfluous to add that the concept of *indemnification* for expropriation cannot be confused with the concept of *price* paid in a sale. The latter is a bilateral agreement under private law, the result of freedom of contract, in which the buyer's obligation must be fulfilled in money. Expropriation is not a contract; it is not a sale, not even a forced one, such as those which take place at public auctions in certain cases; it is of an essentially different order, of public law, dedicated to the good of the community. For these higher motives, the Administration takes private property, and as this method engenders *damage* and not a *price,* it is rectified through an *indemnification.* . . .

The foregoing should influence the interpretation of article 30 of the Constitution, in order not to impose the geometric rigor of a contract upon the process of expropriation, but rather to promote the spirit of equity and justice that governs the institutions of Public Law, tested by the subject matter of this action of unconstitutionality, through the social orientation of Private Law.

And it is fitting to repeat that from among the various criteria for evaluation of land that have been accepted in the countries that have faced land problems, Law 135 has followed the criterion of market value as determined by experts (art. 61, par. 5),. . . .

[The decision was concurred in by all but three of the twenty members of the Court. Two of the dissenting opinions emphasized the separation of powers issues, but all three dissented from the Court's decision on the previous compensation issue. —Eds.]

Assuming that the Colombian Supreme Court had determined to sustain the constitutionality of deferred compensation for landowners under the land reform law, what alternative grounds were available for justifying that result? What would have been the advantage of resting decision on an alternative ground? Why did the Court rest decision on the ground that "previous indemnification" included compensation in bonds or other obligations of the government? If bonds, etc., constitute "previous indemnification," why did the Court discuss the social function of ownership?

VENEZUELA: CONSTITUTION OF 1961

Art. 101. Only for reasons of public purpose or social interest, by means of judicial decision and payment of just compensation, shall the expropriation of any class of property be declared. In the expropriation of land [immovables] for purposes of agrarian reform or of extension or improvement of towns, and in cases determined by law for grave reasons of national interest, the deferment of payment may be established for a determined time, or its partial cancellation may be established by means of the issue of bonds of obligatory acceptance, with sufficient guarantee.

VENEZUELA: AGRARIAN REFORM ACT

Mar. 5, 1960, Gaceta Oficial No. 611
Extraordinario, March 19, 1960, p. 1
(FAO translation)

172. In order to contribute to the financing of the Agrarian Reform under this Act, the constitution of an internal public debt, to be known as the Agrarian Debt, payable by the National Agrarian Institute and guaranteed by the State, is hereby authorized.

173. In accordance with the provisions of the preceding Article, the Directorate of the Institute, subject to compliance with the rules laid down in the Public Credit Act, shall be authorized to issue Agrarian Debt bonds, for the following purposes:

(a) Payment of the cost of property expropriated under this Act;
(b) Payment of the cost of property acquired by amicable agreement and intended for the Agrarian Reform;
(c) Financing of other investments necessary to the Institute.

174. The bonds referred to in the preceding Article shall be of three classes:

1: Class "A," maturing 20 years from date of issue, bearing interest at 3% per annum, the coupons of which shall be acceptable upon maturity for payment of national taxes. These bonds shall be nontransferable, but shall be accepted as security for loans made to expropriated owners by official financial institutions for agricultural or industrial purposes, or in reimbursement of credits obtained by such owners from the said institutions, prior to the publication of this Act, for agricultural purposes. Bonds of this class, the acceptance of which shall be compulsory, shall be applied against payment of the expropriation price of uncultivated properties or properties operated indirectly, as provided in Article 27, paragraph 1, and Article 179, paragraph 1, of this Act. Issues of bonds in this class shall be made in amounts not exceeding 100,000 bolivars each. [1 bolivar = approx. U.S. $.22. – Eds.]

2: Class "B," maturing 15 years from date of issue and bearing interest at 4% per annum. Bonds of this class, the acceptance of which shall be compulsory, shall be applied against payment of the price of expropriated properties other than those mentioned in the preceding paragraph, and of those acquired by negotiation or amicable agreement between the Institute and the owners. Issues of bonds in this class shall be made in amounts not exceeding 100,000,000 bolivars each. The other conditions laid down in respect of Class "A" bonds shall also apply to bonds of this class.

3: Class "C," maturing 10 years from date of issue, bearing annual interest at a rate to be fixed in accordance with the conditions of the bond market, and exempt from income tax. Issues shall be placed directly on the market through the Central Bank. These bonds shall be applied to the financing of other investments of the Agrarian Reform and to payment of the price of properties which, although fulfilling their social function, it has become necessary to acquire or expropriate under Article 33 of this Act, without prejudice to the provisions of the said Article relating to payment in cash for existing useful improvements, livestock and mortgages or privileged debts of the expropriated property, incurred and used for the development and improvement thereof.

175. Each bond shall be provided with a sheet of 20, 15 or 10 coupons respectively according to its period of maturity, and against presentation of which annual interest shall be paid.

176. The interest on and principal of the Agrarian Debt shall be paid by the National Agrarian Institute.

177. When the National Treasury is in a favorable position, the Government may decree the total or partial redemption of bonds prior to the maturity dates prescribed in Article 174, preference being always given to bonds bearing the highest interest and the earliest dates.

178. In accordance with the provisions of Article 174 relating to classes of bonds, payment of the price of properties acquired or expropriated for the purposes of this

Act shall be made by the National Agrarian Institute, without prejudice to the provisions of Article 33, and in conformity with the following scale:

1) Properties the expropriated portions of which do not exceed a value of 100,000 bolivars: in cash;

2) Properties the expropriated portions of which are valued in excess of 100,000 and not exceeding 250,000 bolivars: 40% in cash and 60% in bonds;

3) Properties the expropriated portions of which are valued in excess of 250,000 and not exceeding 500,000 bolivars: 30% in cash and 70% in bonds;

4) Properties the expropriated portions of which are valued in excess of 500,000 and not exceeding 1,000,000 bolivars: 20% in cash and 80% in bonds;

5) Properties the expropriated portions of which are valued in excess of 1,000,000 bolivars: 10% in cash and 90% in bonds;

Provided, that in all cases where the expropriated portions are valued in excess of 100,000 bolivars, the sum paid in cash shall not be less than this figure.

In the *Muñoz* case, page 294, *supra,* it will be recalled that the defendant owner argued that if his land was to be taken, then since his ownership had fulfilled its social function, the land could be taken only under the terms of article 33 of the Venezuelan law. Article 33 provides for payment in cash for livestock, improvements and improvement mortgages, and for payment in Class "C" bonds for the land taken. It will be seen from the foregoing extracts from the Venezuelan law just how significant is the difference between "A" and "C" bonds.

The Colombian Supreme Court justified the deferment of payment (payment in bonds) for uncultivated lands on the ground that ownership was required to perform a social function. Is the Venezuelan compensation scheme similarly pegged to social function considerations? In other words, to the extent that the Venezuelan compensation system is confiscatory, is that confiscation's justification to be found in the social function theory? Does this compensation scheme also reflect an "excessive size" theory of affectability?

CHILE, CONSTITUTIONAL AMENDMENT OF 1967
(As further amended through 1973)

Art. 10, par. 10. *The right of property in its various forms.* The statute law will establish the means of acquiring property, of using, enjoying and disposing of it, and the limitations and obligations that allow the assurance of its social function and that make it accessible to all. The social function of property includes whatever is required by the general interests of the State, public purpose and health, the best exploitation of productive sources and energies in the service of the community and the elevation of living conditions of the general public.

When the national community interest requires, the law may nationalize or reserve to the State exclusive domain over natural resources, capital goods or others, which [the law] declares to be of preeminent importance for the economic, social or cultural life of the country. It shall also incline toward the appropriate distribution of ownership and the constitution of family property. . . .

No one can be deprived of his or her property except by virtue of a general or special law that authorizes the expropriation for reasons of public utility or social interest, specified by the legislator. The expropriated owner shall always have the right to indemnification, whose amount and conditions of payment shall be determined equitably, taking into consideration the interests of the collectivity and of those expropriated. The statute law shall determine the rules for fixing indemnification, as well as the tribunal that shall hear claims concerning the amount, which shall in each case decide according to law, the form of discharging this obligation, and the suitable times and manner in which the expropriating agency shall take material possession of the expropriated property.

In the case of expropriation of rural land, indemnification shall equal the current valuation for purposes of property taxation, plus the value of improvements not there included, and it may be paid partly in cash and the balance in installments over a term not to exceed 30 years, all in the form and on conditions which the law determines. . . .

The small agricultural property, worked by its owner, and housing inhabited by its owner cannot be expropriated except by payment of prior compensation. . . .

Should agrarian bonds be payable in fixed amounts, set at the time of expropriation, or should the amounts of deferred compensation be adjusted for inflation when they are actually paid? Two countries of Latin America that have experienced severe inflation are Chile and Brazil. The Chilean land reform law of 1967 includes these provisions:

> 43. Compensation for expropriation shall be paid partly in cash and the balance in the Agrarian Reform bonds established by this law, and in conformity with the rules laid down in the following articles. Said bonds shall be received at their nominal value. . . . [Improvements shall be paid for in cash.]

> 45. In cases of expropriation [based on excessive size, corporate ownership, voluntary sales, or for certain reclamation projects] , compensation shall be paid 10% in cash and the balance in class "A" Agrarian Reform bonds. Notwithstanding this provision, if the expropriated estate has been abandoned, the cash payment shall be 1%, and if the estate has been poorly exploited, the cash payment shall be 5%; the balance, in either such situation, shall be paid in class "C" Agrarian Reform bonds. . . .

> 48. In case of expropriation [for purposes of an irrigation project] of an estate with respect to which there is in effect, a declaration of inexpropriability in accordance with article 20, the owner . . . shall be paid 33% in cash, and the balance in class "B" Agrarian Reform bonds. . . .

[Note: "A" bonds mature in 25 years, "B" bonds in 5 years, and "C" bonds in 30 years. All bear interest at 3%, calculated on the amount of each payment as it becomes due, adjusted as noted below. —Eds.]

132. . . . Each class of bonds shall be divided in two series. Each class of bonds to be given to the owner in payment of the balance of compensation shall be given in the proportion of 70% of bonds of the first series and 30% of bonds of the second series.

The value of each annual installment payment on bonds of the first series shall be readjusted proportionally to the variation of the index of consumer prices, determined by the Directorate of Statistics and Censuses, between the calendar month preceding the issue of the bonds and the calendar month preceding that in which the respective installment payment becomes due. The annual payments of bonds of the second series shall not be readjusted. [The 3% interest figure is to be readjusted in the amount of 50% of the proportionate readjustment percentage applied to the principal of bonds of the first series.]

Similarly, Article 157, par. 1 of the Brazilian Constitution was amended in 1969 to read as follows:

For purposes of this article, the Union may promote the expropriation of rural property through payment of just compensation, fixed according to criteria established by law, in special public bonds, with a clause of exact monetary correction, redeemable in a maximum period of 20 years in successive annual groups, ...

What is the argument for including such a sliding-scale provision in the terms of land reform legislation? If that argument was persuasive enough for the Chilean Congress to include the quoted provisions of article 132, why did the Congress limit the adjustment, applying it only to 70% of the bonds issued to each owner? Are the arguments on this issue merely a specialized case of the arguments on the general question of the legitimacy of confiscation?

Article 181 of the 1969 Peruvian land reform law provides favorable treatment for expropriated landowners who are willing to invest the proceeds of their compensation in the country's industrialization:

181. Bonds of the Agrarian Debt of classes "A," "B" and "C" shall be accepted at 100% of face value by the State Development Bank when the bonds serve to finance up to 50% of the capital value of a duly qualified industrial enterprise, to which the holder or holders of the Bonds also contribute cash amounting to the other 50% of said enterprise's capital value. The shares of said enterprise shall not be transferred during a period of ten years, except when the proceeds of their sale are invested in another industrial enterprise that is also duly qualified.

Does this provision represent a compromise of one set of purposes of a land reform for the purpose of advancing another set of purposes? (The agrarian bonds are all long-term — from 20 to 30 years — and all bear rather low interest — from 4% to 6%.)

E. SIMPSON, THE EJIDO: MEXICO'S WAY OUT
Pp. 219-28 (1937)

In the matter of agrarian bonds and indemnification in expropriations for ejidos, as in the case of all other aspects of the agrarian reform, there has been a very considerable amount of patching up and making over the laws. . . .

The government is authorized to issue Agrarian Public Debt, twenty-year 5 per cent bearer bonds to the extent of 50 million pesos in series as and when required. Amortization is by annual drawing when the market quotation of the bonds is equal to or greater than par at the time of the drawing (January of each year). Whenever the market value is less than par, bonds are retired by purchase in the open market.[50]

In case of nonpayment of interest (due at the end of each calendar year), or of the nonpayment of bonds favored in a drawing, both bonds and interest coupons may be used at their face value to pay "any federal taxes not especially pledged." Agrarian bonds are receivable at any time, whether drawn or not, at par in payment for public lands; for the payment of rentals or the purchase price of lands granted to villages and subdivided among their inhabitants; for guarantee deposits in any case where bonds of the public debt are permitted in place of cash, and for the payment of certain taxes. Also, agrarian bonds may be offered as collateral in the National Bank of Agricultural Credit up to 66 per cent of their commercial value.

Any person whose land has been expropriated for the purpose of ejido dotations may solicit indemnification from the Ministry of Agriculture within one year after official notification of such expropriation. The basis of indemnity in all cases is the assessed tax value of the land in question plus 10 per cent and allowances for the value of any improvements made after the date of assessment. Those dissatisfied with the evaluation placed on their lands have the right to request a review of their case before the District Courts.

Finally, it should be recalled in connection with this summary of the laws governing compensation in agrarian expropriation cases, that the decree of December 23, 1931, which reformed the original agrarian decree of January 1915 and denied the right of

---

[50]This "foxy" measure, not introduced in the law until December 29, 1928, is to be credited to the Portes Gil administration. It means in practice that agrarian bonds are always retired by purchase in the open market, since they have never been quoted at anywhere near par, much less at more than par. [Footnote by Simpson renumbered.] In 1938, holders of agrarian bonds were authorized to exchange them for ordinary government bonds of 40-year maturity. In 1951, during the Alemán administration, the law was amended to provide that small property owners whose land was taken in violation of their rights under certificates of inaffectability, and who had secured favorable administrative decisions on their claims against the government, were required to accept the same type of 40-year bonds in settlement. Flores, "Financing Land Reform: A Mexican Casebook," in *Masses in Latin America* at 331, 340 (I. Horowitz ed. 1970). [Eds.]

landowners to be granted *amparos* in agrarian cases involving the dotation of lands to villages, expressly states that the only legal recourse open to landowners affected by such dotations is to petition the government for indemnification and that solely in the manner set forth in the agrarian debt laws. . . .

. . . About the only conclusion that can be drawn on the basis of any calculation possible at present is that the agrarian debt, whether by that term is meant the potential debt for land already expropriated or what might with some awkwardness be called the potentially potential debt for the possibly 12.7 million hectares of crop land and anywhere from 25 to 40 million hectares of other types of land yet to be expropriated, is very large. Indeed, so large is the debt compared with Mexico's fiscal resources that one may say without fear of contradiction that it will never be acknowledged in an amount even approximating its entirety and that part which is acknowledged will not be paid at more than a fraction of its face value.

Some support for the foregoing statement may be found in the fact that of the total of approximately 9.7 million pesos of bonds amortized, less than 16 per cent have been retired at their face value, either in cash or in payments for certain classes of taxes, national lands, and so forth. The remaining 84 per cent has been amortized by purchases in the open market at prices far below the face value of the bonds. (The quotation on agrarian bonds at the present time — June 1934 — is around twelve centavos.) The failure of the government in recent years to pay interest regularly on the bonds outstanding has, of course, greatly facilitated the business of buying the bonds in the open market.

In the final analysis, the attitude the government will take with reference to its liabilities assumed and yet to be assumed under the laws governing indemnification in agrarian expropriation cases will be determined by the position eventually adopted toward the whole problem of the ejido. Attention has already been drawn to the fact that some of the older and more conservative of the revolutionary leaders have advocated, as part of their general policy of bringing the distribution of ejido lands to a speedy close,[51] that in the near future the agrarian bond mill should be stopped and that the government should undertake to pay in cash for any further expropriations necessary to complete the program of giving land to villages. . . .

. . . When the new Agrarian Code was enacted in March, 1934, nothing at all was said about payment in cash for initial ejido grants and even the provision regarding payment for *ampliaciones* was quietly omitted. If the younger group of *agraristas* now actively pushing the distribution of ejido lands "to the last man and the last village" has its way, the payment for expropriated lands in bonds will continue to be the order of the day. When these bonds will be redeemed, if ever, is another matter. It has already been suggested by one of the prominent leaders in the revolutionary group that the government will probably have to extend the date of maturity for agrarian bonds anywhere from twenty to sixty years. It may even come to pass that, while the laws are kept on the books as a gesture of international good-will and while bonds will

---

[51] After 1931, the government stopped issuing agrarian bonds. See J. Maddox, *Land Reform in Mexico* (American Universities Field Staff, 1959). The discrepancy in the text may be explained by the fact that Simpson's field work was largely concluded in 1931. [Eds.]

continue to be handed out to those with an appetite for unravelling red tape, the bonds will never be redeemed and the problem of compensation for lands expropriated for ejidos will be solved by the simple process of allowing it to sink deeper and deeper in the morass of bureaucratic inaction until finally it disappears altogether. . . .

In justifying its position with reference to the right to interpret the phrase *mediante indemnización* as permitting the state to indemnify owners of expropriated properties by the method of deferred payment (that is, in bonds) instead of in cash at the time of the making of such expropriations, the government has pointed first to the new conceptions of property established in Article 27 of the constitution and, second, to the doctrine of social necessity. As long as the protection and preservation of private property was conceived as the be-all and end-all of society, it was natural to consider that the right of expropriation was a right to be exercised with the utmost caution. Article 27, however, "in keeping with modern theories," is based on the assumption that "individual private property is social in nature for it is society which creates the right of private property and not private property which creates society." Under this conception expropriation becomes a right which the state exercises with as much freedom as social needs may demand. The point of departure, the entity to be protected, is society and not the individual. Whereas it is desirable whenever possible that, in expropriating private property, payment should be made previous to or at the time of the act, the state is by no means bound to follow this procedure. It may – and that is clearly the implication of the word *mediante* in Article 27 – if social necessity so dictates and if the financial resources of the nation so determine, defer payment.

In answer to the third charge of the *hacendados* to the effect that the bonds offered in payment for land taken for ejidos were without value, the government has held that, whereas it is true that these agrarian bonds cannot be sold in the open market for their face value, it cannot be claimed for this reason that the bonds were worthless. They may be used to pay certain taxes and in a variety of other ways in government transactions. Moreover, on the bonds which have been issued, interest payments have been kept up with at least a fair degree of regularity. Nor must it be forgotten that the government, although under no obligation to do so, has repeatedly extended the period within which petitions for bonds could be made by landowners whose properties have been affected under the ejido laws. The fact that the landowners have, for the most part, refused to avail themselves of this privilege and have consistently declared on all and sundry occasions that the bonds are worthless, is precisely one of the principal reasons why the bonds do not, and cannot, increase in value.

E. FLORES, TRATADO DE ECONOMIA AGRICOLA

Pp. 335-36, 344-45 (1961)

Only 170 [Mexican] national claimants were indemnified; they had presented 381 claims for the expropriation of an area of 222,797 hectares, which equals .55% of the total of 40 million hectares distributed up to [1959]. The compensation amounted to 24,426,800 pesos, which were paid in bonds of the public agrarian debt. [At present one peso equals $.08 in United States money. The inflation in Mexico has been somewhat more rapid than that experienced in the United States, so that earlier equivalences to the dollar were higher. —Eds.] .

The redemption of those bonds was achieved by purchases in the market, at quotations which fluctuated between 5% and 16% of their nominal value; or by accepting them, also with a penalty, in payment of certain taxes; or by exchanging them, in certain cases, for ordinary bonds of the internal public debt of 40 years.

In addition, an unspecified number of influential large owners were indemnified with bonds of the public internal debt; or compensated either in rural or urban lands or in cash; or even in all three of these forms. The area of lands obtained in this manner (as well as the amount of the compensations) is unknown, but it can be conjectured that, as in the foregoing case, it represents an insignificant fraction of the total redistributed lands. The rest of the lands given to *ejidatarios* [beneficiaries] were expropriated without compensation.

Based on the Law of January 6, 1915, and on Article 27 of the Constitution, around two million hectares (1,936,729), property of North American citizens, were affected, to which the owners attributed in their claims a total value of $56 million. With respect to lands owned by other foreigners, the government indemnified their owners by means of private agreement. An indeterminate number of foreign properties were acquired and continue to be acquired by means of mutually satisfactory agreements of sale.

The Mexican Government paid $12.5 million [U.S.], between 1938 and 1955, for lands expropriated from North American citizens in the period 1927-40, which was the critical stage of the Revolution. Although the United States insisted vigorously on the traditional principle of "adequate, prompt payment in cash," finally, as we have seen, the indemnification was agreed upon on a compromise basis, taking into account Mexico's possibilities for payment.

In such a way the third original goal of the agrarian reform was fulfilled, thus preventing the interference of foreign powers from making impossible the immediate application of laws designed to renew the economic structure of the country.

Once more the principle of International Law was confirmed that establishes, without departing completely from traditional norms, that the duty to compensate can be delayed and subordinated to the possibility of payment. This compromise appears to be just in the face of the double necessity of offering a reasonable degree of protection to the property of foreigners and of encouraging the State to maintain the reform even when the payment of compensation turns out to be greater than the State's immediate financial possibilities.

With respect to common, current and isolated expropriations, the rule of prompt and full indemnification is valid; but, on the other hand, with respect to the agrarian reform, given the importance of its objectives and its collective and impersonal character, indemnification must be adjusted to the possibility of payment by the debtor State, not only with respect to the value of the expropriated property but also with respect to the time required for payment.

It was suggested earlier that changes were impending for the traditional standard of international law requiring "prompt, adequate and effective" payment of compensation to foreign owners whose property is expropriated. The old standard is ably criticized in Dawson and Weston, " 'Prompt, Adequate and Effective': A Universal Standard of Compensation?," 30 *Fordham L. Rev.* 727 (1962). See also Karst, "Land Reform in International Law," in *Essays on Expropriations* at 41 (R. Miller and R. Stanger, eds. 1967). The reasons for bending the old rule are obvious. The expropriating state is typically underdeveloped, in desperate need of capital, and quite unable to make immediate compensation in cash. These factors are recognized in the Draft Convention on the International Responsibility of States for Injuries to Aliens, a model multinational treaty prepared by two North American scholars at the request of the International Law Commission. This draft states in Article 10, section 4, that a taking for purposes of general economic and social reform is not wrongful if compensation is paid "over a reasonable number of years," provided that "a reasonable part of the compensation due is paid promptly, and a reasonable rate of interest is paid on the balance." See Sohn and Baxter, "Responsibility of States for Injuries to the Economic Interests of Aliens," 55 *Am. J. Int'l L.* 545 (1961). Would the Colombian or Venezuelan laws on deferred compensation meet the standards of the Draft Convention?

----

3. Valuation of Expropriated Property

The Colombian land reform law of 1961 contained the following provision, which was later amended:

61. When the Institute after survey of a particular area considers acquisition of certain lands necessary to fulfill the social and public utility purposes set forth in Article 54, it shall proceed in the following manner:

1. It shall issue a summons to the owner or his agent in person, or if this proves impossible, through the procedure laid down in the relevant regulatory decree, to attend in person or send a representative so that a thorough survey may be made of the land concerned, including, if necessary, the taking of measurements.

Landowners must allow the aforesaid survey to be made and in the event of their opposing or hindering it, the Institute may use compulsion, imposing successive fines of up to five thousand (5,000) Colombian pesos.

2. Once the Institute and the owner of the portion of the farm which is to be compulsorily acquired have reached an agreement and have classified the land in accordance with Articles 55 and 58, the Institute shall have an estimate made by the experts of the body of appraisers which the Augustín Codazzi Geographical Institute shall form for this purpose; on the basis of the estimate the Institute shall proceed with negotiations to determine the purchase price to be paid in accordance with Article 62 of this Act.

3. If no agreement is reached regarding the price and classification of the land or if the owner refuses to sell voluntarily, the Institute shall issue a resolution laying

down the classification of the land, specifying the technical and economic considerations on which it is based; the Institute shall then order expropriation proceedings to be taken. This action shall be notified in person to the owner or to his agent or legal representative.

If such notification cannot be given in person, it shall be made by using the procedure set forth in the decree issuing regulations under this Act. The order made by the Institute shall be placed before the appropriate Administrative Disputes Court *(Tribunal de lo Contencioso Administrativo)* for decision as regards the classification of the land and its expropriability, if the owner of the land so requests within the five days following the notification. The Court, following the procedure laid down in the regulatory decree and after hearing the opinion of three experts appointed one by each of the parties plus one appointed by the Augustín Codazzi Geographical Institute, shall approve or alter the classification of the land and determine its expropriability.

4. Once the expropriation order has been issued, it shall be placed before the appropriate Circuit Judge *(Juez del Circuito)*. Notwithstanding the provisions of the first paragraph of Article 67, the Institute may enter a request to take immediate possession of the land whose expropriation it has ordered, depositing with the *Banco de la República* the equivalent of the value of the expropriated land in Class B Agrarian Bonds in the case of uncultivated land, or the cash amount that must be paid as a first instalment in the case of other types of land. For this purpose alone the value of the land shall be considered as that established in the estimate made by the Augustín Codazzi Geographical Institute; the estimate shall be attached to the request for expropriation.

It shall be understood that the Institute shall pay interest at the rate established in this Act on the unpaid value in accordance with the expropriation order from the date on which it enters into possession of the land.

5. Valuation for the expropriation proceedings shall be carried out by three experts appointed as follows: one, by the Colombian Land Reform Institute, another by the owner of the land and the third by the Augustín Codazzi Geographical Institute. If any objection is raised by any of the parties to the experts' finding and if the Judge upholds any such objection, three other experts shall be appointed in the prescribed manner, their finding being final.

In any matters not expressly laid down in this Act, the experts shall act in accordance with the relevant rules of the Code of Civil Procedure.

What standards are provided in the Colombian law to guide the valuation of expropriated property? The Supreme Court of Colombia, in upholding the constitutionality of deferred compensation, stated at the end of its opinion that the property taken was to be evaluated at market value. Does the provision cited by the Court (article 61, par. 5) justify that statement? If not, what is the origin of the assumption that market value governs the valuation process? What *does* article 61 provide, in place of a substantive standard for valuation?

A. LOPEZ MICHELSEN, HACIA UNA VERDADERA REFORMA
QUE COMPLETE LA "REVOLUCION EN MARCHA"

in *Tierra: 10 Ensayos Sobre La Reforma Agraria en Colombia*
at 85, 96-99 (1961)

. . . What is the spirit of the Agrarian Reform? First to try to buy in every case within a principle of bargaining. In his statement, Doctor Arias says that there will be expropriation only exceptionally, that this law contains barely a potential authorization to expropriate, but that in the majority of the cases, the land will be purchased. . . .

But even in cases of expropriation one must return to the commercial criterion resulting from the law of supply and demand, to market prices, because the law says that the proceedings will be carried on by means of an evaluation in which the expropriated owner names one expert, the Agrarian Reform Institute names another and the Augustín Codazzi Institute a third. I have said previously that the result was going to be perhaps even higher prices than those which would be arrived at through direct negotiation. It was only a hypothesis; I said: the expert, as happens in every case in which he represents the owner, will put the value in the clouds; the expert of the Agrarian Reform Institute will make a relatively low valuation and the Augustín Codazzi Institute will step in to make an intermediate estimate, so that the land will be acquired at prices exactly equal to those of the market. Well then, I was mistaken. It turns out the Augustín Codazzi Institute values property higher than the commercial prices. [The speaker mentions some high valuations which the Augustín Codazzi Institute has recently made.] And I ask myself: what is going to happen to the agrarian reform on the day when instead of having the Augustín Codazzi Institute play the part of the balancer, the owner becomes the balancer, since the Augustín Codazzi Institute makes the highest valuation, the owner the medium valuation and the Agrarian Reform Institute the lowest valuation. . . .

I have read various Agrarian Reforms. . . . A series of provisions conditioning the form of valuations always exist in order to avoid speculative factors. Our distinguished friend the Minister of Agriculture in his erudite study, shows how the value of the land in Colombia bears no relation to its productivity, in the greater number of cases. Land is like a money box; land is sought for purposes of maintaining valuation; . . . and ultimately land, according to the Tax Reform of last year, has been placed in conditions such that it may be declared at two, three or four times more than its real value during this year for the purpose of avoiding future taxable gains. So the price of land in Colombia is not as it might be in the United States, an economic relation between what it can produce for whoever might acquire it and what it might be worth in commerce. Thus we see the paradox that the best land in the United States, in the State of Illinois, is worth $400 to $500, or rather 4,500 pesos, at the exchange rate of nine pesos to the dollar [the value of the peso in 1974 was 25 to the dollar — Eds.], while in Colombia we see similar lands at 10,000, 15,000 and 20,000 pesos, according to the Augustín Codazzi Institute itself. [The speaker quotes Article 25 of the Venezuelan Agrarian Reform Law, and also a similar provision in a draft land reform law prepared for Peru with the assistance of members of the faculty of Cornell University.]

. . . I should like to go further, to mention the classes given in American universities concerning Agrarian Reform. Here I have some lectures of Professor Rosenstein Rodan, a professor of Massachusetts Institute of Technology. . . . [His students] are taught with respect to Agrarian Reform, that compensation should never be greater than 60% or 70% of the product [presumably the capitalized product —Eds.] of the expropriated estates. Where would expropriation in Colombia be if the criterion were the acquisition of properties for 60% or 70% of their product, at the time of the acquisition on the part of the State? . . .

I should like the defenders of the project, when they answer these objections, to show me the case of some other country where the announcement of an agrarian reform has produced so much enthusiasm, so much demand and so much prosperity for the landowners.

O. MORALES BENITEZ, REFORMA AGRARIA – COLOMBIA CAMPESINA

Pp. 269-70 (1962)

With respect to valuations, there is Article 3 of Law 20 of 1959. Said provision was adopted in order to forward a policy of colonization. It is proper to reproduce it, as well as Article 2, since they show very great similarities in their statements of this problem of land. The text of the two articles is as follows:

[Article 2 outlines the purposes of the 1959 Statute, which are similar to those of the Agrarian Reform Law of 1961.]

"Article 3. The distributions of land to which this law refers are declared to be of public purpose and social interest.

"By executive resolution of the Ministry of Agriculture shall be determined . . . the lands that may be expropriated [for the purposes stated in Article 2], by means of judicial proceeding and appropriate compensation. The value of this compensation shall not exceed 30% above the registered value [for land tax purposes] on December 31 of the year prior to the initiation of the expropriation action."

It should not be forgotten, also, that the Government has been proposing this Agrarian Reform to the country for several months. Therefore, it may be presumed that the owners have used the opportunity given them by Law 81 of 1960 and its regulatory Decree to place a commercial value on their lands, if they consider the tax registry values to be out of adjustment. This Law, which refers to taxes, has tried to avoid burdening owners heavily — with respect to capital gains — if their estates have not been correctly valued in the tax registry, in case they should later sell their lands. It was a good occasion avoiding any misadjustment of the price. . . .

One need not be a very acute interpreter to notice the similarity that exists between the ends and purposes announced in the two transcribed articles of the Law of 1959 and the object of the projected Social Agrarian Reform, which is announced in six points in the first article.

FR. GONZALO ARROYO, S.J., LETTER TO OTTO MORALES BENITEZ
October 29, 1962

in O. Morales Benítez, *Reforma Agraria – Colombia Campesina* at 275 (1962)

Unless enormous sums of money are available, which I do not believe to be the case in Colombia, an agrarian reform that compensates the old owners for the commercial value of lands will be very *limited* and *partial* in practice. A true solution to the problem of the *campesino* will not be obtained. The reason is that a true redistribution of incomes in favor of the *campesino* class is needed, so that the latter can be incorporated into the productive process. . . . In addition, on behalf of the thesis of tax registry value the fact may be advanced that the value of land is inflated above its real productivity, owing to the concentration of lands in a few hands. Still a third argument might be added: If landowners have paid taxes to the State in accordance with the tax registry value, they should also be compensated in accordance with this same value and not with the commercial price of the land.

The ambiguities in the Colombian Law concerning valuation were clarified seven months after the Law's enactment by an administrative regulation (Decreto No. 1904, 1962, art. 1), limiting the appraisers to values not exceeding 130% of the assessed tax valuation for the previous year, following the precedent recommended by Dr. Morales Benítez.   Professor Albert Hirschman called this regulation "perhaps the strongest [provision] of the whole body of new legislation . . . ."[52]

In 1963, however, after the change in administrations (from Liberal to Conservative), the rule was changed to permit an owner to make a new estimate for land valuation purposes, which valuation also serves for determining the land's value in cases of expropriation. Excessive valuations for tax purposes do not bind the acquiring agency. Decreto No. 2895, Nov. 26, 1963; Decreto No. 181, Feb. 1, 1964. This scheme is incorporated by reference into the 1968 amendment to article 61 of the basic land reform law.

E. SIMPSON, THE EJIDO: MEXICO'S WAY OUT
Pp. 225-26 (1937)

The vast majority of the landowners affected by the agrarian laws have undoubtedly felt that they have been very badly treated. They have held, quite

---

[52] *Journeys Toward Progress* 152 (1963).

naturally, that the whole system of compensation for expropriated lands is grossly unjust on the [ground] . . . that, in view of the chaotic and often confiscatory system of taxation, it has been the traditional and accepted practice in many states in Mexico to declare rural properties at something less than their real value and that, hence, indemnification on the basis of 110 per cent of the tax valuation is unfair. . . .

In reply to the charges and complaints of the landlords, the revolutionary government has said in effect that so far as the basis used in the evaluation of expropriated properties is concerned, if the *hacendados* have found this unfair, they have no one to blame but themselves. What could be more just than to take the hacendados' own statements, sworn before the tax authorities, of the value of their properties? Is the government in any way responsible for the fact that the landlords chose to undervalue their properties in order to defraud the government of taxes? Moreover, the landlords have been given repeated opportunities to rectify the valuation they have placed on their lands. Nevertheless, they have refused to take advantage of the government's efforts to make it possible for them to declare their properties at their true worth.

Can the government be blamed for this?[53] Finally, the government has pointed out that it is an acknowledged fact that the pre-revolutionary market values of farm properties were greatly exaggerated and dependent upon artificial tariff barriers and the exploitation of the peon. Since the revolution these values have been deflated and the post-revolutionary market values are probably not far from the fiscal values which the *hacendados* saw fit to place on their properties during their heyday.

VENEZUELA: AGRARIAN REFORM ACT

Mar. 5, 1960, Gaceta Oficial No. 611 Extraordinario,
March 19, 1960, p. 1 (FAO translation)

25. In evaluating rural properties to be acquired in whole or in part for valuable consideration for the purposes of the Agrarian Reform, the following factors shall be taken into consideration:

---

[53]"The Mexican Commissioners further stated that since 1914 the Government had given the owners various opportunities to rectify the fiscal value [of their property.] On the 19th of September of that year a law was passed to determine the value of real property in the Republic, and provided that said assessment would serve as a basis to establish the value in case of expropriation. Later the Constitution of 1917 established the same basis. The owners, however, did not correct their declarations at the time, nor have they up to the present time; as in spite of the fact that a regulation of the decree of October 11, 1922, was issued the 30th of May of the present year [1923], its object being also to determine the value of real property in the country, the owners continued to resist complying with the legislation in that regard.

"Under these circumstances, the Mexican Government believes that the owners have had the opportunity of placing themselves in a position not to suffer damage, and if any of them have not wished to take advantage of this opportunity granted them by the law, it is their own fault." Proceedings of the United States-Mexican Commission, p. 34. [Footnote by Simpson, renumbered.]

(a) The average production over the six years immediately preceding the date of acquisition or of the request for expropriation.

(b) The declared or assessed official value for tax purposes under enactments relating thereto.

(c) The acquisition price of the property in the last conveyances of ownership carried out during the ten-year period prior to the date of valuation, and the acquisition prices of similar properties in the same region or zone in the five-year period immediately preceding the date of the expropriation request or purchase proposal;

Provided, that although in evaluating properties the above-mentioned factors shall primarily be taken into account, any other factors which may be useful in fixing a just price and all those mentioned in the Act relating to Expropriation in the Public or Social Interest, shall also be taken into consideration.

Provided, further, that the valuation shall include, in addition to the value of the land, the value of the buildings, installations, chattels, equipment and improvements existing thereon.

Provided, finally, that the determination of value shall take into account only the actual fair value of the property, to the exclusion of any consideration of possible damages or disadvantage or of the sentimental value of the property.

Paragraph (c) of article 25 of the bill that became the Venezuelan law was originally drafted to refer to "the price at which the property was acquired ... in a period included between three and ten years preceding" the taking. What purpose would be served by inserting such a provision in place of the provision finally adopted?[54]

What purposes are served by Venezuela's list-of-factors approach to valuation, as compared to Colombia's failure to specify the factors to control valuation? Was it wise for the draftsmen of the Venezuelan law to use the word "production" in article 25(a) rather than "productivity"?[55]

---

4. Some Concluding Questions about Confiscation

a. Granted the nearly universal confiscatory nature of the reforms which we have considered, why is it that such pains have been taken to disguise the fact?[56]

b. The principal early Civil Code in the Soviet Union (Civil Code of the R.S.F.S.R. of 1922)[57] provided for compensation at market-value for property expropriated. The market price principle has been displaced generally by fixed prices — government

---

[54] See Comment, "Expropriation and the Venezuelan Law of Agrarian Reform," 6 *Colum. J. Transnational L.* 273, 296 (1967).

[55] The initial draft referred to "productivity." See *id.* at 295 n. 105.

[56] See Karst, "Latin-American Land Reform: The Uses of Confiscation," 63 *Mich. L. Rev.* 327, 369-72 (1964).

[57] The Civil Code was revised in 1964.

controlled prices. Buildings are expropriated at prices fixed by appraisals for tax or insurance purposes.[58] Cuba's 1963 law authorizing expropriation of medium-sized agricultural holdings also provides for compensation. See Le Riverend, p. 338, *supra,* and note this comment on Cuba: "No one has been more explicit or more unequivocal [than Fidel Castro] in assuring and reassuring the small peasants that the Second Agrarian Reform [1963] was the last and that henceforth their status would be fully respected." L. Huberman and P. Sweezy, *Socialism in Cuba* 115 (1969).

Why does a communist government adopt the principle of compensation? Is there any practical distinction between the wholesale takings of property associated with a social revolution and takings thereafter by the revolutionary government in power which would justify the decision to compensate for takings only in the latter case?

E. Expropriation: Institutions and Processes

Every modern Latin American land reform statute has created a specialized agency, empowered to carry out the reform. This agency, usually called the Agrarian Reform Institute, is charged with commencing expropriation proceedings, taking title to lands, compensating owners, and distributing rights in land to eligible campesinos. Even with the strongest support from the rest of the government, the Institute has a formidable task. In fact, many such Institutes have fallen victim to a variety of strategies of counterattack available to the opponents of land reform. In his long and bitter criticism of "counterreform" masquerading as land reform, Ernest Feder describes some of these strategies: The Institute may be underfinanced; its directorate may be dominated by landholders or politicians associated with them; "militant" staff members or directors may be transferred to positions where they are ineffective; other government agencies, jealous of their own prerogatives, may be less than cooperative; the Institute's staff, or its top executive leadership, may be accused of mishandling funds, or of ties to the revolutionary left, so that they spend their efforts in defending themselves; even physical threats may be made against zealous staff members or their families.[59]

Feder's list of horribles is a caricature, but like a good caricature, it outlines the essential contours of the problem of the embattled land reform Institute.[60] Latin American society is not alone in its propensity to assume that the enactment of a law is a sufficient response to a massive social problem; recent experience in the various anti-poverty programs in the United States suggests that the phenomenon is widespread. But this tendency is particularly marked in Latin America, where the difficulties are compounded by a serious shortage of trained middle-level managerial

---

[58]V. Gsovski, 2 *Soviet Civil Law* 79, 80-81 (1949).

[59]Feder, "Counterreform," in *Agrarian Problems and Peasant Movements in Latin America* 173, 192-98 (R. Stavenhagen ed. 1970).

[60]For a discussion of the ineffectiveness of the Colombian land reform agency, INCORA, see Findley, "Ten Years of Land Reform in Colombia," 1972 *Wis. L. Rev.* 880, 903-15.

personnel. In order to administer a complicated land reform law like Chile's 1967 law, a skilled bureaucracy is needed. In Mexico and Bolivia, de facto reform came about before any bureaucratic structure had been created; the agrarian bureaucracy in both those countries performed a clean-up operation on the aftermath of revolution. Land reform without revolution, however, appears to demand a substantial investment in administration – and an Institute that is vulnerable to all the attacks described in Feder's article.[61]

One of the chief institutional necessities of land reform is thus the establishment and nourishment of an agency to carry out the reform's essential functions, and the defense of such an agency against political undermining. The role of the lawyer in that process obviously is a limited one, and yet a legislative draftsman who foresaw the issues raised by Feder might make some suggestions relating to governmental structure – that is, recommendations for building into the land reform law some protection against political attack. What suggestions of this kind would you make, if you were counsel to a legislative committee that was drafting a land reform?

The rest of this section deals with two persistent issues in Latin American land reform: the role of the judiciary, and the problem of delay.

---

1. The Judiciary: Ordinary Judges and Agrarian Tribunals

J. THOME, THE PROCESS OF LAND REFORM IN LATIN AMERICA

1968 *Wisconsin Law Review* 9, 20-21*

Traditionally, the civil courts have had jurisdiction over questions and conflicts affecting property rights. The property law principles themselves are derived from the Civil Codes, which by and large reflect 19th century liberal ideas of the supremacy of the individual and the free exercise of private property rights. In recent times, however, a growing focus on "functional" principles of law has resulted in constitutional amendments and special legislation that restrict individual rights vis-à-vis those of the community. Examples are laws regulating rural leasing arrangements, transfer of property, and, in recent years, land reform laws. Consequently, these new principles and laws are often in direct conflict with certain dispositions of the Civil Code. While land reform and similar laws, because of their "special" character and subsequent enactment, would prevail over the prior Civil Code provisions, the influence and prestige of the Civil Code cannot be overlooked. Because of the nature of legal tradition and education in Latin America, where great emphasis is still placed on the general principles of law contained in the Civil Codes, judges are sometimes prone to interpret social reform laws in accordance with their own longheld views on

---

[61] In Cuba the National Agrarian Reform Institute, INRA, was initially staffed by members of Castro's Rebel Army, which provided a national administrative base for INRA's operations. See E. Boorstein, *The Economic Transformation of Cuba* 43-54 (1968).

*Copyright 1968, University of Wisconsin.

what law is really about. Even more important than legal principles or theory, however, is the manner in which law enforcement institutions, including the courts, operate in rural areas or the smaller cities. Not uncommonly, judges, mayors, and police chiefs are subject to the influence of large landowners and others with local vested interests. The reasons are simple: judges, police chiefs, and other local officials in Latin America are notoriously underpaid and provided with inadequate working facilities; judges in smaller cities are usually isolated from each other for months or years at a time – there are no annual conferences or conventions; and finally, their tenure may well depend on maintaining their local political contacts and friendships. Not surprisingly, then, while adequate social and economic legislation (such as labor and water laws) is not difficult to find in Latin America, in many cases it is ignored, inefficiently enforced, or implemented in a manner that unduly favors a given element of society. But in any case, civil litigation is a long, drawn out, and expensive process that few *campesinos* can afford.

In an effort to avoid these problems, as well as to create specialized or more sympathetic quasi-judicial institutions, many countries have limited the role of the regular courts in the rural areas or eliminated them altogether from the land reform process. Special agrarian courts have been established, or the whole land reform process has been entrusted to an administrative agency, or the courts have been restricted to reviewing narrow and specifically defined questions of law. Yet, as in the case of Bolivia, many of the same problems still persist: partiality is not hard to find, and land reform cases are often as long and complicated, if not more so, than other civil litigation.

A major factor responsible for the length of land redistribution cases is the procedure adopted by many land reform laws for purposes of expropriation and title distribution. Perhaps because of political realities that forced concessions or compromises or because of the *civilista* (overly legalistic) backgrounds of the lawyers who drafted these procedural laws, they are often extremely complicated, are full of legal formalities and loopholes, and have various stages of review that may reach to the president of the nation. In Colombia, for instance, at least 12 steps are required for a full expropriation including approval by the President of the Republic and judicial review by both administrative and civil courts. Not until the initiation of the last stage does the land reform agency enter into possession of the land – usually not less than two years after the initiation of the proceedings. Only then can the agency initiate the complex and also lengthy process of actually redistributing the land in question.

It will be recalled that Zapata's Plan of Ayala referred to "venal justice," by which was meant judges under the domination of those who would lose the most from Mexico's agrarian revolution. Article 27 of the 1917 Mexican Constitution reflected a similar concern, immunizing the expropriation process from judicial review.

In theory, the two major questions involved in a taking – the land's affectability and the compensation due to the owner – are separable; it would be quite consistent for the law to subject one of those issues to judicial determination or judicial review, but leave the other to an unreviewed administrative determination. In Venezuela, we have seen, expropriation is a judicial proceeding: as in the *Muñoz* case, the Institute brings an action in an ordinary civil court, alleging the grounds of affectability of the estate in question. The court determines that issue, and also sets the value of the property for purposes of compensation. While the *Muñoz* case suggests that an administrative determination of affectability is unlikely to be overturned by a court, there is some reason for belief that the Venezuelan judges have been more inclined to assert their independence on the issue of compensation.

How does the Colombian law differ from the Venezuelan, with respect to the role of the judiciary in determining the issues of affectability and compensation?

And in Mexico, since 1947, what is the judiciary's role in this process? which of the issues — affectability or compensation — lends itself better to judicial determination? Why?

The following extract from Professor Joseph Thome's article on the 1967 Chilean law shows that both the draftsmen of the law and the agency charged with administering it have been especially sensitive to issues of judicial review.

J. THOME, EXPROPRIATION IN CHILE UNDER THE FREI AGRARIAN REFORM

19 *American Journal of Comparative Law* 489, 507-09 (1971)

... When the acquisition is based on excess size, "corporate" ownership, or voluntary offers to CORA [the land reform agency], the landowner is paid 10 percent in cash and the balance in twenty-five-year Class "A" bonds. Nevertheless, if CORA can show that a property so acquired was either abandoned or inadequately exploited, then the form of compensation is the same as for properties expropriated because of abandonment or poor exploitation: 1 percent or 5 percent in cash respectively, with the balance in thirty-year Class "C" bonds. (As explained, an expropriation on grounds of abandonment or poor exploitation per se gives the landowner recourse to judicial review, not available under other grounds, and may delay the process for years; also, CORA prefers to acquire properties through amicable settlements with landowners, rather than following the entire expropriation process to its lengthy and costly conclusion.) . . .

Judicial Review: The Agrarian Tribunals

[The 1967 law] established one trial agrarian tribunal in each province (for a total of twenty-five) and ten appeal agrarian tribunals. These have exclusive jurisdiction over all conflicts arising from application of the law, particularly questions of expropriation. Each trial tribunal has one judge and two agronomists, while the appeal tribunals are staffed by two regular appeal judges and one agronomist.

This special court system was a conscious attempt to keep all land reform conflicts out of the regular civil court system, which is notoriously slow and conservative. To get the expropriated properties into CORA's possession as quickly as possible, [the law] stipulates that there are *no* appeals from judgments of the Agrarian Appeal Tribunals. Furthermore, the technical expertise of the members of the agrarian tribunals and their concentration on agrarian reform conflicts, together with special procedural rules, were supposed to ensure a more rapid process while guaranteeing the basic rights of affected individuals.

In practice, however, these goals have not been fully achieved. The Supreme Court, for instance, was quick to accept jurisdiction over land reform conflicts where the landowners claimed that the transitory articles of [the 1967 law] were unconstitutional even though these cases were being heard before Agrarian Tribunals. Although the Court in these and most other cases found that the applications of [the law] did not violate the constitution, nevertheless the appeals did postpone the taking of possession of the affected properties by CORA.

The goal of obtaining more technical and relevant judgments through the use of agronomists as judges has not worked well either. The agronomists, faced with the procedural complexities of a trial, have tended to unhesitatingly follow the lead of the judicial members of the tribunals.

Nor has the goal of a quick trial been attained. The principle that makes all trial proceedings in Chile extremely slow has not been eliminated from the supposedly summary proceedings of the agrarian courts: judges are passive; they only act when petitioned to do so by one of the parties. While it was foreseen that an entire process before the agrarian court would only take thirty-two days, in reality it is more likely to last several months or even years.

For reasons already discussed, CORA usually uses excess size and voluntary offers as expropriation grounds, both of which are rarely susceptible to judicial review by the Agrarian Tribunals. The bulk of the judicial review by the Tribunals, then, involves other matters which are not so important and which do not interrupt the taking of possession by CORA. These include claims that CORA assigned a compensation scheme different from that stipulated by law, that the required reserve right was not granted, and that the assessment by CORA of the "improvements" was erroneous.

Findings from the province of Valparaíso show that relatively few expropriations result in cases before the Agrarian Tribunals. Of the twenty-six expropriations in Valparaíso between July 1967 and March 1969, only six were contested in these courts.

The Bolivian land reform law of 1953, in article 166, establishes single-judge agrarian courts, to be manned by special judges as in Chile. There is no requirement that such a judge be a lawyer; many have been law students. Since much of the legal process of the Bolivian land reform has taken the form of confirmation of titles in persons who have occupied lands informally, is the use of special agrarian judges especially appropriate there? Do you agree with the Chilean legislative solution of appointing agronomists to agrarian tribunals along with lawyers? If you had to do without one or the other, agronomists or lawyers, which would you keep on these courts? Should the Bolivian agrarian judges be lawyers? Agronomists? Does the

Muñoz case suggest that perhaps Venezuela has established de facto agrarian judges, that is, the agronomists whose report was so readily accepted by the court?

---

2. Delay

The problem of delay is not wholly separate from the issue of judicial review, as Professor Thome has noted. But courts are by no means the only institutions responsible for delays in the reform process. Almost every writer on land reform agrees that an effective reform must be both massive and rapid, for economic and social reasons no less than political ones. But delay, the enemy of reform, has been built into some land reform legislation. We return to Ernest Feder, who notes the importance of speed in carrying out a land reform, and then comments:

> Compare this with the snail's pace with which reform *must* proceed in Peru. [Feder is talking about Peru's 1964 law, not the much tougher 1969 law. —Eds.] A careful calculation leads to the conclusion that the total time required by law before the agency can even begin to turn over estate land to the peasants (that is, not including the time required for the declaration of the area as priority zone nor the time needed for the actual land distribution and settlement itself) amounts to no less than thirteen months as a rock-bottom minimum, and it can be of unpredictable length if estate owners take advantage of the various legal maneuvers which the law authorizes, to postpone or set aside the expropriation of their estate which the law authorizes![62]

Other factors inevitably produce delay. An agronomist's report may need to be made in order to determine whether ownership has fulfilled its social function, as in the *Muñoz* case. Indeed, such a report may be meaningful only in comparison with an agricultural census that classifies lands. It is even arguable that the very decision to expropriate lands on an owner-by-owner basis — whatever the grounds for expropriation — involves time-consuming procedures that are a luxury beyond the institutional means of a reforming government. (The alternative, presumably, would be something quite revolutionary, such as wholesale takings by zone, irrespective of the level of cultivation, the size of estates, etc.) In fact, as we might expect, Feder calls the usual approach a "piecemeal" approach, which he says is doomed to failure.[63] Is it possible to have a land reform based, for example, on the social function theory, and to avoid reform-killing delays? Or is the notion of due process for landowners somehow inconsistent with an effective reform?

Sometimes the process seems a bit undue. Consider this example from Colombia: In one case there was a two-year delay between the Institute's initial determination to acquire the land and the court's disposition of the case on review of the Institute's

---

[62]Feder, note 59 *supra,* at 182.

[63]*Id.* at 183.

ultimate decision to expropriate. In that case, the court finally decided that the Institute had not complied with the formalities established by law; thus, the entire proceeding (determination to acquire, negotiations for purchase, and agency decision to expropriate) had to be commenced anew. The defect in the Institute's action was that it had failed to affix a copy of the notice of intention to expropriate to the principal house located on the land — although personal notice had been given to the landowner, and although the proper papers had been recorded in the local land registry.[64]

One way to reduce delays in the judicial process is to authorize a "quick-taking" procedure, in which the agency takes land and then argues about compensation. Most laws authorizing such a taking require the agency to make a deposit of some amount of money in court pending determination of the issue of compensation. (Obviously, once a taking has been accomplished, and campesinos have been settled on the land, the issue of affectability is largely academic. No one would expect a court to order newly-settled families off the land on the ground that the taking was improper. In practice, what is being argued about is, as in the *Muñoz* case, the level and quality of compensation. In the *Muñoz* case, the social function issue was argued by the defendant not to prevent the taking but to bring the case within article 33.) Professor Thome comments on the 1967 Chilean law's quick-taking provision, and shows how it has often been nullified in practice.

J. THOME, EXPROPRIATION IN CHILE UNDER THE FREI AGRARIAN REFORM

19 *American Journal of Comparative Law* 489, 510-12 (1971)

Although no exact data are available on the length of expropriation processes, a fair idea can be obtained by comparing the date of the expropriation decree for each property and the date of the organization of an *asentamiento* [campesino settlement] on it. . . . [V]ery few of the properties expropriated under [the 1967 law] had reached the asentamiento stage by October 1968. CORA, as of this time, was still concentrating on constituting asentamientos on those properties expropriated under [a 1962 law] between January 1965 and June 1967. Yet . . . 208 of the 478 properties so expropriated were as of October 1968 still waiting for the constitution of an asentamiento.

Some of these delays in taking possession can be traced to CORA itself. CORA has often waited until almost a year (the maximum period allowed by the law) after the date of the expropriation decree before depositing the amount required for taking possession. This was probably due to scarcity of funds, though the endemic inflation in Chile may also have played a role — the longer payment of a fixed cost can be

---

[64]The case is discussed, and the slowness of the Colombian procedure trenchantly criticized, in J. Thome, *Limitaciones de la Legislación Colombiana para Expropiar o Comprar Fincas con Destino a Parcelación* (Centro Interamericano de Reforma Agraria, mimeo, 1965).

delayed, the cheaper it becomes. CORA officials admit that it has often taken a long time to set the necessary valuation figures, particularly as regards "improvements." This may have been due to a shortage of sufficiently trained personnel, or to extended negotiations with affected owners.

Many of the difficulties with quick-taking, however, are the results of legal loopholes in [the 1967 law]. CORA could not take possession until it deposited with the Superior Civil Court the amount of cash compensation (1-10 percent of the valuation), and until the judge ordered the inscription of title in CORA's name at the appropriate Registry of Property. Landowners, aided by the conservative nature of most civil court judges in Chile, were quick to object to CORA's deposit on the grounds that valuations were incorrect. Many judges accepted these complaints for consideration, which then became subject to regular civil court procedures, notorious for their complexity and length. In many cases, appeals to higher courts occurred. Not until a final judgment was made could CORA enter possession of the property.

In the face of such problems, the Government introduced an amendment to [the 1967 law]. It was passed, and Law 17.280 of January 17, 1970 substituted new Articles 39, 40, and 41 for the original ones. . . . Among many important changes, the new articles provide that the deposits will be made at the appropriate Municipal Treasuries rather than at the Civil Courts; that in the absence of any tax assessment on the land, CORA will set its own assessment for the purpose of determining the deposit (subject to subsequent tax assessment by Internal Revenue Service); that CORA can obtain the inscription of titles of expropriated properties by presenting the necessary documents at the Registry of Property, rather than doing this through a judge; and that after complying with the above conditions CORA can enter possession of its own accord, and can request and obtain the assistance of the local public authorities. In addition, the new Article 41 provides that possession is no longer to be delayed by the existence of unharvested crops and establishes a new compensation scheme to take care of this situation.

Finally, the new Law establishes that all expropriations pending at the time of its enactment are subject to its provisions, thus enabling CORA to start all over again, under better conditions, to acquire possession of properties in the process of expropriation.

F. Land Distribution: Problems of Structure and Operation

1. Individual v. Collective Ownership

The "new agrarian structure" which emerges from a land reform may simply be the substitution of many little estates for a few great ones. For several reasons, the leaders who have carried out land reforms in Latin America have been reluctant to cut the beneficiaries entirely free. From the very beginning in Mexico, there has been tension between the proponents of individual ownership and management and the proponents of various forms of cooperative or collective systems. Basically, the latter position rests on certain assumptions about rural society in Latin America — in particular, about the need for a kind of paternal guidance and control of the *campesino*. These assumptions have been explored in Chapter I, and are considered again in Chapter VI.

The issue of paternalism is at the heart of questions concerning the form and content of the rights to be distributed in a land reform. It must be faced in deciding whether to distribute individual parcels or shares in a cooperative organization; whether to permit free transferability of the interest which the beneficiary receives or to impose restrictions on alienation, etc.[65] In deciding these questions, legislative planners must make the best possible accommodation of competing considerations such as: the level of agricultural production; political demands for "land," which may mean title, or something like it, to one who has no training in the sophistications of intangible property; the adjustment of agriculture to the rest of the economy. Ideology, too, plays a significant role here. The institutions which emerge from this process are not textbook models, but resultants of the forces which push various politicians to act. The materials in this section should be read partly as an exercise in historical reconstruction.

N. WHETTEN, RURAL MEXICO

Pp. 182-84, 202-04 (1948)*

Definition of the Ejido

The term "ejido" (pronounced a-heé-do), as now used in Mexico, refers to an agrarian community which has received and continues to hold land in accordance with the agrarian laws growing out of the Revolution of 1910. The lands may have been received as an outright grant from the government or as a restitution of lands that were previously possessed by the community and adjudged by the government to have been illegally appropriated by other individuals or groups; or the community may merely have received confirmation by the government of titles to land long in its possession. Ordinarily, the ejido consists of at least twenty individuals, usually heads of families (though not always), who were eligible to receive land in accordance with the rules of the Agrarian Code, together with the members of their immediate families.

The term "ejidatario" refers to an individual who has participated as a beneficiary in a grant of land in accordance with the agrarian laws. The totality of ejidatarios participating in a given grant, together with their families and the lands which they received, constitute an ejido. Thus the term "ejido" refers to a community, while "ejidatario" refers to a specific individual.

The total population of an ejido might vary from less than one hundred inhabitants

---

[65] See Findley, note 60 *supra*, at 916, for discussion of "the new paternalism" in the relationship between INCORA and the beneficiaries of the Colombian land reform.

*Copyright 1948 The University of Chicago Press, reprinted by permission of the publisher.

to several thousand. In the smaller villages where ejidos have been established or in newly settled villages resulting directly from the formation of an ejido, the ejido and the village with its surrounding lands are almost coextensive, though not entirely so. There are almost always a few families in the village, however small, who are ineligible to benefit from the agrarian laws. These may be small shopkeepers or other persons whose traditional occupation is not farming. Their interests might be closely bound up with the ejido, but they would not be considered members of it. Other residents of the village who do not belong to the ejido are those families who were already in possession of small private holdings of their own and for this reason did not quality to receive land under the agrarian laws. In the larger villages and towns there might be two or more ejidos in the same village; or the ejido population might constitute only a fraction of the total population of the town.

The lands of any given ejido do not always form a contiguous block. They are often interspersed with the remnants of the pre-existing hacienda from which the ejido lands were taken. Ordinarily, when lands were expropriated, the hacendado was permitted to select the land he wished to retain, and he often chose irregularly shaped areas in order to include what he regarded as the most desirable for his purpose. . . .

Types of Farm Organization

There are two principal types of farm organization among the ejidos. These are what might be termed "individual" and "collective." These two types as differentiated here apply only to the crop lands, since, according to the Agrarian Code, all pasture lands, woodlands, and other noncrop lands in all ejidos are held and used in common and can never be divided among the individual ejidatarios unless opened up for cultivation. In this sense all ejidos use at least part of their lands in common. However, with reference to the crop land only, ordinarily a given ejido may be classified into one of the two types.

The Agrarian Code stipulates that the president of the Republic shall determine the type of farm organization in the ejidos in accordance with the following principles (Art. 200):

I. Lands which constitute economic units requiring the joint efforts of all the ejidatarios for their cultivation should be worked on a collective basis.

II. Ejidos whose crops are intended for industrial uses and which constitute agricultural zones whose products are homogeneous within an industry shall also be worked on a collective basis. In this case the crops which should be grown shall be specified.

Collective organization may also be adopted in other ejidos whenever technical and economic studies show that in this way better living conditions can be obtained for the peasants, and its establishment is feasible.

In all other cases the ejidatarios of a given ejido have been more or less free to choose the type of farm organization they wanted to follow, although their decisions have no doubt been strongly influenced, in some instances, by the persuasions of the officials of the Ejido Bank, who could withhold credit unless the type of organization appeared feasible to them.

The Individual Ejido

An overwhelmingly large proportion of the ejidos are of the individual type. This means that each ejidatario is allotted a plot of farm land *(parcela)* which he tills in his own way with the help of his family. These plots of crop land on the average for the entire country consist of 4.4 hectares. . . . The collective ejidos are found mostly in the northern areas and in the Gulf states. Only 3.6 percent in the central region are operating collectively, and only 5.9 percent in the south Pacific. The officials of the [Ejido Bank] are firmly convinced that almost all the ejidos which operate collectively are co-operating with the bank. If this is true, it would mean that, of the 14,683 ejidos appearing in the census of 1940, only about 5 percent are operating collectively, while 95 percent operate on an individual basis.

E. SIMPSON, THE EJIDO: MEXICO'S WAY OUT

Pp. 318-34 (1937)

Circular 51 – Simple Collectivism

For almost eight years after the promulgation of the basic agrarian decree of January 1915 no especial attention was given to the matter of ejido social and political organization. When specific questions arose the National Agrarian Commission dealt with them in circulars sent to the State Agrarian Commissions or to the municipal and state political authorities as the case demanded. It was not until October 11, 1922, however, that the Commission in its Circular No. 51, attempted to set forth a really comprehensive plan for the ordering of the political, social, and economic life of the ejidos.

Circular 51 opens with a statement of what in the opinion of the National Agrarian Commission were basic principles: (a) The distribution of land to villages is only the first step in the work of the National Agrarian Commission. The Commission must also assume the responsibility for "regulating the development of the ejidos and directing their progress." It is its duty to work out a program of ejido exploitation "in accordance with the level of social development and the state of agricultural evolution" of the villages and to nominate the authorities who will be charged with putting this program into action. (b) "Just as the development of the technical instruments of modern industry brought to an end small industry and produced capitalism, so also, the evolution of agricultural technology tends to abolish small scale agriculture, for there is an unsurmountable incompatibility between small scale agriculture and mechanization. . . ." (c) It follows, therefore, that if Mexican rural life is to derive the greatest possible benefit from modern methods of machine production, the ejido villages must be organized along strictly cooperative and communal lines.

Moreover, "organization of the type in question . . . must not be left to the initiative of the peasants, impoverished by prolonged exploitation," but the National Agrarian Commission itself "must undertake to control the functioning and even to impose the installation" of cooperatives. By proceeding in this fashion the Commission will not only be adjusting its action to the "current of human progress . . . which dictates that social action shall take precedence over the egoism of personal convenience and that public rights shall be enriched each day at the expense of private rights," but will also be achieving the desideratum "of putting an end to the divorce existing between the . . . productive forces which tend to be collective and the totally antiquated regime of individual private property."

When a village receives its ejido lands either in provisional or definitive possession it becomes the duty of the Administrative Committee to divide the lands into the following classes: (a) an urban zone or *fundo legal*; (b) agricultural lands proper – actual and immediately potential *(de pronto cultivo)*; (c) forest, pasture, and brush lands; and (d) a section of not less than five hectares of cultivable land for each school in the community. The agricultural lands are to be cultivated in common and for this purpose the Committee is to apportion the work and assign to each of the ejidatarios his particular task. The forest, brush, and pasture lands are to be reserved for the use of the whole community under the direction of the Committee. The products of all sorts derived from ejido lands exploited communally are to be distributed as follows: 85 percent is to be divided among the ejidatarios in the manner which they themselves shall determine; 10 percent is to be placed in a fund for cooperative development to be used to purchase agricultural machinery, work animals, and so forth; and 5 percent is to be reserved for the payment of taxes and for urban and other improvements.

A most important section of the Circular states: "The cultivable lands . . . [as well as] the forest, brush and pasture lands in no case shall be subject to lease, mortgages, antichresis, embargo or sale."

The last four articles of Circular 51 state the principles on the basis of which the National Agrarian Commission through its Department of Ejido Development is to organize the ejido cooperatives. These principles are: (a) "distribution of profits in proportion to work contributed"; (b) "equal rights for members . . . following the formula: 'one member one vote' "; and (c) the right of one-fifth of the members of the society to exercise at any time the privileges of initiative, referendum and recall.

Cooperatives are to be governed by the Ejido Administrative Committee enlarged by the addition of three members. The National Agrarian Commission through its Department of Ejido Development is to assume responsibility for organizing cooperatives in each of the ejido villages and supervising their operations "until they are able to prosper without official aid," and for the establishing of regional unions of cooperatives which, in turn, are to be brought together in a single national association.

With the promulgation of Circular 51 the ejido villages were launched upon a career of what, for lack of a better term, may be called simple collectivism. Ejido lands were to be held and worked in common – all for one and one for all, and no questions raised concerning mine and thine. Ejido villages, like their prototypes of Colonial days, were to be the wards of the nation. State and municipal authorities might levy taxes, but there, for all practical purposes, their rights over the ejido lands ended. Economic and social control of ejidos was to be vested immediately in Ejido Administrative Committees. But the powers of these Committees were to be strictly limited by the guarantees of initiative, referendum and recall on the one hand, and the direct intervention and supervision of the National Agrarian Commission on the other.

Thus the program in theory. Thus the vision of simple collectivism. For three years the National Agrarian Commission struggled to translate theory into action; vision into reality. Then, in 1925, nine months after Calles took office as president, came the day of accounting. Circular 51 was tried, judged and sentenced to that large and overflowing ash-can especially reserved in Mexico for *proyectos* of social reform. Why? What was the trouble? Was there something wrong with the program of the common chicken in the communal pot?

The Law of Ejido Patrimony – (Fairly) Rugged Individualism

According to the sponsors of the law which took the place of Circular 51, there were wrongs aplenty and enough trouble to threaten the whole agrarian reform with wrack and ruin and the country with starvation to boot. In a speech before the Chamber of Deputies on September 12, 1925, the Minister of Agriculture, Luis L. León, summarized the charges against the program then in effect as follows: (a) In point of fact, there was hardly an ejido in the country in which the lands were worked communally in the manner required by Circular 51. The regular procedure, as everyone knew, was for a village just as soon as it got its lands to allot them in severalty. Thus the regulations of the National Agrarian Commission were being openly flouted and the ejidatarios by this very action had clearly demonstrated their lack of faith in the communal method. (b) It was a generally acknowledged fact that production on the lands distributed under the agrarian laws had fallen below that which had been hoped for. (c) There was a pervading sense of insecurity among the ejidatarios. This was partly to be explained by the constant threats of the *hacendados* and the malicious rumors that the government was abandoning the agrarian reform, but the main reason for the peasants' uneasiness and discontent was to be found in the character of the control exercised over the ejidos by the local Administrative Committees. These Committees had come to be dominated by the most ambitious and, often most unscrupulous individuals who did not hesitate to pursue their personal gain to the sacrifice of the collective welfare. In many communities no sooner did the ejidatarios get their crops planted on their little parcels than the local politicians would decide to have a reallotment. In a word, the peasants had been rescued from the tyranny of the *hacendados* only to become the victims of the *caciquismo* (bossism) of the Ejido Administrative Committees. . . .

Summary of the Law of Ejido Patrimony
[Enacted in 1925 – essentially the same as the present
governmental structure of the ejido. – Eds.]

1. *Village Agrarian Authorities.* . . . Under the Law of Ejido Patrimony (Agrarian Code), the Ejido Administrative Committee is abolished and in its place are two new

local agrarian authorities: the Ejido Commissariat (*Comisariado Ejidal*) and the Board of Vigilance (*Consejo de Vigilancia*). The Ejido Commissariat, the principal governing authority in the village, is composed of three members in good standing in the community duly elected by a majority vote. The term of service is for two years,[66] unless (as the law ominously provides) the members are previously removed for due cause. The functions of the Commissariat are to represent the village before the administrative and judicial authorities; to administer and to seek to improve the ejido lands in general and to be directly responsible for the exploitation of the common properties (pastures, forests, and so forth, and the water rights which, as will be noted shortly, are not subject to division); to call meetings of the ejidatarios; and to carry out the instructions of the community and those dictated by the Agrarian Department and the National Bank of Agricultural Credit or their representatives.

As its name suggests, the principal function of the Board of Vigilance is to see that the Ejido Commissariat behaves properly. To this end it is empowered to revise the accounts of the Commissariat, to order the calling of meetings of the Ejido Assembly when in its judgment this is necessary or when 20 per cent of the ejidatarios so request and to report to the Agrarian Department any irregularities in the financial or other operations of the Commissariat. The Board of Vigilance, like the Commissariat, is composed of three members elected to hold office for two years [now three years — Eds.].

2. *National Agrarian Authorities.* Authority over and responsibility for the organization and supervision of ejido communities is vested in the first instance in the Agrarian Department. . . .

3. *The Division of Ejido Lands.* At the time of the execution of the presidential decree granting or restoring ejido lands to a village, these lands must be immediately divided up in the manner prescribed by (the present) law.

In dividing up the village lands the following areas are not subject to parcelization: (a) an "urban zone" including a special lot set aside for the rural school and its experimental field; (b) pasture and timber lands; and (c) special areas (*cajas, bolsas y lotes bordeados*) which constitute "a natural, physically nondivisible unit and require for [proper] cultivation the collective intervention of all the ejidatarios."

All the rest of the land (that is, the crop land, actual and potential) granted to the village must be apportioned among the individual ejidatarios and the law sets forth in some detail the manner in which this is to be done with a view to insuring justice and fair dealing to all concerned. In no case may any individual be given a tract of land smaller than the area defined in the presidential resolution making the grant, or, in default of such definition of the area stated in the agrarian laws in force at the time the grant is made.

If any of the land subject to division is left over after each ejidatario receives his tract, a "reserve zone" is formed from which the sons of ejidatarios upon coming of age, or people from neighboring villages having insufficient lands, may receive parcels.

In those cases, on the other hand, where it is found that there is not enough land to give each head of a family his proper share, the law provides that an effort shall be

---

[66]The term is now three years. [Eds.]

made to work out a plan whereby with the financial help of the federal government, the states, the Bank of Agricultural Credit and of the ejidatarios themselves new lands shall be made available for cultivation by clearing some of the ejido pasture and timber lands, building irrigation works, and so forth. However, if this is not feasible, the Agrarian Department shall declare a "deficit of parcels" and shall institute proceedings for an additional expropriation and dotation from surrounding private properties.

4. *Definition of Property Rights.* In defining the nature of the property rights vested in the villages receiving lands under the ejido laws, the Law of Ejido Patrimony (Agrarian Code) restates and reaffirms the principles laid down in the decree of January 1915 and in Article 27 of the constitution in the following words: "The agrarian rights which shall be acquired by centers of population shall be imprescriptible and inalienable and therefore cannot in any case or in any form be ceded, conveyed, hypothecated or made the subject of lien in whole or in part."

Exceptions to the foregoing statement are: (a) the renting of pasture rights, the granting of concessions for the exploitation of timber lands and the sale of irrigation waters when these acts are approved by the Ejido Commissariat and the Agrarian Department as contributing to the best utilization of the pasture and timber lands and other products held in common by the villages; (b) the surrendering of properties of whatever kind when it is necessary to expropriate these properties for the purpose of creating urban zones, constructing means of communication, building irrigation works of public interest, or exploiting natural resources belonging to the nation. No such expropriation of the type in question may be made except by specific presidential resolution and after previous compensation for the economic value of the properties affected either in lands of equal quality or in cash, in the order named.

Property rights in the separate ejido parcels of crop land vested in the individual ejidatarios are also imprescriptible and hence cannot be alienated[67] or made the subject of lien. Neither may the beneficiaries of ejido parcels rent them or work them on shares or "make any other contract which implies the indirect exploitation of the land."

An ejidatario may be deprived of his ejido parcel either temporarily or permanently under certain conditions. Temporarily: if he leaves the community for more than six months without permission of the Commissariat, or if he cultivates his parcel in a manner prejudicial to the interests of the community. Permanently: if he attempts to sell, mortgage, lease, rent, or in any other form or fashion alienate his property; for failure to cultivate his land for a period of two consecutive agricultural years; if he does not contribute promptly to the funds for the payment of taxes or for any other purpose related to the ejido and approved by the Assembly; or, because of "mental derangement, alcoholic degeneration or imprisonment for a period greater than two years providing that there are no members of his household (*familiares*) to take charge of his parcel." Women who possess parcels by reason of being heads of families may be

---

[67]However, ejidatarios living in separate communities may make exchanges of their parcels upon receiving the approval of the ejido Assemblies and the Agrarian Department. [Footnote by Simpson, renumbered.]

deprived of them if they change their civil status "providing that in their new situation the family [still] enjoys the use of a parcel."[68]

Each case of deprivation must be considered on its merits and no individual can be deprived of his land by the Ejido Assembly without fully justified cause and until the case has been reviewed and a definitive judgment handed down by the Agrarian Department. Parcels declared "free" in the manner just indicated automatically return to the community and their disposition is determined by the Assembly with the approval of the Agrarian Department.

Ejido parcels may be bequeathed and inherited, and for this purpose each proprietor of a parcel is required to register a list of succession indicating the person who shall become the head of the family in the event of his death.[69] The list of succession may not include individuals who already have parcels or those who reside in other ejido communities. If there be no one who fulfills the requirements for inheritance, the property reverts to the community and becomes subject to a new adjudication.

The undivided ejido lands — pasture, timber lands and the special areas referred to above — are reserved for the common use of all the ejidatarios. This use may take the form of privileges granted to individual ejidatarios (to cut timber, pasture, cattle, and so forth); or of communal exploitation; or of commercial and industrial exploitation by concession to ejidatarios or outsiders. In the latter cases the proceeds in kind or in money must be placed in the ejido common fund (see below). Rights to irrigation waters are vested in the community in its corporate capacity and the use of these waters is subject to the regulation by the Commissariat in accordance with the rules of the Agrarian Department and the Ministry of Agriculture.

5. *Taxes.* The municipal, state, and federal governments are prohibited from imposing more than one predial tax on ejido properties. Taxes shall be imposed upon the fiscal value of the properties, but in no case may they exceed 5 per cent of the annual production of the ejido. Fiscal responsibility for the individual parcels rests on the individuals concerned but fiscal coaction can be brought to bear only upon the crops in cases of delinquency. For the corporate ejido lands the fiscal responsibility is joint and common.

6. *The Common Fund.* Each ejido community must establish a fund (*fondo común*) to be constituted from special quotas determined by the Assembly and paid by each ejidatario and from the products derived from the exploitation of the

---

[68] Although they do not accurately describe the relationship of the ejidatario to his parcel, as a matter of convenience and to avoid awkward legal circumlocutions, the terms "proprietor," "possessor," "owner," etc., are used in this and other paragraphs in referring to ejido parcels. *Usufructuary* is probably a better indication of the real nature of the property rights involved. [Footnote by Simpson, renumbered.]

[69] It is not without significance that the Law of Ejido Patrimony was originally called the Law of "Family" Patrimony. It was clearly the intention of those who framed the law to make the family unit the depository of ejido parcel property rights and not the individual ejidatario. Also, the law extends somewhat the ordinary concept of family and provides that in the case of the death of the beneficiary of an ejido parcel "the rights to the same shall pass to the person or persons whom he maintained, even though they were not his relatives *(parientes)* provided that they had lived with him as members of his family." [Footnote by Simpson, renumbered.]

common lands. This fund is to be used for the purchase of machinery, work animals, and equipment for general improvements such as irrigation works, and for certain other purposes. . . .

At bottom — curious as it may sound to those who have been fed on stories of "red Mexico" — the Law of Ejido Patrimony represented a flight from communism. In the eyes of the group which came into power with Calles, the conception of the ejido and the program for its organization contained in the Circular 51 *was* communism and, moreover, communism imported directly from Moscow. Now, in the judgment of these gentlemen, communism was not for Mexico. Or, at any rate, not agrarian communism. They had no idea (as had the authors of Circular 51) of "putting an end to the divorce existing between the productive forces which tend to be collective and the totally antiquated regime of individual private property." On the contrary, they believed that the ultimate goal of the reform was private property — private property more justly distributed, private property controlled in the interest of the public, but private property nonetheless. The ejido was not to be an end in itself and certainly not a communistic end. Rather the ejido was looked upon simply as one of several possible methods of redistributing land, a stepping-stone to individualistic ownership and modified laissez-faire. Holding these views it was but natural that the Calles group should have found good and sufficient reasons — in "human nature" in "economic realities," and in "common sense" — for discarding the program of Circular 51. The Law of Ejido Patrimony, from the point of view of its sponsors, was a reasonable and necessary step in the development of the agrarian reform. For its opponents, the law was a specious attempt to mix oil with water, a desertion and a betrayal of the ideals of the revolution.[70]

BOLIVIA: LEGISLATIVE DECREE NO. 03464 RELATIVE TO AGRARIAN REFORM

2 August 1953 (FAO translation)

78. Peasants who have been subject to a feudal work and exploitation system, in their capacity of servants, dependents, labourers, tenant-farmers, *agregados,* outside workers, etc., and who are over 18 years of age, married males over 14 years of age and widows with children who are minors shall, upon the proclamation of this Decree, be declared the owners of the parcels at present in their possession and cultivated by them, until the National Agrarian Reform Service shall grant them all that they are reasonably entitled to in accordance with the definitions of the small property or shall compensate them in the form of collective cultivation of lands enabling them to meet their family needs. . . .

---

[70] The most thorough recent analysis of the ejido system is S. Eckstein, *El Ejido Colectivo en México* (1966). [Eds.]

82. On the lands of a latifundium cultivated under the colonization system, the tenant farmers and agricultural workers of such latifundium having completed a period of residence of two years or more, calculated retrospectively as from the date of proclamation of this Legislative Decree, shall have a preferential right to a grant.

When the initial grant is made, an area of not less than ten per cent of the total of the individual allotments shall be reserved for collective cultivation by the community.

An area equivalent to or larger than that received by each tenant farmer shall be made available for the school field.

83. In cases referred to in Article 82 the following procedure shall be followed in determining the right to assignable areas:

a) If sufficient land is available, a grant shall be made to each family at the rate of one grant unit. Where there remains cultivable land in excess, it shall be considered as vacant land to be granted to peasants of medium and small properties who are without land and who live in the same district or in the neighbourhood up to a distance of six kilometers from the latifundium concerned. If residual land still remains after the grants referred to in the preceding Article have been made, the community may extend the area of lands for collective cultivation.

b) If the lands are not sufficient to afford a grant unit to each family, the assignable areas shall be reduced to the necessary extent so as to satisfy the claims of all those who, by law, have a preferential right to such land. Peasants who receive insufficient grants of land shall have the right to new grants in other available areas. . . .

92. In those regions where adequate land affected by this Legislative Decree exists, allocation to each family shall be made at the rate of a unit of grant having an area equivalent to that of the small property. [See Art. 7, p. 328, *supra.* — Eds.] In regions where there is not sufficient land, the area assignable to each family shall be reduced accordingly, so as to satisfy the claims of all persons having a right to land.

93. In those regions where reductions in the units of grant are necessary, they shall be made by the National Service for Agrarian Reform.

R. PATCH, BOLIVIA: U.S. ASSISTANCE IN A REVOLUTIONARY SETTING

in *Social Change in Latin America Today*
at 108, 128 (1960)*

It was these provisions of the decree that opened the way for multiplying the small subsistence plots or *minifundios*. As the framers of the decree foresaw clearly, in those densely populated areas which stood in greatest need of land redistribution, there was

---

*New York: Harper and Row for the Council on Foreign Relations, 1960. Reprinted by permission of the publisher.

simply not enough land to give each family an allotment even approaching the prescribed "small holding." By reducing the defined minimum holding in order to satisfy all *campesinos* legally entitled to receive land, the decree made a gesture toward appeasing the greatest possible number of *campesinos*. But it thereby made the sub-subsistence *minifundio* the dominant pattern in the more densely populated regions. Agricultural production and marketing have not recovered from this drastic change. That is the root of many of Bolivia's economic straits today.

K. ROSENN, PUERTO RICAN LAND REFORM: THE HISTORY OF AN INSTRUCTIVE EXPERIMENT

73 *Yale Law Journal* 334, 343-47 (1963)*

The heart of the Land Authority's program, the proportional profit farm, was designed to assure the profits of the soil to its Puerto Rican tillers, who might hopefully develop a sense of ownership in the land, while avoiding the loss of efficiency and productivity which many feared would accompany the breaking up of the large sugar corporations. In conception, it was a unique blend of socialism and capitalism, preserving the profit motive for both management and labor, while ownership of the land remained in the Puerto Rican Government. The farms were to be organized in areas where considerations of efficiency made division of large estates inadvisable. The Authority was directed to rent farms of 100 to 500 acres (though larger farms might be leased if justified by efficiency) to qualified farm managers, who were to reside on the farm and manage it in return for five to fifteen per cent of its profits. The lessee-manager was granted the power to hire and fire employees, but was required to pay his employees the going wage rate in the area plus a proportion of the farm's net profits.[71] Each employee's share was to be calculated in direct proportion to the total amount of wages paid that employee for his labor on the farm during the fiscal year.

---

*Reprinted by permission of The Yale Law Journal Company and Fred B. Rothman & Company.

[71] 28 L.P.R.A. §§461, 463 (1955). Unfortunately, privately managed proportional profit farms never materialized. The Land Authority soon found that no financially responsible person would lease land on which he had to accept the risk of loss, grant usufructs of small plots to the people living on the land, pay the going wage rate in the area, and restrict his profits to 15%. . . . Rather than not organize proportional profit farms, the Land Authority hired experienced men to manage the farms and paid them a salary plus a share of the profits. In addition, the authority agreed to assume financial responsibility for any losses of the farm. The Authority called these managers "lessees" because the Land Law directed that the proportional profit farms be rented, but these men were "lessees" in name only. . . .

While eminently sensible, the Authority's assumption of direct control was plainly *ultra vires* until 1946, when two amendments were made to the Land Law. The first provided that the lessee could be paid a current salary and a bonus of 1 to 10% of the farm's profits. Laws of Puerto Rico 1946, Act No. 272. The second amendment stated that "lessee" meant simply the person who administered the farm and did not have tenurial connotations. 28 L.P.R.A. § 462 (1955).

To most observers, the first five years of the Land Authority's operation glowed with promise. But at this point, the Populares [the political party in power] began a slow, yet accelerating, withdrawal from the elaborate program established by the Land Law. Between 1948 and the present, the Land Authority has acquired no additional land and the resuscitated 500 Acre Law has once more been relegated to the statutory scrap heap. Plainly, by 1947 the Populares had realized that their tenurial program, even with the formation of proportional profit farms, was bringing Puerto Rico little closer to their primary goal of full employment with higher living standards. And they realized the political pressures for social change were insufficient to compel a full-scale program of dubious economic wisdom. Henceforth, the attention of the Populares has been riveted upon the economic possibilities presented by the island's industrialization.

Certainly there are historical reasons peculiar to Puerto Rico which partially account for the reversal in the Populares' attitude. Demobilization after World War II meant a loss of wartime revenues and a sharp drop in employment. The budgetary surplus from the extraordinary rum taxes had been quickly consumed, and Puerto Rico's financial resources were sorely limited. Also by this time, the political pressures for land reform had been largely dissipated. The desire for tenurial reform was chiefly a manifestation of dissatisfaction with the power and practices of the large sugar companies, rather than a desire by the *agregado* [farm laborer or sharecropper] for a farm of his own. While a few of the sugar companies had had their lands expropriated,[72] the majority of the companies were curbed in other ways — by regulation of them as public utilities, by passage and enforcement of minimum wage laws, and by termination of their disparate tax treatment. And *agregado* resettlement plus legislation protecting homesteads mitigated fear of company evictions.

In the absence of strong political pressures for land redistribution, the Populares, starkly confronted with a drastic shortage of insular resources, could chart their future course in economic terms — how best to allocate governmental efforts for the island's development. The island's population had far outgrown any likelihood that agriculture could serve as a viable basis for a national economy. Productivity rates, which would be jeopardized by further fragmentation of landholdings, were already dangerously low. Furthermore, substitution of mechanized for antiquated methods of farming was necessary if productivity was to be improved. Yet mechanization necessarily implied larger land holdings and a smaller agricultural work force.

While large enough to achieve the economies of scale needed for improved

---

The Land Authority from the start has exercised almost complete control over the operation of the farm. The administrators or "lessees" are employees of the Authority and are responsible to regional supervisors. The Authority purchases fertilizer and seeds, rents and repairs the equipment used on the farms, supplies credit, handles the negotiation of collective bargaining agreements, and keeps all records and accounts of the farm's operation. The only responsibility of the administrator is the direct supervision of the workers and day-to-day management. . . . [Footnote by Rosenn, renumbered.]

[72] Of the 33 corporations which held more than 500 acres, seven were subjected to expropriation, while five others sold part or all of their land to individuals. Edel, "Land Reform in Puerto Rico," *Caribbean Studies*, Jan. 1963, p. 48. [Footnote by Rosenn, renumbered.]

agricultural productivity, even the proportional profit farms found mechanization difficult. When a government engages in agriculture in overpopulated and under-employed areas, its reluctance to invest in machinery is considerable, for dislocated and unemployed agricultural workers represent votes. The proportional profit farms were not only reluctant to mechanize and modernize outdated agricultural methods, but also hired more workers than were needed and permitted a good deal of featherbedding. As a result of the failure to mechanize, and high management costs, the total profits of the farms were disappointing when compared with the large profits of the sugar companies before 1940. From 1944 to 1948, the proportional profit farms earned $544,000, less than the United States paid these farms for quota sugar under the Sugar Act in 1948 alone. When the price of sugar began to fall in 1947, as sugar producing areas such as the Philippines and Hawaii began to resume normal exports after the war, some of the farms had substantial losses. The bulk of the losses, which amounted to $353,000 in 1948, is attributable to prohibitive labor costs, poor sugar yields, and poor management.

The Populares began to realize that the proportional profit farms were to a large extent performing a make-work function analogous to that performed by some of the New Deal Agencies in the United States, such as the Civilian Conservation Corps or the Works Progress Administration. The cost of subsidizing this alternative form of relief fell almost entirely on the poor agricultural worker, since the profits of the farms were distributed in direct proportion to the wages each worker earned. The Populares also realized that little could be expected from agriculture in supplying more jobs for the large number of unemployed, given the need for mechanization. Furthermore, the scarcity of funds made it difficult to justify continuing the sizeable expenditures involved in the complex of land reform activities. It became increasingly apparent that little would be produced on *agregado* plots and individual farms without sizeable aid in the way of credit, fertilizer, seed, equipment, marketings, and education in improved agricultural techniques. Successful agrarian reform required far more than expenditures for the redistribution of land. And land tenure reform was clearly not an answer to Puerto Rico's developmental needs.

J. CHONCHOL, ANALISIS CRITICO DE LA REFORMA AGRARIA CUBANA

in *El Trimestre Económico,*
Vol. XXX(1), No. 117, p. 69, 117-26 (1963)

[This long and very informative article describes in detail the early days of the Cuban land reform. The author, an economist and Minister of Agriculture in the Chilean government of President Allende, was in Cuba during the first years of the revolution, as a member of an advisory team of the Food and Agricultural Organization of the United Nations. In this article, Chonchol makes a number of interesting points, including the following: From June of 1959 to the end of 1960, the government created around 800 agricultural cooperatives of all kinds. These were cooperatives in name only, since they had neither "a defined organization, a statute, a determined number of members, nor cooperative leaders." Toward the end of 1960, however, the government created over 600 sugarcane cooperatives, covering nearly half of the sugar producing land in the country, and including virtually all the best land devoted to such uses. These cooperatives, of vital importance because of the dominance of sugar in the Cuban economy, were regulated by a "General Regulation of Sugarcane Cooperatives" issued by the Agrarian Reform Institute (INRA) in May of 1960. The Regulation provided, among other things, that the members of each cooperative would receive an advance on their share of the earnings in the form of wages, and that 80 per cent of the net income of each cooperative would be set aside for the building of houses and other buildings during the first five years of the cooperative's existence. A member could withdraw voluntarily, or exchange his or her rights, but could not sell the rights in the cooperative. Presumably this meant that a withdrawal involved relinquishing one's rights. The administrator of each cooperative was to be designated by INRA, at least "until the cooperatives may be perfectly organized and their members may have acquired the experience necessary for their administration." INRA had not yet relinquished this power. The sugarcane coopera-tives generally had 200 to 300 workers each, and from 1,000 to 1,500 hectares of land. What was involved was a change from large-scale capitalist enterprise to large-scale cooperative enterprise, so that the principal change has been a change of management. The shortage of trained management personnel has been one of the most serious problems of the sugar cooperatives.]

[Chonchol also describes the formation in 1961 of the National Association of Small Farmers (ANAP). This association grew out of various associations devoted to particular crops such as rice, tobacco, coffee, potatoes, etc. "The general regulation of ANAP, as distinguished from that of the Sugarcane Cooperatives issued in 1960, contains considerations not only of economic organization, but also of clear political content. In effect, ANAP is defined as an organism in support of the Revolution and aimed at organizing, unifying and orienting the small farmers in the application of the agrarian program of the Revolution." Membership in ANAP is virtually obligatory for any small farmer who needs credit, since credit is channeled through ANAP. Nevertheless, some 43 per cent of the farm land of Cuba remained outside the "socialist sector" (Sugarcane Cooperatives, People's Farms and ANAP). The author apparently believes that it is the ultimate purpose of the government to use ANAP as a means for organizing small producers into some form of collective production, but that the government was reluctant to press this plan for fear of losing the political support of the small farmers. Chonchol goes on to describe and evaluate the People's Farms as follows:]

The People's Farm is a state farm which is considered property of the Nation, such as the large nationalized industrial enterprises. Its basic structural characteristics were defined, at the beginning of 1961, by the president of INRA, Commander Fidel Castro, with the following words, which had to appear in large letters at the principal entrance of every farm:

"This Farm belongs to the People; on it indispensable food for our population is produced, many workers decently obtain their sustenance; families also enjoy the right to housing, education, medical assistance, a social circle, electricity and water, without charge. The income which is obtained from it is invested in this very center or in the establishment of other similar ones throughout the country." . . .

The People's Farms were organized in the first months of 1961, taking as their fundamental base the old livestock and rice latifundios, in addition to other kinds of farms intervened by INRA. ["Intervention" is the government's assumption of management control. — Eds.] All these farms, when they were geographically close, were regrouped in much larger new units called People's Farms. . . .

For each Farm there was designated an administrator and an accountant. . . . In general, the level of preparation of the administrators initially designated was that of practical peasants who previously were administrators of traditional farms, small producers, agricultural workers and, in certain cases, agricultural teachers or agronomists. Of course in all these appointments a decisive factor was the political confidence which the various authorities of INRA had in the persons designated, an aspect which often brought about the appointment as farm administrators of people little prepared for the task. . . .

On May 17, 1961, two years after the promulgation of the Agrarian Reform Act and less than five months after the organization of the People's Farms was initiated, there were in all Cuba 266 such farms which occupied a total area of 2,433,449 hectares. [This was approximately the same area as that covered by farms of members of ANAP. — Eds.] The average area of these farms was greater than 9,000 hectares. This average does not reflect the complete reality with respect to size, since although it is hard to find farms of less than 4,000 hectares, there are many which have more than 15, 20 or 25 thousand hectares. . . .[73]

With respect to the workers on the farms, in a census carried out in May of 1961, it was determined that altogether there were 96,498 workers on these farms in all Cuba, of whom 27,321 were permanent and 69,177 transient.

If this figure is compared with the total area occupied by the farms, one immediately notices the low occupational level of the People's Farms in relation, for example, to that of the Sugarcane Cooperatives. In effect, in the latter there were at this same period, a ratio of 6.6 hectares per cooperative member and 4.8 hectares per worker, considering both permanent cooperative members and transient laborers. In spite of the fact that this occupational level of the best lands in Cuba shows that still they are far from realizing the degree of intensification possible, it is still immensely superior to that of the People's Farms: 89.1 hectares per permanent worker and 25.2 hectares per worker generally, including the transients and permanent workers together. . . .

. . . The People's Farms that have been organized in Cuba constitute a production structure which, without doubt, presents some advantages. However, to our way of thinking, the disadvantages involved in their organization are greater than the advantages. . . .

---

[73] Gutelman reports that in 1966, "there were 575 state farms [People's Farms], . . . whose area varied from 13,000 to 100,000 hectares." Gutelman, "The Socialization of the Means of Production in Cuba," in *Agrarian Problems and Peasant Movements in Latin America* at 347, 362 (R. Stavenhagen ed. 1970). [Eds.]

The principal advantage of the People's Farms is that, because they are State exploitations, integrally financed by the State with their salaried workers receiving the same wage and other benefits regardless of the production level and income of the farm, it is possible, without great opposition from the workers, to raise crops in which the country is interested, though they may not be commercially remunerative. These crops may be important to assure certain supplies or to permit the long-range functioning of large factories that may be under-utilized . . ., for the purpose of making available certain fundamental elements for making concentrated food for livestock (corn), etc. . . .

A second advantage of the People's Farms is the one already mentioned, concerning the possibility of having centers of production in the hands of the State designed fundamentally to develop certain norms which permit the regulation of the market supply. . . .

Other advantages also exist in this formula, such as that invoked by the President of INRA, that the People's Farm gives equal economic and social conditions to all workers, whatever the natural conditions of the respective agricultural enterprises. Without doubt, from a certain point of view it could be argued that equality of conditions signifies a lack of incentive to progress, but there cannot be any doubt that a living minimum wage for all the workers of the country, despite the fact that the conditions in which some work may be less favorable than those of others, is one of the fundamental requisites of social justice and respect for the individual person.

It is also true, on the other hand, that equality of opportunities and the correction of natural disadvantages might be achieved through means of which the Cuban Agrarian Reform seems not to have thought. [For example, variable taxation.] . . .

But with these advantages in mind, let us see what are the disadvantages presented by the formula of the People's Farm in the concrete reality of today's Cuba. [The author's study concluded in 1961. — Eds.]

In the first place, it is an expensive formula. As the People's Farms have been conceived, they require large investments which weigh heavily on the State's budget. This is perhaps one of the reasons why there has been no attempt at this stage to transform all the collective agriculture of the country, including the Sugarcane Cooperatives, into People's Farms.

A second disadvantage, which tends to aggravate the danger just pointed out, is the too-great size of all the farms. . . .

This excessive size presents . . . the possibility of a deficient distribution of investments. . . .

Another inconvenience of this excessive size for each farm is the practical impossibility of carrying out an efficient administration and control. Theoretically the large agricultural enterprise should have the same economic advantages as the large industrial enterprise: maximum specialization of different groups of workers, chain operations, mass production, reduction of general administrative expenses, economic yield at a low unit cost of the product obtained, etc. In practice, nevertheless, the process of agricultural production is much more complex, variable and insecure, owing especially to the operation of a series of unforeseeable natural factors which are often difficult to control.

[In addition, Chonchol notes that the central government has been unwilling to assign sufficient personnel to operate these farms, even where trained personnel may be available — which they normally are not.]

Insufficiency of administrative personnel and excessive centralism (since every People's Farm must deal directly in all its actions with the General Administration of People's Farms in Havana) create very serious problems, especially of delays in the delivery of funds, which sometimes retard payments to the workers or the carrying out of certain indispensable labors.

There are other inconvenient aspects of the excessive size of the People's Farms such as the high cost of transport and distribution within each farm, the impossibility of an efficient control of animals, etc., but it is not worth the trouble to enter into an analysis of these aspects.

It should also be pointed out, finally, that this excessive size has not only economic consequences, but also unfavorable social consequences. The principal social disadvantage is that only with great difficulty can the salaried workers obtain some concept of their participation in the farm other than as mere salaried workers. Indeed, on a State farm, they have more guarantees than before, but psychologically they continue to be salaried workers without active participation in the enterprise.

What has been said makes us think that the myth of the People's Farm — that by virtue of its being a great enterprise of the State in a socialist economy it "is a superior formula of production" — will be seen to be very seriously denied in the concrete reality of the Cuban situation.

R. DUMONT, CUBA: SOCIALISM AND DEVELOPMENT

Pp. 50-56 (Lane translation, Grove ed. 1970)*

I outlined to Che [Guevara] the necessity of increasing the work put out without increasing base salaries just as fast, and proposed that members of cooperatives participate in the building of their houses without pay, especially during the second half of the year, which is the slow season on the farms. This would have allowed full employment to be attained more quickly, and would have allowed the diffusion of technical knowledge to have been the most meaningful part of the project. Since their owners would have had to make a noticeable sacrifice, their houses would have been appreciated much more and therefore would have been kept up much better, and above all they would have cost less within the framework of this "beaver" policy.

I also proposed that the members of cooperatives *invest work in them,* during the season when heretofore they had been out of work. A part of this work would be "paid for" in the form of shares of stock as members of a cooperative. There is no real cooperative without a minimum of contributions by members. They had scarcely any money at this point, but still had a great deal of leisure time, for there was still unemployment; they could thus contribute by working According to my plan, these shares would have borne interest, and thus would have constituted a form of *forced savings.* They would have been redeemed in cash — which was necessary, so as to stress their real value — only when members left the cooperative. I stressed my general impression, received from members of cooperatives, that they did not appear to be *a part of an enterprise that really belonged to them.*

Instead they felt that they had become salaried employees of the government, quasi-functionaries, and for this reason some of them were already not putting forth their best efforts.

If someone in a small collective based on autonomous work malingers, it is friends and neighbors who suffer from your negligence, and they'll make you aware of this. But if it's a question of the State, the collective entity is immense and far away. It is generally admitted, even in the U.S.S.R. today, that everyone can steal from it without going against generally accepted moral standards. The few lazy louts earned as much as the others in 1960, and I therefore found that there were even more of them in 1963. In my opinion, this participation, which corresponded to what a member of a cooperative classically contributed, would reinforce the social capital and would give the members the impression that the cooperative really belonged to them, *a sense of co-ownership*, and a personal attachment to their work collective.

Che reacted violently: "You have put too much emphasis on the sense of ownership that is to be given to members of cooperatives. In 1959, there was a marked tendency here toward 'Yugoslavism' and workers' councils. It is not a sense of ownership that they should be given, but rather a *sense of responsibility*. In this way, the necessary changes in policy will be easier." Che later emphasized that it was an *ideological* error to have set up cooperatives, which were acceptable only in the case of Russian or Hungarian peasants, but not at all acceptable in the case of Cuban agricultural workers, who were really proletarian. Because of this, these workers don't feel that they are working for themselves, but instead only for an entity, the State, that was still too abstract in their minds, even though it had been rebaptized "all the people." In 1963, Titoism was considered real heresy in Havana.

Che therefore outlined a position that was very interesting in principle, a sort of ideal vision of Socialist Man, who would become a stranger to the mercantile side of things, working for society and not for profit. He was very critical of the industrial success of the Soviet Union, where, he said, everybody works and strives and tries to go beyond his quota, but only to earn more money. He did not think the Soviet Man was really a new sort of man, for he did not find him any different, really, from a Yankee. He refused to consciously participate in the creation in Cuba "of a second American society, even if everything belongs to the State." Charles Bettelheim rightfully emphasizes how dangerous it could be to set up institutions where *only the motivation of personal interest* would enter into play.

From another angle, *counting at present only on devotion*, not on a work collective with familiar faces, but on the whole of society more or less poorly envisaged, is to try to go on to communism immediately, like the Chinese in 1958; at the very least, it means skipping certain steps. And the Cuban economic difficulties of 1960-1968 suffice to show how inefficient this is, and therefore how dangerous. In short, Che was far ahead of his time — in thought, he had already entered a communist stage, which I did not think possible even in the Soviet Union of 1980. Advancing the timing in this fashion interferes with the functioning of the motor, and keeps certain of its developments from being truly adapted to the concrete situation in 1964.

Protestants had the merit of renewing the sense of personal responsibility that the old form of Catholicism had not stressed highly. Socialism needs to revive a sense of responsibility; but to believe that these moral stimulations can replace material recompense is *to deliberately and uselessly repeat the whole cycle of errors of the other socialist countries*, for which they have already paid quite dearly. *To have departed from the cooperative formula too much*, though it dominates the agriculture of the socialist countries, *was to my mind the basic error of the Cuban leaders*, and we shall see the many consequences of this.

I have already told about that other day, August 26, 1960, spent with Fidel, this time in his aluminum house in the middle of the Ciénaga de Zapata (how hot it was!) . . . . After having heard the essence of what I had to say, he outlined his project to me.

All farms other than sugar-cane plantations, and all cattle ranches, were to be organized into people's farms — *granjas del pueblo*. He justified this by the advantages that would accrue because of the centralization of machines so as to ensure their full employment, and I vainly insisted on the full employment of men first of all. When he foresaw an area of two to three thousand caballerías, 27,000 to 47,000 hectares, for each *granja*, I gave a start of surprise. Taking from Fidel's hands the sketch on which he had already located the cowshed and its grazing lands here, the pig-sty there, and then the fields to grow crops, I drew lines to divide it into twenty or so *autonomous* groupings: each with its personnel, stock of cattle, and appropriate materiel. His *granja* would thus have been only a sort of *federation* of production units "on the human scale," each of them an individual unit with management of it within the capacities of the existing cadres. The group would have had at its disposal only the largest machines, bulldozers, and a part of the combines.

Why this decision to make a regular practice of establishing not real State farms but overlarge administrative farms? — a lack of proportion that would increase freight rates and general expenses, that would complicate the management of these farms, and prevent their being properly controlled. Giantism is not an article of Marxist faith, which merely condemns — rightly — the microfundium, which is an obstacle to modern technique. It is sought after, however, by socialist neophytes.

Fidel seems to have garnered from his reading about the Soviets the fixed idea that the cooperative is only an *inferior* form of production, that of a small group. Only the State farm represents the *superior* form of ownership, that of the people as a whole. Is it the magic of words, or the hope of surpassing others, that thus prevents the real problems — that of healthy management, of an efficient and rational economy — from assuming their rightful place? Many other experts will be able to [marshal] ample warning, more enlightened than my own, against such a risky decision, but it will be in vain: *Fidel's* decision has been made.

E. BOORSTEIN, THE ECONOMIC TRANSFORMATION OF CUBA

Pp. 45-46 (1968)*

The large cattle ranches were organized into "direct administration farms" run by INRA; at the beginning of 1961 they became *Granjas del Pueblo* or "People's Farms," a form of state farm. The leaders of the Revolution feared that if the cattle were divided up among small farms the protein-hungry peasants would quickly eat them and deplete the supply. They had had experience with this when they were still in the Sierra, and almost all the cattle they had distributed had somehow managed to "break a leg" and require slaughtering. To have formed cooperatives from the large ranches in which a few cowboys took care of thousands of cattle would have been to form a class of rich cooperators.

The lands of the large sugar estates were used to form cane cooperatives. Cooperatives were also set up for the production of rice, tomatoes, henequen, charcoal (the main cooking fuel in the countryside), and other products. But the term cooperative was a misnomer. The administrators of the cooperatives were not elected by the members, but appointed by INRA. And although in theory remuneration of the members was to depend on the profits of the cooperative, in practice it quickly became a system of wage payments. Pay could not be held up indefinitely while someone undertook the impossible task of setting up or straightening out books and determining profits. Remuneration based on profits would have required a developed system of accountancy and accountancy depends on literacy, on the ability of most people to make out bills, reports and records.

Toward the beginning of 1961 the cooperatives other than cane began to be changed into People's Farms, and in 1962 the cane cooperatives were also changed. Here and there a few cooperatives were left; but the People's Farms became the basic form of organization of Cuba's socialized agriculture.

There were other points in favor of People's Farms beside the fact that the cooperatives were never able to work as cooperatives. The farms varied greatly in soil location, and ownership of cattle, machinery, and equipment. If the farms were organized and run as cooperatives, these variations would produce differences in profits and arbitrary differences in remuneration. There would be rich cooperatives and poor cooperatives; people working in different cooperatives would often find themselves doing equal work and getting unequal pay.

And with the great dependence of the whole Cuban economy on the export of sugar and the imports purchased with the proceeds — a situation that has no equivalent among the other socialist countries — Cuba's socialized farms cannot be allowed the degree of choice about what to produce that is normal for cooperatives. The government must be able to tell them how much sugar to produce.

Before the revolution, Cuba's economy depended mainly on sugar production and North American tourism. In the first few years following 1959, the revolutionary government sought to diversify agriculture, and generally to deemphasize agriculture in favor of industrialization. After about five years, it had become apparent that this policy would not work without abandonment of the government's broad social welfare programs. An acute shortage of foreign exchange coincided with strong encouragement from the Soviet Union to convince the Cuban government to do an about-face, and to concentrate on sugar production. Cuba would supply sugar to all the countries of the socialist bloc. 1970 was set as the target year for reaching a record harvest of ten million tons of sugar. (The highest pre-revolution figure had been seven million tons, in 1952, when many Latin American export economies were prospering as an indirect result of the Korean War.) In the event, 1970 saw a harvest of around 8 1/2 million tons of sugar, well short of the goal but still the highest in Cuban history. Castro's July 26 speech in Havana, discussing the failure to reach the goal of ten million tons, laid blame on errors in planning and inefficiencies of organization, particularly in the industrial aspect of sugar production. (He said that enough cane had been harvested to produce ten million tons of sugar.) The entire speech is printed in English translation in *The New York Review of Books*, September 24, 1970, p. 18.

What are the implications of a policy of heavy concentration on sugar production for agricultural organization? Specifically, to what extent is the People's Farm system a necessary implication of that policy? Are Chonchol's criticisms of the People's Farms apt for an economy so focused on sugar? See generally M. Gutelman, *L'Agriculture Socialisée à Cuba*, ch. 3 (1967).

The tensions between individualism and collectivism noted in the foregoing materials found at least a temporary resolution in Chile under the Frei administration (1964-70). Both before and after the 1967 land reform law, the standard means for settling campesinos on land distributed to them was the *asentamiento*. Literally, the word means settlement; in Chile, it is a specialized term for a legal community which owns agricultural land and organizes its cooperative operation. Heads of families were assigned work days; profits of the farm were distributed in proportion to days worked. An elected five-man committee was in charge of operations; a government-employed technician lived on the farm, and consulted with the committee concerning the agricultural plan. (The land reform agency retained a limited veto power over the plan.) The aim of the asentamiento system was to turn over ownership of the land to the campesinos at the end of a three-year period. The assignments of land at that time were to be made in individual parcels; however, if all the members agreed, the asentamiento could be continued as a cooperative. For discussion of a proposal similar in aim to the Chilean asentamiento system, see Dorner and Collarte, "Land Reform in Chile: Proposal for an Institutional Innovation," 19 *Inter-Am. Econ. Affairs* 3 (1965).

The asentamiento was thus a production cooperative, set within the framework of a capitalist market in agriculture. In the event, the Chilean land reform agency tended not to turn over individual titles to the beneficiaries. While in theory the cooperative's profits were to be distributed according to a point system based on such things as number of days worked, cooperative attitude, etc., in fact there was great pressure to divide any profits equally among members of a given asentamiento. Monthly advances (against the anticipated annual distribution of profits) were paid to members, even in cases in which the asentamientos produced little or no profit; these advances were calculated in an amount just exceeding the minimum wage established by national law, and in practice they turned out to be much like wages. If there were no profits at the end of the year (as was often the case during the early years of an asentamiento), the advances were kept, and became an effective subsidy from the land reform agency. Some asentamientos that were producing well appeared to be losing money; because the official prices for crops were set at low levels, it sometimes became more profitable to hide crops and sell them to private buyers who were paying higher prices.

The message that land-reform beneficiaries were responding to market forces was not lost on the administration of President Allende (1970-73). His government was a coalition government, however, and different parts of the coalition had different views as to agrarian policy. Some administration officials favored a new type of organization to replace the asentamiento, the Agrarian Reform Center (CERA). In the minds of some members of the government, the CERA was to be the forerunner of a collective in the nature of a state farm; in the minds of most potential land-reform beneficiaries, however, the CERA was not a desirable substitute for the asentamiento, given that agriculture remained part of a market economy.

The military junta which overthrew President Allende in 1973 has now spoken on these same issues. Land, says General Pinochet (head of the junta), is to be placed entirely in a free-market system. Both the CERA and the asentamiento are to give way to the distribution to individuals of full title to small plots of land. This distribution had begun within three months of the September 1973 *golpe*. Furthermore, landowners whose land had been expropriated for purposes of the land reform are to be allowed to buy state lands, using their agrarian bonds as payment. Finally, "the state guarantees the permanent inexpropriability of farms of 40 hectares or less," and will not even expropriate larger estates for a number of years. In the first year of the military government, it has been estimated, more than a million hectares (some 13% of all the land that had been assigned to the asentamientos) had been returned to their previous owners. About 50,000 hectares of asentamiento land (0.6%) had been given to individual campesinos who were beneficiaries of the reform.[74]

The asentamiento was the Frei government's response to the need for education in modern agricultural techniques as a support for land distribution. A more general moral can be drawn here: Even an authoritarian revolutionary government needs the participation of large numbers of people in the accomplishment of its goals. (Cuba's attempt to achieve a ten-million-ton sugar harvest in 1970 illustrates the point; the cane was cut by office workers, students, housewives — because the government had convinced people generally of the importance of the task.) The institutional framework that emerges from a major social reordering like a land reform should be

---

[74] Latin America, vol. 8, no. 1, pp. 5-6 (1974); vol. 9, no. 5, p. 39 (1975).

designed to achieve maximum participation by persons at the bottom of the social-economic scale. Thus the redistribution of land is only the first of a land reform's objectives; the subsequent development of the agricultural sector requires not merely institutions that coerce and reward, but also institutions that instruct.

We return to the issue of paternalism. Opponents of land reform, says Ernest Feder,

> do not believe that the peasantry is "ripe" for land reform . . . and they insist that the peasants must first be shown and educated how to farm. This is laughable since the peasants — not the landed elite — have done the farm work for centuries.[75]

Are land reformers guilty of the same error, when they insist upon gradual turnovers of rights in land, to be preceded by a trial period for beneficiaries or a period of guidance for them? Who is an elitist?

Is the Mexican solution preferable to the Chilean asentamiento? In what sense is the ejido a vehicle for community cooperation, or for rural education? See Karst and Clement, "Legal Institutions and Development: Lessons from the Mexican Ejido," 16 *U.C.L.A. L. Rev.* 281, 284-93 (1969).

---

2. Title Problems and the Transferability of Beneficiaries' Interests

K. KARST AND N. CLEMENT, LEGAL INSTITUTIONS AND DEVELOPMENT: LESSONS FROM THE MEXICAN EJIDO

16 *U.C.L.A. Law Review* 281, 293-97 (1969)

No ejidatario has full title to his land, in the sense of the power to dispose of it. Ejido parcels are inalienable by sale or mortgage; they are imprescriptible; and they cannot even be rented except for certain cases that are obvious candidates for exceptional treatment. But there are degrees of title, and degrees of certainty of connection to the land. In about 10 per cent of the ejidos, there never has been a final decision by the national government granting the land to the ejido. And of the 90 per cent that do have a final grant of land to the community, only about 5 per cent have had a distribution to their individual members of what are called "titles."[76] Such a title is a certificate describing the ejidatario's land and stating that he is entitled to work it, subject to the Agrarian Code. In an ejido in which no such titles are distributed, the land is nonetheless parceled out to the ejidatarios. Since an ejidatario cannot sell his land, what difference does it make whether he has received a title certificate?

---

[75] Feder, "Counterreform," in Stavenhagen (ed.), *Agrarian Problems and Peasant Movements in Latin America* 173, 183 (1970).

[76] . . . In a given ejido, all members have title certificates or none do. [Footnote by Karst and Clement, renumbered.]

One ejido that illustrates the difference is El Bajo. This ejido, like that of El Medio [these are fictitious names] is associated with a town of about 4,000 population, about 20 miles from Guadalajara. The ejido is composed of some 210 ejidatarios, twice the membership of the ejido of El Medio. The ejido is sharply divided into two factions; suspicion is rife; community cooperation essentially does not exist; no one is optimistic about the future. The town is an unhappy place.

In the ejido of El Bajo, no one has a title certificate. Of course everyone knows which land is "his" — which land he can cultivate this year. But there is no certainty that the same land will be his to cultivate next year. For although the land has been parcelled out in what is called "economic" parcelization,[77] the parcels are precariously held. In El Bajo, this uncertainty of tenure rights has in fact been exploited by a dishonest ejido leadership group, which sought to oust some ejidatarios from the parcels they had been working, and to replace them with the leaders' friends. In 1966, after the harvest, the president of the ejido . . . held a ceremony in his home. In exchange for some cartons of beer, he purported to transfer the rights to work several parcels of land. When the victims complained, an official of the Agrarian Department telephoned the president, informed him that his actions were illegal, and told him to return the parcels to their former occupants. Since the regular ejido elections were to be held within a month, no punishment was visited on the president; the newly-elected comisariado did, however, seek the restoration of several thousand pesos of ejido funds that the old president had "lost." Of course, it would be hard to construct foolproof institutional protections against the disappearance of funds in the hands of the ejido leadership. But prevention of this kind of effort to transfer land illegally would be easy: just distribute certificates of title to the ejido parcels.

Before we ask why that step has been taken only in a sprinkling of the ejidos in Mexico, we want to take note of another source of insecurity of tenure in the ejido system. Ironically, this second reason for insecurity stems from a set of rules that are designed to be protective. Paternalism is an old theme in Latin America, with roots in both the Iberian and the pre-Columbian cultures. In this context, paternalism has resulted in a prohibition against selling or renting an ejido parcel. The ejidatario was to be protected against his own economic mistakes or misfortunes — protected from land speculators who might buy his rights and then resell to large landowners, thus reconstituting the hacienda. Yet there are often compelling reasons why an ejidatario might rationally prefer to rent or sell: he may prefer a job in the city; or he may wish to work for a time as a farm laborer for a wage, as so many Mexican farmers did in the United States until the termination of the *bracero* program.

Whatever the cause, violations of the rule against renting have been widespread. The general pattern has been to let these rentals go unpunished, no doubt because of the severity of the sanction — divestiture of the ejidatario's rights if the ejidatario fails to work his parcel personally for two successive years. Nonetheless, violations of the no-renting rule have been so common over the past decade that a colorable case can be made for divesting a very substantial proportion of ejidatarios of the right to cultivate

---

[77]The term is used in contrast to "legal" parcelization, in which title certificates are distributed. [Footnote by Karst and Clement, renumbered.]

their parcels. An ejido president who wished to favor his friends at the expense of others would have no trouble finding violators to victimize.

The distribution of title certificates would not, in theory, protect ejidatarios from the evils of this kind of selective enforcement. Even an ejidatario with a title certificate is subject to divestiture for an illegal rental. And, also in theory, divestiture can take place only upon the order of the President of Mexico, after a hearing and recommendations by the Agrarian Department. If the ejidatario does have a title certificate, the latter procedure is assured in practice, for his certificate (and the accompanying registration of the parcel in his name) must be cancelled. If he has no certificate, however, — if he simply works a parcel that he has been allowed to occupy in an "economic" parcelization — then it is always arguable by the ejido leadership that the parcel never has been granted to him in any definitive way. The inertial weight of officialdom in such a case leans against the ejidatario, who must appeal his displacement through the various levels of the Agrarian Department. Thus the distribution of title certificates would, even in cases of selective enforcement of the rules against renting or selling, be a practical protection against the corruption of an ejido's leaders.

Still, the distribution of title certificates is not made. Why not? The usual answer is that there is not enough land for final distribution in parcels that meet the minimum-size requirements of the Constitution.[78] If the government were to distribute such parcels, the argument goes, there would be many farmers who would be left out. The solution has been to keep the minimum-size rule, and to avoid doctrinal inconsistency by leaving all but a few ejidos in the country without title certificates for the occupants of their parcels.[79]

We believe, however, that there is a reason for maintenance of the present system that goes beyond doctrinal neatness and beyond concerns about those who might be dispossessed if titles were distributed. It would be possible, after all, to forget the minimum-size rule and to distribute certificates to all those who are now occupying the land; the certificates in El Medio, for example, cover parcels well below the legal minimum. The main reason why distribution is not made, we think, is that insecurity of tenure performs an important political function.

Before we state our thesis about the political utility of tenure insecurity, we must digress briefly to examine the controls that outside organizations exercise over the management of the ejido. It is only a slight exaggeration to say that nothing is decided finally within the ejido if anyone wishes to complain. The Agrarian Code is full of explicit provisions authorizing the Agrarian Department, the Secretary of Agriculture or the Ejido Bank to intervene in ejido affairs: elections, adjudications, and disputes over the use of ejido funds. The losing party can almost always appeal to some agency

---

[78] Article 27, para. x, provides for a minimum grant of 10 hectares of "humid" or irrigated land. [Footnote by Karst and Clement, renumbered.]

[79] Other reasons are also asserted for failing to distribute certificates of title to ejido parcels. It would be expensive to survey the lands and to prepare the legal documentation of the titles. A less persuasive argument is that it would be unwise to distribute inalienable title certificates to ejidatarios who are not good farmers, freezing the land in the hands of unproductive owners. [Footnote by Karst and Clement, renumbered.]

outside the ejido, but judicial review of administrative decisions relating to the ejidos is extremely limited. The ejidatario knows, in other words, that the outside authorities have the final word. And for "outside authorities" usually we can read agencies associated with the PRI, the government party.

More than a decade ago, Carlos Manuel Castillo outlined the negative consequences of these outside controls: the ejido leadership is drained of responsibility, and the ejidatarios look to the outside authorities to solve all their community problems; the possibility of a reversal of every ejido decision produces continuous conflict within the ejido; delay is institutionalized — and all this in addition to the usual problems relating to the quality of absentee decision-making. Insecurity of tenure, in other words, is only one aspect of the general insecurity that infects ejido affairs.

The political utility of this insecurity is easy to see. The ejidatarios are kept dependent on the agencies of the government, and that dependency is readily converted into political support. The ejido leadership represents the ejido in the League of Agrarian Communities, a local branch of the National Farmers Confederation, which is, in turn, a division of the PRI. It is well understood that the ejido — and especially members of the comisariado — can expect more favorable treatment from government agencies when they have been cooperating with the party. Such cooperation takes many forms, from "voluntary" participation in political rallies to returning strong PRI majorities in local and national elections. The results of this arrangement are that the PRI can count on the unswerving support of the ejido sector, and the members of the comisariado can count on having a relatively free hand in managing the internal affairs of the ejido. As long as the comisariado stays within locally accepted rules of behavior, its members can use the lack of title certificates to keep ejidatarios "in line" and also for their own personal benefit or the benefit of some of the agrarian authorities.

The result of this institutionalization of insecurity is not all bad. The ejido system has been a success in maintaining political stability in the countryside, and certainly the absence of violence is an essential precondition for development. As the shooting fades deeper into history, though, the continued costs to the development process implicit in this manner of maintaining political stability may come to appear excessive. An inverted cone of near bribery helps to perpetuate a maldistribution of income; a system of government by outsiders' discretion saps both individual and community responsibility; and even production is hindered. Insecurity of tenure is both a symptom and an aggravating cause of a more pervasive insecurity that inhibits the ejidatario's decisions concerning saving, investment and innovation.

The transferability of an ejido parcel is a current question of great interest in Mexico. It is widely asserted that violations of the nontransferability provisions of the Agrarian Code are constant and widespread:

It has been estimated that in the State of Morelos 60% of the ejido parcels are rented out. The Yaqui Indians rent their communal lands, obtained by way of restitution.[80]

The same phenomenon, although on a smaller scale, is reported in Bolivia and in Venezuela, where there are restrictions on transferability which are less strict than those in the Mexican Law. Some reasons for these unauthorized transfers are suggested in the foregoing article by Karst and Clement. Other reasons may also emerge. A parcel may be so tiny as not to provide enough income to support a family. The beneficiary may be willing to rent his parcel to a so-called "speculator" — one who rents several parcels and hires various beneficiaries to work for him as *peones* or day laborers. The beneficiary may even be able to earn more as a laborer than he could earn exploiting his own parcel.

Thus there are modern proposals, echoing the Reform of Juárez, that the ejido parcels be granted in full ownership, with the right to transfer them freely. Similar proposals have been made, and followed, from time to time in the case of Indian community lands in the United States. One unhappy result, occasionally seen in the United States, may be that land buyers will buy up the newly-transferable parcels at relatively cheap prices, taking advantage of the beneficiaries' sudden needs for cash (for an illness, a wedding, etc.) with the result that the land becomes concentrated again. At the very least, ejido parcels might be allowed to be concentrated to the point that an owner might feed his family from the produce of his land. Economically speaking, it is hard to see what would be wrong with that result. But even consolidating the ejido parcels into minimum-size units would almost certainly have the effect of freeing large numbers of people to leave the villages for the cities, which are already crowded with the unemployed — and frequently unemployable — rural dispossessed. Even Mexico, for all its economic growth, is not immune to the grave political consequences that are a risk of any serious effort to rationalize or restructure the ejido. As a consequence, successive Mexican governments have done nothing along these lines, although there continues to be much talk (outside governmental circles) of freeing the *ejidatario* from his condition as "glebe serf," "bound to the land."

---

3. Payment by Beneficiaries; Other Obligations

E. SIMPSON, THE EJIDO: MEXICO'S WAY OUT

Pp. 218-19 (1937)

The first thought of the revolutionary leaders, or at least of those associated with the Carranza regime, was that the villages themselves should pay for the land they received. The original agrarian decree of January 1915, to be sure, stated that lands for dotation to villages should be "expropriated for the account of the National

---

[80] Fernández y Fernández, "Propiedad Privada Versus Ejidos" (1954) in Palomo Valencia (ed.), *Historia del Ejido Actual* 19, 23 (1959).

Government," and that "interested parties who believed themselves injured" could present demands for compensation to the courts. Article 27 of the 1917 constitution assumed with equal definiteness the Nation's responsibility for the payment of properties expropriated for the purpose of ejido grants. But nothing was said in either the decree of 1915 or in Article 27 about the manner in which payments were to be made or whether the government was to assume final as well as initial responsibility for such payments. From other sources, however, it is clear that it was the original intention for the government, in the case of properties expropriated for ejido grants, to undertake only the functions of a financial intermediary.

The principal evidence in support of the foregoing assertion is to be found, first, in the already mentioned Circular No. 34 of the National Agrarian Commission (issued on January 31, 1919) requiring the inhabitants of villages petitioning for lands to agree in writing "to pay the Nation the value of the lands which they were going to receive by dotation, in accordance with the indemnity which the Nation must pay to the proprietors of the land expropriated"; and, second, in the original enabling act of January 10, 1920, that authorized the creation of the Public Agrarian Debt. This decree (which is still in force) states in Article 6 that for the payment of the bonds and coupons attached thereto, issued to indemnify owners of properties expropriated for ejidos, the government will apply all the revenues coming into the Treasury from the sale of ejido lands to the residents of the respective localities. The plain implication of Article 6 is that it was intended that the villages receiving ejido lands would, sooner or later, reimburse the government for the outlays for land made on their behalf.

When Obregón came into power one of his earliest political moves was to have the National Agrarian Commission rescind Circular No. 34. Although no change has ever been made in the sections of the decree of January 10, 1920, quoted above, generally speaking since Obregón's action removing Circular 34 from the books, there has been no further recognition of even the possibility of villages paying for ejidos.

The Mexican experience of non-payment by land reform beneficiaries has been followed almost everywhere, with the exception of various schemes of colonization in countries which have not seen fundamental land reforms, such as Argentina and Uruguay. Are there any arguments in favor of requiring some eventual payment from the beneficiaries, even though they may not be able to pay anything at the time their parcels are distributed to them? Is there any reason why a campesino might want to make at least a token payment?

Articles 156-60 of the Bolivian land reform law of 1953 provide for payment of compensation to landowners in agrarian bonds that are secured by mortgages on the expropriated land. The mortgages are designed to enforce the obligation to pay for the land, imposed on the land's recipients by article 10. The Bolivian government has no present intention of enforcing article 10, and has never even printed the agrarian bonds, in order not to alarm the land reform's beneficiaries.

There are other kinds of obligations which may be imposed on beneficiaries, relating to the manner in which they exploit their parcels. Some such obligations are suggested by the Venezuelan law: Article 67 requires the beneficiary to undertake to work his parcel personally or with his family; other articles contemplate both the providing of technical services and some form of supervision over the way the beneficiary cultivates his land. (Articles 78, 80, 122-24)

The lawyer's interest in such efforts centers on the creation of institutions to make them work. Suppose that a beneficiary burns the weeds on his parcel instead of using the approved methods of clearing. What kinds of sanctions can be imposed on him? Money fines? Reprimands? Forfeiture of his rights to the parcel? None of these seems satisfactory. It may be more practical to offer rewards for proper behavior than to impose sanctions for violations.

All of these supervisory efforts depend on the creation and maintenance of an effective corps of agricultural extension agents, something which does not now exist in adequate numbers in any country in Latin America. Is the solution to be found, as in Chile, in resident technicians who live in the asentamientos? Or is it to be found, as in Cuba, in the collective organization and management provided by the People's Farms? Or are all such arrangements doomed at least to short-term failure?

The extension scheme which now seems most favored is tied to the system of agricultural credit. "Supervised credit" refers to a loan in which the lender takes some responsibility for overseeing the application of the loaned funds. When an agricultural bank grants credit under such a system, it offers its own program of technical assistance to the borrower. The next section thus deals not only with traditional credit problems, but also with some of the extension service problems, which are necessarily associated with supervised credit for land reform beneficiaries.

---

4. Agricultural Credit

N. WHETTEN, RURAL MEXICO

Pp. 204-07 (1948)*

From the standpoint of financing the agricultural activities of these individually operated ejidos, there are a great many difficulties which present themselves. These stem from a variety of factors, among which are (1) the small size of the plots, (2) the relatively poor quality of the land, (3) the culturally retarded status of the ejidatarios. The size of the holding is, in general, too small to be operated economically. With only 4.4 hectares of farm land, on the average, and much of this either too dry or too mountainous for efficient cultivation, there is little specialization of crops, little use of farm machinery and lack of full employment on the part of the entrepreneur and his family. The general tendency in such cases is for the ejidatario to raise only subsistence crops, usually corn, whether the land is suited for this or not, in the fear of going hungry if he fails to grow what he eats. Ordinarily, his methods of production are backward, and, without a great deal of supervision, he is likely to produce little beyond his subsistence needs. Even with a great deal of supervision, it is questionable whether the return he could realize on his surplus products would be sufficient to compensate a credit agency for providing the necessary supervision. This is the problem with which the [Ejido Bank] is confronted. In order to get a clear conception of the difficulties involved, we shall examine them with reference to the procedure of the bank.

First, in order for the society to receive credit from the bank, a plan of operations for the year must be prepared and approved. Ideally, these would be worked out, first, by each ejidatario for his own plot, then co-ordinated with those of the other members of his credit society, so as to present the bank with a composite plan in requesting specified funds for the society as a whole.

Since membership in the societies carries joint liability, it is quite important that each one know what the others request, so that this may be approved, modified, or rejected by the group in accordance with their knowledge of his needs, capacities, and resources. Actually, it does not work out that way. Many of the ejidatarios lack the experience and the cultural development for working out any such plan. When they meet to discuss the plan in a general assembly, jealousy and rivalry arise, with the result that, regardless of needs or ability to repay, the local officials are reluctant to assign less funds to one individual than to another for fear of unpleasant repercussions. This usually means that the local representative of the bank must consider each case individually, approve each plan separately, and make allotments of credit accordingly. This is almost an impossible task to perform adequately, since there are, on the average, 27 societies per zone and 67 ejidatarios in a society. This would give the local bank representative an average of about 1,809 ejidatarios to look after individually and many of these would be widely scattered.

A second major problem is concerned with the actual dispensing of funds after the plans of operation have been approved and the credit allotted. Again the ideal method would be for the bank to deal only with the member-delegate of a given society and let him distribute the funds among the members; but the bank has found that in most cases the member-delegate is not prepared to shoulder such responsibility. Sad experience has resulted from giving cash to the ejidatarios, since, like children, they often spend it for frivolities rather than for production purposes. For this reason the bank urges its local representatives to ascertain the needs of the ejidatarios and to grant loans to them in the form of supplies and equipment, such as seed, plows, and oxen, instead of giving them the cash. This procedure is very time consuming and costly, however, since the needs of each one must be considered and acted upon separately.

A third problem lies in the growing and marketing of the crop. Ordinarily, the plots are too small to warrant the purchase or use of modern farm machinery, and most of the ejidatarios probably are not even aware that such machinery exists. They use the same primitive methods that have been in use for centuries. In a few instances societies have purchased machinery jointly for the use of their members, but such cases are exceptional. In the last few years the bank has alleviated the machinery problem somewhat by establishing an agency known as the Department of Agricultural

Services. About 16,000,000 pesos were invested in farm machinery from the United States which was placed in conveniently located "machinery centers." The machinery is owned by the bank. Work requiring the use of machinery is then performed at the request of the ejidatarios who pay the bill on a cost basis. . . .

Little uniformity exists in the products from the individual ejidos. Ordinarily, each ejidatario uses his own judgment as to when and what to plant and how to tend the crop. There are no uniform grades for products of a given area, and this makes for difficulty in marketing. The lack of warehouses is also a hindrance to any attempt at marketing the crops co-operatively or holding them for favorable prices. As a rule, the ejidatario lives at, or near, subsistence level, and he is eager to get a return for his crop as quickly as possible. He does not think through the economics of marketing but often bargains away whatever crop he thinks he will be able to spare long before it is ready for harvesting. The *acaparadores* ("monopolizers") have been a plague in rural Mexico for generations, and they are still going strong.

The Ejido Bank is struggling with the problem of convincing the ejidatario that his interests are being jeopardized by such practices and is trying to displace the *acaparador* by more efficient marketing procedures; but when each ejidatario is concerned only with his own little plot and bargains individually, he plays into the hands of the *acaparadores*.

A fourth problem, and one of the most serious, concerns the collecting of debts on loans. Theoretically, all members are supposed to bring their payments to the member-delegate and let him make the society's payments to the bank in a lump sum. It does not work out that way, however. Ejidatarios simply do not bring in their payments. In some cases, as indicated above, the ejidatario has already promised his crop, gets what little money is due him as soon as the crop is harvested, and spends it without considering the debt he owes. Other ejidatarios, sometimes through carelessness in tending their crops, sometimes through factors beyond their control, do not receive enough from their harvests to subsist upon and pay debts in addition. Still others are influenced by propaganda against the Ejido Bank, which not infrequently sweeps through the ejidos, to the effect that ejidatarios need not repay any debts to the bank, since these are government funds and should be given to them as a part of the fruits of the Revolution, just as was done in the case of the land. In one state which the author recently visited, the governor was elected to office on the platform that he would see to it that the ejidatarios would not need to repay their loans. Thus the bank often finds itself under the necessity of trying to collect from each ejidatario individually, necessitating numerous calls, thus greatly augmenting administrative expenses. In many areas these expenses have become so high that operations have had to be suspended entirely.

The problems described above have tended to limit the operations which the bank feels it can safely undertake with the ejidos operating on an individual basis. This is emphasized by statistics showing that the three agencies of Torreón, Ciudad Obregón and Los Mochis, in which practically all the ejidos were operating on a collective basis, received 65.4 per cent of all funds loaned by the bank in 1943. These three agencies included only 11.5 per cent of all ejidatarios operating with the bank.

E. SIMPSON, THE EJIDO: MEXICO'S WAY OUT

Pp. 377-79 (1937)
The Special Nature of the Ejido Credit Problem

Even if Mexico at the beginning of the agrarian reform had possessed a system of agricultural credit and even if this system had been adapted to the needs of small farmers, it is doubtful that it could have been made to serve the ends of the ejidatarios. For so special are the legal, economic and social problems presented by this class of farmers created by the revolution that, for all practical purposes, they lie outside the field of any customary type of either private or public banking enterprise. The problem of providing ejidatarios with funds to work their newly acquired lands and market their products has been, and is, a problem of creating an entirely new type of credit structure.

In the first place it must be recalled that both as a matter of fact and as a matter of law the vast majority of the ejidatarios have very little, if any private capital. As a matter of fact, because by definition those who receive ejidos are drawn from the vast body of "the miserable and the disinherited"; as a matter of law, because no person who possesses "commercial or industrial capital of more than 2,500 pesos," or land "equal to or greater in extension than a [ejido] parcel" may benefit under the ejido laws.

Second, ejido parcels are "imprescriptible and inalienable . . . and therefore in no case and in no form whatsoever may they be ceded, conveyed, rented, hypothecated, or made subject to lien in whole or in part." Moreover, ejido lands may not be the object of seizure as the result of a suit, law, decree, order or otherwise by any authority private or official, whether Federal, State or Municipal. All of which means that practically the only security an individual ejidatario can offer a loan is his crop; and even with respect to this crop there are certain restrictions which render this security of doubtful value to an ordinary bank.

Finally, to the legal and economic peculiarities of the problem of providing credit for the ejidatario there must be added certain complicating factors of a social and political nature. It must be constantly held in mind that the great mass of Mexico's rural population has for centuries been living outside of and divorced from the institutions and procedures of modern economic life, and is, for the most part, profoundly ignorant of financial and credit operations of any type.[81] The problem of credit for the ejidatario in its simplest form, therefore, is one of education. They must be taught the meaning of loans, notes, bonds, checks, shares, warehouse receipts,

---

[81] Most of the lower strata of the farmers have, of course, had some experience with the widespread system of crop-advances by which the *hacendados* have traditionally provided their renters, tenants, resident laborers and sometimes even neighboring "independent" small farmers with seeds, plows, work animals and small amounts of cash. Familiarity with this personalistic and usurious system, however, can hardly be regarded as knowledge of credit operations. Indeed, the system may be said to foster attitudes — servile dependence and lack of responsibility and initiative — just the opposite of those demanded for the successful working of modern methods of financing agricultural operations. . . . [Footnote by Simpson, renumbered.]

interest rates — in a word, they must be taught first that there is such a thing as agricultural credit, and, second, how this mysterious thing works.

But there is also another type of training the lack of which makes it difficult to introduce obviously indicated types of credit organization. The legal set-up of the ejido being what it is, it would seem that some form of cooperative society with collective responsibility would be the most satisfactory means for financing agricultural operations. Any attempt, however, to proceed along these lines meets the obstacle of what the prominent agrarian leader, Luis León has described as the "lack of spiritual preparation." "The Mexican peasants," writes León, "are still too individualistic . . . . As the result of their experience as an exploited class they feel a profound lack of confidence in any undertaking in which they cannot see complete compensation for their work clearly guaranteed. . . . They have no interest in collective work unless they are sure of its advantages." From this point of view, then, agricultural credit for the ejidatario becomes a question of education of a somewhat more complicated type — education, that is, in cooperative enterprise, mutual confidence, and in the meaning of moral responsibility in business transactions.

K. KARST AND N. CLEMENT, LEGAL INSTITUTIONS AND DEVELOPMENT: LESSONS FROM THE MEXICAN EJIDO

16 *U.C.L.A. Law Review* 281, 290-92 (1969)

The reason for ejidatario suspicion of government agencies lies primarily in the history of the National Bank of Ejido Credit, a bank owned and managed by the government, whose object is to make loans[82] to ejidatarios. The Ejido Bank has, in the past, often failed to recover payment of its loans to ejidatarios, so that the loans have come to be regarded by many as subsidies. Since that is plainly not a basis on which the Bank can serve all the ejidos in the country, it is also widely assumed that the Bank's local offices have selected the recipients of credit (or subsidy) with political considerations in mind. The connection of the Bank's local officials to local politics is a source of suspicion among the ejidatarios, even though the most serious abuses are now past. Furthermore, many ejidatarios complain that the dealings of the Bank's local officials frequently have been dishonest.[83]

Still, private bank sources of agricultural credit are normally closed to the ejidatario, for several reasons. First, since his farm is small, the administrative costs associated with short-term credit are prohibitively high. Second, since he possesses

---

[82]The loans may be in cash or in kind (e.g., seed and fertilizer). [Footnote by Karst and Clement, renumbered.]

[83]One such practice has worked this way: The ejidatario is quoted one price for, say, fertilizer; at the time of delivery, he is required to pay a higher price; the difference is described as a "personal service charge." An ejidatario might elect to pay this charge, since the total cost of fertilizer on credit might still be lower than the cost of borrowing from the local moneylenders. But the result would be more ill will toward the Bank. [Footnote by Karst and Clement, renumbered.]

little capital and cannot mortgage his land, he has virtually no security to offer except for his crops.[84] The result is that a private bank is unlikely to be willing even to extend short-term credit; long-term credit is out of the question. Consequently, the ejidatario must borrow either from the Ejido Bank or from the local moneylender. (In a given town, there will usually be one or two individuals who do most of the non-bank lending.) In [an ejido near Guadalajara] nearly all the credit comes from moneylenders, even though their rates may be as much as double the rates of the Ejido Bank. Since the ejidatarios are not unaware of this rate differential, other explanations must be sought for their reliance on the local private moneylenders.

Four such explanations reinforce the distrust of the Ejido Bank noted earlier. First, much of the credit from the Bank is now given in specie: seed, fertilizer, insecticides; if the Bank is late in delivering these inputs, as it is with distressing frequency, the ejidatario may miss the best time for planting or performing other operations.[85] Second, the Bank has recently insisted that its borrowers buy crop insurance; this insurance has been poorly explained to the ejidatarios, and in any case is not especially attractive to a farmer in an area of adequate rainfall such as Jalisco. Third, the local moneylender makes no demands on the borrower with respect to the way in which he conducts his farming operations (the recent practice of the Ejido Bank is to tie its loans to extension services in a program of "supervised credit") and is willing to lend additional money for personal needs unrelated to the ejidatario's farming (illness, a wedding, etc.).[86]

Finally, the Ejido Bank, in theory, deals only with local credit "societies," groups of five or more ejidatarios who form cooperative borrowing associations.[87] In practice, the Bank deals with individual borrowers. Nonetheless, the form of a cooperative is retained, and there is always the lingering fear that one ejidatario will have to make good for another's defaults. The Bank has long since given up trying to make those joint obligations stick, but its past attempts to do so have given the very name "society" a bad sound in the ears of many ejidatarios.

---

[84] Money to be loaned as agricultural credit is scarce enough that private banks can find borrowers who can offer better security. The banks prefer not to have to chase down a borrower's crop when repayment time comes. [Footnote by Karst and Clement, renumbered.]

[85] A frequent complaint from ejidatarios is that the Ejido Bank charges them for inputs that come too late to be used at all. [Footnote by Karst and Clement, renumbered.]

[86] One story from [an ejido near Guadalajara] suggests that bureaucrats of the Ejido Bank, like bureaucrats everywhere, are strongly motivated to look good on paper. The Bank offered to sell the ejido one or two tractors, with the selling point that the tractors would eliminate a lot of hard work relating to plowing and weeding. The number of tractors made available to the ejidos in an official's district may be an important statistic when his superior reviews his personnel file. The ejidatarios quite properly turned down the offer, since they are not now working more than about half the year. They had no interest in going into debt to pay for a machine that would give them still more time to be idle. [Footnote by Karst and Clement, renumbered.]

[87] The objective is to keep the Bank's administrative costs down. [Footnote by Karst and Clement, renumbered.]

R. STAVENHAGEN, SOCIAL ASPECTS OF AGRARIAN STRUCTURE IN MEXICO

in R. Stavenhagen (ed.), *Agrarian Problems and
Peasant Movements in Latin America* at 225, 253-54 (1970)*

The *ejido* is thus integrated in a wide network of bureaucratic and political relationships. This system may, of course, bring a number of benefits to the *ejidatarios*, by channeling to them the goods and services that the government distributes. But it also contributes to the vulnerability of the *ejido's* independence and its capacity for autonomous decision and action as a social unit, by exposing it to official authoritarianism and paternalism, bureaucratization and, particularly, corruption.

Specific cases which it has been possible to study in the rural areas show that corruption is not an "endemic malady" in *ejido* organization, but that when it appears it is generally stimulated from above and outside the *ejido*. It would thus seem that the bureaucratic bourgeoisie (the "new class" of which Djilas speaks in another context) finds in the *ejido* a fertile field for the application of its acquisitive instincts.

There are plenty of examples which would document these generalizations. Let us simply point, among others, to a special kind of problem which has become very important in the development of the *ejido* sector. Sufficient, cheap and timely credit is an essential element in agricultural production. The National Ejido Credit Bank was created over thirty years ago to cater to the needs of the *ejidos*. But as we have already pointed out, its resources are insufficient to satisfy more than a minority of *ejido* farmers. Its activities are channeled mainly toward economically profitable cash crops in the highly productive areas (sugar cane, cotton). Due to various reasons and through different mechanisms, in certain areas the Bank has taken over the control of agricultural production in the *ejidos* through the establishment of agricultural calendars, the distribution of fertilizer, the use of heavy machinery, the management of industrial transformation units such as sugar mills and cotton gins, and the acquisition, stocking and sale of harvests. In these areas, the *ejidatarios* often lose control over the product of their labor and over their own labor force; they become, as it were, wage workers for the Bank on their own plots. Their relations with the Bank, instead of stimulating entrepreneurial capacity among the *ejidatarios*, in fact transform them into passive dependents. The *ejidatario*, instead of planning and caring for his crops, seeks a daily wage for his subsistence. And the local Bank agency handles accounts and distributes profits after the harvest has been sold, with hardly any intervention on the part of the *ejidatarios*.

It is not strange, therefore, that under these conditions the *ejidatario* often ends up at the close of the agricultural cycle in debt to the Bank. Complaints are frequent by *ejidatarios* about fraud, larceny, fictitious costs which are charged against their accounts, inputs of low quality, technical and financial aid which arrives at the wrong time after undue delays, and so forth. And the Bank, in turn, frequently does not recuperate its loans and its balance sheets show large deficits in the management of its

*Reprinted by permission of the publisher, Doubleday & Company, Inc. Copyright © 1970 by Rodolfo Stavenhagen.

accounts, which are all due to the same causes. Some students of the agrarian question maintain that the Bank is no more than a subsidizing agency for the *ejidatario*, because it seems to be managed more by political than purely financial criteria. Others, however, point to the fact that in many areas the Bank's operations involve the *ejidatario* in a cumulative process of decapitalization and that certain types of legislation (such as the law which establishes compulsory areas for the cultivation of sugar cane in order to supply the sugar mills) prevent the *ejidatarios* from breaking this vicious circle.

Note on Supervised Credit Programs

In Mexico and in other countries (notably Chile and Venezuela), money supplied in part by the Alliance for Progress has been deposited with lending agencies for the purpose of establishing programs of supervised credit Essentially, these programs combine credit with extension services in the hope of securing a better rate of repayment, thus reducing the drain on the countries' resources which is implicit in the old system of subsidies disguised as credit.

The Venezuelan program operates as follows: The *campesino* — often, but not necessarily, a beneficiary of the land reform — prepares a plan for the improvement or cultivation of his parcel, with the aid of an extension agent assigned to his village or district. The request for a loan is submitted to a local committee, composed of village leaders, the extension agent, etc. This committee must approve the request, and is to consider primarily the personal characteristics of the borrower — his good faith and the likelihood of his doing his best to fulfill his contract. The technical aspect of his proposal is confided largely to the extension agent, and to the credit committee in the local office of the Agricultural Bank, which has the main responsibility for deciding on requests for credit. Loans are granted for periods of from six to eighteen months, and at interest rates, depending on the size of the loan (the greater the loan, the higher the interest), of from three to six per cent. Security may be given in the form of a mortgage of the borrower's interest in his land, or of his equipment, or probably most frequently a pledge of the next crop. The supervision of the borrower's operation takes the form of regular visits by the extension agent, who checks to see that the plan which he has helped to formulate is being carried out. Sanctions for failure to carry out the plan are limited to the usual lender's remedies — termination of the loan, recourse to the security, etc.[88]

Another scheme is being tried in Mexico, also with the aid of money from the Alliance. The Bank of Mexico has established a fund designed to guarantee up to 90% of loans made by private banks to farmers. There is no political pressure on the private banks to permit borrowers to escape their obligations to repay; on the contrary it is hoped by the scheme's proponents that the private lenders will exercise some degree of supervision over the loaned funds. The program's critics on the political left claim that

---

[88] Banco Agrícola y Pecuario (Venezuela), *Manual de Crédito Supervisado (AID)* (1962).

it is designed to give still another advantage to the "small property owners" – or, as they see it, to relatively wealthy farmers.

G. Epilogue: The "Results" of Land Reform in Latin America

Land reform legislation has been adopted in a majority of the countries of Latin America. In most of these countries, the legislation has been carried out in varying degree; a handful of countries have actually experienced land reform. Even in the latter countries, land reform has meant different things at different times and in different places. For Pedro Martínez in Mexico,[89] land reform was one thing; for Juan Paredes in Cuba,[90] it was something else. To speak of the results of land reform in Latin America is thus to speak in the abstract of phenomena that are disparate – not merely distributed along some imaginary continuum of revolutionary purity, but distributed in so many dimensions as to make generalization extremely hazardous.[91] Nonetheless, no one – not even a lawyer – can think without generalizing, and to round out this chapter, we look briefly at one regional evaluation, and at one single-country evaluation.

Solon Barraclough's discussion is cast in the conditional tense: what *would* a land reform bring to a Latin American country? His predictions, however, are supported with evidence from the countries that have experienced land reform; thus what appears to be a hypothetical discussion is an evaluation of the results of past and ongoing land reforms. Next, Ronald Clark, also an economist, sums up his evaluation of the relation between land reform and economic development in Bolivia.

The quotation marks in this section's title suggest some skepticism about the degree of confidence with which one may speak of the results of land reform in Latin America. The skepticism does not merely rest on the old lament about the unreliability of statistics. More fundamentally, the problem is that in each country that has seen land reform, the evaluator has no "control group" – no parallel history – against which to measure the country's real history. To ask, "What would Mexico have become without a land reform?" is to ask an unanswerable question. (We note that there are those who would say that in fact the Mexican Revolution was a sugar pill and not the real vaccine. We do not mean to enter into that dispute here.)

There are, finally, aspects of a vast social phenomenon like a land reform that defy yardsticks and balance scales. Here, evaluation is necessarily unscientific, at least to the extent that science implies measurement, and thus statistics. In *A New Refutation of Time*, Jorge Luis Borges says:

---

[89] Oscar Lewis' book, *Pedro Martínez* (1964), details the life of a campesino in Morelos who was a follower of Zapata, and later a beneficiary of the land reform.

[90] See J. Yglesias, *In the Fist of the Revolution: Life in a Cuban Country Town,* ch. 5 (1968).

[91] Doreen Warriner's careful country-by-country analysis implicitly makes the point, as does the analysis of Barraclough and Domike, quoted earlier in this chapter, of seven Latin American countries that had not experienced land reform.

The fifth paragraph of the fourth chapter of the treatise *Sanhedrin* of the Mishnah declares that, as far as the Justice of God is concerned, whoever kills one man destroys the world. If there is no plurality, whoever would annihilate all mankind would be no more culpable than primitive and solitary Cain – an orthodox point of view – nor more universal in his destructiveness – which may be magical. That is the way I understand it, too. Clangorous general catastrophes – conflagrations, wars, epidemics – are a single grief, multiplied in numerous mirrors illusorily.[92]

It may be, conversely, that to give hope – and thus life – to one family in the *altiplano* is to create the world. If that suggestion is too romantic for lawyers or other institution-builders, perhaps the suggestion can be clothed in respectable sociologese: Land reform's most significant product is upward mobility. Richard Patch's three sentences, which close the chapter, are at least as meaningful as any supply curve.

S. BARRACLOUGH, AGRICULTURAL POLICY AND STRATEGIES OF LAND REFORM

in I. Horowitz (ed.),
Masses in Latin America
at 95, 154-63 (1970)*

Effects of Agrarian Reform on Agricultural Production

It was shown that the present land-tenure structure is associated with an inefficient use of land and labor, with low rates of investment in agriculture and with few opportunities or incentives to adopt new technologies. To what extent would redistributing the rights and benefits of land ownership in favor of the small producers and to landless tenants directly change this situation?

The answer seems to be that increases in agricultural production resulting from a mere redistribution of rights in land would be rather limited. Access to additional land is only one of the many factors limiting agricultural development. It can not be assumed that removing this limitation – and doing nothing more – would cause a great upsurge in production.

Good agricultural land resources are relatively scarce in the regions of heaviest rural population, such as the Altiplano. In such regions the physical possibilities of expanding greatly the areas of more intensive production have a calculable upper limit, at least until some of the other obstacles to agricultural growth are removed. In most areas of intensively cultivated small plots and large extensively used properties (the latifundia-minifundia complex) the shortage of available land would probably keep

---

[92] J. Borges, *A Personal Anthology* 52 (1967).

*Copyright © 1970 by Irving Louis Horowitz. Reprinted by permission of Oxford University Press, Inc.

production from increasing by more than a maximum of 50 per cent above present levels even after many years of using only traditional technologies.

In practice, agricultural production might not change very much at all in the short-run as a direct result of redistribution in some rural areas. Where land reform has been rapid and at times anarchic — as was the case in post-revolutionary Mexico and Bolivia — some lines of production temporarily decreased. Livestock numbers declined, for example, when campesinos sold or ate breeding stock. Sales of some industrial crops also dropped because of general economic dislocation. There is little evidence, however, that food crop production was greatly affected even in these revolutionary reform areas. The ICAD study of Guatemala indicates that during that country's brief experience with rapid large-scale reform there were temporary production and marketing problems for export crops but a marked increase in corn production for consumption. The rural population consumes more food staples, eggs, meat and vegetables following a land reform, thereby reducing their commercial marketings to the cities. This happened to an important degree in Bolivia and to some extent more recently in Cuba. Reform programs that include real incentives for farmers to increase both production and marketing can be expected to avoid most of this difficulty.

Over a longer period, tenure reform can be expected to show much greater effects on production. These effects, however, are not so much from making more land available to the peasants as from changing incentives, services, and marketing facilities. In this respect, the effects of reform could conceivably even be negative if the limited entrepreneurial and organizing functions of the previous landlords were not adequately replaced by the state or by new local institutions.

In considering the productivity problem in relation to reform little has been said concerning possible economies or diseconomies of scale. The omission was deliberate. In the first place, as was pointed out earlier, the very concept of the farm operating-unit has only very limited applicability in the traditional agricultural structure. The large properties are often not operating-units at all but a complex of producing and consuming units under a central administration that may be more political than economic.

Secondly, the real economies of scale in agriculture are associated with particular functions such as plowing, planting, harvesting, marketing, transport, and processing. These functions are all separable one from another. They are not necessarily strictly associated with property rights or even with the farm unit itself; cooperatives, custom work, and numerous other institutional arrangements can be used to obtain economies of scale in different production, processing or marketing functions. The redistribution of tenure rights does not necessarily mean the division of large properties into individual family farms. The *ejidos* in Mexico, the proportional profit farms in Puerto Rico, the state farms in Cuba and the *asentamientos* in Chile are all examples of other alternatives in a land reform process.

Finally, there simply is no convincing evidence concerning economies or diseconomies of scale in relation to size of farm in Latin American agriculture. One reason for this is that operating units and property units do not coincide, nor do census-defined operating units and the multitude of smaller sharecropper and laborers' units that are included in the larger estates. Another is the difficulty of agreeing on what efficiency criteria to use in evaluation. Should labor be counted as a cost valued at current wage rates when there are no alternative job opportunities? If not, what "shadow prices" should be used? What is the cost of land when market values include prestige, political power, social status, credit security, capitalized subsidy payments and its value as a hedge against inflation? Finally, many advantages of scale are offset by disadvantages such as absentee management and problems of labor organization. The net result is that existing studies of economies of scale in the study countries show highly confusing and contradictory conclusions.

Reform and Income Distribution

A second relationship between agrarian reform and agricultural development is to be found in income distribution. There is no question that a real reform can redistribute income to the benefit of the campesinos by absolving them of the tributes and rents by which landlords now expropriate most of the peasants' surplus above subsistence. In Bolivia, for example, peasant incomes and consumption rose after the reform even where production was unaffected. Of course, peasant incomes will not increase if the payments to the landlord are simply made to the state or tradesmen following reform, but this is unlikely. It was seen that in Chile a redistribution of the income now going to the large farmers could theoretically double peasant incomes. In the *asentamientos* [land settlements] organized under the present reform program, peasant incomes have actually increased by about this amount. Without greater agricultural production and accelerated out-migration, however, incomes resulting from reform would be dissipated by population increase within a generation or so.

While there is no question that reform usually can increase peasant incomes, the direct effects on development are more difficult to assess. The demand for industrial goods will undoubtedly be stimulated. But whether this greater domestic market in turn stimulates industrial growth or merely increases imports and inflation depends on the nation's economic and social structure. The beneficial results often claimed for a wider income distribution presuppose changes in national economic policy.

Whether the more widely distributed post-reform incomes help spark development by changing propensities to invest depends on such a host of variables that generalizations are also impossible about this point. If the incomes of the large landlords previously spent on consumption or relatively non-productive capital were redirected into high priority investments either by the state or other groups, this would obviously stimulate economic growth. But there is no a priori assurance that a simple redistribution of land and income would have this result. The land reform would have to be accompanied by tax and fiscal reforms. Otherwise peasant increased consumption might more than offset indirectly increased investments.

Nonetheless, the conclusion seems reasonable that the seigneurial distribution of income is as antagonistic to economic development in Latin America as it has been in other regions in which large plantations and near-feudal conditions prevailed.

Agrarian Reform and Social Structure

Agrarian reform by definition alters the relationships between groups in the use of land – land-tenure institutions are changed. To the extent that reform is effective, rural social structure will be modified, the combination of institutions in rural areas will be different. The traditional "patronal" system is eliminated with much that it implies for social organization if the reform is a real one and not only a slogan. As a consequence the local political structure will change. So too will the social incentives to produce, to invest, to innovate and to migrate.

We know very little, however, about just what these changes will be in Latin America or by what social mechanisms they take place. Clarence Senior attempted to evaluate this for La Laguna region in Mexico. There have been several partial studies of individual communities affected by reforms. There have also been various studies of the effects of reform on rural social structures in other parts of the world. Obviously the degree of social change will depend in part on the nature of the reform, whether it is part of a more thoroughgoing social revolution or is merely limited to local land tenure institutions. It will also depend on the initial situation, on the local social systems prevailing when the reform takes place.

In Bolivia, many observers have reported greatly increased interest in education on the part of the peasants since reform, following the elimination of the old patrons. The author believes he can see a marked difference in the attitudes toward education and political participation in the Bolivian Aymara communities where the hacendados were eliminated and those across lake Titicaca in Puno. Maddox reports an increased propensity to invest and become entrepreneurs on the part of former large landowners in Mexico after the revolution. Many of us visiting the new Chilean asentamientos think we see a dramatic change in the peasants' desires to produce, to build up farm capital, to improve their farming methods, and to educate their children.

While there is wide agreement among students of agrarian reform that the changes in social structure and incentives are possibly the most important of any in their long-term consequences for future development, there has been surprisingly little systematic testing of this hypothesis. The current ICAD evaluations of the reforms in Mexico, Bolivia, and Venezuela should permit a firmer understanding of what the changes in local social systems have been and how they occurred.

Agrarian Reform and Agricultural Policy

The connections between agrarian reform and agricultural policy are more direct and obvious. A profound land reform eliminates the large landowners as the principal policy clientele. If the reform is a real one and not a token program, their hold on local political power is broken. At the national level they cease to be an important interest group either in advocating policies for their own benefit or influencing the policies of other groups. Connections with the large landowning families are no longer an important prerequisite for political recruitment. New channels of political communication are opened between national centers of power and rural groups. Both political structure and political inputs are altered.

Following reform, agricultural policy as a consequence can be expected to change both in content and in terms of the benefited clientele. The "strategy" of development will no longer call for the large landowners to be the principal modernizers and the capital accumulators. In all probability, however, the new agricultural development "strategy" will not rely only on the campesinos either. The State may take practically all of the initiative in both technical change and capital formation. Or it may leave these functions to new groups of commercial farmers and investors. Or the State may share these responsibilities with campesino and new commercial groups. Which of these alternatives is adopted may depend somewhat on the ideology of the reform movement. It will undoubtedly depend much more on how much representation the campesinos have managed to attain in the new political structure and how well they are organized to press their interests.

Following reform in Mexico, for example, agricultural policy, especially after 1940, became much more development-oriented than before the revolution. The new clientele of agricultural policy, however, does not seem to have been so much the campesinos as the commercial farmers. The larger investors, and the medium- and small-sized commercial operators (the "kulaks") became the new principal beneficiaries of agricultural policies.

In Bolivia and Puerto Rico much the same tendencies as in Mexico are apparent — large commercial operators and medium and small commercially oriented farmers are the new clientele of agricultural policy. In Cuba on the other hand, it seems that the former landless agricultural workers have been among the chief beneficiaries of reform, as have some of the small producers.

In all of these countries, however, the State has assumed a primary role in agricultural development. National technical assistance programs and credit agencies are the chosen vehicles for agricultural modernization. In Chile, for example, present agrarian reform plans call annually for training about 1,000 new agricultural agents of one kind or another to work directly with the campesinos and to take the leadership in agricultural development (the various state agencies combined employed a total of less than 1,000 agents working directly with farmers in 1964). If one reviews the experiences of Egypt, Italy, Japan, Puerto Rico, Venezuela, Yugoslavia, Rumania, or Poland following reform, the same tendencies are evident.

What were the changes in political structure in these countries? To what extent were these a result of agrarian reform and to what extent were they a cause of it? Do the changes in political structure "explain" the new agricultural policy orientations?

We can only pose these questions here. Our hypothesis is that if the reform really redistributes control of the good land among the peasants, they will become a more important political force. Peasant organizations become feasible. Peasants will be a major interest group. National political parties become concerned with peasant problems. Communications between peasant groups and the State improve. Recruitment from peasant ranks increases. As a result, agricultural policy is altered to take this new clientele into account.

Even if the peasants are not fully incorporated into the political system immediately, and their lack of education and traditional social inferiority makes this difficult, national agricultural policy is still likely to become more conducive for development. The small- and medium-sized farmers, urban investors, middle class tradesmen and government officials replace the former landlord elite. History shows many examples of successful development strategies benefiting primarily these new clienteles, even though the campesinos still get a relatively poor deal from official policies. I know of no examples, however, where development strategy was able to rely principally on aiding the traditional large landowners.

Paradoxically, where orderly land reform is possible through normal political processes, it is less necessary for accelerated development than where it is not. Thus land reforms are commonly the consequence of riots, demonstrations, and revolutions (anomic interest groups), or of outside pressures such as defeat in a war, that have led to a breakdown of the established political and social systems.

If our reasoning is correct, in most situations large-scale land reform is revolutionary in that it changes political structures. Unless there have already been sufficient modifications of political structure to permit the groups pressing for agrarian reform to make their interests effective, reform can not be expected to take place through the established political system. But if the political system has evolved sufficiently to make reform a possible policy "output" so should it be possible to redirect other agricultural policies, even without land reform.

Historical perspective shows agrarian reform to be more a result than a cause of development. As economic development and urbanization progress, and pressures mount to change the traditional rural society there are increasing social and political stresses and tensions. Agricultural policies are increasingly inconsistent with development requirements. At this point, the traditional agrarian structure becomes an obstacle to continued rapid development and agrarian reform can be said to be "necessary."

Land-tenure institutions may be reformed abruptly early in the development process, as they were in Mexico and Bolivia, or the changes may be delayed until development is well under way as they were in Cuba and Chile. Tenure reforms may be revolutionary and violent, they may be rapid but relatively orderly, or they may take place only slowly as rural manpower is absorbed into other activities, accompanied by increasing agricultural productivity and growing competition for workers among landowners. What is certain is that the traditional agrarian structure with its peculiar land tenure institutions will be modified sooner or later as development takes place.

One cannot say that land reform per se is either a sufficient or always a necessary condition for accelerated economic growth, even where traditional agrarian structures prevail. After all, there is ample historical evidence of expanding material wealth being created by slaves and serfs as well as free farmers. More than anything else, rapid development requires firm and capable leadership in modernizing the economy and in providing the appropriate economic organizations and incentives to produce and invest.

Taken by itself, land-tenure reform may neither stimulate nor retard economic growth, at least in the short-run. It may be a prerequisite, however, for new groups to displace the traditional elites — to enable the "modernizers" to mobilize the resources and the efforts required for a big push. In any case, the direct effects of land-tenure reform on agricultural development will be most evident through the reorientation of agricultural policies, policies that before land reform served the interests of the larger landowners almost exclusively.

R. CLARK, LAND REFORM AND PEASANT MARKET PARTICIPATION ON THE NORTHERN HIGHLANDS OF BOLIVIA

44 *Land Economics* 153, 171-72 (1968)

In the case of Bolivia the land reform on the north highlands accomplished three things quickly. One, the increased access to land realized by the peasants was equivalent to redistribution of opportunities to earn a cash income. Two, restructuring of the market system began immediately after the redistribution of land, but because it was not accomplished instantaneously, bottlenecks were created and the marketing of agricultural produce in the urban centers fell off. Nevertheless, the process was begun which would eventually lead to the creation of a marketing system in which the peasantry would play a more important role than before 1952. Three, for the first time those who were producing on the land began to spend for consumption items within the rural sector, not just in La Paz or in foreign countries as the landlords had done.

The peasants, most of whom had never before worked their lands as owner-operators, needed time to adjust to this new situation. Perhaps the most important thing the peasant had to accept was that the land reform was a fact and that it would not be undone by a counter-revolution. Two things — a combination of *revolution and land reform* carried out by the government through the peasant unions, and *time* — were necessary to increase the horizons and expectations of the peasantry. This was only to be expected of people who had worked for centuries as serfs on land belonging to others. In particular, time was needed to increase the number of rural families experiencing the new incentives, attitudes and motivations, all of which derived primarily from the development and use of individual managerial talents.

There are indications that what has taken place so far in the rural sector on the north highlands has increased the possibilities for economic development in other sectors of the economy. For example, a greater number of markets with an increased number of peasants participating in them on a cash basis signifies a greater frequency of contact between peasants and buyers from the city. A result of this is that new channels of communication are created. Markets and commercial contacts can be a source of change in attitudes and of expansion of social, political and economic horizons among the peasantry. The expansion of economic horizons leads to new wants, purchases, and consumption patterns. It also acts as a stimulus to the manufacture of commodities for a mass market.

Greater frequency of peasant transactions within the framework of a money economy has increased the extent to which specialization of functions can develop within the rural sector and also between the rural sector and the rest of the economy. When peasant transactions are based largely on barter, opportunities for trade and specialization are reduced considerably, especially in terms of the sales of products of one sector against those of another, and in terms of possibilities for creating regional or national markets for agricultural or manufactured goods. It is in relation to this latter point that considerable change has taken place in Bolivia; national markets for agricultural and non-agricultural products have been created since the land reform.

Development within the agricultural sector has been stimulated by the creation of new markets for agricultural products in precisely those areas where the land reform took place. These small but growing markets for agricultural products are for all kinds of fruits, vegetables, coffee, wheat products (such as bread and noodles), sugar, rice, corn and corn flour, wheat flour, and soft drinks and beer. Admittedly, the per capita consumption of these food products is still low, but the tastes for these products have been created and increased consumption and sales in the future will be more a function of increases in income than new market creation.

The creation of new markets for manufactured goods is even more impressive than that for agricultural products. Widely consumed, locally manufactured goods are plastic and leather shoes, clothing of all kinds, materials, wools and threads, agricultural implements, and the many small items for the home such as doors, windows, beds, tables, chairs, plates, glasses, cups, utensils of all kinds, hand tools, etc. It is the producers of these domestically produced goods who now have access to a wider market than before, assuring to some degree the chances that the domestic production of these goods will continue and grow.

Generally, it can be concluded that the landholding structure and tenure relations which characterized Bolivia before the land reform forced the peasant to produce largely for himself and to consume a minimum of goods not produced on his own lands. This inhibited the development of markets of adequate size for light manufactured goods, domestic or otherwise, which acted as a brake on the development of a manufacturing sector, thus contributing to the slow growth of the country. In this respect the pre-reform landholding structure was inimical to economic development, for the consumption demands of the relatively few landlords could never have created a market of sufficient size to promote development. However, with the redistribution of land — that is, a redistribution of opportunities to earn a cash income from the land — and the greater participation of the peasantry in a money economy, regional and national markets have been created which has given and may continue to give a significant impetus to economic development over the coming years.

"They moved from a caste to a class; true, it was a class at the bottom of the now truncated pyramid, but still it was an upward step in the sense that they could now be mobile within the system. It was no longer wise to use the word *indio* in Bolivia. The word is *campesino*, peasant or rural folk, without the racial attribution."[93]

---

[93] R. Patch, "Land Reform in Bolivia," in *The Progress of Land Reform in Bolivia* 5, 6 (1963).

A decade after Patch wrote those words, the word *indios* has reappeared in Bolivia, chosen by members of the indigenous population as a term of pride to describe themselves. The opportunity to make that choice is as important as any other result of the Bolivian land reform.

Chapter IV

LAW AND INFLATION

The developmental process in a number of Latin American countries has been accompanied by chronic, severe inflation. Though inflation is currently a world-wide economic phenomenon, Latin America's experience with it is unique in that some of the region's nations have been persistently undergoing intense inflationary pressures for several decades. A recent study of inflation in 53 countries for which price data were available between 1949 and 1965 placed six countries in a class by themselves, far surpassing the other 47 countries. One of the six was Korea, which had been a battlefield during the early part of the period under study. The other five – Argentina, Bolivia, Brazil, Chile, and Uruguay – had no war to blame for their inflations. And from 1960 to 1965 the four countries in the study with the highest inflation rates were exclusively South American: Brazil averaged 58 percent a year, followed by Uruguay with 32 percent, Chile with 25 percent, and Argentina with 24 percent.[1] This is not to suggest that inflation has been endemic to all of Latin America; indeed, as Table 2 shows, some parts of Latin America have displayed notable price stability.

The materials in this chapter will focus on three of the South American countries most hard pressed by inflation – Argentina, Brazil, and Chile. All have had long inflationary histories, and all have experienced dramatic increases in the intensity of inflation during the post-World War II efforts to promote rapid economic development. The purposes of the chapter are several. One is to explore facets of the interrelationship between law and development in an economic context. Inflation is both a technique of financing development and a means of redistributing wealth. Billions of dollars worth of assets are transferred from one societal group to another through the mechanism of the price level, despite the law's protection of property and guarantee of fairness.[2] Legislation and doctrine, conceived under the assumption of relative price stability, may function poorly or not all in an inflationary milieu. In subjecting legal institutions to severe stress, inflation raises basic questions about the role of the legal system in providing security and equality.

Secondly, the wealth of case material affords an opportunity to observe Latin American courts in action in basic areas of the civil law, such as contracts and torts.

---

[1] Adekunle, "Rates of Inflation in Industrial, Other Developed, and Less Developed Countries, 1949-1965," 15 *IMF Staff Papers* 531 (1968).

[2] It has been estimated for the United States in 1971 that each one per cent of unanticipated inflation would transfer $32 billion from creditors to debtors. G. Bach, *The New Inflation* 24 (1973).

TABLE 2

ANNUAL CHANGES IN COST OF LIVING INDEX IN LATIN AMERICAN COUNTRIES, 1949-65

(In Per Cent)

Country	1949	1950	1951	1952	1953	1954	1955	1956	1957	1958	1959	1960	1961	1962	1963	1964	1965
Argentina	28.37	33.33	33.33	37.50	4.55	4.35	12.50	12.96	24.59	31.58	114.00	27.10	13.60	27.83	24.30	22.20	28.50
Bolivia	6.52	22.45	33.33	23.75	102.53	122.69	79.17	181.25	115.56	3.09	20.00	11.67	7.46	5.56	-0.66	10.60	2.99
Brazil	0	4.00	7.69	25.00	20.00	19.05	20.00	21.67	19.18	14.94	37.00	35.04	38.38	52.34	75.38	85.67	61.42
Chile	18.86	15.07	22.25	26.73	18.18	76.92	73.91	57.50	25.40	26.58	39.00	11.51	7.74	13.77	44.21	45.99	28.00
Colombia	6.67	20.83	8.62	-3.17	8.20	9.09	-1.39	7.04	14.47	14.94	7.00	3.74	9.01	2.48	32.26	17.07	3.65
Costa Rica	8.45	10.39	7.06	-3.30	1.14	2.25	4.40	1.05	1.04	3.09	0	1.00	2.97	2.88	3.74	2.70	0
Dominican Republic	-4.21	0	8.79	0	-1.01	-2.04	0	1.04	5.15	-1.96	0	-4.00	-3.12	9.68	7.84	1.82	-1.79
Ecuador	1.15	-3.41	11.76	3.16	0	3.06	1.98	-4.85	0	2.04	0	2.00	3.92	2.83	5.50	4.35	2.50
El Salvador	10.34	15.62	16.22	-2.33	7.14	4.44	4.26	1.02	-4.04	5.26	-1.00	0	-2.02	0	1.03	2.04	0
Guatemala	7.69	7.14	4.44	-2.13	3.26	2.11	2.06	1.01	-1.00	1.01	0	-2.00	0	2.04	0	0	-1.00
Honduras	4.00	5.13	9.76	-2.22	2.27	5.56	8.42	-3.88	-2.02	3.09	1.00	-1.98	2.02	0.99	2.94	4.76	3.64
Mexico	6.38	4.00	13.46	15.25	-2.94	6.06	15.71	3.70	5.95	12.36	2.00	5.88	0.93	0.92	0.91	2.70	3.51
Nicaragua	5.56	19.61	19.67	1.37	12.16	8.43	13.33	-2.94	-4.04	5.26	-3.00	-2.06	0	1.05	0	4.17	3.00
Peru	13.33	13.73	10.34	6.25	8.82	5.41	5.13	4.88	8.14	7.53	13.00	7.96	7.38	5.34	7.25	10.81	16.46
Uruguay	4.88	-4.65	14.63	14.89	5.56	12.28	7.81	7.25	14.86	17.65	40.00	38.57	22.16	10.97	20.53	43.22	56.39
Venezuela	7.23	1.12	7.78	1.03	-1.02	0	-1.03	2.08	-3.06	5.26	5.00	3.81	-2.75	-0.94	0.95	0.94	1.89

Source: IMF Financial Statistics, as compiled in Adekunle, *supra.*

The cases provide useful caveats to certain of the broad generalizations about civil law judges and legal institutions made during the first two chapters.

Thirdly, the problems of an inflationary economy are presently very much our own problems. There is much that the U.S. lawyer can learn from the study of Latin American legal institutions about the role of law in controlling inflation and adapting to it.

The interaction of inflation and legal institutions cannot be examined in the abstract, apart from the basic economic concepts connected with inflation. The materials thus include a number of excerpts from the works of economists as well as more traditional legal sources.

A. Inflation and Its Measurement

The term "inflation" is normally used in two senses: to describe higher price levels and to explain the forces generating price increments. When used in the second — causal — sense, inflation generally refers to an expansion of money and credit in excess of real growth in gross national product (monetary inflation), substantial deficits in governmental budgets (fiscal inflation), and/or labor cost increments in excess of productivity (wage inflation).[3] Monetary and fiscal inflation are frequently referred to as "demand-pull" inflation — or, put somewhat crudely, too much money chasing too few goods. Wage inflation is frequently referred to as "cost-push" inflation — or, again put somewhat crudely, too little productivity for too much money. Of course, these are not the only forces that can generate inflationary pressure. Many other factors such as exchange devaluations, import-substitution industrialization, and scarcities of important commodities can be important factors.

When used in the first sense — describing higher price levels — inflation generally refers to price increments stemming from these inflationary pressures. But inflation is far from an exact concept, and there is no precise way to measure it. The two most commonly used yardsticks are the cost of living index and the wholesale price index. The former attempts to measure changes over time in the prices of equivalent goods and services that are consumed during the normal course of living; the latter attempts to measure changes in the wholesale prices paid for a selected list of products. Neither of these indexes covers the entire economy; important items such as land, stocks, and taxes lie beyond their scope. The only index which cuts across the entire economy is an implicit one derived from the process of deflating the gross national product (GNP). Each component of the GNP is deflated for a given year or quarter by the price indexes deemed most appropriate for that component. These are generally the subindexes of the wholesale price index and cost of living index, or special indexes, such as a construction or farm product index. After deflation, the components are

---

[3]M. Gainsbrugh & J. Backman, *Inflation and the Price Indexes* 1, (Nat'l Indus. Conf. Bd., Studies in Business Economics, No. 94, 1966).

aggregated to obtain a constant money GNP. The GNP deflator is obtained by dividing the current money GNP by the constant money GNP.[4]

Table 3 shows the official cost of living indexes from Argentina, Brazil, and Chile from 1965 to 1972. The Table shows that Argentina's cost of living index jumped from 925.3 in 1971 to 1,466.2 in 1972, a rise of 58 percent. What does this signify? What lies behind these index numbers? How are they derived, and what do they purport to measure?

Some of the main problems of constructing a price index are apparent if one hypothesizes an island with a monetary unit of the clam and an economy with only five commodities: bananas, eggs, grass skirts, liquor, and fish. Let us assume that in 1972 and 1973 the following prices prevailed:

Item	1972	1973
bananas (bunch)	1 clam	2 clams
eggs (doz.)	2 clams	2 clams
grass skirts	10 clams	15 clams
liquor	5 clams	10 clams
fish	2 clams	3 clams

With these price data, we might construct a crude price index for our island. One unit of each of the five products cost 20 clams in 1972; the same quantity of goods cost 32 clams in 1973, an increase of 60 percent. If we take 1972 as our base year and let it equal 100, we can construct a simple price index that would look like this:

$$1972 - 100$$
$$1973 - 160$$

Looking at this index, we might conclude that the cost of living on our island has increased by 60 percent from 1972 to 1973. But has it? This simple index implicitly gives greatest weight to the items whose prices have increased the most, i.e., grass skirts and liquor. But these items may constitute a relatively small or large part of a typical islander's expenditures. To refine our index we need to know something about the quantities purchased by our island's inhabitants. For this purpose index makers generally rely on a market basket survey. A representative group is queried about its expenditure patterns, and the results of this market basket survey are used to weight the components of the price index.

Suppose that at the beginning of 1972 we had taken a market basket survey that revealed that in the previous year the typical islander bought 30 bunches of bananas, 20 dozen eggs, 4 grass skirts, 26 bottles of liquor, and 20 fish. Using these quantities as weights, it is apparent that it cost 480 clams in 1973 to purchase the same market basket that cost 280 clams in 1972.

---

[4] A readily intelligible explanation of the varieties of price indexes is W. Wallace, *Measuring Price Changes: A Study of the Price Indexes* (Fed. Res. Bank of Richmond 1970).

TABLE 3

COST OF LIVING INDEXES IN BUENOS AIRES, RIO DE JANEIRO AND CHILE
(Annual Averages)

Year	Buenos Aires 1960 = 100		Rio de Janeiro 1965-7 = 100		Chile 1958 = 100	
	Index	Percentage of Change	Index	Percentage of Change	Index	Percentage of Change
1965	283.8	—	70.5	—	449.3	—
1966	374.3	31	99.6	41	573.0	27
1967	482.8	29	130	31	747.1	30
1968	560.0	16	159	22	946.1	34
1969	604.7	7	194	22	1,236.1	30
1970	686.9	13	238	22	1,532.8	24
1971	925.3	34	286	20	1,839.3	20
1972	1,466.2	58	333	16		

Sources: Argentina — Instituto Nacional de Estadística y Censos
Brazil — Conjuntura Econômica
Chile — Dirección de Estadística y Censos

Item	1972	1973
bananas	30 × 1 = 30	30 × 2 = 60
eggs	20 × 2 = 40	20 × 2 = 40
grass skirts	4 × 10 = 40	4 × 15 = 60
liquor	26 × 5 = 130	26 × 10 = 260
fish	20 × 2 = 40	20 × 3 = 60
Total	280	480

The formula used for constructing a weighted aggregative price index is largely a function of the question to be answered. A price index is commonly expected to show how much it would cost in the current period to purchase the same market basket purchased in the base period. The formula most widely used to construct an index that answers that question is one devised by Etienne Laspeyres in 1864:

$$I_2 = \frac{\Sigma p_2 q_b}{\Sigma p_b q_b} \times 100$$

where I_2 is the value of the index number in the second year added to the value in the base year; p_b represents prices of individual items in the base year; p_2 represents the prices of individual items in the second year; q_b represents the quantities purchased the base year; and Σ is the standard symbol for summation. This index is the weighted ratio of two expenditures: the hypothetical current expenditure divided by the actual base period expenditure. Both weights and the base are fixed. Plugging the data from our hypothetical island into this formula,

$$I_2 = \frac{480}{280} \times 100 = 171.4$$

If we set our base year of 1972 at 100, our index would look like this:

$$1972 - 100$$
$$1973 - 171.4$$

This index would tell us that the cost of living rose by 71.4 percent on our island during 1973.

Price indexes have also commonly been designed to answer how much it would have cost during the base period to purchase the consumer's current market basket of goods. The formula most widely used to construct an index that answers that question was devised by H. Paasche in 1874:

$$I_2 = \frac{\Sigma p_2 q_2}{\Sigma p_b q_2} \times 100$$

This formula differs from the Laspeyres in that it shows the ratio of actual current expenditures to a hypothetical base period expenditure. An annual increase of 70 percent on a Paasche index means that the consumer's current market basket costs 70 percent more than it would have cost during the base period. Since the Paasche index always compares current expenditures with the base period, year-to-year comparisons are misleading. For example, if our island's Laspeyres index number for 1973 doubled for 1974, it would be appropriate to interpret the index as showing that the cost of island living during that year rose by 100 percent.

$$1972 - 100$$
$$1973 - 171.4$$
$$1974 - 342.8$$

But such an interpretation of a Paasche-type index would be incorrect. A Paasche-type index with the above values would tell us that 1974's market basket cost 3.42 times as much as it would have cost in 1972. But it does not tell us that the cost of living doubled from 1973 to 1974. The particular selection of commodities being priced changes from 1973 to 1974, distorting direct comparison of current prices with any year but the base year.

There are numerous technical problems connected with price indexes. One basic difficulty in constructing a weighted price index is that consumers typically change the mix of their market baskets in response to changes in relative prices. If the price of eggs remains the same while the price of fish rises, consumers may purchase more eggs and less fish. Obviously, a market basket survey requires periodic updating if it is to reflect current expenditure patterns, particularly in a society undergoing rapid inflation. Another problem is the representiveness of the group sampled in the market basket survey. In the United States, the Bureau of Labor Standards' Consumer Price Index, which is based upon a survey of the expenditure patterns of urban wage earners and clerical workers, is currently criticized as unrepresentative of the society as a whole. In Latin America the cost of living index tends to be based on expenditure patterns of even narrower groups of workers in a single city. Though these market baskets may differ substantially from the rest of the country, such indexes are widely used on a national basis to correct for inflation. Moreover, there is always the danger that a government which feels that its prestige and political power are in good measure a function of its ability to control inflation will pressure index makers into lowering the rates of inflation being reported.[5] Still another constant source of difficulty is isolating quality changes in products. If a 1975 car costs $150 more than a similarly equipped 1974 car, how much of the increment should be attributed to quality improvement, such as safety devices or design changes? Should the new pollution control devices be considered an improvement or deterioration in quality?

B. Economic Development and Inflation

1. The Monetarist-Structuralist Debate

The causes and cures for inflation, as well as its relationship to economic growth, are matters of considerable debate in Latin America. The controversy, particularly during the late 1950's and early 1960's, tended to divide economists and planners into two opposing camps — the "monetarists" and the "structuralists." As Dudley Seers put it, "At the heart of the controversy . . . are two different ways of looking at economic development, in fact two completely different attitudes toward the nature of social change, two different sets of value judgments about the purposes of economic activity and the ends of economic policy, and two incompatible views on what is politically possible."[6]

The following study by a North American economist summarizes the monetarist and structuralist positions, synthesizing the principal arguments of the leading proponents of each school.

---

[5] This has been a perennial complaint in Chile, and is becoming a serious problem in Brazil. For example, the British newsletter "Latin America" recently reported that private statistical analysts consider the actual inflation rate in Brazil during 1973 was between 20 and 30 percent, though the government admitted only to 14 percent. Jan. 11, 1974, p. 14. Even the Estado de São Paulo, the leading conservative newspaper in Brazil, has criticized the government's underreporting of the rise of the cost of living. Eurico Penteado, "Indices Do Custo de Vida e Erros Das Interpretações," Estado de São Paulo, Jan. 31, 1973, p. 32, col. 3; Estado de São Paulo, Jan. 17, 1973, p. 14. For a discussion of some of the problems of the Brazilian price indexes, see Rosenn, "Adaptations of the Brazilian Income Tax to Inflation," 21 *Stan. L. Rev.* 58, 97-101 (1968).

[6] "Inflation and Growth: The Heart of the Controversy," in W. Baer and I. Kerstenetzky (eds.), *Inflation and Growth in Latin America* 89 (1964).

W. BAER, THE INFLATION CONTROVERSY IN LATIN AMERICA: A SURVEY

2 *Latin American Research Review* 3, 4-19 (1967)

The Monetarist Case

It is the position of the "monetarists" that inflation is prejudicial to economic growth in the long run. Inflation leads to distortions in the allocation of resources. In an inflationary milieu there is a tendency for savings to be put into unproductive investments like real estate or housing or the accumulation of inventories, since these are assets that best protect the saver against price increases. This allocation of investment resources does not increase the productive capacity of the country, and thus hampers the long-run capacity of the country to maximize its economic growth rate. Even if productive investment takes place under inflationary conditions, this investment will tend to be channeled more into projects with a short gestation period. Other projects will be avoided, since under inflationary conditions (when there is uncertainty about the rise in prices from one year to the next; in most inflations the rate varies from month to month and year to year) it is hard to predict changes in the costs of inputs and thus it is difficult to make long-term investment plans. The emphasis on short-gestation investment projects will also tend to introduce a distortion or imbalance in the development of the industrial structure of the economy.

Inflation also causes difficulties in the balance of payments. Since Latin American countries generally operate under a system of fixed exchange rates (these are adjusted only periodically, and political pressures often make devaluation difficult even when recognized as economically necessary), inflation encourages imports and discourages exports. Given a fixed exchange rate, rising internal prices will make imported goods more attractive, while rising costs will tend to discourage exports. As the balance of payments of the country worsens, there will be speculation against the currency in the expectation of a devaluation, thereby increasing the pressures on the balance of payments.

Although continuing inflation will sooner or later force the country to devalue, devaluations will not necessarily come in quick successions; in order to protect its international position the country will resort to direct exchange and/or import controls. Such a situation will discourage foreign investments, since foreign capital will be hesitant to invest in a country whose inflationary and balance of payments difficulties threaten to block the repatriation of their earnings.

In most Latin American countries undergoing inflationary pressures, severe price distortions will appear, leading to further maldistribution of resources and creating bottlenecks that can hamper the growth of the economy. In most major countries of Latin America (e.g., Argentina, Brazil and Chile), the government controls the prices of public utilities (both privately- and publicly-owned) and sets maximum prices on basic foodstuffs. Since inflations are never politically popular, the government will be hesitant to raise the rates of the controlled price sector. Raising the rates on railroads, buses, electricity, telephones, milk, meat, etc. exposes the government to public criticism much more than producing a budget deficit. Usually utility rates and controlled food prices will be allowed to rise with a substantial time lag and the increases are often substantially below the rise of the general price level. Because costs are rising faster than their prices, private utilities will not expand and/or modernize their services, many of which will soon begin to experience breakdowns. . . .

In many Latin American countries control of basic food prices in the midst of inflation has caused perennial shortages. The experience is generally the following: the price of milk is controlled; the general price level is rising; milk prices are not allowed to rise. After a while the producers and/or distributors of milk will assume that the price of milk will have to be raised soon. As a speculative move, they will hoard their milk supply (in the case of milk the "hoarding" might consist of increased cheese or butter production which can be better hoarded), and severe shortages will occur in the cities. Social tensions will rise to the point where the government will either have to interfere directly to get milk to the market (which, in the long run might discourage the production of milk altogether) or they will have to raise the price. Generally, the latter will happen. But the perennial shortages causing social tensions and possibly discouraging investment in the modernization of milk production will not prove beneficial for the smooth development of the economy and the society.

In the publicly-owned utility sector, a refusal to raise prices in an inflationary situation will produce large deficits of public companies. For example, this can be found in the public transportation systems of Argentina, Brazil, and Chile. The government will cover the deficit of these companies. These deficit covering expenditures will then contribute to the general government budget deficit and further feed the inflation.

In some countries price controls extend to financial markets. That is, one will find a legal maximum on interest rates. In Brazil, for example, the maximum interest rate a bank can charge is 12 percent. Since in most inflationary countries the yearly inflation rate is substantially above the maximum legal interest, the real rate of interest will be negative (this is so even if one takes into account that banks will circumvent the maximum interest charge permissible through various types of service charges). The net result will usually be a general scramble for the "free money," personal connections rather than rigorous economic criteria will determine who gets the loans, investment decisions of firms based on strict calculations of the best returns on alternative projects or alternative production techniques will disappear; in short, interest rates as a guide to the efficient allocation of investment funds will disappear, and this will have a prejudicial effect on the growth of the economy.

Another source of inefficiency occurs through the appearance of illusory profits. In the accounting of a firm, part of the receipts are put aside in a depreciation fund, i.e., a fund that will ultimately be used to replace machinery. In most Latin American countries firms calculate depreciation on the basis of the original (historical) cost of the machine, i.e., its costs in local currency when it was purchased (in some countries the laws force firms to do this). In an inflationary economy the new machine will cost substantially more than the original machine in local currency (even when discounting the possible improvements in the new machine), and the depreciation fund based on historical cost will not accumulate enough money to replace the machine. In other words, firms should be charging much more to the depreciation fund; they should be charging an amount geared to actual replacement costs. If this is not done, the total profits of firms will appear much larger than they really are. If these profits are paid out as dividends, the firm will "decapitalize" itself, i.e., it will not accumulate enough funds to replace its equipment. The failure to recognize these "illusory profits," which is common even in countries with long historical experiences in inflation, can lead to severe difficulties. It can cause investments to decline and also a decline in the efficient functioning of the existing productive capacity that can prejudice growth in the long run.

Monetarist Policies

Given all these distortions and balance of payments difficulties resulting from the inflationary process, the monetarist considers it a *sine qua non* for economic development that the economy be rid of inflation and all the concomitant distortions. Since he sees the root of inflation as an overabundant creation of money supply through substantial government deficits and easy credit policies, he will recommend stringent anti-inflationary policies via the curtailment of government expenditures and/or increased collection of taxes to eliminate deficits; the severe tightening up of credit; the elimination of inflationary subsidies; the control of wage increases, which is a necessary complement to control of credit increases; and the elimination of subsidized exchange rates, if there existed a system of multiple exchange rates. The rationale for a control of wage increases (real wages falling because wage increases continue to lag behind price increases) is twofold. On the supply side, it is argued that with credit controls, declines in real wages will increase the profit rate of the capitalist, who needs increased profits to replace credit, now in short supply, as a source of short-term working capital and as a source of long-term expansion. On the demand side, wage restraint will lower the excess demand, which is the basic cause of inflation. Of course, a lower wage level, by decreasing aggregate demand, might discourage the capitalist's use of retained earnings for investment activities, thereby causing a slowdown in economic growth.

The monetarist admits that these policies might have a dampening effect on the rate of economic growth. But once the economy is rid of its distortions, once the price level is stable, once the balance of payments is put in order thereby making it unnecessary to continue foreign exchange controls, both domestic and foreign capital will resume their investment activities and once more a healthy growth rate without distortions will be attained. The stagnation accompanying stabilization policies is considered a short-run sacrifice that the country must make to "clean up" its economy.

The Structuralist Position

The structuralist states that the problem of inflation in Latin America should be viewed against the broad sweep of socioeconomic developments in the region. In the last three decades Latin American societies have undergone substantial degrees of urbanization and industrialization. These trends have resulted in socioeconomic pressures and frictions that manifest themselves in part through inflation.

The friction that initially received most attention by the structuralist school was the inelasticity of the agricultural supply for domestic consumption. With a high rate of growth of the urban population, demand for food by the urban centers has risen substantially. The rise in the demand for food will provoke a rise in the relative price of domestically consumed food products. Unlike what one would expect in a market-responsive economy, the rise of the relative price of food products will not provoke a strong response in the food producing sector; in some countries there might be a slight rise and in others none at all, as a result of the more favorable relative prices. The reason for this small response is the socioeconomic structure prevailing in many Latin American countrysides. The latter are dominated by either large non-capitalistic latifundios, which are not interested in profit maximization, or by minifundios which barely eke out a living and are scarcely integrated into the larger market economy. It should be noted that as long as most of the countries were predominantly rural economies, as long as the vast majority of the population lived in the agricultural sector, the problem of food supply did not arise because the bulk of the rural population was self-sufficient in food products. In the cities, however, the new proletariat is completely dependent on marketed food products, and the demand pressure for food is considerable.

With the lack of a supply response from the agricultural sector, the food shortages of the cities will continue and even worsen. The cost of living of the workers (a large proportion of the city workers' budget is made up of food products; in Brazil it amounts to about 45 percent) in the cities will rise, the subsistence wage will rise, and the cost of production to industries will increase, because in many industries in Latin America wages constitute a large item of total costs (especially in the lighter industries, such as textiles, food products, etc.). The rise in industries' cost of production will result in a rise in the price of domestically manufactured products. Local manufacturers usually have no trouble in passing on increased costs to consumers since they usually have monopolistic powers, i.e., each industry, having a small market, is usually dominated by only a handful of firms. Thus agricultural inelasticity will bring on a continual upward spiral of wages and prices.

Some countries, like Brazil, do not fit into the strict agricultural inelastic pattern as outlined by the initial structuralists. The rate of growth of output of foodstuffs in these countries has kept pace more or less satisfactorily with the rate of growth of the population. Structuralists will argue that this is due to the agricultural frontier possessed by large countries. Even though output in the traditional food producing areas does not rise, increased demand will stimulate production in the frontier region. But this, argue the structuralists, will also have an inflationary impact. Considering the large migration of the population to the cities, the producing areas are farther and farther away from the consuming areas. With poor transportation facilities, antiquated food distribution systems, the cost of food will rise and the net results will be the same as those in countries (like Chile) that were taken as the original models for the theory.

Agricultural inelasticity is complemented by what has been called import inelasticity. Many Latin American countries have suffered from acute balance of payments difficulties due to the slow growth of their traditional exports (accompanied in certain cases by a decline in the terms of trade, i.e., the ratio of export to import prices) in the face of an accelerated growth of their imports. The world market for many traditional Latin American exports has expanded at a very slow pace due to a low income elasticity of demand for such products in advanced countries, partially due to the introduction of synthetic substitutes, and also due to the preferences that some African and Asian countries have obtained in the European market. The urbanization-industrialization process, however, raises considerably the import requirements of most Latin American countries. The net result is a deficit in the current account of the balance of payments, which is not financed by autonomous capital inflows. The latter have been very small in the post-World War II period.

The tendency for continued balance of payments difficulties exhausts foreign exchange reserves, and sooner or later these countries will have to resort to direct import controls — quantitative import restrictions and/or foreign exchange restrictions. Control of imports, implying the cutting down of imports to the size of export receipts, will create shortages of many formerly imported goods. The relative domestic price of these goods will rise and thus contribute to the inflationary forces. Of course, balance of payments difficulties will sooner or later force countries to devalue their currencies; this will also have the effect of an immediate upward push on the price level, especially if imports consist of many consumer goods, including basic foodstuffs, which the agriculturally inelastic country might be forced to import.

The rise of the relative prices of imported goods due to their shortage has in many countries been part of the stimulus toward the import-substitution of these goods, i.e., the domestic production of formerly imported goods. Import substitution has two initial inflationary effects. The cost of local production is high due to limited markets that prevent firms from benefiting from economies of scale, and due to the fact that the efficiency of newly created industry is of necessity low in the early stages of production. The creation of import substitution industries also implies a period of investment in new firms during which labor and capital are employed to create new productive capacity. For a while, however, the investment activity generates income without producing marketable goods. Here again, we have an inflationary force, but it is self-correcting: once the gestation period of the investment is over, new goods will appear on the market.

A third line of argument explaining the Latin American inflationary phenomenon is closely related to the initial structuralist considerations, though it has not received as extensive a treatment in the literature as the agricultural inelasticity phenomenon. The high rate of urbanization and industrialization in most Latin American countries has substantially increased the sphere of necessary government activities. An urban-industrial society needs substantially more infrastructure investment than a pre-dominantly rural one. There are increased needs for better roads, port facilities, power projects, schools, health services, to complement the growing urban-industrial sector. Substantial lags in the construction of these services could severely prejudice the growth of the new industrial sector. High urbanization rates also require more government attention to the construction of low income housing, urban transportation, etc. In other words, the investment responsibilities of the government in the short run increase at a rapid pace. Lack of government investment in these infrastructure facilities can severely increase social tensions in the cities and hamper the smooth growth of industry.

How should the government finance these investment activities? Although it might be feasible in the short run to overhaul tax laws in order to increase government revenues to finance investment projects, most Latin American societies are saddled with antiquated, inefficient and sometimes corrupt tax collecting bureaucracies. The habits of the latter do not change rapidly and the possibilities of effective administrative reforms at an early date are limited. Thus many governments have difficulties in finding adequate finance for the necessary projects and face a dilemma. In the short run investment needs in infrastructure are necessary to produce adequate economic growth, but the overhaul of the tax collecting bureaucracy is a longer-run proposition. Given this dilemma, many Latin American governments have gone ahead with their investment projects, financing them through deficits. The inflation due to this phenomenon can be considered one type of taxation. That is, through deficit financing, the government attracts factors of production (labor and capital) to government projects from other sectors. The degree to which prices rise faster than wages due to this deficit and lower the real income of salaried people has been called forced savings. If we consider saving as that part of the real national product that is not consumed (in a full employment situation), inflation leads to increased savings by causing the country to consume less, save more and therefore invest more.

Structuralist Policies

Structuralists vehemently oppose the policy prescriptions of the monetarists. The elimination of the deficit recommended by the monetarists can be achieved either by increasing tax revenues or by cutting government expenditures. Since the former is usually more difficult in the short run, the latter policy will prevail. Government will curtail its investment expenditures. This will not only have a dampening effect on urban-industrial growth to the extent that government investment activities have a powerful effect on the economy, but it will also interfere with private industrial growth, since a lag of infrastructure investment behind private industrial investment creates bottlenecks that can substantially slow the general growth rate. Credit restrictions will harm the growth of the private industrial sector. Thus the monetarist policies affect mainly the most dynamic sector of a Latin American economy, industry, and cause general economic stagnation.

The structuralists argue that the monetarist policies will produce industrial stagnation, which might possibly cure the symptoms of the economic malady, i.e., the rise of the general price level, without getting at the roots of the problem. The latter implies a structural change of agriculture, making it more productive and responsive to the price mechanism. Monetarist stabilization programs do not deal with this problem. Another structural change required is a diversification of the commodity structure of exports and the continuation of import substitution, thereby dealing with the import inelasticity root of the inflation. Monetarist programs would halt import substitution industrialization, and credit restrictions would not help to diversify exports. It is also said that a slowdown of industrial production due to a stabilization program raises the per unit fixed costs of firms (overhead costs are spread among fewer units of goods produced) and that the industries with their monopolistic powers might raise prices and thus produce an automatic counter-stabilization force. Finally, monetarist policies would halt the process of forced savings, which financed many necessary infrastructure projects, and produce long-run inflationary bottlenecks.

To the monetarist argument that stability would attract domestic and foreign capital to invest in sound and profitable activities, the structuralist answers that if a monetarist stabilization program produces stagnation and hence excess capacity, one can hardly expect foreign capital to want to create new capacity where excess capacity already exists. Also, the social tensions created by a stabilization program would hardly convince the investors of the long-run political stability of an economic stabilization program; the monetarist replies that the social tensions created by an inflation are worse than those created by a stabilization program.

Monetarists claim that inflation causes balance of payments difficulties, while structuralists claim that balance of payments difficulties cause inflation. Structuralists sometimes claim that Latin American inflations are not the cause of balance of payments difficulties. The export of products such as coffee, cotton, cocoa, have their prices determined either in the international market through the forces of demand and supply, or through international agreements, e.g., the International Coffee Agreement. Thus, no matter what happens internally to the price level, the international price (say, dollar price) is a given. The monetarist will grant this, but will reply that, given fixed exchange rates, increased domestic prices and fixed prices for export products will squeeze the exporters' profits and they will tend to turn from producing an export crop to producing for the domestic market, where prices are flexible in the upward direction. Whether or not this happens is a matter of fact. For a number of reasons (especially due to the support programs) this has not happened in most Latin American countries. Again, the structuralist will emphasize that the foreign problem is due to the small growth of markets for traditional exports rather than due to the fact that Latin American countries are pricing themselves out of the market. . . .

It seems, however, that further debate without some hard empirical-analytical work will not advance our knowledge. The empirical work will probably show that many of the contentions of the monetarists concerning the inevitable evils of inflation are not necessarily going to occur; while the claims of the structuralists will also have to be qualified by the more complex reality. The structuralists might discover that the latifundio image of agriculture for all of Latin America is not the complete reality, and that ideologically conceived agrarian and other reforms might thus not solve the basic problems. The monetarists might discover that their greatest fear of a runaway inflation — à la Germany 1923 — will not necessarily occur in societies where the purchasing power of money was never stable, where money was never considered to be a store of value, but only a means of exchange.

2. The Pointless Spiral View

A somewhat different perspective about the nature of the inflationary process in Latin America is provided by W. Arthur Lewis, a distinguished economist, in an address to the Conference on Inflation and Economic Growth held in Rio de Janeiro in January of 1963.

W. A. LEWIS, CLOSING REMARKS

in W. Baer & I. Kerstenetzky (eds.), *Inflation and Growth in Latin America* 21-24 (1964)*

. . . [W]hat stands out most clearly in my mind is the importance of distinguishing between factors which cause prices to start to rise, and spiral processes which keep prices rising on and on far beyond any level that you can justify in terms of the original cause. Our economics have become much more unstable since 1945 than they ever were before. I use the word unstable in the technical sense, to indicate that if for any reason prices move from what may in some sense be an equilibrium level, there are no forces to bring them back. On the contrary, powerful forces at once take over to send prices rising and rising and rising to levels for which there is no justification in the original cause which started them off.

The mechanism is familiar to us all, and is not confined to Latin America. Every country in the world, including the Soviet bloc, has either experienced it, or views it with apprehension. It has three contributing parts: wages, budgetary deficits, and devaluation, and it runs somewhat as follows. First comes the original cause, which starts the mechanism working. This may be a rise in the price of domestic foodstuffs, or a rise in import prices, or an increase in the quantity of money, or a rise in the price of exports, or anything you like, provided it is something which raises the cost of living. Then the mechanism starts. Wages rise, and this raises prices more, wages more, prices more, and so on. Secondly, in those countries where the marginal ratio of government receipts to national income is below the average ratio, the price rise opens up a budget deficit, because government costs rise faster than government revenues. This gives an extra twist to the spiral. Then thirdly the rise in prices forces devaluation, and this raises import prices proportionately to the devaluation and domestic prices in somewhat smaller proportion, so a third twist is given to the spiral. So what with wage pressures, budget deficits, and devaluation, prices may rise continuously and at a high rate for reasons which have nothing to do with the original cause.

Failure to distinguish between the original cause and the spiral mechanism can only cause confusion. If one asks why prices rise by 25 percent per annum in Chile, it is confusing to be told that this is because agricultural output is growing less rapidly than the demand for agricultural products. Chile is only one of 50 countries where agricultural demand is growing more rapidly than supply. The difference between Chile, where prices increase by 25 percent per annum, and India, where prices increase

---

*Reprinted by permission of the publisher, Yale University Press.

by only 2 percent per annum, is not a difference in the elasticity of supply of agricultural output, which is equally low in both countries, nor a difference in the rate of growth, which is higher in India than in Chile. The difference is that Chile is in the grip of the spiral processes to a much greater degree than India.

The spiral is not confined to Latin America; all the world's continents are having to cope with it. Yet it seems to have gotten much more out of hand in some Latin-American countries than in the rest of the world. If during 1963 the cost of living were to rise by, say, 10 percent in, say, Nigeria or Ceylon, one could not confidently predict that this would set off spiral processes which would raise the general price level in Nigeria or Ceylon by 30 percent in three years. But it seems that one could safely predict such a result in some Latin-American countries. Some Latin-American economists assert that this is because their people have acquired expectations of continuously rising living standards which make them more aggressive than the peoples of Asia or Africa. I do not believe this to be so. I do not think that Latin-Americans are more anxious to have a rising standard of living than Nigerians or Ceylonese. The difference is in the expectations, not about the standard of living, but about how prices will behave. A Nigerian is used to seeing prices rise, and then fall again; in fact, if you ask a Nigerian farmer what is likely to happen to agricultural prices, he is even now more likely to predict that they will fall than to predict that they will rise. This is in sharp contrast to those Latin-American countries where today no person under 40 years of age can remember any time when prices fell continuously over a period of two years. A country's expectations depend on its history, and the intensity of the spiral depends on its expectations. Prices rise much faster in Chile or Brazil than they do in Nigeria or Ceylon mainly because Chileans and Brazilians expect prices to rise much faster.

I think we are all agreed that this is a terrible state to be in, because this kind of inflation is quite pointless. One can argue for an inflation which sets out to achieve a deliberate purpose, such as to acquire more resources for a government which is engaged in military operations, or to bring about a change in the distribution of income such that proportionately more resources will be devoted to productive investment. . . .

But the spiral has neither these purposes nor these effects. Once the whole community has been subjected to a high rate of inflation over long periods, nobody is caught by inflation any more. There are no unprotected contractual incomes any more. Even pensioners and professors of economics learn to keep up. So the spiral has all the usual evil effects of inflation without achieving anything useful. I think we are all agreed that, whatever may be the original fundamental causes which start prices rising, the spiral itself adds nothing and should be eliminated if this is at all possible.

Now, in order to eliminate the spiral you have to get at its fundamental cause and stop wages chasing prices. But you must also deal with its secondary contributor, the budgetary deficit.

A budget deficit is not a necessary part of a spiral and does not, in fact, contribute to the spiral as it is experienced in the advanced industrial countries. In most of those countries a rise in the general price level leads, on the contrary, not to a budgetary deficit, but to a budgetary surplus. This is because the marginal ratio of government receipts to national income exceeds the average ratio. These governments take 25 to 35 percent of national income, but their marginal rates of direct taxation exceed 50 percent, and many of their indirect taxes are well over 50 percent on the goods for which demand rises most rapidly. Hence, as national income increases, their revenues rise faster than their civilian expenditures, and, in the absence of increases in military expenditures, the Minister of Finance is every year in the happy position of having to announce tax cuts in order to avoid an ever-increasing budget surplus. Most underdeveloped countries are in the opposite situation. Their marginal tax rates are too low; too many taxes are fixed in money, instead of being on a proportionate basis; and prices of public utilities are slow to adjust. So a general increase in prices raises the governments's cost faster than its revenues, and the resulting deficit makes the spiral worse than it would otherwise be. This seems to be of enormous importance in the bigger Latin American inflations. Without the budgetary deficit the wage spiral by itself might raise prices by 5 or even 10 percent per annum. Increases of 20 percent per annum and more over long periods must mainly be due to the secondary contribution of the budgetary deficit.

To explain how the spiral can produce a budgetary deficit is not to explain why these large budgetary deficits are tolerated year after year. This seems to be a specifically Latin-American phenomenon. Public opinion in India or Nigeria would be shocked by the idea of a large budget deficit every year, financed by creating new money, but public opinion in many Latin-American countries seems to accept the right of the government to print money as it likes. . . .

---

3. The Purposeful Spiral View

T. DAVIS, INFLATION AND STABILIZATION PROGRAMS: THE CHILEAN EXPERIENCE

in W. Baer & I. Kerstenetzky (eds.). *Inflation and Growth in Latin America*
360, 362-63 (1964)*

[N]othing is more evident than the fact that the inflation in Chile, as elsewhere in Latin America, is of the "repressed" type, with controls over the key prices in the economy, especially interest rates, exchange rates, and public utility prices, and is far from what Sir Roy Harrod has referred to as "pure wage-price spiraling." The controls have been imposed precisely for the purpose of redistributing income via the inflationary mechanism, in order to benefit the dominant political groups at the expense of the politically inert.[7] Thus, the Chilean inflation is far from neutral, not

---

*Reprinted by permission of the publisher, Yale University Press.

[7]Elsewhere I have contended that:

. . . greater monetary stability presumably would benefit the following groups: the export industries (since the permitted increase in the price of foreign exchange usually fails to keep up

simply a tax on cash balances resulting from pure wage-price spiraling, but rather a conscious policy that constitutes a common "second-best" for . . . the conservatives (that) have the power to block increased direct taxation; the Radicals and the Left (that) have sufficient power to block any attempt to reduce the real wages of government employees and organized labor permanently; . . . (and) the private sector (or at least the larger firms) . . . (that have) sufficient power to insist that loans to the (larger firms in) the private sector expand *pari passus* with those to the government. Stabilization programs are politically feasible only when it appears to these groups that inflation might conceivably "get out of hand"; but opposition reappears when the rate of inflation has been reduced to what historically seems to constitute "safe" levels.

---

4. Inflation as an Alternative to Revolution

A. HIRSCHMAN, JOURNEYS TOWARD PROGRESS

Pp. 221-23 (1963)*

. . . The Chilean experience does not provide much support for . . . [the thesis that inflation is the only alternative to stagnation], but it supplies some basis for a more unusual one: that inflation can serve to head off revolution or be considered as an alternative to civil war. We shall take up these two assertions in turn.

Inflation and Revolution. . . .

[I]nflation is a particularly conspicuous problem since it is constantly noticed by both housewives and statisticians: consequently, it may engage a disproportionate amount of public attention in comparison to other less immediately harassing, but perhaps more fundamental, problems. From this point of view, inflation has often been held to divert attention from these basic "smouldering" problems. But the Chilean experience

---

with the rise in domestic factor prices); the smaller firms in important and reasonably competitive industries, such as food processing, textiles, leather products, and wood products, which firms obtain direct access to bank credit only at a positive real interest rate; and finally the unorganized laborer and the self-employed person in small-scale industry and agriculture, who bear a disproportionate burden of the generally regressive inflation tax. The explanation for the failure of these groups to constitute a political force proportional to their numbers or to the fraction of total output contributed by their efforts is rather obvious. These are the foreign and the migrant, the unorganized and the unlettered, the distant (from the capital) and the remote (from urban centers). A government that would attempt to rely upon such a fragmented base for support in implementing a stabilization program and thereby alienate the "middle sectors," would immediately be threatened by the totalitarian extremes. Tom E. Davis, "Eight Decades of Inflation in Chile 1879-1959: A Political Interpretation," *J. Pol. Economy* (Aug. 1963). [Footnote by Davis, renumbered.]

suggests that inflation may also serve as a combined fever thermometer and divining rod for these other problems. Persistent inflation, especially when refractory to traditional therapy, encourages a search for those more deep-seated troubles in the economic and social structure which might be held responsible for the inflation. Even though the causal connections established in this way may sometimes be contrived or tenuous, there is considerable *independent* value in having such a search undertaken, especially when other troubles do not ordinarily signal their existence until it is "too late" in some sense. In other words, action to correct them may take place earlier with the stimulus of inflation than without it. It is tempting here to cite the exemplary monetary stability enjoyed by Cuba until 1958; this fact certainly contributed to the impression in some circles that nothing much could be wrong in such a country. No such false sense of security could ever arise in Chile where the inflation has led to a scrutiny of the country's principal institutions from the system of land tenure to social security and from the status of foreign capital to the political structure. If revolution comes to Chile, it certainly will not be for want of warning!

Inflation and Civil War.

. . . the Chilean inflation has been explained by "what the Chileans themselves often call the 'struggle' or even 'civil war' between the country's major economic interest groups." Is this a mere figure of speech or can this vaguely sensed relationship between inflation and civil war be more precisely defined?

Let us first note one general similarity between inflation and civil war: both frequently result from miscalculation. The provocative nature of the first step or the response is due to the fact that the challenger or the respondent overestimate their strength. Many civil wars have been intended as coups or revolutions, and an inflation is frequently brought underway by a group which wrongly believes that it can get away with "grabbing" a larger share of the national product than it has so far received. An overestimate of strength on the part of at least one group, and usually of several, is thus a characteristic cause of both civil war and inflation. Such miscalculation is in turn likely to be caused by poor inter-group information and communication, a situation typical of rapidly changing societies with hitherto fairly rigid class barriers.

Inflation and civil war both being responses to essentially similar social situations, it is tempting to think of inflation as a substitute for civil war. This goes counter to the Lenin dictum that there is no surer way to revolutionize a society than to "debauch its currency." In this well-worn, though perhaps apocryphal, phrase so frequently and enthusiastically quoted by American bank presidents, inflation is seen as a stepping-stone to revolution. No doubt in some cases the disruptions and psychological scars inflicted by prolonged and acute inflation have helped set the stage for revolutionary change. But this should not keep us from realizing that through the device of inflation society gains precious time for resolving social tensions that otherwise might reach the breaking point right away. This would certainly be confirmed by many a Minister of Labor who has settled or prevented a strike by granting inflationary wage increases. . . .

The advocates of monetary stability frequently make it quite clear that what they really want is to do away with all this shadow-boxing implied by successive rounds of "illusory" wage and price increases. Why not have a real good fight right here and now? The 1950 report of the International Monetary Fund to Chile says as much:

> The apparent anonymity and impersonality of any action taking place through credit should not be allowed to obscure its real significance. A credit restriction to be effective must force businessmen to sell goods at prices lower then they had anticipated, oftentimes at a loss; *it must make it financially impossible for them to increase wage rates*, and it must cause a certain minimum amount of unemployment.

No wonder that many a government, faced with this kind of advice, prefers the illusion to last and the inflation to continue a while longer!

Inflation then offers an almost miraculous way of temporizing in a situation in which two or more parties who are psychologically not ready for peaceable compromise appear to be set on a collision course. It permits them, as we have seen before, to maintain a militant and hostile stance while playing an elaborate, largely non-violent, game in which everybody wins sham victories. The result is of course that nothing is resolved – no one has attained his objectives except the perhaps not unimportant one of gratifying his hostility. The realization of having been cheated by inflation may then heighten bitterness and hostility, and this could make an eventual clash more likely (Lenin's thesis). But it is also possible that after having played the game a few times, the parties will realize its futility or that a new element will appear which makes a lull, truce or settlement possible. If that should turn out to be the case in Chile, inflation will have provided that country with additional room for social maneuvering during a particularly critical and disruptive period of its development.

---

5. "Forced Savings" and Wage Policies

Like land reform, inflation is a highly charged political issue, operating to confiscate and redistribute wealth within a society. In Latin American countries with chronic inflationary problems there are constant struggles among various economic interest groups, both public and private, to increase their share of national income at the expense of other groups. Expansion of the monetary income of certain groups via creation of additional means of payment will produce a rise in price levels reflecting this redistribution of income. Other groups whose real income has been reduced as a result of this redistribution will exert pressure to redress the balance, thereby provoking further monetary expansion and additional price increases.

Real incomes of all groups fluctuate widely during inflation. Rarely will anyone be able to maintain income stability in real economic terms. Salaries, wages, and prices are typically raised only after a period of time has elapsed. During this interval the wages of other groups or the prices of other goods and services continue to mount. Certain groups are at real income peaks, while others are at the lowest point in the cycle. But no matter how transitory they may be, these peaks tend to represent the minimum redistributive justice each group feels it has a right to expect, even though it is clearly impossible to maintain all groups at these peak levels without substantial growth in the national product.

It is possible, of course, to imagine an inflation in which every person's income is so protected that price increases effect no redistribution of income. All contracts, pension plans, insurance policies, loans, taxes, salaries, etc. might be equipped with escalator clauses that automatically adjusted income for inflation. Even currency might be so adjusted, depending on its date of issue. Such an inflation could theoretically spiral on without ever reaching a new equilibrium since it would hurt no particular group. On the other hand, no group should have an interest in its continuance, for it would benefit no one in particular. But for this type of inflation to occur, all prices and all incomes would have to move simultaneously so that no real effects would be felt during adjustment lags − a highly unlikely possibility.

As Professor Baer suggests, inflation is a useful technique for financing development only if it produces "forced savings," which accrue if wage levels rise less rapidly than the general price level. The extent to which this has occurred in Argentina, Brazil, and Chile has varied considerably, depending on the politics of the regime in power. During the first half of Perón's initial reign, the real wages of Argentine workers soared. Between 1950 and 1961 real wages declined sharply, rising again to 1949 levels by 1965.[8] Brazilian wage data are spotty, but industrial wages from 1949 through 1959 appear to have risen well above the inflation rate. However, from 1959 to 1967 the real minimum monthly wage declined rather steadily and substantially. Since 1967 wages have risen slightly more than has the inflation rate.[9]

From 1937 to 1956 Chilean white collar workers had their salaries escalated in accordance with the cost of living. The yearly readjustment was made by "Mixed Salary Commissions," which received little guidance from the legislature as to the basis for such adjustments. In 1941-42 and 1949-50 white collar workers received salary increments well in excess of the rise in the cost of living index. By 1953 the minimum salary had risen to 18 times the 1936-38 average, while the cost of living climbed but 12 times.[10]

Since 1960 Chilean wages have generally risen well ahead of the inflation rate.[11] However, one of the first acts of the military junta that ousted the Allende regime was

[8] C. Díaz Alejandro, *Essays on the Economic History of the Argentine Republic* 129, 538 (1970); R. Alexander, *Labor Relations in Argentina, Brazil, and Chile* 228-29 (1962).

[9] See W. Baer, *Industrialization and Economic Development in Brazil* 121 (1965); Rosenbaum & Tyler, "Introduction: An Overview," in *Contemporary Brazil: Issues in Economic and Political Development* 20 (H. J. Rosenbaum & W. Tyler eds. 1972). After the 1964 military revolution, the government enforced a policy of limiting wage readjustments to an amount sufficient to re-establish the average real wage during the preceding 24 month period. Recent legislation has modified that policy slightly, to permit an allowance for productivity increases and to try to restore preexisting wage levels.

[10] A. Hirschman, *Journeys Toward Progress* 186 (1963).

[11] For the fluctuation in the real value of the minimum wage from 1940 to 1966, see Saavedra, "Key Factors in Chilean Economic Development," in *Economic Development Issues: Latin America* 59, 79 (Comm. for Economic Development Supplementary Paper No. 21 (1967). More detailed wage data appear in P. Gregory, *Industrial Wages in Chile* (1967) and F. Pazos, *Chronic Inflation in Latin America* 63-94 (1972).

to rescind a 200 percent wage increase decreed by Allende. Since the inflation rate increased to an awesome 709 percent from June 1973 to June 1974, it would appear that Chile is in for a period of belt-tightening in which wages will rise less rapidly than prices.[12]

How should legal institutions be adapted to inflation? Should the *courts* ignore inflation entirely unless specifically directed to do otherwise by the legislature? Should legal theories be devised to ease the injustices to litigants wrought by inflation? If so, what kinds of theories are to be preferred? To what extent should courts consider the inflationary effects of their own decisions? What kinds of adjustments should *legislatures* enact to adapt legal institutions to inflation? Can the coercive force of law be used effectively to contain inflation? These questions are the central concern of the materials of this chapter.

C. Nominalism v. Valorism

There has been a longstanding doctrinal dispute between "nominalists" — who hold that for the purpose of discharging legal obligations, the value of money should be presumed constant — and "valorists" — who hold that legal obligations should be discharged only upon payment of a sum which corresponds to the real economic value of the sum lent, the service rendered, the commodity sold, or the injury suffered. The enormous convenience of nominalism, which avoided the difficulties of inquiring into the relative economic values of goods and services over time, ultimately resulted in its widespread acceptance over valorism during the 17th and 18th centuries.[13] The Napoleonic Code, which heavily influenced the Civil Codes of Argentina, Brazil, and Chile, was profoundly nominalist in character.[14]

While it functions quite well in a stable economy, nominalism works great hardships in a chronically inflationary economy. Legal systems depend on money to perform essentially three functions. Money can be (1) *a means of payment,* facilitating the exchange of goods and services; (2) *a measure of value,* permitting a common method of determining the value of goods and services; and (3) *a store of value,* facilitating

---

[12] N.Y. Times, Dec. 16, 1973, Sec. E, p. 4, cols. 3-5; N.Y. Times, July 7, 1974, Sec. 4, p. 1, cols. 3-5.

[13] See F. Mann, *The Legal Aspect of Money* 78-82 (3d ed. 1971).

[14] This orientation was most explicit in Article 1895, which provides: "The obligation which results from a loan of money is always only the numerical sum enunciated in the contract. If there has been an increment or diminution in specie before the time of payment, the debtor must repay the numerical sum lent, and must repay only that sum in the specie in effect at the time of payment."

Though the 1853 draft of the Chilean Civil Code flirted with valorism with respect to monetary loans, the 1855 version which was enacted into law adhered firmly to the nominalist principle. See Ramírez Luco, "Un Remedio para la Inflación," in *Primer Congreso Nacional de Abogados Chilenos, El Derecho ante la Inflación* 131, 134 (1955).

savings and deferred payment of obligations.[15] After so many years of sustained inflation the currencies of Argentina, Brazil, and Chile have ceased to function as either a measure or store of value, forcing the legal systems to develop alternative ways to perform these vital functions. This has resulted in a tempering of nominalist notions in a number of areas in which the strain has been most readily apparent.

D. Contractual Adaptations to Inflation

Contracts whose performance or payment is deferred over a considerable period of time, such as construction contracts, long-term loans, rentals, insurance policies, annuities, and installment sales, can be seriously affected by inflation. Without an inflation adjustment mechanism in economies like Argentina, Brazil, or Chile, banks specializing in home mortgages found that it cost them more to keep loans on the books than they were receiving in monthly interest and amortization payments. Widows ruefully realized that the proceeds of insurance policies were insufficient to buy even a new dress. Half-finished construction projects dotted the landscape as contractors operating on fixed-cost contracts went bankrupt. Short-run public reactions were predictable. Sources of long-term credit quickly dried up, and what little remained was allocated through very high interest rates — or through governmental priorities or favors. Insurance purchases declined, and existing policies were allowed to lapse. New construction starts declined drastically. People avoided long term contracts of any sort.

---

1. Gold Clauses

Lawyers have long been confronted with the problem of drafting long term contracts which would protect their clients from inflation. One of the oldest and most popular techniques has been a clause stipulating payment of the obligation in gold coin or its equivalent. Prior to the 1930s, the gold clause constituted part of the boiler plate of long term contracts in the United States and was also widely used in Western Europe and Latin America.[16]

But the great depression of the 1930s produced widespread abandonment of the gold standard and the adoption of legislation abrogating the gold clause. For example, Brazil adopted the following statute.

---

[15] See Doucet, "Le Franc du 8 Mars 1803 au 27 Décembre 1958," in P. Durand (ed.), *Influence de la Dépréciation Monetaire sur la Vie Juridique Privée* 1, 2-3 (1961).

[16] A. Nussbaum, *Money in the Law National and International* 225-27 (Rev'd Ed. 1950).

BRAZIL: DECREE NO. 23.501 OF NOVEMBER 27, 1933

The head of the Provisional Government of the United States of Brazil,

Considering that it is the essential and exclusive function of the state to create and defend its currency . . .

Considering that the decreeing of compulsory tender of paper money as a measure of public order is an inherent attribute of sovereignty of the State;

Considering that once paper money has been deemed compulsory tender, the law which has decreed it cannot be derogated by private agreements which tend to dilute its effects, stipulating means of payment which result in the repudiation or the depreciation of this currency to which the State has guaranteed suitability for legal tender equal to metallic; . . .

Considering that in almost all nations the nullity of the gold clause and other artificial processes of payment which imply an aversion to the means in circulation has been decreed; . . .

Considering that in France even prior to the law of June 25, 1928, the case law since 1873 has firmly declared the nullity of the gold clause as contrary to the public order of the regime of compulsory tender except for international payments . . .;

Considering that the case law of England has also manifested itself against the gold clause . . . in the case of Feist v. The Company . . .;

Considering that the United States, in the Joint Resolution sanctioned last June 6th, declared null any clause which affords the "obligee a right to require payment in gold or a particular kind of coin or currency, or in an amount in money of the United States measured thereby" and determined that "every obligation previously contracted which contains such a provision shall be discharged upon payment, dollar for dollar in any coin or currency that is legal tender"; . . .[17]

Considering, therefore, that any clause, agreement or artifice which is intended to remove the creditor from the regime of paper money as compulsory tender . . . can have no legal validity in Brazilian territory; . . .

Decrees:

Art. 1. Any stipulation of payment in gold, or in a determined specie of money or any means tending to deny or restrict the effects of the compulsory tender of *mil réis*[18] paper, is null.

---

[17] The Portuguese takes some liberty with the English original, which reads: "Every obligation, heretofore or hereafter incurred, whether or not any such provision is contained therein or made with respect thereto, shall be discharged upon payment, dollar for dollar, in any coin or currency which at the time of payment is legal tender for public and private debts." [Eds.]

[18] The *real* (pl. réis) was a Portuguese and Brazilian currency unit. In 1942 the cruzeiro (1000 réis or mil réis) became the official currency unit of Brazil. Reflecting the continuous currency depreciation, a new cruzeiro (1000 cruzeiros) replaced the cruzeiro in 1967. The adjective "new" was dropped in 1970. [Eds.]

Art. 2. As of the publication of this decree, the stipulation of payment in money which is not the official currency, by its legal value, is forbidden under penalty of nullity in contracts executable in Brazil. . . .[19]

Question

What is the purpose of prohibiting the use of gold clauses? Consider these explanations for the decision in the United States:

(a) Preamble to the U.S. Joint Resolution:

Whereas the existing emergency has disclosed that provisions of obligations which purport to give the obligee a right to require payment in gold or a particular kind of coin or currency of the United States, or in an amount of money of the United States measured thereby, obstruct the power of the congress to regulate the value of the money of the United States, and are inconsistent with the declared policy of the Congress to maintain at all times the equal power of every dollar, coined or issued by the United States, in the markets and in the payment of debts.

(b) Norman v. B. & O. R. Co., 294 U.S. 240, 316 (1935):

We are concerned with the constitutional power of the Congress over the monetary system of the country and its attempted frustration. Exercising that power, the Congress has undertaken to establish a uniform currency, and parity between kinds of currency, and to make that currency, dollar for dollar, legal tender for the payment of debts. In the light of abundant experience, the Congress was entitled to choose such a uniform monetary system, and to reject a dual system . . . .

(c) J. Dawson, "The Gold Clause Decisions," 33 *Mich. L. Rev.* 647, 669-70, 673-76 (1935):

The objective of the gold-clause legislation is to ensure complete parity in value between two kinds of *United States currency,* and to preserve their equality in debt-discharging power. To understand the extension of the currency powers of Congress that is involved in the gold-clause decisions, it is necessary to

---

[19] Subsequent legislation excluded two important areas of contract from the provisions of Decree No. 23.501. Law No. 28 of February 15, 1935 created an exception for contracts to import merchandise, while Decree Law No. 6.650 of June 29, 1944 excluded "obligations contracted abroad in foreign currency to be executed in Brazil." This legislation was consolidated by Decree-Law No. 857 of September 11, 1969, which further expanded the list of exceptions to include any contracts in which the debtor or creditor is a foreign resident and domiciliary, as well as any modification or transference of such contracts, even if both parties are Brazilian residents or domiciliaries. However, rental contracts payable in foreign currency are valid only if registered with the Banco Central. See generally J. Chacel, M. Simonsen, & A. Wald, *Correção Monetária* 22-26 (1970). [Eds.]

approach them from still another point of view, by considering the scope of prior legal-tender legislation.

The legal-tender acts of the Civil War period were in a sense an attempt to "regulate the value" of money. They provided in substance that the Treasury notes there authorized were to be a legal tender for the discharge of all "debts," public and private (with enumerated exceptions). All "debts" expressed in fixed sums of money . . . could then be discharged by payment of the nominal sum fixed in legal tender notes. The economic effect of the legislation . . . was equivalent to a "regulation of the value" of money. Creditors were obliged to accept paper money in payment of "debts" arising through the sale of land, goods or services, in spite of the loss they might suffer through the intervening depreciation . . . .

The joint resolution of June 5, 1933, must therefore be understood as an effort to preserve parity in value between different types of United States currency . . . . In holding that devaluation policies are hampered by the use of gold clauses in private contracts, the Supreme Court has not only recognized a perfectly apparent fact but has reached the conclusion which a number of foreign countries at various times have reached. . . .

The devaluation policy has not resulted in a prompt and spontaneous rise of internal commodity prices. Until a corresponding rise has occurred the enforcement of the gold clause in private contracts would result . . . in the creditor's "unjust enrichment." The value of gold has been deliberately and artificially raised by the Government, in the course of a concerted effort to induce a general rise in prices. . . . [T] he gain to creditors would represent an increment owed not to their own industry or to an equivalent value contributed by them, but to governmental action undertaken in the public interest.

The gold clause is now invalidated in private contracts for the long future, and not merely for the time being. If and when internal prices rise above their present level, the holders of private gold-clause obligations cannot hope for compensation. . . . But no real hardship to them will result unless and until internal prices rise above the world price of gold, as defined in terms of the old standard. If they rise to exactly that point, the gold that creditors demand will be worth no more to them than the currency they receive and debtors will presumably be willing to pay gold coin rather than paper money. If internal prices rise *beyond* that point some hardship may arise. But so long as the national currency remains tied to gold, this hardship will be traceable to reliance by creditors on a commodity whose world price is subject to all the influences of ordinary supply and demand and is subject also to political control. It is only in the event that the gold standard is wholly abandoned that the claims of such creditors should provoke sympathy and initiate a movement for their protection.

The outlawry of the gold clause in private obligations seems, then, to be fully justified by considerations of expediency. Nor need there be regret on account of its immediate effects on money obligations. Monetary history has provided no basis for the widespread faith in gold as a stable index of value. The events of the last decade have done much to shake that faith. To insist now upon strict enforcement of gold-clause obligations would not only place an intolerable restraint on governmental control of the monetary system but would preserve a legal device that can no longer perform its economic function. In England and the United States metallic coin has been largely displaced as a medium of exchange by bank credit. In countries where paper currency still serves as the principal monetary medium, an increasing governmental control of the financial structure makes possible a more effective control of monetary values. Within the framework of the gold standard great fluctuations in the value of money are possible. Against these fluctuations the gold clause can provide no protection.

Argentina never enacted legislation similar to the Brazilian Decree No. 23.501 or the U.S. Joint Resolution. But controversy over similar questions raged nevertheless. In *Bustillo, Susana Carlota Pacheco Santamarina de* v. *Café Paulista,* 1953-III J.A. 89, 70 La Ley 399 (1953), the Supreme Court of Argentina invalidated a clause in a lease which stipulated that if the value of the peso declined by more than 40 percent during the life of the lease, the lessor was entitled to secure an equivalent readjustment in the rent. The court reasoned that the legal tender statute constituted an important norm of public law and as such could not be undermined by private law — *i.e.,* contractual agreements between private parties. The distinction between public and private law, which has little relevance to the North American lawyer, is fundamental to the Latin American and European jurist, even though the utility and clarity of the dichotomy are coming under increasing attack.[20]

The Court's decision in the *Bustillo* case, rendered during the first Perón era, has been subjected to severe criticism by commentators.[21] In November 1959, the Sixth National Conference of the Argentine Bar approved a resolution in favor of the validity of contractual stabilization clauses; the Third National Congress of Civil Law at Córdoba in October of 1961 and the Sessions of Civil Law at Santa Fe in November of 1963 did likewise.[22] By 1964 it was dismissed as "an isolated and obsolete precedent" by an author who stated categorically: "The validity of monetary or economic stabilization clauses is unquestioned in civil and commercial juridical relations."[23] Nonetheless, the issue continued to be litigated.

[20] For a helpful explanation, see Merryman, "The Public Law-Private Law Distinction in European and United States Law," 17 *J. Public L.* 3 (1968).

[21] See A. Wald, *A Cláusula de Escala Móvel* 115 (2d ed. 1959); López Olaciregui, "Validez de las Cláusulas Convencionales que Preven la Desvalorización de la Moneda," 1953-III J.A. 89.

[22] The resolutions are reproduced in the Appendix to Guastavino, "El Derecho Civil ante la Inflación," 116 La Ley 1080, 1111-13 (1964).

[23] *Id.* at 1093-94.

BENTIVOGLIO v. ARANA DE JORDAN, L.I.

Supreme Court of Justice, Province of Buenos Aires (Argentina)
129 La Ley 779, 1967-VI J.A. 528 (1967)

[An urban lease entered into between the parties contained the following clause:

The rent is set at 1,800 pesos a month, effectively paid a month in advance, or at 55 grams of pure gold (oro mil), also paid a month in advance, at the domicile of the landlord. . . . The landlord has the option to demand payment in pesos of the national currency or in gold, without the fact of opting first for one signifying that later on the other may not be demanded and thus alternatively and/or successively.

[Prior to the landlord's opting for payment in gold, the tenant instituted the present action, seeking to invalidate the gold clause. The court of the first instance sustained the clause, but the appellate court reversed. The landlord then appealed to the provincial Supreme Court.]

La Plata, September 26, 1967. – Is the Appeal of the inapplicability of the law well founded?

Dr. Bouzat [dissenting] stated: . . .

The number of . . . stabilization clauses, which tend to assure an equilibrium in the performances for which each of the contracting parties is responsible – or better yet to safeguard the creditor from the deteriorating effects produced by inflation on his credit – are multiplying. The gold clause, in its various manifestations (gold coin; gold ingot; gold value) responds to such interest. Those who postulate them see them as a form of safeguarding mutuality in contract through the exercise of private autonomy. . . . On the other hand, those who deny their validity, invoke principles of public economic law and argue from values derived from the field of economic policy. . . .

In this dispute I take . . . the negative thesis. . . .

First of all it should be noted that clauses – such as the one in issue here – through which one stipulates the delivery of gold specie, as well as those in which gold is taken as an index of adjustment of the extent of the monetary obligation (gold value clause), fulfill . . . an identical regulatory function. The two aim to guarantee the creditor against the fortuitous fall in the purchasing power of paper money. . . .

[T]he introduction of clauses like that which concerns us here, affects the efficacy of a monetary system . . . inasmuch as it aims or *tends to displace the unit of value* which the law itself has imperatively enacted or – worse yet – *obstructs the development of a state policy which* – regardless of its effectiveness – *tends to regulate the economic cycle.* . . .

Under metallic monetary systems with the rule of complete convertibility, paper money fulfilled only the function of a representative note of the metallic specie stated on it, which, in the coffers of the issuing entity, served to cover the notes in circulation. Under such conditions one could not raise the problem that concerns us here, for the value (buying power) of such mercantile money (gold or silver) was established according to the same valid principles as other goods, that is, through the relationship of the costs of real production, measured in hours of work, in accordance with the classic concept. . . .

The appearance of non-redeemable notes (legal tender), with the consequent possibility of creating means of credit and bank money independent of the amount of savings, . . . interrupted the peaceful balance between the metallic reserves of the issuing institute and the representative notes in circulation. . . . This occurred in the country in 1914, when inconvertibility [was declared] . . . .

Law 12.155, by which the Central Bank of the Republic was created, replaced the former monetary system, maintaining the regimen of inconvertibility through a transitory arrangement (Art. 58) suspending the . . . obligation to exchange on demand its bank notes for gold or foreign reserves. . . . Both norms were substantially preserved by decree 13.126 of October 1957 (Arts. 24 and 27); . . . [thus], the statute regarded as transitory will continue to prevail permanently as it has for the last thirty years.

Under this system, the gold reserves and holdings of the Central Bank do not act as a cover for the circulating paper. They constitute a regulatory fund available as an appropriate instrument to realize specific objectives of the institution: to regulate the volume of bank credit and the means of payment, to promote the development of savings and investment, to stimulate the ordered growth of the national income, to regulate the possible effects of fluctuations of the balance of payments, etc. (Art. 1, Decree-law 13.126/57).

Therefore the national monetary unit appears unconnected with any metallic content. There is no other national currency than the peso, which the Central Bank issues as an exercise of the monopoly conferred on it by Art. 35 of law 12.155. . . .

. . . [I]f the distinction between money and goods constitutes the fundamental base of the legal monetary analysis, if money and goods are the opposite poles of the economic process and both essentially antithetical, if a monetary system is not conceived that does not advocate an ideal unit, if in contemporary economics the indirect regulation of the economic cycle through measures of monetary policy forms a current measure of the politico-economic action of the state, if such a unit of value constitutes the common denominator of the national wealth, . . . finally, if money also appears as a symbol of sovereignty, and the Constitution has reserved to the highest instances of the federal power "to print money and fix its value," forbidding the exercise of similar powers to the provinces (Art. 108, Constitución Nacional), it is incongruous to admit that the same legal order authorizes the citizens to subvert the imperatively sanctioned monetary system by the exercise of the autonomy of the private will.

Consequently, I judge that . . . the question of the legitimacy of stabilization clauses . . . [must be considered apart] from the narrow scope of the Civil Code in order to [give effect to] the principles of public economic law that regulate the issuance and circulation of money and its entire regime.

Since the time in 1546 when Dumoulin developed a . . . nominalist theory based on the notion of "valor impositus,". . . the argument has been reiterated that the nullity of the gold clause is derived from its incompatibility with a regimen that accords legal tender to inconvertible notes, considering that such a clause implies a fraud on the law that establishes legal tender. . . .

Fundamentally, the stipulations that engage us subvert the economic order . . .; they contribute, in certain cases, to the aggravation of the inflationary process (Pedersen Jorgen, "Teoría y Política del Dinero," Madrid, 1946, p. 218; M. Vassenor, "Le droit des clauses monétaires et les enseignements de l'Economie Politique" en Revue Trimestrelle de Droit Civil, 1952, p. 431) or they make the development of a state policy to control prices difficult. . . .

The circumstance that the State itself, via legislation, recognizes the relevance of monetary devaluation for the purposes of periodically readjusting the payments owed . . . is not inconsistent with the foregoing considerations. The periodic adjustment of the values of federal or state bonds, as a function of indices referring to gold or to foreign currency (case of the Empréstito Nueve de Julio) or to the price level of determined products (the bonds of Yacimientos Petrolíferos Fiscales [the government oil company]); the periodic revision of wages in order to accompany the increase in the cost of living (the case of the escalating essential minimum wage); the recognition of the "increased costs" in the public works contract; or the right to solicit judicial fixation of new urban and rural rents after the passing of a determined time since the celebration of the lease . . . , all constitute measures inspired in objectives of social or economic order that shape a determined legislative policy (upon whose merit it is not for judges to pronounce). . . . [These measures] may not be invoked to validate, by analogy, the agreements between private parties tending to remove for some of the parties the inherent risk of the eventual fall of the currency's buying power. They are considered by the legislator as effective instruments to accomplish objectives of general interest. Some are responses to considerations of simple utility; others [to considerations] of justice, whose evaluation is the exclusive province of the public power. . . . On the other hand, clauses of stability inserted by parties in their private agreements follow exclusively an individual interest, which must yield before the exigencies of general needs and public order (Art. 21 of the Civil Code). . . .

Because of the foregoing considerations I vote [to affirm the decision of the appellate court].

Dr. Nápoli said: . . . [B]y providing that [the free convertibility provision] of article 41 will not go into effect until a special decree so provides, article 58 of law 12.155 does no more than suspend the obligation that this rule imposes on the Central Bank of the Republic to exchange on demand "national currency . . . for gold, or at the option of the bank, for foreign currency reserves." This suspension of the conversion of notes to gold or foreign exchange by no means implies the prohibition of the free market for gold. In order words, nothing prevents the debtor from acquiring gold outside the Central Bank in order to satisfy his obligation.

Furthermore, it is not necessary that he actually deliver gold, since in any case, if it is impossible to acquire gold, the issue is juridically resolved by delivery of the quantity of currency of legal tender sufficient to attain the contractual measure.

Thus, parties that utilize the "gold clause" do not propose to alter or render ineffective the legal tender [provisions] of national paper money, but rather to assure the equivalent metallic value.

Referring directly to the question of whether a gold clause is void during a period of inconvertibility, Schoo points out that some legal tender statutes decree the obligatory receipt of paper currency at its nominal value despite any agreement to the contrary, while others, on the other hand, restrict themselves to decreeing the obligatory receipt of paper currency without making special reference to the gold clause. The situation — he adds — is then quite distinct in the two cases: in the first, one will have to be content with the receipt of depreciated currency, but in the second, . . . one must consider the question . . . whether the rule of legal tender that attributes to inconvertible currency the power to satisfy [legal obligations] is, by its proper nature, [a rule] of public law which cannot be modified, or a [rule] of private law which may be modified by contract. The majority of the treatise writers that sustain the nullity . . . of the gold clause in the face of legal tender . . . argue that the goals of this measure would not be accomplished if people avoided paper currency. It would then be superfluous to prohibit expressly agreements contrary to legal tender, since this is a regimen of public and not private order. If legal tender is designed to make paper notes the money for all contracts — the unit of measure to which all the values that form the object of exchange become equal — it is not within the powers of the contracting parties to modify the nominal value of this means of payment, by agreements relating the calculation of the value of the obligation to a metallic or foreign value substituted for the note of national currency.

. . . Schoo is of the opinion that it would be more correct to frame the issue in terms of whether the gold clause contravenes such provisions that prescribe the acceptance of monetary amounts which are not gold, and he concludes . . . that the answer is negative, as long as the obligation will always be discharged by delivery of legal tender notes, even though not for their nominal value, but for current market value. . . .

Returning to law 12.155, it is worth reiterating that none of its norms prohibit the gold clause. Article 38 provides only that "the notes of the Bank will be legal tender in all the territory of the Republic of Argentina at their expressed amount," but without fixing a determined metallic value. Articles 41 and 58 [provide] that notes are not convertible into gold or foreign currency reserves. That is to say, they regulate the conduct of the holders of the notes with the bank as regards redemption, without affecting [in any way] the relations between private contracting parties about the manner of satisfying their monetary obligations.

. . . [T]he ex-minister of the Treasury, Dr. Federico Pinedo, [confirmed this thesis] in the Chamber of Senators of the Nation, explaining the features of the draft of the abovementioned law:

The government has maintained with profound conviction that the juridical problems of gold are not in issue. . . . If today the peso is valued in terms of gold in contractual relations in proportion to what gold costs in the open market, this law will do nothing to modify this situation. . . . Fixing the value of the peso in terms of gold in satisfying obligations must logically arise when one fixes the legal relationship between gold and paper currency, and not when one makes a simple commercial operation of a sale from one party of gold which does not differ except in magnitude from other gold sale transactions that we make every day. . . . The government's wishes have been limited to restricting the problems with which it was faced: the regulation of a monetary system, the fixing of precise rules for the management of the banks, reliable measures for the mobilization of credits, the possibility of orderly adjustment of accounts. . . .

The concerns, related to the loss of public confidence in the national monetary currency as well as the increase in inflation, that have been wielded to oppose the validity of the gold clause . . . did not motivate the legislator . . . to dictate the banking law 12.155. . . .

The "gold clause" does not affect, as the court of appeals erroneously maintained, the legal regimen of rentals. . . .

The contract signed by the litigants is not intended to substitute gold for money as a means of payment, but only to assure the stabilization of the sum total of rent during the life of the lease. . . . Nor does it seek to elude the prescriptions of the law, but rather to use them in order to avoid the deterioration of the stipulated price. . . .

For all that has been expressed, I vote to grant the appeal. . . .

[Dr. Ramírez Gronda and Dr. Bremberg concurred in Dr. Nápoli's opinion.]

Dr. Granoni said:

I concur with Dr. Nápoli in the solution given to the problem raised in the complaint.

As Schoo reminds us ("La Cláusula Oro," p. 384), Argentine tribunals have been inclined to admit the validity of the gold agreement and by extension, to situations, such as in the pleadings, where the object of the debt is not constituted precisely by gold coins of the stipulated system of the country, but rather for uncoined gold itself (gold performance clause). . . .

While fixing the value of currency is an attribute of public power (art. 67, sec. 10 of the National Constitution), it cannot be so considered in an absolute sense. The state only declares that the currency represents so much in transactions; it guarantees its type (if metallic) and its eventual convertibility (if paper); it fixes . . . [foreign exchange rates] ; but it can only do so within the area of extrinsic (or nominal) value of the currency, as distinguished from its intrinsic exchange value which is governed by the same economic phenomenon (law of supply and demand) that regulates all other values and is independent, as such, from the will of the legislator. . . .

Equally relative is the concept of the stability of the value of currency, for which the public power itself . . . continually resorts to marginal differentials and corrective indices in order to avert [the effects of] currency depreciation. [These include, *inter alia:*] . . . the issuance of bonds for reactivation of Yacimientos Petrolíferos Fiscales, . . . [which are readjusted in accordance with the] average wage received by the workers of that enterprise; . . . the Central Bank of the Republic on the 26th of March of the current year has consented to a readjustment clause for the National Mortgage Bank based upon nominal salaries . . . in order to slow the decapitalization which that credit agency has been suffering and at the same time to attract national and foreign savings for the construction of housing.

If the public sector itself resorts to these expedients in its contractual relations in order to avert the effects of monetary depreciation, I believe it only just to permit clauses provided for by creditors to preserve their credits.

[Dr. Demo also concurred in Dr. Nápoli's opinion, but added a separate opinion which is omitted.]

In accordance with what has been said, the majority grant the defendant's appeal of the inapplicability of law and revoke the appealed decision. . . .

Notes

1. Curiously, neither the majority nor the dissent mentioned the 1953 Federal Supreme Court opinion in *Bustillo v. Café Paulista, supra.*

2. The *Bentivoglio* decision has received extensive and generally favorable case notes at 1967-VI J.A. 529 by Morello and Troccoli, and at 129 La Ley 779 by Casiello.

---

2. Escalator Clauses

ASSIS V. FAKIANI

Tribunal of Alçada Civil of São Paulo (3d Chamber) (Brazil)
No. 121. 366, 409 Rev. Trib. 233 (1969)

. . . This concerns an action to collect a mortgage debt . . . in which the parties have established monetary correction to adjust the value of the debt [in accordance with coefficients derived from a price index].

The judgment of the court below considered this clause valid, and the defendant appealed, seeking its cancellation on the theory that the agreement contravenes Decree No. 23.501 of 1933, which instituted paper money as legal tender.

The appellant is incorrect. . . .

Caio Mário da Silva Pereira ("Instituições de Direito Civil," Vol. II, pp. 115 et seq.) examines the matter exhaustively and shows that the regime of legal tender is in force in the sense that the legal tender currency in circulation must be accepted at face value in the discharge of obligations. . . . But, he continues, . . . monetary clauses, among which one includes monetary correction, . . . are technically valid and recommendable. Their adoption cannot be judicially rejected, for nominalist theory, considered in rigid terms, does not conform with the ideal of justice in times of monetary instability such as inflation. And, he concludes: one must maintain the principle requiring the creditor to receive the paper money in circulation. But that should not be fatal to a clause by which the parties protect themselves against fluctuations in value, so long as there is no rejection of legal tender and lack of respect for its power to discharge obligations by its nominal value.

In accordance with this exposition, the appeal is denied. . . .

Martiniano de Azevedo, dissenting . . . .

The thesis of the opinion is seductive, but in my view gets ahead of the legislature.

The principle of nominalism governs all obligations which have as their object the payment of a sum of money. . . . To be sure, there are exceptions, and these have increased in recent years. However, in the absence of an express provision of law, nominalism and legal tender prevail. Naturally, the creditor suffers the consequences of the loss in value of money, as Washington de Barros Monteiro teaches in his "Direito das Obrigações," Vol. 1, p. 80.

Since the adoption of a monetary correction clause is not yet authorized in loan contracts between individuals, in my view the appellant has the undeniable right to discharge upon payment of the nominal value in currency. The question is one of public order, which cannot, with all due respect, be disregarded by agreement between creditor and debtor.

Now that inflation is controlled and our currency is coming upon better days, this is not the time to break with traditional principles indispensable to the stability of transactions. . . .

Questions

1. Are all escalator clauses inconsistent with the principle of compulsory legal tender?

2. Is there any difference between an escalator clause and a value-commodity clause, i.e., rental of a farm in exchange for half the wheat crop?

SALAS V., MIGUEL

Supreme Court of Chile
63 R.D.J. 141 (2d Part, 4th Sect.) (1966)

[In 1964 Miguel Salas Vergara sold a building for 20,400 escudos, payable in the following manner: 2,550 escudos at the time of the signing of the contract, with the balance spread over the next three years. The amounts of the unpaid installments were to be adjusted in accordance with the official price for wheat, but in no event were they to fall below their nominal values. In addition, these installments bore 8 percent annual interest on the readjusted sums.

[The buyer considered this contract usurious, and swore out a complaint against the seller for violation of article 472 of the Penal Code, which makes it a crime to charge interest in excess of the maximum permitted by law. (Law 16.464 fixes a maximum of one fifth more than the average bank rate in the preceding semester, and considers as interest all stipulations which augment the quantity the debtor must pay. In 21 of the years between 1940 and 1969 the maximum legal rate has been negative, *i.e.,* below the rate of inflation.[24]) The trial judge considered the complaint well-founded and ordered the seller's arrest.

[The seller sought relief by means of amparo in the Court of Appeals, which sustained the court below. The seller then appealed to the Supreme Court.[25]]

. . . 2. The contractual readjustment of the unpaid balance of the price for the sale of the property referred to in the deed of July 31, 1964 . . . does not constitute the crime of usury established and punished by Article 472 of the Penal Code, because readjustment cannot be considered as the furnishing of value at an interest rate which exceeds the maximum permitted by law. Rather, it is clearly the manner of determining the just price of the real property sold.

3. Consequently, . . . the recourse of amparo must be granted. . . .

Notes

1. The Court of Appeals of Santiago recently upheld the conviction for usury of a moneylender whose loan agreements provided for a readjustment of the loan value in accordance with the cost of living index. With one judge dissenting, the Court considered the inflation adjustment as interest. Wagemann Ehrenfeld, Julio, 67 R.D.J. 42 (2d Part, 4th Sec. 1970).

2. Brazilian legislation has specifically provided for the use of escalator clauses in numerous situations, such as leases, construction contracts, bonds, convertible debentures, insurance, and certain types of mortages. See generally, J. Chacel *et al, A Correção Monetária* (1970).

3. The country with the richest, most extensive, and probably most confusing case law and commentary about the validity of index or escalator clauses is France, where numerous fine distinctions have been drawn and redrawn. For a recent summary in English of the vagaries of French treatment of the problem, see Levy, " 'Sliding Scale' or 'Indexation' Clauses in French Law," 16 *Am. U.L. Rev.* 35 (1966). See also, Hauser, "The Use of Index Clauses in Private Loans," 7 *Am. J. Comp. L.* 350 (1958); Vasseur, "French Monetary Depreciation and Methods Used to Remedy it," 30 *Tulane L. Rev.* 73 (1955).

4. Index clauses have been used in the United States, primarily in labor contracts and long term leases. Occasionally they are used in pension plans, royalty agreements, and annuity contracts, but their use is nowhere near so extensive as in countries with more serious inflationary problems. Their validity has been assumed, despite a dearth of case law. See generally, Dawson and Coultrap, "Contracting By Reference to Price Indices," 33 *Mich L. Rev.* 685 (1935); McClintock, "The Probable Legal Consequences

---

[24] B. Gesche Muller, *Jurisprudencia Dinámica: La Desvalorización Monetaria y Otros Problemas en el Derecho* 120 (1971).

[25] This statement of facts is drawn from 1 *Revista de Derecho Privado* 70 (1966).

of Inserting Price-Index Clauses in Long-Term Corporate Obligations," 18 *Hastings L. J.* 959 (1967); Dach, "Validity Price-Index Clauses under the Gold Coin Joint Resolution," 13 *Geo. Wash. L. Rev.* 328 (1945).

Question

Suppose that a client asked you to draft a contract with an escalator clause. How would you proceed if you represented:

(a) a labor union negotiating a two-year wage contract with an automaker. See generally, Backman, "Cost of Living Escalator Clauses — Here and Abroad," 10 *Lab. L.J.* 615 (1959).

(b) a landlord leasing an apartment for a three-year term.

(c) an insurance company leasing a building for ten years to a department store. See generally Denz, "Lease Provisions Designed to Meet Changing Economic Conditions," 1952 *U. Ill. L. For.* 344.

(d) a contractor negotiating to construct a huge office building for a bank.

(e) a coal company negotiating a five-year requirements contract with an electric utility.

Suppose you were an Argentine, Brazilian, or Chilean legislator faced with the question of whether to outlaw the use of index clauses. How would you vote and why? In answering this question, consider the following three extracts.

L. FULLER & R. BRAUCHER, BASIC CONTRACT LAW

P. 79 (1964)*

Do sliding scale prices and rents aggravate, or restrain, fluctuations in price levels? Do they make the upward and downward swings of business activity more or less violent? Apparently little thought has been given to this question. One might argue that these arrangements will tend to accentuate whatever trend of prices, upward or downward, exists at the moment. If a contract contains a fixed price, it can serve as a center of inertia that will hold back the current movement of prices. On the other hand, if contracts are generally so drafted that their price terms are geared to the market, every change in price levels is immediately reflected throughout the nation's economy.

Against the view that flexible pricing aggravates and magnifies price trends, at least two counter-arguments can be made. In the first place as has already been

---

pointed out, flexible pricing avoids the disruptions involved in breach of contract, law suits, and lengthy negotiations between parties whose interests have become sharply opposed. In other words, flexible pricing tends to keep the wheels turning, and may thus mitigate the severity of a downward swing. In the second place, where prices are fixed by some automatic but flexible standard, the periodic renegotiation of price is avoided. This in turn reduces the "psychological factor" that plays so important a role in the business cycle. Where a lease expires during a period of rising prices, in negotiating a new lease the parties are apt to assume that prices will continue to rise, and fix the rent somewhat above the amount current conditions would make appropriate. This act, repeated throughout the economy, tends to make a reality of the prediction on which it is based, and accelerates the upward swing. Where rent moves up and down automatically with current business conditions, the influence of this factor is eliminated.

F. MANN, THE LEGAL ASPECT OF MONEY

Pp. 160-63 (3d ed. 1971)*

The problem of legislative policy, to which protective clauses and, in particular, gold clauses give rise, has been appreciated for many centuries, but is still unsolved.

So long as monetary stability prevails, these clauses are unnecessary. In the event of monetary disturbances, however, they are liable to become intolerable on account of their strong inflationary tendencies. Consequently, a country in which such clauses are frequent, will abolish them at the very moment when they are meant to prove their worth. The idea that their abrogation is *a priori* obnoxious, has rightly been described as "narrow-minded and utterly unsound." An idea in the opposite sense is a more serious proposition and would have much more to commend it. Indeed, there can be no doubt that it was only because gold clauses were (and are) rare in this country [Great Britain], that Parliament could, since 1931, afford not to interfere with them.

Yet it is a curious fact that no legislator, however wide he tried to cast his net, has ever succeeded in eliminating protective clauses altogether. In the United States of America index clauses as well as promises to pay foreign currency have remained valid, and the same applies to promises to deliver commodities other than gold; to make the illegality of gold clauses an article of faith (as is being done in the United States), yet to permit, for example, the index clause, certainly does not disclose consistency of thought. Similarly in France index clauses and promises to deliver commodities other than gold are often valid. In post-war Germany, it is true, the Western Allies have abolished index clauses along with gold and similar clauses, but contracts for the delivery of commodities or even the payment of a variable sum of money determined by the price of commodities have remained valid. It must be recognized that no legislator can eliminate barter. If he makes it too difficult for the parties to make

---

*© 1971 Oxford University Press, reprinted by permission of The Clarendon Press, Oxford.

monetary obligations subject to such protection as may be required, he will merely drive them into barter transactions of a somewhat old-fashioned type. In the case of agricultural rents or mortgages a solution on these lines will be readily found, but even in other cases a skillful draftsman will often succeed.

In these circumstances the question arises whether, accepting the hopelessness of his task and the fortuitous character of his measures, the legislator should refrain altogether from attempting to abolish protective clauses. The question should not be put, and certainly cannot be answered, dogmatically. Much will depend on the circumstances prevailing in the country concerned. The danger of inflation, inherent in the maintenance of protective clauses, and the danger of creating too pronounced a distinction between classes of creditors may be too pressing to be ignored. On the other hand it must be realized that inflationary tendencies cannot be stemmed by legal weapons in general or the abolition of protective clauses in particular, and that, to encourage savings and investments, it is justifiable and necessary to create, and not at the crucial moment to disappoint, a sense of security and confidence. But in no event should the creditor's disillusionment be increased by arbitrarily limiting the abolition to particular types of protective clauses.

For these reasons it is submitted that the legislator should arrive at a deliberate decision about protective clauses of all types in times of economic stability and that he should abide by that decision in times of crisis; in no case should the judiciary assume, on this point, the functions of the legislature. That decision, it is further suggested, will not necessarily have to be uniform, but may have to differentiate both between various types of protective clauses and between various types of transactions, and should be secured by appropriate constitutional guarantees. Nothing would be more discreditable or contrary to public policy than for a legislator to allow protective clauses, if only by implication, thus to create the impression that they afford effective protection, yet in a critical situation to abrogate them almost automatically and perhaps haphazardly.

R. HAUSER, THE USE OF INDEX CLAUSES IN PRIVATE LOANS

7 *American Journal of Comparative Law* 350, 362-63 (1958)

Firstly, it is questionable that even a general adoption of the index clause would, in practice, contribute greatly toward spiraling the inflation. In an excellent paper delivered to the American Economic Association, Dr. Poole notes that there may well be a cushioning effect by virtue of the very increase in the use of such clauses. The index chosen by any given group or parties to a contract will vary according to their particular economic needs, and it is probable that, in their totality, the indices chosen will tend to neutralize each other. Some will tend to encourage consumption, others not. Indeed, even for those that tend to increase consumption patterns, the end effect may well be an eventual increase in the cost of borrowing money, so that investment will be ultimately discouraged.[26] Second, the expected rise in consumption will depend on which groups are receiving the additional sums via the operation of the index clause . . . . It would seem fair, then to conclude that the inflationary effects of a general use of the index clause are quite unknown; the few studies attempted in France have never reached any definitive statement on the inflationary aspects of indexation. Even if we assume that indexation does cause some long term upward price movement, it is important to realize that it is also an antirecession measure, and that any such measure, such as an easy money policy, results in some upward trend. This may be the price we pay to prevent a downward cycle.

What is more important to the lawyer, and to many economists, is the issue of an equitable distribution of the increased wealth resulting from the boom, and an equally equitable division of the costs that inflation may bring. Congress has assured one particular economic group its share in the increased wealth through direct legislation: parity for farmers. Union strength has assured most industrial workers the same through the demand for an indexed wage scale. The entrepreneurial class supposedly shares directly via higher prices and greater profits. Those groups that remain, the white collar worker, the small noninstitutional lender, and the pensioned, fixed income group, find themselves sharing little of this boom prosperity; indeed, they are often adversely affected, not able to maintain the status quo as prices continue to rise. This gain of one group at the expense of another caused René Capitant, the French jurist, to call this situation a classic example of "unjust enrichment." We submit that these groups should not be denied any legitimate and legal avenue of protection under the guise of an anti-inflationary policy, while the stronger, more powerfully organized groups continue to enjoy the advantages of their privileged protections. This would be an inequitable economic situation, and certainly an unjust result.

---

3. Foreign Currency Clauses

A third kind of stabilization clause is one calling for payment in foreign currency. Sometimes a creditor is given the option of demanding repayment in one of several currencies, or the obligation may be linked to a number of currencies, such as the European unit of account.[27] Contracts calling for payment in foreign currency have been regularly upheld by Argentine and Chilean courts, though payment in national currency at the exchange rate in effect when the obligation becomes due has been substituted for actual payment in foreign currency.[28] On the other hand, Brazil, as has

---

[26]This would be particularly true in light of the Federal Reserve Board's restrictive monetary policies in inflationary periods. [Footnote by Hauser, renumbered.]

[27]See Silard, "Maintenance-of-Value Agreements in International Transactions," 5 *L. & Pol. Int'l Bus.* 398 (1973); Note, "The Unit of Account: Enforceability under American Law of Maintenance of Value Provisions in International Bonds," 71 *Yale L. J.* 1294 (1962).

[28]Atlas, S.A. v. Valentine, 105 La Ley 691 (CN Com., Arg., Sala C 1961); Giménez Zapiola y Cía. v. Astengo, 106 La Ley 333 (Capel Rosario 1961); Schwarz v. Cortázar, 60 R.D.J. 169 (2d Part-Court of Santiago 1963).

been indicated, has prohibited the use of foreign currency for domestic contracts. Does such a prohibition make sense?

Consider Professor Harberger's observations on the Chilean experience. In explaining why Chilean prices rose much faster in 1959 than one would have expected on the basis of the increase in the money supply, he noted that in late 1958 and early 1959, when Chile instituted a tight money policy, new bank regulations were adopted permitting commercial banks to receive deposits and make loans in dollars.

> The ostensible motive for these new regulations was to make it possible for the banks to induce Chileans to repatriate capital which they had invested abroad, by offering the convenience of a hedge against inflation "right here at home," and by offering attractive interest rates on time deposits in dollars. There resulted an expansion of over $70 million in the amount of dollar deposits, which initially had been negligible in magnitude. More than half of this increase represented not repatriation of dollars held abroad but multiple expansion of dollar deposits by the Chilean banking system. The dollar became a sort of second currency in Chile, in which loans, transactions, and deposits were made just as in domestic currency. In a sense, the dollar was "more money than money," for while it satisfied the other motives for holding cash just as well as the peso, it provided a hedge against inflation which the peso did not provide.[29]

---

4. Judicial Efforts to Mitigate Inflation's Effects on Contracts

Argentine and Brazilian courts have been confronted with a barrage of lawsuits arising from contracts in which a surge in the rate of inflation has made one party's performance far more onerous than expected at the time of the contract's formation. (Curiously, reported Chilean case law is remarkably devoid of such litigation.) In the absence of positive legislation relieving such improvident contractors,[30] the courts have been confronted with a series of dilemmas. Should the courts deny all such claims for relief until the legislature directs them to do otherwise? If the courts are going to intervene to bail out one of the parties, what should be the doctrinal basis for doing so? Should the courts expand the traditional concept of *force majeure* or impossibility? Should they imply a clause to the effect that the parties would have intended to relieve an obligor of a performance that had become unduly onerous because of inflation? What kinds of remedies should the courts employ? Rescission? Revocation? Termination? Should the courts attempt to modify the terms of the

---

[29] Harberger, "Some Notes on Inflation," in W. Baer & I. Kerstenetzky (eds.) *Inflation and Growth in Latin America* 319, 334 (1964).

[30] Not until 1968 did Argentina modify its Civil Code to deal with these problems on a general basis. *Infra,* p. 481. Brazil has statutorily authorized contractual revisions only in limited cases, such as government construction contracts. *Infra,* pp. 475-76.

contract to make it "fair?" Should they offer the other party the option of accepting such a modification or having the contract terminated? Or should they simply adjust the damage remedy to cushion the pecuniary effects of nonperformance? To what extent should it matter whether the contract is executory, partially executed, or fully executed?

(a) The Theory of Imprevision

FERRARI ET AL. v. ESTANCIAS SANTA ROSA, S.A.

National Chamber of Civil Appeals of the Federal Capital, Division A (Argentina)
1965-IV J.A. 413, 118 La Ley 330 (1965)

[This case and a similar one, *Félix Sola v. Colonias y Estancias El Rodeo,* 1964-III J.A. 600, are by-products of the Perón dictatorship's attack on an enormous industrial and landholding complex called the "Bemberg Group." The heirs of the Bemberg estate were charged with tax evasion and fined more than $10,000,000, an unprecedented sum. The group was also alleged to have violated the antitrust laws by monopolizing the beer industry. Special legislation was passed ordering liquidation of many of the group's companies, and in 1954 several of the group's ranches were expropriated. Any compensation due was offset by tax claims. These properties, valued at more than $100,000,000, were restored to their former owners in 1959 by the Frondizi government.]

2d Instance. — Buenos Aires, November 29, 1964.

Dr. Llambías said:

1st — On July 2, 1951 Teodoro Ferrari, agent for the plaintiffs, and Drs. Juan P. Oliver and Daniel A. Llambí, acting as liquidators of Santa Rosa Estancias, S.A., [a company] in liquidation, agreed to a memorandum sales contract . . . which the defendant promised to sell the land called "San Martín," located in Chascomus, to Dr. Ferrari, for a total price of 743,120.63 pesos at 1,000 pesos per hectare. This price was to be paid: 223,000 pesos when the sales contract was signed, 148,000 pesos before August 16 of the same year in exchange for turning over possession, and the balance on the date of signing the deed, which would be after 180 days, in the presence of a notary to be designated by the seller.

Immediately upon taking possession of the land the purchaser repeatedly requested from the defendant's attorney the prompt signing of the deed to the property. . . .

[The deed was not signed, primarily because of the arbitrary attitude of government officials, who refused to furnish necessary certificates. On April 26, 1961 the buyer's heirs requested that the defendant sign the deed.] Since that intimation produced no result, they brought this complaint, which the trial judge granted.

The defendant . . . [raises three points on appeal. We omit discussion of the defendant's first point — that the sale was involuntary — which the court rejected for failure of proof.] b) there was *force majeure* that prevented the debtor from fulfilling the obligation and thus released him from it; c) such *force majeure* had led to the condition of "imprevision" which excused the nonfulfillment of the obligation, since the monetary devaluation that had taken place between July 1951 and the present made the seller's position excessively onerous; he would receive, through no fault of his own, [money] which no longer had the value [it] had in 1951. For this reason, good faith would require the unpaid price to be readjusted to a figure ten times higher. . . .

3d — [*Impossibility; force majeure*] The appellant's reference to the *force majeure* that had prevented it from signing a deed for several years carries no weight in this case. [The purpose of this suit] . . . is not to enforce a responsibility arising from some wrongful action of the seller. If, . . . for example, damages were claimed by the buyer for the delay in signing the deed, it would be understandable for the defendant to allege *force majeure* in order to avoid the obligation to indemnify. But since that claim has not been made in this lawsuit, and since the appellant admits that by the year 1961 the obstacle to signing the deed had disappeared, there is no doubt that [the argument based on] *force majeure* has no function here whatsoever. . . .

4th — *Theory of imprevision.* In this respect the appellant maintains that the long delay of the pending sale transaction had made the fulfillment of the agreement excessively burdensome for it, since it would be required to accept 50% of the price in pesos worth about one-tenth their value at the time of the contract. It thus adduces the so-called "theory of imprevision" as a cause for termination of the unexecuted transaction.

I do not doubt the efficacy of the theory of imprevision as a cause for rescission of long-term juridical relationships. The law cannot permit a future unforeseen event, that displaces the general assumption which is the basis of a contract of continuing execution, to ruin one of the contracting parties, when that party's performance becomes excessively burdensome, by requiring him to continue performing at a loss in the future. As Spota says, it is not possible to view impassively the ruin of a merchant whose only mistake is that he did not foresee the unforeseeable. . . . The truth is that when one contracts, the rights of the contracting parties are determined in relation to a belief shared by them about a number of basic assumptions that have not been explicitly stated, because it has not been thought that any difference would arise concerning them. . . .

Thus, when in the life of the lasting juridical relationship that links the parties, absolutely unforeseeable events occur which skew the economic framework of the contract, making the payment of one of the contracting parties enormously burdensome, he may insist on the rescission of the contract. . . .

Although new in its formulation by modern juridical science, this idea of the theory of imprevision is very old. It was already touched upon by the Roman jurisconsults, . . . but above all it is in the work of the canonists where one may observe the theory of imprevision: in the *Decretum Gratian,* in the Summa Theologica of St. Thomas Aquinas, and in Bartolomeo of Brescia. The glossators did not occupy themselves with the point, but the school of the post-glossators did so profusely, with Bartolus at the head. . . . But it should not be thought that this doctrine was known only in Italy, since one sees it discussed and applied from the 16th century forward in

France, by Alciato, and also in Spain and Savoy. If Alciato had already traced a very exact scheme of the theory of imprevision, all his precision was acquired through Italian doctrine and jurisprudence at the end of the 16th century and beginning of the 17th century. Two authors in particular contributed to his writing, Cardinals Mantica and de Luca. The latter is particularly interesting because, by giving numerous decisions of the Court of the Rota, he allows us to see beyond the workd of the theoreticians into the practical jurisprudence of the ecclesiastical tribunals. For Cardinal de Luca, there are two conditions for the applicability of the phrase "rebus sic stantibus": a) the contract must have duration over a period of time or be subject to a future event; b) the change occurring in the facts must result in a flagrant injustice.

As for the Germans, the old idea of the phrase "rebus sic stantibus" [in these circumstances] also made itself known, through Grotius and Pufendorf. During the course of the 18th century, German jurists frequently dealt with this matter and even made various attempts at theoretical construction regarding the nature, function and effects of that phrase. But at the end of that century and the beginning of the 19th century, the dominance of individualistic liberal thought made the doctrine less favorable to the admission of the theory, which no longer is the subject of close study and which, when it is referred to by authors, is regularly mentioned in order to limit its range of application. Finally, at the end of the 19th century . . . the thread of the tradition has been taken up again.

I have briefly related the historical antecedents which may be found, with one or another variation, in so many expressions of the abundant literature inspired by this theme, within and without our country, in order to show how the theory of imprevision is engrained in the very heart of the law. In our environment, the appearance of the doctrine of the authors is practically unanimous regarding the applicability of the theory of imprevision. . . .

The fact which brings into operation the theory of imprevision, considered by itself, must include the characteristics of inevitable accident or *force majeure*. Thus, it must be unforeseeable, inevitable, creating an obstacle to performance of the obligation and not be the responsibility of the obligor. Some authors, Ripert among them, add that the fact must affect an entire category of obligors, but such a condition would discount an unfortunate contingency because it is purely personal. It is hard to see why, in such a situation, one should tolerate the flagrant injustice of which Cardinal Luca spoke. . . .

In order for the theory of imprevision to come into play, the fact in question must cause an excessive burden in the exaction of the payment owed. To determine when the burden becomes excessive "is a matter left to the prudent discretion of the trier of fact," says Messineo. . . .

Finally, contracts affected by the theory of imprevision are, to my mind, those which involve, by their very nature, a continuing juridical relation among the contracting parties. . . .

The *effects* of the theory of imprevision are summed up in the *rescission*[31] of the juridical relation that bound the parties. But it must be precisely a rescission that dissolves the tie for the future only, leaving intact the effects produced up to that time. . . . The contract was valid; therefore, it obligated the contracting parties until they were discharged by the declaration of rescission, when it was proven that because of the substantial change that had occurred, the old contract had died. What survived was a complex of rights and obligations, apparently contractual, but in truth lacking the pure consent of both contracting parties. Still, rescission is not unavoidable; if the party favored by the change in circumstances agrees to modify the terms of the contract (cf. art. 1467 of the Italian Code), . . . the "flagrant injustice," which was the *raison d'être* for the breaking of the contract, disappears. The judicial revision upholding the contractual regime in all aspects not at odds with justice is substituted for the rescission asserted as a right by the injured party.

After this theoretical exposition that has seemed necessary in order to make clear the just solution of the case at hand, it is now proper to project the conclusions reached with respect to the case.

Undoubtedly the unexpected prolongation of the contractual tie . . . imposed on the contracting parties has resulted in an excessively onerous performance by the seller, who, according to the terms of the contract should receive, in payment of half the price, a value equivalent to 5% of the value of the land sold. Therefore, . . . one condition of the theory of imprevision is present: excessive onerousness.

On the other hand, this case does not fulfill the condition relating to the juridical relation of periodic performance or one dependent on a future act. For the memorandum sale agreement . . . is the instrument of an instantaneous contract (as is the contract of sale), a feature which does not disappear by virtue of the inclusion of installment payments. This affects the power to demand payment . . . [rather than signifying the existence of a continuous right as opposed to a non-continuous right (the court draws the distinction metaphorically — "flowing rights" v. "non-flowing rights")]. The nature of this contract forecloses the possibility of determining [the existence] of fractional performance as is possible in contracts to be performed over a period of time [*e.g.*, leases]. The only alternatives are to respect the entire contract or to destroy it in its entirety. The latter [solution] in this case would certainly be unjust to the buyer, to whom would be returned currency devalued by 1000%, despite his having nothing to do with the delay. In juridical relations calling for performance over a period of time, the solution is different, because, to the claim of rescission by the injured party, the one who benefits may impose a claim for [judicial] revision of the future terms of the contract. . . . This Division of the court has had occasion to state that the processes of inflation or deflation that often afflict the economy of a country "may not displace the basic principles of each juridical institution, on pain of putting the entire juridical order into crisis" (causa 58.733). Thus judges must prevent those evils from damaging the juridical structure of the Nation, maintaining the incidence of

---

[31] The court uses the term "rescisión" as if it meant termination of the contract (normally "resolución"). In Argentina, as in the United States, the juridical effects of the remedies are distinct. [Eds.]

the risk of the contract with the party who, by the nature of things, should undergo that risk (decision of this division "in re": "Voss C. Mijalovich," Rev. La Ley, vol. 97, p. 38 [fallo 44.301]).

5th — By virtue of the foregoing, I vote [to affirm] . . . .

Doctor *Borda* said:

Although I am substantially in agreement with the erudite opinion of Dr. Llambías, it it necessary to point out a doctrinal difference which, as will be seen, does not influence the conclusions.

I think, in fact, that the theory of imprevision is applicable not only to contracts to be performed periodically but also to those of postponed execution. This seems clear to me because what justifies the revision of the contract is an unforeseeable and substantial alteration in the motivating conditions (the basis of the juridical act,[32] according to German terminology) that breaks the contractual balance, so that maintenance of the original conditions is repugnant to equity. And this may happen as well in contracts to be performed over a period of time as in those of delayed execution. Messineo says in this respect: "Observe that the remedy for the effects of an excessive burden finds its *raison d'être* in the time that passes between the formation of the contract and the moment of its execution. The application of the remedy to cases of contracts with continued or periodical execution depends on the fact that in these contracts a difference of time is established between the formation of the contract and the various phases of execution of the same; therefore, the right of termination is conceded to the debtor not on the basis of the continuity or periodic nature, of a contract, but on the basis of the deferment of its execution" (Tratado de Derecho Civil y Comercial, t. IV, p. 527).

. . . [I]n modern doctrine opinion is almost unanimous that the theory of imprevision is also applicable to contracts of delayed performance. . . . This is also the express solution of the Italian Civil Code (Art. 1467),[33] which speaks of contracts of

---

[32] The term "juridical act" is a fundamental concept in the civil law and is the subject of a large body of legal scholarship. It has been defined as an act "by which the party or parties declare their intention of effecting changes in legal relations and to which the law attaches the power of producing such changes. The [juridical act] . . . is wider than the term contract or even agreement. It includes, *e.g.,* a notice to quit given to a tenant, a declaration by which one party avoids a contract on the ground of fraud, the grant of authority to an agent, the making of a will, etc." I *Manual of German Law* 42 (Brit. For. Off. 1950), quoted in A. Von Mehren, *The Civil Law System* 467 (1957). See also, J. Merryman, *The Civil Law Tradition* 81-3 (1969). [Eds.]

[33] Article 1467. Contract for mutual counterperformances. In contracts for continuous or periodic performances or for deferred performance, if extraordinary and unforeseeable events make the performance of one of the parties excessively onerous, the party who owes such performance can demand dissolution of the contract, with the effects set forth in article 1458. [That article provides that dissolution shall have retroactive effects, except for contracts of continuous or periodic performance. As to the latter, dissolution does not extend to performance already rendered.]

Dissolution cannot be demanded if the supervening onerousness is part of the normal risk of the contract.

A party against whom dissolution is demanded can avoid it by offering to modify equitably the conditions of the contract.

Article 1468. Contracts with obligations of one party only. In the case contemplated in the

continued or periodic performance or of delayed performance, and it was also the solution proposed by the Third National Congress of Civil Law in Córdoba in 1961, which approved the following recommendation: "In commutative[34] bilateral contracts of delayed or continued performance, if the payment owed by one of the parties becomes excessively onerous because of extraordinary and unforeseeable events, the affected party may ask for termination of the contract" (Tercer Congreso Nacional de Derecho Civil, v. 2., p. 778).

I do not dissent from the decision proposed by Dr. Llambías for this reason. In the present case, we are dealing with a sale with payment in installments; but, when the contractual time period ran out, stipulated as 180 days, no economic imbalance had been produced, and the succeeding delay took place for reasons that had nothing to do with the purchaser. Even supposing that the delay was due to reasons of *force majeure,* this should not weigh upon the buyer, who from the moment fixed for execution of the deed had to have the money he owed liquid and uninvested.

Thus, I adhere to the previous vote.

Dr. de Abelleyra said:

My thinking coincides with that of Dr. Borda, insofar as he sustains that the doctrine of imprevision is applicable to contracts of extended performance as well as to those of delayed performance.

... [But] in order for the theory to enter into the analysis of the problem, it was necessary to prove – and this was not done – that the contract price was not related to the value of the thing sold at the precise moment when completion of the contract was possible.

In this respect, [a report in the trial record] does not refer to the price of the land, but to our currency in relation to the US dollar, between the months of July 1951 and November 1962. In regard to [certain expert testimony], besides the fact that [the valuation] was carried out by someone [who was not properly qualified] ..., it takes into account the values in 1963 when it was made, and not those during 1959 or 1960 when it was possible to fulfill the contract. ...

Because of the foregoing agreement, the appealed decision is affirmed. . . .

---

preceding article, if the contract is one in which only one of the parties has assumed obligations, he can demand a reduction in his performance or a modification of the manner of performance, sufficient to restore it to an equitable basis.

Article 1469. Aleatory contracts. The provisions of the preceding articles (1467 f.) do not apply to contracts which are aleatory by their nature or by the intention of the parties. [As translated in M. Beltramo et al., *The Italian Civil Code* 372-73 (1969).] [Eds.]

[34] A commutative contract is a non-gratuitous contract in which both of the parties can reasonably estimate at the time the contract is made the cost of performance which they are obligated to render. The civilians use the category of commutative contracts to distinguish from aleatory contracts, such as insurance, in which one of the parties does not know, at the time the contract is made, whether (or precisely how much) it may have to pay to satisfy its contractual obligation. [Eds.]

REYES, JUAN C., SUC. v. BRONSTEIN, JOSE V. Y OTROS

National Chamber of Civil Appeals of the Federal Capital (Argentina)
1966-II J.A. 223, 121 La Ley 367 (1965)

2d Instance — Buenos Aires, Dec. 30, 1965. Is the appealed decision in accordance with law?

Dr. Fleitas said:

. . . On Nov. 30, 1954, Bernard Olstein, José Volif Bronstein, and Abraham Krasuk agreed to sell to [their tenant], Juan C. Reyes, unit 12, apartment letter "A" on the fifth floor of the building on Avenida Callao 1763/73 . . . [in accordance with the provisions of a rent control law giving the tenant the preferential right to purchase the apartment]. In conformance with the agreement of sale . . . and the valuation made by the Dirección General Impositiva . . . in 1951, the price was fixed at 133,600 pesos, which was to be paid in the following manner: 13,360 pesos . . . [at the time of the signing of the agreement to sell]; 53,440 pesos at the signing of the deed; and the balance of 66,800 pesos — to be guaranteed by a first mortgage to be executed by the buyer at the signing of the deed — in 10 trimestral quotas of 6,680 pesos each . . . plus 8% annual interest on the unpaid balance. In addition, the buyer was to pay 450 pesos per month as rent until execution of the deed, which was to take place within 120 days following the signing of the agreement to sell. For such purpose, Reyes was to appear before the designated notary when first notified by telegram; if he did not, the annual interest of 8% on the balance owed would begin to run, as well as the periods for the payment of amortization quotas, with the consequent cessation of the payment of the agreed upon rent and the assumption by the buyer of his corresponding share of the common expenses [i.e., condominium maintenance] in accordance with the percentage established by the Dirección General Impositiva.

On April 27, 1955, prior to the formalization of the sale, Reyes died. After probate proceedings, his son, César Reyes, was declared his sole and universal heir, assuming the contract rights. Such were things on August 10, 1955, when the plaintiff's sister, Elena Reyes de Navarro Loveira brought suit against . . . [the landlords] for recognition of her preferential right to purchase the apartment (on the ground that she is the tenant) and to declare the above mentioned agreement to sell a nullity. . . . [This suit, which dragged out in the courts until December of 1960, was unsuccessful. In the meantime the landlords had been refusing to accept rent from either César Reyes or Elena Reyes de Navarro Loveira. Soon after the judgment in Mrs. de Navarro Loveira's action became final, the landlords sent Reyes a telegram declaring the agreement to sell rescinded and offering to refund 26,720 pesos (twice the amount of the down payment). This offer was rejected by Reyes.]

Here things stood when on October 19, 1962, almost eight years after signing the agreement to sell (when the value of the apartment was notably superior to the price stipulated), Reyes brought suit against the sellers for the deed. The sellers opposed the suit and counterclaimed for rescission and annulment of the agreement to sell. . . .

[T]he decision below allowed the complaint and rejected the counterclaim. The defeated party appealed from this pronouncement. . . .

[The court rejected two of the appellants' claims — that they had the right to rescind the agreement of sale unilaterally, and that the appellee's contract rights did not survive the death of Juan C. Reyes.]

. . . Because of the great disparity between the considerations, the defendants also argue . . . that the plaintiff would be unjustly enriched. As proof of this defense, . . . [they point to the valuation of 2,571,300 pesos placed upon the apartment in June of 1964, and] invoke reasons of morality and equity.

It seems clear to me that the prerequisites for a successful action of "in rem verso," in accordance with the generality of our doctrine, are not made out here; one cannot affirm for example, the inexistence of juridical, legal, or legitimate cause [*causa*— analogous to consideration] for the enrichment of the plaintiff and the consequent impoverishment of the defendants. . . .

But the error of the appellants in the legal theory as to the issue involved in this lawsuit (the result of circumstances totally unimputable to them — subsequent to the execution of the contract — which has created a decided disparity in values) does not prevent this court, by virtue of the principle "iura novit curia," from analyzing the case in light of the principles of the "theory of imprevision". . . .

[B]ecause of the principles that make up . . . [the theory of imprevision,] the complaint cannot be sustained. First of all, . . . that we are not confronted with a contract to be performed periodically is no barrier to the application of the clause "rebus sic stantibus," for [*rebus*] also applies to contracts of deferred performance (concurring votes of Drs. Borda and Abelleyra in . . . [*Ferrari et al. vs. Estancias Santa Rosa, S.A.*] . . . .

Furthermore, the pleadings contain the prerequisites for allowing the theory of imprevision, if one recalls that: a) the long delay in the performance of the contract was due to extraneous causes not imputable to the sellers. [Moreover, such causes were] completely unforeseeable (death of the buyer, handling of the probate proceedings, and the subsequent claims by the sister . . ., all combined with a dizzying process of monetary devaluation); b) that at no time prior to the sending of the telegram on January 18, 1961 had the defendants been found in default with respect to the obligations placed upon them by the agreement to sell; c) that the apartment still continues to be occupied by "intruders retaining it illegally," as the plaintiff admits . . .; and d) that even if the plaintiff accepts the deed for the property with the "intruders" who occupy it (who are his relatives), the disproportion that already exists in consideration had acquired such magnitude that the acceptance of the complaint would involve a real deprivation to the owners, which is even more evident if one remembers that they had to take care of the common expenses of the building, "which greatly exceed the price of 133,600 pesos stipulated in the contract."

The Supreme Court of the Nation has said that in the exercise of the judicial duty, concern for justice cannot be laid to one side. . . . It is precisely this concern . . . that unhesitatingly brings me to propose the reversal of the decision on appeal.

Keep in mind that in 1954 the owners, because of state intervention in sales [of rent-controlled property] . . ., had a very restricted freedom to contract, such that the tenants had a preferential right to buy at a price fixed by administrative authorities, always far below the real value of the property. Under such regime . . ., the agreement of sale . . . for a price of 133,600 pesos, was made. It would be a miscarriage of justice, to order the sellers, eleven years later, to receive this amount . . . when the property has a present value of 4,650,000 pesos.

Also, as I said in the opinion of this court in "La Ley," t. 113, p. 724, citing the decisions of the Supreme Court of the Nation . . ., our legal order must be interpreted in such a manner that its provisions are in accord with the principles and guarantees of the National Constitution. . . . It is evident, in my opinion, that the decision on appeal, in as much as it grants the complaint, signifies the total destruction of the right of property of the defendants, which Article 17 of the Constitution guarantees and protects. . . .

For these reasons I vote in the negative, rejecting the complaint and supporting the counterclaim in as much as it seeks the termination of the agreement of sale, which means that the defendants shall return to the plaintiff, within a period of ten days, the sum of 13,360 pesos. . . .

Dr. Chichero said:

. . . I will only add, with the object of eliminating a possible ambiguity, that no contradiction exists between the case now decided and the result in the case "Sola, Félix v. Colonias y Estancias El Rodeo," in which the court to which I belong rejected the seller's counterclaim for termination of the contract through invocation of the clause "rebus sic stantibus." . . .

In that case, as in this, supervening circumstances led to an evident disparity between the reciprocal considerations, . . . upsetting or undermining the economic structure of the transaction, with significant prejudice to the seller. But the difference between that . . . [case and this was that] the impossibility of fulfilling the obligation to deliver the deed within the agreed time . . . was not only foreseen by the seller, but the sale of the property in question was the means availed of to shield it from a third party's maneuvers intended to dispossess it illegitimately. That is to say, the risk that gave rise to the disparity in the basis of the bargain, far from having been unforeseeable, was precisely what motivated the seller to make the contract. And when the risk is the determining motive for contracting, it is inappropriate to speak of the equivalence of consideration, presupposed or desired by the parties. The supervening onerousness is part of the normal risk of the legal transaction.

I also point out that while in both cases the factors which delayed formalization of the contract were not imputable to the contracting parties, in the case to which I am referring, those factors were not foreign to the person of the vendor. The situation in the case at bar is the opposite, for the causes of the nonperformance appear to be intimately connected with the person of the buyer.

With these brief explanations, I join in the opinion of Dr. Fleitas and also cast my vote in the negative.

. . . [T]he appealed decision is revoked and the complaint is rejected. The counterclaim, in as much as it refers to termination of the agreement of sale is granted, by virtue of which the defendants shall return the sum of 13,360 pesos which they received to the plaintiff party within a period of 10 days from the date of this decision. . . .

Questions

1. Are the *Ferrari* and *Reyes* cases inconsistent?

2. For the purposes of the theory of imprevision should the following contracts be treated differently?

    (a) prepayment of a ten-year magazine subscription;

    (b) a whole life insurance policy;

    (c) a ten-year requirements contract to supply gasoline at a fixed price;

    (d) a thirty-year home mortgage;

    (e) purchase of a farm with payments spread over a five-year period.

3. Should it make a difference whether the contract is executory or executed?

4. Should the court simply abrogate the contract, or should it make a new contract for the parties?

5. Is the theory of imprevision a useful doctrine for affording relief from inflation-induced distortions in contracts in Argentina, Brazil, or Chile?

The Argentine military government recently made the theory of imprevision part of the Civil Code.

LAW 17.711 OF APRIL 22, 1968

A.L.J.A. 1968-A, p. 498, 508

(65) Substitute for Article 1198 the following:

Article 1198. — Contracts must be celebrated, interpreted, and executed in good faith and in accordance with what the parties probably intended or could have intended, operating with care and foresight.

If, in bilateral commutative contracts and in nongratuitous and commutative unilateral contracts with deferred or continued performance the performance of one of the parties becomes excessively onerous because of extraordinary and unforseeable events, the prejudiced party may demand the termination of the contract. The same principle shall apply to aleatory contracts when excessive onerousness results from causes extraneous to the very risk of a contract.

In contracts of continued performance termination shall not affect that which has already been performed.

Termination shall not be granted if the prejudiced party has been at fault or in delay.

The other party may prevent termination by offering to improve the effects of the contract in an equitable manner.

Questions

1. Would you have voted for adoption of this amendment?

2. To what extent does this provision borrow from Articles 1467-69 of the Italian Civil Code, set out in footnote 33, *supra*?

3. Upon what hypothetical set of facts would the theory of imprevision apply to an aleatory contract?

4. How would the *Ferrari* and *Reyes* cases be decided under this amendment?

This amendment has been the subject of extensive commentary in Casiello, "La Teoría de la Imprevisión en la reciente reforma del Código Civil," 131 *La Ley* 1491 (1968).

NOTE ON THE THEORY OF IMPREVISION IN BRAZIL

The theory of imprevision made its debut much earlier in Brazil than in Argentina, emerging at the beginning of the depression as part of the case law. It was not a response to the phenomenon of inflation; instead it was utilized to relieve a party from a contractual obligation that had become exceedingly onerous because of commercial uncertainties stemming from Brazil's revolution of 1930 and the sharp decline in the exchange rate.[35] Acceptance of the doctrine has been the work of the commentators and the courts. While a draft of a new Code of Obligations has adopted the theory, only in isolated instances has imprevision crept into legislation. It became an important doctrinal device to mitigate the effects of inflation only in the area of construction contracts. Particularly during the decade of the 1940's, when the prices of construction materials soared, a number of Brazilian courts permitted either the revision or abrogation of construction contracts on the theory of imprevision,[36] despite the explicit mandate of Article 1246 of the Brazilian Civil Code.[37] With the exception of public construction contracts, however, the tendency of the case law has

---

[35] Carlos Conteville & Cia. v. Maison F. Eloi and Cia., S.A. e Rene Charlier, 100 Rev. Dir. 178 (1930; aff'd 77 Rev. For. 87 (1938 STF). See generally A. Fonseca, *Caso Fortuito e Teoria da Imprevisão* (3rd Ed. 1958).

[36] *E.g.,* Santos Filho & Cia. v. Rodrigues Tavares, 151 Rev. Trib. 712, 68 Arch. Jud. 344 (5th Cam. Civ. of Court of Appeal of Fed. Dis. 1943); Durante v. Teixeira, 166 Rev. Trib. 786, 104 Rev. For. 269 (3d Cam. Civ. Court of Appeal Fed. Dis. 1945). But see Processo M.T.I.C.N. 231.800-44, 2 Rev. Dir. Admin. 812 (Fasc. II 1945).

[37] Article 1246 provides: The architect or builder who contracts to build in accordance with plans accepted by the owner, shall not have the right to demand an increment in the price, even if salaries or materials become more expensive, or there has been an alteration or increase in the amount of work specified in the plans, unless such increment or alteration is done in accordance with written instructions from the owner and exhibited by the architect or builder.

been to accept the doctrine of imprevision in theory but deny its application in practice on the ground that inflation is quite foreseeable in Brazil.[38]

PREFEITURA MUNICIPAL DE SANTOS v. DANIEL DOMINGOS & IRMÃOS, LTDA.

Supreme Federal Tribunal of Brazil (Third Term)
RE No. 57.832, 41 R.T.J. 709 (1966)

Report

Minister Prado Kelly: — The case comes summarized in the decision on page 184 [of the record]:

"The case arises from a request for readjustment of a construction contract *(empreitada)* entered into by the appellant and the appellee to perform public works and effectuated after competitive bidding in which there were express restrictions with respect to the calculations serving as the basis for fixing the price. In order to justify its request for readjustment, the appellant invokes the supervenience of a 61% increase in the minimum wage, which is exactly the reduction in profits stemming therefrom requested in this action.

"Understanding that the "theory of imprevision is an extraordinary exception to the obligatory performance of contracts," and admitting, however, its applicability to "administrative contracts," the judgment of the court of the first instance emphasized the diversity between its basis in private law and administrative law, where it springs from the principle of "continuity of public service," agreeing with Laubadere and other modern authors that there are three basic requisites of the "state of imprevision" (unforeseeability, involuntariness of the causative fact, and the extreme onerousness of the financial disequilibrium of the contract). . . .

"[The court of the first instance found that the first and third of the above mentioned requirements were not satisfied.] The signing of the contract coincided with the promulgation of Decree 45.106A, which raised the minimum wage throughout the country. Since the periodic revisions of the minimum wage are always preceded by intense debate in the public communications media between the

---

[38]*E.g.*, Constructora Inmobíliaria Comercial S.A. v. Orlando France et al., RE No. 48.487, 36 R.T.J. 104 (3d Term STF 1965) (Construction contract signed in 1957); Beckhauser et ux v. Pascoa Ceccato, RE No. 55.425, 35 R.T.J. 597 (1st Term STF 1965) (Construction contract signed in 1957); ECAL v. Araujo Pereira, A.C. No. 34.076, 10 Rev. Juris. Guan. 208 (5th Cam. Civ. 1964) (Contract for sale of apartment by insolvent construction firm made in 1961); Banco Americano de Crédito S.A. et al. v. Espólio de Pinto de Macedo et al., Embargos no A.C. No. 24.992, 13 Rev. Juris. Guan. 183 (3rd Group of Cam Civ. 1965) (Contracts for sale of apartment by insolvent construction firm made in 1956 and 1957); Auerback et al.v. Coelho Pinto, A.C. No. 17.083, 210 Rev. For. 143 (5th Cam Civ. Guan. 1961) (Construction contract to be performed in 1956-1958); Lustman et al. v. da Costa Barros, RE 62.480, 41 R.T.J. 725 (1st Term STF 1967) (Construction contract signed in 1962).

governmental authorities and the representatives of interested classes, one has to infer that the salarial increase decreed on 12/27/58, to take effect on 1/1/59, was a fact already foreseen by the parties prior to the signing of the contract whose revision is intended. . . .

"The plaintiff implies in its complaint that although foreseeable or foreseen, the salarial increase could not enter into its calculations, for the 'ground rules of the competition' required that the proposals of the competitors contain the present price of the works to be executed.

"Although this is correct, the argument is invalid because the plaintiff, in this hypothesis, would have agreed to perform work for a price which would be shortly obsolete.

"However, it is with relation to the third requirement that the lack of merit of the claim of the complaint appears most clearly. It has already been said that the existence of prejudice in the execution of the work is insufficient. This corresponds to a contingency of commercial activity, whose onus is normally borne by the contractor. The State, which is not a partner in the contractor's profits, does not have to be one in his losses.

"Revision of the price in a construction contract is admissible only when the amount of prejudice is intolerable and ruinous.

"The plaintiff did not prove, nor even allege, that the prejudice resulting from the obligation had produced a deep financial crisis. The prejudice alleged, the sum of Cr$501.353,70, represents only part of the expected profit, amounting to 20% of the budget. . . . The plaintiff only failed to receive about half of its expected profit, which does not translate as an intolerable and ruinous prejudice."

But the facts and legal relations were viewed through another prism in the decision of the 5th Civil Chamber of the Tribunal of Justice, which sustained the action: (p. 184).

"As Hélio Lopes Meireles points out in his excellent work, Direito de Construir (p. 267 and 282), the doctrine and the case law have come to admit the application of the referred to clause [*rebus sic stantibus*] in construction contracts in general, there being no reason to refrain from applying it in cases of construction contracts with the Public Power.

"The administration has the duty to make arrangements . . . for the just application of public moneys. Precisely because it is made within rules imposed upon the interested parties (as occurred in this case in which the basis for calculation of the price in the competition were determined in accordance with prices then in effect for material and labor), this just application carries with it a counterpart. Inasmuch as the Public Power ought not to pay more, it also ought not to pay less than the job at hand is really worth. . . .

"The exclusion of the possibility of a competitor defending himself against future price fluctuations, imposed by the [bidding] competition . . . in the presentation of the proposal, means that in view of the change in the value of labor, determined through a supervening legal disposition, the request for readjustment will be granted, with application of the clause of *rebus sic stantibus* via simple verification of real prejudice, without the necessity of the aspect of calamity that the doctrine requires for cases of common contracts.

"Moreover, this has been the understanding of the Governments of the State and Municipality of São Paulo in . . . Decrees 26.439 of 9/19/56 and 3.465 of 2/22/57, in which norms were established for the revision of prices in construction contracted with them. This attitude conforms with ethics and the principles of good faith from which the Public Power should not depart, and encounters support in the lessons of the doctrinists. . . ."

The City Government of Santos appealed specially, invoking lines (a) and (d) of the Constitutional permission.[39] The learned Attorney General has stated:. . . .

"6. On the merits, the better doctrine and the majority of the cases have come to admit readjustment for unforeseeable facts in these construction contracts.

"It is true that in this case the judge of the first instance did not deny hypothesis of readjustment in construction contracts; rather he denied it when pleaded for an increase in the minimum wage, because this did not appear to be an unforeseeable fact.

"7. However, even though it is true that the minimum wage has been periodically increased, it is not easy for contractors to increase their price for an increase in the minimum wage which has not yet been conceded or securely provided for.

"8. This appeal should be granted. . . ."

That is the report.

Vote

Minister Prado Kelly (Reporter) — I vote to deny the appeal.

Despite the brilliance and juridical information revealed in opposing senses in the excellent decisions of the first and second instances, the material does not present the opportunity for the extreme appeal, either through line (a), or through line (d) of the constitutional permission.

As to the first: (a) the opinion [of the 5th Civil Chamber] accepted as proven factual circumstances concerning the "imprevisibility" and the rupture of the "financial equation" inherent in the contract (contrary to what was accepted in the judgment [of the first instance]). . . . On these points the case law criterion expressed in words of *Súmula* 279 applies ["For the simple re-examination of proof the special appeal will not lie."]; (b) the said opinion reasonably interpreted the rule of *pacta sunt servanda* (safeguarded in article 1246 of the Civil Code), as well as the clause *rebus sic stantibus,* which is implicit in agreements, and took advantage of the aid ministered by the state and municipal laws of São Paulo, — rendering the appeal inadequate in the light of what *Súmula* 400 recommends. ["A decision which has given a reasonable interpretation to the law, even though not the best, does not authorize a special appeal via letter *a* of article 101 (III) of the Federal Constitution."]

---

[39] The special appeal is derived from the writ of error of the United States Judiciary Act of 1789. At this time the Supreme Federal Tribunal's jurisdiction to hear special appeals was set out in Article 101 (III) of the 1946 Constitution, which permitted review of final judgments "(a) when the decision is contrary to a provision of this Constitution, or to the text of a treaty or federal law; . . . (d) when the interpretation of the federal law invoked in the appealed decision differs from that given to it by any other courts or the Supreme Federal Tribunal itself. . . ." [Eds.]

[The jurisdictional basis of the appeal grounded on letter *d* was also denied for failure to comply with a procedural rule of the court in transcribing portions of decisions to show a case law divergency. The other members of the court unanimously accepted the report of Minister Prado Kelly and denied the appeal.]

Questions

1. Is there any justification for treating public construction contracts differently from private contracts in applying the theory of imprevision?

2. To what extent is application of the theory of imprevision inconsistent with competitive bidding on public works?

3. Does this decision render Article 1246 of the Brazilian Civil Code (set out in footnote 37, *supra*) meaningless?

4. Under the standards articulated by the Argentine courts, would application of the theory of imprevision to this case be appropriate?

Public works contracts with the Brazilian Federal Government are now governed by a recent statute providing criteria for price revision.

BRAZIL: DECREE LAW NO. 185 OF FEBRUARY 23, 1967

... Art. 2. The services and works which are the responsibility of the various organs of the Federal Government shall be paid when adjusted or contracted with third parties through a General Table of Unitary Prices, variable for the different regions of the country, but identical for all the organs.

Art. 3. The General Table of Unitary Prices shall be calculated ... on the basis of real costs of services and works ... by a permanent Commission, constituted from representatives of the different organs of each Ministry. ...

§3. The General Table of Unitary Prices shall be annually revised, in whole or in part, or every time that the economic picture so recommends. ...

Art. 5. Contracts for works and services for the organs of the Federal Government may contain clauses for price revision, as long as the conditions for revision have been previously stipulated in the acts inviting the respective competitions. ...

Art. 6. The revisions of contractual unitary prices or part of the total value of the contract shall be calculated according to the following formula:

$$R = .90 \times \frac{Ii-Io}{Io} \times V$$

R is the value of readjustment sought;

Io is the price index verified in the month the proposal which led to the contract was presented;

Ii is the arithmetical average of the monthly indexes in the period which is to be adjusted;

V is the contractual value of the work or services to be readjusted. . . .

§4. When dealing with a contract for labor in the execution of works or services, readjustments will only be permitted when the burden stems from an act of the State, principally a wage modification. . . .

BRAZIL: DECREE NO. 60.407 OF MARCH 11, 1967

. . . Art. 1. In the application of Decree Law No. 185 of February 23, 1967, the following maximum limits for readjustments shall be observed:

I — in the case of a contract signed when the cited decree law was in effect, the total of the readjustments cannot exceed the value of the initial contract by 35%;

II — in case a contract in force on the date of the publication of the referred to decree-law, the total readjustments cannot exceed (R + 35%) of the value of the initial contract, R being the percentage value of the readjustment on the date of publication of the decree-law. . . .

Art. 2. Having reached the maximum values defined in Article 1, the public administration shall proceed with rescission of the contract for works or services unless the contractor is ready to terminate without readjustment in work or service.

. . . §1. In case of rescission based upon the disposition of this article, there shall be no indemnification beyond payment for services executed.

. . . §2. In exceptional cases in the judgment of the Minister of State continuance with the work may be authorized even though the percentage of readjustment exceeds that provided for in this article. . . .

Question

Do Decree Law No. 185 and its implementing regulation seem like a fair way to allocate the burdens of inflation? If not, how would you redraft it?

For a recent criticism of the failure of Argentina to adopt similar legislation to protect the government contractor from inflation, see Giadone and Pensavalle, "Las Variaciones de Costos y la Depreciación Monetaria en el Contrato de Obra Pública," 131 *La Ley* 1445 (1968).

(b) Lesión

Literally, the term *lesión* or *lesão* means injury or wound. In legal parlance it has come to mean the disadvantage suffered by one party to a juridical act, typically an agreement of sale. Thus anyone who buys at a price in excess of the "real" or "just" value, or sells at less, is said to have suffered a *lesión*. No jurisdiction permits annulment of contracts solely on the basis of *lesión;* however, some civil codes do permit abrogation or modification of contracts for *lesión enorme* or *lesión enormísima* — great, or very great, *lesión*. For example, the French Civil Code permits the seller (but not the buyer) of real property to rescind within two years of the date of the sale if the purchase price is less than 5/12 of the fair value. The buyer can avoid rescission by paying a total of 90 per cent of the property's fair value. Articles 1674-1684.

The doctrine of *lesión,* whose origin can be traced to Roman law and perhaps beyond, was deliberately rejected by the draftsmen of the Argentine and Brazilian Civil Codes. The principal reason for doing so, according to Vélez Sársfield, the author of the Argentine Civil Code, was that ". . . we should cease to be responsible for our actions if the law should permit us to make amends for all errors or all our imprudences. Free consent given without fraud, error or duress, and with the solemnities required by law, should make contracts irrevocable."

The Chilean Civil Code, however, adopted the Napoleonic Code's concept of *lesión,* albeit in a modified form.

CIVIL CODE OF CHILE (1855)

Book Four — Of Obligations in General and of Contracts
Title XIII — Of the Contract of Purchase and Sale

§13 — Of the Rescission of the Sale for *Lesión Enorme*
Art. 1888. The contract of purchase and sale can be rescinded for *lesión enorme*.
Art. 1889. The seller suffers *lesión enorme* when the price he receives is less than half the just price of the thing which he sells; and the buyer, in turn, suffers *lesión enorme* when the just price of the thing he buys is less than half the price he pays for it.
Just price refers to the time of the contract.
Art. 1890. The purchaser against whom rescission is declared may, in his discretion, consent to it or make up the difference in the just price, with a deduction of one tenth; and the seller in the same situation, may, in his discretion, consent to the rescission or return the price received in excess of the just price, plus one-tenth.
Interest or gains *(frutos)* are not owed except from the date of the complaint, nor can anything be sought for the expenses which the contract has occasioned.

Art. 1891. The action of rescission for *lesión enorme* shall not lie for sales of movables, nor for those sales made by the Ministry of Justice.

Problem

On December 31, 1951 Juan signs an agreement to sell his farm near Santiago de Chile to Paulo for 500,000 pesos. One-fifth of the price is paid at the time of the signing of the agreement to sell, and the balance is to be paid in four annual installments of 100,000 pesos each. The deed is to be delivered when the final installment is paid. Paulo faithfully observes the terms of the agreement, and upon tendering the last payment on December 31, 1955, requests a deed for the farm.

Though 500,000 pesos corresponded to the fair market value of the farm at the end of 1951, such is not the case at the end of 1955. The cost of living index for Santiago has risen in the following fashion:

Year	Index	% Increase
1951	100	—
1952	112	12%
1953	174.7	56%
1954	298.7	71%
1955	549.6	84%
1956	758.4	38%

Base: 1951 year end=100

Assuming that the value of the farm at least accompanies the increase in the cost of living, is Juan entitled to rescind the contract because of *lesión enorme*: (a) on a nominalist theory? (b) on a valorist theory? If so, how much more would Paulo have to tender to be able to receive the deed to the farm?

PERLWITZ, EMILIO, v. ZAMBRANO, MANUEL

Supreme Court of Chile
65 R.D.J. 210 (2d Part, 1st Sec.) (1968)

[In January 1953 the plaintiff signed an agreement of sale in which he promised to sell nine lots to the defendant. The price was set at 820 escudos (or 820,000 pesos), payable in installments. When the defendant paid the final installment on January 10, 1958, the plaintiff refused to execute the deed. After years of procrastination and litigation, on April 2, 1965 a deed to the lots in favor of the defendant was finally executed by judicial fiat.

[Thereupon, the reluctant seller instituted this action to rescind the sale because of *lesión enorme*. The lower courts held for the defendant. and the plaintiff appeals to the Supreme Court.] . . .

2. Article 1889 of the Civil Code establishes that the seller suffers *lesión enorme* when the price which he receives is less than one half the just price of the property he sells; and adds in its second clause that: "The just price refers to the time of the contract." The purpose of this provision is to prevent rescission for *lesión enorme* if for any reason the just price varies subsequent to the sale.

3. . . . [T]his precept does not expressly contemplate the case in which the sale has been preceded by an agreement of sale. This raises the question . . . whether just price refers to the time of celebrating the purchase and sale [the signing of the deed] or the signing of the agreement of sale.

4. . . . [T]o fix the genuine meaning and limits of this legal norm, it is indispensable to interpret it in accordance with the norm which creates and regulates the agreement to sell. . . .

6. . . . [S]ince the agreement of sale is a contract or convention which produces obligatory effects and has the force of law for the contracting parties, its stipulations are inalterable and govern the promised contract. It is, then, in the agreement of sale that the parties definitively and minutely agree on all of its peculiarities and characteristics. . . .

7. Therefore the judges below correctly applied the precept in question . . ., relying principally on the following reasoning to dismiss the complaint: "*Lesión* is a defect of consent, for annulment of the juridical act results from consideration of the correspondence in values alone . . .; it must be considered, then, objectively in relation to the equivalence of the performances [adequacy of consideration]. If this is so, the proportionality must be judged at the moment of formation of consent. The second section of Article 1889 of the Civil Code provides nothing else when it says 'the just price refers to the time of the contract', that is, to the moment which produces a meeting of wills as to the thing and the price." . . . [T]he "time of the contract" cannot refer to the signing of the deed, but rather to the date the agreement came into being, which does not always or necessarily coincide with the required solemnities. . . .

8. This thesis is corroborated by the legislature itself . . . in a law, which although of a recent date, constitutes a valuable illustration, for it was designed to govern situations entirely similar to the case at bar. . . . Law 16.742 of February 8 of the present year provides in Article 85: "For the purposes of Article 1889 of the Civil Code, in purchase and sale contracts entered into to fulfill agreements of sale for lots which are part of a subdivision made pursuant to the Law of Construction and Urbanization, it shall be understood that the just price refers to the time of the celebration of the agreement of sale when said price is paid in accordance with the terms of the agreement."

9. That [the price was to be paid via a down payment at the time of the signing of the agreement of sale with the balance in monthly installments] acquires transcendent importance in the present controversy . . ., [for it indicates that] the parties had foreseen subsequent variations in the value of the lots being sold, and had taken

precautions against this eventuality or risk through this down payment, which consolidated the equivalence of their reciprocal performances.

10. . . . [T] he promised buyer performed all of his obligations, so that it is also a fact that the promised seller received . . . the entire price much earlier than he should have, and that he delayed considerably delivery of the public deed. . . .

11. The money which the appellant collected as the price for that which he promised to sell had at that time an effective value much superior to what it represented on the day on which the sale was effectuated due to the constant depreciation of our monetary unit. . . .

12. . . . [I]n the form in which it has been presented, the appeal must fail, because in order to determine accurately the just price for the purpose of indicating whether *lesión enorme* existed, one would have to consider the purchasing power of the sums received by the appellant at the time of receipt. If one considers only the nominal quantity, as the appellant contends, the buyer would be forced to accept devolution of the same sum in depreciated currency . . ., which would not only artificially destroy the real equivalence of performances provided for by the parties, but would also contravene the most elemental principles of justice and equity. . . .

14. . . . [T] he contract of sale should have been celebrated on July 7, 1959 when [the buyer instituted suit against the seller for the equivalent of specific performance]. However, as has been seen, the [deed] could only be effectuated after the passage of several years because of the seller's obstinate resistance to fulfillment of his obligation. Now, using this delay, for which he is exclusively responsible, to rescind the contract, the seller is trying to take advantage of his own fault. This is totally unacceptable. . . .

15. The preceding leads us once again to the ineluctable conclusion that the just price of the thing sold cannot refer to the date of the celebration of the contract of sale, which appears in the public deed as April 2, 1965, . . . but rather . . . to the time of the agreement of sale. . . .

Questions

1. What is the relevance of a 1968 statute to the intent of the legislature in 1855, when the Civil Code was adopted?

2. What alternative is there to returning the purchase price in depreciated currency?

3. How effective is the doctrine of *lesión enorme* in protecting against contractual disequilibrium stemming from inflation or deflation?

Notes

1. The *Perlwitz* case would appear to be a departure from a prior line of Chilean Supreme Court cases, such as *Jungk S., Alicia y otra v. Wagner Sch., Rose Marie*, 58 R.D.J. 47 (2d Part, 1st Sec. 1961). It also represents a departure from French statutory and case law, which regards the relevant date for determination of whether

there has been *lesión* as the day of the completion of the sale. Law of Nov. 28, 1949; Wahl, "La Lésion dans les Promesses Unilatérales de Vente," 26 *Revue Trimestrielle de Droit Civil* 571 (1927). It has been suggested that one strong motive for adopting this date "was undoubtedly the desire to relieve the vendors of land against the effects of inflation." Dawson & Cooper, "The Effect of Inflation on Private Contracts: United States, 1861-1879," 33 *Mich. L. Rev.* 852, 865 fn. 186 (1935). For a discussion of some of the other problems raised by the operation of *lesión* in the inflationary milieu of Chile, see E. Navarette Cerda, *La Lesión Enorme en el Cumplimiento de la Promesa de Venta* (1965); Barriga Errázuriz, "La Inflación en sus Relaciones con los Contratos de Tracto Sucesivo, de Compraventa y de Promesa de Venta y con la Lesión Enorme," *Primer Congreso Nacional de Abogados Chilenos, El Derecho ante la Inflación* 156 (1955).

2. In recent decades there has been a decided retreat from the individualism that stamped Brazilian civil law. One characteristic of this retreat has been the gradual return of the doctrine of *lesión*. It has crept back into Brazilian law through legislation making it a criminal offense to "obtain or stipulate in any contract, abusing the pressing necessity, inexperience or levity of the other party, a patrimonial profit in excess of one-fifth of the current or just value of the performance rendered or promised." Decree-Law № 869 of November 18, 1938, as amended by article 4(b) of Law № 1.521 of December 26, 1951. It has also been proposed in articles 62-64 of the Draft of a Code of Obligations (Anteprojeto de Código de Obrigações). See C. Silva Pereira, *Lesão nos Contratos* 151-69 (2d ed. 1959).

3. Much the same development has occurred in Argentina, where prior to support in positive law, several Argentine courts implicitly invoked *lesión* to set aside contracts where the consideration was grossly inadequate. See J. Carranza, *El Vicio de Lesión en la Reforma del Código Civil* 23-30 (1969).

Argentina has recently amended its Civil Code, borrowing from Article 138 of the German Civil Code a more generalized and subjective concept of *lesión*. Law 17.711 of April 22, 1968, A.L.J.A. 1968-A, p. 498, 507, amended Article 954 of the Civil Code to read:

> Acts vitiated by error, *dolo,* violence, intimidation, or simulation can be annulled.
>
> One can also demand the nullity or modification of juridical acts when one of the parties, exploiting the necessity, levity, or inexperience of the other, thus obtains an evidently disproportionate and unjustified patrimonial advantage.
>
> Without proof to the contrary, it shall be presumed that such exploitation exists in the case of a notable disproportion in consideration.
>
> Calculations shall be made according to the values at the time of the act, and the disproportion must continue to exist at the moment of the complaint. . . .
>
> The plaintiff has the option of demanding the nullity or the equitable readjustment of the agreement, but the first of these actions shall be transformed into an action for readjustment if offered by the defendant in answer to the complaint.

Question

How should a case like *Perlwitz* be resolved under this statutory provision?

(c) An Overview of the Judicial Role: a Critique by Dawson and Cooper

In a series of articles published in 1934-35, Professors John Dawson and Frank Cooper thoughtfully analyzed the doctrinal and policy problems confronting courts in according relief to contracting parties because of inflation.[40] These articles were primarily concerned with judicial reaction to the German inflation of the early 1920's, and the inflation resulting from the U.S. Civil War. The depreciations of the German mark and Confederate currency were far more colossal and short-lived than the chronic monetary depreciation of Argentine, Brazilian, or Chilean currency.[41] Moreover, price indexes of those eras were far more rudimentary than those presently available. Consider to what extent Dawson and Cooper's conclusions about the role of courts during inflation also apply to the present-day chronic, yet "controlled," inflations of the South American countries.

J. DAWSON AND F. COOPER, THE EFFECT OF INFLATION ON PRIVATE CONTRACTS: UNITED STATES, 1861-1879, PART II

33 *Michigan Law Review* 852, 898-922 (1935)

The attitudes that courts should adopt toward the legal problems raised by a major inflation are necessarily influenced by some broad considerations of policy. They should hesitate to develop private law doctrines along lines that would conflict with the language or purpose of monetary legislation or imperil the larger interests of society. At the same time they should be aware that their attitudes toward monetary

---

[40] Dawson, "Effects of Inflation on Private Contracts: Germany, 1914-1924," 33 *Mich. L. Rev.* 171 (1934); Dawson and Cooper, "The Effect of Inflation on Private Contracts: United States, 1861-1879," 33 *Mich. L. Rev.* 707, 852 (Parts I and II, 1935).

[41] Between mid-1861 and January 1865 the Confederate dollar lost all but 1/50 of its value; it became wholly worthless after the surrender of the Confederacy. German currency collapsed completely under the strain of reparations payments and their psychological repercussions. In December 1918 the mark was quoted at 8.28 to the dollar; two years later it stood at 73 to the dollar. The pace of depreciation accelerated sharply in 1922. In July it took 493.22 marks to purchase a dollar, and by December, 7,589.27 marks were required. In 1923 the bottom (and the sides) fell out of the mark market. In August the dollar was quoted at 4,620,455 marks; one month later it stood at an astronomical 98,860,000 marks.

issues have important economic consequences. Whether they decide to assume the initiative in restoring a disturbed equilibrium or to insist instead on literal enforcement of all money contracts, they should be prepared to face the broader questions of policy that are inevitably involved. . . . [S]ome of the factors of policy which might present obstacles to the development of judicial remedies . . . [are]: (1) the legal-tender quality of money; (2) the public interest in preserving the purchasing power of money; . . . (4) policies involved in the allocation of risk; (5) the public interest in the security of transactions; (6) the choice between legislative and judicial remedies.

1. *The Legal Tender Quality of Money*

The first and most important barrier to judicial relief against the effects of inflation is legal-tender legislation. . . . [T]he legal-tender acts passed in the North during the Civil War were a deliberate and large-scale sacrifice of private claims to the national interest. When their constitutionality was once established, all "debts" that had been expressed in fixed sums of money (without gold or other stable-value clauses) became at once exposed to the risk of fluctuations in the purchasing power of money. Nor was the experience of Northern creditors in the greenback period by any means unique. In the German inflation of the last decade, legal-tender legislation stood as an insuperable obstacle to the general revision of money debts until the mark had approached its bottom level, a trillion to one. In the French inflation after the Great War legal-tender legislation had a similar effect, less striking only because the depreciation of the currency never went so far. In general it may be expected that governments resorting to an irredeemable paper currency will by legislation attach the legal-tender quality. The primary purpose of such legislation is usually to ensure the circulation of paper currency; but if the currency depreciates, the inevitable effect is to destroy a substantial share of accumulated wealth which takes the form of claims of money. . . .

If courts refused to enforce legal-tender legislation in periods of extreme inflation, their action would tend to a limited extent to arrest the process of depreciation. Debtors would then be unable to pay off debts in paper money at its nominal par. If some reliable and stable standard of value could be found as a substitute for the national currency, the nominal sum due would increase as the purchasing power of money declined. Debtors would then be deprived of the incentive for borrowing which they have in periods of continuing monetary depreciation. They would no longer have the assurance that the money repaid would be worth less than the money borrowed. For the class of borrowers, such as manufacturers and industrialists, who are in the strongest position to profit by this unequal exchange, the removal of this incentive would have some effect in restricting the credit inflation which often accompanies over-issues of paper money.[42]

---

[42] This suggestion assumes that lenders of money can be found who are willing to assume the risk of depreciation between the date of the loan and the date of repayment. Not many private persons would be willing to assume this risk if further depreciation were in prospect. It is chiefly from commercial banks that the impulse to further credit inflation would come, and their willingness to lend would depend on whether they were able to shift their loss onto some other agency. [Footnote by Dawson and Cooper, renumbered.]

In other respects, however, the repudiation of the legal-tender quality would probably have but little effect on the main course of monetary depreciation. The stabilization of contracts, achieved by this means, would not attack the root causes of inflation — usually found in budgetary deficits of the government. If the government was forced by its financial necessities to continued over-issues of paper money, the depreciation would continue at very nearly the same rate. Private persons who found themselves in the possession of such money would be just as anxious as before to dispose of it in return for property of more stable value; that is to say, the "flight from the currency" (an important secondary source of inflation) would continue. It is clear, then, that nullification of legal-tender legislation cannot be justified on the ground of the deflationary effect of such action. Whatever moral justification there might be would be found in the desire to prevent intolerable injustice and hardship to private creditors, whose claims were being swallowed up in the gulf of monetary ruin. . . .

There is no factual evidence directly showing the importance of the legal-tender attribute in maintaining the circulation of currency. . . .

Nevertheless, experience would seem to indicate that the debt-discharging power is of great practical importance in sustaining the official currency through periods of depreciation. The inflation in the Confederate states during the Civil War demonstrates that the pressure of an aroused public opinion can go far in ensuring the acceptance of depreciated money, at least during the early stages of depreciation. On the other hand, a rapid and extreme depreciation may, as in Germany, drive an irredeemable paper currency out of circulation, even though the legal-tender attribute is attached. Up until the final collapse of the currency, however, it seems that legal-tender legislation is an important factor in ensuring its circulation. That this is the assumption of legislatures is shown by the prompt resort to such legislation whenever depreciation is in prospect. . . .

. . . One must conclude, in spite of the absence of factual evidence, that the legal-tender quality must be preserved by courts, at least until the public interest in the continued circulation of the currency is greatly reduced or wholly destroyed. Although constitutional grounds for a direct attack on legal-tender legislation might be found, it would have to be postponed to a very late stage of monetary depreciation and even then might jeopardize the government's position at a critical time.[43]

After all these concessions have been made, it is important to emphasize that the field of operation for legal-tender legislation is limited. It purports to apply only to "debts"; it declares that "debts" will be discharged by payment of the nominal sum due in legal-tender money; its evident purpose is to ensure the *circulation* of legal-tender money by forcing its acceptance at par. There is nothing in the language of legal-tender legislation to indicate a purpose of "regulating the value of money." . . . It

---

[43] Particularly at a late stage of depreciation, the financial necessities of the government may make the issue of legal-tender money the only practicable form of governmental borrowing. The impaired credit of the government is apt to make this type of forced loan the only method of maintaining it in operation. However much one might deplore the resultant injustice to individuals, a court should hesitate before destroying the only remaining claim on the wealth of citizens. [Footnote by Dawson and Cooper, renumbered.]

must be emphasized, therefore, that legal-tender legislation has nothing to do with the value at which money shall circulate or with the processes by which the quantum of any "debt" is determined, either by contract, statute, or judgment. The legislation does not preclude a recognition by courts of changes in the value of money that have in fact occurred. Indeed, during the greenback period and again during the American inflation of the Great War, such changes were recognized by courts and given whatever effect was required by general rules of private law. It is only where the amount of a "debt" has been finally and conclusively fixed that legal-tender legislation intervenes to enforce its discharge through payment or tender of the specified sum in legal-tender money.

The limited effect of legal-tender legislation may be suggested by reverting to the problem of specific performance during periods of inflation. Suppose, for example, that a contract is made for the sale of land for $10,000; that at the time of the contract this represents approximately the fair value of the land; and that monetary depreciation subsequently increases the nominal value to $40,000. If equity were to refuse specific performance unless the purchaser consented to a proportionate increase in the price, it would *in effect* hold that $10,000 in depreciated paper money was not legal tender for the discharge of the purchaser's debt. But the result would be explained in terms of the power of courts of equity to prevent hardship and ensure adequacy of consideration. In other words, the nominal sum fixed by the parties would not be a measure of the performance which equity would exact of the purchaser. Being free to redefine the "debt" to conform to its own standards of fairness, a court of equity could remove the case entirely from the operation of legal-tender acts.

If "change of conditions" were urged as a ground for outright rescission at law or in equity, a court would be free in the same way to determine whether the purpose of the contract had been frustrated by intervening monetary depreciation. Although the "debt" due from the purchaser could be discharged by payment of the sum of money promised, the question would still remain whether the nominal sum in paper money was the contemplated equivalent for the other party's performance. Nor does there seem to be any theoretical objection to the further step, taken by German courts in the intermediate stage of the German inflation, of attaching a *condition* to the grant of rescission, so that rescission would be denied if the purchaser consented to a "reasonable" increase in price. The obstacle to the development of rescission remedies, then, does not lie in legal-tender legislation. It is to be found in the limited range of existing private law doctrines and in the practical difficulties which have prevented the recognition of monetary fluctuations as a "change of conditions." . . .

We feel justified in concluding, then, that the readjustment of private contracts in periods of monetary depreciation is precluded only at certain points and to a limited extent by legal-tender legislation. The next obstacle that must be considered, not wholly unrelated to the legal-tender quality, is the public interest in preserving confidence in the national currency.

2. *The Public Interest in Preserving the Purchasing Power of Money*

If it could be shown that judicial revision of private contracts accelerated the depreciation of money or impaired the national credit, the sacrifice of private claims might be required by an overriding public interest.

In the preceding section it was argued that the legal-tender quality is in practice so important that its repudiation would be dangerous, even though constitutional reasons could be found. But the question now raised involves something more than the repudiation by courts of the legal-tender quality of money. The question is somewhat broader, whether *any* recognition by courts of the decreased purchasing power of money would shake public confidence in the monetary system and accelerate the decline in the purchasing power of money.

This question was discussed in an interesting book by a French writer, published in 1922. He proposed for judicial use a theory of "frustration of purpose," essentially the same as the Anglo-American theory of "frustration of the venture." He felt forced to admit, however, that a large-scale judicial revision of private contracts would constitute "an official recognition of the bankruptcy of the currency" and would "precipitate the monetary bankruptcy of the country." He considered this to be particularly true in the field of simple money obligations, such as mortgages, bonds, and Treasury obligations (though it would seem that legal-tender legislation would be a sufficient answer here to any claim for revision). His conclusion was that in most classes of transactions courts should not create a popular impression that the currency had depreciated, though some room for judicial activity might remain.

This argument seems wholly unconvincing.... If a major depreciation is under way, its effects on private transactions will become apparent long before any claim for judicial relief has any prospect of success. In the language of the New York Court of Appeals in a case from the greenback period, "Why should a court be the only place where men must affect an ignorance of what all men know?"

There would be more substance to this objection if it appeared that an upward revision of money obligations would increase the volume of money in circulation and thereby indirectly promote a further rise in prices. It seems clear that in most cases the objective of judicial relief would be to increase the sum of money required for a debtor's performance. This is most apparent where an affirmative decree is rendered for the payment of a larger nominal sum in paper money. It is also clear that the same purpose would underlie a condition attached to specific performance or to the grant of rescission, where the condition could only be satisfied by payment of a larger sum of money. Even if rescission were unconditional, the release of the vendor would have the effect of enabling him to secure a larger sum of money for the goods or services he had agreed to sell.

But there seems to be no reason to think that a direct or indirect increase in the sums due on particular contracts would increase the total volume of money in circulation or tend to force up prices in general. The process involved would be merely a transfer of purchasing power from one class of persons to another. The debtors from whom a larger sum was extracted would have less money to spend on other commodities or services. As in the case of direct attack on legal-tender legislation, the practical effect would be to remove an important incentive for going into debt. The only generalized result would seem to be a limited check on the tendency toward credit inflation which often accompanies the depreciation of money. . . .[44]

4. *Policies Involved in the Allocation of Risk*

More serious attention must be paid to the factor of risk-assumption, which becomes a primary factor in administering both legal and equitable remedies for "change of conditions." The difficulties in assessing the effect of this factor arise from what may be called its double origin. The allocation of risk depends in first instance on the actual intentions of contracting parties and on the range of risk which was expressly assumed in their agreement. Beyond this, however, lie important elements of risk which attach irrespective of conscious states of mind. For reasons of convenience or basic economic policy risk may be *imposed* as a matter of law.

The problem of defining the limits of risk-assumption underlies many fields of tort and contract law and is resolved in terms of legal concepts which in appearance have little in common. In contract law the problem of risk-assumption is most clearly perceived, perhaps, in cases of impossibility of performance and "frustration of the venture." In such cases judicial relief is invoked on the ground of supervening events which lay outside the contemplation of the parties at the time of the contract and which have defeated the purposes they had in mind. To dispose of such cases courts must not only scrutinize with care the language and economic setting of the particular contract; they must also consider the broader factors of policy which dictate an allocation of risk independently of agreement.

In periods of relative stability fluctuations in the value of money undoubtedly lie within the range of ordinary business risks. . . . [I]n most fields of enterprise unfavorable price-movements are peculiarly the type of hazard against which parties must protect themselves. For this general position the initial justification is that prices are *known* to be unstable. The prices of particular commodities are known to be unstable because the pressures of competition are chiefly concentrated at the point of price. A like reason why the stability of the price structure cannot safely be relied on is the fact, also well known, that the value of money in general is subject to important fluctuations. Beyond this, as a further justification for the position usually taken, is a factor of convenience – the extreme practical difficulty of substituting new standards of value for the monetary standards that have undergone an intervening change. The main reason, however, is probably one that depends neither on factors of convenience

---

[44] It should be pointed out here, as it was above, note 43, that a still more effective check on the tendency of debtors to go into debt is the reluctance of creditors to extend credit without some guarantee against depreciation in purchasing power. Since commercial banks are the chief class of creditors who may be eager to take such risks, and since commercial banks would not ordinarily be directly involved in contracts for the sale of goods or services, the economic effect of judicial remedies here would probably be even more limited than would the effect of nullifying legal-tender legislation. [Footnote by Dawson and Cooper, renumbered.]

nor on what the parties knew or could have ascertained; this reason is the basic assumption in an individualistic economy that the processes of competition should be allowed free operation wherever competition does not involve too great waste. Since agreement on price is the "heart" of competition, judicial interference with free competitive price-fixing is thought to be almost as hazardous as legislative price-regulation.

It follows that for private law doctrines to be applied to inflation problems, the influence on prices of purely monetary factors must clearly emerge as a factor independent of ordinary influences of supply and demand. In periods of moderate inflation this distinction is difficult to make. . . . [T]he influences moving from the side of *money* would be hard to separate from those moving from the side of *commodities*. The effect of inflation differs greatly as between different commodity groups. Where markets are highly organized, as in the case of stocks and bonds, wheat, corn, and other agricultural commodities, current prices represent a speculative discount, not only of conditions of supply and demand, but of the future course of the currency itself. It appears, then, that judicial relief could not be expected on any general basis, until indices of the general price-level had made it abundantly plain that the nominal rise in prices was in reality a drastic change in the value of money. . . .

How much weight should be given this element of conscious risk-assumption cannot be decided by arm-chair speculation. It must be remembered that the effects of inflation are dramatized for courts by its concrete effects on particular private contracts. It is only when a series of private transactions are thrown hopelessly out of balance that courts might be persuaded to intervene. In the German inflation, for example, courts reluctantly granted the rescission remedy when vendors, if forced to perform, would have suffered *losses* approximately equal to the agreed purchase price. When such situations become common, it is plain that the assumed foundations of many commercial transactions have been destroyed.

A willingness to give relief in particular classes of contracts need not necessarily lead to a general overhauling of all commercial relations. Indeed, the decisions of German courts during the German inflation can be criticized from a social point of view, precisely on the ground that they did not go far enough. The class of cases in which indulgence was first shown was the sale of goods or services, where a continuing expenditure of money was required for the vendor's performance. The rapid rise in costs of labor and materials caused enormous losses and made plain the disproportion between money price and other performance. It was natural that this type of case should first attract attention. But remedial measures in this field gave protection to the economic group (i.e., manufacturers and industrialists generally) who were receiving the greatest gains from inflation. On the other hand, the class of wage-earners and salaried workers suffered incredible hardships, against which courts were powerless to relieve.

The factor of risk-assumption operates differently on different types of contracts. No prediction can be made as to the emphasis it will receive in each instance. In general, however, it may be said that severe monetary depreciation, when its effects on private contracts have become plain, can properly be distinguished from other forms of economic risk. The forces which lead to a major movement of prices lie far outside the foresight or control of private individuals. When monetary fluctuations lie within a narrower range considerations of policy and convenience may induce courts to withhold relief. But when they are reflected in large numbers of private transactions, through an extreme disproportion between the performances on either side, the doctrines of risk-assumption do not seem to require a strict enforcement of all commercial contracts.

5. *The Public Interest in the Security of Transactions*

It is the effect of judicial remedies on the security of transactions that should lead courts to hesitate. In general the resistance to the development of "change of conditions" doctrines has been rightly based on the conviction that too wide an extension of such doctrines might imperil the sanctity of contract and produce a general insecurity. Recent extensions have tended more and more to release obligors from strict and literal performance of contract obligations. At every point where further extensions are urged, the central question is whether such extensions can safely be permitted.

The concept of the "security of transactions" is one of those short-hand descriptions of complex social phenomena with which lawyers must deal and which must influence their thinking in a variety of situations. It is nonetheless significant or suggestive because the idea itself cannot be clearly and specifically defined.

At the outset it should be pointed out that monetary fluctuations greatly alter the economic setting in which the "security of transactions" must be visualized: In any period of monetary instability there is a powerful tendency in *newly framed transactions* toward contracting on shorter term, with an avoidance of long-term commitments. Where monetary depreciation proceeds at the rate reached in the German post-war inflation, vendors of goods and services attempt to move as far as possible onto a cash basis. Where some interval between contract and performance is unavoidable, the "open-price" contract may be used to remove most of the risk of intervening monetary change. . . .

But this is by no means the whole picture. A large volume of transactions must inevitably be carried over from earlier periods of relative stability. Many others, arising after depreciation has set in, will not be drafted so flexibly that readjustment can be quickly secured without litigation. It is clearly impossible, furthermore, to eliminate the extension of credit in a modern industrial society, or to place commercial contracts completely on a cash basis. Unless the parties have protected themselves against monetary fluctuations by stable-value clauses (e.g., through the use of price-indices), some dispute is bound to arise. The question then becomes this: Can legal doctrines, formulated from case to case in ordinary litigation, provide the clear guide to conduct that is especially needed in the general chaos of a major inflation?

The experience of Germany in the inflation of the last decade provides the richest materials for an answer to this question. On the basis of that experience alone, the answer must be negative. Contemporary writers testify to the widespread confusion and uncertainty resulting from the doctrines of the Reichsgericht [Germany's highest court]. Vendors of goods and services were naturally reluctant to perform when the intervening depreciation of money had reduced the money price to a fraction of the real value it possessed at the time of the contract. They eagerly welcomed judicial doctrines which offered some prospect of release from burdensome and unprofitable contracts. Repudiation became the order of the day. The controversies that then arose would have involved protracted and expensive litigation, whose eventual outcome was uncertain. The practical result was to tip the scales heavily in favor of the large industrial concerns, which had grown enormously in power and influence through the processes of the inflation itself.

The experience of Germany is not conclusive. . . . Nevertheless, the difficulties faced by German courts in the development of remedial principles can be anticipated in any legal system overwhelmed by a major inflation. The formulation of law through ordinary litigation is a cumbersome and protracted process. The accidents of litigation affect the form that judicial utterances may take. In periods of economic stability the advantages of judge-made law may outweigh the waste, delay, and uncertainty involved in awaiting the outcome of private litigation. But in periods of rapid economic change, the imperative need for speed and clarity outweigh most other considerations. By the time a case has been carried through trial and appellate courts to a final and decisive conclusion, the whole economic setting may have changed; a solution proper in the beginning may have become meaningless or clearly inappropriate for the situation as it has meanwhile developed.

If courts are to extend the scope of remedial doctrines in inflation cases they must be prepared to act rapidly and decisively. It is not possible to formulate arithmetical tests for determining the degree of dislocation necessary for judicial relief, or to anticipate in advance all the situations that might arise. But it can be expected that the factors of policy involved be weighed as fully as possible in advance and the main lines of development mapped out.

If judicial relief is to be given, what form should it take? The argument in earlier sections of this article pointed to two main conclusions — first, that in cases where specific performance is normally granted a mere refusal of the remedy or the attaching of strict conditions is ineffective as a device for alleviating the hardship caused by inflation; and second, that a reduction in the damages recoverable against defaulting vendors leads to serious complications and encourages repudiation. The main device left for relieving against monetary change is, therefore, rescission, which is incidentally the usual remedy in kindred cases of impossibility and "frustration of the venture."

Should the courts go further and attempt by direct or indirect means to revise money obligations, so as to prevent general dislocation and preserve continuity in commercial relations? It is conceivable that American courts might follow the example of the German Reichsgericht, and attempt an indirect revision of the price-term by granting rescission *unless* a reasonable increase in price were agreed to. Courts of equity have employed the conditional refusal of specific performance as a means of exerting pressure toward voluntary price-revision in specific performance cases. In courts of law there seems to be no doubt as to the power to render judgments conditional in form, though the power itself has been sparingly exercised and no authority has been found for its use in cases of impossibility or "frustration." In some cases, where the parties have proceeded rather far with performance and the price-term relates to a relatively unimportant element in the whole contract, a direct or indirect revision might be preferable to outright rescission.

But attempts to revise money obligations meet exaggerated difficulties in periods of inflation. The spread of price-changes as between different commodity groups, the rapid fluctuations within particular groups, and the conflicts of interest which appear as between debtor and creditor, all offer special grounds for refusing to "make new contracts for the parties." Even in periods of monetary stability courts of equity have not met with signal success in their attempts to revise the price-term as an incident to specific performance. The extreme inflations experienced by Germany in the last decade and by the Southern states during the Civil War gave eloquent testimony to the disruption in economic processes which impedes the formulation, in courts of law, of substitute standards of value. Difficulties of the same type, though less exaggerated in degree, are encountered in periods of moderate inflation. To impose the burden of price-revision on trial courts would lead to intolerable confusion and delay, which can scarcely be justified by the gain in continuity and stability of existing commercial relationships.

6. *The Choice Between Legislative and Judicial Remedies*

When monetary depreciation has proceeded far the choice finally presented is one between legislative and judicial remedies. Some central questions of policy and of legal method are involved in this choice. The course taken in any legal system will depend ultimately on certain basic presuppositions and on inherited traditions as to legal method.

After the overwhelming catastrophe of the German inflation, courts declared themselves ready to undertake a general revision of all money obligations by the technique of ordinary private litigation. But the problems involved were soon found to be too complex for solution by this means. The whole field of mortgage obligations and long-term bonds was withdrawn from the operation of private law rules and revised by statute at a flat rate, with the aid of a generalized scale of money values covering most of the inflation period. Important classes of money obligations remained, however. The effort of courts was here directed to attaining more exact results than could be achieved by the generalized language of statute. The total product of this effort has been described by one eminent critic as multiplied waste and confusion.[45] Confusion there was, and protracted uncertainty. But it is believed that the whole blame cannot be rested on courts for assuming the initiative in the fields expressly remitted to their charge. A large share of the resulting litigation arose from the complexity and obscurity of the revalorization acts. In the field of judicial revalorization, much of the difficulty was due to the universal havoc wrought by inflation on the whole economic and legal order. Legislation could have provided more generalized standards for the revision of money obligations; the uncertainties inherent in a system of judicial precedent could have been largely removed, at the expense of a more exact justice in an enormous mass of particular cases. For the effort of German courts to reconstruct an economic system through the resources of a developed and refined legal science, an American lawyer would be inclined not to criticize, but to pay them a high tribute.

The Confederate inflation resulted, like the German, in complete catastrophe. The initial impetus for the reconstruction of monetary values came there from legislation. But the language of the scaling acts was so general and their standards so crude that the main burden was thrown on the courts. Wholly unprepared for their task, with but little experience as a guide, the Southern courts showed remarkable insight into the economic and legal problems created by extreme inflation. Before the Supreme Court of the United States intervened to invalidate the main method employed in the scaling acts, Southern courts succeeded in liquidating most of the outstanding indebtedness expressed in Confederate money.

In an inflation less extreme than the German or the Confederate inflation, it is unlikely that American legislatures would act before the destruction of values had brought widespread and intolerable injustice. If legislation were employed, it is doubtful whether generalized tests could be framed that would be more precise or illuminating than tests derived from general rules of private law.[46] In any event, such legislation would encounter constitutional obstacles which would require extreme care in drafting. Such legislation would probably have to be drawn in such form as to project the courts into calculations of the value of *money*, at a time when economic data provided no satisfactory index of the value of money in general.

A prediction that remedial measures would come first in this country from courts and not from legislatures does not by any means imply that the doctrines of private

---

[45] Nussbaum, *Die Bilanz der Aufwertungstheorie,* pp. 15-18 (Recht und Staat, 1929). It is there pointed out that one weekly series of selected "revalorization decisions" published in Germany attained a total of 424 decisions in 1926, 609 in 1927, and 563 in 1928; and that the decisions published by Zeiler had totaled 1530 by May 1929. It was estimated that at least 2,864,217 actions were brought in Prussia alone prior to January 1928, and that in Prussian courts of first instance 849 judges were required for the decision of revalorization questions. In the "revalorization senate" of the Berlin Kammergericht (an intermediate court of appeal), 18 judges were employed and throughout Germany several hundred judges were added to the regular judicial personnel for the decision of revalorization cases. [Footnote by Dawson and Cooper, renumbered.]

[46] See, for example, the *loi Failliot* passed in France on January 21, 1918, allowing rescission of some types of contracts for the sale of goods wherever the expenses or losses through performance

law can adequately protect private contracts against the effects of inflation. Judicial remedies, like legislation, would come at a late stage, when most of the damage had been done. The only effective protection of contracts against monetary fluctuation seems to lie in the widespread adoption of stable-value clauses, particularly through the use of price-indices.

E. Inflation Adjustments in Damage Awards

1. Tort Damage Awards

(a) Readjustment of Pensions

GUZMAN ET AL. v. EMPRESA DE LOS FERROCARRILES DEL ESTADO

Court of First Instance, Santiago (Chile)
60 R.D.J. 407 (2d Part, 1st Sect. 1963)

[The plaintiff's husband was killed in a train accident in 1934. Suit was brought against the railroad, and on Sept. 10, 1942 the railroad was finally ordered to pay a pension of 500 pesos a month to the plaintiff for the rest of her life or until she remarried. The railroad was also ordered to pay a monthly pension of 400 pesos to the deceased's daughter until she married and a similar pension of 400 pesos to the deceased's son until he reached his majority. The daughter married on Oct. 30, 1948 and the son reached his majority on January 28, 1953. The plaintiff remained a widow at the time the action was filed in 1959.

[The complaint seeks revision of all three pensions to the extent they failed to keep pace with increments in the cost of living index, retroactively back to 1934, plus interest. The official cost-of-living index shows that the purchasing power of Chilean currency fell by 99.4% between the date of the accident and September of 1959. A 500-peso pension was worth about $21 in 1934; by 1959 the dollar value had fallen to a little under fifty cents; it is presently worth less than a mill.]

"greatly exceed those which could reasonably have been foreseen at the time the contract was made." Dalloz. 1918. 4. 261.

Legislative relief could of course be undertaken on a narrower scale for certain specified types of contracts, such as contracts of employment on public enterprises or contracts for maintenance and support. Here it would be possible to readjust money obligations in terms of cost-of-living indices, since a large share of the expenditure by the obligees would be on commodities listed in a cost-of-living index. In the later stages of the German inflation contracts for maintenance and support were selected for special treatment, and legislation was passed authorizing officials to modify money obligations of this type in accordance with "equity." Law of Aug. 18, 1923 (*Reichsgesetzblatt,* 1923, 1, 815). [Footnote by Dawson and Cooper, renumbered.]

Decision of the First Instance, Santiago, November 28, 1959

... 6th. The defendant's argument of res judicata must be rejected. In the opinion of this court [this argument rests on] a mistaken view of the present controversy. There is no decision that has pronounced on the right of the appellants to the readjustment they now seek. This question was not decided by the preceding decision [between these parties], nor could it have been decided, since it arises from events that occurred after that case [was decided].... [H]ere a new matter is brought forth, the right of readjustment. The reason for the claim is not the same. In the earlier case it was the wrongful act; in the present case, it is revaluation of the currency. Nor is the relief sought the same in both cases. In the former, it was a compensatory payment. In this action it is the numerical adjustment, in conformance with the currency's fluctuation, of the payment already ordered.

7th. The defenses of payment and prescription appear equally based on that same mistaken understanding of the true procedural nature of this case. If what is sought in the complaint is a readjustment that the [railroad] ... has not paid and resists paying, the defense of payment based on the prompt discharge of the decreed pension installments has no relation [to the issue]. The defense of prescription is based on article 2332 of the Civil Code, according to which actions for injury or fraud are prescribed [terminate if not commenced] within four years from the perpetration of the act. As in the present case the basis of the claim is that which was set forth and not the wrongful act, the prescription [provided in article 2332] cannot be accepted;

8th. Therefore there remains only to see whether the renewed action is or is not according to law. The defendant enterprise has said that such an action has no foundation in positive national legislation now in force. That is correct. But that fact has resulted in presenting [to the courts] a contentious question which must be decided even though no express law exists to resolve it. A similar case is allowed and contemplated in our juridical order, since the procedural lawmaker [*i.e.,* the Congress in legislating about judicial procedure] ordered that every final decision must contain a statement of the laws, and in the absence thereof, of the principles of equity, upon which the judgment is based (article 170, No. 5th, of the Code of Civil Procedure). Very well, if equity alone can be the basis of a decision, the present case is a typical example of the applicability of that situation. For one could not sanction, on the pretext of the absence of positive law on the subject, the injustice which the plaintiffs have suffered in the decrease of the purchasing value of the pensions they acquired through judicial decision in reparation of the damage caused them by the accidental death of the head of their family. The amount of the compensatory life pension collected presently by Dona Berta Guzmán – five hundred pesos a month – is a joke. While one cannot fix responsibility on individuals for the acute inflationary process nor for the lack of legislative solution to its unsettling effects on economic life, the courts, as organs whose purpose is to apply the law, can and should afford the law's protection [and] re-establish normality in cases ... like the present one, which are supported by the most elemental principles of equity. Finally, this [policy] also should be considered with respect to unjust enrichment. . . . Considering the pension that the defendant is paying Doña Berta Guzmán, the money which it is giving her is in real terms but a tiny proportion of the amount that was fixed in the judgment considered in relation to the value of the exchange rate at that time. In other words, the defendant is retaining almost all that value which . . . it would be disbursing if the phenomenon of monetary depreciation had not taken place; . . .

11th. The recovery of interest is not permissible, since in accordance with the law, income payments or periodical pensions do not produce interest.

By reason of these considerations, . . . *it is declared* that the complaint is allowed except in regard to the recovery of interest, which is disallowed, and except in regard to the award of costs against the defendant party. . . .

[The court ordered the defendant to readjust the widow's pension in accordance with the official cost-of-living index. Similarly the daughter's and son's pensions were ordered readjusted retroactively for the terms of their respective spinsterhood and minority.

[The defendant appealed, alleging that the decision contravened fundamental legal principles, especially that of res judicata. The Court of Appeals of Santiago reversed the judgment for violation of the principle of res judicata.

[The Chilean Supreme Court sustained the Court of Appeals, adding that even if the decision of the court of first instance did not contravene the principle of res judicata, "in our law it is not possible to include monetary depreciation as a source of obligations . . ." 60 R.D.J. at 418-19.]

Questions

1. Upon what theory did the Court of First Instance order revision of the pension?

2. Do you agree with the Court of Appeals that the principle of res judicata bars the suit for readjustment?

3. Would the use of lump-sum damage awards obviate the effect of currency depreciation in wrongful death suits?

Note

The Chilean Supreme Court has more recently permitted monetary depreciation to be taken into account in a tort suit. In *Cohen, Mario César,* 66 R.D.J. 203 (2d Part, 4th Sect. 1969) the Supreme Court affirmed reversal of a damage award on direct appeal to permit an inflation adjustment. See generally B. Gesche Muller, *Jurisprudencia Dinámica: la Desvalorización Monetaria y otros Problemas en el Derecho* 48-52 (1971).

Argentina uses lump-sum damage awards.[47] Brazil does not, and consequently has had to confront the problem of pension readjustment. Prior to September 1939 Brazilian law permitted the courts a choice of three types of remedies to reimburse accident victims for loss of future earnings: (1) a lump-sum settlement, (2) a monthly pension paid by the defendant, and (3) the funding of an annuity.[48] Concern that recipients of lump sums were squandering the money and that monthly pensions were sometimes in default led to the adoption of Articles 911 and 912 of the Brazilian Code of Civil Procedure which provide:

> Article 911. In the determination of the indemnification arising from a wrongful act, lost earnings shall be converted into an annuity or pension by means of the payment of capital which, at the legal rate of interest, will assure the payments owed.
> Article 912. The indemnification referred to in the previous article shall be fixed, if possible, in the principal action, and it shall include the legal costs, attorney's fee, and pension payments already due, along with the respective interest. The judgment must provide for the application of the capital in securities of federal public debt for the production of income.
> This capital shall be inalienable during the life of the victim, reverting to the obligor after the victim's death. If the victim dies as a consequence of the wrongful act, the capital shall serve to maintain those persons to whom the victim owed a duty of support, taking into account the probable life of the victim. In this case, the capital shall revert to the obligor only after the obligation of support ceases.[49]

Such a system may make sense in a country inclined towards both paternalism and monetary stability, but in Brazil, which has historically been inclined only to the former, it was highly prejudicial to plaintiffs. The certificates of the public debt bore an annual interest of only five percent, paid semestrally. Moreover, the government's poor payment record was notorious.[50] With interest rates rising as high as five or six percent a *month,* the ritual of the compulsory purchase of government bonds paying a fixed annual interest of five percent must have seemed ludicrous. The high inflation rates of the 1960's provided an overwhelming incentive to settle out of court.

Originally, the pension was calculated on the basis of the plaintiff's earnings at the time of the accident, which typically would have occurred several years prior to final adjudication. Hence, the pension was generally only a fraction of what the plaintiff would have been earning at the time it was decreed. Since legal interest of six percent hardly made up the difference, the defendant had a substantial vested interest in

---

[47]See A. Orgaz, *El Daño Resarcible* 151 (1960); Martínez de Grecco et al v. San Vicente, 62 La Ley 451 (2d Appel. Cham. of La Plata 1950).

[48]See P. Miranda, 13 *Comentários ao Código de Processo Civil* 171 (2d ed. 1969).

[49]As amended by Decree-Law No. 4.565 of August 11, 1942.

[50]See Ministério do Planejamento e Coordenação Econômica, Aspectos Macroeconômicos, Política Monetária e Mercado de Capitais (Versão Preliminar) 48 (March 1967).

delaying the litigation as much as possible. After much vacillation, the courts finally took the position that the amount of the pension must be calculated on the basis of what the victim would have been earning at the date of final decision.[51] But this was only a start on the problem.

The following cases show the Brazilian courts struggling to make the system of tort indemnification set up by the Code of Civil Procedure operate sensibly and equitably during chronic inflation.

RÊDE FERROVIÁRIA FEDERAL S.A. v. PAMPILLON

Supreme Federal Tribunal of Brazil (Third Term)
R.E. 58.252, 38 R.T.J. 215 (1966)

[The plaintiff lost a leg in a train accident. The trial court held the defendant responsible, fixed plaintiff's disability at sixty percent and ordered the defendant to pay a pension that would accompany changes in the minimum wage. The 4th Civil Chamber of the Tribunal of Justice of the State of Guanabara modified the decision, limiting the pension to $Cr 3.800, sixty percent of the minimum wage in effect at the time of the accident. It also dispensed with the requirement that the pension be funded by the deposit of government bonds because the defendant was a wholly-owned government corporation. 1 Rev. Juris. Guan. 136 (Ano I 1961). The Group of the Civil Chambers revised the decision of the 4th Chamber to reinstate the sliding-scale pension that would accompany changes in the minimum wage and required the defendant to purchase sufficient securities to fund the pension. The defendant appealed specially to the Supreme Court.]

Vote of Minister Hermes Lima (Reporter):

The appeal will lie in part. Fixing the indemnification as a value corresponding to a variable minimum wage corresponds . . . to a just indemnification. This Court has decided in this sense in RE 42.900 of 6/27/61, whose headnote states:

Fixing an indemnification based upon the minimum wage and its later variations corresponds to the dominant understanding of the Supreme Court.

. . . As to the formation of capital in certificates of public debt in order to yield the disposable income for the monthly payments, that is unimportant, for the Federal Railroad is an autarchy in which the Union [the Federal Government] is the exclusive stockholder. The securities would be those of the Union itself. Hence adoption of the criterion of self-funding the monthly pension does not violate the law. The deposit of

---

[51] Súmula da Jurisprudência Predominante do Supremo Tribunal Federal No. 314 and cases cited therein.

policies of the public debt would serve to guarantee this pension. However, since the guarantee lies in securities of the Union itself, there is no reason to obligate the Railroad [to secure] them in order to attend to an indemnification which is, in the final analysis, guaranteed by the Federal Government itself. It will probably be easier to receive the self-funded pension.

Vote of Minister Gonçalves de Oliveira (President):

It would really be an inequity for the accident victim to receive an indemnification permanently based on a fixed minimum wage with the tremendous inflation which Brazil is undergoing. . . .

In relation to the deposited capital, . . . [the self-funded pension] is the best form, for the accident victims will be paid at the counters of the Railroad more advantageously and punctually than at the counters of the National Treasury. . . .

Decision

In accordance with the record, the decision was the following: to hear the appeal and to grant it, in part, in accordance with the vote of the Reporter. Unanimous. . . .

FAZENDA DO ESTADO v. DA LUZ

Tribunal of Justice of São Paulo (Sixth Civil Chamber)
No. 163.135, 393 Rev. Trib. 168 (1968)

. . . In 1957 the Treasury of the State was ordered to deposit capital which would assure the payment of a monthly pension corresponding to NCR$ 2.92, then equivalent to 79% of the minimum wage, because of the reduction in the working capacity from an accident suffered by the plaintiff on the state railroad.

In his present complaint the plaintiff seeks a revision in the prior judgment to permit him to receive a pension accompanying the present levels of the minimum wage. [The value of his pension at the time of this appeal was about U.S. $.71, while the minimum wage was about U.S. $40.00.]

. . . [T]he decision below, which partially sustained the suit, cannot be allowed to stand.

Indemnification for a wrongful act is basically conducted in two ways: (a) the payment of a pension, and (b) the deposit of capital [to fund an annuity.] Although the Code of Civil Procedure (Art. 911 and 912) has adopted the second solution, the case law has been permitting option for the first when there is security of execution.

If the judgment is to render periodic payments, no obstacle exists to revision of the amount in order to prevent the disequilibrium . . . resulting from the inflationary process. Such a solution, which in Germany has found support beyond discussion in Art. 323 of the Procedural Statute . . ., has not been shown offensive to the case law nor to our national doctrine. However, in cases in which the payment of indemnification has been made in the form provided for in Arts. 911 and 912 of the Code of Civil Procedure, there is no opportunity for the requested revision. This is because the deposit of capital extinguishes the obligation of the responsible party. The deterioration of the creditor's situation because of inflation is entirely unrelated to the debtor, who has already paid. Thus, in such circumstances, any readjustment for monetary depreciation is unworkable. The situation of the plaintiff, however lamentable, is one which only the legislature can correct. . . . São Paulo, December 11, 1967. [One of the three judges dissented.]

Question

Is there any theory on which the court might order readjustment in the rate of return on the government securities?

(b) The Concept of the Adaptable Debt

O. GOMES, TRANSFORMAÇÕES GERAIS DO DIREITO DAS OBRIGAÇÕES

Pp. 109-13 (1967)

The distinction between a *pecuniary debt* and an *adaptable debt*[52] has practical interest in view of the distortions to the principle of the nominal value of money. . . . When the object of the debt does not consist in the delivery of a sum of money, . . . it is unjust to apply the *principle of nominal value.*

It is the nature of what is owed that permits one to distinguish between a pecuniary and an adaptable debt. One obliged to pay a certain quantity as a purchase price of a determined good contracts a *pecuniary debt,* for the precise object of the debt is the delivery of an agreed upon sum of money. . . . One required to make monetary payments of support is obliged to assure the creditor a sum necessary to his maintenance in the conditions fixed, so that if the purchasing power of money varies, the quantity of money has to be altered to conserve its initial value. In these debts, money is taken into account, not as an object, but as a measure of value. It is easy to

---

[52] The term *Wertschuld* was created in 1925 by Authur Nussbaum to distinguish obligations of value from monetary obligations. In the Civil law countries the distinction has been much elaborated and the expressions "deuda de valor," "dívida de valor," "debito di valore," and "créances de valeur" are familiar juridical terms. Because he felt the term "value-debt" was obscure, Professor Nussbaum decided to translate the concept as "adaptable debt." See A. Nussbaum, *Money in the Law National and International* 180 (Rev. Ed. 1950). [Eds.]

perceive the distinction, considering that the person obliged to support another may give lodging and sustenance in his own house. Thus, the obligation of support does not necessarily consist in the delivery of a sum of money, but in allocating the conditions of sustenance to those who require them. On the other hand, those who discharge their obligation giving lodging and sustenance will spend increasing amounts if money should depreciate for one cannot admit that in monetary terms the performance remains an inalterable sum. The readjustment of performance in an adaptable debt is justified, as Ascarelli has lucidly clarified, because its object is constituted not by a determined sum of money, but rather by a value which may correspond in diverse moments to varying sums of money in relation to the variations in the general level of prices, that is to say, to the oscillations in the purchasing power of money.

In contradistinction to what occurs with pecuniary debts, the nominal sum of money in adaptable debts is a simple expression corresponding to one of the ways in which it may be liquidated; consequently, one cannot apply the *principle of nominal value.*

... [T] he State attributes to money an invariable *nominal* value, permanently equal to itself, an imposed value which cannot be corrected by private parties in order to adjust it to its real value, not even through a clause of comparison with foreign money.

Such is the *principle of nominal value.* Adhered to in all of the Codes since that of Napoléon as one of the rules to which pecuniary debts are subordinated, it signifies that "the quantity of money owed at the time of payment is determined by its correspondence to the quantity of money at the moment in which the debt was constituted, in relation to an ideal basic unit, with other considerations having little importance." However, this principle has never been applied in absolute terms. . . . Generally speaking, its solidarity disintegrates in times of monetary crisis when expedients are sought to prevent the consequences of its application. One tries to expand the concept of an *adaptable debt.* . . . In short, one tries to adapt the law of obligations to monetary depreciation, seeking via prophylactic or therapeutic measures, the contractual equilibrium which monetary nominalism corrodes and destroys when depreciation reaches an unbearable degree. . . .

. . . [I] t is undeniable that the elaboration [of the concept of the adaptable debt] is due to the necessity of justifying the revaluation of the subject of certain performances in view of the diminution of the real value of the money in which they are expressed.

There is no conceptual uniformity; the notion varies according to the exigencies of the monetary picture and the criteria which the writers prefer. . . . [B] ut the preferable notion is that which characterizes [adaptable debts] as obligations whose object does not originally constitute a nominal sum, but depends upon the circumstances or future elements, variable and exterior to the juridical relationship. However, they do not constitute a homogeneous category. Mugel has separated them into three groups: (1) credits of reparation; (2) credits of reimbursement; and (3) credits of unjust enrichment. In the first category are included the obligations of indemnity; in the second, those which have as the object reimbursement for expenses . . . , those subsequent to the dissolution of a contract, such as interest for delay, and those of the price in expropriation; in the third category, the debt stemming from unjust enrichment, whose sum must be calculated at the moment of the condemnatory judgment and not that of the date of the enrichment.

However, the area in which adaptable debts appear is much broader, for those also qualifying include, among others, those which result from: the obligation of support, acquisition, condominium, a dividing wall, an irregular usufruct, payment of insurance, and a return of advancement made to heirs. . . .

ROCHA v. CIA. ULTRAGAZ S/A

Tribunal of Justice of São Paulo (Third Civil Chamber) (Brazil)
No. 153.858, 377 Rev. Trib. 194 (1967)

[The victim, a minor who worked as a shoeshine boy, was run over and killed in 1955. In accordance with Art. 912 of the Brazilian Code of Civil Procedure, the judgment entered against the defendant required it to deposit 130,000 cruzeiros, which at 6% a year, would yield a monthly pension of 650 cruzeiros, corresponding to half the amount the boy contributed to his mother. In 1955 $Cr 650 was worth about nine to nineteen U.S. dollars, depending on whether the official or free-market exchange rate is used. By 1966 the value of 650 cruzeiros had fallen to about thirty cents. The boy's mother brought suit for revision of the pension. In the court below the judge had sustained the defense of res judicata.]

[Opinion of the Court]

This case concerns an adaptable debt, not a pecuniary debt. The judgment had and has a supportive character. . . . The pension was fixed in consideration of the purchasing power at the time of the accident, when the minor shoeshine boy only earned 50 cruzeiros a day. Today such a quantity will not even pay for half of one shoe shine. And since it is an adaptable debt and not a pecuniary debt, Art. 912, after creating an obligation of support stemming from a wrongful act, took into account one more element, the probable life of the victim. The liquidation must have already considered the income of the deceased during his probable life and not just on the day on which he was run over. . . .

Then, if the revision is calculated on new facts which were not foreseen at the time, the three identities of "res," "persona" and "causa petendi" do not exist. The indemnity is no longer in issue. What is in issue is its being brought up to date. What is intended is not a new indemnity but simply the obtaining of a quantity which has the same purchasing power. Consequently, the object of the litigation is quite different, varying with respect to the "res" and the "causa petendi." Res judicata does not exist. . . .

Moreover, laws vary greatly with respect to escalator clauses or the adoption of the theory of adaptable debts. The Italians, for example, have simplified the concept of an adaptable debt. . . .

In this subject Brazil has been evolving greatly, applying monetary correction via various laws in expropriation, fiscal debts, the values of rents, earnings and salaries, in workmen's compensation, and attempting an escalator clause in adaptable debts in general.

The lessons of Tullio Ascarelli, Caio Mário da Silva Pereira, Santiago Dantas, and Arnold Wald . . . [citations omitted] are gaining an echo, and rightfully so during the economic and financial vicissitudes which have been going on in our country.

Therefore, res judicata does not apply, and prosecution of the action is permitted. . . .

São Paulo, May 31, 1966.
[One judge dissenting.]

Note

Súmula 490 of the Brazilian Supreme Federal Tribunal now states: "The pension corresponding to compensation for civil responsibility must be calculated on the basis of the minimum wage in effect at the time of the judgment and shall be adjusted to later variations."

Questions

1. Is characterizing the underlying tort obligation as an adaptable debt helpful in deciding how to allocate the losses arising from monetary depreciation?

2. Is there any justification for placing the burden of monetary depreciation on the defendant in *Rocha v. Ultragaz?*

3. Recently, courts have started to utilize Readjustable Treasury Obligations, see pp. 527-29, to fund pensions. *E.g.,* Viaçao Nove de Julho Ltda. et al. v. Cromopel-Comércio e Indústria de Papel e Papelao S/A, A.C. No. 169.923, 395 Rev. Trib. 183, 186 (1st Civ. Chamb. S.P. 1968). Will this solve the problem?

4. At what time does an adaptable debt become converted into a pecuniary debt? Suppose the plaintiff's car is damaged in an accident. The car is repaired and the plaintiff pays the garage bill of $400. Is that sum an adaptable or pecuniary debt? In the past few years the question has produced a huge number of almost equally divided cases in Argentina. The cases are collected in Malvar, *Deudas de Valor y de Dinero. La Desvalorización Monetaria y el Proceso, Oportunidad para Alegarla,* 1968-VI J.A. 138-39. In Pardi v. Gruninger, A.C. No. 157.127, 222 Rev. For. 149 (1966), the Fifth Chamber of the Tribunal of Justice of the State of São Paulo (Brazil) permitted monetary correction of a tort damage award, reimbursing the plaintiff for the present value of expenses incurred in 1963. In doing so the court noted:

It is true that monetary correction, in the expressed text of the law, only applies to tax debts and the updating of compensation in the process of expropriation. But in accordance with the criteria of the case law, there is no obstacle to updating the value of other debts. Without it, debtors, themselves remiss, would benefit from monetary depreciation. Litigation would be a great source of profits, for those defeated would benefit from the loss and the value of money.

Here, if this loss of value is an onus to which citizens are subject, there is no reason that the successful plaintiff should support it rather than the vanquished defendant. . . . The winner ought not bear the onus of monetary depreciation.

Would it be fairer to divide the loss?

5. Does the U.S. have a problem similar to that of Brazil and Chile with respect to inflation and damage awards? See Bernstein, "The Need for Reconsidering the Role of Workmen's Compensation," 119 *U. Pa. L. Rev.* 992, 996 (1971).

6. Does the use of lump-sum awards in tort suits eliminate the need for consideration of price level changes in determining the proper amount of damages to be awarded? Consider the U.S. cases collected in the annotation, "Changes in cost of living or in purchasing power of money as affecting damages for personal injuries or death." 12 *ALR* 2d 611 (1950); Note, "Fluctuating Dollars and Tort Damage Verdicts," 48 *Colum. L. Rev.* 264 (1948); Note, "Damages for Loss of Future Income: Accounting for Inflation," 6 *U.S.F. L. Rev.* 311 (1972).

(c) Obsolescence of Fixed-Sum Damage Limitation Provisions

Protracted and severe inflation has rapidly rendered statutes containing limitations expressed in a fixed sum of pesos or cruzeiros hopelessly out of date. Elevators are equipped with brass plaques solemnly warning that overloading will be punished by a fine of what is now the equivalent of a few cents. Jurisdictional limitations on damages that could be awarded practically put certain courts out of business until legislatures finally got around to revising them. Legislative lag in adjusting damage limitation provisions can produce most vexing problems for courts, including those of the United States, as the following case illustrates.

TRAMONTANA v. S.A. EMPRÊSA DE VIAÇÃO AÉREA RIO GRANDENSE

350 F.2d 468 (D.C. Cir. 1965), cert. denied, 383 U.S. 943

McGowan, Circuit Judge: . . .

I

Vincent Tramontana was killed on February 26, 1960, when the United States Navy airplane in which he was traveling on naval orders collided over Rio de Janeiro,

Brazil, with an airplane owned and operated by a Brazilian airline. At the time of his death, Tramontana was a member of the United States Navy Band, which was on an official tour of Latin America. The record does not show his permanent duty station, but he resided with his wife, appellant here, in Hyattsville, Maryland. The Navy plane in which he was travelling when he was killed was en route from Buenos Aires in Argentina to Galeão, Brazil. Appellee Varig Airlines is a Brazilian corporation having its principal place of business in Brazil but carrying on its transportation activities in many parts of the world, including the United States. The Brazilian plane was on a regularly scheduled commercial flight from Campos, Brazil, to Rio de Janeiro when the accident occurred.

Almost two years after her husband's death, appellant instituted this action in the District Court against Varig and its predecessor, alleging that negligence in the operation of the Brazilian plane had caused her husband's death. She explicitly based her claim for recovery on certain provisions of the Brazilian Code of the Air which provide a cause of action for injury or death resulting from negligent operation of aircraft in Brazil. She claimed damages of $250,000. Service was made on Varig Airlines, which concededly is subject to suit in the District of Columbia. Varig filed an answer to appellant's amended complaint and the same day moved for summary judgment dismissing the complaint or, in the alternative, for summary judgment in respect of so much of appellant's claim as exceeded the U.S. dollar equivalent of 100,000 Brazilian cruzeiros. Varig relied on Article 102 of the Brazilian Code, which limits liability for injury or death in aviation accidents to that amount. The District Court, with Varig's consent, entered judgment in favor of appellant in the amount of $170.00, the current dollar value of 100,000 cruzeiros. It awarded judgment in favor of Varig "for all of the plaintiff's claim which exceeds the sum of One Hundred Seventy Dollars ($170.00)." From this latter judgment Mrs. Tramontana appealed.

II

The only question now before us is whether Brazil's limitation on the damages recoverable for death sustained in airplane accidents occurring there is to be applied in this suit in the District of Columbia. Appellant appears to concede that her cause of action, if any, was created by, and arises under, a provision of Brazilian law enacted coincidentally and in conjunction with the damage limitation. She argues, however, that the forum law regarding damages for wrongful death occurring in the District of Columbia, *i.e.*, unlimited recovery, should govern that aspect of her claim. Initially, she accepts the applicability of the traditional conflict of laws rule in personal injury cases that the *lex locus delicti*, the law of the place where the injury occurred, generally governs in a suit brought elsewhere, but she asserts that a court sitting in the District of Columbia should adopt the familiar exception to the effect that the forum will refuse to apply the otherwise applicable foreign law if it is contrary to some strong public policy of the forum. Appellant asserts the existence of a strong policy of the District of Columbia in favor of unlimited recovery for wrongful death, which she claims is evidenced by Congress' repeal in 1948 of the $10,000 maximum until then contained in the local wrongful death statute. She points also the fact that only thirteen states still limit recovery for wrongful death, and that none imposes a ceiling as low as that contained in the Brazilian Air Code. She cites the Warsaw Convention, which governs generally accidents involving international air carriers and which now permits recovery up to $8,292, as constituting in essence an international standard of fairness in such matters.[53] And, finally, she relies on the New York Court of Appeals decision in Kilberg v. Northeast Airlines, Inc., 9 N.Y.2d 34, 211 N.Y.S.2d 133, 172 N.E.2d 526 (1961), as a persuasive precedent for the position she urges us to adopt. Another contention, which we treat separately hereinafter, is that the Brazilian limitation should be disregarded because of the striking decline which has taken place in the value of the cruzeiro in terms of the dollar. . . . Our conclusion that the District Court properly applied the Brazilian limitation rests upon an examination of the respective relationships of Brazil and the District of Columbia with the accident, and with the parties here involved; and a consideration of their respective interests in the resolution of this issue.

The interest underlying the application of Brazilian law seems to us to outweigh any interest of the District of Columbia. Not only is Brazil the scene of the fatal collision, but Varig is a Brazilian corporation which, as a national airline, is an object of concern in terms of national policy. To Brazil, the success of this enterprise is a matter not only of pride and commercial well-being, but perhaps even of national security. The limitation on recovery against airlines operating in Brazil was enacted in the early days of commercial aviation,[54] no doubt with a view toward protecting what was then, and still is, an infant industry of extraordinary public and national importance. The Brazilian limitation in terms applies only to airplane accidents, unlike the Massachusetts provision rejected in *Kilberg,* which was an across-the-board ceiling on recovery for wrongful death in that state. The focus of Brazilian concern could hardly be clearer.

We have seen nothing that would suggest that Brazil's concern for the financial integrity of her local airlines should be deemed to be less genuine now than when Article 102 was enacted, simply because of the depreciation of the cruzeiro. The failure to amend that provision may reflect a conscious desire to avoid enlarging the potential liability of local airlines during a period of general economic difficulty. It may represent an unwillingness to contribute to the inflationary spiral by adjusting "prices" fixed by statute, which the government can control. Or it may be attributable in part to both motives. In any event, we are not persuaded that the fact of inflation itself — with the result that 100,000 cruzeiros are worth now considerably less than when the limitation was enacted — should be deemed to render obsolete Brazil's legitimate interest in limiting recoveries against her airlines.

---

[53] Both Brazil and the United States are signatories to the Convention, but its coverage is limited in terms to claims by or on behalf of passengers of the carrier against which recovery is sought. [Footnote by the court, renumbered.]

[54] The Brazilian Code of the Air, including Article 102, was enacted in 1938. Air transportation has become increasingly important in Brazil, both because of the size of the country, and because of the relative inadequacy of surface transportation. [Footnote by the court, renumbered.]

III

A separate facet of appellant's public policy argument is that the Brazilian limitation on recovery for wrongful death should be disregarded entirely because of the recent marked decline in the dollar value of the Brazilian cruzeiro. Brazil's current economic problems are a matter of common knowledge, including the fact that inflation has depreciated the Brazilian currency by more than 600 per cent since the accident occurred in 1960. This development undoubtedly contributes to the appeal of appellant's argument, but it does not, in our view, warrant a result different from that we would reach had the value of the cruzeiro in terms of the dollar remained unchanged.

Brazil's interest in the protection of the financial integrity of its most important means of domestic transportation almost certainly has not been diminished by the decline in the value of its currency. Indeed, its concern may well have increased in proportion to the rate of domestic inflation. A reluctance to reflect that decline in those prices that are subject to direct government control would be wholly understandable. . . . Moreover, an unpredictable and virtually immeasurable factor would be imported into the decision of international conflict of laws cases if the otherwise applicable law were subject to being displaced because of the recent history of the relative values of the currencies involved. Courts would be called upon in each case to determine at what point a declining rate of exchange of a foreign currency made application of the foreign law intolerable. Should Brazilian law be disregarded if the cruzeiro had depreciated only 300 per cent? or 50 per cent? Victims of the same negligence might recover widely differing amounts, depending, not on where they lived — a not irrelevant factor, as we have suggested — but on *when* they sued.

Considerations of comity among sovereign nations certainly have relevance in this context. International balance of payments problems have a way of assailing the weak and the strong alike, and it is not only the underdeveloped nations who feel the sometimes rapidly fluctuating effects upon their exchange rates of both domestic and international economic factors, over some of which at least they have little or no control. If the courts of one country make the applicability of the law of another turn on the way the exchange balance happens to be inclined at the moment, a speculative and highly artificial element would be intruded into those considerations normally recognized by civilized nations as germane in the choice of applicable law. And the forum so motivated, whether it knows it or not, wields a two-edged sword.

One further question remains, though it is one not raised by the parties.[55] The District Court converted the 100,000 cruzeiro ceiling on recovery into dollars at the rate of exchange prevailing on October 14, 1963, the date of the entry of its judgment. Although New York, alone among jurisdictions in this country, and England appear to

---

[55] Appellant's argument has been that, because the judgment in dollars reflects a striking weakness of the cruzeiro *vis-à-vis* the dollar as of the day of its entry, the forum should disregard the Brazilian limitation entirely and apply its own law. It has not asked, even alternatively, that the conversion rate used in the judgment be that either of the date of the accident or of the initial enactment of the Brazilian Air Code. [Footnote by the court, renumbered.]

follow a rule that recovery in tort is to be measured in terms of the rate of exchange on the date of the wrong, we think the District Court applied the sounder rule. This "day of judgment" rule has the support of the authors of the *Restatement (Second), Conflict of Laws* § 612a, (Tent. Draft No. 11, 1965), and is in accord with the Supreme Court's most recent decision on the point, Die Deutzche Bank Filiale Nurnberg v. Humphrey, 272 U.S. 517, 47 S.Ct. 166, 71 L.Ed. 383 (1926). It has been endorsed by the majority of writers who have considered the problem.[56] And it has been applied by both the Second Circuit and the United States District Court in Maryland in tort cases. Shaw, Savill, Albion & Co. v. The Fredericksburg, 189 F.2d 952 (2d Cir. 1951); The Integritas, 3 F.Supp. 891 (D.Md. 1933). The rule provides the plaintiff with the dollar equivalent of the amount he would recover if he had sued in the country whose law determines his right to recover, and it thereby ensures that he neither suffers nor benefits from the fact that he chose another forum in which to litigate his claim.

The judgment appealed from is Affirmed.

FAHY, Circuit Judge (concurring).

I concur in the opinion of Judge McGowan for the court that the forum law regarding damages for wrongful death occurring in the District of Columbia does not govern this case, and that the Brazilian limitation of recoverable damages applies. However, were it not for the fact that plaintiff seems to concede that should the District of Columbia limitation not apply the limitation found in the Brazil Air Code governs the amount of recovery, I would leave the amount of recovery open for determination upon the basis of more ample information as to what the Brazilian law, as applied by the courts of Brazil, would permit to be recovered in this case.

Notes

1. After this case was heard, the U.S. Court of Claims, pursuant to a reference by Congress, recommended an award of $25,000 to the families of each of the 18 members of the Navy band who perished in the crash. Armiger et al. Estates v. U.S., 339 F.2d 625 (Ct. Cl. 1964). This recommendation was founded upon equitable rather than legal considerations.

2. In 1938 the official exchange rate was U.S. $1 = $Cr 17.62, making $Cr 100,000

---

[56] See, *e.g.,* Mann, *The Legal Aspect of Money* 315 (1953); Nussbaum, *Money in the Law* 372 (1950); Evan. "Rationale of Valuation of Foreign Money Obligations," 54 *Mich. L. Rev.* 307 (1956); Fruenkel, "Foreign Moneys in Domestic Courts," 35 *Colum. L. Rev.* 360 (1935); Note, 40 *Harv. L. Rev.* 619 (1927). Compare Gluck, "The Rate of Exchange in the Law of Damages," 22 *Colum. L. Rev.* 217 (1922); Note, 65 *Colum. L. Rev.* 490 (1965). *Cf.* Aratani v. Kennedy, 115 U.S. App. D.C. 97, 317 F. 2d 161, 323 F. 2d 427 (1963), cert. granted, 375 U.S. 877, 84 S. Ct. 147, 11 L. Ed. 2d 110, motion for reference granted, 376 U.S. 936, 84 S. Ct. 790, 11 L. Ed. 2d 657 (1964). [Footnote by the court, renumbered.]

worth roughly U.S. $5,675. Would this have been a more appropriate standard than that employed by the court?

3. Would it have been appropriate for the court to employ monetary correction based on a coefficient derived by the Brazilian government for back tax debts?

4. Law No. 4.221 of May 8, 1963 substituted a damage limitation provision of 150 times the highest minimum wage (then $Cr 21,000) for the $Cr 100,000 provision in the 1938 Code of the Air. Should this change in the law have affected the court's decision?

5. Judge Fahy's hesitation about applying the damage limitation provisions of Article 102 would appear to be justified, particularly when the provision is seen in context.

BRAZIL: DECREE LAW 483 OF JUNE 8, 1938 (CODE OF THE AIR)

Responsibility to Third Parties

Art. 96. The provisions relating to the responsibility of the transporter to third parties shall cover any airplanes, be they public or private, national or foreign, which fly over Brazilian territory.

Art. 97. Any damage to persons or property found on the earth's surface caused by a plane in flight, or from the maneuvers of taking off or landing, shall give rise to a right of compensation.

Art. 98. Any damage caused by an object or substance which falls from a plane, or which was projected therefrom . . . shall be compensated for under the same conditions.

Art. 99. Damages caused by a plane at rest shall be governed by ordinary law.

Art. 100. Joint responsibility for the damages to which the preceding articles refer shall be imposed upon:

(a) the person in whose name the plane was registered;

(b) the person who was using or exploiting the plane;

(c) whoever on board the plane caused the damage. . . .

Art. 101. Any persons jointly liable shall have a subrogation action against the one who caused the damage.

Art. 102. The joint responsibility for each accident shall be limited to:

(a) a maximum of [100,000 cruzeiros] per person for bodily injury or death;

(b) in case of injury or destruction of property, its just value.

Sole Paragraph: The person held liable cannot take advantage of these limits if the interested party proves that the damage was caused by *dolo*.

[Articles 127 to 132, which deal specifically with liability for airplane collisions, contain no provisions restricting liability.]

Article 131. Communication of the collision to the authorities of the closest airport to the accident is required in order for the limits of responsibility provided in this Code to prevail, provided the planes are under Brazilian jurisdiction. . . .

Because of the poor draftsmanship in this statute, there has been considerable controversy as to whether the damage limitation provisions of Art. 102 apply to an airplane collision where the plaintiff was not a passenger in the defendant's airplane. There is a strong doctrinal current against limited liability. See T. Azeredo Santos, *Direito da Navegação* (Marítima e Aérea) 409-17 (1964); *Aguiar Dias*, 2 *Da Responsabilidade Civil* 826-27 (4th ed. 1960); Lemos Sobral, *A responsabilidade civil no abalroamento aéreo*, 132 Rev. For. 36 (1950); Vale, *O Nôvo Código Brasileiro do Ar*, 223 Rev. For. 12, 19-20 (1968). The controversy has finally been settled by the new Brazilian Code of the Air, Decree Law No. 32 of November 18, 1966, as amended by Decree Law No. 234 of February 28, 1967. Article 132 of the new statute establishes a limit of 400 times the highest prevailing minimum wage in Brazil for a wrongful death or injury stemming from a negligent aircraft collision.

------

2. Expropriation Awards

The combination of severe inflation and dilatory payment of eminent domain awards has typically produced a substantial amount of disguised confiscation in the expropriation process. Brazilian and Argentine governments have notoriously adopted the policy of take now, pay later. Unfortunately for the expropriated owners, the civil codes dealt with the problem of delay in payment of monetary obligations by providing only for the payment of legal interest. With the inflation rate soaring beyond the legal interest rate, the longer the expropriating agency delays payment, the cheaper the real cost of the property becomes. Insufficient budgetary appropriations, which are characteristic of inflationary economies,[57] and procedural rules permitting lengthy dilatory appeals, are the chief culprits. Brazil in particular has been slow in paying victims of expropriation; the reports contain numerous decisions in which compensation for condemned property has remained unpaid for twenty years or more.[58]

------

[57]Werner Baer has observed, ". . . [I]n an inflationary milieu the policy maker finds himself in a dilemma. It is difficult for him to be realistic and make expenditure projections assuming a higher rate of inflation the following year, since this would admit the government's impotence in controlling the growth of inflation. Even projecting under the assumption of the same rate of inflation would admit the government's impotence in reducing the rate of inflation. So, at best, a government can project assuming the same rate of inflation or a smaller rate. Many times projections are based upon the assumption that prices will remain unchanged." W. Baer, *Industrialization and Economic Development in Brazil* 83-84 (1965).

[58]*E.g.*, Emprêsa Territorial Vila Niterói Ltda. v União Federal, RE 63.091, 43 R.T.J. 277 (1967); Nemésio Raposo et al. v. União Federal, RE 54.221, 34 R.T.J. 91, 84 R.D.A. 174 (1965); União Federal v. Cia. Viação São Paulo-Mato Grosso et al., AC 5.637 (embs.), 217 Rev. For. 100 (TFR 1964).

As will be recalled from the preceding chapter on land reform, despite constitutional provisions requiring prior and full compensation, expropriated parties have frequently received something less. The materials in this section show some of the problems the courts have faced in seeking to preserve eminent domain awards from inflationary confiscation.

OLÍMPIA DO VALE PIMENTAL CALDAS v. SURSAN

Tribunal of Justice of the State of Guanabara (5th Civil Chamber) (Brazil)
A.C. No. 20.663, 211 Rev. For. 150 (1965)

[On Oct. 30, 1962 the court affirmed on the basis of the following opinion of the trial court.]

Olímpia do Vale Pimental Caldas and her husband . . . have instituted this action of unjust enrichment *(enriquecimento sem causa)* against the State of Guanabara and the Superintendency of Urbanization and Sanitation (SURSAN), with cumulative damages and the specific object of securing payment of the present value of buildings at 168, 170, 176, and 178 of Rua Marques de Sapucai and 134 Rua Julio do Carmo. Alternatively, in view of the manifest disinterest of the expropriating power and the prescription occurred in its execution, [the plaintiffs seek] reversion of these properties to their dominion inasmuch as since 1949 they have been diligently but unsuccessfully trying to receive payment of the judicially determined compensation. This has resulted in the impoverishment of the plaintiffs and the consequent illicit enrichment of the expropriator through . . . the inflationary process.

The defendants have contested the action, arguing preliminarily res judicata, and on the merits taking the position that [a] the constitutional precept of prior and just compensation has not been infringed because the value has been judicially fixed and besides, [b] the transfer of possession of the properties has not been effectuated. Moreover, there is no time limit fixed for the payment of the *precatório*,[59] which has already been sent; so the action lacks substance. Delay in the execution would not amount to unjust enrichment, presenting only a case for application of article 1061 of the Civil Code.[60] . . .

In effect, what the plaintiffs intend is the updating of the final value determined in the expropriatory action, or the declaration that the expropriation has no effect, with the properties reverting to their dominion.

Such a reversion . . . [is inconsistent] with the cause and purpose of expropriation. . . . Even in its alternative form, the action is devoid of substance.

---

[59] The *precatório* is a letter of remittitur sent by the judge to the president of the court to requisition payment of a judgment against the public treasury. [Eds.]

[60] Article 1061 of the Civil Code provides: "Damages in obligations for the payment in money consist of the interest for delay and costs. . . ." Article 1062 provides: "The rate of interest for delay, when not agreed upon, shall be six percent per annum." [Eds.]

It is undeniable that sporadic judicial decisions, in an indirect fashion, have attended to the complaint for completing payment of the price after the lapse of a long period between fixing the price and fulfillment of the obligation to pay it.

As a rule, they are based on the transient phenomenon of inflation, which debases the value of the delayed price, prejudicing the expropriated party and bringing . . . an illicit enrichment to the expropriator.

However, the law cannot be subverted by such transitory phenomena, even if foreseen, nor by artificial concepts or constructs to discipline delay in executions, if the law itself has already provided for the delay of the debtor.

The basic constitutional principle of prior and just compensation . . . is preserved by the regular transmission of the expropriatory action, which had its own normal term. [This proceeding] entered the phase of execution upon the sending of the *precatório,* which is the order of payment directed against the budgetary appropriation destined to cover judgments.

It is incomprehensible how the budget of the administrative entity responsible for the payment lacks sufficient funds to cover it. One can admit the possibility of an insufficiency in the corresponding budget, but not in the following budget, whose funds result from the sum of verified obligations. [Provision for unsatisfied judgments is routinely made in the next year's budget.]

This is incomprehensible even if the chronological order of the obligations has not been complied with. If so, notwithstanding, the remedy to cure this vice is in the Constitution itself, which even includes sequestration as one of the measures to assure payment.

With the right thus safeguarded, it is up to the expropriator to make it effective, above all because expropriation is irreversible after the judgment unless there is a supervening rescissory action, and because interest for delay has already entered into the just price to compensate for retarding execution of the obligation of payment.

It should be emphasized that the expropriated party continues to exploit the property economically since the transfer of possession has not been effectuated.

Hence, there is a presumption that no other damage has occurred other than that resulting from the . . . inflationary increase in value of the properties.

But this increase in value does not figure in unjust enrichment because the expropriator does not enjoy the fruits of the thing, and since it [*i.e.,* the interest for delay] has already been added to the composition of the judgment itself, it also follows that the defendant [the plaintiffs in this action] has no right to update the price. . . .

ESTADO DE GUANABARA v. PARADAS

Tribunal of Justice of the State of Guanabara (4th Civil Chamber) (Brazil)
AC 44.009, 13 Rev. Juris. Guan. 284 (Ano V 1966)

. . . The appellee brought an ordinary action for . . . damages against . . . [the State of Guanabara], alleging that by Mun. Decree 6.897 of Dec. 28, 1940, his property on 187 Rua Teófilo Ontoni was expropriated by the old prefecture of the then Federal District.[61]

On October 13, 1952 the compensation to be paid him was fixed at Cr$ 470.240 by the decision of the distinguished Supreme Court.

Despite the plaintiff's pursuance of the judgment's execution, the necessary *precatório* having been sent on 7/17/1963, until the present time no payment has been made.

The [plaintiff's theory] . . . is that the inertia of the government in satisfying its obligation to pay the price of the expropriation, causing him grave prejudice, constitutes the fault *(culpa)* referred to in Article 159 of the Civil Code,[62] making the State of Guanabara, successor to the old city government, responsible for the reparation due.

The State contested the complaint, arguing res judicata . . . and sustaining the thesis that its obligation is limited to payment of interest for the delay.

. . . [The court below], considering . . . that according to the master's report . . . the present value of the property is Cr$ 9.100.000, and that the [plaintiff] . . . has continued and continues in possession, enjoying its fruits, decided in favor of the plaintiff. The defendant was ordered to pay the plaintiff compensatory interest (damages) . . . corresponding to the difference between the sum of the value fixed in the expropriation action (Cr$ 470.240) and the earnings derived until transference of possession, and the updated value of the property (Cr$ 9.100.000). . . .

Despite the brilliance of the answer and the reasons set out in the appeal, the appellant does not prevail.

There is no offense to the principle of res judicata, for the judgment which decreed the expropriation is unaffected.

New facts have arisen which profoundly alter the situation of the parties. First, there is the failure of the old prefecture, succeeded by the State, to effectuate the expropriation decreed thirteen years ago. Second, there is the notorious devaluation of the cruzeiro, in catastrophic proportions, reducing the purchasing power of the money to practically zero, a fact which has been recognized by the government itself when it established monetary correction . . . in the collection of debts owed to it.[63]

Rio de Janeiro, Sept. 13, 1965.

---

[61] In 1960 the federal capital was transferred to Brasília, and the Federal District, comprising the city of Rio de Janeiro, became the State of Guanabara. [Eds.]

[62] Article 159 provides: "Whoever, by voluntary act or omission, negligence, or imprudence violates a right or causes prejudice to another, is obliged to repair the damage.

Proof of fault *(culpa)* and the calculation of damages are governed by the provisions of this Code, Arts. 1518 to 1532 and 1537 to 1553. . . ." [Eds.]

[63] The reference is to Art. 7 of Law No. 5357 of July 16, 1964, p. 527 *infra,* which instituted monetary correction of back tax debts. Since then, the principle of monetary correction has been extended to all sums owed the federal government, plus interest at 12 percent per annum on the original sum. Law 5.421 of April 25, 1968. [Eds.]

Dissenting Vote of Salvador Pinto Filho:

... What the plaintiff seeks is ... damages for the delay in the payment of the price and not — according to his statement — complementation of the price in order to adjust the value of the property to economic reality at the moment of payment, which has been delayed for various years.

Here, according to the dominant case law of the illustrious Supreme Court — *Súmula* 416 — for delay in the payment of the price of an expropriation complementary compensation in addition to interest will [not] lie.

Such interest implies precisely compensation for damages for the delay in payment of pecuniary debts, which is the legal principle.

... If the economic conditions of the country create inequitable situations, such as that set out in the complaint, the solution is to reform the legislation in force in order to avoid them, such as has already been done with relation to monetary correction for expropriation suits.

Thus I would reform the decision to limit the compensation to interest for the delay. . . .

Questions

1. What measure of damages did the court employ? Is there any rational basis for deducting the earnings of the property prior to transference of possession from plaintiff's recovery?

2. Would the result have been different if the court had employed the theory of an adaptable debt?

3. Would the theory of an adaptable debt have been conceptually neater than allowing a second suit for damages? Consider Wald, Opinion of the Attorney General of the State of Guanabara in AC 45.825, 13 Rev. Juris. Guan. 413, 416 (Ano V 1966):

Since the Constitution has determined that compensation stemming from expropriation must be just and prior, the better doctrine is that which considers the case as a true adaptable debt, readjustable in accordance with variations in the cost of living, carrying with it in judgment the value initially fixed, but admitting transformation of the corresponding cruzeiro value.

Compensation stemming from expropriation is an adaptable debt, in accordance with the teaching of Pontes de Miranda . . . and Ascarelli . . ., admitting revision of its correspondence or monetary translation in order to maintain the purchasing power at which it was initially fixed.

And it is Pontes de Miranda who clarified . . . that indemnifications are adaptable debts until the moment they are paid, admitting readjustment to the variations of the cost of living. . . .

The case law of São Paulo has taken the same direction in various opinions, based upon the distinction between adaptable and pecuniary debts, admitting that delay in payment by the expropriator justifies a new indemnification stemming from the delay. . . .

4. Would it be preferable for the legislature to provide that the condemnation proceeding is void if the expropriator fails to pay the compensation awarded within 30 days after final judgment? Compare §§ 1251 and 1252 of the California Code of Civil Procedure.

Notes

1. In 1965 the Brazilian legislature finally moved to remedy the situation by adding the following sentence to the basic condemnation statute: "After the lapse of more than a year from the date of valuation, the judge or court, prior to final decision, shall determine monetary correction of the value set." Law No. 4.686 of June 21, 1965. This cryptic, poorly drafted amendment has generated a great deal of litigation. Only recently has the case law firmed up, permitting application of monetary correction to all pending cases, as well as those on direct appeal, where there has been a delay of more than a year between the valuation and payment, and the judgment has not been executed. *E.g.*, Constantino et al. v. Prefeitura Municipal de São Paulo, R.E. 63.395, 52 R.T.J. 711 (STF *en banc* 1969). The troublesome phrase "final decision" has now been firmly construed to refer to the permanent transfer of title following verification that payment has been made. The cases are collected in Ferraz, "Desapropriação: Indicações de Doutrina e Jurisprudência,"22 *Rev. Dir. Procur. Geral* 344, 418-21 (1970).

2. Disturbed by the sizeable judgments resulting from monetary correction of long unpaid eminent domain awards, Brazil's Congress on July 2, 1971, enacted Law No. 5.670, denying application of monetary correction to periods predating legislation specifically authorizing its use. The effect of this statute is to prevent monetary correction from going back further than June 1965 in eminent domain cases. Despite vigorous dissent, the Supreme Federal Tribunal has recently upheld the constitutionality of this statute. E.R.E. 69.304 (STF *en banc*, Nov. 24, 1971), cited in R.E. 72.904, 61 R.T.J. 540, 541 (STF 2d Term 1972).

3. The Supreme Court has reversed *Súmula* 416 and now permits the former owner to bring a separate action for damages resulting from delay in payment of an expropriation award. Universidade do Estado da Guanabara e Estado da Guanabara v. Boudroux, R.E. 66.807, 100 R.D.A. 117 (1st Term S.T.F. 1969); Estado da Guanabara v. Borges, R.E. 65.053, 101 R.D.A. 199 (1st Term S.T.F. 1969). The lower courts now routinely convert separate damage suits into successful requests for monetary correction. E.g., Soares Nunes v. Estado da Guanabara, 47.912, 14 R.J.G. 166 (8th Cam. Civ. T.J. GB. 1966); Embargos 47.962, 20 R.J.G. 235 (1st Group Cam. Civ. T.J.GB. 1967).

As the following cases illustrate, the Argentine courts have struggled with many of the same problems without the benefit of a statute.

ADMINISTRACION GRAL. DE VIALIDAD NACIONAL v. POJTICOVA DE FOITH

Federal Chamber of Appeals of La Plata *(en banc)* (Argentina)
1962-VI J.A. 488, 108 La Ley 685 (1962)

La Plata, October 9, 1962. Dr. *Fernández del Casal* said:

The appellant complains that the decision on appeal has fixed as the price of the expropriated property a value that does not take into account the devaluation or loss in buying power of the currency occurring after possession of the expropriated property was taken.

This, in my opinion, is equivalent to impugning the appraisal because it was made with reference to the [date of] taking of possession, principally when in his initial pleading the owner of the expropriated property demanded delivery of a sum of money which, at the moment of payment, represents the just price of the property taken.

I consider the appellant's claim justified. . . .

Originally, reference to the date of taking possession for the valuation of the expropriated property had a scope and purpose completely different from those later given to it.

That rule was adopted by the Supreme Court in times when the buying power of money was stable, and its purpose was simply to prevent the owner from benefitting in the valuation placed on the expropriated property as a result of the [public] work itself . . . or to permit the owner to take advantage of the increase in valuation after the beginning of the expropriation process or of the authoritative measures that ordered it, so long as the rise in valuation was not caused by speculation from the prospect of the realization of the public work. . . .

When the inflation began and the courts had to decide how compensation for expropriations should be fixed, they continued to use the same rule without reflecting that it was more reasonable to let the valuation refer to the time the expropriation was completed. . . .

In those [earlier] times of stability, it did not matter whether one date or the other was taken as a point of reference for valuation. The essential thing was to use a definite and constant norm.

The criterion of indifference appears clearly in the opinion of the Supreme Court that is the "leading case" in opposition to monetary revaluation in expropriation cases: "There can be no doubt," said the Supreme Court, "that by the end of the process values have changed, but [these may be] as much upward as downward. The value of real property in the city of Buenos Aires is not in a process of regular and definite increase. . . . The justness of the rule selected, which is reasonable in itself, is reinforced by the fact of its constant and uniform application." . . .

The justice of revaluation has been generally unrecognized by national case law. One reaction is noted in the damage and injury cases, revaluation being accepted in all cases via the opinion of jurists and foreign decisions. The principle has even made its way into modern constitutional texts in relation to the incomes of retired ex-public employees. . . .

The 5th National Conference of Lawyers, meeting in the city of La Plata in 1960, unanimously approved a resolution recommending to the government "readjustment in the discharge of adaptable debts, especially, in compensation for damages in contractual and extracontractual matters, expropriation, etc." . . . "[T]he notorious and universal fact of monetary depreciation, understood as a loss in the buying power of money, should be compensated as a means of safeguarding the patrimonial rights of the individual, a conclusion which is based on the constitutional provision on the inviolability of property and the principles of full reparation, responsibility and equity."

In my opinion, these conclusions are consonant with the true constitutional doctrine. It is not believable that the National Constitution, in according its fundamental guarantees − which are nothing but limitations of the powers of the public authorities − meant to leave them to the whim of those same organs whose power it wanted to constrain. If these organs could hand out discretionary rules for the judicial determination of values or neutralize their effectiveness through the equally discretionary management of the currency, through issuance of money, the guarantees referred to would be merely illusory. . . . [Unlike the U.S. Constitution, Argentina's Constitution contains no guarantees of "just" compensation. Instead, Article 17 simply states: "Expropriation for reasons of public utility must be authorized by law and previously compensated." Nevertheless the court infers the requirement of "just compensation" from the principle of justice and the meaning of the term "previously."]

When dictating the provision of art. 619 of the Civil Code[64] − which is taken as a basis for affirming the nominalism of the codifier −, it is clear that the legislator did not provide for the adjustment of pecuniary debts to the real value that they had on the date of the juridical act [i.e., when contracted] because he considered devaluation morally impossible. The proof of this is in the note to the article referred to, which says: "We abstain from projecting laws to settle the much debated question regarding the obligation of the debtor, when there has been an alteration in the currency, because that alteration would have to be ordered by the national legislative body, *an almost impossible occurrence.*" After enumerating the provisions of European legislation containing the same solution as the legal text, the note continues: "If the intrinsic value of money is altered − says the Code of Austria − the person who received it must reimburse the full value that it had at the time of the loan. If one had

---

[64] Article 619 of the Argentine Civil Code provides: "If the debtor's obligation is to deliver a sum of a particular kind or quality of national currency, the obligation is discharged by delivering the money specified, or another kind of national currency at the rate of exchange prevailing in the place on the day which the obligation matures." [Eds.]

to promulgate a law, supposing the alteration of currencies, we would accept the article of the Austrian Code."

It is thus a question of one of those typical lacunae — admitted in this case by the legislator — which are produced when a rule is inapplicable because it embraces too much or carries with it consequences that the legislator would not have enacted had he known or suspected them. In such a case . . . the judge must find for himself the rule for the decision, developing the law according to his own fundamental idea. . . .

It is fitting to note that the present monetary depreciation has not been caused by reasons of *force majeure* or through facts foreign to the will of the state; rather it has been provoked by planning an economic-social policy that fatally leads to gravely inflationary situations such as that which presently afflicts the country. . . .

The solution held in this vote — that of valuation on the closest possible date to that of payment — adequately contemplates, to my way of seeing, the correct interpretation of the constitutional guarantee of property and more especially, of the requirement that payment be prior to expropriation. . . .

I do not believe that lack of proof regarding the amount of the increase in valuation is an obstacle to allowing the [appeal]. . . . I understand that such proof is not indispensable since the case law has determined that the changes in money's buying power belong in the sphere of notorious facts; that is, they constitute a fact which the judges know without either of the parties having to bring forward any proof in that respect ("judicial notice rule"). . . .

Since the adjustment to which the owner of the expropriated property has a right does not refer to the real increase in the value of the property, but rather to the decrease in buying power of money, it seems to me just to take heavily into account the index numbers of the cost of living in general, which manifest that decrease.

This solution is all the more just since neither of the parties has claimed an increase or decrease in the real value of the property.

I regard it most prudent, within the relative approximation which can be aspired to in any valuation, to take into account the official figures on the cost of living index, . . . currency in circulation, the means of payments, and the coefficient established for the revaluation of real assets by the regulating decree of capital gains tax law.[65] I omit the exchange rate of the national currency in relation to foreign money — which gives a quantitatively smaller result — because the country does not have a truly free money market. It is known that the international value of the peso is greater than its internal value due to the severe control of imports and to the intervention of the Central Bank in regulating the value of the peso, by purchasing and selling various foreign currencies at times it considers opportune.

---

[65] To adjust for inflation on real estate sales, article 16 of the Capital Gains Tax Regulations then in force permitted the taxpayer to increase his cost basis by 25% for each year he held the asset. This inflation adjustment was initially limited to the period between date of purchase and Dec. 31, 1960, and was subsequently extended to Dec. 31, 1966. Since 1972 the inflation adjustment has been linked to a coefficient fixed annually by the Income Tax Bureau in accordance with the wholesale prices of nonagricultural products. Law 19.414 of Dec. 31, 1971, Art. 5. [Eds.]

The index number of the cost of living in the month of October 1959 is 3,091.6 . . . and that of the month of July of the present year, 5,223. . . .

Applying the formula:

$$\frac{N\text{-}n \times 100}{n}$$

in which N is the latest number index, and n the previous one, with which we want to compare N, we have:

$$\frac{5223\text{-}3091.6}{3091.6} \times 100 = 69$$

which indicates the percentage increase in the cost of living between the dates indicated.

Applying the revaluation coefficient for real assets provided for by art. 16 of the regulating decree of the capital gains tax law . . . — that is, 25% a year for a period of two years and 10 months, one arrives at a 70% increase.

Comparing the figures of currency in circulation — 85,366 million pesos in October 1959 . . . and 141,442 million in July of the current year . . . one arrives at 75% [65.6% — Eds.].

Adopting the figures that correspond to the total means of payment — including money created through bank credit — 124,361 pesos in October of 1959, and in May of 1962 (latest published figure, 207,235 pesos, Boletín de Estadísticas del Banco Central) . . . we arrive at 68% [66.6% — Eds.].

Taking into account all those circumstances, I regard it as prudent to fix the increase in value taking place since the taking of possession until the present at 70%. Applying this proposition to the value fixed by the appraisal of 25,400 pesos by the Appraisal Tribunal (Tribunal de Tasaciones), results in 17,780 pesos, which added to the previous amount, increases to 43,180 pesos, which I conceive to be the equitable value to attach to the expropriated property. . . .

Dr. *Mallea* said:

I concur in the rule laid down in the opinion of Dr. Fernández del Casal, insofar as it accepts [the proposition] that the effects of the present severe monetary depreciation should be taken into account in fixing compensation for expropriation.

. . . [I]f the State has at hand the necessary means to prevent the process of expropriation from suffering delays which are seriously prejudicial to the property owner due to the uncontained devaluation, such as adequately bringing together [the dates of] dispossession, appraisal, . . . and provisional or final payment, there is no good reason for not charging the state with the consequences of its own negligence, conforming to the general principles of imputability. . . .

It must also be borne in mind that in the law . . . [of expropriation] the moment when the fair value of the property expropriated must be fixed has not been determined. . . . Such determination must be made by the appraising body with reference to the [date of appraisal] . . ., since the parties, particularly the . . . expropriator, can obtain judgment and execution . . . in short order.

This rule conforms, within the practical possibilities of the lawsuit, to the constitutional rule of immediate payment, and eliminates or strongly tempers the expressed consequences of the monetary devaluation. . . .

On the other hand, the adoption of a simple percentage increase in valuation, calculated in accordance with an index of general devaluation of money in circulation, as proposed in the complaint, is not admissible, for it lacks precision and an objective legal basis.

The increase in value should be established for each particular concrete case, taking into account the effect of monetary depreciation on the property . . . The percentage of increase is not the same in all circumstances, for the phenomenon of inflation strikes with varying intensity. . . . Hence it is infeasible to consider the same coefficient based on general cost of living tables at a determined moment as a certain and computable effect in all cases.

I am of the opinion, then, that in the particular case at bar . . ., in order to be just and in accordance with the aforementioned principles, given the long time that has elapsed since the appraisal – December 1960 – it is fitting to require a new appraisal [based on the property's present value] . . . .

Dr. *Esteves* [dissenting] said:

The Supreme Court of Justice of the Nation, through a constant and unvarying line of decisions . . . and the most important courts of the entire country have established the firm principle that the compensation for expropriation is set with reference to the value of the property and the damages caused at the date of dispossession.

I find no reason nor circumstance that now authorizes departure from the decisional rule . . ., which is based on a very reasonable interpretation of the legal texts and followed inexorably by this court in the midst of the most dreadful inflationary process that ever afflicted the country. But in any event, . . . if a re-examination of the matter is desired, this is neither the case nor the time to do so. And I say this because the small amount in dispute will prevent review by the Supreme Court. This said, let us enter into an examination of the question. The National Constitution requires in its art. 17 that expropriation for reasons of public utility must be previously indemnified, and leaves the extent of reparation to statutory law. According to what has been enacted, this encompasses only "the objective value of the property and the damages which are the direct and immediate consequence of the expropriation" (art. 11, law 13.264). Articles 18 and 19 of law . . . 13.264 establish that when the amount corresponding to the real property tax valuation (which may be increased up to 30%) has been deposited, the expropriator will obtain possession, and upon notification of the deposit, transference of the property will be declared.

From what has been said it follows that the date of dispossession is the point of reference for fixing compensation, because the dominion of the expropriated party ceases the moment that the expropriation is executed. In every case only the price is argued. . . .

The inflationary process constitutes a real national calamity and affects the economic life of all the inhabitants equally and that of the State itself, which, to cite only one example – closely tied to this matter – is hurt in multimillion figures with respect to the collection of the real property tax. . . .

I do not understand either how the effects of legal tender (art. 26, law 13.571) can be ignored and how one can confer on the expropriated party an insurance against inflation that is not authorized by any legal text and which is not possessed by the instalment seller, the lender of money, or the depositor of the Savings Bank (Caja de Ahorro). Neither is it held by the worker, employee, public functionary or retired person, nor by the judges themselves whose recompense is guaranteed by the Constitution itself (art. 96). Such an insurance is not held by the common litigant who after a long ordinary suit obtains a sum which has retained no equivalence to that which he originally sued for. Finally, [such insurance] is not held by the State when it collects devalued sums owed it in fines, charges, taxes and other [similar] concepts, or receives amortizations for long range development or housing loans, which most of the time do not justify the collection costs. . . .

The situation cannot be even remotely compared with the devaluation of the mark, nor do the concepts elaborated with respect to it apply. While this devaluation was due exclusively to a conscious maneuver of the German government, our monetary devaluation is accompanied by an intense struggle . . . in search of stabilization, for which the Nation has sacrificed important quantities of foreign currency reserves.

Consequently, I vote to declare contrary to law the grievance brought by the appellant, based on the devaluation of the currency. . . .

Dr. *Rivarola* said:

. . . I do not believe the circumstance that it is more difficult to take this case to the Supreme Court because of the small amount of money involved in the judgment, is an argument which will impede reconsideration of the problem, especially when we consider that in the several hundred cases decided by the court in the last two years, there are very few which amount to a million pesos. On the other hand, this is the first case in which the question of monetary depreciation appears put forth in the complaint itself, a requirement which the court en banc (with my disagreement and that of Dr. Masi) previously decided necessary for [the question] to be considered. . . .

In many cases about extra-contractual responsibility one sees the tendency to diminish the debtor's responsibility in the face of negligence during the process of the lawsuit. The case *sub judice* was begun in 1952 and possession taken in 1959.

One must take into account these two stages: in the first, before [transference] of possession, one could not require from the defendant that which was against his own interest, . . . and that he urge at the time of a housing crisis his eviction from the very house where he was living. . . .

In the second stage, there were common interests in the prompt termination [of the litigation] . . . . But, whether because of the overload of cases, or through the tortuous procedure established, it is common for expropriation proceedings to [delay several years in the courts], which makes one think that the fault of the creditor is minimal and should not be considered in this case. . . .

There are various means of according the expropriated party just compensation, such as increasing the rate of interest to give it a clearly compensatory aspect, on utilizing the cost of living indexes contained in the official publications, or the official norms of revaluation. Remanding the case for a new valuation in the respective court has, in my opinion, the inconvenience that the new price may be influenced by the fact that the same work has already been done. I find it most prudent and objective in this case to take the index of revaluation for real assets provided for in art. 16 of the regulatory decree of the law of capital gains, which estimated that sum at 25% annually. . . . [T]his amounts to the 70% proposed by Dr. Fernández del Casal, to whose other basic statements I adhere. . . .

Therefore, . . . through the majority of opinions, . . ., it is resolved to declare that it is proper to take into account the loss in the buying power of money in fixing the compensation owed to the owner by the expropriating party.

That in the present case the compensation that should be credited to the owner for the expropriation of the affected property amounts to . . . the sum of 43,180 pesos. Let the proceedings return to the original court in order that the remaining unsettled questions may be considered.

Questions

1. What response may be made to the equal protection argument of Dr. Esteves — that no other group is accorded the protection of the law against economic loss stemming from inflation?

2. Dr. Fernández del Casal's opinion articulates three criteria in addition to the cost of living index, generally considered to be the best indicator of money's purchasing power, for adjusting the value of the expropriated property: (1) the increase in the amount of currency in circulation, (2) the increase in the means of payment, and (3) the coefficient for revaluation of real assets for capital gains taxation. Presumably, if Argentina had had a freely fluctuating exchange rate during the operative period, that too would have been thrown into the crucible. What relevance do these factors have to correcting the value previously placed upon the expropriated property?

In answering this question consider the following:

(a) Kaldor, "Monetary Policy, Economic Stability and Growth," in *N. Kaldor, 1 Essays on Economic Policy* 128-29 (1964):

It cannot be emphasized too strongly that there is no direct relationship in a modern community between the amount of money in circulation (whatever definition of "money supply" is adopted in this connection) and the amount of money spent on goods and services per unit of time. To proceed from the one to the other it is necessary to postulate that changes in the supply of money leave the frequency with which money changes hands (the so-called "velocity of circulation of money") unaffected, or at least that any consequential change in the velocity of circulation is limited to some predictable fraction of the primary change in the supply of money. There are no valid grounds however for any such supposition. The velocity of circulation of money (or what comes to the same thing, the ratio which cash balances bear to the volume of turnover of money payments, per unit of time) is not determined by factors that are independent either of the supply of money or the volume of money payments; it simply reflects the relationship between these two magnitudes. In some communities the velocity of circulation is low, in others it is high, in some it is rising and in others it is falling, without any systematic connection between such differences or movements and the degree of inflationary pressure, the rate of increase in monetary turnover, etc. Such differences can only be explained in terms of historical developments rather than psychological propensities or of institutional factors, while the movements in the ratio can only be accounted for by the varying incidence of the policies pursued by the monetary authorities. In countries where the authorities pursue a restrictive policy, the ratio tends to fall, and *vice versa.*

(b) The terms "money supply" (or "money stock") and "means of payment" are not exactly terms of art; perhaps it is simply that the state of the art is such that economists do not always use these terms to refer to the same things. Money supply or stock usually refers to currency in circulation plus the adjusted demand deposits of the commercial banks. Milton Friedman and his followers have also included time deposits of commercial banks on the theory that they are such close substitutes for money that one is likely to err less by including than by excluding them. See Teigen, "The Demand for and Supply of Money" in *W. Smith & R. Teigen* (eds.), *Readings in Money, National Income, and Stabilization Policy* 44, 56 (1965).

"Means of payment" typically refers to much the same thing as money — that which can be used to satisfy monetary obligations. As used by the Argentine Central Bank, "means of payment" would appear to include outstanding currency (domestic and foreign), gold, and sight deposits at commercial banks.

(c) A recent study of the dynamics of the Argentine inflation from 1945 to 1962, using multiple regression analysis, found that four independent variables produced statistically significant explanations for price level changes: (1) the annual rate of change of the money supply in the hands of the public, (2) the annual rate of change of hourly money-wage rates in industry, (3) the annual rate of change in the exchange rate, and (4) the annual rate of change in real available supplies. The data suggested the following conclusions, where other things are equal:

(i) A one-percent increase in the money supply in the hands of the public will result in an increase in the level of prices of slightly more than one percent for rural and imported products, and of roughly one percent for the overall wholesale price index.

(ii) A one-percent increase in hourly industrial money-wage rates will result in an increase of one-half of one percent in the prices of domestically manufactured goods.

(iii) A devaluation of 10 percent will increase the level of wholesale prices by roughly 3 percent.

(iv) A one-percent increase in aggregate real supply will lead to a one-percent drop in the price level.

C. Diaz Alejandro, Exchange-Rate Devaluation in a Semi-Industrialized Country 116-122 (1965).

PROVINCIA DE SANTA FE v. NICCHI

Supreme Court of Justice of Argentina
1967-IV J.A. 115, 127 La Ley 164 (1967)

Buenos Aires, June 26, 1967.

1st — In this action for expropriation brought by the province of Santa Fé against Carlos A. Nicchi, expropriation was allowed and the Province was ordered to pay the sum of 199,575 pesos, plus the coefficients of monetary devaluation between the time of the defendant's answer and the date of payment, according to indexes established by the Secretary of the Treasury of the Nation, with interest and costs. The inclusion of the factor for monetary devaluation motivates this appeal by the plaintiff [Province], based on the prior decisions of the Court.

2d — The Court has previously decided that compensation must cover the value of the [expropriated] property on the date of dispossession, without allowing any compensation for the monetary devaluation taking place between that date and the date of judgment. . . .

3d — This Court, as presently composed, does not share that position. In expropriation the State exercises a juridical power recognized by the Constitution, but the exercise of that power, authorized by reason of public utility, supposes the sacrifice of a right that also has a constitutional basis, obliging due compensation for the expropriated party.

4th — Compensation which is not just is neither constitutional nor legal. (National Constitution, art. 17; Civil Code, art. 2511.) And compensation is just when it restores to the owner an economic value equal to that of which he is deprived, as well as any damages that are the direct and immediate consequences of the expropriation.

5th — To indemnify is, in sum, to free from all damages through a complete compensation. And such complete compensation is not achieved if the damage persists to any extent. For that reason this Court has said that the indemnification must be full: the objective value of the [expropriated] property must suffer no diminution or deterioration of any kind, nor can the owner suffer any damage to his property which is not thoroughly and promptly compensated.

6th — This is so because expropriation, as legislated in our National Constitution, is an institution conceived to reconcile public and private interests. And such reconciliation does not occur if the latter are substantially sacrificed to the former and if the owner is not compensated for the loss of his property, *i.e.,* offered an economic equivalent that permits him, if possible, to acquire another property similar to the one he loses by virtue of [the expropriation].

7th — In order to maintain inviolate the principle of just indemnification in the face of continued depreciation of the currency, the value of the expropriated property must be fixed on the day of the final decision, assuming that the property is then transferred and that payment follows that decision without appreciable delay. If it were not so, it would then be necessary to protect the right of the expropriated party to compensation for harm resulting from the unjustified delay.

8th — . . . [I] t follows nonetheless that one cannot automatically and indiscriminately apply to all kinds of expropriations an index which corrects for currency devaluation. For purposes of indemnification, [the court] must keep in mind the nature and the alternative uses of the expropriated property, whose value does not always increase — even in periods of inflation — but rather sometimes decreases.

9th — The foregoing is not to say, as the lower court said, that the appraised value should be increased by a factor based on currency devaluation, applying the cost-of-living indexes of the National Directorate of Statistics and Censuses. Such a procedure is equally inadmissible, because the plain and simple application of general indexes of the growing cost of living would produce a new violation of the principle of "just" indemnification. Not all property follows a curve similar to that of the increase in the cost of living. There are [some property values] which in recent years have suffered a decline. . . . It is obvious, therefore, that if it were a question of the expropriation of such properties, it would be inappropriate to increase the indemnification on the ground of currency depreciation. [Such a judicial solution would] authorize an injustice in depreciation of the State's interest. . . . Judges should weigh in each case the nature of the property under consideration and its characteristics, and estimate its real value at the time of decision.

10th — Strict application of this criterion would, without doubt, necessitate a new expert appraisal before the decision in each instance, which would mean a long, troublesome proceeding with serious effects on the litigation. The problem, therefore, should be resolved by application of this principle: Once the existence of damage (but not its amount) has been fixed, it is the judge's responsibility to decide the amount reasonably. In doing so, he can take into account the official statistics on the increase in the cost of living, keeping in mind those other elements of judgment which influence every concrete case and which often will suggest the application of indexes lower than those resulting from the aforementioned statistics.

Therefore, . . . the appealed decision is affirmed as to the principle it decides, and modified in terms of paragraphs 7 through 10 of this opinion. The case is remanded to the court below for proceedings in accordance with this Court's opinion. . . . — *Eduardo A. Ortiz Basualdo.* — *Roberto Z. Chute.* — *Marco A. Risolía.* — *Luis C. Cabral.* — *José F. Bidau* (in a separate opinion).

Separate opinion. — *Considering: 1st* — The case law of this Court for many years held that the devaluation of currency should not be considered in determining the appropriate indemnification to be awarded in cases of expropriation. This result is explained by the desire to uphold juridical principles that have appeared immutable, especially the unvarying line of cases establishing that the time to calculate the value of expropriated property was the moment when possession was taken by the [State]. From that moment forward the owner lost his power over the property, and it would be unjust for him to suffer the depreciation of any subsequent decline in its value, or benefit from an increase in its value. Any damages resulting from delay in [fixing the amount due to the owner] were compensated by the appropriate interest charges.

2d — One may explain the persistence of this doctrine in spite of the phenomenon of inflation (which has a long history) by reference to the double hope that the latter could be slowed down or that the legislature would attend to its juridical implications.

3d — In view of the persistence of that phenomenon, along with the extremes it has now reached, it is no longer possible to uphold juridical principles that have become fictions. . . .

5th — In reality, the ideal solution (to keep the owner from suffering loss of value) would be to award him whatever is necessary to acquire another property analogous to [to expropriated property]. In such a case we could not lose sight of the monetary factor under consideration. . . .

9th — Regarding the method of calculating the effect of monetary devaluation, the undersigned is in agreement with the procedure indicated in paragraphs 8, 9 and 10 of the majority opinion, with which he agrees fully. The writer offers this opinion only for the purpose of explaining his change of view, since he had previously maintained the opposite, both in this Court and in the Federal Chamber of Appeals of the Capital. . . . — *José F. Bidau.*

Questions

1. Suppose the government had requisitioned a ship during the Suez crisis of 1956-57, when the price of ships had risen extraordinarily. A valuation of 800,000,000 pesos was placed upon the ship at that time. Let us further suppose that in 1960, when the case is finally appealed to the Supreme Court, the price of similar ships has fallen to 600,000,000 pesos despite an interim rise in the wholesale price index of 50 percent. How much indemnification should the shipowner receive under the Argentine approach? Under the approach of the 1965 Brazilian statute set out on pp. 534-35, *infra.*

2. Which approach seems preferable?

3. Argentine law permits a former owner to bring an action to recover the property taken from him by eminent domain in the event that it ceases to be used for the public purpose for which it was condemned. A condition of bringing this action (called *retrocesión*) is that the former owner repay the amount which he received for the property. Should that amount be subject to monetary correction or revaluation? The Argentine Supreme Court recently held that currency depreciation should not be taken into account in a *retrocesión* action. Ortega v. Dirección Gral. de Fabricaciones Militares, 1968-V J.A. 240, 131 *La Ley* 153 (1968). Do you agree?

Notes

1. A comparison of the Argentine and Brazilian experiences with eminent domain and inflation appears in Rosenn, "Expropriation, Inflation and Development," 1972

Wis. L. Rev. 845. For succinct discussions of eminent domain in Argentina, Brazil, Chile, Mexico, Peru, and Venezuela, *see* A. Lowenfeld (ed.), *Expropriation in the Americas* (1971).

2. Chilean condemnation procedures were revised in 1967 by government decree to take overt advantage of the confiscatory effects of the inflationary process. Compensation for eminent domain is determined by alternative procedures: the negotiated settlement and the contested suit.

If the owner and the government reach an agreement on the amount of compensation, the government takes possession and title upon payment of 20 percent in cash. The balance is payable in two annual installments. If no agreement is reached, valuation is set by three experts designated by the government from a special list. The owner can appeal this valuation to the courts, but the government secures possession and title upon deposit of 20 percent of the amount set by its panel of experts. Whether set by the court or the panel of experts, the balance of the compensation is payable in five annual installments.

Under either method the unpaid installments bear interest at the rate of six percent annually. These unpaid balances are also subject to a curious inflation adjustment. Sixty percent of the unpaid balance is adjusted upwards either by a coefficient derived from the official cost of living index, or the percentage increase in the minimum wage, whichever is the lower. Since both cost of living index and the minimum wage are set by the government at rates widely believed to be below the actual inflation rate, and only 60 percent of the unpaid balance is corrected for inflation or the government's wage policy (which may be much less the rate of inflation), the condemnee has a portion of his award confiscated by inflation whichever method of condemnation is employed. Burke, "Law and Development: The Chilean Housing Program," 2 *Lawyer of the Americas* 333, 351-52 (Part II, 1970).

3. As has been seen in the discussion of land reform, still another effect of inflation on expropriation arises in the context of agrarian reform programs in which bonds rather than cash are used to compensate the expropriated party. The extent to which such bonds are protected against monetary depreciation varies considerably among Latin American nations. *See* pp. 341 ff. *supra.*

F. Adapting Credit Transactions to Chronic Inflation

1. The Use of Inflation Adjustments in Government Bonds

One result of Brazil's 1964 military *coup d'état* was the delegation of considerable power to a group of technocratic economists who considered the strategy of financing development through inflation counterproductive. Instead they preferred to generate the needed resources through taxation, borrowing, private savings and investment. But rather than try to eradicate inflation as quickly as possible, a strategy they considered disastrous for economic growth, these economists introduced a gradual stabilization program.[66]

A crucial part of that gradual stabilization program was the institutionalization of monetary correction to neutralize some of the redistributive effects of inflation and permit the nominal operation of existing legal institutions regulating and structuring credit transactions. Monetary correction adjusts for declines in the purchasing power of money by multiplying original monetary values by coefficients derived from price indexes.

Bonds of the Brazilian government paying five or six percent annual interest had long been a most unattractive investment, and by 1964, when the inflation rate was in excess of 90 percent, the voluntary market for government bonds was practically nonexistent.[67] To recreate a bond market, Brazil's new military regime passed the following law.

BRAZIL: LAW NO. 4357 OF JULY 16, 1964

Article 1. The executive is authorized to issue Obligations of the National Treasury up to a limit of CR$ 700 billion, in conformity with the following conditions . . .:

(a) Maturity between three and twenty years;

(b) Minimum interest rate of six percent a year, calculated on the updated nominal value; . . .

§ 1. The nominal value of the Obligations shall be updated periodically as a function of variations in the purchasing power of national currency. . . .

§ 2. The unitary nominal value in terms of updated currency . . . shall be declared trimestrally. . . .

§ 7. The difference between unitary nominal value and the updated currency amount . . . does not constitute taxable income for individuals or legal entities. . . .

The National Economic Council has implemented this statute by utilizing coefficients derived from the wholesale price index for monetarily correcting the face values of these Treasury Obligations. These bonds have greatly aided the Brazilian government finance budgetary deficits through non-inflationary means. By 1965 about half the budgetary deficit was financed by Readjustable Treasury Obligations. Between

---

[66] This program is described in Kafka, "The Brazilian Stabilization Program, 1964-66," 75 *J. Political Economy* 596 (Supp. Part II, Aug. 1967) and its results are analyzed in M. Simonsen, *Inflação: Gradualismo X Tratamento de Choque* (1970).

[67] For many years the government had been resorting to "compulsory loans," which were virtually indistinguishable from taxes since the government failed to repay them.

1965 and 1968 the amount of these bonds in circulation increased from 293 billion old cruzeiros to 3,570 billion, an increase in real terms of 556 percent.[68]

Undoubtedly, the popularity of readjustable obligations has partly been due to extremely powerful incentives that from several viewpoints were also very burdensome for the National Treasury. For example, in November 1965 the government issued Decree-Law 1, which gave buyers of readjustable obligations two alternatives until May 1966: they could opt either for the monetary-correction clause, or for readjustment of the value of the obligation by an increase in the dollar exchange rate, using US$1=NCr$ 1.85 as the base (the decree-law was promulgated when the dollar rate was already NCr$ 2.20). After May 1966 one-year obligations would yield 6 percent per year. Since the dollar was readjusted to NCr$ 2.70 in February 1967, purchasers of obligations at par between February and May 1966 received a nominal yield of

$$\frac{2700}{1850} \times 1.06\text{-}1 = 55 \text{ percent per year.}$$

This was a burdensome rate for the Treasury, since the inflation of the period did not reach 40 percent per year.

The conditions of Decree-Law 1 were extremely favorable to those who bought readjustable obligations with foreign capital. However the exchange rate varied, obligations bought before May 1966 had a guaranteed one-year yield of

$$\frac{2.20}{1.85} \times 1.06\text{-}1 = 26 \text{ percent}$$

in dollars, since the obligations' base for readjustment was the dollar at NCr$ 1.85 and the effective exchange rate was already NCr$ 2.20.[69]

Two additional reasons for the success of Readjustable Treasury Bonds have been (i) their huge purchases by the National Housing Bank out of funds supplied by a national pension fund (Fund for the Guaranty of Service) and (ii) tax incentives.[70] Were it not for these artificial stimuli, it is questionable whether Readjustable Treasury Bonds would have had much public acceptance, given the notoriously unreliable

---

[68] The nominal values were taken from J. Chacel et al, *supra* note 19, at 112 and deflated by Conjuntura Econômica's general price index.

[69] Simonsen, "Inflation and the Money and Capital Markets of Brazil," in *The Economy of Brazil* 133, 157-58 (H. Ellis ed. 1969). Several subsequent similar exchange rate stimuli to the purchase of Readjustable Treasury Bonds are described in Sant'ana, "As Obrigações Reajustáveis do Tesouro Nacional e a Técnica Operacional de sua Utilização no Mercado de Capitais," 4 *Apec Estudos Econômicos Brasileiros* 148 (1969).

[70] *E.g.*, Law 4.357 of July 16, 1964, art. 3, § 8 gave taxpayers the option of paying a five percent tax on the sums resulting from compulsory monetary correction of their fixed assets, or subscribing to twice these sums in nontransferable Readjustable Treasury Obligations.

Of the 3,570 billion old cruzeiros outstanding in Readjustable Treasury Obligations at the end of 1968, 907.7 billion cruzeiros, or a little more than one fourth, were attributable to the National Housing Bank, the Fund for the Guaranty of Service, and alternative tax payments.

payment record of past Brazilian governments and the substantially higher yields offered by bills of exchange and other credit instruments.[71]

In 1953 Chile authorized the Banco del Estado de Chile to issue readjustable bonds paying not more than 6½% annual interest for housing and agricultural purposes.[72] Those issued for agricultural purposes were to be adjusted annually in accordance with the price of a measure of wheat or some other agricultural product or group of products determined by the Bank, while those issued for construction purposes were to be readjusted annually in accordance with the price of concrete or some other measure related to construction prices. Unfortunately, the system of readjustment has had no practical application.[73]

In 1962 Argentina issued tax-exempt bonds paying 7 percent annual interest as an emergency measure. To assure their public acceptability, the government found it necessary to include a clause adjusting the face value and interest in accordance with the decline in the value of the peso with relation to gold.[74]

In December 1972 Argentina issued tax-exempt bonds paying 7% annual interest, plus monetary correction. The nominal amount of the bond is to be adjusted in accordance with variations in the wholesale price index for nonagricultural products, less 5%. The 5% reduction in the inflation adjustment is supposedly "equal to the average inflation rate experienced by the majority of countries with so-called stable currency."[75]

Why is the rate of inflation abroad relevant to the rate of monetary correction payable on internal debt obligations of the Argentine government?

---

2. The Development of Inflation Adjustments in Private Sector Lending

M. SIMONSEN, BRAZILIAN INFLATION: POSTWAR EXPERIENCE AND OUTCOME OF THE 1964 REFORMS

in *Economic Development Issues: Latin America* 261, 301-05
(Comm. for Economic Development Supplementary Paper No. 21, 1967)

A chronic and violent inflation obviously produces deep distortions in the credit

---

[71] For example, in January 1973 a one-year Readjustable Treasury Obligation was paying only 19.6 percent a year, versus 28.2 percent for a one-year bill of exchange and 22 percent for a three-year real estate bill. Conjuntura Econômica, Aug. 1973, p. 88.

[72] D.F.L. No. 357 of July 25, 1953.

[73] See Moreno, "Sistemas Legales de Reajustes en los Valores Monetarios," 2 *Rev. Der. Econ.* 57, 64 (No. 6) (1964). Another form of readjustable bond is issued for agrarian reform purposes. Class A bonds are readjusted annually in accordance with the official cost-of-living index; however, for the purpose of calculating the three-percent annual interest paid by these bonds, only half the readjustment is added to nominal value. See Thome, "Expropriation in Chile under the Frei Agrarian Reform," 19 *Am. J. Comp. L.* 489, 508 (1971).

[74] Decree No. 6590, 1962 Anuario de Legislación, p. 188.

[75] Law 19.978 of November 28, 1972.

market of a country. At the outset, it is the borrowers who first profit, since they pay back their borrowings in devalued currency. However, this so-called "debtor's profit" is eventually frustrated by the lenders, who begin to include inflation in their forecasts. They raise their interest rates in anticipation of further inflationary pressures. But since there often are legal ceilings on these rates, inflation drives the real and the nominal interest rates far apart.

In Brazil's case, a 1933 "Usury Law" prohibits loan contracts with interest rates of more than 12 percent a year. Though this is certainly a very high rate during periods of monetary stability, it obviously becomes ridiculously inadequate when the inflation rate reaches 50 percent or more. However, various devices have been used to get around the Usury Law. Lawyers and finance experts always find legal formulas to replace the words "loan" and "interest." They respect the form of the law, but disobey the content.

Aside from the legal problems involved, however, another problem arises with interest rates when a country goes into such a steep inflation as that experienced by Brazil. Forecasting the rate of inflation — and hence the interest rates that should be charged — becomes very difficult, particularly over fairly long periods of time. This naturally makes long-term lending extremely unattractive and cuts down the supply of money available for such loans. . . .

The interest on bank deposits, both demand and time deposits, is controlled by the monetary authorities and cannot exceed a very small limiting rate. Some banks used to pay additional interest rates to some long-term depositors, but this is an irregular operation which now tends to disappear. The natural consequence has been the almost complete disappearance of time deposits. These deposits, which in 1950 represented about one-fourth of total banking deposits, are reduced today to an extremely small fraction — less than 5 percent — of the total.

In making loans, the commercial banks until fairly recently, did obey the limits of the Usury Law, even though inflation already had reached 20 percent a year. Obviously, the banks could do this because they paid even smaller interest rates to their depositors. Lately, however, the barriers of the Usury Law have been wholly surmounted. This has been achieved by three main devices, sometimes in combination:

Under-the-table interest. This is the crudest device; it consists of charging extra interest without any accounting entries either in the bank's or the borrower's books.

Overcharge of banking fees. This is the most common device. Besides the interest rate, the bank charges the borrower several fees — for opening the account, for collection of bills, etc. Such fees (duly inflated) raise the actual interest rate far above the limits of the Usury Law.[76]

---

[76]The service fee collected by the Banco do Estado de Minas Gerais, one of Brazil's major banks, totalled 24% annually during the 1962-1967 period. This fee was openly collected and registered in all loans. Silveira, "Interest Rate and Rapid Inflation: The Evidence from the Brazilian Economy," 5 *J. Money, Credit & Banking* 794, 795 (1973). [Eds.]

Linked accounts. This device — the most sophisticated of the three — consists of tying a loan to a time deposit until the debt is paid off. The borrower takes out a loan much larger than he needs and deposits part of this money in the bank. Since the interest rate paid on such deposits is far less than the rate charged for the loan, the effective interest rate is far above that appearing in the contract. For the banks, this type of loan has the inconvenience of causing an increase in compulsory deposits, at the order of the Central Bank. Since the account of the bank deposits increases artificially, bankers naturally prefer to use the other devices.

The fact that banks charge effective interest rates far above the Usury Law is a question of supply and demand. It would be impossible to keep supply and demand in equilibrium if the interest rates, under inflationary conditions, were limited to the legal 12 percent. It must be said that the effective rates presently charged are still below the pace of inflation, which means that the real interest is negative. Also, the present rates are not sufficiently high to balance the supply and the demand for loans. Because credit is rationed, a certain margin of demand remains unsatisfied. It is obvious, however, that the situation would have been more unbalanced if the Usury Law had been effective.

Let us now examine the medium-term credit market. The demand for this type of credit has increased extraordinarily in recent years with the development of the consumer durable-goods and capital-goods industries, especially with the development of the automobile industry. These industries, in order to broaden their markets, had to turn to installment selling on terms up to 18 or 24 months. But commercial banks, because they were unable to attract time deposits, were not in a position to grant medium-term loans. After a certain period of difficulties, the problem was solved by the so-called "credit and finance companies" through the use of some perfectly legal devices to get around the Usury Law. These were successful in attracting medium term funds equivalent to time deposits.

The finance companies have developed two main methods of operation — participation accounts and bills of exchange (Letras de Cambio).

The first method consists of substituting participation-account partnership contracts for deposits and loans. Under the Brazilian Commercial Code, partnerships can be set up without the formalities required for other types of firms, which exempts these from the usual bureaucratic red tape. Above all, they are very flexible. In the formation of a participation fund, the finance company itself is the open partner and time depositors are the hidden ones. The resources of the fund are then used in new participation-account partnerships, in which the borrowers of the company are the open partners and the fund is the hidden one. In reality, there is only a change of label. Deposits and loans take the name of participation-account partnerships and the interest rates take the name of profits. This change of words, however, allows escape from the Usury Law regulations, because the earnings of participation-account partnerships are considered profit, not interest. Thus, finance companies are able to pay their depositors (officially known as "participants") interest rates around 40 percent a year. The borrower pays this rate, plus an extra amount to cover the expenses and a margin of profit for the finance company.

The second system, employing bills of exchange, is even more ingenious. The borrower exchanges promissory notes for bills of exchange drawn by him and accepted by the finance company.[77] The due dates of the bills of exchange are scheduled in such a way that before the due date of each an equivalent amount of promissory notes brought in by the borrower become due. Thus the finance company assures the payment of the bills it has accepted through the previous falling due of bills received by it. The company charges no interest for this operation — which would make no sense in this case — but merely an acceptance fee. Up to then, the borrower simply exchanged promissory notes for bills of exchange. However, since the bills of exchange are considered as securities it is possible to sell them at a discount in the capital market. Thus, the borrower keeps the money he requires. (In practice, a company that resells the securities buys them from the borrower and resells them to the public.)

For the purchaser of the security, interest is replaced by the discount thereof and, once again, this substitution allows escape from the Usury Law regulations. In this way, a one-year security that is resold for 74 percent of its nominal value (that is, with a 26 percent discount) assures the purchaser an implicit interest of 26/74, or 35.1 percent per year. The borrower, who exchanged his promissory notes for bills of exchange, indirectly pays this implicit interest rate, plus a series of taxes and commissions. . . .

Loans from finance companies can legally extend up to 24 months, though in practice they rarely exceed 18 months. While this solves in part the problem of medium-term credit, it does not touch the problem of long-term credit. With the exception of certain governmental institutions, such as the National Bank for Economic Development (BNDE), there is no available supply in Brazil of long-term loans.

D. TRUBEK, LAW, PLANNING, AND THE DEVELOPMENT OF THE BRAZILIAN CAPITAL MARKET: A STUDY OF LAW IN ECONOMIC CHANGE

Pp. 23-25
(Yale Law School Studies in Law and Modernization No. 3)
Reprinted from Bull., Nos. 72 & 73,
N.Y. Univ. Grad. School of Bus. Admin., April 1971

The *letra* [*de câmbio* or bill of exchange] seemed to have three basic disadvantages. First, it was based on a discount which reflected an *anticipation* of inflation. Despite the fact that real returns were consistently negative, the government seemed to feel that this technique built an inflationary bias into the system of finance. Secondly, the *letra* system increased the overhead costs of finance. While the *letra* substituted for

---

[77]Instead of promissory notes Brazilian firms often use the "duplicatas," a special bill tied to commodity sales, created by Brazilian commercial laws. [Footnote by Simonsen, renumbered.]

bank time deposits, it brought into being a costly parallel set of financial institutions. Finally, the *letra* provided only short term financing, while the government saw long-term finance as a necessity if industrial expansion was to be financed through the debt-asset system.

Minister of Finance Bulhões diagnosed the situation as follows:

> "Between 1960 and 1963, entrepreneurs invested relatively little and resorted heavily to credit.... The solution consists of reducing loans, and increasing corporations' own working capital and shareholder capital.... Firms heavily in debt must reduce loans in favor of an increase in share capital.... As long as we insist on basing the expansion of firms on short-term credit ... we can be sure that inflation will always be a danger and promising economic development a dream."

The government encountered serious obstacles to reforming these "distortions." The art of juggling the three goals adopted by the Castello Branco Government — stabilization, reform, and development — was a subtle one, and nowhere did it appear more difficult, nor more important, then in the field of corporate finance. In this area, all the goals seemed to interrelate, and yet measures designed to achieve one purpose might threaten the achievement of another.

Thus, the government believed that one of the main causes of the inflation had been an excessive expansion of short term credit to business; one major aim of stabilization policy, therefore, had to lie in reducing this credit. However, the government at the same time wished to increase the growth rate, and this required a rapid recuperation of industrial growth; yet the credit squeeze threatened to cut back production. Indeed, given the traditional reliance of many firms on government credit at negative interest rates, this policy could precipitate a serious recession.

The basic solution adopted to resolve this dilemma was to develop a *selective* credit expansion policy that would channel resources to the most important areas, and at the same time attempt to take selective fiscal measures that would increase the flow of personal savings to corporations through the capital market. Since achievement of the latter goal required structural reforms, the capital market policy reflected the merging of the government's three-fold efforts at stabilization, reform and development....

Thus a major aspect of the government's policy was to develop instruments and mechanisms which would increase the amount of savings elicited through the debt-asset system, and to assure that these resources would be channelled to business in the form of long-term debt or equity....

Many provisions of the [Capital Markets Law] eliminated legal barriers to market development. Typical and noteworthy among these were the authorization of monetary correction for debt instruments and bank deposits, and the introduction of authorized but unissued shares. Prior to the Capital Markets Law, lenders were not allowed to index loans to foreign currency or to the price level, nor to charge more than 12% interest. The *letra* circumvented these prohibitions, protecting the lenders against inflation, but could only be used for short-term loans. Thus the legal prohibitions were thought to create a bias in favor of short-term lending. The Capital Markets Law attempted to end that bias by authorizing monetary correction on loans over one year.

Another "distortion" caused by legal barriers were obstacles to issuance of *convertible debentures*. Brazilian company law did not permit companies to authorize shares prior to subscription. This deterred the creation of convertible debentures, since this instrument requires authorized but unissued stock which can be taken by debenture holders upon conversion. By allowing authorized but unissued shares, and explicitly sanctioning convertible debentures, the Capital Market Law attempted to remove another obstacle to long term corporate finance.

BRAZIL: LAW № 4.728 OF JULY 14, 1965
(THE CAPITAL MARKETS LAW)

Article 26 — Share corporations may issue debentures or obligations in bearer form or registered indorsable obligations with a clause of monetary correction, provided that the following conditions are observed:

I.   Period to maturity equal to or greater than one year;
II. Correction effected in periods of not less than three months in accordance with coefficients approved by the National Economic Council for the correction of fiscal obligations;[78]
III. Subscription by financial institutions specially authorized by the Banco Central, or placing in capital market through the intermediary of said institutions.

§ 1 — The issuance of debentures pursuant to the provision of this article shall have as a maximum limit the amount of the net worth of the company, established pursuant to the terms established by the National Monetary Council.

§ 2 — The National Monetary Council shall issue, for each type of activity, standards with regard to:

a) limit upon the issuance of debentures, observing the maximum established in the foregoing paragraph;
b) technical and economic-financial analysis of the issuing company and of the project to be financed with the resources of the issue, which is to be carried out by the financial institution which subscribes to or places the issue;
c) minimum coefficients or indices of earning capacity, solvency, or liquidity which the issuing entity is to satisfy;
d) stabilization of the debentures in the market by the financial institutions which participate in the placement.

§ 3 — The differences in principal amount resulting from the correction of the principal amount of the debentures issued pursuant to the provisions of this article do not constitute taxable income for income tax purposes, nor do they require the supplementing of the stamp tax paid upon the issuance of the debentures. . . .

---

[78] These are derived from the wholesale price index. [Eds.]

Article 27 — Companies with an economic purpose[79] may draw, issue or accept bills of exchange or promissory notes whose principal is subject to monetary correction, provided the following conditions are observed:

I.   Period to maturity equal to or greater than one year and within the maximum limit established by the National Monetary Council;
II. Correction pursuant to the coefficents approved by the National Economic Council for the correction attributed to Treasury Obligations;
III. They be destined for placement in the capital market with the acceptance or co-obligation of financial institutions authorized by the Central Bank.

§ 1 — The provisions of Article 26, § 3 apply to the monetary correction of the instruments referred to in this article.

§ 2 — The bills of exchange and promissory notes referred to in this article, shall contain the monetary correction clause in their text.

Article 28 — The financial institutions which satisfy the general conditions established by the Central Bank for this type of operation may assure monetary correction to deposits with a fixed term of not less than one year, and which are non-withdrawable during the entire term.

§ 1 — The rules approved by the National Monetary Council being observed, the financial institutions to which this article refer may contract loans with the same conditions of correction, provided that:

a) they are for a minimum period of one year;
b) the total of the corrected loans does not exceed the amount of the corrected deposits referred to in this article;
c) the total remuneration of the financial institutions in such transactions shall not exceed the limits established by the National Monetary Council.

§ 2 — The deposits and loans referred to in this article may not be corrected beyond the coefficients established by the National Economic Council for the correction of Treasury Obligations.

§ 3 — The differences in face amount resulting from the correction, pursuant to the provisions of this article, of the principle amount of deposits, do not constitute taxable income for purposes of income tax.

Questions

1. Is the monetary correction scheme set out in the Capital Markets Law fairer and more practical than the prior system of making an implicit allowance for inflation in the interest or discount rate?

2. Would your answer be any different if the corporation issuing the obligation with monetary correction were a public utility?

---

[79]This limitation excludes nonprofit or charitable enterprises. [Eds.]

3. Suppose a corporation wished to issue a convertible debenture with monetary correction. If you were a representative of the Central Bank entrusted with approving such a security, what kinds of provisions would you insist upon to protect creditors and shareholders?

4. Would a bond or note containing a monetary correction clause be a negotiable instrument under U.S. law? See McClintock, "The Probable Legal Consequences of Inserting Price-Index Claims in Long-Term Corporate Obligations," 18 *Hastings L.J.* 959, 967-71 (1967).

Note

The Capital Markets Law has had only limited success in two of its principal objectives: (1) increasing the length of periods for which credit is extended in Brazil and (2) instituting the use of credit instruments whose nominal instrument rate varied with the rate of inflation actually verified by the price indexes. Lenders are still reluctant to extend credit for more than a year or two, and the government has been forced to reduce the minimum period for monetarily correctible credit instruments from one year to six months. Brazilian borrowers have been reluctant to accept short-term loans whose costs are uncertain until the time set for repayment. Instead, they have preferred to pay pre-fixed monetary correction plus interest. There has been no rush to issue convertible debentures with monetary correction, partly because the Central Bank only recently issued regulations on the subject, and partially because of the complexity of such an endeavor. See generally, J. Chacel et al, *Correção Monetária* 114-17 (1970).

---

3. Housing Finance and Monetary Correction

Rapid urbanization and (in the case of Brazil) population growth, coupled with a lack of long-term credit and rent controls that deprived landlords of a fair return on investment, produced huge housing deficits in Argentina, Brazil, and Chile.[80] Chronic, severe inflation dried up most mortgage financing and savings deposits in these countries, forcing most home purchasers into self-financing arrangements, and placing ownership of a decent home beyond the reach of the bulk of the population.

Both Brazil and Chile have resorted to the use of inflation adjustments in the

---

[80] See generally Instituto de Investigaciones Económicas y Financieras de la CGE, "La Vivienda en la Argentina; Aspectos Económicos, *Estudios Sobre la Economía Argentina* (No. 2, Aug. 1968), p. 54, (No. 5, Aug. 1969), p. 66; Lefcoe, "Monetary Correction and Mortgage Lending in Brazil: Observations for the United States," 21 *Stan. L. Rev.* 106 (1968); Burke, "Law and Development: The Chilean Housing Program," 2 *Lawyer of the Americas* 173 (1970).

financing of housing. In an imaginative effort to stimulate the construction of desperately needed housing units, Brazil in 1964 organized a national housing system around the principle of monetary correction. A national housing bank (BNH) was set up to serve as a conduit for the investment and application of funds in residential housing. The BNH's resources are derived from a national pension fund (FGTS) administered by the bank, and by the sale of real estate bills to private investors. In addition, banks and other savings institutions are permitted to pay monetary correction as well as interest on deposits. These funds receive an annual return of about 7-8 percent plus tax-free monetary correction, calculated in accordance with coefficients derived from the wholesale price index. All borrowers were initially required to repay their loans with the same type of monetary correction, which was triggered every time the government changed the minimum wage (normally about once a year). However, before two years had elapsed the number of borrowers in arrears on their monthly mortgage payments had reached alarming proportions. One reason for the large number of defaults was apparent: the wholesale price index rose 76 percent from February 1964 to February 1965, while the highest minimum wage rose by only 57 percent. Consequently, the Bank adopted a program permitting low-cost housing loans to be readjusted on the basis of the percentage increment in the minimum wage, while retaining the wholesale price index as the yardstick for higher cost housing.[81]

To make up the difference between actual payments and what should have been paid if the original plan of monetary correction had been adhered to, the BNH readjusted the term of the mortgage. To meet the complaint that payments might go on forever, the Bank set a limit of one and one-half times the original mortgage term. To insure against possible losses resulting from this limitation on repayment obligations, the Bank set up a Compensation Fund for Salary Variations. Borrowers paid one monthly installment into the Fund in exchange for the Fund's guaranty to liquidate any balance remaining at the end of the expanded term of the mortgage.

There was great dissatisfaction with this scheme, and much of the dissatisfaction was psychological in origin. Low-income mortgagors had difficulty understanding the intricacies of a constantly shifting mortgage payment and term, and lacked the economic sophistication to comprehend the concept of monetary correction. In 1969 the Bank felt constrained to replace this program with the Plan of Salary Equivalence *(Plano de Equivalência Salarial).* Under this new plan, which is optional for borrowers, the maximum number of mortgage payments is fixed (though the borrower may prepay), and all payments to the Compensation Fund by the borrower are eliminated. The system of monetary correction for low-income borrowers is geared to the minimum wage. If wages rise faster than the wholesale price index over the life of the mortgage, the borrower will wind up paying more cruzeiros than he would have under the original program. But if the contrary trend continues, the Compensation Fund of the Bank will in effect subsidize the low-income borrower.[82]

---

[81] Banco Nacional de Habitações, Resolution No. 5/66.

[82] See BNH Resolution 36/69, discussed in 24 *Conjuntura Econômica* No. 3, p. 65 (March 1970) (Vol. 17, No. 3, p. 37 of the English language version).

Despite these difficulties, the Brazilian housing program has been extraordinarily successful in attracting funds and stimulating the construction of a vastly increased number of housing units. Part of the credit for the success of the housing program goes to much-needed reforms in the mortgage, civil construction, and rent control laws,[83] but a large part of the program's success stems from the monetary correction mechanism.[84]

Chilean DFL No. 2 of July 31, 1959 set up a housing system rather similar to Brazil's. The law created the concept of a savings quota bearing 3 percent annual interest plus an annual readjustment in accordance with the wage index.[85] Loan balances are also readjusted in accordance with the same index. But while Chile has been fairly successful in capturing savings,[86] the system, or perhaps lack thereof, has worked poorly.

Until recently, the government savings and loan system has been hopelessly confused and economically unsatisfactory. Over twelve different savings plans were available, at least in theory. Terms, interest rates, and down payments varied arbitrarily. Though savings was to be a major condition for obtaining a loan, the granting of loans was not in fact closely related to an aspirant's savings record. Loans did not constitute an effective response to the demand for housing. Finally, loans were not adequately tailored to meet the costs of borrowers.[87]

The system was restructured in 1967 to remedy some of these weaknesses, but some of the problems persist. One of the chief problems is the heavy default rate. It has been estimated that approximately 80 percent of the 150,000 borrowers are behind on at least one payment, and that the average arrearage is ten payments. Collection procedures are chaotic, and the government has thus far been politically incapable of insisting upon its mortgage rights.[88]

G. Inflation and Income Taxation

As was suggested at the start of this chapter, inflation frequently operates as an implicit tax, transferring wealth to a government from its citizens. Inflation also

---

[83] Lefcoe, *supra* note 80, at 112-14; Iorio, "A Correção Monetária nos Financiamentos Habitacionais Brasileiros" (translated as Monetary Correction in Brazilian Housing Loans), 12 *APEC, A Economia Brasileira e suas Perspectivas* 243, 249 (1973).

[84] *Id.*

[85] See Moreno, *supra* note 73, at 65-70.

[86] See Saavedra, "Key Factors in Chilean Economic Development," in *Economic Development Issues: Latin America* 59, 82-83 (Comm. for Economic Development Supp. Paper No. 21, 1967).

[87] Burke, *supra* note 80, at 353.

[88] *Id.* at 360-63.

distorts existing tax structures, and the failure to correct these distortions may produce a breakdown in the tax system, gross inequities, and severe misallocations of resources. This section explores the causes of these distortions, and the techniques which have been developed to correct them.

K. ROSENN, ADAPTATIONS OF THE BRAZILIAN INCOME TAX TO INFLATION

21 *Stanford Law Review* 58, 65-74 (1968)

Inflation-Induced Distortions of Business Income

Business income was traditionally computed for tax purposes in accordance with accounting conventions designed to reflect annual variations in a firm's financial position. In a stable economy these conventions would reasonably reflect a firm's economic variations, but in the context of the Brazilian inflation, application of these accounting conventions so greatly distorted the concept of taxable income that the income tax became, in real economic terms, a tax on capital as well as on income.

One of the principal sources of distortion stemmed from [inadequate] depreciation. . . . Fixed assets were valued at historical cost and annual deductions for depreciation or amortization were limited to a fixed percentage of the asset's historical cost. Assuming there had been no quality improvement, the sum of the deductions for depreciation over an asset's useful life plus salvage value should theoretically have permitted replacement of the asset. But computation of the depreciation deduction on the basis of historical cost during a severe inflation meant that a firm could depreciate during an asset's useful life only a small fraction of the amount necessary to replace it. Denial of a deduction for the difference between the historical cost depreciation allowance and the replacement cost created fictitious profits, because a firm was not allowed to write off fully its real costs. Moreover, inflation-induced underestimation of the salvage value produced another fictitious profit whenever an asset was sold.[89]

A second principal source of distortion lay in techniques of inventory valuation. The tax law has required that inventory be valued at the lower of original cost and current market value. Given Brazil's steadily rising prices, inventory has had to be valued at original cost. The Brazilian tax authorities have interpreted the law to permit the use of accounting techniques like FIFO (First In First Out) or average cost, but have refused to permit the use of LIFO (Last In First Out), which would have reduced

---

[89] Suppose a firm has an asset that it purchased for 100, with an estimated useful life of 10 years and an estimated salvage value of 10. Also suppose that the total rate of inflation during the 10-year period is 100 percent and that the asset's replacement cost varies directly with the inflation rate. If the asset were sold for 20 at the end of its useful life, the gain of 10 (the difference between the sale price and the salvage value) would have been considered at taxable income. Actually it represents a fictitious profit due to underestimation of the salvage value. [Footnote by Rosenn, renumbered.]

the overstatement of profits.[90] The taxation of profits resulting from appreciation of inventory prices imposed an unreasonably heavy tax burden on Brazilian firms; a certain amount of inventory must be maintained in every going concern, yet some firms might require a net liquidation of inventories in order to pay their tax liabilities.

A third source of distortion has been the use of the accrual method for reporting gains and losses. Though not required to by the tax law, most firms producing goods for sale have found it necessary to keep their books on an accrual basis. Time lags in the receipt of payment for goods will cause part of a firm's profits to be fictitious, though any harm will normally be offset by the time lags between receipt of income and payment of tax. Similarly, a firm receiving advance payments, such as a magazine publisher who receives a prepaid 5-year subscription, will underreport the real value of its income by allocating equal portions (perhaps less normal interest) over the entire period for which the advance payments are received.

A fourth source of distortion has been the tax law's failure to recognize that firms that maintained part of their assets in cash or its equivalent, or lent money at negative interest rates, suffered real losses from the inflation. In order to offset inflation's steady erosion of the real value of working capital, firms were constantly forced to transfer a portion of their normal profits to working capital. Nonetheless, tax law failed to allow a deduction for that portion of receipts applied simply to maintain working capital at its previous real level. Lending institutions or other credit firms frequently found themselves in the uncomfortable position of having lent money at an interest rate well below the inflation rate. Not only did the tax law fail to give such taxpayers a deduction for their real losses, but it taxed the nominal interest income as well. Conversely, firms able to borrow at real negative interest rates realized gains because of inflation. Yet the tax law failed to recognize this gain as taxable income, treating the nominal interest paid as a deductible expense.

Finally, the capriciousness of the incidence of inflation constituted another distortive element. Some firms were affected much more by inflation than others, producing inequitable discriminations in effective tax rates. For example, a firm whose fixed assets consisted primarily of machines that had to be replaced every few years was much more adversely affected by inflation than a firm whose fixed assets consisted primarily of land or buildings. Similarly, a firm that operated primarily with its own capital was more adversely affected by inflation than a firm that operated primarily with borrowed capital.[91] . . .

---

[90] Suppose a firm's entire inventory consists of three identical widgets purchased at different times and prices. The first was purchased at T_1 for Cr\$ 1,000; the second at T_2 for Cr\$ 2,000; and the third at T_3 for Cr\$ 3,000. It then sold one item at T_3 for Cr\$ 3,500. FIFO accounting would require a showing of a "profit" of Cr\$ 2,500 (Cr\$ 3,500 minus Cr\$ 1,000); average cost accounting would show a profit of Cr\$ 1,500 (Cr\$ 3,500 minus Cr\$ 2,000), and LIFO would show a profit of Cr\$ 500 (Cr\$ 3,500 minus Cr\$ 3,000). The first two accounting methods will clearly overstate profit, since the real cost of the product at T_1 is Cr\$ 3,000; this was its cost at T_1 in terms of T_3 cruzeiros, and this is the present cost of replacing the item. [Footnote by Rosenn, renumbered.]

[91] This would not be true if the borrowed capital had to be repaid in a hard foreign currency or was subject to a monetary correction clause. [Footnote by Rosenn, renumbered.]

Inflation-Induced Distortions of Personal Income

The taxable income of an individual in Brazil is the difference between his gross income and certain exemptions and deductions. Personal income taxation has also been seriously distorted by inflation, primarily due to: (1) the fixing of personal exemption levels and progressive tax brackets in nominal terms; (2) the taxation of negative interest income; and (3) the taxation of illusory capital gains from transfers of real property.[92] ...

Exemption levels and tax brackets must be continually adjusted to prevent inflation from making substantial changes in effective tax rates and thus distorting the allocation of tax burdens implicit in the legislative determination of such levels and brackets. But exemption levels and tax brackets were adjusted in Brazil only after intervals of several years, during which effective tax rates increased sharply. Even after adjustment, the new brackets and exemption levels generally failed to accompany the inflation rate. Similarly, real marginal tax rates on certain brackets more than doubled between 1951 and 1965. To be sure, this was, at least partially, a deliberate policy designed to increase tax receipts. But though one would expect corresponding increases in tax yields because of this theoretical elasticity, in practice real receipts from the personal income tax did not even increase proportionately with the nation's real income. This lag is largely attributable to increased evasion by upper bracket taxpayers and by the agricultural sector; this has further distorted the incidence of the income tax.

The second principal source of distortion of the personal income tax caused by inflation has been the taxation of negative interest income. Individuals suffered the same distortion as companies from the failure of the income tax to permit creditors to receive a deduction for receipt of negative interest income and to require debtors to recognize a corresponding gain. Individuals who reported interest income from the usual sources — bank deposits, government bonds, discount on *letras de câmbio*, ... — in almost all cases were taxed on illusory gains.

The third principal source of distortion stemmed from the capital gains tax imposed on net profits from the sale of real property by individuals. Though the Brazilian income tax normally does not tax individuals on capital gains, starting in 1946 an exception was made for the gains resulting from transfers of real property. . . . Real estate values rose rapidly during the inflation, producing substantial nominal profits on real estate transactions. However, in real terms most of the profit on these transactions was fictitious.

Distortion of Total Tax Receipts

The growth in real income and the sharp increases in effective tax rates since 1948

---

[92] Individuals are not taxed on gains from sales of capital assets in Brazil, with the temporary exception of gains from real estate transactions. This difference from American tax law apparently follows from the Brazilian concept of personal income as recurrent receipts from a productive source. *See World Tax Series, Taxation in Brazil* 107, 188-89 (1957). [Footnote by Rosenn, renumbered.]

should have produced a dramatic rise in tax receipts. However, the real increment in total receipts from the income tax amounted to even less than it would have if the rates had remained constant and the cruzeiro stable during these years.

In addition to providing a great spur to evasion, the income tax law also offered a great incentive to delay payment of taxes. Until November 1962 the penalty for delay in payment of taxes due was only 10 percent plus 1 percent a month interest, or a maximum of 22 percent in a year. Moreover, the total penalty, regardless of the number of years payment was delayed, could not exceed 50 percent of the tax owed. With the inflation rate averaging more than 30 percent between 1959 and 1961, one could realize a nontaxable gain of more than 8 percent a year by delaying tax payment. Even after 1962, when the 10 percent penalty was applied cumulatively every 6 months, the maximum penalty for delay totaled only 32 percent a year. With an inflation rate in excess of 50 percent by 1962, it remained profitable to borrow one's back taxes from the government.

The government was also hurt by the time lag between earning of income and payment of taxes. Taxes were not due until the following year when the cruzeiros in which they were payable were worth considerably less than the cruzeiros in which the income was earned. Although this loss was reduced somewhat by an increase in withholding levels, the withholding system itself generated further distortion. The withholding tax fell most heavily on the salaried middle-class and lower-middle-class groups, who were most seriously hurt by the inflation. The withholding system forced them to pay their income tax in current cruzeiros, while the higher income groups were able to pay their taxes in the cruzeiros of the following year. With inflation raging at more than 90 percent in 1964, the effective rate for income not subject to withholding earned in 1963 was reduced by as much as 45 percent by virtue of the time lag between receipt of income and payment of the tax. Thus, the effect of withholding provisions was to make the income tax less progressive by increasing the effective tax rates of lower and middle income groups relative to the higher income groups.

The Effects of Failure to Provide Inflation Adjustments

What were the consequences of inflation's distortions of real income? Most important was subjection of Brazilian taxpayers, both individuals and business firms, to unreasonably heavy tax burdens. This was particularly acute with regard to business income, which consisted principally of fictitious profits. A recent study by Werner Baer and Mario Simonsen showed that the great bulk of the reported profits of Brazilian firms have been illusory, existing only upon balance sheets. More than 43 percent of the reported profits of 20 large industrial corporations in 1962 could be attributed to nonaccounted-for depreciation. More than half the reported profits of some 7,000 Brazilian firms from 1958 to 1962 were attributable to the maintenance of the real value of inventories. Taxation of firms on these illusory profits meant a very steep effective tax rate, which increased with the inflation rate. In addition, an examination of the balance sheets of 2221 firms disclosed that these companies held 77 percent of their net assets in working capital. With an inflation rate of approximately 80 percent in 1963, these firms would have had to earn a net nominal profit after taxes of 61.6 percent on their assets (valued as of the beginning of the year) just to maintain the same real level of working capital. But to do so firms would have had to subject themselves to a very steep excess profits tax, rising as high as 50 percent on certain profits. Moreover, certain corporations were subjected to an additional 30 percent tax on increases in reserves in excess of their paid-in capital stock. Since a large percentage of gross receipts of a firm would be used to replenish working capital, and since receipts so used would be considered "profit," these amounts would appear as retained earnings on the liability side of the balance sheet and thus would be subject to this tax.

The unreasonableness of Brazilian tax rates impelled Tito Rezende, former Director of the Income Tax Department, to publish a series of 10 articles in 1962 in a São Paulo newspaper under the title "Fiscal Madness in Brazil." He demonstrated, *inter alia,* that an individual taxpayer in the highest progressive rate bracket was being subjected to an income tax amounting to 118 percent of his nominal income. Dr. Rezende also calculated that a corporation with a capital of Cr$10,000,000 that had earned Cr$25,000,000 of taxable income in 1961 would have a tax bill of Cr$27,916,000 (111.66 percent of taxable income) if all its shares were bearer shares and the entire profit were distributed. . . .   These unreasonably high levels of real tax rates exaggerated the predisposition of many Brazilian firms and individuals to understate their income for tax purposes. The tradition that one ought to pay taxes has never been firmly implanted in Brazilian soil, and the exorbitant real rates attributable to the inflation have served as both an incentive and rationalization for defrauding the taxing authorities.

Another by-product of the failure to permit inflation adjustments has been the decapitalization of Brazilian firms. Accountants generally maintained corporate books on the same nominal basis as required by the tax laws. Relatively few firms were aware of how large a percentage of their profits were illusory and unwittingly decapitalized themselves by unrealistic dividend policies. Payment of taxes on illusory profits helped speed the process of decapitalization. . . .

Still another effect of failure to provide income tax adjustments for inflation has been a noticeable lag in replacement of worn out or obsolete equipment. . . . To be sure, this phenomenon is not solely attributable to the income tax, but the failure of the tax law to provide business firms with adequate depreciation deductions has certainly been a contributing factor.

R. ALEMANN, ECONOMIC DEVELOPMENT OF ARGENTINA

in *Economic Development Issues* 1, 22
(Comm. for Econ. Develop. Supp. Paper No. 21, 1967)
[These paragraphs appear in reverse order in the original]

The deterioration in tax administration engendered a vicious circle. As tax evasion increased, the authorities, in need of ever-increasing amounts of money to counteract inflation, increased tax rates, tightened controls, and multiplied taxes – all of which did nothing except intensify tax evasion.

Tax ethics in Argentina, before inflation set in, were no better or worse than in the majority of the southern European countries, and perhaps they were better than in some of them. But as a result of the actions of the authorities, a feeling quickly spread that tax evasion was justified. The Argentine taxpayers became convinced that their only protection against a cheating government, which was debasing through inflation the value of their incomes and properties, was to use any method compatible with personal security to lower their contribution to the government.

BRAZIL: LAW № 4.357 OF JULY 16, 1964

Art. 3. Monetary correction of the original value of fixed assets of corporate bodies . . . shall be obligatory from the date of this law, in accordance with the coefficients established annually by the National Council of Economy, so that they express the variation in the purchasing power of the national currency, between the month of December of the last year and the annual average for each of the preceding years.

Paragraph 2. Within 90 (ninety) days from the date of this law, corporate entities must readjust their share capital by monetarily correcting the value of the fixed assets as shown in the last balance sheet.

Paragraph 3. The result of the monetary correction effected obligatorily each year, shall be shown as a separate account in the deferred liabilities . . . until capitalized. . . .

Paragraph 7. The income tax [upon revaluation gains] is reduced to 5% (five percent) and shall be paid in 12 (twelve) monthly installments.

Paragraph 8. Payment of the tax referred to in the preceding paragraph shall be dispensed with if the taxpayer prefers to acquire [Readjustable Treasury] Obligations . . . at a corrected nominal value corresponding to twice the amount of tax due. . . .

Paragraph 12. Bonds purchased under the terms of this article shall be nominative and nontransferable for a period of 5 (five) years. . . .

Paragraph 14. In calculating annual depreciation . . . for income tax purposes, the purchase value shall be considered the [monetarily corrected] original value of the assets. . . .

Article 7. Fiscal debts arising from failure to pay taxes, additionals or penalties on the due date and which are not effectively liquidated within the calendar quarter in which they should have been paid, shall have their value corrected monetarily in proportion to the variations in the purchasing power of the national currency. . . .

Paragraph 6. Fines and interest for delayed payment provided for in current legislation as a percentage of the fiscal debt, shall be calculated on the respective amount corrected monetarily under the terms of this article.

Paragraph 7. Taxpayers who settle their fiscal debts within 90 (ninety) days from the date this law takes effect shall enjoy a 50% reduction in the value of fines applied. . . .

Questions

1. To what extent does this law eliminate fictitious profits from taxation?

2. Is there any justification for requiring corporations to pay a five-percent tax on revaluation gains? Suppose a firm lacked sufficient liquid funds to pay the tax due upon revaluation?

3. One result of this law was an enormous increase in the nominal value of Brazilian corporations. From October 1964 through September 1965 monetary correction produced an increase in the capital of Brazilian firms of 4.4 trillion cruzeiros, which in nominal terms amounted to 137 percent of the total capitalization of all Brazilian corporations at the start of that period. Are there any practical consequences other than tax resulting from this revaluation?

4. What alternative method might have been employed to value fixed assets?

5. What techniques are being employed by the drafters of this statute to use the legal system to promote developmentally oriented behavior?

Notes

1. After more than a decade of occasional revaluations, Argentina has recently adopted the Brazilian approach and placed monetary correction of fixed assets for depreciation purposes on a permanent basis. Law No. 19409 of Dec. 31, 1971, as regulated by Decree 3225 of May 30, 1972, art. 70.

2. Chile has employed a much broader mechanism to eliminate taxation of fictitious profits, as the following statute reveals.

CHILE: LAW Nº 15.564 OF FEBRUARY 14, 1964

Article 35 . . . [Companies] declaring their actual income [in contradistinction to those taxed according to an estimate] shall adjust their net worth annually into current money in accordance with the variations experienced by the consumer price index between the month prior to the date of the balance sheet and the same month of the previous year. The consumer price index will be that fixed by the National Directorate for Statistics and Census. For the purposes of this provision, the taxpayer's net worth shall mean the equity which exists in his favor representing the difference between the assets and current liabilities in the respective balance sheet, without taking into account the profit or loss of the fiscal year, after previous deduction from assets of the intangible, nominal, temporary . . . items which do not represent actual investments.

The increase in value resulting from revaluation . . . will not be subject to tax and will be considered as net worth for all legal effects from the day following the date of the balance sheet, both in respect to the taxpayer and to the shareholder or partners, said difference in value being applied successively in the following order:

1. Revaluation of depreciable elements of fixed assets up to an amount equal to readjusting their net value in proportion to the time they have remained in the enterprise during the respective fiscal year, in accordance with the index referred to in the first subparagraph. However, when fixed assets include assets acquired with credits in foreign currency which are totally or partially unpaid, the value of the assets corresponding to the unpaid balance on the date of the balance sheet must be adjusted separately according to the rate of exchange in force on that date, instead of using the consumer price index. Said readjustment will not be applied to the amount of revaluation of net worth which is determined according to rules in the first subparagraph.

2. Revaluation of securities adjusted to the most recent stock exchange quotations given in the fiscal year.

If there has not been such a quotation during the fiscal year, the value of cost or acquisition duly realized of said elements will be revalued according to the index referred to in the first subparagraph.

3. Charge or deduction from profits for the same fiscal year up to the remaining balance of the revaluation of net worth, this charge or deduction not being permitted to exceed 20% of the net taxable income for the same year, calculated before effecting this operation.

The total of revaluation should be used to increase the operating capital of the enterprise; therefore, it should neither be distributed nor invested for purposes aside from the concern's operations, but may only be capitalized.

GRUPO DE ASESORES DEL MINISTERIO DE HACIENDA, LA REVALORIZACION

5 *Revista de Derecho Económico* 135, 140-141 (Nos. 19 and 20, 1967)

In effect, the Chilean method starts from the basis that revaluation ought to be conceded only insomuch as there exist actual investments in the firm. In other words, one considers that investment in assets effectuated by means of credits does not deserve revaluation in that whatever loss the firm suffers by not revaluing its assets will be compensated for by the gain realized in the form of a reduction in real terms of current liabilities. This result is justified by affirming that in an inflation the debtor benefitted while the creditor is prejudiced due to the diminution in the value of debts. As we shall comment on later, one cannot be certain of this general supposition.

If the limitation of 20% did not exist, and if the above mentioned supposition were correct, the Chilean system would represent a complete and effective revaluation. However, it is notorious that creditors in a chronic inflation protect themselves, exacting high interest at short terms such that debtors do not benefit from the inflation. In these circumstances one should not punish debtors by denying them revaluation of their assets. The result is that the Chilean system of revaluation has an impact that varies according to the relationship of net worth to the amount of fixed assets and securities which each firm has; hence some succeed in replacing losses suffered on debt items, inventories, and cash, while others cannot even though they have not enjoyed benefits stemming from inflation. For example, generally a service firm has few fixed assets so that any deduction from revaluation of net worth can be considered, in large part, as a recompense for losses in cash and debts. On the other hand, another firm which is industrial or commercial, is unable to take advantage of the same recompense because it first has to replace the devaluation of its fixed assets and inventory; that is to say, the industrial or commercial firm does not defend itself against inflation where debts and cash are concerned. The limitation of 20% avoids too great an exaggeration of this discrimination among sectors.

In 1966 Brazil adopted a law intended to eliminate balance sheet distortions and the taxation of fictitious corporate profits. Is it superior to the Chilean approach? Does it succeed in its objectives?

BRAZIL: DECREE-LAW № 62 OF NOVEMBER 21, 1966

. . . Art. 4. In balance sheets closed as of January 1st, 1967, companies obliged to maintain books of account may monetarily correct these accounts:

I – fixed assets and their respective funds for depreciation, amortization and depletion;

II – net worth . . .;

III – credits and obligations in foreign currency, or in national currency subject to correction by legal or contractual stipulation.

Art. 5. The monetary correction of the fixed assets shall be . . .

I – based on the monthly wholesale price indices . . .;

II – investments in shares or portions of the capital of other companies shall be monetarily corrected at their original acquisition cost, which shall not be altered in the case of receipt, without payments, of shares or portions distributed as dividends.

Art. 6. Net worth shall be monetarily updated in accordance with . . . coefficients which translate the variation of the purchasing power of the national currency between the month of the balance-sheet to be corrected and the month of the closing balance-sheet of the previous business period.

Art. 7. If the company has credits or obligations in national currency, the principal of which is subject to monetary correction in the terms of a legal or contractual stipulation, it shall register at the date of the balance-sheet, the monetary variations which may have occurred, in relation to the credit or debit balance at which they are registered.

Paragraph 1. If the company has credits or commitments in foreign currency, it shall register the variations in value in national currency, calculated at the rate of exchange in force at the date of the balance-sheet, observing the stipulation in the following paragraph.

Paragraph 2. The variations in accounts of the assets and liabilities shall be registered up to the limit of the increase in assets resulting from the correction, after the corrections of the account referring to net worth have been compensated.

Art. 8. The cross entries corresponding to the correction made in the accounts of the assets and liabilities shall be debited or credited to the account "monetary correction of the balance sheet."

Paragraph 1. The cross entry of the corrections of the fixed assets shall correspond to the net increase in the accounts of the assets resulting from the correction, after registration of the variations in the depreciation, amortization and depletion funds and deduction of the corrections or revaluations previously made.

Paragraph 2. If the final balance of the "monetary correction of the balance sheet" account is a debit, it may be transferred in whole or in part to the profit and loss account of the fiscal year.

Paragraph 3. The amount of the debit balance not offset by the profits of the fiscal year shall be transferred to the subsequent year or years, in the form of losses to be compensated.

Art. 9. If the final balance of the "monetary correction of the balance sheet" account is a credit, it shall be offset, obligatorily, by the losses of the financial year or those transferred from previous years which are pending compensation for tax purposes.

Paragraph 1. The credit balance not absorbed by the losses shall be added to the actual profit of the financial year, in an amount corresponding to the following values:

a) amount of the depreciation, amortization and depletion funds, calculated on the basis of monetary correction of the fixed assets and which have been registered as cost or expenditure in the business year;

b) monetary correction of the fixed assets sold during the business year and which have been computed as a cost of these assets in order to determine the profit earned on the transaction;

c) monetary correction or exchange adjustment of the credits referred to in Art. 7, corresponding to portions of the principal which have been effectively received during the financial year.

Paragraph 2. The additions to the actual profit shall be made successively, in the order of the letters of the preceding paragraph, up to the total of the credit balance of the "monetary correction of the balance sheet" account.

Paragraph 3. Any balance remaining after the additions to the profit referred to in the preceding paragraphs shall be transferred to the following financial year. . . .

K. ROSENN, ADAPTATIONS OF THE BRAZILIAN INCOME TAX TO INFLATION

21 *Stanford Law Review* 58, 90-92 (1968)

The basic principle underlying this statute [Decree Law No. 62] is that a firm operating with its own capital suffers a real loss from inflation, while firms fortunate enough to operate with the unprotected capital of third parties derive a real gain from inflation. These gains and losses within a firm should be offset against each other, and any balance should be added to or subtracted from taxable income. Normally, the higher a firm's equity ratio, the more valuable the deduction afforded by Decree Law No. 62.

The mechanics of Decree Law No. 62 may emerge more clearly by considering a simplified hypothetical balance sheet. Let us suppose a firm with the following balance sheet:

Assets	Liabilities
Cash (C)	Current liabilities (L)
Receivables (R)	Hard-currency loans (F)
Hard-currency credits (H)	Net worth (N)
Fixed assets (A)	

Let us further assume that the firm's fixed assets were all purchased on the date of the closing of the balance sheet for the prior year so that the coefficient of monetary correction *(c)* will be the same for the fixed assets and for net worth. Let us also assume the exchange rate differential *(e)* is the same for all the foreign loans and credits. The calculation of the *balancette* can then be represented by:

$$c(N - A) + e(F - H).$$

Since $N - A = C + R + H - L - F$, the amount that can be deducted or added to profits can, when one goes through the computations, be written as:

$$c(C + R - L) + (e - c)(F - H).$$

. . . If the firm has no deferred credits or deferred liabilities, the deduction permitted by Decree Law No. 62 will correspond to what is necessary to preserve working capital (in the traditional accounting sense of the difference between current assets and current liabilities) from inflationary erosion.

The balance sheet correction provided for in Decree Law No. 62 is obligatory for all mixed companies controlled by the government, but optional for all other corporations. . . .

[M]uch of the taxation of business firms on illusory gains stemming from inflation will be eliminated [by Decree Law No. 62]. Even distortions caused by the increase in replacement costs of inventories will be partially eliminated, for the annual correction for working capital will include amounts necessary to maintain inventory real values. Taxation on sales transactions, however, will still use historical cost as the basis in determining profits, but trying to correct values on inventory that is constantly turning over poses enormous practical problems.[93] Moreover, the heavy taxation of inventory gains may have been an important factor in explaining the failure of Brazilian firms to accumulate excessive inventory during many inflationary years. A more thorough and simpler method of eliminating taxation of these nominal profits would be the adoption of LIFO inventory accounting. The optional status of Decree Law No. 62 will also generate some inequities, for firms operating primarily with borrowed capital will find it disadvantageous to correct their balance sheets and will refrain from doing so. It would seem preferable to require all firms to make the calculations, despite the serious strains such computations are likely to place on accounting departments.

Notes

1. Regulations implementing Decree Law No. 62 were never implemented because of fear that revenue loss would be too great. The statute was substantially diluted by Decree-Law No. 401 of December 30, 1968, as amended by Decree-Law No. 433 of January 23, 1969, which permitted revaluation beyond the limits of monetary correction for land and construction components of corporate fixed assets upon payment of a tax of 15 percent of the additional revaluation, or purchase of Readjustable Treasury Obligations in double that amount. It also permitted deduction from taxable income of a reserve for the maintenance of a firm's "own working capital" free from monetary depreciation, but conditioned this deduction upon purchase of non-transferable Readjustable Treasury Bonds in an amount equal to 15 percent of the deduction taken during fiscal years 1969 and 1970, and limited use of this deduction to a maximum of 20 percent of the income tax that would have otherwise been payable.

2. Failure to permit asset revaluation in the course of protracted inflation has been particularly pernicious for public utilities in countries such as Brazil where rates have been calculated as a percentage of historical cost. The extremely low returns offered by these utilities have made it hard to attract new funds needed for expansion, while

---

[93] During the Fourth Republic, France permitted business firms to reduce the value of their inventories (and thus taxable profits) by an amount corresponding to the cost of replenishing at current prices inventories necessary for the continued functioning of the firm. This inflation adjustment for essential inventories generated a host of administrative problems concerning the essentiality of inventories and was strongly criticized for permitting large quantities of real income to escape taxation. *World Tax Series, Taxation in France* 312-13 (1966). [Footnote by Rosenn, renumbered.]

inadequate depreciation allowances have made internal financing of expansion equally difficult. One result has been frightfully poor utility service. Electrical, telephone, and train service in Brazil during the 1960's has been charitably described as "deplorable."

Another result is more subtle. This short sighted attitude toward public utility control can also contribute to an inflationary spiral. As Professors Cavers and Nelson explained:

> (1) Control of utility prices results in a lag behind the general price inflation. This makes outside financing both more necessary and more difficult; as the lag increases, it finally produces operating deficits. (2) These industries are then transferred to the public sector of the economy if the operating deficits are hopeless; at least the public sector must provide expansion funds if the industry cannot. (3) The spread between prices charged by these industries and other prices continues or even widens, thereby reducing the internal flow of expansion funds or increasing deficits. (4) Funds to meet deficits and for expansion are obtained in part or entirely by the creation of new money and new bank reserves. (5) This further stimulates inflation and pushes still other public utility enterprises over the brink. *Electric Power Regulation in Latin America* 43-44 (1959).

Though Brazilian governments prior to 1964 refused to modify legislation calculating the basic rate structure on historical cost, principally because of fear of adverse political reaction, they appeared quite willing to accommodate the large foreign-owned power companies by permitting additional rates for increased operating expenses, preferential foreign exchange rates for debt service and profit remittance, and government loans at increasingly negative interest rates. The fascinating story of this subsidization by subtrefuge is carefully told in J. Tendler, *Electric Power In Brazil: Entrepreneurship in the Public Sector* 43-79 (1968).

The military regime of Castelo Branco, which was not so concerned about political popularity, openly permitted the power companies to adjust their cost bases and depreciation reserves for inflation. Decrees No. 54.936, 54.937, and 54.939 of November 4, 1964.

Questions

1. Is it fair to permit inflation adjustments for business income but deny them for personal income?

2. Are inflation adjustments for personal income administratively feasible?

3. Does the use of inflation adjustments in a progressive income tax make the tax structure more regressive or progressive?

4. Does the use of inflation adjustments make the tax structure more equitable?

5. Do inflation adjustments necessarily neutralize the countercyclical stabilizing effect of a progressive income tax?

In answering the questions above, consider the following comment.

COMMENT, INFLATION AND THE FEDERAL INCOME TAX

82 *Yale Law Journal* 716, 718-20, 738-43 (1973)*

It would be impractical, however, to adjust for the precise amount of inflation which might have occurred between the purchase and sale of an asset.[94] One possible approximation would be to account for all inflation which occurred during the year of purchase, and to ignore all inflation during the year of sale, regardless of the particular dates of the two transactions. This system would, however, be subject to abuse[95] and therefore inflation during a particular calendar year should be accounted for only if the property was held by the taxpayer throughout the year.

Thus, if stock purchased for $1000 is sold for $1200 after fifteen percent inflation has occurred, $1150 of the sale price represents approximately the same value as did $1000 in the year of purchase and so merely restores the taxpayer's original cost. Only the remaining $50 would be taxable. More generally, taxable gain on any such transaction could be computed by use of a "floating basis" which would increase on the last day of each taxable year by the rate of inflation during the preceding year, as long as the taxpayer had held the asset during the entire year. This basis would thus at any given time reflect the approximate recovery cost of the original asset. An asset purchased for $A would therefore have a basis of $A(1+i) after a total of i percent inflation, and a sale for $B at that time would result in a taxable gain of $B−A(1+i). This gain will be called the *net property gain*.

This new adjusted basis would be used for many purposes other than the calculation of gain. For example, even if the nominal sale price of an asset exceeds its nominal cost, a real loss has occurred if the former is less than the inflated basis, since the increase in price has not been sufficient to compensate for inflation. . . .

[I]nflation does have a greater effect on property gains (which include capital gains) than it does on wage income. The net property gain figure is in nominal dollars

---

*Reprinted by permission of The Yale Law Journal Company and Fred B. Rothman & Company.

[94] Because of the large number of items that must be sampled, actual calculation of day-to-day inflation would not be feasible. In any event, the daily figure would be meaningless because its inherent inaccuracy would certainly dwarf the magnitude of the daily changes in the figure.

Both problems could be avoided by the allowance of a pro rata adjustment to the annual inflation figure, based on the exact number of days during the particular year that an asset was held. Alternatively, a quarterly or semiannual adjustment could be allowed. In fact, depreciation during the year of purchase of an asset is now based on the "half year convention." . . . [Footnote in original, renumbered.]

[95] An asset purchased on December 31 and sold for the same price the next day would give the taxpayer a loss measured by the inflation during the entire preceding year. [Footnote in original, renumbered.]

of the year the asset is sold, with the same value as an equal amount of wage income received during the same year. . . .

Inflation Neutrality and Tax Policy

Although many of the proposed technical adjustments which correct for inflation may be administratively feasible, there are other more important grounds for evaluating such a thorough revision of the Code. This section will suggest some of the effects inflation neutrality would have on horizontal and vertical equity, revenue yields, and macroeconomic stabilization.

Two preliminary observations should, however, first be made. The present system clearly allows Congress to increase taxes by inaction, since the real tax burden increases every year for which Congress does not lower tax rates. Of course, Congress does periodically adjust brackets so as roughly to cancel out the real increases in tax burdens due to inflation; but these periodic revisions are enacted with great fanfare as "tax cuts," even though they may merely cancel years of hidden tax increases. An inflation-neutral system should therefore enhance the accountability of government for both tax increases and reductions, since all enactments would then be in real terms. The second point is simply that the effects of the present system are haphazard. If some of the effects of inflation were deemed desirable, they could be achieved more equitably by annual amendments of a real tax system. But few presently concern themselves with the obscure — but very real — effects of inflation.

Horizontal Equity

The basic argument for relying on real rather than nominal income rests on the concept that individuals with the same real income should be taxed at the same real rate. Because of its reliance on nominal dollars, the present system fails to meet this condition in two respects. First, an individual with a constant real income may be taxed at different rates at different points in time. Moreover, measurement of income in nominal terms produces inequities between individuals having identical real incomes at the same point in time. For example, two taxpayers with the same real income will be taxed differently depending on their relative indebtedness. Similarly, taxpayers who own property may have their real income overstated because present depreciation and the calculation of gain or loss is based on historical cost. . . .

Vertical Equity

Here the basic issue is whether a system of real income taxation enhances the progressivity of the Code. This question will require analysis of the various components of income.

Inflation theoretically results in a more regressive tax structure. This is true because the marginal rate of taxation increases with taxable income at a diminishing rate, and thus the real tax burden on individuals in the upper brackets does not increase as rapidly as that on those in the lower brackets. At the extreme, an individual who pays no tax on a nominal income of $2000 will face an infinite increase in his real tax burden when inflation draws him into the taxpaying ranks. To the extent, then, that a system of real income taxation would prevent taxpayers from being pushed into higher brackets by illusory income gains, the benefits would be distributed inversely with the size of taxable income, and the progressivity of the income tax would be enhanced.

However, real income taxation might in other ways increase the regressivity of the Code. This redistributional effect would be caused by the relative holdings by different income groups of monetary assets, capital assets, and depreciable property. Indeed, it may well be that the rich would be the chief beneficiaries of a system of real income taxation.

The poor hold a smaller proportion of their wealth in net monetary assets (*i.e.,* debt claims against others, less indebtedness) than do the rich, and thus gain relative to the rich from inflation. An inflation-neutral system of income taxation would reduce this redistributional effect of inflation by according the rich greater loss deductions.

Similarly, net capital gains as a percentage of total income increases for higher income classes. Some commentators, recognizing this fact, have justified the present system's taxation of illusory capital gains as a type of wealth tax which enhances progressivity.

Unless the preferential rates accorded to long-term capital gains were withdrawn, the chief beneficiaries of the floating basis adjustment would be upper income taxpayers who hold most capital assets. . . . Finally, the use of a floating basis adjustment will increase the annual depreciation allowances for accelerated as well as straight line depreciation. Accelerated depreciation will therefore be even more "accelerated" than at present, and the economic distortions inherent in the use of such methods will be magnified. It should be emphasized that mere superimposition of the floating basis system on the present methods of computing depreciation will overcompensate owners of depreciable assets whenever there is a positive *real* interest rate, *i.e.,* a market interest rate greater than the rate of inflation. Furthermore, the overcompensation is greatest for accelerated depreciation methods. The implications for vertical equity are clear, because the benefits of accelerated depreciation again accrue primarily to the rich and to corporations. It therefore appears that if the floating basis adjustment for depreciation were adopted, it should be accompanied by some limitation on the use of accelerated depreciation.

Revenue Effects

Under the present system, the tax liability of each taxpayer, and hence aggregate federal tax revenues, increase annually in real terms. Three recent econometric studies have estimated that a one percent aggregate increase in adjusted gross income will increase federal tax revenue by approximately 1.4 percent. But the proposed system of real income taxation will result in revenues increasing at just the rate of inflation, thereby remaining constant in real terms, for increases in total income which are not due to real economic growth. It is not clear whether the prices of goods and services purchased by the government have increased at a rate faster than the rate of overall inflation. If they have, annual real tax increases may be necessary in order for the government to maintain the present level of services; even if the costs of government increase no faster than the overall rate of inflation, annual real tax increases will be necessary for any expansion. The present rapidly increasing demand for public services, as indicated by the federal budget which is rising much faster than the rate of inflation, seems to indicate that for one reason or another the real costs of government are increasing.

This, in itself, does not decide the issue for or against a system of real income taxation. Any of the revenue losses under such a system could be recovered by increasing tax rates. The critical issue is whether the political difficulty of obtaining congressional approval for such explicit tax increases, when combined with a need for increasing revenues, justifies a system of hidden annual increases.

Still, the magnitude of the revenue "lost" through an inflation-neutral system should not be underestimated. Only one change among all those proposed — the reduction of the interest deduction to reflect income from reduced real debt obligations — would increase tax yield; revenue losses would result from all the other proposed changes. An important loss would arise from the fact that an inflation-neutral system would increase a host of fixed dollar deductions, exemptions, and exclusions as well as the widths of marginal rate brackets. Although the size of any particular exemption, deduction, or exclusion may only increase by a small amount per individual taxpayer, the aggregate sums may be quite large. . . .

Macroeconomic Stabilization

A progressive income tax is one of the major tools of government fiscal policy. It is often called an automatic stabilizer because it cushions fluctuations in national income. During periods of boom, tax revenues rise more rapidly than aggregate income, thus dampening aggregate demand. Recession, on the other hand, automatically moves the budget toward greater deficits and fiscal stimulus as revenues fall.

Real income taxation has been criticized because it will reduce this effect of the tax structure: Tax yields will not rise as quickly as they do now from inflationary shocks, nor will they fall as rapidly in periods of recession.

While this criticism is somewhat valid, the importance of automatic stabilizers should not be exaggerated. The built-in flexibility of the Code can only reduce a small fraction of the fluctuation in aggregate income. Discretionary fiscal and monetary policy will still be necessary to achieve the proper balance of full employment and moderate inflation.

It should also be remembered that a system of real income taxation remains a progressive income tax system. The progressivity of the income tax system, however, will be maintained in real rather than nominal terms. Exogenous shocks to the economy will still generate increasing real tax revenues which will partially offset aggregate fluctuations.

A system of inflation-neutral taxation may even aid in the pursuit of macroeconomic objectives. There is some evidence that constant real rates might reduce the short term pressure of wage inflation: Wage earners who are assured that their net after-tax real take home pay will not be eroded by higher real tax rates should not have as great an incentive to make exorbitant wage demands.

H. Wage and Price Controls

Law has frequently been utilized as an instrument to combat inflation. There are a wide variety of stabilization measures that rely on the force of law for implementation. Standard stabilization techniques such as increasing tax revenues and contracting credit have already been referred to in prior sections. More controversial, but nevertheless frequently employed, are direct controls over wages and prices.

A glance at tables 2 and 3, *supra,* suggests that wage and price controls, which have been used extensively in Argentina, Brazil, and Chile, have had little success in damming the inflationary tide. Price controls have been widely circumvented and evaded. Political pressures to permit wages to rise at least as fast as the cost of living have been exceedingly difficult to resist. Black markets and shortages have been common by-products of the attempt to control prices by governmental decree.

But this does not mean that controls have been wholly ineffective. The reported rates of inflation might have been much higher in the absence of such controls. And the patterns of income distribution and allocation of resources would have been quite different. This section briefly explores some of the results of wage and price controls in South America.

S. MORLEY, THE ECONOMICS OF INFLATION

Pp. 137-38 (1971)*

Almost inevitably comments about the wisdom of some form of government intervention in price and wage setting arise during an inflation. The rationale for these comments is the identification of rising prices as the cause of inflation. To stop the inflation, therefore, the government need only decree the end of price increases. This confuses the symptom with the cause. As Milton Friedman has stated, it is as if the doctor attempted to cure a patient's fever by stopping the mercury in the thermometer from rising. Yet it is possible that the rise in prices in response to excess demand could be moderated by some form of price-wage guidelines or controls.

What we mean by a wage-price policy is some intervention by the government to force labor and management to make decisions they would not otherwise have made.

---

*Reprinted by permission of the Dryden Press.

Consider the difficulties in applying such a policy. The government has to know what the appropriate price should be and how it should change over time. Suppose, for example, that the government had set a target rate of inflation of 4 percent. Does this mean that all prices should be rising by 4 percent? Not at all. If there is any real growth going on in the economy, some products are expanding. Even in the absence of any greater than normal price increases in the raw material costs or wages, prices may rise in the industry because of diminishing returns. How much they rise depends on just how hard it is to expand output. In a growing economy the demand for different products grows at different rates, and the ability to supply that increased demand varies with industries. The government would have to know each industry's supply curve to determine the justifiable price increase it should be granted. Another problem immediately comes to mind. What signal does the market have for raising output other than profits? If demand rises in an industry, prices are raised, profits increase, and business in that industry is prompted to expand its facilities and to increase its output. The short-run rise in prices is the legitimate signaling device of the market economy by which more output will later be supplied. If the government short-circuits the signal, no extra output will be forthcoming. This is all right if government sets the right price. If it sets one that is too low, the substitute for inflation is a smaller total output and perhaps rationing. One sees examples of this in public utilities and cities with rent controls. Prices set at artifically low levels have created long-run shortages in electric power, natural gas, and housing.

---

1. Wage Controls in Chile

E. M. BERNSTEIN, WAGE-PRICE LINKS IN A PROLONGED INFLATION

6 *International Monetary Fund Staff Papers* 323, 349-51 (1958)

Wage and salary adjustments, usually in the form of massive increases for large classes of employees, have been made periodically in Chile. The primary purpose of the adjustments has been to compensate for increases in the cost of living. For example, at the time of exchange reform of July 1953, legislation was adopted to compensate for the rise in the cost of living expected to result from the depreciation of the import rate for foodstuffs and other cost of living items. The legislation also extended the system of family allowances for workers. Massive adjustments of wage rates were made in 1954 and 1955 in an attempt to compensate for the price rises of 1953 and 1954.

Legislation existing in 1955 provided for the periodic adjustment of salaries of white-collar workers and government employees by amounts corresponding roughly to the increase in the cost of living during the previous year. Salary adjustments generally were made in January each year. The mechanism of the wage and salary revisions differed for (1) manual workers in industry, commerce, mining, and services, (2) white-collar workers in the private sector, and (3) government employees. Agricultural workers usually received annual adjustments in January; these adjustments were measured roughly by the revision each year of the minimum wages fixed by legislation. For employees in the private sector, yearly revisions were made in the minimum wage legislation. Nonagricultural laborers generally obtained, at the expiration of their collective contracts, a wage adjustment commensurate with the increase in the cost of living during the previous year. Some workers in the private sector (particularly employees of some of the larger mining companies) also had contracts providing for automatic wage revision when the cost of living index rose more than a certain percentage – generally 5 per cent – in any month. Government workers were entitled to salary increases of 25-90 per cent (the percentage depending on the level of their salaries) of the estimated rise in the cost of living index during the previous year. Each adjustment in wages and salaries resulted in a similar increase in the amounts of social security contributions paid by employers and the Government in certain fixed percentages of total wages.

Early in 1956, steps were taken, as part of a comprehensive exchange reform and stabilization program, to break the wage-price spiral. Under the previous law requiring automatic increases in salaries and wages, an increase of about 80 per cent was due in 1956, based on changes in the cost of living. This law was abrogated, however, and on January 23, 1956 the Congress approved a new law limiting automatic wage and salary adjustments.

CHILE: LAW 12.006 OF JANUARY 20, 1956

Article 1. The general readjustment of salaries for all public or quasi-public . . . employees during 1956 shall not exceed 50%, nor be less than 44% of the rise in the cost of living, as determined by the Central Bank and the National Statistical Service for 1955 and the first two weeks of January, 1956.

If these indices are different, their average shall be used.

For the purposes of this provision, salary shall be understood to include all types of remuneration that is readjustable in accordance with existing legislation.

Employees whose salary is paid in gold or foreign currency shall not benefit from this readjustment.

Article 2. The minimum wage *(sueldo vital)* for 1956 shall be that prevailing on December 31, 1955, increased by 50% of the rise in the cost of living, calculated in accordance with the provisions of article 1.

Article 3. During 1956 . . . [governmental and nongovernmental employees], as well as persons receiving retirement pay or pensions . . ., who have no governmentally recognized dependents, shall receive only two-thirds of the increase provided for in this law. . . .

Article 4. The daily wages of governmental . . . laborers shall be readjusted by a percentage equivalent to 50% of the increase in the cost of living, as calculated in accordance with article 1.

The daily wages of laborers in private industry and commerce shall be readjusted, at the date of expiration of their respective contracts, by a percentage equivalent to 50% of the increase in the cost of living determined by the Central Bank and the National Statistical Service for the period governed by said contracts. . . .

These provisions shall not apply to firms which have had a system of readjusting wages for the increase in the cost of living and which have increased the remuneration of their laborers by more than 50% of the rise in the cost of living during 1955 and the first two weeks of January, 1956. . . .

Article 9. The President of the Republic is authorized to increase gradually during 1956 the present family subsidy for laborers up to 1800 pesos per dependent. . . .

Article 11. During 1956 the prices fixed for articles of primary necessity and habitual use or consumption on November 16, 1955, may be increased only by Supreme Decree agreed upon by the ministers of the Treasury and Economy, upon prior study of costs, general expenses, and legitimate profits. . . .

The price increases authorized in conformance with the preceding paragraphs may not exceed on any single article a total of 40% of the price in effect on November 16, 1955, with the exception of imported articles or those whose manufacture requires imported raw materials, or which exceed the above limit for other reasons.

The President of the Republic is authorized to subsidize articles of primary necessity with funds derived from exchange rate differentials. This compensation shall be made directly or through an increase in family allowances. . . .

Article 13. The rents of offices and commercial and industrial locations cannot be increased during 1956 over the levels in force on November 16, 1955.

During 1956 urban housing rents may not be increased by more than 5% of the rent in force on November 16, 1955. . . .

Article 16. Those responsible for sales at prices in excess of those fixed in accordance with this law shall be punished by fine and . . . [in the case of third offenders] imprisonment. . . .

Article 22. Starting December 31, 1956 every disposition which establishes a legally required system of readjustment for wages, salaries, and pensions, with the exception of benefits corresponding to years of service, is repealed. . . .

Article 26. The provisions of this law shall apply as of January 1, 1956. . . .

Questions

1. Does this law seem an equitable and rational technique for breaking Chile's wage-price spiral?

2. In what ways is the Chilean government here utilizing the formal legal system? What advantages does the legal determination of wage and price levels have over market determination?

3. Paradoxically, the pre-existing Chilean system of annual mandatory wage increases of 25-90 percent of the prior year's increase in the cost of living for all civil servants had been justified "on two fairly convincing anti-inflationary grounds: (1) In previous years, pay increases had often exceeded cost-of-living increases and to hold them to percentages reaching only up to 90 percent of such increases was considered

helpful; and (2) the Minister of Finance had been spending such a grotesque proportion of his time on resolving continuous salary demands of civil servants that he had been unable to concentrate on the task of fighting the inflation."[96]

To what extent is Law 12,006 likely to exacerbate these problems in the following year?

4. Brazil's post 1964 wage stabilization has been built upon a general formula designed to yield a real wage equal to the average real wage during the preceding two years, plus an additional amount corresponding to a productivity increase. The nominal wage paid in each of the preceding 24 months prior to readjustment is multiplied by the corresponding price index coefficient for that month to determine the average real wage. Since inflation was expected to continue after readjustment, thereby immediately starting the erosion of real purchasing power once again, the formula also provided for a further salary increase of one-half the amount of inflation forecast for the next twelve months. Does this seem like a fairer and more rational approach than that used by Chile in 1956?

SINDICATO INDUSTRIAL DE OBREROS "LABORDE HNOS' "

Supreme Court of Chile
53 R.D.J. 15 (2d Part, Section 3, 1956)

1. On December 30, 1955 an arbitral award ended a labor dispute between the Laborde Brothers Company, a shoe manufacturer, and the Industrial Workers Union of the firm. Among other things the award provided: "Wages . . . shall be increased by 80 percent," and "This award shall govern for a year starting as of January 1, 1956."

. . . [T] he union asks this Court to declare articles 4 (clause 2) and 26 of Law 12,006 . . . inapplicable to it on the ground that these articles are contrary to article 10 (10) of the Constitution.[97] . . .

2. The asserted inapplicability of those provisions is based on the theory that they "would establish a retroactive limitation on the increase in remuneration accorded by the aforesaid arbitral award and the deprivation of the rights of the workers of the

---

[96] A. Hirschman, *supra* note 10, at 186-87.

[97] The Chilean Constitution at that time provided:

Article 10. The Constitution ensures to all inhabitants of the Republic: . . .

(10) The inviolability of all property without distinction.

No one can be deprived of property under his control, nor of any part thereof, nor of any right which he may have therein, except by judicial pronouncement or by expropriation for public purpose, in accordance with law . . . .

The exercise of the right of property is subject to the limits or rules required for the maintenance and progress of social order, and in this sense, the law may impose obligations or servitudes for public use in the general interest of the State, of the health of its citizens, and of public welfare. [Eds.]

union to receive their entire wage increase." These rights are alleged to have been incorporated in the patrimony of the workers since the date of the arbitral award, December 30, 1955, despite its not being enforceable until the following January 1. These are personal rights or credits according to article 578 of the Civil Code, and article 583 of the same text bestows on their possessors a kind of property, protected by the guarantee of Article 10 (10) of the Constitution, [which preserves] the inviolability of all property without distinction. Furthermore, it is alleged that the right was acquired on December 30, 1955, or in any event, on January 1, 1956, when article 625 of the Labor Code, which made an arbitration award binding on the parties . . . was in force. At that time Law 12,006 had not been enacted; . . . hence, the retroactive application of the legislative mandate represents a deprivation prohibited by the Constitution.

3. In accordance with the provisions of article 86 of the Constitution, upon which this appeal is based, this tribunal is responsible for determining whether articles 4 (clause 2) and 26 of Law 12.006 are contrary to the constitutional precept.

4. The first of these . . . is one more of the numerous laws which readjust wages to the conditions of life, today imposing a maximum limit, just as previously they established a minimum wage for workers and a minimum salary for employees. The manner in which this new provision would contravene the right of property is unstated. . . .

5. It has been said and repeated often that the nonretroactivity of the civil law is not a constitutional norm, and therefore, a legal provision is not by itself inapplicable just because it is retroactive; however, it can be nonapplicable if it contravenes the right of property. . . .

6. Law 12.006 is a body of provisions . . . intended to confront the problem of inflation. It deals with a complex of factors which determine the increase in the cost of living. . . . On one hand, it tries to brake increases in wages, salaries, pensions, subsidies, etc., while on the other hand, it tries to do the same for the prices of goods of primary necessity, food, housing, clothing, and others. The law takes things in the state in which it finds them; it does not try to give or take from some to benefit others. It does not interfere with relations between capital and labor, nor modify the *status quo* in that respect. It takes from everyone — capitalists, workers, producers, and consumers — what it deems necessary to achieve its purpose. . . .

As a natural consequence of these provisions, it is hoped that although wages and salaries may be numerically less, in reality they will be equal, and that in the long run [these provisions] will benefit everyone. . . . The basis of the law is a balance of burdens; far from affecting any right guaranteed by the Constitution, the law is tailored to its mandates.

7. The plaintiffs allege that they have previously obtained a higher wage increase for the following year, an increase which they are being deprived of in violation of a constitutional rule.

This allegation is not entirely correct. The shoe workers will not be deprived of their entire raise, but only of that portion inconsistent with the legislative mandate, that is, that in excess of 46.5 percent of their prior wage. But this does not contravene the Constitution, because there are no acquired rights in the face of public order. The general ordering of society directed towards the fulfillment of essential goals admits of no interference from other interests and requires the immediate execution of the new law, over all other rules.

The authors are explicit in these respects. "Confronted with the exigencies of public order," says Josserand, "private interests must give way. One cannot value acquired rights which oppose public order. In such case, neither can one speak of the retroactivity of a law; . . . in conformity with social necessities, one applies it immediately, without anything more . . . ." (Civil Code, Vol. I, page 81).

8. Just as the shoe workers claim that the day before or 23 days before they had acquired a right which must be respected, by analogy it would be valid for all the salaried workers in the country . . . [to claim] that they had acquired rights in prior years to greater readjustments than article 22 of the new law accorded them. To admit the appellants' claim would create an unjust discrimination between the great bulk of the workers and a benefitted few, which would constitute a privilege for the latter that no constitutional norm can support.

9. . . . Even if the law had affected acquired rights, it would not for this reason be inapplicable, for the Constitution authorizes burdening citizens with direct or indirect public obligations. This provision permits depriving the appellants of their excess readjustment . . . without curtailing the inviolability of private dominion.

For these reasons . . . the appeal [of the union] . . . is rejected.

Questions

1. Is the Court's opinion unnecessarily broad? Does it amount to a disclaimer of the power of judicial review?

2. If real property rights had been cut off by retroactive legislation, do you expect that the Court would have written a very different opinion?

---

2. Rent Control in Brazil

K. ROSENN, CONTROLLED RENTS AND UNCONTROLLED INFLATION: THE BRAZILIAN DILEMMA

17 *American Journal of Comparative Law* 239, 241-42, 244-51, 267 (1969)

. . . Rent control was reinstituted as a wartime emergency measure freezing all residential rentals at the levels in force at the end of 1941. All expiring leases were extended and eviction was limited to cases of nonpayment of rent, breach of an important contractual obligation, or the landlord's retaking the premises for his personal use.

This statute and its successors, popularly known as the *Lei do Inquilinato*, (literally, "law of tenancy") contained no provisions for preserving a fair return to the landlord on his investment, nor did they attempt to prevent the real value of rentals from being eroded by inflation or increased expenses. Rather they were conceived of as temporary emergency measures that would expire by their own terms in a year or two. But like many a convict on death row, rent control has been granted a seemingly endless succession of reprieves.

Since tenants who paid their rent could not be evicted, landlords were locked into leases which became progressively more disadvantageous. . . .

The first thaw in the rent freeze imposed in 1942 did not come for four years. But instead of attempting to restore the decline in real rental values suffered during the prior four years, when the cost of living had risen by almost 170 percent, the 1946 statute permitted only 20 percent rent increases for leases predating 1935 and 15 percent increases for those predating 1942.

Much more startling was the failure of the Brazilian legislature to permit another general revision until 1963. In the interim the cost of living soared by a fantastic 3200 percent. . . . [T]he adjustments permitted [in 1963] were far too little and too late. Law No. 4240 permitted rent increases by either mutual consent or judicial arbitration, provided the adjustments remained within statutory limits, ranging from a minimum of 10 percent for leases begun in 1962 up to a maximum of 200 percent for leases predating the end of 1950. . . .

The quantum of the confiscatory component of rent control and the inadequacy of the 1963 adjustments can be seen more vividly by taking the specific case of an apartment rented in 1945 for Cr$1950 (worth U.S. $100 at the then prevailing exchange rate)[98] Assuming that the landlord was an ordinary citizen rather than a widow or charity, that the original tenant remained the same, and that the tenant had not voluntarily consented to paying a higher rent, no rent adjustment would have been permitted prior to July of 1963. In the interim the dollar value of the original rent (Cr$1950) would have been reduced from U.S. $100 to U.S. $3.07. Even with the 200 percent increase conceded by Law No. 4240, the dollar value of the rent would have been only $9.21. . . .

The law and socio-economic reality have frequently marched to different drums in Brazil. Long accustomed to dancing to several simultaneous samba rhythms, Brazilians have become equally adept at marching to the simultaneous but distinct tempos of law and socioeconomic reality. Twisting the formal legal structure to expediency, which to some extent occurs in all cultures, has in Brazil been developed into an artful and

---

[98] . . . To some extent comparisons between exchange rates and the inflation rate are misleading, particularly since multiple exchange rates were in effect in Brazil for much of this period. However, in the long run the Brazilian exchange rate has tended to parallel the domestic inflation rate and the transition to dollars is useful to convey the magnitude of Brazilian inflation to the non-Brazilian reader. [Footnote by Rosenn, renumbered.]

highly prized national institution called *jeito* (literally, a "knack" or "way").[99] To presume that rent control operated only along the formal statutory lines sketched above would be to omit one of the most fascinating aspects of the interaction between law and inflation.

As the economic squeeze became tighter, more and more landlords resorted to the para-legal solution of the *jeito*. The failure to create a specialized agency to administer rent control, as has been done in other countries like the United States, facilitated circumvention of the formal legal structure. From its inception the *Lei do Inquilinato* permitted the landlord to retake the premises for his personal use.

Probably the most commonly employed *jeito* was the fabrication of a personal or family need for the leasehold. The simple threat to bring an eviction action on such grounds proved quite effective in persuading tenants to make supplemental rental payments, for the courts placed the burden of proving the insincerity of the request upon the tenant, *a priori* an almost impossible task.

Another favorite device for eliminating unwanted tenants was to refuse to accept rent payments; then to turn around and sue to evict the tenant for failure to pay rent. Since it was often difficult for the tenant to offer any clear proof that he had tendered his rent, this simple ruse worked with surprising frequency. Even though a tenant could always toll the action by formally offering to pay the rent due, plus attorney's fees and costs, within five days after institution of the suit, a substantial number of cases held that repeatedly curing delays in the payment of rent in this fashion constituted an abuse of the right *(abuso de direito)*, justifying eviction. This line of cases was finally overturned by the legislature in 1956 because of notorious abuses by landlords. But this repeal gave many tenants the green light to delay rental payments in order to pay in devalued currency. In 1964, the legislature tried to change the color of the light by limiting the tenant's right to cure delays to just two opportunities, but the President vetoed the provision on the ground that landlords would again systematically refuse to accept rent.

Several other techniques have also been invoked. Some landlords conveyed their property to a third party (ofttimes a straw) who would retake the premises for his personal use. Others evicted their tenants by bringing actions based upon plans to remodel the structure of their premises. And where tenants had sublet, landlords often induced the original tenants to rescind their leases, depriving the sublessees of any legal rights to resist eviction.

Predictably, these uses and abuses of legal loopholes generated a prodigious amount of litigation. To counterbalance some of the landlord's leverage, the legislature created a veritable tenant's arsenal. A tenant was granted the right to recover penalties ranging from 12 to 24 months rent from a landlord who evicted him on the basis of insincere allegations. Failure to furnish a receipt for rent, attempts to charge rents greater than those permitted by the *Lei do Inquilinato,* or the failure to use retaken premises for the

---

[99] See Rosenn, "The Jeito: Brazil's Institutional Bypass of the Formal Legal System and its Developmental Implications," 19 *Am. J. Comp. L.* 514 (1971). [Eds.]

purposes alleged in the eviction proceeding were all made criminal offenses punishable by fine and imprisonment. Though the number of convictions has been small, the statute undoubtedly has given the tenant psychic comfort. In addition, the tenant was armed with the preferential right to purchase the property if the landlord decided to sell. This option gave the tenant substantial leverage because the selling price written in the deed or agreement to sell was generally much understated for tax purposes; hence it became quite common for the owner to buy off the tenant prior to negotiating any sale of the premises. However, probably the most important means of self defense available to the tenant was delay. Even modest efforts on the tenant's behalf by any competent lawyer could tie up eviction-proceedings for years. . . .

By the mid-1950's it had become quite clear to most landlords that it was extremely unwise to enter into any new lease without taking some precaution against the risk that both the lease and inflation may continue indefinitely. Since the *Lei do Inquilinato* from 1950 to 1964 set no limits on new rentals that could be charged, but indefinitely extended their term, landlord reaction tended to assume three forms. Some landlords asked rentals that were initially exorbitant on the theory that they would probably average out as reasonable rentals over the life of the lease. Others tried to protect themselves by clauses providing for periodic increments in the rent; two year leases with a clause raising the rent 10 or 15% per year were fairly typical in this period. And despite doubts about their lawfulness, due to the peculiar language employed in the legal tender statute, a number of landlords began to use escalator clauses tied to the cost of living index. While an occasional case invalidated such clauses, the dominant tendency of the case law has been to uphold them. By 1958 the practice of inserting clauses automatically increasing the rent periodically had become so widespread that the legislature felt constrained to restrict their use in residential rentals to a maximum increment of 5% per annum. . . .

The actual effects of the *Lei do Inquilinato* are difficult to calculate. It had become such a legislative hodgepodge by 1964 that no fewer than 18 different regimes regulating rentals were in force simultaneously. Which regime governed the rental varied with the date and term of the lease, the characteristics of the landlord, the size and location of the premises, and which judge happened to be hearing the case. . . .

One result was the creation of a multiplicity of classes or tenants. Some, by virtue only of the length of their tenancy, were paying merely nominal rents. Others, who had occupied their leaseholds just as long, were paying much higher rentals because their landlord happened to be a spinster or a charitable institution. Still others, who had the misfortune to have arrived on the scene more recently, were paying exorbitant rentals, for the excess demand for rental housing was channelled into the uncontrolled sector. Such discrimination among classes of tenants wholly unrelated to ability to pay cannot be justified on any rational basis. Indeed, the discrimination was most severe against youth and recent immigrants, whose ability to pay was probably considerably less than that of older tenants. Little wonder that the great bulk of those recently arrived on the urban scene have been forced to reside in the rapidly proliferating *favelas,* squatter settlements which surround Brazil's major cities.

The combination of rent control and inflation effected a rather substantial redistribution of income from landlords to tenants. . . . Moreover, there would appear to be no justification for the windfall received by the landlord whose uncontolled building rents for a considerably higher price because of the channelling of excess demand into the uncontrolled sector. Rent control is a very clumsy redistributive device. In theory it would have been far preferable to have taxed landlords (as well as the rest of the society) fairly on their incomes and grant direct rent subsidies to impecunious tenants as has been done in Great Britain.

Another pernicious result of rent control was the discouragement of the construction of new rental housing units. Despite one of the highest rates of population growth in the world, the rate of new housing starts in Brazil's principal cities declined drastically. While a good part of this decline is undoubtedly attributable to the drying up of sources of long term financing, failure to preserve a fair rate of return to landlords in the face of severe inflation has also played an important role. . . .

Rent control has also spurred the rapid deterioration of existing rental housing. The steady decline in real rental income and the steady increase in the cost of repairs and improvements gave landlords a substantial disincentive to maintain their buildings properly. Since rents were fixed with regard to the quality of the accommodations furnished, many landlords tried to maximize their net incomes by letting their property run down.

Nevertheless rent control has had a salutary effect in restraining the reported inflation rate. The Getúlio Vargas Foundation's cost-of-living index for Rio de Janeiro, which is generally considered to be the best reflector of Brazil's inflation rate, until 1966 accorded rent a weight of 20 percent. From 1958 to 1966 the rental component of the index rose only 56.73 percent as fast as the rest of the index, which means that, if the other factors remained constant, the reported inflation rate would have been about 10 percent higher without rent control. This percentage would have been much higher prior to 1958 when the rental component in Rio's cost-of-living index was based entirely upon the rent control statutes, reflecting only legally authorized elevations in rent controlled housing. Since a host of legal obligations and expectations have been linked to this index, rent control has plainly acted to brake Brazilian inflation. Rent control may also have had a beneficial effect on the economy by discouraging investment in real estate, which tended to channel funds into more productive investments such as industrial expansion. . . .

Brazil's long experience shows that rigid rent control can, for a time, help anchor the inflationary balloon and restrain real estate speculation. But like a narcotic, it becomes difficult to kick, even when it is apparent that its side effects have become extremely deleterious to the organism. Eventually, landlords, lawyers, and courts managed to adapt it to inflation, though not before perpetrating a great deal of injustice and disrespect for the formal legal system.

Brazil has yet to create a favorable climate to foster investment in rental property. The life of laws regulating rentals has been neither logic nor experience; it has only been short. The continual shift from one statutory scheme to another has hardly been conducive to the creation of an atmosphere in which investors are likely to make long-term commitments.

The key to total elimination of rent control probably lies in the success of the government's national housing program, which has financed the construction of some

350,000 new residences in its first four years of operation. However, given a population growth rate of slightly better than 3 percent per year, even this concentrated effort by the government to stimulate housing construction has not even been sufficient to prevent the existing shortage from becoming more acute. With a population presently estimated at about 90 million, Brazil would have to construct about 482,000 new housing units per year (assuming the present occupancy rate of 5.6 persons per unit) just to prevent the 8 million unit deficit from growing. Reimposition of controls upon new rentals will only aggravate the existing deficit and will ensure the perpetuation of economic distortions and substantial inequities. . . .

Questions

1. What does the Brazilian experience with rent control suggest about the suitability of long-term price controls to curb inflation?
2. What are the developmental implications of promoting paralegal institutions like the *jeito?*

---

3. Chilean Price Controls and Competition

D. FURNISH, CHILEAN ANTITRUST LAW

19 *American Journal of Comparative Law* 464, 465-69, 482-83, 486-87 (1971)

In the early 1950's the issue of a definitive direction for Chilean economic policy came to a head. It had become obvious by then that inflation and other traditional economic afflictions . . . were going to persist even into more "normal" times. . . . The price-control mechanism had become entrenched in Chilean economic policy by then, imposed through relatively sophisticated cost-study and other techniques. In addition, long term imposition of controls had engendered many attendant adjustments, such as direct subsidies to producers, protective tariffs, negative-real interest credit through official government agencies, discriminatory exchange rates favoring the import of primary materials and capital goods, and cooperation between producers to "protect" themselves.

The Klein-Saks Mission, . . . [a team of foreign economists hired by the Chilean government] soon argued that price controls were impossible to enforce and skewed the Chilean economy badly where they did have an effect. Efficiency, the ultimate protection for the consumer, would never be fostered so long as the producers responded to factors other than competition. In place of price controls, Klein-Saks recommended a free economy policed by anti-monopoly legislation and the possibility of taking down tariff barriers whenever domestic prices went too high on a given item.

A proposed antitrust statute, substantially drawn from United States law, was prepared but apparently never received serious consideration. . . .

Klein-Saks' economic teachings may not have been lost on all Chileans, however. The successful presidential candidate in 1958 was Jorge Alessandri, a conservative who immediately set about overhauling Chile's economic system, incorporating many of the same measures advocated by the Klein-Saks Mission. . . .

Alessandri's major concern in 1958 was the *Radical* party, which had held the presidency from 1938 to 1952, a period during which it drafted and implemented most of the institutions of Chile's *dirigiste* state. Primarily an urban middle-class party whose constituency was in salaried employees, the *Radicales* in 1958 retained a strong congressional block and might have been expected to resist proposals which would do away with wage, price, and other controls that had generally been administered to provide the urban dweller not only the necessities of life at relatively low cost but also, for those growing numbers of white-collar Chileans staffing the bureaucracy, the money with which to purchase them. The *radical* years had seen deficit spending, loose administration of credit, multiple exchange rates, and the growth of protective tariffs, in addition to the comprehensive controls on wages and prices. Under these conditions, inflation had become Chile's greatest public issue. . . .

Alessandri proposed to substitute a program of fiscal responsibility, credit restrictions, a unified exchange rate, and new access to imports of capital goods and raw materials to keep wholesale prices down. At the same time, he proposed a free-market competition in prices, with controls being removed on most items. Although the proposals represented a great shift in economic policy, apparently no real philosophical confrontation arose over the exchange. . . . Alessandri made his changes easier to embrace by submitting them as additions to the system existing at the time, rather than trying to supplant it. . . .

[The Alessandri regime in 1959 enacted an antitrust law that] follows the general traditions of most Western antitrust laws. . . . [But] article 181 specifically leaves most of the *dirigiste* structures in effect. This in spite of the fact that the regime of price and other controls is in many ways basically inimical to the theory behind antitrust. There is more than philosophical tension in a confrontation between antitrust and price controls such as that which occurred in Chile. By 1959, when Law No. 13,305 was passed, the interventionist policies initiated two decades before had evolved into a working environment for commerce and industry. Economic processes must go on under whatever regime is in force, and where the burden presses too heavily compensatory institutions and procedures may evolve to shift the weight of the burden or avoid it altogether. Often, amelioration may come in the form of official acts. Licensing, discriminatory tax and finance structures, preferential tariff and distribution systems, and a whole congeries of other controls which could sometimes be manipulated to advantage and at worst usually helped to make the system bearable, were familiar to men who had operated under them for as long as twenty years. In short, although Chile's price-control regime may have taken away competitive pricing as a variable, it probably compensated by creating other possibilities for getting ahead in the system.

The substantive effect of article 181, in leaving the price-control environment largely unaltered, at the time when other articles [of the antitrust law] commanded price competition, was probably to negate the prospect of a true competitive economy and of the very goals for which Chile's antitrust law was presumably written. Article 181 retained a system designed to run the economy without price competition. . . .

. . . [O]ver a period of time, it became apparent that whatever success the Alessandri government was enjoying in keeping prices down, it was not having an overall salutary effect on the Chilean economy, despite the President's original emphasis on economic growth along with stopping inflation. The unified exchange rate, maintained over almost three years despite pressures which left the official rate 45% under parity according to one estimate, encouraged increased imports. Chile's balance of payments suffered under the burden of its over-valued currency and relaxed controls. Wages and salaries were permitted to increase at a faster pace than prices, squeezing producers, manufacturers, and distributors. In short, Alessandri's program bought short-term price stability at the cost of economic stagnation, and he was forced to abandon that course by mid-1962, having hung on so long only against rising pressures for change back to price and wage controls which permitted inflation. . . .

Alessandri first had occasion to use the price-control agency in 1960, when a major earthquake shook south-central Chile. Prices were frozen for what was originally labelled the "emergency period." . . . After February, 1963, the Alessandri government had a more comprehensive system of price controls than any prior administration. Price controls utilized by Alessandri thereafter included the simple price-freeze, but generally permitted price increases within each calendar year up to a specified percentage of the price existing at previous year's end, this limit usually corresponding to the prior year's rate of inflation. Another Alessandri control, ostensibly introduced for greater statistical security, required all price increases on uncontrolled items to be approved by the price-control agency (DIRINCO) before they went into effect. Approval was supposedly automatic, but bureaucratic delays often helped to hold "free" prices down an extra period of time.

Alessandri, who had assumed office as the architect of the new Chilean competitive economy, bowed out instead as the perfector of the price-control system of the interventionist state. By 1964, the antitrust provisions . . . were of virtually no practical importance . . .

Perhaps the lesson of antitrust's failure is not so much that antitrust was inappropriate to Chile, as that Alessandri's objective of a free-market economy was inappropriate, or at least politically impossible. . . .

Chile today has many restraints on free competition, a high percentage of which are imposed by the government. This should not be surprising.

Chile is a small country, in economic terms, beset by problems of continuing inflation and unequal distribution of income. Thus it has long been preoccupied with controlling inflation and stabilizing the economy in such a way that growth and development will result, with minimum hardship to the populace at large. As a unitary market, Chile's economic potential will not justify many production and distribution operations of the scale currently expected for viable economic efficiency. As in other Latin American countries, the executive class is limited in numbers, traditional in composition, and oftener than not related by blood and marriage to one another in a society which encourages cooperation among friends and family. To ask for competition in such an environment is often to ask for the impossible: in most key industries under five (often one or two) producers supply the domestic market while operating well below optimum percentage of capacity.

Competition might come in the form of foreign investors and companies unencumbered by the allegiances and customs of the domestic economy, but to date Chile has taken a protective stance vis-à-vis its domestic producers and has permitted foreign investors in only under strict inhibiting rules and regulations. Competitive imports (except for a short time in Alessandri's administration) generally have not been allowed, because of the state's unequivocal commitment to fostering a domestic industrial and manufacturing sector as the best means to achieve proper levels of employment, stability and growth. Even more important than the theory involved, and perhaps even surpassing the basic economic characteristics and potential of the country in importance, is the momentum built up over time by an interventionist system. A bureaucracy is created, people learn to live within the system by means including cooperation among industrialists for purposes of dealing with the government. To attempt to instigate competition under those circumstances is to launch a craft against a strong current, created not only by those with vested interests in price controls, but by government policies concerning credit, labor and wages, import-export questions, licensing and other areas where policy and practice have evolved to fit a scheme including price controls.

Chile's unsuccessful experiment with antitrust may have had a salutary effect on its administration of price controls and the interventionist state, however. Whatever price controls may have been at the time they were initiated in Chile, they are today an instrument of some subtlety and range in their application. This may be due to the fact that the price-control system is one designed by an administration which began with a free-market economic philosophy. Thus the theory of price control probably advanced from the concept of a technique for direct confrontation of effects like inflation to the concept of an instrument which might be employed in varying ways to affect basic causes of economic ills. Price controls no longer take the form of across-the-board price freezes (save in exceptional situations) and price control administrators in DIRINCO, the agency primarily responsible, are as apt to speak of resource allocation and planning, stability and growth, redistribution of income, or curbs on oligopoly power as they are to refer to inflation and consumer prices. . . .

Questions

1. To what extent does a well-functioning antitrust law obviate the need for price controls?

2. The Furnish article suggests that securing favorable government treatment is an alternative to open competition in the marketplace in Chile. What obstacles to regional economic integration do you foresee in this substitution of legal allocation for marketplace allocation?

Note

The new Chilean military regime has abruptly terminated price controls and is attempting to return to a free market economy. N.Y. Times, January 13, 1974, Sec. 1, p. 9.

---

4. Controlling Prices in Brazil through Fiscal Incentives

K. ROSENN, ADAPTATIONS OF THE BRAZILIAN INCOME TAX TO INFLATION

21 *Stanford Law Review* 58, 85-89 (1968)

Disillusioned with the excess profits tax as an anti-inflationary measure, the Castelo Branco government . . . [turned instead to] a completely different approach — rewarding with tax favors firms that increased productivity while maintaining prices. . . . This approach was introduced in February 1965 by Portaria No. 71, an ultra vires ruling issued jointly by the Ministers of the Treasury, Industry and Commerce, and Planning. It gave certain advantages in importation, obtention of credit, and collection of the excise tax to industrial firms voluntarily agreeing to maintain prices until the end of the year. The hope was that this approach might help break the prevailing inflationary mentality.

The approach was extended and enacted into the income tax law in June 1965 . . . Industrial and commercial firms able to show that they had increased sales by at least 5 percent over 1964 levels and had not increased prices on the internal market by more than 15 percent between February 28, 1965, and December 31, 1965, were granted the following tax benefits:

(1) reduction of the regular income tax rate on 1965 income from 28 to 20 percent;

(2) reduction of *regular* taxable income for 1965 by an amount necessary to maintain the real level of working capital . . .;

(3) reduction of the 5 percent tax on fiscal 1966 revaluations of fixed assets to 2 percent; and

(4) exemption from the 15 percent tax on increases in reserves in excess of paid-in capital for fiscal 1966.

Firms that increased prices by more than 30 percent between February 28 and December 31, 1965, were penalized by taxation at 35 percent instead of the normal 28 percent. Only if they could show that the portion of the price rise above 30 percent resulted from an increase in the costs of imported raw materials or from a rise in the costs of raw materials furnished by a government-controlled firm, could such firms avoid the penalty.

Law No. 4.862 of November 1965 was a legislative extension of Portaria No. 71.

Firms that had fulfilled their pledges under the Portaria and were willing to make a similar pledge for 1966 were rewarded in tax year 1966 by:

(1) taxation of 1965 profits at 18 rather than 28 percent;
(2) taxation of 1966 revaluations of fixed assets at 2 rather than 5 percent; and
(3) exemption from the 15 percent tax on 1966 increases in reserves.

A good many firms that had gone along with the terms of Portaria No. 71 balked at assuming a new commitment for 1966. Most had agreed to go along with the government's policy of voluntary price restraints upon the assumption that the government would do its part in controlling inflation by curtailing expansion of the money supply. But despite the government's predictions of a 25 percent increment, the means of payment actually increased by close to 75 percent in 1965. This miscalculation by the government meant that the proposal that businesses limit price increases to 10 percent for all of 1966 was wholly unrealistic.

In order to avoid the breakdown of the stabilization program whenever the government's prediction of the inflation rate turned out to be embarrassingly far off the mark and to mold the multiplicity of laws and regulations that characterized price-control stimuli into a more coherent system, the government enacted Decree Law No. 38. This statute eliminated most of the voluntary character from the fiscal incentive program and shifted the burden of predicting price levels from the government to the business firms.

Under this law firms maintaining the average of their price increases at a level 30 percent below the increase in the general price index from October 1966 to the end of December 1967 were taxed in 1968 at 20 percent less than the normal income rate. Firms raising their average prices on the internal market during this period by more than 10 percent above the increase in the general price index were penalized by a fine of 2 percent of their gross receipts during the time their prices were elevated. . . .

The attempt to use the income tax to induce firms to maintain current price levels has created great difficulties. The amount of paperwork generated is enormous. A firm must fill out tables showing monthly price changes on each of its products. Sales data on each product must also be given, so that the various products can be weighted and a monthly price index for the firm calculated. This firm price index must then be compared with the wholesale-price index. While this may not involve a great burden for a small single product factory, the amount of paperwork imposed on a department store is enormous. The effort involved in trying to prove that a rise in prices was justified is even greater. Brazil does not have enough trained inspectors to enforce the basic provisions of its income tax, and the added task of enforcing this kind of legislation severely aggravates the problem.

Decree Law No. 38 was badly conceived for two other reasons. A firm must guess how much the wholesale-price index will rise before deciding whether to raise its prices. Yet, the wholesale-price index is calculated after this decision is made. If the firm guesses incorrectly, it is subject to a 2 percent tax on gross receipts during the period its prices remained above the general price index. Many firms have found it much simpler, and in some cases much cheaper, to raise their prices 2 percent more than they would otherwise have done, and make no attempt to comply.

Moreover, the wholesale-price index would not seem to be the ideal measuring stick for industrial and commercial firms; this is an output index, and an input index should have been used. The government's concern ought to be directed toward firms raising prices disproportionately to costs, and these costs may vary substantially from the wholesale-price index. For example, a wage increase will not be directly reflected in the wholesale-price index, but a large part of a firm's costs may be salaries. Thus selection of an output index may unreasonably ask firms to absorb increased costs.

Question

What advantages do you see in using a carrot instead of a stick approach to produce desired economic behavior?

Chapter V

LEGAL INSTITUTIONS IN THE
CARACAS BARRIOS:
A LAW-IN-SOCIETY CASE STUDY

In this chapter we explore the internal law and legal institutions of some marginal urban squatter settlements (*barrios*)[1] of the city of Caracas, Venezuela, as the substance and shape of that law and those institutions have been illuminated by a field study conducted during 1966 and 1967. Law students might pursue the subjects of this chapter for a variety of reasons, but we emphasize four objectives;

(1) Here, as in some parts of the chapter on land reform, we shall look at the development process from the bottom. Our concern will be with the internal norms and sanctions operating in the barrios, as they may affect development decisions at the lower levels on the social and economic scales. We return to these issues in Chapter VI.

(2) The internal barrio norms and sanctions being studied are not limited to those formally established by Venezuela's national legal system. Thus the materials of the chapter raise questions about the meaning of "law" itself. This is an issue much debated in the literature of legal philosophy and in the literature of the anthropology of law. In this short chapter, we shall not presume to reduce such profound questions to a formula. Yet it will be useful to ask, with respect to a number of internal barrio institutions, whether or not they should be called "law."

(3) Some barrio institutions are unquestionably "legal." The chapter thus examines the birth and evolution of some small-scale legal institutions, in the light of some standard hypotheses about the basic functions of law. These questions, too, are considered more fully in Chapter VI.

(4) We shall consider some ways in which a lawyer might appropriately contribute to social research on law-related subjects.

In 1966, two lawyers and an educational sociologist, all from the United States, together with several Venezuelan colleagues (principally from the discipline of Sociology), began a study of the customary law, or informal legal system, of some of

---

[1] The word *barrio* means "neighborhood" in Spanish. In Venezuela the word refers to a marginal squatter settlement. A non-barrio neighborhood in Caracas is called an *urbanización*.

the marginal urban squatter settlements in and around Caracas. The study's main objective was to describe the norms and sanctions governing the lives of the barrio residents in four substantive areas of law. The legal areas chosen were: family obligations, rights in land and housing, protection of the person, and simple contractual relations. (A social scientist might chide the directors of the study for being culture-bound, since three of those areas may have seemed "basic" partly because they are in the standard first-year curriculum of a U.S. law school. A reply that the subjects are also regarded as basic in Latin American law schools might simply confirm the social scientists' worst suspicions.) As the study progressed, its participants found themselves increasingly interested in the institution of the *junta* — the leadership group that is present in many barrios — as a resolver of disputes and a lawmaking body. So the barrio junta was added to the list of subjects to be studied. For each subject area, the study aimed at (a) describing norms and sanctions in the barrios studied; (b) analyzing the barrio residents' attitudes and conduct in the subject area in relation to characteristics such as age, sex, education and employment; (c) describing the operations of the juntas that were found in the barrios studied; and (d) refining hypotheses for further studies (*e.g.*, an analysis of changes in norms resulting from rural-urban migration, or a comparison with parallel norms in a middle-class urban community). Field work for the study was completed in 1967.

The present chapter is not an exhaustive analysis of the data produced by the Caracas barrio study.[2] Rather we shall focus on a few problem areas that have been selected in view of the objectives stated at the outset of the chapter. But even so limited an analysis cannot be made until we have passed through a stage that is more purely descriptive. Thus we begin with some materials that generally describe the barrios of Caracas, and we seek to place this description in the context of a growing social-science literature on marginal urban squatter settlements in Latin America.

A. The Barrios of Caracas

The runways at the Caracas airport run East and West, because there is no alternative. The airport runs along a strip of flat land edged by high mountains (8000 feet) on the south and by the Caribbean on the north. The deplaning visitor encounters the tropics: warm, moist air and lush vegetation. But to get to the main city, the visitor must leave the coast and drive fifteen miles up through a mountain pass and down into the Valley of Caracas. Here, at an altitude of 2500 feet, the stifling air of the coast is gone, replaced by an "eternal spring" that is more than a promotional slogan.

The Valley, also on an east-west axis, is about twenty miles long, and ranges from one to five miles in width. It is virtually filled by the city of Caracas. Several smaller valleys open out to the south, and they too are rapidly filling. The northern edge of

---

[2] The study is reported fully in K. Karst, M. Schwartz and A. Schwartz, *The Evolution of Law in the Barrios of Caracas* (1973), from which part of this chapter is taken.

the city plays out against the steep mountain range that separates the city from the coast. By 1966, Greater Caracas had reached a population of nearly 1,800,000,[3] almost one-fifth of the national population. In 1950, the comparable figure was just under 800,000. The City's population is growing at a rate of 6.6% per year; for Venezuela as a whole, the annual population growth rate is 3.4%. The best estimates are that in 1990 Caracas will be a city of 3.5 to 4.0 million inhabitants.[4] The Valley, of course, does not get any bigger. Land prices in Caracas are already very high, and will go higher as high-rise apartments replace single-family residences. In 1966, some 35% of the city's residents lived in multi-family buildings, and 40% lived in "regular" (non-barrio) single-family units. In 1990, these percentages are expected to shift markedly, to 65% in multi-family units and 10% in "regular" single-family units.

Both in 1966 and 1990 percentages, it will be seen, leave 25% of the population unaccounted for. These 25% (the percentage is ultra-conservative) live, and their 1990 successors are expected to live, in the barrios, most of them squatting on land for which they do not have title, in houses built without building permits. The land they occupy is, for the most part, marginal in a physical sense — located mainly on hillsides, but also tucked away in such places as the banks of a stream running below street level, or under a viaduct, or even alongside a new freeway. Some barrios are within easy walking distance of centers of employment and commerce, but others lie on the fringes of the city. A smaller barrio may include only 100 houses; a very large one will house more than 2000 families. Some barrios have active community leadership groups (juntas) and some have none at all. Some barrios have existed for more than thirty years, and surely some new ones will be forming while we study this chapter. There are over 400 barrios in Caracas.

The diversity of the Caracas barrios is such that it would be misleading to speak of the typical barrio; it is a commonplace in Caracas as in other Latin American cities that two adjoining squatter settlements may have characteristics that not only measure quite differently on the social scientists' various scales, but also produce different "feels" for residents and casual visitors alike. The descriptions that follow should be read with these cautionary words in mind.

---

1. Formation of the Barrios

References to marginal urban squatter settlements can be found in sixteenth-century descriptions of cities as diverse as London and Mexico City. Even the modern phenomenon of marginal settlements in Latin America is one that has been with us for some time:

Marginal settlements have leaped into prominence since World War II. The *favelas* of Rio, however, date from the 1890's, and one suspects that peripheral

---

[3] *Statistical Abstract of Latin America, 1967* p. 64 (UCLA Latin American Center, 1968).

[4] 1990 estimates are from the Oficina Ministerial del Transporte, made in connection with the planning of the Caracas subway.

clusters of squatters' or rural-type dwellings are a traditional urban feature, particularly in the Indian countries.[5]

(a) Population Growth and Migration Patterns

The reason for the squatter settlements' leap into prominence is their explosive growth during the past two decades.

Professor Morse's summary includes these examples:

— In Lima the *barriada* population grew from about l00,000 in 1958 (10% of the city population) to about 400,000 in 1964 (20%).

— In Rio de Janeiro the population of the *favelas* grew from about 203,000 in 1950 (8.5% of city pop.) to about 600,000 in 1964 (16%). By 1960 their growth rate was three to four times that of the city as a whole. . . .

— In twelve communes of Greater Santiago the number of *callampa* family dwellings appeared to hold steady from 1952 (16,502 dwellings) to 1961 (16,042 dwellings). This is explained by (1) the campaign of the government Housing Corporation, greatly accelerated in 1959, to eradicate *callampas*, and (2) the tendency of new *callampas* to be smaller and even more provisional, thus escaping enumeration.[6]

(It will be seen that each country has its own distinctive name for the phenomenon called "barrio" in Venezuela; to the above list we can add such names as the *villa miseria* of Buenos Aires, the *barriada de emergencia* of Panama City, and the *colonia proletaria* of Mexico City.)

High national rates of population growth obviously cannot fully explain these increases in the populations of marginal settlements. The additional explanation lies in a dramatic acceleration of rural-to-urban migration, as Latin America shares a worldwide tendency typically related to improved communications between the metropolis and the provinces. Most studies of Latin American marginal settlements show that the resident heads of families are largely rural in origin, but that most of them have lived for a while in the city before coming to the barrios where they now live. One frequent pattern looks something like this: The young couple from a small town come with their child to the city to live with relatives. The family moves to the barrio after a few years of city residence, and further children are born after the move to the barrio. Those few rural migrants who do move directly into the barrio tend to live with relatives, or at least to learn of the availability of land or a house from relatives who already live in the barrio. The pattern of migration thus rests in great part on the flow of information about housing opportunities.

---

[5] Morse, "Recent Research on Latin American Urbanization: A Selective Survey with Commentary," 1 *Latin Am. Research Rev.* 35, 49 (1965).

[6] Morse, *supra* note 5, at 50.

(b) Invasions and the Formation of Barrios

To speak of the "availability" of land is to use a neutral term to describe a situation that normally is characterized by conflict and often results in violence. Squatters, by definition, live on land owned by someone else. Most of the Caracas barrios, like most marginal settlements elsewhere in Latin America, have originated in "invasions" — rapid (even overnight) occupations by groups of settlers who may or may not have been organized for the occasion. While some such invasions are tolerated and even encouraged by government officials, others are resisted by the government, to the point of destruction of the settlers' houses. It is not unusual to hear of a squatter settlement that has been constructed overnight, torn down by the police the next day, constructed again the following night, destroyed again, and reconstructed until the authorities tire of fighting:

> In Lima, after months of planning, thousands of people moved during one night to a site that had been secretly surveyed and laid out. They arrived with the materials to build a straw house, all their belongings, and a Peruvian flag. They were determined and, in several cases, returned to sites two and three times after police burned their belongings and beat and killed their fellows . . . .[7]

When title to vacant land is clearly held by a private individual, the governments have tended to be rather firmly committed to protecting the land against invasion by squatters. When the land is held by the church, or by some branch of the government itself, official tolerance is more likely, as it is when the title to "private" land is disputed among several claimants.

(c) Formation of the Caracas Barrios

For many of Latin America's great cities, large-scale migration and large marginal squatter settlements are phenomena that date from around World War II; we noted earlier that some of Rio's *favelas* are much older. In Caracas there were barrios in substantial numbers by 1930. But the critical dates in the formation of the Caracas barrios are 1958-60. The military dictatorship of Marcos Pérez Jiménez had sought, during the 1950s, to end the existence of the barrios that had already formed in Caracas, and to prevent the formation of new barrios. From 1954 to 1958, the government built apartment houses, including 85 *superbloques* (giant 15-story apartment buildings) to house 180,000 people. The government's solution to the barrios was the bulldozer. On a given morning, policemen and trucks would arrive at the barrio; an official would direct the loading of the residents' belongings onto the truck; policemen would deal with any objections; when the belongings and the residents had been removed to the new apartments, the houses were demolished. Nevertheless, in 1958, after these upheavals, the barrio population in Caracas was still 220,000.

---

[7]Mangin, "Latin American Squatter Settlements: A Problem and a Solution," 2 *Latin Am. Research Rev.* 65, 69 (1967).

After the overthrow of Pérez Jiménez in January 1958, a provisional junta governed for a year; elections were held in December, 1958, and President Rómulo Betancourt took office two months later. During its brief period of government, the junta put into operation an Emergency Plan, providing for payment of a minimum "wage" to unemployed workers in Caracas. The Plan also provided materials and other assistance for public-works projects in the barrios in what seemed at the time to be a makeshift political response to the revolutionary potential of the urban poor. Around the same time the Plan was activated, the police and the military stopped preventing the formation of new barrios. Thus the principal barrier blocking migration to Caracas was removed, and the system of unemployment compensation for workers in Caracas was a special attraction to migrants. The building materials provided by the government were often pilfered and converted, by this private initiative, into an investment in barrio housing rather than public works. The total city population grew by 400,000 in a single year. By 1966, the residents of the barrios totaled nearly half a million.

---

2. A Physical Description of the Barrios

It is possible to find some barrios in Caracas that lie on flat land, but the overwhelming majority of the barrios occupy hillsides. The small valleys that open from Caracas to the south are, of course, separated by hills and ridges, most of which are covered with barrios. The hilly eastern and western ends of the main valley are dominated by barrios, and some older barrios occupy low hills right in the middle of the city. The slopes vary in steepness of grade, but nearly all barrio residents live on hills. Perhaps they lack the spectacular panoramas of the Rio *favela* that served as a setting for the movie *Black Orpheus*, but the views of the Valley of Caracas from many barrios are beautiful in the eye of any beholder.

The close-up view of the barrio, on the other hand, has varied widely, depending on the observer. Here is an evaluation by a Venezuelan professor of architecture and urbanism, apparently written late in 1965 or early in 1966:

> Today's *rancho*[8] is in Venzuela what *villa miseria* is in Argentina, *favela* in Brazil, [etc.] .... These words usually describe spaces that are enclosed by four wall surfaces for which various materials that would otherwise be leftovers are used, such as packing-box wood, tin plate, soft board, and paper, with a roof of

---

[8] The word *rancho* is used in Venezuela to refer to a house in a barrio. More precisely, a rancho is a house built of materials like those in Dr. Sanabria's description, typically of pasteboard or packing-box walls and a roof of corrugated zinc. Some descriptions use the term ranchos as synonymous with the term barrios, but the barrio is a settlement, and the rancho is an individual house. In 1967 there were a great many houses in the barrios that did not fit Dr. Sanabria's earlier description, as the Caracas barrio study shows. In popular usage (*outside* the barrios, it should be noted), all houses in barrios are called ranchos. Inside the barrios, one usually speaks only of a *casa*, a house. The word rancho is, in fact and in law, a pejorative term. Later in this chapter, for example, we shall consider a national statute that forbids the rental of ranchos, using the term in its more precise narrow sense. Throughout this chapter, we use the word in that sense. [Eds. note.]

the same materials; that is, the most primitive form of human refuge one can think of, where a number of people live in a state of overcrowding. In them they cook, eat, rest, and sleep, thereby emphasizing the problems caused by overcrowding. Their floor is the plain earth. They have neither sewers nor water service . . . .

. . . A great number of the shacks do not have windows, and access to them is only through tortuous paths, which are narrow and steep. Garbage collection is made only in places of relatively easy access to vehicles. In general, garbage is thrown down the hills, which stimulates the proliferation of flies and disease. At the same time, in the Metropolitan Area only about 3 percent of the dwellings lack electricity for lighting. Most *ranchos* have refrigerators, television, and other modern appliances. This incongruity becomes even more incredible if we add to it the fact that a high percentage of *rancho* inhabitants own cars.[9]

Physical descriptions of marginal squatter settlements such as the one just quoted abound in the literature. They are often accompanied by either an assumption or an explicit argument that the barrios must be eradicated. Within the past few years, however, the literature has taken a turn toward optimism about the squatter settlements.[10] Social scientists have found that the barrios are performing a number of useful functions — that they are, in the words of John Turner, (a) "a manifestation of normal urban growth processes under historically abnormal conditions" (*i.e.*, abnormally rapid urban growth); and (b) "both the product of and the vehicle for activities which are essential in the process of modernization."[11] These differences in attitudes toward marginal squatter settlements are reflected in different physical descriptions. The image of the "festering sore" is still strong, but among serious students of the barrios it is fading.

The barrio study that is the subject of this chapter showed that in July 1967 some 60% of the houses in the ten barrios surveyed had concrete block walls. While there appears to be a positive correlation between the age of the barrio and the quality of its houses, it is doubtful that there was a dramatic change in the 1½ years between the writing of the quoted description and the 1967 survey. What is the explanation of the differences in reactions? Perhaps, as time has passed and eradication of the barrios has seemed less likely, there has been an unconscious resignation, a decision to live with the barrios. Perhaps the directors of the 1967 survey were unduly influenced by the more recent social-science optimism, so that their sampling was unconsciously biased toward the "better" barrios. The important thing to keep in mind is that we are still talking about the barrios' *physical* characteristics. If observers can differ so in their descriptions of relatively objective matters such as the materials used in houses, it should not be surprising that they differ in their reactions to more intangible qualities

---

[9]Sanabria, "Urbanization on an Ad Hoc Basis: A Case Study of Caracas," in G. Beyer, (ed.), *The Urban Explosion in Latin America* at 337, 341-42 (1967). Copyright 1967 by Cornell University. Used by permission of Cornell University Press.

[10]The literature is reviewed in Mangin, "Latin American Squatter Settlements: A Problem and a Solution," 2 *Latin Am. Research Rev.* 65 (1967).

[11]J. Turner, *Uncontrolled Urban Settlement: Problems and Policies* 4, 5 (1966).

of barrio life such as the sense of security or the degree of commitment to "urban" values.

The 1966-67 study produces this composite picture of a mythical "typical" Caracas barrio: The barrio fills a dish-shaped area on a hillside, between two small ridges that run from the top of the hill to the bottom. On the opposite side of each ridge, there is another barrio, with a different name. At the bottom of the hill runs a paved street. At a right angle to the street, a short paved street runs up the hill, into the barrio, for about 50 yards. Beyond the end of this short street, no automobile can pass. There are, however, a few paved stairways that go about two-thirds of the way up the hillside. Halfway up one of these stairways, the pedestrian crosses a level paved walkway that goes in a semicircular path from one side of the barrio to the other. At the top of the stairway there is another such paved path. The resulting pedestrian grid resembles the pattern of the aisles of an open-air amphitheater. Within the grid, the houses are very close together; at the bottom, near the main street, the houses have common walls, and some of them are two-story buildings. Concrete walls and concrete ceilings characterize the houses in the lower, more dense sector. Toward the top of the hill, the houses are of poorer construction, and many of them are shacks (ranchos) with packing-box sides and zinc roofs; the housing density decreases.

Almost all the houses have electricity; the exceptions are the shacks at the top of the hill. One-fourth of the houses have television sets. The national government has provided not only the heavy equipment and building materials for constructing the paved walkways and stairways, but also pipes for bringing water to the barrio. The houses nearest the street are individually connected to the public water system; the upper reaches of the barrio are served by faucets used commonly by anyone who needs water. For the past month, a construction project has been underway in the barrio: the junta has secured the government's cooperation in building a sewage system. Work proceeds every day, but is especially active on the days when the heavy equipment is available, and on weekends. Sewers were installed in the lower portions of the barrio several years ago, and the current project will serve the middle levels. Residents of the upper level will be without sewers for at least two years. The only telephones are in stores that front on the street that runs along the lower edge of the barrio.

An elementary school was built for the barrio five years ago; it is now overflowing, and the school authorities are considering closing the first grade in order to add a sixth grade. Older children must take the bus to their secondary school; the bus stops in front of the barrio. There is no police station in the barrio; the nearest station is a fifteen-minute drive away. There is no dispensary in the barrio, nor is there a pharmacy. The nearest church is two miles away.

The barrio, with a population of 2500, has 450 houses. Its total area is less than ten acres. In the barrio, there are many little stores that sell basic food items, soft drinks and beer, and commodities like soap and small housewares. On the main street at the bottom of the hill there is a bakery, an auto mechanic's shop, a barber shop, and a grocery store that is larger than the little stores on the hillside.

3. Patterns of Barrio Life

While variations among the barrios' physical characteristics are clearly visible — notably in the adequacy of housing, which is closely related to the age of the barrio — the variations in those invisible qualities that comprise a barrio's "atmosphere" are even more pronounced. Of course the physical setting itself contributes much to a barrio's atmosphere; some barrios on the edge of the city have a distinctly rural feel, while others more centrally situated are blending into the city socially as well as architecturally. Such features as crime rates and community organization also vary widely, even among barrios that look indistinguishable. Despite these variations, though, there is considerable consistency from one barrio to another when the observer inquires into such social phenomena as family living patterns, education and employment.

(a) Family Living Patterns

Later in this chapter we shall look more closely at the subject of family obligations, and so we reserve much of our descriptive material for that discussion. For the present, it will suffice to say that while an anthropologist would classify the barrio family as matrifocal — with the strongest and most lasting ties between mother and children — still the great majority of families (four out of five families in the 1967 survey) are headed by men. In 78% of the households, husbands were living in stable unions with their wives. The median number of children living in the house, according to the 1967 survey, was four. A substantial number of households departed from the nuclear-family-only pattern of occupancy, principally by subtracting the male head of the household or by adding other relatives (parents, brothers and sisters, nieces and nephews). In about 60% of the homes where there were children, all children had the surname of the present husband of the mother. In another 27% all children had the mother's surname.

The average household numbers six occupants. In a barrio near one of the city's centers, the typical house completely fills a parcel of land that is some seven meters wide and ten meters long. Living in the barrio usually means living close to the neighbors; it almost certainly means living very close to the others in the same house. In the barrio, nearly everyone is acquainted with everyone else. In a large barrio, of course, that statement cannot be true, but even in a barrio of 10,000 residents one is apt to know many more of one's neighbors than does the resident of a middle-class neighborhood of comparable size.

(b) Education

While about one-quarter of the heads of families are illiterate (in the 1967 survey), the median had gone to school through the fourth, fifth or sixth grade. Only one out of ten heads of families had gone to secondary school or its equivalent, such as a special commercial school. The children surveyed had more schooling: Only three percent of school age or beyond were illiterate; nearly one out of three had attended secondary school or its equivalent. (These figures are conservative; for example, they count a sixth-grade student who is planning to go to secondary school the same as a child who has completed the sixth grade and quit school.) The statistics about education are reflected in the everyday conversation of the barrio residents. While they tend to have only modest expectations for themselves in the way of socio-economic advancement, they are very optimistic about their children. Education is seen as the road to progress for the individual and for the community.

The barrio residents read the newspapers and watch television; virtually every family has a small radio. Two music-and-news radio stations in Caracas specialize in public-service announcements about the barrios. A typical announcement would be: "Radio Rumbo calls on the responsible authorities to act on the petition of the Barrio Brisas de Pro Patria for immediate establishment of a dispensary." Such an announcement suggests a certain sophistication on the part of the barrio residents, who have mastered some of the public-relations techniques of the modern urban political system. Later we shall consider the barrio junta's place in this system.

(c) Employment

Only one household in ten reported that no one in the house was employed. If the head of the family was unemployed (as was often the case when the head of the family was a woman), then children or other relatives supported the household. Employment ranged over a variety of occupations, but centered on five categories: skilled labor (*e.g.*, auto mechanic, building-trades specialist), unskilled labor (including drivers of Caracas's fixed-line jitney cabs), low-level white-collar employment, domestic employment, and government employment (*e.g.*, policeman, messenger for federal agency).

(d) Community Life

One feature of underemployment that falls in the "silver lining" category is the ready availability of labor for the barrio's communal work projects. While these projects do draw most of their support on the weekends, still men are around during the week, and thus able to participate. The major projects are supported quite widely; often on a Sunday afternoon, there is a large turnout of men both young and old for several hours of work, and the sharing of some cases of beer. Beer has become a kind of ritual drink for such occasions. The homeowner who wishes to add a room to his house must wait until he can afford the materials — and the beer to be supplied to any relatives or friends who help him. It is not too much to say that beer is a kind of social cement in the barrios. The chief evening entertainment for men is to sip a few cans of beer at a barrio store, perhaps in conjunction with a few games of *bolas criollas*, a game like ninepins. Age groupings are far less rigid in the barrios — and less rigid throughout Venezuela — than they are in middle-class North American society. The swapping of stories at the local shop will often be well-attended by boys who drink soft drinks, plus the sips of beer that may be allowed them. On other nights, the same boys may be roaming around the barrio, or, if they are teenagers, roaming around other parts of the city that are reachable on foot or by bus.

Women's social lives are more restricted in the evenings. Generally, they stay home, or visit nearby neighbors, or perhaps attend a government-supported sewing class. Young women who work outside the barrio as nurses or clerks may go out of the barrio for the evening, say, to the movies, but even they tend to stay close to home at night. An older woman, especially one who was born in a small town, may leave the barrio only infrequently — to do the weekly shopping at a free market, or to go to church.

A value that ranks very high in the barrio is *respeto*: respect, dignity, seemliness. One shows (or demands) *respeto* in many ways. If an outsider comes to the barrio looking for a parcel of land and there is none available, the junta will write a "To whom it may concern" letter for the newcomer, asking that land be provided by the junta in another (unspecified) barrio. The letter is meaningless, apart from its value in showing the newcomer that he or she is regarded by the junta as a person, as someone worth helping. A resident who blares his radio at midnight is not showing *respeto*; but the provocation has to go on for a long time before the neighbors complain, for they must treat the offender with *respeto*.[12] A young man whose younger sister has been having an affair with a man says: "He has to take her out of my parents' house wearing veil and crown or I'm ready to kill him or to be killed by him." Later on, as we discuss the conflict-resolution role of the barrio junta, we shall return to this theme.

B. The Study: Objectives and Methods

The Caracas barrio study that began in 1966 was initially conceived by lawyers, although it soon became an interdisciplinary effort. One well-known historian commented, on learning of the study, that a lawyer who turns to anthropology is rather like Madame Pompadour trying to become Florence Nightingale. But the lawyers who co-directed the study continue to insist that they did so as lawyers, not as pseudo-social scientists. In this section we shall be concerned first with the question whether there is any utility in the participation of lawyers in such studies, and secondly with the research methods employed in the Caracas study.

---

1. Lawyers as Participants in Social Research

(a) Styles of Legal Research

Legal research, until very recently in the long history of western legal systems, consisted almost entirely in library work. To a lawyer, "research" meant tracking down authoritative documents that controlled the disposition of the issues being

---

[12] An exact parallel is found in the experience of Lisa Peattie in her book *The View from the Barrio* (1968), extracted *infra,* describing a barrio in Ciudad Guayana, Venezuela.

examined. Creative legal analysis was the imaginative assembly and interpretation of texts: constitution, statute, precedent judicial decision, scholarly treatise. There were early exceptions to this pattern. A notable English example of such an exception was the work of Lord Mansfield, who labored mightily and successfully to make the common law governing commerce useful in relation to the practice of merchants. Still, the generalization we have made about legal research is a fair one, at least until the end of the 19th century. Around that time, some legal thinkers began a systematic analysis of the functions of legal rules in society. The work of these scholars, mostly European, came to be called by the ungainly name of sociological jurisprudence. By the 1920s, the stage was set for the "legal realism" movement in the United States. A realist would ask questions like these: Who really makes the effective decision? What are the real criteria for judgment? What, if any, are the effective sanctions applied against departure from an authoritative norm?

Law teaching in this country continues to this day to be concerned with mastery of doctrinal principles, but the legal realists have won at least a partial victory in the law schools. Virtually every course now goes beyond doctrinal analysis into some study of the operation of rules and principles in their social (economic, etc.) contexts. The movement has carried even beyond this point, into the study of "the legal process." Implicit in such a study is a conception of law as more than a set of principles, more than a legislature or a court system. Law so conceived is, in fact, a *process* by which the organized society creates, modifies and applies its authoritative norms (its legal rules). A modern course on Contracts thus may properly be concerned not only with the Uniform Commercial Code and the decisions of courts, but also with the practices of retail sellers or construction contractors and with the practices of lawyers who create and apply law as they draft agreements and help negotiate the non-judicial settlement of contract disputes.

Similarly, modern law reform activity frequently depends heavily on assumptions about the way the legal process is in fact operating in a given economic or social context. One who drafts a model consumer credit code cannot fail to consult with bankers and other lenders, not only because those people are an effective legislative pressure group but because they have information that bears on the potential utility of any proposed reform. Thus "law-in-action" research, so long neglected, now is much in vogue, and not only among academic lawyers.

The Caracas barrio study differed from these recent studies of law in social context in two obvious respects: (1) The Caracas study presented the problem of cultural bias, for its directors were North Americans. We may note parenthetically that a similar study conducted entirely by Venezuelan lawyers and social scientists would raise at least similar problems; few such scholars come from the barrios. (2) The Caracas study did not concentrate on the operation of the rules of the national legal system in the barrios. Rather, it started with an inquiry into the effective norms and sanctions in the barrios, and only then turned to the question of the penetration of the external legal system into the barrios. This question of focus — whether the researcher begins with a statute or a set of judge-made rules, asking, "how do these rules work in practice?" or instead begins with the question, "What are the rules that are operating?" — reflects more than a formal choice. The researcher's beginning point will have much to do with both the substance and flavor of the research product. In field research as in every other area where lawyers work, the most critical stage of analysis is in the formulation of the questions to be asked. Lawyers should heed the computer-specialist's lament: "Garbage in, garbage out."

(b) The Caracas Study: Goals of the Lawyer Participants

What should lawyers expect to learn from a study such as the Caracas barrio study? A prominent Venezuelan lawyer expressed the view, at the outset of the study, that there was no law in the barrios, since the barrios were "a jungle." Implicit in his comment are some fundamental assumptions about the nature of law. He knew, of course, that in the barrios people lived together and normally did not kill one another or steal or set fires to houses. There were, even in that lawyer's view, some social controls operating to keep the barrios from dissolving into destruction and chaos. By "law," he must have meant statutes, judges, lawyers. It can be admitted that a great many barrio residents have never seen a judge or a lawyer; it can even be admitted that an on-duty policeman is a rarity in most barrios. But the same might be said of a residential neighborhood in London or Seattle. What our lawyer had in mind, no doubt, was that disputes and other relations among the barrio residents normally are not settled or governed by resort to lawyers and courts. But if, in a squatter community where no one has a legal title to his parcel of land, nonetheless the residents respect one another's "rights" to land, is it accurate to say that there is no law of property? A fundamental thesis of the Caracas barrio study is that there exists in the barrios something that appropriately may be called law, even though it is not a directly-connected branch of the national system of substantive and procedural law.

Thus the first goal of the study was a description of an informal legal system, bearing some similarity to the efforts of an anthropologist to describe the customary law of a primitive society. A lawyer might find such a description useful for the perspectives it might offer concerning what is basic in a legal system, or concerning the way a norm becomes law. The directors of the study, trained in the Anglo-American system, repeatedly saw parallels between the development of the customary law of the barrios and the evolution of the early English common law. A development-minded lawyer might focus on that aspect of "institution-building" that relates to the legal system itself: How does a particular person or group come to hold legislative or adjudicative authority? (We speak intentionally of authority rather than power; a legal system, in our view, requires legitimacy as well as force.) Is there a positive correlation between "law and order" (in the sense of popular compliance with rules prohibiting disfavored conduct) and the community's sense of sharing in the formulation of the rules?

These are ambitious questions, and no single study is likely to produce answers on so high a level of abstraction. But social research monographs very often conclude with calls for "further study." It may not be too much of an oversimplification to say that the goal of social research is the progressive refinement of hypotheses about subjects that are constantly changing, even as they are being studied.

The Caracas study had one additional characteristic that might recommend it to a lawyer who wished to learn about the process of development. The study focused on institutions at the lowest level of the social-economic scale, not on exchange controls or regional common markets or industrial promotion legislation. This was a study of "grass roots" development, if one may speak of grass roots in the city. Even a national planning agency's lawyers have much to gain from increased awareness about the barrio residents and their views on questions of right and obligation.

(c) The Caracas Study: The Lawyers' Contributions

The more serious question concerning a lawyer's participation in a study like this one relates not to what the lawyer can hope to gain from it, but rather to what he or she can contribute that is distinctive. We have noted that the lawyer's formal training, even in an era dominated by legal realist thought, has continued to emphasize library research. The kind of barrio study most congenial to that training would be a study of legislation that might be brought to bear on barrio problems.[13] An able lawyer's critical analysis of existing or proposed legislation, in the light of the social situation, can be of enormous value to everyone who must deal with barrio affairs. What we are asking at this point, however, is whether a lawyer should feel justified in going outside this analytical framework into an effort to describe the social situation itself. Most legal writing in North American law reviews is concerned with law in its social context; but most lawyer-authors have felt constrained to take their assumptions about the context from the work of social-science professionals. There is a natural and quite proper reluctance to pretend competence in another's field.

The lawyer's diffidence might be expected to be especially pronounced in the area of the Caracas barrio study. The social-science literature on marginal squatter settlements in Latin America is growing rapidly.[14] Furthermore, the subject of norms and values is one that falls within the professional provinces of political scientists, sociologists, anthropologists and social psychologists. How can a lawyer hope to make a contribution to this literature?

Both training and experience make the lawyer familiar with the kinds of issues that regularly arise out of certain standardized relationships. Thus a lawyer member of a research group investigating a law-related subject might be expected to identify some problem areas worth studying. When the research is carried out in a foreign country, however, there is a danger that confronts all social researchers: The experience of the

---

[13] One excellent study of this type is Manaster, "The Problem of Urban Squatters in Developing Countries: Peru," 1968 *Wis. L. Rev.* 23.

[14] The Mangin and Morse articles, *supra,* both contain long bibliographies. For additional bibliographical lists on marginal squatter settlements, see T. Ray, *The Politics of the Barrios of Venezuela* 191-206 (1969); Cornelius, "The Political Sociology of Cityward Migration in Latin America: Toward Empirical Theory," in F. Rabinovitz & F. Trueblood, (Eds.), 1 *Latin American Urban Research* 95 (1971); Morse, "Trends and Issues in Latin American Urban Research, 1965-1970," 6 *Latin Am. Research Rev.* no. 1, p. 3 (Part I), and no. 2, p. 19 (Part II) (1971).

researcher is necessarily forced into conceptual categories, and those categories may be next to useless if they are not attuned to the system of thought prevailing in the community under investigation. A researcher who speaks of his or her "data" seems to be talking about raw facts. But behind the data lie row upon row of assumptions about a society's structure and workings, about the likelihood that individuals can meaningfully be placed in the categories used in carrying out the study, about the very meaning of the words used in the streams of communications running from principal investigators through survey-takers or participant observers to the people being studied, and then back again.

To be more specific: A lawyer can be expected to have some expert ability to recognize certain patterns in standard relationships such as "marriage" or "tenancy" or "credit purchase." But North American lawyers had better be skeptical about our ability to transfer our special skills to another culture. The three kinds of relationships just noted represent different positions on a figurative scale of ease-of-transfer-of-skills. It takes no special insight to see that the cluster of relationships called marriage may, in a Caracas barrio, differ radically from the parallel cluster of relationships in a middle-class North American community. A North American lawyer would be more willing to trust his or her "feel" for the issues that might arise from a tenancy in a barrio, and perhaps still more willing to predict the kinds of problems that might arise from a sale on credit by a barrio storekeeper. The vital thing to remember is to stay alert to the difficulties of research in another culture even when the matter being studied looks most like its domestic counterpart.

Still, training in one legal system is an aid to the identification of substantive issues that may arise in another. The lawyer member of a social research team may thus be conceived as a walking checklist of topics for preliminary exploration. But a lawyer's training is not limited to the substance of legal rules and principles. Being a lawyer implies a professional concern with the institutional forms that condition the resolution of disputes and the making of law. Here, too, there is the danger of the culture-blindness that anthropologists call ethnocentrism. The very existence of a judge, for example, calls to the mind of a common lawyer much of the tradition of judges and judging in our system, only part of which may have relevance for the investigation of conflict resolution in another culture. Yet the lawyer's training may aid in the definition of issues for research. For example: The rules of jurisdiction that govern courts in Illinois, state or federal, are not apt to have much specific transfer value when a lawyer studies the dispute-settling powers of the junta in a Caracas barrio. But an acquaintance with the concepts of personal jurisdiction and subject-matter jurisdiction would be helpful in such a study, focusing the researcher on some features of the process of conflict resolution that properly can be called "basic," at least in systems that have established certain persons or groups as authoritative settlers of disputes.

Thus far, the two suggested kinds of contributions for lawyers to make to social research have related, respectively, to the law's substantive content and to the institutional structure through which the substantive law is created and applied. But these two factors are not the whole legal system, as the following quotation from Lawrence Friedman makes clear:

A working legal system can be analyzed further into three kinds of components. Some are *structural*. By structural, we mean the institutions themselves, the forms they take, and the processes they perform. Structure includes the number and type of courts; presence or absence of a constitution; presence or absence of federalism or pluralism; division of powers between judges, legislatures, governors, kings, juries, and administrative officers; modes of procedure in various institutions; and the like.

Other elements in the system are *cultural*. These are the values and attitudes which bind the system together and which determine the place of the legal system in the culture of the society as a whole. What kind of training and habits do the lawyers and judges have? What do people think of the law? Do groups or individuals willingly go to court? For what purposes do people turn to lawyers, for what purposes do they make use of other officials and intermediaries? Is there respect for law, government, tradition? What is the relationship between class structure and the use or non-use of legal institutions? What informal social controls exist in addition to or in place of formal ones? Who prefers which kind of controls, and why?

These aspects of law — the legal culture — influence all of the legal system. But they are particularly important as the source of the demands made upon the system. It is the legal culture, that is, the network of values and attitudes relating to law, which determines when and why and where people turn to the law, or to government, or turn away.

Still other components are *substantive*. This is the output side of the legal system. These are the "laws" themselves — rules, doctrines, statutes and decrees, to the extent that they are actually used by the rulers and the ruled, and, in addition, all other rules which govern, whatever their formal status.

The three elements together — structural, cultural, and substantive — make up a totality which, for want of a better term, we can call the legal system. The living law of a society, its *legal system* in this revised sense, is the law as actual process . . . .[15]

The lawyer who participates in social research on a legal subject can help social scientists identify what *is* cultural by helping to explain the system's structural and substantive elements. Furthermore, the lawyer can help to focus the investigation of a legal system's cultural aspects (*e.g.*, attitude research) on issues that are relevant to the structure and substance of the system. (We should not be carried away by the symmetry of Professor Friedman's vocabulary. He would be the first to state that his categories are not water-tight. But his three elements are useful as suggestions of areas of emphasis in examining a legal system.)

The latter point — that a lawyer can help to make social research on "legal culture" relevant to the law's structural and substantive aspects — itself betrays a tendency of

[15] L. Friedman, "Legal Culture and Social Development," in L. Friedman & S. Macaulay, *Law and the Behavioral Sciences,* 1003-04. Copyright 1969 by The Bobbs-Merrill Company Inc. Reprinted by permission. All rights reserved.

thought that pervades the culture of the legal profession. We are action-oriented. Our legal journals are full of articles that not only describe and analyze, but also prescribe. A lawyer who is a member of a social research team will find it hard to avoid thinking about the ways in which his or her work can contribute to the betterment of the communities being studied. The dangers to objectivity of such an attitude are easy to see. An action orientation is apt to distort the researcher's observations and analysis; it carries with it an irreducible minimum of paternalism. The question, What can I do for these poor unfortunates? implies a built-in prejudice about the society under study. Of course there is nothing wrong with thinking about people as people rather than as data; the opposite attitude is not only unfeeling, but also apt to produce highly organized statistical half-truths. The point is simply a cautionary one: lawyers and others who do social research must try to avoid letting their prescriptive inclinations interfere with understanding. One can "accept" a state of facts for purposes of making an adequate description without resigning oneself to the existing situation. Remedial action is most likely to succeed if it is based on accurate fact assumptions.

---

2. The Methods of the Study

As our earlier references to "the 1967 survey" have implied, the Caracas barrio study included a survey, by questionnaire interviews, of barrio residents. Survey research, long the province of sociologists, has come to be a standard tool for all the social sciences. And social-science evidence has found an increasing acceptance in the lawmaking process, both legislative and judicial, in this country as well as others. A congressional committee considering the reform of the bail system in the federal courts naturally turns to the social scientists; so does a court that must decide on the content of the Equal Protection Clause in the context of educational opportunity. Thus it behooves lawyers to become acquainted with the rudiments of social-science research techniques. We include a description of the methods of the Caracas barrio study party for this rather general purpose; more specifically, this methodological discussion is included to assist the student in evaluating the assertions made later in this chapter about the study's results.

(a) Participant Observation

The study was not limited to the questionnaire. It also rested on the observations of three graduate students who lived in three different barrios during the summer of 1967. Such participant observation has always been the anthropologist's primary research method. The three students (two of them law students, the other an anthropology-oriented student of Latin American studies) were all fluent in Spanish. Two were former Peace Corps volunteers who had done work in Ecuador, the Dominican Republic and Panama; the third was a Chilean. Each of the participant-observers involved himself to the maximum possible extent in the life of his barrio, helping with community projects such as road building, a barrio census, or even the planning of a fiesta. Throughout the summer, the students met at least weekly with one of the study's directors; experiences were shared and subjects for further exploration were suggested.

The participant-observers focused on the same general subject areas that were covered by the questionnaire, so that their observations were a useful cross-check on the results of the survey. Furthermore, since some of the topics under study were found to be too sensitive for inclusion in a structured questionnaire interview, the students living in the barrios were asked to do some delicate probing of certain issues that had been left out of the questionnaire form. They also followed particular events and transactions, in the classical case-study method. They made a special effort to become acquainted with the operations of the various barrio juntas, to provide an inside view of that institution to complement the picture produced by the survey of the barrio residents' attitudes toward the junta.

The advantages of participant observation over a survey are apparent: The survey's success depends to a great extent on the ability of the researchers to formulate questions that will produce meaningful results when the answers are tabulated. A survey must be adjusted to the requirements of some system of tabulation. Inherent in such an adjustment is the forcing of raw facts into categories that are invented before the data are gathered. The potential distortion can be reduced by the use of pre-tested pilot questionnaires, but after all reasonable precautions have been taken there remains a danger that the categories of potential response to the survey's questions will be too much the researcher's and not enough the categories of thought of the interviewees. Furthermore, living in a community permits the researcher the kind of depth of understanding that often is described with words like "feel" or "flavor." Few of those intangible qualities come across in the answers to a questionnaire.

No one suggests that participant observation is free from the danger of distorted description. The presence of the observer as a disturbing factor is undeniable; the literature of anthropology includes repeated references to the problem. And even a distortion-free description of a community would be just that — a description. Survey research offers possibilities for analytic comparison of individuals in a manner that is "scientific" beyond the capacities of participant observation. The Caracas study, as planned from the beginning, contemplated a survey of individuals as well as the placement of observers in some barrios.

(b) The Survey: Drafting the Questionnaire

The first draft of the questionnaire was written a full year before the survey was to be taken. Although the first draft was in English, it was written jointly by Venezuelans and North Americans. Successive drafts (there were seven in all) were all in Spanish — in Venezuelan Spanish. The first Spanish draft questionnaire was tested in a pilot barrio, where about 100 interviews were taken by two experienced Venezuelan researchers. On the basis of this test, it was decided to cut the interview's length severely. Where the pilot questionnaire took about an hour and a half to complete, the final version was completed in 45 minutes or less. Another reason for cutting was the resistance of some interviewees in the pilot barrio to questions they thought improper, *e.g.*, some questions about marriage relations.

At the same time, it was decided to change the form of many of the questions from an open-ended-response to a closed-response form. An open-ended question is one like this: "What do you think of the junta in this barrio? The answers to such a question, of course, will scatter widely. The question might be closed, using a form like this: "Has the junta in this barrio been, in your opinion, very good, good, ordinary, bad, or very bad?" Such a form requires the respondent to make a choice; he cannot answer that the junta has been good with respect to road-building, but unsatisfactory in pursuing the goal of an elementary school. Thus the closed question forces the data into the researcher's categories more than does the open-ended question. Answers to the open-ended question, however, are much harder to tabulate. The decision in the Caracas barrio study was to make most of the questions closed, and to rely on the participant observers to provide many of the data that might be supplied by a more open-ended survey. Some of the "closed" questions really turned out to be a bit open-ended, however; a list of categories would conclude with the category, "Other (specify)." And a substantial number of questions relating to marriage obligations were left completely open-ended. (*E.g.*, "Suppose that a man and a woman live together, that is, that they are *unidos*. How do you think the man should behave, that is, what obligations does the man have to fulfill? And what else?")

There were ten parts to the questionnaire, which ran for 23 mimeographed pages. The ten parts covered the following material:

1. Personal data about the interviewee and his or her family. Migration history; age, sex, education and employment of each member of the household.
2. History of affording housing to relatives or others; willingness to do so in the future. Expectations that relatives or others would house the interviewee in case of need; history of such a case. Persons who are now contributing to the maintenance of the house.
3. Occupancy of land and house. Who owns the land, the house? How was the land obtained? Title disputes, if any; sense of security about future occupancy. Rental arrangements. Past or expected investment in housing (added room, improved roof, etc.). Expectations about devolution of property upon death.
4. Commercial relations, emphasizing short-term credit and remedies in case of a merchant's cheating.
5. Theft in the barrio. Past experience, past and expected remedies.
6. Cash borrowing. Terms of repayment, interest, creditors' remedies.
7. Physical security. Involvement of members of the family in fights; obligation to aid a relative in a fight. Sense of security within the barrio. Relations with the police.
8. Marriage obligations of husband and wife; effect of legal marriage on obligations; informal sanctions against infidelity. Pregnancy of an

unmarried daughter: parents' sanctions, legal or otherwise; attitudes toward abortion, contraception.

9. The barrio junta. Activities, residents' evaluations of the junta's work. Attitudes toward cooperation.

10. General matters: Income of the household; type of housing construction; location of house within the barrio.

These subjects, it will be seen, were not explored in an order dictated by the outline of the study. The income question, for example, logically belongs with questions about employment. It was put at the end because it might spoil the interviewer's rapport with the interviewee if it came early. People with clipboards and papers look "official"; interviewers in other studies have reported that the interviewees thought they were tax officials or other representatives of the government. The questions about marriage were put near the end of the questionnaire for the same reason. A few women interviewees were unhappy with these questions, and one of them asked the student who was conducting the interview what a nice girl like her was doing in a survey like this. The questionnaire was constructed in such a way as to follow every sensitive subject with a neutral one.

Apart from the testing of the questionnaire in the pilot barrio, the study directors sought the advice of a number of social scientists in the United States and Venezuela. The seventh and final draft was a major revision that took account of the helpful and detailed criticisms of some Venezuelan sociologists who were not members of the research team but who generously offered their assistance.

(c) The Survey: Selecting the Barrios

Budget considerations dictated that the survey be limited to around 600 interviews. It was decided initially to aim for about 500, averaging 50 each in ten barrios. The barrios to be surveyed were not chosen at random; instead, it was decided to select ten barrios that displayed a range of various characteristics that might bear some significant relations to the barrios' internal legal system. Thus it was necessary to construct a rudimentary typology of the barrios: a list of kinds of characteristics that might differentiate one barrio from another. This task was effectively performed by two Venezuelan members of the research team. They began with six potential variables (barrio characteristics): population size, area, public services (water, electricity, sewers, schools), community organization (existence of a junta and degree of its activity), terrain (suitability for stable housing), and distance from centers of employment and commerce.

Data concerning approximately half the barrios in Caracas were obtained from a variety of official and unofficial sources. (Two special censuses of the barrios had been carried out by government agencies in 1959 and 1966.) These data were reduced to a code in which each factor was assigned a weight from 0 to 3. Each factor was tested for its degree of correlation with the others. Not surprisingly, area and population had a high positive correlation; the factor of area was thus eliminated from the typology.

The factor of terrain was also eliminated. Finally, the factor of community organization was eliminated on the ground that the data about the existence of juntas were so incomplete as to preclude confidence in their accuracy. The three factors remaining, and those used in the initial screening of the barrios, were thus (1) population size, (2) the quality of public services, and (3) proximity to centers of employment and shopping.

Each of these three factors was assigned a value from 1 to 3. A very large barrio that had good public services and was quite close to the urban centers would thus be assigned a code of 111; a small barrio with poor public services and located on the city's fringes would have a code of 333. The possible combinations in this scheme, of course, total 27. In fact, on the basis of a sample of some 200 barrios, some 24 types were found; of these, only 16 types were represented by more than two barrios in the sample. The selection of ten barrios was aimed at producing a variety of types within this framework. It was also decided to try to make some minimal use of other factors, including some that had been discarded, *i.e.*, seeking to include some barrios with strong community organization and others with little or none, and also seeking some diversity in barrio terrain and in the age of the barrios surveyed.

The final selection of ten barrios was based on visits to scores of barrios by one of the research directors, along with some Venezuelan researchers. No one should minimize the magnitude of such physical-logistical problems in survey research. Most of an entire week was spent in this final process of driving around and talking to barrio residents, inspecting the characteristics of housing and public services, and the like.

(d) The Survey: Sampling

Within each barrio to be surveyed, the interviewees were chosen on a systematic basis. In the largest barrio (some 2000 houses), the sample was 7.5% of all households in the barrio, for a total of 150 interviews. In the smallest barrios, the sample surveyed was more than 30% of the households. The overall sample in all ten barrios came out to be about 15%. A 20% sample, for example, was secured by going to every fifth house on every street or pathway, and counting two-family buildings as two households. A 28% sample would be obtained by going to every third house, then every fourth house, then every third house, etc. The interviewers were acquainted with the dangers of biasing the sample, such as by omitting a particular house because it looked like a disagreeable place for an interview or for some other reason. The instructions to the interviewers at the orientation session gave great emphasis to the need for maintaining the purity of the sample's systematic nature. If a resident was away from the house, the interviewers were instructed to return later in the same day to secure the interview; barrio residents rarely leave their houses unattended for long periods, and this method was normally successful in preserving the sample.

(e) The Survey: Conducting the Interviews

Two teams of interviewers, 23 in all, had been selected. All were sociology students in the Andrés Bello Catholic University in Caracas; all were experienced in survey-taking, and about half had worked previously on surveys in barrios. Fourteen were women and nine were men. At a lengthy orientation session, each question on the questionnaire form was explained and discussed; the session ended with some brief role-playing in which the most experienced interviewers enacted the parts of interviewer and interviewee.

It was decided to attempt to survey each barrio in a single day. The purpose of this strategy was to permit the interviewers to take all their interviews before the residents of the barrio became acquainted with the survey questions, so that they knew the "right" answers. The week chosen for the survey began with two days of holiday; Monday and Tuesday of that week were the days of celebration of the 400th anniversary of the founding of the city of Caracas. The week was chosen deliberately, in the hope that a number of men would be at home. The expectation was that no fewer than one-third of the interviewees would be men; as it turned out, over 40% were men. (A measure of middle-class misunderstanding of the barrios was the warning, solemnly given by some Venezuelan social scientists, that the survey should not be taken on a holiday, since most of the men would be drunk that day. No such difficulty was reported by the interview teams.) Fortunately for the success of the survey, the interviews (622 in all) were completed in five days; by Friday afternoon, all the questionnaire forms had been returned to the team leaders. The very next night, Caracas was hit by a severe earthquake that took over 200 lives and disrupted normal activities in the city for several weeks. It is a safe bet that no reliable interviewing could have been carried on for fully a month after the earthquake.

The survey teams found the barrio residents to be very cooperative. Often the barrio junta helped to introduce the interviewers, or otherwise to make their work easier. The rejection rate was under four percent. In one barrio with a "rough" reputation, the residents warned the interviewers not to go down a certain pathway. The team leader, who had been told to err on the side of caution in such matters, told his interviewers to avoid the area; thus the sample in that barrio was slightly biased. The survey directors wanted the survey to study the problem of physical security, not to be part of it.

(f) The Survey: Coding and Data Processing

The questionnaires were collected, and each form was given a number that designated the barrio, the interviewer, and the interview's arbitrary number within its barrio. Next, a numerical code was adopted, assigning a number to each of the possible responses to each question. For closed-ended questions, the code was implicit in the structure of the questions. Open-ended questions presented a different problem, and required an "empirical code": the classification of the answers actually given to these questions, and the assignment of a code number to each category identified. The open-ended question on a man's obligations to the woman with whom he is living, quoted earlier, provides an example. The empirical code for this question, made on the basis of reading a sample of fifty completed questionnaire forms, included these categories:

Bring home money (food, clothes)
Behave well (be serious, stay home, don't get drunk)

Fidelity
Respect the woman
Love and affection, avoid arguments, be nice, don't hit the woman
Marry the woman
Educate the children
Take care of the children, be affectionate to them, discipline them
Other
Inadequate answer (*e.g.*, fulfill the duties of the home)

(Provision was made for coding multiple answers, combining two or more of the above.) The use of "Other" as a catchall category illustrates one hazard of open-ended questions: not all of the data on the questionnaires will survive the coding process, for it would be nearly useless to have a category which fit the responses of, say, two persons.

Once the code was established, a team of coders (composed of some of the same students who had acted as interviewers) went through all 622 questionnaires, entering numbers on standard code sheets for all the responses. Once again, the open-ended questions pose a problem: the coder must evaluate the answer on the questionnaire, and try to fit it into one of the categories in the empirical code. (Some of these difficulties are removed later on in the processing of the data, when the survey directors, after seeing the figures that result, decide to combine categories for purposes of analysis.) The code sheets were given to a punch-card operator, who punched three cards for each interview. The punched cards were put through a computer for a preliminary print-out of the data, and "impossible" responses (*e.g.*, the printing of the number 7 when the code provided only for responses up to the number 4) were checked and corrected. A computer programmer wrote a program that permitted the cross-tabulation and correlation of the responses, and a final print-out was obtained from a more sophisticated computer. When a survey researcher says, "64% of those surveyed said . . .," that is a shorthand way of referring to a process such as the one described here.

C. The Study: Rights in Land and Housing

If the barrios really were a jungle, then a person's occupation of a house would depend on the day-to-day ability to defend possession. The difference between such a condition and the conditions that almost universally govern human society is in some sense *law*, whether or not any rules are reduced to writing or formally adopted by the community. In the Caracas barrios, as nearly everywhere else, families live in houses, secure in the expectation that their neighbors are not on the point of dislodging them. This section examines the content of the law of the barrios about housing.

---

1. Patterns of Ownership

Who owns the land? Our earlier mention of land invasions suggests that much of the land occupied by barrios is owned by persons other than the occupants. In many Caracas barrios the ownership of the land is uncertain. When General Juan Vicente Gómez died in 1935, the government "inherited" his enormous landholdings; as a result, a considerable extension of hillside land in Caracas has been government-owned for a generation. Even much of that land has been the subject of litigation, as various levels of government have made their claims. Similarly, a considerable proportion of the private land in these marginal areas has been claimed by more than one would-be owner. Some barrio residents have bought their land from the city or from private owners. In the 1967 survey, some 21% of the respondents answered that the land on which they lived was owned by them, or their spouses, or other relatives; these responses were concentrated in three of the oldest barrios. A similar percentage (19%) identified other private individuals as the owners of their land, and some 14% said the land was owned by the city or the government. But nearly half of the respondents said that they did not know who owned the land. These figures are little more than a statistical reflection of what it means to use the expression "squatter community." By definition, the squatter lives on someone else's land; the barrio residents who now own their land are more appropriately called ex-squatters.

Most Venezuelan lawyers, like their North American counterparts, would conclude from this picture of uncertain titles that there is little security of tenure in the barrios. One rather general hypothesis of the Caracas barrio study, confirmed by the study's results, was that such a conclusion was not justified. More than four out of five of the interviewees in the Caracas survey said that they (or their spouses, or relatives) owned the *houses* they were occupying. The rest rented their houses. In the newer barrios, nearly all the occupant families owned their own houses. In the oldest barrios, the percentage of renters increased to as high as 40% in one central-city barrio. The older barrios are blending into the city, and titles are becoming regularized. (The percentages of "Don't know" answers to the question of land ownership were low in the old barrios.) In such a barrio, an occupant who does not own the land on which he or she is living is not likely to own the house, either; instead, the occupant is renting from another person who owns both the house and the land. In the newer barrios, ownership of the house and the land tend to be divided. Later we shall discuss the implications of these data for the barrio residents' sense of security about their houses.

---

2. Acquisition of Land and Houses

While the "typical" barrio was formed in a land invasion, only one-sixth of the respondents in the 1967 survey reported that they had acquired their land by occupation. The percentages were substantially higher in the newer barrios, reaching 57% in the very newest, which was only five months old at the time of the survey. The point is not that the older barrios were formed more peacefully, but that the present occupants of the older barrios have acquired their occupancy rights by orderly purchase or rental from earlier occupants.

At the outset of a barrio's existence, the barrio junta assigns parcels of land for the construction of houses. The junta may or may not be authorized by the municipal government to perform this task. Lots are measured — say, 7 by 10 meters in a barrio that is close to the city's commercial and employment centers, and perhaps 15 by 20 meters in a more rural setting. A new arrival asks the junta's permission to occupy a lot, perhaps showing a letter from a municipal office authorizing the person to move into the barrio. As a barrio becomes established, a weakening junta may abandon this power to designate where new arrivals may live, but a strong junta will retain the power as a device to screen out persons thought to be undesirable.

Even in the oldest barrios, where the greatest number of housing turnovers can be expected to have occurred, a majority of the residents have built their own houses, as distinguished from buying them. Frequently a new resident in a new barrio will have paid for the parcel of land the junta has designated — not buying the title from the owner, whoever that may be, but buying the service of a man who has leveled a portion of the hillside so as to convert it into a parcel on which a house can be built.

---

3. The Content of an Owner's Rights

The one-out-of-five barrio resident who owns his or her land, of course, has the usual rights of an owner; title is registered in the appropriate land registry. Our interest here is in the rights of the barrio resident who does not own the land, but who says that he or she owns his house. It is easy for a lawyer in Venezuela or in the United States to conceive of such a division of ownership rights; the "bundle of rights" notion has its precise parallel in the civil law; in Spanish, it is even called the "haz de derechos." Three out of five of the residents own their houses but not their land. What does it mean to "own" one's house when one is a squatter?

The most obvious feature of ownership is the right to undisturbed possession. In fact, challenges to an owner-occupant's right to remain in a house are rare. All but 11% of the respondents in the 1967 survey said that no one had ever disputed their rights to build on the land or live in their houses. The percentage of affirmative replies to this question was relatively high (24%) only in the brand-new barrio that was five months old at the time of the survey. Most of the residents of this barrio[16] had taken their land by occupation. Disputes about the right to occupy a parcel occur, if they occur at all, primarily during the early days of the barrio's existence. After a short time, virtually all such disputes cease, and possession is peaceful. Occasionally someone will turn up who claims to represent the true owner of the land (the 11% figure above

---

[16]The barrio is named Cuatricentenario, in honor of the 400th anniversary of the founding of Caracas, celebrated in 1967.

represents these incidents), but the nearly universal reaction to such an appearance has been to reject any demand for removal from the premises, or for payment for the land.

Thus, the central fact about a squatter-owner's rights is that nothing happens to disturb his or her occupancy. The neighbors respect each other's rights; the sense of "yours" and "mine" is accepted and enforced. The enforcement typically happens in one of the rare disputes over boundaries between adjoining neighbors. In such a case, the junta's decision settles the issue. Boundary disputes, like other disputes about the rights of squatter-owners, tend to arise early in the barrio's history and then to cease.

In the oldest barrios, where most houses share common walls with the houses next door, boundary disputes are nearly a physical impossibility. But analogous issues about an owner's rights do arise. For example, suppose that one resident begins to excavate into the hill behind his house for the purpose of adding a room. His neighbor to the rear may be afraid that the digging will undermine his house, and may call on the barrio junta to insist on a retaining wall, or to stop the digging altogether. Such a dispute, like a boundary dispute, falls clearly within the junta's customary jurisdiction.[17]

Other claims to rights in land are not infrequently brought before the junta. Sometimes it is hard for a resident to reach his house without passing over the lot of another resident; the typical case would be that of the uphill neighbor who needs to pass over the downhill neighbor's lot. Usually, no trouble would arise. If the two neighbors have a falling out, however, the downhill man may threaten violence to the uphill man who tries to cross his lot. In such a case, the junta may order that a right-of-way be given. A common law court would call such an arrangement an "easement by necessity." (This problem is apt to be as temporary as the usual boundary dispute. Even if the neighbors perpetuate their feud, the matter may be resolved by the building of a common concrete stairway.)

The barrio house-owner's right to transfer the house is universally recognized by the barrio residents. The owner can sell the house or give it away, and the transferee's right to occupy will not be challenged. (If the house should remain vacant for a period of several months, then the junta may assign another family to occupy it. Even a longer period of vacancy would be respected, however, if it were understood that the transferee had been delayed in taking possession by, say, illness.) Alternatively, the owner may rent the house; about one house in five in the barrios is rented. There are legal restrictions on barrio rentals, both in the national legislation and in the customary law of the barrios. We shall discuss these restrictions later in this section.

If a house-owner's occupancy were precarious, we should expect the owner's death to produce some instability. In fact, the nearly universal result upon the death of the owner of a barrio house is the assumption of ownership rights by members of his or her family. The responses to the 1967 survey showed that almost everyone expected to be able to designate the successor to his or her house. And over 98% said they expected to leave their belongings, including their houses, to relatives. While nine out of ten barrio residents had taken no action to assure their families of the right of succession, about half of them expressed the intention to do so, unsually in vague

---

[17]We discuss the junta's dispute-settling functions in greater detail in section E of this chapter.

terms about "signing a document" of some sort. A few who said they had no intention of taking any action to assure the passage of their property to their children remarked that there was no need to do so, since the children were legitimate. That view, which may have been held by others who did not volunteer a reason for their lack of intention to make a will or otherwise try to control the succession to their property, reflects an awareness of the national legislation about inheritance.

---

4. Rental Arrangements

The rental of a rancho is specifically prohibited by national law. The content of this prohibition is found in the Regulations for the Rent Control Law and for the Legislative Decree on Eviction. These regulations, adopted in 1960, were an early legislative product of the Betancourt government. Their text, in relevant part, follows:

> Art. 21. The rental of dwellings known as ranchos is neither permitted nor valid, nor is the rental, in general, of urban or suburban dwellings which do not possess minimum elementary conditions of health and habitability. The existence or non-existence of such conditions shall be determined by the appropriate sanitary authority, in conformity to the respective laws, regulations and municipal ordinances.
>
> Art. 22. Persons who, on August 1, 1960, occupied ranchos or dwellings such as those mentioned in Article 21 are not obligated to make rental payments from that date forward. Payments which may have been made for that purpose are considered unjust, and therefore subject to restoration.
>
> Art. 23. [A person who thinks that he is entitled to be relieved of rental payments under Arts. 21 and 22 may apply to the Directorate of Tenancy for a certificate that he need not pay rent.]
>
> Art. 24. Landlords of the dwellings referred to in Art. 21 who consider that their dwellings do not fit the presuppositions of that Article, or that such presuppositions have ceased to exist, may offer proof of such circumstances to the Directorate of Tenancy, by showing credentials of habitability of the property as issued by the appropriate sanitary authority, ... The Directorate shall [consider the representations of the tenant] and shall [in the proper case] give to the landlord a certificate of compliance with the requirements [of health and habitability], which certificate shall serve, in turn, as a certificate of revocation of the remission from the obligation to pay rent granted to the tenant . . . . [The certificate shall fix the date from which the landlord is entitled to collect rent.]

Thus the tenant of a rancho — in the narrow and pejorative sense of the term "rancho" — need not pay rent, and if such payments are made, theoretically the tenant has a right to recover them. The owner, however, can seek to persuade the authorities that the house is properly constructed; if it is, the owner can get a certificate (*certificado de bienhechura*) authorizing the collection of rent from the tenant.

The regulations, it will be seen, rely on agencies of the government for their enforcement; there is no place in the regulatory scheme for the barrio junta to play any role. In other respects, however, a strong junta will be exercising jurisdiction over matters relating to rights in land, and it is not surprising that some juntas assert the additional power to police illegal rentals of ranchos. The form of the policing is simple; the junta prevents the landlord from evicting the tenant for nonpayment of rent. One member of a junta put it this way: An owner who rents his rancho doesn't need it, and someone who needs it should have it. Presumably this attitude was not what motivated the government to prohibit the rental of ranchos; the regulation seems instead to have been adopted in order to discourage the business of building ranchos in order to rent them. Still, the two purposes often lead to the same result: relieving the tenant from paying rent. So the public authorities have not obstructed the juntas from assisting.

Thus a tenant can move into a rancho, paying the first month's rent; instead of going through the procedure of getting a certificate from the government, the tenant can simply inform the junta, which will provide protection from the landlord's harassment. Some juntas have made similar efforts to stop builder-speculators who construct ranchos and then sell them, but the junta's power to reach such cases is more limited. Ranchos can be built, sold and occupied practically overnight, and the junta will not be disposed to evict the buyer once a family is in the rancho.

The proportion of rented houses appears to be correlated positively with the age of the barrio; in the 1967 survey, there were many rented houses in the oldest barrios (up to 40%), while in the two barrios most recently formed, the percentages of renters were 0% and 1.7%, respectively. Since by far the greater number of ranchos are in the newer barrios, it appears that popular practice is in accord with the national legistation. The rancho is for the most part a temporary dwelling, to be lived in by the owner until he or she can modify the building progressively by adding a cement floor, block walls, and a concrete roof.

The terms of the typical rental arrangement are simple, and unwritten. The tenant must pay rent; one who fails to pay must vacate. (About one-quarter of the tenants do not follow this pattern; most of them appear to be living in houses owned by relatives.) Other conditions are rare, but a substantial number of renters assume that their landlords could evict them for causing damage to the house, or for using the house for an illicit purpose. Only in a handful of cases has an owner sought to raise the rent during a tenant's occupancy; the usual pattern seems to be that the landlord does not make improvements for the tenant, and therefore does not ask for an increase in rent.

---

5. Security of Tenure

Implicit in much of the preceding discussion is an assumption that the barrio residents feel secure in the occupancy of their houses. The main source of the tenure security found in the barrios is undoubtedly the respect shown by the residents generally for their neighbors' ownership interests, and the expectation that each barrio's residents will stand together against the ownership claims of outsiders.

Ultimately, the barrio people know how impolitic it would be for the national government to dislodge any substantial number of them. In fact, only 11% of the residents have ever been faced with a claim of payment for their land by a purported owner. Since eight out of nine have never been presented with such a claim, it is no wonder that their sense of tenure security is strong.

The 1967 survey asked this question of residents who did now own the land on which their houses were located: "If the owner of the land came and asked you to pay him, what would you do?" The answers demonstrate the strength of the barrio residents' expectations of permanence:

18.0%   We would move
3.0%   The owner would have to pay us the value of the house
48.5%   We would pay for the land (without conditions), or we would pay if everyone else did
5.9%   We would pay for the land if he could prove he was the owner
7.9%   We would pay for the land if he would set a fair price (or give us time to pay, etc.)
1.0%   We would do whatever the junta said to do
2.6%   We would reach an agreement (without specifying either the sale of the house or the purchase of the land)
3.3%   We would go to the authorities (or the police, etc.)
9.8%   Don't know

Thus the great majority expected to be able to work out a compromise arrangement in order to stay where they were. The majority's willingness to pay for their land, given the unlikelihood that the courts or other officers of government would evict them, may seem altruistic. Another explanation may be the barrio residents are at least vaguely aware of the system of land title registration, and that they want the added security of a formally recognized title.

In Peru, the Barriadas Law of 1961 provides for the state to expropriate the land on which pre-1960 occupants live, and for the adjudication of title to an occupant in return for payment (in installments) to the state of the value of the lot. (Land values are calculated as of the time just before the barriada was formed, to avoid requiring the squatting resident to pay for the increase in value that has resulted from the barriada's establishment.)[18] Should the occupants be required to pay for their land? Does your answer depend on whether the former owner was a private individual or the government itself? There are analogies here to some of the issues we have seen in our discussions of rural land reform. Are those analogies complete, or would it be consistent to oppose requiring land-reform beneficiaries to pay for their land while favoring such a requirement for urban squatters who are granted title? Should those two positions more properly be reversed?

Another question in the 1967 survey asked whether the resident would expect to be paid for the house in the event that the government should decide to take his land

---

[18]Manaster, "The Problem of Urban Squatters in Developing Countries: Peru," 1968 *Wis. L. Rev.* 23, 48-55.

to build a road. Some 92% of the respondents answered affirmatively. And over 34% said they would expect the government to pay them for their *land*, in similar circumstances; since only 21% have title to their land, there are some who think the government would place a compensable value on their right to occupy someone else's land.

The barrio residents have come there principally for the purpose of owning their own homes. One barrio resident spoke of his decision to move to the barrio: "I used to come by here every day. Everyone's ambition is to live under his own roof, not in an apartment that belongs to someone else. You have to ask permission for everything — to bring up a bed, to change a plug. Besides, I want to have something to leave to the children, a little house, or something like that." The mixture of pride and practicality in that statement has its concrete expression in the improvements made to barrio houses. The 1967 survey asked this question of owners of houses: "Have you added any important additions to the house? If so, what?" (An "important addition" was defined narrowly: a concrete roof, cement-block walls, a cement floor, or another room.) Eliminating the barrio that had been in existence only five months, we find these responses:

25.8%   No
36.9%   Yes, one such improvement
20.0%   Yes, two such improvements
17.3%   Yes, three or more such improvements

So about three quarters of the barrio homeowners surveyed had made at least one major investment in their houses, and over 37% had made at least two such improvements. Furthermore, more than 71% said that they were planning to make an improvement of this kind in the future. These results are visible to the eye. The houses in the newest barrios are ranchos, of carton and zinc construction. The older the barrio the better are its houses. The oldest barrios blend into the city physically; cement-block walls are covered with stucco and painted in pastel colors. One who visited Caracas in 1963 and again in 1967 would see a dramatic change in the way the barrios looked. And these observations are confirmed by the 1967 survey, which showed markedly better housing construction in the older barrios than in the newer ones. In Aesopian language, one of the Venezuelan sociologists who worked in the barrio study described this slow-but-steady investment process as *un trabajo de hormigas*, a work of ants.

Rented houses, on the other hand, are improved far less frequently; some 74% of the renters reported no important improvements. Thus, the key to motivation to investment in barrio housing appears to be the occupant's ownership of the house. Ownership of the land seems not to be significant in this process, since the percentages are nearly the same in the various barrios, regardless of the presence of a substantial number of residents who have title to the land.

In what sense does the barrio resident's security of tenure rest on law? What are the relevant *substantive* components of the barrios' legal system? What are that system's relevant *structural* and *cultural* components, for purposes of analyzing the security of tenure?

---

6. Implications for Government Policy

What conclusions should be drawn by government planners from the results of the 1967 survey? Would you favor a program on the Peruvian model for distributing land titles to the barrio residents? What should be the highest priority projects for those planners concerned with the physical condition of the barrios? Should the law prohibiting rental of ranchos be enforced vigorously? Repealed? Are there implications in the survey's results for the choice, frequently posed (at least theoretically) by planners, between eradication of a barrio (with substitution of high-rise housing) and its rehabilitation?

D. The Study: Family Obligations

1. The Extended Family

Studies of rural-urban migration around the world have identified the family as an institution that provides support for the migrant. This comment on the *barriadas* of Lima is typical:

> . . . it is always the family which provides the greatest source of security for the inhabitants of these areas. Even when very unsettled and living in overcrowded conditions, the family is always the mainstay of its members.[19]

While most residents of the Caracas barrios have not come directly from the countryside, a similar support function for the family can be observed there. Very frequently, the motive for choosing a particular barrio as the place to reside is the presence in that barrio of another member of the new resident's family. The kinship network is one important means of communicating the availability of land in a new barrio, or the availability of a house in an old one. It is not surprising to find that usually a barrio resident has relatives living in the same barrio. Many residents who have built their own houses have been assisted in the task by relatives. And those who have given or received lodging in a time of need report that their benefactors and beneficiaries in such situations have been relatives.

The following description of the kinship network in a Venezuelan barrio comes not from Caracas, but from Ciudad Guayana. Nonetheless, for our purposes, it is accurate in most important respects. The author, Lisa Redfield Peattie, is an anthropologist.

---

[19]Matos Mar, "The 'Barriadas' of Lima: An Example of Integration into Urban Life," in P. Hauser (Ed.), *Urbanization in Latin America* 170, 175 (1961).

L. PEATTIE, THE VIEW FROM THE BARRIO

Pp. 40-51 (1968)

The social world of Barrio La Laja is not that of an isolated village or small community in which everyone knows everyone else. People are always moving in and out; nearly a quarter of the barrio's adults had been there less than a year; and at no time does each person there know all the others personally, or by name. There is no single institution or group of institutions in the barrio to which all residents belong. Moreover, everyone in the barrio has connections — economic, kinship, social — outside the barrio. Each person's field of social relations includes part, but not all, of the barrio, the proportion varying greatly according to age, length of residence, economic role, and number of kin. At the same time each person's field of social relations spreads outside the barrio as well, some to a much greater extent than others.

The social world of the barrio is in some ways typically urban in form. It is perhaps even more striking, therefore, that relations based on kinship or assimilated to kinship are dominant in the social network. People are likely to have relatives living nearby. In this barrio, to which nearly half the adults have migrated within the last five years, two-thirds of the households are connected by kinship with at least one other household in the barrio. People, especially women, interact with their kin. People aid their kinsfolk economically. Kinship terms are used in address much more generally than they are in the United States at any social level. One greets a kinsman as "cousin" or some other appropriate term rather than by name.

The kinship model is extended to other relationships. It seems natural to treat a person, especially a younger person, with whom one is on any basis of intimacy, as though he or she were a kinsman. A neighbor's child may be addressed as "son" or "daughter," two little girls who play together habitually come to address each other as "sister."

Moreover, to these biological kin are added one's *compadres* and *comadres*, a group of chosen kinsfolk. For each child, a parent will choose three pairs of godparents, one for the little baptismal ceremony performed in the house by laymen, one for the formal church baptism usually held when the child is three years old or so, and one for the first communion. The godparents have certain obligations to the godchild, most notably in the case of the first communion godparents, the buying of the elaborate costume which is de rigueur on this occasion; but, although the Church defines the godparent-godchild relationship as primary in the situation, La Laja places in practice most stress on the relationship established through *compadrazgo* between the child's own parents and his ritual parents. The importance placed on the relationship is symbolized in the way they always address each other, not by name but as *compadre* or *comadre*.

Since it has often been thought and said that kinship relations tend to become less important in the urban setting, this situation might be thought of as anomalous, an evidence of a transition still incomplete from rural to urban life. But there may be more to it than that. Among the working-class population of Panama City and of Mexico City, among Puerto Rican migrants to New York, kinship relations seem to be at least as important and perhaps more important than among their rural counterparts. The work of such social researchers as Michael Young has exposed strong kinship networks in segments of British urban society. But in addition, a look at the nature of the kinship networks in such urban areas suggests that they may in fact be shaped by the necessities of urban life: that they are a folkish plant which springs up from the very city pavements.

In taking a look at kinship in La Laja, the primary unit used will be the household. "The family" seems hardly to exist as a social unit with discrete boundaries; certainly in La Laja there is nothing comparable to those kinship groups functioning as corporate entities which are reported for some African societies. Kinship ties are extended bilaterally; husband and wife each continue to have their own kinship networks. People may speak of "the Rodrigues" as of a social unit, but such a naming seems to designate a sort of conspicuous clot of kinship relations, connecting with other such clots rather than a distinct group for which one can easily enumerate members and nonmembers. The household, on the other hand, is a unit rather clearly defined at any point of time by the units of physical cohabitation, except for a few marginal cases in which a single aged parent is living in a separate house next door to grown children and may be considered as forming for some purposes part of a single household with them. It is not, of course, a unit with long-term boundaries; since people join not only by birth but also by affiliation for social and economic reasons, or, on the other hand, move out to join other households or to establish households of their own. Nor is the kinship structure fully described by an enumeration of households, for the households are, as already noted, more generally than not connected to others by kinship. The grouping called in the barrio "the Campos" (that is, the Campos "family") includes the personnel of four households, totaling thirty-six persons more or less, in which the maternal generation consists of six sisters; two other households are related to this core.

But as a point from which to begin, the household is a convenient unit. An analysis was made of the composition of La Laja's eighty households, and this was supplemented by interviewing on values and practices with regard to family and household organization in an attempt to analyze the principles which seem to govern household structuring. The following "principles" attempt to describe how families are actually structured in terms of the cultural and social factors which seem involved in giving them their characteristic form.

1) Normally, a household consists of persons related to each other by blood or marriage.

Of the eighty households of La Laja, six violate this rule. Four of the cases involve the taking-in of older unmarried persons with no kin living nearby: two old men, unrelated, live together; two other households consist of small nuclei of related single men and another bachelor friend; in one household an extremely poor old woman living with her grandchild has taken in an even poorer beggar woman. One family has an adoptive child of no blood relationship to them (adoption of kinship-related children is not rare). In the sixth case, an older male house-owner had been sharing his house for a month with a young couple, unrelated to him, with their two children. In all other cases, the people living in a single household were in some way related by kinship.

2) The primary axis of kinship structure is the relationship between a mother and her children, her own or adoptive.

Men, it is felt, ought to support and care for their children but women "have to" care for their children. The children have a reciprocal obligation, not quite so strong, to care for their mother. Although both these reciprocal obligations seem to imply both an element of practical aid and one of sentiment, the parent-child relationship seems to be more weighted on the side of practical care and support, that of child to parent more on the side of sentiment. Poetry about mothers is especially read by and at times composed by more educated persons; however, a group of *clase obrero* teenagers in publishing a weekly newpaper also inserted a number of examples of literature on this theme. When my husband was killed in an automobile accident while I was living in the barrio, two people commented that one must be able to adjust to anything; "one can *even* adjust to the death of one's mother."

Women may have and rear children without a husband. If a young woman has children while living in her parents' home and later marries a man other than the father of her first children, she will ordinarily bring the children with her to the marriage. (There are some exceptions to this, in which the tie between mother and child has been extended and transferred to the mother's mother; adoption by the mother's sister also seems not uncommon.) When marriages break up, as they not rarely do, the children always stay with the mother. Usually, the women and children also retain the house. Thus, in the working-class household the woman is typically the effective head of the household, even if

3) the man, when and if present, is formally the *jefe familia* or "head of the family." He should be treated with respect by both wife and children. He may strike his wife as well as his children. However, conspicuous wife-beating is not common, and women can and do leave men who drink or mistreat them. One of the few cases of real violence in La Laja during the time I was living there was when a grown daughter cracked her father's head open when he tried to beat her mother.

4) Ordinarily, a couple with an established marital relationship, whether legalized or common-law union, should establish a household of their own. This applies with especial force to the combination of parents and married children.

Only four households in La Laja contain more than one married pair. In one, the principal nuclear family has added to it the man's first cousin with his wife and children. In another, the husband's sister and her husband share the household with the principal pair; the "extra couple" have no children. The third is a case in which the wife's brother, with his wife and children shares the house. In only one case are the two married pairs of successive generations. Here a grown daughter's common-law husband (He has legally recognized her child) lives in the household with his wife, his wife's parents, and his wife's siblings. This situation has been of short duration and seems unstable; it appears that it will be resolved either by the younger couple getting their own house or by their relationship breaking up. There are plenty of three-generation households in La Laja, but with the exception cited, either the first or second generation or both is a *mujer sola* — a woman without husband either in law or common law. . . .

Since living with the parental generation is not a valid alternative, as it is the preferred one in some societies, it follows that something of a solid economic base is essential to a marriage; the couple has to pay a separate rent. It would appear that some stable relationships evolving toward marriage break up before they even get started, so to speak, in the practical and economic difficulties of establishing a separate household. The man then drifts away, and the girl is left, perhaps with a child or two, living in her parents' house.

5) There is considerable separation between the world of men and of women. In the evenings a man is likely to be drinking beer with his male friends, while his wife visits with her women friends on her front doorstep or on theirs. The world of men is more *en la calle* — the world of the bars, movie theaters, etc.; women are more likely to stay close to home.

6) Siblings in general have egalitarian and mutually supporting relationships. The tie between sisters is likely to be especially strong, perhaps because of the greater common focus on the home.

7) Marriage is conceived of as an alliance between individuals rather than family groups.

In a "proper" marriage the young man asks the parents of his intended spouse for their permission, but this custom seems often honored in the breach, and there seems to be none of the reciprocal exchange of calls and gifts which in some Latin American societies makes marriage establish relationships between the family groups of the two married persons. It seems to be possible for a marriage to survive the active hostility of the parental generation, for the mother of one young woman in the barrio still does not speak to her daughter's (legally married) husband after five years and two children. This attitude does not seem to cause any serious problems, for the mother regards her daughter's marriage, while a mistake, as her business; and the husband puts no obstacles in the way of his wife's considerable visiting and economic aid to the mother. The married couple and the mother live at about ten houses' distance from each other.

It is not uncommon for marriage to take place by having the girl "go off" with the man; this may be followed by legal marriage, or it may not. Church marriage is of distinctly higher social prestige than a merely legal marriage, and the latter higher than common-law residence, but aside from this status gradient there seem few social sanctions on failure to legalize. Church marriages are uncommon in La Laja. People say that they are expensive, by which they presumably mean not so much the ceremony itself as the outlay in dress and festivities which the status implications of a church wedding bring to it. Women in La Laja also comment that a church marriage is bad because it permits no divorce. It is a contract with no escape clause in a society where separation often seem appropriate.

It may be seen that there is a general correlation between the status implications of the marriage form, the formality in legal and ritual terms of the marriage, and the degree of masculine dominance implied. At one extreme is the middle-class-style legalized marriage with the husband clearly the *jefe familia*, the house and property generally his, and the husband's economic and social role highly status-defining for his wife and children. At the other is the definitely matrifocal family of the working class, organized around a woman and her children; the house (probably the only substantial property) is the woman's, and "husbands" attach themselves peripherally for longer or shorter periods, and with greater or smaller degrees of definiteness. This structure is perfectly acceptable socially in La Laja, but it is clearly seen as of lower social status than the first. The status gradient here suggested seems clearly implied by other behavior; for example, there appears to be a distinct tendency for those who get married in church to practice other behavior characteristic of the middle class, such as keeping their children particularly clean and well dressed.

Marriages, especially common-law ones of the matrifocal type, may be, and are, terminated by either party. "He left me for another woman." "He drank much and I decided to spend the rest of my years in peace with my children." A woman unhappy with her husband may hang on until her children are somewhat grown and then take advantage of the solidarity of mother and children to rely on their mutual support. . . .

In some societies, family groups are important economic units; this is particularly true in peasant agricultural societies, where it is the family that runs the farm which is the basis of life. In La Laja, there is no need for the family to stick together to manage property; property, besides personal clothing and effects, consists at best of ownership of a house and furniture, perhaps crucial to a woman with children to care for but not to the husband. There is no necessary economic collaboration through sex division of labor, for men can in a pinch cook or eat out and women can in a pinch earn a living. Compare the Eskimo, where a man with no woman to sew furs and prepare food for him is in almost as serious a plight as the woman with no man to hunt for her. In La Laja, husband and wife move in distinct worlds — neither requires the other. In the absence of corporate kin groups, marriage cannot be used to cement a useful alliance between families; there is no process analogous to the transfer of the marriage cattle which in African tribal society mobilizes the kin groups to pressure husband and wife to maintain a difficult relationship. In La Laja the bilateral extension of kinship ties is likely to be a dispersive factor, if anything, as kinsfolk of husband and wife make their claims for aid which conflict with the claims of the nuclear family. In many societies, ranging from some Mexican Indian villages to the American young-corporation-executive suburb, there is a game of status which is played in couples; it is the husband and wife together who do the things which move one up through the system. For the working-class world of La Laja, in which people are scrambling to "defend themselves," as people put it, such considerations do not apply. . . .

It seemed to me, therefore, that the "matrifocal family" arises naturally out of the conditions of lower-class life, whether in Venezuela or elsewhere, especially under conditions of high unemployment; the steady job is seen as relevant in providing men with status and roles which might become the foci for stabilizing the conjugal relationship.

Thus, it is not remarkable that marriages in La Laja are not likely to be particularly stable or permanent. It is more remarkable that about half the households of La Laja consist of more or less stable nuclear family groups — a married (legally or in custom) pair and their children — with or without the addition of other kinsfolk. . . .

. . . If the family is not an economic unit, and partly for this reason may hardly be said to exist as "a unit" at all, what is the reason for the family ties which link the majority of La Laja's households together? Why do the people of La Laja, moving about in the labor market as so many individual labor units, still form a network of social ties largely defined by kinship? If *the* family is not crucial, why are familial relationships so important?

Let us start from a summary of the nature of these relationships. The social structure of La Laja may be described most generally as a series of partly overlapping networks of highly personalized kinship relations and of personal relations often made into quasi-kinship through *compadrazgo*. Kinship relations are developed bilaterally. There is a good deal of choice in the kinship ties to be stressed; beyond the tie between mother and children, defined around the physical dependence of the young child, it is open to a given individual to select, in large part, which of the many possible kinship relations he is to develop into strong ties. This selection then is made with regard to considerations of the pleasures and advantages, including economic advantages, of a particular association compared to others. This element of individual choice, taken together with the bilaterality of the system, reduces the tendency of the kinship system to produce distinct corporate groups and exaggerates the tendency of the system to produce networks of relationship. Then, to the real kinsfolk are added additional ties and relationships of chosen, fictitious kinsfolk through the *compadre* system.

It must be recalled again that kinship networks of similar form are reported for groups similarly placed in the economic order in places as diverse culturally as Mexico City and New York. The basis of these networks of kinship and kinship-like relations seems to lie in the very structure of the economic situation which makes for that sort of matrifocal family structure often looked at by the middle class observer as "weak" or lacking in form. In the urban setting the kinship and quasi-kinship network is a basis of economic security – perhaps not a solid basis, but the basis that is available.

People who work at unskilled labor in an economy to which they are necessarily marginal as individuals, and which has a continuing high rate of unemployment, can rarely accumulate capital. When they are working their continuance at work is unsure, and they are often out of a job. Out of a paying job, there is little they can do to make a living; one cannot in such a setting live off the land or by farming. There is, for the people of La Laja, no organized public welfare system to which to turn. If you are desperate the town council might tide you over with a small gift. With luck you might get on the list to receive occasional packages of American surplus food. But there is no "welfare" in the American sense.

A person's kinsmen, then, are the people to whom one can turn for support. A young man who is out of a job will find a brother, an aunt, a cousin who will house and feed him while he looks for work to turn up. A household with no current income being brought in by any of its members directly will draw on other related households of kin who do have some access to cash. Thus, the two sisters who lived next door to me with their children survived for months on what might have been censused as "no income"; the children were neither healthy nor well-dressed, but they did not starve. At times one or the other of the two women would have work doing washing or ironing. The rest of the time they were "helped" by the grown daughter of one of them who worked as a cleaning woman for me, and who, since her husband worked intermittently, was able to detach some of her earnings for her mother, and by another sister who lived in the house behind them and whose husband, a ship's cook, would have had a good income if he had not drunk so much of it. In La Laja, with one out of three adult males out of a job, and nearly half the population under thirteen, only one person out of six had any regular income. The other five-sixths were apparently living — if precariously — off the employed segment. It was the social networks in which kinship relations are basic which made this possible.

The sort of kinship structure seen in La Laja, then, seems to operate as a system of social and economic welfare in an environment otherwise uncertain in the extreme. Its very looseness makes it possible for any given individual to maximize his possibilities for eliciting help. He will join the household kin group at a particular time most able to take care of him; he will make the kinship claim to the relative who at the time he needs help is most likely to be able to give him help. This welfare function of the kinship network in turn serves to draw kinsfolk into physical proximity; because claims are made in quite personalized terms it is hard to assert a claim in the absence of personal contact and a personally developed relationship.

---

2. Husband and Wife

The 1967 Caracas barrio survey showed a family living pattern similar to the one described by Peattie: the great majority of households (about 78%) included a nuclear family of husband, wife and children. (In 46% of the households, only the nuclear family was present; in the others, other relatives were also present.) Among the couples living together, about half described their status as married by law, and the other half were *unidos*, living in common-law unions. The early drafts of the survey questionnaire contained questions designed to measure the stability of marital unions, but those questions were eliminated when the pilot survey showed them to be offensive to the interviewees. Some sense of the degree of stability can be obtained, however, from an examination of the surnames of the children in the households surveyed. In 60% of the households, we have noted, *all* of the children had the same surname as the current husband of the mother. It would be surprising to find such a phenomenon in a household where a series of husbands had been present to father the woman's children. In another 27% of the cases, all the children had the surname of the mother. This pattern suggests the absence of a stable marital union, but is not conclusive; some such cases may reflect awareness of the national law of legitimacy and recognition.

Apart from the survey, the 1967 study contemplated that the participant-observers living in the barrios would take special note of subjects dropped from the questionnaire because of their sensitivity. The observers reported many statements by men of half-formed intention to leave their wives, but few instances where such an intention was carried into action. Every barrio seems to have its celebrated cases of individuals, both men and women, whose marital turnover rate is high. Many a middle-class Venezuelan thinks of such a case as the barrio norm. But these cases are the subject of gossip within the barrio precisely because they do not fit the usual pattern of barrio family life. As we have seen, the principal motive for moving to a barrio is home ownership, which implies some expectation of family stability.

(a) The Husband's Obligations

This question was asked in the 1967 survey:

Suppose a man and woman live together, that is, they are *unidos*. How do you think the man should behave? That is, what obligations does the man have to fulfill?

The interviewers were instructed to keep sounding out the respondents, asking, "What else?" Most of the responses were thus multiple, identifying several obligations. By far the most prominent answer, both as a first response (46%) and taking all responses cumulatively (79%), was that the husband must bring home money, food, clothes and the like. The husband's primary obligation, as it is perceived by men and women alike, is to be the breadwinner. This perception is borne out by the figures on contributions to the household's expenses. In the overwhelming majority of cases, the husband who is present in the house provides the chief support for the household. Concern for this obligation to support the wife was expressed indirectly in the answers to a question that seemingly was not related. The questionnaire, in its section on norms of sexual behavior of unmarried young people, asked whether it would be more serious or less serious for an underage girl to have sexual relations with a boy who is also a minor than it would be if the young man had reached majority. More than seven out of ten respondents answered that the case would be more serious, chiefly because a boy under age could not be compelled to marry and support the girl. (Of the 11% who answered that the case would be less serious, 7% appeared to understand the question as calling for a moral judgment, saying that it would be less serious — *menos grave* — for a boy under age, since he would not know what he was doing. Thus the "more serious" view probably is held even more widely than the seven-out-of-ten figure indicates. One moral here is that a closed-end question needs to be made very explicit, in order to avoid such ambiguities.)

The two obligations perceived for the husband that share the runner-up position, far behind the duty to support the wife, are these:

Behave well (be serious, stay home, don't cause scandal, don't get drunk)
Take care of the children, be affectionate to them, discipline them, etc.

Each of these responses was given by about one-third of the interviewees, most frequently in the latter case as a second or third (prompted) response. Fidelity was mentioned by fewer than 2% of the respondents and by only 2 out of 239 men). The issue of the husband's sexual fidelity was raised explicitly, however, in a series of questions carefully constructed to avoid asking directly for the respondent's own views. The responses show a considerable intolerance for the husband who brings another woman to live in the same house, but an easing of this intolerance in the case of the "other woman" who lives in another barrio. The open-ended questions, with their empirically coded responses, are as follows:

Suppose a man lives in a house with a woman, and that he brings a second woman to live in the same house. What do you think would happen?

2.1%   The first woman would accept the situation.
1.2%   Some would accept it, others not.
29.2%   The first would throw the second one out.
5.4%   One of the two would have to leave.
28.7%   Expressions of disgust, but without answering adequately (*e.g.*, they would fight)
15.5%   The first would leave.
11.5%   The first would throw out the man (or both the man and the second woman).
4.2%   Resort to the authorities (the law, etc.).
2.3%   Don't know..

What would the neighbors do? Do you think they would continue visiting the house?

62.5%   No
25.8%   Yes
1.2%   Some yes, some no
4.1%   Sometimes yes, sometimes no (or it depends)
.8%   Other
5.6%   Don't know

Would the neighbors continue to have anything to do with the man in this case?

52.2%   No
31.3%   Yes
1.4%   Some yes, some no
5.9%   Sometimes yes, sometimes no (or it depends)
3.1%   Other
6.2%   Don't know

And if the man brought the second woman and had her live in the same barrio, or lived with another woman in the same barrio, what do you think would happen?

21.3%   The first woman would accept the situation. (Of women respondents, 24.4% gave this answer. The figure for men was 15.8%.)
2.5%   Some would accept it, others not.
1.3%   The man would have to choose one.
26.0%   Expressions of disgust, without answering adequately (*e.g.*, they would fight).
28.1%   The first woman would abandon the man.

    1.1%   Resort to the authorities.
    1.1%   If they were married, the first would divorce the man.
 13.9%   The first would try to make the second woman leave the barrio
            (or throw her out).
    4.6%   Don't know

And would the neighbors continue seeing the man in this case?

 38.6%   No
 45.6%   Yes
    1.7%   Some yes, some no
    5.7%   Sometimes yes, sometimes no (or it depends)
    1.0%   Other
    7.4%   Don't know

And what would happen if he had another woman in another barrio?

 40.5%   The first woman would accept the situation. (Of women
            respondents, 45.1% gave this answer. The figure for men was
            32.1%.)
    2.7%   Some would accept it, others not.
    1.2%   The man would have to choose one.
 10.9%   Expressions of disgust, without answering adequately (*e.g.*, they
            would fight).
    1.0%   Resort to the authorities.
 12.8%   The first would abandon the man (or throw him out, or leave).
    1.0%   If they were married, the first woman would divorce the man.
    5.6%   Don't know.
 24.4%   If she doesn't know about it, it doesn't matter.

And would the neighbors continue seeing the man in this case?

 22.7%   No (men: 26.1%; women: 19.9%)
 65.7%   Yes (men: 62.2%; women: 68.2%)
   .2%   Some yes, some no
   3.3%   Sometimes yes, sometimes no (it depends)
   .5%   Other
   7.6%   Don't know

    Are the husband's obligations, if any, as illuminated by these responses, properly considered to rest in law?
    Other obligations of the husband mentioned in the multiple responses to the basic open-ended question were these:

 11.9%   Respect the woman
 14.4%   Love and affection for the woman, avoid arguments, be nice,
            don't hit the woman, etc.
   5.6%   Marry the woman
 21.2%   Educate the children (send them to school)

If the latter response is added to the previous mentioned one about taking care of the children, then about half of the respondents are seen to have expressed the view that a "common-law" husband has obligations toward the children beyond the providing of support for the household. Some interviewees would be counted twice in this process, but it is clear that some obligation toward the children is the second most important one perceived for the husband.

(b) The Wife's Obligations

The 1967 questionnaire posed a similar open-ended question about the obligations of the woman in the same informal-union situation. The coded multiple responses are:

Total Responses	First Responses	
10.8%	7.4%	Same obligations as the man
64.1%	39.0%	Take care of the home, make the meals, wash, iron, market, etc.
51.4%	29.0%	Look after the husband, be considerate, etc.
21.0%	9.0%	Respect the husband, obey him, avoid arguments.
9.3%	2.8%	Stay home
4.6%	2.1%	Fidelity
44.7%	6.7%	Take care of the children
2.6%	.8%	Work outside the home if she can
7.7%	3.3%	Other

The obligation mentioned most frequently is something like a reciprocal of the husband's obligation to support the wife and children. One way to read these results would be to conclude that in the barrios material concerns are thought to be the most important in marriage. An alternative possibility is that the word "obligations" carries with it a cold and contractual sound, calling to mind duties of this kind. Also, a barrio, like other communities that are relatively poor, is a place where abstractions are apt to play a role in conversation that is secondary to things that can be seen and touched; the duty to wash and iron, like the duty to bring home dinner, is a duty that is easy to define.

The foregoing responses might be taken to mean that fidelity is not a highly prized virtue in barrio women. However, the participant observers who lived in barrios all reported that the classical double standard was very much at work there. One observer's report includes several direct quotations from barrio men to the effect that a single sexual transgression by a woman was sufficient ground for abandoning her. (One highly speculative guess would explain the absence of responses about fidelity to the questionnaire's inquiry into the woman's obligations as a reflection of the fact that a wife's infidelity is in some literal sense unthinkable.)

(c) The Effect of Legal Marriage

This question was put to the barrio residents in 1967:

And if they get married by law, do you think that then the man would have new obligations to fulfill, now that he is legally married? If yes, which?

The response was 68% negative. (For the woman's obligations, the answers were 72% negative.) The affirmative answers were scattered: more respect for the wife; stay with the wife; be faithful. The most interesting affirmative response was that the man would have the same obligations, "but with greater responsibility." This response was so frequent (about 10%) that it was added to the empirical code for the questionnaire, even though the answer had not been anticipated when the questionnaire was prepared. A person who gives this answer appears to be assuming that the legal system will enforce some marital obligations when the couple are civilly married which will not be enforced when they are living together in an informal union. Both in theory and in practice, that is a dubious assumption. "Common-law" husbands have a legal obligation to support their wives; and a barrio wife's enforcement in court of her support rights is not a realistic expectation, whether or not she is legally married. (Child support is something else again, as we shall see in the next section.)

In any case, as we have seen, there is no widely-shared perception of a duty on the part of a "common-law" husband to marry his wife in a civil or church ceremony. When the respondents answered that it was important to try to persuade young people who were having sexual relations to marry, they were not necessarily talking about a civil marriage or a church marriage, but instead seemed to have in mind persuading the couple to set up their own household as husband and wife, with or without a ceremony. Of course, as Peattie says about her barrio in Ciudad Guayana, a formal marriage is more prestigious, particularly for the woman. This concern for *respeto* is one we shall see again as we discuss the various roles of the barrio junta.

(d) Termination of Marriage: Support, Child Custody and Division of Property

In an informal union, of course, there need be no "grounds" for termination of the union. But among the barrio residents who are *unidos*, there is a fairly clear sense of at least some justifications for ending the relationship. While the husband's infidelity appears to be widely tolerated if it is not too blatantly carried on in front of the wife, the standard for the wife is not at all flexible — at least not in the conversation of barrio residents. The most widely accepted "ground" for a wife's decision to terminate an informal union is physical brutality by the husband, either toward the wife or toward her children. Nonsupport appears not to be an independent ground; a man who decides to stop supporting his family ordinarily leaves the household; there is no occasion for the wife to make a decision in such a case.

Upon the termination of an informal union, the children nearly universally stay with the mother, or with her family. (It is common for the maternal grandmother to take the children under such circumstances, and even to keep them when the wife forms another union with a new husband.) The notion of an obligation on the departing husband to support his children is not well developed. It will be recalled that in about 40% of the cases the children did not all bear the same surname as the resident spouse of the mother. Yet, out of nearly 600 responses, only 26 households (4.4%) reported that a nonresident father was contributing anything to the maintenance of the household; in 515 cases (86.6%), no one other than those living in the house was contributing.

The most important item of property to be allocated upon the termination of a union is, of course, the house. If the husband has built the house or bought it, then the common practice treats the house as his, to be disposed of as he may choose. The typical case in which the husband is thought to have no such right is the case in which the wife (and perhaps some children by a previous union) had been living in a house when the husband moved in. And even in this case, it is possible to find examples of acquiescence by the wife in the husband's power to control the property. One such case, reported by an observer who was living in a barrio in 1967, was the following: A woman lived in a house with a man and two children from a previous union, aged 16 and 9. The land on which her house was built had been given to her, and she had paid for the materials and had the house built. The man with whom she was living regularly came home drunk and beat her and her children. She was afraid to leave the children alone in the house, for fear of what he might do to them; some of the beatings were administered with a machete. This situation had been in progress for several months. The woman said to the observer that she thought the house was her property, but that she did not expect to be able to get the man to leave, even though he was then unemployed and not contributing to the household. (In the section on the barrio junta, later in this chapter, we shall return to this case as we discuss the junta's "judicial" jurisdiction.) The woman assumed that her only remedy was to leave with her children, abandoning the house to the man. In this case, what are the dispositive features of the barrio's law of property?

---

3. Parent and Child

The barrio population, like the national population of Venezuela, is young. A 1965 estimate placed some 50% of Venezuela's population under 15 years of age, and about two-thirds of the population under 25. (In 1965, about 31% of the population of the United States was estimated to be under 15.) The average barrio household in the 1967 survey included four minors. And a walk through any barrio confirms the impression left by these statistics: children everywhere.

Many of the children are the product of informal unions. In 1961, when the Venezuelan Congress was considering new legislation to protect such children, the framers of the new law reported these national statistics: From 1947 to 1956, the percentage of "illegitimate" births (births outside formal marriage) dropped from 60% to 56% of the total births in Venezuela. Since the ratio of informal unions to legal marriages is higher in the barrios than for the nation at large, it seems conservative to estimate that at least half the children in the barrios are illegitimate in this formal sense.

Illegitimate birth is seen as a problem in the barrio, but only for the mother who has no man to support her child. Even in such a case, abortion is almost universally (96.1%) rejected as a solution when the issue is presented in the abstract. (This ideal norm breaks down in practice. At the huge Caracas maternity hospital, in 1964 there was one abortion for every four live births.) In fact, contraception is rejected by a large majority (nearly 69%) of both men and women in the barrios surveyed in 1967 — similarly in the abstract.

In the barrios, both parents of natural children accept the obligation to care for the children, at least during the time when the parents are living together. But a nonresident father may or may not expect to support his children, once he has left the household. One analogue to this latter phenomenon is the absence of any sense of obligation on the part of a man who casually fathers a child by a woman with whom he is not living. The prevailing attitude in this situation appears to be that the mother should expect to support the child herself or with the aid of her family (and especially her mother).

Education of the children is high on the list of parental aspirations. But educational opportunity is partly a function of the system of support for the household. If there is no man in the house, even young children may have to work. And even in a barrio that has easy access to a school (thus eliminating the cost of bus fare), sending the children to school implies the expense of dressing them adequately. Despite these obstacles, as we have seen, the barrio children are, on the average, better educated than their parents by a margin of several years of schooling. The husband's perceived obligation to educate the children of an informal union appears to be commonly fulfilled.

The recognition of children by their natural fathers is an explicit goal of national legislative policy. A 1961 law required the directors of public maternity hospitals (where as many as one-third of all births may occur) to encourage a declaration of paternity by the father. (Ley Sobre Protección Familiar, Gaceta Oficial, No. 26,735, Dec. 22, 1961, art. 2.) The statistics of the 1967 survey tell us that in nearly 60% of the barrio households surveyed, all the children carried the surname of the present spouse of the mother. But those figures do not establish that the fathers have formally recognized their natural children. The same law restates the duty of natural parents to support their children. The problem in the case of a non-supporting nonresident father is one of enforcement; few barrio mothers are able to contemplate a lawsuit, and few are even willing in such a case to seek the aid of the Venezuelan Children's Council (CVN), a government agency whose primary responsibility is child welfare and which is authorized to institute judicial proceedings to compel parents to support their children.

The CVN also is empowered to intervene in family affairs in cases of child neglect, such as a case in which small children are left alone for long periods. The final remedy in such a case would be for the CVN to place the children in a foster home or in an institution for children. One of the observers in the 1967 study reported a particularly aggravated case of neglect, involving the worst kind of filth and real hunger. When he asked a barrio resident why no action had been taken, this was the response: "The junta won't do anything because [the president] is incompetent, [another officer] is too busy, and the rest don't much care. The neighbors won't because it's too much trouble. Once you report the matter to the Consejo del Niño [CVN], you have to show up for hearings and trials, and it's too time-consuming." The observer adds this to his report: "I felt there was also the reluctance to act as a fink since they are all poor and don't want to be unfair to a neighbor. Nevertheless, all who knew of the case were shocked by the conditions." Question: What is the *law* of child neglect in this barrio? (Can this question be answered without further specification of the meaning of "law" as it is used here?)

Both the 1967 questionnaire and questions of the participant observers produced frequent and rather sentimental references to children. The statement quoted earlier about the urge to have a little house to leave to one's children typifies such remarks. The statement is reinforced by the survey's results in the area of inheritance. The barrio resident who owns a house expects to be able to dispose of it upon his or her death, and expects further to leave the house to members of the family. The questionnaire asked the latter question in an open-ended way. Here are the question and the responses:

If you died, to whom would you leave your belongings (the house) as inheritance?

70.5%	Children
9.2%	Spouse
8.5%	Children and spouse
9.8%	Other relative
0.3%	Other person
0.8%	Other answer
0.8%	Don't know

The "natural objects of the bounty" of the barrio resident, then, appear to be children first of all. In the case of a barrio father who leaves the household, we have seen that this sense of obligation weakens considerably. In the case of the barrio mother, the obligation is strong and enduring.

E. The Study: The Barrio Junta

1. Formation; Structural Characteristics; Patterns of Cooperation

T. RAY, THE POLITICS OF THE BARRIOS OF VENEZUELA

Pp. 43-45 (1969)*

The barrio junta is a small committee consisting of between seven and nine

---

*Originally published by the University of California Press; reprinted by permission of The Regents of the University of California.

residents. Its declared function is to represent the barrio before the city officials and try to obtain basic community facilities. Juntas exist or have existed in every barrio. They are considered a natural part of its early existence, as natural as ranchos and dirt roads, the result of the conviction shared by most families that a barrio can realize its role as a new community within the city only when it has an organized body to represent it.

To form the junta a public meeting is called, in the evening or on a Sunday. Representatives from about half of the families attend. They probably have had disappointing experiences with juntas in other barrios: big plans and promises but no results. Nevertheless, most of the families feel that this is a new start and that maybe this time they will get a good junta; consequently they are animated. The meeting is opened by the invasion leader, who is accompanied by several of his lieutenants and probably by two or three important outsiders, often government officials. He talks of the needs of the community, and the men and women of the barrio express their views. There is common agreement that the most urgent are water and electricity. The subject of the junta is then brought up, and one of the principals declares that it must be nonpartisan and ready to "fight for the progress of the barrio." When nominations are called for, the leader is the first to be proposed for the presidency. He is duly elected by a raising of hands, and his lieutenants are then elected to fill lesser offices. The remaining members are undistinguished residents known and liked by a number of families and with no partisan ties. Usually at least two are women. The officers of the junta are typically president, vice-president, secretary, treasurer, secretary of sports, and secretary of culture; the other members are simply called *vocales*. . . .

At this first public meeting, the junta members announce their intention of going to the Municipal Council to inquire about the possibilities of getting water. They mention other projects as well; a school, a dispensary, and a police house are all discussed, and the residents voice their support of them. The people leave the meeting in an optimistic mood; the future looks bright.

A week later, at a second public meeting, the junta reports that the officials have expressed their interest in helping as soon as possible. The wait for results begins. When it becomes obvious that the expected assistance is not forthcoming, more meetings are held at which the junta explains the delays. Gradually the attendance diminishes, and the president stops calling them. This state of inactivity can exist for months or even a few years. Disenchanted junta members drop out and new ones are added. Unless the junta is smart or lucky enough to divert the community's attention from obtaining water to another feasible project, thus justifying its continued existence, it eventually ceases its efforts and fades into retirement or disbands completely. Subsequently, when the prospects for success are better, a new group is formed or the old reemerges.

As the foregoing extract from Ray's book suggests, the public-works function is the most important one the barrio junta performs. Not only does the junta represent the barrio to the government and other outside agencies. It also organizes the barrio residents in cooperative labor; those who do not work are expected to make small cash contributions toward the community's projects, and the junta collects these "voluntary" payments. Typically, the junta will organize a small project, say, the grading and paving of a road at the barrio's entrance, or the laying of water pipes. Ray continues:

> This cooperative action on the part of the community members is known among lower class Venezuelans, in both the city and countryside, as a *cayapa*. A cayapa is usually a spontaneous movement that results when a community believes that a major physical problem can be solved through its own efforts. Since the enthusiasm and spirit of cooperation which give a cayapa its momentum are generally short-lived, its effectiveness is limited, and it usually disbands as soon as its goal is realized, if not sooner. Whereas a cayapa can usually complete a job that requires only a Sunday or two of work, such as installing a water system or repairing a road, it cannot complete a more difficult job that requires months of planning and labor, such as building a school or laying an extensive sewer system.[20]

In dealing with the government agencies that provide such things as building materials, the junta is aided substantially if its leaders are agents of the right political parties. (The governmental structure in Caracas is sufficiently complex that different parties may have independent capacity to aid a barrio.) This phenomenon, not unknown in the history of certain large cities in the United States, results in a high correlation between the degree of activity by the junta and its intensity of political orientation. In one very large barrio studied in 1967, all the members of the junta said when interviewed that politics had nothing to do with the way the junta operated. However, all but one of them were members of Acción Democrática (then in control of the Presidency, and of the government of the Federal District, which includes the portion of Caracas where the barrio was located), and the junta's president was on the payroll of the Ministry of Public Works.

There is no Venezuelan statute prescribing a method for electing members of a barrio junta, or fixing the junta's term of office. Some juntas are associated with regional or national associations (which, in turn, are arms of national political parties), and thus may adopt the model constitutions published by the associations. But in most barrios, elections are held irregularly, principally to fill vacancies in the office of president. Many barrio residents, and even members of the junta, assume that the period of a junta's term is two years, or one year. In practice, however, a successful junta — and that means a successful president — will hold office for a longer time. The president may resign because he becomes too occupied with his non-barrio job, or because of ill health; more typically, he will resign because he is tired of being president, or because his popularity has decreased. An unsuccessful president may resign after only a few months in office.

"Successful," in this context, means able to accomplish the junta's goals, primarily in the field of public works. Thus the cooperation of a government agency may be crucial to the junta's continuation in office. At least as important to the junta's success

---

[20]T. Ray, *The Politics of the Barrios of Venezuela* 47 (1969).

is its ability to convince the barrio's residents that they should join in cooperative projects. The judgment of nearly all writers on marginal squatter settlements in Latin America is that this cooperation is easier to secure in the more recently settled barrios, and becomes harder as the barrio gets older, more prosperous, and more integrated into the city. William Mangin exemplifies this analysis in his summary of the later history of a "typical" Lima *barriada*:

> Belongingness and integration tend to be replaced by coresidence. The original settlers are swallowed up by the growing population, and some of them move out. The need for unity in defense against outside threats to the *barriada* lessens, and internal tensions increase. Many more people rent, and many of the older inhabitants, who were pleased with their situation at first, begin to complain of the surroundings, quarrel with their neighbors, and comment unfavorably on new arrivals . . . . Many individuals also develop new, or reinforce old, relationships with outsiders on the basis of such ties as kinship, region, occupation, and politics.
>
> The association takes on a more political character and, even though personality and regionalism continue to be important in the local elections, national politics and national issues play a larger part. The original leaders often move out (in which case they may or may not continue to exert influence) or, following a time-honored Peruvian tradition, a reform faction accuses them of stealing money and they, in turn, can choose to fight, flee, or sulk. As the *barriada* becomes more a part of Lima the association usually loses power.[21]

Occasionally it is suggested that the barrio residents' early inclination toward cooperation is a remnant of rural or small-town patterns of cooperative work. That is a plausible explanation — although we have seen that most barrio residents have lived in the city for a time before coming to their present homes. But other explanations may also be valid. The practicing lawyer knows that the first clause to draft in a partnership agreement is the dissolution clause. The very newness of a venture instills an optimistic, cooperative frame of mind. Most barrio residents, we have seen, come there with the expectation of something better than what they have left behind. The new ranchos are not the refuge of the desperate, but symbols of hope. Furthermore, the residents must come together at the outset for purposes of defense or consolidation. As the barrio becomes established, at the same time the residents are, as Mangin notes, strengthening their ties to the world outside, so that they are more inclined to take a "what's-in-it-for-me" position when asked to cooperate. Talton Ray notes that no one seems to himself to be so foolish as a barrio resident who works alone on a community project while his neighbors are watching.

The residents of the newer barrios almost all know that a junta exists. In the older barrios, not only are greater numbers of residents ignorant of the existence of a junta; even those who do know of the junta tend to characterize it as "inactive" or "not very active." And yet, even in the older barrios, cooperation remains the norm among the

---

[21] Mangin, "Mental Health and Migration to Cities: A Peruvian Case," 84 *Annals of the N.Y. Academy of Sciences* 911, 914 (1960).

residents, at least in the sense that they say cooperation is a good idea. In response to an open-ended question in the survey ("What do you think a resident of a barrio should do to improve it?"), some 62% answered that one should cooperate, unite, etc. (About 6.5% answered, "Nothing.") The positive answers were in a lower proportion in the older barrios, and, curiously, in the newest of all. Perhaps during the very first months of this barrio's existence, the residents were so busy getting their own houses constructed that they had not yet identified community needs that demanded cooperation. Some 25% of the residents of this new barrio answered, to the above question, "Let everyone work (build) on his own account; let everyone leave others alone, etc." The average percentage for this answer in all the barrios surveyed was 14%.

Just under a third (31%) of the interviewees in 1967 said that they (or their spouses) would accept a position in the junta if it were offered. Of the 62% who answered negatively to this question, some 38% thought it necessary to volunteer a reason for declining: "I don't have time," or "I am too old," or "I can't read." While only 3% were willing to say that residents of the barrio should not cooperate with the junta, more than one-quarter reported that they had not, in fact, ever cooperated. While these figures do not form an entirely consistent pattern, it seems fair to say that community cooperation is generally accepted as an obligation among the barrio residents, and specifically that cooperation with the junta is widely considered to be appropriate, at least in the abstract.

In the larger barrios, sectionalism is a persistent problem. The barrio junta tends to be dominated by the residents of the older sectors, located nearest the city streets. The people on top of the hill feel left out of the barrio's community activities, and excluded from the benefit of cooperative projects, and with good reason. They *are* left out. At the time of the 1967 study, these feelings were crystallizing in some barrios, producing new and separate juntas, and even the adoption of new names to identify barrios that were emerging in these excluded sectors. One of the participant-observers lived in the upper portion of a barrio called La Charneca. While he was there, the residents of his zone established a new junta for a barrio which they named not Alta Charneca but Colinas de las Acacias. Las Acacias is the name of an upper-middle-class urbanization on the other side of the hill. The idea behind the new name was not so much to identify the hilltop barrio with Las Acacias as it was to emphasize its independence from La Charneca. La Charneca is an old barrio, whose lower portions are practically indistinguishable from the rest of the city. The junta in La Charneca has become little more than a political club. The barrio has a reputation as a high-crime area. On the top of the hill, though, there is now a new barrio, with a new junta; community cooperation is the order of the day.

---

2. Lawmaking and Dispute Resolution

If the junta's public-works activities can be characterized as executive functions, the junta also has some functions that can be called legislative and judicial. In the preceding sections on rights in land and family obligations, we have seen some of the reach of the junta's power, and some of its limitations. The most important legislative functions of the junta relate to its supervision of rights in land. As we have seen, the junta, immediately after it is organized, assumes the power to measure and designate parcels of land to be occupied by newly arriving residents. Even after the barrio is well established, new residents are added, either building on unoccupied parcels or acquiring already-built houses by purchase or rental. The junta may seek to control new building, but it does not have jurisdiction to decide whether a new arrival can buy or rent an existing house. Any effort to enforce such a decision would be regarded as an unwarranted interference with the property rights of the seller or landlord. The exception to this pattern, we have noted before, is the case of the illegal rental of a rancho. A strong junta will intervene in such a case, not to prevent the tenant from occupying but to prevent the landlord from evicting the tenant for nonpayment of rent.

Another legislative function, closely related to the public-works responsibilities of the junta, is the designation of places for the barrio residents to deposit trash and garbage. This is not a trivial matter. Certainly no one who lives in a barrio thinks of trash disposal as a minor problem. Here, as in the designation of lots for new residents to occupy, the legislative function of the junta blends into its dispute-resolving functions. Disputes about trash disposal can be of long duration, since each day produces its own new opportunities for trouble; in contrast, a boundary dispute is normally settled once and for all.

The foregoing discussion suggests that much of the junta's lawmaking is accomplished in its handling of particular cases that come before it for action. That suggestion is not misleading. Most of what might be called the barrios' distinctive contribution to their own legal system (that is, the portions of the effective law governing the barrios that do not derive directly from the national legal system) is, in fact, a kind of common law. Not all of this law is junta-made law, by any means; the section on family obligations made clear that in some areas of law, both the establishment of the rule and the sanction for disobedience were quite independent of anything the junta might do. When the junta does make law, however, it normally does so case by case. While its "judicial" decisions are not recorded formally – most juntas keep only the most sketchy records – nonetheless precedents are remembered. Even the most general conversation with a member of a junta about the norms enforced by the junta is sure to call up illustrative examples of previous cases.

The dispute-resolving functions of the junta vary from barrio to barrio, in positive correlation to the junta's strength and level of activity in promoting community cooperation. A junta that is not organizing road-building or other public-works activity is not likely to be inclined to try to resolve individual disputes, nor would such a junta's decisions be respected.

Even in an active junta, there is a rather well-defined sense of the limits of the junta's "judicial" jurisdiction. The clearest case for the junta to resolve is the case of the boundary dispute; and as we have seen, other claims based on rights in land are frequently brought before the junta. But just as these issues seem clearly to fall within the junta's dispute-settling power, so some other kinds of disputes seem plainly to fall outside the junta's province. Family quarrels, for example, are something that the junta normally will not touch, even in cases that might seem extreme to an outsider.

Recall the case discussed earlier concerning the woman whose husband was beating her and her children. In that case, the woman presumably was entitled to protection by some agency, even a court. But her only *effective* remedy would have been to go to the junta, and she knew they would not intervene. In a few cases of family squabbles, a strong junta will take action, but those cases are rare, and they tend to involve disturbance of the neighbors. Thus, if a husband and wife quarrel in such a way as to become a nuisance (we use the word in both its legal and its popular sense), the junta may order them out of the barrio. Even if they owned their house, such an order would be effective, for the municipal council would not interfere with the junta's decision, absent some special influence on behalf of the excluded persons.

Another kind of case in which the junta usually will not offer protection is the case of theft, or physical assault. Crimes such as these are regarded as the jurisdiction of the police, even in relatively isolated barrios. Often, of course, the junta will be the ones to call the police, and there is some reason to believe that the police are more ready to respond to such a call than they might be if they were called by someone else. Some juntas, during the period of greatest influx into Caracas, just after the fall of Pérez Jiménez, organized vigilante committees, but practically all of those groups are now defunct. Persistent troublemakers who engage in fights, or in open violation of the prevailing moral code, may be ordered out of the barrio. This sanction, however, is very rarely invoked, and not at all in barrios where the residents have legal title to their land.

The picture of the junta that emerges from this brief analysis is one of limited effectiveness. The reasons for these limitations are explored in the following passage from Peattie's book. Her anecdotes parallel the reports of the participant-observers in the 1967 Caracas study.

L. PEATTIE, THE VIEW FROM THE BARRIO

Pp. 57-60 (1968)

One way of describing the situation as to informal social controls in La Laja is to say that the social structure is too loosely meshed to cage anyone, that it is generally impossible to mobilize in the community a group large enough or united enough to force any sanction on the deviate. He who is disapproved of is disapproved of by individuals and clusterings of individuals; they may stare and they may talk, but the obstreperous individual will still find others to be his supporters, and he will be barred from no community facilities.

Moreover, in the highly personalized social structure of La Laja, an attempt to express disapproval of another's behavior cannot appear in such a social context as to be read as 'social sanction.' It is perceived as personal disagreement and quarrelsomeness, and as such is subject itself to social disapproval. A family 'of respect' is one which 'doesn't get involved' in quarrels with its neighbors.

The ideal of being a family 'of respect' which 'doesn't get involved' in fights is not an easy ideal to put into practice. People in La Laja live so close to their neighbors that their radios and domestic quarrels are bound to be heard. Their numerous and undisciplined children are continually impinging on their neighbors by petty theft, stone-throwing, and simple invasions of privacy and peace. Many families keep domestic animals which roam into others' yards. The technical and economic level of living is such as to make for a constant stream of petty borrowings of ice, small food items, and small money loans. More serious still, the weakness of the conjugal relationship means that a husband or wife is fairly likely to find some neighbor presenting a sexual rival. Thus, it takes some effort to be a family which 'doesn't get involved.'

Certain social techniques have been developed to make this easier. One is that of using children as intermediaries. That it is always a child who comes to borrow a lime or an egg or to ask to buy a *medio's* worth of ice from the lucky owner of a refrigerator might be seen as a particular instance of the general practice of having children run errands at the store. But the fact that a child is sent to ask a favor — a car ride to town for a sick family member, for example, or, bearing a small, closely folded note, to ask for a loan of money — seems to be a way of avoiding either an embarrassing refusal or direct hostility. Another technique is the general practice, at least by parents who take the child-rearing role seriously, of immediately disciplining a child seen annoying a neighbor.

Aside from this, there is a strong and explicit reluctance to say anything to a neighbor who may be carrying on some annoying activity. An example may illustrate. During my stay, the little junta supposed to represent communal needs in the barrio and to organize group action to solve them carried on a long discussion of the pig problem. The problem was that the pigs in the barrio, instead of being kept penned, were left to wander about to scavenge as much of their food as possible. They made the streets and public spaces dirty and disorderly. There was no difference of opinion within the junta over this situation's representing a problem; on this all agreed. The question was: What to do about it? Long discussion proposed action by the police, San Félix sanitary authorities, etc., but failed to present any clear means for ensuring that the pigs would be penned. A young American community development worker listening to the discussion was nonplussed. 'Well,' he said, 'you say there are only six pigs in the barrio now, and two of them belong to one person. That means that only five families are letting pigs roam. Why don't you just go to those five families and in the name of the community ask them to pen up their pigs?' The suggestion was greeted with general and total rejection. 'Oh, we couldn't do that.'

Other examples of this kind of situation show the lack of local social machinery for controlling the noncollaborative, the annoying, the offensive, or the immoral.

When a considerable group of men were working as unpaid volunteers to finish the barrio's water line, there were other men in the barrio who took no hand in the work. Some sat playing cards in plain sight of a team working away in the hot sun. They did not appear ill at ease in the situation, nor was any attempt made, that I could see, to sanction them for their nonparticipation, beyond a friendly invitation to join the job.

One man in the barrio, otherwise liked and respected, formed the habit of playing his radio at top volume every morning from about 5:00 A.M. until he left for work at twenty minutes to six. Although several neighbors spoke to the writer of their annoyance at being thus awakened every day, and although (perhaps because?) on good terms with the radio's owner, they were unwilling to speak to him about his conduct. Similarly, when the bar played music late at night and again early in the morning, and when one evening a group of people experimented with a loudspeaker emitting ear-splitting racket into the street, no one felt it proper to object (until, finally, I did — in the last case — and had my plea immediately and courteously heeded).

A young man in the barrio began to drink one week and, as his mood built up, to make gross remarks to his neighbors, especially the girls. His state and his remarks were the subject of general comment and of very strong disapproval, but no attempt was made to take him in hand.

A man on my street found it quite possible to leave his wife, seven months pregnant and with three older children, and to start living with another woman in the same block, refusing to contribute in any way to the support of the first family, although his wife's landlady was threatening eviction for nonpayment of rent. His conduct was certainly regarded generally as irresponsible and reprehensible, but the social disapproval was not such as to make him either help his wife pay the rent or move further away with his new woman.

A corollary of the weakness of informal social controls in the barrio is the fact that when people *do* 'involve themselves' in quarrels with their neighbors, they are quite likely to call in the police. The woman owner of the bar across the street from me was adamant in her determination to avoid disorderly behavior in her bar, and should any drinker resist when she proposed to eject him she would not hesitate to go into town and get the paddy wagon, be the obstreperous young man one of the local boys or not. Of the five cases in which to my knowledge the police were called into the barrio in the first year of my stay (before the bar came in to bring with it a somewhat higher incidence of police intervention), only one involved the arrest of someone from outside the barrio (an attempted housebreaker) on the complaint of an insider, and three involved disputes between kinsfolk, one of whom called the police to arrest the other. The first of these was a case in which a woman called the police to protect her mother by arresting the son-in-law who was beating the mother. In another case a woman had the young son of her husband's first cousin arrested for throwing a stone at her. The last of the cases was one in which a young man called the police to arrest his common-law wife. The police may be called not only to deal with the personal but to deal with what looks, at least, like the trivial. The houseowner behind me threatened to call the police to arrest a neighbor whose little boy had thrown a stone making a hole in his thin sheet aluminum roof, an event not only minor but also very common, owing to the conjunction of very thin roofing with a passion for stone-throwing by little boys.

The barrio council, in asking the police to patrol the barrio in the evenings, especially on weekends, to keep down noise and disorder from intoxicated young men, was not proposing an enforcement method strange to the barrio. The lack of well-organized mechanisms of informal social control makes it natural for the barrio to resort to the impersonal mechanisms provided by the larger society, even in fairly trivial or rather personal cases.

What would have been new in the arrangement proposed by the barrio council was the community-interest framework of the enforcement. Indeed, the development of a barrio council may be looked at from one point of view as a groping toward some way of dealing with individual behavior from a level more general than that of personal opposition.

This description by Peattie raises again some questions we have seen repeatedly in this chapter. When is it appropriate to say that a community norm has become law? What is the nature of "law" when there is no sanction to enforce it? What must be present within a community before customary norms develop enforcing sanctions? Is there any practical difference between a community norm that carries no sanction and an enacted national statute that is unenforceable? To what extent does popular observance of a norm rest on a sense of popular participation in (or approval of) the norm's formulation? Similar questions, it will be seen, might be asked with respect to a variety of legal systems, from the customary law of a remote tribe to the practices of wheat traders in Chicago to the law governing relations among nations to the law that effectively governs a North American urban ghetto.

Chapter VI

PERSPECTIVES ON
LAW AND DEVELOPMENT

The preceding chapters frequently have raised questions about the interrelation between the legal process and the process of development in Latin America. The focus in each of these discussions, however, has been the particular subject area at hand. This concluding chapter does not summarize the foregoing materials, but uses a selective rearrangement of them to help construct an approach to the understanding of the role of law in Latin American development.

As the words "help" and "approach" suggest, no one today would sensibly argue that we have anything like a comprehensive theory that explains the interrelation of law and development in general, or in Latin America, or even in a single society. Yet there are some general themes that appear and reappear whenever one analyzes the interactions of the legal process and the process of development. This chapter develops four of those themes, in the light of the materials of chapters II through V. The themes are: security, legitimacy, community and inequality.

A. Security

1. The Varieties of Security

Bentham said that security was "the principal object of law," an "inestimable good, the distinctive index of civilization."[1] But what is security? Imagine a house built on a geological fault. Is that house secure? The question is put, of course, not as a test of knowledge about earthquakes, but as a beginning exploration of the meaning of the question itself.

Almost anyone, asked our hypothetical question about security, will begin to wonder what earth movements are going to take place under the house. Would that information answer the question of security? Suppose we could predict earth movements with a degree of accuracy approximating today's weather forecasting. What difference would that make to our question about security? Suppose we knew precisely when earth movements would take place, what their intensities would be, and what effects the movements would have on the house. Would we then speak of security?

---

[1] P. 308 *supra.*

The question of security is a question of probability; it is the inverse of the question of risk, which every law student encounters in studying the law of torts. Risk is a prediction; when we speak confidently of "certainties," we have left the area of law in which risk is a crucial factor of decision, and entered the world of intention. If we *knew* what would happen to the house, we should not speak of risk or security; we should simply say what would happen. In an omniscient Mind, the concept of security would be without meaning. The question of security, then, implies the presence of some observer who predicts the future on the basis of imperfect information. Our question about the security of the house is meaningful only if we posit an observer: perhaps the owner, or a prospective buyer, or some hypothetical observer who has a different store of information about what will happen. (The law of torts invents such an imagined observer, the "reasonable" man or woman, who both calculates risks and weighs them.) Security is not an objective reality but a state of mind. Our beginning question was a false one. Houses are neither secure nor insecure; people are.[2]

The word "security" is sometimes used to refer to a generalized sense of well-being that comes from the absence of danger. In this sense, one may find security in a variety of ways, some of which may even be contradictory. Thus, one may feel secure — and to feel secure is to *be* secure, even though someone else may perceive the metaphorical banana peel in one's path — because of a supreme self-confidence, or, alternatively, because of confidence that a patron will offer protection. Bentham, however, wrote of a more specific sort of security: the predictive states of mind, the *expectations,* that result from assurances given by the law of property and contracts. One who labors under contract can expect payment, not merely because the employer is trustworthy, but also because the organized society has provided a regularized means of enforcing contracts. Once the laborer is paid, he or she can expect to keep the value earned, because society similarly protects property. Property and contract are not things, but legal relations — which is to say, *promises* by the organized community to take certain kinds of action whenever various combinations of events occur. In Bentham's view, people work and save and invest only because of the expectations — the security — guaranteed by law.

Bentham's model of "development" (the term would have seemed odd to him) was thus a market model. For Bentham, humanity's natural tendency toward prodigality was overcome by a social system of rewards; law protected the fruits of industry, and so people were encouraged to choose to engage in development-oriented activity. A contrasting model of development is more candidly coercive; a leadership group that is strong enough simply orders individuals to produce in specified ways, and allocates their product as it sees fit; those who are uncooperative are punished. Enthusiasts for a market system, in their more lyrical moments, tend to see the two models as presenting the contrast between freedom and coercion. But in any unsentimental view of the market, one of its chief developmental virtues is precisely that it provides discipline. In a pure market system, most people *must* produce; their range of effective choice does not extend to the decision to remain idle. Furthermore, the market's own

---

[2] The idea that what people believe about authority is as important as the "true" facts is a staple of modern literature. One example is Genet's play, "The Balcony."

mechanisms depend on coercion. Bentham's comments about law are, in the last analysis, statements about the potential application of the state's coercive power.

The place of law in a market economy was more fully articulated by Max Weber. In the following extract, Professor David Trubek elaborates Weber's analysis with some of his own.[3]

D. TRUBEK, MAX WEBER ON LAW AND THE RISE OF CAPITALISM

1972 *Wisconsin Law Review* 720, 740-43*

In his economic sociology, Weber stressed the importance for capitalist development of two aspects of law: (1) its relative degree of *calculability*, and (2) its capacity to develop *substantive* provisions — principally those relating to freedom of contract — necessary to the functioning of the market system.

The former reason was the more important of the two. Weber asserted that capitalism required a highly calculable normative order. His survey of types of law indicated that only modern, rational law, or logically formal rationality, could provide the necessary calculability. Legalism supported the development of capitalism by providing a stable and predictable atmosphere; capitalism encouraged legalism because the bourgeoisie were aware of their own need for this type of governmental structure.

Legalism is the only way to provide the degree of certainty necessary for the operation of the capitalist system. Weber stated that capitalism "could not continue if its control of resources were not upheld by the legal compulsion of the state; if its formally 'legal' rights were not upheld by the threat of force." He further specified that: "[T]he rationalization and systematization of the law in general and . . . the increasing calculability of the functioning of the legal process in particular, constituted one of the most important conditions for the existence of . . . capitalistic enterprise, which cannot do without legal security."

Weber never worked out in detail a model of capitalist production which might explain why legal calculability was so important to capitalist development. I have developed such a model, and I believe that underlying Weber's repeated emphasis on legal calculability is a vision similar to this latter-day ideal type.

The essence of the model is the conflict of egoistic wills, which is an inherent part of competitive capitalism. In pure market capitalism of the type idealized in micro-economics texts, each participant is driven to further his own interests at the expense of all other participants in the market. Theoretically, the profit motive is insatiable, and is unconstrained by any ethical or moral force. Thus, each actor is

---

[3] See also Rheinstein, "Introduction," in M. Rheinstein (ed.), *Max Weber on Law in Economy and Society* xxv (1954) (hereinafter cited as *Weber*). Cf. Macaulay, "Non-Contractual Relations in Business: A Preliminary Study," 28 *Am. Soc. Rev.* 55 (1963), suggesting that the functions of contract law are often served by other non-legal devices, and that businessmen in the United States normally do not rely on legal sanctions for the enforcement of contracts.

*Copyright 1972 University of Wisconsin.

unconcerned with the ramifications of his actions on the economic well-being of others.

At the same time, however, economic actors in this system are necessarily interdependent. No market participant can achieve his goals unless he secures power over the actions of others. It does little good, for example, for the owner of a textile plant to act egocentrically to further his interests if at the same time he cannot be sure that other actors will supply him with the necessary inputs for production and consume his product. If suppliers do not provide promised raw materials, if workers refuse to work, if customers fail to pay for goods delivered, all the ruthless, rational self-interest in the world will be of little value to the textile producer in his striving for profits.

Now if all the other actors were nice, cooperative fellows, our textile manufacturer might not have to worry. Others would play their roles in the scheme and he would come out all right. But this may not always happen because they are, by hypothesis, as selfish as he is. Thus, they, too, will do whatever leads to the highest profit; if this means failing to perform some agreement, so be it. And since one can assume that there will frequently be opportunities for other actors to better themselves at the expense of providing him with some service or product necessary to the success of his enterprise, our hypothetical businessman lives in a world of radical uncertainty.

Yet, as Weber constantly stressed, uncertainty of this type is seriously prejudicial to the smooth functioning of the modern economy. How can the capitalist economic actor in a world of similarly selfish profitseekers reduce the uncertainty that threatens to rob the capitalist system of its otherwise great productive power? What will permit the economic actor to predict with relative certainty how other actors will behave over time? What controls the tendency toward instability?

In order to answer these questions, Weber moved to the level of sociological analysis. The problem of the conflict between the self-interest of individuals and social stability – what Parsons calls "the Hobbesian problem of order" – is one of the fundamental problems of sociology, and, to deal with it, Weber constructed his basic schemes of social action. Weber recognized that predictable uniformities of social action can be "guaranteed" in various ways, and that all of these methods of social control may influence economic activities. Actors may internalize normative standards, thus fulfilling social expectations "voluntarily." Or they may be subjected to some form of "external effect" if they deviate from expectations. These external guarantees may derive from some informal sanctioning system or may involve organized coercion. Law is one form of organized coercion. All types of control may be involved in guaranteeing stable power over economic resources; factual control of this type, Weber observed, may be due to custom, to the play of interests, to convention, or to law.

As I have indicated, however, Weber believed that the organized coercion of *law* was necessary in modern, capitalist economies. While internalization and conventional sanctions may be able to eliminate or resolve most conflict in simpler societies, it is incapable of serving this function in a way that satisfies the needs of the modern exchange economy. For this function, law, in the sense of organized coercion, was necessary. Weber stated:

[T]hough it is not necessarily true of every economic system, certainly the modern economic order under modern conditions could not continue if its control of resources were not upheld by the legal compulsion of the state; that is, if its formally "legal" rights were not upheld by the threat of force.

Why is coercion necessary in a market system? And why must this coercion take legal form? Finally, when we speak of *legal* coercion, do we mean state power, regardless of how it is exercised, or do we mean power governed by rules, or legalism?[4] Weber gives no clear-cut answer to these questions. The discussion suggests answers but the issues are not fully developed. And the most crucial question, the interrelationship between the need for coercion and the model of legalism, is barely discussed at all. However, I think answers to the questions can be given which fit coherently with other aspects of his analysis.

Coercion is necessary because of the egoistic conflict I have identified above. While Weber never clearly identified this conflict, he himself was aware of it. Some principle of behavior other than short term self-interest is necessary for a market system. Tradition cannot function to constrain egoistic behavior because the market destroys the social and cultural bases of tradition. Similarly, the emerging market economy erodes the social groupings which could serve as the foci for enforcement of conventional standards. Indeed, the fact that the type of conflict I have described comes into existence is evidence of the decline of tradition and custom. Only law is left to fill the normative vacuum; legal coercion is essential because no other form is available.

A second reason why the necessary coercion must be legal is tied to the pace of economic activity and the type of rationalistic calculation characteristic of the market economy. It is not enough for the capitalist to have a general idea that someone else will more likely than not deliver more or less the performance agreed upon on or about the time stipulated. He must know exactly what and when, and he must be highly certain that the precise performance will be forthcoming. He wants to be able to predict with certainty that the other units will perform. But given the potential conflict between their self-interests and their obligations, he also wants to predict with certainty that coercion will be applied to the recalcitrant. The predictability of performance is intimately linked to the certainty that coercive instruments can be invoked in the event of nonperformance.

In this context, it becomes clear why a calculable legal system offers the most reliable way to combine coercion and predictability. Here the model of legalism and the model of capitalist dynamics merge. A system of government through rules seems inherently more predictable than any other method for structuring coercion. Convention is inherently too diffuse, and, like custom, was historically unavailable given the market-driven erosion of the groups and structures necessary for effective constraint of egoism. Like Balzac, Weber saw how the decline of family, guild, and Church unleashed unbridled egoism. Pure *power,* on the other hand, is available in the sense that the state is increasingly armed with coercive instruments. But untrammeled

---

[4] Trubek is using this term to refer to formal legality, not an excessive concern with legal formalities. [Eds.]

power is unpredictable; wielders of power, unconstrained by rules, will tend not to act in stable and predictable ways. Legalism offers the optimum combination of coercion and predictability.

It is here that the significance of legal autonomy can be seen. Autonomy is intimately linked to the problem of predictability. The autonomous legal system in a legalistic society is an institutional complex organized to apply coercion only in accordance with general rules through logical or purely cognitive processes. To the extent that it truly functions in the purely logical and, consequently, mechanical manner Weber presented, its results will be highly predictable. If it is constantly subject to interference by forces which seek to apply coercion for purposes inconsistent with the rules, it loses its predictable quality. Thus Weber observed that authoritarian rulers (and democratic despots) may refuse to be bound by formal rules since:

> They are all confronted by the inevitable conflict between an abstract formalism of legal certainty and their desire to realize substantive goals. Juridical formalism enables the legal system to operate like a technically rational machine. Thus it guarantees to individuals and groups within the system a relative maximum of freedom, and greatly increases for them the possibility of predicting the legal consequences of their actions.

Where Bentham had emphasized the security which law provides for private *property,* Weber thus emphasized the security of *transactions* in a market that was relatively free. Some measure of the importance Weber attached to the security of transactions is suggested by this remarkable statement: "All of the 'public peace' arrangements of the Middle Ages were meant to serve the interests of exchange."[5] Despite this extravagant claim, the law of torts and the criminal law obviously serve other purposes. Murder is a crime even in societies whose economies are primitive; people value the security of the person, and property security as well, for reasons that have scarcely anything to do with a system of exchange. ". . . [M] an, by an instinct which he shares with the domestic dog, . . . will not allow himself to be dispossessed, either by force or fraud, of what he holds, without trying to get it back again."[6]

Questions

1. Chapter IV examined some of the lawmaking adaptations of Latin American judges and legislators to periods of rapid inflation.

(a) In various ways, this adaptive lawmaking was designed to promote security. Which legal mechanisms were aimed at property security? Which were aimed at transaction security?

------

[5] *Weber* 196.
[6] O. W. Holmes, Jr., *The Common Law* 168 (1881).

(b) The various mechanisms discussed in Chapter IV can be described as reactions of the legal system to changes in the economic environment. Can they also be seen as instruments designed to affect that environment, *i.e.*, to promote development? What kinds of developmental decision-making are contemplated by the creators of these new legal arrangements? The decision to save? The decision to allocate savings to productive investment? How might such decisions be influenced by the inflation-adjustment mechanisms we have seen?[7]

(c) In the context of inflation, which types of security are the most important for the legal system to seek to achieve? Why?

(d) Which of the adaptive legal mechanisms are well designed for their security-promoting purposes? Which are rather less well designed for those purposes? To what extent are these lawmaking successes or failures the result of lawyers' craftsmanship? What are the characteristics of good legal craftsmanship in this context?

(e) Do these adaptive legal mechanisms illustrate Trubek's analysis, or contradict it? In what particulars?

(f) Can the law provide security for both creditors and debtors in a period of inflation? Is every argument based on the value of security really only a disguise for an assertion of self-interest? Or are there some implications of the principle of security that are neutral in this political sense? Can any principle of security be written into law for *developmental* purposes without abandoning neutrality?

2. Weber emphasized the importance of law in promoting the security of transactions in a depersonalized market — a market that largely ignores individuals' characteristics *as* individuals, looking instead at the qualities and prices of the goods and services they bring to the market.

(a) In a system of exchange that is heavily influenced by patronage and personal "connections," are legal protections of calculability important?

(b) Does such a system of exchange rest on the security of transactions? Does a patronage system provide alternative forms of security? What is it that is calculable (or not) in such a system?

(c) Could a patronage system of exchange respond to the problems posed by inflation? Are there some kinds of transactions that are beyond the capacity of a patronage system to make secure? If so, what are the characteristics of such transactions? Do the answers to these last questions imply a distinctive role for the kind of legal security emphasized by Weber?

3. In Chapter V we saw that about three-quarters of those residents of the Caracas barrios who owned their houses had made significant improvements to their houses. It was suggested that this pattern of steady investment rested on security of tenure.

(a) It is commonly said that investment implies the taking of some risk. What, precisely, does the barrio resident risk in adding concrete-block walls to his or her house? Does such investment require a particular time perspective? A willingness to trust others?

---

[7] See D. Trubek, *Law, Planning, and the Development of the Brazilian Capital Market* (1971).

(b) What specific risks threaten a barrio resident's tenure? What potential actions, by what people, constitute those risks?

(c) In the face of these risks to a barrio resident's tenure, what actions or processes provide the security that promotes investment? In what sense can these actions or processes be called "law"?

4. We first discussed Bentham's views on security in connection with the subject of land reform. A latter-day Bentham might argue that if the residents of the Caracas barrios should be protected in their security of tenure, so should the owners of the great agricultural estates.

(a) Does such an argument rest on a particular assumption about the motivations that underlie ownership? Is it proper to make the same assumptions about such motivations both for barrio residents and for *hacendados*?

(b) Do Bentham's views on property security rest on assumptions about the freedom of the market? Are those views less valid if there is, for example, no free market in agricultural land?

(c) What led Bentham to argue that the principle of property security extended even to the Russian serf-owner's property interest in human beings? Does the abolition of serfdom or slavery involve an invasion of the interest in property security?

(d) Before abolition, were slaves secure? Consider the degree of security of a slave as to property, transactions, family stability and even bodily integrity. Is the principle of property security finally nothing more than an apology for the status quo? Is the principle thus anti-developmental? What about the barrio residents, and their investment in housing?

5. The word *amparo* means "protection," and thus suggests that the principle of security has played a part in creating the judicial institutions bearing that name. To Brazilians, that relationship is even more obvious; their analogue to the amparo is called a writ of security

(a) What specific kinds of interests are protected by the amparo and the writ of security? Against what specific risks?

(b) Does the amparo imply a particular model of development? What assumptions about the development process underlie the principle that the government should "obey the rules"?

(c) Is it consistent – or possible – for the legal system to be used at the same time as (i) an instrument for the government to control behavior for developmental purposes, and (ii) a limitation on governmental arbitrariness?[8]

(d) If the government does not "obey the rules," and refuses to limit its own arbitrariness, may there be an impairment of its ability to use the legal system to control private behavior for developmental purposes? Are the answers to this question and the preceding question consistent?

---

[8] See Trubek, "Toward a Social Theory of Law: An Essay on the Study of Law and Development," 82 *Yale L. J.* 1, 18-21 (1972).

2. Rule v. Discretion

"Modern" societies, it is sometimes said, have embraced "universalism," while traditional societies are characterized by "particularism." A particularistic social system defines an individual's place in the system not according to universal, objective, impersonal criteria of *performance,* but according to the individual's own *qualities.* The family is the particularist system *par excellence;* the market typifies a universalist system. Parents love their children because they are their children; the market's fickle affections follow the calls of demand and supply.

Most of the world's legal systems are highly universalist in form. In the Western legal tradition, universalism begins in Roman law. The universalist spirit pervades the Code Napoléon, and thus the codes that are the heart of private law throughout Latin America. In theory, the law applies to everyone; burdens and benefits are allocated according to prescribed objective criteria. The very idea of law implies, for most Latin Americans as for most Europeans and North Americans, a formal system of rights and obligations defined by ascertainable rules and enforced by a regularized official system of sanctions. (Within such a univeralistic system, there is room for particularistic legal relations; marriage, for example, is what Weber called a "status contract," altering a total relationship and imposing certain kinds of mutual obligations that are owing because of the spouse's quality as spouse, not his or her performance according to generalized criteria.)

The universalism of the Code Napoléon obeyed the explicit instructions of Napoléon himself. The Code, he said, must be written in language that any literate person could understand. (And, upon learning that the first academic commentary on the Code had been published, he is supposed to have said, "Mon Code est perdû" – "My Code is lost.") One who knew his rights under the French law would think of himself as a Frenchman.

The very idea of rights assumes a system characterized by rule, not discretion. Furthermore, rights exist only when there is a system of conflict resolution based on principled adjudication, as distinguished from fiat on the one hand or bargaining on the other. A model of development that emphasizes participation is thus oriented toward a "rights" mentality, for a system of rules and an effective enforcement mechanism are basic to the security on which participatory development depends.

Correspondingly, there are no effective rights if a state is too weak or too corrupt to enforce them on a principled basis. A bribe, to take the clearest example, causes the disregard of universalist criteria and the undermining of a system of rights. The expectations formally defined by law do not provide security if resources are distributed, or conflicts settled, in favor of those who can pay the highest bribes. Furthermore, "[r]esources are frequently misallocated when the criterion of the private gain of the allocator is employed."[9] Thus even a top-down approach to development is undermined by corruption. The point need not be belabored; it is

---

[9] Rosenn, "The Jeito: Brazil's Institutional Bypass of the Formal Legal System and its Developmental Implications," 19 *Am. J. Comp. L.* 514, 543 (1971).

sufficient to say that in *any* system, to the extent that security based on law is instrumental to development, corruption is anti-developmental.[10]

Ironically, corruption itself is often a response to conditions of insecurity. If strangers are suspect, then the world of market transactions is cold and forbidding. A bribe turns a transactional relationship into a "moral" relationship — although the word "moral" may be jarring in this context — by defining a new particularist moral community.[11] Such a community is functionally analogous to the community created when one person becomes the godparent *(padrino)* of another's child, making the two "co-parents" *(compadres)*,[12] bound to each other in quasi-familial loyalties that imply, among other things, some forms of economic support.

Nor is corruption the only form of particularist/personalist response to the insecurities of an open society. No society is more open and transactional than the Hobbesian society of "war of all against all," where order is always precarious. Feudalism was a reaction to the insecurities of such a world, founding order and security on a base that combined the landlord-tenant relationship with that of patron and client. Similarly, the patronage system of the Latin American hacienda offered a kind of security that the state was unable to provide. Once a patronage system is installed, it is not easily dislodged by a more universalist order. Patronage de-emphasizes principled decision according to rule, and emphasizes discretionary justice and "connections." In such a climate, security is not to be found in rules, but in personal relationships. Knowing one's rights matters less than knowing one's friends.

The relation of patron and client was formally recognized in Roman law; like marriage in our own law, the patron-client relation was an island of particularism in a universalist legal system.[13] Rules existed for such a relation — not merely defining its boundaries, but governing some aspects of the relation itself. One critical rule was that a patron could not sue his client, nor vice-versa; they must work out their disputes in such a way as to maintain the relationship for the future. Discretion, not principled adjudication, is the model of conflict resolution in a patronage system. Where the Weberian model of the market looks to universal rules as the guarantee of the security of transactions, the patronage model looks to the patron's decree as a means of preserving the security of the relationship. The patron's decree may be partly or wholly based on custom — and thus on rule. But even in such a case, the parties tend to perceive that a principled resolution of the dispute is the product of the patron's discretionary choice. A court of law focuses on single transactions; it closely examines the past, applies the rules, and makes injured parties whole; one side wins, and the

[10] See *infra* at pp. 700-02. Correspondingly, where the security based on law is absent, it may be possible for corruption to promote development precisely by undermining some of the features of the legal system that produce insecurity. Or, corruption may safeguard against the worst effects of an ineffective economic policy, performing the "valuable function of a hedge." See Leff, "Economic Development Through Bureaucratic Corruption," 8 *Am. Behavioral Sci.* No. 3, p. 11 (Nov. 1964).

[11] See Bailey, "The Peasant View of the Bad Life," *Advancement of Science*, Dec. 1966, pp. 399-409, reprinted in T. Shanin (Ed.), *Peasants and Peasant Societies* 299, 304-05 (1971).

[12] The corresponding feminine forms of these words are *padrina* and *comadre*.

[13] Much of the Anglo-American law of fiduciary duty has its roots in this body of Roman law.

other loses; for the future, security lies not in the personal relations of plaintiff and defendant, but in the market mechanisms, as underpinned by law. In a "multiplex" relationship,[14] where legal questions are dominated by one's place in the relationship, disputes are diffuse, focusing less on the normative evaluation of particular transactions than on the healing of the entire relationship for the future.[15] (The metaphor of healing is a reminder that in our own legal system, one of the fundamental problems of the criminal law lies in the question whether to respond to anti-social conduct with the particularist — and patronizing — medical model of "treatment" or the more transactional/universal legal model of punishment.)

Development itself may seem to demand an emphasis on discretionary governmental controls — particularly where developmental strategies are heavily influenced by the top-down model. The dangers of corruption in such a system are acute,[16] as Latin Americans have known from the earliest days of the colonial bureaucracy. Weber assumed that the rise of a state bureaucracy would inevitably press toward an increasing universalism, with ever-growing emphasis on calculable rules. In Latin America, however, governmental administration has, from the very beginning, been incorporated into the prevailing system of patronage.[17] Nepotism, for example, which seems almost sinful in the Anglo-American world, is widely regarded in Latin America as a social duty. Monopoly privilege is at least as old as the Conquest; Queen Isabella sought from the outset to limit the exploitation of the New World to her own subjects — not even to Spaniards generally, but to subjects of Castile. In Latin America, it is sometimes said, mercantilism never died. Given this history, it has been argued that the very idea of "rights" in Latin America is meaningful largely in terms of group privileges, as distinguished from individual rights. Legal universalism is thus seen as a dream — and perhaps a North American dream at that — rather than even a potential reality in Latin America.[18]

Questions

1. The foregoing discussion identifies two models of organization and conflict resolution, which can be loosely summarized under the headings of "rule" and "discretion." Any legal system will, of course, be a blend of both.

---

[14] The term is Max Gluckman's. See his *The Judicial Process among the Barotse of Northern Rhodesia* 15-24 (1955).

[15] In other particularistic relationships not characterized by clear superior-inferior roles, the alternative to discretionary decision-making by the superior is not adjudication but negotiation.

[16] See Myrdal, "The 'Soft State' in Underdeveloped Countries," 15 *U.C.L.A. L. Rev.* 1118 (1968). Discretion need not imply caprice, if discretion is exercised for the purpose of achieving specified goals. But the goals stated for development planners are notoriously diffuse ("economic growth," etc.), and thus susceptible to unprincipled manipulation.

[17] See S. Stein and B. Stein, *The Colonial Heritage of Latin America* 67-81 (1970).

[18] See Wiarda, "Toward a Framework for the Study of Political Change in the Iberic-Latin Tradition: The Corporative Model," 25 *World Politics* 206 (1973).

(a) Was the *Muñoz* case[19] (the Venezuelan case dealing with the grounds for expropriation of a landowner's two estates) decided according to rules? Does it instead fit the pattern of discretion? What are the distinctive characteristics of decision according to rule?

(b) What kinds of risks are reduced by a system of rule, as distinguished from discretion? What are the necessary conditions for a system of rule? Under what circumstances might a formal system based on rule turn out to produce less security than a system of patronage?

(c) In a society in which there are sharp cleavages between the "haves" and the "have-nots," would we be apt to find the haves urging devotion to rule, and the have-nots insisting on systems of discretionary justice? Is the principle of devotion to rule merely a mask for preserving the status quo? In answering these questions, contrast two types of rules: (i) rules guaranteeing property security against governmental interference; (ii) rules establishing a minimum wage, or providing for social security benefits financed by taxation of the wealthy.

(d) Does development depend on innovation and even improvising, which will be incompatible with a system of rules? What kind of rules? (Consider, for example, the rules protecting the holders of patents and copyrights.)

(e) Assuming that a legal system includes major ingredients of both rule and discretion, is it important for developmental purposes to identify clearly the boundary between the two areas? Why?

(f) If some legal issues should be decided according to rule, and others left to discretion, where should the following subjects be placed: Penal justice? (The substantive definition of crimes? The disposition of offenders?) Commercial law? Regulation of currency exchange rates? Expropriation of land for purposes of land reform? (Does decision according to rule mean, in the land reform context, compensation of owners at full market-value rates?) What are the characteristics of a legal subject area that make it appropriate for assignment to the area of rule? For assignment to the area of discretion?

2. A system of patronage, we have seen, offers its own kinds of security that do not depend on the enforcement of universalistic rules.

(a) Under a system of rules, security depends on one's ability to know the rules. What is the analogous knowledge that one must have in order to be secure under a system of patronage?

(b) Is a patronage system anti-developmental? (i) Does such a system inhibit trade? (Consider the experience of colonial monopolies.) (ii) Does a patronage system inhibit investment? (iii) Does a patronage system inhibit innovation? Such a system sets great store by the preservation of existing relationships. What kinds of innovation might be threatening to a patronage system?

3. Executive discretion is limited by the application of such judicial controls as the amparo or the writ of security, which purport to be institutions designed to protect the "rule of law."

---

[19] P. 294, *supra.*

(a) *Are* these institutions wholly rule-oriented? Or do they contain elements of discretion?

(b) If a Mexican court is forbidden to make any general pronouncement of law in an amparo proceeding, in what sense is its decision a decision according to rule? Does principled adjudication imply explanation of decisions?

(c) Is the "rule of law" a protection against oppression? Consider the question alternatively from the standpoints of (i) an executive official who wants to dispense justice and otherwise hand out favors as a matter of grace, and (ii) persons who are economically powerless, and who see judicially-protected freedoms — particularly market freedoms — as weapons in the hands of the economically powerful.

---

3. Security as Self-Confidence: the Willingness to Take Moderate Risks

The risks and uncertainties of investment are compounded, in the development process, by the risks and uncertainties of innovation: the decision to seek employment in a new city, the decision to plant a new crop. It is, in fact, unpredictability that chiefly makes people fear the unfamiliar. Much of what passes for fatalism, and for an acceptance of the status quo as the natural order of things, surely arises out of the need for security.

Decision-making theorists distinguish between *risk* and *uncertainty*. *Risk* is taken to refer to the case in which an objective probability can be assigned to an event's occurrence or nonoccurrence. *Uncertainty* refers to the case in which, since information is lacking, it is not possible to assign a probability to the event's occurrence or nonoccurrence. Suppose there are ten marbles in a bag. If we know that seven marbles are red and three are blue, we know there is a 70 percent probability (risk) that, after a thorough shake, the first marble drawn "blind" from the bag will be red. If we did not know how many marbles there were of each color, we should face a situation not of risk but of uncertainty; we could only guess. "We dispel uncertainty with information."[20]

In the world that lies beyond the comfortable abstractions of imaginary colored marbles, it may not be so easy to separate the questions of uncertainty and risk. Consider the farmer who is told that strawberries would be more profitable than the corn he has been growing all his life. The agricultural extension agent may reduce uncertainty by telling the farmer about such things as the amounts of water needed for growing strawberries; the farmer can then make his own calculation of the risk of inadequate rainfall, as tempered by the probability of access to irrigation water. But suppose the farmer asks, "Who will buy my crop, and at what price?" Is that question directed at uncertainty, or at risk? A reply might focus on the nature of market forces,

---

[20]W. Scott and T. Mitchell, *Organization Theory: A Structural and Behavioral Approach* 170 (1972). We should not be carried away with this distinction. One also dispels risk with information, as, by peeking at the marbles, or by learning exactly how marbles behave in a shaken bag.

and predictions about supply and demand;[21] alternatively, it might focus on a government agency's promise to buy at a guaranteed minimum price. Either reply involves the farmer in some rational calculation, and some plain guessing. Thus we should not be surprised if the farmer's decision turns out to be importantly influenced by factors that have little to do with objective calculations: his values and his perception of his own role. These states of mind will have been formed long before the farmer has even begun to think about replacing corn with strawberries. "Minds appear not to need making up; it is un-making them which takes time and evidence."[22]

The role of law in affecting an individual's willingness to take the risks (and face the uncertainties) implicit in developmental activity is itself far from certain. Yet at least four kinds of connection are identifiable: Law appears to play a significant part in (a) affecting (reducing *or* increasing) the objective risks of developmental activity; (b) affecting (reducing *or* increasing) the degree of uncertainty of those risks; (c) affecting (reinforcing *or* undermining) the values that underpin developmental activity; and (d) shaping individuals' perceptions of themselves. We have dealt with the first of these roles for law in analyzing the varieties of security, and with the second one in our treatment of the theme of rule v. discretion. The third role for law relates to the legitimacy of change, and will be discussed in the next section of this chapter. In the present discussion, we shall look at the way in which the legal system affects developmental decision-making by affecting the self-perception of individual men and women.

The paradox of law and change, like all paradoxes, is "only seeming contradiction."[23] Law is not only compatible with social change, but indispensable to it:

> The behavior of both individuals and organizations changes constantly. However, during any given period when some elements are changing, others must remain stable, or there will be a loss of identity. For example, the specific behavior of an individual or bureau may be quite different on Tuesday from what it was on Monday, but the rules governing that behavior may be the same on both days.[24]

However revolutionary a change may be, in political or other terms, some underlying principles of law are crucial to the prevention of individual or social breakdown. We shall return to this theme at the level of organizational breakdown when we examine into the problem of legitimacy. For now, we are concerned with the importance of law

---

[21] The calculation of market risks may be a sophisticated process. There is a story about Brazilian farmers that has achieved the status of a folk tale. Government extension agents would tell farmers that prices for corn were high, and so many farmers would plant corn instead of onions. The price of corn would fall, and the price of onions would rise. The agents would then tell the farmers to plant onions because of the high price. The more alert farmers, so the story goes, learned to plant the opposite of what the extension agents recommended.

[22] Audley, "What Makes Up a Mind?" in F. Castles, D. Murray and D. Potter (eds.), *Decisions, Organizations and Society* 56, 62 (1971).

[23] Brown, "The Open Economy: Mr. Justice Frankfurter and the Position of the Judiciary," 67 *Yale L. J.* 219 (1957).

[24] A. Downs, *Inside Bureaucracy* 167 (1967).

in providing the predictability necessary as a stable underpinning for changes in individual behavior.

We begin with the fact that no decision-making, not even economic decision-making, is wholly a rational process. The following excerpt from Professor H. A. Simon's influential article points the way toward a redefinition of "economic man."

H. SIMON, THEORIES OF DECISION-MAKING IN ECONOMICS AND BEHAVIORAL SCIENCE

49 *American Economic Review* 253, 272-24 (1959)

The decision maker's information about his environment is much less than an approximation to the real environment. The term "approximation" implies that the subjective world of the decision maker resembles the external environment closely, but lacks, perhaps, some firmness of detail. In actual fact the perceived world is fantastically different from the "real" world. The differences involve both omissions and distortions, and arise in both perception and inference. The sins of omission in perception are more important than the sins of commission. . . .

Perception is sometimes referred to as a "filter." This term is as misleading as "approximation," and for the same reason: it implies that what comes through into the central nervous system is really quite a bit like what is "out there." In fact, the filtering is not merely a passive selection of some part of a presented whole, but an active process involving attention to a very small part of the whole and exclusion, from the outset, of almost all that is not within the scope of attention.

Every human organism lives in an environment that generates millions of bits of new information each second, but the bottleneck of the perceptual apparatus certainly does not admit more than 1000 bits per second, and probably much less. Equally significant omissions occur in the processing that takes place when information reaches the brain. . . . [T]here are hosts of inferences that *might* be drawn from the information stored in the brain that are not in fact drawn. The consequences implied by information in the memory become known only through active information-processing, and hence through active selection of particular problem-solving paths from the myriad that might have been followed. . . .

A real-life decision involves some goals or values, some facts about the environment, and some inferences drawn from the values and facts. The goals and values may be simple or complex, consistent or contradictory; the facts may be real or supposed, based on observation or the reports of others; the inferences may be valid or spurious. . . . The resemblance of decision making to logical reasoning is only metaphorical, because there are quite different rules in the two cases to determine what constitute "valid" premises and admissible modes of inference. . . .

We can find common ground to relate the economist's theory of decision making with that of the social psychologist. The latter is particularly interested, of course, in social influences on choice, which determine the *role* of the actor. In our present terms, a role is a social prescription of some, but not all, of the premises that enter into an individual's choices of behavior. Any particular concrete behavior is the result of a large number of premises, only some of which are prescribed by the role. In addition to role premises there will be premises about the state of the environment based directly on perception, premises representing beliefs and knowledge, and idiosyncratic premises that characterize the personality.

Simon has used the term "role" in the sociologist's sense: it is by definition a cluster of norms — expectations — that attach to a person who occupies a particular position in relation to another. When we speak of one's role as parent, or employee, or citizen, we are speaking of a set of expectations released by occupancy of the position. Many of those expectations are defined by law. In our present context, we are concerned with the willingness to assume those roles associated with developmental activity. Innovation is unlikely from one who cannot conceive of himself or herself as an innovator; leadership requires acceptance of the role of leader; even investment depends on expectations about oneself. The model of participatory development in particular demands the widespread diffusion of developmental roles.

The law's contribution to this process is varied, and often subtle. Law, it has been remarked, is conservative in the way that language is conservative; it establishes categories of thought which are transcended only with great difficulty.[25] Law also contributes to stability by legitimizing existing arrangements, as we shall see in the next section of this chapter. But perhaps the law's most serious potential inhibition on social change lies in its impact on individuals' self-perception. If the legal system causes people to think that they are incapable of changing, then they *are* incapable. Widely shared self-confidence may not be a sufficient condition for participatory development, but it is a necessary condition.[26]

Self-confidence tends to be part of a circular process: nothing succeeds like success. The circles also work in the other direction: insecurity breeds insecurity; dependency breeds dependency. A strategic place for the law to intervene in these circles is the definition of citizenship — not merely the formal definitions to be found in constitutions and statutes, but also the effective definitions, given reality by the legal system's actual workings. A person who has been consistently treated as a ward will not easily become independent. Thus a primary aim for the law in promoting

---

[25] See Wasserstrom, "Lawyers and Revolution," 30 *U. Pitt. L. Rev.* 125, 129 (1968). The same can be said of any social institution; there is an innate tendency of an institution to maintain itself, through its policies of recruitment and socialization. Institutional change thus implies a degree of disintegration.

[26] See the discussion of inequality, *infra* at pp. 691-710.

participatory development is to give large numbers of individuals the dignity of responsibility.[27]

We alluded earlier to the competition in criminal justice between the theories of "treatment" and punishment. An outstanding Norwegian lawyer-sociologist has remarked that the medical model of treatment is now in the ascendancy largely because of society's collective psychic need for seeming predictability; if deviant behavior can be brought within the scope of our theories of behavioral science, it will seem predictable and thus less threatening.[28] In the medical model, of course, the doctor knows best; the offender-patient does not have rights and responsibilities, but a regimen, prescribed on the basis of the doctor's discretionary judgment.[29] The offender may emerge from the process as less of a threat to society, but a treatment-oriented legal system will have done little to train the offender as a self-confident and responsible decision-maker.[30] The issue provides another perspective on the question, raised earlier, that must always be asked in analyzing the relation of law to predictability and security: Predictability for whom? Participatory development, we have seen, requires a particular answer to this question. The law provides an institutional base for rational developmental decision-making at all levels of the society. In the model of participatory development, individuals are regarded not as clients or patients, but as citizens.

The symbolism of citizenship is thus far from empty. Land reform is, in one important dimension, a political response to the yearnings of rural people for a share in the dignity long associated with the ownership of land. So, too, the amparo and the writ of security are declarations that the state is not above the rules, but can be called to account by the individual citizen. Even for the land-reform beneficiary whose "title" must be described with quotation marks, and even for the citizen who is too poor to contemplate bringing an action in amparo, these promises of universal citizenship are significant as symbols that they are persons, members of the national community. That is scarcely the end of participatory development, but it is an essential beginning.

Beyond the symbolism of citizenship, the law contributes to self-confidence mainly by ordering an individual's surroundings in such a way that he or she perceives them to be rationally manipulable. A body of written law, merely by existing, promotes such a "rational" view of life to some extent; some persons, at least, are aware of the authoritative documents (statutes, regulations, etc.) as a system that is, on the whole, coherent and internally consistent. (Indeed, the average person in a "modern" society probably thinks of the law as being somewhat more coherent and consistent than it is

---

[27] The point is by no means limited to capitalist development. In Cuba, the institution of popular tribunals appears to have been motivated in part by similar considerations. See Berman, "The Cuban Popular Tribunals," 69 *Colum. L. Rev.* 1317 (1969).

[28] W. Aubert, *Elements of Sociology* 144 (1967, reprinted 1970).

[29] But if the doctor prescribes "punishment" as "treatment," a court may step in to limit the doctor's discretion. See *In Re Maddox*, 351 Mich. 358, 88 N.W. 2d 470 (1957).

[30] The point is dramatically made in Anthony Burgess' novel, *A Clockwork Orange*. Herbert Morris has persuasively argued that the right to be treated as a person implies a right to be punished rather than "treated." Morris, "Persons and Punishment," 52 *The Monist* 475 (1968).

in fact.) This view of law emphasizes law's qualities as a body of discernible rules and principles. Two generations of "legal realism" have taught us, however, to beware any view of law that does not emphasize its qualities as a process. In studying the criminal law, for example, the realists do not look so much to the substantive statutory definitions of crime as to such phenomena as police investigation methods, prosecutorial discretion, plea bargaining, probation reports, and the effective lengths of "indeterminate" sentences. The substantive criminal law thus appears, as one professor used to describe it, as "an island of technicality in a sea of discretion." Such perspectives on law are not only useful but indispensable. But in our zeal to be realistic, we should not overlook the obvious and central fact that an enormous portion of every legal system in the "developed" world is exceedingly coherent and knowable. (Our own legal education, which still centers on developing analytical skills, is misleading in this respect, for it consistently focuses on problem situations, while most transactions and relationships are "easy cases.") Consider, in contrast, this comment on Brazil — which is surely one of Latin America's leaders, both in the rate of growth of gross national product[31] and in the sophistication of the legal system.

K. ROSENN, THE JEITO: BRAZIL'S INSTITUTIONAL BYPASS OF THE FORMAL LEGAL SYSTEM AND ITS DEVELOPMENTAL IMPLICATIONS

19 *American Journal of Comparative Law* 514, 538-41 (1971)

This formal legal system has had all the earmarks of a modern, developed institutional structure. Official determinations of rights and obligations have been based upon application of impersonal, universalistic principles by professionals trained in the system. However, this formal system failed to penetrate very far into Brazilian society. With the exception of the elite and the small, emerging middle class, the great bulk of the population has remained largely unaffected by the formal legal structure. Their disputes have been resolved by the *patrão, paterfamilias* or local custom.

Even today penetration of the formal legal system is quite limited. Improvements in modern communications and transportation have done surprisingly little to reduce Brazil's vastness and enormous regional disparities. Approximately half this huge country still lies in remote and inaccessible areas, for all practical purposes outside the market economy. Much of the rural interior still is only nominally under the control of the formal authorities. Though the situation is slowly changing, especially since the military takeover, what Jacques Lambert wrote in the mid-1950's is essentially valid today:

---

[31] In Seers' definition, p. 2, *supra,* this economic growth may or may not be justifiably called "development." The Brazil of the "economic miracle," it will be remembered, is also the Brazil of the "Death Squads" and the repression of political dissent. See Carl, "Erosion of Constitutional Rights of Political Offenders in Brazil," 12 *Va. J. Int'l. L.* 157 (1972).

But when one leaves the "new country" in which the Government's action is exercised directly, federal and even state legislation is weakened by intervention of local authorities, whose command is more respected than that of the distant Government. The man of the interior is accustomed to go to the local authorities to seek protection against laws which he does not know and fears, instead of going to functionaries of the Central Government to ask them to apply the law. In spite of centralizing institutions, the old Brazil effectively continues decentralized, because the uniform . . . law is not respected or even known.

The system has been built upon compromise, with the local bosses delivering the rural vote to federal and state authorities in exchange for ample extra-legal autonomy. Though the municipalities have lacked legal autonomy, as a practical matter incumbent heads of municipalities have been free to "render justice to one's friends and to apply the law to one's adversaries." . . .

Penetration of the formal system into even the modern, urban sectors is greatly hampered by difficulties in ascertaining its provisions. Caligula was reputed to have had his laws and decrees posted high off the ground where none of the populace could read them. The Brazilian method is not so obvious, but it is nearly as effective. Discovering the governing law in Brazil is still as perplexing and difficult a task today as in colonial times. The myriad forms of the federal government's positive law — the Constitution, amendments, institutional acts, complementary laws, decree-laws, laws, decrees, regulations, resolutions, ordinances, *portarias,* circulars, instructions, etc. — are published in the *Diário Oficial,* an official gazette. (There are corresponding publications at the state level.) However, the federal *Diário Oficial* is unindexed, undigested, and occasionally unreadable. Only recently has a decent unofficial index for legislation been published. While there is a semi-official collection of laws and decrees, the *Coleção das Leis do Brasil,* the precarious indexing is on a volume by volume basis. Whether one finds a particular law or decree frequently depends upon luck and the caption's phraseology. Even at the federal level, there is no official codification integrating the multiplicity of legislative pronouncements on any given subject. While an attempt is made from time to time to bring the plethora of income tax statutes together into an official compilation, it is incomplete, sometimes incorrect, and quickly obsolete.

Instead of amending basic code provisions, Brazilian practice has been to adopt supplemental legislation, which, in turn, is amended and reamended. Generally one is forced to read a host of separate statutes and decrees regulating a given subject (and many others as well) and then undertake the jigsaw job of piecing together the provisions still in force to arrive at the governing law.[32] For example, so many

---

[32] For an interesting tour of the technical aspects of elaborating Brazilian laws, as well as collection of horrors of past efforts, see H. Fernandes Pinheiro, *Técnica Legislativa* (2nd ed. 1962). While private compilations, such as the *Vademecum Forense* and the *Carteira da Revista Forense,* collect most of the basic statutes and some of the decrees, they are far from complete. Though there are occasional footnotes for cross reference and some integration of successive legislative pronouncements on the same subject, the reader is not spared the bulk of the task of integrating the jumble of conflicting and complementary laws. [Footnote by Rosenn, renumbered.]

different rent control laws were enacted between 1942 and 1964 that no fewer than 18 different regimes regulating rentals were simultaneously in force.

Laws are frequently drafted with such haste that clarifying legislation follows hard on the heels of the original statute, producing generalized confusion. Thus Decree-Law No. 62 of November 21, 1966, a carefully and intelligently conceived statute, authorized firms to effect monetary correction of their balance sheets starting with fiscal year 1968. But the law was not self-executing. It depended upon issuance of regulations by the Treasury, and the regulations were never issued. Just before 1968 expired, a hastily concocted and poorly conceived statute, Decree-Law No. 401, was promulgated as a substitute for Decree-Law No. 62. In less than six months, Decree-Law No. 401 was amended and clarified by no fewer than five decree-laws and one *portaria.*[33]

Many decisions of important tribunals, including the nation's highest court, remain unpublished. Since there is no doctrine of *stare decisis* (though the introduction of the *Súmula* in 1964 was a step in that direction),[34] it is common to find numerous decisions on both sides of a given question. Indexing of reported cases depends on the terminology employed in the headnote; it is unreliable and sketchy at best. One looks in vain for comprehensive digests, Shepard's, a key number system, CCH or PH type services, or an index to legal periodicals. To be sure, cases are not as important in civil law jurisdictions, and Brazil is far ahead of most of her neighbors in indexing and reporting cases. Nevertheless, the system falls far short of what is available in the neighboring civil law jurisdiction of Argentina.

Hence it is quite common to discover that the authorities charged with administering a particular body of law are unaware of significant changes in the statutory or case law. Inertia, ignorance, and inability to keep abreast of rapid-fire legal change frequently combine to produce substantial differences between the formal norm and the law actually being applied.

Legislative confusion about rent control can cause disputes between landlords and tenants that are wasteful and frustrating; millions of ordinary people are directly affected by such laws, and their views of the entire legal system can easily be affected by single instances of regulatory chaos. And while the accountants and managers of firms required to correct monetary values in their balance sheets are in no sense a cross-section of the Brazilian population, they are an especially significant group, considered from the standpoint of market-oriented developmental activity. If such persons are persuaded that the law, like the peace of God, "passeth understanding," it is natural for them to turn to the *despachante,* the professional go-between who expedites dealings with governmental agencies for a fee. The world — or, that part of

---

[33] . . . Theoretically, a *portaria,* an administrative pronouncement, cannot modify the terms of a law. However, since this one modifies the law intelligently, no one complains. It is simply another example of the ubiquitous *jeito.* [Footnote by Rosenn, renumbered.]

[34] See p. 104 n. 25, *supra,* for a description of the *Súmula.* [Eds.]

the world regulated by law — may be seen to be rationally manipulable, but manipulable by the *despachante*, not the citizen. When personalist connections are seen to triumph over a system of rules, the self-confidence necessary for participatory development is undermined. Security-as-self-confidence is thus partly derived from security-as-predictability.[35]

Questions

1. It is sometimes said that a high degree of social mobility promotes development; participatory development in particular appears to be promoted by mobility, at least in the sense of the potential actor's perception that improvement is possible. How does law affect such perceptions?

2. We have seen how the willingness to take moderate risks rests on an underlying security; the discussion has emphasized the role of law in providing security in a market system. Is risk-taking inhibited in a patronage/connections system? Would it be useful to distinguish between the risks of investment and the risks of innovation? Which of these development-oriented activities (investment or innovation) is the greater threat to a system of patronage and connections?

3. Submissiveness to other people, we have seen, is antithetical to participatory development.

(a) In devising the "new agrarian structure" to succeed a taking of land in a land reform, what form or forms of rights in land might be recommended, by way of encouraging independence and self-confidence?

(b) The "no reelection" rule, applied to the Mexican ejido, requires the replacement of ejido officers every three years. How does this rule bear on the issue of submissiveness v. independence? In terms of this issue, what are the trade-offs to be considered in evaluating a proposal to repeal the "no reelection" rule?

4. Perhaps the most obvious example of successful participatory development considered in these materials has been the construction and improvement of houses in the Caracas barrios. Can that pattern of investment be explained as resting on a system of "knowable" legal rules? Even if the rules in question were never reduced to writing? Was that housing investment in fact the result of the security of a patronage/connections system, rather than security based on rules?

---

[35] An alternative view of these same phenomena might be that exposure to inconsistent norms provides training in dealing with the unexpected, and is thus conducive to self-confidence. Or, if the *despachante* is perceived as the agent of the citizen who employs him, arguably this system of manipulation of the bureaucracy may breed self-reliance in the citizen, and a corresponding willingness to take risks. Which of these views seems more useful in studying the relation of law to the development process?

B. Legitimacy

In Chapter III, the discussion of the Bolivian land reform is entitled: "Land Reform First, Then Law." There is a sense in which it is true that the effective land reform in Bolivia occurred when the campesinos occupied the great estates, ejecting both owners and administrative foremen. But a great deal of formal legal activity has taken place in the two decades since those first heady days of revolution. Land reform has been formalized through the confirming of legal titles in the names of thousands of people, many of whom participated in the initial occupation of the lands. This process of title confirmation was not a legalistic nicety, but a political necessity. The campesinos did not merely want to work the land and keep the resulting profits; they wanted titles. Speaking more abstractly, we might say that they had power, and sought legitimacy for the exercise of that power. It made a difference to the campesinos that their occupancy of the lands was *rightful*.

The case of the Bolivian campesinos can be explained as a variation on the theme of security. Legitimacy was important to them because it lent greater weight to the expectation that they could continue to occupy the lands and work them for their own accounts. Similarly, when the successful authors of a military coup seek the blessings of the nation's highest court for the person they have installed as President, we may assume that the exercise is designed to improve the new government's security of tenure. Yet the legitimacy of domination has other significance for the development process. To the extent that the state must perform an organizing role, it must have the power to translate the decisions of its leaders into action by large numbers of people. No government can govern effectively for any protracted period "out of the barrel of a gun." If government is to play an important part in the development process, masses of people must be willing to accept the government's commands just because they *are* the government's commands.

---

1. The Varieties of Legitimacy

Discussions of legitimacy always begin with Max Weber; to lend this discussion the legitimacy of tradition, we shall not depart from the pattern.

R. BENDIX, MAX WEBER: AN INTELLECTUAL PORTRAIT

Pp. 297-300 (1960)*

In Weber's view beliefs in the legitimacy of a system of domination are not merely philosophical matters. They can contribute to the stability of an authority

---

*© 1960, 1962 by Reinhard Bendix. Reprinted by permission of Doubleday & Company, Inc.

relationship, and they indicate very real differences between systems of domination. Like all others who enjoy advantages over their fellows, men in power want to see their position as "legitimate" and their advantages as "deserved," and to interpret the subordination of the many as the "just fate" of those upon whom it falls. All rulers therefore develop some myth of their natural superiority, which usually is accepted by the people under stable conditions but may become the object of passionate hatred when some crisis makes the established order appear questionable. Weber saw only three principles of legitimation — each related to a corresponding type of "apparatus" — that have been used to justify the power of command:

(1) *Legal domination* exists where a system of rules that is applied judicially and administratively in accordance with ascertainable principles is valid for all members of the corporate group. The persons who exercise the power of command are typically *superiors* who are appointed or elected by legally sanctioned procedures and are themselves oriented toward the maintenance of the legal order. The persons subject to the commands are *legal equals* who obey "the law" rather than the persons implementing it. These principles apply also to the "apparatus" that implements the system of legal domination. This organization is continuous; its officials are subject to rules that delimit their authority, institute controls over its exercise, separate the private person from the performance of official functions, and require that all transactions be in writing in order to be valid.

(2) *Traditional domination* is based on the belief in the legitimacy of an authority that "has always existed." The persons excercising the power of command generally are *masters* who enjoy personal authority by virtue of their inherited status. Their commands are legitimate in the sense that they are in accord with custom, but they also possess the prerogative of free personal decision, so that conformity with custom and personal arbitrariness are both characteristic of such rule. The persons subject to the commands of the master are *followers* or *subjects* in the literal sense — they obey out of personal loyalty to the master or a pious regard for his time-honored status. The "apparatus" appropriate to this system consists either of personal retainers — household officials, relatives, personal favorites — in a typically patrimonial regime,[36] or of personally loyal allies — vassals, tributory lords — in a feudal society. In their official capacity personal retainers are subject to the customary or arbitary commands of their master, so that their sphere of activity and power of command is a mirror-image of that master at a lower level. By contrast, in a feudal society, officials are not personal dependents but socially prominent allies who have given an oath of fealty and who have independent jurisdiction by virtue of grant or contract. The distinction between feudal and patrimonial rule and the juxtaposition of customary and arbitrary commands under both systems pervades all forms of traditional domination.

(3) *Charismatic domination.* Personal authority also may have its source in the very

---

[36] A patrimonial regime is one in which government is considered to be part of the ruler's private domain, in the sense of property. Government officials are thus the equivalent of the ruler's personal servants; their offices "originate in the household administration of the ruler." R. Bendix, *Max Weber: An Intellectual Portrait* 335 (1960). See also p. 33 n. 40, *supra.* [Eds.]

opposite of tradition. The power of command may be exercised by a *leader* — whether he is a prophet, hero, or demagogue — who can prove that he possesses *charisma* by virtue of magical powers, revelations, heroism, or other extraordinary gifts. The persons who obey such a leader are *disciples* or *followers* who believe in his extraordinary qualities rather than in stipulated rules or in the dignity of a position sanctified by tradition. Under a charismatic leader officials are selected in terms of their own charisma and personal devotion, rather than in terms of their special qualifications, status, or personal dependence. These "disciple-officials" hardly constitute an organization, and their sphere of activity and power of command depends upon revelation, exemplary conduct, and decision from case to case, none of which is bound by rules or tradition but solely by the judgment of the leader.

In history these "pure types" of domination are *always* found in combinations, but Weber insisted that clear concepts are needed to analyze such combinations in terms of their legal, traditional or charismatic elements. The first step is to show how these more or less heterogeneous elements are combined in different historical configurations such as feudalism or the modern state. On this basis Weber believed it was possible to show that certain incompatibilities in a system of domination are related to modifications of the institutional structure and to changed beliefs in legitimacy. For example, a fully consistent charismatic leadership is inimical to rules and tradition, but the disciples always wish to see the leader's extraordinary capacities preserved for everyday life. As the disciples have their way, rules and traditions develop that denature the charisma they consciously mean to serve. In this way one may analyze the tendencies by which one system of domination can change in the direction of another.

Yet change is not necessarily a change from one type of domination to another. Each system of domination possesses certain built-in safeguards of its own identity, which result from the belief in the legitimacy of the relation between rulers and ruled. It follows that every system of domination will change its character when its rulers fail to live up to the standards by which they justify their domination and thereby jeopardize the beliefs in those standards among the public at large. Under legal domination the "superior" is himself subject to law, and he can undermine the beliefs sustaining the legal order if he uses formal compliance to extend his domination indefinitely. Under traditional domination the "master" can undermine belief in sacred tradition if he uses his arbitrary powers of command to put himself above the tradition that confers these powers upon him. Similarly, the charismatic leader forfeits his authority when he fails to prove himself in the eyes of his disciples.

Legitimacy, like security, is a state of mind. It is, however, a state of mind that is largely shared throughout a community; power cannot be said to be legitimate when only scattered members of the community believe it to be so. Legitimacy, then, is interlocked with issues of consensus and community — which we explore in the next section of this chapter — no less than with issues of security. The present section differs from those which precede and follow it, not by treating different social phenomena, but by offering a different perspective. Thomas Reed Powell once remarked that "the legal mind" was a mind capable of thinking about something that was inextricably linked to something else, without thinking about the something else. The phenomenon, far from being exclusive to lawyers, is implicit in the process of thought. What is important is to avoid those omissions that mislead.

---

2. Legitimacy in Latin America

The "crisis of legitimacy" in Latin America is by no means a new historical development. Consider the following extract from Professor Richard Morse's article in the light of Weber's three types of legitimacy. What role does Morse see for the kind of legitimacy that is founded on rules of law?

R. MORSE, THE HERITAGE OF LATIN AMERICA

in L. Hartz (ed.), *The Founding of New Societies*
Pp. 123, 161-64 (1964)*

The extent of the politico-administrative crisis faced by the independent Spanish American nations of 1830 can be appreciated when we recall our model of the Thomist-patrimonial state. The lower echelons of administration had operated by the grace of an interventionist, paternal monarch, thoroughly sanctioned by tradition and faith. His collapse straightway withdrew legitimacy from the remnants of the royal bureaucracy. It was impossible to identify a substitute authority that would command general assent. Decapitated, the government could not function, for the patrimonial regime had developed neither: (1) the underpinning of contractual vassalic relationships that capacitate the component parts of a *feudal* regime for autonomous life; nor, (2) a rationalized *legal* order not dependent for its operation and claims to assent upon personalistic intervention by the highest authority.

Although legitimacy was withdrawn from the hierarchies of government and society by independence, no revolutionary change occurred. "Thus the social and spiritual structure of the past is preserved under new forms; its class hierarchy, the privileges of special bodies ... the values of the Catholic religion and Hispanic tradition are maintained. At the same time its political and legislative forms and its international status change." ...

The collapse of the supreme authority activated the latent forces of local oligarchies, municipalities, and extended-family systems in a struggle for power and prestige in the new, arbitrarily defined republics. These telluric creole social structures were direct heirs of social arrangements proliferated in the conquest period but held in check by the patrimonial state. Now again they seized the stage. The *caudillo* of the independence period, controlling a clan-like or an improvised retinue through

---

charismatic appeal, was the latter-day version of the conquistador. In the absence of developed and interacting economic interest groups having a stake in constitutional process, the new countries were plunged into alternating regimes of anarchy and personalist tyranny. The contest to seize a patrimonial state apparatus, fragmented from the original imperial one, became the driving force of public life in each new country.

There is abundant testimony that Spanish America universally suffered a collapse of the moral order during the early decades of independence. The face of anarchy was somewhat masked, however, by that ancient habit of legalizing and legitimizing every public act which had been so important a cement to the former empire. Each new country duly produced its constitutional convention and one or more Anglo-French-type constitutions. The political mechanism which emerged was generally a biparty system. Party programs faithfully reflected the rhetoric of Western parliamentary politics, though not without occasional shrewd adaptation to local situations. Although only an elite was politically active (as was the case in the England of 1830 for that matter), party adherence frequently reflected an alignment of "conservative" landed and monied interests, high clergy, and former monarchists against the "liberal" professionals, intellectuals, merchants, and those with a creole, anticlerical and anticaste outlook. Given a static rather than a dynamic social system, however, the game of politics became a naked contest for power.

Chile was an example perhaps unparalleled of a Spanish American country which managed, after a twelve-year transitional period, to avoid the extremes of tyranny and anarchy with a political system unencumbered by the mechanisms and party rhetoric of an exotic liberalism. . . . Because the landholding class had been infiltrated by mercantile groups partly composed of recent immigrants from northern Spain, the elite represented a spectrum of moderately diverse economic interest. A Valparaíso businessman, Diego Portales, was shrewd enough to identify and coordinate those interests within a constitutional system having an aura of native legitimacy. The centralizing 1833 Constitution which bore his influence created a strong executive without stripping the congress and courts of countervailing powers. The first president had the aristocratic bearing which Portales himself lacked; a staunch Catholic and brave general who stood above party factionalism, he helped to legitimize the office itself. The first several presidents each served double five-year terms. The official candidate was generally victorious and hand-picked by his predecessor. Thus the structure of the Spanish patrimonial state was re-created, with only those minimum concessions to Anglo-French constitutionalism that were necessary for a nineteenth-century republic which had just rejected monarchical rule.

From our broad premises and from the specific case of Chile we may infer that for a newly erected Spanish American political system to achieve stability and continuity it had to reproduce the structure, the logic, and the vague, pragmatic safeguards against tyranny of the Spanish *patrimonial state*. The collapse of monarchical authority meant that this step required the intervention of strong *personalist* leadership. The energies of such leadership had to flow toward investing the state with suprapersonal *legitimacy*. The ingredients of legitimacy, in turn, were native psychocultural *traditions*, leavened or perhaps merely adorned by the *nationalism* and *constitutionalism* which had become watchwords of the age.

The usual political trajectory of a Spanish American nation can be plotted as one or another form of breakdown or short circuit in this model. The most notorious form is personalist leadership that constitutes its own untransferable legitimacy. In a telluric setting of moral and institutional collapse, the instances of personalism ranged from the superb, intellectually informed, yet tragically frustrated political genius of a Bolívar all the way to careers dominated by sheer enactment of impulse, such as those of the Argentine *caudillo* Facundo described by Sarmiento; or the Bolivian president who commanded his aides to play dead like poodles, and who had his ministers and generals troop solemnly around the table on which his mistress stood naked. . . .

At this point we may summarize some of the presuppositions, limiting conditions, and possibilities for political change in the Latin-American countries as they advance into the genuinely "national" phase of their history. However heavily the Western, industrial world – or, for that matter, the Communist, industrial one – may impinge upon these countries, quickening their pace of life, engendering new hopes, wants, and fears, introducing new programs, equipment, technology, and wares, it seems probable that any changes wrought will in some way eventually accommodate to a number of enduring premises that underlie Latin-American political life.

The first point is that *now as in the past the sense that man makes and is responsible for his own world is less deep or prevalent than in many other lands.* The Latin American may be more sensitive to his world, or more eloquently critical of it, or more attached to it. But he seems less concerned with shaping it. The natural order looms larger than the human community. The old tradition of "natural law" has not atrophied as it did in the United States. The individual conscience is presumed more fallible, the process of voting less consequential than in the northern democracies. The regime of voluntary, rationalized political association, of seesaw bi-party systems, of quasi-rational legislative procedure has a fitful existence after almost a century and a half of "republican" life.

These characteristics, some will argue, are generic to all "underdeveloped" countries. Scales of political maturity have been devised for ranking the emergent nations of Latin America, Africa, and Asia. Granted that Latin America has much in common with other "developing areas," the point stressed in this essay is that Latin America is subject to special imperatives as an offshoot of postmedieval, Catholic, Iberian Europe which never underwent the Protestant Reformation. In its shaping of the present, such a past differs substantially from a Confucian or a Mohammedan or an African tribal past.

To Spanish American society Talcott Parsons applies the rubric "particularistic-ascriptive pattern" and in so doing differentiates it explicitly from, for example, Chinese society. In Spanish America, he observes, the larger social structures, beyond kinship and local community, tend "to be accepted as part of the given situation of life, and to have positive functions when order is threatened, but otherwise to be taken for granted."

Such societies tend to be individualistic rather than collectivistic and non- if not anti-authoritarian. . . . The individualism is primarily concerned with expressive interests, and hence much less so with opportunity to shape the situation through achievement. There tends to be a certain lack of concern with the remoter framework of the society, unless it is threatened. Similarly, there is no inherent objection to authority so long as it does not interfere too much with expressive freedom, indeed it may be welcomed as a factor of stability. But there is also not the positive incentive to recognize authority as inherent that exists in the cases of positive authoritarianism. The tendency to indifference to larger social issues creates a situation in which authority can become established with relatively little opposition.

The second point, implied in the quotation just given, is that *the Latin-American peoples still appear willing to alienate, rather than delegate, power to their chosen or accepted leaders,* in the spirit long ago condoned by sixteenth-century Hispano-Thomist thought. Yet the people retain also a keen sense of equity, of natural justice, and their sensitivity to abuses of alienated power. It may be that the classic image of the Latin-American "revolution" is the barracks coup by an insurgent *caudillo* against an incumbent whose authority lacks legitimacy. But the more significant if more infrequent uprising is that having a broad popular base and no clearly elaborated program beyond reclamation of sovereignty that has been tyrannically abused. Socioeconomic change of a truly revolutionary character which may occur in the wake of such movements tends to be improvised under leadership that desperately seeks to legitimate its authority.

The third point, therefore, is that *the present "National" Period is marked by a renewed quest for legitimate government.* The regimes of the last century did not, by and large, attain legitimacy. Most have not yet done so. A "legitimate" revolution in Latin America needs no sharp-edged ideology; it need not polarize the classes; it need not produce an immediate and effective redistribution of wealth and goods. The regime it produces need not be conscientiously sanctioned at the polls by a majority vote. . . .

On the other hand, a legitimate revolution probably necessitates generalized violence and popular participation, even though under improvised leadership and with unprogrammed goals. It needs to be informed by a deep even though unarticulated sense of moral urgency. It needs to be an indigenous movement, unencumbered by foreign support. It needs charismatic leadership of special psychocultural appeal. Even with all their bluster and blunder, Perón and Fidel Castro have such appeal.

Questions

1. Weber (who began his career as an academic lawyer) differentiates between "legal domination" and "traditional domination." In what sense are the two separate? Suppose a legal system which protects private property, including the power to designate heirs upon death. Ownership in such a system is a form of legitimated power — as the Bolivian campesinos knew when they demanded title to the lands they were working. When children inherit rights of ownership from a parent, do they not "enjoy personal authority by virtue of their inherited status"? If it be argued that the owner of a property interest is not a ruler, and does not give commands, we may recall

the comments of Morris Cohen:[37] the essence of property is control over access to things — which implies the power to command services from anyone else who seeks access. In a system of private property, does the chief difference between "legal" and "traditional" domination lie in the capacity of a "legal" system to conceal the fact of domination?

2. In a system characterized by "legal domination," why is it that so many people obey rules of law because they *are* rules of law? A statute that results from an intricate political compromise may be something less than a model of reasoned lawmaking or even technical draftsmanship. (Land reform legislation — at least in a country in which there is some intention to carry out the legislation — is an illustration.) Despite a widespread awareness that a statute is merely a crystallization of the political process, once a law is enacted, something happens to the way very large numbers of people think about it. It is no longer merely a set of policies and administrative mechanisms; it is The Law. Such feelings are to be found among all sorts of people, including social scientists as well as men and women "in the street." What accounts for such special feelings about law?

3. In the "charismatic" and "traditional" forms of domination, according to Weber, law is legitimated — justified — either by reference to the leader's personal qualities (the "gift of grace") or by reference to the master's traditional authority. What legitimates law in the "legal" form of domination?[38]

4. At the end of the extract of Morse's article, he points to a "renewed quest for legitimate government" in Latin America, and identifies Juan Perón as the sort of charismatic leader capable of bringing off a "legitimate revolution." In Chapter II, we suggested that it was no accident that the Argentine amparo was judicially adopted as a national institution shortly after the overthrow of the Perón government. Does the Argentine amparo reflect a quest for legitimacy? If so, what kind of legitimacy? Are the amparo and strong charismatic leadership compatible? Or are Weber's various types of legitimacy mutually exclusive? (Recall Bendix's italicized remark: "In history these 'pure types' of domination are *always* found in combinations. . . .")

5. Does the model of "legal domination" imply a system of judicial review of governmental action? If judicial review does exist, how does it contribute to the legitimacy of government?[39]

6. In this chapter's earlier discussion of security, we asked whether it was possible to use the legal system simultaneously as (i) a means for government to promote development by controlling behavior and (ii) a limitation on governmental power. Does the principle of legitimacy through "legal domination" suggest a perspective in which those two objectives may be seen to be consistent?

7. When the Supreme Court of Argentina is called upon to give formal recognition to a President installed by military coup, are the generals seeking legitimacy on the basis of "legal domination"? On the basis of "traditional domination"? Does it matter

---

[37] P. 315, *supra*.

[38] See Trubek, "Max Weber on Law and the Rise of Capitalism," 1972 *Wis. L. Rev.* 720, 732.

[39] See C. Black, *The People and the Court*, ch. II (1960), for a discussion of the role of the United States Supreme Court in legitimizing governmental action.

which kind of legitimacy is sought? Are there implications for judicial review in the form of legitimacy sought by successful revolutionaries? Are the "tightrope" experiences of the highest courts of Brazil and Argentina explainable on the basis of the generals' concerns for legitimacy? (Recall Stalin's famous question: "How many divisions has the Pope?")

8. In Chapter III, it was suggested that in the Mexican land reform, the restitution theory played an important role in providing legitimacy for expropriations that ultimately proved confiscatory. In Weber's terms, what sort of legitimacy was provided? In the midst of the revolutionary upheaval of 1910-20, what difference did it make whether takings of land were considered legitimate or not?

9. In Chapter V, it was noted that a barrio junta's effective power to adjudicate disputes depended on its being active in organizing public works projects, representing the barrio to outside agencies, etc. *Cf.* S. Lipset, *The First New Nation: the United States in Historical and Comparative Perspective* 52 (1963): "All claims to a legitimate title to rule in new states must ultimately win acceptance through demonstrating effectiveness. . . . [Claims to legitimacy] are subjected on the part of the populace to a highly pragmatic test — that is, what is the payoff?" Does this "payoff" principle apply to all the Weberian forms of legitimacy, or only to "charismatic domination"? Does the newness of a community — say, a "new nation," or a new Caracas barrio — affect the answer to this question?

It is also relevant to ask: Payoff for whom? The army? The elite? The "people"? What sort of payoff matters? A global increase in gross national product? A redistribution of income? An increase in personal liberty? Speaking of the Brazilian military regime, a contemporary Brazilian social scientist writes:

> It has been able to generate policies and to define goals quite effectively and simultaneously to legitimate itself in the society at large through the symbolic appeal of strengthening the Fatherland. At another level, perhaps a more basic one, the regime seeks to gain legitimacy . . . through economic achievements. In a peculiar parody of those analytical schemes that posit a strict conditioning effect between economy and polity, the only answer given to protest against repression comes in economic development figures. The language of human rights is in this sense translated into GNP growth rates.[40]

10. If a revolutionary regime is self-legitimating, as Kelsen suggests,[41] what accounts for phenomena such as the following? (a) Fidel Castro's rather legalistic speech at his trial in 1953.[42] (b) The compensation provisions of agrarian legislation in Mexico, Bolivia and Cuba. (c) The 1961 amendment to the Venezuelan Constitution (following the 1958 overthrow of Pérez Jiménez), authorizing deferred compensation for lands taken for the agrarian reform.

---

[40] Cardoso, "Associated-Dependent Development: Theoretical and Practical Implications," in A. Stepan (Ed.), *Authoritarian Brazil* 142, 174 (1973).

[41] P. 190, *supra.*

[42] See p. 336, *supra.*

3. Law and the Symbols of Government in Village and Nation

Morse suggested that a key ingredient of what he called a "legitimate revolution" was popular participation. Are there certain forms of legitimacy that are more conducive than others to participatory development, as we have earlier defined it? Much of our discussion of legitimacy up to this point has centered on the legitimacy of the national government. But, as we have implied in our comments and questions about such diverse phenomena as barrio juntas and land titles for land reform beneficiaries, the problem of legitimacy is pervasive, existing wherever some people exercise power over others. Many of the questions already asked are relevant to issues of legitimacy at the level of the local community, as the following extract from Professor Paul Friedrich's paper shows.

P. FRIEDRICH, THE LEGITIMACY OF A CACIQUE

in M. Swartz (ed.), *Local-Level Politics: Social and Cultural
Perspectives,* 243, 248-49, 253-54, 258-59, 261-64 (1969 ed.)*

The word "cacique" (pronounced kah-sée-ke) comes ultimately from the Arawak Indian language but is now used throughout the Spanish-speaking world, including Spain itself. Consonant with the size of this universe and the diversity of social conditions, the meaning of the word varies enormously — from the militaristic boss of a national state, to a conservative, upper-class, and paternalistic landlord, to the chief of a small band of South American hunters and gatherers, to the religious leader of a Zuñi pueblo. But these and most other referents share at least several component or constituent meanings: strong individual power over a territorial group held together by some socioeconomic or cultural system. Moreover, most although certainly not all of the referents of "cacique" imply detachment or freedom from the normative, formal, and duly instituted structure of government.

In Mexico the term and the phenomenon of cacique are centuries old, deeply and perhaps ineradicably built into the traditions and the way of life and the idioms of Mexican Spanish. With particular reference to Mexico, this article defines a cacique as a strong and autocratic leader in local and regional politics whose characteristically informal, personalistic, and often arbitrary rule is buttressed by a core of relatives, "fighters," and dependents, and is marked by the diagnostic threat and practice of violence. These caciques bridge, however imperfectly, the gap between peasant villagers and the law, politics, and government of the state and nation, and are therefore varieties of the so-called "political middleman." . . .

[*Eds. note:* The heart of this paper is a detailed analysis of the operations and functions of one cacique, fictitiously named "Pedro Caso," in "Durazno," a village in

---

*Reprinted by permission of Aldine Publishing Company.

Michoacán, in southwest Mexico. In extracting this paper, we emphasize those parts of Friedrich's discussion that bear directly on the relation of law to the legitimacy of this cacique and his close associates. We omit, for example, Friedrich's discussion of religion and the traditional norms of the Tarascan community.]

Pedro played many roles in his village, particularly in its economy. He had learned agricultural skills as a boy and had spent some thirteen years working the soil like a peasant, but during the early 1950's, partly because of a back injury, he shifted gradually to illegal sharecropping (i.e., renting ejido plots from men too lazy or drunk to cultivate them), to usurious moneylending, and to buying standing maize before the harvest (his second wife eventually became one of the village's four outstanding moneylenders and maize-buyers). As the appointed local representative of the national Ejido Bank and as the accomplice of the local capitalists, Pedro was instrumental in excluding most outside credit, which in a sense could be interpreted as protecting the community against the fixed rates of interest and the inexorability of collection on loans made by "outside exploiters." By 1956 his total income from these capitalistic enterprises, from his 40-odd acres (owned, rented, and ejidal), and from his official jobs, probably totaled well over 50,000 pesos a year, making him the third-wealthiest person in the pueblo (his mother's brother was first and his mother was fifth). Nevertheless, his adobe house, though comparatively well-appointed inside (with concrete floor and a gas oven), did not look materially different from the others strung along the street. His main "luxury" was a scorn of tortillas and a subsistence mainly on dairy products and meat. Most of his surplus income went into the education of his seven children in schools in the state and national capitals, and into outside political investments in the state chapter of the Masons, and the coffers of the huge national Party of Institutional Revolution (PRI), which is financed primarily by 3 to 5 per cent of its membership, including − in Scott's terminology − "the ambitious officers of farm groups."

Pedro's political, legal, and governmental functions were also diverse. He spoke relatively well in public but, like his uncle, did so only on rare occasions, such as the visit of a government inspector or during a crisis of political support. His specialty was relating the provisions of the national agrarian legislation, particularly about twenty key sections of the *Código Agrario,* to the partly illegal and politically muddled realities of the local ejido. As covert arbiter, Pedro − within his home − settled minor squabbles, judged cases of violence that were often technically criminal under law, and acted as matchmaker after elopement and bride-capture (he was one of the two men in Durazno who knew by heart the lengthy Tarascan speech requesting reconciliation). In this ritually demanding jural role, his main objectives were to settle and judge in accordance with local mores, to distribute compensations and punishments over as wide a field as possible, and to protect his fellow villagers from prosecution under state and federal law − with the attendant court expenses, fines, and jail sentences. The extreme informality and usual effectiveness of his arbitration certainly reduced public questioning of his legitimacy, although it came nowhere close to eliminating it. . . .

The case of Pedro raises questions about legitimacy precisely because he is clearly illegitimate in many ways. To begin with, one is not elected cacique, nor does a cacicazgo depend on instituted, public, or democratic selection. Indeed, as the leaders of an ideologically extremist faction in the minority, with commitments to violence, Pedro and the three uncles who preceded him could never have won a free election, and the expedient informality of Pedro's local cacicazgo contradicts the notion of "a mandate from the people." This failure verifiably to represent his community flies in the face of the model precedent set by his uncle, Primo Tapia, the charismatic revolutionary who on several occasions was delegated to perform major tasks and was elected as "the representative" by public assemblies of the Durazno community or by large contingents of agrarians from the Pazacu Tarascan towns.

The fact that Pedro was not elected and that his rule is temporally unrestricted also contradicts the higher ideal of the Mexican Revolution and the Mexican nation that the succession of chiefs in a community should be orderly, regular, and solemnized through a public process of election and institution. (For example, all official documents close with the exhortation: "No Re-election! Effective Suffrage!") It is true that Pedro, in a manner of speaking, was elected president of the regional committee for thirteen years, and that he went through the ritual of nomination and election as alternate (suplente) to the national senator, but these were personal achievements and hardly affected the non-representative character of his rule within Durazno.

In the second place, Pedro's status as a cacique is not legitimized or enhanced by charisma in either of its two most usual senses; the religious and the personalistic. He lacks the persuasive idiom, the magnetic personality, the ideological fervor, and the other less apparent qualities that rally followers to a strong faction or a revolutionary movement. Most villagers acknowledge his learned skills and acquired contacts, but I doubt that even a large minority submits to him because of a firm belief in his extraordinary powers as a person. The position in which he has matured has called forth and cultivated a set of personal traits that – if not always antithetical – at least differ sharply from those of Primo Tapia, whose rude but eloquent phrase and bold vision of an anarchist-agrarian future "touched the sensitive parts" of a restless and landless peasantry.

Pedro tries to legitimize his status through the progressive ideology of the national party and speaks – albeit vaguely – of material progress, agrarian reform, and public education. This attempted legitimation, nevertheless, blatantly contradicts his own behavior, which has been effective in cutting down the local teaching staff, in excluding capital investment from without, and in the illegal reallocation of almost two dozen plots of ejido land from usufruct by "original agrarian fighters" who struggled with Tapia, to younger relatives and dependents of the dominant faction of which Pedro is now cacique. . . .

. . . The village has been controlled with little respite by the members of one "political family," a loosely knit name group that is called the "Casos" but also includes many de las Casas, and others, affiliated by blood or marriage.

This continuity in power, this effective rule by one or two of the most able and ambitious within a half-fictive kinship group, has reached the point where the Casos declare it a right and natural state of affairs; and many villagers either agree or have resigned themselves. . . . Although standing at a low moral level, the Caso dynasty illustrated what one political philosopher has called "the normative power of the factual." . . .

[Friedrich concludes that Caso has enhanced his legitimacy through demonstrated performance – particularly in areas where he can demonstrate aptitudes such as facility with the Agrarian Code, resolution of personal conflicts, toughness as a competitor, and contacts with outside politicians. Compare Professor Lipset's remarks about "payoff," quoted earlier. – Eds.]

Unlike the elders and chiefs of many prerevolutionary villagers, whose legitimacy could be defined almost exclusively in terms of local values, the agrarian cacique has always conspicuously attempted to validate his power by appeals to higher political and governmental levels of leaders, institutions, and ideas. Pedro tries to legitimize his role by describing his friendship with politically powerful persons: compadres in nearby county seats, and "very good friends" such as the former state senator, . . .

Both caciques [Caso and another named Otón] try to perpetuate the dying fires of agrarian ideology through invoking the dimly remembered charisma of its heroes. They appeal to semi-legends such as Emiliano Zapata, and exaggerate their roles in the "struggle," and their subscription to the socialistic dogmas of "the Center" in Mexico City. Both men exploit every opportunity to underscore their personal friendship with the man who still enjoys the greatest charisma in Michoacán, and perhaps in Mexico: the former president, Lázaro Cárdenas. The charisma of the great agrarian caciques and caudillos, past or distant or both, casts a spotty reflection of legitimacy on the bureaucrats and minor party officials of fully institutionalized agrarianism. And inasmuch as Durazno is an agrarian community, it is primarily the Caso and Pérez leaders who – if only occasionally – articulate its new ideals in public assemblies, in discussions before the town hall, and in private homes.

Leaders such as Pedro and Otón legitimize their rule in two directions. Just as they demonstrate to the local peasants their connections with higher levels, so they present themselves before state politicos and higher administrators as indigenous revolutionaries, grass-roots agrarians, and the like. To create this image as "Indian revolutionaries" they exploit to the limit their knowledge of Tarascan, their participation in the revolt, their de facto "control" of Durazno and contiguous pueblos, and the incontrovertible fact that both men have resided almost continuously in their indigenous community (with the obvious exception of Pedro's thirteen years as a student and teacher); in contrast, a damning charge against Pedro's uncle, Pérez, that dates from the 1930's, is that he moved to the state capital and "disacknowledged his own people." The ideological leverage of such posturing is enormous in a state political machine whose radicalism – perhaps the most extreme and articulate in Mexico – consists to a large degree of championing the lowly Indian and forcing through massive expropriations of land for the benefit of the (Indian) peasant. Thus Pedro can persuasively claim to represent his Indians, although actually rather unresponsive to their needs; he is primarily responsible to the Cárdenas machine in his activities, his beliefs, his personal alliances, and his political combinations. In terms of the logic of legitimacy, his position depends on decomposing and realigning the constituent meanings of responsibility and representation. . . .

Durazno is a "typical" agrarian community in that ever since the sanguinary revolt and reform of the 1920's its leaders have broken and flouted the criminal law on assault and homicide. Tapia ordered many assassinations; Otón personally shot down five villagers with his pistol; and Pedro both planned and committed political killings. Yet by a singular dialectic the legitimacy of such caciques is argued mainly in terms of laws that have been enacted formally and are "on the books." The reason for this seeming paradox in agrarian politics is that statutory law itself is sharply divided into, first, the criminal and civil codes of the state and nation and, second, the large corpus of national legislation and executive decrees that affect agrarian reform and the administration of the ejidos. This agrarian legal corpus was thought out and formalized by jurists and agrarian experts before its "tumultuary and giddy" introduction into peasant villages. Even early and initiatory caciques such as Primo Tapia created considerable authority through their "reasoned elaboration" of the premises and mandates of major national laws, notably the Agrarian Law of 1915, Article 27 of the Constitution of 1917, and the Agrarian Regulatory Law of 1922. Agrarista villagers depended on Tapia's familiarity with the welter of often conflicting statutes and the state-level rules of procedure for agrarian expropriation. The solitary Roca leader with some legal training served a similar function during the enforcement of the Law of Ejidal Patrimony of 1925, as did Pedro and one of his cousins during the Cárdenas presidency, when Durazno — equipped with telephones and typewriters — was a regional headquarters for agrarian litigation. For forty years the Durazno caciques have vehemently and logically insisted that, by effectuating a reform and supervising an ejidal economy, they have been not only obeying but actively executing the law of the land. Their arguments are often legalistic in the pejorative sense of strutting the letter of the law or in manipulating its wording for contrary ends. By 1956 Pedro was Durazno's most expert interpreter and defender (and perverter) of the two score or so most relevant sections of the total of 1,063 sections in the Agrarian Code. Although in part weakened by misinterpretation, the provisions of the code did seriously affect land use by laying down rules for the administration of the ejido and the selection of its officers, and by explicitly stating many of the principles by which the village had been living for over thirty years. For example, during a tense and dramatically ironic session of the ejido, Pedro quoted verbatim Article 165, according to which peasants acquired rights in any plot by working it for two years — although everyone in the meeting knew that for the two-year minimum the original ejidatarios had been prevented by force from tilling their plots.

Despite such partial and occasional perversions, the Durazno ejido operated largely in accordance with the intent of the agrarian reform. The primacy of ejidal economics, and the political awareness of many of its peasants, had made infringements of the Agrarian Code a delicate and sometimes explosive matter. Covert infractions were denounced vigorously by the opposition, attracting the attention and the inspectors of the national government. Caciques such as Otón and Pedro contravened agrarian laws often enough, but they also limited and often disguised their actions because these selfsame laws were a main source of their legitimacy. The two men, like their agrarian predecessors, were in the quasi-Hobbesian position of equating or confusing the legitimate with the legal, and of justifying, validating, and falsely rationalizing their rule because of its logical relations to the agrarian law of the land.

Questions

1. In what sense is "Pedro Caso" legitimate in terms of "traditional domination"? In terms of "legal domination"? In terms of "charismatic domination"?

2. Does Caso draw legitimacy *from* law, or does his position as cacique give legitimacy *to* the law that he dispenses, or both?

3. Does Caso care about the legitimacy of his rule, or is that something that only visiting social scientists care about?

4. Does the experience of the village of "Durazno" support a governmental strategy of participatory development, as distinguished from maintenance of a patronage/connections system? What kinds of developmental change would make Pedro Caso irrelevant? Consider this comment in an Appendix to Friedrich's paper:

> As a rather vague postscript, I would add that the assassination of Otón and the enormous growth of the Pazacu industrial and commercial complex and the governorship of Madariaga [the new Governor of the State of Michoacán] have all contributed to a drastic change in the politics of Durazno. Insofar as I could judge during a short visit in 1967, a cacique had not emerged to replace the deceased Pedro, and control was shared by many families and individuals.

5. Friedrich notes that part of Caso's legitimacy was drawn from the "higher levels" of Mexican government and society: from connections with various state and local politicians, and from the Agrarian Code itself. Recall also Morse's suggestion[43] that in Latin America, "legalism" serves as proof of the legitimacy of the official who is preoccupied with formalities. Is legitimacy always based on the notion of some "higher law"? In the form of legitimacy Weber called "legal domination," it is easy to see the "higher law" idea at work; such a notion is the essence of constitutionalism in the Western liberal tradition. What of "traditional" and "charismatic" domination? Do they also rest ultimately on a similar notion of some higher authority?

6. Is a "top-down" theory of legitimacy, as suggested in the preceding question, consistent with participatory development? Might a development-oriented government, for example, use propaganda to encourage widespread participation in various kinds of developmental activity? (It is said that the use of anesthetics during childbirth was resisted by women in England until Queen Victoria set a national example by using them herself.)

7. Is the whole notion of legitimacy — and of law itself — merely a confidence game designed to lull people into approval of the status quo? If law is in some sense self-legitimizing, and if law lends legitimacy to the existing order, is it the enemy of social change? Thurman Arnold's book, originally published in 1935, is an entertaining

---

[43] P. 63, *supra.*

example of the school of criticism called "legal realism." Is the following extract realistic?

T. ARNOLD, THE SYMBOLS OF GOVERNMENT

Pp. 33-35, 44, 49 (1962 ed.)

The thing which we reverently call "Law" when we are talking about government generally, and not predicting the results of particular lawsuits, can only be properly described as an attitude or a way of thinking about government. It is a way of writing about human institutions in terms of ideals, rather than observed facts. It meets a deep-seated popular demand that government institutions symbolize a beautiful dream within the confines of which principles operate, independently of individuals. . . .

. . . It is part of the function of "Law" to give recognition to ideals representing the exact opposite of established conduct. Most of its complications arise from the necessity of pretending to do one thing, while actually doing another. . . .

The principles of law are supposed to control society, because such an assumption is necessary to the logic of the dream. Yet the observer should constantly keep in mind that the function of law is not so much to guide society, as to comfort it. Belief in fundamental principles of law does not necessarily lead to an orderly society. Such a belief is as often at the back of revolt or disorder. . . .

"Law" is primarily a great reservoir of emotionally important social symbols. It develops, as language develops, in spite of, and not because of, the grammarians. Though the notion of a "rule of Law" may be the moral background of revolt, it ordinarily operates to induce acceptance of things as they are. It does this by creating a realm somewhere within the mystical haze beyond the courts, where all our dreams of justice in an unjust world come true. Thus in the realm of the law the least favored members of society are comforted by the fact that the poor are equal to the rich and the strong have no advantage over the weak. The more fortunately situated are reassured by the fact that the wise are treated better than the foolish, that careless people are punished for their mistakes. . . .

. . . "Law" represents the belief that there must be something behind and above government without which it cannot have permanence or respect. Even a dictator cannot escape this psychology of his time. He does not quite believe in his own government unless he is able to make gestures toward this prevailing ideal. It is child's play for the realist to show that the law is not what it pretends to be and that its theories are sonorous, rather than sound; that its definitions run in circles; that applied by skillful attorneys in the forum of courts it can only be an argumentative technique; that it constantly seeks escape from reality through alternate reliance on ceremony and verbal confusion. Yet the legal realist falls into grave error when he believes this to be a defect in the law. From any objective point of view the escape of the law from reality constitutes not its weakness but its greatest strength. Legal institutions must constantly reconcile ideological conflicts, just as individuals reconcile them, by shoving inconsistencies back into a sort of institutional subconscious mind. If judicial institutions become too "sincere," too self-analytical, they suffer the fate of ineffectiveness which is the lot of all self-analytical people. They lose themselves in words, and fail in action. They lack that sincere fanaticism out of which great governmental forces are welded. . . .

An official admission by a judicial institution that it was moving in all directions at once in order to satisfy the conflicting emotional values of the people which it served would be unthinkable. It would have the same effect as if an actor interrupted the most moving scene of a play in order to explain to the audience that his real name was John Jones. The success of the play requires that an idea be made real to the audience. The success of the law as a unifying force depends on making emotionally significant the idea of a government of law which is rational and scientific.

Questions

1. Social change implies conflict. Is the legitimacy of any change enhanced by orderly resolution of the conflicts brought about by the change? Underneath Arnold's exterior of tough realism may there beat the heart of a believing, participating citizen?

2. Arnold suggests that a belief in law-as-principles may lead to disorder and revolt. Castro's "History Will Absolve Me" speech might be cited as supporting evidence; so might the various direct-action techniques (sit-ins, etc.) that characterized the U.S. civil rights movement of the 1960s, and even some of the violence done in the name of "revolution." Is there a sense, however, in which the role of lawyer is fundamentally inconsistent with the role of revolutionary?[44]

C. Community

The ideas of "law" and "community" are logically interdependent. Law exists only within a community, and all communities are characterized — even defined — by the existence of community-wide bodies of law. To speak of the functions of law in a community is merely to speak of the functions of law. In this section, however, we narrow the focus, emphasizing the role of law in persuading people to think of themselves as members of communities. While we shall be concerned with the problem of *compliance* — "the readiness of individuals to act in conformity with the norms of society"[45] — we shall be even more concerned with two other problems: (i) *cohesion:*

---

[44] See Wasserstrom, "Lawyers and Revolution," 30 *U. Pitt. L. Rev.* 125 (1968).

[45] P. Cohen, *Modern Social Theory* 138 (1968, reprinted 1972).

a social unit's "resistance to division or secession";[46] and (ii) *solidarity:* "a readiness to act in concert for certain purposes."[47]

---

1. Latin American Development and the Varieties of Community

Emile Durkheim contrasted two types of solidarity: (i) a traditional or primitive "mechanical" solidarity, in which people are bound together by uniform practices as well as shared values and beliefs; and (ii) a more modern or complex "organic" solidarity, based on the social interdependence that results from increased differentiation, notably the division of labor. The rise of "organic" solidarity does not mean the disappearance of shared values; a society so characterized would, for example, share those values that underlay its very differentiation: reciprocity, exchange-oriented cooperation, etc. The inferences that Durkheim drew from his model of social evolution have been subjected to heavy criticism and need not detain us just now.[48] The model itself does approximate historical reality, at least at the level of abstraction used in our statement of the model. And whatever else the model may imply, it surely means that development does not dispense with the problem of solidarity. To the extent that development requires cooperation, it plainly requires the would-be cooperators to agree, at least tacitly, that they are cooperating. Furthermore, as we have seen in our discussion of security, even a market system, in which individual actors seek to serve their own interests, demands a minimum of agreement and mutual trust.[49]

Recently, some social scientists have begun to use the term "moral community" to describe the group of persons to whom obligations are owed and from whom rights can be claimed. F. G. Bailey, writing of certain peasant villages in India, gives us this definition:

> In everyday language this is the distinction between "we" (the moral community) and "they" (the outsiders). For those who follow Durkheim the adjective "moral" is perhaps redundant, since the society (or community) is co-extensive with moral action. Nevertheless, I retain the adjective to emphasize the continuous judgment of right and wrong which characterizes interactions within a community. Beyond the community such judgments do not apply: to cheat an outsider is neither right nor wrong: it is merely expedient or inexpedient.

---

[46]*Id.* at 131.

[47]*Id.* at 135.

[48]See generally E. Durkheim, *The Division of Labor in Society* (1964 ed.). For a summary of recent critical evaluations of this aspect of Durkheim's work, see Cohen, note 45 *supra,* at 226-32.

[49]Parsons, "Institutional Aspects of Agricultural Development Policy," 48 *J. Farm Econ.* 1185, 1189 (1966). See also Kozolchyk, "Toward a Theory on Law in Economic Development: The Costa Rican USAID-ROCAP Law Reform Project," 1971 *Law and the Social Order* 681, 737-51.

It is also difficult to draw a boundary around a particular moral community, for each one varies according to the [person] who is chosen as the point of reference.[50]

It will be noted that this definition, by emphasizing rights and obligations, reinforces our statement that "law" and "community" are defined by the same boundaries. Even if development is perceived in strictly economic terms, it implies "learning to deal fairly with strangers"; the legal process has an obvious role to play in broadening the scope of the moral community. If it is appropriate to speak of "national integration"[51] as a developmental goal, then that goal also demands that the system of rights and obligations be expanded into a truly national system. (We note parenthetically that the concept of "integration" is potentially misleading. A society can be integrated in a variety of different ways; no social system is more integrated, for example, than the classical hacienda. Development — a form of change — in fact implies *dis*integration of some social structures and their replacement with others. If, however, the term "integration" is intended to convey the idea of the lowering of class barriers and an increased social mobility, then it surely is an important developmental goal. We shall return to the issue later in this chapter, as we deal with the subject of inequality.)

Expressions such as "the moral community" are useful shorthand references, but they should not obscure the fact that social phenomena always resist being classified neatly in such either-or terms. Thus, even in the southern-Italian peasant village where Edward Banfield found the dominant social principle of action to be "amoral familism" — the maximizing of the nuclear family's short-run advantage, to the near-exclusion of other goals — examples of varying degrees of trust are also to be found: credit is sometimes extended; sharecroppers work land on two-year contracts.[52] The boundaries of "the" moral community are not clear-cut; one may regard another as within the moral community for some purposes, but not for others. It is precisely this lack of rigid boundaries that permits us to conceive of expanding the moral community in some circumstances.

Latin American society illustrates the difficulty of assigning definite boundaries to the moral community. Just as Latin American governmental structures have been called a "living museum," in which all sorts of ancient and modern systems of government coexist,[53] so Latin American society is at the same time characterized by Durkheim's simple, traditional "mechanical" solidarity and his modern, complex "organic" solidarity. The following two extracts are complementary. Professor Percy Cohen's rather abstract discussion is focused not on the problem of solidarity but on

---

[50] Bailey, note 11 *supra,* at 302-03 n. 5. Reprinted by permission of British Association for the Advancement of Science.

[51] As the term is normally used, it means "the bringing together of the disparate parts of a society into a more integrated whole," to make "a closer approximation of one nation." Wriggins, "National Integration," in M. Weiner (Ed.), *Modernization: The Dynamics of Growth* 181 (1966).

[52] E. Banfield, *The Moral Basis of a Backward Society* 52 (paperback ed. 1967).

[53] See C. Anderson, *Politics and Economic Change in Latin America,* ch. 4 (1967).

the problem of "functional integration" — "the way in which different sets of norms, values, role-structures, institutions, beliefs and symbols, which are characteristic of a social system, are interrelated."[54] He is concerned with the degree to which these various social processes reinforce each other (or stay out of each other's way) at the level of conduct. Furthermore, on the psychological level, Cohen is concerned with the consistency of a culture's ideas, norms and symbols. As you read this extract, consider its implications for the sense of community. Professor Howard Wiarda speaks more directly to the Latin American experience. His characterization of Latin America in terms of "the corporative model" may be extreme, but it is provocative in the context of a set of teaching materials emphasizing participatory development.

P. COHEN, MODERN SOCIAL THEORY

Pp. 152-54 (1968)*

. . . In very simple societies, most of the members participate, jointly, in a variety of institutional contexts — political, economic, ritual, etc. — and almost every (adult) member participates in almost all of these. This is another way of saying that all relationships are "multiplex" — they are governed by a number of obligations and interests — and that there is a low degree of differentiation in the society, so that all members of it are members of all institutions. Furthermore, most relationships are immediate, rather than mediated — that is, most members interact with one another directly — and where they are mediated, the span of mediation is fairly narrow, or, to put it another way, the "interactive distance" is not great. Finally, interactions are frequent. In these circumstances the different sets of norms, beliefs, etc., are likely to be brought into close relationship with one another. Any incompatibilities between norms will be readily experienced by those who are beset by them. *And because the different norms are embedded in the same concrete relationships, particularly those of kinship, each set tends to reinforce the others:* for example the norms of property ownership and usage will be affected by those of religious ritual and belief, and vice versa, because those who participate in common ritual activities may also have common interests in property.

Finally, because each member of society tends to participate in the whole round of activities, and therefore internalizes all or most of the norms, ideas and symbols of the culture, these will be contained within the individual minds of each member of society; and since each member will be in constant interaction with each other, there will be constant reinforcement and standardization of the different cultural items. These two conditions — "total" internalization and constant interaction — favour the creation of a consistent or patterned relation between the different items of culture at the ideational level. . . .

---

[54] Cohen, note 45 *supra*, at 148-49.

*© 1968 by Percy S. Cohen, Basic Books, Inc., Publishers, New York.

This is the picture – or model – of functional integration in a simple social system. In a complex system – or in a model of a complex system – one finds all the opposite characteristics. First, relationships are highly specific – the personnel with whom one interacts in one institutional sphere may be totally different from those with whom one interacts in other spheres – so that the norms of different types of relationship can be kept fairly separate from one another. This being the case, if different norms are potentially in conflict with one another, the actors may not, for the most part, necessarily experience conflict with any regularity, so that the pressure for compatibility is not great. The second important characteristic of complex systems is the high degree of specialization of roles and of institutional "segregation"; because of these, the norms of each sphere tend to be relatively autonomous; and this autonomy is facilitated by the fact that one interacts with different personnel in different contexts: if one does not interact with one's kinsmen in industrial organizations it is relatively simpler to keep the norms of kinship and organizational management separate from one another. Thirdly, each individual interacts with only a small proportion of the "total society," and many or most interactions are mediated through a long chain of relationships; this means that there is less pressure for uniformity of norms and ideas. This difference may be partly offset by the existence of bureaucratic structures and media of mass communication which tend to standardize many practices over a wide social field; but this standardization does not necessarily affect the "private" sectors of life, or those sections in which some degree of choice, initiative or creativity are considered desirable. Fourth, each person participates in only a fairly small part of the total number of available activities, so that only a small part of the existing culture is internalized in any one mind; this means that there is little or no psychological possibility of creating some pattern-consistency between different ideas, norms, symbols, etc. And even if the individual mind does tend to create some consistency between the different cultural items which it internalizes, the set of items internalized by any one mind will be different from that internalized by another. Furthermore, because the individual is, to some extent, drawn into different sectors of activity which are segregated from one another, the different parts of the self are possibly compartmentalized, so that the internal strain to consistency may, for this reason, be low. This does not mean that in highly complex social systems there is little function integration. What it does mean is that *particular* parts of complex systems may be tightly integrated, but that these "tight systems" may be only loosely related to one another. . . .

H. WIARDA, TOWARD A FRAMEWORK FOR THE STUDY OF POLITICAL CHANGE IN THE IBERIC-LATIN TRADITION: THE CORPORATIVE MODEL

25 *World Politics* 206, 217-19, 221-23 (1973)*

. . . [A] good starting point for the discussion is to picture the Iberic-Latin nations

---

*© 1973. Reprinted by permission of Princeton University Press.

as structured horizontally in terms of distinct and fairly rigid layers and vertically in terms of a number of corporate elites and *intereses,* with the Crown or the central state apparatus controlling and guiding its various components. Historically, each corporate entity as well as each "class" in the hierarchy had its own responsibilities, status, and special privileges *(fueros),* corresponding to natural law and to God's just ordering of the universe. Men were expected to accept their station in life; there could thus be little questioning of the system and little mobility. Little change could or did take place. The Crown rested at the apex of the socio-political pyramid, regulating, through its power over financial affairs and its authority to grant charters and legal recognition, the corporate and group life that swirled about it. These units related to each other through the central administration, rather than directly or across class lines. The Iberic-Latin model of political authority is thus essentially a traditional-patrimonialist one, where the wealth of the realm, its subjects, etc., are all a part of the ruler's own domain. . . .

Though the separation from the mother countries in the early nineteenth century brought on a severe politico-administrative legitimacy crisis,[55] no sharp changes occurred in the basic structure of society. Indeed, the wars of independence were largely conservative movements, designed to preserve corporate privilege and elite, centralized rule against the revolutionary, democratizing currents then at work. The apex of the pyramid had been lopped off, but the underlying base and the governing mores and institutions remained intact. Once the legitimacy vacuum created by the withdrawal of Spanish and Portuguese authority had been filled by the creole aristocracies, *caudillos,* and armies, the traditional structure reasserted itself. New institutional arrangements were grafted on; but in essence the hierarchical patterns of class and caste, the system of *fueros* and corporate privilege (now extended to include the national armies), the seigneurial system of *patrón-clientela* relations, the power of the Church and of a preeminently Catholic religio-political culture, the patrimonialist political structure — all these elements of Iberic-Latin tradition were mainly unaffected by independence. . . .

In keeping with the Catholic-Thomistic conception, society and the state in the Iberic-Latin context are thought of as an organic whole with a profoundly moral purpose. Attempts are thus made, through personal and family ties, the *compadrazgo,* and personal identification with the leader, to construct various linkage mechanisms so that a sense of "belonging" is engendered and all are integrated into the prevailing structure. Branches, associations, and official syndicates now exist for nearly everyone. The national system is often conceived of in terms of the family metaphor — implying strong, benevolent leadership, assigned, accepted duties, privileges, status and a purpose greater than the sum of its individual parts. It is now the state, replacing the Crown, that serves as the instrument of national integration, incorporating diverse groups, guilds, and interests, and functioning as the regulator and filter through which the legitimacy of new social and political forces is recognized and through which they

---

[55]This statement is misleading if it is applied to Portuguese America, where it was the son of the king of Portugal who declared the independence of Brazil in 1822. Brazil continued to operate under a monarchy until 1889. [Eds.]

are admitted into the system. Power tends to be concentrated in the executive and in the bureaucratic-patrimonialist state machinery; the President is viewed as the personification of the nation with a direct identification with and knowledge of the general will of his people. The bureaucracy serves to dispense the available goods, favors, and spoils to the deserving. The traditional *patrón*-client relationship thus remains strong, with the government and its many agencies playing the role of national *patrón*, replacing the *caudillos* and local *hacendados* of the past. The same paternalistic *clientela* system persists, dressed up in new and more "modern" forms, but retaining its traditional substance and mode of operation.

The same traditional hierarchical, corporative, elitist, and authoritarian orientation and structure is also still present today, modified by twentieth-century changes but by no means destroyed by them. Politics still centers around the old, hierarchically organized and vertically compartmentalized system of corporate *intereses* and elite groups, now expanded and broadened somewhat to include the newer elements, but still authoritarianly controlled from the top and linked together directly through the government. The "corporative framework" thus refers to a system in which the political culture and institutions reflect a historic hierarchical, authoritarian, and organic view of man, society, and polity. In the corporative system the government controls and directs all associations, holding the power not only to grant or withhold juridical recognition (the *sine qua non* for the group's existence) but also access to official funds and favors without which any sector is unlikely to succeed or survive. Group "rights," or *fueros,* hence take precedence over individual rights; similarly, it is the "general will" and the power of the state that prevail over particular interests. The government not only regulates all associations and corporate bodies, but also seeks to tie those that have earned their place in the existing system into a collaborative effort for integral national development. Obviously the system works best where the number of interests is small and within a context of shared values, but it is not necessarily incompatible with a growing pluralism of ideologies and social forces.

In the virtually inherently corporative systems of the Iberic-Latin nations, the effort is made to ameliorate social and political conflict — to deal with it bureaucratically rather than to provoke divisiveness and breakdown. Administration supersedes politics in both theory and practice; thus, society is represented functionally, in terms of its component segments, and organized bureaucratically, with the government seeking to maintain the proper balance between the various interests and to coordinate them into the state apparatus. Political issues are dealt with more through the process of elite integration and the granting of access to the spoils and privileges that accrue with acceptance into the system, rather than through program enactment and implementation. The greatest need is social and political solidarity; there can be no room for divided loyalties, autonomous political organizations, or challenges to the system's fundamental structure. The personnel of government may shift, new groups and ideas may be assimilated, and the elites may rotate in power (thus giving the appearance of change more than its substance); but the essentials of the socio-political order and the base on which it rests must remain steadfast. The newer groups may be co-opted, but they cannot challenge or seek to topple the system *per se.* Those that do are likely to be crushed — unless their goal is merely the limited one of trying to demonstrate a power capability and the right to be admitted as a bargaining agent in the larger system. This kind of limited and usually carefully-orchestrated violence may be tolerated, even accepted; a movement aimed at toppling the entire structure, in contrast, can expect to and will probably be suppressed.

Considerable change can and does take place within the corporative system, but it usually comes from the top downward rather than as a result of grass roots pressure from below. . . .

Questions

1. Consider the last two sentences of the extract from Cohen's book. Is Wiarda saying in his article that Latin American society exemplifies the possibility suggested by Cohen, *i.e.,* a collection of tightly knit groups, loosely connected to each other in the larger society? It may be useful, in considering this question, to distinguish between "horizontal" and "vertical" ties in the society. Wiarda emphasizes the weakness of horizontal ties, and the strength of vertical ones; it is the vertical connections that matter, he says, in a system of patronage and group rights. Within a given society, are the strengths of vertical and horizontal ties inversely proportional? Can the relative importance of vertical ties in Latin America, for example, be explained by the relative weakness of horizontal ones? The emphasis in such a model would be on the use of "connections" — and, above all, the extended family, including *compadres* — for defensive purposes. In such a world, one's home would be one's castle in all the medieval fullness of that metaphor.

2. The foregoing questions suggest a way in which the notion of community intersects with the notion of security. Does the notion of community also intersect with that of legitimacy? How?

3. With respect to a given transaction or relationship, if A regards B as a member of the moral community, will B necessarily so regard A? If the answer is negative, may it still be true that if, over a period of time, A consistently treats B as a member of the moral community, B's inclination to reciprocate will be increased? Why?

4. Does participatory development require a sense of community that is inconsistent with Wiarda's "corporative model" of community? Consider the following kinds of developmental activity in relation to this question: (a) the construction of houses in a Caracas barrio; (b) the formation and operation of an agricultural production cooperative; (c) the contribution of labor or money to the installation of a system of water pipes in a Caracas barrio; (d) the decision to send one's children to school rather than have them work and contribute to the household income. If the answer to the above question is not the same for all of these forms of activity, what are the characteristics that distinguish one case from another?

---

2. Law and the Sense of Community

Durkheim saw the criminal law, and punishment in particular, as serving one dominant function: not correction of the offender, not restitution to the victim, not deterrence of future crime – but the maintenance of the vitality of "the common conscience." (This common conscience is the sum of those shared values on which "mechanical" solidarity is founded.) Punishment, which Durkheim admitted was largely non-reflective – "a passionate reaction of graduated intensity" – was above all designed to "heal the wounds made upon collective sentiments," by expressing the intensity of the community's aversion to assaults on those sentiments.[56]

Law in the form of punishment can be seen as a means to force the recalcitrant into being members of a community, at least by passively accepting the community's thou-shalt-nots. But, as Durkheim's discussion of punishment illustrates, the law also persuades people that they are a community in other ways that are less blatantly coercive. Merely by existing, a body of law asserts that the group to which it applies is, to the extent of the law's reach, a community. The qualifying phrase, "to the extent of the law's reach," is important. Two examples will make the point: (a) A shareholder's membership in the community called the corporation is limited to corporate affairs. Rights and duties within that community, defined by the external law and by the corporation's internal lawmaking apparatus (charter, by-laws, directors' and shareholders' decisions), are in fact the definition of the community itself. If one shareholder punches another in the nose, the act may violate a norm, but it is a norm of a different community. (b) National laws that have not "penetrated"[57] into a rural area (see Rosenn's discussion of Brazil, extracted above[58]) surely persuade no one in that area that he or she is a member of a national community. The law's community-defining function, then, depends on both its formal coverage (its asserted area of jurisdiction) and its effective reach.

Napoléon's insistence that the Code bearing his name be written in understandable language represented more than mere annoyance at lawyers' technicality. Like Justinian before him and Haile Selassie in our own time, he wanted a national body of law for the purpose of unifying a nation. The law was to be a teacher, not only as to its substantive content of rights and obligations, but also as to the citizenship implied in the very existence of such a body of law. The Code, in defining a *national* system of rights and obligations, would define a national "moral community." What Napoléon sought was a community based on legal universalism, to replace the system of patronage that had defined the community of the old regime. Our previous discussion of rule v. discretion is thus relevant not only to the problem of security, but also to the problem of community. The question to be asked is not whether either model (rule v. discretion, universalism v. personalism) provides security, or community;

---

[56] See Durkheim, note 48 *supra*, at 68 ff.

[57] See Freidman, "Legal Culture and Social Development," in L. Friedman and S. Macaulay, *Law and the Behavioral Sciences* 1000, 1014-15 (1969).

[58] P. 646, *supra*.

instead, the important questions are (i) what kinds of security or community are provided in each, and (ii) which legal areas should be governed by universal rule, and which by personalist discretion? The second question, we have seen, is highly value-laden; its answer depends very much on the kind of society one wants.

There is as much circularity in the causal connections between law and community as there is in the corresponding connections between law and security, or between law and legitimacy. If some degree of consensus is necessary for the emergence of a social or legal norm, then it is also true that the existence of a norm itself tends to produce consensus. Equally, if some willingness to trust strangers is necessary before people will bring their disputes to court for decision according to law, then it is also true that the existence of a system of decision by law promotes the willingness to trust strangers. We have suggested that a strategic place to break into the law-security causal circle is at the point of the definition of citizenship. The argument rested in part on the symbolism of citizenship, and its effect on the self-perception of the individual actor. A similar argument is even more obviously apt in the context of one's self-perception as a member of a community — as Napoléon knew.

The nations of Latin America are not "new nations." Yet most of their governments are still concerned with the promotion of a sense of national identity. If *indigenismo* in Mexico often seems concerned less with the health and nutrition of today's indigenous peoples, and more with the glorification of yesterday's, the government's motivations are understandable and perhaps even pardonable. But the problem of maintaining national identity, though still serious in some countries, is on the wane everywhere in Latin America. Even in Peru, the Spanish language is taking over at an accelerating rate, largely as the result of urbanization. Every Latin American country has a large body of formal national law on the books — and has had, at least from the mid-19th Century. Still, the vertical segmentation highlighted by Wiarda[59] persists, stubbornly resisting the establishment of truly national legal universalism. The moral communities, in other words, are national communities only with respect to a relatively limited number of kinds of transactions and relationships.

A perspective that emphasizes participatory development, however, permits us at least to speculate that a "horizontally" oriented idea of community may grow at a grass-roots level, with legal institutions playing their expected role: defining communities, providing channels for group effort, providing training in cooperation and in leadership. If the residents of a new Caracas barrio organize a junta, they presumably do so not merely for the purpose of defense against the police, or to secure water lines or paved streets. They seek, among other things, the security that comes from the sense that the barrio is a community — which may, indeed, be related to their needs for defense and public services, since there is strength in numbers. The very struggle for existence that characterizes a barrio's early days provides a "community of memories"[60] that endures throughout the barrio's separate existence as a barrio. Barrio residents who are cooperating to improve their barrio see themselves

---

[59] Pp. 670-73, *supra*.
[60] *Weber* 340.

as part of a moral community that runs well beyond the limits of the family. In learning a system of rights and obligations as to each other, they inevitably learn about the abstract idea of rights and obligations that run "horizontally," which abstraction is transferable to other contexts.

We have suggested that legal institutions not only define communities, but also are capable of providing channels for cooperation and structures for the exercise of leadership within groups. The other side of the coin, of course, is that legal institutions may also obstruct cooperation and stifle leadership. After raising some questions about the relation of law to the sense of community, we turn to the problems of leadership, and then to some broader problems inherent in cooperation.

Questions

1. Cohen describes the transition from a "simple" society to a "complex" one as a process of transformation from (i) a situation in which "all members of [the society] are members of all institutions" to (ii) a situation in which relationships are specific and roles are specialized. This evolution can also be pictured as a transition from a society composed of a single community to one characterized by the coexistence of a large number of communities. In a complex society, each individual is simultaneously a member of many communities, some separate and some overlapping; only very rarely will any two individuals be members of precisely the same set of communities. If "law" and "community" define each other, then does not each individual in a complex society carry around his or her own personalized set of laws? What becomes of the notion that "modern" societies tend to be characterized by legal universalism? (Recall Ganivet's suggestion, p. 60, *supra,* that the Spaniard's ideal is for each person to carry around his or her own *fuero,* giving permission to do as the individual pleases.)

2. Suppose that the "penetration" of law is not regionally selective, as in the example of rural Brazil, but selective along the lines of socio-economic status? Suppose, for example, that (i) a knife fight between two urban slum dwellers is always ignored by the police, while attacks on shopkeepers are always vigorously pursued, or that (ii) an hacendado's property rights are strictly enforced against a tenant, but not vice-versa. Is the community-defining force of the formal law weakened in such situations? Why?

3. Do Weber's three categories of legitimacy ("traditional," "charismatic" and "legal" domination) all require a sense of community? What kinds of shared values, or agreed-upon interests, are required for each? Does "legal" domination rest upon a sharing of purposes or values (Durkheim's "mechanical" solidarity) or upon a more transactional consensus about the complementarity of interests (Durkheim's "organic" solidarity), or neither, or both?

4. In what sense does the action of amparo (or the writ of security) promote community? Does the decision to go to court constitute an implicit assertion by the plaintiff about his or her membership in a community? Which community? May such a decision also represent the breakdown of another community? Suppose that one

resident of a village brings a lawsuit against another? Can the same action contribute both to "integration" and to "disintegration," depending on one's perspective?

---

3. Law and Leadership

Throughout this chapter we have been concerned with ways in which institutions, particularly legal institutions, influence behavior. A central theme of the chapter has been that the law affects conduct not only directly, through the application of coercion and reward, but also indirectly, through its influence on individuals' perceptions and evaluations of themselves. For the child, the self-image is taken almost exclusively from others; as one grows, one's self-image is constantly adapted, so that at any one time it reflects both "autonomy" (which is to say, the influence of the self-image previously developed) and the influence of the current (assumed) judgment of others. The "others" who influence a person's self-image, of course, are not all the other people he or she may meet; only some of those people are leaders, or, in the language of the sociologists, "significant others":

> ... [T]he key mechanism by which institutions form persons involves the circle of significant others which the institution establishes. This is important because it in due course leads, for full institutional members, to changes in the generalized other [*i.e.,* the individual conscience – Eds.]. By internalizing the expectations of institutional heads, ... [individuals] come to control themselves – to pattern and to enact their roles in accordance with the constraints thus built into their characters.[61]

The creation of new leadership positions, and the recruitment and training of new leaders, both promote development and result from development. Some forms of development require cooperation, and some forms of cooperation demand the leader's coordinating role. And as a society becomes progressively more complex, its leadership functions must be divided and further subdivided; not even a totalitarian state can escape this necessity. We shall consider the institutional context of cooperation in the next section. At present we are concerned primarily with the role of legal institutions in establishing and maintaining leadership relations.

Our previous discussion of legitimacy was, in large measure, an elaborate response to the question: Why do people allow themselves to be led? Weber's categories of domination are an effort to classify leadership relations. But the subject of legitimacy is broader than the subject of leadership. One may speak, for example of the legitimacy of a farmer's occupancy of a plot of land; yet it would be odd to describe that issue as one involving leadership. Not all power relations, in other words, are leadership relations. Nor is the converse even true; there are leadership positions that do not involve the exercise of power: the "figurehead" leader is known in many cultures. Normally, however, leaders do not merely symbolize power, but exercise it.

---

[61] H. Gerth and C. Mills, *Character and Social Structure* 173 (paperback ed. 1970).

Law is related to this process both as cause and as effect; law maintains the institutions that leaders lead, and those same institutions make law.

The reasons why members of a community will participate in the community's activities are ultimately reducible to two: they believe either that participation is their duty or that it is to their advantage. Leadership, then, draws on both of Durkheim's types of solidarity: (i) Families, tribes, nations – all these typically offer a strong built-in sense of generalized obligation to the community, growing out of the sharing of *values*. (ii) Mutual *interests* underlie many other kinds of cooperation such as the cooperative grading of a road in a barrio, or the cooperative marketing of dairy products. It should not be assumed that a community built on the solidarity of shared values can count on its members to cooperate in any and all matters. One who is willing, under some circumstances, to die for one's country may nonetheless balk at paying a particular tax. Still, it is this kind of solidarity that comes first to mind when one speaks of "the moral community." Indeed, a community's shared values can be said to underpin some forms of solidarity based on mutual interests, as F. G. Bailey recognizes in these comments about the leadership relation in some peasant villages in India:

> Leader-follower relationships within a moral community have a degree of hardness and calculation of self-interest: when the relationship crosses the boundaries of the moral community, wariness hardens into suspicion and double-dealing. Within the moral community the peasant understands the range of possible action; within limits, he knows what his opponent will do, because he and his opponent (whether leader or follower) share certain basic values; furthermore the relationship is seen to be regulated by councils . . . or superior leaders. But outside the moral community none of these controls apply: official action is unpredictable; values are not shared; and adjudicative institutions like courts of law, are not part of the peasant moral community but are regarded as instruments or weapons to be used in the contest. Within the moral community, one looks carefully to see if the leader is fulfilling his side of the bargain: outside the moral community, one knows that a bargain will not be fulfilled, and one must therefore insure oneself by anticipatory cheating.[62]

All the reservations earlier expressed about the concept of "the moral community" are equally appropriate here. Every community is a moral community, including the coldest and most thoroughly "transactional" relationships of the market. If government agents, for example, are mistrusted, nonetheless there are some things that are "not done," even when dealing with them. Perhaps it is true that the morality of transactions and mutual interests tends to be perceived as a matter of expediency and reciprocity, while the morality of shared values tends to be perceived as a matter of duty, but *both* duty and expediency infuse the morality of either sort of relationship. The leader, then, appeals to both the sense of duty and the sense of expediency in persuading his or her followers to act. As the basis for community shifts its center of

---

[62] Bailey, note 11 *supra,* at 307-08. Reprinted by permission of British Association for the Advancement of Science.

gravity away from a hypothetically "pure" shared-values solidarity toward a "pure" solidarity of mutual interests, the leader's emphasis may be expected to shift accordingly, toward a lesser reliance on exhortations about moral duty and a greater reliance on appeals to expediency. An effective leader, however, will ignore neither of these approaches.

A system of law, in fact, blurs the distinctions between interests and values, by converting many expedient relationships into relationships based on duty. One follows the legitimate leader (or the legitimate order) not so much out of a rational calculation of the relative advantages of compliance and noncompliance, but because of a sense of duty to follow.

Law's role in relation to the leadership function is thus first and foremost a legitimizing role, and we shall not repeat our previous discussion of legitimacy. But law also structures the institutions that leaders lead, and in so doing can either ease the task of leadership or complicate it. Further, institutional structures, embodied in law, can either promote or retard the training of new leaders. The questions that follow emphasize these latter two themes.

Questions

1. Leaders in all cultures regularly complain that they cannot be effective because too many other people must be consulted before anything significant can be done. What are the tradeoffs to be considered in designing an institution — say, an agricultural cooperative to manage lands distributed in a land reform — that influence the selection of decision-making mechanisms? Are there some issues that should be decided only by a governing body, or a manager? Some that should be decided only by unanimous vote of the members? What are the types of characteristics that determine where issues should be placed along this continuum?

2. Are the same factors controlling when the size of the organization is vastly greater? Consider this comment on Brazilian public administration:

> In a recent interview, the present Minister of Education, Jarbas Passarinho, complained that no sooner had he taken office than his subordinates began appearing with "urgent" documents that required his signature — permission to unload 156 pieces of paper and a lease of a home for an inspector of secondary education in the Northeast.[63]

What are the consequences for *leadership* of such concentration of power?

3. In a Mexican ejido, the leadership is elected for a three-year term, and may not be reelected; this rule of the Agrarian Code derives from the "no reelection" tradition of the origins of the 1910 Revolution. Can such a rule be effective in preventing a cacique from arising? (Consider the case of "Pedro Caso.") Does the no-reelection rule aid in the training of leaders, or hinder it? Suppose that it takes nearly three years for

---

[63] Rosenn, note 9 *supra,* at 526.

an inexperienced ejido president to become acquainted with the demands of the job? Is the informal practice of the Caracas barrios preferable, allowing effective leaders of the juntas to continue in office indefinitely?

4. Earlier we suggested that the cooperative grading of a road in a Caracas barrio was an example of solidarity based on mutual interests. Is there also a sense in which the leader of such a project can draw on the solidarity of shared values? (Consider Bailey's comments about cooperation inside the moral community in peasant villages in India.) Is the boundary of the moral community, with respect to a particular transaction or relationship, simply the area within which behavior is predictable? Is "community" just a sub-category of "security"?

Before leaving the subject of leadership, we introduce one more theme, which is particularly important in Latin America: the role of local leadership in connecting local communities with the world outside. The smallest, most compact, most "mechanically" solid community is part of larger communities — with the ever-decreasing exceptions represented by certain tribal cultures in the very remote jungles of South America. One perspective on the leaders in small communities views them as brokers who link those communities with the national societies. "Pedro Caso" performed such a function, in his own not-so-attractive way. So do the politically-connected members of a Caracas barrio's junta. The corporative tradition in Latin America reinforces these vertical relationships, which are the functional descendants of older forms of patronage. So viewed, the local leader transmits national norms (including law) downward. Equally importantly, he or she becomes upwardly (and, in geographical terms, outwardly) mobile, through continued contacts with wider communities. And the process of brokerage is itself a training process. Such a "politician-entrepreneur" "must learn to operate in an arena of continuously changing friendships and alliances, which form and dissolve with the appearance of new economic or political opportunities."[64] In other words, the local leader learns the transactional morality of the market — which is itself one of the national norms that penetrates the local community.

---

4. Law and Cooperation

P. COHEN, MODERN SOCIAL THEORY

Pp. 146 (1968)*

. . . Cooperation is a deliberate and voluntary effort to facilitate the performance of

---

[64]Wolf, "Aspects of Group Relations in a Complex Society: Mexico," 58 *Am. Anthropologist* 1065, 1072 (1956).

*© 1968 by Percy S. Cohen, Basic Books, Inc., Publishers, New York.

tasks by others in return for similar services. There are various forms of it. In the simplest, the cooperation inheres in the specific activity itself: for example, if two or more men farm land which they own jointly. In more complex forms of cooperation the return of services may be delayed: one farmer may assist another to clear a field in the expectation that reciprocal assistance will be given at some other time. In some cases cooperation can be contractual and its obligations specified, in others the arrangement may be diffuse and open.

Cooperation is a form of reciprocity; but not all reciprocity is cooperation: to buy goods or to barter them, is a form of reciprocity but it is not necessarily cooperation. Cooperation is also a form of interdependence; but many forms of interdependence are not strictly cooperative: industrial managers and workers are interdependent, but they do not cooperate. Both reciprocity and interdependence are compatible with conflict; but to cooperate is to renounce conflict. This does not mean that those who cooperate cannot also be in conflict with one another; they can indeed, but the issues of conflict must be separate from that of cooperation. Two brothers may cooperate in work, but may be rivals for the favours of the same woman. But they cannot work together and, at the same time, aim to prevent one another from succeeding in the goals of the work activity; this is obvious.

Discussions of social phenomena always risk being misunderstood, for they face an especially acute problem of perspective. Professor Cohen, when he says that industrial managers and workers do not cooperate, must be thinking of the relevant "task" as, for example, the fitting of handles onto automobile doors. The managers do not perform that task — although they might be said to facilitate its performance. But if the "task" were identified as the production of automobiles, there would be nothing wrong with saying that managers and workers cooperate. In this discussion, we shall be concerned with the role of law in promoting or retarding cooperative effort, seen at either of these levels of abstraction. Cohen's summary emphasizes three qualities of cooperation: reciprocity, interdependence and the renunciation of conflict. Any legal system is designed to promote all three.

It is important to distinguish between cooperation and consensus. Two men may cooperate in pulling a car out of a muddy path — a farmer who wants to unblock the path for his tractor, and a man who wants to impress his ladyfriend. The only consensus required by cooperation is agreement about the nature and extent of each cooperator's duties. One writer puts it this way: "Consensus is agreement on the content of behavior, while cooperation necessitates agreement only on the form of behavior."[65] (For "content," presumably we should read "purposes.") Nevertheless:

> Cooperation, in its most extreme form, and when it is not sporadic or purely spontaneous, must involve a high degree of commitment to norms and, usually, to certain moral values. There are several reasons for this. Firstly, regular and

---

[65] I. Horowitz, *Three Worlds of Development: The Theory and Practice of International Stratification* 501 (2d ed. 1972).

successful forms of cooperation demand a high degree of predictability of conduct. Secondly, cooperation demands that those involved should renounce certain goals or defer certain gratifications. Neither of these conditions can be met without a high degree of normative prescription which must, in the long run, be buttressed by moral values.[66]

Law in the form of direct coercion is seldom effective to produce sustained active group effort; a group of people may be coerced to dig a ditch, but not to form a partnership or a credit cooperative.[67] And yet it is the latter kind of group effort — cooperation — that is critical to development. Professor Manning Nash makes this comment about the Indian peasants of Mexico and Guatemala:

> They do not lack economic rationality, the matching of means and ends for best outputs; they do not hedge economic activity with a host of traditional barriers; they do not despise wealth and hard work; and they exhibit the free market where each man follows his own economic interest. Thus they have the values, the markets, the pecuniary means of exchange, the ability to calculate, and the interest in economic activity. . . . What is lacking is the social organization of an entity like the firm, an autonomous, corporate group dedicated to and organized for economic activity.[68]

It need hardly be added that cooperation is, if anything, even more necessary to that style of development which rejects market mechanisms in favor of collective systems of production and distribution. If coercion will not produce cooperation,[69] what will?

We return to Durkheim's two forms of solidarity. There may be a strong sense of mutual responsibility within a family. The primitive European law of loans, building on this sense, made members of a kinship group jointly liable in delict (tort) for the failure of a member to repay a loan to an outsider.[70] But cooperative joint borrowing from Mexico's Ejido Bank has been a failure, foundering on the unwillingness of one ejidatario to be responsible for another's share of the loan, when each is producing and selling on his or her own account. It is hard in even the most "advanced" economies to get people to accept responsibility for others in such a transactional context. This excursion into the dismal world of lending and borrowing illustrates a major point to be made about cooperation in the context of development within a market system: The cooperation that matters — cooperative work, cooperative investment — is more easily initiated on the basis of solidarity of mutual interests ("organic" solidarity) than

---

[66]Cohen, note 45 *supra,* at 147.

[67]Coercion is to be distinguished from rewards or other similar inducements in this context; for example, tax incentives seem far more apt for encouraging the formation of cooperatives than does the threat of punishment. It is fair to emphasize the incentive aspects of such a scheme even though the entire tax system can also be seen as a form of coercion.

[68]Nash, "Indian Economies," in *Social Anthropology* (vol. 6, Handbook of Middle American Indians, 1967) at 87, 98.

[69]Of course, if cooperation is by definition voluntary, it is a contradiction in terms to speak of using coercion to produce cooperation.

[70]*Weber* 115.

on the basis of solidarity of shared values ("mechanical" solidarity). Thus it is no surprise that the ability of a Caracas barrio junta to organize cooperative work in the barrio declines with the passage of time. The barrio residents are not members of a single closed community, but instead are members of any number of communities, of which the barrio is merely one. They may have some vague sense of loyalty to the barrio *as* a barrio, but their willingness to cooperate in barrio improvements is directly proportional to their perception of personal advantage in the improvements. (These are not unusually selfish people; how many urban residents are loyal to "dear old 20th Street"?)

Cooperation for a community development project, for example, must appeal to the interests of members of the community in these ways: The project must be understandable; it must be seen to benefit the whole community, and not just the privileged few (and particularly not just the would-be organizers); it must seem attainable with reasonable effort; it must be expected to produce a payoff either immediately or in the rather near future. All of these qualities are variations on the theme of trust; Gerritt Huizer found that trust was inhibited by the "social climate" in one peasant village in El Salvador, to the impediment of two community development projects.

G. HUIZER, COMMUNITY DEVELOPMENT, LAND REFORM AND POLITICAL PARTICIPATION

28 *American Journal of Economics and Sociology* 159, 160-62 (1969)

Both the sanitation and road-improvement projects appeared to be ideal community development efforts since they corresponded with strongly felt needs of the villagers who had to get water from contaminated wells some distance away and who suffered also when the rainy season made it difficult to reach even the nearest towns. In addition, both projects looked ideal with regard to contributions from the government. For the sanitary drinking water system several kilometers of pipes were being supplied by the government. The latter was also contributing technical supervision and help in collecting the water at a well in the nearby mountains. The villagers only had to contribute manual labor which, because of chronic underemployment in rural El Salvador, was abundantly available. A similar arrangement was offered for the road work. Initially the villagers did not respond actively, however. . . .

The most striking factor certainly was distrust. Once a confidential relationship with the villagers had been established, they revealed their strong conviction that the sanitation project would not benefit them but would rather serve the local large landholder, whose big house was not far from the center of the village. In their experience, government employees and landlords always organized such things together. The people also resented having to work without pay while the officials who made them do so earned (compared with a rural day laborer) relatively high salaries. Most of these officials are, moreover, known to enjoy additional incomes as absentee landowners. Along with all these factors was the further one of those government agents (mostly engineers, but including the social educator who was an ex-Army major) treating the villagers, not as responsible citizens whose collaboration was being sought with reasonable arguments, but as inferior beings who were merely to be told what they should do. This attitude was strongly resented by the villagers, but since no open opposition was tolerated, people withdrew in silence and simply did not show up for work.

The spirit of distrust and resentment was expressly related to such past experiences as the bloody repression of a peasant revolt in 1932, still well remembered in 1955, although rarely mentioned and then only in a low voice at somebody's home. It was said that thousands of peasants had been killed in those days and that since then public gatherings of more than five peasants was not allowed. It is known that the formation of peasants' organizations in El Salvador is legally forbidden. . . .

It will be clear that in this kind of authoritarian social climate to create an atmosphere favorable to voluntary cooperation is very difficult.

The theme of trust and the theme of self-respect are not new to these pages; the law's role in promoting both these states of mind has been explored at length, and we refer back to those discussions.[71] In addition, the law may affect the willingness to cooperate or the effectiveness of cooperation through its structuring of the institutions in which people cooperate. Certain issues reappear wherever cooperative forms of activity are carried on: the selection of managers; the process of review by the members of the managers' decisions; the determination of members' contributions; and the allocation of the fruits of cooperation. The latter two issues are intimately connected, for they are aspects of the problem of incentives, a problem that is critical in collective economies, but also present in some degree in any form of cooperation. The following is a very short extract from a long speech given by Fidel Castro in 1968. The first paragraphs refer to the remarks of a previous speaker who had spoken on behalf of a group of students.

CASTRO, CREATING WEALTH WITH POLITICAL AWARENESS, NOT CREATING POLITICAL AWARENESS WITH MONEY OR WEALTH

in M. Kenner and J. Petras (eds.), *Fidel Castro Speaks*
406, 416-17, 419 (Grove ed. 1972)*

. . . They have said that material incentives do not matter to them, that what does matter is the awareness of their duty, and that their behaviour is not motivated, nor

---

[71] Pp. 641-49, 674-80, *supra.*

will it be motivated, by money; their acts are motivated not by material incentives, but by their conscience and their sense of duty. . . . With this they express their confidence in the future, their confidence in the possibility of a communist society, their confidence in a society where all work for all and all receive what they need. They said that they were not going to work by the clock, but that their work day would be dictated by their conscience. . . .

They expressed the opinion that the Revolution will not use the tool of material incentives as the instrument for raising productivity, for raising the level of accomplishment. Of course this does not mean that in our society all citizens — not by any means — have reached these levels of conscience; there are many who have achieved this, but there are many who still have not done so. . . .

And we should not use money or wealth to create political awareness. To offer a man more to do more than his duty is to buy his conscience with money. To give a man participation in more collective wealth because he does his duty and produces more and creates more for society is to turn political awareness into wealth.

As we said before, communism, certainly, cannot be established if we do not create abundant wealth. But the way to do this, in our opinion, is not by creating political awareness with money or with wealth, but by creating wealth with political awareness, and more and more collective wealth with more collective political awareness.

In commenting on this speech a year later, two sympathic observers added:

> Time alone will tell whether Fidel is right. In the meantime, it is obvious that the Revolution cannot afford to rely exclusively on political and moral incentives. And since it has renounced the method of material incentives, it will have to resort to organization and discipline — what we have called the semi-militarization of work.[72]

Partly fulfilling this prophecy, in 1971 Cuba adopted a new Vagrancy Law (*Ley Contra la Vagancia,* officially translated as the Law on "Loafing"), which provides criminal penalties for prolonged absenteeism from work. Penal sanctions, however, are a last resort; shorter periods of absenteeism place the absentee in a "pre-criminal" status. The language of the law emphasizes the goal of rehabilitation.[73]

Questions

1. Does Castro's speech appeal to his audience's sense of shared values, or of mutual interests, or both? Can it be said that Cuba's 1971 Vagrancy Law seeks to

---

[72] L. Huberman and P. Sweezy, *Socialism in Cuba* 153 (paperback ed. 1970).

[73] The law is carefully analyzed, and assessed in the light of Cuban developmental goals, both economic and political, in Kennedy, *"Cuba's Ley Contra la Vagancia — The Law on Loafing,"* 20 U.C.L.A. L. Rev. 1177 (1973). See generally R. Bernardo, *The Theory of Moral Incentives in Cuba* (1971).

promote both of these kinds of solidarity? (Recall Durkheim's views on the functions of punishment.[74]) Is it proper to define cooperation, as Cohen does, as "voluntary" effort?

2. In a market system, what, specifically, does the law of contracts contribute to the process of cooperation? Obviously, a system of private contract rests on the "organic" solidarity of mutual interests. Does it also rest on the "mechanical" solidarity of shared values? If so, what are the values in question, and how does the law contribute to their sharing? May it be that the law's greatest long-term contribution to predictability – and thus to cooperation, as well as to security – lies in its promotion of shared values? (Recall Bailey's comments on leadership and predictability within the moral community.[75])

3. Cohen says that cooperation may be either "contractual" (with obligations specified) or "diffuse and open." What is an example of such diffuse cooperation? May such cooperation rest on a legal base?

4. Is it true that the deferment of gratification requires "a high degree of normative prescription which must, in the long run, be buttressed by moral values"?[76] May one not decide to defer gratification on the basis of calculation of his or her interests? Is the key to the quoted statement to be found in the phrase, "in the long run"?

5. Suppose you are asked to design an agricultural production cooperative, to be operated by the beneficiaries of a land reform. Assume that agriculture is part of a market economy. Will the issue of "incentives," as presented by Castro's speech and the Cuban Vagrancy Law, affect your choice of institutional forms? How, specifically, will the issue arise? What legal-institutional tools are available for its resolution?

---

5. Conflict and Community

Any activity implies risk to existing interests; change of the kind that merits the name "development" guarantees the disturbing of some aspects of the existing order. Professor Eric Wolf illustrates the point in this comment on the impact of what is sometimes euphemistically called "national integration" on the traditional community of shared values in a Mexican village:

> Confronted by these contrasts between the mobile and the traditional, the nation-oriented [leader-brokers] and the community-oriented, village life is riven by contradictions and conflicts, conflicts not only between class groups but also between individuals, families or entire neighborhoods. Such a community will inevitably differentiate into a number of unstable groups with different orientations and interests.[77]

"Community," then, does not imply the absence of conflict. Particularly where

---

[74] P. 674, *supra.*

[75] P. 678, *supra.*

[76] Cohen, quoted at p. 682, *supra.*

[77] Wolf, note 64 *supra,* at 1073.

solidarity rests on mutual interests, or "complementarity,"[78] community promises to produce inequality and resentment: managers and workers are the neo-classic case, and "industrial conflict" is the child of their organic solidarity. If law has any substantive content that is distinctively its own, that content lies in the procedures which all legal systems provide for the resolution of disputes. We shall first try to specify what conflict is and is not, and then turn to an examination of the role of law as manager of conflict. Once again, we begin with Professor Cohen.

P. COHEN, MODERN SOCIAL THEORY
Pp. 146-47 (1968)*

Conflict implies deliberate attempts to prevent the attainment of goals by others. At its most extreme it takes the form of struggle. Conflict itself involves a relatively low degree of normative definition of role performance between the conflicting parties; when men seek to outwit one another, to eliminate one another from a contest, or to interfere directly with one another's attempts to attain particular goals, they gain advantages by adopting courses of action which are not expected and which cannot therefore be prescribed within roles. This does not mean that conflict necessarily occurs without any normative constraint. Usually, the opposite is the case; in most forms there are very specific normative constraints within which conflict occurs; when spouses quarrel, there are some things which are not said and done; when entrepreneurs compete, certain practices are not adopted; when managers and workers bargain over wages they may use the strike and lock-out, but they try to avoid destruction of property and physical violence; when combatants go to war, they adhere to certain rules in the use of weapons, in the treatment of prisoners, and so on. In the first example, the restraints are built into the moral character of the relationship: usually spouses experience guilt when resorting to certain practices in their quarrels. But in the other examples the adherence to norms is clearly in the interests of the conflicting parties; neither side may wish the conflict to spread or take forms which become unmanageable. When the advantages of adhering to such norms are no longer weighed against the disadvantages the norms may come to have morally binding significance. But whether this occurs or not, the adherence to norms necessarily sets limits to the relationship of conflict; it is therefore correct to say that conflict, *in its most extreme form,* involves the renunciation or absence of normative constraint.

---

[78] This term is used in Aubert, note 28 *supra,* at 78 ff., to describe the relation formed when people come together on the basis of mutual interests, *e.g.,* employer and employee. It is to be distinguished from those "affective" communities which rest on close personal association and shared values. Precisely because affective communities suppress conflict, when conflict does surface it tends to be pronounced, or even violent. See Cohen, note 45 *supra,* at 136-37. Marriage is based on such an affective community; so might be a group of political revolutionaries.

*©1968 by Percy S. Cohen, Basic Books, Inc., Publishers, New York.

Cohen's italics emphasize that conflict is the polar opposite of cooperation only when conflict is total; the entrepreneurs in his example, for instance, may well cooperate in the maintenance of market institutions. Conflict becomes total only in very rare situations; even modern "total war" is not total. Indeed, conflict regularly performs the function of highlighting the fact that the contending parties agree on certain values: Cohen's hypothetical two brothers, who contend for the favors of a woman, agree in their high estimation of the lady; competing entrepreneurs, or contending workers and managers, agree on the value of money; the list is as endless as the list of potential conflicts. Thus conflict does not imply the total absence of consensus, or even the total absence of solidarity; people who are arguing are at least communicating. Nor does a community's cohesion (its resistance to fragmentation) depend on the absence of conflict. Indeed, a complex and highly differentiated national society derives cohesion precisely from the fact that a large number of divisions (potential conflicts) intersect, forming a patchwork pattern, rather than coinciding. (A concomitant of this increased national cohesion, of course, is the breakdown of cohesion in smaller units, as Wolf makes clear in his discussion of Mexican villages.)

Law in this analysis is not so much the preventer of conflict as the manager of conflict. The settlement of specific disputes by peaceful means is surely the oldest function of law, responding to the most basic of social needs. But law also relates to conflict in more sophisticated ways, providing the channels that direct conflict into paths that are not socially disastrous. Law not only defines the limits on tactics (*e.g.,* the law of unfair trade practices, or the Geneva Convention), but also establishes and maintains institutions through which conflicts may be carried on peacefully (*e.g.,* the market, the legislature). In the latter sense, the enactment or nonenactment of a specific statute may itself be the point of contention between the conflicting parties; in such a case — a land reform law would be one example[79] — law and conflict are related in a circle of mutual causation. More generally and more subtly, law not only defines permissible tactics in conflict, but also plays an important part in defining our substantive goals in life. So viewed, law not only forbids certain things that are "not done," but also, through its structure and content, inhibits us from even conceiving of some kinds of possible social arrangements. It is in this sense that law "is conservative in the same way in which language is conservative."[80]

The settlement of particular disputes according to established norms may be contrasted with various other approaches to conflict resolution. Two such approaches are particularly relevant here; one is negotiation, and another is dispute settlement within a system of patronage. Negotiation may or may not involve the presence of a

---

[79] It bears repeating that the enactment of a law is not the same thing as the accomplishment of a land reform.

[80] Wasserstrom, note 25 *supra.* Compare Holmes' famous comment that a decision under the due process clause of the 14th Amendment would "depend on a judgment or intuition more subtle than any articulate major premise." Lochner v. New York, 198 U.S. 45, 74, 76 (1905) (dissenting opinion). It is relatively easy for us to see what an earlier era's inarticulate major premises were, and extraordinarily difficult to discern our own.

third-party mediator. A mediator should not be confused with an arbitrator; arbitrators judge and resolve disputes; mediators seek to bring parties together in a process of negotiation. What are the distinctions between the functions of mediators and those of judges or arbitrators?[81] Where a mediator tries to reconcile the parties (usually by a compromise solution), a judge decides which of them is right and which is wrong. Mediation looks ahead, to the preservation of the relationship between the parties; adjudication looks backward, sorting out the facts of the past. Mediators avoid normative judgments, while such judgments are the essence of adjudication; thus, while adjudication focuses on facts and values, mediation/negotiation focuses on the adjustment of interests. Indeed, since people do not like to think of themselves as compromising about "matters of principle,"

> conditions are, generally speaking, less favourable for mediation than for other forms of conflict-resolution when the conflicts are characterized by disagreements about normative factors.[82]

Finally, unlike mediation, which reaches agreements without explanation, adjudication presses the judge to state the basis of his or her decision: the norms that apply, and the reasons why they do apply; thus the act of adjudicating itself "makes a precedent," leaving an impression on the normative order.[83]

Dispute settlement within a system of patronage may partake of some of the characteristics of negotiation, but "negotiation" would scarcely be an acceptable characterization of such a process. The client does not negotiate with the patron; he supplicates. When the patron settles claims as between himself or herself and the client, the degree to which customary or other "rules" influence the settlement is determined by the patron. The patron may also decide disputes between two clients; here, although a patriarchal sort of justice may be done, and no "rules" formally acknowledged, there is an inevitable pressure in such a case toward decision according to established norms. As soon as a third party is called in as arbiter of any dispute, the dispute tends to become one about facts or norms or both. The arbiter — even a patron — cooperates in this process, for the purpose of lending additional legitimacy to his or her decision. Thus law begets principled adjudication, and adjudication begets law.

Questions

1. Does principled adjudication depend for its success upon the solidarity of shared values? On the solidarity of mutual interests? Is successful negotiation/mediation based merely on the solidarity of mutual interests, or is it also aided by "mechanical" solidarity?

---

[81] See Eckhoff, "The Mediator, the Judge and the Administrator in Conflict-Resolution," 10 *Acta Sociologica* 158 (1966), in J. Aubert (ed.), *Sociology of Law* at 171 (1969).

[82] *Id.* at 174. Of course law may enact norms that set up the machinery for mediation.

[83] See Aubert, note 28 *supra*, at 133-35.

2. If conflict implies an effort to gain advantage over one's competitor by being unpredictable, in what ways do the law's systems of conflict resolution and conflict management contribute to predictability, and thus to the security on which developmental activity depends?

3. If an arbitrator or a judge settles a dispute, does it matter, for the development process, whether the decision-maker simply rules "thumbs-up" or "thumbs-down," or gives reasons for the decision?

4. Is the encouragement of a "rights" mentality consistent with a dispute-settlement style that emphasizes negotiation, or the discretionary decree of a patron?

5. In our earlier discussion of legitimacy, it was suggested that the orderly resolution of conflicts engendered by social change had a legitimizing effect on the change. May it also be true that the mere existence of machinery for such orderly adjudication has such a legitimizing effect?

6. Dispute settlement according to rules requires a considerable degree of trust in the impartiality of the judge or arbitrator, which trust in turn is related to the boundaries of the litigants' moral communities. In what sense does a patronage-style system of dispute resolution similarly rest on trust, and on perceptions about the moral community? Are there, in fact, norms that limit the discretion of the patron in such a system? If so, do those norms relate to the maintenance of the moral community?

7. In a "corporative" system, in which vertical lines of authority and community tend to predominate, will conflicts over basic values tend to be muted by reduced institutional contact between those who disagree? If conflicts over values do arise, and must be resolved according to norms (since conditions are unfavorable for their negotiated settlement), do such conflicts not inevitably press the system toward the model of adjudication/rules? Do such conflicts over values, by posing "either-or" choices in a zero-sum-game situation, threaten community cohesion and tend toward revolution? (In a zero-sum game, one party's gain always implies another's loss.)

8. If a system of discretionary justice exists, and is faced with a large volume of cases to be decided, will there be a tendency for that system to develop rules in order to dispose of cases efficiently? (Weber says that such tendencies are universal among bureaucracies.) If a patron makes a regular practice of deciding conflicts between clients on the basis of rules, will the patron-client relation tend to change in the direction of "legal domination"? Why?

9. Put yourself in the place of the loser in a dispute. Is it easier to take (a) an unfavorable settlement that is negotiated, or (b) an unfavorable decision by a judge? Consider, for example, a lunch-counter operator in the southern U.S. who is forced to desegregate the establishment. Is it sometimes useful to be able to point to a third party as having imposed a decision on one? Even at the cost of having an unfavorable moral judgment passed?

10. Friedrich referred to "Pedro Caso's" role as dispute-settler as "ritually demanding." What does that expression mean? Is all adjudication ritually demanding? For the parties as well as the judge? Is the role of mediator ritually demanding?

11. The amparo and the writ of security are obviously systems for resolving conflicts between individuals and government. Is there a sense in which they are also channels defining the acceptable limits of conflict?

12. Why is a Caracas barrio junta's dispute-settling "jurisdiction" so clearly limited to cases involving land use (including "nuisance")?

13. Why is a junta's decision of such a case influenced by its previous decisions in other similar cases, even though no records are kept of such decisions?

D. Inequality

Until this point, the section headings in this chapter have had a positive, reassuring ring: Security, Legitimacy, Community. In such a context, "Inequality" may seem incongruous. Of course the problem of inequality is a fundamental problem for all the developing countries — but why not deal with it under the heading of "Equality"? The answer is that inequality is a fact, while equality is an ideal. The fact of inequality has pervaded all the complex societies that history has known, but in Latin America it is a dramatically impressive fact that imposes itself on any effort to understand social phenomena.

---

1. Inequality and Development

Increasingly, economists are expressing concern about the anti-developmental effects of inequality. Professor Peter Dorner, speaking positively of the income-redistribution effects of land reform, represents this point of view:

> Fragmentary though it is, the evidence from these countries [Egypt, Taiwan, Bolivia, Chile] does show that large scale land reforms result in substantial income transfers to the poorer rural classes — the farm workers and cultivators. In those instances where case studies have been made, they show increased participation in the money economy following such transfers. The new expenditure patterns appeared to be based on economically rational criteria. If a reform is massive and involves a large percentage of the rural people, the new expenditure patterns will change the national structure of demand and the earning rates of capital in alternative uses. There is likely to be a greater stimulus in the simple consumer-goods industries. These industries are more labour intensive in their production processes and also require a lower input of foreign exchange than the industries producing luxury and semi-luxury products for a relatively small group of wealthy landowners.[84]

Gunnar Myrdal broadens the argument in the following extract from a book that summarizes the policy implications from his larger work, *Asian Drama* (1968).

---

[84] P. Dorner, *Land Reform and Economic Development* 90-91 (1972).

G. MYRDAL, THE CHALLENGE OF WORLD POVERTY: A WORLD ANTI-POVERTY PROGRAMME IN OUTLINE

Pp. 64,68-69 (Pelican ed. 1971)*

Traditionally, Western economists for the most part assume . . . a conflict between economic growth and egalitarian reforms. They take it for granted that *a price has to be paid for reforms* and that often this price is prohibitive for poor countries. . . .

In my opinion, there are a number of general reasons why, contrary to the ordinary conception of a conflict between the two goals of economic growth and greater economic equality, those are often in harmony, and why *greater equality in underdeveloped countries is almost a condition for more rapid growth.*

First, the usual argument that inequality of income is a condition for saving has much less bearing on conditions in underdeveloped countries, where landlords and other rich people are known to squander their incomes for conspicuous consumption and conspicuous investment, and sometimes, particularly (but not only) in Latin America, in capital flight.

Second, since large masses of people in underdeveloped countries suffer from undernutrition, malnutrition and other serious defects in their levels of living, in particular lack of elementary health and educational facilities, extremely bad housing conditions and sanitation, and since this impairs their willingness and ability to work and to work intensively, this holds down production. This implies that measures to raise income levels for the masses of people would raise productivity.

Third, social inequality is tied to economic inequality in a mutual relationship, each being both cause and effect of the other. Greater economic equality would undoubtedly tend to lead to greater social equality. As social inequality is quite generally detrimental to development, the conclusion must be that through this mechanism also greater equality would lead to higher productivity.

Fourth, we cannot exclude from consideration that behind the quest for greater equality is the recognition of the fact that it has an independent value in terms of social justice, and that it would have wholesome effects for national integration.

Myrdal's first point, a refutation of more traditional assumptions about inequality and the propensity to save, is unexceptionable as to some parts of Latin America. But recent experience in Brazil, for example, provides some support for "the usual argument" about the relation of inequality to saving and investment — at least in the context of capitalist development.[85] Myrdal's second point, entirely apt for the Asian context, is only selectively valid in Latin America, applying with great force in a country like Ecuador, and only marginally in, say, Argentina. It is undoubtedly true,

---

*Copyright 1971, Pantheon Books, a Division of Random House, Inc.

[85] See Trubek, "When is an Omelette? What is an Egg? Some Thoughts on Economic Development and Human Rights in Latin America," 67 *Am. J. Int'l L.* 198, 199 (1973):

. . . [Brazil], the nation in Latin America that is experiencing the fastest economic growth

as he says in his third point, that economic and social inequality are mutually causative; the rest of the paragraph, though, is assertion, not proof. Finally, Myrdal's fourth point mainly expresses value preferences — not only the preference for greater equality as an aspect of social justice, but also the preference for national integration, as distinguished, perhaps, from the wrenching disintegration of revolution. We offer these criticisms not by way of rejecting Myrdal's conclusions — which we share, including his value preferences — but by way of highlighting the fact that the negative influence of inequality on economic development is not so "scientifically" established as he suggests. Of course, the preference for equality is built into some definitions of development, as we saw in this book's Introduction.

It seems clear, however, that rigid or closed social stratification — the inequality that is cast in social concrete — does inhibit at least those developmental activities that rest on innovation. The incentive of upward mobility — particularly "partial" mobility[86] — has historically been a powerful motive for innovation itself, and for the adoption of innovations. A closed system puts a premium on conformity, and tends to reconcile people to the values associated with their own strata. Such a system also eliminates the stimulus that competition gives to innovation: people at the top do not need to compete, and people at the bottom cannot compete.[87]

The foregoing paragraph has taken us away from the general question of the inequalities in a social system and into the related but separate question of mobility within the system. A society might contain enormous disparities of wealth, or other forms of power, or prestige, and still be relatively open, so that individuals (or their children) might move upward or downward on these scales. One who favors "equality of opportunity" favors a high degree of social mobility. High mobility appears to relate positively to development not only in its stimulus to innovation, but also in its maximization of human resources; the principle of the "fair competition" is founded in part on the notion that if careers are open to talents, then society will gain from placing the most talented individuals in positions where they can produce most

---

seems to be doing relatively little to preserve "human rights." Thus, for the past six years the Brazilian economy has grown prodigiously. Yet at the same time the citizen's ability to participate in political life has been curtailed, protection of individual rights and liberties has been weakened, and income has been progressively more concentrated in the hands of a small part of the society. On the other hand, both Chile, which [under President Allende] continues to maintain an open political system, protects individual liberties, and Cuba, which has reduced social inequities, have much less impressive economic growth records. Can it be, then, that rapid economic growth in Latin America *requires* political repression and intensified social inequality?

Cf. Fishlow, "Some Reflections on Post-1964 Brasilian Economic Policy," in A. Stepan (ed.), *Authoritarian Brazil* 69 (1973).

[86] The term refers to the situation in which there are some obstacles to upward mobility, which obstacles are susceptible to being destroyed by upwardly mobile people. See Germani, "Social and Political Consequences of Mobility," in N. Smelser and S. Lipset (eds.), *Social Structure and Mobility in Economic Development* at 364, 372 (1966).

[87] See R. La Piere, *Social Change* 373 (1965).

effectively. A sense of opportunity, too, while it produces some kinds of frustrations,[88] also reduces those frustrations that tend toward disruption of a complex society;[89] in this sense, to the extent that stability is conducive to development, it is arguable that a high degree of social mobility is developmentally positive.

Despite these common-sense assumptions and arguments, the precise ways in which social mobility relates to development are far from clear. In the first place, there are a surprising number of different ways of measuring social mobility; the writer of one paper sums up this point in a section with the intimidating title, "Nineteen Ideas Behind the Label 'Social Mobility.' "[90] Another writer flatly asserts that

> there is and can be no fixed and determinate general relationship between measures of economic growth and indexes of social mobility, either over time in one country or between countries at a point in time.[91]

It is undeniably true that social mobility of a relatively high degree is to be found in the societies that have experienced the greatest degree of economic development. What is not clear is the causal relation; rapid or advanced development seems at least as much a cause of high mobility as its effect. Given the current state of our testable knowledge on this question, it seems sensible, for our present purposes, to accept the conventional wisdom — ideologically inspired or not — that increased social mobility is an important developmental goal, and to return to our main theme of inequality.

---

2. Law and Inequality

Inequality — unlike security, legitimacy and community — is not primarily a state of mind. One can measure and even see and touch a great many kinds of inequality: income, educational level, health, sanitary facilities, housing. Inequalities of power and prestige, however, exist at least partly in people's minds; power and prestige are not things, but relations between people. And if we look beyond the palpable, touchable thing itself (a house, a bicycle) to the ownership of the thing, we see that inequalities of wealth are merely one subclass of the larger category of inequalities of power. Wealth, like security, is a prediction of what someone will do to protect one's relationships with other people in regard to a thing. Bentham lucidly reminded us:

---

[88] The point is that in an open system, the "losers" tend to find fault with themselves.

[89] A sense of opportunity, of course, may be highly disruptive in a simpler, traditional society.

[90] Wilensky, "Measures and Effects of Social Mobility," in Smelser and Lipset, note 86 *supra,* at 98, 106. For example, one may speak of *structural* mobility, in which whole classes or other groups advance in the social hierarchy (as in the case of social revolution), or *exchange* mobility, in which class structures remain relatively fixed, but individuals change places. In another dimension, one may contrast *individual* mobility with *intergenerational* mobility. A good overview of the analytical problem is Smelser and Lipset, "Social Structure, Mobility and Development," in Smelser and Lipset, note 86 *supra,* at 1.

[91] Duncan, "Methodological Issues in the Analysis of Social Mobility," in Smelser and Lipset, note 86 *supra,* at 51.

Property and law are born together, and die together. Before laws were made there was no property; take away laws, and property ceases.[92]

Property inequality, resting on law, is at once a collective promise and a prediction, a series of states of mind. To say that A is wealthier than B is to predict that the organized community will continue to assign to A a greater degree of power over things than it will assign to B.[93]

We emphasize that we do not suggest that inequality exists primarily "in the mind." Power relations exist in fact, despite the difficulty of measuring some of them; wealth inequalities, for that matter, are not even hard to measure. Yet there is utility in approaching the question of inequality from this predictive perspective, which highlights the role of law in the creation, maintenance and reduction of inequality. Furthermore, emphasis on such a state-of-mind approach is useful as a reminder that analysis of the question of inequality necessarily involves selection and classification, both of which are mental constructs. One does not normally raise any question of equality unless the facts or qualities being compared are comparable within a coherent universe of ideas. Ask someone whether a Moon rock is or is not equal to a boa constrictor; even a Zen master might be expected to raise an eyebrow. It is always appropriate to ask: Equal with respect to what? Furthermore, a claim to greater equality, within a social system, normally is a group claim, based on an argument that the existing distribution of rights — the existing classification of persons — is not justified. Since every individual in a complex society is a member of many groups both separate and overlapping, the issue of equality inevitably requires a decision-maker to impose a conceptual grid over life's unruly phenomena. The decision-maker must (a) sort out these phenomena and (b) select some of the claimant's characteristics as relevant, before the issue of equality can even be understood.

If the mental exercise just described seems familiar, the reason is not merely that legal education is devoted almost entirely to analysis of this kind. All decision-making involves a similar analytical process. Our conceptual grids — shaped in part by such mental constructs as law — filter the "facts" in the very process of perceiving them. We noted this phenomenon earlier, when we were considering the effects of law on one's decision whether to take the risks of development-oriented activity. We repeat it here to emphasize that the mental process of selection and classification, so critical to the analysis of inequality, is itself importantly influenced by the same law that underpins the very inequality we are analyzing.

Some inequalities are inescapable in any society. Even Engels commented that

the real content of the proletarian demand for equality is the demand for the *abolition of classes*. [For Engels, it would be redundant to say "economic

---

[92] See the full quotation at pp. 308-09, *supra*.

[93] Inequalities often have a great deal to do with people's perceptions of their own well-being. A high-status individual whose income remains the same may feel the poorer if the incomes of lower-status individuals are raised.

classes." — Eds.] Any demand for equality which goes beyond that, of necessity passes into absurdity.[94]

The following two extracts explore this theme of the inevitability of inequality (social stratification) from two different points of view: first, the implications of the division of labor in a complex society, and second, the implications of a system of norms and sanctions (*i.e.,* law) in any society, complex or not.

P. COHEN, MODERN SOCIAL THEORY

Pp. 59-61 (1968)*

The functionalist theory of social stratification, which has been put forward by Davis and Moore, and, separately by Parsons, derives in fact from Durkheim. What these writers have sought to show is that social stratification inevitably occurs in any complex society, particularly in an industrial society, and that it serves "vital functions" in such societies. This means, in other words, that social stratification is indispensable to any complex society and that any attempt to be rid of it would necessarily require the abandonment of other features of such societies. The argument is as follows. In a society in which tasks are specialized, some of these tasks call for talents which are rare, or are found more abundantly in some individuals than in others. It is necessary that the more talented be attracted to those occupations which require their skills. These occupations demand administrative, entrepreneurial, military, or intellectual skills, which are vital to the society. While anyone can perform unskilled tasks only the talented can perform certain skilled ones; consequently, such tasks must earn higher material and prestige rewards than others; and often they also involve the exercise of greater power. The possession of greater wealth, prestige and power marks off a section of society as a class. Given this, and given the existence of the human family, class privileges will be inherited by one generation from another. But there will also be a certain amount of social mobility; those who are unsuccessful at performing the tasks required of them may lose their class position, while others with exceptional abilities may rise.

The critics of this view, who see in it an apology for the status quo, put forward the following counter-arguments. First, they show that stratification may actually hinder the efficient working of a social system by preventing those with superior, innate abilities from performing certain tasks which are the preserve of a privileged class. Second, they dispute the argument that some tasks are more vital or important to a society than others: the manager is no more vital than the manual labourer, for the one cannot operate without the other. Third, they question the need for large income differentials as a means of attracting men of talent to skilled occupations: they argue,

---

[94] *Marx and Engels: Basic Writings on Politics and Philosophy* 318 (L. Feuer ed., paperback ed. 1969).

*© 1968 by Percy S. Cohen, Basic Books, Inc., Publishers, New York.

in fact, that if occupations require special skills they will usually give more intrinsic satisfaction than those which do not, so that there should be less need to offer higher rewards, not more. Fourth, they cast doubt on the implicit assumption that actual differentials of reward do reflect differences in the skills required for particular occupations: for example, if a surgeon earns twenty times more than a coal-miner, does this mean that the surgeon's skills are twenty times greater or more valuable to society than those of the miner? The final criticism is that a society without social classes is, in principle, possible if it possesses a value-system which encourages a commitment to equality and public service. Such a society may never exist; but this would be more a consequence of existing stratification than of the requirements of a complex society; for the inheritance of privilege, which is the greatest determinant of class position, also ensures its own continuity.

These criticisms appear unanswerable. But this only means that they are true statements, not that they constitute a refutation of the functionalist theory. For it is at least arguable that the two theories are not really incompatible, since they really answer different questions. Davis and Moore, and Parsons, set out to explain why social stratification must exist in all contemporary complex societies, even if they have no history of stratification, and now have an egalitarian ideology. They assume that the division of labour produces inequality of reward, so that even if the present structures of social class were abolished, there would still be inequalities of occupational status to replace the old class structure. The second part of their answer is that without such inequalities of reward there would be no way of ensuring the continuity of a complex division of labour.

The opposing theory is really an answer to the question: why do social classes perpetuate themselves? The answer given is that such perpetuation may have nothing to do with the so-called "needs of society," but may lie within the structure of privilege and of the family. Put in this form the two theories are compatible, for they answer different questions.

R. DAHRENDORF, ON THE ORIGIN OF INEQUALITY AMONG MEN

in R. Dahrendorf (ed.), *Essays in the Theory of Society* 167-69 (1968)*

Human society always means that people's behavior is being removed from the randomness of chance and regulated by established and inescapable expectations. The compulsory character of these expectations or norms is based on the operation of sanctions, i.e. of rewards or punishments for conformist or deviant behavior. If every society is in this sense a moral community, it follows that there must always be at least that inequality of rank which results from the necessity of sanctioning behavior according to whether it does or does not conform to established norms. Under whatever aspect given historical societies may introduce additional distinctions

---

*Reprinted by permission of Stanford University Press.

between their members, whatever symbols they may declare to be the outward signs of inequality, and whatever may be the precise content of their social norms, the hard core of social inequality can always be found in the fact that men as the incumbents of social roles are subject, according to how their roles relate to the dominant expectational principles of society, to sanctions designed to enforce these principles. . . .

. . . Since every society discriminates in this sense against certain positions (and thereby all their incumbents, actual and potential), and since, moreover every society uses sanctions to make such discriminations effective, social norms and sanctions are the basis not only of ephemeral individual rankings but also of lasting structures of social positions.

The origin of inequality is thus to be found in the existence in all human societies of norms of behavior to which sanctions are attached. What we normally call law, i.e. the system of laws and penalties, does not in ordinary usage comprise the whole range of the sociological notions of norm and sanction. If, however, we take the law in its broadest sense as the epitome of all norms and sanctions, including those not codified, we may say that the law is both a necessary and a sufficient condition of social inequality. There is inequality because there is law; if there is law, there must also be inequality among men.

The stylistic parallel between Dahrendorf's last comment about inequality and Bentham's comment about property is perhaps not accidental. Property, after all, is a power of command over persons, as Marx and others before and since have remarked. Furthermore, the power that comes from property — from law — itself can be translated into power over other relationships, including the state. A contemporary Brazilian writer states the point with vigor:

> There is no doubt . . . that control of the State, and, through it, of the other sectors of both the dominant and dominated classes of the society, is the most perfect form for advancing the interests of large-scale capitalism. The repressive apparatus — bureaucratic, juridical and legislative — at the State's disposal is the only instrument capable of guaranteeing and promoting the transformations that maintain the control of large-scale capitalism over the society.[95]

Thus the influence of law, which we saw to be circular in defining issues of inequality, is also circular in creating and maintaining inequality. There is no way out of this situation. A legal right is a power position, and power in a social system includes the power to formulate the rules for the system's future distributions of power. This fact of social life is by no means limited to capitalist power or capitalist systems: the exercise of power is implicit in an industrial society, or indeed in any complex society.

---

[95] Dos Santos, "El Nuevo Carácter de la Dependencia," in *Dos Santos, et al., La Crisis del Desarrollismo y la Nueva Dependencia* at 11, 84 (1969).

R. ARON, PROGRESS AND DISILLUSION: THE DIALECTICS
OF MODERN SOCIETY

Pp. 146 (Pelican ed. 1972)*

Looking back, it is somewhat surprising to find that superior minds pinned their hopes on what were called structural reforms but actually were but juridical regulations controlling the means of production. Why should ownership laws determine the organization of work, the conditions of workers, the level of pay? During the initial stages of modernization, the myth had some relationship to necessary or desirable social changes. If a part of the land in vast agricultural holdings is not cultivated or is badly cultivated, if the owners of land or factories use their profits — which represent a substantial percentage of the national product — for conspicuous spending on luxuries and prestige, a revolt against rights acquires historic significance as well as economic effectiveness. Even in an industrialized country, laws regulating ownership still have ideological significance, because they influence the selection of heads of enterprises and the relationship between the order of production and that of commerce. But, clearly, no property laws can do away with submission to a rational discipline which entails the domination of one man by another, as well as the administration of things.

We shall return to some of the issues raised by Professor Aron in this very suggestive paragraph. Just now, we summarize some key points in the discussion thus far: (1) Any society regulates its members' behavior through a system of norms and sanctions, that is, law. (2) A complex society requires the discipline of command. (3) For both of the preceding reasons, some degree of social inequality is inevitable. (4) Since law implies power relations, law implies inequality; inequality equally implies law. (5) Law *is* power; law *creates* and *destroys* power; law *legitimizes* power — and in each of those overlapping statements, "inequality" may be substituted for "power."

---

3. Inequality and Latin American Development

"Latin America" is an inconveniently large unit for the analysis of issues of inequality. Not only are there great country-to-country differences in social stratification and mobility; there are also enormous differences between, for example, the rural and urban populations; and even those differences are further complicated by the phenomenon of urbanization — the shift of populations to the cities — which is itself a reflection of social as well as geographical mobility. Inequality means one thing in a São Paulo factory, and quite another thing in a classical hacienda in highland Ecuador. Those differences are not only *reflected* in law; they *are* law, as well.

The example of the hacienda is chosen to typify the tradition, at least as old as the Conquest, of the "dual" society, in which virtually all significant lines of division coincide. This Latin American tradition, imported from Spain and Portugal, begins in the techniques of subordination of the indigenous peoples. Many were slaughtered or driven to remote areas, North-American style, and millions died of diseases imported from Europe. But large indigenous populations survived, to become either formally or functionally enslaved. This dual system's lower stratum was not limited to the indigenous population; whites and mestizos were admitted, as were blacks brought in slavery from Africa. As you read the following extract from the Steins' book, consider the role of law in the process they describe.

S. STEIN AND B. STEIN, THE COLONIAL HERITAGE OF LATIN AMERICA: ESSAYS ON ECONOMIC DEPENDENCE IN PERSPECTIVE

Pp. 57-58, 66, 70, 72-75, 80-81 (1970)*

A superficial comparison of Iberian and Ibero-American society about 1700 suggests that Iberians had managed to reproduce in the Mexican and Andean highlands and along the coast of Brazil a replica, or what passed for a replica, of their Old World society: a two-class or two-stratum social structure — an elite of landowners, miners, high bureaucrats, and churchmen, a mass of rural dwellers in Amerindian communities or on haciendas or tropical plantations, and between these two strata a small group of merchants, bureaucrats, minor ecclesiastics. In other words, . . . there existed a social structure typical of an agrarian, pre-industrial, or underdeveloped economy. . . .

It was probably in the seventeenth century that the large landowner emerged in America as the dominant figure of both the colonial society and economy. Landowners (and miners) appeared as quasi-seigneurs, with their own chaplains, their own jails, their own stocks and whips for the deviants under their control, and their own police forces. Yet the New World seigneurs also provided their own form of security for the obedient: subsistence, protection, and social stability. . . .

In practice, the colonial administration, from the ministers of the Council of the Indies and the Board of Trade in the metropolis [Spain and Portugal] to the viceroys, the judges of the viceregal courts *(audiencias),* and the local administrators such as corregidores and their subordinates in the so-called Indian "republics," was a vast system of patronage in which peninsulares [those born in Spain or Portugal] and criollos [born in America] participated. . . .

. . . In theory omnipotent, in practice viceregal authority was somewhat fictitious. It was hedged about by countervailing forces: the audiencia, judicial review of the viceroy's performance at the end of his tenure *(residencia),* and the influence of

---

*Copyright © 1970 by Oxford University Press, Inc. Abridged and used by permission of the authors and the publisher.

corporative bodies with special jurisdiction, such as the ecclesiastical establishment and the merchant guild whose interests the viceroy could not lightly override however respectful the tone in which their demands were phrased. . . .

. . . Whereas in the sixteenth century viceroys were capable grandees [noblemen], in the seventeenth the grandees sought colonial service for the opportunity to create fortunes for themselves, the members of their extended families, and their clients. Instead of imposing solutions, one senses that they strove for consensus among conflicting groups on the basis of bribery not of equity. In this fashion powerful colonial interests in effect manipulated viceroys who found in colonial office economic opportunities lacking in the metropolis. . . .

. . . Venality and corruption became generalized, institutionalized, and legitimized as employment in the colonial bureaucracy became a major source of status and income for the Spanish aristocracy and gentry, their extended circles of relatives, clients, and dependents, and for the sons of the middle class who were able to attend the metropolitan law schools. The interaction of legally sanctioned monopoly and of private interest inevitably produced an atmosphere in which corruption was tolerated and aggressive individualism was concealed or disguised by the apparent functional corporative nature of society. In the context of a society based upon scholastic natural law, liberty was exercised within the corporate body. Those involved in the administration of the colonies found its principles and practice anything but oppressive. And where colonial legislation conflicted with local interest, it could always be suspended or ignored as suggested by the often utilized formula "to be obeyed but not executed." . . .

Thus by about 1700 the characteristic features of the colonial policy were already well established. Public office at all levels was seen as a legitimate instrument to further private interests over public weal. A monarchy extorting a share of a viceroy's spoils of office symbolized, indeed legitimized, venality, encouraged corruption and showed itself demonstrably incapable of controlling malfeasance in office. It is an ironic commentary on the effects of colonial rule that the very term "cacique" — originally applied to Amerinds who served the colonial elite to exploit the Amerindian masses — was to become in Spain the term for a local boss. Furthermore, the local colonial government of town officials, corregidores, and priests emerged as the core of political power that fused the interests of [the] local elite of wealth, power, and prestige. It was expected that the colonial civil service armed with broad discretionary powers would work closely with local interests to enforce the *status quo* by manipulating the colonial law code. To the elite, law became a norm honored in the breach. To the unprivileged, law was arbitrary and alien, therefore without moral force.

———————————

It is precisely this common colonial heritage that is the main justification for treating Latin America as a whole for purposes of discussing the interrelation of law and development. For while the "dual" qualities of society have given way in many areas (geographical and otherwise) of Latin American life, two features of the colonial period have made lasting marks on all Latin American society: (a) the tradition of patronage/personalism/discretion/monopoly privilege — in short, the corporative tradition; and (b) the tradition of disrespect for law/corruption/bossism. In colonial Latin America, these two clusters of social phenomena went hand in glove; they still do. Once a system of monopoly privilege and patronage is installed, it is hard to persuade people to trust the competing system of law-as-principles. Even the functionaries of the legal system find it hard to confide in their own system's ability to function in accordance with the written law. Privilege feeds corruption, which in turn feeds privilege. In such a system, inequality is heightened, for the rich can buy what they need, including all manner of official permissions.

The result for development planning is disastrous. Gunnar Myrdal's argument,[96] based mainly on his experience in South Asia, is largely transferable to Latin America: (a) Governments seek to control private business with a plethora of discretionary administrative controls; almost no important business decision can be taken without some state approval. (b) Heavy positive inducements are given for certain kinds of investment: cheap exchange rates, protection from competition, low interest rates, low prices for public-sector services, tax incentives. (c) Such inducements are so generous for their recipients that they cannot be given out according to general rules, but must be awarded on a discretionary basis; thus there must be a huge "paraphernalia of negative controls" to keep other businesses from entering the area of privilege. Myrdal comments, "This is like driving a car with the accelerator pushed to the floor but with the brakes on."[97] (d) The established and large-scale businesses are in a strategic position to be given these permissions and inducements; monopoly is thus encouraged. (e) The officials who run this system have a vested interest in keeping it in operation: first, the system gives them power; secondly, it gives them wealth:

> Particularly in a setting where caste, family, economic and social status, and, more generally, "connections" mean so much, collusion between business and officialdom becomes a natural tendency. The result is often corrupt. The corrupt then get a vested interest in the system.[98]

Several oft-cited Latin American writers have, over the past decade, developed a theory that might have been called "the new dualism," but in fact has come to be called the theory of "dependency." These writers view Latin American society as part of a polarized international system, dominated by large-scale monopoly capital, which system integrates Latin America into the international economy at the cost of national disintegration and dependency. The dependency in question runs not only from the dependent countries to the dominant (North American and European) countries, but also within a given Latin American country, from the "marginalized" sectors (those who are not associated with the great international corporations) to the dominant sectors (the corporations' proconsuls, including the national governments). In such a system, industrialization does not serve the ends of national development, but the ends

---

[96] See note 16 *supra.* See also G. Myrdal, *The Challenge of World Poverty: a World Anti-poverty Programme in Outline* 225-29 (Pelican ed. 1971).

[97] *Id.* at 226.

[98] *Id.* at 229.

of international monopoly capital and their local-elite representatives. Investment is capital-intensive, so that it provides a minimum of employment. Production is geared toward consumers' goods, even luxuries. Incomes and power within the dependent countries tend toward ever greater concentration.

The literature of dependency is much in vogue, and growing.[99] But the idea of dependency is in the main a new perspective on some very old problems. The Steins' book on colonial Latin America bears a subtitle that emphasizes "economic dependence." What the dependency writers are mainly pointing out is that patterns of domination established long ago in Latin America have been adapted to the world of automated production lines. Here are two examples from this literature that point up the tenacity of systems of patronage and privilege:

> The industrial revolution, from the second half of the 19th century to the great depression of the 1930s, permitted a growing demand for Latin American products, while the region was able to continue importing from Europe, at relatively low prices, manufactured consumers' goods. The enormous riches produced — in which the plantations, the great haciendas and the mines could offer raw materials in exchange for which the elites could obtain their luxury articles, and even provide most of the ordinary necessities of the masses — assured the system great stability, keeping the rural masses under the complete domination of the landholding oligarchy. So long as the system continued expanding, the emergence and growth of the urban middle class could easily be co-opted through a clientelist policy, by means of the "cartorial" state, which could offer to the middle class public employment, more or less idle, in exchange for political support and good social conduct.[100]

> The old clientelist electoral system, that ruled in the countryside in the 19th century and at the beginning of the 20th century, was transferred to the cities, contaminating the new forms of political action. In its own way, populism reproduced these old clientelist operations, in a compromise between urban mass techniques and traditional personalist techniques.[101]

The ability of the tradition of patronage to survive even a populist revolution is demonstrated by the agrarian establishment in Mexico, which we saw in operation in chapter III.

Two points deserve to be noted, to round out these references to the "dependency" writers. *First,* the problem of "restraining the cadres" — keeping leadership groups from consuming too much, and directing a national economy for their own advantage — is a serious problem for every developing country, whether capitalist or

---

[99] A leading article is Sunkel, "Capitalismo Transnacional y Desintegración Nacional en la América Latina," *El Trimestre Económico,* Apr.-Jun. 1971, pp. 571-628. See also the essays collected in Dos Santos, et al., note 95 *supra;* and H. Jaguaribe, et al., *La Dependencia Político-Económica de América Latina* 1970).

[100] Jaguaribe, "Causas del Subdesarrollo Latinoamericano," in *Dos Santos, et al.,* note 95 *supra,* at 201, 210-11.

[101] Dos Santos, "La Crisis de la Teoría del Desarrollo y las Relaciones de Dependencia en América Latina," in Jaguaribe, et al., note 99 *supra,* at 147, 169.

not. *Secondly,* the "urban" or "modernizing" or "transitional" sectors of Latin American society (a) are not so much characterized by dualism as by hierarchy, and (b) offer considerable individual social mobility. We limit our exploration of the first of these points to the following extract from I. Wallerstein's paper.

I. WALLERSTEIN, THE STATE AND SOCIAL TRANSFORMATION

1 *Politics and Society* 359, 362 (1971),
in H. Bernstein (ed.), *Underdevelopment and Development*
277, 280-81 (1973)

The most difficult aspect of limiting consumption by internal cadres is that a regime in power, whatever its ideological self-assessment, is by definition composed of a section of the cadres. Its interests are, to a very large extent, linked with the interests of the cadres as a stratum. Furthermore, its strength, at least in part, is dependent on the support of these cadres.

It can, of course, use physical force up to a point to control these cadres. This technique works for a while. A regime can rely on police force to hold the cadres in line, though this has all the disadvantages the Communist Party of the Soviet Union recognized at its Twentieth Party Congress and since. Or a regime can utilize an upsurge of working-class elements to control the cadres, as in the "cultural revolution" in China. This method, too, has its built-in limitations, as recent attempts made by the Chinese political leaders to curb the excesses of the Red Guards and give more order to the political process have indicated. The use of force against its cadres by a weak regime may lead simply and directly to its overthrow, as has been the case in a number of African states in the post-Independence period.

The regime can also use ideology to keep its cadre in line. Any ideological appeal to self-restraint in consumption by cadres will of course accomplish the end desired, provided the ideological pressure is firm and unremitting but not inflexible. Weber and others have described how Calvinism was thus used in the seventeenth century. But ideological pressure only works as long as faith persists, and the persistence of faith is itself a function of a certain degree of success combined with a certain tension due to ideological opposition plus the existence of a professional body of ideologists – usually, in modern times, within the framework of an ideological party.

Given the limitations of force and ideology to control the cadres, it is no surprise that the regime will fall back on rewards of money, status and power, including the offer of both security and perpetuity of reward. But as this happens, the surplus begins to be consumed by these very cadres; the revolution risks being "betrayed," unless rewards of this kind can be limited.

Our second footnote to the discussion of "dependency" is that Latin America is a "dual" society mainly in its backward rural sectors, where mobility is low. Elsewhere, "dualism" is a misleading oversimplification – as is shown by the condition of the residents of the Caracas barrios – and mobility is rather high. Given high individual mobility, there is little potential for major pressure for radical structural change. Correspondingly, where individual mobility is low, then for an individual to advance, a whole group must be upwardly mobile. It is not surprising that the major pressures for structural change (as distinguished from, say, government's replacing private ownership as the manager of industry) have tended to come in the rural sectors.

---

4. "Substantive" and "Legal" Equality

We introduce our final theme with yet another quotation from the literature of dependency. Speaking of the liberal ideologies of the 19th century, Tomás Vasconi says:

> "Free navigation of the rivers" and "free trade" were the chief instruments of subordination to the system of international domination; "private property" and "freedom to work," the ideological justifications for the exploitation of subordinate groups by the dominant class; "constitutionalism," the "liberal state," "parliament," the political instruments of social domination.[102]

Once again, this is not so much a new interpretation of 19th century history as it is a contemporary echo of 19th century thought. Marx frequently made the same point, often in similarly dramatic fashion. Weber particularized the inquiry, identifying two quite different meanings of the idea of equality: "legal" and "substantive" equality.

MAX WEBER ON LAW IN ECONOMY AND SOCIETY

Pp. 145-46, 355-56 (M. Rheinstein, ed. 1954)*

The ever-increasing integration of all individuals and all fact-situations into one compulsory institution which today, at least, rests in principle on formal "legal equality" has been achieved by two great rationalizing forces, i.e., first, by the extension of the market economy and, second, by the bureaucratization of the activities of the organs of consensual communities. They replaced that particularist mode of creating law which was based upon private power or the privilege granted to monopolistically closed organizations, in which we have recognized the autonomy of associations of a primarily corporate-status nature. This replacement was effected by two arrangements: The first is the formal, universally accessible, closely limited, and

---

[102] Vasconi, "Cultura, Ideología, Dependencia y Alienación," in Dos Santos, et al., note 95 *supra,* at 134, 149.

*Copyright 1954 by Harvard University Press. Reprinted by permission of the publisher.

legally regulated autonomy of association which may be created by anyone wishing to do so; the other consists in the grant to everyone of the power to create law of his own by means of engaging in private legal transactions of certain kinds. The decisive factors in this transformation of the technical forms of autonomous legislation were, politically, the power-needs of the rulers and officials of the state as it was growing in strength and, economically, the interests of those segments of society that were oriented towards power in the market, i.e., those individuals who are economically privileged in the formally free competitive struggle of the market by virtue of their class-position as property owners. If, by virtue of the principle of formal legal equality, everyone "without respect of person" may establish a business corporation or a trust fund, the propertied classes as such have a sort of factual "autonomy," since they alone are able to utilize or take advantage of these powers. . . .

[T]he attitude of every democratic movenent . . . aiming at the minimization of "authority" must necessarily be ambiguous. The demands for "legal equality" and of guaranties against arbitrariness require formal rational objectivity in administration in contrast to personal free choice on the basis of grace, as characterized the older type of patrimonial authority. The democratic ethos, where it pervades the masses in connection with a concrete question, based as it is on the postulate of substantive justice in concrete cases for concrete individuals, inevitably comes into conflict with the formalism and the rule-bound, detached objectivity of bureaucratic administration. For this reason it must emotionally reject what is rationally demanded. The propertyless classes in particular are not served, in the way in which bourgeois are, by formal "legal equality" and "calculable" adjudication and administration. The propertyless demand that law and administration serve the equalization of economic and social opportunities vis-a-vis the propertied classes, and judges or administrators cannot perform this function unless they assume the substantively ethical and hence non-formalistic character of the Khadi. [Weber used the phrase "Khadi justice" to refer to the dispensing of justice, not according to rule, but according to the expediential demands of some external postulates, such as ethics, or religion, or politics. The Khadi was a judge of a particular Mohammedan court. – Eds.]

Equality before the law, and particularly the "legal equality" that assures free access to a market, is, in one view, anti-authoritarian. Such "legal equality" does reduce one form of coercion, that which emanates from the patrimonial leader or the modern state. But, as Weber saw, "it is also obvious how advantageous this state of affairs is to those who are economically in the position to make use of the empowerments. . . . [In such a private economy,] coercion is exercised to a considerable extent by the private owners of the means of production and acquisition, to whom the law guarantees their property and whose power can thus manifest itself in the competitive struggle of the market."[103]

---

[103] *Weber* 189.

One unhappy Latin American illustration of the foregoing abstractions is to be found in the post-Independence legislation that conferred formal equality on the indigenous populations:

> Indians would now be able to divide their communally owned lands and to dispose of them at will; they would have no special taxes or courts; in theory they would participate as citizens with full political rights and responsibilities. No longer would there be Indians and non-Indians, but only rich and poor. Laudable objectives, but to Indian communities this equality threatened the mechanisms that protected them against the skills of those better prepared for the competitive individualism of a Liberal economy and polity. Those reared in the tradition of "enclave" politics were ill-prepared for juridical equality. Amerinds who abandoned their communities were incorporated as wage laborers; as illiterates and domestics, they were conveniently disenfranchised by the new constitutions. Those who remained in their communities sought protection in further isolation, or reacted in hopeless revolt. In Mexico and Peru intermittent criollo-Indian warfare continued throughout the nineteenth century. Here and elsewhere the rural masses sought redress by supporting local magnates, usually landlords – the caciques or caudillos – who promised protection against the central government in return for local allegiance and fidelity.[104]

Formal legal equality is thus consistent with a system of patronage, just as it is consistent with the universalist principles of the market; under either system, it is – to say the very least – consistent with substantive inequality of an extreme degree.

Still, it would be a great mistake to assume that legal equality is either meaningless or pernicious. Complete substantive equality is an illusory goal in human society, for the reasons we have seen. The question at any given time and place must be, not whether full equality can be attained, but what kinds of inequality are acceptable, in view of prevailing social values. The phrase, "at any given time and place," is a critical qualification to any discussion of inequality, for the kinds of disparities that are acceptable will vary according to the society's levels of wealth and its developmental goals. (As to the latter point, compare the inequalities of industrialization in the United States of the late 19th and early 20th centuries with the inequalities of Soviet industrialization under Stalin.) Given the inevitability of substantive inequality – and a particularly high degree of inequality in a developing society – legal equality has a critical psychological role to play in making tolerable the lot of the disadvantaged. Once a person's subsistence needs are satisfied, all deprivation is "relative deprivation." If the decision is made to set a "social minimum"[105] at some point above the subsistence level, the reason is largely psychic: to make the poor more contented. (Or, more to the point, perhaps, to make them less discontented and therefore less

---

[104] Stein and Stein, note 17 *supra*, at 162.

[105] See the discussions of "relative deprivation" and "social minimum" in Michelman, "On Protecting the Poor Through the Fourteenth Amendment," 83 *Harv. L. Rev.* 7 (1969).

threatening.) The harm of inequality is above all a harm to human dignity. Here is Edward Banfield again, speaking of Southern Italian peasants:

> What makes the difference between a low level of living and *la miseria* comes from culture. Unlike the primitive, the peasant feels himself part of a larger society which he is "in" but not altogether "of." He lives in a culture in which it is very important to be admired, and he sees that by its standards he cannot be admired in the least; by these standards he and everything about him are contemptible or ridiculous. Knowing this, he is filled with loathing for his lot and with anger for the fates which assigned him to it. . . .
>
> By the standards of the larger society, the peasant's work, food and clothing all symbolize his degradation. . . . What the peasant lacks is not opportunity for recreation, but opportunity for those particular kinds of recreation — having coffee in the bar in the public square, for example — which are *civile* and which would therefore identify them as persons entitled to respect and admiration.[106]

What appears to be so-called "peasant fatalism" may thus be a lack of self-confidence, produced in considerable measure by the degradations of a particular social system's forms of inequality.[107] Myrdal's argument that low levels of living impair productivity[108] thus may be valid in a way he has not suggested, and at levels of living that are well above those he describes; a reformulation of his argument would emphasize the demoralizing effects of inequality.

At several points in this chapter we have emphasized the importance of the law's influence on the way men and women perceive themselves. The subjects of security and community are scarcely intelligible apart from such questions of self-perception. Repetition of the point here emphasizes that all of the themes of this chapter are intertwined in a single social system. Issues are not circular, but spherical; sorting them out for analysis, however necessary it may be, imperils the kind of understanding that comes from hearing a whole symphony or taking in the sounds and the "atmosphere" in a village. Issues of inequality pervade the problems of security, legitimacy and community; law, in turn, stands in relation to each of these themes both as effect and as cause.

Questions

1. Do the various legislative and judicial mechanisms devised to protect creditors against the effects of inflation represent class legislation? Consider the question of monetary adjustment through the eyes of the victim of a railroad accident, who is awarded a lifetime pension. What is *class* legislation?

---

[106] Banfield, note 52 *supra,* at 63-65.

[107] See Ortiz, "Reflections on the Concept of 'Peasant Culture' and 'Peasant Cognitive Systems,'" in T. Shanin (ed.), *Peasants and Peasant Societies* 322, 327-28 (1971).

[108] See p. 692, *supra.*

2. We saw that the residents of the Caracas barrios are rather "middle-class" in their outlook. Is law one of the causes of such attitudes? What law?

3. Is the amparo, or the writ of security, expressive of Weber's "legal equality"? Is a guarantee of judicial protection against state arbitrariness consistent with demands for "substantive equality"?

4. If law legitimizes power, it legitimizes inequality. Are there any circumstances in which legitimacy depends on the idea of equality? Weber says that "legal domination" implies that the persons exercising power and those subject to their commands are legal equals. May "charismatic domination" also rest on notions of equality? (Recall Morse's suggestion that a "legitimate revolution" demands charismatic leadership in the style of Perón or Castro.)

5. What does Aron mean by his reference to "a revolt against rights"?[109] Engels spoke in similar terms, saying that "the abolition of feudal inequality" led to a bourgeois "equality of rights" (what Weber called "legal equality"), while "the proletarian demand for equality has arisen as the reaction against the bourgeois demand for equality."[110] Is a land reform a reaction against "bourgeois equality"? Is it, as Aron suggests, a revolt against rights? Consider (a) a land reform based on the theory of restitution, or (b) a land reform which distributes legal titles to beneficiaries, as in Bolivia or Venezuela.

6. Inequality has, historically, been a major source of social conflict. May inequality also promote a sense of community? Consider these two comments by an anthropologist who has worked extensively in India:

> That is the essential "function" of hierarchy: it expresses the unity of such a society while connecting it to what appears to it to be universal, namely a conception of the cosmic order, whether or not it includes a God, or a king as mediator. If one likes, hierarchy integrates the society by reference to its values. . . .
>
> Talcott Parsons draws attention . . . to the fact that the distinction of statuses carries with it and supposes equality within each status. Conversely, where equality is affirmed, it is within a group which is hierarchized in relation to others. . . . It is this structural relation that the equalitarian ideal tends to destroy. . . . [E]quality contains inequalities instead of being contained in a hierarchy.[111]

7. Low-level governmental corruption in Latin America has been flippantly called "the democratization of theft" — a way of spreading the financial benefits of power over a large number of functionaries, instead of concentrating them at the apex of the pyramid of privilege. In what sense is corruption the mortal enemy of the process of creating a greater equality in Latin American society?

---

[109] P. 699, *supra.*

[110] Marx and Engels, note 94 *supra,* at 317-18.

[111] Dumont, "Caste, Racism and 'Stratification': Reflections of a Social Anthropologist," in A. Beteille (ed.), *Social Inequality* 337, 354, 360 (1969).

8. Are all of Weber's types of legitimacy ("legal," "charismatic" and "traditional" domination) impaired by governmental corruption? Does the kind of corruption, or the level at which it occurs, matter?

These last two questions are fragments of a larger question, repeatedly raised in this book: To what extent does law's contribution to development rest on the widespread diffusion of respect for law? One cannot discuss the subject of inequality in Latin America without touching the issue of corruption. Nor are the questions of security, legitimacy and community understandable apart from the question of respect for legal institutions. No Latin American ever makes the mistake of ignoring the implications of this larger question. We close with a quotation — in translation, but also in Spanish, because translation wrings out its flavor — from Gabriel García Márquez's story, *La Increíble y Triste Historia de la Cándida Eréndida y Su Abuela Desalmada* (1972). A young girl has been sequestered by a group of missionaries, because her grandmother has been making a handsome profit from the girl's short-term rental. The passage speaks to exploitation and to insecurity, to the problem of community and the problem of legitimacy — in short, to the major themes of this chapter and this book:

The grandmother left no measure untried in attempting to deliver her granddaughter from the custody of the missionaries. Only when all her efforts failed, from the most straightforward to the most devious, did she resort to the civil authority — which was wielded by a military man.

[No hubo un recurso que la abuela no intentara para rescatar a la nieta de la tutela de los misioneros. Sólo cuando le fallaron todos, desde los más derechos hasta los más torcidos, recurrió a la autoridad civil, que era ejercida por un militar.]

APPENDIX A

BRAZIL: STATUTE REGULATING THE WRIT OF SECURITY

Law No. 1.533 of December 31, 1951

The President of the Republic:

I announce that the National Congress decrees and I sanction the following law:

Article 1. The writ of security shall be granted to protect a clear and certain right, not protected by habeas corpus, whenever anyone suffers a violation thereof, or there is a just apprehension of suffering such violation, [through] illegality or abuse of power on the part of an authority. . . .

§ 1. For the effects of this law, administrators or representatives of autarchic entities, and individuals or legal entities with functions delegated by the public power, shall be considered authorities only to the extent of these functions.

§ 2. When the right threatened or violated is that of several persons, any of them may request a writ of security. . . .

Article 4. In case of urgency one may, observing the requirements of this law, bring an action for a writ of security by telegram or radiogram to the proper judge, who may determine that the coercive authority be notified in the same way.

Article 5. The writ of security shall not be granted whenever the case concerns:

I. An act from which an administrative appeal with suspensive effect may be taken without a supersedeas bond;

II. A court order or judicial decision when an appeal has been provided for in the laws of procedure or which may be modified by way of correction [a means of correcting procedural defects in court proceedings];

III. A disciplinary act, except when practiced by an incompetent authority or without observance of an essential formality. . . .

Article 6. The initial petition . . . shall be presented in duplicate, and the documents which support the first copy shall be reproduced in the second copy.

Sole paragraph. In case a document necessary to the proof of an allegation is in a public bureau or establishment, or in the power of an authority which refuses to furnish a certificate of it, the judge shall preliminarily order . . . the production of the original document, or an authentic copy, and shall set a period of ten days for fulfillment of the order. . . .*

Article 7. In acting upon the initial petition, the judge shall order:

I. That the coercive party be notified of the substance of the petition . . . so that

---

*As amended by Law No. 4.166 of December 4, 1962.

**As amended by Law No. 4.348 of June 26, 1964.

within a period of ten days** the coercing party may render information which it deems necessary;

II. That the act which motivated the petition (when relevant to its basic theory) be suspended if the . . . [failure to do so] may make the petition, if granted, ineffective.

Article 8. The initial petition shall be summarily rejected when it is not a case for the writ of security or any of the requisites of this law are lacking.

Sole paragraph. The appeal provided for in Article 12 shall lie from this summary dismissal. . . .

Article 10. At the end of the period referred to in subsection I of Article 7 and having heard the representative of the Public Ministry within 5 days, submissions shall be concluded before the judge, who, independently of a party's motion, shall render a decision within 5 days. . . .

Article 12. From the decision of the judge, denying or granting the writ, the appeal of *agravo de petição** shall lie, assuring the parties the right to oral argument before the proper court. . . .

Sole Paragraph. From a decision [on appeal] granting the writ of security, the judge shall appeal, *ex officio,* without this appeal having a suspensive effect.

Article 13. When the writ is granted and the president of the Supreme Federal Tribunal, the Federal Tribunal of Appeals, or the Tribunal of Justice, orders the judge to suspend execution of the decision, an *agravo de petição* shall lie from this act to the court over which he presides. . . .

Article 16. The petition for the writ of security may be renewed if the decision denying it was not made on the merits.

Article 17. Writ of security proceedings shall have priority over all judicial acts except for habeas corpus. They shall be brought to judgment on appeal in the first session which follows the date on which . . . the reporter has finished the transcript.

Sole Paragraph. The period for [arriving at] the conclusion may not exceed 24 hours, starting from the distribution [i.e., the date the reporting judge receives the case.]

Article 18. The right to request the writ of security expires 120 days from the time the interested party has knowledge of the challenged act. . . .

GETÚLIO VARGAS
Francisco Negrão de Lima

---

*A type of appeal normally taken from a decision which does not determine the merits of a case. This appeal normally has no suspensive effect, though the presidents of the Supreme Federal Tribunal or the Tribunal of Justice can order suspension of execution of the judgment pending appeal. A Wald, *Do Mandado de Segurança na Prática Judiciária* 91 (3d ed. 1968). [Eds.]

APPENDIX B

MEXICO: CONSTITUTION OF 1917 (AS AMENDED, 1968)

Article 107. All controversies mentioned in Article 103 shall follow the legal forms and procedures prescribed by law, in accordance with the following bases:

I. A trial in amparo shall always be granted upon the request of the aggrieved party.

II. The judgment shall only affect private individuals, being limited to according them the relief and protection pleaded for in the particular case, without making any general declaration as to the law or act on which the complaint is based.

A defect in the complaint may be corrected whenever the act complained of is based on laws declared unconstitutional by the case law rule *(jurisprudencia)* of the Supreme Court of Justice.

A defect in the complaint may also be corrected in criminal matters, and in behalf of workers in labor disputes, when there has been an obvious violation of the law against the injured party, who has been left without defense; and in criminal matters, likewise, when the trial has been based on a law not directly applicable to the case.

In amparo proceedings complaining about acts that have or could have the effect of depriving *ejidos,** [indigenous] communities (either *de facto* or *de jure*), or members of an *ejido* or community of title, possession, or the fruits of lands, waters, pastures, and forests, any defect in the complaint must be corrected in accordance with the Regulatory Law of Articles 103 and 107 of this Constitution. In no case shall the claim lapse or fail for procedural inactivity. Nor shall an abandonment be declared when the rights of the *ejidos* or communities are affected.

III. When the complaint is against acts by judicial, administrative, or labor tribunals, the writ of amparo shall be granted only in the following cases:

a) Against final judgments or awards which cannot be modified or revised on ordinary appeal . . . provided that in civil matters, timely objection was made during the course of the trial, and that the issue was preserved on appeal. This requirement will be waived when the amparo is against judgments entered in controversies over civil status, or which affect the order and stability of the family.

b) Against acts which occur during trial which, if allowed to stand, will produce irreparable harm, either out of court or after the conclusion of the trial, provided all available recourses have been exhausted.

c) Against acts which affect persons not parties to the proceedings.

IV. In administrative matters amparo will lie against decisions which cause an injury that cannot be remedied through any appeal, trial, or means of legal defense. It shall not be necessary to exhaust these remedies when their requirements to suspend the contested act are greater than the Regulatory Law for Trials in Amparo.

---

*Village communities to which land has been granted in the Mexican land reform. See Chapter III, at pp. 375-83.

V. A writ of amparo against final judgments or awards, whether the violation [complained of] occurred during the trial or in the judgment itself, shall be applied for directly to the Supreme Court of Justice, [in the following cases:]

a) In criminal matters against final decisions rendered by Federal Judicial Courts, including military courts; if the judicial authorities are the ordinary courts, when the judgments which motivate the filing of the writ of amparo impose the death sentence, or a prison sentence which exceeds the limitation set out in Section 1 of article 20 of this Constitution granting freedom on bond [five years].

b) In administrative matters, when private parties complain of final judgments of Federal, Administrative or Judicial Courts, which cannot be remedied by any appeal, trial or ordinary legal means of defense, within the appellate jurisdictional limitations.

c) In civil matters, when the complaint is against final judgments given in federal or commercial trials, whether the authority rendering the decision is federal or local, or in ordinary actions, within the jurisdictional limitations set out by the law. Amparo against judgments rendered in controversies over civil status, or that affect the order and stability of the family shall be granted only by the Supreme Court.

In federal civil proceedings, any of the parties, including the Federation, in the protection of its patrimonial interests, may invoke amparo against the judgment.

d) In labor matters, when the complaint is against the awards given by federal Central Conciliation and Arbitration Boards in collective disputes; by federal authorities of Conciliation and Arbitration in any conflict, or by The Federal Tribunal of Arbitration and Conciliation of State Workers.

VI. Except for the cases provided for in the preceding section, amparo against final judgments or awards, whether the violation occurred during the proceedings or in the judgment itself, shall be appealed directly to the Collegiate Circuit Court (Tribunal Colegiado de Circuito) of the same jurisdiction as the authority which rendered the judgment or award.

In cases referred to in this section, and in the preceding one, the Regulatory Law for Actions in Amparo will set out the procedure to be followed both by the Supreme Court of Justice and by the Collegiate Circuit Courts. . . .

VII. When a writ of amparo is sought against a law, acts of administrative authorities, or acts at the trial (either outside the trial or after its conclusion), or if persons not parties to the action are affected, application shall be made to the District Judge of the jurisdiction where the act in question was performed, or was to be performed. The procedure shall be limited to the report of the authority in question, and to a hearing for which notice shall be included in the order requesting the report and at which the interested parties shall present any evidence and allegations. The decision shall be rendered at the same hearing.

VIII. Judgments in amparo rendered by District Judges are subject to review. The Supreme Court of Justice will review such judgments in the following cases:

a) When a law is challenged as unconstitutional.

b) In cases encompassed within sections II and III of article 103 of this Constitution.

c) When the constitutionality of federal regulations issued by the President of the Republic under Article 89, Section I, of this Constitution is challenged.

d) When, in agrarian matters, the acts of any authority which affect the nuclei of *ejidos* or communities in their collective rights, or the "small property" [property exempt from taking for land reform purposes].

e) Whenever the responsible authority against whom administrative amparo is granted is federal, within the jurisdictional limitations prescribed by law.

f) Whenever, in criminal cases, the allegation is solely a violation of article 22 of this Constitution [dealing with cruel and unusual punishment, the death penalty, and imprisonment for debt].

In the cases not mentioned above, as well as writs of amparo invoked against acts of administrative authorities under Section VI, subsections 1 and 2 of article 73 of this Constitution, review shall be had in the Collegiate Circuit Courts. Their decisions may not be appealed.

IX. Decisions in direct amparo rendered by the Collegiate Circuit Courts may not be appealed unless the decision involved the unconstitutionality of a law, or established a direct interpretation of a provision of the Constitution, in which case it may be appealed to the Supreme Court of Justice, but review shall be limited exclusively to the adjudication of actual constitutional questions.

A decision of a Collegiate Circuit Court may not be appealed if it is based on a case law rule *(jurisprudencia)* established by the Supreme Court of Justice on the constitutionality of a law or on a direct interpretation of a provision of the Constitution.

X. Contested acts may be enjoined *(suspensión)* in those cases and under conditions and guarantees determined by law, taking into account the nature of the alleged violation, the difficulty of remedying the damages that the aggrieved party might suffer by its performance, damages that the injunction might cause to third parties, and the public interest.

Final judgments in criminal matters must be stayed upon notice of the application for a writ of amparo. In civil matters [such judgments must be stayed] when bond is posted by the complainant to cover liability for damages occasioned by the stay; however, this stay shall be ineffective if the other party posts countersecurity to ensure the restoration of things if amparo is granted, and to pay the ensuing damages.

XI. A stay shall be requested from the responsible authority in cases of direct amparo to the Supreme Court of Justice or to the Collegiate Circuit Courts. In each case the aggrieved party shall notify the responsible authority, within the period fixed by law and under oath to tell the truth, about the petition for amparo, filing two copies of the petition, one for the record and the other to be issued to the opposing party. In all other cases, decisions as to a stay shall be made by the District Courts.

XII. Violation of the guarantees set forth in article 16, and in articles 19 and 20 in criminal matters shall be complained about before the court superior to the one where the violation occurred, or before the appropriate District Judge, and in either case, the decision can be appealed according to the terms prescribed in section VIII.

If the District Judge does not reside in the same place as the responsible authority, the law shall specify the judge before whom the writ of amparo is to be presented, and that judge may provisionally stay the act in question, in those cases, and under the terms established in the same law.

XIII. When the Collegiate Circuit Courts take contradictory positions in amparo cases within their jurisdiction, either the ministers of the Supreme Court of Justice, the Attorney General of the Republic, the courts themselves, or the parties to the actions in which the positions were taken, may denounce the contradiction to the appropriate chamber [of the Supreme Court] to decide which position shall prevail.

If Chambers (Salas) of the Supreme Court of Justice sustain contradictory positions in amparo cases within their jurisdiction, any of these panels, the Attorney General, or the parties to the actions where those decisions were upheld, may challenge the inconsistency before the Supreme Court of Justice, which will decide *en banc* which position shall prevail.

The decision rendered by the Chambers, or the Supreme Court *en banc* in the cases referred to in the prior two paragraphs, shall have the sole effect of determining the case law rule, and shall not affect the specific juridical results in the judgments in the cases where the contradictions occurred.

XIV. Except as stated in the last paragraph of section II of this article, whenever the constitutionality of a law is in issue, when the contested act originated with civil or administrative authorities, proceedings will be discontinued by the inactivity of the aggrieved party according to the Regulatory Law. The discontinuance of the action in amparo shall render the judgment final.

XV. The Attorney General of the Republic, or an Agent of the Federal Public Ministry appointed for that purpose, shall be a party in all suits in amparo, but he may abstain from intervening if, in his opinion, the matter in question lacks public interest.

XVI. If after amparo is granted, the responsible official persists in repeating the contested act, or attempts to evade the decision of the federal authority, he shall be immediately removed from office and taken before the appropriate District Judge.

XVII. The responsible authority will be taken before the appropriate authority whenever he fails to suspend the act when bound to do so, and if he posts bond that is invalid or insufficient, in such cases the responsible authority and bondsman are jointly and severally liable.

XVIII. Bailiffs and jailers who do not receive an authorized copy of the order of imprisonment of an arrested person within the seventy-two hours prescribed by article 19, counted from the day the party was at the disposal of the judge, must notify the judge of this fact at the end of such period, and if the order is not received within three hours, the prisoner shall be released.

Anyone violating the article cited in this provision will be immediately turned over to a competent authority.

Likewise, anyone who, after an arrest, does not take the arrested person before a judge within twenty-four hours, shall himself be turned over to such authority or his agent.

If the detention takes place outside the locality in which the judge resides, sufficient time is to be added to the above period to account for the distance involved.

APPENDIX C

STATUTE OF THE ARGENTINE REVOLUTION

1966 A.L.J.A. 233 (June 28, 1966)

In view of the Act of the Argentine Revolution, taking into account what results therefrom, and

Considering:

That the Government represents all of the people of the Republic, whose devoted assistance is indispensable in order to reach the revolutionary goals and to reconstruct the grandeur of the Nation.

That the Government commands the allegiance of the Armed Forces of the Nation and of the other security and police forces; and, as such, disposes sufficient power to assure peace and public order, and to protect the life and property of the inhabitants. . . .

That the principle of the irremovability of members of the Judicial Power must be maintained as an irreplaceable measure for procuring the full force of the law, whose constant violation has been one of the principal causes of the ills afflicting the Republic;

That since the Government is ruled by the prescriptions of the Goals of the Revolution, the Statute of the Revolution, and the National Constitution, it is essential to have sworn allegiance to those norms;

That the Republic will maintain strict fulfillment of all obligations contracted;

That, in case of headlessness *(acefalía)*, it is necessary to establish the form of proceeding to replace the president.

For all these reasons:

The Revolutionary Junta, in order to fulfill the objectives of the revolution, and in exercise of the constituent power

ORDAINS:

Article 1. – The Executive Power of the Nation shall be exercised by the citizen whom this Revolutionary Junta designates with the title of president of the Argentine Nation. . . .

Article 3. – The Government shall conform its execution of the provisions of this Statute to those of the National Constitution and laws and decrees issued pursuant thereto to the extent they are not opposed to the goals enunciated in the act of the Argentine Revolution.

Article 4. – The Government shall respect all international obligations contracted by the Republic of Argentina.

Article 5. – The President of the Nation shall exercise all the legislative powers that the National Constitution bestows on the Congress, including those which are exclusive to each of the Chambers, with the exception of those provided for in articles 45, 51, and 52 for cases of impeachment of the judges of national tribunals. . . .

Article 7. — The magistrates designated as members of the Supreme Court of Justice and the present members of the inferior tribunals of the Nation shall enjoy the guarantees laid down in article 96 of the National Constitution.

Article 8. — For the purposes of the provisions of articles 45, 51 and 52 of the National Constitution, referring to members of the Court and inferior Tribunals, the Government shall promulgate a law to promote the establishment and functioning of an *ad hoc* impeachment tribunal *(jurado de enjuiciamiento)* for national magistrates.

Article 9. — The Government shall decree with respect to the provincial governments and shall designate their respective governors, who shall exercise the powers conceded by the respective provincial constitutions to the Executive and Legislative powers, and shall carry out their mandates subject to the principles expressed in articles 3 and 5 of this Statute and the instructions of the national government.

With reference to the Judicial Power, the governors may propose, on this one occasion, the total or partial removal of the present judges of the Superior Tribunal of each province, confirming with respect to the other magistrates the guarantees of tenure which are found in each Constitution. For the removal of magistrates, the governors shall establish a regime of a tribunal in conformance with the principles which are established for national magistrates.

Article 10. — In case of the absence from the country of the president of the Argentine Nation, the Executive Power shall be exercised by the Minister of the Interior.

In case of the incapacity or death of the president, his successor shall be designated by a common accord among the commanders in chief of the Armed Forces.

APPENDIX D

VENEZUELA: AGRARIAN REFORM LAW (1960) (excerpts)
Gaceta Oficial, No. 611 Extraordinario, 19 March 1960, p. 1
(FAO translation)

Introductory Title
Principles of the Agrarian Reform

1. The purpose of this Act is to transform the agrarian structure of the country and to incorporate its rural population into the economic, social and political development of the Nation, by replacing the latifundia system with an equitable system of land ownership, tenure and operation based on the fair distribution of the land, satisfactory organization of credit, and full assistance to agricultural producers, in order that the land may constitute, for the man who works it, a basis for his economic stability, a foundation for his advancing social welfare and a guarantee of his freedom and dignity.

2. In view of these purposes, this Act:

(a) Guarantees and regulates the right of private land ownership, in accordance with the principle that such ownership should fulfill a social function, and in accordance with other provisions laid down in the Constitution and in law.

(b) Guarantees the right of any individual or group, capable of farm work and lacking land or possessing insufficient land, to be provided with economically profitable land, preferably in the places of their work or residence, or, when circumstances so require, in duly selected regions within the limits and under the provisions laid down in this Act.

(c) Guarantees to farmers the right to remain on the land they cultivate, under the terms and conditions prescribed by this Act.

(d) Guarantees and recognizes to the indigenous population, which *de facto* maintains tribal or clan status, without diminishing their rights as Venezuelan citizens, as provided in the preceding paragraphs, the right to enjoy the land, forests and waters which they occupy or own in those places in which they habitually reside, without prejudice to their incorporation into national life in accordance with this or other enactments.

(e) Fosters and protects in particular the development of small and medium rural property and of agricultural cooperatives in such a manner as to render them stable and efficient.

For that purpose, the right to small family property is hereby established in accordance with the provisions of this Act governing allocations free of charge.

3. The obligations arising out of the principle that land ownership should fulfill a social function devolve both upon private persons and upon the State.

4. For the purposes of the provisions of Article 2, paragraph *b)*, the State shall gradually incorporate into the economic development of the country those zones or regions which are under-exploited or not suitable for technical and rational

exploitation due to lack of means of communication or irrigation, drainage or other similar works.

For that purpose, it shall put forward integrated development plans of economic or hydrographic regions, provided that in every case hydraulic improvement and agricultural development work shall be executed with a view to integrated development and shall be in accordance with agrarian reform plans.

5. The State shall establish and develop the public services necessary and sufficient for the transformation of the rural class and for aiding the agricultural producers bound by the responsibilities arising from the social function of property to comply with the obligations imposed upon them by this Act.

6. The General Budget Act shall contain appropriate provisions for financing the Agrarian Reform and the agricultural plans arising therefrom.

7. The State shall be required to lay down the bases and conditions necessary for raising the status of hired agricultural labor through satisfactory regulation of such labor and of its juridical status in keeping with the changes which will arise out of the Agrarian Reform.

8. Under conditions established or to be established, foreign nationals shall enjoy equality of rights with Venezuelan citizens and shall be subject to the same obligations in respect of the matters coming under this Act.

9. Persons entitled to request allocations of land may report the existence of lands which do not fulfill their social function.

Such reports shall be filed with the competent local office which shall, within thirty days, initiate the appropriate investigation and inform the person having filed the report.

If the report proves to be justified, the lands shall be subject to acquisition or expropriation, in accordance with the provisions of this Act.

Title I
Agricultural Property
Chapter I
Lands of Public Agencies

10. Lands of the public agencies shall be set aside for the purposes of the Agrarian Reform; in this respect, and without prejudice to the provisions of other special legislation, there shall be considered as such:

(a) Public land;
(b) Rural properties forming part of State lands *(dominio privado);*
(c) Rural properties belonging to the autonomous national agencies;
(d) Rural property having become property of the Nation as a result or consequence of illicit profiteering against the State.

11. Lands belonging to the States and municipalities and to the public agencies thereof shall also be set aside for the Agrarian Reform. Accordingly, the Government shall enter into the agreements necessary therefor.

12. With the exception of the areas reserved for urban and industrial expansion, those specifically excepted in Article 14, and those intended for the common use of inhabitants of towns, all other communal lands shall be set aside for the Agrarian Reform; for this purpose, the Government shall enter into such agreements with the municipalities as it deems appropriate.

13. For the purposes of the provisions of Articles 11 and 12, the formalities prescribed by the Basic Act on National Property in respect of alienation of property shall not be applicable.

14. The areas of rural properties forming the subject of this Chapter and occupied by petroleum or mineral exploitations, and those reserved or destined by the public administration for the establishment of public services or other works, may be set aside for the purposes of the Agrarian Reform when the National Agrarian Institute considers that agricultural activities may be carried out thereon without interfering with the operation of the said activities, and the Government shall so provide.

For such purpose, the Government shall prescribe regulations governing the necessary expropriations for the use of the said areas in accordance with the plans of the Agrarian Reform.

15. The lands set aside for the Agrarian Reform under the provisions of this Chapter shall not be alienated, encumbered, or leased unless the Government finds that they are required for other purposes of public or social policy and so authorizes.

16. In view of the provisions of Article 10 of this Act, the competent authorities shall not approve further requests for leases of public land. Without prejudice to the provisions of Article 69 [on relocation of residents of conservation zones], and provided that no allocation procedure forms an obstacle thereto, any person who duly proves to the National Agrarian Institute that he has occupied public land without let or hindrance for more than one year prior to the promulgation of this Act shall be entitled to be awarded, to the extent and within the limits laid down in Article 29, that part of such land which he is actually cultivating in conformity with the principle of the social function and under the conditions laid down in this Act.

Similarly, the occupation of areas greater than those specified in the Public and Common Land Act shall not give rise to the privileges granted by the said Act to the occupier of such land in respect of the lease or purchase thereof.

17. After agreement with the municipalities, and provided that no interference with the establishment of Agrarian Centers is caused thereby, the National Agrarian Institute shall grant, to those persons who on the date of publication of this Act are cultivating land leased from municipalities in accordance with the principles of the social function, ownership of areas not exceeding the limits laid down in Article 29 of this Act, without prejudice to the provisions of Article 12; in such cases, the plus-value and real improvements shall be paid according to fair expert valuation.

18. Properties belonging to or administered by the State and set aside in conformity with the provisions of this Chapter shall be transferred without charge to the National Agrarian Institute by the Government, which is hereby expressly authorized to take such action; the authorization of the National Congress or other government agency shall not be required to carry out the said conveyance.

After the appropriate agreements have been made, economically exploitable rural properties of the other public bodies and establishments shall be likewise transferred.

Chapter II
Privately-Owned Land
Section I
Social Function of Property

19. For the purposes of the Agrarian Reform, private ownership of land fulfills its social function when it combines all the following essential elements:

(a) The efficient exploitation and profitable use of the land in such a manner as to bring usefully into play the productive factors thereof, according to the zone in which it is located and its special characteristics.

(b) Personal operation and management of, and financial responsibility for, the agricultural enterprise by the landowner, except in special cases of indirect exploitation for good reasons.

(c) Compliance with the provisions governing conservation of renewable natural resources.

(d) Respect of legal provisions governing paid labor, other labor relations questions, and other farm contracts, under the conditions laid down in this Act.

(e) Registration of the rural property in the Office of the National Register of Land and Waters in accordance with appropriate legal provisions.

20. In particular, it shall be considered contrary to the principle of the social function of property and incompatible with the national welfare and economic development for uncultivated or unprofitable properties to exist and to be maintained, especially in economic development regions. Indirect systems of land exploitation, such as those carried out through leasing, the various types of sharecropping, day labor and squatting, shall also be considered contrary to the principle of the social function of property;

Provided, that the State shall in particular impose upon uncultivated or unprofitable properties a graduated tax scale to be prescribed in the appropriate enactments, without prejudice to expropriation in cases provided for under this Act.

21. When a private fragmentation program is planned for a property inhabited or worked by farmers entitled to receive land allocations, fragmentation shall be authorized by the National Agrarian Institute only if due care has been taken to safeguard the interest of such farmers as beneficiaries of the Agrarian Reform.

22. Failure by private landowners to comply with any of the obligations arising out of the social function of property shall constitute sufficient cause for the assignment of the land to the Agrarian Reform and, consequently, such land shall not be immune from expropriation on the grounds laid down in Article 26 of this Act.

23. The State shall provide incentives to those persons who utilize land in accordance with its social function and who thus contribute to the economic development of the country.

Section II
Acquisition of Land

24. Land acquired by the Institute to be used for the Agrarian Reform shall be economically exploitable. Acquisition for valuable consideration may take place only

after a prior favorable technical report indicating that the provisions of this Article are satisfied; the said report shall be included in the file of documents in the appropriate Public Registry Office.

25. In evaluating rural properties to be acquired in whole or in part for valuable consideration for the purposes of the Agrarian Reform, the following factors shall be taken into consideration:

(a) The average production over the six years immediately preceding the date of acquisition or of the request for expropriation.

(b) The declared or assessed official value for tax purposes under enactments relating thereto.

(c) The acquisition price of the property in the last conveyances of ownership carried out during the ten-year period prior to the date of valuation, and the acquisition prices of similar properties in the same region or zone in the five-year period immediately preceding the date of the expropriation request or purchase proposal:

Provided, that although in evaluating properties the abovementioned factors shall primarily be taken into account, any other factors which may be useful in fixing a just price, and all those mentioned in the Act relating to Expropriation in the Public or Social Interest, shall also be taken into consideration;

Provided, further, that the valuation shall include, in addition to the value of the land, the value of the buildings, installations, chattels, equipment and improvements existing thereon;

Provided, finally, that the determination of value shall take into account only the actual fair value of the property, to the exclusion of any consideration of possible damages or disadvantage or of the sentimental value of the property.

Section III
Expropriation

26. Rural properties which fulfill their social function in accordance with the provisions of Article 19 shall be immune from expropriation for the purposes of the Agrarian Reform, except as specifically provided otherwise by this Act.

27. Expropriation shall be resorted to when, at the site of allocation or at neighboring sites, there exists no public land or other rural properties mentioned in Title I, Chapter I, of this Act, or if such land or properties are inadequate or unsuitable, and if the National Agrarian Institute has been unable by any other means to acquire other land equally exploitable from an economic point of view.

Such expropriation shall be applied primarily to such land as fails to fulfill its social function, in the following order of priorities:

1) Uncultivated properties, and, in particular, those of the greatest area; properties exploited indirectly through tenants, sharecroppers, settlers and occupiers; and properties not under cultivation during the five years immediately prior to the initiation of expropriation proceedings.

2) Properties on which private land fragmentation programs have not been brought to completion, provided that if the National Agrarian Institute requests expropria-

tion thereof after the said programs have been initiated, the rights of beneficiaries of such fragmentation already in occupation shall be safeguarded.

3) Crop lands being used for range livestock grazing.

Expropriation of other land shall be resorted to when the above possibilities have been exhausted and there is no other means of solving an agrarian problem of evident gravity; in such cases, the provisions of Article 33 of this Act shall apply.

28. The national parks and forests, forest reserves, protective zones, natural and artistic monuments and wild-life sanctuaries shall be immune from assignment for the purposes of the Agrarian Reform.

29. Land or properties the area of which is not in excess of 150 hectares of the first category, or the equivalent thereof in land of other categories, in accordance with criteria to be laid down in Regulations, shall also be immune from expropriation.

The equivalents referred to in this Article shall be included between 150 and 5000 hectares.

In extreme flood or drought zones, individual maxima shall be fixed in each case by the National Agrarian Institute.

30. Owners of properties under expropriation shall be entitled to reserve for themselves thereon the area defined in Article 29 as immune from expropriation.

Land annexed to the principal reserve and required for proper operation of the property (*e.g.,* pastures, land occupied by buildings, and land covered with high trees and acting as protective zones for water conservation or as wind-breaks), shall not be considered as forming part of the reserved areas referred to in this Article, and shall be the object of an additional reserve, not to exceed 15% of the area of the principal reserve.

The Court may, at the request of the National Agrarian Institute, grant reductions in reserves up to 50% of the area immune from expropriation, on the grounds that the land is situated in a zone of high population density or that it is adjacent to a zone within the purview of the provisions of Article 183. In the case of lands lying near population centers of less than 3000 inhabitants, the reserve may be reduced to one third when such action is necessary to satisfy land allocation requirements. In no case may a reserve be granted in such part of a property as is being cultivated indirectly through a tenancy, sharecropping, fundación or other similar system.

31. Any person owning or acquiring more than one rural property which is expropriated shall be entitled to reserve for himself an area, not exceeding the limits laid down in Article 29, on one such property only.

32. In the cases mentioned in Articles 29 and 30, immunity from expropriation shall lapse in respect of properties and reserves made up of uncultivated or fallow land which has not been cultivated within three years, or on which an efficient stock-grazing enterprise has not been installed within five years from the date on which the land was allocated or the reserve was established, or if during the said period such land has been operated indirectly.

For the purposes of this Act, efficiently operated stock-grazing enterprises shall be those enterprises on which cultivated pastures predominate and on which exist such improvements as fences, stables, or watering troughs, or on which the practice of burning over pastures has been eliminated, so that a maximum herd of stock may be maintained on a minimum land area without adverse biological effect upon the soil or the stock.

33. When it becomes necessary to organize land in a given place, and when the existence thereat of one or more properties forms a technical or economic obstacle to proper execution of the scheme, the total or partial expropriation of such properties shall be authorized even when they fall within any of the classifications specified in Articles 26 and 29 of this Chapter. In order to take such action, the Institute shall be required to prove, during the appropriate judicial proceedings, that the conditions laid down in this Article exist. In such cases, cash payment shall be made for existing useful improvements, livestock, mortgages or preferential debts incurred and used for development and improvement purposes. The balance shall be paid in Class "C" bonds in accordance with the provisions of Article 174 of this Act.

Small or medium landowners whose properties have been totally expropriated under this Article shall be entitled, after the said land has been organized, to obtain, against payment, ownership of a parcel of the said land of a size equal to the largest area allocated.

Total expropriation shall take place where partial expropriation would destroy the economic unity of the property or would render it useless or unfit for the purpose for which it was destined.

34. When the properties are made up of lands of various qualities, the area immune from expropriation shall be determined by taking as one hectare of first-category land the appropriate equivalents to be prescribed by Regulation.

35. Prior to proceeding to the expropriation of a property the National Agrarian Institute shall directly propose an amicable arrangement with the owner. If such amicable arrangement is not reached within a period which may not exceed 90 days, the Institute shall request expropriation; no prior declaration of public interest shall be required, expropriation of land or properties for the purposes of this Act being of such nature.

36. In expropriating properties for the purposes of the Agrarian Reform, the provisions of the Act relating to Expropriation in the Public or Social Interest shall be complied with, except as otherwise provided by this Act, and especially as follows:

1) The request for expropriation, submitted to the Court having jurisdiction over the locality where the property is situated, shall be accompanied by a certificate issued by the competent Public Registry Office relating to tax assessments on the property during the ten preceding years, a report on the general characteristics of the property, and the classification of the property, prepared by the National Agrarian Institute in accordance with Article 29, for the purposes of the reserve mentioned in Article 38.

To this end, the competent Public Registry Office shall be required to furnish such certificates and reports within three working days after the date of request therefor. At the session at which the expropriation request is received, or at the following session, the Court shall take cognizance thereof and shall summon the interested parties to reply thereto.

2) Appeals or other resources against decisions of the trial judge shall lie in second instance before the Federal Court, against the decision of which no appeal whatsoever shall lie.

3) The expropriation request and summons for hearing shall be published twice, at intervals of not more than six days and not less than three days between the first and second publications, by notices affixed in the most public places and published in a daily newspaper of the Capital of the Republic.

4) Within five sessions after the date of the final publication, the persons summoned shall appear before the Court, personally or through an attorney, to file replies to the expropriation request. At the session following the expiration of the said period, an attorney shall be named for persons having failed to appear, and he shall be deemed to have been summoned.

If the attorney thus named fails to appear to be sworn at the first session after his appointment, such appointment shall be taken as having been refused. In such cases, the Court shall proceed to appoint a new attorney in the session immediately following.

5) If the appeal is on formal grounds only, a decision shall be rendered on such grounds at the fifth session following the filing of replies, after oral statements from all parties have been heard. In other cases, without a decree or order of the Court being necessary, a period of 15 working days after the full hearing shall be allowed, to permit the parties to collect and submit the necessary evidence; in no case may a *término de distancia** be granted for the collection of evidence.

6) At the expiration of the period allowed for taking evidence, a hearing shall be called within the two following sessions, at which time the parties shall file their written pleadings; the following session shall be fixed for hearing oral arguments on the points raised therein, provided that no party or the attorney thereof shall be authorized to speak more than once or for more than 30 minutes. After termination of the hearing, the Court shall announce its decision within the five following sessions. The Court may, once only, call a new hearing for further information. Such new hearing shall be held within the five following sessions, and the decision shall be announced within the three sessions following the expiration of the said period.

7) At the session following the filing of replies, the parties shall be present at a time to be fixed by the Court in order to reach an agreement on the price of the property under expropriation. If no such agreement is reached, the Court shall set a time at the following session for the appointment of experts to make a valuation; proceedings in respect thereof, when an appeal has been filed, shall be entered on a separate docket and shall be carried forward independently of the principal action. When the experts designated by the parties to the same case have twice in succession declined to act, the Court shall appoint experts.

---

*Trans. Note: Under Venezuelan law, a delay granted when distances remote from the seat of the Court are involved.

37. When, under the provisions of this Act, expropriation of a property is required for an immediate allocation of land, the prior occupation of the lands and properties in question may be carried out under the conditions laid down in Articles 51 and 52 of the Act in force relating to Expropriation in the Public or Social Interest, taking into account, in respect of the payment of the amount at which the property is evaluated, the provisions of Article 33 of this Act.

38. The owner shall be required to decide upon the location of the land he desires to reserve under the provisions of Articles 29, 30 and 31 prior to the day fixed for the swearing-in of the experts. If he fails to do so at the proper time, the Court shall indicate the location of the reserve prior to execution of the valuation, within a period of ten calendar days after administration of the oath; prior to and during such period, the Court may order the execution of any acts it finds necessary. If, after the interested party has chosen a location, a conflict arises with the agrarian authorities concerning the unsuitability of such location in view of execution of the agrarian scheme, the Court shall decide the question in accordance with the procedure laid down in Article 386 of the Code of Civil Procedure.

39. When it is necessary for the purposes of the Agrarian Reform to assign common land *(tierras baldías)* occupied by third parties carrying out agricultural activities thereon, and the National Agrarian Institute has not reached agreement with the occupiers, the expropriation of the works and improvements shall be requested, and a right shall be recognized to the occupier to retain part of his exploitation, such part being fixed in accordance with the project establishment plans, unless he prefers to be relocated on another parcel assigned him by the National Agrarian Institute. If in the expropriation proceedings the occupier claims ownership of the property and produces proof thereof, the provisions of Article 37 shall apply.

40. If an occupier of public land has failed to establish thereon a useful agricultural enterprise, the National Agrarian Institute shall request of the ordinary Court having jurisdiction in expropriation matters judicial authorization to occupy such land, and shall pay the occupier for the works and improvements he has installed thereon at a fair rate established by experts. In case the occupier claims ownership of the land but fails to present title thereto, the National Agrarian Institute shall request the same measure, and may recognize the occupier as a beneficiary of an allocation under this Act. If, during either expropriation proceedings or final occupation proceedings the occupier has claimed ownership of the land, he shall be entitled to request that the Government make an adjustment or settlement of the matter, unless the Government considers that resort should be had to an administrative claims procedure; such procedures shall be initiated within one year after occupation by the National Agrarian Institute has been authorized. . . .

Title XI
Transitional Provisions

. . . 198. Pending publication of the Regulations provided for in Article 204 concerning classification of land, the following scale of values shall apply:

Land	Points	Hectares
First Category	90-100	150
Second Category	80-89	151-200
Third Category	70-79	201-300
Fourth Category	60-69	301-500
Fifth Category	50-59	501-1000
Sixth Category	40-49	1001-2500
Seventh Category	less than 40	2501-5000

In arriving at the number of points, the following criteria shall be applied:

1) Population density; distance from marketing centers and transportation time: 40 points;

2) Meteorological conditions and existence of surface water utilizable for irrigation: 20 points;

3) Agrological capacity (topography, physical, chemical, and biological condition of the soil): 40 points.

In accordance with the International Classification, the agrological capacity shall be determined by the following conditions:

A) Suitable for culture:
    (a) Without requiring special conservation measures: 40 points;
    (b) Requiring moderate conservation measures: 35 points;
    (c) Requiring intensive conservation measures: 25 points.
B) Suitable for partial or limited culture:
    (a) With limited use and intensive methods: 15 points.
C) Unsuitable for culture but adequate for permanent vegetation:
    (a) Without restriction or use of special methods: 10 points;
    (b) With moderate restrictions: 5 points:
    (c) With severe restrictions: 0 points.

However, the National Agrarian Institute shall be authorized to decide any extreme cases which may arise. . . .

Title XII
Final Provisions

. . . 203. Owners of rural properties shall, within six months of the date of publication of this Act, forward to the Institute a list of the tenants and occupiers present on their properties, indicating the class of culture or type of operation carried on by each, the approximate areas they occupy, period of time installed on the property, rent paid and any other pertinent data;

Provided, that the Institute shall proceed to any investigations it may deem necessary to determine the exact situation of such tenants and occupiers and may, for this purpose, call for the cooperation of national, state and municipal officials and public employees or private persons, who shall be required to furnish such assistance.

204. The Government shall issue the appropriate regulations in view of an equitable technical classification of land, for the purposes of this Act.

INDEX